W9-AYE-917

Teacher Wraparound Edition

GLENCOE FRENCH 1

Bon voyage!

WITH FEATURES BY
NATIONAL GEOGRAPHIC SOCIETY

Conrad J. Schmitt • Katia Brillié Lutz

Glencoe McGraw-Hill

New York, New York Columbus, Ohio Woodland Hills, California Peoria, Illinois

Glencoe

The McGraw-Hill Companies

Copyright © 2004 by The McGraw-Hill Companies. All rights reserved. Except as permitted under the United States Copyright Act, no part of this publication may be reproduced or distributed in any form or by any means, or stored in a database or retrieval system, without the prior permission of the publisher.

Send all inquiries to:
Glencoe/McGraw-Hill
8787 Orion Place
Columbus, Ohio 43240-4027

ISBN 0-07-860941-0 (Teacher Wraparound Edition)
ISBN 0-07-860938-0 (Student Edition)

Printed in the United States of America

1 2 3 4 5 6 7 8 9 10 071 10 09 08 07 06 05 04 03

From the Authors

Itinerary for Success

- ✓ Exposure to Francophone culture
- ✓ Clear expectations and goals
- ✓ Thematic, contextualized vocabulary
- ✓ Useful and thematically linked structure
- ✓ Progressive practice
- ✓ Real-life conversation
- ✓ Cultural readings in the target language
- ✓ Connections to other disciplines . . . in French!
- ✓ Recycling and review
- ✓ **National Geographic Society** panoramas of the Francophone world

Dear French Teacher,

Welcome to Glencoe's **Bon voyage!** French program. We hope you will find that the way in which we have organized the presentation of the French language and Francophone cultures will make the French language more teachable for you and more learnable for your students.

Upon completion of each chapter of **Bon voyage!** your students will be able to communicate in French in a real-life situation. The high-frequency, productive vocabulary that is presented at the beginning of the chapter focuses on a specific communicative topic and covers key situations where students would have to use French to survive. The structure point that follows the vocabulary presentation will enable students to put their new words together to communicate coherently.

After students acquire the essential vocabulary and structure needed to function in a given situation, we present a realistic conversation that uses natural, colloquial French and, most importantly, French that students can readily understand. To introduce students to the culture of France and the Francophone world, the chapter topic is subsequently presented in a cultural milieu in narrative form. Each **Lecture culturelle** recombines known language and enables students to read and learn—in French—about the fascinating cultures of the people who speak French.

Any one of us who has taught French realizes the importance of giving students the opportunity to practice, a factor so often overlooked in many textbooks today. Throughout **Bon voyage!** we provide students with many opportunities to use their French in activities with interesting and varied, but realistic formats. The activities within each chapter progress from simple, guided practice to more open-ended activities that may use all forms of the particular structure in question. Finally, activities that encourage completely free communication enable students to recall and reincorporate all the French they have learned up to that point.

We are aware that your students have varied learning styles and abilities. For this reason we have provided a great deal of optional material in **Bon voyage!** to permit you to pick and choose material appropriate for the needs of your classes. In this Teacher Wraparound Edition we have clearly outlined the material that is required, recommended, or optional in each chapter.

Many resources accompany **Bon voyage!** to help you vary and enliven your instruction. We hope you will find these materials not only useful, but an integral part of the program. However, we trust you will agree that the Student Text is the lifeline of any program; the supporting materials can be used to reinforce and expand upon the themes of the main text.

Again, we hope that your yearlong journey with each of your classes will indeed be a **Bon voyage!**

Bien amicalement,

Conrad J. Schmitt • Katia Brillié Lutz

Teacher Edition

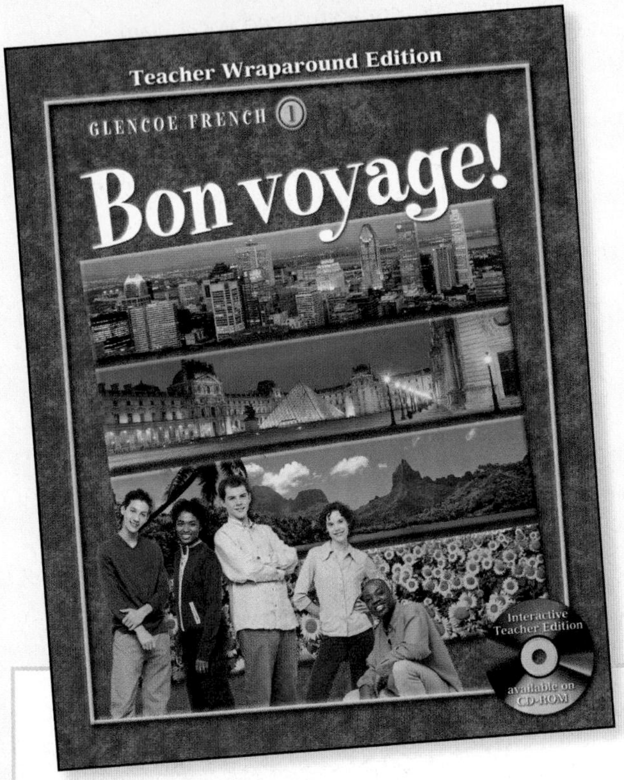

A Guided Tour of the Student Edition T6

A Guided Tour of the Teacher Edition T22

Bon voyage! Resources T26

French Names T30

Classroom Expressions T31

Standards for Foreign Language Learning T32

Student Edition

La francophonie
Why Learn French?
L'alphabet français
Leçons préliminaires

CHAPITRE 1
Une amie et un ami

CHAPITRE 2
Les cours et les profs

CHAPITRE 3
Pendant et après les cours

CHAPITRE 4
La famille et la maison

Révision Chapitres 1–4

NATIONAL GEOGRAPHIC Reflets de la France

LITERARY COMPANION

Littérature 1
La petite Fadette
George Sand

CHAPITRE 5
Au café et au restaurant

CHAPITRE 6
La nourriture et les courses

CHAPITRE 7
Les vêtements

Révision Chapitres 5–7

NATIONAL GEOGRAPHIC Reflets de l'Afrique

LITERARY COMPANION

Littérature 2
«Dors mon enfant»
Elolongué Epanya Yondo

CHAPITRE 8
L'aéroport et l'avion

CHAPITRE 9
La gare et le train

CHAPITRE 10
Les sports

CHAPITRE 11
L'été et l'hiver

Révision Chapitres 8–11

NATIONAL GEOGRAPHIC Reflets du Canada

LITERARY COMPANION

Littérature 3
La Chanson de Roland
Auteur anonyme

CHAPITRE 12
La routine quotidienne

CHAPITRE 13
Les loisirs culturels

CHAPITRE 14
La santé et la médecine

Révision Chapitres 12–14

NATIONAL GEOGRAPHIC Reflets de Paris

LITERARY COMPANION

Littérature 4
Le Comte de Monte-Cristo
Alexandre Dumas

Handbook
InfoGap Activities
Study Tips
Verb Charts
French-English Dictionary
English-French Dictionary
Index

Expand your students' view of the Francophone world

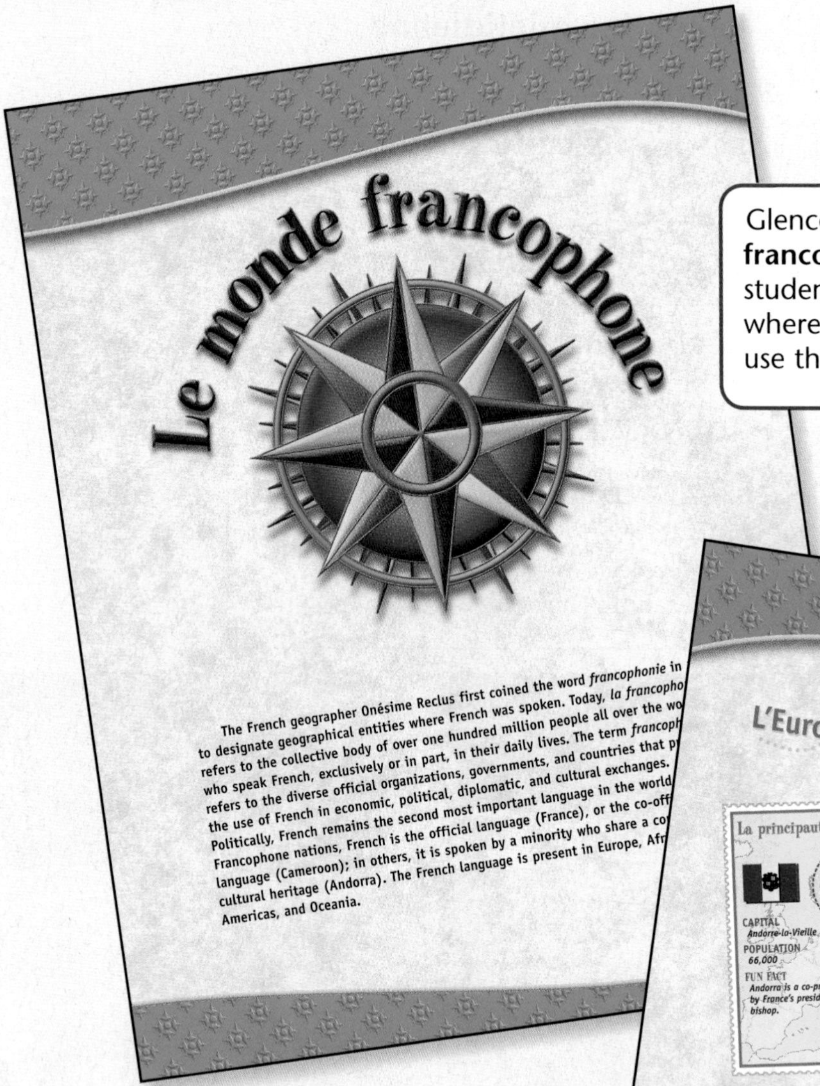
Le monde francophone

The French geographer Onésime Reclus first coined the word *francophonie* in
to designate geographical entities where French was spoken. Today, *la francopho*
refers to the collective body of over one hundred million people all over the wo
who speak French, exclusively or in part, in their daily lives. The term *francoph*
refers to the diverse official organizations, governments, and countries that p
the use of French in economic, political, diplomatic, and cultural exchanges.
Politically, French remains the second most important language in the world
Francophone nations, French is the official language (France), or the co-off
language (Cameroon); in others, it is spoken by a minority who share a co
cultural heritage (Andorra). The French language is present in Europe, Afr
Americas, and Oceania.

Glencoe's **Le monde francophone** will take your students to the many places where they will be able to use their French.

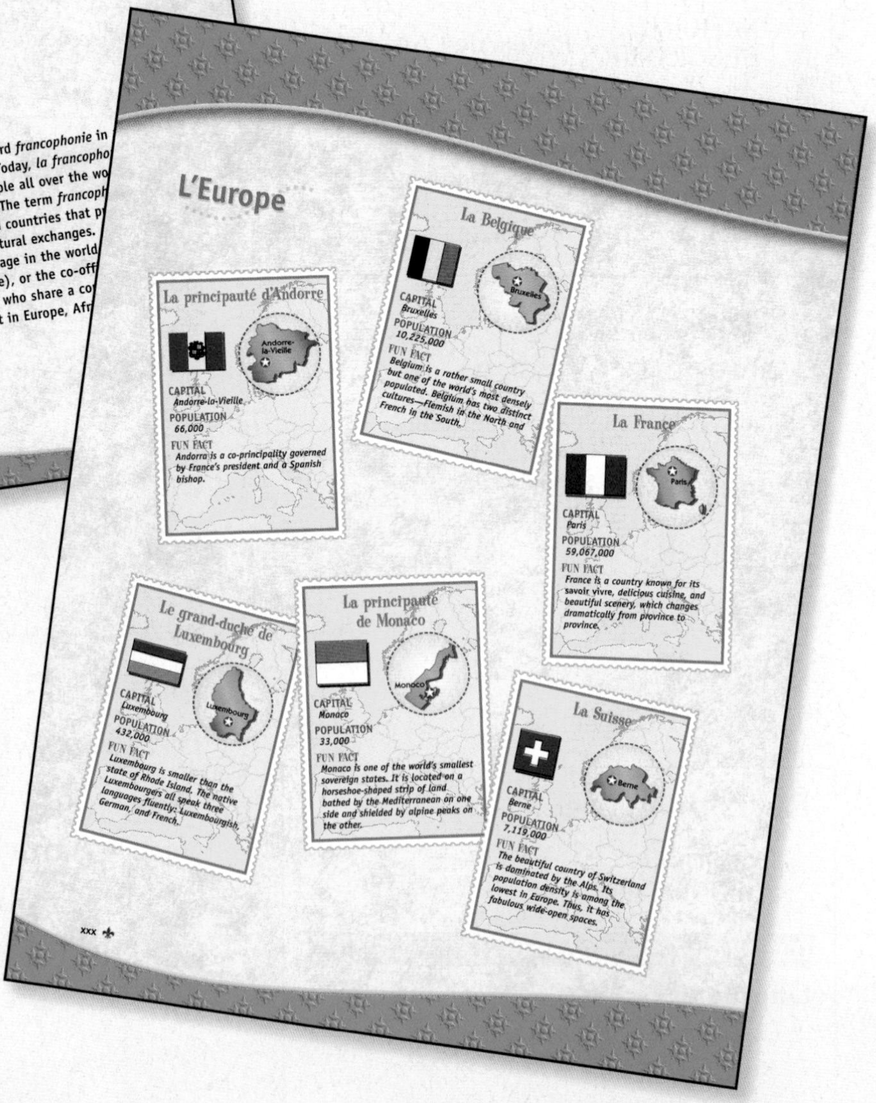
L'Europe

La principauté d'Andorre

CAPITAL
Andorre-la-Vieille
POPULATION
66,000
FUN FACT
Andorra is a co-principality governed by France's president and a Spanish bishop.

La Belgique

CAPITAL
Bruxelles
POPULATION
10,225,000
FUN FACT
Belgium is a rather small country but one of the world's most densely populated. Belgium has two distinct cultures—Flemish in the North and French in the South.

La France

CAPITAL
Paris
POPULATION
59,067,000
FUN FACT
France is a country known for its savoir vivre, delicious cuisine, and beautiful scenery, which changes dramatically from province to province.

Le grand-duché de Luxembourg

CAPITAL
Luxembourg
POPULATION
432,000
FUN FACT
Luxembourg is smaller than the state of Rhode Island. The native Luxembourgers all speak three languages fluently: Luxembourgish, German, and French.

La principauté de Monaco

CAPITAL
Monaco
POPULATION
33,000
FUN FACT
Monaco is one of the world's smallest sovereign states. It is located on a horseshoe-shaped strip of land bathed by the Mediterranean on one side and shielded by alpine peaks on the other.

La Suisse

CAPITAL
Berne
POPULATION
7,119,000
FUN FACT
The beautiful country of Switzerland is dominated by the Alps. Its population density is among the lowest in Europe. Thus, it has fabulous wide-open spaces.

xxx

Maps, facts, and figures will serve as a valuable resource for you and your students throughout your journey.

Awaken your students' interest with an introduction to the chapter theme in a cultural context

Itinerary for Success

- ✓ Exposure to Francophone culture
- ✓ Clear expectations and goals
- ✓ Thematic, contextualized vocabulary
- ✓ Useful and thematically linked structure
- ✓ Progressive practice
- ✓ Real-life conversation
- ✓ Cultural readings in the target language
- ✓ Connections to other disciplines . . . in French!
- ✓ Recycling and review
- ✓ **National Geographic Society** panoramas of the Francophone world

CHAPITRE
11
L'été et l'hiver
Objectifs
In this chapter you will learn to:
✓ describe summer and winter weather
✓ talk about summer activities and sports
✓ talk about winter sports
✓ discuss past actions and events
✓ make negative statements
✓ talk about a ski trip in Quebec
RF 3,00 F 0,46 €
bonnes vacances
Maurice Utrillo Montmartre sous la neige
354

Objectives let students know what they will be able to do at the end of the chapter.

Fine art connection to the chapter topic serves as a springboard for discussion.

Opening photo provides a cultural backdrop for the chapter.

Give students something to talk about with thematic, contextualized vocabulary

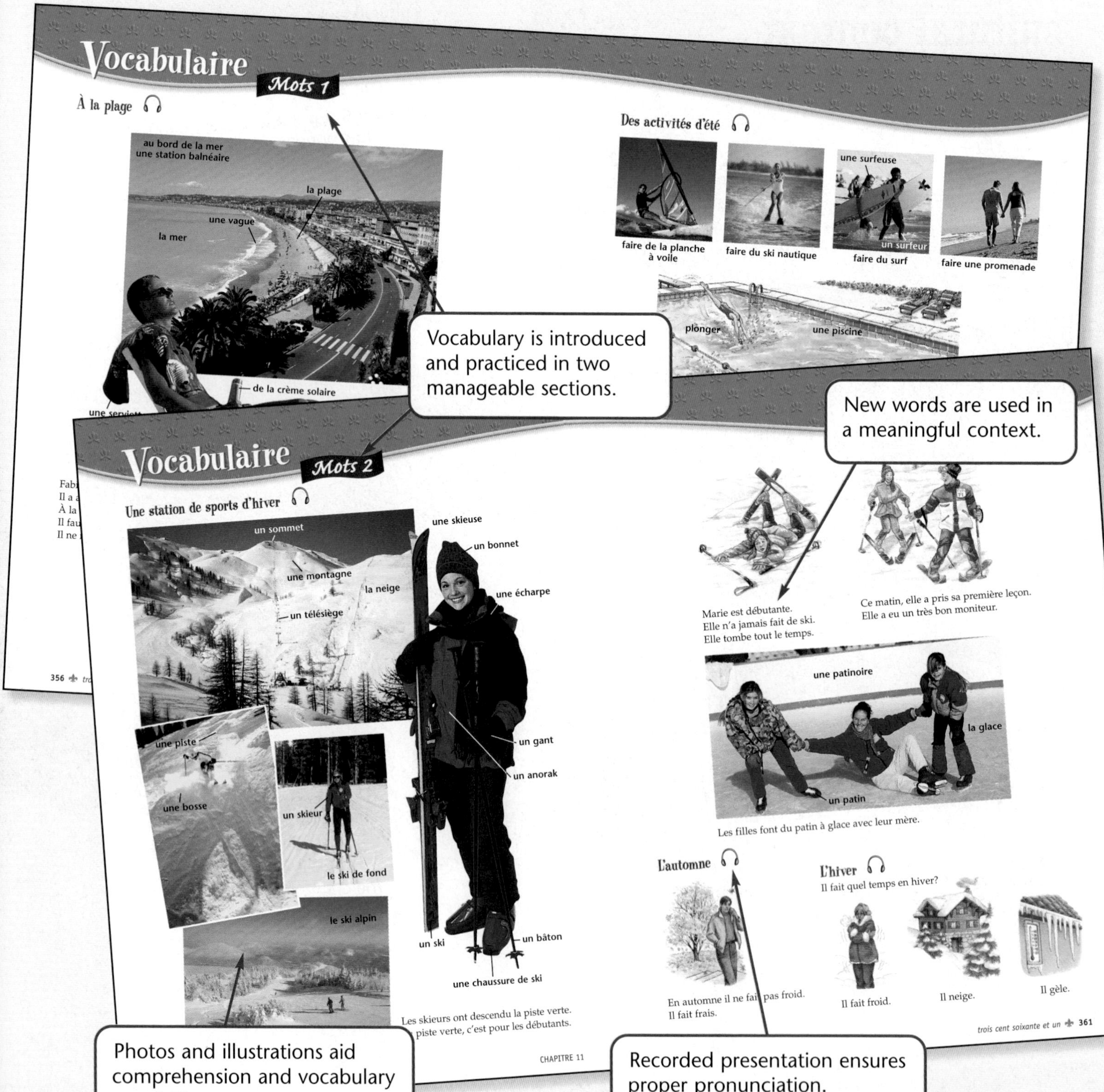

Vocabulary is introduced and practiced in two manageable sections.

New words are used in a meaningful context.

Photos and illustrations aid comprehension and vocabulary acquisition.

Recorded presentation ensures proper pronunciation.

Provide practice for the mastery of new vocabulary

Itinerary for Success

- ✓ Exposure to Francophone culture
- ✓ Clear expectations and goals
- ✓ Thematic, contextualized vocabulary
- ✓ Useful and thematically linked structure
- ✓ Progressive practice
- ✓ Real-life conversation
- ✓ Cultural readings in the target language
- ✓ Connections to other disciplines . . . in French!
- ✓ Recycling and review
- ✓ **National Geographic Society** panoramas of the Francophone world

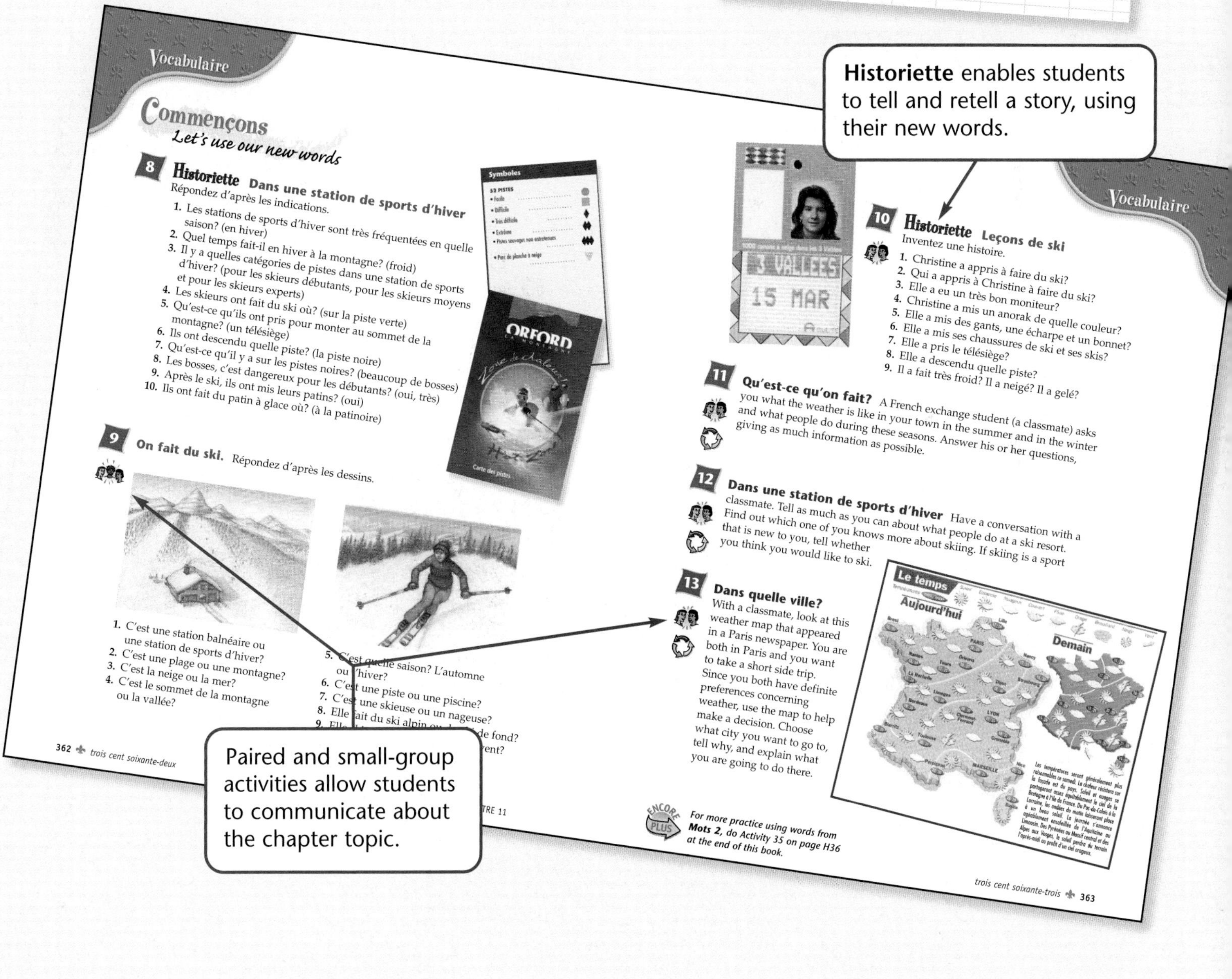

Vocabulaire

Commençons
Let's use our new words

8 Historiette Dans une station de sports d'hiver
Répondez d'après les indications.
1. Les stations de sports d'hiver sont très fréquentées en quelle saison? (en hiver)
2. Quel temps fait-il en hiver à la montagne? (froid)
3. Il y a quelles catégories de pistes dans une station de sports d'hiver? (pour les skieurs débutants, pour les skieurs moyens et pour les skieurs experts)
4. Les skieurs ont fait du ski où? (sur la piste verte)
5. Qu'est-ce qu'ils ont pris pour monter au sommet de la montagne? (un télésiège)
6. Ils ont descendu quelle piste? (la piste noire)
7. Qu'est-ce qu'il y a sur les pistes noires? (beaucoup de bosses)
8. Les bosses, c'est dangereux pour les débutants? (oui, très)
9. Après le ski, ils ont mis leurs patins? (oui)
10. Ils ont fait du patin à glace où? (à la patinoire)

9 On fait du ski. Répondez d'après les dessins.
1. C'est une station balnéaire ou une station de sports d'hiver?
2. C'est une plage ou une montagne?
3. C'est la neige ou la mer?
4. C'est le sommet de la montagne ou la vallée?
5. C'est quelle saison? L'automne ou l'hiver?
6. C'est une piste ou une piscine?
7. C'est une skieuse ou un nageuse?
8. Elle fait du ski alpin ou … de fond?
9. Elle … ent?

362 ✤ trois cent soixante-deux

10 Historiette Leçons de ski
Inventez une histoire.
1. Christine a appris à faire du ski?
2. Qui a appris à Christine à faire du ski?
3. Elle a eu un très bon moniteur?
4. Christine a mis un anorak de quelle couleur?
5. Elle a mis des gants, une écharpe et un bonnet?
6. Elle a mis ses chaussures de ski et ses skis?
7. Elle a pris le télésiège?
8. Elle a descendu quelle piste?
9. Il a fait très froid? Il a neigé? Il a gelé?

11 Qu'est-ce qu'on fait? A French exchange student (a classmate) asks you what the weather is like in your town in the summer and in the winter and what people do during these seasons. Answer his or her questions, giving as much information as possible.

12 Dans une station de sports d'hiver Have a conversation with a classmate. Tell as much as you can about what people do at a ski resort. Find out which one of you knows more about skiing. If skiing is a sport that is new to you, tell whether you think you would like to ski.

13 Dans quelle ville? With a classmate, look at this weather map that appeared in a Paris newspaper. You are both in Paris and you want to take a short side trip. Since you both have definite preferences concerning weather, use the map to help make a decision. Choose what city you want to go to, tell why, and explain what you are going to do there.

For more practice using words from ***Mots 2,*** *do Activity 35 on page H36 at the end of this book.*

trois cent soixante-trois ✤ 363

Historiette enables students to tell and retell a story, using their new words.

Paired and small-group activities allow students to communicate about the chapter topic.

Build communicative competence with thematically linked structure

New structures are presented in simple terms with familiar vocabulary.

Immediate reinforcement shows students how structure works to build meaning.

Structure

Describing more past actions
Le passé composé des verbes irréguliers

1. You have already learned that the past participles of regular verbs end in the sounds /é/, /i/, and /ü/. The past participles of most irregular verbs also end in the sounds /i/ or /ü/, even though they are not spelled the same way.

Infinitif → participe passé /i/		Infinitif → participe passé /ü/	
dire	dit	avoir	eu
écrire	écrit	croire	cru
mettre	mis	voir	vu
permettre	permis	boire	bu
prendre	pris	devoir	dû
apprendre	appris	pouvoir	pu
comprendre	compris	lire	lu
		recevoir	reçu
		vouloir	voulu

J'ai pris des leçons de natation.
J'ai appris à nager.
J'ai eu un bon moniteur.

Tu as lu son livre?
Il a écrit un livre?
Tu as compris ce qu'il a dit?

2. The verbs **être** and **faire** have irregular past participles.

être → été   faire → fait

J'ai fait un voyage à Megève l'année dernière.
J'ai été content d'apprendre à faire du ski.

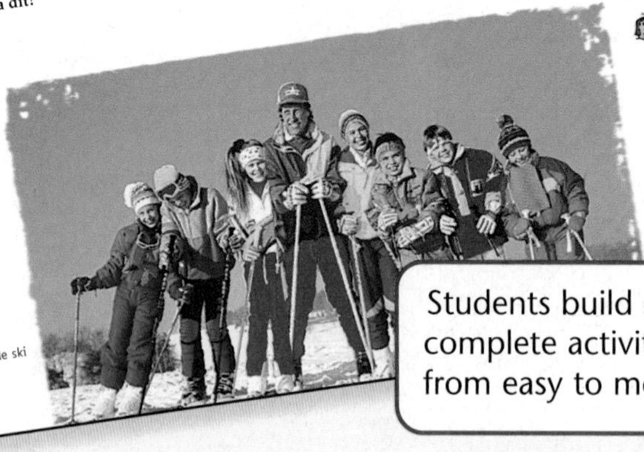
Une classe de ski

364 ✤ trois cent soixante-quatre

Continuons
Let's put our words together

Une vue de la ville de Québec

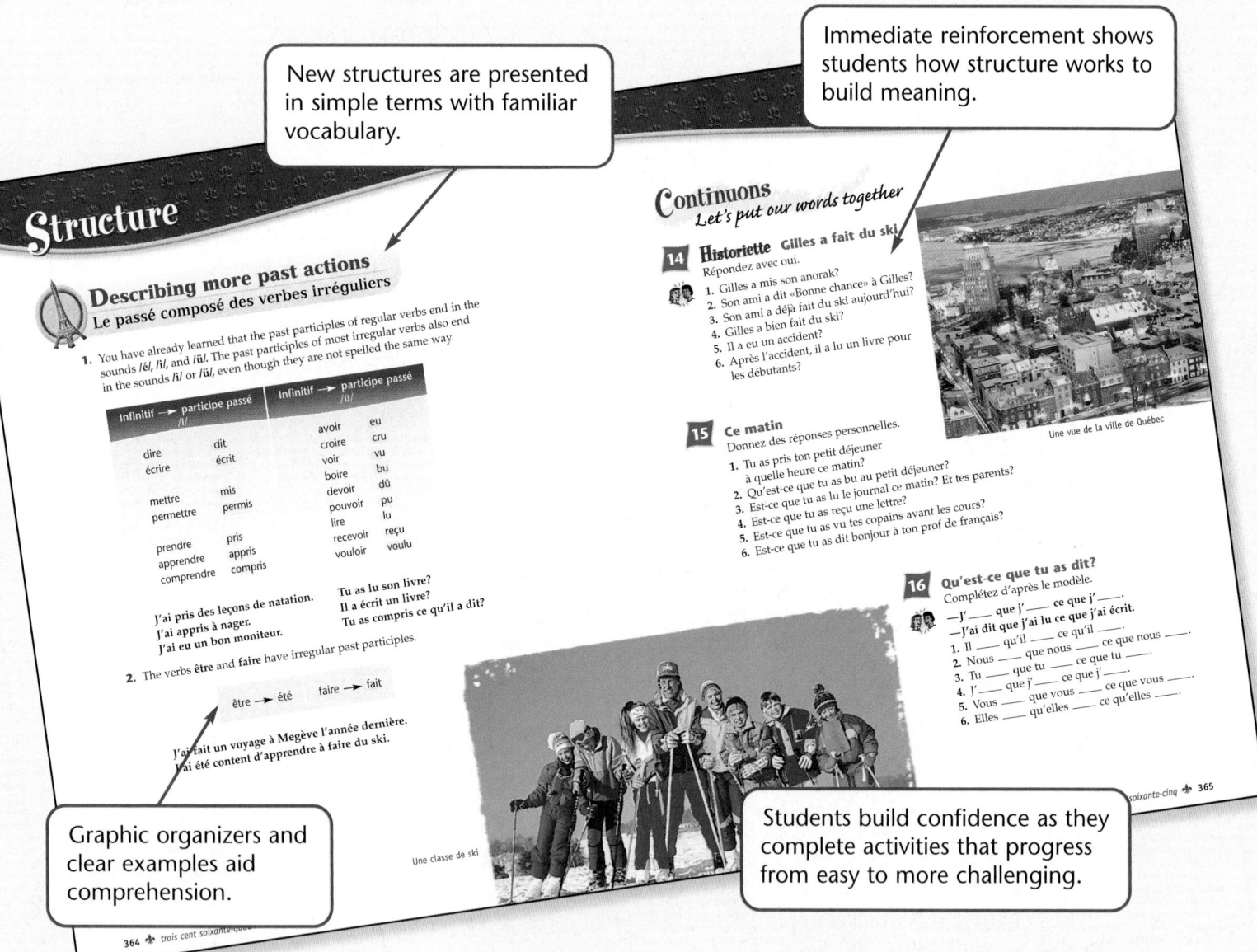

14 Historiette Gilles a fait du ski
Répondez avec oui.
1. Gilles a mis son anorak?
2. Son ami a dit «Bonne chance» à Gilles?
3. Son ami a déjà fait du ski aujourd'hui?
4. Gilles a bien fait du ski?
5. Il a eu un accident?
6. Après l'accident, il a lu un livre pour les débutants?

15 Ce matin
Donnez des réponses personnelles.
1. Tu as pris ton petit déjeuner à quelle heure ce matin?
2. Qu'est-ce que tu as bu au petit déjeuner?
3. Est-ce que tu as lu le journal ce matin? Et tes parents?
4. Est-ce que tu as reçu une lettre?
5. Est-ce que tu as vu tes copains avant les cours?
6. Est-ce que tu as dit bonjour à ton prof de français?

16 Qu'est-ce que tu as dit?
Complétez d'après le modèle.
—J'___ que j'___ ce que j'___.
—J'ai dit que j'ai lu ce que j'ai écrit.
1. Il ___ qu'il ___ ce qu'il ___.
2. Nous ___ que nous ___ ce que nous ___.
3. Tu ___ que tu ___ ce que tu ___.
4. J'___ que j'___ ce que j'___.
5. Vous ___ que vous ___ ce que vous ___.
6. Elles ___ qu'elles ___ ce qu'elles ___.

soixante-cinq ✤ 365

Graphic organizers and clear examples aid comprehension.

Students build confidence as they complete activities that progress from easy to more challenging.

Strengthen proficiency with continuous reinforcement and reentry

Itinerary for Success

- ✓ Exposure to Francophone culture
- ✓ Clear expectations and goals
- ✓ Thematic, contextualized vocabulary
- ✓ Useful and thematically linked structure
- ✓ Progressive practice
- ✓ Real-life conversation
- ✓ Cultural readings in the target language
- ✓ Connections to other disciplines . . . in French!
- ✓ Recycling and review
- ✓ **National Geographic Society** panoramas of the Francophone world

Rappelez-vous que... links what students already know to the new structure being presented.

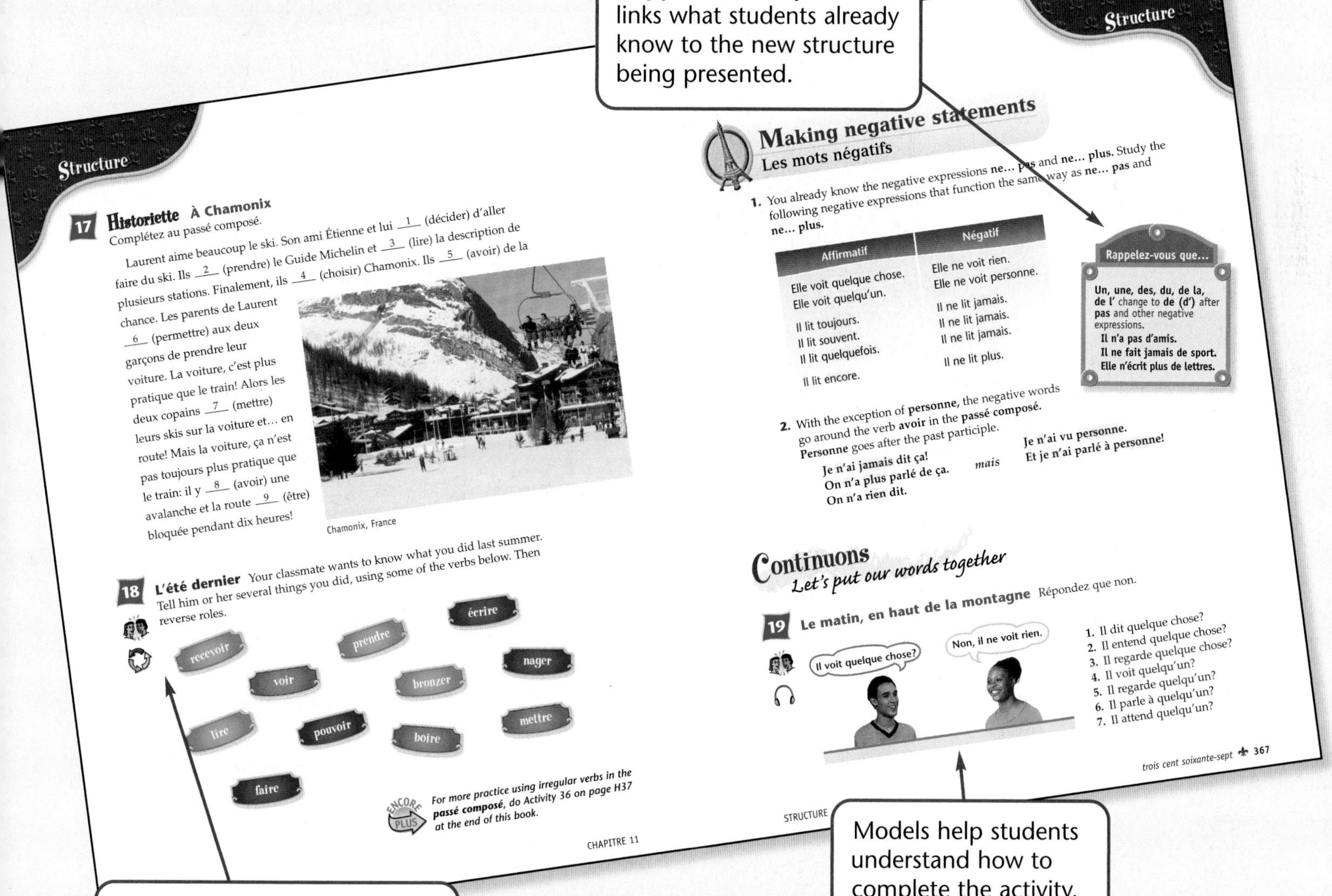

Structure

17 Historiette **À Chamonix**
Complétez au passé composé.

Laurent aime beaucoup le ski. Son ami Étienne et lui __1__ (décider) d'aller faire du ski. Ils __2__ (prendre) le Guide Michelin et __3__ (lire) la description de plusieurs stations. Finalement, ils __4__ (choisir) Chamonix. Ils __5__ (avoir) de la chance. Les parents de Laurent __6__ (permettre) aux deux garçons de prendre leur voiture. La voiture, c'est plus pratique que le train! Alors les deux copains __7__ (mettre) leurs skis sur la voiture et... en route! Mais la voiture, ça n'est pas toujours plus pratique que le train: il y __8__ (avoir) une avalanche et la route __9__ (être) bloquée pendant dix heures!

Chamonix, France

18 L'été dernier Your classmate wants to know what you did last summer. Tell him or her several things you did, using some of the verbs below. Then reverse roles.

recevoir, voir, prendre, écrire, bronzer, nager, lire, pouvoir, boire, mettre, faire

ENCORE PLUS *For more practice using irregular verbs in the* ***passé composé****, do Activity 36 on page H37 at the end of this book.*

CHAPITRE 11

Structure

Making negative statements
Les mots négatifs

1. You already know the negative expressions **ne... pas** and **ne... plus**. Study the following negative expressions that function the same way as **ne... pas** and **ne... plus**.

Affirmatif	Négatif
Elle voit quelque chose.	Elle ne voit rien.
Elle voit quelqu'un.	Elle ne voit personne.
Il lit toujours.	Il ne lit jamais.
Il lit souvent.	Il ne lit jamais.
Il lit quelquefois.	Il ne lit jamais.
Il lit encore.	Il ne lit plus.

Rappelez-vous que...
Un, une, des, du, de la, de l' change to **de (d')** after **pas** and other negative expressions.
Il n'a pas d'amis.
Il ne fait jamais de sport.
Elle n'écrit plus de lettres.

2. With the exception of **personne**, the negative words go around the verb **avoir** in the **passé composé**. **Personne** goes after the past participle.

Je n'ai jamais dit ça!
On n'a plus parlé de ça. *mais* **Je n'ai vu personne.**
On n'a rien dit. **Et je n'ai parlé à personne!**

Continuons
Let's put our words together

19 Le matin, en haut de la montagne Répondez que non.

Il voit quelque chose?
Non, il ne voit rien.

1. Il dit quelque chose?
2. Il entend quelque chose?
3. Il regarde quelque chose?
4. Il voit quelqu'un?
5. Il regarde quelqu'un?
6. Il parle à quelqu'un?
7. Il attend quelqu'un?

STRUCTURE

trois cent soixante-sept 367

Models help students understand how to complete the activity.

Continuous reentry occurs as the chapter vocabulary and topic are used to practice the new structure points.

Engage students in real conversation

Students apply newly learned vocabulary and structures to real-life situations.

Students can watch and participate in the interactive conversation on CD-ROM.

Use realia to expand acquired language skills.

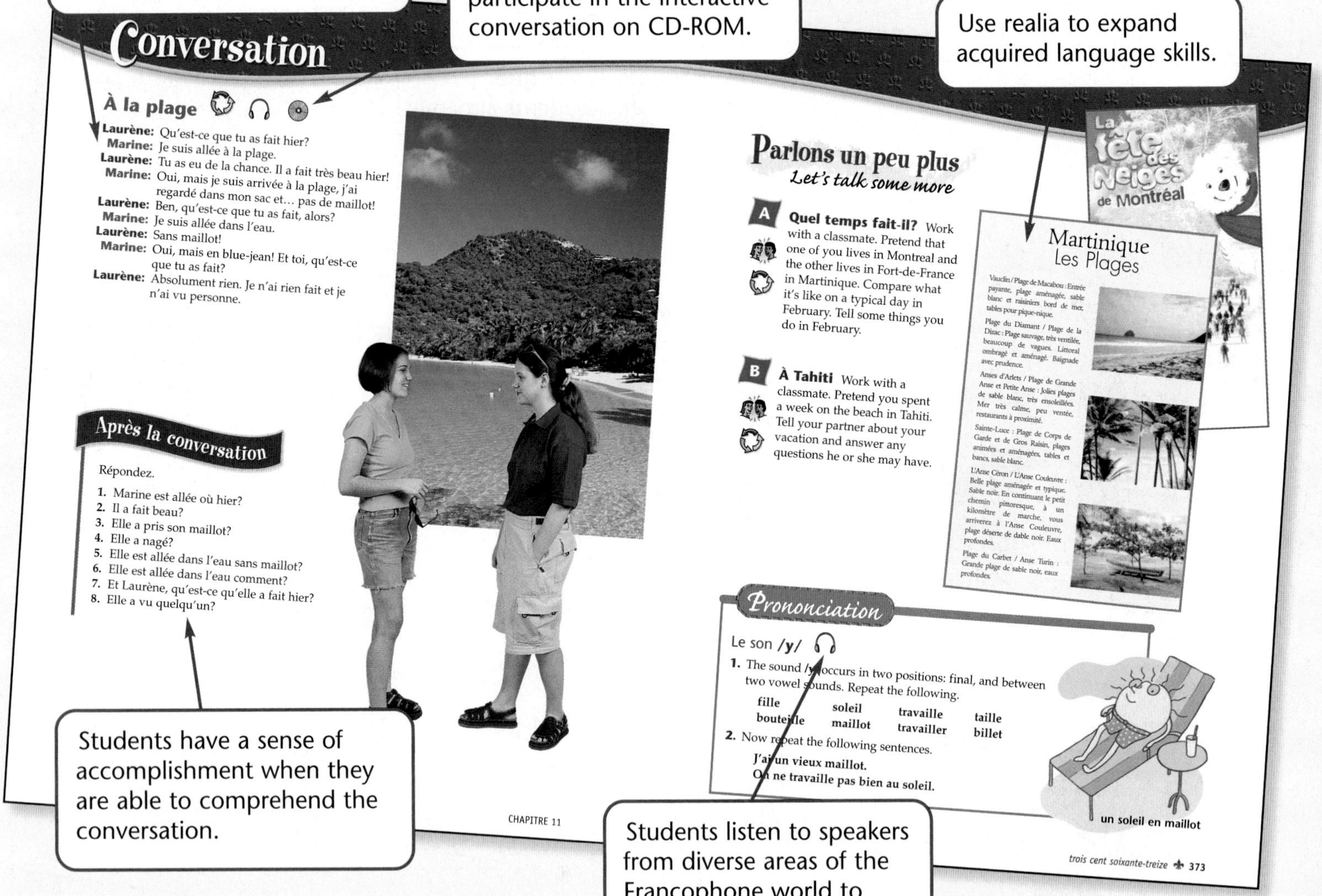

Conversation

À la plage

Laurène: Qu'est-ce que tu as fait hier?
Marine: Je suis allée à la plage.
Laurène: Tu as eu de la chance. Il a fait très beau hier!
Marine: Oui, mais je suis arrivée à la plage, j'ai regardé dans mon sac et… pas de maillot!
Laurène: Ben, qu'est-ce que tu as fait, alors?
Marine: Je suis allée dans l'eau.
Laurène: Sans maillot!
Marine: Oui, mais en blue-jean! Et toi, qu'est-ce que tu as fait?
Laurène: Absolument rien. Je n'ai rien fait et je n'ai vu personne.

Après la conversation

Répondez.

1. Marine est allée où hier?
2. Il a fait beau?
3. Elle a pris son maillot?
4. Elle a nagé?
5. Elle est allée dans l'eau sans maillot?
6. Elle est allée dans l'eau comment?
7. Et Laurène, qu'est-ce qu'elle a fait hier?
8. Elle a vu quelqu'un?

CHAPITRE 11

Parlons un peu plus
Let's talk some more

A Quel temps fait-il? Work with a classmate. Pretend that one of you lives in Montreal and the other lives in Fort-de-France in Martinique. Compare what it's like on a typical day in February. Tell some things you do in February.

B À Tahiti Work with a classmate. Pretend you spent a week on the beach in Tahiti. Tell your partner about your vacation and answer any questions he or she may have.

Martinique
Les Plages

Vauclin / Plage de Macabou : Entrée payante, plage aménagée, sable blanc et raisiniers bord de mer, tables pour pique-nique.

Plage du Diamant / Plage de la Dizac : Plage sauvage, très ventilée, beaucoup de vagues. Littoral ombragé et aménagé. Baignade avec prudence.

Anses d'Arlets / Plage de Grande Anse et Petite Anse : Jolies plages de sable blanc, très ensoleillées. Mer très calme, peu ventée, restaurants à proximité.

Sainte-Luce : Plage de Corps de Garde et de Gros Raisin, plages animées et aménagées, tables et bancs, sable blanc.

L'Anse Céron / L'Anse Couleuvre : Belle plage aménagée et typique. Sable noir. En continuant le petit chemin pittoresque, à un kilomètre de marche, vous arriverez à l'Anse Couleuvre, plage déserte de dable noir. Eaux profondes.

Plage du Carbet / Anse Turin : Grande plage de sable noir, eaux profondes.

Prononciation

Le son /y/

1. The sound /y/ occurs in two positions: final, and between two vowel sounds. Repeat the following.

fille	**soleil**	**travaille**	**taille**
bouteille	**maillot**	**travailler**	**billet**

2. Now repeat the following sentences.

J'ai un vieux maillot.
On ne travaille pas bien au soleil.

un soleil en maillot

trois cent soixante-treize 373

Students have a sense of accomplishment when they are able to comprehend the conversation.

Students listen to speakers from diverse areas of the Francophone world to improve pronunciation.

Heighten students' cultural awareness

Itinerary for Success

- ✓ Exposure to Francophone culture
- ✓ Clear expectations and goals
- ✓ Thematic, contextualized vocabulary
- ✓ Useful and thematically linked structure
- ✓ Progressive practice
- ✓ Real-life conversation
- ✓ Cultural readings in the target language
- ✓ Connections to other disciplines . . . in French!
- ✓ Recycling and review
- ✓ **National Geographic Society** panoramas of the Francophone world

Recorded reading provides options for addressing various skills and learning styles.

Reading strategies help students read with ease.

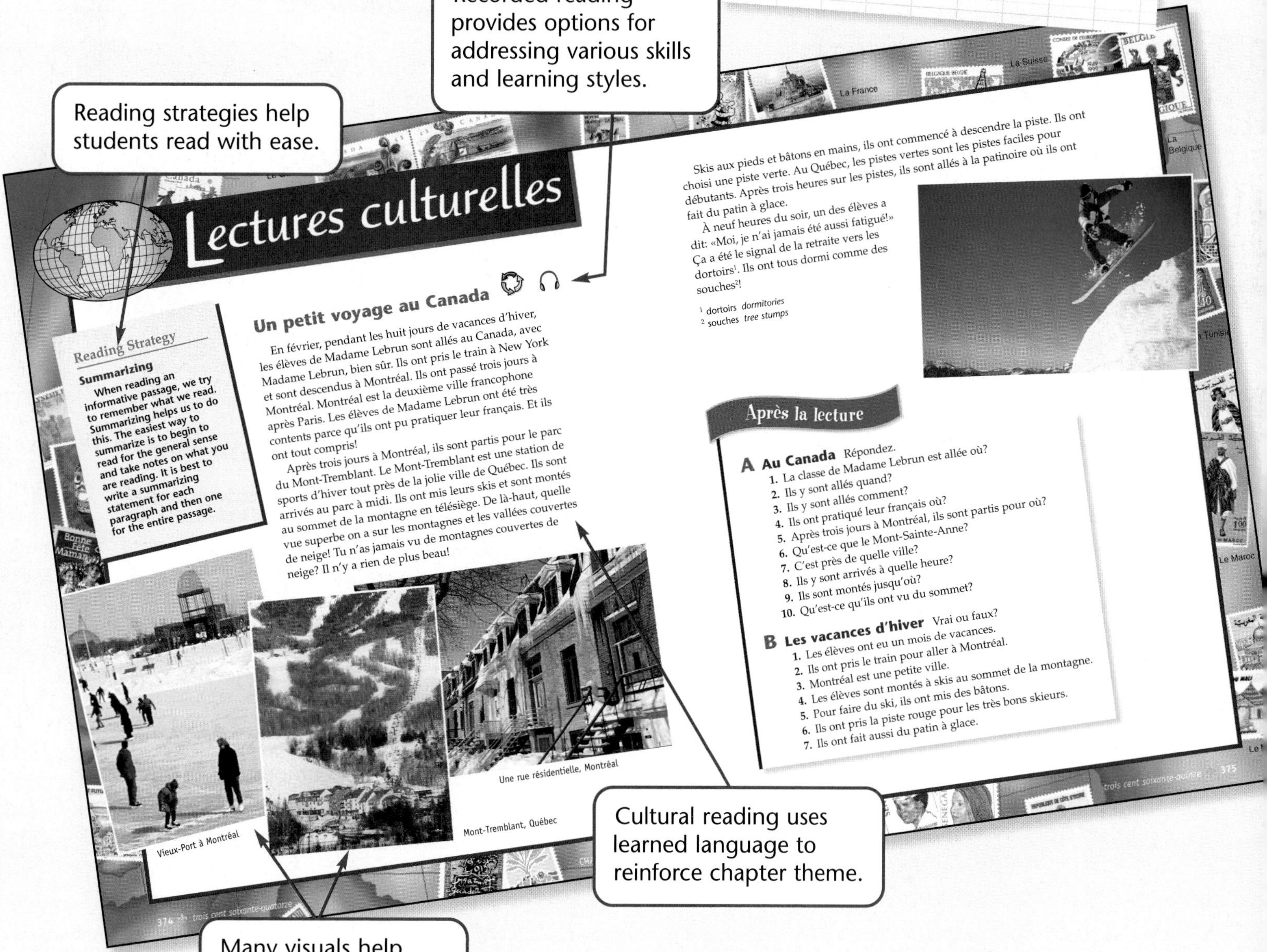

Lectures culturelles

Reading Strategy

Summarizing When reading an informative passage, we try to remember what we read. Summarizing helps us to do this. The easiest way to summarize is to begin to read for the general sense and take notes on what you are reading. It is best to write a summarizing statement for each paragraph and then one for the entire passage.

Un petit voyage au Canada

En février, pendant les huit jours de vacances d'hiver, les élèves de Madame Lebrun sont allés au Canada, avec Madame Lebrun, bien sûr. Ils ont pris le train à New York et sont descendus à Montréal. Ils ont passé trois jours à Montréal. Montréal est la deuxième ville francophone après Paris. Les élèves de Madame Lebrun ont été très contents parce qu'ils ont pu pratiquer leur français. Et ils ont tout compris!

Après trois jours à Montréal, ils sont partis pour le parc du Mont-Tremblant. Le Mont-Tremblant est une station de sports d'hiver tout près de la jolie ville de Québec. Ils sont arrivés au parc à midi. Ils ont mis leurs skis et sont montés au sommet de la montagne en télésiège. De là-haut, quelle vue superbe on a sur les montagnes et les vallées couvertes de neige! Tu n'as jamais vu de montagnes couvertes de neige? Il n'y a rien de plus beau!

Vieux-Port à Montréal

Mont-Tremblant, Québec

Une rue résidentielle, Montréal

374 trois cent soixante-quatorze

Skis aux pieds et bâtons en mains, ils ont commencé à descendre la piste. Ils ont choisi une piste verte. Au Québec, les pistes vertes sont les pistes faciles pour débutants. Après trois heures sur les pistes, ils sont allés à la patinoire où ils ont fait du patin à glace.

À neuf heures du soir, un des élèves a dit: «Moi, je n'ai jamais été aussi fatigué!» Ça a été le signal de la retraite vers les dortoirs[1]. Ils ont tous dormi comme des souches[2]!

[1] dortoirs *dormitories*
[2] souches *tree stumps*

Après la lecture

A Au Canada Répondez.
1. La classe de Madame Lebrun est allée où?
2. Ils y sont allés quand?
3. Ils y sont allés comment?
4. Ils ont pratiqué leur français où?
5. Après trois jours à Montréal, ils sont partis pour où?
6. Qu'est-ce que le Mont-Sainte-Anne?
7. C'est près de quelle ville?
8. Ils y sont arrivés à quelle heure?
9. Ils sont montés jusqu'où?
10. Qu'est-ce qu'ils ont vu du sommet?

B Les vacances d'hiver Vrai ou faux?
1. Les élèves ont eu un mois de vacances.
2. Ils ont pris le train pour aller à Montréal.
3. Montréal est une petite ville.
4. Les élèves sont montés à skis au sommet de la montagne.
5. Pour faire du ski, ils ont mis des bâtons.
6. Ils ont pris la piste rouge pour les très bons skieurs.
7. Ils ont fait aussi du patin à glace.

trois cent soixante-quinze 375

Cultural reading uses learned language to reinforce chapter theme.

Many visuals help students comprehend what they read.

Enrich students' cultural knowledge

Optional cultural readings reinforce the chapter theme.

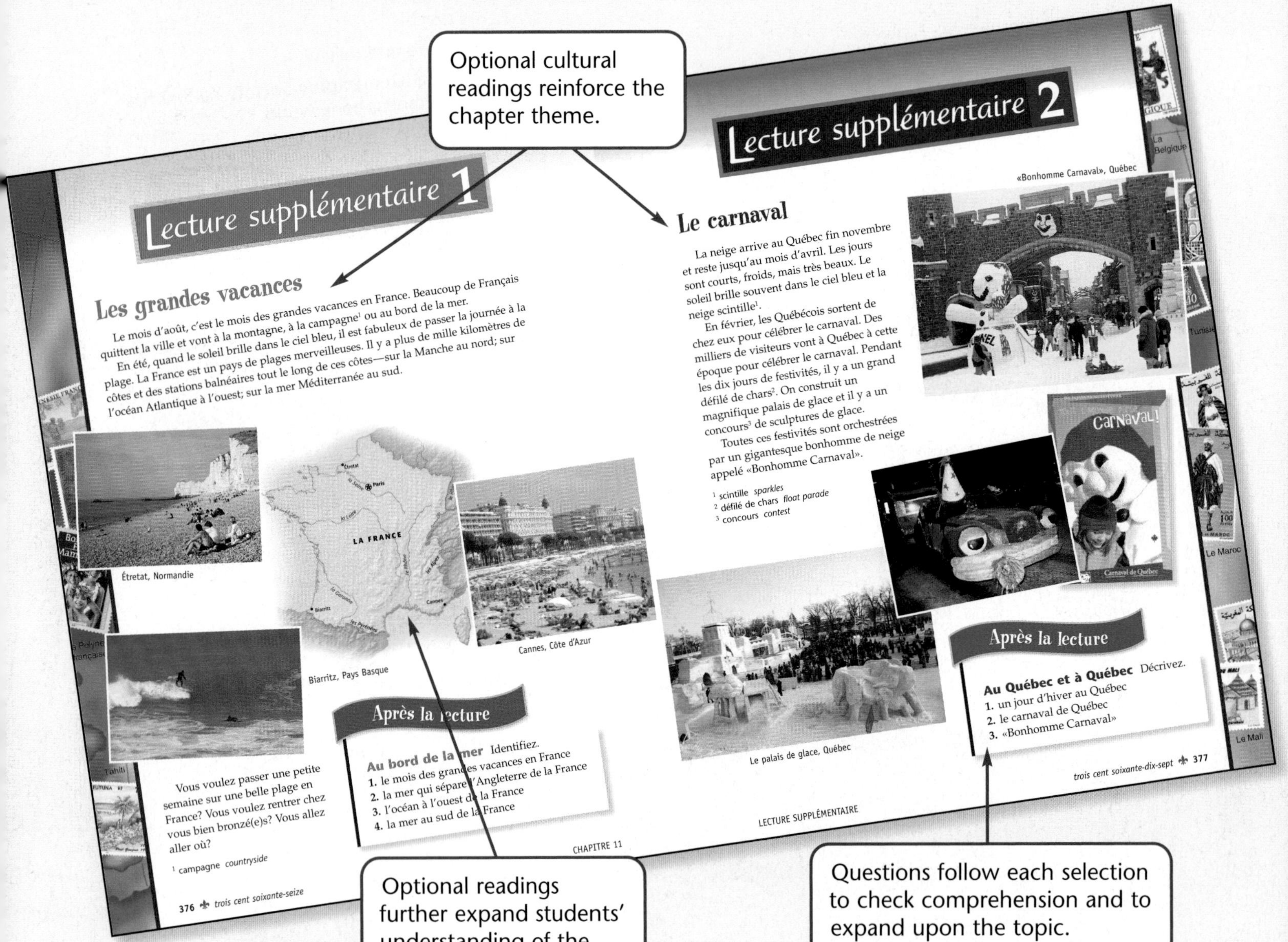

Lecture supplémentaire 1

Les grandes vacances

Le mois d'août, c'est le mois des grandes vacances en France. Beaucoup de Français quittent la ville et vont à la montagne, à la campagne[1] ou au bord de la mer.

En été, quand le soleil brille dans le ciel bleu, il est fabuleux de passer la journée à la plage. La France est un pays de plages merveilleuses. Il y a plus de mille kilomètres de côtes et des stations balnéaires tout le long de ces côtes—sur la Manche au nord; sur l'océan Atlantique à l'ouest; sur la mer Méditerranée au sud.

Étretat, Normandie

Cannes, Côte d'Azur

Biarritz, Pays Basque

Vous voulez passer une petite semaine sur une belle plage en France? Vous voulez rentrer chez vous bien bronzé(e)s? Vous allez aller où?

[1] campagne *countryside*

Après la lecture

Au bord de la mer Identifiez.
1. le mois des grandes vacances en France
2. la mer qui sépare l'Angleterre de la France
3. l'océan à l'ouest de la France
4. la mer au sud de la France

CHAPITRE 11

376 trois cent soixante-seize

Lecture supplémentaire 2

«Bonhomme Carnaval», Québec

Le carnaval

La neige arrive au Québec fin novembre et reste jusqu'au mois d'avril. Les jours sont courts, froids, mais très beaux. Le soleil brille souvent dans le ciel bleu et la neige scintille[1].

En février, les Québécois sortent de chez eux pour célébrer le carnaval. Des milliers de visiteurs vont à Québec à cette époque pour célébrer le carnaval. Pendant les dix jours de festivités, il y a un grand défilé de chars[2]. On construit un magnifique palais de glace et il y a un concours[3] de sculptures de glace.

Toutes ces festivités sont orchestrées par un gigantesque bonhomme de neige appelé «Bonhomme Carnaval».

[1] scintille *sparkles*
[2] défilé de chars *float parade*
[3] concours *contest*

Le palais de glace, Québec

Après la lecture

Au Québec et à Québec Décrivez.
1. un jour d'hiver au Québec
2. le carnaval de Québec
3. «Bonhomme Carnaval»

LECTURE SUPPLÉMENTAIRE

trois cent soixante-dix-sept 377

Optional readings further expand students' understanding of the Francophone world.

Questions follow each selection to check comprehension and to expand upon the topic.

Connect with other disciplines

Itinerary for Success

- ✓ Exposure to Francophone culture
- ✓ Clear expectations and goals
- ✓ Thematic, contextualized vocabulary
- ✓ Useful and thematically linked structure
- ✓ Progressive practice
- ✓ Real-life conversation
- ✓ Cultural readings in the target language
- ✓ Connections to other disciplines . . . in French!
- ✓ Recycling and review
- ✓ **National Geographic Society** panoramas of the Francophone world

Introduction to the **Connexions** provides the background for students to understand the reading.

CONNEXIONS

Les Beaux-Arts

La peinture

One may know a great deal or just a little about art. But almost everyone has at least some interest in art. How often have we heard, "I may not know anything about art, but I certainly know what I like"?

There is no doubt that France has produced many of the world's greatest artists. Do you recognize the names of these famous French artists: Renoir, Monet, Manet, Degas, Seurat, Boudin, Gauguin?

In 1874, two of these painters, Monet and Renoir, were among a group of artists who held a famous exhibition of their works in Paris. The critics laughed at their works and called the artists "Impressionists" to mock one of Monet's paintings entitled ***Impression, soleil levant***. Today, paintings by the Impressionists are among the most admired works in the history of art.

Claude Monet *La pie*

Claude Monet *La route sous la neige à Honfleur*

Les impressionnistes

On dit que les impressionnistes sont les peintres de la vie moderne. Ils ont peint la vie quotidienne[1] des gens (personnes) simples. Pour eux, tous les sujets sont bons. Ils ont peint des parcs, des gares, des usines[2]. Beaucoup de peintres impressionnistes ont préféré quitter leur atelier[3] pour aller peindre en plein air. Les scènes d'été et les scènes d'hiver sont des sujets favoris de plusieurs impressionnistes.

Voici deux tableaux de paysages d'hiver de Claude Monet—*La pie* et *La route sous la neige à Honfleur*.

[1] vie quotidienne *daily life*
[2] usines *factories*
[3] atelier *studio*

Voici maintenant des scènes de plage. Eugène Boudin a peint *La plage de Trouville*.

Ce tableau *Sur la plage* a été peint par l'ami de Monet, Édouard Manet.

Georges Seurat a peint *Les baigneurs à Asnières*. Asnières est dans la banlieue[4] parisienne sur la Seine. Au fond, on voit les cheminées des usines de Clichy. Il fait très chaud et les ouvriers[5] font un petit plongeon dans la Seine.

[4] banlieue *suburbs*
[5] ouvriers *workers*

Eugène Boudin *La plage de Trouville*

Édouard Manet *Sur la plage*

Georges Seurat *Les baigneurs à Asnières*

Après la lecture

A Un peu de géographie Find all the places mentioned where these artists painted.

B Mon tableau favori Pick your favorite painting, describe it, and explain why it is your favorite.

378 ✤ *trois cent soixante-dix-huit*

CHAPITRE 11

trois cent soixante-dix-neuf ✤ 379

Students further their knowledge of other disciplines—in French!

Encourage students to apply what they have learned

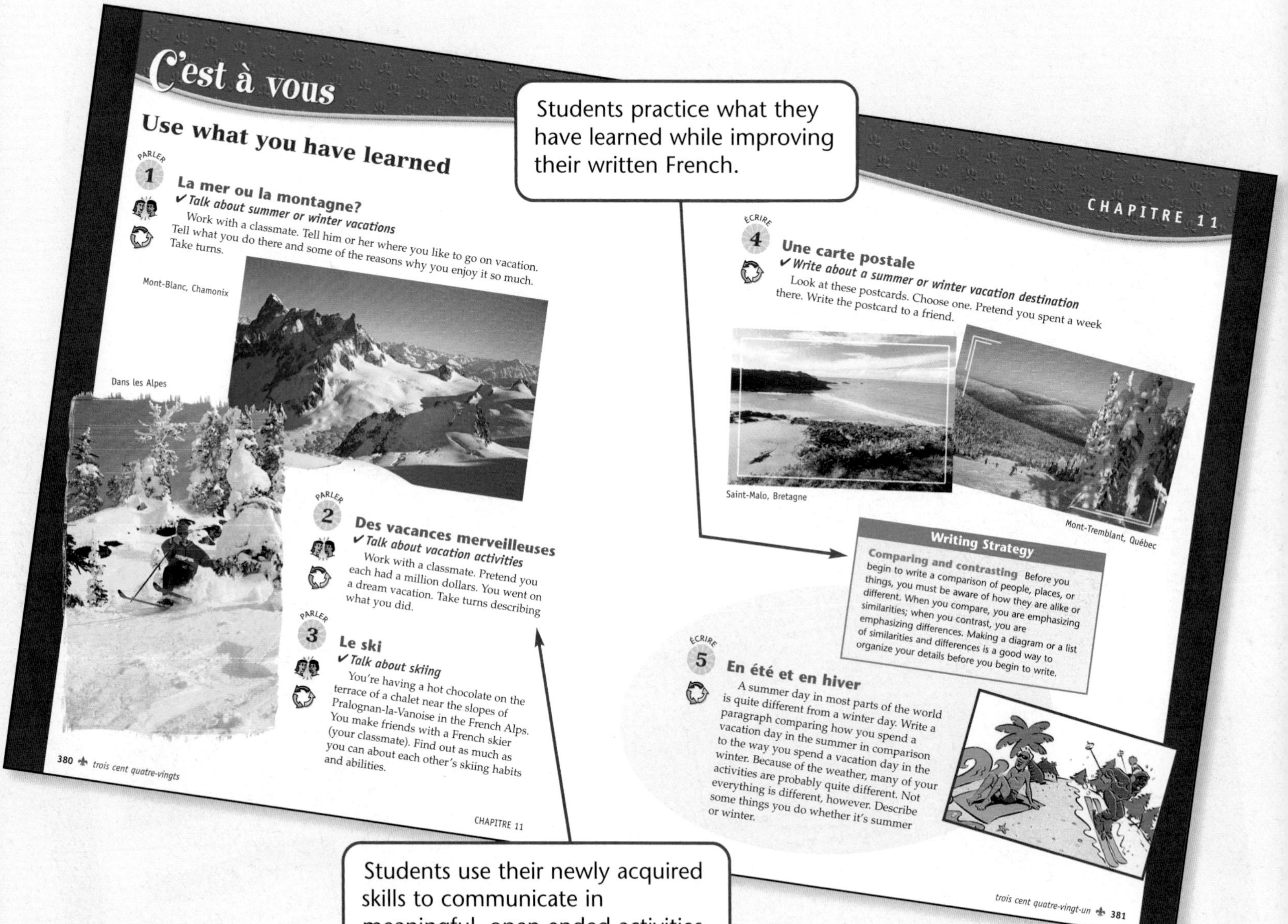
C'est à vous

Use what you have learned

PARLER 1 **La mer ou la montagne?**
✔ *Talk about summer or winter vacations*
Work with a classmate. Tell him or her where you like to go on vacation. Tell what you do there and some of the reasons why you enjoy it so much. Take turns.

Mont-Blanc, Chamonix

Dans les Alpes

PARLER 2 **Des vacances merveilleuses**
✔ *Talk about vacation activities*
Work with a classmate. Pretend you each had a million dollars. You went on a dream vacation. Take turns describing what you did.

PARLER 3 **Le ski**
✔ *Talk about skiing*
You're having a hot chocolate on the terrace of a chalet near the slopes of Pralognan-la-Vanoise in the French Alps. You make friends with a French skier (your classmate). Find out as much as you can about each other's skiing habits and abilities.

380 trois cent quatre-vingts

CHAPITRE 11

CHAPITRE 11

ÉCRIRE 4 **Une carte postale**
✔ *Write about a summer or winter vacation destination*
Look at these postcards. Choose one. Pretend you spent a week there. Write the postcard to a friend.

Saint-Malo, Bretagne

Mont-Tremblant, Québec

Writing Strategy
Comparing and contrasting Before you begin to write a comparison of people, places, or things, you must be aware of how they are alike or different. When you compare, you are emphasizing similarities; when you contrast, you are emphasizing differences. Making a diagram or a list of similarities and differences is a good way to organize your details before you begin to write.

ÉCRIRE 5 **En été et en hiver**
A summer day in most parts of the world is quite different from a winter day. Write a paragraph comparing how you spend a vacation day in the summer in comparison to the way you spend a vacation day in the winter. Because of the weather, many of your activities are probably quite different. Not everything is different, however. Describe some things you do whether it's summer or winter.

trois cent quatre-vingt-un 381

Students practice what they have learned while improving their written French.

Students use their newly acquired skills to communicate in meaningful, open-ended activities.

Check students' progress

Itinerary for Success
- ✓ Exposure to Francophone culture
- ✓ Clear expectations and goals
- ✓ Thematic, contextualized vocabulary
- ✓ Useful and thematically linked structure
- ✓ Progressive practice
- ✓ Real-life conversation
- ✓ Cultural readings in the target language
- ✓ Connections to other disciplines . . . in French!
- ✓ Recycling and review
- ✓ **National Geographic Society** panoramas of the Francophone world

Assessment activities give students a chance to see what they have really learned.

Yellow "sticky" notes direct students to the correct pages for review.

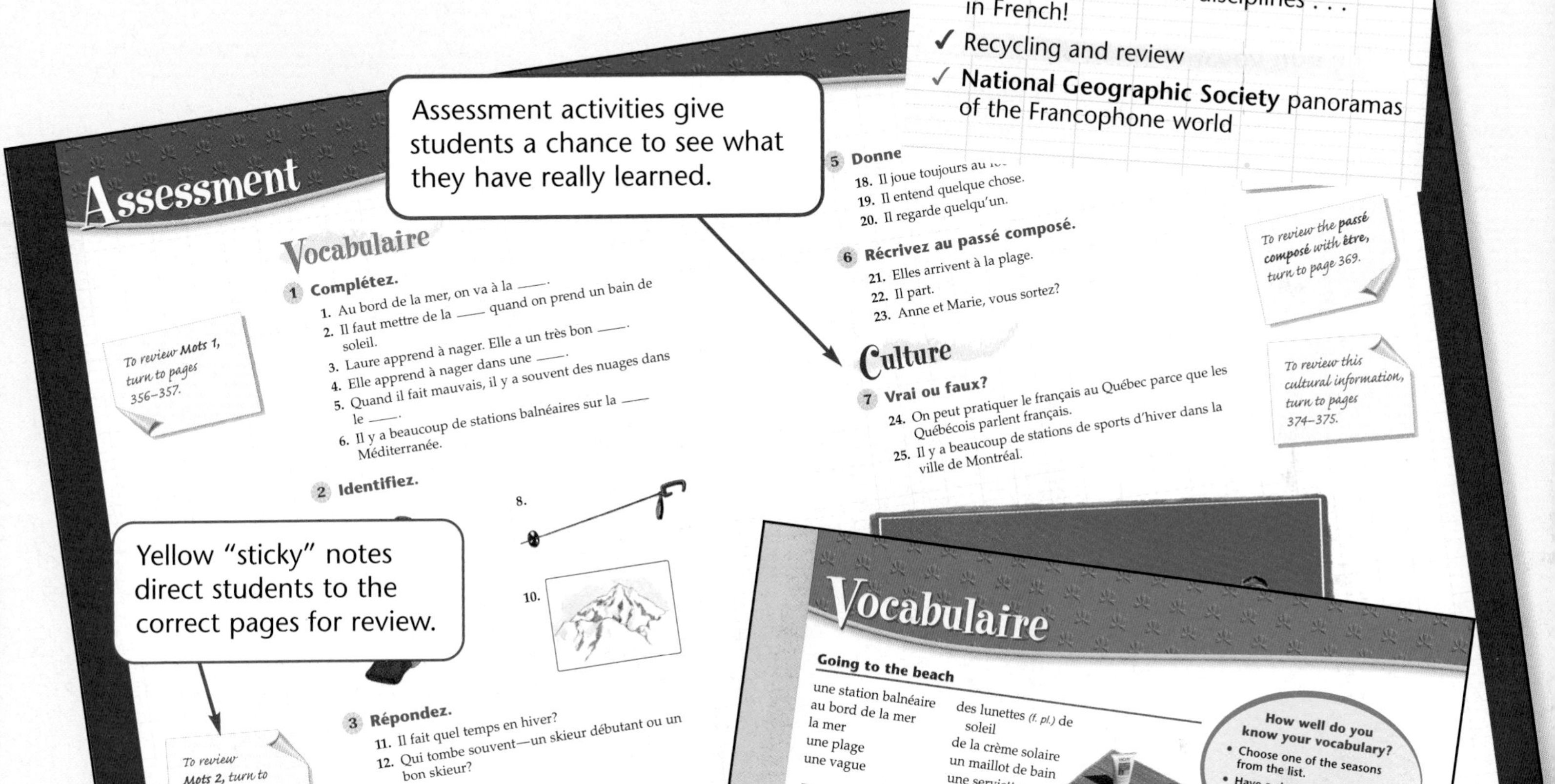

Assessment

Vocabulaire

1 Complétez.
1. Au bord de la mer, on va à la ____.
2. Il faut mettre de la ____ quand on prend un bain de soleil.
3. Laure apprend à nager. Elle a un très bon ____.
4. Elle apprend à nager dans une ____.
5. Quand il fait mauvais, il y a souvent des nuages dans le ____.
6. Il y a beaucoup de stations balnéaires sur la ____ Méditerranée.

To review Mots 1, turn to pages 356–357.

2 Identifiez.

8.

10.

3 Répondez.
11. Il fait quel temps en hiver?
12. Qui tombe souvent—un skieur débutant ou un bon skieur?

To review Mots 2, turn to pages 360–361.

Structure

4 Complétez au passé composé.
13. Il ____ des leçons de natation. (prendre)
14. Il ____ un très bon moniteur. (avoir)
15. Elles ____ un maillot de bain. (mettre)
16. J'____ une carte postale. (écrire)
17. Tu ____ le match? (voir)

To review irregular verbs in the passé composé, turn to page 364.

382 trois cent quatre-vingt-deux

5 Donne
18. Il joue toujours au ...
19. Il entend quelque chose.
20. Il regarde quelqu'un.

6 Récrivez au passé composé.
21. Elles arrivent à la plage.
22. Il part.
23. Anne et Marie, vous sortez?

To review the passé composé with être, turn to page 369.

Culture

7 Vrai ou faux?
24. On peut pratiquer le français au Québec parce que les Québécois parlent français.
25. Il y a beaucoup de stations de sports d'hiver dans la ville de Montréal.

To review this cultural information, turn to pages 374–375.

383

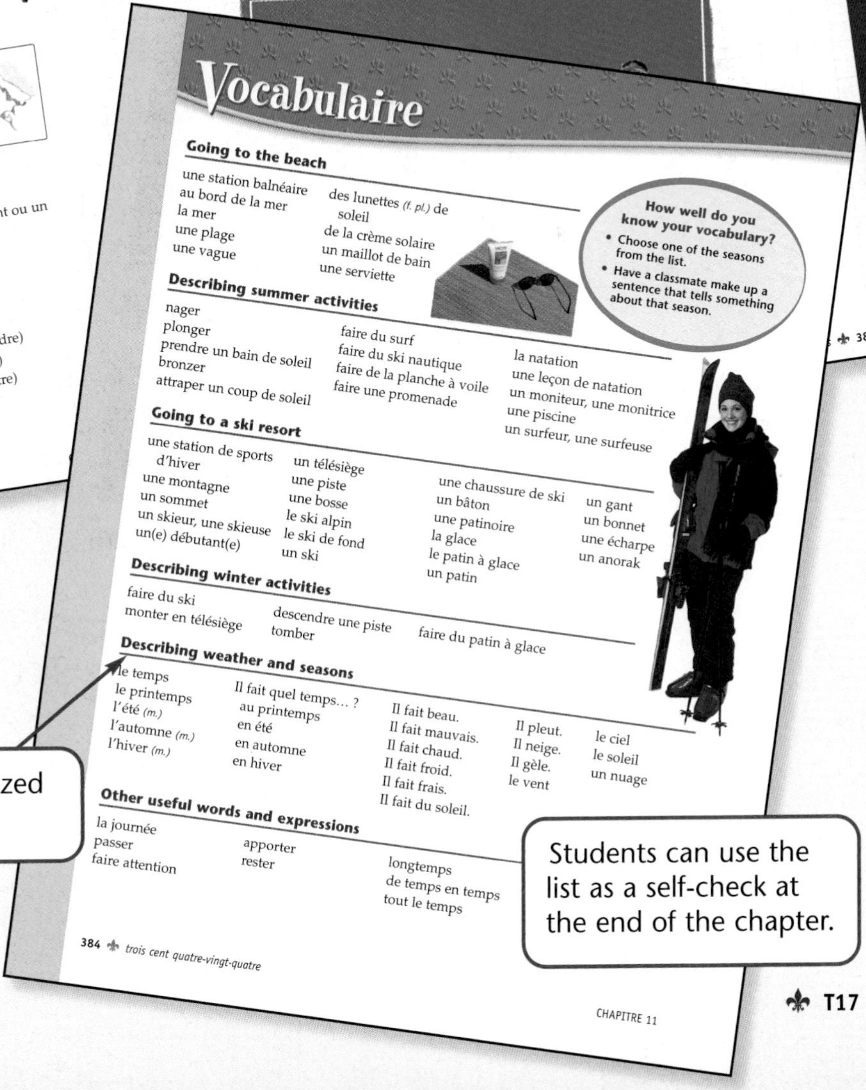

Vocabulaire

Going to the beach
une station balnéaire, au bord de la mer, la mer, une plage, une vague, des lunettes (f. pl.) de soleil, de la crème solaire, un maillot de bain, une serviette

How well do you know your vocabulary?
- Choose one of the seasons from the list.
- Have a classmate make up a sentence that tells something about that season.

Describing summer activities
nager, plonger, prendre un bain de soleil, bronzer, attraper un coup de soleil, faire du surf, faire du ski nautique, faire de la planche à voile, faire une promenade, la natation, une leçon de natation, un moniteur, une monitrice, une piscine, un surfeur, une surfeuse

Going to a ski resort
une station de sports d'hiver, une montagne, un sommet, un skieur, une skieuse, un(e) débutant(e), un télésiège, une piste, une bosse, le ski alpin, le ski de fond, un ski, une chaussure de ski, un bâton, une patinoire, la glace, le patin à glace, un patin, un gant, un bonnet, une écharpe, un anorak

Describing winter activities
faire du ski, monter en télésiège, descendre une piste, tomber, faire du patin à glace

Describing weather and seasons
le temps, le printemps, l'été (m.), l'automne (m.), l'hiver (m.), Il fait quel temps... ?, au printemps, en été, en automne, en hiver, Il fait beau., Il fait mauvais., Il fait chaud., Il fait froid., Il fait frais., Il fait du soleil., Il pleut., Il neige., Il gèle., le vent, le ciel, le soleil, un nuage

Other useful words and expressions
la journée, passer, faire attention, apporter, rester, longtemps, de temps en temps, tout le temps

384 trois cent quatre-vingt-quatre

Vocabulary is categorized to help recall.

Students can use the list as a self-check at the end of the chapter.

- Answer sheets for Assessment are provided in the Transparency Binder.

Take students beyond the text to learn more about culture and language

The **Bon voyage!** Video Program reinforces the themes and language of the text, making it enjoyable and comprehensible for the students.

Students read a synopsis to set the stage for the video.

Students will love getting acquainted with the **Bon voyage!** video characters.

Online activities give students more opportunities to further explore the chapter topic.

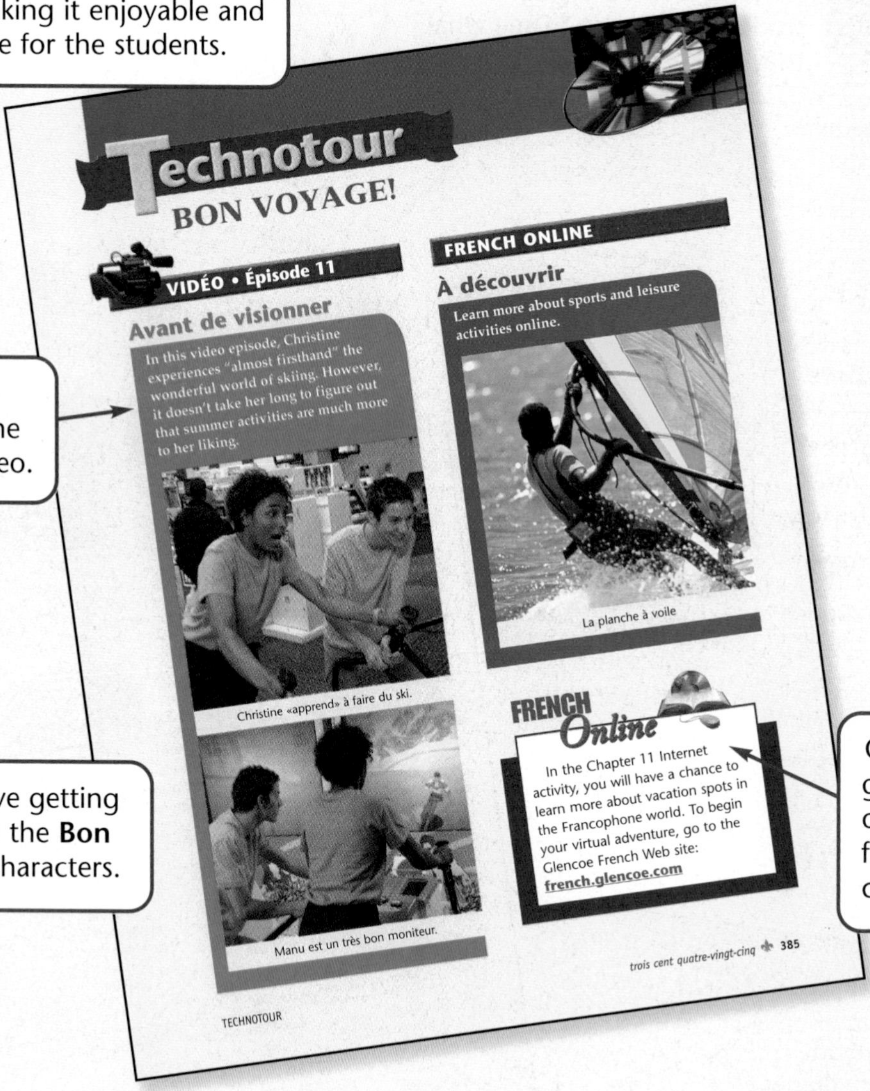
Technotour
BON VOYAGE!

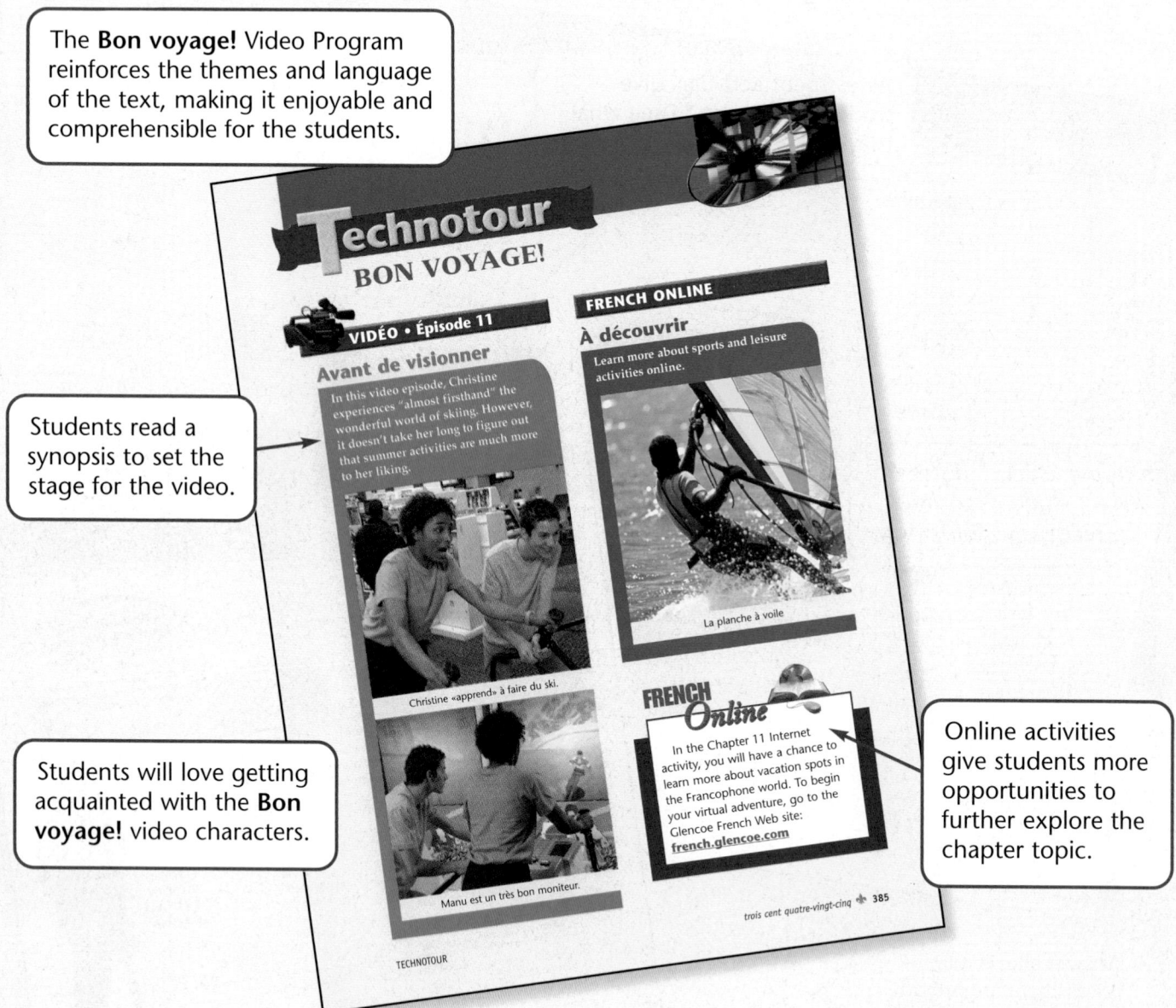

VIDÉO • Épisode 11

Avant de visionner

In this video episode, Christine experiences "almost firsthand" the wonderful world of skiing. However, it doesn't take her long to figure out that summer activities are much more to her liking.

Christine «apprend» à faire du ski.

Manu est un très bon moniteur.

FRENCH ONLINE

À découvrir

Learn more about sports and leisure activities online.

La planche à voile

FRENCH Online

In the Chapter 11 Internet activity, you will have a chance to learn more about vacation spots in the Francophone world. To begin your virtual adventure, go to the Glencoe French Web site: **french.glencoe.com**

trois cent quatre-vingt-cinq 385

TECHNOTOUR

Cultivate an appreciation of the diverse Francophone world with National Geographic Reflets

Itinerary for Success

- ✓ Exposure to Francophone culture
- ✓ Clear expectations and goals
- ✓ Thematic, contextualized vocabulary
- ✓ Useful and thematically linked structure
- ✓ Progressive practice
- ✓ Real-life conversation
- ✓ Cultural readings in the target language
- ✓ Connections to other disciplines . . . in French!
- ✓ Recycling and review
- ✓ **National Geographic Society** panoramas of the Francophone world

Students learn to appreciate the expanse of the Francophone world.

Stunning **National Geographic** photography illustrates the variety of the Francophone world.

Enhance appreciation of literature and culture

Itinerary for Success

- ✓ Exposure to Francophone culture
- ✓ Clear expectations and goals
- ✓ Thematic, contextualized vocabulary
- ✓ Useful and thematically linked structure
- ✓ Progressive practice
- ✓ Real-life conversation
- ✓ Cultural readings in the target language
- ✓ Connections to other disciplines . . . in French!
- ✓ Recycling and review
- ✓ **National Geographic Society** panoramas of the Francophone world

Literary Companion affords students yet another opportunity to apply their reading skills in French.

Literary selections present another view of Francophone culture.

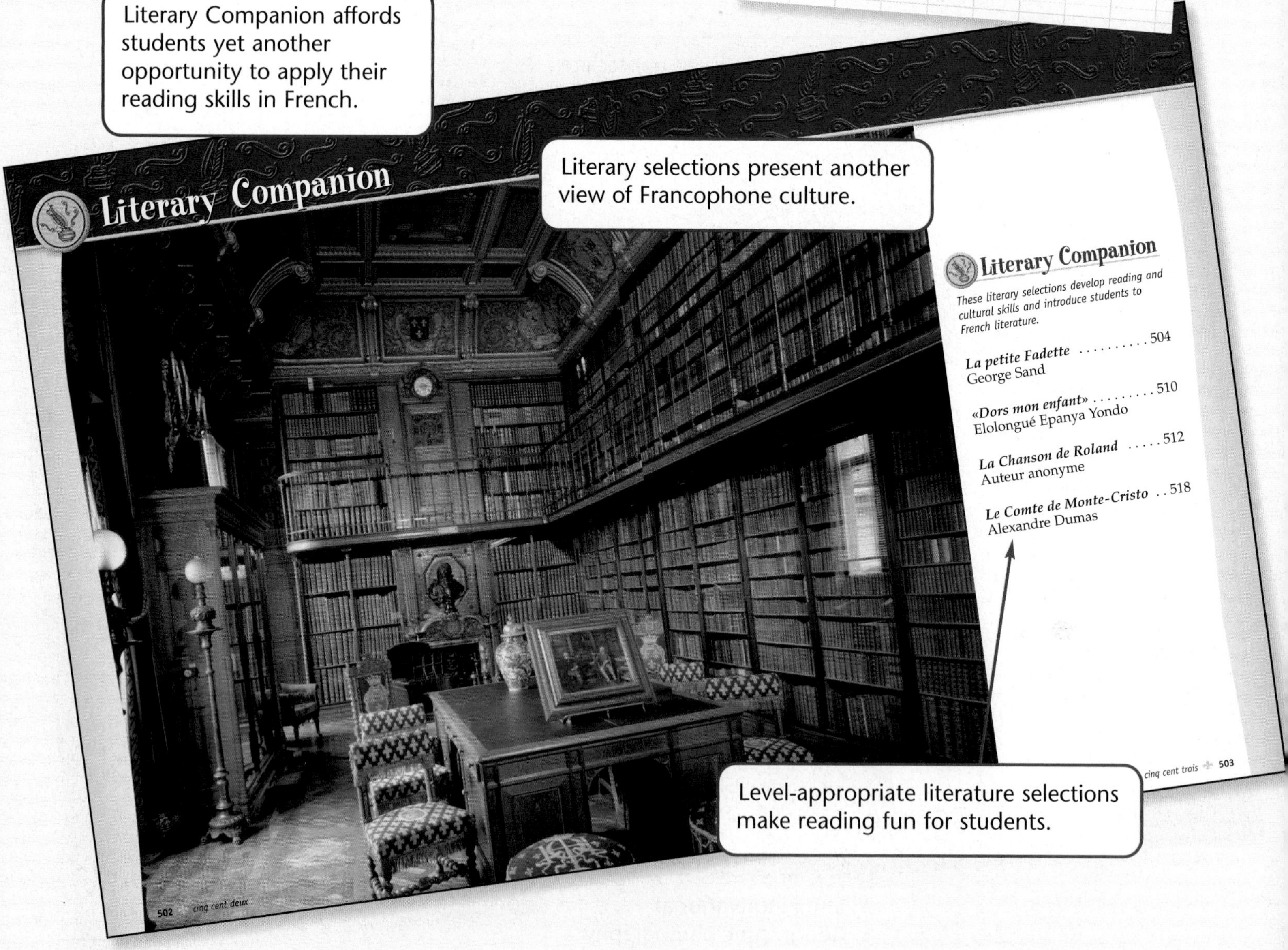
Literary Companion
Literary Companion
These literary selections develop reading and cultural skills and introduce students to French literature.
La petite Fadette 504
George Sand
«Dors mon enfant» 510
Elolongué Epanya Yondo
La Chanson de Roland 512
Auteur anonyme
Le Comte de Monte-Cristo .. 518
Alexandre Dumas
502 cinq cent deux
cinq cent trois 503

Level-appropriate literature selections make reading fun for students.

Pacing and priorities

Each chapter of **Bon voyage!** contains required, recommended, and optional material. **Vocabulaire, Structure,** and **Conversation** sections are always required. The recommended sections include the first cultural reading in **Lectures culturelles, C'est à vous,** and **Assessment. Lectures supplémentaires, Connexions,** and **Technotour** are optional. The following chart provides you with a guide to the number of required, recommended, and optional pages in each of the fourteen chapters.

Chapter Planning in the Student Edition

	required number of pages	recommended number of pages	optional number of pages
Chapter 1	17	7	8
Chapter 2	17	7	8
Chapter 3	17	7	8
Chapter 4	19	7	8
Chapter 5	17	7	8
Chapter 6	17	7	8
Chapter 7	17	7	8
Chapter 8	17	7	8
Chapter 9	15	7	8
Chapter 10	15	7	8
Chapter 11	13	7	8
Chapter 12	15	7	8
Chapter 13	15	7	8
Chapter 14	15	7	8
Total:	226 required	98 recommended	112 optional

Note: Chapters 13 and 14 of **Bon voyage! Level 1** are repeated as Chapters 1 and 2 of **Bon voyage! Level 2** for additional flexibility.

Preview and objectives let you know what to plan for

Spotlight on Culture gives you facts and information about the art and photographs on the page. Your students will think you know everything.

References to the National Standards are made for you.

CHAPITRE 3
Preview
In this chapter, students will learn to talk about their school and afterschool activities. They will also learn to identify, describe, and shop for school supplies. They will learn to use singular forms of -er verbs to communicate in various situations that arise when shopping. They will also learn to express likes and dislikes.
National Standards
Communication
In Chapter 3, students will communicate in spoken and written French to talk about school and afterschool activities. Students will engage in conversations, provide and obtain information, and exchange opinions as they fulfill the chapter objectives listed on this page.
CHAPITRE 3
Pendant et après les cours
Objectifs
In this chapter you will learn to:
talk about what you do in school
talk about what you and your friends do after school
identify and shop for school supplies
talk about what you don't do
tell what you and others like and don't like to do
discuss schools in France
Pierre Auguste Renoir La lecture
80
FRENCH Online
The Glencoe World Language Web site (french.glencoe.com) offers several options that enable you and your students to experience the French-speaking world via the Internet:
• The online Activités are correlated to the chapters and utilize francophone Web sites around the world. For the Chapter 3 activity, see student page 109.
• Games and puzzles afford students another opportunity to practice the material learned
• The Enrichment section offers students an opportunity to visit Web sites related to the theme of the chapter for more information on a particular topic.
• Online Chapter Quizzes offer students an opportunity to prepare for a chapter test.
• Visit our virtual Café for more opportunities to practice and explore the French-speaking world.
80
CHAPITRE 3
Spotlight on Culture
Photograph This photo is of a group of students on a quai along the Seine River in Paris. In this area, there are many stalls of bouquinistes where one can buy old books, drawings, records, etc.
Painting This painting, La lecture, was done by Pierre Auguste Renoir (1841–1919). At the age of twenty-two, Renoir met Monet, Sisley, and Bazille and went to paint with them in the Fontainbleau Forest. Renoir exhibited his paintings in the first exposition of the Impressionists in 1874.
In 1881 he took a trip to Italy where he was completely taken by the works of Raphael. This caused him to distance himself a little from the Impressionists, adopting a somewhat more classical style.
In La lecture, we see a young girl at a table reading. Although Renoir's works dealt with many themes, he did several famous paintings with children, such as Madame Charpentier et ses enfants (1878) and Jeunes filles au piano (1892).
Chapter Projects
Patrick et moi After students have completed the structure section of the chapter, have them undertake a project that compares their day with that of Patrick in the Vocabulaire sections. For example: Patrick habite près de Paris. Moi, je n'habite pas près de Paris. J'habite près de ____. Patrick habite rue Saint-Paul et moi j'habite ____. This can be either a written or an oral project. Patrick appears in both Mots 1 and 2.
Après les cours Have students in your class survey the student body for information about afterschool activities. If the survey is restricted to the activities taught in Mots 1 and 2, students can report back in French. Each person interviewed should initial the interview sheet to avoid repetition.
Une papeterie You may wish to have students set up a papeterie in the classroom where they can take on the roles of cashier and customer. Stock the papeterie with the school supplies learned in the vocabulary sections. Include a toy cash register, play money, and prices for the items. Students may work in pairs or small groups to prepare at least three questions and three answers to include in their dialogue. Give each pair/group a chance to rehearse their "skit" and then have pairs/groups present their vignette to the class.
81

Get some great ideas for fun activities from Chapter Projects.

French Online gives you ideas for expanding your lesson—virtually.

Step-by-step hints help you through the chapter

Resource Manager lets you know which resources you will need for each part of the chapter.

Bellringer Reviews (also available in the Transparency Binder) provide quick checks of previously taught material.

Clear, step-by-step instruction guides your presentation of the lesson.

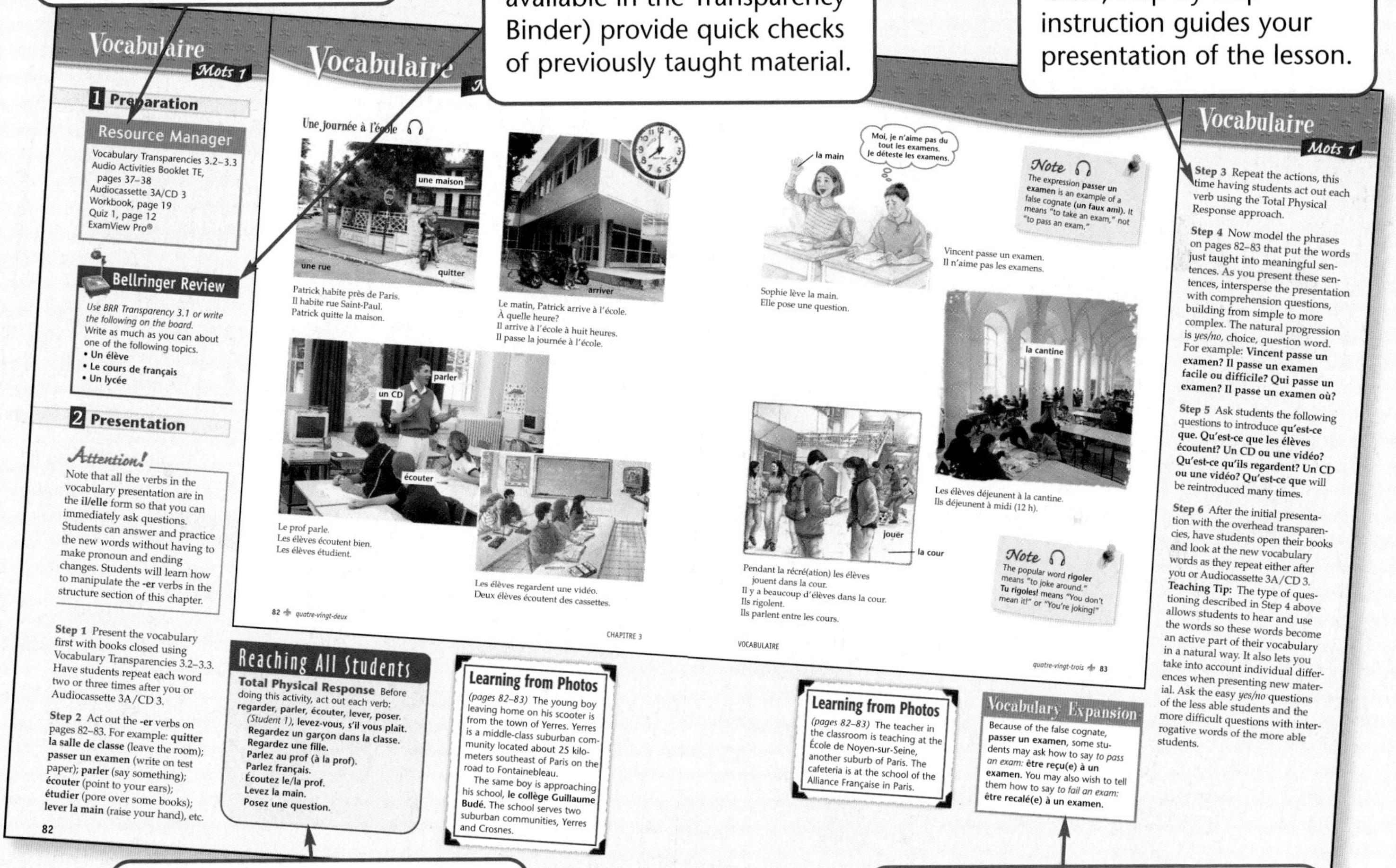

Vocabulaire
Mots 1

1 Preparation

Resource Manager
Vocabulary Transparencies 3.2–3.3
Audio Activities Booklet TE, pages 37–38
Audiocassette 3A/CD 3
Workbook, page 19
Quiz 1, page 12
ExamView Pro®

Bellringer Review
Use BRR Transparency 3.1 or write the following on the board.
Write as much as you can about one of the following topics.
- **Un élève**
- **Le cours de français**
- **Un lycée**

2 Presentation

Attention!
Note that all the verbs in the vocabulary presentation are in the **il/elle** form so that you can immediately ask questions. Students can answer and practice the new words without having to make pronoun and ending changes. Students will learn how to manipulate the **-er** verbs in the structure section of this chapter.

Step 1 Present the vocabulary first with books closed using Vocabulary Transparencies 3.2–3.3. Have students repeat each word two or three times after you or Audiocassette 3A/CD 3.

Step 2 Act out the **-er** verbs on pages 82–83. For example: **quitter la salle de classe** (leave the room); **passer un examen** (write on test paper); **parler** (say something); **écouter** (point to your ears); **étudier** (pore over some books); **lever la main** (raise your hand), etc.

82

Vocabulaire

Une journée à l'école

Patrick habite près de Paris.
Il habite rue Saint-Paul.
Patrick quitte la maison.

Le matin, Patrick arrive à l'école.
À quelle heure?
Il arrive à l'école à huit heures.
Il passe la journée à l'école.

Le prof parle.
Les élèves écoutent bien.
Les élèves étudient.

Les élèves regardent une vidéo.
Deux élèves écoutent des cassettes.

82 quatre-vingt-deux

CHAPITRE 3

la main
Moi, je n'aime pas du tout les examens. Je déteste les examens.

Sophie lève la main.
Elle pose une question.

Vincent passe un examen.
Il n'aime pas les examens.

Note
The expression **passer un examen** is an example of a false cognate (**un faux ami**). It means "to take an exam," not "to pass an exam."

Les élèves déjeunent à la cantine.
Ils déjeunent à midi (12 h).

Pendant la récré(ation) les élèves jouent dans la cour.
Il y a beaucoup d'élèves dans la cour.
Ils rigolent.
Ils parlent entre les cours.

Note
The popular word **rigoler** means "to joke around." **Tu rigoles!** means "You don't mean it!" or "You're joking!"

VOCABULAIRE

quatre-vingt-trois 83

Vocabulaire
Mots 1

Step 3 Repeat the actions, this time having students act out each verb using the Total Physical Response approach.

Step 4 Now model the phrases on pages 82–83 that put the words just taught into meaningful sentences. As you present these sentences, intersperse the presentation with comprehension questions, building from simple to more complex. The natural progression is *yes/no*, choice, question word. For example: **Vincent passe un examen? Il passe un examen facile ou difficile? Qui passe un examen? Il passe un examen où?**

Step 5 Ask students the following questions to introduce **qu'est-ce que. Qu'est-ce que les élèves écoutent? Un CD ou une vidéo? Qu'est-ce qu'ils regardent? Un CD ou une vidéo? Qu'est-ce que** will be reintroduced many times.

Step 6 After the initial presentation with the overhead transparencies, have students open their books and look at the new vocabulary words as they repeat either after you or Audiocassette 3A/CD 3.
Teaching Tip: The type of questioning described in Step 4 above allows students to hear and use the words so these words become an active part of their vocabulary in a natural way. It also lets you take into account individual differences when presenting new material. Ask the easy *yes/no* questions of the less able students and the more difficult questions with interrogative words of the more able students.

Reaching All Students
Total Physical Response Before doing this activity, act out each verb: **regarder, parler, écouter, lever, poser.**
(Student 1), **levez-vous, s'il vous plaît.**
Regardez un garçon dans la classe.
Regardez une fille.
Parlez au prof (à la prof).
Parlez français.
Écoutez le/la prof.
Levez la main.
Posez une question.

Learning from Photos
(pages 82–83) The young boy leaving home on his scooter is from the town of Yerres. Yerres is a middle-class suburban community located about 25 kilometers southeast of Paris on the road to Fontainebleau.
The same boy is approaching his school, **le collège Guillaume Budé.** The school serves two suburban communities, Yerres and Crosnes.

Learning from Photos
(pages 82–83) The teacher in the classroom is teaching at the École de Noyen-sur-Seine, another suburb of Paris. The cafeteria is at the school of the Alliance Française in Paris.

Vocabulary Expansion
Because of the false cognate, **passer un examen,** some students may ask how to say *to pass an exam:* **être reçu(e) à un examen.** You may also wish to tell them how to say *to fail an exam:* **être recalé(e) à un examen.**

Reaching All Students offers alternate activities to meet the diverse needs of your students.

Vocabulary Expansion enriches your vocabulary and suggests extra vocabulary for your students.

Painless presentation of structure makes it easier for you to reach your students

Attention! points out potential problems and gives you tips for avoiding them.

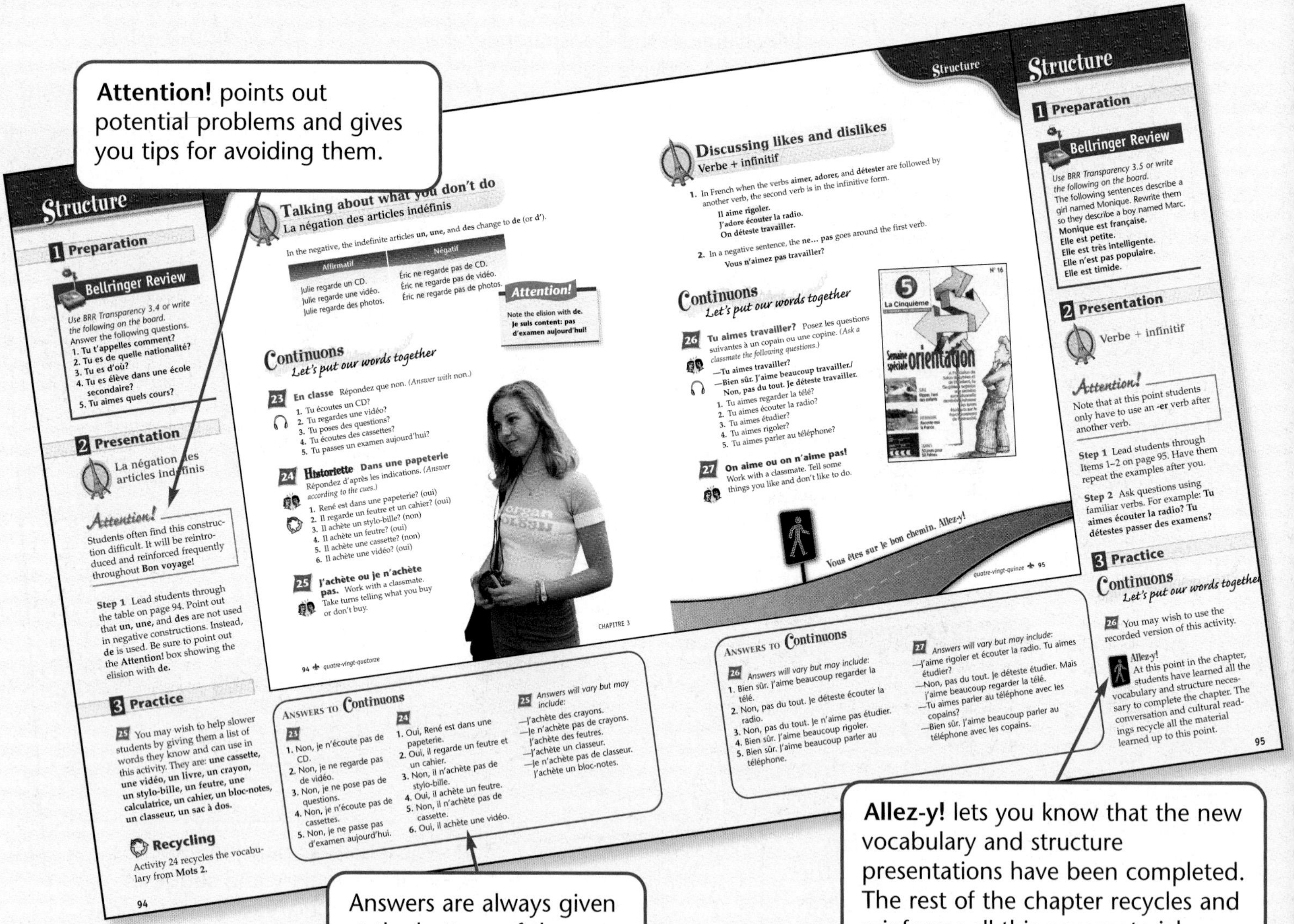
Structure

1 Preparation

Bellringer Review

Use BRR Transparency 3.4 or write the following on the board. Answer the following questions.
1. Tu t'appelles comment?
2. Tu es de quelle nationalité?
3. Tu es d'où?
4. Tu es élève dans une école secondaire?
5. Tu aimes quels cours?

2 Presentation

La négation des articles indéfinis

Attention!
Students often find this construction difficult. It will be reintroduced and reinforced frequently throughout Bon voyage!

Step 1 Lead students through the table on page 94. Point out that un, une, and des are not used in negative constructions. Instead, de is used. Be sure to point out the Attention! box showing the elision with de.

3 Practice

25 You may wish to help slower students by giving them a list of words they know and can use in this activity. They are: une cassette, une vidéo, un livre, un crayon, un stylo-bille, un feutre, une calculatrice, un cahier, un bloc-notes, un classeur, un sac à dos.

Recycling
Activity 24 recycles the vocabulary from Mots 2.

94

Talking about what you don't do
La négation des articles indéfinis

In the negative, the indefinite articles un, une, and des change to de (or d').

Affirmatif	Négatif
Julie regarde un CD.	Éric ne regarde pas de CD.
Julie regarde une vidéo.	Éric ne regarde pas de vidéo.
Julie regarde des photos.	Éric ne regarde pas de photos.

Attention!
Note the elision with de.
Je suis content: pas d'examen aujourd'hui!

Continuons
Let's put our words together

23 En classe Répondez que non. (Answer with non.)
1. Tu écoutes un CD?
2. Tu regardes une vidéo?
3. Tu poses des questions?
4. Tu écoutes des cassettes?
5. Tu passes un examen aujourd'hui?

24 Historiette Dans une papeterie
Répondez d'après les indications. (Answer according to the cues.)
1. René est dans une papeterie? (oui)
2. Il regarde un feutre et un cahier? (oui)
3. Il achète un stylo-bille? (non)
4. Il achète un feutre? (oui)
5. Il achète une cassette? (non)
6. Il achète une vidéo? (oui)

25 J'achète ou je n'achète pas. Work with a classmate. Take turns telling what you buy or don't buy.

94 quatre-vingt-quatorze — CHAPITRE 3

Structure

Discussing likes and dislikes
Verbe + infinitif

1. In French when the verbs aimer, adorer, and détester are followed by another verb, the second verb is in the infinitive form.
Il aime rigoler.
J'adore écouter la radio.
On déteste travailler.

2. In a negative sentence, the ne... pas goes around the first verb.
Vous n'aimez pas travailler?

Continuons
Let's put our words together

26 Tu aimes travailler? Posez les questions suivantes à un copain ou une copine. (Ask a classmate the following questions.)
—Tu aimes travailler?
—Bien sûr. J'aime beaucoup travailler./ Non, pas du tout. Je déteste travailler.
1. Tu aimes regarder la télé?
2. Tu aimes écouter la radio?
3. Tu aimes étudier?
4. Tu aimes rigoler?
5. Tu aimes parler au téléphone?

27 On aime ou on n'aime pas! Work with a classmate. Tell some things you like and don't like to do.

Vous êtes sur le bon chemin. Allez-y!

quatre-vingt-quinze 95

Structure

1 Preparation

Bellringer Review

Use BRR Transparency 3.5 or write the following on the board. The following sentences describe a girl named Monique. Rewrite them so they describe a boy named Marc.
Monique est française.
Elle est petite.
Elle est très intelligente.
Elle n'est pas populaire.
Elle est timide.

2 Presentation

Verbe + infinitif

Attention!
Note that at this point students only have to use an -er verb after another verb.

Step 1 Lead students through Items 1–2 on page 95. Have them repeat the examples after you.

Step 2 Ask questions using familiar verbs. For example: Tu aimes écouter la radio? Tu détestes passer des examens?

3 Practice

Continuons
Let's put our words together

26 You may wish to use the recorded version of this activity.

Allez-y!
At this point in the chapter, students have learned all the vocabulary and structure necessary to complete the chapter. The conversation and cultural readings recycle all the material learned up to this point.

95

Answers to Continuons

23
1. Non, je n'écoute pas de CD.
2. Non, je ne regarde pas de vidéo.
3. Non, je ne pose pas de questions.
4. Non, je n'écoute pas de cassettes.
5. Non, je ne passe pas d'examen aujourd'hui.

24
1. Oui, René est dans une papeterie.
2. Oui, il regarde un feutre et un cahier.
3. Non, il n'achète pas de stylo-bille.
4. Oui, il achète un feutre.
5. Non, il n'achète pas de cassette.
6. Oui, il achète une vidéo.

25 Answers will vary but may include:
—J'achète des crayons.
—Je n'achète pas de crayons.
J'achète des feutres.
—J'achète un classeur.
—Je n'achète pas de classeur.
J'achète un bloc-notes.

Answers to Continuons

26 Answers will vary but may include:
1. Bien sûr. J'aime beaucoup regarder la télé.
2. Non, pas du tout. Je déteste écouter la radio.
3. Non, pas du tout. Je n'aime pas étudier.
4. Bien sûr. J'aime beaucoup rigoler.
5. Bien sûr. J'aime beaucoup parler au téléphone.

27 Answers will vary but may include:
—J'aime rigoler et écouter la radio. Tu aimes étudier?
—Non, pas du tout. Je déteste étudier. Mais j'aime beaucoup regarder la télé.
—Tu aimes parler au téléphone avec les copains?
—Bien sûr. J'aime beaucoup parler au téléphone avec les copains.

Answers are always given at the bottom of the page for easy reference.

Allez-y! lets you know that the new vocabulary and structure presentations have been completed. The rest of the chapter recycles and reinforces all this new material.

Help your students feel confident about their speaking skills

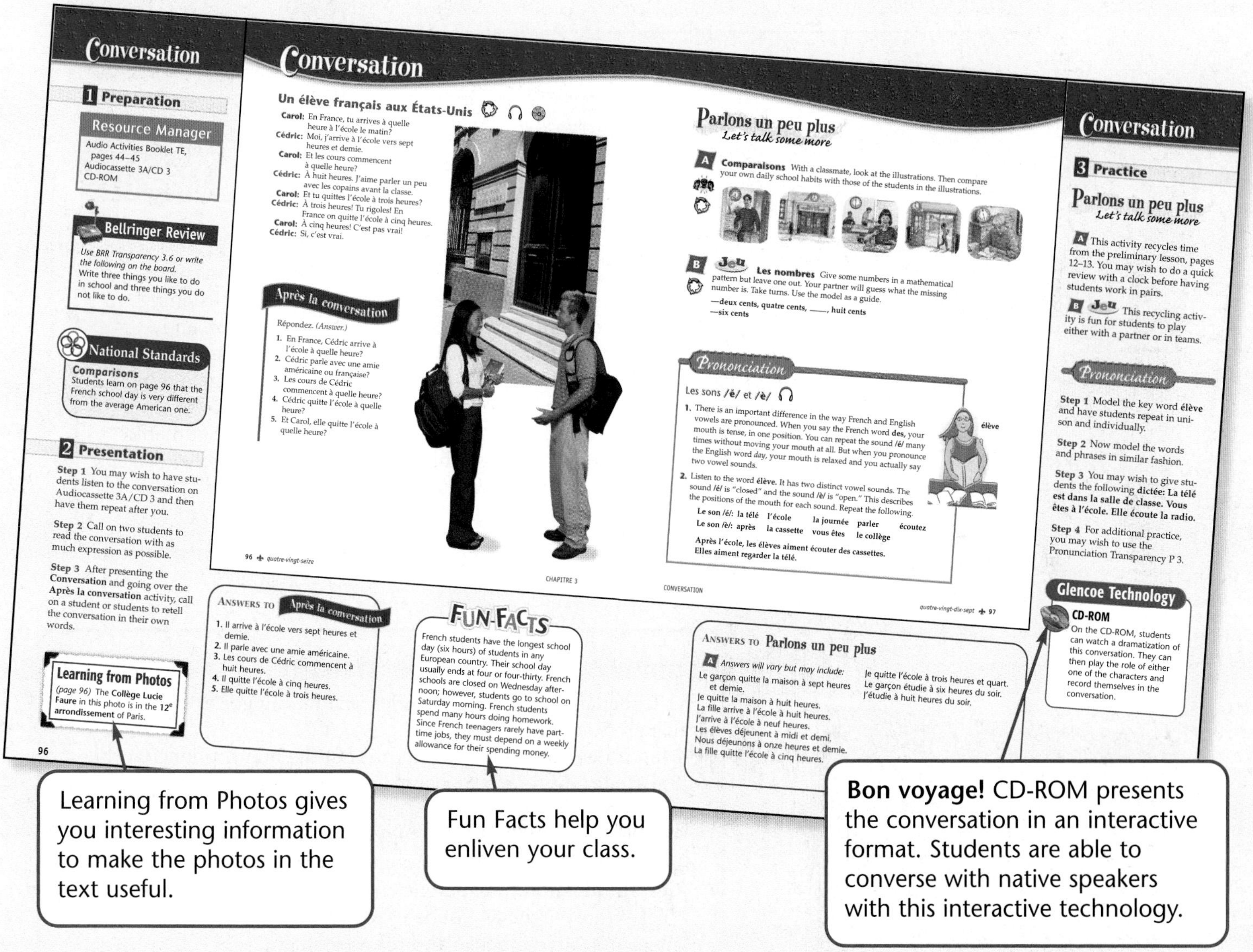

Conversation

1 Preparation

Resource Manager

Audio Activities Booklet TE, pages 44–45
Audiocassette 3A/CD 3
CD-ROM

Bellringer Review

Use BRR Transparency 3.6 or write the following on the board.
Write three things you like to do in school and three things you do not like to do.

National Standards

Comparisons
Students learn on page 96 that the French school day is very different from the average American one.

2 Presentation

Step 1 You may wish to have students listen to the conversation on Audiocassette 3A/CD 3 and then have them repeat after you.

Step 2 Call on two students to read the conversation with as much expression as possible.

Step 3 After presenting the **Conversation** and going over the **Après la conversation** activity, call on a student or students to retell the conversation in their own words.

Learning from Photos

(page 96) The **Collège Lucie Faure** in this photo is in the 12e **arrondissement** of Paris.

96

Conversation

Un élève français aux États-Unis

Carol: En France, tu arrives à quelle heure à l'école le matin?
Cédric: Moi, j'arrive à l'école vers sept heures et demie.
Carol: Et les cours commencent à quelle heure?
Cédric: À huit heures. J'aime parler un peu avec les copains avant la classe.
Carol: Et tu quittes l'école à trois heures?
Cédric: À trois heures! Tu rigoles! En France on quitte l'école à cinq heures.
Carol: À cinq heures! C'est pas vrai!
Cédric: Si, c'est vrai.

Après la conversation

Répondez. *(Answer.)*

1. En France, Cédric arrive à l'école à quelle heure?
2. Cédric parle avec une amie américaine ou française?
3. Les cours de Cédric commencent à quelle heure?
4. Cédric quitte l'école à quelle heure?
5. Et Carol, elle quitte l'école à quelle heure?

96 ✣ *quatre-vingt-seize*

CHAPITRE 3

Parlons un peu plus
Let's talk some more

A Comparaisons With a classmate, look at the illustrations. Then compare your own daily school habits with those of the students in the illustrations.

B Jeu Les nombres Give some numbers in a mathematical pattern but leave one out. Your partner will guess what the missing number is. Take turns. Use the model as a guide.
—deux cents, quatre cents, ____, huit cents
—six cents

Prononciation

Les sons /é/ et /è/

1. There is an important difference in the way French and English vowels are pronounced. When you say the French word **des,** your mouth is tense, in one position. You can repeat the sound /é/ many times without moving your mouth at all. But when you pronounce the English word *day,* your mouth is relaxed and you actually say two vowel sounds.
2. Listen to the word **élève.** It has two distinct vowel sounds. The sound /é/ is "closed" and the sound /è/ is "open." This describes the positions of the mouth for each sound. Repeat the following.

élève

Le son /é/: la télé l'école la journée parler écoutez
Le son /è/: après la cassette vous êtes le collège

Après l'école, les élèves aiment écouter des cassettes. Elles aiment regarder la télé.

CONVERSATION

quatre-vingt-dix-sept ✣ 97

Conversation

3 Practice

Parlons un peu plus
Let's talk some more

A This activity recycles time from the preliminary lesson, pages 12–13. You may wish to do a quick review with a clock before having students work in pairs.

B Jeu This recycling activity is fun for students to play either with a partner or in teams.

Prononciation

Step 1 Model the key word **élève** and have students repeat in unison and individually.

Step 2 Now model the words and phrases in similar fashion.

Step 3 You may wish to give students the following **dictée: La télé est dans la salle de classe. Vous êtes à l'école. Elle écoute la radio.**

Step 4 For additional practice, you may wish to use the Pronunciation Transparency P 3.

Glencoe Technology

CD-ROM
On the CD-ROM, students can watch a dramatization of this conversation. They can then play the role of either one of the characters and record themselves in the conversation.

Answers to Après la conversation

1. Il arrive à l'école vers sept heures et demie.
2. Il parle avec une amie américaine.
3. Les cours de Cédric commencent à huit heures.
4. Il quitte l'école à cinq heures.
5. Elle quitte l'école à trois heures.

Fun Facts

French students have the longest school day (six hours) of students in any European country. Their school day usually ends at four or four-thirty. French schools are closed on Wednesday afternoon; however, students go to school on Saturday morning. French students spend many hours doing homework. Since French teenagers rarely have part-time jobs, they must depend on a weekly allowance for their spending money.

Answers to Parlons un peu plus

A *Answers will vary but may include:*
Le garçon quitte la maison à sept heures et demie.
Je quitte la maison à huit heures.
La fille arrive à l'école à huit heures.
J'arrive à l'école à neuf heures.
Les élèves déjeunent à midi et demi.
Nous déjeunons à onze heures et demie.
La fille quitte l'école à cinq heures.
Je quitte l'école à trois heures et quart.
Le garçon étudie à six heures du soir.
J'étudie à huit heures du soir.

Learning from Photos gives you interesting information to make the photos in the text useful.

Fun Facts help you enliven your class.

Bon voyage! CD-ROM presents the conversation in an interactive format. Students are able to converse with native speakers with this interactive technology.

Bon voyage! Resources

Build proficiency in all language skills

Provide More Practice!

The **Writing Activities Workbook** includes numerous activities to reinforce the material presented in the Student Edition. The activities are varied to provide several ways for the students to practice and apply what they have learned in class. Further reading and writing skills and cultural knowledge with **Mon autobiographie** and **Un peu plus.** The students can prepare for assessment using the Self-Test after each unit.

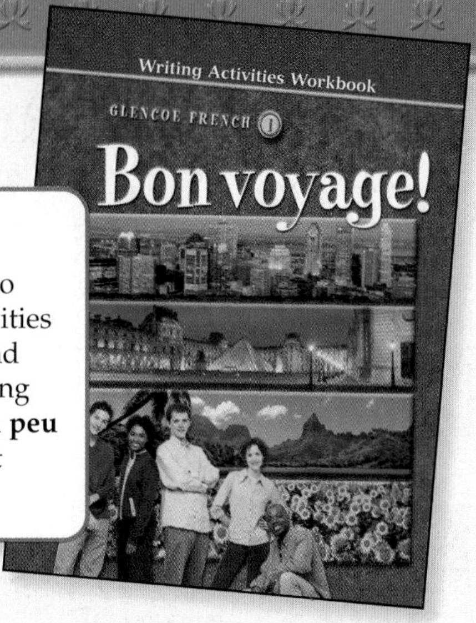

Improve Listening and Speaking Skills!

The **Bon voyage! Audio Program** (available on cassette or on CD) supports the Student Edition with listening practice for the **Mots, Structure, Conversation**, and **Prononciation** sections of each chapter. Many new activities are provided in addition to those signaled in the Student Edition with the earphones. The **Deuxième partie** of each recorded chapter includes more authentic listening selections. The **Audio Activities Booklet** contains worksheets for the students to use with the Audio Program.

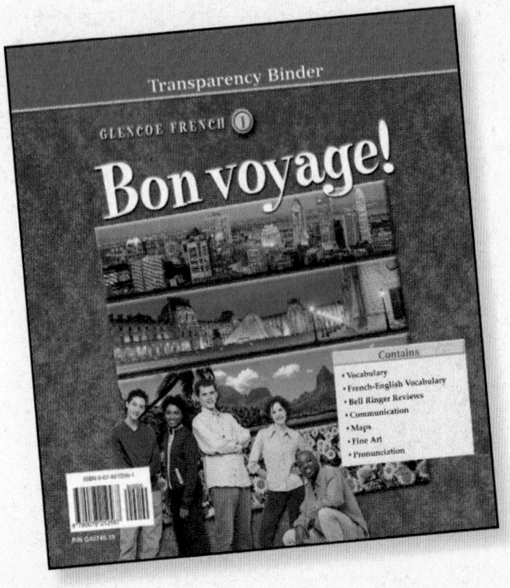

Enhance Your Lessons Visually!

The **Transparency Binder** includes several categories of transparencies:

- **Map** transparencies help you present the Francophone world.
- **Bellringer Review** transparencies provide a quick review activity to begin the class.
- **Vocabulary** transparencies support your presentation of the vocabulary and provide for continued reinforcement.
- **Communication** transparencies illustrate the chapter theme. These transparencies can be used for written and oral communicative practice and for assessment.
- **Assessment** transparencies with answers replicate the Assessment pages of the text so you can review the answers with your students in class.
- **Vocabulary Translations** transparencies provide the French-to-English translations of the chapter vocabulary.
- **Fine Art** transparencies are full-color reproductions of works of famous artists. These transparencies can be used to reinforce cultural topics introduced in the text.

Bring French to life!

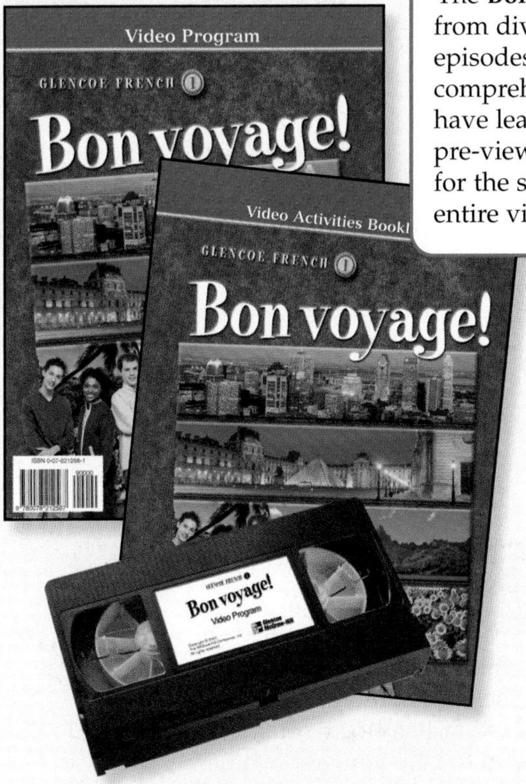

The **Bon voyage! Video Program** features teens from diverse parts of the Francophone world. The episodes follow the text thematically to aid comprehension and to reinforce what the students have learned. The Video Activities Booklet provides pre-viewing, viewing, and post-viewing activities for the students. It also contains the script for the entire video along with culture notes.

TPR Storytelling Booklet stories are written to reinforce the chapter themes and vocabulary. Once you have presented the chapter-specific story, your students will have fun acting it out and retelling it in their own words.

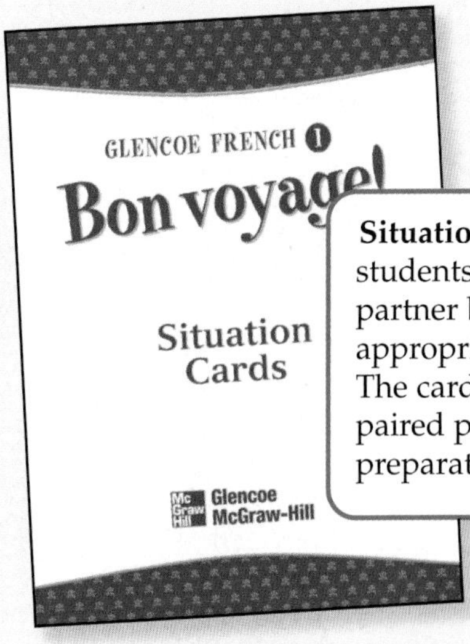

Situation Cards encourage students to communicate with a partner by suggesting a chapter-appropriate situation to discuss. The cards may be used for paired practice, assessment preparation, or assessment.

Interactive Conversation CD-ROM allows students to view the Conversation section of the text on video and to become an active participant in the conversation. They listen and record their own responses within the conversation.

FRENCH Online

Glencoe French Online gives students many opportunities to review, practice, and explore. There are chapter-related activities, online quizzes, and many links to Web sites throughout the vast Francophone world. Go to french.glencoe.com

Assess what they have learned!

The MindJogger Videoquiz Program is a test preparation tool in gameshow format. Students "play" three rounds of the game to review the material they have learned in each chapter. Instructions for playing the game are included in the package.

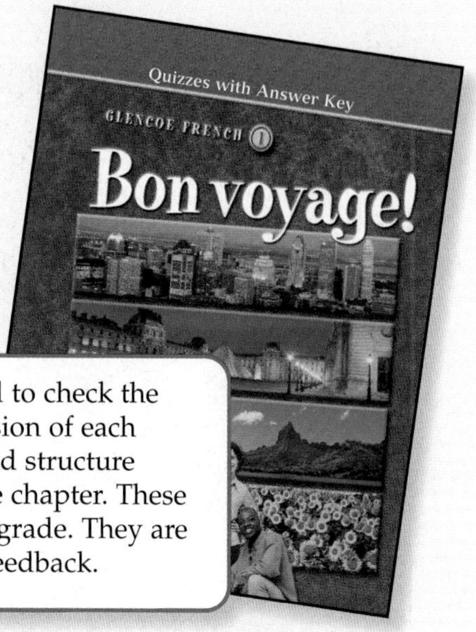

Quizzes are provided to check the students' comprehension of each vocabulary section and structure point presented in the chapter. These are short and easy to grade. They are ideal for immediate feedback.

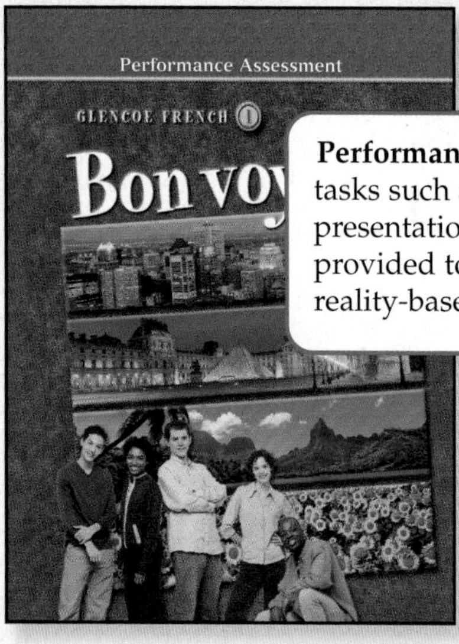

Performance Assessment provides tasks such as interviews, research, presentations, and skits. Rubrics are provided to help you grade these reality-based tasks.

Test Booklet with Answer Key includes chapter tests for Reading, Writing, Listening, (an audio recording of the listening tests is available on CD or on cassette) and Speaking, which can be administered together or separately. In addition to the Chapter Tests, Unit Tests are included to follow each Revision section of the Student Edition. Also included are Chapter Proficiency Tests designed to measure the students' mastery on a more global level.

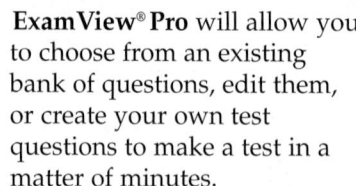

ExamView® Pro will allow you to choose from an existing bank of questions, edit them, or create your own test questions to make a test in a matter of minutes.

We can help make your job easier!

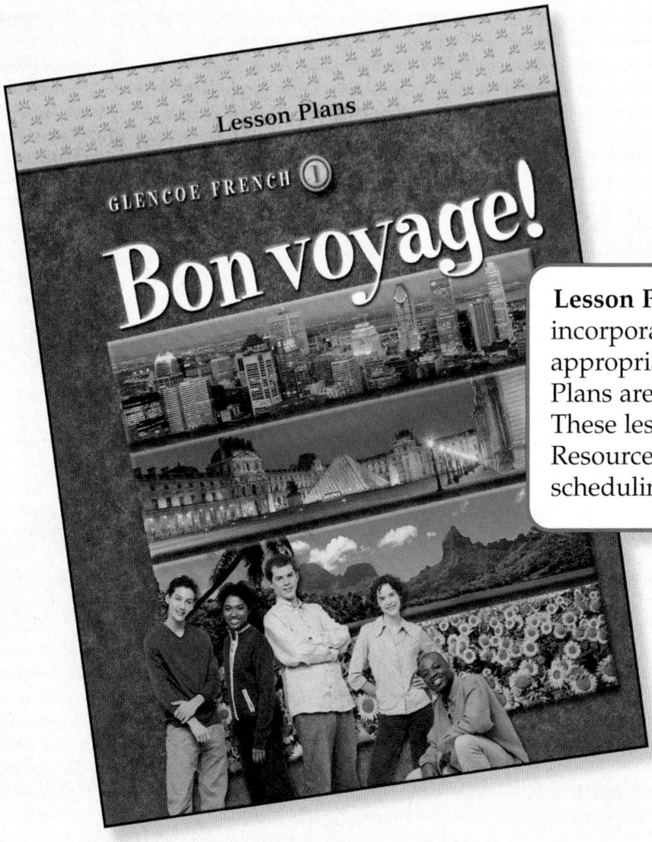

Lesson Plans are written for you. The lesson plans incorporate the Program Resources at their most appropriate point of use. Block Schedule Lesson Plans are provided for classes on the Block Schedule. These lesson plans also incorporate the Program Resources and are flexible for the various block-scheduling configurations.

The **Interactive Lesson Planner** allows you to put your lesson plans into a customized calendar and to adjust them as necessary.

The **Bon voyage! Interactive Teacher Edition (ITE)** is your entire Teacher Wraparound Edition on disk. It includes your printed ancillaries as well. This tool will ease your preparation time and lighten your book bag.

French Names

The following are some French boys' and girls' names that you may wish to give to your students.

Garçons

Alain
Albert
Alexandre
Alexis
André
Antoine
Arnaud
Baptiste
Benjamin
Benoît
Bernard
Bertrand
Bruno
Cédric
Charles
Christian
Christophe
Claude
Clément
Daniel
David
Denis
Didier
Dominique
Édouard
Emmanuel
Éric
Étienne
Fabrice
Florian
François
Franck
Frédéric
Georges
Gérard
Gilbert
Gilles
Grégoire
Guillaume
Guy
Henri
Hervé
Hugo
Jacques
Jean
Jérôme
Joseph
Julien
Laurent
Loïc
Louis
Lucas
Marc
Marcel
Martin
Matthieu
Maxime
Michel
Nicolas
Olivier
Pascal
Patrice
Patrick
Paul
Philippe
Pierre
Quentin
Raoul
Raphaël
Raymond
Rémi
René
Richard
Robert
Roger
Roland
Romain
Sébastien
Serge
Stéphane
Sylvain
Théo
Thierry
Thomas
Tristan
Valentin
Victor
Vincent
Xavier
Yann
Yves

Filles

Alice
Anaïs
Andrée
Angèle
Anne
Annick
Antoinette
Arlette
Béatrice
Bénédicte
Bernadette
Brigitte
Camille
Carole
Caroline
Catherine
Cécile
Chantal
Chloé
Christiane
Christine
Clara
Claire
Claude
Claudine
Colette
Corinne
Danielle
Denise
Diane
Dominique
Dorothée
Élisabeth
Émilie
Emma
Ève
Évelyne
Florence
Francine
Françoise
Gabrielle
Geneviève
Hélène
Inès
Irène
Isabelle
Jacqueline
Janine
Jeanne
Julie
Juliette
Justine
Laura
Laure
Laurence
Léa
Liliane
Lise
Louise
Lucie
Madeleine
Magali
Manon
Marguerite
Marianne
Marie
Marine
Martine
Maryse
Mathilde
Michèle
Mireille
Monique
Morgane
Nadine
Nathalie
Nicole
Océane
Odile
Pascale
Patricia
Pauline
Renée
Sabine
Sandrine
Sarah
Simone
Solange
Sophie
Stéphanie
Suzanne
Sylvie
Thérèse
Valérie
Véronique
Virginie

Classroom Expressions

Below is a list of words and expressions frequently used when conducting a French class.

du papier	paper
une feuille de papier	sheet of paper
un cahier	notebook
un cahier d'exercices	workbook
un stylo	pen
un stylo-bille	ballpoint pen
un crayon	pencil
une gomme	(pencil) eraser
une craie	chalk
le tableau	chalkboard
une brosse	chalkboard eraser
la corbeille	wastebasket
un pupitre	desk
un rang	row
une chaise	chair
un écran	screen
un projecteur	projector
une cassette	cassette
un livre	book
une règle	ruler
un ordinateur	computer
une vidéo	video
un CD	CD

Viens.	**Venez.**	Come.
Va.	**Allez.**	Go.
Entre.	**Entrez.**	Enter.
Sors.	**Sortez.**	Leave.
Attends.	**Attendez.**	Wait.
Mets.	**Mettez.**	Put.
Donne-moi.	**Donnez-moi.**	Give me.
Dis-moi.	**Dites-moi.**	Tell me.
Apporte-moi.	**Apportez-moi.**	Bring me.
Répète.	**Répétez.**	Repeat.
Pratique.	**Pratiquez.**	Practice.
Étudie.	**Étudiez.**	Study.
Réponds.	**Répondez.**	Answer.
Apprends.	**Apprenez.**	Learn.
Choisis.	**Choisissez.**	Choose.
Prépare.	**Préparez.**	Prepare.
Regarde.	**Regardez.**	Look at.
Décris.	**Décrivez.**	Describe.
Commence.	**Commencez.**	Begin.
Prononce.	**Prononcez.**	Pronounce.
Écoute.	**Écoutez.**	Listen.
Parle.	**Parlez.**	Speak.
Lis.	**Lisez.**	Read.
Écris.	**Écrivez.**	Write.
Demande.	**Demandez.**	Ask.
Suis le modèle.	**Suivez le modèle.**	Follow the model.
Joue le rôle de...	**Jouez le rôle de...**	Take the part of . . .
Prends.	**Prenez.**	Take.
Ouvre.	**Ouvrez.**	Open.
Ferme.	**Fermez.**	Close.
Tourne la page.	**Tournez la page.**	Turn the page.
Efface.	**Effacez.**	Erase.
Continue.	**Continuez.**	Continue.
Assieds-toi.	**Asseyez-vous.**	Sit down.
Lève-toi.	**Levez-vous.**	Get up.
Lève la main.	**Levez la main.**	Raise your hand.
Tais-toi.	**Taisez-vous.**	Be quiet.
Fais attention.	**Faites attention.**	Pay attenion.

Attention.	Attention.
Attention, s'il vous plaît.	Your attention please.
Silence.	Quiet.
Encore.	Again.
Encore une fois.	Once again.
Un à un.	One at a time.
Tous ensemble.	All together.
À haute voix.	Out loud.
Plus haut, s'il vous plaît.	Louder, please.
En français.	In French.
En anglais.	In English.

Standards for Foreign Language Learning

Bon voyage! has been written to help you meet the Standards for Foreign Language Learning as set forth by ACTFL. The focus of the text is to provide students with the skills they need to create language for communication. Culture is integrated throughout the text, from the basic introduction of vocabulary to the photographic contributions of the National Geographic Society. Special attention has been given to meeting the standard of Connections with a reading in French in each chapter about another discipline. Linguistic and cultural comparisons are made throughout the text. Suggestions are made for activities that encourage students to use their language skills in their immediate community and more distant ones. Students who complete the **Bon voyage!** series are prepared to participate in the Francophone World.

Specific correlations to each chapter are provided on the teacher pages preceeding each chapter.

Communication

Communicate in Languages Other Than English	**Standard 1.1**	Students engage in conversations, provide and obtain information, express feelings and emotions, and exchange opinions.
	Standard 1.2	Students understand and interpret written and spoken language on a variety of topics.
	Standard 1.3	Students present information, concepts, and ideas to an audience of listeners or readers on a variety of topics.

Cultures

Gain Knowledge and Understanding of Other Cultures	**Standard 2.1**	Students demonstrate an understanding of the relationship between the practices and perspectives of the culture studied.
	Standard 2.2	Students demonstrate an understanding of the relationship between the products and perspectives of the culture studied.

Connections

Connect with Other Disciplines and Acquire Information	**Standard 3.1**	Students reinforce and further their knowledge of other disciplines through the foreign language.
	Standard 3.2	Students acquire information and recognize the distinctive viewpoints that are only available through the foreign language and its cultures.

Comparisons

Develop Insight into the Nature of Language and Culture	**Standard 4.1**	Students demonstrate understanding of the nature of language through comparisons of language studied and their own.
	Standard 4.2	Students demonstrate understanding of the concept of culture through comparisons of the cultures studied and their own.

Communities

Participate in Multilingual Communities at Home and Around the World	**Standard 5.1**	Students use the language both within and beyond the school setting.
	Standard 5.2	Students show evidence of becoming life-long learners by using the language for personal enjoyment and enrichment.

Glencoe's **Bon voyage!** is based on a proven methodology that enables students to understand and to apply a language system. Students are introduced to new material in meaningful contexts and then given a multitude of opportunities to practice and apply what they have learned. The varied presentation and practice and the reinforcement that occurs through the upward spiraling in the text helps teachers reach all levels of students. The clear and succinct explanations and the highly visual aspect of the text make it approachable for students at a range of ability levels and for English Language Learners who cannot rely on complex explanations in English. Special activities in the Teacher Wraparound Edition marked Reaching All Students give suggestions for modifying activities for Universal Access. Teachers have a variety of tools to evaluate what students can do with their language skills each step of the way. The Glencoe methodology follows the same logical sequence of building language proficiency as the California Language Learning Continuum.

On the opening page of each chapter of **Bon voyage!** you will see examples of activities in which your students will be exposed to the required functions, content, and context as stated on the Continuum. A more extensive listing can be found in the Guide to Evaluating Glencoe's **Bon voyage!**

The example below is the correlation to Chapter 1. For each category we list page numbers and activities. Bold numbers indicate the specific activity referred to in the page reference. The italicized *i, p,* and *m* indicate introduced, practiced and learned to mastery. Below is an example of:

Correlations to Continuum

Stage I
Greet and respond. p. 31 (**21**, *p*); Introduce and respond. p. 31 (**21**, *i*); Engage in conversations. p. 32 (**25**, **26**, *i*), p. 34 (*p*), p. 42 (**2**, *m*); Obtain information. pp. 18–19 (*i*), p. 21 (**5**, *p*), p. 33 (**30**, *p*), p. 42 (**3**, *m*); Understand some ideas and familiar details. p. 26 (*i*), p. 30 (**19**, *p*), p. 35 (**B**, *m*); Provide information. pp. 18–19 (*i*), p. 25 (**10**, **11**, *p*), p. 42 (**1**, *m*); Converse in social interactions. p. 31 (**21**, *i*), p. 35 (**A**, *p*); Listen during social interactions and listen to audio or video texts. p. 21 (**5**, *i*), p. 47 (*p*); Write postcards. p. 43 (**4**, *i*), p. 43 (**4**, *p*); Use short sentences, learned words and phrases when speaking and writing. p. 20 (**1**, *i*), p. 31 (**20**, *p*); Understand ideas and familiar details when listening. p. 25 (**12**, *i*); Understand texts enhanced by visual clues. pp. 36–37 (*i*); Understand and convey information about the self and school. p. 23 (*i*), p. 32 (**25**, *p*), p. 43 (**5**, *m*); Understand and convey information on geography and topography. p. 40 (*i*), p. 41 (*p*); Communicate effectively. p. 35 (*B*); Culturally acceptable. p. 43 (**4**); Most important information. p. 43 (**5**)

Stage II
Use and understand learned expressions, sentences, and strings of sentences, questions, and polite commands when speaking and listening. p. 33 (**30**, *i*), p. 42 (**1**, *p*)

Stage III
Clarify and ask for and comprehend clarification. p. 31 (**23**, *i*)

The California Continuum Correlations to **Bon voyage!** appear on the respective chapter opening pages, namely 16, 48, 80, 110, 152, 184, 218, 258, 290, 322, 354, 398, 430, and 462.

About the Authors

Conrad J. Schmitt

Conrad J. Schmitt received his B.A. degree magna cum laude from Montclair State University. He received his M.A. from Middlebury College. He did additional graduate work at New York University.

Mr. Schmitt has taught Spanish and French at all levels—from elementary school to university graduate courses. He served as Coordinator of Foreign Languages for the Hackensack, New Jersey Public Schools. He also taught Methods of Teaching a Foreign Language at the Graduate School of Education, Rutgers University. Mr. Schmitt was Editor-in-Chief of Foreign Languages and ESL/EFL materials for the School Division of McGraw-Hill and McGraw-Hill International Book Company.

Mr. Schmitt has authored or co-authored more than one hundred books, all published by Glencoe/McGraw-Hill or by McGraw-Hill. He has addressed teacher groups and given workshops in all states of the United States and has lectured and presented seminars throughout the Far East, Latin America, and Canada. In addition, Mr. Schmitt has traveled extensively throughout France, French-speaking Canada, North Africa, French-speaking West Africa, the French Antilles, and Haiti.

Katia Brillié Lutz

Ms. Lutz has her **Baccalauréat** in Mathematics and Science from the Lycée Molière in Paris and her **Licence ès Lettres** in languages from the Sorbonne. She was a Fulbright scholar at Mount Holyoke College.

Ms. Lutz has taught French language at Yale University and French language and literature at Southern Connecticut State College. She also taught French at the United Nations in New York City.

Ms. Lutz was Executive Editor of French at Macmillan Publishing Company. She also served as Senior Editor at Harcourt Brace Jovanovich and Holt Rinehart and Winston. She was a news translator and announcer for the BBC Overseas Language Services in London.

Ms. Lutz is the author of many language textbooks at all levels of instruction.

McGraw-Hill Glencoe

The McGraw-Hill Companies

Copyright © 2004 by Glencoe/McGraw-Hill. All rights reserved. Except as permitted by the United States Copyright Act, no part of this publication may be reproduced or distributed in any form or by any means, or stored in a database or retrieval system, without prior permission of the publisher.

The feature in this textbook entitled **Reflets** was designed and created by the National Geographic Society's School Publishing Division. Copyright 2002. National Geographic Society. All rights reserved.

The name "National Geographic" and the yellow border are registered trademarks of the National Geographic Society.

Printed in the United States of America.

Send all inquiries to:
Glencoe/McGraw-Hill
8787 Orion Place
Columbus, OH 43240-4027

ISBN 0-07-860938-0 (Student Edition)
ISBN 0-07-860941-0 (Teacher Wraparound Edition)

1 2 3 4 5 6 7 8 9 071 09 08 07 06 05 04 03

Teacher Reviewers

We wish to express our appreciation to the numerous individuals throughout the United States and the French-speaking world who have advised us in the development of these teaching materials. Special thanks are extended to the people whose names appear below.

Anne-Marie Baumis
Bayside, NY

Claude Benaiteau
Austin, TX

Sr. M. Elayne Bockey, SND
St. Wendelin High School
Fostoria, OH

Linda Burnette
Rockville Junior/Senior High School
Rockville, IN

Linda Butt
Loyola Blakefield
Towson, MD

Betty Clough
Austin, TX

Yolande Helm
Ohio University
Athens, OH

Jan Hofts
Northwest High School
Indianapolis, IN

Kathleen A. Houchens
The Ohio State University
Columbus, OH

Dominique Keith
Lake Forest, CA

Raelene Noll
Delmar, NY

Nancy Price
Fort Atkinson High School
Fort Atkinson, WI

Sally Price
Marysville-Pilchuck High School
Marysville, WA

Bonita Sanders
Eisenhower High School
New Berlin, WI

Deana Schiffer
Hewlett High School
Hewlett, NY

Julia Sheppard
Delaware City Schools
Delaware, OH

James Toolan
Tuxedo High School
Tuxedo, NY

Mary Webster
Romeo High School
Romeo, MI

Marian Welch
Austin ISD
Austin, TX

Richard Wixom
Miller Middle School
Lake Katrine, NY

Brian Zailian
Tamalpais High School
Mill Valley, CA

Table des matières

La francophonie

Le monde francophone ... xxi
Le monde ... xxii
La francophonie ... xxiv
La France ... xxxii
Paris ... xxxiii
Le Canada ... xxxiv
L'Afrique ... xxxv

Why Learn French? ... xxxvi

L'alphabet français ... xxxviii

Leçons préliminaires

Objectifs

In these preliminary lessons you will learn to:

- ✔ *greet people*
- ✔ *say good-bye to people*
- ✔ *ask people how they are*
- ✔ *ask and tell names*
- ✔ *express simple courtesies*
- ✔ *find out and tell the days of the week*
- ✔ *find out and tell the months of the year*
- ✔ *count from 1 to 30*
- ✔ *find out and tell the time*

A Bonjour! ... 2

B Au revoir! ... 4

C Les noms ... 6

D La politesse ... 8

E La date ... 10

F L'heure ... 12

CHAPITRE 1 Une amie et un ami

Objectifs

In this chapter you will learn to:

- ✔ *ask or tell what someone is like*
- ✔ *ask or tell where someone is from*
- ✔ *ask or tell who someone is*
- ✔ *describe yourself or someone else*
- ✔ *talk about students from France and Martinique*

Vocabulaire

Mots 1 18
Comment est la fille? 18
Comment est le garçon? 19
Mots 2 22
Une sœur et un frère 22
Une école et un collège 22

Structure

Les articles au singulier 26
L'accord des adjectifs 28
Le verbe **être** au singulier 30
La négation 33

Conversation

Il est d'où, Luc? 34

Prononciation

L'accent tonique 35

Lectures culturelles

Un garçon et une fille 36
Le français en Afrique 38
Un artiste français 39

Connexions

La géographie 40

C'est à vous 42

Assessment 44

Technotour 47

CHAPITRE 2 Les cours et les profs

Objectifs

In this chapter you will learn to:

- ✔ *describe people and things*
- ✔ *talk about more than one person or thing*
- ✔ *tell what subjects you take in school and express some opinions about them*
- ✔ *speak to people formally and informally*
- ✔ *talk about French-speaking people in the United States*

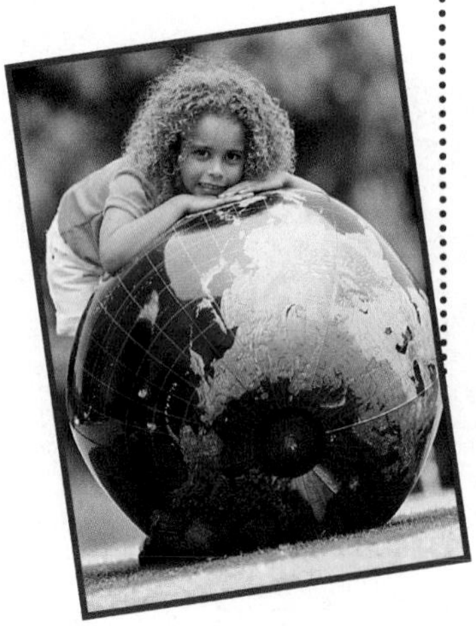

Vocabulaire

Mots 1 50
- Les élèves et les profs 50
- Comment sont les cours? 51

Mots 2 54
- Les matières 54
- En cours de français 55

Structure

- Le pluriel: articles, noms et adjectifs 58
- Le verbe **être** au pluriel 60
- **Tu** et **vous** 64

Conversation

- Quel prof? 66

Prononciation

- Les consonnes finales 67

Lectures culturelles

- Le français aux États-Unis 68
- La scolarité en France 70
- Un message 71

Connexions

- La biologie, la physique et la chimie 72

C'est à vous 74

Assessment 76

Technotour 79

CHAPITRE 3 Pendant et après les cours

Objectifs

In this chapter you will learn to:

- ✔ *talk about what you do in school*
- ✔ *talk about what you and your friends do after school*
- ✔ *identify and shop for school supplies*
- ✔ *talk about what you don't do*
- ✔ *tell what you and others like and don't like to do*
- ✔ *discuss schools in France*

Vocabulaire

Mots 1 82
Une journée à l'école 82
Mots 2 86
Des fournitures scolaires 86
Après les cours 87

Structure

Les verbes réguliers en **-er** au présent 90
La négation des articles indéfinis 94
Verbe + infinitif 95

Conversation

Un élève français aux États-Unis 96

Prononciation

Les sons /é/ et /è/. 97

Lectures culturelles

Une journée avec Jacqueline 98
Qui travaille? 100
Un groupe de rap—Manau 101

Connexions

L'ordinateur 102

C'est à vous 104

Assessment 106

Technotour 109

CHAPITRE 4 La famille et la maison

Objectifs

In this chapter you will learn to:

- ✔ *talk about your family*
- ✔ *describe your home and neighborhood*
- ✔ *tell your age and find out someone else's age*
- ✔ *tell what belongs to you and others*
- ✔ *describe more people and things*
- ✔ *talk about families and homes in French-speaking countries*

Vocabulaire

Mots 1 112
La famille Morel 112
L'anniversaire de Marie 113
Mots 2 116
La maison 116
L'immeuble 116
Les pièces de la maison 117

Structure

Avoir au présent 120
Les adjectifs possessifs 123
D'autres adjectifs 126

Conversation

Ma nouvelle adresse 128

Prononciation

Le son /ã/ 129

Lectures culturelles

Où habitent les Français? 130
Le logement dans d'autres pays 132
Les noms de famille 133

Connexions

Art et histoire 134

C'est à vous 136

Assessment 138

Technotour 141

RÉVISION — **Chapitres 1–4** **142**

NATIONAL GEOGRAPHIC — **Reflets de la France** **148**

LITTÉRATURE 1 — ***La petite Fadette***
George Sand **504**

CHAPITRE 5 Au café et au restaurant

Objectifs

In this chapter you will learn to:

- ✔ *order food or a beverage at a café or restaurant*
- ✔ *tell where you and others go*
- ✔ *tell what you and others are going to do*
- ✔ *give locations*
- ✔ *tell what belongs to you and others*
- ✔ *describe more activities*
- ✔ *compare eating habits in the United States and in the French-speaking world*

Vocabulaire

Mots 1 154
À la terrasse d'un café 154
Mots 2 158
Le couvert 158
Au restaurant 158
Les trois repas de la journée 159

Structure

Le verbe **aller** au présent 162
Aller + infinitif 165
Les contractions avec **à** et **de** 166
Le verbe **prendre** 168

Conversation

Au restaurant 170

Prononciation

Le son **/r/** 171

Lectures culturelles

Au restaurant? Vraiment? 172
Les repas en France 174
Les goûts changent 175

Connexions

L'arithmétique 176

C'est à vous 178

Assessment 180

Technotour 183

CHAPITRE 6 La nourriture et les courses

Objectifs

In this chapter you will learn to:

- ✔ *identify more foods*
- ✔ *shop for food*
- ✔ *tell what you or others are doing*
- ✔ *ask for the quantity you want*
- ✔ *talk about what you or others don't have*
- ✔ *tell what you or others are able to do or want to do*
- ✔ *talk about French food-shopping customs*

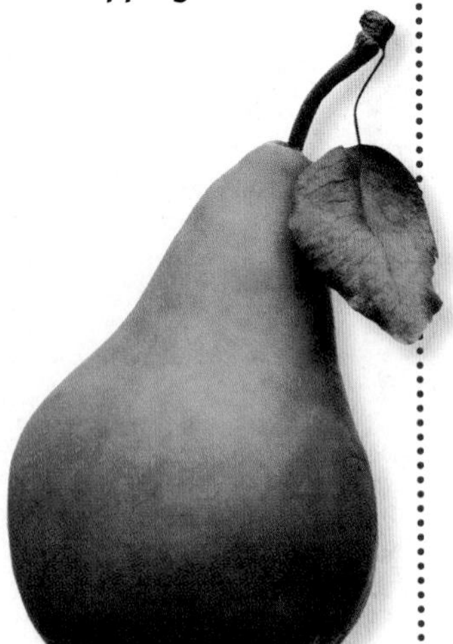

Vocabulaire

Mots 1 186
À la boulangerie-pâtisserie 186
À la crémerie. 186
À la boucherie. 186
À la poissonnerie 186
À la charcuterie. 186
À l'épicerie 186
Mots 2 190
Au marché. 190

Structure

Le verbe **faire** au présent. 194
Le partitif et l'article défini 196
Le partitif au négatif. 198
Les verbes **pouvoir** et **vouloir**. 201

Conversation

Au marché. 204

Prononciation

Les sons /œ́/ et /œ̀/. 205

Lectures culturelles

Les courses 206
Les grandes surfaces 208
Les marchés. 209

Connexions

Les conversions. 210

C'est à vous 212
Assessment. 214
Technotour 217

CHAPITRE 7 Les vêtements

Objectifs

In this chapter you will learn to:

- ✔ *identify and describe articles of clothing*
- ✔ *state color and size preferences*
- ✔ *shop for clothing*
- ✔ *describe people's activities*
- ✔ *compare people and things*
- ✔ *express opinions and make observations*
- ✔ *discuss clothes and clothes shopping in the French-speaking world*

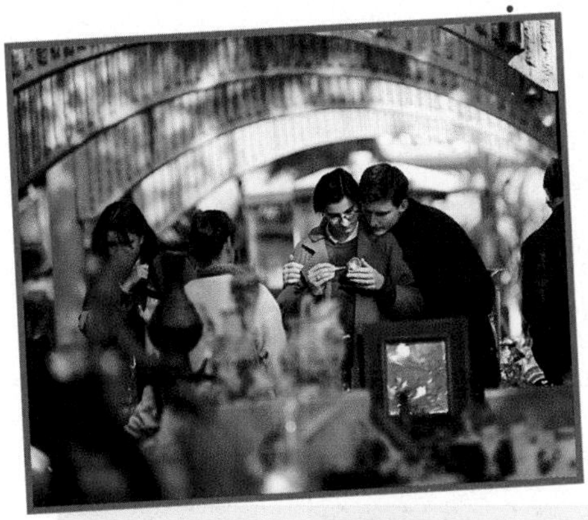

Vocabulaire

Mots 1 220
Les vêtements sport 220
Les vêtements pour hommes. 221
Les vêtements pour femmes 221
Mots 2 224
On fait des courses. 224

Structure

Le verbe **mettre**. 228
Le comparatif des adjectifs 230
Les verbes **voir** et **croire**. 232

Conversation

Dans une petite boutique. 234

Prononciation

Les sons **/sh/** et **/zh/** 235

Lectures culturelles

On fait des courses où, à Paris?. 236
Les vêtements 238
Les tailles. 239

Connexions

La poésie 240

C'est à vous 242

Assessment. 244

Technotour 247

RÉVISION **Chapitres 5–7** **248**

NATIONAL GEOGRAPHIC **Reflets de l'Afrique**. **254**

LITTÉRATURE 2 ***«Dors mon enfant»***
Elolongué Epanya Yondo **510**

AIR FRANCE
le billet électronique
si simple, si pratique

CHAPITRE 8 L'aéroport et l'avion

Objectifs

In this chapter you will learn to:

- ✔ *check in for a flight*
- ✔ *talk about some services aboard the plane*
- ✔ *talk about more activities*
- ✔ *ask more questions*
- ✔ *talk about people and things as a group*
- ✔ *discuss air travel in France*

Vocabulaire

Mots 1 260
À l'aéroport 260
Mots 2 264
À bord 264

Structure

Les verbes en **-ir** au présent 268
Quel et **tout** 270
Les verbes **sortir, partir, dormir,** et **servir** 272

Conversation

On part pour Toulouse 276

Prononciation

Le son /l/ final 277

Lectures culturelles

On va en France 278
Le décalage horaire 280
Un pilote écrivain 281

Connexions

Le climat et le temps 282

C'est à vous 284

Assessment 286

Technotour 289

CHAPITRE 9 La gare et le train

Objectifs

In this chapter you will learn to:

- ✔ *purchase a train ticket and request information about arrival and departure*
- ✔ *use expressions related to train travel*
- ✔ *talk about people's activities*
- ✔ *point out people or things*
- ✔ *discuss an interesting train trip in French-speaking Africa*

Vocabulaire

Mots 1 292
À la gare 292
Mots 2 296
Un voyage en train. 296
Dans le train 296

Structure

Les verbes en **-re** au présent 300
Les adjectifs démonstratifs 303
Les verbes **dire, écrire, lire** 306

Conversation

Au guichet. 308

Prononciation

Les sons /õ/ et /ẽ/ 309

Lectures culturelles

Un voyage intéressant 310
La SNCF 312

Connexions

Des conversions—les horaires. 314

C'est à vous 316

Assessment. 318

Technotour 321

CHAPITRE 10 Les sports

Objectifs

In this chapter you will learn to:

- ✔ *talk about team sports and other physical activities*
- ✔ *describe past actions and events*
- ✔ *ask people questions*
- ✔ *discuss what sports are popular in Canada and in French-speaking Africa*

Vocabulaire

Mots 1 324

Le foot(ball) 324

Mots 2 328

D'autres sports d'équipe 328

Structure

Le passé composé des verbes réguliers 332

Qui, qu'est-ce que, quoi 335

Les verbes **boire, devoir** et **recevoir** au présent 337

Conversation

On a gagné! 340

Prononciation

Liaison et élision 341

Lectures culturelles

Le hockey et le basket-ball 342

Le Tour de France 344

Connexions

L'anatomie 346

C'est à vous 348

Assessment 350

Technotour 353

xiv

CHAPITRE 11 L'été et l'hiver

Objectifs

In this chapter you will learn to:

- ✔ *describe summer and winter weather*
- ✔ *talk about summer activities and sports*
- ✔ *talk about winter sports*
- ✔ *discuss past actions and events*
- ✔ *make negative statements*
- ✔ *talk about a ski trip in Québec*

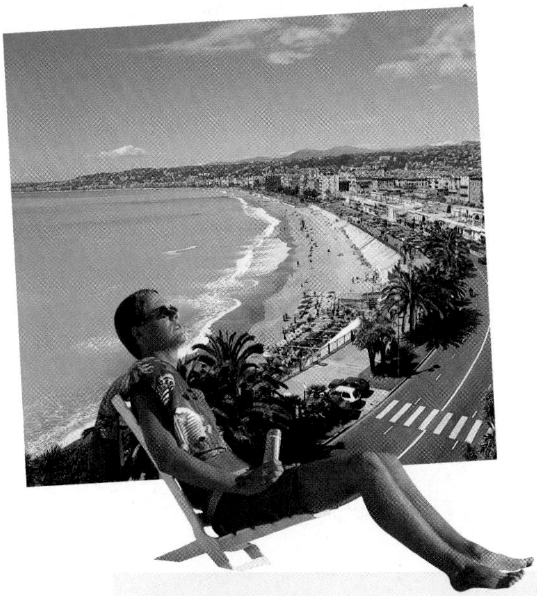

Vocabulaire

Mots 1 356
À la plage 356
Des activités d'été. 357
Le printemps. 357
L'été 357
Mots 2 360
Une station de sports d'hiver 361
L'automne 361
L'hiver 361

Structure

Le passé composé des verbes irréguliers 364
Les mots négatifs 367
Le passé composé avec **être**. 369

Conversation

À la plage 372

Prononciation

Le son **/y/**. 373

Lectures culturelles

Un petit voyage au Canada. 374
Les grandes vacances. 376
Le carnaval 377

Connexions

La peinture 378

C'est à vous 380

Assessment. 382

Technotour 385

RÉVISION — **Chapitres 8–11** **386**

NATIONAL GEOGRAPHIC — **Reflets du Canada** **394**

LITTÉRATURE 3 — ***La Chanson de Roland***
Auteur anonyme **512**

CHAPITRE 12 La routine quotidienne

Objectifs

In this chapter you will learn to:

- ✔ *describe your personal grooming habits*
- ✔ *talk about your daily routine*
- ✔ *talk about your family life*
- ✔ *tell some things you do for yourself*
- ✔ *talk about daily activities in the past*
- ✔ *discuss a French family's daily routine*

Vocabulaire

Mots 1 400
La routine 400
Mots 2 404
Chez les Moulin 404

Structure

Les verbes réfléchis au présent 408
Les verbes réfléchis au passé composé. 413

Conversation

Quelle interro? 416

Prononciation

Les sons /**s**/ et /**z**/ 417

Lectures culturelles

La famille Ben Amar 418
Le petit déjeuner 420

Connexions

L'écologie 422

C'est à vous 424
Assessment 426
Technotour 429

CHAPITRE 13 Les loisirs culturels

Objectifs

In this chapter you will learn to:

- ✔ *discuss movies, plays, and museums*
- ✔ *tell what you know and whom you know*
- ✔ *tell what happens to you or someone else*
- ✔ *refer to people and things already mentioned*
- ✔ *talk about some cultural activities in Paris*

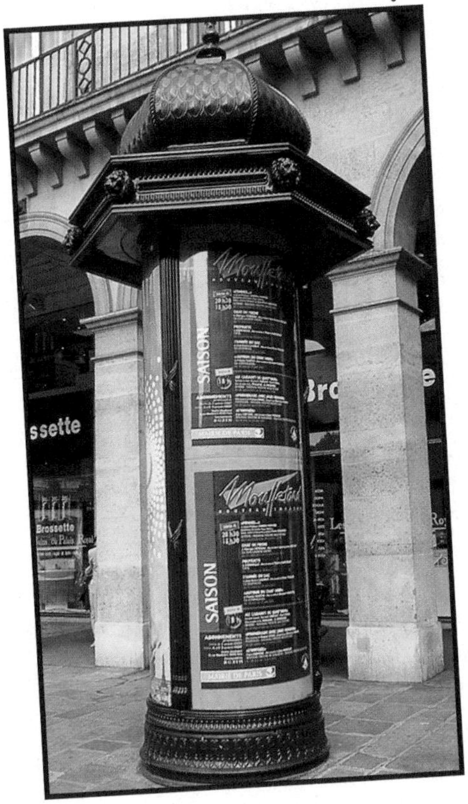

Vocabulaire

Mots 1 432
Au cinéma 432
Au théâtre 433
Mots 2 436
Au musée 436

Structure

Les verbes **savoir** et **connaître** 440
Les pronoms **me, te, nous, vous** 442
Les pronoms **le, la, les** 444

Conversation

On va au cinéma? 448

Prononciation

Le son **/ü/** 449

Lectures culturelles

Les loisirs culturels en France 450
La musique africaine 452

Connexions

La musique 454

C'est à vous 456

Assessment 458

Technotour 461

CHAPITRE 14 La santé et la médecine

Objectifs

In this chapter you will learn to:

- ✔ *explain a minor illness to a doctor*
- ✔ *have a prescription filled at a pharmacy*
- ✔ *tell for whom something is done*
- ✔ *talk about some more activities*
- ✔ *give commands*
- ✔ *refer to people, places, and things already mentioned*
- ✔ *discuss medical services in France*

Vocabulaire

Mots 1 464
On est malade. 464
Mots 2 468
Chez le médecin 468
À la pharmacie 469

Structure

Les pronoms **lui, leur**. 472
Les verbes **souffrir** et **ouvrir** 474
L'impératif. 475
Le pronom **en** 478

Conversation

Chez le médecin 480

Prononciation

Les sons /**u**/ et /**ü**/. 481

Lectures culturelles

Une consultation. 482
Culture et santé. 484
Les services médicaux en France 485

Connexions

La diététique 486

C'est à vous 488

Assessment. 490

Technotour 493

RÉVISION — **Chapitres 12–14** **494**

NATIONAL GEOGRAPHIC — **Reflets de Paris**. **498**

LITTÉRATURE 4 — *Le Comte de Monte-Cristo*
Alexandre Dumas. **518**

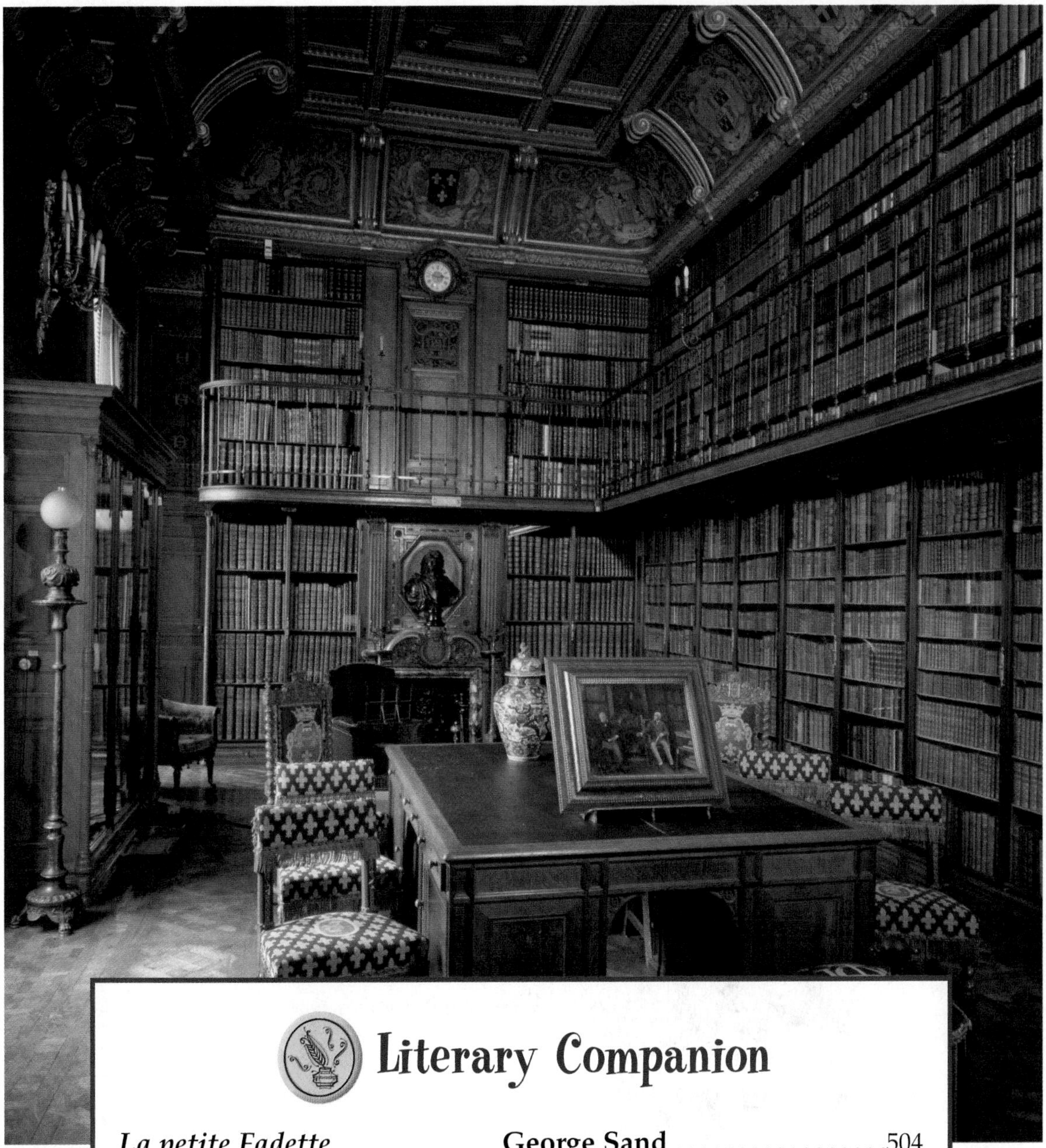

Literary Companion

La petite Fadette George Sand 504

«Dors mon enfant» Elolongué Epanya Yondo 510

La Chanson de Roland Auteur anonyme 512

Le Comte de Monte-Cristo Alexandre Dumas 518

Handbook

InfoGap Activities H2
Study Tips H51
Verb Charts H68
French-English Dictionary H72
English-French Dictionary H96
Index H120

Guide to Symbols

Throughout **Bon voyage!** you will see these symbols, or icons. They will tell you how to best use the particular part of the chapter or activity they accompany. Following is a key to help you understand these symbols.

Audio Link This icon indicates material in the chapter that is recorded on compact disk format and/or audiocassette.

Recycling This icon indicates sections that review previously introduced material.

Paired Activity This icon indicates sections that you can practice orally with a partner.

Group Activity This icon indicates sections that you can practice together in groups.

Encore Plus This icon indicates additional practice activities that review knowledge from current chapters.

Allez-y! This icon indicates the end of new material in each section and the beginning of the recombination section at the end of the chapter.

Literary Companion This icon appears in the review lessons to let you know that you are prepared to read the literature selection indicated if you wish.

Interactive CD-ROM This icon indicates that the material is also on an Interactive CD-ROM.

Le monde francophone

The French geographer Onésime Reclus first coined the word *francophonie* in 1880 to designate geographical entities where French was spoken. Today, *la francophonie* refers to the collective body of over one hundred million people all over the world who speak French, exclusively or in part, in their daily lives. The term *francophonie* refers to the diverse official organizations, governments, and countries that promote the use of French in economic, political, diplomatic, and cultural exchanges. Politically, French remains the second most important language in the world. In some Francophone nations, French is the official language (France), or the co-official language (Cameroon); in others, it is spoken by a minority who share a common cultural heritage (Andorra). The French language is present in Europe, Africa, the Americas, and Oceania.

xxi

Le monde

LE MONDE FRANCOPHONE

Le monde

The areas in color indicate the vast Francophone world.

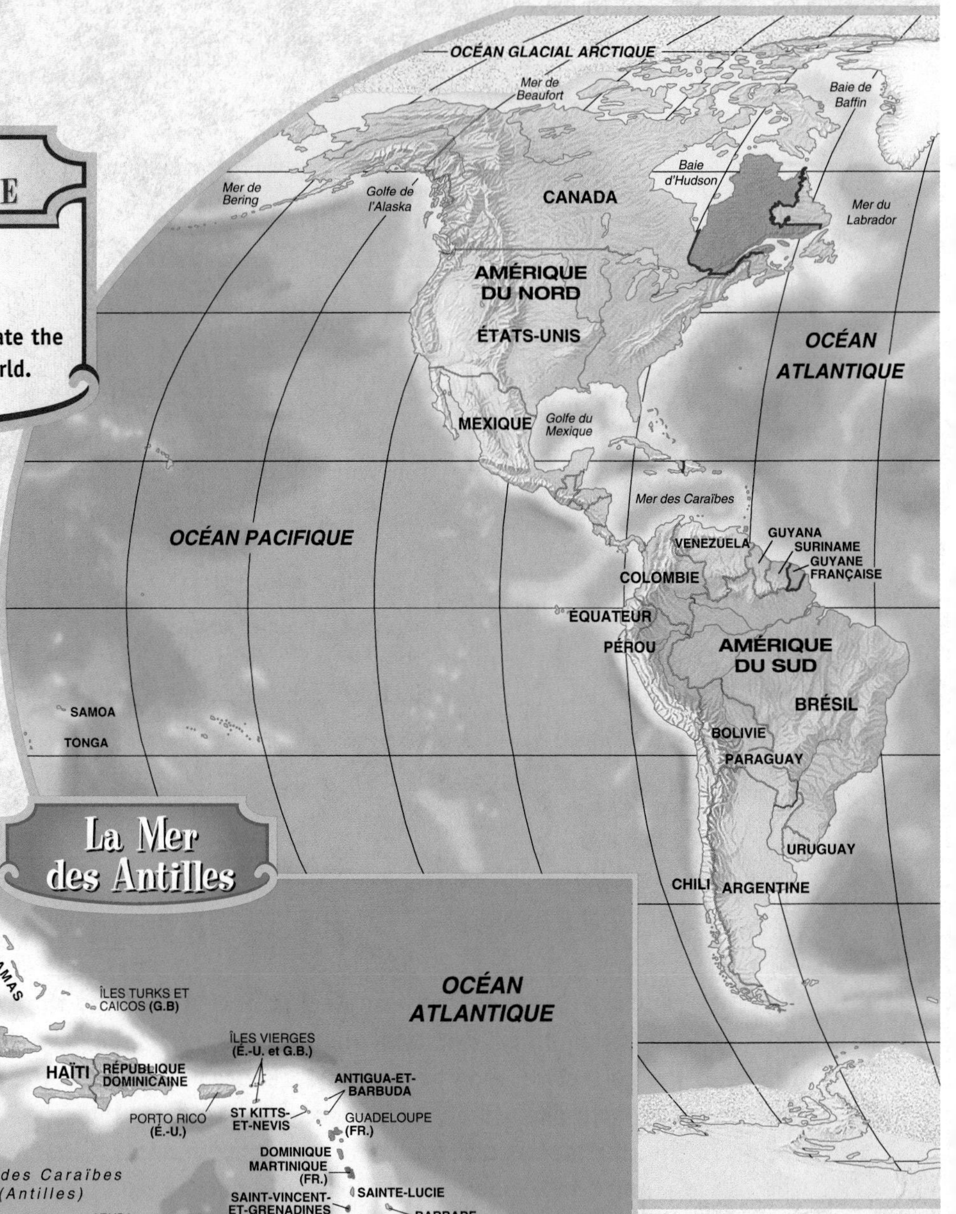

La Mer des Antilles

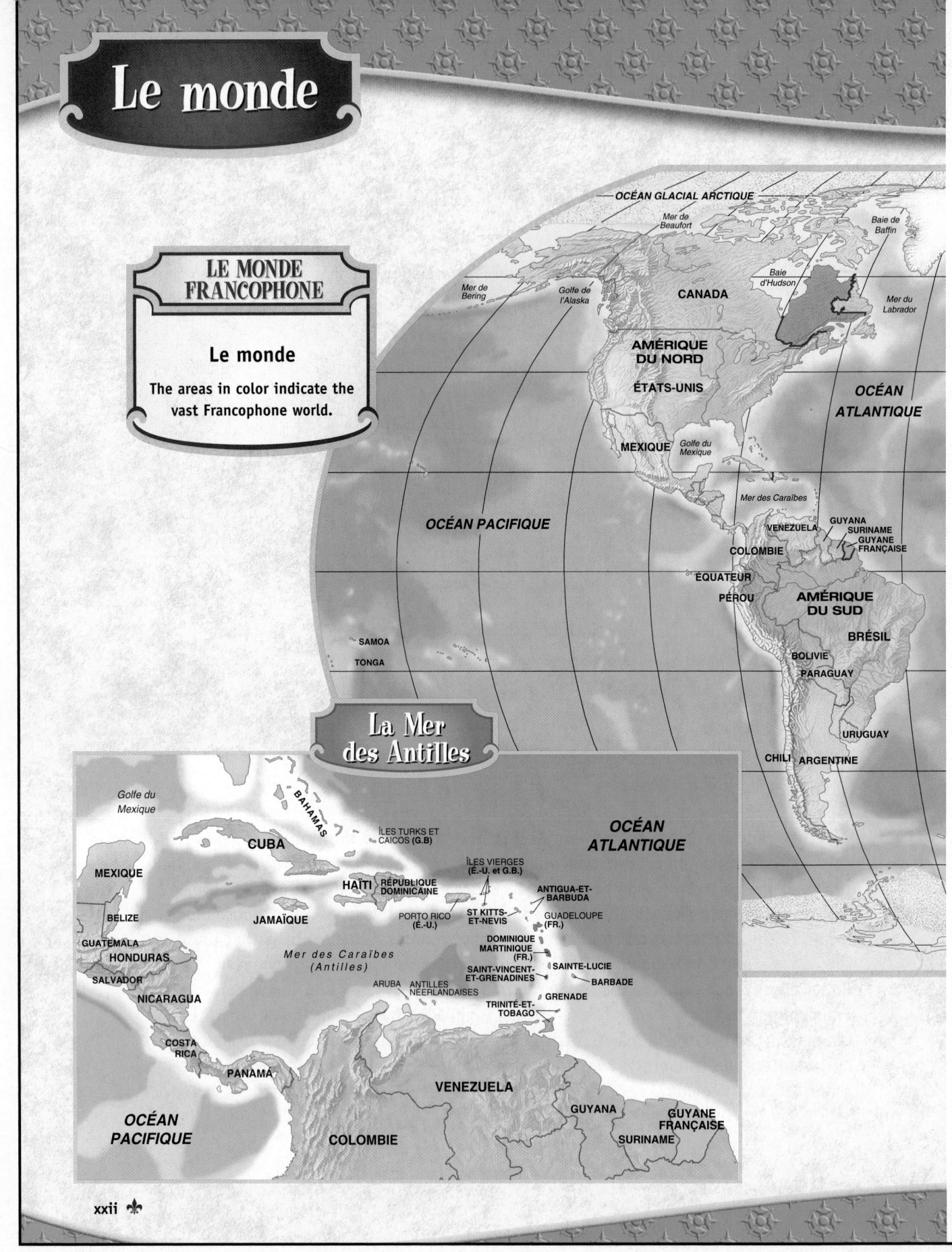

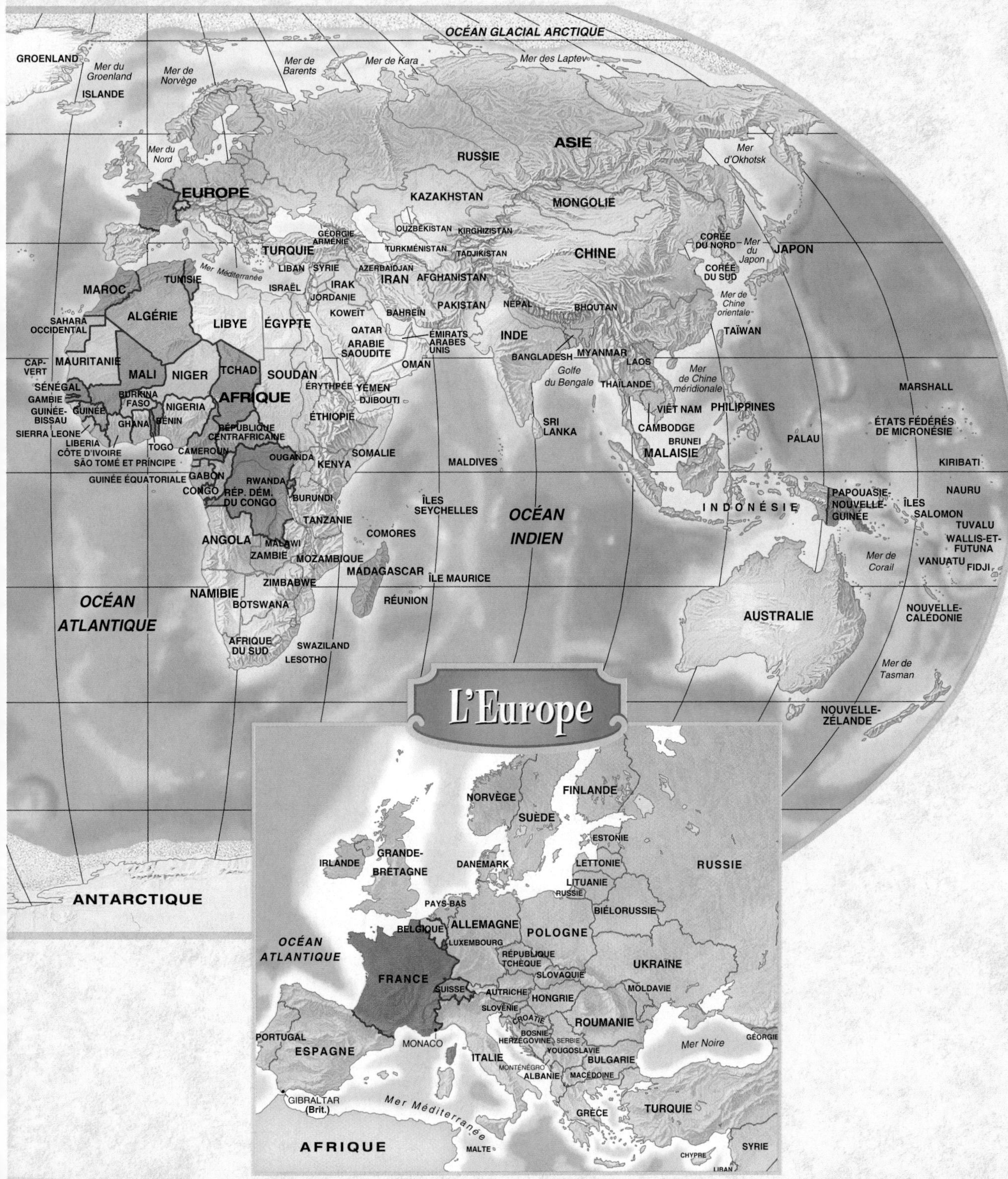
OCÉAN GLACIAL ARCTIQUE
GROENLAND
Mer du Groenland
ISLANDE
Mer de Norvège
Mer de Barents
Mer de Kara
Mer des Laptev
Mer du Nord
RUSSIE
ASIE
Mer d'Okhotsk
EUROPE
KAZAKHSTAN
MONGOLIE
GÉORGIE
ARMÉNIE
OUZBÉKISTAN
KIRGHIZISTAN
TURKMÉNISTAN
TADJIKISTAN
TURQUIE
CHINE
CORÉE DU NORD
Mer du Japon
JAPON
CORÉE DU SUD
Mer Méditerranée
TUNISIE
LIBAN
SYRIE
AZERBAÏDJAN
IRAK
IRAN
AFGHANISTAN
ISRAËL
JORDANIE
MAROC
KOWEÏT
BAHREÏN
PAKISTAN
NÉPAL
BHOUTAN
Mer de Chine orientale
ALGÉRIE
LIBYE
ÉGYPTE
QATAR
ÉMIRATS ARABES UNIS
INDE
TAÏWAN
SAHARA OCCIDENTAL
ARABIE SAOUDITE
OMAN
BANGLADESH
MYANMAR
LAOS
CAP-VERT
MAURITANIE
MALI
NIGER
TCHAD
SOUDAN
Golfe du Bengale
Mer de Chine méridionale
SÉNÉGAL
GAMBIE
GUINÉE-BISSAU
GUINÉE
BURKINA FASO
ÉRYTHRÉE
YÉMEN
THAÏLANDE
MARSHALL
AFRIQUE
DJIBOUTI
VIÊT NAM
PHILIPPINES
NIGERIA
SIERRA LEONE
GHANA
BÉNIN
ÉTHIOPIE
SRI LANKA
CAMBODGE
ÉTATS FÉDÉRÉS DE MICRONÉSIE
LIBERIA
CÔTE D'IVOIRE
TOGO
RÉPUBLIQUE CENTRAFRICAINE
BRUNEI
PALAU
CAMEROUN
SOMALIE
MALAISIE
SÃO TOMÉ ET PRINCIPE
OUGANDA
KENYA
MALDIVES
KIRIBATI
GUINÉE ÉQUATORIALE
GABON
RWANDA
CONGO
RÉP. DÉM. DU CONGO
BURUNDI
ÎLES SEYCHELLES
OCÉAN INDIEN
INDONÉSIE
PAPOUASIE-NOUVELLE-GUINÉE
NAURU
ÎLES SALOMON
TANZANIE
TUVALU
COMORES
WALLIS-ET-FUTUNA
ANGOLA
MALAWI
ZAMBIE
MOZAMBIQUE
Mer de Corail
VANUATU
FIDJI
MADAGASCAR
ÎLE MAURICE
ZIMBABWE
OCÉAN ATLANTIQUE
NAMIBIE
RÉUNION
BOTSWANA
AUSTRALIE
NOUVELLE-CALÉDONIE
AFRIQUE DU SUD
SWAZILAND
LESOTHO
Mer de Tasman
NOUVELLE-ZÉLANDE
ANTARCTIQUE
L'Europe
NORVÈGE
FINLANDE
SUÈDE
ESTONIE
IRLANDE
GRANDE-BRETAGNE
DANEMARK
LETTONIE
RUSSIE
LITUANIE
RUSSIE
PAYS-BAS
BIÉLORUSSIE
BELGIQUE
ALLEMAGNE
POLOGNE
OCÉAN ATLANTIQUE
LUXEMBOURG
RÉPUBLIQUE TCHÈQUE
UKRAINE
FRANCE
SLOVAQUIE
SUISSE
AUTRICHE
MOLDAVIE
HONGRIE
SLOVÉNIE
CROATIE
ROUMANIE
BOSNIE-HERZÉGOVINE
SERBIE
PORTUGAL
MONACO
YOUGOSLAVIE
Mer Noire
GÉORGIE
ESPAGNE
ITALIE
MONTÉNÉGRO
BULGARIE
ALBANIE
MACÉDOINE
GIBRALTAR (Brit.)
Mer Méditerranée
GRÈCE
TURQUIE
AFRIQUE
MALTE
CHYPRE
SYRIE
LIBAN

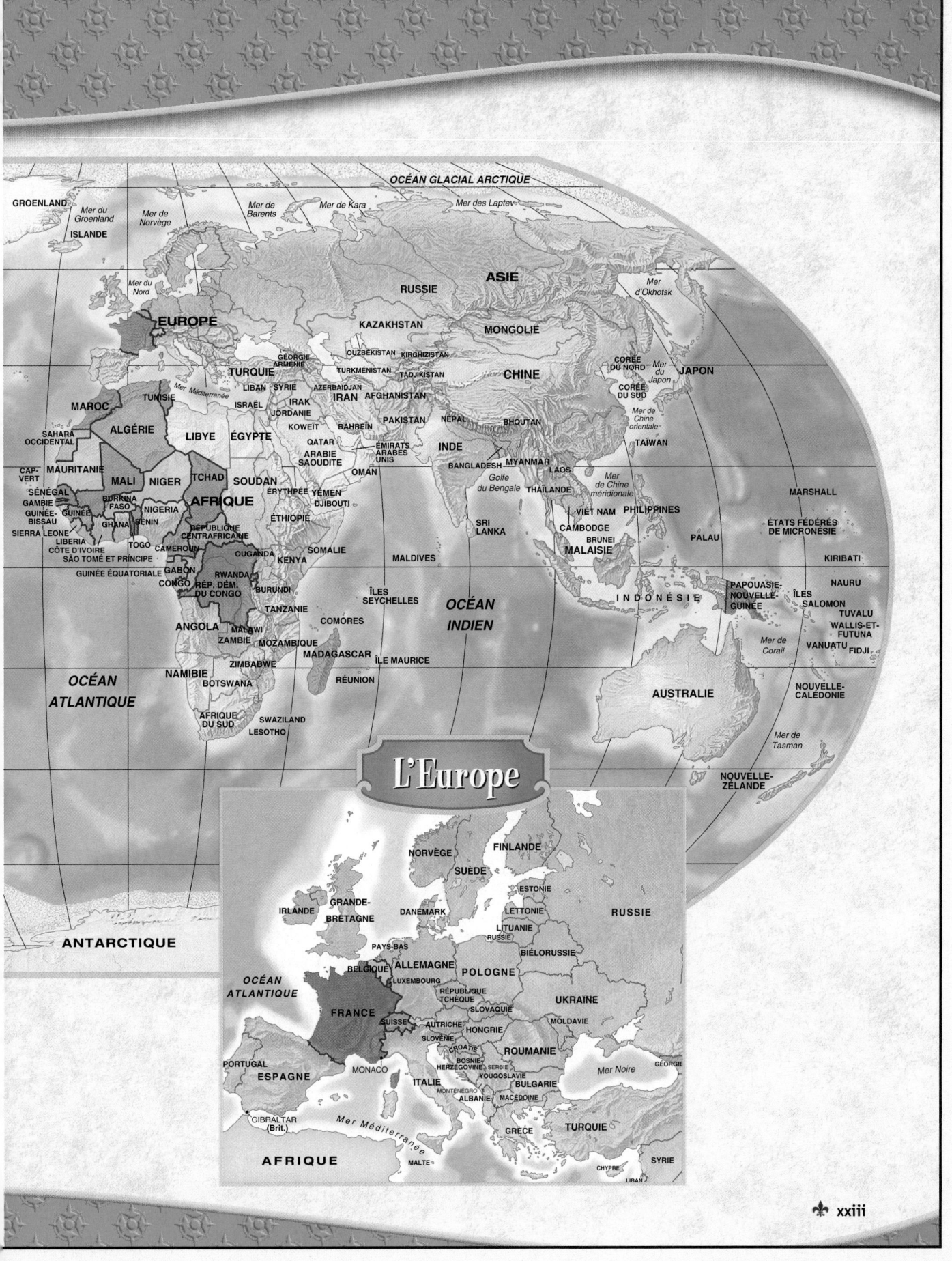

xxiii

La francophonie

L'Afrique

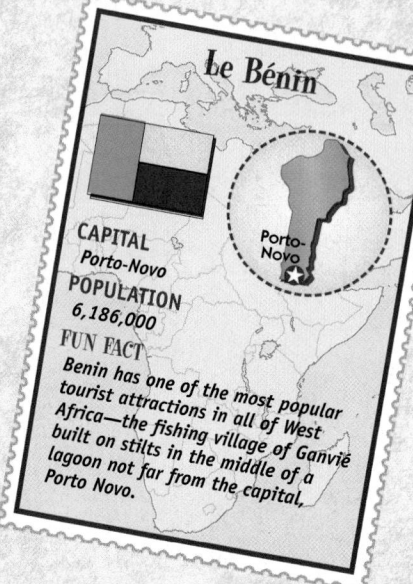

Le Bénin

CAPITAL
Porto-Novo

POPULATION
6,186,000

FUN FACT
Benin has one of the most popular tourist attractions in all of West Africa—the fishing village of Ganvié built on stilts in the middle of a lagoon not far from the capital, Porto Novo.

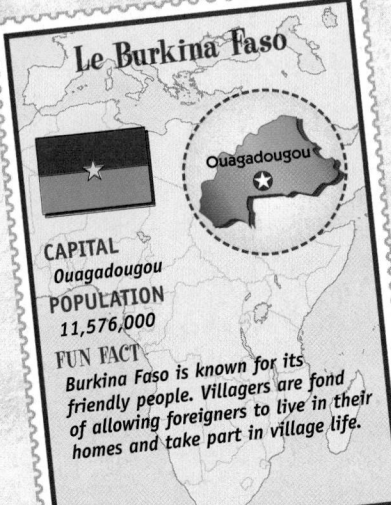

Le Burkina Faso

CAPITAL
Ouagadougou

POPULATION
11,576,000

FUN FACT
Burkina Faso is known for its friendly people. Villagers are fond of allowing foreigners to live in their homes and take part in village life.

L'Algérie

CAPITAL
Algiers

POPULATION
30,774,000

FUN FACT
Algeria is called "the geographic giant" of the Maghreb. It is four times the size of France. Most of the country lies in the Sahara desert.

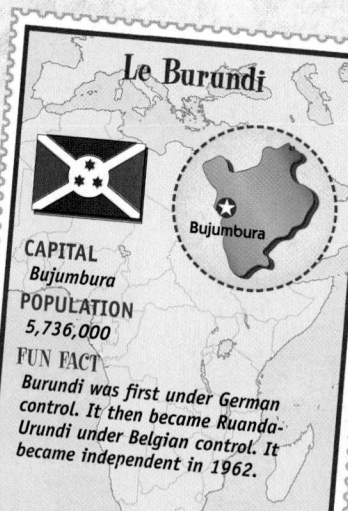

Le Burundi

CAPITAL
Bujumbura

POPULATION
5,736,000

FUN FACT
Burundi was first under German control. It then became Ruanda-Urundi under Belgian control. It became independent in 1962.

Le Cameroun

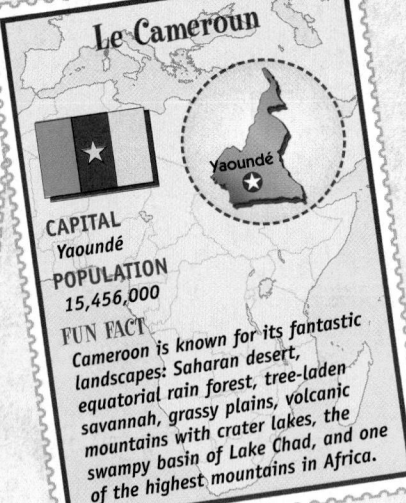

CAPITAL
Yaoundé

POPULATION
15,456,000

FUN FACT
Cameroon is known for its fantastic landscapes: Saharan desert, equatorial rain forest, tree-laden savannah, grassy plains, volcanic mountains with crater lakes, the swampy basin of Lake Chad, and one of the highest mountains in Africa.

xxiv

Les Comores

CAPITAL
Moroni

POPULATION
563,000

FUN FACT
The beautiful Comores Islands in the Indian Ocean are known for their lovely, isolated beaches. These islands are among the few areas in the world where natural beauty reigns.

La République Centrafricaine

CAPITAL
Bangui

POPULATION
3,445,000

FUN FACT
The Central African Republic has two very expensive exports—gold and diamonds.

La République du Congo

CAPITAL
Brazzaville

POPULATION
2,717,000

FUN FACT
Seventy percent of the population lives in the capital city or near the railroad between it and Pointe-Noire about 250 miles to the west.

La République Démocratique du Congo

CAPITAL
Kinshasa

POPULATION
42,200,000

FUN FACT
The population of the Democratic Republic of the Congo is made up of six major ethnic groups which are divided into over 250 subgroups.

La Côte d'Ivoire

CAPITAL
Yamoussoukro

POPULATION
15,818,000

FUN FACT
The Côte d'Ivoire's principal city, Abidjan, is West Africa's most cosmopolitan city and is often referred to as the "Paris of West Africa."

XXV

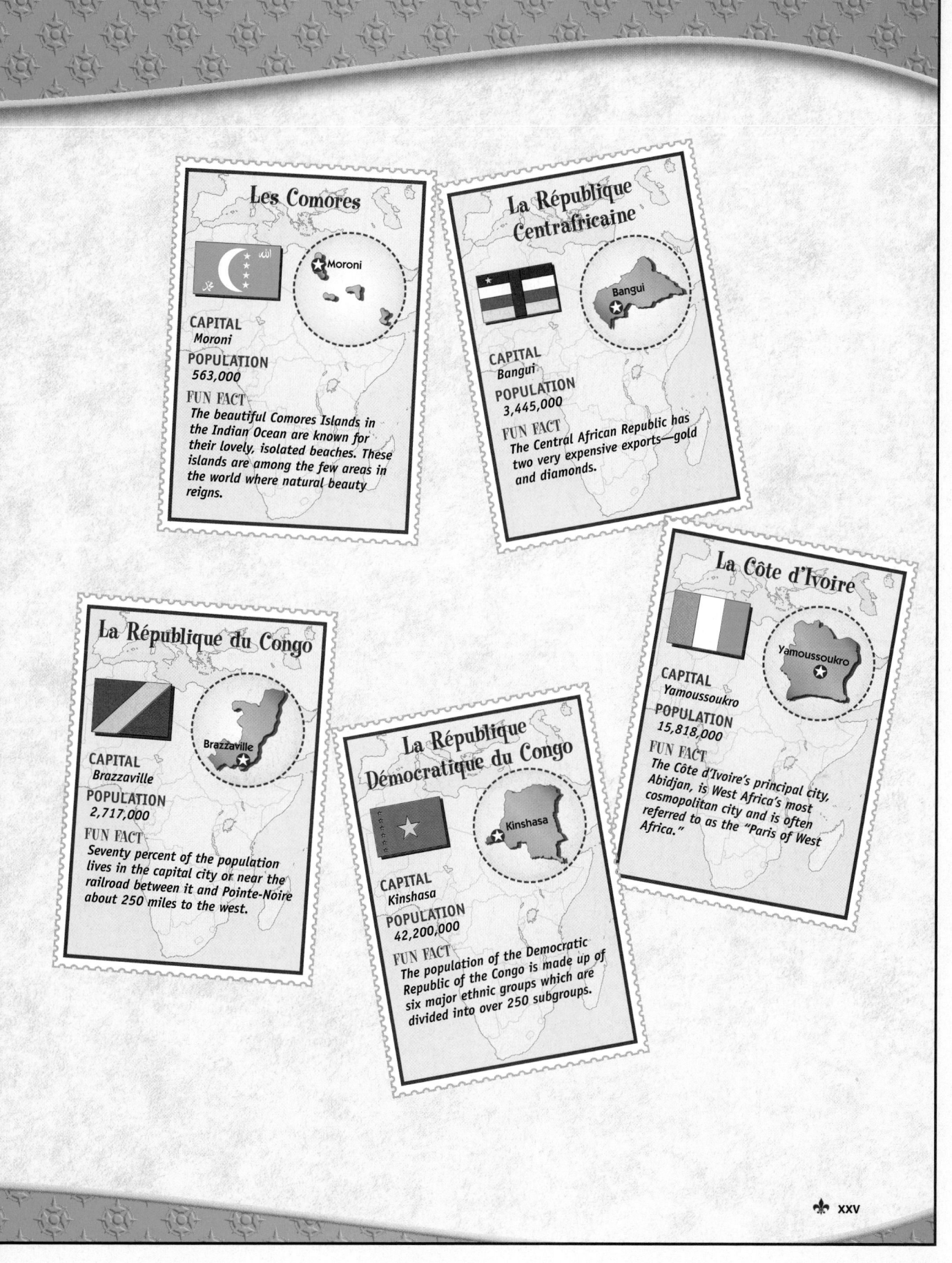

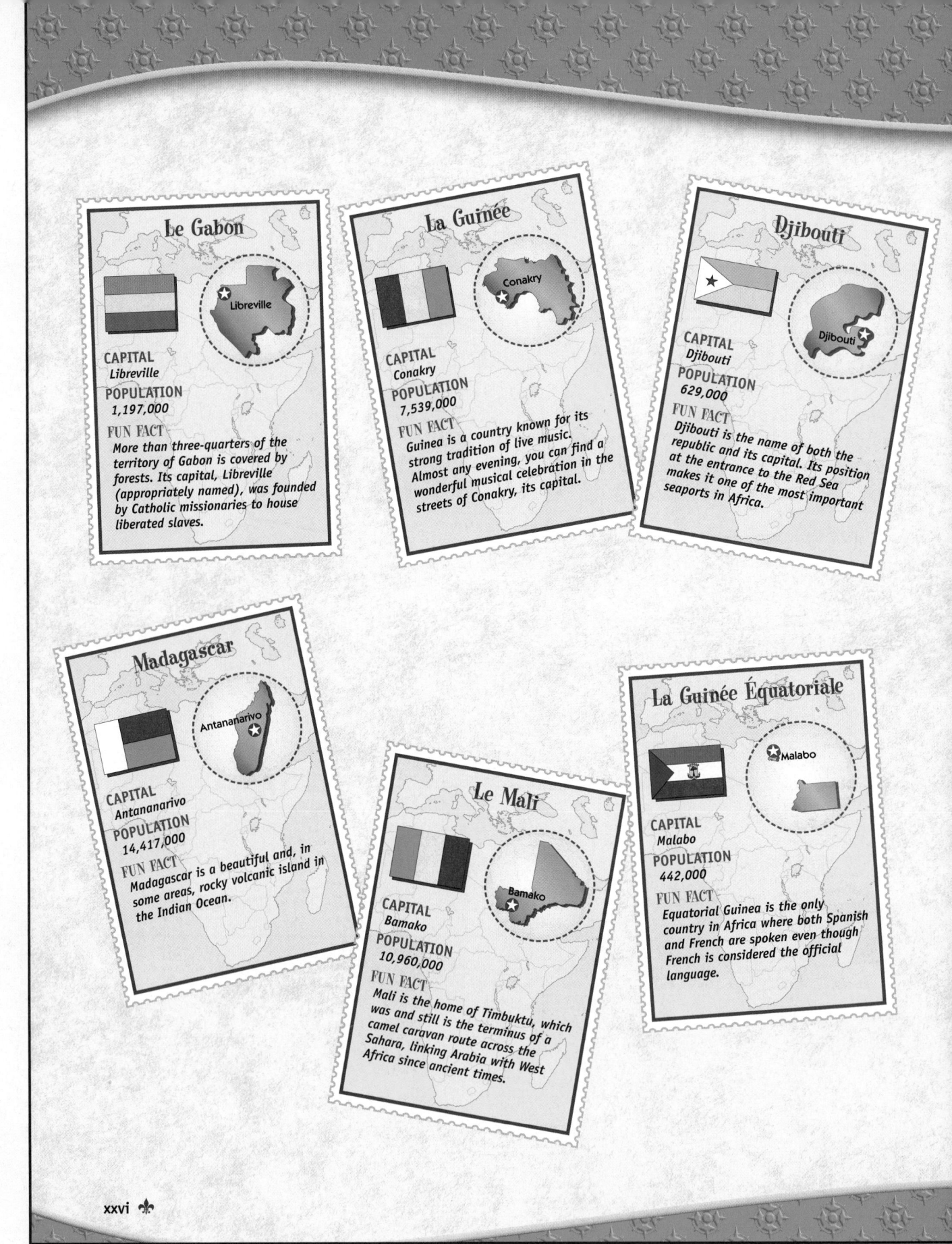

Le Gabon

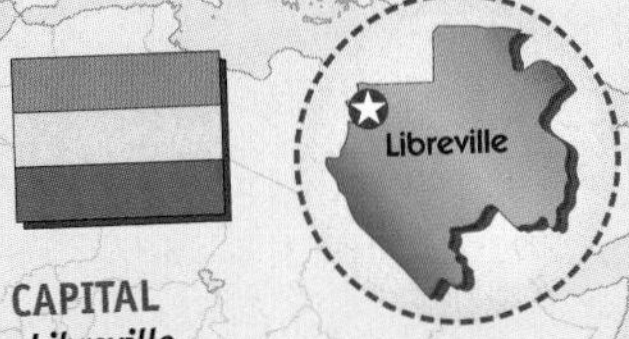

CAPITAL
Libreville

POPULATION
1,197,000

FUN FACT
More than three-quarters of the territory of Gabon is covered by forests. Its capital, Libreville (appropriately named), was founded by Catholic missionaries to house liberated slaves.

La Guinée

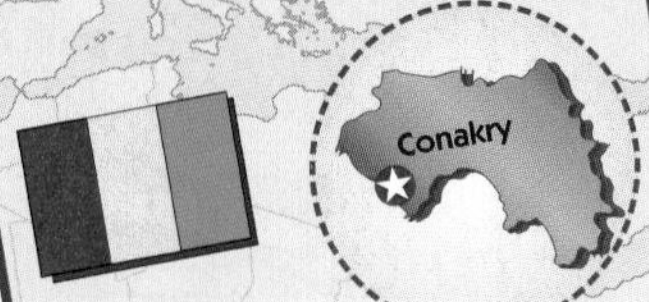

CAPITAL
Conakry

POPULATION
7,539,000

FUN FACT
Guinea is a country known for its strong tradition of live music. Almost any evening, you can find a wonderful musical celebration in the streets of Conakry, its capital.

Djibouti

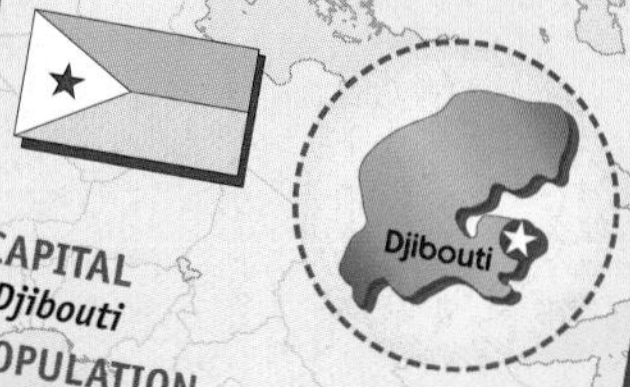

CAPITAL
Djibouti

POPULATION
629,000

FUN FACT
Djibouti is the name of both the republic and its capital. Its position at the entrance to the Red Sea makes it one of the most important seaports in Africa.

Madagascar

CAPITAL
Antananarivo

POPULATION
14,417,000

FUN FACT
Madagascar is a beautiful and, in some areas, rocky volcanic island in the Indian Ocean.

Le Mali

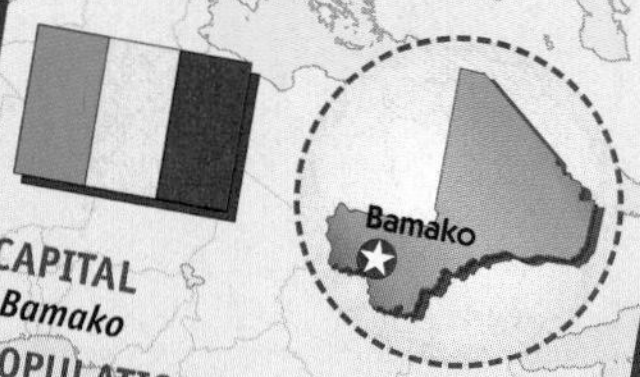

CAPITAL
Bamako

POPULATION
10,960,000

FUN FACT
Mali is the home of Timbuktu, which was and still is the terminus of a camel caravan route across the Sahara, linking Arabia with West Africa since ancient times.

La Guinée Équatoriale

CAPITAL
Malabo

POPULATION
442,000

FUN FACT
Equatorial Guinea is the only country in Africa where both Spanish and French are spoken even though French is considered the official language.

xxvi

L'île Maurice

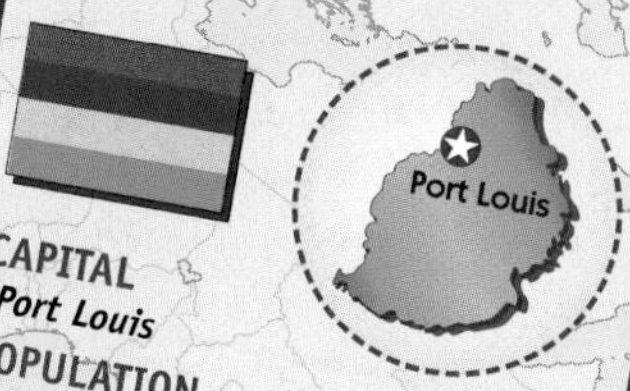

CAPITAL
Port Louis

POPULATION
1,172,000

FUN FACT
Mauritius is a volcanic island in the Indian Ocean known for its natural beauty.

La Mauritanie

CAPITAL
Nouakchott

POPULATION
23,000,000

FUN FACT
Mauritania is a bridge between the Maghreb in the North and sub-Saharan Africa in the South.

Le Niger

CAPITAL
Niamey

POPULATION
9,962,000

FUN FACT
Niger is a starkly dramatic country with its desert terrain. The capital, Niamey, on the fringe of the Sahara, is a city of modern buildings and wide boulevards—where many times you will see camels walking.

Le Maroc

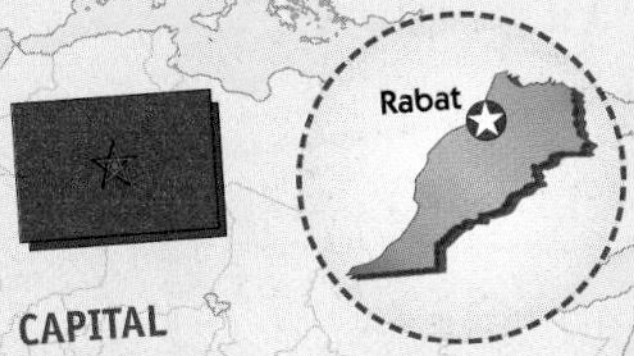

CAPITAL
Rabat

POPULATION
28,248,000

FUN FACT
Morocco is a country of many beautiful, fascinating cities, such as Casablanca, Tangiers, Fez, and Marrakech.

Les Seychelles

CAPITAL
Victoria

POPULATION
80,000

FUN FACT
The Republic of the Seychelles is made up of more than one hundred islands and is a vacationer's paradise. The Seychelles attract people from all over the world.

Le Tchad

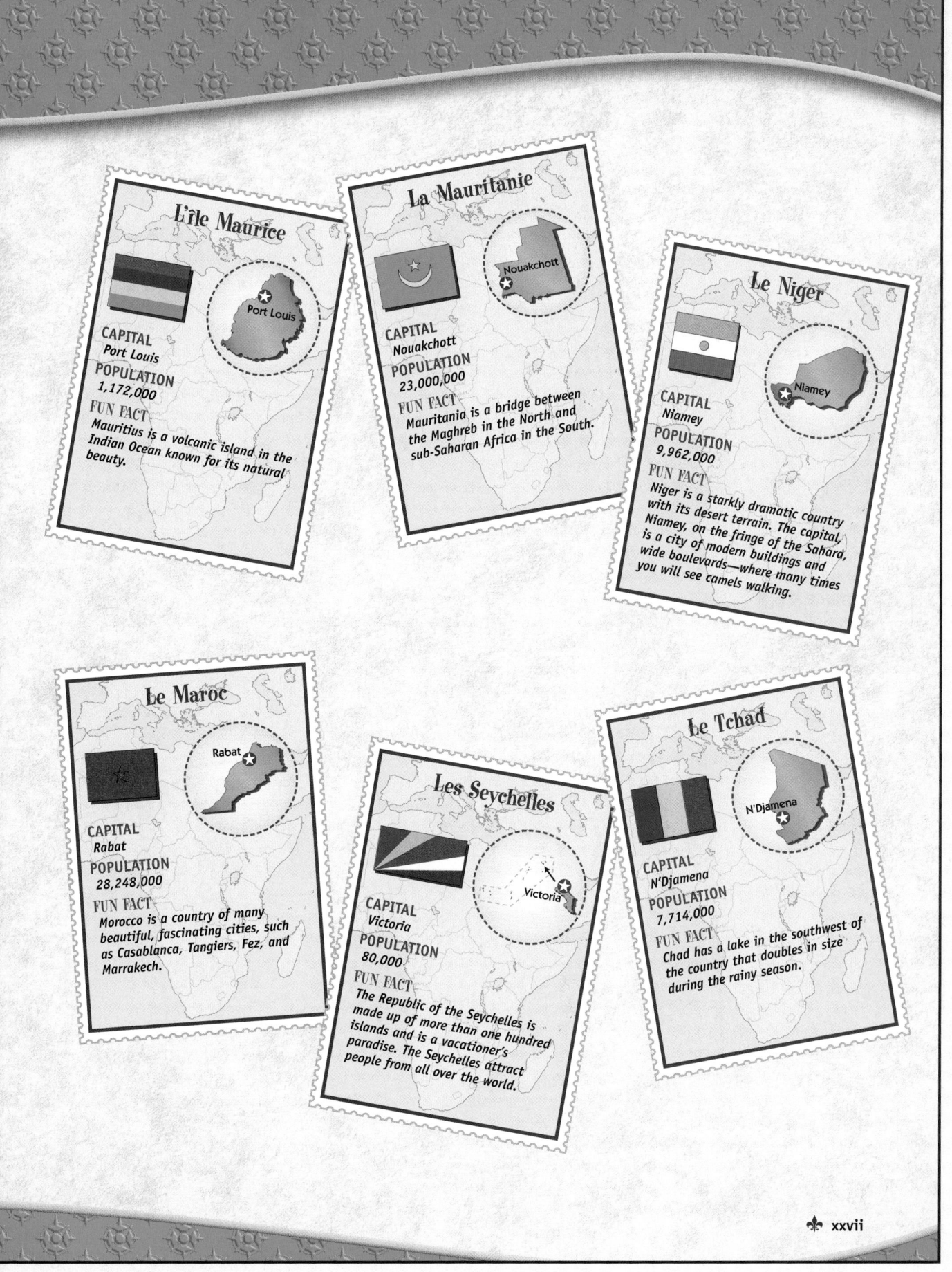

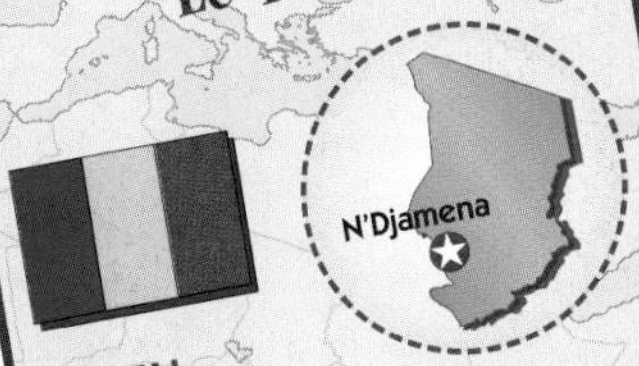

CAPITAL
N'Djamena

POPULATION
7,714,000

FUN FACT
Chad has a lake in the southwest of the country that doubles in size during the rainy season.

Le Rwanda

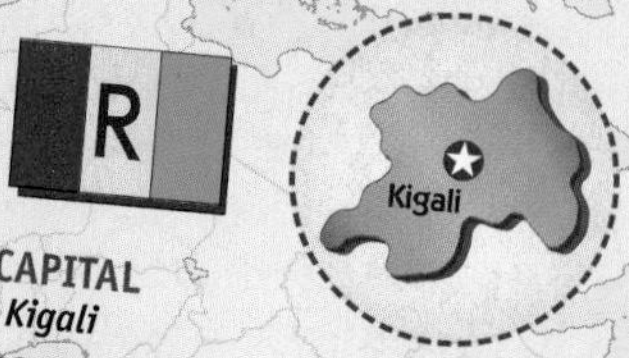

CAPITAL
Kigali

POPULATION
8,155,000

FUN FACT
Ruanda, located in Central Africa, is a country of many lakes. It has one of the densest populations in all of Africa.

La Réunion

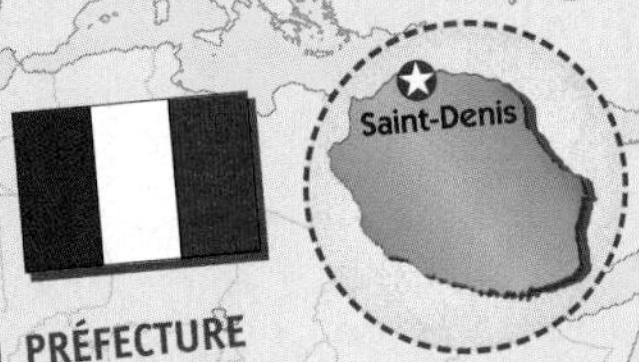

PRÉFECTURE
Saint-Denis

POPULATION
705,000

FUN FACT
Réunion, a French overseas department, is a beautiful island in the Indian Ocean with many beaches. It has a very hot, tropical climate.

Le Sénégal

CAPITAL
Dakar

POPULATION
9,240,000

FUN FACT
Senegal is a country that has a fabulous mix of Afro-French characteristics. More visitors go to Senegal than to any other Western African country.

Le Togo

CAPITAL
Lomé

POPULATION
4,512,000

FUN FACT
Togo is a pencil-thin strip of land whose capital, Lomé, has some of the most beautiful beaches just a block or two from the heart of town.

La Tunisie

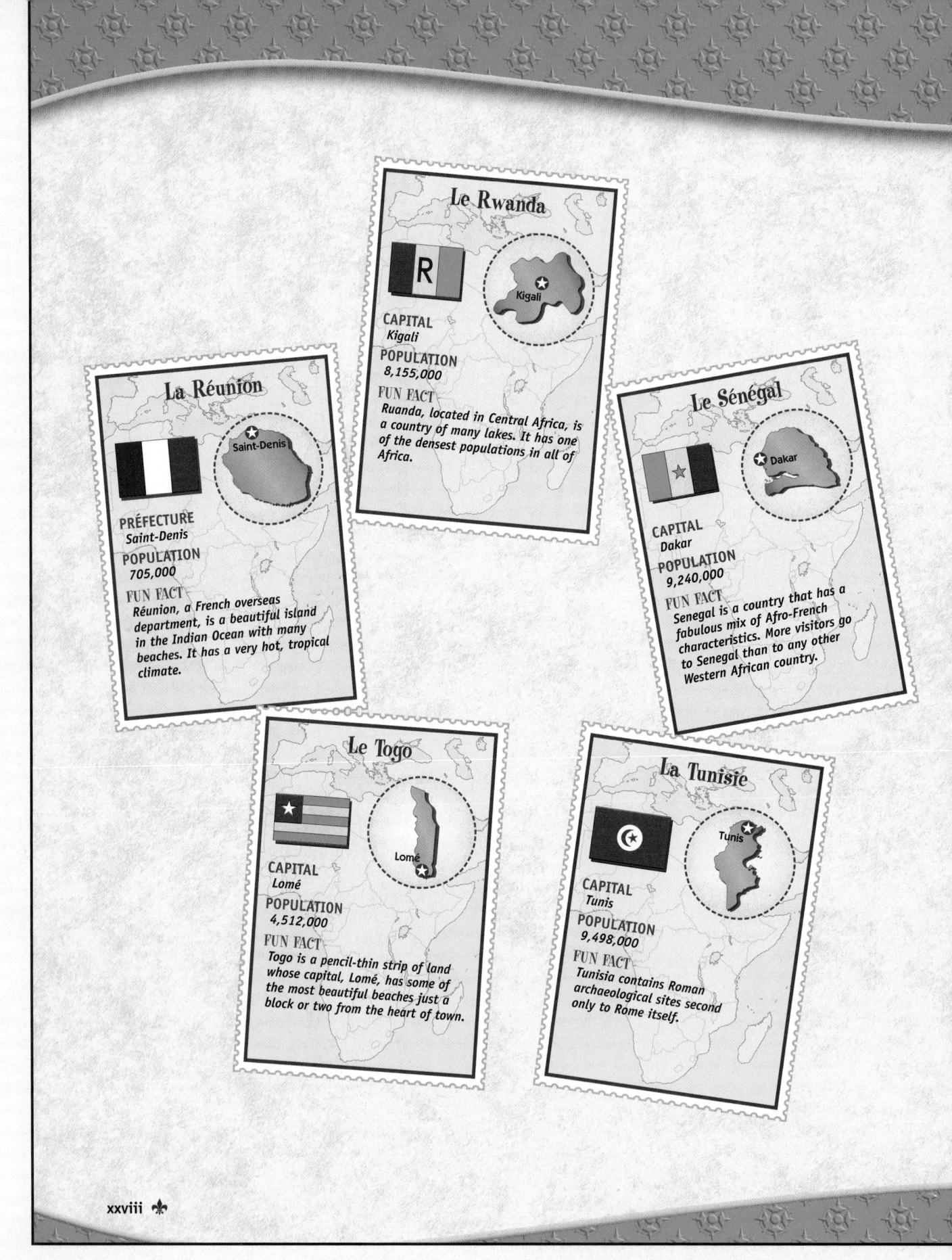

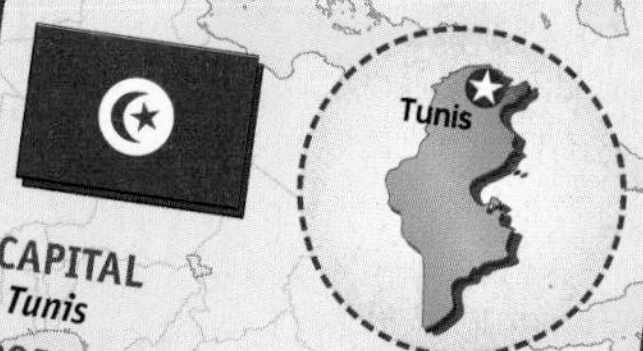

CAPITAL
Tunis

POPULATION
9,498,000

FUN FACT
Tunisia contains Roman archaeological sites second only to Rome itself.

xxviii

L'Amérique du Nord et du Sud

La Guadeloupe

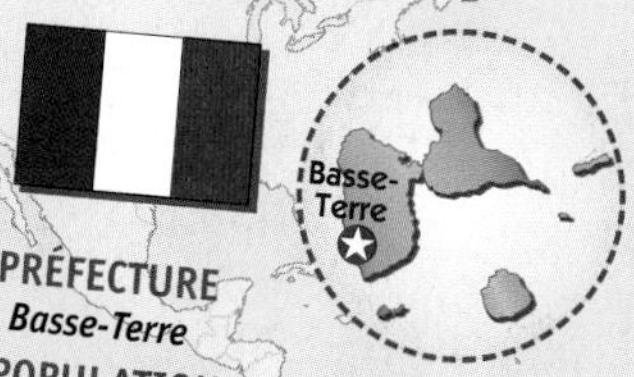

PRÉFECTURE
Basse-Terre

POPULATION
387,000

FUN FACT
Guadeloupe, a French overseas department in the Caribbean, is made up of two major islands in addition to some smaller ones. It is known for its jungle highlands and beautiful seaside resorts.

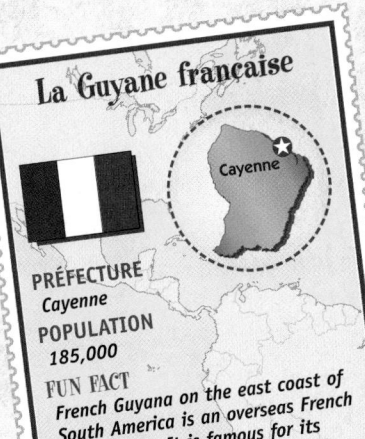

La Guyane française

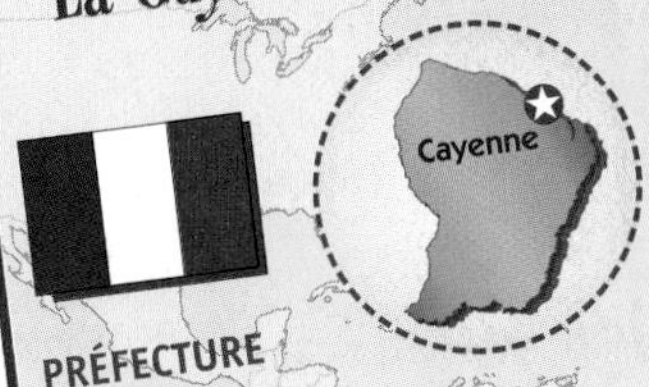

PRÉFECTURE
Cayenne

POPULATION
185,000

FUN FACT
French Guyana on the east coast of South America is an overseas French department. It is famous for its Devil's Island, which once served as a French penal colony.

Haïti

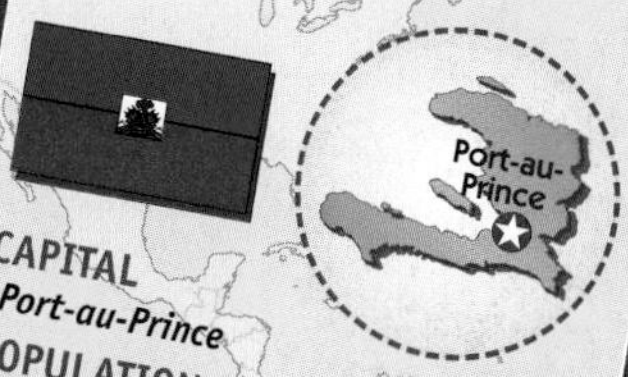

CAPITAL
Port-au-Prince

POPULATION
7,751,000

FUN FACT
Haiti shares the island of Hispaniola with the Dominican Republic. Its friendly people are known for their musical and artistic talents. Haitian primitive art is sought after in art galleries around the world.

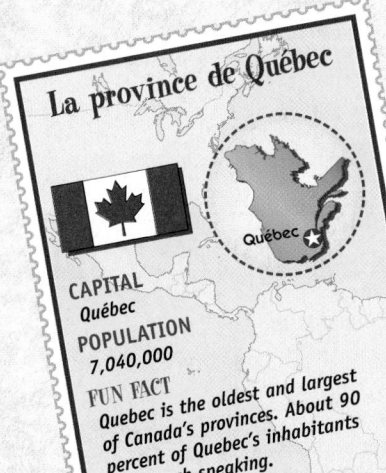

Saint-Pierre-et-Miquelon

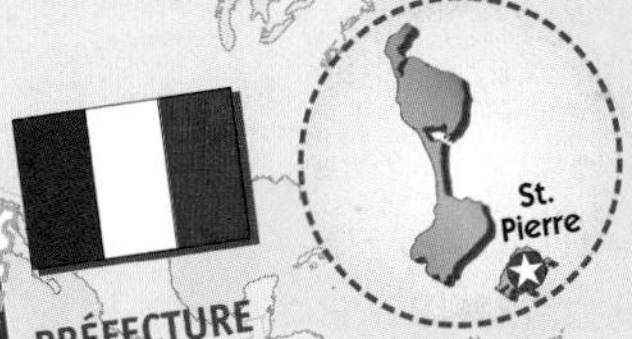

PRÉFECTURE
Saint-Pierre

POPULATION
6,966

FUN FACT
Saint-Pierre-et-Miquelon are two French-speaking islands in the Atlantic Ocean, south of Newfoundland. Many of its residents work in the cod-fishing industry.

La province de Québec

CAPITAL
Québec

POPULATION
7,040,000

FUN FACT
Quebec is the oldest and largest of Canada's provinces. About 90 percent of Quebec's inhabitants are French-speaking.

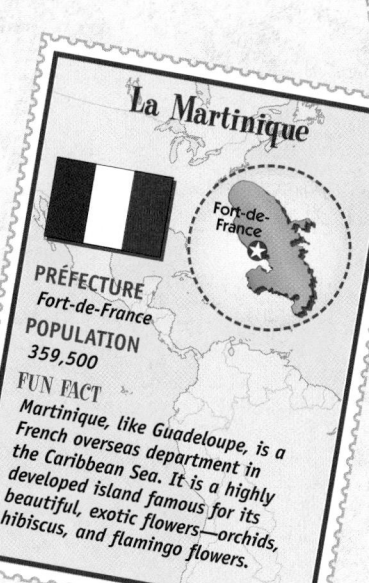

La Martinique

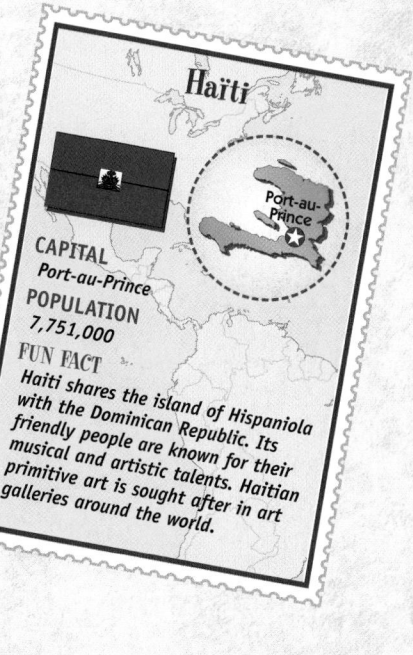

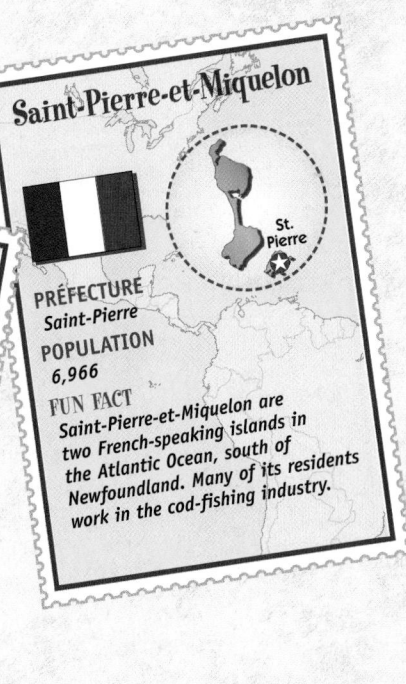

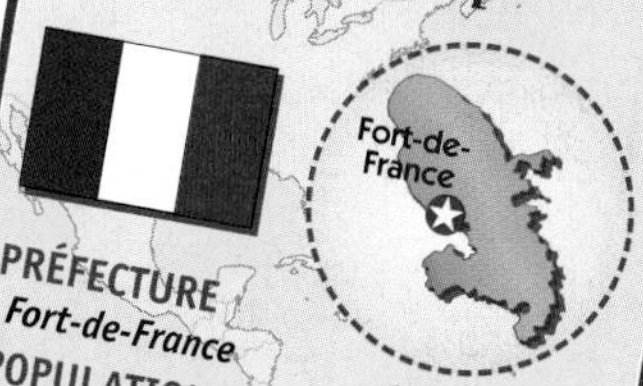

PRÉFECTURE
Fort-de-France

POPULATION
359,500

FUN FACT
Martinique, like Guadeloupe, is a French overseas department in the Caribbean Sea. It is a highly developed island famous for its beautiful, exotic flowers—orchids, hibiscus, and flamingo flowers.

L'Europe

La principauté d'Andorre

CAPITAL
Andorre-la-Vieille

POPULATION
66,000

FUN FACT
Andorra is a co-principality governed by France's president and a Spanish bishop.

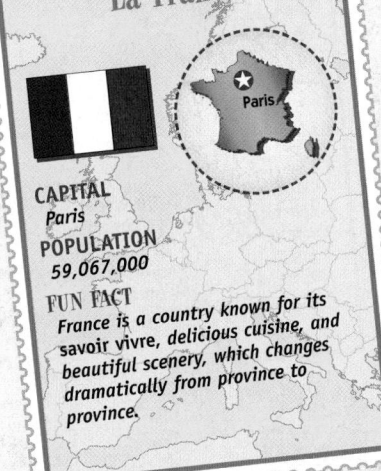

La Belgique

CAPITAL
Bruxelles

POPULATION
10,225,000

FUN FACT
Belgium is a rather small country but one of the world's most densely populated. Belgium has two distinct cultures—Flemish in the North and French in the South.

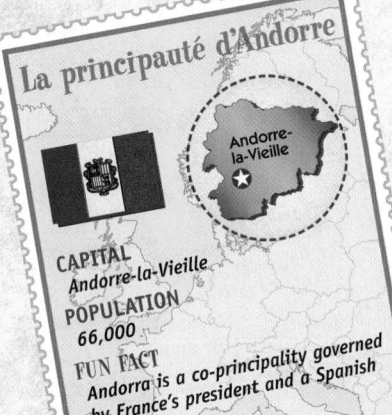

La France

CAPITAL
Paris

POPULATION
59,067,000

FUN FACT
France is a country known for its savoir vivre, delicious cuisine, and beautiful scenery, which changes dramatically from province to province.

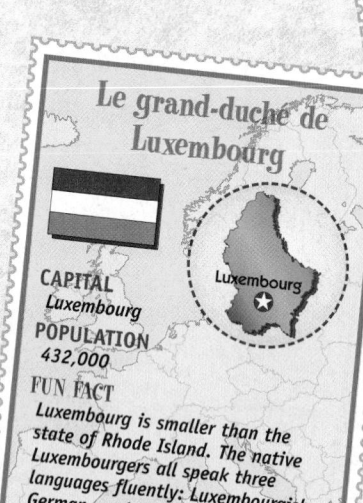

Le grand-duche de Luxembourg

CAPITAL
Luxembourg

POPULATION
432,000

FUN FACT
Luxembourg is smaller than the state of Rhode Island. The native Luxembourgers all speak three languages fluently: Luxembourgish, German, and French.

La principauté de Monaco

CAPITAL
Monaco

POPULATION
33,000

FUN FACT
Monaco is one of the world's smallest sovereign states. It is located on a horseshoe-shaped strip of land bathed by the Mediterranean on one side and shielded by alpine peaks on the other.

La Suisse

CAPITAL
Berne

POPULATION
7,119,000

FUN FACT
The beautiful country of Switzerland is dominated by the Alps. Its population density is among the lowest in Europe. Thus, it has fabulous wide-open spaces.

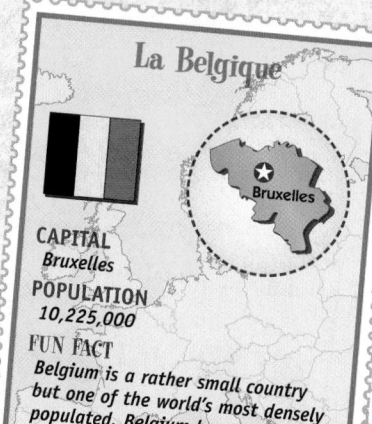

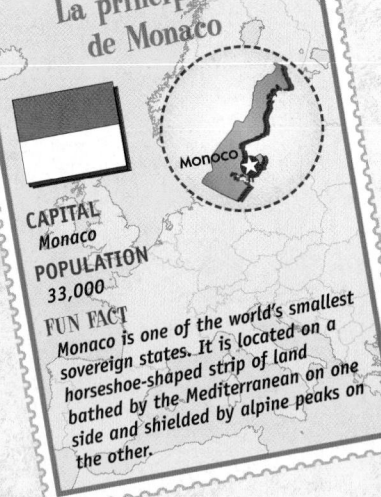

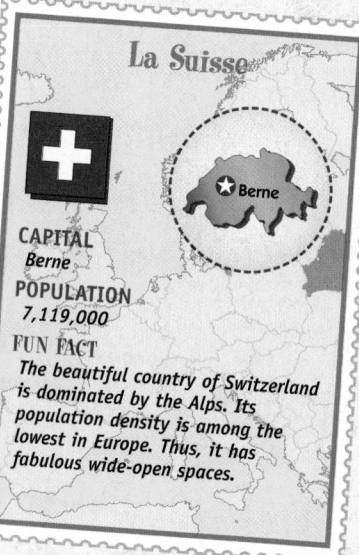

L'Océanie

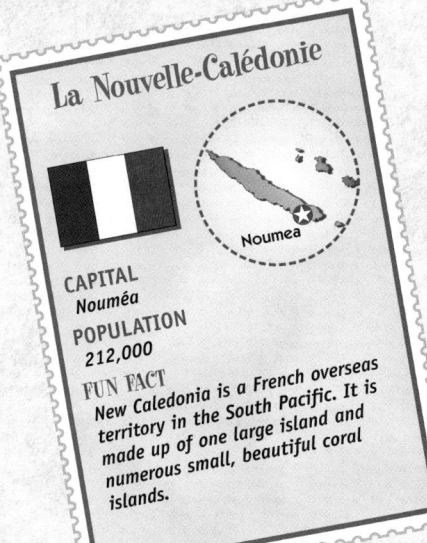

La Nouvelle-Calédonie

CAPITAL
Nouméa

POPULATION
212,000

FUN FACT
New Caledonia is a French overseas territory in the South Pacific. It is made up of one large island and numerous small, beautiful coral islands.

Vanuatu

CAPITAL
Port-Vila

POPULATION
186,000

FUN FACT
The republic of Vanuatu is an archipelago in the South Pacific, made up of forty islands of volcanic origin. Some of the volcanoes are still active.

La Polynésie française

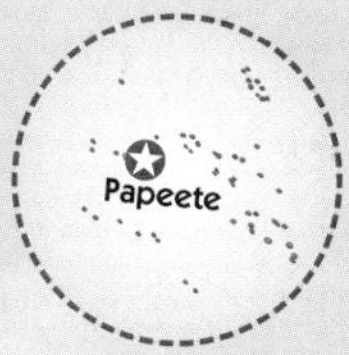

CAPITAL
Papeete

POPULATION
234,000

FUN FACT
French Polynesia is a French overseas territory made up of approximately 130 islands. The islands are known for their volcanic mountains, tropical climate, and beautiful bays and coves.

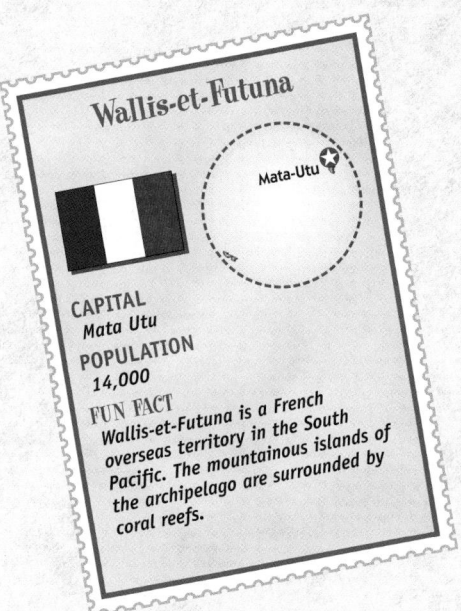

Wallis-et-Futuna

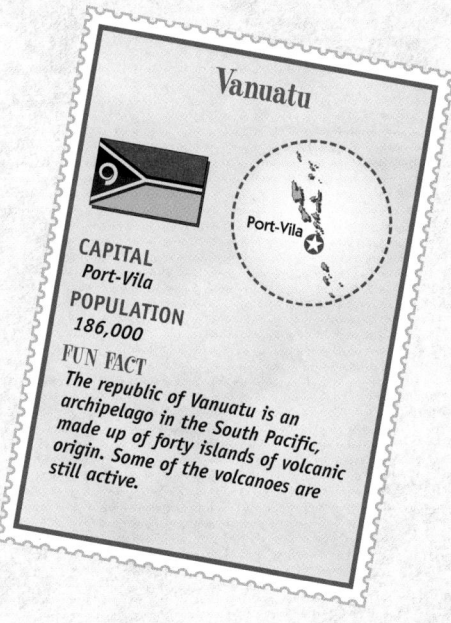

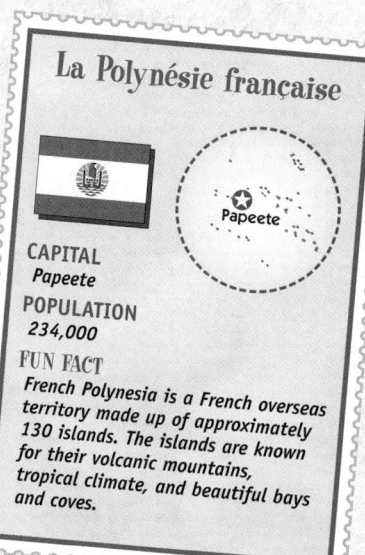

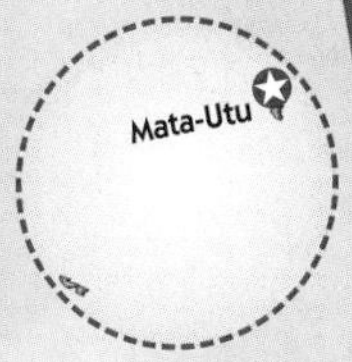

CAPITAL
Mata Utu

POPULATION
14,000

FUN FACT
Wallis-et-Futuna is a French overseas territory in the South Pacific. The mountainous islands of the archipelago are surrounded by coral reefs.

xxxi

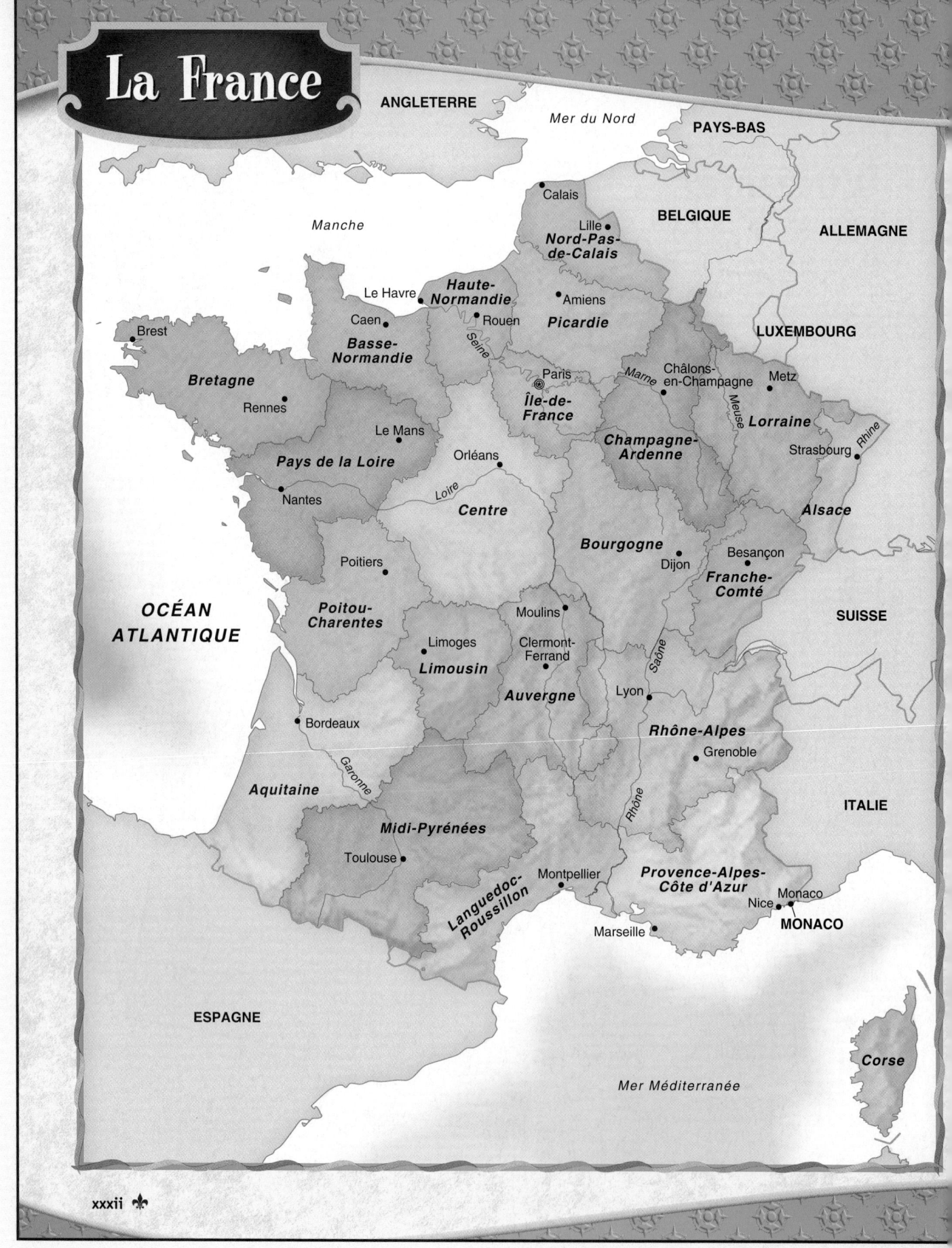

La France

ANGLETERRE
Mer du Nord
PAYS-BAS
Calais
BELGIQUE
Manche
Lille
Nord-Pas-de-Calais
ALLEMAGNE
Le Havre
Haute-Normandie
Amiens
Caen
Rouen
Picardie
Brest
LUXEMBOURG
Basse-Normandie
Seine
Paris
Marne
Châlons-en-Champagne
Metz
Bretagne
Rennes
Île-de-France
Meuse
Lorraine
Le Mans
Champagne-Ardenne
Rhine
Strasbourg
Orléans
Pays de la Loire
Loire
Nantes
Centre
Alsace
Bourgogne
Besançon
Poitiers
Dijon
Franche-Comté
OCÉAN ATLANTIQUE
Poitou-Charentes
Moulins
SUISSE
Limoges
Clermont-Ferrand
Saône
Limousin
Auvergne
Lyon
Bordeaux
Rhône-Alpes
Grenoble
Garonne
Aquitaine
Rhône
ITALIE
Midi-Pyrénées
Toulouse
Montpellier
Provence-Alpes-Côte d'Azur
Languedoc-Roussillon
Monaco
Nice
MONACO
Marseille
ESPAGNE
Corse
Mer Méditerranée

Paris

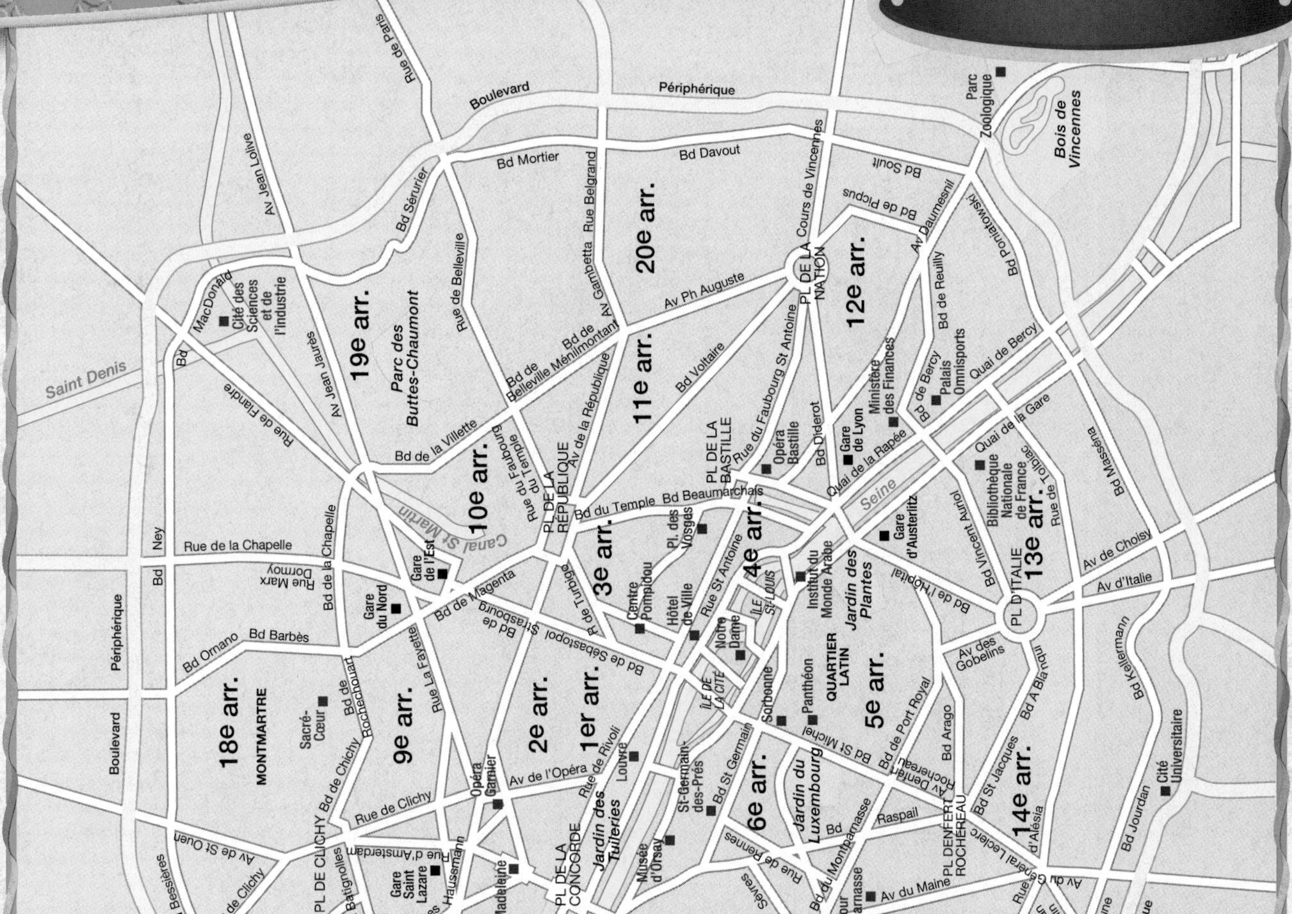

xxxiii

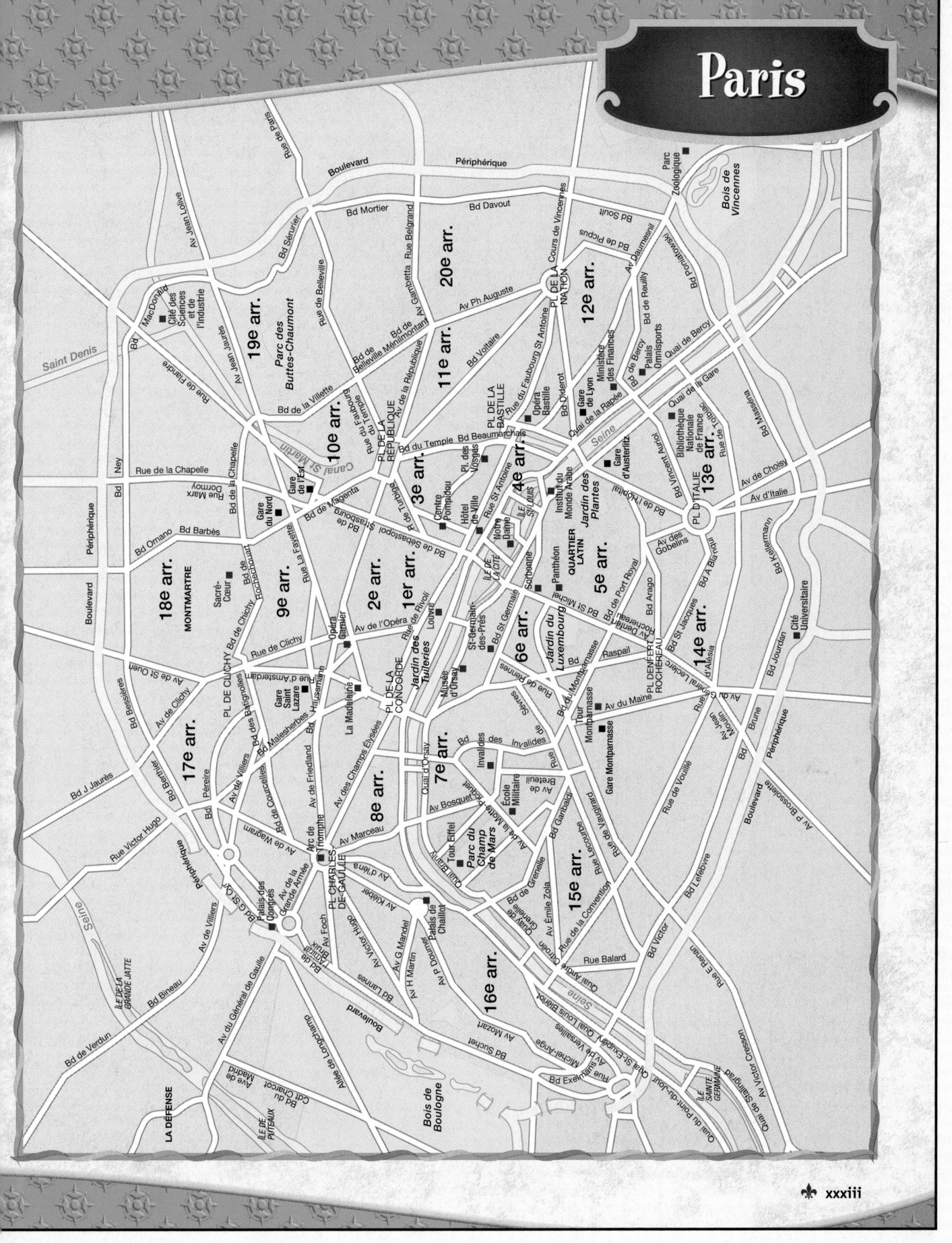

Le Canada

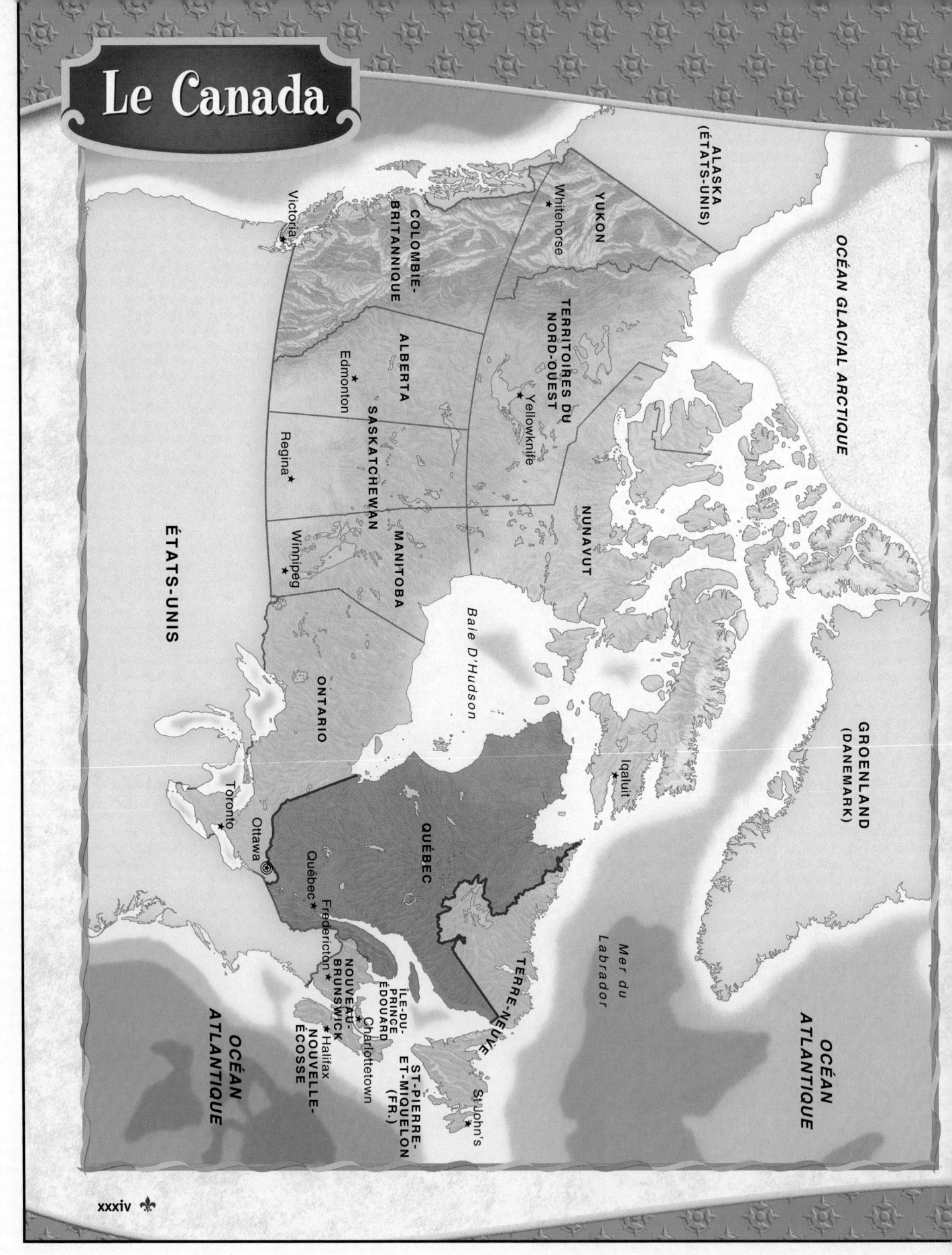

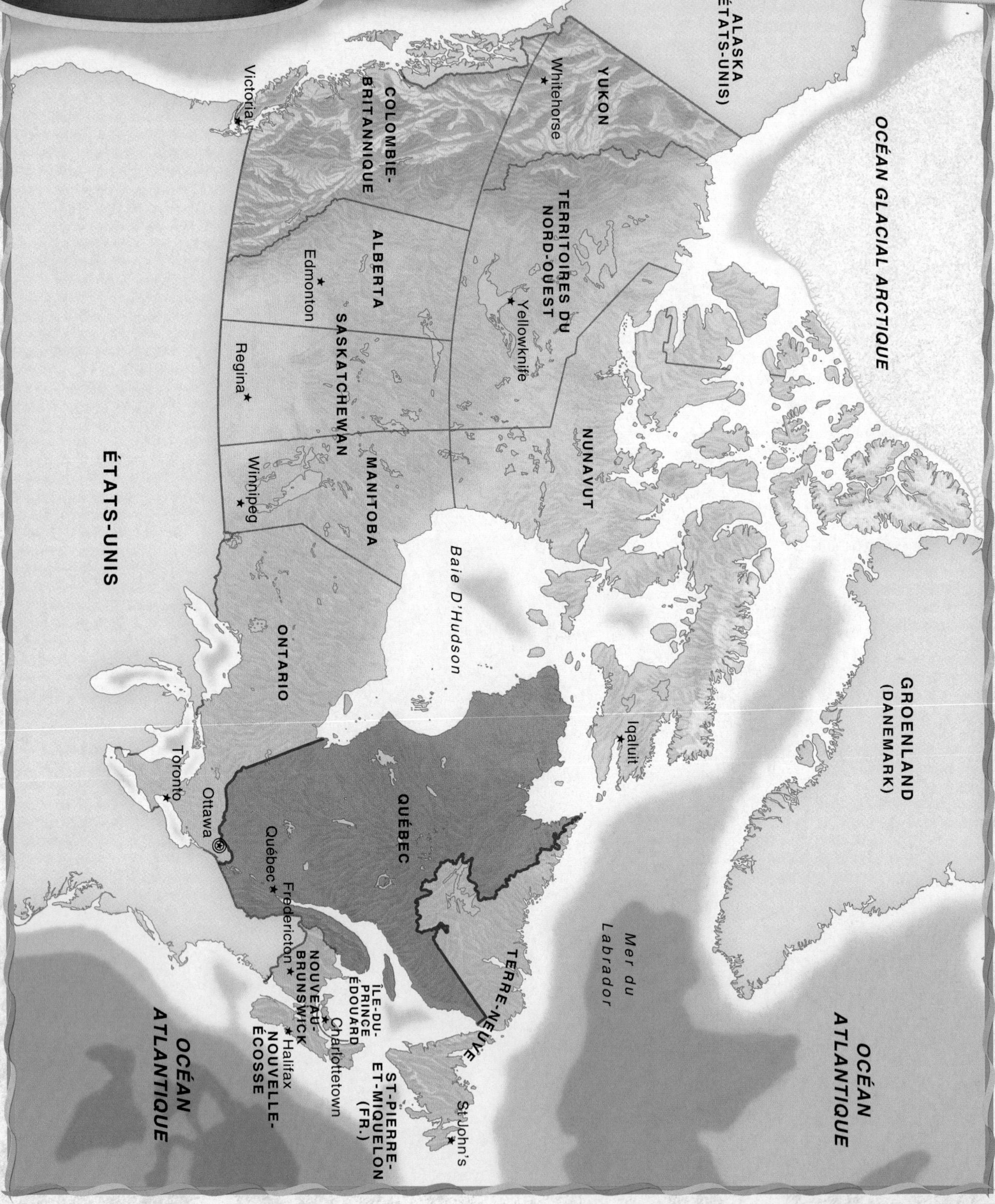

xxxiv

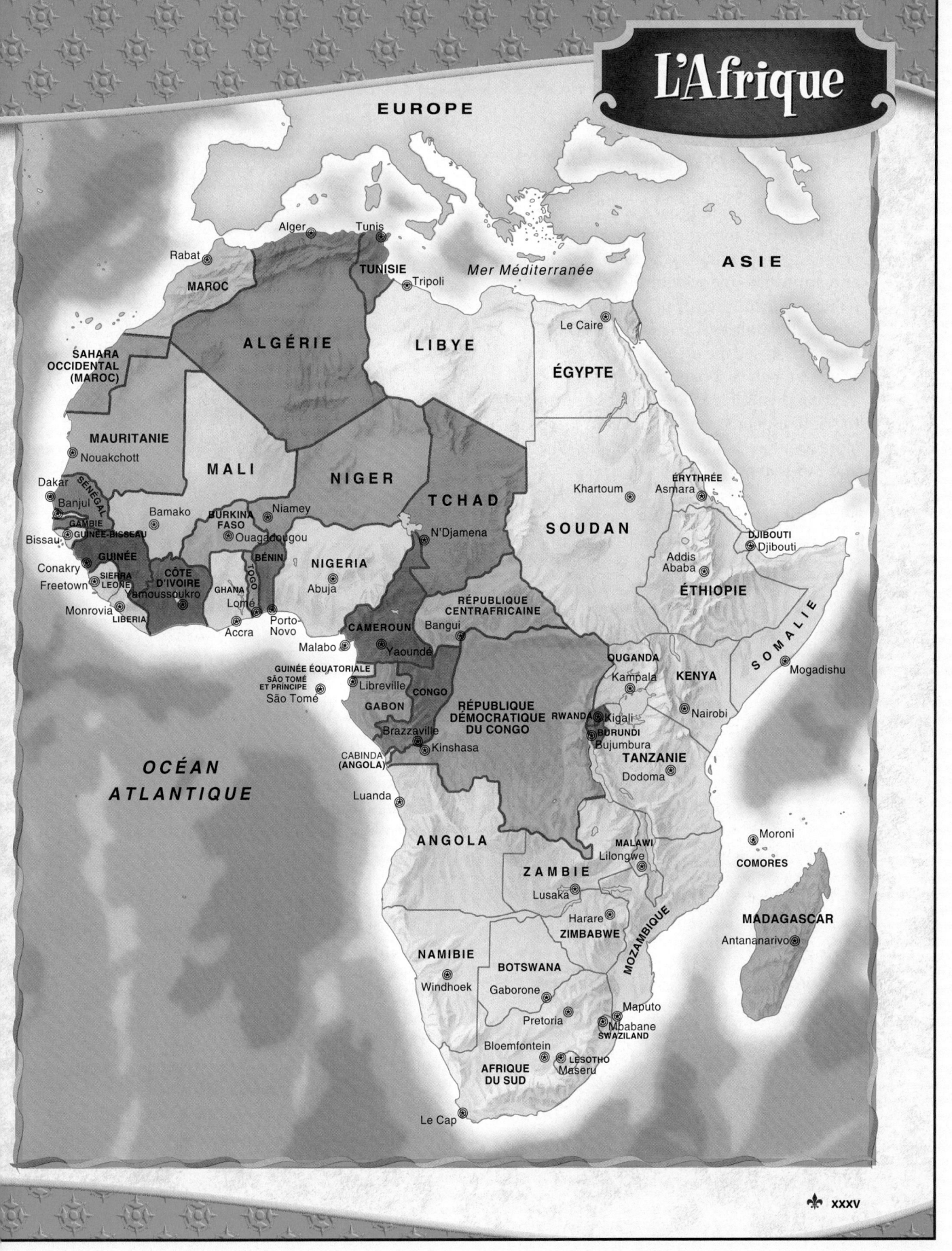

L'Afrique

EUROPE
ASIE
Mer Méditerranée
OCÉAN ATLANTIQUE
Alger
Tunis
Rabat
TUNISIE
Tripoli
MAROC
Le Caire
ALGÉRIE
LIBYE
SAHARA OCCIDENTAL (MAROC)
ÉGYPTE
MAURITANIE
Nouakchott
MALI
NIGER
TCHAD
Dakar
SÉNÉGAL
Banjul
GAMBIE
Bamako
BURKINA FASO
Niamey
Ouagadougou
Bissau
GUINÉE-BISSEAU
N'Djamena
Khartoum
ÉRYTHRÉE
Asmara
SOUDAN
DJIBOUTI
Djibouti
GUINÉE
BÉNIN
NIGERIA
Conakry
SIERRA LEONE
Freetown
CÔTE D'IVOIRE
Yamoussoukro
TOGO
GHANA
Abuja
Addis Ababa
ÉTHIOPIE
Monrovia
LIBERIA
Lomé
Accra
Porto-Novo
RÉPUBLIQUE CENTRAFRICAINE
Bangui
CAMEROUN
Yaoundé
Malabo
SOMALIE
Mogadishu
GUINÉE ÉQUATORIALE
SÃO TOMÉ ET PRINCIPE
São Tomé
Libreville
GABON
CONGO
OUGANDA
Kampala
KENYA
Nairobi
RÉPUBLIQUE DÉMOCRATIQUE DU CONGO
RWANDA
Kigali
BURUNDI
Bujumbura
Brazzaville
Kinshasa
CABINDA (ANGOLA)
TANZANIE
Dodoma
Luanda
ANGOLA
MALAWI
Lilongwe
Moroni
COMORES
ZAMBIE
Lusaka
Harare
ZIMBABWE
MOZAMBIQUE
MADAGASCAR
Antananarivo
NAMIBIE
Windhoek
BOTSWANA
Gaborone
Pretoria
Maputo
Mbabane
SWAZILAND
Bloemfontein
LESOTHO
Maseru
AFRIQUE DU SUD
Le Cap

Why Learn French?

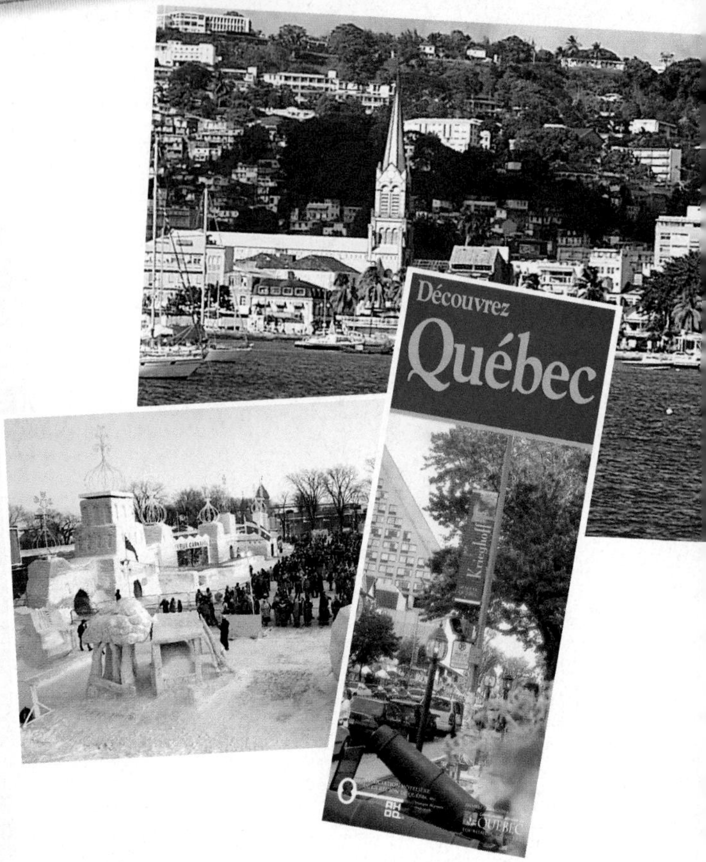

The Francophone World

Culture Knowing French will open doors to you around the world. As you study the language, you will also come to understand and appreciate the way of life, customs, values, and cultures of people from many different countries. Look at the map on page xxii to see the areas of the world in which French is spoken, either as a first or second language. You might be surprised to see that people speak French in places as close to home as Haiti, Martinique, Quebec, and Louisiana.

Learning French can be fun and will bring you a sense of accomplishment. You'll be really pleased when you are able to carry on a conversation with a French-speaking person in French. You will also be able to read French literature, keep up with current events in French magazines and newspapers, and understand French films without relying on subtitles. The French language will be a source of enrichment for the rest of your life.

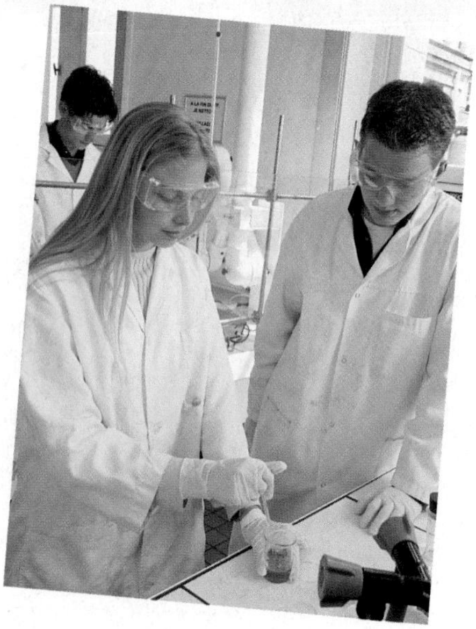

Career Opportunities

Business Your knowledge of French will also be an asset to you in a variety of careers. Many French companies are multinational and have branches around the world, including the United States. Some of the fields in which French companies excel are: clothing and fashion, cosmetics, tourism, agriculture, the automotive and aerospace industries, and technology.

Research France is also a world leader in high-energy physics research and medical genetics. Did you know that French and English are the two major languages of the Internet? French can help you in almost any career path you choose.

Language Link

Another benefit to learning French is that it will improve your English. Once you know another language, you can make comparisons between the two and gain a greater understanding of how languages function. As a result, your use of English will be more effective. You'll also come across many French words that are used in English. Just a few examples are: **rouge, chaise longue, chic, crêpe, à la mode, omelette, chargé d'affaires, déjà vu, détente,** and **laisser faire.** French will also be helpful if you decide to learn yet another language. Once you learn a second language, the learning process for acquiring other languages becomes much easier.

French is a beautiful, rich language that is spoken on many continents. Many people use French on a daily basis as their second language. Whatever your motivation is for choosing to study it, French will expand your horizons and increase your job opportunities. **Vive la langue française! Et bon voyage!**

L'alphabet français

a

***a**mis*

b

***b**é**b**é*

c

***c**irque*

d

***d**eux*

e

*l**e**çon*

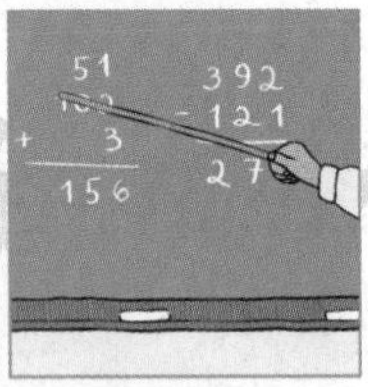

f

***f**enêtre*

g

***g**iraffe*

h

***h**uit*

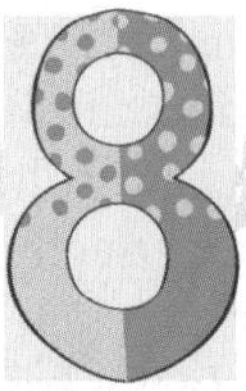

i

***i**gloo*

j

***j**eu*

k

***k**ilo*

l

***l**ivre*

m

***m**aison*

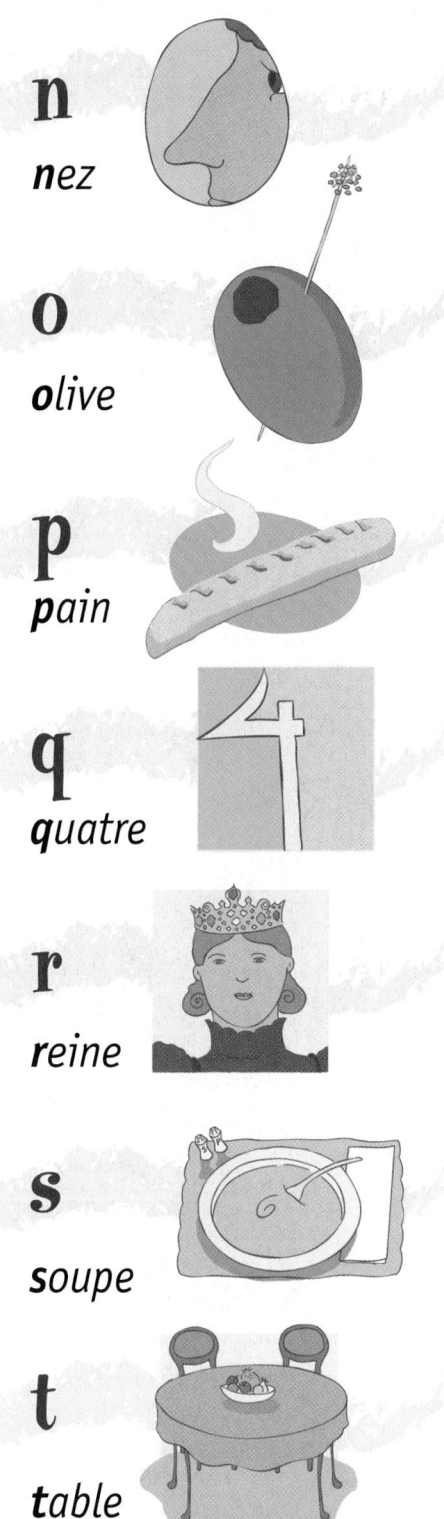

n

***n**ez*

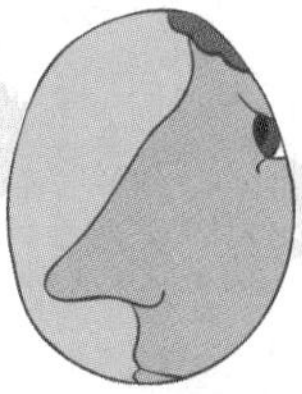

o

***o**live*

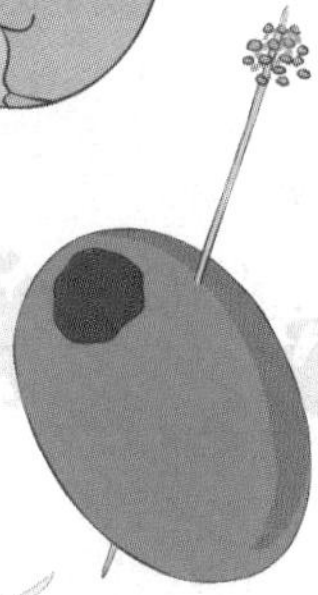

p

***p**ain*

q

***q**uatre*

r

***r**eine*

s

***s**oupe*

t

***t**able*

u

***u**nivers*

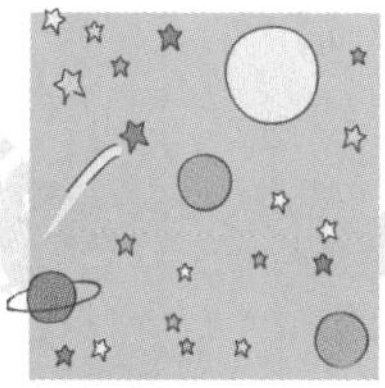

v

***v**iolette*

w

***w**agon*

x

*e**x**tra*

y

***y**eux*

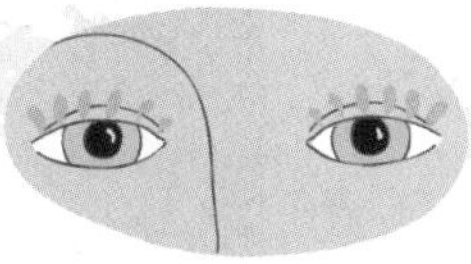

z

***z**èbre*

Preview

In the **Bienvenue** section, students will begin their study by communicating immediately in French. In this preliminary section, they will learn to greet one another, take leave of one another, ask and tell names, express simple courtesies, use days of the week and months of the year, count from 1–30, and tell time.

National Standards

Communication

In this preliminary section, students will communicate in spoken French on the following topics:

- greeting others
- saying good-bye
- being polite
- dates and seasons
- counting
- telling time

Leçons préliminaires

Bienvenue

Objectifs

In these preliminary lessons you will learn to:

- ✓ *greet people*
- ✓ *say good-bye to people*
- ✓ *ask people how they are*
- ✓ *ask and tell names*
- ✓ *express simple courtesies*
- ✓ *find out and tell the days of the week*
- ✓ *find out and tell the months of the year*
- ✓ *count from 1 to 30*
- ✓ *find out and tell the time*

4.

3.

2.

1.

FRENCH Online

The **Glencoe Foreign Language Web site** (french.glencoe.com) offers several options that enable you and your students to experience the French-speaking world via the Internet:

- The online **Activités** are correlated to the chapters and utilize Francophone Web sites around the world.
- Games and puzzles afford students another opportunity to practice the material learned in a particular chapter.
- The *Enrichment* section offers students an opportunity to visit Web sites related to the theme of the chapter for more information on a particular topic.
- Online *Chapter Quizzes* offer students an opportunity to prepare for a chapter test.
- Visit our virtual **Café** for more opportunities to practice and to explore the French-speaking world.

1. Karim Ashour, Tunis, Tunisie
2. Yvonne Senghor, Abidjan, Côte d'Ivoire
3. Jacques Ferrand, Montréal, Canada
4. Thérèse Nguyen, Lyon, France
5. Yves Clémenceau, Fort-de-France, Martinique
6. Ahmed Rashid, Paris, France
7. Vincent Daudet, Rouen, France
8. Élodie Lutz, Strasbourg, France
9. Marie Robert, Marseille, France

Spotlight on Culture

Photographs Throughout their study of French in **Bon voyage!**, students will learn about the many areas of the world where French is spoken. In this preliminary opener, students see photos of young people from representative areas of the Francophone world.

Preview

In this short lesson, which should take less than one class period, students will learn to greet their peers and older people.

Presentation

Greeting people

Step 1 Have students repeat the conversation with as much expression as possible. Begin with books open. Then repeat with books closed.

Step 2 Have students read the conversation aloud in pairs.

Step 3 Use simple drawings of faces to illustrate so-so, content, and very happy. Have students identify the corresponding response to **Ça va?** for each face.

Step 4 Have students stand and greet each other using a brisk, French-style handshake.

Préliminaire A *Bonjour!*

Greeting people

When someone wants to know how you are doing and asks **Ça va?,** there are several different answers you can give.

Ça va.
Bien, merci.
Ça va très bien.
Pas mal, merci.

1 Salut!

Get up from your desk. Walk around the classroom. Say hello to each classmate you meet.

2 Ça va?

Work with a classmate. Greet one another and find out how things are going.

Answers

1 *Students will say* Salut! *(and perhaps shake hands).*

2 *Students will use the greetings in the text. Dialogues may include:*

Salut! / Salut! Ça va?
Oui, ça va. Et toi? / Pas mal, merci.

More greetings

1. **Salut!** is an informal greeting that you can use with people your own age. When you greet an older person, you may use the following expressions.

Bonjour, monsieur.

Bonjour, madame.

Bonjour, mademoiselle.

2. Note that the titles **monsieur, madame,** and **mademoiselle** are almost always used without the last name of the person.

3 Bonjour!

Draw some figures on the board. Some will represent friends your own age and others will represent older people. Greet each of the figures on the board properly.

4 Salutations

Look at these photographs of young people in France and Martinique. As they greet one another they do some things that are different from what we do when we greet each other. What do you notice in the photographs?

Presentation

More greetings

Step 1 Greet each student: **Bonjour, Michel.** Have students answer you appropriately: **Bonjour, madame, (monsieur, mademoiselle).**

Step 2 Name other adults from school (librarian, secretary, etc.) and have students state an appropriate greeting for each.

Attention!

It is suggested that you present these preliminary lessons for oral work only. Writing begins in Chapter 1.

Paired Activity

Have students work in pairs to make up their own exchanges for greeting each other. Call on volunteers to present their skits to the class.

Reaching All Students

Additional Practice Practice greeting the following people.

1. your history teacher.
2. a young saleswoman at the department store.
3. your parents' friend, Mrs. Smith.
4. your neighbor, Mr. Roberts.
5. the principal of your school.

Answers

3 Answers will use the appropriate greetings taught on pages 2–3.

4 Men shake hands, two women or a man and a woman give each other a light kiss on each cheek.

Préliminaire B

Preview

In this lesson, students will learn farewell expressions. **Préliminaire A** and **B** together should take about one classroom period.

Presentation

Saying good-bye

Step 1 Have students look at the photo as they repeat the expressions for leave-taking.

Step 2 Have them read Items 1, 2, 3 aloud or read them to the students. Have the class repeat each word or expression in unison.

Recycling

You are walking down the street in Poitiers, in western France, when you run into one of your French friends (your partner). Greet each other and ask each other how things are going.

Préliminaire B *Au revoir!*

Saying good-bye

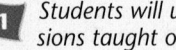

Au revoir, madame.
Au revoir, Christine.

Ciao, Thomas.
À tout à l'heure.
Ciao, Charlotte.

1. A very common expression to use when saying good-bye to someone is **Au revoir.**
2. If you plan to see the person again soon, you can say **À bientôt!** If you plan to see the person very soon, you can say **À tout à l'heure.** If you plan to see the person the next day, you can say **À demain.**
3. An informal expression you often hear is **Ciao.** It comes from Italian and is used in many parts of Europe.

1 Ciao!

Go over to a classmate and say good-bye to him or her.

2 À bientôt!

Work with a classmate. Say **Ciao** to each other and let one another know when you will be getting together again.

3 Au revoir!

Say good-bye to your French teacher. Use **monsieur, madame,** or **mademoiselle,** as appropriate. Then say good-bye to a friend. Use a different expression with each person.

Reaching All Students

Additional Practice Have a student near the front of the room say good-bye to a student seated nearby, using an appropriate expression. Continue around the room, having each student say good-bye to a neighbor using any appropriate expression.

Answers

1. *Students will use one of the expressions taught on page 4.*
2. *Students will say* Au revoir! *or* Ciao!, *followed by either* À bientôt!, À tout à l'heure! *or* À demain!
3. *Students will use two of the expressions taught on page 4.*

Conversation

Salut, Rémi.
Salut, Julie. Ça va?
Ça va. Et toi?
Pas mal, merci.

Au revoir.
Au revoir. À bientôt!

4 Salut!

Work with a classmate. Have a conversation in French. Say as much as you can to each other.

5 Bonjour!

Work with a classmate. One of you will pretend to be an older person. Have a conversation. Say as much as you can to each other.

Préliminaire B

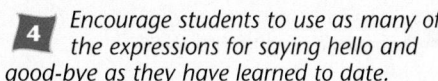

Presentation

Conversation

Recycling

This conversation recombines the greetings and farewells presented in Preliminary Lessons A and B.

Step 1 Have pairs of students present the conversation to the class. They can read it if necessary, but many will probably be able to do it on their own. If they make any changes that make sense, that's fine.

Step 2 Encourage students to use as much expression and as many gestures as possible when presenting the conversation.

Reaching All Students

Additional Practice

- Say the following to a classmate. He or she will answer.
  Salut!
  Ça va?
  Au revoir!
  Ciao!
- Say good-bye to your French teacher. Say you will see him or her tomorrow.
- Say good-bye to a friend. Say that you'll see him or her later in the day.

Answers

4 *Encourage students to use as many of the expressions for saying hello and good-bye as they have learned to date.*

5 *Encourage students to use as many of the expressions for saying hello and good-bye as they have learned to date, being careful to observe the conventions of formality.*

Preview

In this lesson, students will learn to tell their names and ask others their own age for their names.

Presentation

Finding out a person's name

Step 1 Have the students repeat the miniconversation after you with books closed.

Step 2 Then have students open books and read the conversation aloud in pairs.

Step 3 Have one student ask his neighbor's name. The student who responds then asks the next student and so on.

Préliminaire C Les noms

Finding out a person's name

Tu t'appelles comment?
Moi, je m'appelle Nicolas. Et toi?
Je m'appelle Marie.

When you want to find out the name of a person who is about the same age as you, you can ask **Tu t'appelles comment?** However, you would not use this expression with an older person. You will learn the more formal forms at a later time.

1 Tu t'appelles comment?

Get up from your desk. Walk around the room. Find out several of your classmates' names. Let them know your name, too.

Answers

1 *Students will use the question and answer taught on page 6.*

Conversation

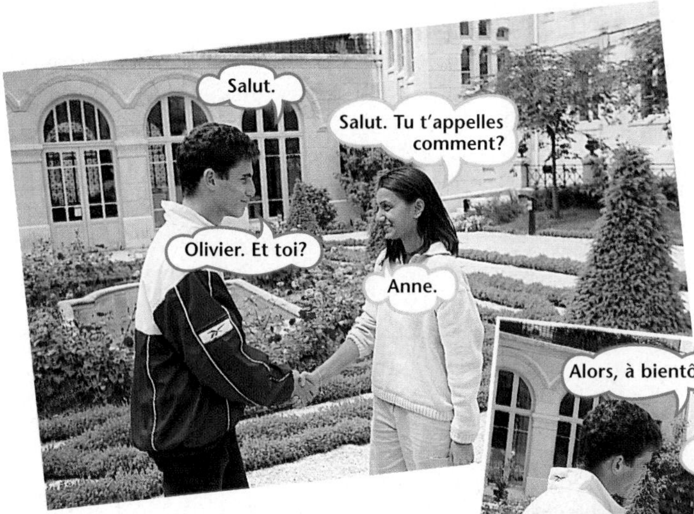

Salut.
Salut. Tu t'appelles comment?
Olivier. Et toi?
Anne.

Alors, à bientôt!
À bientôt, Olivier!

2 Salut!

Have a conversation with a classmate. Find out each other's name, how things are going, and say good-bye to each other.

3 Je m'appelle...

Look at this photograph of young French people introducing each other. Are they doing something that you probably would not do? What is it?

Answers

2 *Encourage students to use as many of the expressions that they have learned to date as possible.*

3 *They are shaking hands.*

Préliminaire C

Presentation

Conversation

Recycling

This conversation recombines greetings, farewells, and introductions.

Step 1 Have pairs of students present the conversation to the class. They can read it if necessary, but many will probably be able to do it on their own. If they make any changes that make sense, that's fine.

Préliminaire D

Preview

In this lesson, students will learn to order a few simple food items. They will also learn the polite expressions one needs to know when dealing with people.

Presentation

Ordering food politely

Step 1 Have the students repeat the dialogue.

Step 2 Have them read the information about *please, thank you* and *you're welcome.* Repeat the expressions several times.

Préliminaire D *La politesse*

Ordering food politely

Expressions of politeness are always appreciated. The following are the French expressions for "please," "thank you," and "you're welcome."

Formal	Informal
S'il vous plaît.	S'il te plaît.
Merci (madame).	Merci.
Je vous en prie.	Je t'en prie.

Préliminaire D

1 La politesse

With a classmate, practice reading the preceding conversation aloud. Be as animated and as polite as you can.

2 Une limonade, s'il vous plaît.

You are at a café in Canada. Order the following things. Your partner will be the server. Be polite when you order.

1. 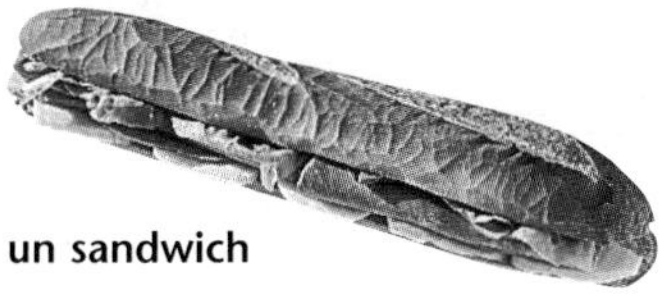
un sandwich

2. 
un coca

3. 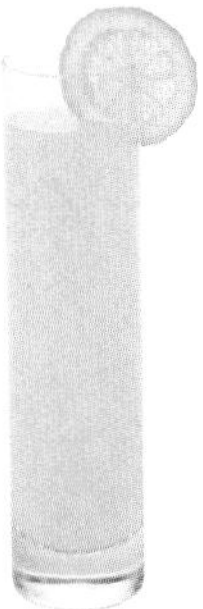
une limonade

4. 
un café

5. 
une pizza

6. 
une saucisse de Francfort, un hot-dog

7. 
une crêpe

1 Expansion: Have the students change the dialogue to an exchange between two classmates at a French Club party:

—Salut, Marie.
—Salut. Une limonade, s'il te plaît.
—Merci.
—Je t'en prie.

About the French Language

- In Canada, the word for lemonade is **une limonade.** In France, it is **une citronnade.** In France, **une limonade** is a carbonated, clear lemon-flavored soda.
- **Un hot-dog** is used in both Canada and France. In France, **une saucisse de Francfort** is also used.

Answers

1 *Monitor students' practice. Then ask for pairs to perform their dialogue for the class.*

2 *Answers will vary, but students should follow the model conversation on page 8 when doing this activity.*

Préliminaire E

Preview

In this lesson, students learn the days of the week, the months, and numbers from 1 to 30. These topics will be reinforced and recycled in later chapters.

Presentation

Telling the days of the week, Telling the months

Step 1 Have students repeat the days of the week and months of the year.

Step 2 Have them give different days of the week and months at random, rather than in a fixed order. Many students know the days of the week when they recite them in a row but don't know the difference between **mardi** and **jeudi,** for example. Having them give the days of the week in other than a set order helps avoid this problem.

Note: Although we will concern ourselves with writing starting in Chapter 1, you may want to point out to students that days and months are not capitalized in French.

Préliminaire E *La date*

Telling the days of the week

To find out and give the day of the week, you say:

C'est quel jour aujourd'hui?
(Aujourd'hui), c'est lundi.
Demain, c'est mardi.

LUNDI	MARDI	MERCREDI	JEUDI	VENDREDI	SAMEDI	DIMANCHE
1	2	3	4	5	6	7
8	9	10	11	12	13	14

1 C'est quel jour?

Answer the following questions in French.

1. C'est quel jour aujourd'hui?
2. Et demain? C'est quel jour?

Telling the months

janvier	mai	septembre
février	juin	octobre
mars	juillet	novembre
avril	août	décembre

Les nombres de 1 à 30

1 un	7 sept	13 treize	19 dix-neuf	25 vingt-cinq
2 deux	8 huit	14 quatorze	20 vingt	26 vingt-six
3 trois	9 neuf	15 quinze	21 vingt et un	27 vingt-sept
4 quatre	10 dix	16 seize	22 vingt-deux	28 vingt-huit
5 cinq	11 onze	17 dix-sept	23 vingt-trois	29 vingt-neuf
6 six	12 douze	18 dix-huit	24 vingt-quatre	30 trente

ANSWERS

1

1. Aujourd'hui, c'est _____.
2. Demain, c'est _____.

Finding out and giving the date

Quelle est la date aujourd'hui?
(C'est) le trente et un août.

LUNDI	MARDI	MERCREDI	JEUDI	VENDREDI	SAMEDI	DIMANCHE
1	2	3	4	5	6	7
8	9	10	11	12	13	14
15	16	17	18	19	20	21
22	23	24	25	26	27	28
29	30	31				

Premier is used for the first day of the month. For other days you use **deux, trois, quatre,** etc.

le premier août
le deux septembre

2 La date, s'il vous plaît.

Answer the following questions in French.

1. Quelle est la date aujourd'hui?
2. Et demain?

le 6 janvier

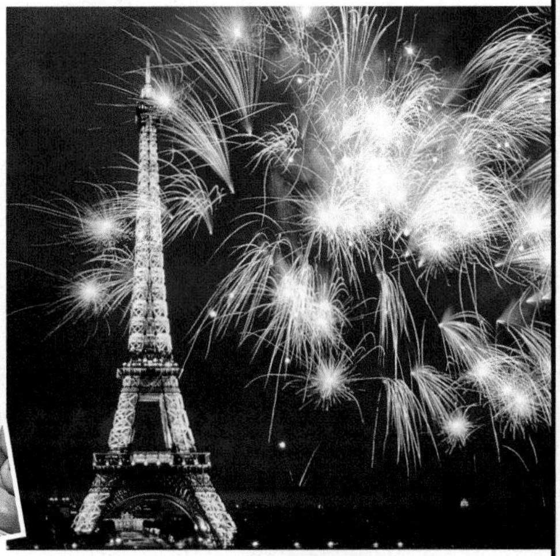

le 14 juillet à Paris

3 En quel mois?

Each of you will stand up in class and give the date of your birthday in French. Listen carefully and keep a record of how many of you were born in the same month. Then tell in French in which month the greatest number of students were born. In which month were the fewest born?

Answers

2

1. C'est le _____.
2. Demain, c'est le _____.

3 *Students will give their birth date.*

They can say: C'est le _____. *or just* le _____.

Presentation

Finding out and giving the date

In this lesson, we have presented the numbers from 1 to 30 so students can say the date. At this point, students should not be expected to know these numbers perfectly. They will be reintroduced in Chapters 1, 2, and 3. It is suggested that you not make students write the numbers.

Preview

In this lesson, students will be introduced to telling time.

Attention!

It is recommended that you teach a few of these time expressions each day rather than present them all at once. A possible plan is:
Day 1: **Il est une heure. Il est deux heures.** (hours)
Day 2: **Il est une heure cinq. Il est deux heures dix.** (after the hour)
Day 3: **Il est une heure moins cinq. Il est deux heures moins dix.** (before the hour)
Day 4: **Il est une heure et demie. Il est deux heures et quart,** etc.

Presentation

Telling time

Step 1 Have students open their books to page 12 or use Vocabulary Transparency BV 8. Have them repeat the time shown on each clock after you.

Step 2 Introduce the question, **Il est quelle heure?** Then ask the time for each clock.

Teaching Tip
Use a toy clock or make your own cardboard clock with moveable hands. Using the clock, ask **Il est quelle heure?** Repeat the question as many times as you can and monitor student responses. Then have a student ask the question and have another respond.

Préliminaire F *L'heure*

Telling time

1. To find out the time, you ask:

Il est quelle heure?

2. To give the time on the hour, you say:

1 h
Il est une heure.

2 h
Il est deux heures.

10 h
Il est dix heures.

12 h
Il est midi.

12 h
Il est minuit.

3. To give the time after the hour, you say:

1 h 05
Il est une heure cinq.

3 h 10
Il est trois heures dix.

4 h 25
Il est quatre heures vingt-cinq.

4. To give the time before the hour, you say:

4 h 50
Il est cinq heures moins dix.

5 h 40
Il est six heures moins vingt.

9 h 35
Il est dix heures moins vingt-cinq.

5. To express time on the quarter hour and half hour, you say:

2 h 15
Il est deux heures et quart.

6 h 45
Il est sept heures moins le quart.

6 h 30
Il est six heures et demie.

6. If you need to specify whether it is A.M. or P.M., you can use the following expressions.

Il est six heures du matin.

Il est quatre heures de l'après-midi.

Il est onze heures du soir.

1 Il est quelle heure?

Look at each clock and give the time.

1. 
2. 
3. 
4. 
5. 
6. 

Reaching All Students

Additional Practice Tell what time it is.

1. 10 h
2. 5 h 35
3. 9 h 15
4. 11 h 25
5. 12 h
6. 7 h 40
7. 2 h 15
8. 1 h 10
9. 9 h 30
10. 4 h 05
11. 11 h 55

Answers

1

1. Il est deux heures moins dix.
2. Il est quatre heures vingt.
3. Il est trois heures et demie.
4. Il est trois heures.
5. Il est dix heures moins le quart.
6. Il est six heures et quart.

Presentation

Conversation

2 Have students read the dialogue below before presenting it on their own.

3 Have students prepare several times on small slips of paper to use in this activity before beginning. Have students switch roles.

Préliminaire F

Conversation

2 Ciao!

Work with a classmate. Greet each other. Find out the time and react as if you have to get going.

3 Il est quelle heure, s'il te plaît?

Get up from your desk and walk around the room. Go up to a classmate. Greet the person quickly and ask the time. Show your classmate a piece of paper with a time on it. He or she will give you the time.

Answers

2 *Students' dialogues should be similar to the model dialogue on page 14.*

3 *Students' dialogues will vary but should include expressions taught on pages 12–13.*

Vocabulaire

Greeting people

Salut!	Ça va?	Bien.
Bonjour!	Pas mal.	Très bien.

Giving titles

Monsieur	Madame	Mademoiselle

Saying good-bye

Au revoir.	À bientôt.
Ciao!	À demain.
À tout à l'heure.	

Finding out a person's name

Tu t'appelles comment?
Je m'appelle…

Being courteous

S'il te plaît.	Je t'en prie.
S'il vous plaît.	Je vous en prie.
Merci.	

How well do you know your vocabulary?

- Choose an expression from the list to begin a conversation.
- Have a classmate respond.
- Take turns.

Telling the days of the week

lundi	jeudi	samedi	C'est quel jour?
mardi	vendredi	dimanche	aujourd'hui
mercredi			demain

Telling the months of the year

Quelle est la date?	avril	août	novembre
janvier	mai	septembre	décembre
février	juin	octobre	
mars	juillet		

Telling time

Il est quelle heure?	Il est midi.
Il est ____ heure(s).	Il est minuit.
du matin	
de l'après-midi	
du soir	

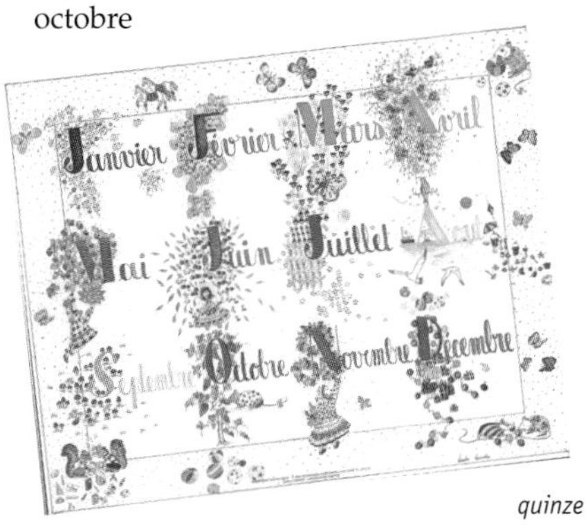

Vocabulary Review

The words and phrases in the **Vocabulaire** have been taught for productive use in this chapter. They are summarized here as a resource for both student and teacher.

Attention!

You will notice that the vocabulary list here is not translated. This has been done intentionally, since we feel that by the time students have finished the material in the lessons they should be familiar with the meanings of all the words. If there are several words they still do not know, we recommend that they refer back to the preliminary lessons or go to the dictionaries at the back of this book to find the meanings. However, if you prefer that your students have the English translations, please refer to Vocabulary Transparency BV 1, where you will find all the words listed here with their translations.

Planning for Chapter 1

SCOPE AND SEQUENCE, PAGES 16–47

Topics

- Asking about others
- Describing yourself and others

Functions

- How to describe people
- How to count from 30–60

Culture

- Nicolas, a student from France
- Valérie, a student from Martinique
- Diane and Karim, students from Africa
- The French artist Toulouse-Lautrec

Structure

- Singular forms of definite and indefinite articles
- Adjective agreement
- Singular forms of the verb **être**
- Negation

National Standards

- Communication Standard 1.1 pages 20, 21, 24, 25, 29, 30, 31, 32, 33, 35, 42
- Communication Standard 1.2 pages 20, 21, 24, 25, 27, 29, 32, 33, 36–37, 38, 39, 40–41
- Communication Standard 1.3 pages 20, 21, 25, 29, 31, 32, 33, 43
- Cultures Standard 2.1 pages 36–37, 38
- Connections Standard 3.1 pages 40–41
- Comparisons Standard 4.1 pages 19, 23, 29
- Comparisons Standard 4.2 pages 36–37, 38

PACING AND PRIORITIES

The chapter content is color coded below to assist you in planning.
■ **required** ■ **recommended** ■ **optional**

Vocabulaire *(required)* *Days 1–4*
- ■ Mots 1
  - Comment est la fille?
  - Comment est le garçon?
- ■ Mots 2
  - Une sœur et un frère
  - Une école et un collège

Structure *(required)* *Days 5–7*
- ■ Les articles au singulier
- ■ L'accord des adjectifs
- ■ Le verbe **être** au singulier
- ■ La négation

Conversation *(required)*
- ■ Il est d'où, Luc?

Prononciation *(recommended)*
- ■ L'accent tonique

Lectures culturelles
- ■ Un garçon et une fille *(recommended)*
- ■ Le français en Afrique *(optional)*
- ■ Un artiste français *(optional)*

Connexions *(optional)*
- ■ La géographie

■ **C'est à vous** *(recommended)*

■ **Assessment** *(recommended)*

■ **Technotour** *(optional)*

RESOURCE GUIDE

Section	Pages	Section Resources
Vocabulaire *Mots 1*		
Comment est la fille? Comment est le garçon?	18 19–21	Vocabulary Transparencies 1.2–1.3 Audiocassette 2A/CD 2 Audio Activities Booklet TE, pages 14–15 Workbook, pages 1–2 Quiz 1, page 1 ExamView Pro®
Vocabulaire *Mots 2*		
Une sœur et un frère Une école et un collège	22 22–25	Vocabulary Transparencies 1.4–1.5 Audiocassette 2A/CD 2 Audio Activities Booklet TE, pages 15–17 Workbook, pages 3–4 Quiz 2, page 2 ExamView Pro®
Structure		
Les articles au singulier L'accord des adjectifs Le verbe **être** au singulier La négation	26–27 28–30 30–32 33	Audiocassette 2A/CD 2 Audio Activities Booklet TE, pages 17–21 Workbook, pages 5–7 Quizzes 3–6, pages 3–6 ExamView Pro®
Conversation		
Il est d'où, Luc?	34	Audiocassette 2A/CD 2 Audio Activities Booklet TE, pages 21–22 CD-ROM
Prononciation		
L'accent tonique	35	Pronunciation Transparency P 1 Audiocassette 2A/CD 2 Audio Activities Booklet TE, page 22
Lectures culturelles		
Un garçon et une fille Le français en Afrique Un artiste français	36–37 38 39	Audiocassette 2A/CD 2 Audio Activities Booklet TE, page 23 Test Booklet, Chapter 1
Connexions		
La géographie	40–41	Test Booklet, Chapter 1
C'est à vous		
	42–43	**Bon voyage!** Video, Episode 1 Video Activities Booklet, Chapter 1 French Online Activities french.glencoe.com
Assessment		
	44–45	Communication Transparency C 1 Quizzes 1–6, pages 1–6 Test Booklet, Chapter 1 ExamView Pro® Situation Cards, Chapter 1 **Marathon mental** Videoquiz

Using Your Resources for Chapter 1

Transparencies

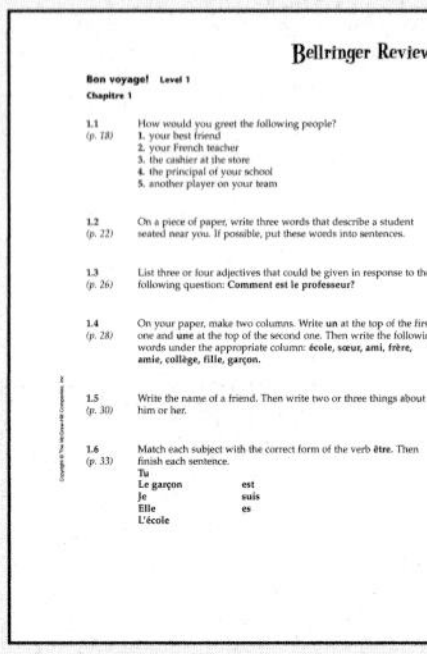

Bellringer 1.1–1.8

Vocabulary 1.1–1.5

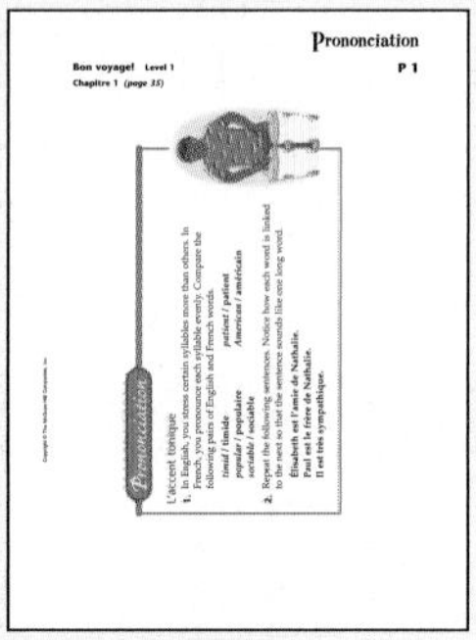

Pronunciation P 1

Communication C 1

Writing Activities Workbook

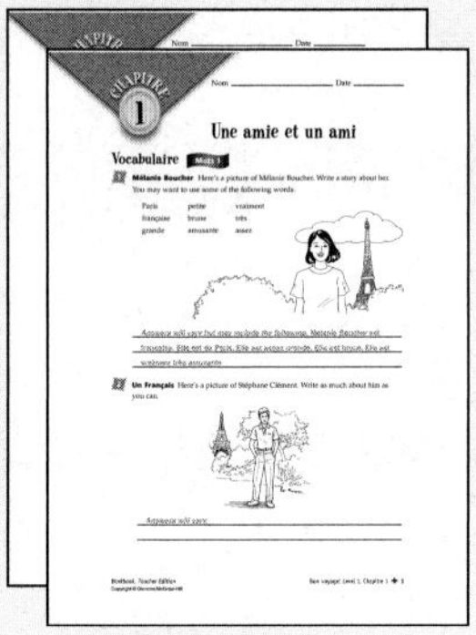

Vocabulary, pages 1–4

Structure, pages 5–7

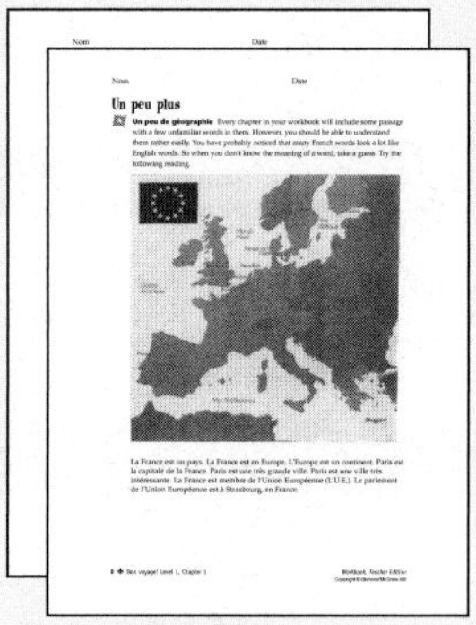

Enrichment, pages 8–10

Audio Program and Audio Activities Booklet

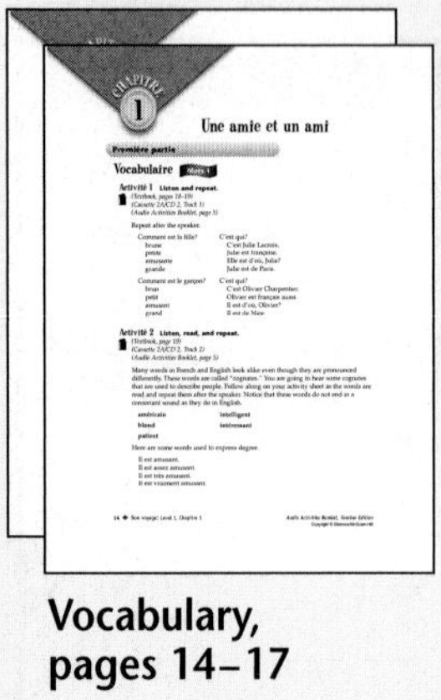

Vocabulary, pages 14–17

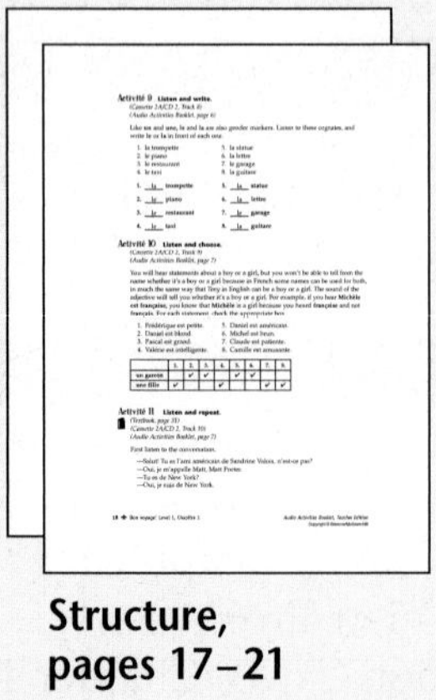

Structure, pages 17–21

Conversation, Pronunciation, pages 21–22

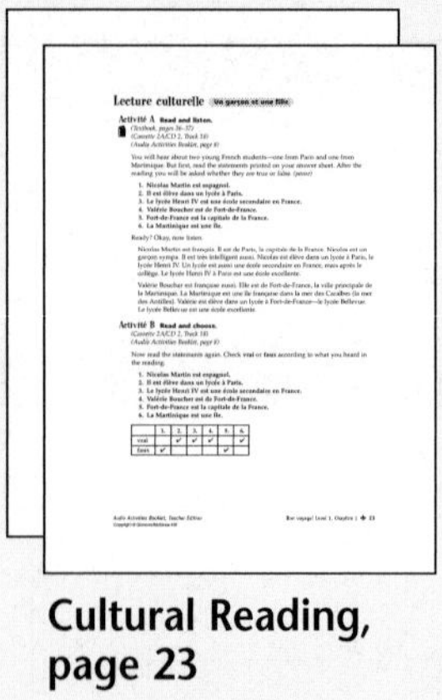

Cultural Reading, page 23

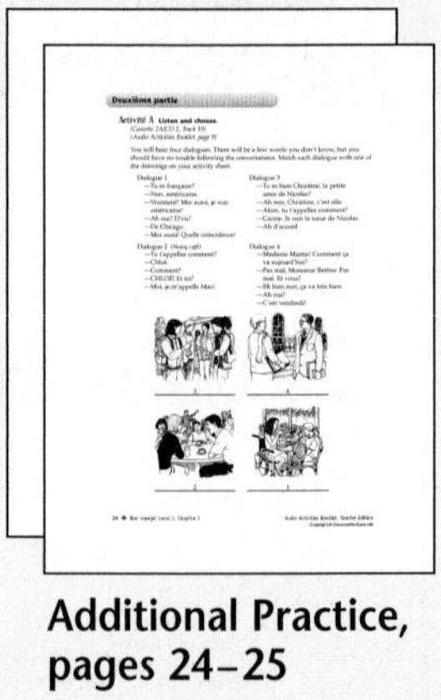

Additional Practice, pages 24–25

Assessment

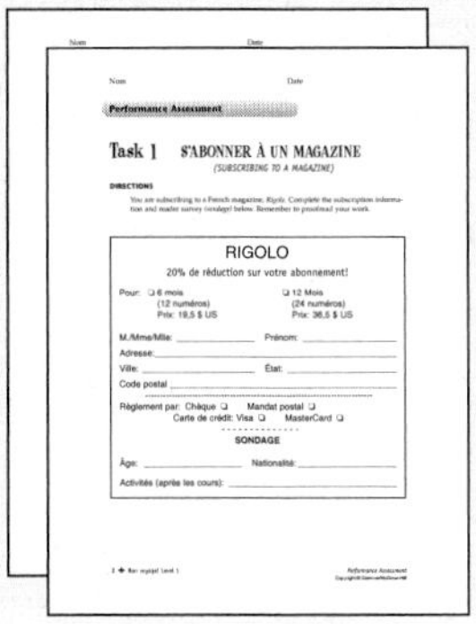

Vocabulary and Structure Quizzes, pages 1–6

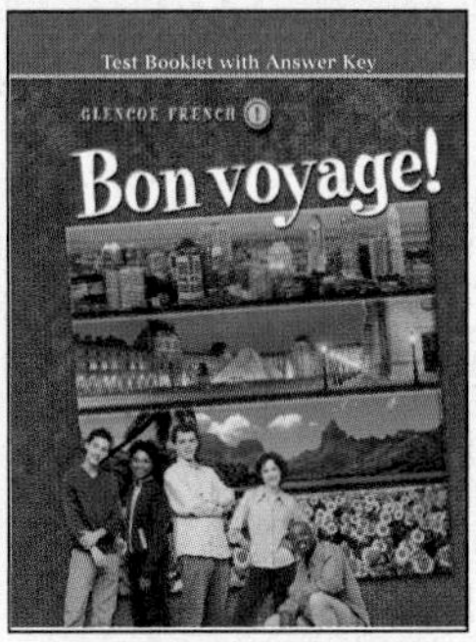

Chapter Tests, Chapter 1

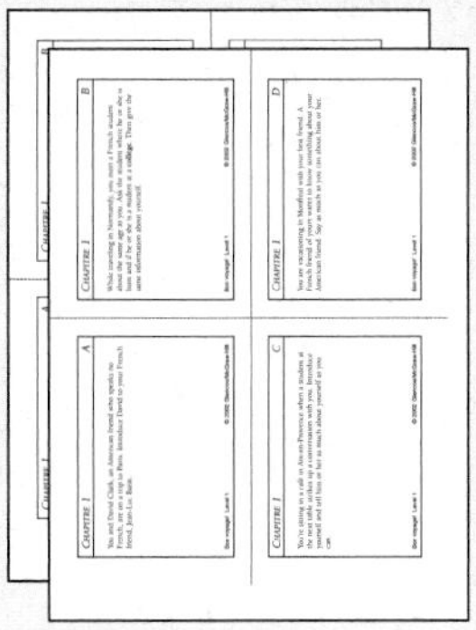

Situation Cards, Chapter 1

Timesaving Teacher Tools

Interactive Teacher Edition

Imagine having your Teacher's Edition and all resources on a CD-ROM. Click on a resource and it appears on your screen, ready to be printed, sorted, or planned.

Interactive Lesson Planner

The Interactive Lesson Planner CD-ROM helps you organize your lesson plans for a week, month, semester, or year. Look at this planning tool for easy access to your Chapter 1 resources.

ExamView Pro®

Test Bank software for Macintosh and Windows makes creating, editing, customizing, and printing tests quick and easy.

Technology Resources

FRENCH Online

In the Chapter 1 Internet activity, you will have a chance to learn more about the geography of the Francophone world. Visit french.glencoe.com.

On the Interactive Conversation CD-ROM, students can listen to and take part in a recorded version of the conversation in Chapter 1.

NATIONAL GEOGRAPHIC SOCIETY

See the National Geographic Teacher's Corner on pages 150–151, 256–257, 396–397, 500–501 for reference to additional technology resources.

Bon voyage! Video and Video Activities Booklet.

Help your students prepare for the chapter test by playing the **Marathon mental** Videoquiz game show. Teams will compete against each other to review chapter vocabulary and structure and sharpen listening comprehension skills.

CHAPITRE 1

Preview

In this chapter, students will learn to describe themselves as well as a friend, using the singular forms of the verb **être** and high-frequency descriptive adjectives. The plural forms of the verb **être** will be presented in Chapter 2 to avoid introducing an overwhelming number of forms in this initial chapter.

National Standards

Communication

In Chapter 1, students will communicate in spoken and written French to:

- identify and describe themselves and others
- find out where people are from and say their nationality

Students will engage in conversations, provide and obtain information, and exchange opinions as they fulfill the chapter objectives listed on this page.

Spotlight on Culture

Photograph The students in this photograph are walking in the Jardin du Luxembourg. The Luxembourg Garden has many fountains, formal gardens, and gravel walks. The beautiful seventeenth-century Palais du Luxembourg is also in the garden.

Painting This painting, ***Enfants jouant au cerceau,*** was done by the French painter Victor Gabriel Gilbert (1847–1933). Gilbert's paintings depict realistic scenes of common people going about their daily activities.

CHAPITRE 1

Une amie et un ami

Objectifs

In this chapter you will learn to:

- ✔ *ask or tell what someone is like*
- ✔ *ask or tell where someone is from*
- ✔ *ask or tell who someone is*
- ✔ *describe yourself or someone else*
- ✔ *talk about students from France and Martinique*

Victor Gabriel Gilbert *Enfants jouant au cerceau*

16

Correlations to Continuum *(see page* i *for code)*

Stage I
Greet and respond. p. 31 (**21**, *p*); Introduce and respond. p. 31 (**21**, *i*); Engage in conversations. p. 32 (**25**, **26**, *i*), p. 34 (*p*), p. 42 (**2**, *m*); Obtain information. pp. 18–19 (*i*), p. 21 (**5**, *p*), p. 33 (**30**, *p*), p. 42 (**3**, *m*); Understand some ideas and familiar details. p. 26 (*i*), p. 30 (**19**, *p*), p. 35 (**B**, *m*); Provide information. pp. 18–19 (*i*), p. 25 (**10**, **11**, *p*), p. 42 (**1**, *m*); Converse in social interactions. p. 31 (**21**, *i*), p. 35 (**A**, *p*); Listen during social interactions and listen to audio or video texts. p. 21 (**5**, *i*), p. 47 (*p*); Write postcards. p. 43 (**4**, *i*), p. 43 (**4**, *p*); Use short sentences, learned words and phrases when speaking and writing. p. 20 (**1**, *i*), p. 31 (**20**, *p*); Understand ideas and familiar details when listening. p. 25 (**12**, *i*); Understand texts enhanced by visual clues. pp. 36–37 (*i*); Understand and convey information about the self and school. p. 23 (*i*), p. 32 (**25**, *p*), p. 43 (**5**, *m*); Understand and convey information on geography and topography. p. 40 (*i*), p. 41 (*p*); Communicate effectively. p. 35 (**B**); Culturally acceptable. p. 43 (**4**); Most important information. p. 43 (**5**)

Stage II
Use and understand learned expressions, sentences, and strings of sentences, questions, and polite commands when speaking and listening. p. 33 (**30**, *i*), p. 42 (**1**, *p*)

Stage III
Clarify and ask for and comprehend clarification. p. 31 (**23**, *i*)

CHAPITRE 1

About the French Language

- In conversational French, the most common way to form a question is to raise one's voice at the end of the sentence. This rising intonation pattern can be used with *yes/no* questions and many question words: **Richard est français?** Note that in spoken French the question word is often placed at the end of a sentence: **Richard est d'où?**
- Another way to ask a question is to begin a statement with **est-ce-que: Est-ce que Marie est française? Où est-ce qu'elle habite?**
- A question can also be formed using inversion: **D'où est Jean?**

In the early chapters, questions are formed in the above three ways. Most frequently, the rising intonation pattern is used. The only form not used in the early chapters is the formal inversion: **Où Robert va-t-il?** We have not used this inversion, since it is not often used in conversation.

Tell your students that they will hear questions in the three ways outlined above. When they ask questions, they can use any option they please.

Chapter Projects

L'école Have one or more students research in as much detail as possible the French educational system. Have students find out what some of the major differences are between schools in the United States and those in France.

Un(e) ami(e) Have students who are interested get a pen pal in a French-speaking country. Have them request a photograph of their pen pal. Students can prepare a bulletin board with the photographs they receive. They can also write a short paragraph about their pen pal to accompany the photograph. Tell students to use only French they know when writing their description. At this very early level, we do not want to encourage students to try to say and write things that are beyond their knowledge.

Les pays francophones Have one or more students do a research project on a French-speaking country or region and prepare a brief introduction to it. Some possibilities include: Martinique, Tahiti, Tunisia, Ivory Coast, Quebec, Morocco, Haiti, French Guyana or any others they choose from pages xxiv–xxxi (French 1A, 1B: pages xviii–xxiii).

1 Preparation

Resource Manager

Vocabulary Transparencies 1.2–1.3
Audio Activities Booklet TE, pages 14–15
Audiocassette 2A/CD 2
Workbook, pages 1–2
Quiz 1, page 1
ExamView Pro®

Bellringer Review

Use BRR Transparency 1.1 or write the following on the board.
How would you greet the following people?
1. your best friend
2. your French teacher
3. the cashier at the store
4. the principal of your school
5. another player on your team

Attention!

You will note that we start the descriptive sentences with the feminine form first using adjectives in which the final consonant sound is heard in the feminine form, but not in the masculine form. Students find it easier to drop the final sound when talking about a boy than to add the sound when talking about a girl. They also find it easier to remember to drop the **e** when writing than to add it.

2 Presentation

Step 1 Present the vocabulary first with books closed using Vocabulary Transparencies 1.2–1.3. You may also wish to use students as "models" as you present many of the descriptive adjectives.

Step 2 Present one word or phrase at a time and build to a complete sentence. For example,

Vocabulaire Mots 1

Comment est la fille?

C'est qui?
C'est Julie Lacroix.
Julie est française.

Elle est d'où, Julie?
Julie est de Paris.

Reaching All Students

Total Physical Response Before doing this activity, make sure students understand each of the following commands by acting them out: **levez-vous, promenez-vous, arrêtez-vous, montrez-moi, asseyez-vous.**

(Student 1), **levez-vous, s'il vous plaît.**
Promenez-vous dans la salle de classe.
Arrêtez-vous.
Montrez-moi un garçon blond.
Montrez-moi une fille blonde.
Montrez-moi un garçon brun.
Montrez-moi une fille brune.
Montrez-moi un garçon amusant.
Montrez-moi une fille amusante.

Comment est le garçon?

brun

petit

amusant

grand

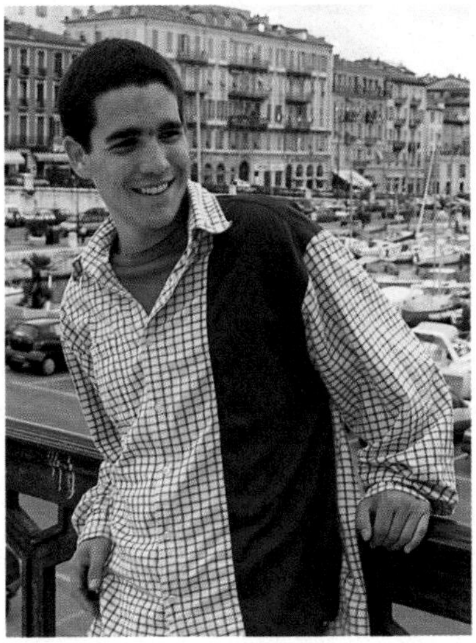

C'est qui?
C'est Olivier Charpentier.
Olivier est français aussi.

Il est d'où, Olivier?
Il est de Nice.

Note

Many words in French and English look alike even though they are pronounced differently. These words are called "cognates." You can use the following cognates to describe people.

américain
blond
patient
intelligent
intéressant

Here are some words used to express degree.

Il est amusant.
Il est assez amusant.
Il est très amusant.
Il est vraiment amusant.

point to Julie as the class says **Julie.** Point to a map of France as you and the class say **française.** Then have the class say the entire sentence: **Julie est française.** Point to each individual on pages 18–19 and model the accompanying word or phrase. Have students repeat each word or phrase in unison.

Step 3 After the initial presentation with the overhead transparencies, have students open their books and look at the new vocabulary words as they repeat either after you or Audiocassette 2A/CD 2.

Step 4 You may wish to ask the following types of questions during the oral presentation of the vocabulary or as the students are reading from their books: **C'est Julie? C'est Julie ou Olivier? Julie est française? Qui est française?** *(as you point to Julie).* **Olivier est français? Qui est français?** *(as you point to Olivier).* **Il est grand ou petit?** These questions that build from very easy to more complex permit you to take into account the varying abilities of your students. Gear the questions to the skill level of each student.

Teaching Tips

- Use gestures to help convey the meaning of words such as: **intelligent, amusant, grand, petit,** or call on students who like to perform and have them pantomime the meaning of each word.
- Use intonation and expression to illustrate the difference between **assez, très,** and **vraiment.**

Learning from Photos

(page 18) The girl in this photo is in Paris. The building in the background is the **basilique du Sacré-Cœur** in the Montmartre area.
(page 19) The boy in the photo is in Nice, the beautiful resort town on the French Riviera (Côte d'Azur). In the background you can see the **port de plaisance,** a yacht marina.

Vocabulary Expansion

When students ask for additional related vocabulary in the very early chapters, it is strongly recommended that you not give them more words at this point. This will complicate or confuse the language concepts being presented. For example, in this section students are using only those adjectives which have a final consonant sound in the feminine form that is dropped in the masculine form.

Attention!

It is extremely important that students be able to use and respond correctly to interrogatives from the early stages of language acquisition. In this chapter, the interrogative words **qui, d'où,** and **comment** are introduced.

3 Practice

Commençons
Let's use our new words

Attention!

When students are doing the **Commençons** activities, accept any answer that makes sense. The purpose of these activities is to have students use the new vocabulary. They are not factual recall activities. Thus, it is not necessary for students to remember specific factual information from the vocabulary presentation when answering. If you wish, have students use the photos on this page as a stimulus, when possible.

Historiette Each time **Historiette** appears, it means that the answers to the activity form a short story. Encourage students to look at the title of the **Historiette,** since it can help them do the activity.

Do these activities first with books closed. Ask the questions and call on a different student to answer each one. Then have students open their books and do the activities again. You may wish to have students work in pairs when doing Activities 1 and 2. They may take turns as one reads the question and the other answers.

3 Notice that Activity 3 reinforces the interrogative word **qui.**

Paired Activity

After completing the activities on pages 20 and 21, reinforce the lesson with the following:

- Have students work in pairs to write sentences describing two other students in the class—one male and one female.
- Have students compare two other students. For example: **Robert est brun. Marc est brun aussi.**

Commençons
Let's use our new words

1 Historiette Une fille française

Inventez une histoire. *(Make up a story.)*

1. Sophie est française ou américaine?
2. Elle est de Paris ou de New York?
3. Elle est brune ou blonde?
4. Elle est amusante?
5. Elle est grande ou petite?

Sophie Legrand

2 Historiette Un garçon français

Inventez une histoire. *(Make up a story.)*

1. Christophe est américain ou français?
2. Il est de Lyon ou de Houston?
3. Il est brun ou blond?
4. Il est amusant?
5. Il est très intelligent?
6. Il est assez patient?

Christophe Gaudin

Bill

Henri

3 Un Français ou un Américain?

Répondez d'après les photos.
(Answer according to the photos.)

1. Qui est américain?
2. Qui est français?
3. Qui est de Paris?
4. Qui est de Los Angeles?
5. Qui est blond?
6. Qui est brun?

Answers to Commençons

1

1. Sophie est française.
2. Elle est de Paris.
3. Elle est brune.
4. Oui, elle est amusante.
5. Elle est grande (petite).

2

1. Christophe est français.
2. Il est de Lyon.
3. Il est blond.
4. Il est amusant.
5. Il est très intelligent.
6. Il est assez patient.

3

1. Bill est américain.
2. Henri est français.
3. Henri est de Paris.
4. Bill est de Los Angeles.
5. Henri est blond.
6. Bill est brun.

4 **Il est... ? Elle est... ?** Look at the following people and say two things about each of them. Then, find out who they are. They are all famous.

5 **C'est qui?** Think of a student in the class. A classmate will ask you questions about the person and try to guess who it is. Take turns.

ENCORE PLUS *For more practice using words from* ***Mots 1****, do Activity 1 on page H2 at the end of this book.*

Writing Development

Have the students write answers to Activities 1 and 2 in paragraph form to illustrate how the answers to all the items tell a story. Have students write the answers to Activity 3; you may wish to have them write two paragraphs, one to describe Bill and one to describe Henri.

Learning from Photos

(page 20) Sophie Legrand is in Paris. The monument behind her is the Arc de Triomphe. Christophe Gaudin is standing in front of a lycée in Lyon. Bill is in Hollywood, California, and Henri is on a street in the **7e arrondissement** of Paris. The monument in the background is the famous Eiffel Tower.

(page 21) These photographs are of Meg Ryan (an American actress), Charles de Gaulle (French general and former head of state), Oprah Winfrey (TV talk show host), and Napoleon Bonaparte (French Emperor).

Attention!

Note that the activities are color-coded. All the activities in the text are communicative. However, the ones with blue titles are guided communication. The red titles indicate that the answers to the activity are more open-ended and can vary more. You may wish to correct students' mistakes more so in the guided activities than in the activities with a red title, which lend themselves to a freer response.

Answers to Commençons

4 *Answers will vary but may include:*

Elle est blonde. Elle est amusante. Elle est américaine. C'est Meg Ryan.
Il est grand. Il est intelligent. Il est français. C'est Charles de Gaulle.
Elle est brune. Elle est assez petite. Elle est vraiment intelligente. C'est Oprah Winfrey.
Il est très petit. Il est français. Il est intéressant. C'est Napoléon.

5 *Answers will vary but may include:*

—Elle est grande ou petite?
—Elle est petite.
—Elle est blonde ou brune?
—Elle est brune.
—Elle est d'où?
—Elle est de New York.
—Elle est amusante?
—Oui, elle est amusante.
—C'est Marie?
—Oui!

Vocabulaire
Mots 2

1 Preparation

Resource Manager

Vocabulary Transparencies 1.4–1.5
Audio Activities Booklet TE, pages 15–17
Audiocassette 2A/CD 2
Workbook, pages 3–4
Quiz 2, page 2
ExamView Pro®

Bellringer Review

Use BRR Transparency 1.2 or write the following on the board.
On a piece of paper, write three words that describe a student seated near you. If possible, put these words into sentences.

2 Presentation

Step 1 Have students close their books. Present the vocabulary, using Vocabulary Transparencies 1.4–1.5 or student models.

Step 2 Model each new word or phrase. Have students repeat each word or phrase after you or Audiocassette 2A/CD 2. Emphasize the difference between **un/une, le/la.**

Step 3 If you have a male student whose pronunciation is good, call him to the front of the room. Say to the class: **C'est Mark.** Explain to students, in English, that Mark is going to tell them something about himself. Then have the student take the role of Mark and read Mark's lines on page 23.

Learning from Photos

(page 22) Carol is shown in front of her high school in Westerville, Ohio. Bruno is shown in front of his collège, le collège Lucie Faure in Paris.

Vocabulaire
Mots 2

Une sœur et un frère

Voilà Nathalie et Luc Simonet.
Nathalie est la sœur de Luc.
Luc est le frère de Nathalie.

Voilà Philippe.
Philippe n'est pas le frère de Nathalie.
Philippe est un ami de Nathalie.

Une école et un collège

Carol est élève dans une école américaine.

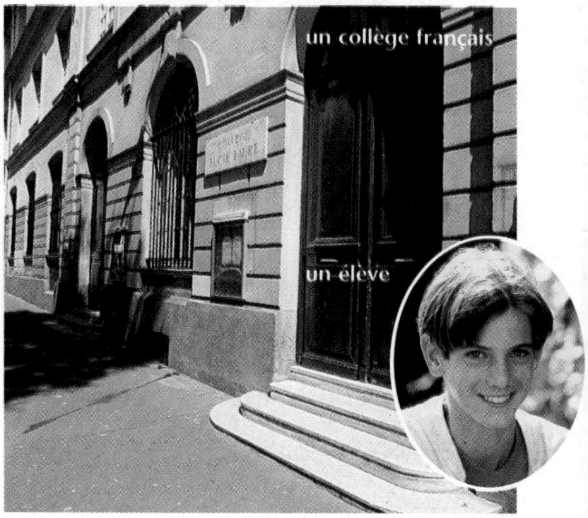

Bruno est élève dans un collège français.
Un collège est une école secondaire en France.

Reaching All Students

Total Physical Response Before doing this activity, make sure students understand the following command by acting it out: **Retournez à votre place.**

(Student 1), **levez-vous, s'il vous plaît.**
Promenez-vous un peu dans la classe
Arrêtez-vous et montrez-moi un ami (un élève).
C'est qui? C'est *(Student 2).*
Promenez-vous encore dans la classe.
Et maintenant, arrêtez-vous.
Montrez-moi une amie (une élève).
C'est qui? C'est *(Student 3).*
Très bien. Et merci.
Retournez à votre place.
Asseyez-vous, s'il vous plaît.

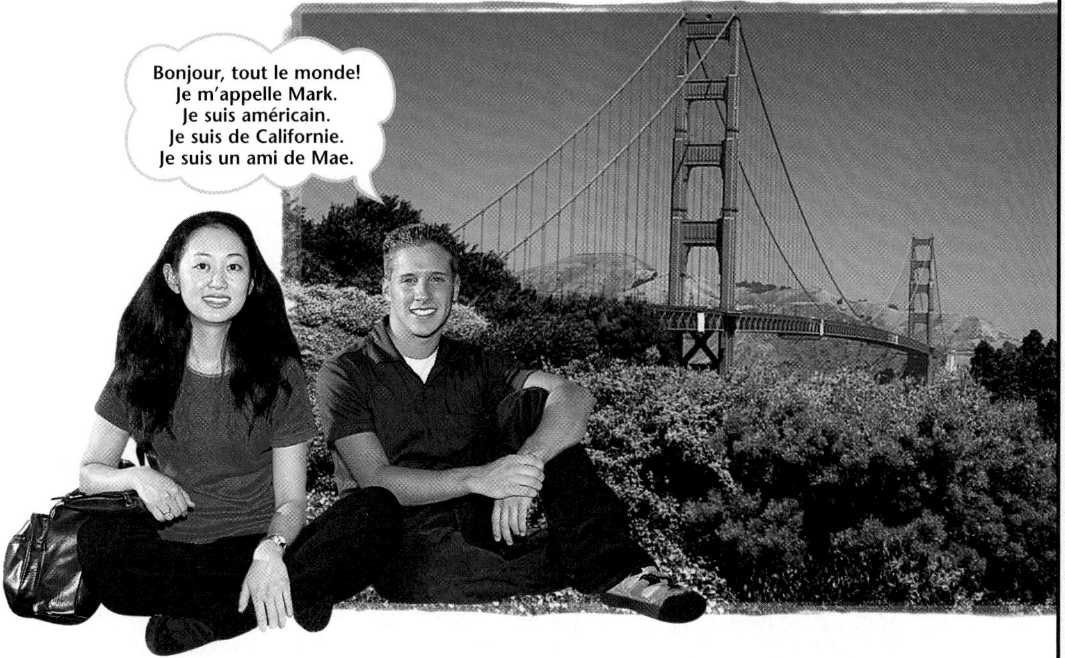
Bonjour, tout le monde!
Je m'appelle Mark.
Je suis américain.
Je suis de Californie.
Je suis un ami de Mae.

Mae est une amie de Mark.
Mae est très sympathique.
Mark est très sympa aussi.

Note

You can also use the following cognates to describe people.

dynamique
énergique
populaire
timide
égoïste
enthousiaste
sociable

Les nombres de 30 à 60

30 trente	35 trente-cinq	40 quarante
31 trente et un	36 trente-six	50 cinquante
32 trente-deux	37 trente-sept	60 soixante
33 trente-trois	38 trente-huit	
34 trente-quatre	39 trente-neuf	

Cognate Recognition

Since students tend to anglicize the pronunciation of cognates, have them first repeat the cognates on page 23 carefully after you with books closed. Then, pronounce them again with books open.

Step 4 Have students give the opposite of the following nouns: **une sœur, une amie, une élève,** etc.

Assessment

As an informal assessment, check for comprehension by asking *yes/no* questions and *either/or* questions. Call on the entire class as well as individual students to respond. For example:

Nathalie est la sœur ou le frère de Luc?
Luc est la sœur ou le frère de Nathalie?
Bruno est élève?
Carol est élève dans une école américaine ou un collège français?
Mae est la sœur ou une amie de Mark?

Attention!

The numbers 1–30 were presented in the **Bienvenue** section. Note that in this lesson we stop at 60. The numbers from 70 to 100 will be presented in the next chapter to avoid teaching too many numbers at once. It is suggested that you not stress the spelling of numbers, since students will very seldom, if ever, have to spell them out in real-life situations.

- Have students repeat the numbers after you.
- Write some numbers from 1–60 in random order on the board and call on individuals to give the number in French.

3 Practice

Commençons
Let's use our new words

6 After students complete Activity 6, have one student summarize all the information about Céline in his or her own words.

7 Have students look at the map as they answer each question. Note that this activity reinforces the interrogatives **qui** and **d'où.**

Learning from Photos

(page 25 top) This photograph is of La place de l'Hôtel de Ville in Lyon. Lyon is the second largest city in France. It is known for its many bridges spanning the Rhône and Saône rivers and its massive stone houses. Lyon is quite a bustling, industrial city. It is also know for its many restaurants and excellent cuisine—**la cuisine lyonnaise.**

Commençons
Let's use our new words

6 Historiette Une élève française Choisissez la bonne réponse.
(Choose the right answer.)

1. ____ est française.
   a. Céline Dupont **b.** Thomas Duhamel
2. Céline est élève dans ____.
   a. une école américaine **b.** un collège français
3. Elle est ____.
   a. de Paris **b.** de Miami
4. Céline est ____ de Karim.
   a. un ami **b.** une amie
5. Karim est ____ de Céline.
   a. un ami **b.** un élève
6. David est ____ de Céline.
   a. la sœur **b.** le frère
7. Céline est ____ de David.
   a. le frère **b.** la sœur

7 Qui est d'où? Répondez d'après la carte.
(Answer according to the map.)

1. Qui est de Bordeaux?
2. D'où est Maïa?
3. Et Olivia, elle est d'où?
4. Et Ahmed, il est d'où?

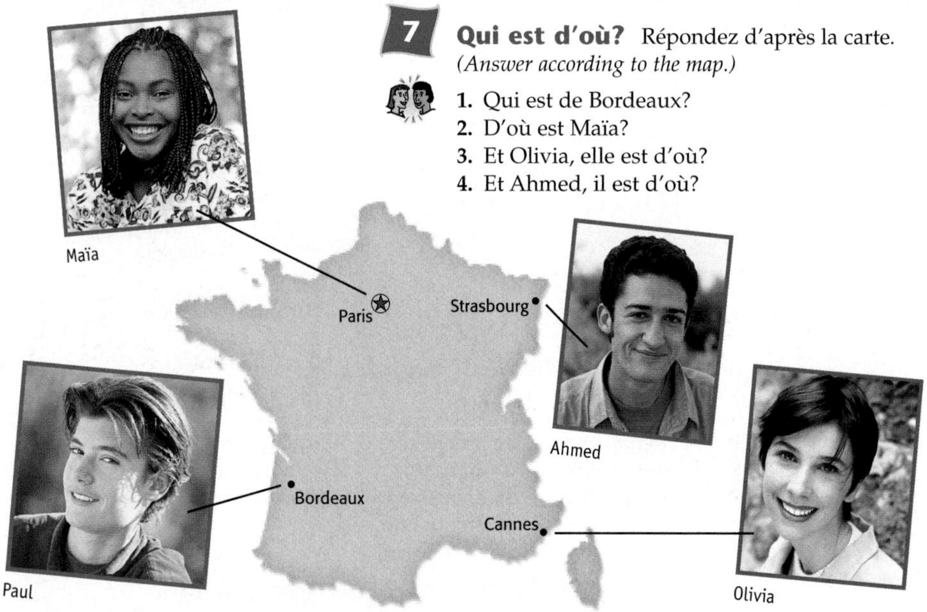

Answers to Commençons

6
1. a
2. b
3. a
4. b
5. a
6. b
7. b

7
1. Paul est de Bordeaux.
2. Maïa est de Paris.
3. Olivia est de Cannes.
4. Ahmed est de Strasbourg.

8 Historiette David Williams, un garçon américain

Inventez une histoire. *(Make up a story.)*

1. Qui est américain, David Williams ou Serge Legrand?
2. D'où est David Williams? Il est de New York ou de Paris?
3. Il est de quelle nationalité? Il est français ou américain?
4. David est élève dans un collège français ou dans une école américaine?
5. Comment est David? Il est timide ou sociable?

Lyon, France

9 Historiette Sophie est vraiment amusante.

Complétez. *(Complete.)*

Sophie Bellecour est de Lyon. Elle est __1__. Elle n'est pas américaine. Sophie est blonde. Elle n'est pas __2__. Elle n'est pas timide. Pas du tout! Elle est très __3__. Elle est très sympa aussi. Elle est __4__ dans un collège à Lyon.

Pascal Denjean

10 Pascal Denjean

Here is a photo of Pascal Denjean. He is a student from Bordeaux. Say a few things about Pascal.

11 Élodie Denjean

The blonde girl in the photo is Élodie Denjean. She is Pascal's sister. She is also a student in Bordeaux. Say a few things about Élodie.

Élodie Denjean

12 Jeu Un nombre secret

Think of a number between 1 and 60. Your partner tries to guess the number you have in mind. Use a hand gesture to indicate whether the number you are thinking of is higher or lower. Continue until your partner guesses the correct number. Take turns.

ENCORE PLUS *For more practice using words from **Mots 2**, do Activity 2 on page H3 at the end of this book.*

Vocabulaire

8 You may wish to do Activity 8 with books closed the first time.

Oral Development: Have one student retell the story in his or her own words.

9 Activity 9 must be done with books open. You may wish to go over it a second time and have one student read the entire activity.

10 and 11 These activities provide an opportunity for students to recycle and recombine all vocabulary they have learned to this point to describe people. Encourage them to write or tell as much as they possibly can about each photo.

Note: Activities 10 and 11 encourage students to use the chapter vocabulary in open-ended situations. It is not necessary to have all students do all activities. Let students choose the ones they wish to do.

12 You may wish to divide the class into two teams to play Activity 12 as a class competition after the students have practiced in pairs.

ENCORE PLUS This *infogap* activity will allow students to practice in pairs. The activity should be very manageable for them, since all vocabulary and structures are familiar to them.

Reteaching

Bring to class a magazine photo of a well-known personality all the students will recognize. Have them describe the person, using vocabulary they know.

Answers to Commençons

8 *Answers will vary but may include:*

1. David Williams est américain.
2. Il est de New York.
3. Il est américain.
4. Il est élève dans une école américaine.
5. Il est sociable (timide).

9

1. française
2. brune
3. sociable
4. élève

10 *Answers will vary but may include:*
Pascal est français. Il est de Bordeaux. Pascal est le frère d'Élodie. Il est élève dans un collège français. Il est brun. Il est petit. Il est intelligent et amusant. Il est assez populaire.

11 *Answers will vary but may include:*
Élodie est française. Elle est de Bordeaux. Élodie est la sœur de Pascal. Elle est élève dans un collège français. Elle est blonde. Elle est grande. Elle est intelligente et amusante. Elle est très populaire.

1 Preparation

Resource Manager

Audio Activities Booklet TE, pages 17–21
Audiocassette 2A/CD 2
Workbook, pages 5–7
Quizzes 3–6, pages 3–6
ExamView Pro®

Bellringer Review

Use BRR Transparency 1.3 or write the following on the board.
List three or four adjectives that could be given in response to the following question: **Comment est le professeur?**

2 Presentation

Les articles au singulier

Step 1 Read Items 1–3 aloud.

Step 2 Have students repeat the examples in Items 2 and 3. Practice the pronunciation of the examples given in the **Attention!** section.

Step 3 Contrast the use of a definite article to refer to a specific person with the indefinite article to refer to any person. Say: **le garçon brun** and have students point to a specific boy in the class. Say: **un garçon brun** and have students look around the class and say: **Qui? Robert ou Luc?** Do the same thing with **une fille.**

Talking about a person or a thing

Les articles au singulier

1. A noun is the name of a person, place, or thing. In French, every noun has a gender, either masculine or feminine. Except for people, you cannot tell what the gender of a noun is by just looking at it. You need other clues.

2. Many words that accompany nouns can indicate gender. They are called "gender markers." **Une** and **un** are gender markers. They are indefinite articles and correspond to *a (an)* in English. **Une** accompanies a feminine noun and **un** accompanies a masculine noun.

LES ARTICLES INDÉFINIS

Féminin	Masculin
une amie	un ami
une sœur	un frère
une école	un collège

3. **Le, la,** and **l'** are definite articles and often correspond to *the* in English.

LES ARTICLES DÉFINIS

Féminin	Masculin
la fille	le garçon
la sœur	le frère
l'amie	l'ami

Attention!

Note that the definite articles **le** and **la** are shortened to **l'** when they accompany a noun that begins with a vowel. When pronounced, the vowel sound is dropped. This is called "elision."

la amie → l'amie
le ami → l'ami

The **n** of the indefinite article **un** is pronounced when it accompanies a noun beginning with a vowel. This is called "liaison."

un‿ami **un‿élève**

Une sœur et un frère

Continuons
Let's put our words together

13 **Historiette** **Olivier et Marie** Complétez avec **un** ou **une.** *(Complete with* un *or* une.*)*

Olivier est __1__ garçon très sympa. Olivier est __2__ ami de Christophe. Christophe est __3__ élève très intelligent. Il est élève dans __4__ école secondaire à New York.

Marie est __5__ amie de Christophe. Marie est __6__ élève intelligente aussi. Marie est __7__ fille vraiment amusante.

14 **Historiette** **Brendan Jones et Sabine Morel**
Complétez avec **le, la** ou **l'.** *(Complete with* le, la, *or* l'.*)*

__1__ garçon, Brendan Jones, est américain, mais __2__ fille, Sabine Morel, n'est pas américaine. Elle est française. Sabine est __3__ amie de Ludovic Girard et __4__ sœur de Luc Morel. Brendan n'est pas __5__ ami de Sabine; il est de Miami et Sabine est de Strasbourg. Brendan est __6__ ami de Karen Miller et __7__ frère de Melissa Jones. Brendan est élève et Sabine est élève aussi. __8__ école de Brendan est à Miami. __9__ collège de Sabine est à Strasbourg.

Strasbourg, France

3 Practice

Continuons
Let's put our words together

13 and **14** These activities must be done with books open. Have one student complete two or three sentences before you call on the next student. If a student makes an error, call on another to give the correct response. Return to the student who made the error and see if he or she can now give the correct response.

Oral Development: After calling on several individuals to complete Activities 13 and 14, have one student do each of the activities in its entirety. Call on other students in the class to ask questions about the information in the activities. This allows them to form their own questions. You can answer the questions or have students answer them.

Learning from Photos
(page 27) Strasbourg is the capital of Alsace. It is a city full of interest, known for its medieval streets with carved timbered houses similar to those of many areas of nearby Germany. This photo was taken in the beautiful district known as **la Petite France,** which is crisscrossed by the river Ill. This river gave its name to the whole region once known as Ill-Sass—thus Alsace.

Answers to Continuons

13
1. un
2. un
3. un
4. une
5. une
6. une
7. une

14
1. Le
2. la
3. l'
4. la
5. l'
6. l'
7. le
8. L'
9. Le

1 Preparation

Bellringer Review

Use BRR Transparency 1.4 or write the following on the board.
On your paper, make two columns. Write **un** at the top of the first one and **une** at the top of the second one. Then write the following words under the appropriate column: **école, sœur, ami, frère, amie, collège, fille, garçon.**

2 Presentation

L'accord des adjectifs

Step 1 Draw two stick figures on the board. Name them Marie and Paul. Point to Marie as you say: **blonde, française, intelligente.** Then point to Paul as you say: **blond, français, intelligent.** Ask students if they hear a difference in the sound and why there is a difference. Remind them that words used to describe males and females are pronounced differently.

Step 2 Model the examples given in the structure explanation and have students repeat the examples after you.

Step 3 To demonstrate that adjectives ending in **e** can refer to feminine or masculine words, have female and male students come to the front of the class. Each pair will hold his or her own adjective card with the same word written on each one. Make statements about each student and then ask questions. For example: **André est sympathique. Yvonne est sympathique aussi. Qui est sympathique? (André) Qui est sympathique aussi? (Yvonne)**

Describing a person or a thing
L'accord des adjectifs

1. An adjective is a word that describes a noun. The highlighted words in the following sentences are adjectives.

   La fille est blonde. Le garçon est blond aussi.
   Jeanne est française. Vincent aussi est français.

2. In French, an adjective must agree with the noun it describes or modifies. Adjectives that end in a consonant such as **blond** and **français** have two forms in the singular. Study the following.

Féminin	Masculin
La fille est blonde.	Le garçon est blond.
La fille est française.	Le garçon est français.
La fille est brune.	Le garçon est brun.
La fille est intelligente.	Le garçon est intelligent.
L'école est grande.	Le collège est grand.

3. Adjectives that end in **e**, such as **énergique** and **sympathique,** are both feminine and masculine.

Féminin	Masculin
Charlotte est très énergique.	Nicolas est très énergique.
Elle est sympathique.	Il est sympathique.

Le garçon est très amusant.

Attention!

When a final consonant is followed by an **e,** you pronounce the consonant. When a word ends in a consonant, you don't pronounce it.

petite	**petit**
française	**français**
intéressante	**intéressant**

Attention!

- You may wish to explain to students that the adjectives in Item 2 can also serve as gender markers because they provide a clue as to the gender of the noun they modify: **L'école est grande.** The **e** on **grande** lets you know that **école** is feminine.
- Explain to students that most French adjectives follow the noun: **La fille blonde est française. Le garcon brun est intelligent.** A few very commonly used adjectives come before the noun. **Petit** and **grand** are examples. **C'est une petite école. C'est un grand collège.**

Continuons
Let's put our words together

15 Historiette Chloé et Adrien Chancel Répondez d'après le dessin. *(Answer according to the illustration.)*

1. Chloé est française ou américaine?
2. Elle est blonde ou brune?
3. Elle est grande ou petite?
4. Elle est amusante?
5. Adrien est le frère de Chloé?
6. Adrien est blond ou brun?
7. Il est grand ou petit?
8. Il est amusant?
9. Chloé est élève dans un collège français ou dans une école américaine?
10. Et le frère de Chloé, il est élève dans un collège français ou dans une école américaine?

16 Historiette Maïa, Emmanuel et moi Complétez. *(Complete.)*

1. Maïa est une amie ___ et ___. (amusant, sympathique)
2. Emmanuel est le frère de Maïa. Il est ___ aussi. Il est ___ et très ___! (sympathique, amusant, sociable)
3. Maïa est ___. (français)
4. Et moi, je m'appelle ___ *(your name)*. Je suis ___. Je ne suis pas ___. (américain, français)
5. Je suis élève dans une école ___ ___. (secondaire, américain)
6. Je ne suis pas élève dans un collège ___. (français)

17 Jeu Devinez. You often hear French teenagers talk about their friends' younger siblings and say something like: **«Oh, la petite sœur de Corinne, elle est vraiment casse-pieds!»** (literally, *a foot-breaker*). Can you guess what expression we use in English?

18 Un ami idéal ou une amie idéale

What are some qualities an ideal friend would have? With a classmate, discuss what you think an ideal friend is like.

Answers to Continuons

15

1. Chloé est française.
2. Elle est brune.
3. Elle est petite.
4. Oui, elle est amusante.
5. Oui, Adrien est le frère de Chloé.
6. Il est brun.
7. Il est grand.
8. Oui, il est amusant.
9. Elle est élève dans un collège français.
10. Il est élève dans un collège français.

16

1. amusante, sympathique
2. sympathique, amusant, sociable
3. française
4. *(student's name)*, américain(e), français(e)
5. secondaire, américaine
6. français

17

casse-pieds *a nuisance, pain in the neck*

18 *Answers will vary but may include:*
Une amie idéale est amusante et sympa. Un ami idéal est amusant et patient. Une amie idéale est vraiment intéressante. Un ami idéal est vraiment intéressant aussi.

Structure

3 Practice

Continuons
Let's put our words together

15 You can do this activity with books closed and then with books open.

Expansion
- Have one student read all of Activity 15. Then have another student retell the story in the activity in his or her own words.
- Have students substitute the names of students in the class for the names in the activity and have them ask the questions about people in their class.
- Have students give a description of Chloé and another description of Adrien in their own words.

Recycling

Activity 18 recycles and recombines the vocabulary from Chapter 1.

Assessment

As an informal assessment, give students a masculine or feminine adjective and have them describe someone in the class using that adjective. For example, you say **blonde.** Students must say: **Marie est blonde.**

Reaching All Students

For the Younger Students Using large cards labeled with feminine adjectives, call girls to the front of the class to hold the cards. Pronounce the words in unison with the class. Give the boys cards with the letter **e** crossed out. Ask them to stand next to the girls to form the masculine adjective forms. Now pronounce the masculine forms of the words.

1 Preparation

Bellringer Review

Use BRR Transparency 1.5 or write the following on the board.
Write the name of a friend. Then write two or three things about him or her.

2 Presentation

Le verbe être au singulier

Step 1 Before presenting the verb **être,** have students do the following:

- point to themselves as they say **je**
- look at a neighbor as they say **tu**
- point to a boy as they say **il**
- point to a girl as they say **elle**

Step 2 Present the verb forms in Item 1. Write them on the board and have students repeat them.

Step 3 Have students look at the illustrations as they read the sentences in Item 2 aloud.

Step 4 Read the explanatory material in Item 3 to the students and have them read the sentences in unison.

19 **C'est qui?** Work with a classmate. Say three things that describe someone in the class. First your partner will tell you whether you're describing a boy or a girl. Then, he or she will guess who it is. Take turns.

—**brun, grand, amusant**
—**C'est un garçon. C'est Marc.**

Identifying people and things
Le verbe être au singulier

1. The verb *to be* in French is **être.** Study the following forms.

ÊTRE	
je	suis
tu	es
il	est
elle	est

2. You use **je** to talk about yourself.

You use **tu** to address a friend.

You use **il** to talk about a boy or a man.

You use **elle** to talk about a girl or a woman.

3. You also use **il/elle** when referring to things.

Le collège? Il est grand.
L'école? Elle est petite.

Answers to Continuons

19 *Answers will vary but may include:*
Petite, intelligente, brune. C'est une fille. C'est Anne.
Petit, patient, blond. C'est un garçon. C'est Marc.

Reaching All Students

Additional Practice Tell where a student is seated in the classroom, using his or her name and **devant** or **derrière. Marie est devant Mark.** First have students replace the noun subject with the correct subject pronoun: **Elle est devant Mark.** Then increase the difficulty by asking: **Où est Marie?** Have students respond with the correct subject pronoun**: Elle est devant Mark.**

Continuons

Let's put our words together

20 **Historiette** **Sylvie Latour** Voici une photo de Sylvie Latour. Décrivez Sylvie d'après les indications. *(Here is a photo of Sylvie Latour. Describe Sylvie using the cues.)*

1. canadienne
2. blonde
3. amusante et intelligente
4. sociable
5. de Montréal

21 **En France** Répétez la conversation. *(Repeat the conversation.)*

22 **Historiette** **Matt Porter** Parlez de Matt. *(Say all you can about Matt.)*

23 **Pardon!** Répondez d'après le modèle. *(Answer according to the model.)*

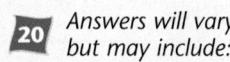

1. Je suis de Nice.
2. Je suis d'Antibes.
3. Je suis de Lille.
4. Je suis de Strasbourg.

Answers to Continuons

20 *Answers will vary but may include:*
1. Elle est canadienne.
2. Elle est blonde.
3. Elle est amusante et intelligente.
4. Elle est sociable.
5. Elle est de Montréal.

22 *Answers will vary but may include:* Il est sociable et amusant. Il est brun. Il est de New York. Il est très énergique et populaire aussi.

23
1. Pardon, tu es d'où?
2. Pardon, tu es d'où?
3. Pardon, tu es d'où?
4. Pardon, tu es d'où?

Structure

3 Practice

Continuons

Let's put our words together

20 This activity reviews the third-person form presented in the vocabulary. Have students read the answers aloud, telling about Sylvie.

21 The purpose of this miniconversation is to let students hear, see, and use the singular forms of the verb **être** in context before they use them on their own. Read the conversation to the class, or use Audiocassette 2A/CD 2, having students repeat after you or the recorded speaker. Next, ask several students to take the roles.

22 This activity reinforces once again the third person. Students will now tell all about Matt, based on what they learned about him in the conversation in Activity 21.

23 You can do this activity as a paired activity. Note that it gives students practice using the **je/tu** exchange.

3 Practice *(continued)*

25 This activity gives students the opportunity to hear the **tu** form and respond with **je.**

27 This activity makes students use all singular forms of **être.** Have them write the activity in paragraph form.

Learning from Photos

(page 32) Marseilles is the third largest city in France after Paris and Lyon. It has been an important port in the Mediterranean for over 2,500 years since it was first settled by the Greeks. This photo was taken from le Vieux Port, a very popular area in the city that has changed little over time. The church on the hill is the basilique de Notre-Dame-de-la-Garde, built in 1853 and consecrated in 1864.

Memory Aid

Dramatize the negative concept on page 33 by comparing the **ne... pas** construction with a sandwich. The **ne... pas** is the bread, and the verb is the filling for the sandwich.

About the French Language

When teaching the negative on page 33, you may wish to point out to students that in spoken French today, the **ne** is rarely used. **Je suis pas français. Elle est pas très sociable!**

In **Bon voyage!** we do use the **ne** in all activities and practice material. However, we do omit the **ne** in some very colloquial conversations to make them more realistic.

24 **Je suis...** Donnez des réponses personnelles. *(Give your own answers.)*

Je m'appelle __1__ *(name)*. Je suis de __2__ *(place)*. Je suis __3__ *(nationality)*. Je suis __4__ *(occupation)*.

25 **Une interview** Posez des questions à un(e) ami(e). *(Ask a friend the following questions.)*

1. Tu es français(e) ou américain(e)?
2. Tu es d'où?
3. Tu es élève dans une école secondaire?
4. Tu es sociable ou timide?

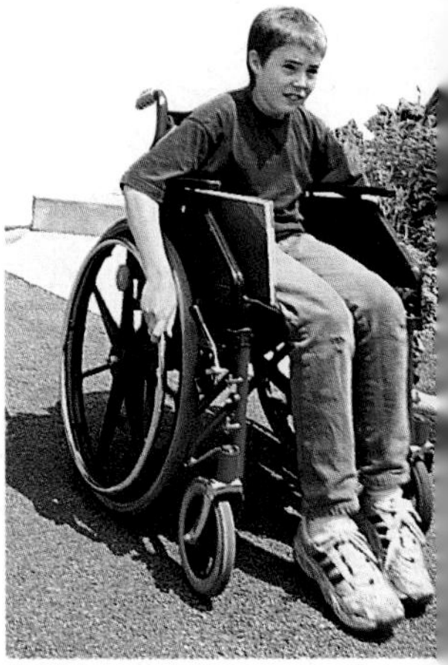

Rémi Tonon

26 **Rémi** Voici une photo de Rémi Tonon. Il est de Nîmes. Posez des questions à Rémi d'après le modèle. *(Ask Rémi questions according to the model. Your partner will answer as if he were Rémi.)*

français
—Rémi, tu es français?
—Oui, je suis français.

1. de Nîmes
2. élève dans un collège de Nîmes
3. sociable
4. intelligent

27 **Historiette** **Antoine Delcourt** Complétez. *(Complete.)*

Voici Antoine Delcourt. Il __1__ français. Il est de Marseille. Moi aussi, je __2__ de Marseille. Marseille __3__ un port important en France. Antoine __4__ élève dans un collège à Marseille. Le collège est assez grand. Et toi, tu __5__ français(e) ou américain(e)? Tu __6__ d'où? Tu __7__ élève dans une école secondaire? L'école __8__ petite?

Marseille, France

Answers to Continuons

24 *Answers will vary but may include:*
Je m'appelle *(name)*. Je suis de *(place)*. Je suis américain(e). Je suis élève.

25 *Answers will vary but may include:*
1. Je suis américain(e).
2. Je suis de (Seattle).
3. Oui, je suis élève dans une école secondaire.
4. Je suis (sociable/timide).

26
1. Rémi, tu es de Nîmes?
   Oui, je suis de Nîmes.
2. Rémi, tu es élève dans un collège de Nîmes?
   Oui, je suis élève dans un collège de Nîmes.
3. Rémi, tu es sociable?
   Oui, je suis très sociable.
4. Rémi, tu es intelligent?
   Oui, je suis assez intelligent.

27
1. est
2. suis
3. est
4. est
5. es
6. es
7. es
8. est

Making a sentence negative
La négation

To make a sentence negative in French, you put **ne... pas** around the verb. Note that **ne** becomes **n'** before a vowel.

Affirmatif	Négatif
Je suis américain.	Je ne suis pas français.
Tu es amusant.	Tu n'es pas timide.
Il est sociable.	Il n'est pas égoïste.
Elle est de Lyon.	Elle n'est pas de Paris.

Continuons
Let's put our words together

28 Non, Justine n'est pas américaine.
Mettez à la forme négative. *(Change to the negative.)*

1. Justine est américaine.
2. Elle est de San Francisco.
3. Et moi, je suis français(e).
4. Je suis de Paris.
5. Je suis élève dans un collège à Paris.

Lycée Henri IV, Paris

29 Tu es français(e)? Donnez des réponses personnelles. *(Give your own answers.)*

1. Tu es français(e)?
2. Tu es de Lyon?
3. Tu es timide?
4. Tu es l'ami(e) de Justine?

30 Un petit ami ou une petite amie A classmate will pretend that he or she has a new boyfriend or girlfriend. Ask as many questions as you can to find out who it is.

ENCORE PLUS *For more practice using the verb **être**, do Activity 3 on page H4 at the end of this book.*

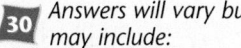

Vous êtes sur le bon chemin. Allez-y!

Answers to Continuons

28
1. Justine n'est pas américaine.
2. Elle n'est pas de San Francisco.
3. Et moi, je ne suis pas français(e).
4. Je ne suis pas de Paris.
5. Je ne suis pas élève dans un collège à Paris.

29 *Answers will vary but may include:*
1. Non, je ne suis pas français(e). Je suis américain(e).
2. Non, je ne suis pas de Lyon. Je suis de _____.
3. Non, je ne suis pas timide. Je suis très sociable.
4. Non, je ne suis pas l'ami(e) de Justine. Je suis l'ami(e) de _____.

30 *Answers will vary but may include:*
—Elle est américaine?
—Oui, elle est américaine.
—Elle est sociable?
—Non, elle n'est pas sociable. Elle est assez timide.
—C'est Anne?
—Oui!!

Structure

1 Preparation

Bellringer Review

Use BRR Transparency 1.6 or write the following on the board.
Match each subject with the correct form of the verb **être.** Then finish each sentence.

Tu	
Le garçon	**est**
Je	**suis**
Elle	**es**
L'école	

2 Presentation

La négation

Step 1 Explain how to make sentences negative by choosing a student to read the affirmative statements on page 33. After each one, model the corresponding negative statement.

Step 2 Repeat the procedure. This time, model the affirmative statements and have the class say the negative version in unison.

Learning from Photos

(page 33) Le lycée Henri IV is located in the Latin Quarter near the Sorbonne. It is one of the most prestigious lycées in all of France.

Allez-y!

At this point in the chapter, students have learned all the vocabulary and structure necessary to complete the chapter. The conversation and cultural readings that follow recycle all the material learned up to this point.

1 Preparation

Resource Manager

Audio Activities Booklet TE, pages 21–22
Audiocassette 2A/CD 2
CD-ROM

Bellringer Review

Use BRR Transparency 1.7 or write the following on the board.
On a sheet of paper, answer the following questions in the negative.

1. **Tu es français(e)?**
2. **Tu es égoïste?**
3. **Paris est une ville américaine?**
4. **Un collège est une école primaire?**

2 Presentation

Step 1 Tell students they are going to hear a conversation between Sophie and Luc, who are meeting each other for the first time.

Step 2 Ask students to open their books to page 34. Have them follow along as you read the conversation or play the recorded version on Audiocassette 2A/CD 2.

Step 3 Have students work in groups of two to practice the conversation. Then have several groups present it to the class.

Step 4 After presenting the conversation, go over the **Après la conversation** activity. If students can answer the questions with relative ease, move on. Students should not be expected to memorize the conversation.

Conversation

Il est d'où, Luc?

Sophie: Luc, tu es de Paris, non?
Luc: Non. Je ne suis pas de Paris.
Sophie: Tu es d'où, alors?
Luc: Je suis de Cannes.
Sophie: Tu es de Cannes… sur la Côte d'Azur?
Luc: Oui.
Sophie: C'est super, la Côte d'Azur!

Après la conversation

Répondez. *(Answer.)*

1. Luc est de Paris?
2. Il est d'où?
3. Où est Cannes?
4. Comment est la Côte d'Azur?

Answers to Après la conversation

1. Non, Luc n'est pas de Paris.
2. Il est de Cannes.
3. Cannes est sur la Côte d'Azur.
4. La Côte d'Azur est super.

Learning from Photos

(page 34)

- This photo is of Vieux Port in Cannes. In the nineteenth century, Cannes became a winter resort for the British aristocracy seeking refuge from the cold. Today, Cannes is a year-round resort but is most popular in the summer. The famous International Film Festival takes place in Cannes every May.

Parlons un peu plus
Let's talk some more

A **Au café** You've just met a student your own age at a café in Antibes, near Cannes. Have a conversation to get to know each other better.

Antibes, France

B **Jeu** **Tu es... !** Play a guessing game. Think of someone in the class. Pretend you are this person and describe yourself. Your classmates have to guess who you are.

Prononciation

L'accent tonique

1. In English, you stress certain syllables more than others. In French, you pronounce each syllable evenly. Compare the following pairs of English and French words.

timid / **timide**	*patient* / **patient**
popular / **populaire**	*American* / **américain**
sociable / **sociable**	

2. Repeat the following sentences. Notice how each word is linked to the next so that the sentence sounds like one long word.

Élisabeth est l'amie de Nathalie.
Paul est le frère de Nathalie.
Il est très sympathique.

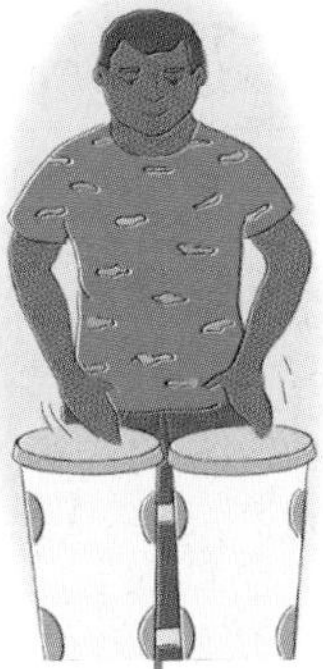

Answers to Parlons un peu plus

A *Answers will vary but may include:*

—Salut!
—Salut! Tu t'appelles comment?
—Je m'appelle David.
—Et je m'appelle Sylvie.
—Tu es de quelle nationalité?
—Je suis française.
—C'est très intéressant. Tu es élève?
—Oui, je suis élève dans un collège à Paris.

B *Answers will vary but may include:*

—Je suis très intelligente et amusante.
—Tu es Élizabeth?
—Non, je ne suis pas Élizabeth. Et je suis de San Francisco.
—Tu es Anne?
—Oui, je suis Anne.

3 Practice

Parlons un peu plus
Let's talk some more

A Have students work in pairs. You may wish to choose a pair of students to do this activity for the class.

B **Jeu** This recycling activity is fun for students to play either with a partner or in teams.

Glencoe Technology

CD-ROM

On the CD-ROM, students can watch a dramatization of this conversation. They can then play the role of either one of the characters and record themselves in the conversation.

Prononciation

Step 1 Have students repeat the words after you or the recording on Audiocassette 2A/CD 2.

Step 2 Have students open their books to page 35. Call on individuals to read the sentences carefully.

Step 3 All model sentences on page 35 can be used for dictation.

Learning from Photos

(page 35) Antibes is located halfway between Cannes and Nice. The fortifications seen here in the old city were built by the military architect Vauban. The area around Antibes is known for its flowers, particularly roses that are used to make perfume. Antibes is also a resort.

Resource Manager

Audio Activities Booklet TE, page 23
Audiocassette 2A/CD 2

National Standards

Cultures
This short, simple reading introduces students to two of their peers in two very different areas of the French-speaking world.

Comparisons
The readings make some comparisons between schools in the French-speaking world and those in the United States.

Communication
Students can say as much as they can in their own words about Nicolas Martin and Valérie Boucher.

Presentation

Pre-reading

Step 1 Have students locate Paris and Martinique on the world map, page xxii (French 1A, page xvi). You may wish to have students look at the photos on pages 36–37 now.

Step 2 Read and discuss the Reading Strategy. Have students name some cognates that they have encountered already.

Step 3 Have students scan the reading quickly and silently.

Lectures culturelles

Reading Strategy

Cognates
Words that look alike and have similar meanings in French and English are called "cognates." Look for cognates whenever you read in French. Recognizing cognates can help you figure out the meaning of many words in French and will help you understand what you read.

Un garçon et une fille

Un Parisien

Nicolas Martin est français. Il est de Paris, la capitale de la France. Nicolas est un garçon sympa. Il est très intelligent aussi. Nicolas est élève dans un lycée à Paris, le lycée Henri IV. Un lycée est aussi une école secondaire en France, mais après[1] le collège. Le lycée Henri IV à Paris est une école excellente.

[1] après *after*

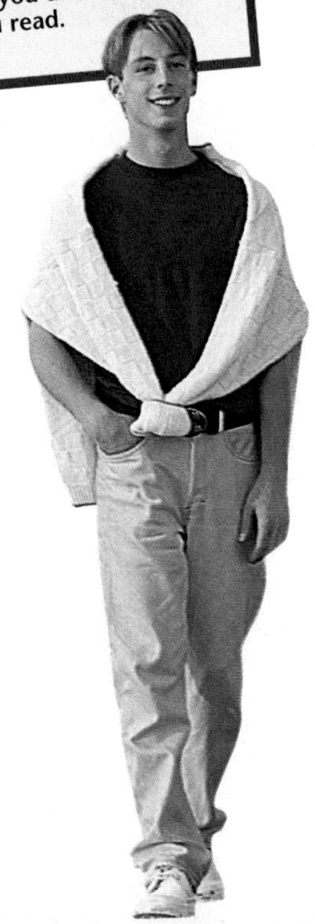

Lycée Henri IV, Paris

Learning from Photos

(page 37) Martinique is a beautiful island in French Antilles. Martinique is a volcanic island. Fort-de-France, its major city, is home to about one third of the island's 360,000 inhabitants. The Bellevue district mentioned in this reading is a very pleasant district of the city located in the hills.

Une Martiniquaise

Valérie Boucher est française aussi. Elle est de Fort-de-France, la ville[2] principale de la Martinique. La Martinique est une île[3] française dans la mer des Caraïbes (la mer des Antilles). Valérie est élève dans un lycée à Fort-de-France—le lycée Bellevue. Le lycée Bellevue est une école excellente.

[2] ville *city* [3] île *island*

Fort-de-France, Martinique

Après la lecture

A Un Parisien Répondez. *(Answer.)*

1. Nicolas Martin est de quelle nationalité?
2. Il est d'où?
3. Quelle est la capitale de la France?
4. Comment est Nicolas?
5. Il est élève où?

B Une Martiniquaise Vrai ou faux? *(True or false?)*

1. Valérie Boucher est espagnole.
2. Elle est de Pointe-à-Pitre.
3. La Martinique est une île portugaise.
4. Valérie est élève dans une école américaine.

Reading

Step 1 Lead students through the **Lecture** on pages 36-37 by reading it aloud. Have students repeat each sentence after you.

Step 2 After every two or three sentences, ask questions such as: **D'où est Nicolas Martin? Comment est Nicolas? Il est élève dans une école américaine?**

Step 3 Call on some students to read aloud individually. After a student has read about three sentences, ask questions of other students to check comprehension.

Post-reading

Have students do the **Après la lecture** activities on page 37 orally after reading the selection in class. Then assign these activities to be written at home. Go over them again the following day.

Après la lecture

A Either allow students to refer to the story to look up the answers or use this activity as a testing device for factual recall.

B **Expansion:** After doing Activity B, you may wish to have students correct each false statement made in the activity. For example: **1. Valérie Boucher est française.**

Answers to Après la lecture

A

1. Nicolas Martin est français.
2. Il est de Paris.
3. Paris est la capitale de la France.
4. Nicolas est sympa et intelligent.
5. Nicolas est élève dans un lycée à Paris.

B

1. F 3. F
2. F 4. F

Fun-Facts

When a student graduates from a lycée in Martinique he or she may attend a university in France, but many students go to the University of the West Indies in Schœlcher, a suburb of Fort-de-France.

National Standards

Cultures
This selection familiarizes students with two French-speaking countries in Africa.

Presentation

Step 1 Have students read the selection quickly as they look at the photos that accompany it.

Step 2 Ask what they learned about Côte d'Ivoire and Tunisia.

Après la lecture

A Either allow students to refer to the story to look up the answers or use this activity as a testing device for factual recall.

Learning from Photos

(page 38 top) Known as the "Paris of West Africa," Abidjan has a population of 2.5 million today compared to 100,000 in 1951. Once a favorite showcase in Africa, the Côte d'Ivoire has recently been facing some severe economic and political problems. Abidjan is a beautiful city with modern skyscrapers in the central district called le Plateau and posh residential streets in Cocody and les Deux Plateaux. Until 1983, Abidjan was the capital of the Côte d'Ivoire until the then president moved it to his native village of Yamoussoukro, which continues as the capital in name only.

Lecture supplémentaire 1

Le français en Afrique

Abidjan, Côte d'Ivoire

Bonjour! Je m'appelle Diane Koffi. Je suis d'Abidjan. Abidjan est la ville principale de la Côte d'Ivoire. La Côte d'Ivoire est un pays[1] d'Afrique Occidentale[2]. C'est un pays francophone[3].

Moi, je m'appelle Karim Ashour. Je suis tunisien. Je suis de Tunis, la capitale de la Tunisie. La Tunisie est un pays nord-africain sur la mer Méditerranée. La langue officielle de la Tunisie est l'arabe. Le français est la deuxième[4] langue.

[1] pays *country*
[2] Occidentale *Western*
[3] francophone *French-speaking*
[4] deuxième *second*

Tunis, Tunisie

Après la lecture

A Diane Complétez. *(Complete.)*

1. Diane Koffi est d'____.
2. Abidjan est la ville principale de la ____.
3. La Côte d'Ivoire est un pays d'____ Occidentale.

B Karim Vrai ou faux? *(True or false?)*

1. Karim Ashour est une fille.
2. Karim est algérien.
3. Karim est de Tunis.
4. Tunis est la capitale de la Tunisie.
5. La Tunisie est en Europe.
6. La langue officielle de la Tunisie est le français.

Learning from Photos

(page 38 bottom) Tunis, the capital of Tunisia, is an attractive city with many boulevards. This photo is of the Place de la Victoire, and the gate, la porte de France, is one of the seventeen gates that formed the original medieval ramparts that were, for the most part, torn down at the end of the last century. Tunisia gained its independence from France in 1956. Rather than repudiate the French contribution, Tunisia has integrated it; thus one can find there an interesting blend of Islamic and occidental cultures.

Answers to Après la lecture

A
1. Abidjan
2. Côte d'Ivoire
3. Afrique

B
1. F
2. F
3. V
4. V
5. F
6. F

Un artiste français

Henri de Toulouse-Lautrec est un peintre français. Il est d'Albi, une petite ville dans le sud de la France. La famille d'Henri est noble et assez riche.

Le jeune Henri est très petit. Il est boiteux[1]. Le petit garçon souffre de beaucoup de[2] fractures. Mais le jeune Henri possède un grand talent. Il adore la peinture[3].

Un sujet favori de Toulouse-Lautrec est la vie[4] parisienne.

Un autre sujet favori de Toulouse-Lautrec est le cirque. Le clown est très amusant, n'est-ce pas?

[1] boiteux *lame*
[2] beaucoup de *many*
[3] peinture *painting*
[4] vie *life*

Albi, France

Après la lecture

A Un peintre français Répondez. *(Answer.)*

1. Qui est Toulouse-Lautrec?
2. Il est d'où?
3. Comment est la famille Toulouse-Lautrec?
4. Comment est le jeune Henri?
5. Il souffre de beaucoup de fractures?
6. Il adore la peinture?
7. Il adore le cirque?

B Stratégie de lecture Trouvez les mots apparentés dans la lecture. *(Find the following cognates in the reading.)*

1. family
2. talent
3. rich
4. subject
5. possess
6. favorite
7. circus
8. painter

Answers to Après la lecture

A

1. Toulouse-Lautrec est un peintre français.
2. Il est d'Albi.
3. La famille est noble et assez riche.
4. Il est très petit et boiteux.
5. Oui, il souffre de beaucoup de fractures.
6. Oui, il adore la peinture.
7. Oui, il adore le cirque.

B

1. la famille
2. le talent
3. riche
4. le sujet
5. possède
6. favori
7. le cirque
8. le peintre

Lecture supplémentaire 2

Attention!

The readings on pages 38–39 are optional. You may skip them completely, have the entire class read them, have only several students read them and report to the class, or assign either of them for extra credit.

Presentation

Step 1 Have students read the selection to themselves.

Step 2 Now have students do the **Après la lecture** activities.

Learning from Photos

(page 39) The beautiful, small city of Albi is on the banks of the river Tarn. The city is dominated by towering red walls. The famous Albi episcopate today houses a museum with the world's best collection of works by Toulouse-Lautrec.

Art Connection

Many of the works of Toulouse-Lautrec depict life in Montmartre in his day. However, the circus was another theme that fascinated Toulouse-Lautrec from the first moment he was taken to the circus at age sixteen by the painter of animals René Princeteau. Toulouse-Lautrec loved to paint the clowns, acrobats, and circus riders **(écuyères)**.

National Standards

Connections
This reading establishes a connection with another discipline—geography. Knowledge students already have from previous study of the subject will enable them to read this selection with ease as they increase their vocabulary in French and learn more about the geography of France.

Attention!

The readings in the **Connexions** section are optional. They focus on some of the major disciplines taught in schools and universities. The vocabulary is useful for discussing such topics as history, literature, art, economics, business, science, etc. You may choose any of the following ways to do the readings in the **Connexions** sections.

Independent reading Have students read the selections and do the post-reading activities as homework, which you collect. This option is least intrusive on class time and requires a minimum of teacher involvement.

Homework with in-class follow-up Assign the readings and postreading activities as homework. Review and discuss the material in class the next day.

Intensive in-class activity This option includes a pre-reading vocabulary presentation, in-class reading and discussion, assignment of the activities for homework, and a discussion of the assignment in class the following day.

CONNEXIONS

Les sciences sociales

La géographie

Geography is the study of the earth. It deals with all the earth's features, such as mountains, rivers, and seas. It is also the study of where people live and how the earth's features affect their lives. It is a subject that has interested human beings since the earliest of times.

Look at the map of France. Notice how many geographical terms you are able to recognize in French. See how easy it is to read about geography in French.

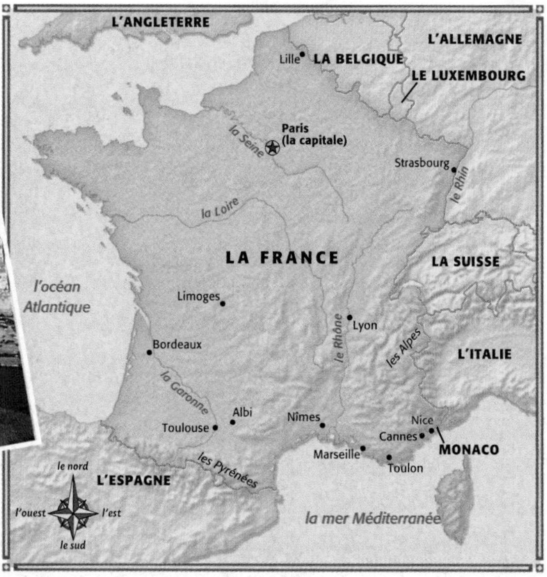

Le Rhône à Avignon

La Seine à Paris

Learning from Photos

(page 41 top) The musée du Louvre in Paris is one of the most famous museums in the world. The Louvre once served as the palace of the French kings. It was first built as a fortress in the thirteenth century. The glass pyramid seen in the photo serves as a new entrance to the Louvre. The large pyramid is surrounded by three smaller pyramids. Designed by the architect I. M. Pei, it was commissioned by the former president François Mitterrand and unveiled in 1989. The startling contrast between the modern glass pyramid and the classical architecture of the Louvre caused a furor, as did the Eiffel Tower when it was first unveiled. The initial outrage has faded, as it did with the Eiffel Tower.

- Orleans on the Loire River is about an hour's train ride from Paris. This city is famous because it is the home of the French heroine Joan of Arc (Jeanne d'Arc), who saved the city from the English and Burgundian armies in 1429.

La France

Villes

La France est en Europe. La France est un pays important dans le monde[1]. La capitale, Paris, est une ville culturelle. Lille, dans le nord, est une ville industrielle. Marseille, dans le sud, est un port important sur la mer Méditerranée.

Fleuves

Il y a[2] cinq fleuves[3] en France. La Seine passe à Paris. La Seine est un fleuve très calme. La Loire est un fleuve très long. Le Rhin forme une frontière naturelle entre la France et l'Allemagne. Le Rhône est un fleuve important: c'est une grande source d'énergie électrique. La Garonne est un fleuve assez violent.

[1] monde *world* [2] Il y a *There are* [3] fleuves *rivers*

Musée du Louvre, Paris

La Loire à Orléans

Après la lecture

Un peu de géographie

Vrai ou faux? *(True or false?)*

1. La France est un continent.
2. Paris est une ville industrielle.
3. Lille est dans le sud de la France.
4. Marseille est un port.
5. La Seine est un fleuve violent.
6. La Loire est un fleuve très long.
7. Un fleuve forme une frontière naturelle entre la France et l'Allemagne.

CONNEXIONS

Presentation

Les sciences sociales

La géographie

Step 1 Have students read the introduction in English on page 40.

Step 2 Have students read the selection quickly or have them skim it.

Step 3 You may wish to have them find and repeat all the cognates. Explain to students that there are two important strategies to use when reading unfamiliar material—learn to recognize cognates and try to derive meaning from context.

Après la lecture

Have a student read the sentence aloud and indicate whether it is true or false. Call on more able students to correct the false statements.

FRENCH Online

The Internet activity for Chapter 1 is a map activity that reinforces the material presented in this reading. Students are asked to identify some major French cities and geographical features. Maps and worksheets for this activity are available at the Glencoe Foreign Language Web site: french.glencoe.com

Answers to Après la lecture

1. F
2. F
3. F
4. V
5. F
6. V
7. V

Assessment

You may wish to give the following quiz to students who have done the **Connexions** section.
Find the following information.

1. **Les noms de trois fleuves en France**
2. **Une ville industrielle**
3. **Une grande source d'énergie électrique**
4. **Un port sur la mer Méditerranée**

Use what you have learned

1 Preparation

Bellringer Review

Use BRR Transparency 1.8 or write the following on the board.
Copy the following sentences, supplying the missing words.

1. _____ est le professeur.
2. C'est _____? C'est Marie!
3. Chantal Dubois est _____.

Recycling

These activities allow students to use the vocabulary and structure from this chapter in completely open-ended, real-life situations.

2 Presentation

Encourage students to say as much as possible when they do these activities. Tell them not to be afraid to make mistakes, since the goal of these activities is real-life communication. If someone in the group makes an error, allow the others to politely correct him or her. Let students choose the activities they would like to do.

You may wish to divide students into pairs or groups. Encourage students to elaborate on the basic theme and to be creative. They may use props, pictures, or posters if they wish.

C'est à vous

Use what you have learned

PARLER **1**

Un ami

✔ ***Describe a male friend and answer questions about him***

Work with a classmate. Here's a picture of Vincent Terrier, a friend of yours from Paris, France. Say as much as you can about him. Answer any questions your partner may have about Vincent.

PARLER **2**

Une élève

✔ ***Ask a female friend questions and tell her about yourself***

Jeanne Marin (a classmate) is a new girl in your school. She is from Montreal, Canada. You want to get to know her better and help her feel at home. Find out as much as you can about her. Tell Jeanne about yourself, too.

Jeanne Marin

Saint-Tropez, France

PARLER **3**

Dis donc, c'est qui?

✔ ***Ask someone questions about another person***

You and a friend (a classmate) are at a sidewalk café in Saint-Tropez, on the French Riviera. You see an attractive girl or boy sitting a few tables away. It just so happens that your friend knows the person. Ask your friend as many questions as you can to find out about the boy or girl you're interested in.

Learning from Photos

- *(page 42 middle)* This photo was taken in Montreal, the major city of Quebec. Montreal is the second largest French-speaking city in the world.
- *(page 42 bottom)* St. Tropez was once a small fishing village like many other villages in the south of France. Today it is a village whose harbor is full of yachts. The resort is completely closed down in the winter, but there is a tremendous influx of people in the summer.

Answers to C'est à vous

1 *Answers will vary but may include:*

—C'est Vincent Terrier.
—Il est sympa?
—Oui, il est sympa et patient, aussi.
—Il est d'où, Vincent Terrier? Il est de New York ou de Paris?
—Il est de Paris.
—Alors, il est français!
—Oui!

ÉCRIRE

4 Un ami français

✔ Write a postcard to a friend about yourself

Here's a postcard you just received from a new pen pal. First read his message. Then answer it. Give Christophe similar information about yourself.

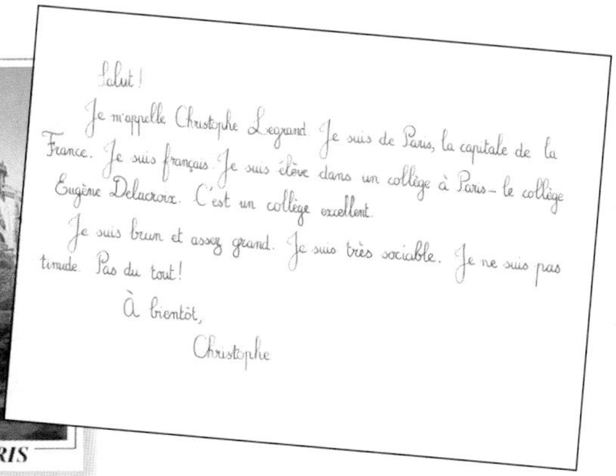

Salut!

Je m'appelle Christophe Legrand. Je suis de Paris, la capitale de la France. Je suis français. Je suis élève dans un collège à Paris— le collège Eugène Delacroix. C'est un collège excellent.

Je suis brun et assez grand. Je suis très sociable. Je ne suis pas timide. Pas du tout!

À bientôt,

Christophe

Writing Strategy

Freewriting One of the easiest ways to begin any kind of personal writing is simply to begin—to let your thoughts flow and write the first thing that comes to mind. Sometimes as you think of one word, another word you know will come to mind. If you get stuck, take several minutes to think of another word or phrase you have already learned. Brainstorming and freewriting are often methods for generating ideas when writing about yourself.

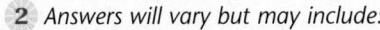

ÉCRIRE

5 Moi

On a piece of paper, write down as much as you can about yourself in French. Your teacher will collect the descriptions and choose students to read them to the class. You'll all try to guess who's being described.

Answers to C'est à vous

2 *Answers will vary but may include:*

—Tu t'appelles comment?
—Jeanne. Je suis de Montréal.
—Et moi, je m'appelle Paul. Je suis américain. Je suis élève dans une école secondaire à ____. Tu es élève?
—Oui, je suis élève dans un collège à Montréal.
—Le collège, il est grand?
—Non, le collège n'est pas grand. Il est très petit!
—Alors, à bientôt, Jeanne!
—À bientôt, Paul!

3 *Answers will vary but may include:*

—Le garçon brun, c'est qui?
—C'est Luc. Il est très sympathique.
—Il est français?
—Non, il n'est pas français; il est ____.
—Il est élève?
—Oui, il est élève dans un collège à ____.
—Il est timide?
—Non, il n'est pas timide. Il est vraiment sociable!

C'est à vous

Writing Development

Have students keep a notebook or portfolio containing their best written work from each chapter. These selected writings can be based on assignments from the Student Textbook and the Writing Activities Workbook. The two activities on page 43 are examples of writing assignments that may be included in each student's portfolio. In the Workbook, students will develop an organized autobiography **(Mon autobiographie).** These workbook pages may also become a part of their portfolio.

Writing Strategy

Freewriting Have students read the Writing Strategy on page 43. If students have difficulty thinking of words to describe themselves, have them use the vocabulary list on page 46.

Learning from Photos

(page 43) No other building in Paris is more associated with the history of the city than Notre-Dame on the Île de la Cité. Construction was started in 1163 and continued for 170 years. The cathedral is particularly noted for its three magnificent portals in the front, its two rose windows, gargoyles, and flying buttresses.

Assessment

Resource Manager

Communication Transparencies
Quizzes
Test Booklet
ExamView Pro®
Situation Cards
Performance Assessment
Marathon mental Videoquiz

Assessment

This is a pre-test for students to take before you administer the chapter test. Note that each section is cross-referenced so students can easily find the material they have to review in case they made errors. You may wish to collect these assessments and correct them yourself or you may prefer to have the students correct themselves in class. You can go over the answers orally or project them on the overhead, using your Assessment Answers transparencies.

Glencoe Technology

MINDJOGGER

You may wish to help your students prepare for the chapter test by playing the MindJogger game show. Teams will compete against each other to review chapter vocabulary and structure and sharpen listening comprehension skills.

Assessment

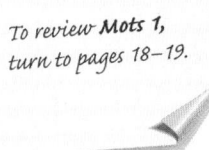

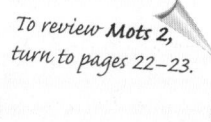

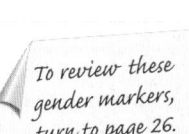

Paris, France

Vocabulaire

*To review **Mots 1**, turn to pages 18–19.*

1 Répondez d'après la photo. *(Answer according to the photo.)*

1. Jeanne est française ou américaine?
2. Elle est de Paris ou de Boston?
3. Elle est blonde ou brune?

*To review **Mots 2**, turn to pages 22–23.*

2 Choisissez. *(Choose.)*

4. Guillaume est ___ dans un collège français.
   a. ami **b.** élève
5. Guillaume est ___ de Françoise.
   a. le frère **b.** la sœur

Structure

To review these gender markers, turn to page 26.

3 Complétez avec «un» ou «une». *(Complete with* un *or* une.*)*

6. Sylvie est élève dans ___ collège français.
7. Sylvie est ___ fille très sympa.
8. Paul est ___ ami de Sylvie.
9. Paul est ___ garçon sympa aussi.

4 Complétez avec «le», «la» ou «l'». *(Complete with* le, la, *or* l'.*)*

10. ___ fille, Sylvie, est de Lyon.
11. Jean-Pierre est ___ frère de Sylvie.
12. ___ école de Sylvie est grande.

To review agreement of adjectives, turn to page 28.

5 Complétez. *(Complete.)*

13. C'est une école assez ___. (petit)
14. Martine est une fille très ___. (dynamique)
15. Le garçon ___ est amusant. (américain)
16. Robert est un élève ___. (intelligent)

Answers to Assessment

1
1. Jeanne est française.
2. Elle est de Paris.
3. Elle est brune.

2
4. b
5. a

3
6. un
7. une
8. un
9. un

4
10. La
11. le
12. L'

5
13. petite
14. dynamique
15. américain
16. intelligent

Assessment

6 Complétez avec «être». *(Complete with* être.*)*

17. Dominique, tu ____ français?
18. Oui, je ____ de Bordeaux.
19. La fille blonde, elle ____ américaine?
20. Non, elle ____ canadienne.

To review the verb ***être,*** *turn to page 30.*

7 Répondez au négatif. *(Answer in the negative.)*

21. Alain Gérard est américain?
22. Il est timide?
23. Alain est le frère de Julie?

To review making a sentence negative, turn to page 33.

Culture

8 Choisissez. *(Choose.)*

24. Un lycée est ____ secondaire en France.
 a. un collège **b.** un élève **c.** une école
25. La ville principale de la Martinique est ____.
 a. Bellevue **b.** Fort-de-France **c.** Paris

To review this cultural information, turn to pages 36–37.

Grand-Rivière, Martinique

Learning from Photos

(page 45) Grand-Rivière is a small village located on the northern coast of Martinique. The fishermen's boats painted in bright colors are called **des yoles.**

Answers to Assessment

6

17. es
18. suis
19. est
20. est

7

21. Non, Alain Gérard n'est pas américain.
22. Non, il n'est pas timide.
23. Non, Alain n'est pas le frère de Julie.

8

24. c
25. b

Vocabulaire

Vocabulary Review

The words and phrases in the **Vocabulaire** have been taught for productive use in this chapter. They are summarized here as a resource for both student and teacher. This list also serves as a convenient resource for the **C'est à vous** activities on pages 42–43. There are approximately twelve cognates in this vocabulary list. Have students find them.

Attention!

You will notice that the vocabulary list here is not translated. This has been done intentionally, since we feel that by the time students have finished the material in the chapter they should be familiar with the meanings of all the words. If there are several words they still do not know, we recommend that they refer back to the **Mots 1** and **2** sections in the chapter or go to the dictionaries at the back of this book to find the meanings. However, if you prefer that your students have the English translations, please refer to Transparency V 1.1, where you will find all these words with their translations.

Vocabulaire

Identifying a person or thing

un garçon
une fille
un ami
une amie
un(e) élève
un frère
une sœur
une école
un collège
être

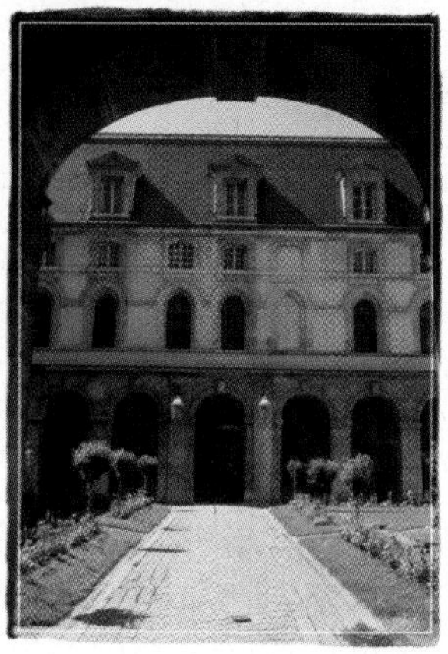

Describing a person

petit(e)
grand(e)
brun(e)
blond(e)
amusant(e)
patient(e)
intelligent(e)
intéressant(e)
sympa(thique)
timide
énergique
égoïste
dynamique
populaire
sociable
enthousiaste

Stating nationality

français(e)
américain(e)

How well do you know your vocabulary?

- Choose five words that describe a good friend.
- Use these words to write several sentences about him or her.

Finding out information

Qui?
D'où?
Comment?
C'est qui?
De quelle nationalité?

Expressing degrees

assez
très
vraiment

Other useful words

voilà
aussi
secondaire

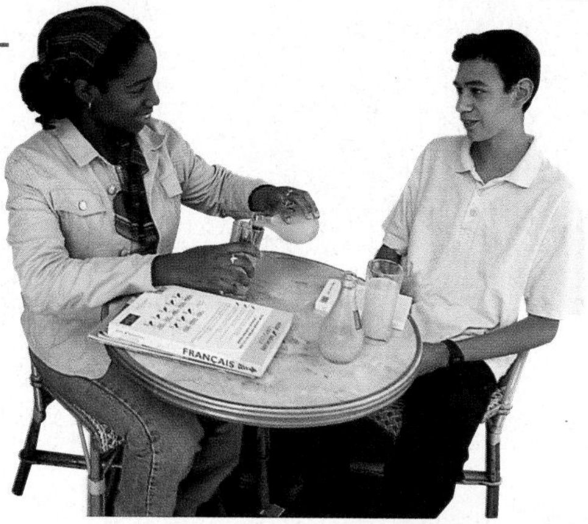

Technotour

BON VOYAGE!

VIDÉO • Épisode 1

Avant de visionner

In this video episode, Vincent and Chloé, each hoping to get a great shot of le Sacré-Cœur, bump into each other on the steps below the church.

Vincent et Chloé à Montmartre

Une vue splendide de Paris

FRENCH ONLINE

À découvrir

Learn more about le Sacré-Cœur and la place du Tertre—the heart of Montmartre—online.

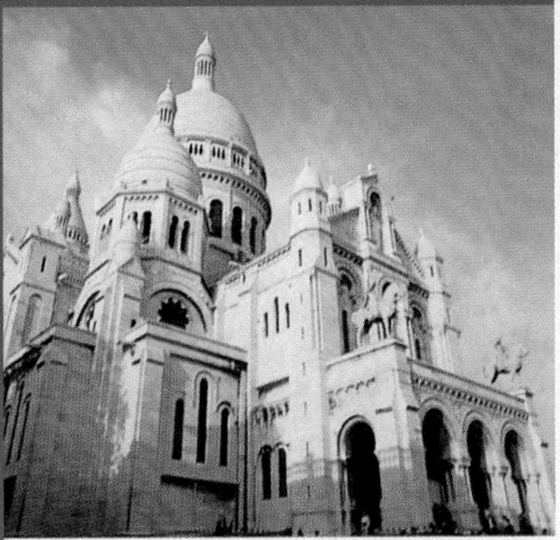

La basilique du Sacré-Cœur

FRENCH Online

In the Chapter 1 Internet activity, you will have a chance to learn more about the geography of the Francophone world. To begin your virtual adventure, go to the Glencoe French Web site: **french.glencoe.com**

Overview

This page previews two key multimedia components of the **Glencoe French** series. Each reinforces the material taught in the chapter in a unique manner.

VIDÉO

The Video Program allows students to see how the chapter vocabulary and structures are used by native speakers. For maximum reinforcement, show the video episode as a final activity for Chapter 1.

The two photos on the left show highlights from the Chapter 1 video episode. Before viewing the episode, you may want to present the characters in the photos to your students and have them describe each one, using the adjectives from the chapter. See the Video Activities Booklet for detailed suggestions for using this resource.

FRENCH Online

- The **À découvrir** photo shows le Sacré-Cœur in Paris. Students can go online to the Glencoe French Web site for additional information about la basilique du Sacré-Cœur, the spot where Vincent and Chloé meet up in this first video episode.
- Teacher Information and Student Worksheets for this activity can be accessed at the Web site.

Video Synopsis

In this first episode, we meet two of the five main characters who are filming videos for the Internet site of the International Youth Institute in Paris. Vincent Martin is from Paris, France. He is sixteen years old and his specialty is producing video. He is in Montmartre as the video opens and bumps into Chloé Samson. She is from Lyon, France. She is seventeen years old and her area of specialty is art and design. They are making their way through the throngs of tourists, strolling through the place du Tertre filming and watching the artists. They both end up on one of the landings on the steps below the church where each hopes to take a great shot of the Sacré-Cœur. Chloé is quite surprised to see Vincent. They laugh and fool around, and as they race up the stairs toward the Basilique, Vincent films Chloé who motions to the city of Paris behind her. The video then breaks into some shots of Paris in all its splendor.

Planning for Chapter 2

SCOPE AND SEQUENCE, PAGES 48–79

Topics

- Describing people
- School subjects

Functions

- How to describe people
- How to describe and express opinions about school subjects
- How to count from 70 to 100

National Standards

- Communication Standard 1.1 pages 52, 53, 56, 57, 59, 60, 62, 63, 65, 67, 74
- Communication Standard 1.2 pages 52, 53, 56, 57, 59, 60, 62, 63, 66, 69, 70, 71, 73
- Communication Standard 1.3 pages 52, 56, 57, 59, 60, 75
- Cultures Standard 2.1 pages 68–69, 70, 71
- Cultures Standard 2.2 page 57
- Connections Standard 3.1 pages 72–73
- Comparisons Standard 4.2 pages 68–69, 70
- Communities Standard 5.1 page 75

Culture

- Discussing Haitian, Canadian, and Cajun influences in the United States
- Schools in France
- An e-mail from Nicolas, a Parisian student on vacation in Biarritz

Structure

- Plural forms of articles, nouns, and adjectives
- Plural forms of the verb **être**
- **Tu** and **vous**

PACING AND PRIORITIES

The chapter content is color coded below to assist you in planning.

■ required ■ recommended ■ optional

Vocabulaire *(required)* *Days 1–4*

- ■ Mots 1
  - Les élèves et les profs
  - Comment sont les cours?
- ■ Mots 2
  - Les matières
  - En cours de français

Structure *(required)* *Days 5–7*

- ■ Le pluriel: articles, noms et adjectifs
- ■ Le verbe **être** au pluriel
- ■ **Tu** et **vous**

Conversation *(required)*

- ■ Quel prof?

Prononciation *(recommended)*

- ■ Les consonnes finales

Lectures culturelles

- ■ Le français aux États-Unis *(recommended)*
- ■ La scolarité en France *(optional)*
- ■ Un message *(optional)*

Connexions *(optional)*

- ■ La biologie, la physique et la chimie

■ **C'est à vous** *(recommended)*

■ **Assessment** *(recommended)*

■ **Technotour** *(optional)*

RESOURCE GUIDE

SECTION	PAGES	SECTION RESOURCES
Vocabulaire *Mots 1*		
Les élèves et les profs Comment sont les cours?	50 51–53	Vocabulary Transparencies 2.2–2.3 Audiocassette 2B/CD 2 Audio Activities Booklet TE, pages 26–27 Workbook, page 11 Quiz 1, page 7 ExamView Pro®
Vocabulaire *Mots 2*		
Les matières En cours de français	54 55–57	Vocabulary Transparencies 2.4–2.5 Audiocassette 2B/CD 2 Audio Activities Booklet TE, pages 27–29 Workbook, pages 12–13 Quiz 2, page 8 ExamView Pro®
Structure		
Le pluriel: articles, noms et adjectifs Le verbe **être** au pluriel **Tu** et **vous**	58–60 60–63 64–65	Audiocassette 2B/CD 2 Audio Activities Booklet TE, pages 30–32 Workbook, pages 14–16 Quizzes 3–5, pages 9–11 ExamView Pro®
Conversation		
Quel prof?	66	Audiocassette 2B/CD 2 Audio Activities Booklet TE, pages 32–33 CD-ROM
Prononciation		
Les consonnes finales	67	Pronunciation Transparency P 2 Audiocassette 2B/CD 2 Audio Activities Booklet TE, pages 33–34
Lectures culturelles		
Le français aux États-Unis La scolarité en France Un message	68–69 70 71	Audiocassette 2B/CD 2 Audio Activities Booklet TE, pages 34–35 Test Booklet, Chapter 2
Connexions		
La biologie, la physique et la chimie	72–73	Test Booklet, Chapter 2
C'est à vous		
	74–75	**Bon voyage!** Video, Episode 2 Video Activities Booklet, Chapter 2 French Online Activities **french.glencoe.com**
Assessment		
	76–77	Communication Transparency C 2 Quizzes 1–5, pages 7–11 Test Booklet, Chapter 2 ExamView Pro® Situation Cards, Chapter 2 **Marathon mental** Videoquiz

Using Your Resources for Chapter 2

Transparencies

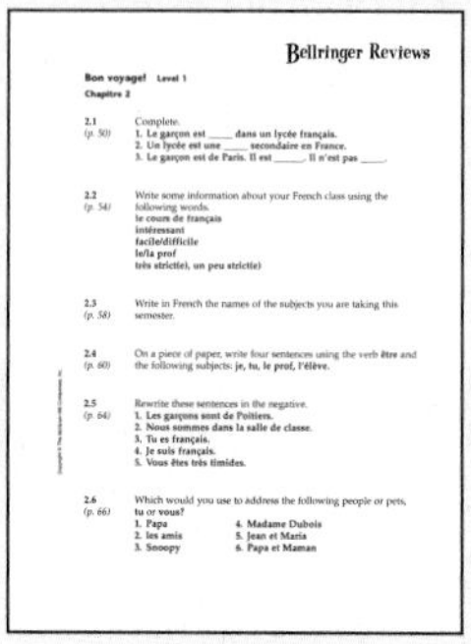

Bellringer 2.1–2.8

Vocabulary 2.1–2.5

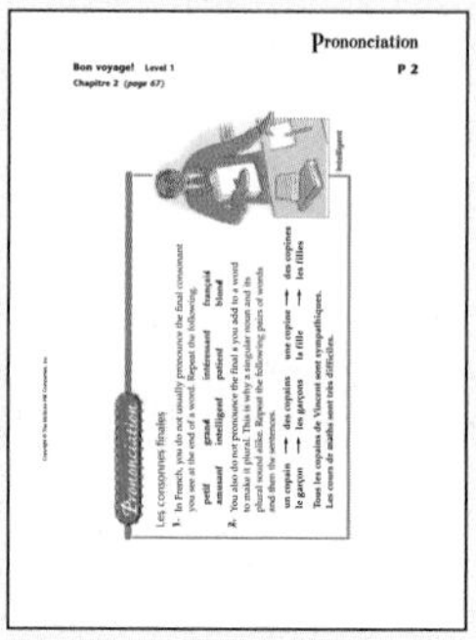

Pronunciation P 2

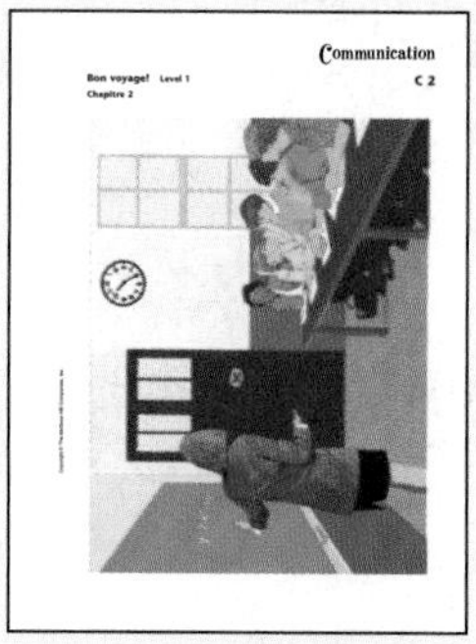

Communication C 2

Writing Activities Workbook

Vocabulary, pages 11–13

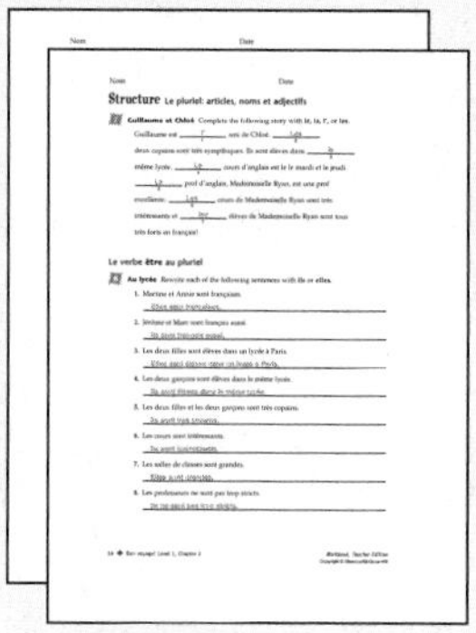

Structure, pages 14–16

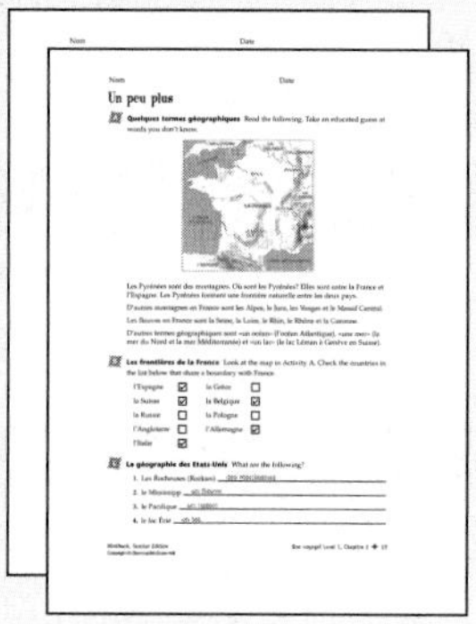

Enrichment, pages 17–18

Audio Program and Audio Activities Booklet

Vocabulary, pages 26–29

Structure, pages 30–32

Conversation, Pronunciation, pages 32–34

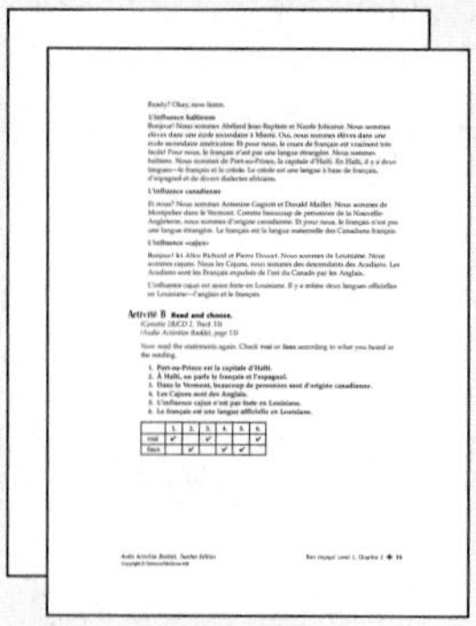

Cultural Reading, pages 34–35

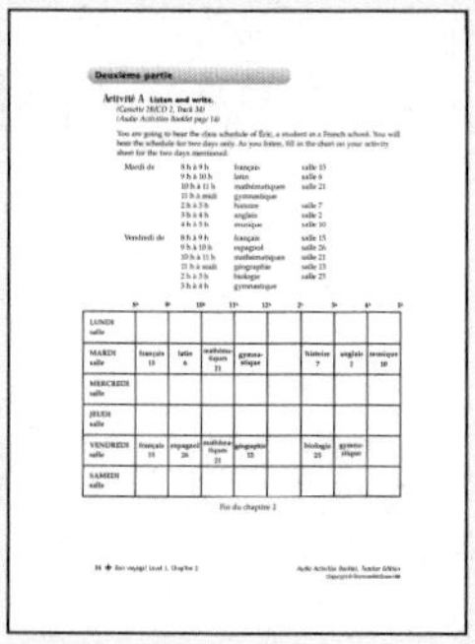

Additional Practice, page 36

Assessment

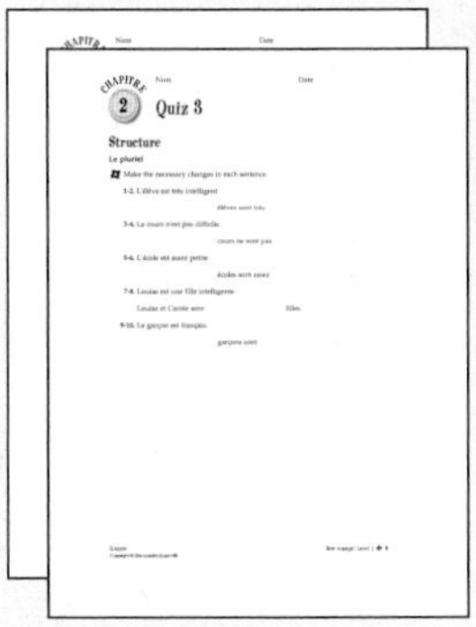

Vocabulary and Structure Quizzes, pages 7–11

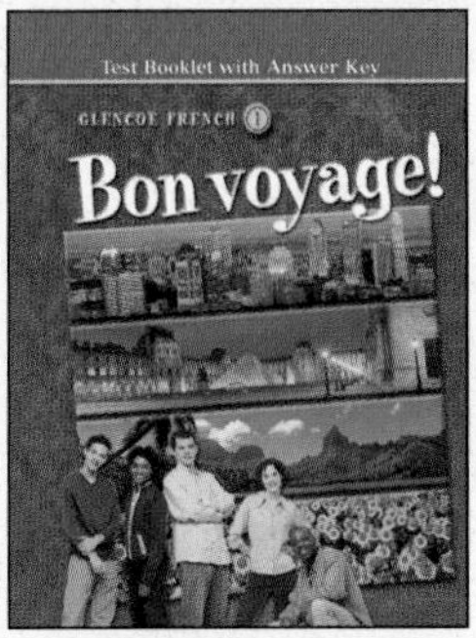

Chapter Tests, Chapter 2

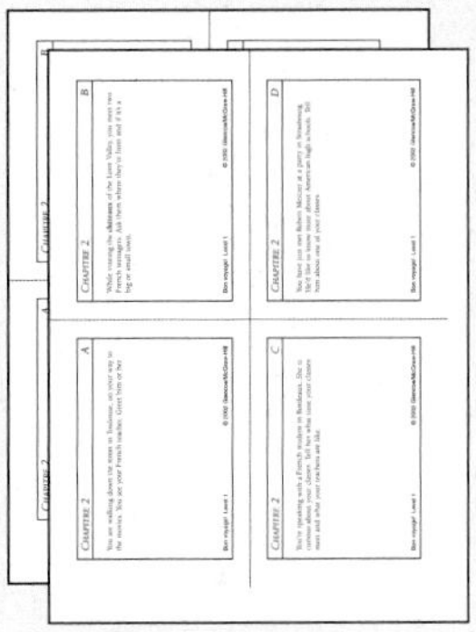

Situation Cards, Chapter 2

Timesaving Teacher Tools

Interactive Teacher Edition

Imagine having your Teacher's Edition and all resources on a CD-ROM. Click on a resource and it appears on your screen, ready to be printed, sorted, or planned.

Interactive Lesson Planner

The Interactive Lesson Planner CD-ROM helps you organize your lesson plans for a week, month, semester, or year. Look at this planning tool for easy access to your Chapter 2 resources.

ExamView Pro®

Test Bank software for Macintosh and Windows makes creating, editing, customizing, and printing tests quick and easy.

Technology Resources

FRENCH Online — In the Chapter 2 Internet activity, you will have a chance to learn more about schools in the Francophone world. Visit french.glencoe.com.

On the Interactive Conversation CD-ROM, students can listen to and take part in a recorded version of the conversation in Chapter 2.

NATIONAL GEOGRAPHIC SOCIETY — See the National Geographic Teacher's Corner on pages 150–151, 256–257, 396–397, 500–501 for reference to additional technology resources.

Bon voyage! Video and Video Activities Booklet.

Help your students prepare for the chapter test by playing the **Marathon mental** Videoquiz game show. Teams will compete against each other to review chapter vocabulary and structure and sharpen listening comprehension skills.

CHAPITRE 2

Preview

In this chapter, students will learn to describe people and things, using the plural forms of articles, adjectives, and the verb **être.** (The singular forms were taught in Chapter 1.) Active vocabulary from Chapter 1 is recycled in this chapter as new descriptive adjectives and school-related terms are presented.

National Standards

Communication

In Chapter 2, students will communicate in spoken and written French to:

- obtain and provide information about their friends and courses
- talk about themselves

Students will engage in conversations, provide and obtain information, and exchange opinions as they fulfill the chapter objectives listed on this page.

Attention!

Cognates Since the vocabulary in this chapter has to do with school and school subjects, there are many cognates. The large number of cognates will help students learn the new words quickly. However, cognates often present a pronunciation problem. Since they are so similar to the English words, students will often anglicize the pronunciation. Take care to model the pronunciation of cognates very carefully. However, the cognates do give students the feeling that they are progressing rapidly in their language acquisition.

CHAPITRE 2

Les cours et les profs

Objectifs

In this chapter you will learn to:

- ✔ *describe people and things*
- ✔ *talk about more than one person or thing*
- ✔ *tell what subjects you take in school and express some opinions about them*
- ✔ *speak to people formally and informally*
- ✔ *talk about French-speaking people in the United States*

Pierre Bonnard *Écriture de fille*

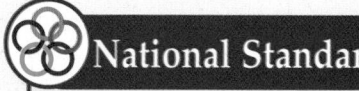

48

Correlations to Continuum *(see page i for code)*

Stage I
Greet and respond. p. 55 (*i*); Express likes and dislikes. p. 51 (*i*), p. 59 (**13**, *p*); Obtain information. p. 57 (**9**, *p*); Understand some ideas and familiar details. p. 56 (**8**, *p*); Converse in face-to-face social interactions. p. 63 (**22**, *p*); Listen during social interactions and listen to video texts. p. 74 (**2**, *p*), p. 79 (*p*); Write notes, lists, poems, postcards, and short letters. p. 71 (*i*), p. 75 (**3**, *p*); Use short sentences, learned words and phrases, and simple questions and commands when speaking and writing. p. 53 (**4**, *p*), p. 60 (**14**, *p*); Understand ideas and familiar details when listening. p. 66 (*p*); Understand texts enhanced by visual clues. pp. 72–73 (*p*); Understand and convey information about self, school, likes and dislikes, campus life. pp. 50–51 (*i*), p. 52 (**3**, *p*), p. 74 (**1**, *m*); Communicate effectively with some hesitation and errors, which do not hinder comprehension. p. 74 (**1**); Demonstrate culturally acceptable behavior for Stage I functions. p. 65 (**24**); Understand most important information. p. 75 (**5**)

Stage II
Understand and express important ideas and some detail. p. 56 (**7**, *i*), pp. 68–69 (**C**, *p*); Describe and compare. pp. 50–51 (*i*), p. 67 (**A**, *p*), p. 74 (**2**, *m*); Write letters. p. 71 (*i*); Use and understand learned expressions, sentences, and strings of sentences when speaking and listening. p. 52 (**2**, *i*), p. 74 (**1**, **2**, *p*);

Stage III
Express and understand opinions. p. 51 (*i*), p. 60 (**15**, *p*); Use strings of related sentences when speaking. p. 74 (**2**, *i*)

Stage IV
Understand and convey information on the sciences. p. 72 (*i*), pp. 72–73 (*p*); Write journals and letters. p. 75 (**4**, *i*)

CHAPITRE 2

Spotlight on Culture

Photograph This photo shows some students and a teacher at the lycée Janson de Sailly. Janson de Sailly is an excellent lycée in the **16e arrondissement** of Paris.

Painting This painting by Pierre Bonnard is entitled ***Écriture de fille.*** Bonnard (1867–1947) studied law but realized at a young age that he would devote his life to art. He did paintings in oil and watercolor. He also produced posters and lithographs and designed stage sets. Many of his paintings deal with family life, and he produced many portraits of women and children as well as other themes.

Chapter Projects

La scolarité en France Have students do a research project on the educational system in France. Have them find information on the following types of schools: **l'école maternelle, l'école primaire, le collège, le lycée, l'université, les grandes écoles.**

1 Preparation

Resource Manager

Vocabulary Transparencies 2.2–2.3
Audio Activities Booklet TE, pages 26–27
Audiocassette 2B/CD 2
Workbook, page 11
Quiz 1, page 7
ExamView Pro®

Bellringer Review

Use BRR Transparency 2.1 or write the following on the board.
Complete.

1. **Le garçon est _____ dans un lycée français.**
2. **Un lycée est une _____ secondaire en France.**
3. **Le garçon est de Paris. Il est _____. Il n'est pas _____.**

2 Presentation

Step 1 Have students close their books. Present the vocabulary, using Vocabulary Transparencies 2.2–2.3. Have students repeat the words and sentences in **Mots 1** after you or play the recording on Audiocassette 2B/CD 2.

Step 2 Prepare large cards on which you have written plural adjectives and nouns from **Mots 1.** Have pairs of students hold up a card together. Now ask *yes/no* and *either/or* questions referring to the pairs of students: **Pierre et Alexandre sont élèves? Karine et Stéphanie sont françaises ou américaines?**

Step 3 Have students repeat words in isolation first and build to complete sentences. For example: **le cours, facile, difficile. Le cours est facile. Le cours n'est pas difficile.** Then ask questions using the new words.

Vocabulaire

Mots 1

Les élèves et les profs

Karine et Stéphanie sont françaises.
Pierre et Alexandre sont français aussi.

Les quatre copains sont de Rouen.
Ils sont élèves dans le même lycée.
Ils sont tous très sympathiques.

Reaching All Students

Total Physical Response Before doing this activity, act out the following commands to make sure students understand them: **marchez lentement, marchez vite.**
(to one or more students)

Levez-vous.
Promenez-vous dans la salle de classe.
Marchez vite.
Et maintenant, marchez lentement.
Arrêtez-vous.
Montrez-moi un garçon.
Montrez-moi deux garçons.
Montrez-moi deux garçons bruns.
Montrez-moi une fille.
Et maintenant, montrez-moi deux filles.
Promenez-vous dans la salle de classe et montrez-moi tous les garçons blonds.
Et maintenant, continuez. Promenez-vous dans la salle de classe et montrez-moi toutes les filles blondes.
Merci, _____, retournez à votre place et asseyez-vous.

Comment sont les cours?

Le cours de français est facile.
La prof n'est pas trop stricte. Juste un peu.

Mais les cours de sciences sont vraiment difficiles. Toi, tu es d'accord ou pas?
Non, je ne suis pas d'accord. Pour moi, les cours de sciences sont très faciles.

Vocabulaire
Mots 1

Step 4 After presenting the vocabulary orally, have students open their books and read the new vocabulary words as they repeat either after you or Audiocassette 2B/CD 2. Intersperse questions throughout the reading to continue to elicit oral responses.

Cognate Recognition

Ask volunteers to identify words in **Mots 1** that are cognates **(le prof, le cours, la classe, difficile, facile, sciences, stricte).**

Teaching Tip: Use a French beret or a small American flag as you demonstrate the difference in pronunciation between French and English words.

Vocabulary Expansion

You may wish to give students some additional classroom words such as:

un pupitre	**une brosse**
une fenêtre	**une craie**
une porte	**un projecteur**
un tableau	**un ordinateur**

However, it is recommended that you limit the amount of additional vocabulary.

About the French Language

In French, **la classe** refers to the number of students. **Le cours** refers to the subject matter.

La classe est petite.
Le cours est intéressant.

Reaching All Students

Visual-Spatial Learners Have students look at the expressions on the students' faces to help convey the meaning of **difficile** and **facile.** You can also use a gesture to help convey the meaning of **difficile;** wipe your brow and make a hand motion, then say **facile, pas difficile,** and shake your head to indicate *not.*

3 Practice

Commençons
Let's use our new words

Attention!

When students are doing the **Commençons** activities, accept any answer that makes sense. The purpose of these activities is to have students use the new vocabulary. They are not factual recall activities. Thus, it is not necessary for students to remember specific factual information from the vocabulary presentation when answering. If you wish, have students use the photos on this page as a stimulus, when possible.

Historiette Each time **Historiette** appears, it means that the answers to the activity form a short story. Encourage students to look at the title of the **Historiette,** since it can help them do the activity.

1 and **2** Do Activities 1 and 2 orally with books closed. Then have students read them for additional reinforcement.
Expansion: Call on one student to answer all the questions. Then have another student retell the **Historiette** in his or her own words.

3 Go over Activity 3 once orally, asking questions of individual students. Have them open their books and read it for additional reinforcement. Now reverse the process. Have students close their books and give them the response. Have them ask you the questions.

Commençons
Let's use our new words

Rennes, France

Des lycéens de Rennes

1 Historiette
Deux copines françaises

Inventez une histoire. *(Make up a story.)*

1. Léa et Touria sont françaises ou américaines?
2. Elles sont copines?
3. Elles sont de Rennes?
4. Elles sont élèves dans le même lycée?
5. Le lycée est à Rennes?
6. Elles sont dans la salle de classe?

2 Historiette
Deux copains français

Inventez une histoire. *(Make up a story.)*

1. Paul et Jamal sont français ou américains?
2. Ils sont copains?
3. Ils sont amusants?
4. Ils sont sympathiques?
5. Ils sont de Rennes?
6. Ils sont élèves dans le même lycée?

FRENCH Online
For more information about Rennes and other cities in France, go to the Glencoe French Web site: french.glencoe.com

3 Le cours de français
Donnez des réponses personnelles. *(Give your own answers.)*

1. Qui est le/la prof de français?
2. Il/Elle est sympa?
3. Il/Elle est strict(e)?
4. Il/Elle est de quelle nationalité?
5. Le cours de français est facile ou difficile?
6. Pour toi, les cours de sciences sont faciles ou difficiles?

Answers to Commençons

1 *Answers will vary but may include:*
1. Léa et Touria sont françaises.
2. Oui, elles sont copines.
3. Oui, elles sont de Rennes.
4. Oui, elles sont élèves dans le même lycée.
5. Oui, le lycée est à Rennes.
6. Oui, elles sont dans la salle de classe.

2 *Answers will vary but may include:*
1. Paul et Jamal sont français.
2. Oui, ils sont copains.
3. Oui, ils sont amusants.
4. Oui, ils sont sympathiques.
5. Oui, ils sont de Rennes.
6. Oui, ils sont élèves dans le même lycée.

3 *Answers will vary but may include:*
1. Mme Moreau est la prof de français.
2. Oui, elle est sympa.
3. Non, elle n'est pas stricte.
4. Elle est française.
5. Le cours de français est vraiment facile.
6. Les cours de sciences sont difficiles.

4 **Le prof idéal ou la prof idéale** Work with a classmate. Share ideas as to what you look for in an ideal teacher. Let your classmate know whether you agree with him or her. You may want to use some of the following words.

intéressant | sympathique | patient | strict
intelligent | amusant | enthousiaste | dynamique

Un cours de français aux États-Unis

For more practice using words from **Mots 1**, do Activity 4 on page H5 at the end of this book.

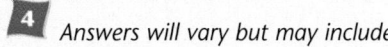

Vocabulaire

4 Have students do Activity 4 as a miniconversation. Encourage them to use as much expression as possible.

Learning from Photos

(page 52) Rennes is the capital of Brittany. Rennes is a very friendly city with many quaint medieval streets. It also has two universities.

Writing Development

Have students write the answers to Activity 3 in a paragraph. They will see that these answers tell a story.

You may also wish to have students close their books and write a short paragraph about their French class.

ENCORE PLUS This *infogap* activity will allow students to practice in pairs. The activity should be very manageable for them, since all vocabulary and structures are familiar to them.

Learning from Photos

(page 53) Have students look at the photo and say as much as they can about it. They should describe the class, the teacher, and each student in the photo.

Answers to Commençons

4 *Answers will vary but may include:*

—La prof idéale est amusante et dynamique.
—Non, la prof idéale n'est pas amusante et dynamique. Elle est intelligente et patiente.
—La prof idéale n'est pas trop stricte!
—Non, la prof idéale n'est pas trop stricte! Juste un peu.

Reaching All Students

Additional Practice After completing the activities, have students work in pairs. One makes incorrect statements about the French class and the teacher. The other corrects him or her. For example:

La classe de français est grande.
La classe de français n'est pas grande.

1 Preparation

Resource Manager

Vocabulary Transparencies 2.4–2.5
Audio Activities Booklet TE, pages 27–29
Audiocassette 2B/CD 2
Workbook, pages 12–13
Quiz 2, page 8
ExamView Pro®

Bellringer Review

Use BRR Transparency 2.2 or write the following on the board.
Write some information about your French class using the following words.
le cours de français
intéressant
facile / difficile
le/la prof
très strict(e), un peu strict(e)

2 Presentation

Step 1 Have students imitate the pronunciation of the words on page 54 as carefully as they can. Since they are almost all cognates, students will have a tendency to mispronounce them.

Step 2 Call two students to the front of the room. Select two who have fairly good pronunciation. Have them open their books to page 55 and read the words in the speech bubble to the class, as if they were the people in the illustration. This procedure helps students grasp the meaning of **nous.**

FUN-FACTS

In France, public school students have to buy their own textbooks in a bookstore. Books are not provided by the school.

Vocabulaire Mots 2

Les matières

Les sciences naturelles

la biologie
la chimie
la physique

Les mathématiques (Les maths)

l'algèbre
la géométrie
la trigonométrie
le calcul

Les langues

le français
l'italien
l'espagnol
l'allemand
l'anglais
le latin

Les sciences sociales

l'histoire
la géographie
l'économie

D'autres matières

la littérature
l'informatique
la gymnastique
la musique
le dessin

Reaching All Students

Total Physical Response Before doing this activity, act out **levez la main** to be sure students understand the expression.

TPR 1
Les élèves d'espagnol, levez la main.
Les élèves de maths, levez la main.
Les élèves de biologie, levez la main.
Les élèves de latin, levez la main.
Les élèves d'histoire, levez la main.
Merci, tout le monde.

TPR 2
Levez-vous tous.
Si vous êtes élèves d'allemand, asseyez-vous.
Si vous êtes élèves de physique, asseyez-vous.
Si vous êtes élèves de dessin, asseyez-vous.
Si vous êtes élèves de trigonométrie, asseyez-vous.
Si vous êtes élèves de français, asseyez-vous.

En cours de français

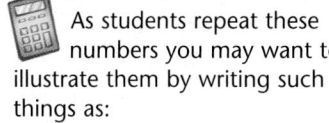

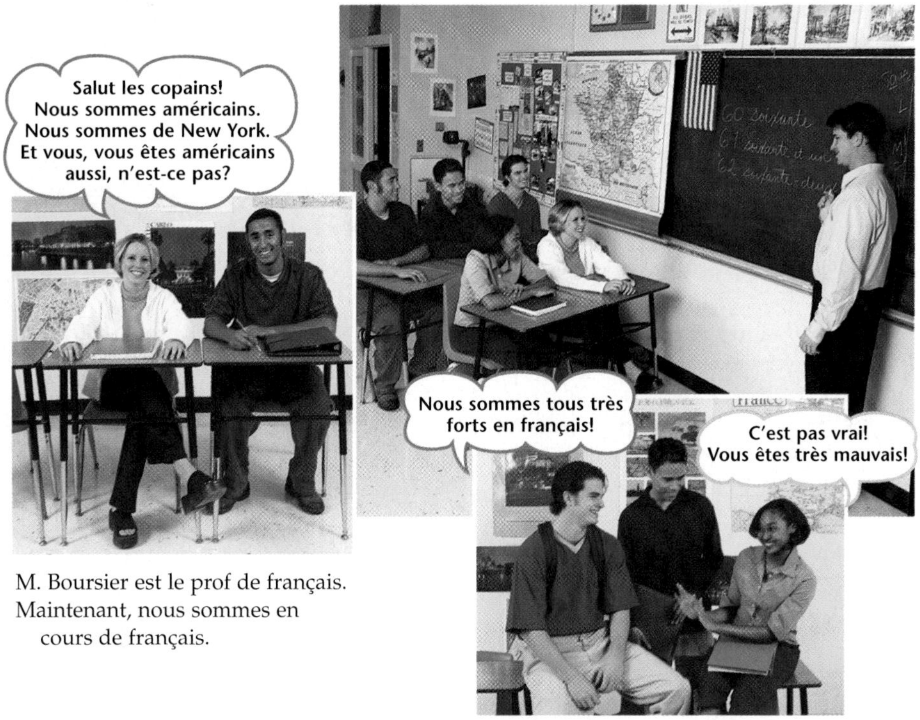

Salut les copains!
Nous sommes américains.
Nous sommes de New York.
Et vous, vous êtes américains aussi, n'est-ce pas?
Nous sommes tous très forts en français!
C'est pas vrai!
Vous êtes très mauvais!

M. Boursier est le prof de français.
Maintenant, nous sommes en cours de français.

Les nombres de 70 à 100

70 soixante-dix	80 quatre-vingts	90 quatre-vingt-dix
71 soixante et onze	81 quatre-vingt-un	91 quatre-vingt-onze
72 soixante-douze	82 quatre-vingt-deux	92 quatre-vingt-douze
73 soixante-treize	83 quatre-vingt-trois	93 quatre-vingt-treize
74 soixante-quatorze	84 quatre-vingt-quatre	94 quatre-vingt-quatorze
75 soixante-quinze	85 quatre-vingt-cinq	95 quatre-vingt-quinze
76 soixante-seize	86 quatre-vingt-six	96 quatre-vingt-seize
77 soixante-dix-sept	87 quatre-vingt-sept	97 quatre-vingt-dix-sept
78 soixante-dix-huit	88 quatre-vingt-huit	98 quatre-vingt-dix-huit
79 soixante-dix-neuf	89 quatre-vingt-neuf	99 quatre-vingt-dix-neuf
		100 cent

Step 3 Go around the room, pointing to two students at a time and say **vous.** Have someone point to himself or herself and someone else and say **nous.**

Step 4 Les nombres de 70 à 100 Have students repeat the numbers. Then write numbers on the board in random order and have students say them aloud.

Attention!

- The gender of words such as **l'espagnol, l'italien,** etc., is indicated in the reference vocabulary list on page 78.
- Note that the **n'** is omitted in **C'est pas vrai!,** since this is what everyone would say in informal conversation.

Math Connection

As students repeat these numbers you may want to illustrate them by writing such things as:

$60 + 10 = 70$
$4 \times 20 = 80$
$4 \times 20 + 11 = 91$

Students will learn mathematical terms in **Connexions,** Chapter 5, pages 176-177.

Reaching All Students

Additional Practice Have students make a list of their courses and indicate whether they consider each one **facile** or **difficile.** They can then tell about the class, using **intéressant** affirmatively or negatively.

Assessment

As an informal assessment, check for comprehension by asking *yes/no* questions and *either/or* questions. Call on the entire class as well as individual students to respond. For example:

L'espagnol est une langue? Le calcul est une science sociale?

Vocabulary Expansion

You may wish to give students some informal words they can use to describe something in a positive or negative way.
positive: **chouette, super, extra, génial**
negative: **moche**
Terrible can have either a positive or negative meaning depending on the tone of voice.

3 Practice

Commençons
Let's use our new words

5 This activity can be done with books open. Note that it serves as an introduction to the plural, since it contrasts **est/sont** and singular and plural forms of nouns and adjectives.

7 **Expansion:** After doing Activity 7, have students look at the photo on page 56. Use the activity as a model to ask the following questions:

Les élèves sont de quelle nationalité?

Ils sont élèves dans un lycée français?

Ils sont en cours de chimie?

Le cours de chimie est facile ou difficile?

Les élèves sont forts en chimie?

8 Students should be able to recognize the cognates used in Activity 8, but they are for passive recognition only. Students should not be expected to learn or produce this receptive vocabulary. You may wish to have them say the words once.

Commençons
Let's use our new words

Un cours de chimie à Paris

5 Sciences ou langues? Vrai ou faux? *(True or false?)*

1. La chimie est une science.
2. L'histoire et la géographie sont des mathématiques.
3. Le calcul est une langue.
4. Le latin et l'espagnol sont des langues.
5. Pour vous, le français est un cours obligatoire.

6 Des cours faciles et difficiles Donnez des réponses personnelles. *(Give your own answers.)*

1. Le cours de français est facile ou difficile?
2. Pour toi, quels sont les cours faciles?
3. Quels sont les cours difficiles?
4. Tu es fort(e) en français?
5. Tu es fort(e) en sciences?
6. Tu es très fort(e) en quelle matière?
7. Tu es assez mauvais(e) en quelle matière?

7 Historiette Des élèves américains Inventez une histoire. *(Make up a story.)*

1. Les élèves sont de quelle nationalité?
2. Ils sont élèves dans une école secondaire américaine?
3. Ils sont en cours de français?
4. Le cours de français est facile ou difficile?
5. Les élèves sont forts en français?

8 C'est quel cours? Identifiez le cours. *(Identify the course.)*

1. la littérature, la grammaire anglaise
2. la conversation, la culture française
3. un poème, une pièce de théâtre, une fable
4. un microbe, un animal, une plante, un microscope
5. un cercle, un rectangle, un triangle, un parallélogramme
6. un piano, un violon, un concert, un opéra
7. les montagnes, les villes, les villages, les capitales, les océans
8. la peinture, la sculpture, les statues, les artistes
9. une disquette, un moniteur, un microprocesseur, un bit

Answers to Commençons

5
1. V
2. F
3. F
4. V
5. F

6 *Answers will vary but may include:*
1. Le cours de français est difficile.
2. Les cours faciles sont le dessin et la musique.
3. Les cours difficiles sont le latin et la physique.
4. Oui, je suis fort(e) en français.
5. Non, je ne suis pas très fort(e) en sciences.
6. Je suis très fort(e) en informatique.
7. Je suis assez mauvais(e) en économie.

7 *Answers will vary but may include:*
1. Les élèves sont américains.
2. Oui, ils sont élèves dans une école secondaire américaine.
3. Oui, ils sont en cours de français.
4. Le cours de français est assez facile.
5. Oui, les élèves sont assez forts en français.

8
1. C'est le cours d'anglais.
2. C'est le cours de français.
3. C'est le cours de littérature.
4. C'est le cours de biologie.
5. C'est le cours de géométrie.
6. C'est le cours de musique.
7. C'est le cours de géographie.
8. C'est le cours de dessin.
9. C'est le cours d'informatique.

9 Comment est la classe?

With a classmate, look at the illustration. Take turns asking each other questions about it. Use the following question words: **qui, où, quel cours, à quelle heure, comment.**

LUGAGNE-DELPON Olivier
257 r Lecourbe 15e 01 45 58 96 30
LUGAGNE DELPON Paul
4 r Chevert 7e 01 44 05 55 31
LUGAGNE-DELPONT Véronique
15 r Marie et Louise 10e 01 43 41 37 85
LUGAN Benoît
34 pl Marché St-Honoré 1e 01 42 97 55 05
» **Bernard et Gabrielle**
5 bd Grenelle 15e 01 45 75 47 83
» **Bruno et Stéphanie** Bat A2
64 r Compans 19e 01 40 18 13 57
» **Hermann**
11 r Vasco de Gama 15e 01 45 55 44 35
» **Jacques** 75 av Ledru Rollin 12e 01 43 47 84 57

10 Le numéro de téléphone

Look at this page from the Paris phone book with a classmate. Give a telephone number. Your classmate will tell whose number it is. Then reverse roles.

11 Jeu Quelle matière?

Work with a classmate. Think of a school subject and use whatever means necessary (voice, hands, drawings) to help your partner guess which subject it is.

Un cours de dessin à Paris

ENCORE PLUS *For more practice using words from **Mots 2**, do Activity 5 on page H6 at the end of this book.*

Vocabulaire

11 Students may want to use the words from Activity 8 to do Activity 11. They may also consider describing the teacher of the class that they have in mind.

Teaching Tip: You may wish to divide the class into two teams to play Activity 11 as a class competition after the students have practiced in pairs.

FUN-FACTS

Note that French phone numbers have ten digits. The first two digits are the regional code. The prefix for Paris is 01. The numbers are given as follows: **le zéro un, quarante-deux/trente-trois/zéro un/dix-huit**

Assessment

As an informal assessment, ask individual students the following questions: **Qui est le prof de français? Qui sont deux élèves dans le cours de français? Comment est le cours de français, facile ou difficile?**, etc.

ENCORE PLUS This *infogap* activity will allow students to practice in pairs. The activity should be very manageable for them, since all vocabulary and structures are familiar to them.

Answers to Commençons

9 *Answers will vary but may include:*

—Qui est la prof?
—La prof est Madame Haddad.
—C'est quel cours?
—C'est le cours de français.
—Le cours de français est à quelle heure?
—Le cours de français est à neuf heures.
—Comment est la professeur?
—Elle est petite, brune, et sympathique.

10 and **11** *Answers will vary.*

Reaching All Students

For the Younger Students Use pictures or props (an equation for algebra, a globe for geography, art pencils for drawing, etc.). Ask students *either/or* questions. For example: **C'est un cours de dessin ou un cours de littérature? C'est un cours de géographie ou un cours d'algèbre?**

Learning from Photos

(pages 56–57) The photos of the chemistry and art classes were taken at the lycée Janson de Sailly. Have students look at these photos. Encourage them to write or tell as much as possible about each photo.

1 Preparation

Resource Manager

Audio Activities Booklet TE, pages 30–32
Audiocassette 2B/CD 2
Workbook, pages 14–16
Quizzes 3–5, pages 9–11
ExamView Pro®

Bellringer Review

Use BRR Transparency 2.3 or write the following on the board.
Write in French the names of the subjects you are taking this semester.

2 Presentation

Le pluriel: articles, noms et adjectifs

Step 1 If you wish to present the grammar point deductively, have students close their books. On the board, write the singular forms of the nouns from Item 1 on page 58. Now ask students to supply the plural forms. (They know the plural forms of the articles from the vocabulary presentation in **Mots 1.**) Then have students open their books and read Items 1 and 2.

Step 2 Have students zero in on the fact that there is only one plural form for the indefinite articles **(des)** and one for the definite articles **(les).**

Step 3 Have students read the model sentences aloud in Item 3.

Structure

Talking about more than one person or thing
Le pluriel: articles, noms et adjectifs

1. The articles you know **(un/une, le/la/l')** are singular markers. The plural forms of these articles are plural markers. Study the following.

LES ARTICLES INDÉFINIS

Masculin		Féminin	
Singulier	Pluriel	Singulier	Pluriel
un garçon	des garçons	une fille	des filles
un‿ami (n)	des‿amis (z)	une amie	des‿amies (z)
un collège	des collèges	une école	des‿écoles (z)

LES ARTICLES DÉFINIS

Masculin		Féminin	
Singulier	Pluriel	Singulier	Pluriel
le garçon	les garçons	la fille	les filles
l'ami	les‿amis (z)	l'amie	les‿amies (z)
le collège	les collèges	l'école	les‿écoles (z)

2. In French, you form the plural of most nouns by adding an **s.** This **s,** however, is not pronounced. It is the article **les** or **des** that lets you know the noun is plural: **un prof → des profs; la prof → les profs.**

3. When a noun is plural, any adjective that describes or modifies it must also be in the plural. You form the plural of most adjectives in French by adding an **s.** The **s** is not pronounced.

Singulier	Pluriel
La classe est petite.	Les classes sont petites.
La prof est patiente.	Les profs sont patientes.
Le lycée est grand.	Les lycées sont grands.
Le prof est intéressant.	Les profs sont intéressants.

Note: You do not add an **s** if the word already ends in **s.**
un cours **des cours**

About the French Language

You may wish to point out to students that the plural articles do not indicate gender. However, if there is an adjective with the noun, the adjective may provide a clue as to the gender of the noun.

Class Motivator

Levez la main! Give students a word orally. Have them raise one hand if it is singular, two hands if it is plural. For example: **le cours, les garçons.**

Continuons
Let's put our words together

12 **Ils sont comment?** Mettez au pluriel. *(Put in the plural.)*

—Le garçon est blond.
—Les garçons sont blonds.

1. La fille est blonde.
2. Le garçon est brun.
3. La sœur de Valentin est amusante.
4. Le frère de Stéphane est égoïste.
5. Le prof est intéressant.
6. Le cours est assez difficile.
7. La salle de classe est petite.
8. L'ami de Paul est vraiment sympathique.
9. L'élève est très intelligent.
10. L'ami de Valérie est amusant.

Deux lycéennes de Yerres, France

13 **Pour toi...** Citez... *(Name . . .)*

Pour moi, deux matières très intéressantes sont ____ et ____.

1. deux matières très intéressantes
2. deux cours très intéressants
3. deux écoles excellentes
4. deux élèves populaires
5. deux professeurs stricts
6. deux filles très intelligentes
7. deux garçons très sympas
8. deux élèves fort(e)s en géographie
9. deux élèves assez mauvais(es) en musique

3 Practice

Continuons
Let's put our words together

12 and **13** These activities can be done with books closed, open, or both. You may wish to write the answers to Activity 12 on the board so students can see the silent **s.**

Learning from Photos

(page 59) Yerres is a middle-class suburb of Paris. Have the students describe the girls in the photo.

FUN-FACTS

Both girls in this photo are riding **un scooter.** French teenagers cannot drive a car until they are eighteen (sixteen if they have a special permit and are accompanied by an adult). However, they can drive smaller vehicles such as mopeds and motorbikes (**vélomoteurs** and **cyclomoteurs**).

Answers to Continuons

12

1. Les filles sont blondes.
2. Les garçons sont bruns.
3. Les sœurs de Valentin sont amusantes.
4. Les frères de Stéphane sont égoïstes.
5. Les profs sont intéressants.
6. Les cours sont assez difficiles.
7. Les salles de classe sont petites.
8. Les amis de Paul sont vraiment sympathiques.
9. Les élèves sont très intelligents.
10. Les amis de Valérie sont amusants.

13 *Answers will vary but may include:*

1. Pour moi, deux matières très intéressantes sont ____ et ____.
2. Pour moi, deux cours très intéressants sont ____ et ____.
3. Pour moi, deux écoles excellentes sont ____ et ____.
4. Pour moi, deux élèves populaires sont ____ et ____.
5. Pour moi, deux professeurs stricts sont ____ et ____.
6. Pour moi, deux filles très intelligentes sont ____ et ____.
7. Pour moi, deux garçons très sympas sont ____ et ____.
8. Pour moi, deux élèves fort(e)s en géographie sont ____ et ____.
9. Pour moi, deux élèves assez mauvais(es) en musique sont ____ et ____.

Recycling

Activity 15 recycles the adjectives from Chapter 1.

1 Preparation

Bellringer Review

Use BRR Transparency 2.4 or write the following on the board.
On a piece of paper, write four sentences using the verb **être** and the following subjects: **je, tu, le prof, l'élève**

2 Presentation

Le verbe être au pluriel

Step 1 Have students keep their books closed as you write **je, tu, il/elle** on the board with the appropriate forms of **être.** Remind the students that they learned the singular forms of the verb **être** in Chapter 1, page 30.

Step 2 Now write in **ils/elles** and ask students if they remember the corresponding verb form (from the **Mots 1** section). Do the same with **nous sommes** and **vous êtes.** (The difference between **tu** and **vous** for informal and formal terms of address will be explained in the next structure section, page 64. For now, use **vous** in its plural meaning only.)

Learning from Realia

(page 60) Have students guess the meaning of the saying on this greeting card.

14 **En commun** Inventez des points communs.
(Make up what these people have in common.)

Caroline et Marie
Elles sont amusantes, fortes en algèbre...

1. Laurent et Christian
2. Isabelle et Sandrine
3. Romain et Christophe
4. Marine et Nathalie
5. Loïc et Mathias

15 **Comme moi** Work with a classmate. Tell your partner what you and your friends have in common. Your partner will agree or disagree.

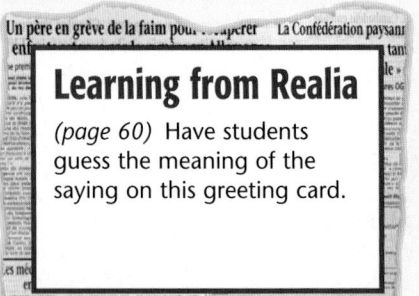

Sue et Jennifer sont sociables... comme moi.
Moi, je ne suis pas d'accord. Elles ne sont pas sociables du tout!

Les vrais amis sont amis pour la vie

Talking about more than one
Le verbe être au pluriel

1. You have already learned the singular forms of the verb **être.** Now study the plural forms.

ÊTRE

Singulier	Pluriel
je suis	nous sommes
tu es	vous‿êtes
il/elle est	ils/elles sont

Answers to Continuons

14 *Answers will vary but may include:*

1. Laurent et Christian—Ils sont très amusants et assez sociables.
2. Isabelle et Sandrine—Elles sont fortes en sciences et vraiment intelligentes.
3. Romain et Christophe—Ils sont mauvais en dessin.
4. Marine et Nathalie—Elles sont énergiques, populaires, et très fortes en français.
5. Loïc et Mathias—Ils sont vraiment intéressants, assez forts en anglais, et très forts en trigonométrie.

15 *Answers will vary but may include:*

—John et Cheryl sonts mauvais en mathématiques... comme moi.
—Moi, je ne suis pas d'accord. Ils ne sont pas mauvais en mathématiques du tout!
—Nathalie et Émily sont populaires et fortes en chimie... comme moi.
—Moi, je suis d'accord. Elles sont très populaires et fortes en chimie!

Structure

2.

You use **nous** when referring to yourself and another person or other people.

You use **vous** when talking to several people.

You use **ils** when referring to two or more males or to a group of males and females.

You use **elles** when referring to two or more females.

Savez-vous que... ?

You also use **ils/elles** when referring to things.

Les cours? Ils sont très faciles.

Les salles? Elles sont petites.

Step 3 Using groups of students in front of the class, convey the meaning of **nous** (include yourself in the meaning), then **vous, ils,** and **elles.** If there is enough space, have the groups stand in front of the chalkboard and write the appropriate subject pronoun above each group in large letters.

Step 4 Have students open their books and lead them through Items 1 and 2 on pages 60–61.

Reaching All Students

Kinesthetic Learners Some students learn by moving and doing. Have individuals and various groups made up of two, three, or four students stand in different locations in the room. Some groups should be all one sex, some mixed. Choose one base sentence such as **Il est amusant.** Have different students apply this sentence to various groups or individuals to whom they point, changing subject pronoun, verb, and adjective as necessary. For example: **Elles sont amusantes. Vous êtes amusantes. Je suis amusant(e). Nous sommes amusants.**

Musical Rhythmic Learners Have students make up a rap melody to sing.

Moi, je suis américain(e) et toi, tu es américain(e).
C'est ça!
Nous sommes américain(e)s, tous (toutes) les deux.
Et vous? Et vous?
Vous êtes de quelle nationalité?

3 Practice

Continuons

Let's put our words together

Attention!

Note how these activities develop from simple to more complex.

16 Students hear but do not have to produce the **nous/vous** forms.

17 Students use only the **ils/elles** forms based on what they heard in the conversation.

18 Students hear **vous** and learn that when they hear **vous** they will respond with **nous.**

ENCORE PLUS This *infogap* activity will allow students to practice in pairs. The activity should be very manageable for them, since all vocabulary and structures are familiar to them.

Attention!

Note that the activities are color-coded. All the activities in the text are communicative. However, the ones with blue titles are guided communication. The red titles indicate that the answers to the activity are more open-ended and can vary more. You may wish to correct students' mistakes more so in the guided activities than in the activities with a red title, which lend themselves to a freer response.

Continuons

Let's put our words together

16 Vous êtes d'où? Répétez la conversation. *(Repeat the conversation.)*

17 Historiette Ils sont américains. Complétez d'après la conversation. *(Complete according to the conversation.)*

Les deux garçons __1__ américains. Ils ne __2__ pas de New York. Ils __3__ de Boston. Boston __4__ une grande ville américaine.

Les deux filles ne __5__ pas américaines. Elles __6__ françaises. Elles __7__ de Toulouse. Toulouse __8__ une grande ville française.

18 À vous Répondez en utilisant **nous.** *(Choose a partner and answer for both of you using* nous.*)*

1. Vous êtes américain(e)s?
2. Vous êtes d'où?
3. Vous êtes élèves dans une école secondaire?
4. Vous êtes dans la classe de quel professeur?
5. Vous êtes fort(e)s en français?

ENCORE PLUS ***For more practice using the verb être, do Activity 6 on page H7 at the end of this book.***

Answers to Continuons

16 *Students will repeat the conversation.*

17

1. sont
2. sont
3. sont
4. est
5. sont
6. sont
7. sont
8. est

18 *Answers will vary but may include:*

1. Oui, nous sommes américain(e)s.
2. Nous sommes de ____.
3. Oui, nous sommes élèves dans une école secondaire.
4. Nous sommes dans la classe de ____.
5. Oui, nous sommes fort(e)s en français.

19 **Des questions** Posez des questions et répondez d'après le modèle. *(Ask and answer questions according to the model.)*

américaine / française
—Vous êtes américaines ou françaises?
—Nous sommes françaises.

1. martiniquaise / américaine
2. petit / grand
3. sociable / timide
4. brune / blonde

20 **Historiette** **L'ami de Christophe**
Complétez en utilisant **être.** *(Complete with* être.*)*

Je ___1___ un ami de Christophe. Christophe ___2___ très sympa et très amusant. Nous ___3___ français, Christophe et moi. Nous ___4___ de Cancale, un petit village breton (en Bretagne). Cancale ___5___ vraiment très pittoresque.

Nous ___6___ élèves dans un collège. Où ___7___ le collège? À Dinard. Tous les deux, nous ___8___ forts en anglais. La prof d'anglais, Mlle Fielding, ___9___ anglaise. Elle ___10___ de Liverpool. Elle ___11___ assez stricte et le cours d'anglais n'___12___ pas facile. Mais les élèves de Mlle Fielding ___13___ très intelligents!

Dinard, Bretagne

21 **Vous êtes américains?** Complétez la conversation. *(Complete the conversation.)*

—Vous ____ américains, n'est-ce pas?
—Oui, nous ____ américains. Nous ____ de ____.
—Vous ____ élèves dans une école secondaire?
—Oui, et nous ____ très forts en français.
—Vraiment? Qui ____ le/la prof de français?
—C'est ____.
—Il/Elle ____ comment?
—Il/Elle ____ ____.

22 **Tous les deux** Work with a classmate. Discuss things you have in common.
—Nous sommes sympathiques, intelligent(e)s, fort(e)s en...

Structure

19 Now students must interact using both **vous** and **nous.**

20 **and** **21** Now that all forms have been practiced, students will have to use all forms in these activities. Activities 20 and 21 are more difficult than Activities 16–19.

22 Students make up sentences on their own.

Learning from Photos

(page 63) Dinard is a lovely resort town in Brittany on the estuary of the Rance River.

Writing Development

After going over Activities 20 and 21, you may wish to have students write a summary of the information in each activity.

Answers to Continuons

19

1. Vous êtes martiniquaises ou américaines? Nous sommes américaines.
2. Vous êtes petits ou grands? Nous sommes petits/grands.
3. Vous êtes sociables ou timides? Nous sommes sociables/timides.
4. Vous êtes brunes ou blondes? Nous sommes brunes/blondes.

20

1. suis
2. est
3. sommes
4. sommes
5. est
6. sommes
7. est
8. sommes
9. est
10. est
11. est
12. est
13. sont

21

êtes
sommes
sommes, *(name of a city)*
êtes
sommes
est
Madame/ Monsieur ____
est
est, strict(e)/sympa/intéressant(e)

22 *Answers will vary but may include:*

—Nous sommes sociables, amusant(e)s et fort(e)s en dessin.
—Et nous ne sommes pas timides!
—Nous sommes très mauvais(es) en informatique et en algèbre.
—Oui, et nous sommes très mauvais(es) en latin!

1 Preparation

Bellringer Review

Use BRR Transparency 2.5 or write the following on the board.
Rewrite these sentences in the negative.

1. **Les garçons sont de Poitiers.**
2. **Nous sommes dans la salle de classe.**
3. **Tu es français.**
4. **Je suis français.**
5. **Vous êtes très timides.**

2 Presentation

Tu et vous

Step 1 Have students open their books to page 64. Explain how the two forms of "you" are used, leading students through the examples on page 64. Explain that **tu** is also used when talking to a pet.

Step 2 You may wish to present **tu** and **vous** using puppets or stuffed animals. Show a puppet of a child when using **tu** and a puppet of an adult when using **vous.** Show both puppets when teaching the plural usage of **vous.** Hold up the puppets as students ask **tu** and **vous** questions.

FUN-FACTS

Explain to students that most languages make the **tu/vous** distinction when addressing people. English once had a **tu** form—*thou:*
thou shalt not
thy will be done
for thine is the kingdom

Talking to people formally or informally
Tu et vous

1. As you already know, there are two ways to say *you* in French: **tu** and **vous.** You use **tu** when talking to a friend, a person your own age, or to a family member.

Éric, tu es trop timide!

Maman, tu es d'accord?

2. You use **vous** when talking to several people.

3. You also use **vous** when talking to an older person, a person whom you do not know very well, or anyone to whom you wish to show respect.

Vous deux, vous êtes d'accord?

Monsieur, s'il vous plaît! Vous êtes le professeur de musique?

Continuons

Let's put our words together

23 **Vous êtes français?** Regardez les photos et posez la question.
(Ask the people in the photographs if they are French.)

1.

2.

3.

4.

5.

6.

24 **D'autres questions** Ask the same people other questions. You may want to use some of the following words or expressions: **d'où, de quelle nationalité, d'accord, patient, fort en.**

Vous êtes sur le bon chemin. Allez-y!

3 Practice

Continuons

Let's put our words together

23 This activity can be done in pairs. One student calls out the number of a picture and the other student asks the question. The first student may answer for the person or people in the picture. Then the partners reverse roles.
Expansion: Ask the following people in your class if they are French:
1. le prof
2. une élève blonde
3. un élève brun
4. une fille
5. deux garçons

Learning from Photos

(page 65) Ask students to describe the people in the photos on page 65 using the French they already know. For example, for Photo 1: **Elle est petite. Elle est brune.**

Recycling

Activity 24 recycles and recombines the vocabulary and structures from Chapter 1.

Allez-y!
At this point in the chapter, students have learned all the vocabulary and structure necessary to complete the chapter. The conversation and cultural readings that follow recycle all the material learned up to this point.

Answers to Continuons

23
1. Tu es française?
2. Tu es français?
3. Vous êtes françaises?
4. Vous êtes française?
5. Vous êtes français?
6. Vous êtes français?

24 *Answers will vary but may include the following questions and the appropriate answers:*
Tu es (vous êtes) d'où?
Tu es (vous êtes) de quelle nationalité?
Tu es (vous êtes) d'accord avec le professeur?
Le prof est très patient. Tu es (vous êtes) d'accord?

1 Preparation

Resource Manager

Audio Activities Booklet TE, pages 32–33
Audiocassette 2B/CD 2
CD-ROM

Bellringer Review

Use BRR Transparency 2.6 or write the following on the board.
Which would you use to address the following people or pets, **tu** or **vous?**

1. Papa	**4. Madame Dubois**
2. les amis	**5. Jean et Maria**
3. Snoopy	**6. Papa et Maman**

2 Presentation

Step 1 Tell students they are going to hear a conversation between Paul and Anne.

Step 2 Have students repeat the conversation after you once or twice, or have them listen to the recording on Audiocassette 2B/ CD 2. Have the whole class repeat and then ask individual students to repeat.

Step 3 After presenting the conversation, go over the **Après la conversation** activity. If students can answer the questions with relative ease, move on. Students should not be expected to memorize the conversation.
Note: To convey the meaning of **Je suis complètement nul,** say **nul, zéro.**

Learning from Photos

(page 66) The students in this photo are at the lycée Janson de Sailly. Ask students to look at the photo and describe each of the three characters, using the French they know.

Conversation

Quel prof?

Paul: Vous êtes dans la classe de Mme Martin?
Anne: Non, nous sommes dans la classe de M. Lepic.
Paul: M. Lepic?
Anne: Ben oui, le prof de maths.
Paul: Ah oui. Comment il est?
Anne: Un peu strict, mais sympa.
Paul: Oui, mais toi et Samuel, vous êtes forts en maths.
Anne: Ben, toi aussi.
Paul: Moi? Je suis très mauvais en maths. Je suis complètement nul!

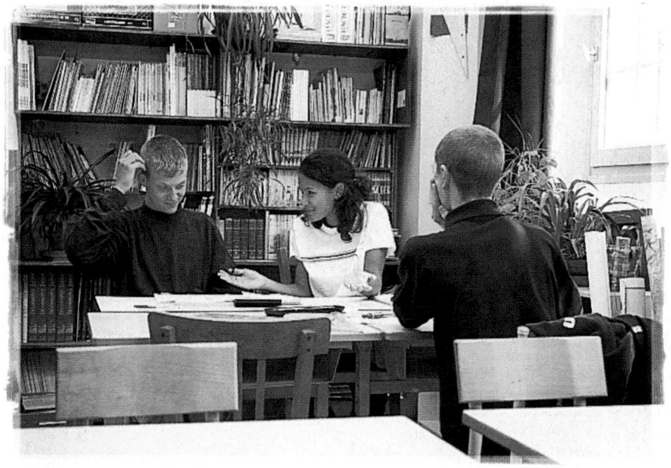

Après la conversation

Répondez. *(Answer.)*

1. Anne et Samuel sont dans la classe de Mme Martin?
2. Ils sont dans la classe de quel professeur?
3. Qui est M. Lepic?
4. Il est comment?
5. Samuel et Anne sont forts en maths?
6. Et Paul, il est fort en maths?

Answers to Après la conversation

1. Non, ils ne sont pas dans la classe de Mme Martin.
2. Ils sont dans la classe de M. Lepic.
3. M. Lepic est le professeur de maths.
4. Il est un peu strict, mais sympa.
5. Oui, ils sont forts en maths.
6. Non, il n'est pas fort en maths.

Reaching All Students

Musical/Rhythmic Learners
Tell students to listen carefully to the CD and pay particular attention to the tone of voice of the speakers. When listening to any conversation, the tone of voice can greatly help with comprehension.

Parlons un peu plus
Let's talk some more

A **D'accord ou pas?** Make a chart like the one below. List all your classes and rate them. Then compare your chart with that of a classmate.

—Pour moi, le cours de français n'est pas difficile. Tu es d'accord?
—Oui, je suis d'accord. / Non, je ne suis pas d'accord. Pour moi, le cours de français est très difficile.

Cours	Pas difficile	Assez difficile	Très difficile
le français	✓		
l'algèbre			✓

B **Jeu** **Quel cours?** Work with a classmate. He or she gives you one word about a class. Guess what class it is. If you're wrong, your partner will give you another hint until you can guess the class. Take turns.

Prononciation

Les consonnes finales

1. In French, you do not usually pronounce the final consonant you see at the end of a word. Repeat the following.

petit	**grand**	**intéressant**	**français**
amusant	**intelligent**	**patient**	**blond**

2. You also do not pronounce the final **s** you add to a word to make it plural. This is why a singular noun and its plural sound alike. Repeat the following pairs of words and then the sentences.

un copain → **des copains**   **une copine** → **des copines**
le garçon → **les garçons**   **la fille** → **les filles**

Tous les copains de Vincent sont sympathiques.
Les cours de maths sont très difficiles.

intelligent

3 Practice

Parlons un peu plus
Let's talk some more

A Have students work in pairs. You may wish to have the students work in teams and interview other teams to report their findings back to the class. Make a chart on the board like the one in the book and record the findings for the class as a whole.

B **Jeu** This recycling activity is fun for students to play either with a partner or in teams. **Note:** You may wish to refer students to Activity 8, page 56, for additional ideas.

Prononciation

Step 1 Using Pronunciation Transparency P 2, model the word **intelligent.** Have students say it in unison and individually. Write the word on the board and ask students what they notice about its pronunciation. *(The last letter is silent.)* Explain that this is common in French.

Step 2 Now lead students through Items 1–2 on page 67, modeling the examples. Call on individuals to read the sentences carefully.

Step 3 For additional pronunciation practice, use Audiocassette 2B/CD 2: **Pronunciation** and the Audio Activities Booklet, Teacher Edition, pages 33–34.

ANSWERS TO Parlons un peu plus

A *Answers will vary but may include:*

—Salut!
—Pour moi, le cours de biologie est assez difficile. Tu es d'accord?
—Oui, je suis d'accord.
—Pour moi, le cours d'informatique n'est pas difficile. Tu es d'accord?
—Non, je ne suis pas d'accord. Pour moi, le cours d'informatique est très difficile.

Glencoe Technology

CD-ROM

On the CD-ROM, students can watch a dramatization of this conversation. They can then play the role of either one of the characters and record themselves in the conversation.

Resource Manager

Audio Activities Booklet TE, pages 34–35
Audiocassette 2B/CD 2

Bellringer Review

Use BRR Transparency 2.7 or write the following on the board.
Make sentences from the following words.

1. **filles / Paris / sont / ne / les / de / deux / pas**
2. **cours / difficile / est / pas / le / français / de / n'**
3. **suis / je / accord / oui / d'**

National Standards

Cultures

This reading and the related activities on pages 68–69 about the Francophone population in the United States give students an understanding of the importance of learning French.

Communities

This selection familiarizes students with Francophone influence in communities in the United States.

Presentation

Pre-reading

Step 1 Have students locate Haiti and Quebec on the world map, pages xxii–xxiii (French 1A, 1B: pages xvi–xvii). On a map of the United States, have students locate Vermont, Florida, and Louisiana. You may want to have students look at the photos on pages 68–69 now.

Step 2 Read and discuss the Reading Strategy on page 68. Have the students tell you what the titles in the reading selection mean.

Le Québec

Lectures culturelles

Reading Strategy

Using titles

Always look at titles and subtitles before you begin to read. They will help you figure out what a reading selection is about. Having an idea of what a reading is about will help you guess the meaning of unfamiliar words and therefore understand better as you read.

Deux copains haïtiens

Une plage près de Port-au-Prince, Haïti

Deux amis de Montpelier

Le français aux États-Unis

L'influence haïtienne

Bonjour! Nous sommes Abélard Jean-Baptiste et Nicole Jolicœur. Nous sommes élèves dans une école secondaire à Miami. Et pour nous, le cours de français est vraiment très facile! Pour nous, le français n'est pas une langue étrangère[1]. Nous sommes haïtiens. Nous sommes de Port-au-Prince, la capitale d'Haïti. En Haïti, il y a[2] deux langues—le français et le créole. Le créole est une langue à base de français, d'espagnol et de divers dialectes africains.

L'influence canadienne

Et nous? Nous sommes Antonine Gagnon et Donald Maillet. Nous sommes de Montpelier dans le Vermont. Comme beaucoup de personnes de la Nouvelle-Angleterre[3], nous sommes d'origine canadienne. Et pour nous, le français n'est pas une langue étrangère. Le français est la langue maternelle des Canadiens français.

[1] étrangère *foreign*
[2] il y a *there are*
[3] Nouvelle-Angleterre *New England*

Reaching All Students

For Students of Varying Abilities

When asking comprehension questions, you can gear easy questions to the slower learners and more difficult questions to the faster learners.

Easy:
- **Abélard est élève?**
- **Et Nicole est élève?**

Intermediate:
- **Abélard Jean-Baptiste et Nicole Jolicœur sont élèves?**
- **Ils sont élèves dans une école à Miami?**

Difficult:
- **Abélard et Nicole sont élèves où?**
- **Comment est le cours de français pour Abélard et Nicole?**

L'influence «cajun»

Bonjour! Ici Alice Richard et Pierre Doucet. Nous sommes de Louisiane. Nous sommes cajuns. Nous les Cajuns, nous sommes des descendants des Acadiens. Les Acadiens sont les Français expulsés[4] de l'est du Canada par les Anglais.

L'influence cajun est assez forte en Louisiane. Il y a même[5] deux langues officielles en Louisiane—l'anglais et le français.

[4] expulsés *expelled* [5] même *even*

Deux élèves de Louisiane

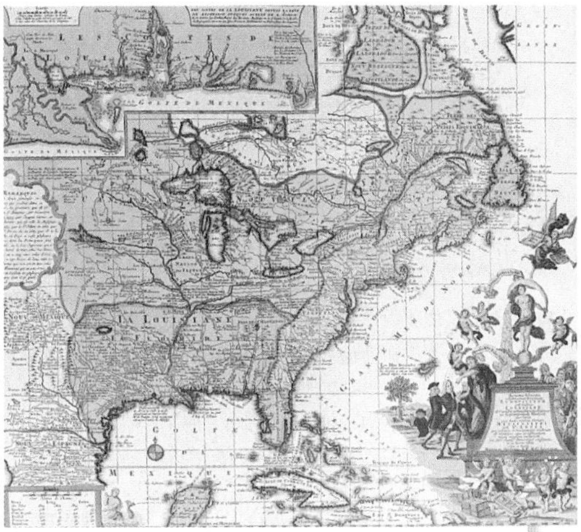

Après la lecture

A Les Haïtiens

Répondez. *(Answer.)*

1. Abélard Jean-Baptiste et Nicole Jolicœur sont d'où?
2. Pour Abélard et Nicole, le français est facile?
3. Ils sont de quelle nationalité?
4. Le créole est à base de quelles langues?

B Les descendants des Canadiens français Répondez. *(Answer.)*

1. D'où sont Antonine et Donald?
2. Montpelier est dans quel état?
3. Il y a beaucoup de personnes d'origine canadienne en Nouvelle-Angleterre?
4. Quelle est la langue maternelle des Canadiens français?

C Les Cajuns Répondez. *(Answer.)*

1. Qui sont les Cajuns?
2. Quelles sont les deux langues officielles en Louisiane?

Step 3 Have students scan the reading quickly and silently.

Reading

Step 1 Read one paragraph aloud to students as they follow along in the book. Call on an individual to read two or three sentences.

Step 2 After every two or three sentences, ask questions to check comprehension.

Step 3 Call on some students to read aloud individually. After a student has read about three sentences, ask questions of other students to check comprehension.

Post-reading

Have students do the **Après la lecture** activities on page 69 orally after reading the selection in class. Then assign these activities to be written at home. Go over them again the following day.

Note: Students may listen to a recorded version of the **Lecture culturelle** on the audio program (Cassette 2B/CD 2).

Après la lecture

A, B, and C Allow students to refer to the story to look up the answers, or you may use these activities as a testing device for factual recall.

Learning from Photos

(pages 68–69) Have students look at the photos on pages 68–69 and describe the teens in their own words.

Answers to Après la lecture

A

1. Abélard Jean-Baptiste et Nicole Jolicœur sont de Port-au-Prince.
2. Oui, pour Abélard et Nicole, le français est facile.
3. Ils sont haïtiens.
4. Le créole est à base de français, d'espagnol et de divers dialectes africains.

B

1. Antonine et Donald sont de Montpelier.
2. Montpelier est dans le Vermont.
3. Oui, il y a beaucoup de personnes d'origine canadienne en Nouvelle-Angleterre.
4. La langue maternelle des Canadiens français est le français.

C

1. Les Cajuns sont des descendants des Acadiens.
2. Les deux langues officielles en Louisiane sont l'anglais et le français.

National Standards

Cultures
This selection familiarizes students with secondary education in France.

Attention!

This reading is optional. You may skip it completely, have the entire class read it, have only several students read it and report to the class, or assign it for extra credit.

FUN-FACTS

School is obligatory in France from age 6–16. The educational system is divided into three parts:

- **Premier degré; écoles maternelles** *(preschool);* **écoles primaires** *(elementary)*
- **Second degré; collèges (classes de la 6e à la 3e)** *(middle or junior high school)*
  Lycée-classes de la 2nd a la terminale *(high school)*
  There are two types of **lycées: les lycées professionnels** *(prepare students for a trade)* and **les lycées d'enseignement général et technologique** *(prepare students for a profession)*
- **Enseignement supérieur: universités, écoles spécialisées,** and **grandes écoles.**
  Le baccalauréat (le bac) is the exam one must pass before entering the university.

FRENCH Online

To learn more about schools in the Francophone world, see the Chapter 2 Internet activity at the Glencoe French Web site listed on page 79.

Lecture supplémentaire 1

La scolarité en France

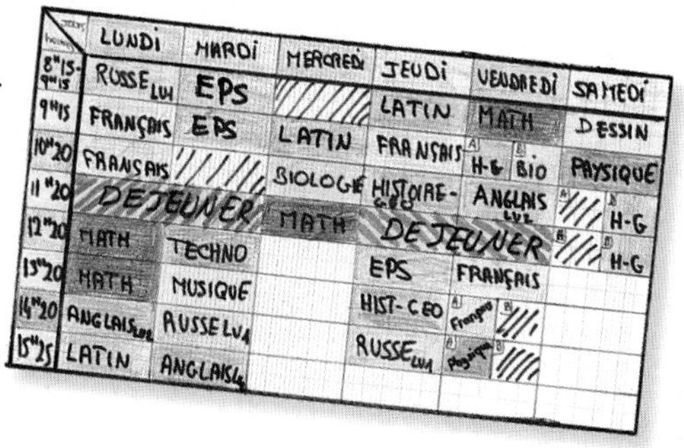

Le collège en France est une école secondaire. Les élèves sont des collégiens. Le collège est obligatoire pour quatre ans.

Après[1] le collège, le lycée est aussi une école secondaire, mais pour trois ans. Les élèves sont des lycéens. Il y a[2] deux diplômes d'études secondaires—un diplôme professionnel après deux ans et le baccalauréat après trois ans. Le baccalauréat ou «le bac» est nécessaire pour entrer à l'université.

Voici l'emploi du temps de Louise Belleroche. Elle est en troisième, l'équivalent de *ninth grade.* Il y a combien de[3] cours en troisième en France?

[1] Après *After* [2] Il y a *There are* [3] combien de *how many*

Lycée Pasteur, Neuilly, France

Après la lecture

A La scolarité Vrai ou faux? *(True or false?)*

1. En France un collège est une petite université.
2. Le collège n'est pas obligatoire.
3. Le lycée est une école secondaire.
4. Le «bac» est un diplôme universitaire.
5. Le «bac» est nécessaire pour entrer à l'université.

B L'emploi du temps de Louise Répondez. *(Answer.)*

1. Il y a combien de cours?
2. Le cours de maths est quels jours? À quelle heure?
3. Et le cours d'anglais?
4. Et le cours de français?
5. Et le cours de biologie?
6. Et le cours d'histoire/géographie?
7. Et le cours de dessin?

Answers to Après la lecture

A

1. F
2. F
3. V
4. F
5. V

B

1. Il y a douze cours.
2. Le cours de maths est à 12 h 20 le lundi, à 11 h 20 le mercredi, et à 8 h 15 le vendredi.
3. Le cours d'anglais est à 14 h 20 le lundi, à 15 h 25 le mardi, et à 10 h 20 le vendredi.
4. Le cours de français est à 9 h 15 le lundi, à 9 h 15 le jeudi, et à 12 h 20 le vendredi.
5. Le cours de biologie est à 10 h 20 le mercredi et à 9 h 15 le vendredi.
6. Le cours d'histoire/géographie est à 10 h 20 et 13 h 20 le jeudi, à 9 h 15 le vendredi, et à 10 h 20 le samedi.
7. Le cours de dessin est à 8 h 15 le samedi.

Un message

Salut! Je m'appelle Nicolas Vidal. Je suis de Versailles, une ville[1] dans la banlieue[2] parisienne. Je suis élève dans un lycée. Mais maintenant, je ne suis pas à Versailles. Je suis à Biarritz avec la famille de Guillaume Cartier. Guillaume et moi, nous sommes copains. Nous sommes élèves dans le même lycée. Mais maintenant, pas de profs, pas de cours! Nous sommes libres[3]! Nous sommes en vacances à Biarritz. Biarritz est une petite ville très pittoresque à la frontière espagnole. Pour moi, les vacances, c'est toujours super. Tu es d'accord?

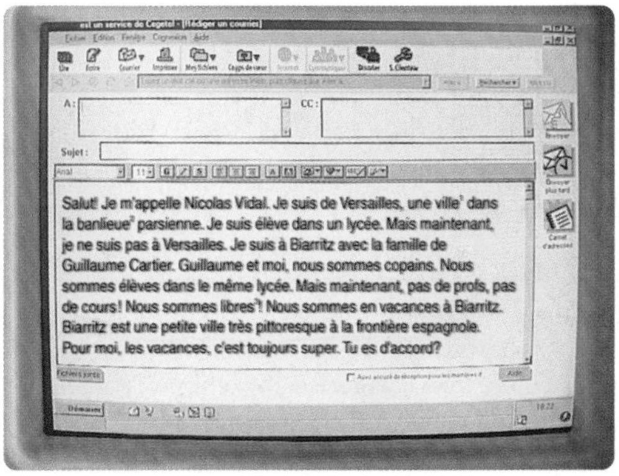

[1] ville *town* [2] banlieue *suburbs* [3] libres *free*

Biarritz, France

Versailles, France

Après la lecture

A Deux copains Répondez. *(Answer.)*
1. D'où est Nicolas?
2. Où est Versailles?
3. Où est Nicolas maintenant?
4. Il est à Biarritz avec qui?
5. Les deux garçons sont copains?
6. Les deux copains sont en vacances? Où?

B Un peu de géographie
Vrai ou faux? *(True or false?)*
1. Versailles est sur la Côte d'Azur.
2. Versailles est dans la banlieue parisienne.
3. Biarritz est aussi dans la banlieue parisienne.
4. Biarritz est à la frontière espagnole.
5. Biarritz est en Espagne.
6. Biarritz est en France.

Attention!

This reading is optional. You may skip it completely, have the entire class read it, have only several students read it and report to the class, or assign it for extra credit.

Learning from Photos

(page 71 top) Of all the Atlantic beaches in France, Biarritz is the most frequented. Its location at the entrance to the **Pays Basque** makes it very attractive. The pine forests of the Landes to the north merge with the craggy coast of the **Pays Basque** to the south.
(page 71 bottom) Versailles, a suburb of Paris, is famous for the palace and gardens of Louis XIV, King of France from 1643–1715. The palace is now a national museum. After World War I, the Treaty of Versailles was signed in 1919 in the palace's Hall of Mirrors.

La Belgique

La Tunisie

Maroc

Le Mali

ANSWERS TO *Après la lecture*

A
1. Nicolas est de Versailles.
2. Versailles est dans la banlieue parisienne.
3. Nicolas est à Biarritz.
4. Il est à Biarritz avec la famille de Guillaume Cartier.
5. Oui, les deux garçons sont copains.
6. Les deux copains sont en vacances à Biarritz.

B
1. F
2. V
3. F
4. V
5. F
6. V

CONNEXIONS

National Standards

Connections
This reading establishes a connection with another discipline—science. It allows students to draw from material they have most probably learned in their biology, physics, and chemistry classes. At the same time they increase their vocabulary and learn to talk about a scientific topic in French.

Attention!

The readings in the **Connexions** section are optional. They focus on some of the major disciplines taught in schools and universities. The vocabulary is useful for discussing such topics as history, literature, art, economics, business, science, etc. You may choose any of the following ways to do the readings in the **Connexions** sections.

Independent reading Have students read the selections and do the post-reading activities as homework, which you collect. This option is least intrusive on class time and requires a minimum of teacher involvement.

Homework with in-class follow-up Assign the readings and post-reading activities as homework. Review and discuss the material in class the next day.

Intensive in-class activity This option includes a pre-reading vocabulary presentation, in-class reading and discussion, assignment of the activities for homework, and a discussion of the assignment in class the following day.

CONNEXIONS

Les sciences naturelles

La biologie, la physique et la chimie

Sciences are an important part of the school curriculum. If you like science, it would be fun to be able to read some scientific material in French. You will see how easy it is. It's easy because you already have some background in science from your science courses. In addition, many scientific terms are cognates.

La biologie

La biologie est l'étude des organismes vivants. En biologie, il y a trois catégories importantes: l'anatomie, la zoologie et la botanique. L'anatomie est l'étude du corps humain. La zoologie est l'étude des animaux et la botanique est l'étude des plantes.

La botanique est l'étude des plantes.

La zoologie est l'étude des animaux.

Learning from Photos

(page 72)

- The photo on the left is of a rain forest in Martinique. In the northern part of the island, there is a great deal of lush, tropical vegetation, fields of pineapples, banana trees, towering cliffs, and deep gorges. As you can tell from this photo, the clouds often hang right over or engulf the rain forest.
- The animal in this photograph is a lemur (**un maki** in French) from Madagascar. The lemurs have an extremely long tail and they abound in Madagascar. Madagascar is an island nation in the Indian Ocean. The two languages spoken there are **Malgache** and French. Another small island, **Nosy-Bé,** is also a part of Madagascar. The French were in Madagascar as early as 1643, but it was not declared a French colony until 1896. General Gallieni served as governor-general from 1896–1903. Madagascar got its independence in 1960.

Note: You may wish to have only students who are interested in science read this selection. The reading should be quite easy, since there are many cognates and students already know all the information from their science courses.

La physique et la chimie

La physique est l'étude de la matière et de l'énergie. La chimie est l'étude des caractéristiques des éléments.

Les savants

Dans un laboratoire, le savant (le biologiste, le chimiste ou le physicien) observe et analyse des phénomènes scientifiques. Le biologiste, par exemple, observe et analyse des microbes[1], des cellules, des bactéries et des virus à l'aide d'un microscope.

[1] microbes *germs*

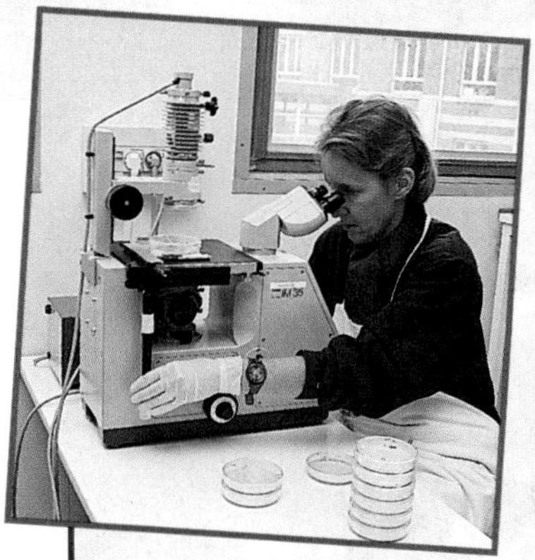

Une biologiste

Learning from Photos

(page 73)

- The scientist at work in the photo at the top of the page is at the prestigious Institut Pasteur. Students will learn more about Louis Pasteur and the Institute he founded in Chapter 14.
- The science students in the photo at the bottom of the page are in a science lab at the lycée Janson de Sailly.

Après la lecture

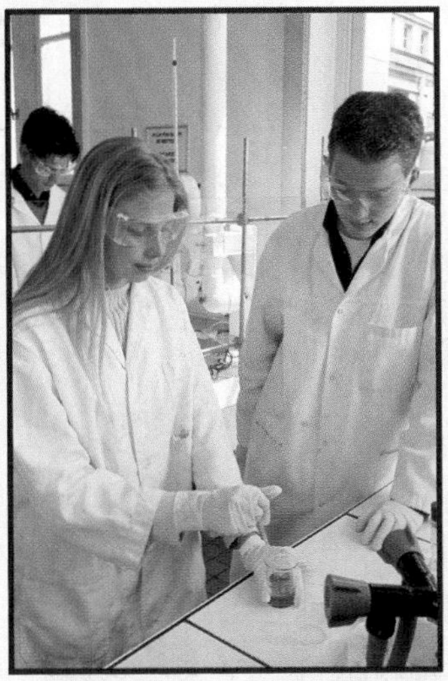

Des élèves dans un laboratoire à Paris

A Des termes scientifiques

Préparez une liste. *(Make a list of scientific terms you recognize in the reading.)*

B C'est quelle science? Répondez. *(Answer.)*

1. l'étude des animaux
2. l'étude des plantes
3. l'étude de la matière et de l'énergie
4. l'étude du corps humain

C Stratégie de lecture Note that the words in each of the following groups are all related to one another. If you know the meaning of one word, you can guess the meanings of the others. Can you figure them all out?

1. la biologie, un(e) biologiste, biologique
2. analyser, une analyse, analytique
3. un microbe, microbien
4. une bactérie, bactérien
5. un virus, viral

ANSWERS TO Après la lecture

A *Answers will vary but may include:*
les sciences, la biologie, organismes, l'anatomie, la zoologie, la botanique, la physique, l'énergie, éléments, un laboratoire, le physicien, phénomènes, microbes, cellules, bactéries, virus, un microscope

B
1. la zoologie
2. la botanique
3. la physique
4. l'anatomie

C
1. biology, biologist, biological
2. to analyze, an analysis, analytical
3. microbe, microbial
4. bacteria, bacterial
5. virus, viral

Use what you have learned

Bellringer Review

Use BRR Transparency 2.8 or write the following on the board.
Say everything you can about your favorite class in school. Include descriptions of the class, the teacher, and the students.
Mon cours favori est le cours de _____.

Recycling

These activities allow students to use the vocabulary and structure from this chapter in completely open-ended, real-life situations. They also give students the opportunity to reuse the vocabulary and structure from Chapter 1.

Presentation

Encourage students to say as much as possible when they do these activities. Tell them not to be afraid to make mistakes, since the goal of these activities is real-life communication. If someone in the group makes an error, allow the others to correct him or her politely. Let students choose the activities they would like to do.

C'est à vous

Use what you have learned

L'école internationale de Paris

PARLER **1** **Nous**

✔ Describe yourself and someone else

Work with a classmate. You are at an international student gathering in France. You and your partner introduce yourselves to the other students. Try to get to know one another better. You may use the following as a guide:

- say who you are
- give your nationality
- tell where you're from
- give the name of your school
- describe some of your qualities or faults

PARLER **2** **L'école idéale**

✔ Talk about school

Work with a classmate. Describe what for each of you is an ideal school. Say as much as you can about the teachers, classes, and students. Determine whether or not you share the same opinions.

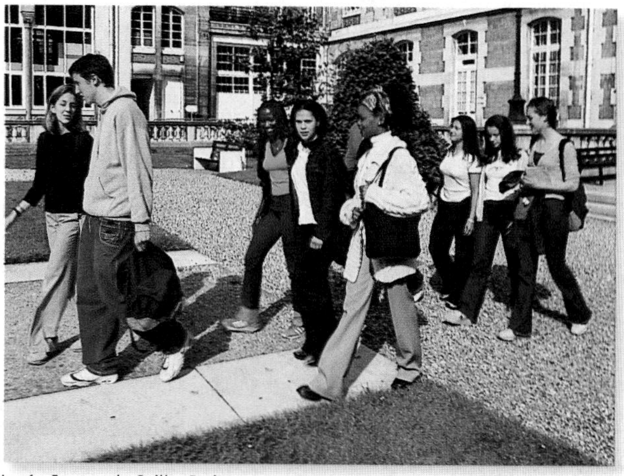
Lycée Janson de Sailly, Paris

Answers to C'est à vous

1 *Answers will vary but may include:*

—Je m'appelle Jean.
—Et je m'appelle Catherine.
—Je suis américain.
—Et je suis américaine, aussi.
—Je suis de Chicago.
—Et je suis de New York.
—Je suis élève à l'école Washington.
—Je suis élève à l'école Central.
—Je suis très sociable.
—Et je suis vraiment timide!

2 *Answers will vary but may include:*

L'école idéale est intéressante. Les profs sont un peu stricts, mais ils sont sympas, aussi. Les cours sont intéressants. Les cours ne sont pas très difficiles. Ils sont assez faciles. Les élèves sont dynamiques et intelligents.

Career Connection

Teaching is an excellent way to use one's knowledge of a foreign language and culture. Have your students interview you about the education and training that was necessary for you to obtain your position. Be sure to mention your travel and study abroad experiences or any specialized workshops that you attended. At this level, the interview will be in English.

C'est à vous

ÉCRIRE

3 Un message

✔ Write about your classes and friends

You answer an e-mail message from a student in France who wants to know about your life in the United States. Give him or her as many details as possible about your classes and your friends.

Collège de Montois, Noyen-sur-Seine

Writing Strategy

Keeping a journal There are many kinds of journals you can keep, each having a different purpose. One type of journal is the kind in which you write about daily events and record your thoughts and impressions about these events. It's almost like "thinking aloud." By keeping such a journal, you may find that you discover something new that you were not aware of.

ÉCRIRE

4 Les cours et les professeurs

You've been in school for about a month. You've had a chance to get to know what your courses are like and to become familiar with your teachers. Create a journal entry about school. Try to write about your classes, the days and times of each, what the class is like, who the teacher is, and what he or she is like. When you have finished, reread your journal entry. Did you discover anything about your courses or your teachers that you hadn't thought of before?

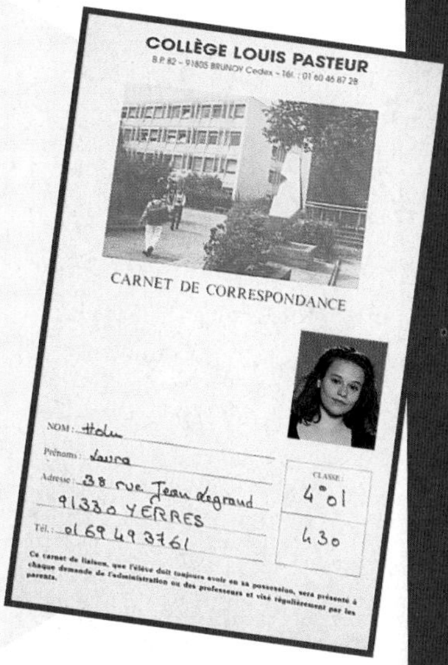

Writing Development

Have students keep a notebook containing their best written work from each chapter. These selected writings can be based on assignments from the Student Textbook and the Writing Activities Workbook. The two activities on page 75 are examples of writing assignments that may be included in each student's portfolio. In the Workbook, students will develop an organized autobiography **(Mon autobiographie).** These workbook pages may also become a part of their portfolio.

FUN-FACTS

In many areas of the United States, there are communities of French-speaking people. Some are recent arrivals and some have been here for a century or more. In Florida, there are large communities of Haitians and people from the French Antilles. The same is true in the New York area, which also has many people from West Africa.

For hundreds of years there has been a great deal of French-Canadian influence in the states of New England and Cajun influence in Louisiana.

There are many lesser-known French communities in the United States. For example, people of French ancestry occupy fifth place among the ethnic groups in Texas. French settlements were made at Fort Saint Louis and Galveston Island.

Have students do some research and find out if there are any French communities near you. Have them find out as much information as possible about these people, their descendants and their traditions.

Answers to C'est à vous

3 *Answers will vary but may include:*

L'école est vraiment super! Les amis sont très intéressants et dynamiques. Pour moi, les cours difficiles sont la biologie, la chimie, et l'algèbre. Pour moi, les cours assez faciles sont l'anglais et le français. La prof de chimie est très, très stricte! Mais la prof de français n'est pas trop stricte. Elle est assez sympa. Je suis mauvais(e) en chimie mais fort(e) en français.

Learning from Photos

Have students describe the three photos on pages 74–75. Have them describe the people in the photos as well as the setting of each photo.

Resource Manager

Communication Transparencies
Quizzes
Test Booklet
ExamView Pro®
Situation Cards
Performance Assessment
Marathon mental Videoquiz

Assessment

This is a pre-test for students to take before you administer the chapter test. Answer sheets for students to do these pages are provided in your transparency binder. Note that each section is cross-referenced so students can easily find the material they have to review in case they made errors. You may wish to collect these assessments and correct them yourself, or you may prefer to have the students correct themselves in class. You can go over the answers orally or project them on the overhead, using your Assessment Answers transparencies.

Glencoe Technology

MINDJOGGER

You may wish to help your students prepare for the chapter test by playing the MindJogger game show. Teams will compete against each other to review chapter vocabulary and structure and sharpen listening comprehension skills.

Assessment

Vocabulaire

To review ***Mots 1****, turn to pages 50–51.*

1 Choisissez. *(Choose.)*

1. Christophe et Julien sont amis. Ils sont ____.
   a. frères **b.** sœurs **c.** copains
2. Les deux garçons sont ____ dans un lycée français.
   a. élèves **b.** profs **c.** cours
3. Le cours de français n'est pas difficile. Le cours de français est ____.
   a. strict **b.** facile **c.** comique
4. La prof n'est pas très stricte. Juste ____.
   a. difficile **b.** d'accord **c.** un peu

To review ***Mots 2****, turn to pages 54–55.*

2 Vrai ou faux? *(True or false?)*

5. L'algèbre et la musique sont des sciences naturelles.
6. L'économie est une langue.
7. Pour les élèves américains, l'anglais est un cours obligatoire.
8. L'allemand est une science sociale.

Structure

To review plural articles, nouns, and adjectives, turn to page 58.

3 Mettez au pluriel. *(Put in the plural.)*

9. Le copain de Lucie est amusant.
   ____ copain____ de Lucie sont amusant____.
10. La sœur de Monique est intelligente.
   ____ sœur____ de Monique sont intelligente____.
11. L'ami de Frédéric est français.
   ____ ami____ de Frédéric sont français____.
12. Le prof de biologie est strict.
   ____ prof____ de biologie sont strict____.
13. La fille brune est américaine.
   ____ fille____ brune____ sont américaine____.

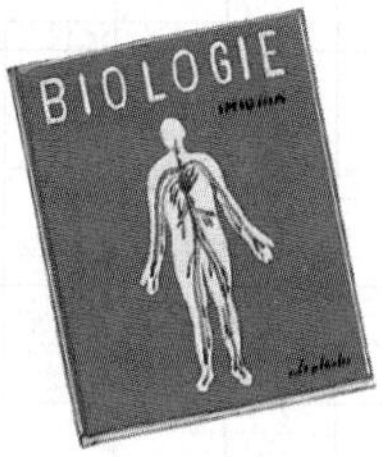

Answers to Assessment

1

1. c
2. a
3. b
4. c

2

5. F
6. F
7. V
8. F

3

9. Les, -s, -s
10. Les, -s, -s
11. Les, -s, Ø
12. Les, -s, -s
13. Les, -s, -s, -s

4 Complétez avec «être».
(Complete with être.*)*

14. Nous ____ élèves dans une école secondaire américaine.
15. Ils ____ élèves dans un lycée français.
16. Vous ____ élèves où?
17. Les élèves de Madame Fauvet ____ intelligents.
18. Qui ____ le prof de géométrie?

To review the verb ***être****, turn to page 60.*

Culture

5 Choisissez. *(Choose.)*

19. En Haïti, il y a deux langues—le français et ____.
    a. l'anglais **b.** le créole **c.** l'espagnol
20. Il y a beaucoup d'influence «cajun» en ____.
    a. Nouvelle-Angleterre **b.** Haïti **c.** Louisiane

To review this cultural information, turn to pages 68–69.

La Nouvelle-Orléans, Louisiane

Learning from Photos

(page 77) New Orleans is a lovely city in Louisiana. This photo was taken in the French Quarter of New Orleans, a neighborhood which draws many tourists. French influence is very strong in Louisiana. Many **Acadiens** (French settlers who were expelled from Canada by the English in 1755) went to Louisiana, which was still a French territory at that time. The term "Cajun" is a deformation of the French word **acadien.**

Answers to Assessment

4

14. sommes
15. sont
16. êtes
17. sont
18. est

5

19. b
20. c

Vocabulary Review

The words and phrases in the **Vocabulaire** have been taught for productive use in this chapter. They are summarized here as a resource for both student and teacher. This list also serves as a convenient resource for the **C'est à vous** activities on pages 74–75. There are approximately twenty-three cognates in this vocabulary list. Have students find them.

Attention!

You will notice that the vocabulary list here is not translated. This has been done intentionally, since we feel that by the time students have finished the material in the chapter they should be familiar with the meanings of all the words. If there are several words they still do not know, we recommend that they refer back to the **Mots 1** and **2** sections in the chapter or go to the dictionaries at the back of this book to find the meanings. However, if you prefer that your students have the English translations, please refer to Transparency V 2.1, where you will find all these words with their translations.

Vocabulaire

Identifying a person or thing

un professeur
un(e) prof
un copain
une copine
un lycée
une salle de classe
un cours
une classe
une matière

Identifying school subjects

les sciences naturelles
- la biologie
- la chimie
- la physique

les mathématiques, les maths *(f. pl.)*
- l'algèbre *(f.)*
- la géométrie
- la trigonométrie
- le calcul

les langues *(f. pl.)*
- le français
- l'espagnol *(m.)*
- l'italien *(m.)*
- l'allemand *(m.)*
- l'anglais *(m.)*
- le latin

les sciences sociales
- l'histoire *(f.)*
- la géographie
- l'économie *(f.)*

d'autres matières
- la littérature
- l'informatique *(f.)*
- la gymnastique
- la musique
- le dessin

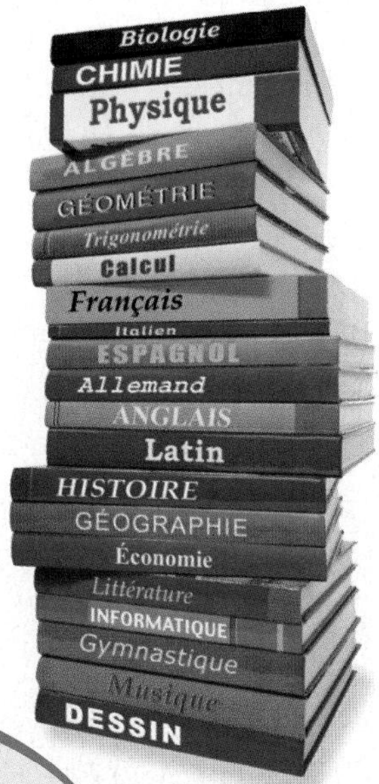

Describing teachers, students, and courses

facile
difficile
strict(e)
intéressant(e)
fort(e)
mauvais(e)

Agreeing and disagreeing

Tu es d'accord?
Oui, je suis d'accord.
Non, je ne suis pas d'accord.
C'est vrai.
Ce n'est pas vrai. C'est pas vrai.

Other useful words and expressions

en cours de (français, maths, etc.)
même
tous
trop
juste un peu

How well do you know your vocabulary?

- **Choose your favorite school subject. Choose words to describe this subject.**
- **Use these words to describe the subject and your teacher.**

Technotour

BON VOYAGE!

VIDÉO • Épisode 2

Avant de visionner

In this video episode, Vincent is at the lycée Louis-le-Grand, interviewing students there about their teachers and courses.

Vincent et une amie, Élodie, au lycée Louis-le-Grand

Manu et Vincent en cours de chimie

FRENCH ONLINE

À découvrir

The lycée Louis-le-Grand is situated in the heart of Paris. Learn more about Paris online.

L'île de la Cité, le centre historique de Paris

FRENCH Online

In the Chapter 2 Internet Activity, you will have a chance to learn more about schools in the Francophone world. To begin your virtual adventure, go to the Glencoe French Web site:
french.glencoe.com

Technotour

Overview

This page previews two key multimedia components of the **Glencoe French** series. Each reinforces the material taught in the chapter in a unique manner.

VIDÉO

The Video Program allows students to see how the chapter vocabulary and structures are used by native speakers. For maximum reinforcement, show the video episode as a final activity for Chapter 2.

The two photos on the left show highlights from the Chapter 2 video episode. Before viewing the episode, you may want to present the characters in the photos to your students and have them describe each one using the adjectives from the chapter. Now show the Chapter 2 video episode. See the Video Activities Booklet for detailed suggestions for using this resource.

FRENCH Online

- The **À découvrir** photo shows a photo of Paris. Students can go online to the Glencoe French Web site for additional information about some of the more famous areas of Paris, such as the Île de la Cité.
- Teacher Information and Student Worksheets for this activity can be accessed at the Web site.

Video Synopsis

In this episode, Vincent begins by giving us a tour of Île de la Cité, the historic center of Paris, and St-Germain-des-Prés, a famous cultural center. We move on to the Latin Quarter, where his school, le lycée Louis-le-Grand, is located. Vincent joins the students walking through the arched hallway near the front entrance. He stops to interview several of them. He films them as they discuss their favorite courses. The video then shows Vincent in chemistry class working with a partner. His partner is another of the main characters—Manu Chentouf. He is from Algeria and he is seventeen years old. We are not sure just what his specialty is. However, we see him here doing a chemistry experiment—as only Manu knows how to do it!

Planning for Chapter 3

SCOPE AND SEQUENCE, PAGES 80–109

Topics

- School activities
- Afterschool activities
- School supplies

Culture

- Jacqueline, a student from Paris
- Discussing differences between school in the United States and France
- Antoine, a student from Montreal
- Manau—a rap group; music in the French-speaking world

Functions

- How to identify and describe school supplies
- How to count from 100 to 1000

Structure

- The present tense of regular **-er** verbs
- Negative of indefinite articles
- Verb + infinitive

National Standards

- Communication Standard 1.1 pages 84, 85, 89, 91, 92, 93, 94, 95, 97, 104, 105
- Communication Standard 1.2 pages 84, 85, 88, 89, 91, 92, 93, 94, 95, 96, 97, 99, 100, 101, 103, 104, 105
- Communication Standard 1.3 pages 84, 85, 88, 91, 92, 93, 105
- Cultures Standard 2.1 pages 96, 97, 98–99, 100, 101
- Cultures Standard 2.2 page 101
- Connections Standard 3.1 pages 102–103
- Comparisons Standard 4.1 pages 102–103
- Comparisons Standard 4.2 pages 97, 105
- Communities Standard 5.1 page 105

PACING AND PRIORITIES

The chapter content is color coded below to assist you in planning.

■ required ■ recommended ■ optional

Vocabulaire *(required)* *Days 1–4*

- ■ Mots 1
  - Une journée à l´école
- ■ Mots 2
  - Des fournitures scolaires
  - Après les cours

Structure *(required)* *Days 5–7*

- ■ Les verbes réguliers en **-er** au présent
- ■ La négation des articles indéfinis
- ■ Verbe + infinitif

Conversation *(required)*

- ■ Un élève français aux États-Unis

Prononciation *(recommended)*

- ■ Les sons **/é/** et **/è/**

Lectures culturelles

- ■ Une journée avec Jacqueline *(recommended)*
- ■ Qui travaille? *(optional)*
- ■ Un groupe de rap—Manau *(optional)*

Connexions *(optional)*

- ■ L'ordinateur

■ **C'est à vous** *(recommended)*

■ **Assessment** *(recommended)*

■ **Technotour** *(optional)*

RESOURCE GUIDE

SECTION	PAGES	SECTION RESOURCES
Vocabulaire *Mots 1*		
Un journée à l´école	82–85	Vocabulary Transparencies 3.2–3.3 Audiocassette 3A/CD 3 Audio Activities Booklet TE, pages 37–38 Workbook, page 19 Quiz 1, page 12 ExamView Pro®
Vocabulaire *Mots 2*		
Des fournitures scolaires Après les cours	86 87–89	Vocabulary Transparencies 3.4–3.5 Audiocassette 3A/CD 3 Audio Activities Booklet TE, pages 39–41 Workbook, pages 20–21 Quiz 2, page 13 ExamView Pro®
Structure		
Les verbes réguliers en **–er** La négation des articles indéfinis Verbe + infinitif	90–93 94 95	Audiocassette 3A/CD 3 Audio Activities Booklet TE, pages 41–44 Workbook, pages 22–25 Quizzes 3–5, pages 14–16 ExamView Pro®
Conversation		
Un élève français aux États-Unis	96	Audiocassette 3A/CD 3 Audio Activities Booklet TE, pages 44–45 CD-ROM
Prononciation		
Les sons **/é/** et **/è/**	97	Pronunciation Transparency P 3 Audiocassette 3A/CD 3 Audio Activities Booklet TE, pages 45–46
Lectures culturelles		
Une journée avec Jacqueline Qui travaille? Un groupe de rap—Manau	98–99 100 101	Audiocassette 3A/CD 3 Audio Activities Booklet TE, page 47 Test Booklet, Chapter 3
Connexions		
L´ordinateur L´ordinateur travaille!	102 103	Test Booklet, Chapter 3
C'est à vous		
	104–105	**Bon voyage!** Video, Episode 3 Video Activities Booklet, Chapter 3 French Online Activities french.glencoe.com
Assessment		
	106–107	Communication Transparency C 3 Quizzes 1–5, pages 12–16 Test Booklet, Chapter 3 ExamView Pro® Situation Cards, Chapter 3 **Marathon mental** Videoquiz

Using Your Resources for Chapter 3

Transparencies

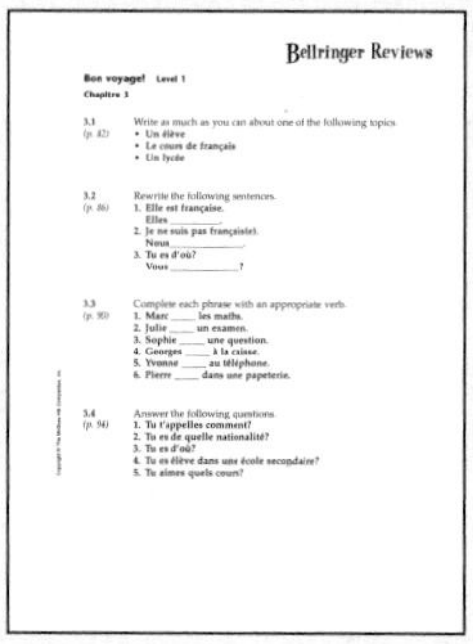
Bellringer 3.1–3.8

Vocabulary 3.1–3.5

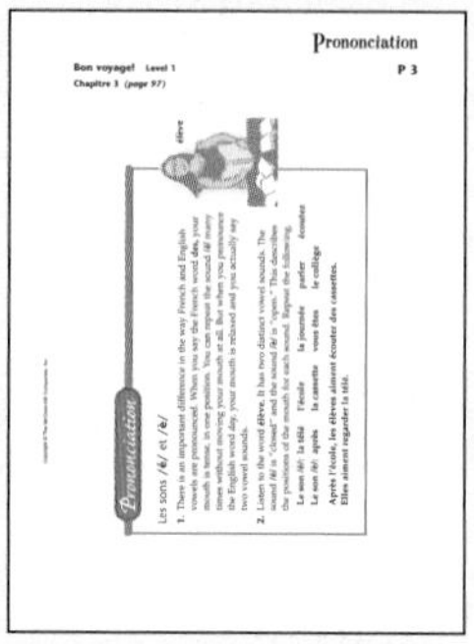
Pronunciation P 3

Communication C 3

Writing Activities Workbook

Vocabulary, pages 19–21

Structure, pages 22–25

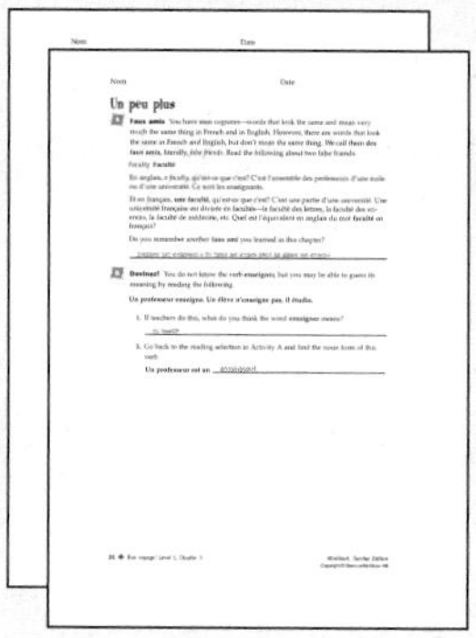
Enrichment, pages 26–28

Audio Program and Audio Activities Booklet

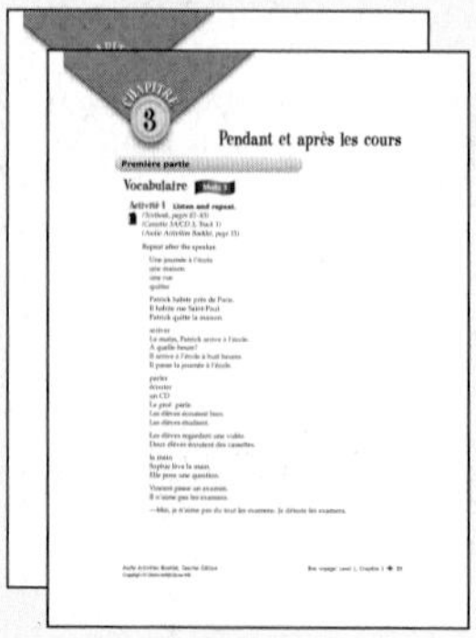
Vocabulary, pages 37–41

Structure, pages 41–44

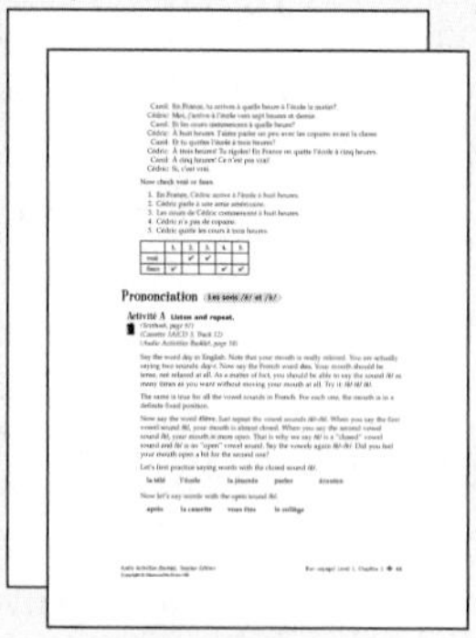
Conversation, Pronunciation, pages 44–46

Cultural Reading, page 47

Additional Practice, page 48

Assessment

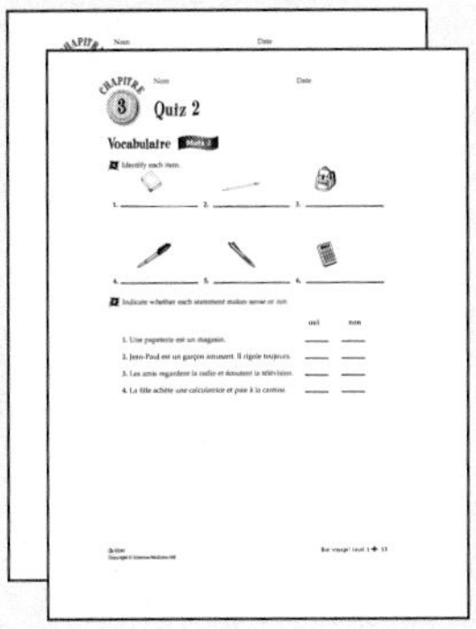

Vocabulary and Structure Quizzes, pages 12–16

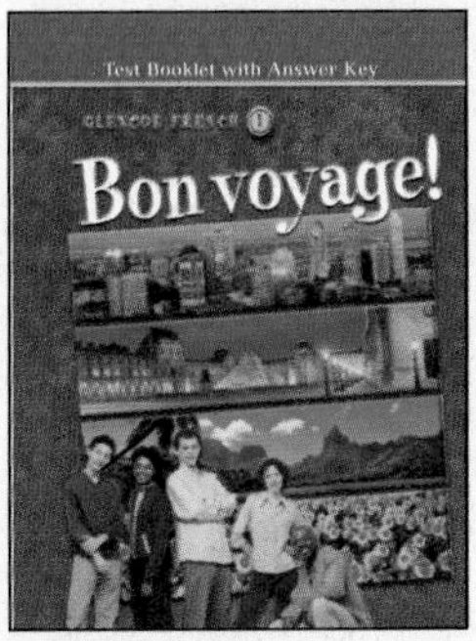

Chapter Tests, Chapter 3

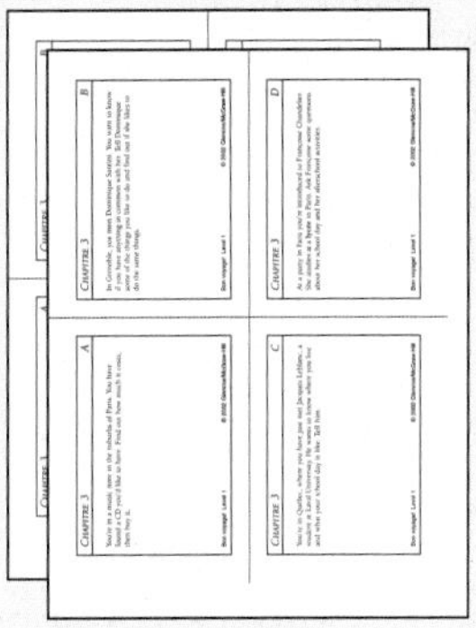

Situation Cards, Chapter 3

Timesaving Teacher Tools

Interactive Teacher Edition

Imagine having your Teacher's Edition and all resources on a CD-ROM. Click on a resource and it appears on your screen, ready to be printed, sorted, or planned.

Interactive Lesson Planner

The Interactive Lesson Planner CD-ROM helps you organize your lesson plans for a week, month, semester, or year. Look at this planning tool for easy access to your Chapter 3 resources.

ExamView Pro®

Test Bank software for Macintosh and Windows makes creating, editing, customizing, and printing tests quick and easy.

Technology Resources

FRENCH Online

In the Chapter 3 Internet activity, you will have a chance to learn more about schools in the Francophone world. Visit french.glencoe.com.

On the Interactive Conversation CD-ROM, students can listen to and take part in a recorded version of the conversation in Chapter 3.

NATIONAL GEOGRAPHIC SOCIETY

See the National Geographic Teacher's Corner on pages 150–151, 256–257, 396–397, 500–501 for reference to additional technology resources.

Bon voyage! Video and Video Activities Booklet.

Help your students prepare for the chapter test by playing the **Marathon mental** Videoquiz game show. Teams will compete against each other to review chapter vocabulary and structure and sharpen listening comprehension skills.

CHAPITRE 3

Preview

In this chapter, students will learn to talk about their school and afterschool activities. They will also learn to identify, describe, and shop for school supplies. They will learn to use singular forms of **-er** verbs to communicate in various situations that arise when shopping. They will also learn to express likes and dislikes.

National Standards

Communication
In Chapter 3, students will communicate in spoken and written French to talk about school and afterschool activities. Students will engage in conversations, provide and obtain information, and exchange opinions as they fulfill the chapter objectives listed on this page.

CHAPITRE 3

Pendant et après les cours

Objectifs

In this chapter you will learn to:

- ✓ *talk about what you do in school*
- ✓ *talk about what you and your friends do after school*
- ✓ *identify and shop for school supplies*
- ✓ *talk about what you don't do*
- ✓ *tell what you and others like and don't like to do*
- ✓ *discuss schools in France*

Pierre Auguste Renoir *La lecture*

Correlations to Continuum *(see page i for code)*

Stage I
Engage in conversations. p. 89 (**11**, *p*); Express likes and dislikes. p. 95 (**26**, *p*), p. 95 (**27**, *m*); Obtain information. pp. 86–87 (*i*), p. 91 (**15**, *p*), p. 104 (**1**, *m*); Provide information. p. 105 (**4**, *m*); Converse in face-to-face social interactions. p. 97 (**A**, *p*), p. 105 (**2**, *m*); Listen during social interactions and listen to audio or video texts. p. 109 (*p*); Write lists. p. 88 (**7**, *i*); Use short sentences and learned words and phrases when speaking and writing. p. 84 (**1**, *p*), p. 105 (**3**, *m*); Understand ideas and familiar details when listening. p. 96 (*p*); Understand texts enhanced by visual clues. pp. 102–103 (*p*); Understand and convey information about school and likes and dislikes. pp. 82–83 (*i*), p. 92 (**17**, *p*); Demonstrate culturally acceptable behavior for Stage I functions. p. 104 (**1**); Understand most important information. pp. 98–99

Stage II
Understand and express important ideas and some detail. p. 93 (**22**, *p*); Describe and compare. p. 93 (**21**, *p*); Use and understand learned expressions, sentences, strings of sentences, and questions when speaking and listening. p. 85 (**6**, *p*), p. 105 (**4**, *p*); Demonstrate increasing fluency and control of vocabulary. p. 105 (**2**); Show no significant pattern of error when performing Stage I functions. p. 105 (**4**)

Stage III
Clarify and ask for and comprehend clarification. p. 85 (**4**, *p*); Express and understand opinions. p. 83 (*i*)

CHAPITRE 3

Spotlight on Culture

Photograph This photo is of a group of students on a **quai** along the Seine River in Paris. In this area, there are many stalls of **bouqinistes** where one can buy old books, drawings, records, etc.

Painting This painting, ***La lecture,*** was done by Pierre Auguste Renoir (1841–1919). At the age of twenty-two, Renoir met Monet, Sisley, and Bazille and went to paint with them in the Fontainbleau Forest. Renoir exhibited his paintings in the first exposition of the Impressionists in 1874.

In 1881 he took a trip to Italy where he was completely taken by the works of Raphael. This caused him to distance himself a little from the Impressionists, adopting a somewhat more classical style.

In *La lecture,* we see a young girl at a table reading. Although Renoir's works dealt with many themes, he did several famous paintings with children, such as ***Madame Charpentier et ses enfants*** (1878) and ***Jeunes filles au piano*** (1892).

Chapter Projects

Patrick et moi After students have completed the structure section of the chapter, have them undertake a project that compares their day with that of Patrick in the **Vocabulaire** sections. For example: **Patrick habite près de Paris. Moi, je n'habite pas près de Paris. J'habite près de ____. Patrick habite rue Saint-Paul et moi j'habite ____.** This can be either a written or an oral project. Patrick appears in both **Mots 1** and **2.**

Après les cours Have students in your class survey the student body for information about afterschool activities. If the survey is restricted to the activities taught in **Mots 1** and **2,** students can report back in French. Each person interviewed should initial the interview sheet to avoid repetition.

Une papeterie You may wish to have students set up a **papeterie** in the classroom where they can take on the roles of cashier and customer. Stock the **papeterie** with the school supplies learned in the vocabulary sections. Include a toy cash register, play money, and prices for the items. Students may work in pairs or small groups to prepare at least three questions and three answers to include in their dialogue. Give each pair/group a chance to rehearse their "skit" and then have pairs/groups present their vignette to the class.

Vocabulaire *Mots 1*

1 Preparation

Resource Manager

Vocabulary Transparencies 3.2–3.3
Audio Activities Booklet TE, pages 37–38
Audiocassette 3A/CD 3
Workbook, page 19
Quiz 1, page 12
ExamView Pro®

Bellringer Review

Use BRR Transparency 3.1 or write the following on the board.
Write as much as you can about one of the following topics.
- **Un élève**
- **Le cours de français**
- **Un lycée**

2 Presentation

Attention!

Note that all the verbs in the vocabulary presentation are in the **il/elle** form so that you can immediately ask questions. Students can answer and practice the new words without having to make pronoun and ending changes. Students will learn how to manipulate the **-er** verbs in the structure section of this chapter.

Step 1 Present the vocabulary first with books closed using Vocabulary Transparencies 3.2–3.3. Have students repeat each word two or three times after you or Audiocassette 3A/CD 3.

Step 2 Act out the **-er** verbs on pages 82–83. For example: **quitter la salle de classe** (leave the room); **passer un examen** (write on test paper); **parler** (say something); **écouter** (point to your ears); **étudier** (pore over some books); **lever la main** (raise your hand), etc.

Vocabulaire *Mots 1*

Une journée à l'école

Patrick habite près de Paris.
Il habite rue Saint-Paul.
Patrick quitte la maison.

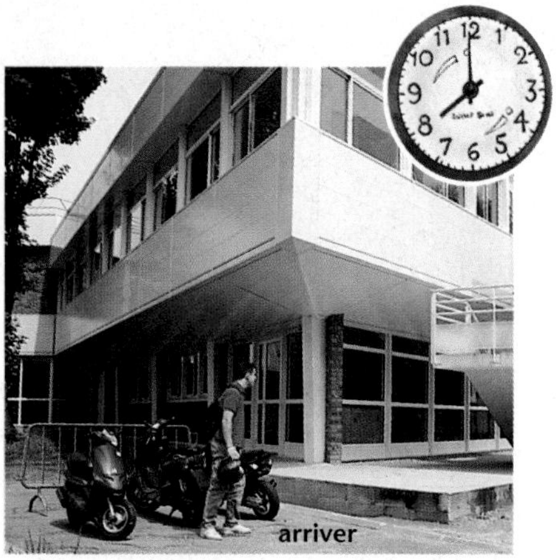

Le matin, Patrick arrive à l'école.
À quelle heure?
Il arrive à l'école à huit heures.
Il passe la journée à l'école.

Le prof parle.
Les élèves écoutent bien.
Les élèves étudient.

Les élèves regardent une vidéo.
Deux élèves écoutent des cassettes.

Reaching All Students

Total Physical Response Before doing this activity, act out each verb: **regarder, parler, écouter, lever, poser.**

(Student 1), **levez-vous, s'il vous plaît.**
Regardez un garçon dans la classe.
Regardez une fille.
Parlez au prof (à la prof).
Parlez français.
Écoutez le/la prof.
Levez la main.
Posez une question.

Learning from Photos

(pages 82–83) The young boy leaving home on his scooter is from the town of Yerres. Yerres is a middle-class suburban community located about 25 kilometers southeast of Paris on the road to Fontainebleau.

The same boy is approaching his school, **le collège Guillaume Budé.** The school serves two suburban communities, Yerres and Crosnes.

Moi, je n'aime pas du tout les examens. Je déteste les examens.

la main

Vincent passe un examen.
Il n'aime pas les examens.

Note 🎧

The expression **passer un examen** is an example of a false cognate (**un faux ami**). It means "to take an exam," not "to pass an exam."

Sophie lève la main.
Elle pose une question.

la cantine

Les élèves déjeunent à la cantine.
Ils déjeunent à midi (12 h).

jouer

la cour

Note 🎧

The popular word **rigoler** means "to joke around." **Tu rigoles!** means "You don't mean it!" or "You're joking!"

Pendant la récré(ation) les élèves
jouent dans la cour.
Il y a beaucoup d'élèves dans la cour.
Ils rigolent.
Ils parlent entre les cours.

VOCABULAIRE

quatre-vingt-trois ✤ 83

Learning from Photos

(pages 82–83) The teacher in the classroom is teaching at the École de Noyen-sur-Seine, another suburb of Paris. The cafeteria is at the school of the Alliance Française in Paris.

Vocabulary Expansion

Because of the false cognate, **passer un examen**, some students may ask how to say *to pass an exam:* **être reçu(e) à un examen.** You may also wish to tell them how to say *to fail an exam:* **être recalé(e) à un examen.**

Step 3 Repeat the actions, this time having students act out each verb using the Total Physical Response approach.

Step 4 Now model the phrases on pages 82–83 that put the words just taught into meaningful sentences. As you present these sentences, intersperse the presentation with comprehension questions, building from simple to more complex. The natural progression is *yes/no*, choice, question word. For example: **Vincent passe un examen? Il passe un examen facile ou difficile? Qui passe un examen? Il passe un examen où?**

Step 5 Ask students the following questions to introduce **qu'est-ce que. Qu'est-ce que les élèves écoutent? Un CD ou une vidéo? Qu'est-ce qu'ils regardent? Un CD ou une vidéo? Qu'est-ce que** will be reintroduced many times.

Step 6 After the initial presentation with the overhead transparencies, have students open their books and look at the new vocabulary words as they repeat either after you or Audiocassette 3A/CD 3.
Teaching Tip: The type of questioning described in Step 4 above allows students to hear and use the words so these words become an active part of their vocabulary in a natural way. It also lets you take into account individual differences when presenting new material. Ask the easy *yes/no* questions of the less able students and the more difficult questions with interrogative words of the more able students.

3 Practice

Commençons
Let's use our new words

Attention!

When students are doing the **Commençons** activities, accept any answer that makes sense. The purpose of these activities is to have students use the new vocabulary. They are not factual recall activities. Thus, it is not necessary for students to remember specific factual information from the vocabulary presentation when answering. If you wish, have students use the photos on this page as a stimulus, when possible.

Historiette Each time **Historiette** appears, it means that the answers to the activity form a short story. Encourage students to look at the title of the **Historiette,** since it can help them do the activity.

2 This activity focuses attention on the interrogative words. Read the model sentence. Call on a student to read the first question. Have the same student answer the question. Let him or her answer first with a complete sentence to practice all the new words, but then have the student answer again giving just the word or expression that responds to the interrogative word.

3 **Expansion:** You may wish to have more able students ask questions about this completed narrative: **Qui est une élève excellente?**

Commençons
Let's use our new words

1 Historiette Un élève parisien

Inventez une histoire. *(Make up a story.)*

1. Fabien est de Paris?
2. Il habite rue Jacob?
3. Il quitte la maison à quelle heure?
4. Il passe la journée où?
5. Il déjeune à la cantine?

Un lycéen français

2 Toujours des questions

Répondez. *(Answer.)*

Le matin, les élèves arrivent à l'école à huit heures.

1. Qui arrive à l'école?
2. Ils arrivent où?
3. Ils arrivent à quelle heure?
4. Ils arrivent à l'école le matin ou à midi?

Les élèves déjeunent à la cantine à midi.

5. Qui déjeune?
6. Les élèves déjeunent où?
7. Ils déjeunent à la cantine à quelle heure?

3 Historiette En classe

Complétez. *(Complete.)*

En classe la prof ___1___ et les élèves ___2___. Anne est une élève excellente. Elle ___3___ beaucoup. Sophie est dans la même classe. Elle ___4___ la main et ___5___ une question.

Vincent ___6___ un examen. Les examens sont difficiles. Vincent n'___7___ pas les examens. Il ___8___ les examens.

Answers to Commençons

1 *Answers will vary but may include:*

1. Non, Fabien n'est pas de Paris.
2. Oui, il habite rue Jacob.
3. Il quitte la maison à sept heures.
4. Il passe la journée à l'école.
5. Oui, il déjeune à la cantine.

2

1. Les élèves arrivent à l'école.
2. Ils arrivent à l'école.
3. Ils arrivent à huit heures.
4. Ils arrivent à l'école le matin.
5. Les élèves déjeunent.
6. Les élèves déjeunent à la cantine.
7. Ils déjeunent à la cantine à midi.

3

1. parle
2. écoutent
3. étudie
4. lève
5. pose
6. passe
7. aime
8. déteste

Vocabulaire

4 **Pardon!** Préparez une petite conversation d'après le modèle. *(Prepare a short conversation according to the model.)*

Sandrine écoute une cassette.
Pardon? Qu'est-ce qu'elle écoute?

1. Sandrine écoute un CD.
2. Sandrine regarde une vidéo.
3. Sandrine lève la main.
4. Sandrine pose une question.
5. Sandrine passe un examen.
6. Sandrine adore les vidéos.

5 **Historiette** **Dans la cour** Répondez. *(Answer.)*

1. Les élèves sont dans la cour?
2. Ils sont dans la cour pendant la récréation?
3. Ils parlent entre les cours?
4. Ils jouent où?
5. Ils rigolent avec les copains?
6. Ils déjeunent dans la cour?

6 **En classe** With a classmate, look at the illustration. Take turns saying as much as you can about it.

ENCORE PLUS *For more practice using words from* ***Mots 1****, do Activity 7 on page H8 at the end of this book.*

4 This activity can be done as a paired activity. The activity makes students use the interrogative **qu'est-ce que.**

5 Have a student retell the information given in this activity in his or her own words.

6 Have students work in pairs. The first student will say something about the illustration. The next student will say something else. For added practice, you may wish to have students give an incorrect description to allow their partner to disagree and correct.
Expansion: Have students volunteer to do this activity in front of the class.
Teaching Tip: You may wish to call on more able students to make up questions about the illustration in Activity 6. They can also call on someone to answer the question.

Writing Development

Have the students write answers to Activities 3 and 5 in paragraph form to illustrate how the answers tell a story.

Assessment

As an informal assessment, after you have presented the vocabulary in **Mots 1** and after completing the activities in the **Commençons** section, you can show the overhead transparencies again and call on students to say whatever they can about any of the illustrations or photographs.

Answers to Commençons

4

1. Pardon? Qu'est-ce qu'elle écoute?
2. Pardon? Qu'est-ce qu'elle regarde?
3. Pardon? Qu'est-ce qu'elle lève?
4. Pardon? Qu'est-ce qu'elle pose?
5. Pardon? Qu'est-ce qu'elle passe?
6. Pardon? Qu'est-ce qu'elle adore?

5 *Answers will vary but may include:*

1. Oui, les élèves sont dans la cour.
2. Oui, ils sont dans la cour pendant la récréation.
3. Oui, ils parlent entre les cours.
4. Ils jouent dans la cour.
5. Oui, ils rigolent avec les copains.
6. Oui, ils déjeunent dans la cour.

6 *Answers will vary but may include:*
Il est quatre heures de l'après-midi et les élèves sont dans un lycée à Paris. Les élèves écoutent le prof. Une fille lève la main. Elle pose une question.

1 Preparation

Resource Manager

Vocabulary Transparencies 3.4–3.5
Audio Activities Booklet TE, pages 39–41
Audiocassette 3A/CD 3
Workbook, pages 20–21
Quiz 2, page 13
ExamView Pro®

Bellringer Review

Use BRR Transparency 3.2 or write the following on the board.
Rewrite the following sentences.

1. **Elle est française.**
   Elles _______.
2. **Je ne suis pas français(e).**
   Nous _______.
3. **Tu es d'où?**
   Vous _______?

2 Presentation

Step 1 Have students close their books. Model the new vocabulary on pages 86–87 using Vocabulary Transparencies 3.4–3.5. Have them repeat each word or expression two or three times.

Step 2 Identify the school supplies your students are actually using. Have the class repeat each item after you once or twice. Ask **Qu'est-ce que c'est?** and have a student respond.

Step 3 Have students repeat the short conversation with the clerk in the illustration on page 87.

Vocabulaire

Mots 2

Des fournitures scolaires

Qu'est-ce que c'est?
C'est un cahier.

Class Motivator

Qu'est-ce qu'il y a dans le sac à dos? Bring an empty backpack to class. Pass the backpack around the room. As each person gets the backpack, he or she puts a school supply in it, names it, and tells what else is in the backpack. **Il y a un crayon dans le sac à dos.** If someone has already put a certain item in the pack, the others can still put in the same item. However, the other students now have to say how many notebooks, pens, etc., are in the backpack. The last student has to name everything in the pack. (Hint: You may allow students to look in the pack if they need help remembering.)

Après les cours

Le sac à dos, c'est combien, s'il vous plaît?
Vingt dollars cinquante.
la caisse
payer
un magasin

Lucette travaille après les cours.
Elle travaille dans une papeterie.
Combien d'heures par semaine?
Dix heures.

Sylvain regarde un sac à dos.
Il demande combien coûte le sac à dos.
Il achète le sac à dos.
Il paie à la caisse.

Les nombres de 100 à 1 000

100	cent	400	quatre cents
101	cent un	500	cinq cents
102	cent deux	600	six cents
200	deux cents	700	sept cents
220	deux cent vingt	800	huit cents
300	trois cents	900	neuf cents
350	trois cent cinquante	1000	mille

Après les cours, Patrick ne travaille pas.
Il rentre à la maison l'après-midi.
Il rentre chez lui.

Il écoute la radio.
Il parle un peu au téléphone.

Step 4 Have students repeat the sentences on page 87. As they do, intersperse with questions such as the following, building from simple to more complex sentences:

Sylvain achète le sac à dos?
Qu'est-ce que Sylvain achète?
Qui achète le sac à dos?
Sylvain achète le sac à dos où?

Have students answer with the complete sentence or sometimes have them use just the specific word or expression that responds to the question word.

Step 5 After presenting the vocabulary orally, have students open their books and read the new vocabulary aloud. You can have the class read in chorus or call on individuals to read. Intersperse with questions such as those outlined above.

Attention!

Les nombres It is recommended that you not hold the students responsible for writing out numbers, since this is something they will seldom or never do in real-life situations. You may merely wish to point out that **deux cents** has an **s** only when **cent** is not followed by another number. This point, of course, is up to the discretion of the teacher.

Reaching All Students

For the Younger Students Have students prepare a catalogue/advertisement for a stationery store using the school supply vocabulary they have learned in **Mots 1** and **Mots 2.** Tell students to label each item in French. They may also give prices in euros or dollars. (Have students check the exchange rates for France and Canada.)

Vocabulary Expansion

You may wish to teach the students the verb **gagner. Lucette gagne cinquante dollars par semaine.** You can ask: **Elle gagne combien d'argent? Elle gagne vingt dollars ou cinquante dollars?** This will teach the meaning of **argent.**

About the French Language

In the illustration on page 87, the salesperson says dollars because the scene is set in Quebec, Canada. In the **Lecture supplémentaire** on page 100, students will make comparisons about part-time jobs for students in Canada, the U.S., and France. They will learn why they are not very common in France.

3 Practice

Commençons
Let's use our new words

7 Have a contest to see who has written the most words for this activity.

Learning from Photos

(page 88) You may wish to ask the following questions about the photo.

La fille travaille dans une papeterie?
La papeterie est à Montréal?
La fille est sociable ou timide?
Qu'est-ce qu'elle regarde?
Elle travaille à la caisse?

Writing Development

Have students write the answers to Activity 10 in a paragraph to illustrate how the sentences tell a story.

Commençons
Let's use our new words

7 **Des fournitures scolaires** Préparez une liste de fournitures scolaires. *(Make a list of important school supplies.)*

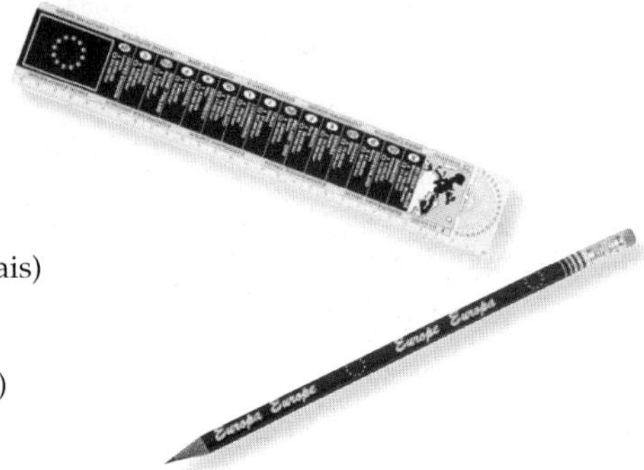

8 **Historiette Loïc est français.** Répondez d'après l'indication. *(Answer according to the cues.)*

1. Loïc est français ou américain? (français)
2. Il habite où? (près de Paris)
3. Il travaille après les cours? (non)
4. Il rentre chez lui après les cours? (oui)
5. Qu'est-ce qu'il écoute? (la radio)
6. Qu'est-ce qu'il regarde? (une vidéo)
7. Il parle au téléphone? (oui)
8. Avec qui? (les copains)

Une papeterie, Montréal, Canada

9 **Historiette Dans une papeterie** Inventez une histoire. *(Make up a story.)*

1. Catherine est canadienne?
2. Elle travaille après les cours?
3. Elle travaille combien d'heures par semaine?
4. Elle travaille dans une papeterie?
5. Où est la papeterie?
6. Qu'est-ce qu'il y a dans une papeterie?
7. Il y a beaucoup d'élèves dans la papeterie?
8. Un garçon paie à la caisse?
9. Un cahier coûte combien?

Answers to Commençons

7 *Answers will vary but may include:*

un cahier, un bloc-notes, un crayon, un stylo-bille, un feutre, une gomme, une règle, un livre, un classeur, une calculatrice, une feuille de papier, un sac à dos

8

1. Loïc est français.
2. Il habite près de Paris.
3. Non, il ne travaille pas après les cours.
4. Oui, il rentre chez lui après les cours.
5. Il écoute la radio.
6. Il regarde une vidéo.
7. Oui, il parle au téléphone.
8. Il parle avec les copains.

9 *Answers will vary but may include:*

1. Oui, Catherine est canadienne.
2. Oui, elle travaille après les cours.
3. Elle travaille dix heures par semaine.
4. Oui, elle travaille dans une papeterie.
5. La papeterie est à Montréal.
6. Il y a des cahiers, des bloc-notes, et des classeurs dans la papeterie.
7. Oui, il y a beaucoup d'élèves dans la papeterie.
8. Oui, un garçon paie à la caisse.
9. Un cahier coûte deux dollars cinquante.

10 **Historiette** **À la papeterie** Choisissez la bonne réponse. *(Choose the correct completion.)*

1. Sandrine ___ dans une papeterie.
   a. étudie **b.** habite **c.** travaille
2. Elle ___ à un client au téléphone.
   a. écoute **b.** parle **c.** paie
3. Les élèves ___ des fournitures scolaires dans la papeterie.
   a. travaillent **b.** rentrent **c.** regardent
4. Un garçon ___ un cahier.
   a. regarde **b.** joue **c.** rentre
5. Il ___ une calculatrice pour le cours de maths.
   a. passe **b.** quitte **c.** achète
6. La calculatrice ___ six dollars canadiens.
   a. paie **b.** habite **c.** coûte
7. Le garçon ___ à la caisse.
   a. quitte **b.** coûte **c.** paie

11 **Pour la rentrée des classes** Work with a classmate. It's back-to-school time and you're buying the school supplies below. Take turns being the customer and the salesperson.

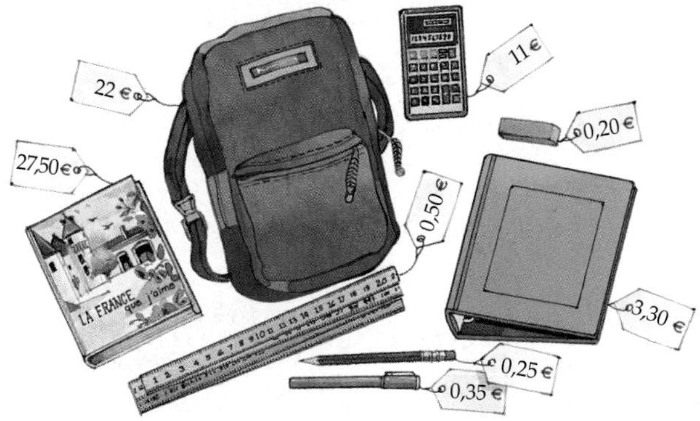

12 **Jeu** **Qu'est-ce que c'est?** Work with a classmate. Have your partner close his or her eyes. Hand your partner a school supply. Have your partner guess what it is. Take turns.

ENCORE PLUS *For more practice using words from **Mots 2**, do Activity 8 on page H9 at the end of this book.*

10 Have individual students read the entire sentence, including the correct completion word.
Expansion: Ask the more able students to make up original sentences using the word choices that do not fit in the blanks. For number 1, they could say: **Sandrine étudie à la maison. Sandrine habite à Montréal.**

11 Have students work in pairs. The first student will ask the price of the item, the second student will respond with the price given. Make sure each student has the opportunity to role-play both the customer and the salesperson before ending this activity. Have students volunteer to role-play this activity for the class.

12 **Jeu** This is a good activity to use at the beginning or the end of the class period.

ENCORE PLUS This *infogap* activity will allow students to practice in pairs. The activity should be very manageable for them, since all vocabulary and structures are familiar to them.

Attention!

Note that the activities are color-coded. All the activities in the text are communicative. However, the ones with blue titles are guided communication. The red titles indicate that the answers to the activity are more open-ended and can vary more. You may wish to correct students' mistakes more so in the guided activities than in the activities with a red title, which lend themselves to a freer response.

Answers to Commençons

10

1. c
2. b
3. c
4. a
5. c
6. c
7. c

11 *Answers will vary but may include:*

—Bonjour, madame.
—Bonjour, mademoiselle.
—Le classeur, c'est combien, s'il vous plaît?
—Le classeur coûte trois euros trente.
—Le sac à dos, c'est combien, s'il vous plaît?
—Le sac à dos coûte vingt-deux euros.

1 Preparation

Resource Manager

Audio Activities Booklet TE, pages 41–44
Audiocassette 3A/CD 3
Workbook, pages 22–25
Quizzes 3–5, pages 14–16
ExamView Pro®

Bellringer Review

Use BRR Transparency 3.3 or write the following on the board.
Complete each phrase with an appropriate verb.

1. **Marc _____ les maths.**
2. **Julie _____ un examen.**
3. **Sophie _____ une question.**
4. **Georges _____ à la caisse.**
5. **Yvonne _____ au téléphone.**
6. **Pierre _____ dans une papeterie.**

2 Presentation

Les verbes réguliers en -er au présent

Step 1 Draw two stick figures on the board, labeling one Mireille and the other Didier. Write the verbs **parler, travailler,** and **étudier.** Have students make up sentences about either Mireille or Didier. This reviews the **-er** verbs from the vocabulary presentation.

Step 2 Lead students through Items 1–4 on page 90. Write the present tense forms of **parler** and **aimer** on the board. Point to the pronouns **je, tu, il, elle, ils, elles** as you pronounce the forms. Students should come to realize that although the forms are spelled differently, they are pronounced the same.

Structure

Talking about people's activities
Les verbes réguliers en -er au présent

1. A word that expresses an action or a state is a verb. **Parler** (*to speak*), **écouter** (*to listen to*), and **aimer** (*to like*) are verbs in the infinitive form. They are called regular verbs because they all follow a regular pattern. Their infinitives end in **-er.**

2. French verbs change endings with each subject. To form the stem to which the endings are added, you drop the **-er** from the infinitive.

Infinitive	Stem
parler	parl-
écouter	écout-
aimer	aim-

3. You add the ending for each subject to the stem. Note that, although the endings for the **je, tu, il,** and **ils** forms are spelled differently, they are pronounced the same.

	PARLER	AIMER
je parl -e	je parle	j' aime
tu parl -es	tu parles	tu aimes
il/elle parl -e	il/elle parle	il/elle aime
nous parl -ons	nous parlons	nous‿z aimons
vous parl -ez	vous parlez	vous‿z aimez
ils/elles parl -ent	ils/elles parlent	ils‿z/elles‿z aiment

4. You will see and hear the word **on** a great deal. **On** has several meanings, such as "we," "they," and "people." **On** always takes the **il/elle** form of the verb. In spoken French, people use **on** more often than **nous.**

On parle français en France.
On travaille beaucoup.
On‿n arrive à l'école le matin.

Attention!

There is elision when **je** or **ne** is followed by a verb that begins with a vowel or silent **h.**

J'habite à Paris. **Je n'habite pas à Lyon.**
J'aime les maths. **Je n'aime pas les sciences.**

There is a liaison with all plural subject pronouns and a verb that begins with a vowel or silent **h.** The **s** on the pronoun is pronounced as a **z.**

nous‿z étudions **vous‿z aimez** **ils‿z habitent**

Reaching All Students

Additional Practice After completing Activity 15 on page 91, tell students you are going to give them some action words. Let them suggest that you all do it, using the pronoun **on.** For example:

Regarder une vidéo? On regarde une vidéo?

étudier **rigoler**
arriver à l'école **déjeuner**

Attention!

The structure activities on **-er** verbs on page 91 develop from simple to more complex. Activity 13 reviews the **il/elle** form used in the vocabulary presentation. Activity 14 contrasts the third person singular and plural. On page 92, Activity 17 has students interact from **tu** to **je,** Activities 18 and 19, from **vous** to **nous.** Activities 20–22 have students use all forms.

Continuons
Let's put our words together

Un cours de français aux États-Unis

13 **Historiette** **Un Américain**
Inventez une histoire. *(Make up a story.)*

1. Kevin est français ou américain?
2. Il habite à Paris ou à Chicago?
3. Il parle anglais ou français?
4. Il étudie quelle langue?
5. Il parle beaucoup en classe?
6. Il travaille bien à l'école?

14 **Historiette** **Les élèves ou les profs?** Suivez le modèle. *(Follow the model.)*

—Qui arrive à l'école le matin?
—Les élèves et les profs arrivent à l'école.

1. Qui parle en classe?
2. Qui écoute quand le prof parle?
3. Qui écoute des cassettes?
4. Qui passe des examens?
5. Qui étudie beaucoup?
6. Qui lève la main?
7. Qui pose des questions?
8. Qui rigole dans la cour?

15 **Aux États-Unis** Un(e) élève français(e) pose des questions à un(e) élève américain(e). *(You are a French student. Ask a classmate about life in the United States.)*

1. On arrive à l'école à quelle heure?
2. On quitte l'école à quelle heure?
3. On travaille beaucoup à l'école?
4. On aime beaucoup les examens?
5. On travaille après les cours?
6. On écoute des CD?
7. On regarde la télé?
8. On parle au téléphone?

Step 3 Point out that the oral forms of the **-er** verbs are quite easy. However, they do present a spelling problem. You may wish to emphasize this by writing the endings in a different color chalk. Then ask students to note which endings remain silent and which ones are pronounced.

3 Practice

Continuons
Let's put our words together

Teacher Note: It is suggested that you go over all activities in class before assigning them as independent practice.

13 **Expansion:** After completing this activity, have several students combine the sentences into a short narration. For example, **Kevin est américain. Il habite à Chicago. Il parle anglais.,** etc.

14 This activity reviews **qui.** It also points out that **qui** with a singular verb form is used to elicit plural responses.

Answers to Continuons

13 *Answers will vary but may include:*

1. Kevin est américain.
2. Il habite à Chicago.
3. Il parle anglais.
4. Il étudie le français.
5. Oui, il parle beaucoup en classe.
6. Oui, il travaille bien à l'école.

14

1. Les élèves et les profs parlent en classe.
2. Les élèves écoutent quand le prof parle.
3. Les élèves écoutent des cassettes.
4. Les élèves passent des examens.
5. Les élèves étudient beaucoup.
6. Les élèves lèvent la main.
7. Les profs et les élèves posent des questions.
8. Les élèves rigolent dans la cour.

15 *Answers will vary but may include:*

1. On arrive à l'école à neuf heures moins le quart.
2. On quitte l'école à trois heures et demie.
3. Oui, on travaille beaucoup à l'école.
4. Non, on n'aime pas beaucoup les examens.
5. Oui, on travaille après les cours.
6. Oui, on écoute des CD.
7. Oui, on regarde la télé.
8. Oui, on parle au téléphone.

2 Presentation *(continued)*

16 This miniconversation lets students hear, see, and say the first- and second-person singular forms of **-er** verbs before they use them actively in Activity 17. Read the conversation and have students repeat after you. Then ask for volunteers to take the parts.

18 This activity gives students practice using the interrogative **Qu'est-ce que** and the **nous** form of the verb. Have students look at one another to make this exercise more realistic.

Reaching All Students

Additional Practice Ask students questions such as the following about your own class:

Qui arrive à l'école à sept heures?
Qui étudie beaucoup?
Qui écoute en classe?
Qui parle beaucoup en classe?
Qui habite près de l'école?
Qui parle espagnol?
Qui étudie le dessin?

16 Tu parles français? Répétez la conversation. *(Repeat the conversation.)*

Sue: Tu n'es pas français, toi?
Luc: Non, je ne suis pas français.
Sue: Mais tu parles français!
Luc: Bien sûr que je parle français.
Sue: Et comment ça, si tu n'es pas français?
Luc: Mais je suis belge.
Sue: Ah, c'est vrai. On parle français en Belgique.

Bruxelles, Belgique

17 Historiette À votre tour! Donnez des réponses personnelles. *(Give your own answers.)*

1. Tu habites dans quelle ville?
2. Tu quittes la maison à quelle heure le matin?
3. Tu arrives à l'école à quelle heure?
4. Est-ce que tu parles français avec les copains?
5. Tu aimes quelles matières?
6. Tu aimes quels profs?
7. Tu détestes quelles matières?
8. Tu travailles après les cours?
9. Tu parles beaucoup avec les copains au téléphone?
10. Tu regardes la télé?

18 Pardon? Posez des questions d'après le modèle. *(Ask questions according to the model.)*

Nous écoutons des CD.
Pardon? Qu'est-ce que vous écoutez?

1. Nous détestons les examens.
2. Nous regardons la télé.
3. Nous regardons des magazines.
4. Nous écoutons la radio.
5. Nous aimons l'école.
6. Nous étudions l'espagnol.

Answers to Continuons

17 *Answers will vary but may include:*

1. J'habite à ____.
2. Je quitte la maison à sept heures.
3. J'arrive à l'école à sept heures et demie.
4. Oui, je parle français avec les copains.
5. J'aime le français, la littérature et l'informatique.
6. J'aime la prof de français et le prof de géographie.
7. Je déteste l'histoire et la biologie!
8. Oui, je travaille après les cours.
9. Non, je ne parle pas beaucoup avec les copains au téléphone.
10. Oui, je regarde la télé.

18

1. Pardon? Qu'est-ce que vous détestez?
2. Pardon? Qu'est-ce que vous regardez?
3. Pardon? Qu'est-ce que vous regardez?
4. Pardon? Qu'est-ce que vous écoutez?
5. Pardon? Qu'est-ce que vous aimez?
6. Pardon? Qu'est-ce que vous étudiez?

19 **Nous tous** Donnez des réponses personnelles en utilisant **nous.** (*Give answers about you and your classmates. Use* nous.)

1. Vous arrivez à l'école à quelle heure le matin?
2. Vous quittez l'école à quelle heure l'après-midi?
3. Vous passez combien d'heures à l'école?
4. Vous aimez les cours?
5. Vous écoutez bien quand le professeur parle en classe?
6. Vous aimez ou vous détestez les examens?

20 **Historiette** **À l'école** Complétez. (*Complete.*)

Nous __1__ (arriver) à l'école à sept heures et demie. Et vous, vous __2__ (arriver) à quelle heure? Avant les cours, j'__3__ (aimer) parler un peu avec les copains. On __4__ (rigoler). Mais en classe, non! On __5__ (travailler) beaucoup. Moi, j'__6__ (écouter) bien quand les profs __7__ (parler). Et toi, tu __8__ (travailler) beaucoup aussi? Tu __9__ (passer) des examens? Tu __10__ (aimer) les examens ou pas?

21 **Une journée typique** Work with a classmate. Tell each other about a typical school day. Find out what activities you have in common.

22 **Tu travailles ou pas?** Get together in small groups and find out who works after school in your group. Find out where, how many hours a week, etc. Here are some words you may want to use.

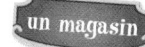

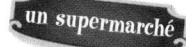

un restaurant
un fast-food
une station-service
un magasin
un supermarché

ENCORE PLUS *For more practice using* ***-er*** *verbs in the present, do Activity 9 on page H10 at the end of this book.*

Answers to Continuons

19 *Answers will vary but may include:*

1. Nous arrivons à l'école à sept heures et demie.
2. Nous quittons l'école à trois heures et quart.
3. Nous passons huit heures à l'école.
4. Oui, nous aimons les cours.
5. Oui, nous écoutons quand le professeur parle en classe.
6. Nous détestons les examens.

20

1. arrivons
2. arrivez
3. aime
4. rigole
5. travaille
6. écoute
7. parlent
8. travailles
9. passes
10. aimes

21 *Answers will vary but may include:*

—J'arrive à l'école à sept heures et demie. Et toi?
—Moi, j'arrive à l'école à huit heures moins le quart.
—Je déteste l'anglais et les maths!
—Je déteste l'histoire et l'algèbre!
—Tu travailles après les cours?
—Oui, je travaille après les cours. Et toi?
—Je travaille après les cours, aussi.

Structure

22 **Expansion:** You may wish to conduct a classwide poll and tabulate the results. This would be an excellent resource to use with the **Lecture supplémentaire 1,** page 100.

Learning from Photos

(pages 92–93) Belgium has two distinct cultures: Flemish and Walloon. The Flemish speak Flemish and inhabit the northern half of the country. The Walloons speak French. Brussels, the capital, is officially a dual-language area. This photo is of **la Grand-Place. La Grand-Place** is one of the most ornate market squares in Europe. There is a daily flower market, as seen in the photo, and on Sundays there is also a bird market.

About the French Language

Note that **la Grand-Place** is spelled without an **e.** It is suggested that you not give students the written name at this point.

ENCORE PLUS This *infogap* activity will allow students to practice in pairs. The activity should be very manageable for them, since all vocabulary and structures are familiar to them.

1 Preparation

Bellringer Review

Use BRR Transparency 3.4 or write the following on the board.
Answer the following questions.

1. **Tu t'appelles comment?**
2. **Tu es de quelle nationalité?**
3. **Tu es d'où?**
4. **Tu es élève dans une école secondaire?**
5. **Tu aimes quels cours?**

2 Presentation

La négation des articles indéfinis

Attention!

Students often find this construction difficult. It will be reintroduced and reinforced frequently throughout **Bon voyage!**

Step 1 Lead students through the table on page 94. Point out that **un, une,** and **des** are not used in negative constructions. Instead, **de** is used. Be sure to point out the **Attention!** box showing the elision with **de.**

3 Practice

25 You may wish to help slower students by giving them a list of words they know and can use in this activity. They are: **une cassette, une vidéo, un livre, un crayon, un stylo-bille, un feutre, une calculatrice, un cahier, un bloc-notes, un classeur, un sac à dos.**

Recycling

Activity 24 recycles the vocabulary from **Mots 2.**

Talking about what you don't do
La négation des articles indéfinis

In the negative, the indefinite articles **un, une,** and **des** change to **de** (or **d'**).

Affirmatif	Négatif
Julie regarde un CD.	Éric ne regarde pas de CD.
Julie regarde une vidéo.	Éric ne regarde pas de vidéo.
Julie regarde des photos.	Éric ne regarde pas de photos.

Attention!

Note the elision with **de.**
Je suis content: pas d'examen aujourd'hui!

Continuons
Let's put our words together

23 En classe Répondez que non. *(Answer with* non.*)*

1. Tu écoutes un CD?
2. Tu regardes une vidéo?
3. Tu poses des questions?
4. Tu écoutes des cassettes?
5. Tu passes un examen aujourd'hui?

24 Historiette Dans une papeterie
Répondez d'après les indications. *(Answer according to the cues.)*

1. René est dans une papeterie? (oui)
2. Il regarde un feutre et un cahier? (oui)
3. Il achète un stylo-bille? (non)
4. Il achète un feutre? (oui)
5. Il achète une cassette? (non)
6. Il achète une vidéo? (oui)

25 J'achète ou je n'achète pas. Work with a classmate. Take turns telling what you buy or don't buy.

Answers to Continuons

23

1. Non, je n'écoute pas de CD.
2. Non, je ne regarde pas de vidéo.
3. Non, je ne pose pas de questions.
4. Non, je n'écoute pas de cassettes.
5. Non, je ne passe pas d'examen aujourd'hui.

24

1. Oui, René est dans une papeterie.
2. Oui, il regarde un feutre et un cahier.
3. Non, il n'achète pas de stylo-bille.
4. Oui, il achète un feutre.
5. Non, il n'achète pas de cassette.
6. Oui, il achète une vidéo.

25 *Answers will vary but may include:*

—J'achète des crayons.
—Je n'achète pas de crayons. J'achète des feutres.
—J'achète un classeur.
—Je n'achète pas de classeur. J'achète un bloc-notes.

Discussing likes and dislikes
Verbe + infinitif

1. In French when the verbs **aimer, adorer,** and **détester** are followed by another verb, the second verb is in the infinitive form.

   Il aime rigoler.
   J'adore écouter la radio.
   On déteste travailler.

2. In a negative sentence, the **ne... pas** goes around the first verb.

   Vous n'aimez pas travailler?

Continuons
Let's put our words together

26 Tu aimes travailler? Posez les questions suivantes à un copain ou une copine. *(Ask a classmate the following questions.)*

—Tu aimes travailler?
—Bien sûr. J'aime beaucoup travailler./ Non, pas du tout. Je déteste travailler.

1. Tu aimes regarder la télé?
2. Tu aimes écouter la radio?
3. Tu aimes étudier?
4. Tu aimes rigoler?
5. Tu aimes parler au téléphone?

27 On aime ou on n'aime pas! Work with a classmate. Tell some things you like and don't like to do.

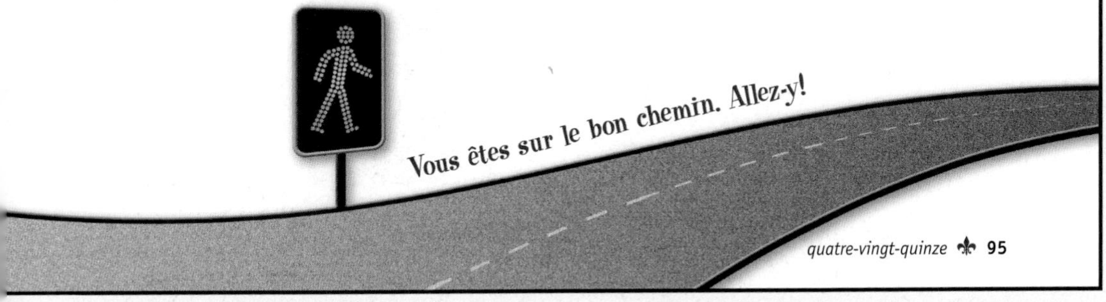

Structure

1 Preparation

Bellringer Review

Use BRR Transparency 3.5 or write the following on the board.
The following sentences describe a girl named Monique. Rewrite them so they describe a boy named Marc.
Monique est française.
Elle est petite.
Elle est très intelligente.
Elle n'est pas populaire.
Elle est timide.

2 Presentation

Verbe + infinitif

Attention!
Note that at this point students only have to use an **-er** verb after another verb.

Step 1 Lead students through Items 1–2 on page 95. Have them repeat the examples after you.

Step 2 Ask questions using familiar verbs. For example: **Tu aimes écouter la radio? Tu détestes passer des examens?**

3 Practice

Continuons
Let's put our words together

26 You may wish to use the recorded version of this activity.

Allez-y!
At this point in the chapter, students have learned all the vocabulary and structure necessary to complete the chapter. The conversation and cultural readings recycle all the material learned up to this point.

Answers to Continuons

26 *Answers will vary but may include:*
1. Bien sûr. J'aime beaucoup regarder la télé.
2. Non, pas du tout. Je déteste écouter la radio.
3. Non, pas du tout. Je n'aime pas étudier.
4. Bien sûr. J'aime beaucoup rigoler.
5. Bien sûr. J'aime beaucoup parler au téléphone.

27 *Answers will vary but may include:*
—J'aime rigoler et écouter la radio. Tu aimes étudier?
—Non, pas du tout. Je déteste étudier. Mais j'aime beaucoup regarder la télé.
—Tu aimes parler au téléphone avec les copains?
—Bien sûr. J'aime beaucoup parler au téléphone avec les copains.

1 Preparation

Resource Manager

Audio Activities Booklet TE, pages 44–45
Audiocassette 3A/CD 3
CD-ROM

Bellringer Review

Use BRR Transparency 3.6 or write the following on the board.
Write three things you like to do in school and three things you do not like to do.

National Standards

Comparisons
Students learn on page 96 that the French school day is very different from the average American one.

2 Presentation

Step 1 You may wish to have students listen to the conversation on Audiocassette 3A/CD 3 and then have them repeat after you.

Step 2 Call on two students to read the conversation with as much expression as possible.

Step 3 After presenting the **Conversation** and going over the **Après la conversation** activity, call on a student or students to retell the conversation in their own words.

Learning from Photos

(page 96) The **Collège Lucie Faure** in this photo is in the **12e arrondissement** of Paris.

Un élève français aux États-Unis

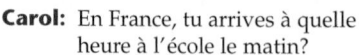

Carol: En France, tu arrives à quelle heure à l'école le matin?
Cédric: Moi, j'arrive à l'école vers sept heures et demie.
Carol: Et les cours commencent à quelle heure?
Cédric: À huit heures. J'aime parler un peu avec les copains avant la classe.
Carol: Et tu quittes l'école à trois heures?
Cédric: À trois heures! Tu rigoles! En France on quitte l'école à cinq heures.
Carol: À cinq heures! C'est pas vrai!
Cédric: Si, c'est vrai.

Après la conversation

Répondez. *(Answer.)*

1. En France, Cédric arrive à l'école à quelle heure?
2. Cédric parle avec une amie américaine ou française?
3. Les cours de Cédric commencent à quelle heure?
4. Cédric quitte l'école à quelle heure?
5. Et Carol, elle quitte l'école à quelle heure?

Answers to Après la conversation

1. Il arrive à l'école vers sept heures et demie.
2. Il parle avec une amie américaine.
3. Les cours de Cédric commencent à huit heures.
4. Il quitte l'école à cinq heures.
5. Elle quitte l'école à trois heures.

Fun Facts

French students have the longest school day (six hours) of students in any European country. Their school day usually ends at four or four-thirty. French schools are closed on Wednesday afternoon; however, students go to school on Saturday morning. French students spend many hours doing homework. Since French teenagers rarely have part-time jobs, they must depend on a weekly allowance for their spending money.

Parlons un peu plus
Let's talk some more

A **Comparaisons** With a classmate, look at the illustrations. Then compare your own daily school habits with those of the students in the illustrations.

B **Jeu** **Les nombres** Give some numbers in a mathematical pattern but leave one out. Your partner will guess what the missing number is. Take turns. Use the model as a guide.

—deux cents, quatre cents, ____, huit cents
—six cents

Prononciation

Les sons **/é/** et **/è/**

élève

1. There is an important difference in the way French and English vowels are pronounced. When you say the French word **des,** your mouth is tense, in one position. You can repeat the sound /é/ many times without moving your mouth at all. But when you pronounce the English word *day*, your mouth is relaxed and you actually say two vowel sounds.
2. Listen to the word **élève.** It has two distinct vowel sounds. The sound /é/ is "closed" and the sound /è/ is "open." This describes the positions of the mouth for each sound. Repeat the following.

Le son /é/:	**la télé**	**l'école**	**la journée**	**parler**	**écoutez**
Le son /è/:	**après**	**la cassette**	**vous êtes**	**le collège**	

Après l'école, les élèves aiment écouter des cassettes.
Elles aiment regarder la télé.

3 Practice

Parlons un peu plus
Let's talk some more

A This activity recycles time from the preliminary lesson, pages 12–13. You may wish to do a quick review with a clock before having students work in pairs.

B **Jeu** This recycling activity is fun for students to play either with a partner or in teams.

Prononciation

Step 1 Model the key word **élève** and have students repeat in unison and individually.

Step 2 Now model the words and phrases in similar fashion.

Step 3 You may wish to give students the following **dictée: La télé est dans la salle de classe. Vous êtes à l'école. Elle écoute la radio.**

Step 4 For additional practice, you may wish to use the Pronunciation Transparency P 3.

Glencoe Technology

CD-ROM
On the CD-ROM, students can watch a dramatization of this conversation. They can then play the role of either one of the characters and record themselves in the conversation.

Answers to Parlons un peu plus

A *Answers will vary but may include:*
Le garçon quitte la maison à sept heures et demie.
Je quitte la maison à huit heures.
La fille arrive à l'école à huit heures.
J'arrive à l'école à neuf heures.
Les élèves déjeunent à midi et demi.
Nous déjeunons à onze heures et demie.
La fille quitte l'école à cinq heures.
Je quitte l'école à trois heures et quart.
Le garçon étudie à six heures du soir.
J'étudie à huit heures du soir.

Resource Manager

Audio Activities Booklet TE, page 47
Audiocassette 3A/CD3

Bellringer Review

Use BRR Transparency 3.7 or write the following on the board.
Write the question word or phrase associated with each of the following. For example: **le matin = quand?**

1. le prof
2. à la maison
3. à huit heures
4. l'après-midi
5. vingt dollars

National Standards

Cultures

The reading on pages 98–99 gives students some insights into some aspects of the school life of their counterparts in the French-speaking world.

Comparisons

The reading makes some comparisons between schools in France and those in the United States.

Presentation

Pre-reading

Step 1 Have students scan the reading quickly and silently.

About the French Language

You will see *Latin Quarter* written in French with both lowercase and capital letters. We have followed the style of Hachette in their **Guides-Voir** series. The **l** of **Quartier latin** is lowercase.

Lectures culturelles

Reading Strategy

Using pictures and photographs

Before you begin to read, look at the pictures, photographs, or any other visuals that accompany a reading. By doing this, you can often tell what the reading selection is about before you actually read it.

Une journée avec Jacqueline

Jacqueline est une élève française. Elle habite rue Jacob à Paris. La rue Jacob est dans le Quartier latin, tout près de[1] la Sorbonne. La Sorbonne est une université célèbre[2] à Paris. Le Quartier latin est un quartier très fréquenté par les étudiants d'université et les lycéens.

[1] tout près de *very near*
[2] célèbre *famous*

Une librairie, boulevard Saint-Michel, Paris

La Sorbonne, Paris

Learning from Photos

(page 98 top) The bookstore is on the **Boul'Mich'**—student slang for the **boulevard Saint-Michel.** There are many bookstores on the boulevard. They sell all types of books, including large sections of textbooks since French students have to buy their own books for school.

(page 98 bottom) The Sorbonne is one of the oldest universities in Europe. It was founded in 1253 by the canon Robert de Sorbon as a theological college for sixteen students. The university buildings were restored by Cardinal Richelieu in the seventeenth century. The Sorbonne is the hub of the Latin Quarter. It has been and continues to be one of France's principal institutions of higher learning.

Jacqueline est élève au lycée Louis-le-Grand. Le matin, elle quitte la maison à sept heures et demie. Les cours commencent à huit heures. Jacqueline passe la journée au lycée. Comme tous[3] les lycéens, Jacqueline travaille beaucoup, à Louis-le-Grand et à la maison. À la récréation, Jacqueline retrouve[4] des copains dans la cour. Ils parlent et ils rigolent un peu. À midi, ils déjeunent à la cantine. Ils ne rentrent pas à la maison pour déjeuner.

Jacqueline quitte le lycée à cinq heures de l'après-midi. Et vous, vous quittez l'école à quelle heure?

[3] Comme tous *Like all*

[4] retrouve *meets, gets together with*

Lycée Louis-le-Grand, Paris

Après la lecture

A Une élève française Répondez. *(Answer.)*

1. Qui est Jacqueline?
2. Elle habite où?
3. Jacqueline quitte la maison à quelle heure?
4. Les cours commencent à quelle heure?
5. Elle retrouve des copains où?
6. À midi, elle rentre chez elle pour déjeuner?
7. Elle déjeune avec qui?
8. Elle quitte le lycée à quelle heure?

B Paris Trouvez les informations dans la lecture. *(Find the information in the reading.)*

1. la rue où Jacqueline habite
2. le nom d'une université célèbre à Paris
3. un quartier de Paris fréquenté par les étudiants et les lycéens
4. le nom du lycée de Jacqueline

Reading

Step 1 Have students close their books. Relate the story on pages 98–99 in your own words. Follow up by asking a few questions about what you said.

Step 2 With books open, have the class repeat two or three sentences after you. Ask comprehension questions.

Step 3 Go over the story a second time, calling on some students to read aloud individually.

Post-reading

Have students do the **Après la lecture** activities on page 99 orally after reading the selection in class. Then assign these activities to be written at home. Go over them again the following day.

Note: Students may listen to a recorded version of the **Lecture culturelle** on the audio program (Audiocassette 3A/CD 3).

Learning from Photos

(page 99) The lycée Louis-le-Grand is near the Sorbonne on rue Saint-Jacques. This lycée is the most prestigious in France, along with the lycée Henri IV. The school was founded in 1530 by François I as the **Collège des trois langues.** Students learned Latin, Greek, and Hebrew as well as other subjects favored by the academics at the Sorbonne. Molière, Voltaire, and Robespierre studied at the Louis-le-Grand. Today's buildings date from the seventeenth century.

Fun-Facts

The Latin Quarter has been the student quarter of Paris since the days of the great twelfth-century scholar Abélard. It got the name **Quartier latin** because in those days all classes were conducted in Latin.

Answers to Après la lecture

A

1. Jacqueline est une élève française (parisienne).
2. Elle habite rue Jacob à Paris.
3. Jacqueline quitte la maison à sept heures et demie.
4. Les cours commencent à huit heures.
5. Elle retrouve des copains dans la cour.
6. Non, elle ne rentre pas chez elle. Elle déjeune à la cantine.
7. Elle déjeune avec des copains.
8. Elle quitte le lycée à cinq heures de l'après-midi.

B

1. Jacob
2. la Sorbonne
3. le Quartier latin
4. Louis-le-Grand

National Standards

Cultures
This selection familiarizes students with the afterschool habits of teens in Quebec and France.

Comparisons
This selection also compares the afterschool life of a teen in the United States with that of a teen in Quebec and France.

Attention!

This reading is optional. You may skip it completely, have the entire class read it, have only several students read it and report to the class, or assign it for extra credit.

Learning from Photos

(page 100) In 1966, the city of Montréal undertook the development of a **Cité souterraine.** It stretches more than thirty kilometers and its well-lit passages protect people from the severe winter weather and summer heat. This underground city includes hotels, offices, theaters, movies, boutiques, restaurants, and ice-skating rinks.

Lecture supplémentaire 1

Qui travaille?

Le centre commercial «Place de la Cathédrale»

Antoine est canadien. Il est québécois. Il est de Montréal, la deuxième ville francophone du monde après Paris. Après les cours, il travaille dans une papeterie pour gagner un peu d'argent[1]. Il travaille dix heures par semaine. La papeterie où il travaille est dans le centre commercial[2] «Place de la Cathédrale». C'est un très grand centre commercial souterrain[3].

Un restaurant fast-food, Montréal

Aux États-Unis et au Québec aussi, un grand nombre d'élèves travaillent après les cours. Ils travaillent dans un magasin, dans un supermarché ou dans un restaurant fast-food (de restauration rapide). Ils gagnent de l'argent pour acheter des CD, des cassettes, un blue jean. En France, non. Très peu de collégiens ou de lycéens travaillent après les cours. C'est assez rare. Certains travaillent, mais seulement pendant les vacances. Mais… ils sont à l'école jusqu'à cinq heures de l'après-midi!

[1] gagner un peu d'argent *to earn a little money*
[2] centre commercial *mall*
[3] souterrain *underground*

Après la lecture

Au Québec Exprimez d'une autre façon.
(Express another way.)

1. Antoine est *du Canada.*
2. Montréal est la *seconde* ville francophone du monde.
3. Antoine travaille après *l'école.*
4. C'est un *immense* centre commercial.
5. Aux États-Unis, *beaucoup* d'élèves travaillent.
6. *Pas beaucoup* de lycéens français travaillent après les cours.

Answers to Après la lecture

1. canadien
2. deuxième
3. les cours
4. très grand
5. un grand nombre
6. Très peu

Un groupe de rap–Manau

Quand les collégiens ou les lycéens français rentrent à la maison l'après-midi, qu'est-ce qu'ils écoutent? Eh bien, ils écoutent la même musique que les élèves américains. Ils écoutent du rap, par exemple.

Manau, c'est un groupe de rap très populaire chez les collégiens français. Et Manau n'est pas un groupe de rap ordinaire. C'est un groupe de rap «celtique». Les instruments de musique sont la cornemuse[1], le violon, la harpe… Les chansons[2] de Manau parlent de mythes et légendes celtes avec des druides et des dolmens.

Les deux garçons du groupe, Cédric et Martial, sont copains. Le musicien, c'est Cédric: Cédric est le compositeur de la musique. Et le texte, c'est Martial: Martial est l'auteur des paroles[3].

Les deux garçons sont de la région parisienne. Mais les mères[4] de Cédric et Martial sont de Bretagne. Comme beaucoup de Bretons, elles sont d'origine celtique. Le nom du premier[5] album de Manau? *Panique Celtique!*

[1] cornemuse *bagpipes*
[2] chansons *songs*
[3] paroles *words*
[4] mères *mothers*
[5] premier *first*

FRENCH Online
For more information about music in the Francophone world, go to the Glencoe French Web site: french.glencoe.com

Un dolmen près de Carnac, Bretagne

Après la lecture

Un groupe de rap Vrai ou faux? *(True or false?)*

1. Les collégiens français n'écoutent pas la même musique que les élèves américains.
2. Manau, c'est un groupe de rap ordinaire.
3. Les chansons de Manau parlent de l'école.
4. Cédric et Martial sont de Bretagne.

Answers to Après la lecture

1. F
2. F
3. F
4. F

FRENCH Online

Encourage students to take advantage of this opportunity to learn more about music in the French-speaking world. Perhaps you can do this in class or in a lab if students do not have Internet access at home.

Lecture supplémentaire 2

Presentation

Step 1 Have students read the selection to themselves.

Step 2 Now have students do the **Après la lecture** activity on page 101. **Expansion:** Have students change the false statements to make them true.

Step 3 You may wish to ask students to bring to class any music they may have from the French-speaking world.

History Connection

Brittany did not become part of France until 1532. Although few Bretons desire secession, many still feel a sense of Breton nationalism. The Breton language is related to Welsh and, until recently, was dying out except among some older people. However, today the language is being revived and there are schools that teach in Breton as well as Breton language publishing houses. This has led to a rebirth of Breton folklore, music, and art.

Learning from Photos

(page 101) The menhirs and dolmens were left by primitive tribes, who lived in the area some four thousand years before Christ. Their use still remains a mystery, but it is believed they had a religious significance. Menhirs are stones that stand upright. The word menhirs come from the Breton **men** meaning *stone* and **hir** meaning *long*. The dolmens such as we see here in the photo have the form of a table. Dolmen also comes from Breton **men** *(stone)* and **dol** *(table)*.

CONNEXIONS

National Standards

Connections

This reading establishes a connection with computer science. Since most students today are very familiar with computers they should find it very easy to use computer terms in French and thus increase their French vocabulary.

Comparisons

This introduction to computer vocabulary in French is very useful for reading advertisements or instructions concerning the use of computers.

Attention!

The readings in the **Connexions** section are optional. They focus on some of the major disciplines taught in schools and universities. The vocabulary is useful for discussing such topics as history, literature, art, economics, business, science, etc. You may choose any of the following ways to do the readings in the **Connexions** sections.

Independent reading Have students read the selections and do the post-reading activities as homework, which you collect. This option is least intrusive on class time and requires a minimum of teacher involvement.

Homework with in-class follow-up Assign the readings and post-reading activities as homework. Review and discuss the material in class the next day.

Intensive in-class activity This option includes a pre-reading vocabulary presentation, in-class reading and discussion, assignment of the activities for homework, and a discussion of the assignment in class the following day.

CONNEXIONS

La technologie

L'ordinateur

Some years ago computers began to revolutionize the way people conduct their lives. They have changed the way we view the world. Computers have a place in our homes, in our schools, and in the world of business.

If you are interested in computers, you may want to familiarize yourself with some basic computer vocabulary in French. Then read the information about computers on the next page.

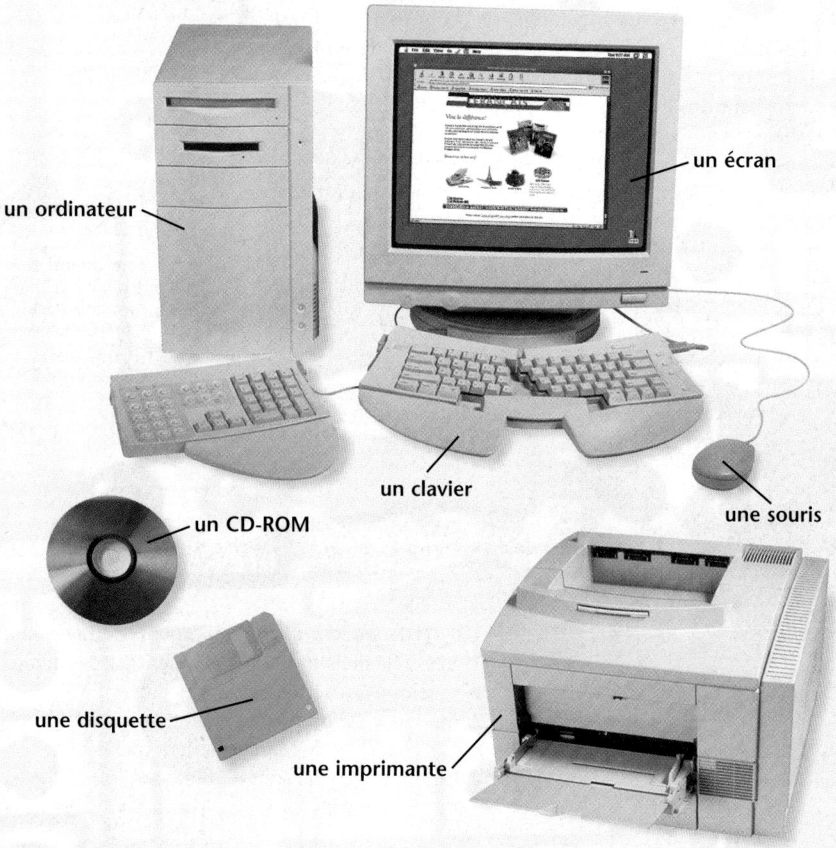

CAREER CONNECTION

Explain to students that a knowledge of computer vocabulary in French could be an asset in careers in business and finance. Have them do some research to find out what U.S. companies have offices in French-speaking countries.

L'ordinateur travaille!

Le hardware et le software

Un ordinateur exécute très rapidement les instructions d'un programme. Le hardware, c'est la partie électronique de l'ordinateur. Le software, c'est la partie programmation de l'ordinateur. Les logiciels sont des programmes. Un programme ou un logiciel est un groupe d'instructions. Un document est un fichier. L'ordinateur stocke des données[1]. On sauvegarde les documents importants sur une disquette. On utilise un modem pour connecter l'ordinateur à une ligne téléphonique. Grâce au[2] modem, un ordinateur est en liaison avec Internet et échange des informations dans le monde[3] entier.

Internet

Grâce à Internet, le monde entier est accessible. Le nombre des sites est infini. On télécharge[4] des informations sur l'histoire, l'économie, l'art, la musique et toutes sortes de domaines intéressants. Quand on navigue sur Internet, on est capable d'envoyer[5] un e-mail, parler avec des amis sur d'autres continents… Il n'y a pas de limites!

[1] données *data*
[2] Grâce au *Thanks to*
[3] monde *world*
[4] télécharge *download*
[5] envoyer *to send*

Après la lecture

A En français, s'il vous plaît.
Trouvez les mots suivants dans la lecture.
(Find the following words in the reading.)

1. hardware
2. software
3. program
4. file
5. modem
6. surf the net
7. e-mail
8. telephone line
9. site
10. save

B Une page Web Look at the monitor on page 102. If you have access to the Internet either at home or at school, go to french.glencoe.com

Answers to Après la lecture

A
1. le hardware
2. le software
3. un programme (un logiciel)
4. un fichier
5. le modem
6. naviguer sur Internet
7. un e-mail
8. une ligne téléphonique
9. un site
10. sauvegarder

Connexions

Presentation

La technologie
L'ordinateur

Step 1 Most students will be familiar with these computer terms in English. Model the terms in French and have students repeat after you.

Step 2 If there is a computer in your classroom, have students name the equipment in French.

Step 3 You may wish to have students find and repeat all the cognates in the reading selection. Explain to them that there are two important strategies to use when reading unfamiliar material—they should learn to recognize cognates and derive meaning from context.

Step 4 Ask students to scan the reading on page 103 and make a list of words they do not know the meaning of.

Step 5 As a whole-class activity, go over the words students have listed, asking other students to guess their meaning based on the context.

Après la lecture

A This is a skimming activity designed to provide practice in reading for specific information. Do this activity orally.

B Tell students that the monitor on page 102 shows the Glencoe World Language Home page. At the Web site there are Internet activities designed to accompany and reinforce the material presented in each chapter of the textbook. (See student page 109 for a description of the Internet activity for this chapter and page 80 of this Teacher Wraparound Edition for more information about the content of the **Glencoe World Language Web site.**

Use what you have learned

Bellringer Review

Use BRR Transparency 3.8 or write the following on the board.
Answer the questions in complete sentences.

1. **Tu arrives à l'école à quelle heure?**
2. **Qui parle beaucoup en classe?**
3. **Tu quittes l'école le matin ou l'après-midi?**
4. **Tu habites où?**
5. **Tu aimes passer des examens?**

Recycling

These activities allow students to use the vocabulary and structure from this chapter in completely open-ended, real-life situations.

Presentation

Encourage students to say as much as possible when they do these activities. Tell them not to be afraid to make mistakes, since the goal of these activities is real-life communication. If someone in the group makes an error, allow the others to politely correct him or her. Let students choose the activities they would like to do.

You may wish to divide students into pairs or groups. Encourage students to elaborate on the basic theme and to be creative. They may use props, pictures, or posters if they wish.

C'est à vous

Use what you have learned

PARLER

1

Dans une papeterie

✔ Identify and shop for school supplies

With a classmate, take turns playing the parts of a student and a salesperson in a stationery store. Here are a few exchanges you may want to use.

—Où sont les _____, s'il vous plaît?
—Là-bas.
—Merci.
—_____, c'est combien?
—_____ euros.
—On paie à la caisse?
—Non, ici.

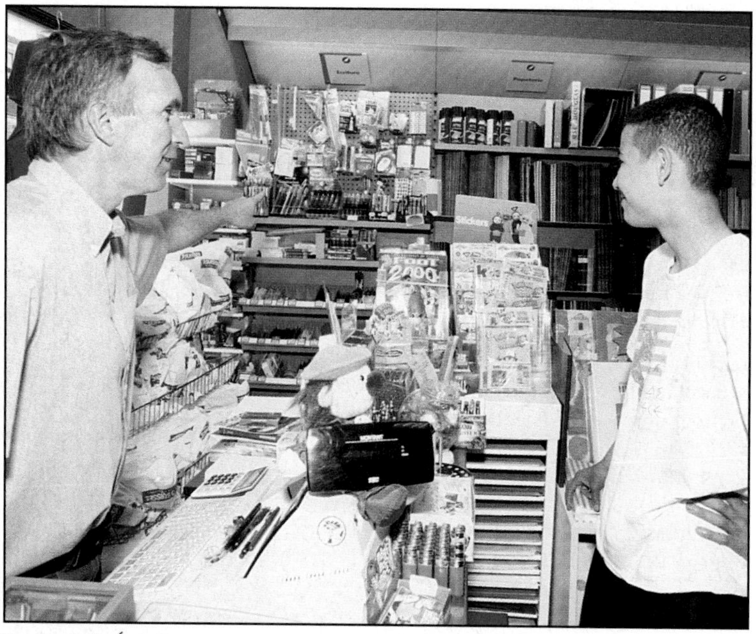

Une papeterie, Évry, France

Answers to C'est à vous

1 *Answers will vary but may include:*

—Où sont les calculatrices, s'il vous plaît?
—Là-bas.
—Merci.
—La calculatrice, c'est combien?
—Dix-huit euros.
—On paie à la caisse?
—Oui.

Learning from Photos

(page 104) This stationery store is in Évry. Évry is **une ville nouvelle** in the **banlieue parisienne.** Students will learn about the **villes nouvelles** in Chapter 12. Have students identify everything they can in the photo of the **papeterie.**

PARLER

2 Au café

✔ Talk about school life in the United States

You're seated at a café in Provins. You're chatting with a French student (your partner). He or she has some questions about school life in the United States. Have a conversation. Be sure to answer his or her questions.

Un café, Provins, France

ÉCRIRE

3 Une journée typique

✔ Write about a typical school day

You can now go back to the e-mail you sent your new friend on page 75 and add more details about what a typical school day is like in the United States.

Writing Strategy

Preparing for an interview An interview is one way to gather information for a story or a report. A good interviewer should think about what he or she hopes to learn from the interview and prepare the questions ahead of time. The interview questions should be open-ended. Open-ended questions cannot be answered by "yes" or "no." They give the person being interviewed more opportunity to "open up" and speak freely.

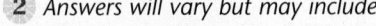

PARLER ÉCRIRE

4 Interview avec Charles Bauchart

Your first assignment for the school newspaper is to write an article about a new exchange student, Charles Bauchart, from Fort-de-France in Martinique. To prepare for your interview with him, write down as many questions as you can. Ask him about himself, his school, and his friends in Martinique. After you have prepared your questions, conduct the interview with a partner who plays the role of Charles. Write down your partner's answers. Then organize your notes and write your article.

Answers to C'est à vous

2 *Answers will vary but may include:*

—Tu arrives à l'école à quelle heure le matin?
—J'arrive à l'école à huit heures moins le quart. Et toi, tu arrives à l'école à quelle heure?
—J'arrive à huit heures. Et tu quittes l'école à quelle heure?
—Je quitte l'école à trois heures et demie.
—Ce n'est pas vrai! Je quitte l'école à cinq heures de l'après-midi!

3 *Answers will vary but may include:*

L'école est vraiment super! Les amis sont très intéressants et dynamiques. J'arrive à l'école à sept heures et demie, et je déjeune à la cantine à midi. Le prof de chimie est très, très strict! Mais la prof de français n'est pas trop stricte. Elle est assez sympa. Je suis mauvais(e) en chimie mais forte(e) en français. Mardi je passe un examen de français. Je déteste les examens!

C'est à vous

Writing Strategy

Preparing for an interview Have students read the Writing Strategy on page 105. Now give the students the following pair of questions and have them decide which is open ended.

Tu étudies l'anglais?
Qu'est-ce que tu étudies?

National Standards

Communities

It is a rather recent phenomenon to see French directions on products in the United States. Have students begin to notice and seek out French descriptions or directions on products. They will be able to find quite a few in stationery, clothing, and home appliance stores. Have students bring in some examples.

History Connection

Have students look at the photo of the café in Provins on page 105. You may wish to explain that during the Middle Ages, the little town of Provins near Paris was the third most important city in France after Paris and Rouen. It originated as a Roman campsite, and under the Counts of Champagne it became the economic capital of the province. It has been famous for growing roses since the days of the Crusades.

Resource Manager

Communication Transparencies
Quizzes
Test Booklet
ExamView Pro®
Situation Cards
Performance Assessment
Marathon mental Videoquiz

Assessment

This is a pre-test for students to take before you administer the chapter test. Answer sheets for students to do these pages are provided in your transparency binder. Note that each section is cross-referenced so students can easily find the material they have to review in case they made errors. You may wish to collect these assessments and correct them yourself, or you may prefer to have the students correct themselves in class. You can go over the answers orally or project them on the overhead, using your Assessment Answers transparencies.

Glencoe Technology

MINDJOGGER

You may wish to help your students prepare for the chapter test by playing the MindJogger game show. Teams will compete against each other to review chapter vocabulary and structure and sharpen listening comprehension skills.

Assessment

Vocabulaire

To review ***Mots 1****, turn to pages 82–83.*

1 Choisissez. *(Choose.)*

1. Sandrine ____ la maison à sept heures et demie.
   a. quitte **b.** arrive **c.** habite
2. Les élèves passent ____ à l'école.
   a. la cantine **b.** la prof **c.** la journée
3. Leïla pose une ____.
   a. rue **b.** question **c.** maison
4. Vincent ____ des cassettes.
   a. écoute **b.** quitte **c.** passe
5. Le prof ____ et les élèves écoutent bien.
   a. travaille **b.** regarde **c.** parle

To review ***Mots 2****, turn to pages 86–87.*

2 Identifiez. *(Identify.)*

6. 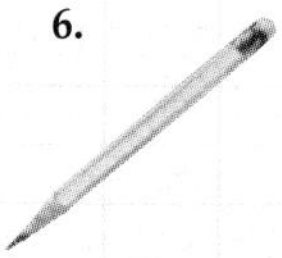
7. 
8. 
9. 
10. 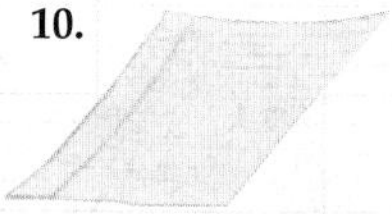

Structure

To review ***-er*** *verbs in the present tense, turn to page 90.*

3 Complétez. *(Complete.)*

11. Les élèves ____ à l'école le matin. (arriver)
12. Nous ____ entre les cours. (parler)
13. Je ____ à la cantine avec les copains. (déjeuner)
14. Luc ____ la télé après les cours. (regarder)
15. Tu ____ beaucoup à la maison? (travailler)
16. On ____ français en France. (parler)

Answers to Assessment

1

1. a
2. c
3. b
4. a
5. c

2

6. un crayon
7. un stylo-bille
8. un livre
9. une calculatrice
10. une feuille de papier

3

11. arrivent
12. parlons
13. déjeune
14. regarde
15. travailles
16. parle

4 Mettez à la forme négative. *(Make each sentence negative.)*

17. Sandrine achète un crayon à la papeterie.
18. Elle regarde une calculatrice.
19. Ils achètent des livres.
20. Les élèves passent un examen aujourd'hui.

To review indefinite articles in the negative, turn to page 94.

5 Choisissez. *(Choose.)*

21. On aime ____ la télé.
    a. regardent b. regarder c. regarde
22. Je déteste ____.
    a. travailler b. travaille c. travaillons

To review the use of verbs with infinitives, turn to page 95.

Culture

6 Vrai ou faux? *(True or false?)*

Une rue du Quartier latin, Paris

To review this cultural information, turn to pages 98–99.

23. La Sorbonne est une université célèbre à Paris.
24. La Sorbonne est dans le Quartier latin.
25. En France, les élèves quittent le lycée à trois heures de l'après-midi.

Learning from Photos

(page 107) This photo was taken on the corner of Saint-Séverin and rue de la Harpe in the Quartier latin. The surrounding area has several pedestrian-only streets that have inexpensive restaurants, many of which are Greek, Tunisian, or Italian, and more recently some Thai and Vietnamese restaurants.

Answers to Assessment

4

17. Sandrine n'achète pas de crayon à la papeterie.
18. Elle ne regarde pas de calculatrice.
19. Ils n'achètent pas de livres.
20. Les élèves ne passent pas d'examen aujourd'hui.

5

21. b
22. a

6

23. V
24. V
25. F

Vocabulary Review

The words and phrases in the **Vocabulaire** have been taught for productive use in this chapter. They are summarized here as a resource for both student and teacher. This list also serves as a convenient resource for the **C'est à vous** activities on pages 106-107. There are approximately twelve cognates in this vocabulary list. Have students find them.

Attention!

You will notice that the vocabulary list here is not translated. This has been done intentionally, since we feel that by the time students have finished the material in the chapter they should be familiar with the meanings of all the words. If there are several words they still do not know, we recommend that they refer back to the **Mots 1** and **2** sections in the chapter or go to the dictionaries at the back of this book to find the meanings. However, if you prefer that your students have the English translations, please refer to Vocabulary Transparency 3.1, where you will find all the words listed with their translations.

Vocabulaire

Getting to school

une maison	habiter
une rue	arriver
quitter	

Discussing classroom activities

passer la journée	étudier
parler	lever la main
écouter	poser une question
regarder	passer un examen

Discussing recess and lunch activities

la récré(ation)	jouer
la cour	rigoler
la cantine	déjeuner

How well do you know your vocabulary?

- Identify the words and expressions that describe what you do at school and after school. Make two lists.
- Use as many words as you can from one of your lists to write a story about either your school activities or what you do after school.

Discussing afterschool activities

rentrer à la maison	parler au téléphone
écouter la radio	travailler

Identifying school supplies

Qu'est-ce que c'est?	un stylo-bille	une calculatrice
des fournitures *(f. pl.)* scolaires	un feutre	une feuille de papier
	une gomme	un sac à dos
un cahier	une règle	une cassette
un bloc-notes	un livre	une vidéo
un crayon	un classeur	un CD

Shopping for school supplies

un magasin	acheter	coûter
une papeterie	payer	C'est combien?
la caisse	demander	Ça coûte combien?

Other useful words and expressions

aimer	pendant	le matin	combien de (d')
détester	entre	l'après-midi	beaucoup de (d')
après	chez	À quelle heure?	

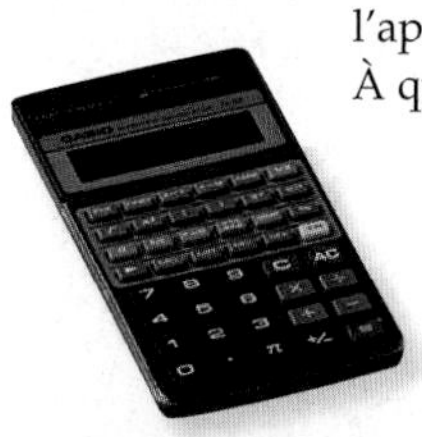

Reaching All Students

For the Younger Students

- Students love to talk about their teachers. If you are willing, have them use adjectives they have learned that they feel describe you and your class.
- Have students dramatize or pantomime the following words: **arriver, quitter, parler, déjeuner, lever la main, étudier, écouter, passer un examen, poser une question, parler au téléphone, écouter la radio, payer, demander.**

Technotour
BON VOYAGE!

VIDÉO • Épisode 3

Avant de visionner

In this video episode, Amadou and Christine shop for school supplies before Christine's dance class at the École de Danse in the Marais.

Amadou et Christine dans la rue après les cours

Amadou et Christine dans la papeterie

FRENCH ONLINE

À découvrir

Learn more about the Marais area of Paris online.

La place des Vosges est dans le quartier du Marais, tout près de l'école de danse de Christine.

FRENCH Online

In the Chapter 3 Internet activity, you will have a chance to learn more about schools in the Francophone world. To begin your virtual adventure, go to the Glencoe French Web site:
french.glencoe.com

Technotour

Overview

This page previews two key multimedia components of the **Glencoe French** series. Each reinforces the material taught in the chapter in a unique manner.

VIDÉO

The Video Program allows students to see how the chapter vocabulary and structures are used by native speakers. For maximum reinforcement, show the video episode as a final activity for Chapter 3.

The two photos on the left show highlights from the Chapter 3 video episode. Discuss the photos with your students before viewing the episode. See the Video Activities Booklet for detailed suggestions for using this resource.

FRENCH Online

- **The À découvrir** photo shows **la place des Vosges** in the **Marais** section of Paris. Students can go online to the Glencoe French Web site for additional information about this interesting area of Paris.
- Teacher Information and Student Worksheets for this activity can be accessed at the Web site.

Video Synopsis

In this episode, we are introduced to two more main characters of the video. Amadou Kouyate is from Mali. He is seventeen years old and his specialty is music. Christine Deloir is from Martinique. She is sixteen years old and, as you will see in this video episode, her specialty is dance.

Amadou and Christine meet after school and buy some school supplies. Christine leaves to go to her African dance class at the **Centre de danse du Marais,** also called the **Café de la Gare.** She does her video web report on the various dance classes at the dance studio.

Planning for Chapter 4

SCOPE AND SEQUENCE, PAGES 110–141

Topics

- Family
- Home and neighborhood
- Age

Functions

- How to talk about your family
- How to describe your home and neighborhood
- How to express age
- How to express what belongs to you and others

National Standards

- Communication Standard 1.1 pages 114, 115, 118, 119, 120, 121, 122, 124, 125, 127, 129, 136
- Communication Standard 1.2 pages 114, 115, 118, 119, 120, 121, 122, 124, 125, 127, 128, 129, 131, 132, 133, 135, 136
- Communication Standard 1.3 pages 114, 115, 118, 119, 120, 121, 124, 125, 137
- Cultures Standard 2.1 pages 130–131, 132, 133, 136
- Cultures Standard 2.2 pages 130–131, 132
- Connections Standard 3.1 pages 134–135
- Comparisons Standard 4.2 page 133
- Communities Standard 5.1 page 137

Culture

- Housing in France
- The Duval family's apartment in Paris
- Housing in other French-speaking countries
- Family names
- **Reflets de la France**

Structure

- The verb **avoir** in the present tense
- Possessive adjectives
- Other adjectives

PACING AND PRIORITIES

The chapter content is color coded below to assist you in planning.
■ required ■ recommended ■ optional

Vocabulaire *(required)* *Days 1–4*

- ■ Mots 1
  - La famille Morel
  - L´anniversaire de Marie
- ■ Mots 2
  - La maison
  - L'immeuble
  - Les pièces de la maison

Structure *(required)* *Days 5–7*

- ■ **Avoir** au présent
- ■ Les adjectifs possessifs
- ■ D´autres adjectifs

Conversation *(required)*

- ■ Ma nouvelle adresse

Prononciation *(recommended)*

- ■ Le son **/ã/**

Lectures culturelles

- ■ Où habitent les Français? *(recommended)*
- ■ Le logement dans d'autres pays *(optional)*
- ■ Les noms de famille *(optional)*

Connexions *(optional)*

- ■ Art et histoire

■ **C'est à vous** *(recommended)*

■ **Assessment** *(recommended)*

■ **Technotour** *(optional)*

RESOURCE GUIDE

Section	Pages	Section Resources
Vocabulaire *Mots 1*		
La famille Morel L'anniversaire de Marie	112 113–115	Vocabulary Transparencies 4.2–4.3 Audiocassette 3B/CD 3 Audio Activities Booklet TE, pages 49–50 Workbook, pages 29–30 Quiz 1, page 17 ExamView Pro®
Vocabulaire *Mots 2*		
La maison L'immeuble Les pièces de la maison	116 116 117–119	Vocabulary Transparencies 4.4–4.5 Audiocassette 3B/CD 3 Audio Activities Booklet TE, pages 51–52 Workbook, pages 31–32 Quiz 2, page 18 ExamView Pro®
Structure		
Avoir au présent Les adjectifs possessifs D'autres adjectifs	120–122 123–125 126–127	Audiocassette 3B/CD 3 Audio Activities Booklet TE, pages 53–55 Workbook, pages 33–35 Quizzes 3–5, pages 19–21 ExamView Pro®
Conversation		
Ma nouvelle adresse	128	Audiocassette 3B/CD 3 Audio Activities Booklet TE, page 56 CD-ROM
Prononciation		
Le son **/ã/**	129	Pronunciation Transparency P 4 Audiocassette 3B/CD 3 Audio Activities Booklet TE, pages 57–58
Lectures culturelles		
Où habitent les Français? Le logement dans d´autres pays Les noms de famille	130–131 132 133	Audiocassette 3B/CD 3 Audio Activities Booklet TE, pages 58–59 Test Booklet, Chapter 4
Connexions		
Art et histoire	134–135	Test Booklet, Chapter 4
C'est à vous		
	136–137	**Bon voyage!** Video, Episode 4 Video Activities Booklet, Chapter 4 French Online Activities french.glencoe.com
Assessment		
	138–139	Communication Transparency C 4 Quizzes 1–5, pages 17–21 Test Booklet, Chapter 4 ExamView Pro® Situation Cards, Chapter 4 Performance Assessment, pages 1–8 **Marathon mental** Videoquiz

Using Your Resources for Chapter 4

Transparencies

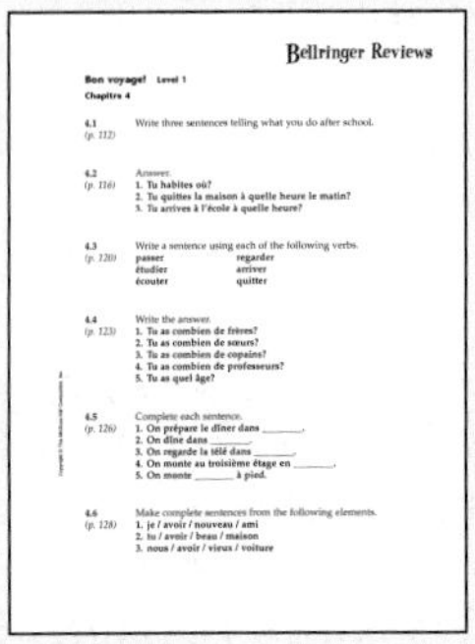
Bellringer 4.1–4.7

Vocabulary 4.1–4.5

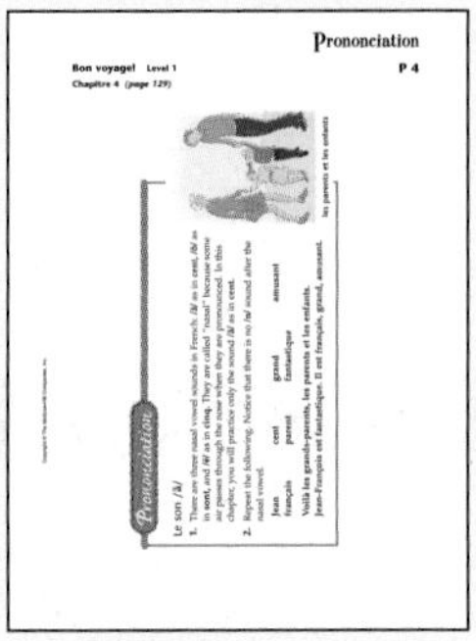
Pronunciation P 4

Communication C 4

Writing Activities Workbook

Vocabulary,
pages 29–32

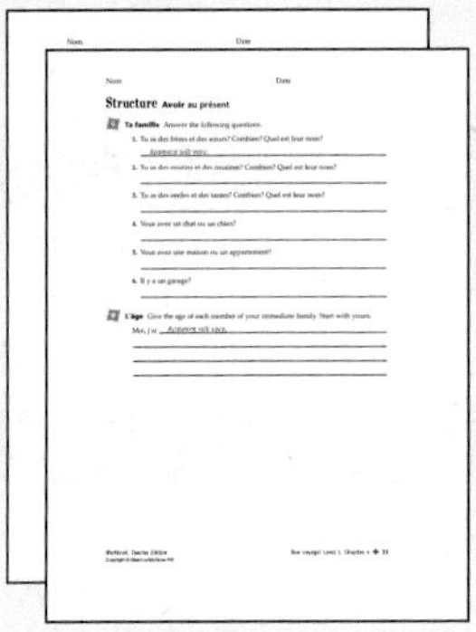
Structure,
pages 33–35

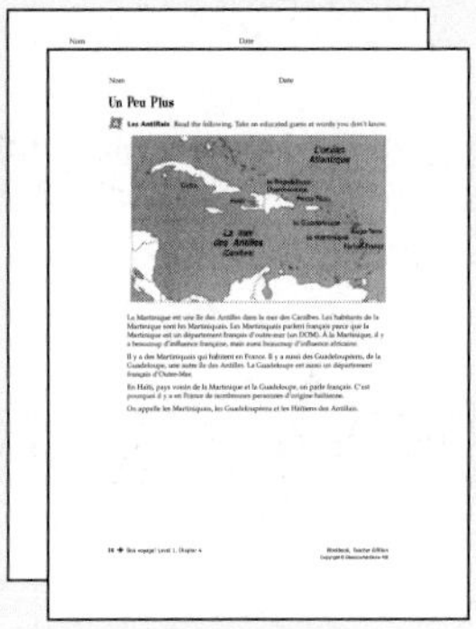
Enrichment,
pages 36–38

Audio Program and Audio Activities Booklet

Vocabulary,
pages 49–52

Structure,
pages 53–55

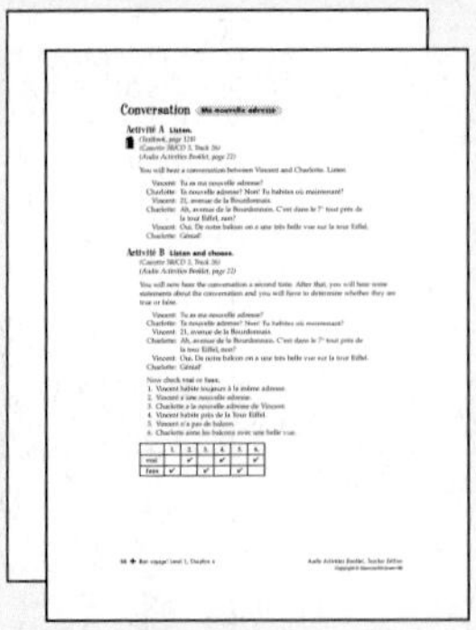
Conversation,
Pronunciation,
pages 56–58

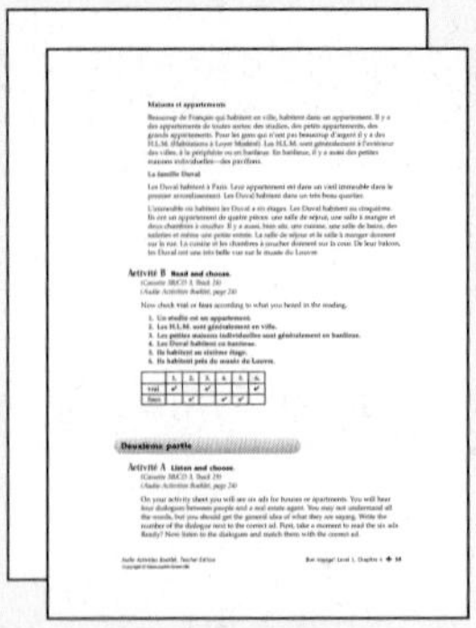
Cultural Reading,
pages 58–59

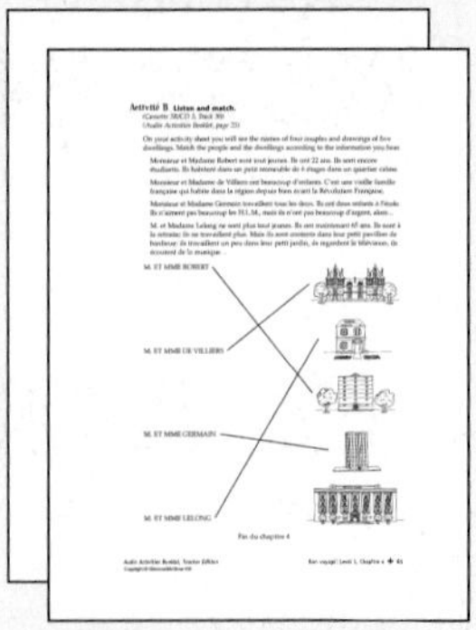
Additional Practice,
pages 59–61

Assessment

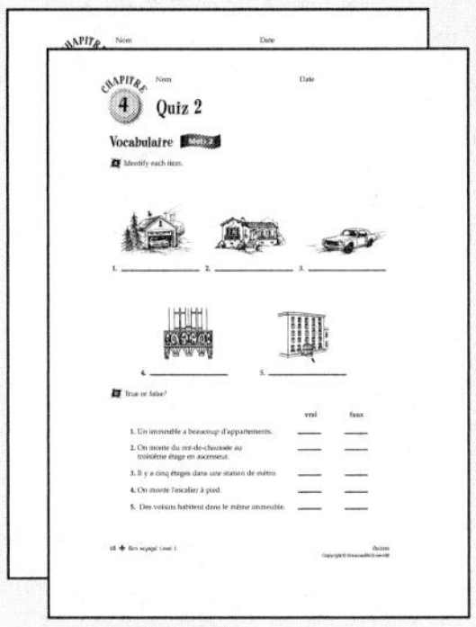

Vocabulary and Structure Quizzes, pages 17–21

Chapter Tests, Chapter 4

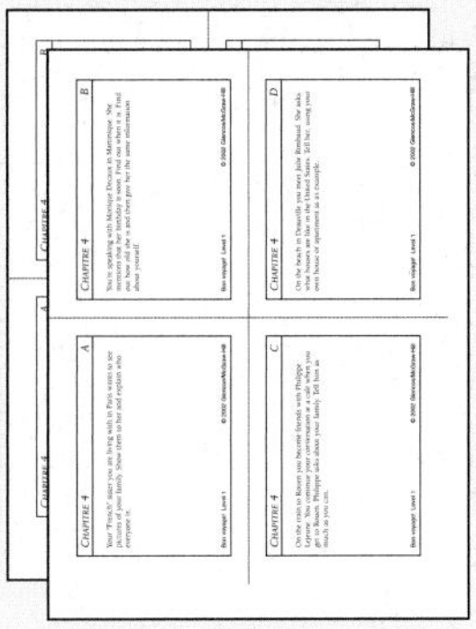

Situation Cards, Chapter 4

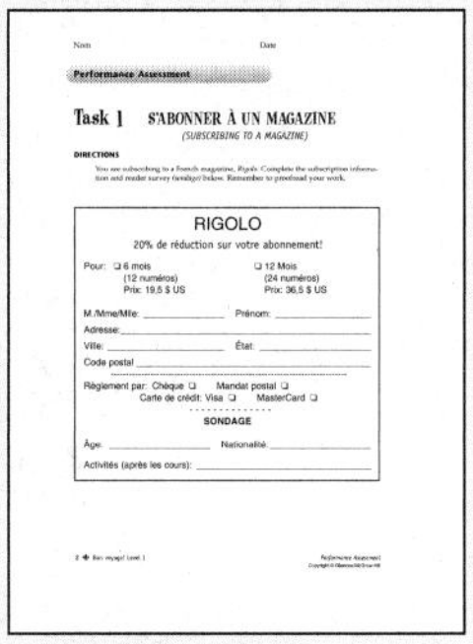

Performance Assessment, pages 1–8

Timesaving Teacher Tools

Interactive Teacher Edition

Imagine having your Teacher's Edition and all resources on a CD-ROM. Click on a resource and it appears on your screen, ready to be printed, sorted, or planned.

Interactive Lesson Planner

The Interactive Lesson Planner CD-ROM helps you organize your lesson plans for a week, month, semester, or year. Look at this planning tool for easy access to your Chapter 4 resources.

ExamView Pro®

Test Bank software for Macintosh and Windows makes creating, editing, customizing, and printing tests quick and easy.

Technology Resources

FRENCH Online

In the Chapter 4 Internet activity, you will have a chance to learn more about renting or buying a house or an apartment in a French-speaking country. Visit french.glencoe.com.

On the Interactive Conversation CD-ROM, students can listen to and take part in a recorded version of the conversation in Chapter 4.

NATIONAL GEOGRAPHIC SOCIETY

See the National Geographic Teacher's Corner on pages 150–151, 256–257, 396–397, 500–501 for reference to additional technology resources.

Bon voyage! Video and Video Activities Booklet.

Help your students prepare for the chapter test by playing the **Marathon mental** Videoquiz game show. Teams will compete against each other to review chapter vocabulary and structure and sharpen listening comprehension skills.

CHAPITRE 4

Preview

In this chapter, students will learn to talk about their family and home. To do this, they will learn vocabulary associated with family members and housing. They will learn to use the verb **avoir** to describe what kind of family and house they have. They will also learn possessive adjectives and some irregular adjectives.

National Standards

Communication

In Chapter 4, students will communicate in spoken and written French on the following topics:
- Describing their family
- Describing some family activities
- Describing their house

Students will obtain and provide information about these topics and engage in conversations concerning their own family and families throughout the French-speaking world.

CHAPITRE 4

La famille et la maison

Objectifs

In this chapter you will learn to:

- ✔ *talk about your family*
- ✔ *describe your home and neighborhood*
- ✔ *tell your age and find out someone else's age*
- ✔ *tell what belongs to you and others*
- ✔ *describe more people and things*
- ✔ *talk about families and homes in French-speaking countries*

Pierre Auguste Renoir *Madame Charpentier et ses enfants*

110

Correlations to Continuum (*see page* i *for code*)

Stage I
Engage in conversations. p. 122 (**16**, **17**, *p*); Understand some ideas and familiar details. p. 121 (**13**, **14**, *p*); Provide information. p. 115 (**5**, *p*); Listen during social interactions and listen to audio or video texts. p. 141 (*p*); Use authentic materials such as newspaper ads and fine art. p. 119 (**11**, *i*), pp. 134–135 (*p*); Write lists and short letters. p. 129 (**B**, *i*), p. 137 (**3**, *p*); Use short sentences, learned words and phrases when speaking. p. 115 (**6**, *p*); Understand ideas and familiar details when listening. p. 128 (*p*); Understand texts enhanced by visual clues. pp. 130–131 (*p*); Understand and convey information about houses. p. 119 (**10**, *i*); Understand and convey information on monuments, cultural and historical figures, places, and fine art. pp. 134–135 (*p*); Communicate effectively with some hesitation and errors, which do not hinder comprehension. p. 125 (**24**); Understand most important information. p. 137 (**5**)

Stage II
Understand and express important ideas and some detail. p. 136 (**2**, *p*); Describe and compare. p. 127 (**26**, *p*); Write letters. p. 137 (**4**, *p*); Use and understand learned expressions, sentences, strings of sentences, and questions when speaking. p. 129 (**A**, *p*); Create simple paragraphs. p. 118 (**8**, *i*), p. 137 (**5**, *p*); Understand important ideas and some details in highly contextualized authentic texts when reading. p. 136 (**1**, *i*); Demonstrate increasing fluency and control of vocabulary. p. 125 (**24**)

Stage III
Use strings of related sentences when speaking. p. 125 (**24**, *p*); Understand and convey information about history and art. pp. 134–135 (*i*)

Stage IV
Read short literary texts. pp. 504–506 (*i*), pp. 506–509 (*p*)

CHAPITRE 4

Spotlight on Culture

Photograph The family in this photo is getting ready for a family picnic while spending some time in the Carcassonne area.

Painting This painting is ***Madame Charpentier et ses enfants*** by Pierre Auguste Renoir. (For more information on Renoir, please see pages 80–81.) Renoir painted ***Madame Charpentier et ses enfants*** in 1878 when he was still very much influenced by the Impressionists, before his trip to Italy in 1881.

Learning From Photos

(pages 110–111) You may wish to ask the following questions about this photo after students have finished this chapter.

Il y a combien de personnes dans la famille Lefèbre?
Ils ont une belle maison ou un appartement?
Ils habitent dans une maison privée?
Ils quittent la maison ou ils rentrent à la maison?
Les Lefèbre ont une voiture?
Leur voiture est dans le garage?
M. et Mme Lefèbre ont combien d'enfants?
Leur fils a quel âge?
Et leurs filles, elles ont quel âge?
Ils sont comment, leurs enfants?

Chapter Projects

Deux personnes célèbres Have students think of at least two famous people. Students will pretend they are working for a magazine such as ***Paris Match*** or ***Pointes de vue*** and describe the people, explain where they live, and tell something about their homes. Have them present the information as if it were an article for the magazine. Encourage them to include some photographs in the article.

Des cartes Have students find out if the local card store, stationery store, or supermarket has greeting cards in French. If they are not too expensive, have each student buy one and prepare a bulletin board of French language greeting cards. Or have them draw or create their own greeting cards on a computer.

Ma maison Have students make a floor plan of their house or apartment and give a "tour" to other classmates.

Vocabulaire
Mots 1

1 Preparation

Resource Manager

Vocabulary Transparencies 4.2–4.3
Audio Activities Booklet TE, pages 49–50
Audiocassette 3B/CD 3
Workbook, pages 29–30
Quiz 1, page 17
ExamView Pro®

Bellringer Review

Use Transparency 4.1 or write the following on the board.
Write three sentences telling what you do after school.

2 Presentation

Step 1 Have students close their books. Present the vocabulary using Vocabulary Transparencies 4.2–4.3. Have students repeat the names and relationships of the Morel family after you or the recording on Audiocassette 3B/CD 3. Be sure that they pronounce the words as carefully as possible.

Step 2 Ask the following questions as students look at the transparencies: **C'est la famille Morel? C'est la famille Morel ou la famille Martin? C'est quelle famille? Les Morel ont deux enfants? Ils ont une fille? Ils ont un fils? Ils ont deux enfants ou trois enfants? Ils ont combien d'enfants? Ils ont un chien? Ils ont un chat?**

Step 3 After the initial presentation with the overhead transparencies, have students open their books and look at the new vocabulary words as they repeat either after you or Audiocassette 3B/CD 3 for additional reinforcement.

Vocabulaire
Mots 1

le chien

Voici la famille Morel.
M. et Mme Morel ont deux enfants—un fils et une fille.
Les Morel ont un chien.
Leur chien est adorable.
La famille Morel n'a pas de chat.

le chat

Reaching All Students

Total Physical Response Draw a family tree on the board, writing in the name of each family member.

(Student 1), **levez-vous, s'il vous plaît.**
Allez au tableau.
Regardez l'arbre généalogique.
Prenez la règle.
Montrez-moi Luc.
Montrez-moi le père de Luc.
Montrez-moi la tante de Luc.
Montrez-moi sa sœur.
Et son oncle.
Montrez-moi le cousin de Luc.
Montrez-moi ses grands-parents.
Retournez à votre place, s'il vous plaît.

L'anniversaire de Marie 🎧

> Tu as quel âge, Marie?

une bougie un gâteau un cadeau

> Moi? J'ai quinze ans. Aujourd'hui, c'est mon anniversaire.

C'est quand, l'anniversaire de Marie?
C'est le deux août.
Tout le monde a un cadeau pour Marie.
Il y a beaucoup de cadeaux.

Marie donne une fête pour son anniversaire.
Elle invite ses amis et ses cousins.

Note 🎧

In French, some of the words for family members are cognates. Can you guess who these family members are?

une tante	un oncle
une cousine	un cousin
une nièce	un neveu

Here are some words for other family members.

une belle-mère *stepmother*
un beau-père *stepfather*
une demi-sœur *half sister*
un demi-frère *half brother*

About the French Language

- In French, **les** is used with the family name to refer to the entire family. No **s** is added to the last name as is done in English. You use the **les** before the family name: **les Dupont, les Lefèbre, les Senghor**.

- Family relationships: In French, *half brother* and *half sister* are **demi-frère** and **demi-sœur**. (Note that there is no **e** on **demi** in **demi-sœur**.) Many people would say **mon frère** or **ma sœur** for *stepbrother* or *stepsister* and let it go at that. As for stepparents, **ma belle-mère** and **mon beau-père** are sometimes heard, but these terms are more commonly used for *mother-in-law* and *father-in-law*. (**Ma belle-mère** or **mon beau-père** might be used for a stepparent if the natural parent were still alive, but if the latter were deceased, the stepparent might be referred to as **ma mère** or **mon père**, depending on the personal situation.) To be precise about a step relationship, a French person would say: **le mari de ma mère, la femme de mon père, le fils (la fille) du mari de ma mère, le fils (la fille) de la femme de mon père.** ⚜

Vocabulary Expansion

You may wish to give students the following additional words:
un(e) jeune chien(ne), un chiot *a puppy*
un(e) petit(e) chat(te), un chaton *a kitten*
un jumeau, une jumelle *a twin*
l'aîné(e) *the oldest*
le cadet, la cadette *the youngest*
une carte d'anniversaire *birthday card*

Reaching All Students

Total Physical Response Dramatize very quickly the meaning of **écrivez**.
 Si vous avez un frère, levez-vous.
 Et maintenant, asseyez-vous.
 Si vous avez une sœur, levez la main.
 (Student 1), vous avez une sœur?
 Levez-vous, s'il vous plaît.
 Allez au tableau.
 Prenez la craie.
 Vous avez une sœur, n'est-ce pas?
 Écrivez son nom au tableau.

Elle a quel âge? Écrivez son âge.
Elle habite où? Écrivez son adresse.
Merci, (Student 1). Mettez la craie ici, s'il vous plaît.
Et maintenant, retournez à votre place et asseyez-vous.

3 Practice

Commençons

Let's use our new words

1 and **2** These activities can be done with books closed, open, or once each way.

Writing Development

Have students write answers to Activities 1 and 2 in paragraph form to illustrate how the answers to the items tell a story.

Learning from Photos

(page 114) Have student pairs create a description of the brother and sister. Have them tell what they look like, where they are students, what their strong and weak subjects are, what they do after school, etc. The pairs can write descriptions or share their description orally.

Reaching All Students

For the Younger Students When doing Activity 3, you may wish to have younger students make their own dictionary page. For example: **grand-père = le père de mon père.**

Vocabulaire

Commençons

Let's use our new words

1 Historiette La famille Senghor

Inventez une histoire. *(Make up a story.)*

1. Madame Senghor est la femme de Monsieur Senghor?
2. Monsieur Senghor est le mari de Madame Senghor?
3. La famille Senghor est française?
4. M. et Mme Senghor ont deux enfants? Ils ont un fils et une fille?
5. Les enfants ont quel âge?
6. Quelle est la date de l'anniversaire de la fille?
7. Il y a combien de personnes dans la famille Senghor?
8. Les Senghor ont un chien ou un chat?

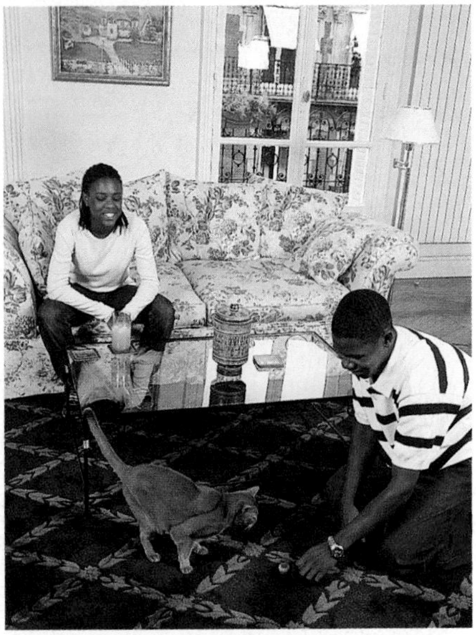

Marie et Blaise Senghor habitent à Paris.

2 Historiette L'anniversaire de Francine

Répondez d'après les indications. *(Answer according to the cues.)*

1. Elle a quel âge, Francine? (quinze ans)
2. C'est quand, son anniversaire? (aujourd'hui)
3. Quelle est la date aujourd'hui? (le deux août)
4. Qu'est-ce que Francine donne pour son anniversaire? (une fête)
5. Elle invite qui à la fête? (ses amis et ses cousins)
6. Qu'est-ce que tout le monde a pour Francine? (beaucoup de cadeaux)
7. Il y a un gâteau pour Francine? (oui)
8. Le gâteau a des bougies? (oui, quinze)

3 La famille

Complétez. *(Complete.)*

1. Le frère de mon père est mon ____.
2. La sœur de mon père est ma ____.
3. Le frère de ma mère est mon ____.
4. La sœur de ma mère est ma ____.
5. Le fils de mon oncle et de ma tante est mon ____.
6. La fille de mon oncle et de ma tante est ma ____.
7. Le père de ma mère est mon ____.
8. Et la mère de mon père est ma ____.

Answers to Commençons

1 *Answers will vary but may include:*

1. Oui, Madame Senghor est la femme de Monsieur Senghor.
2. Oui, Monsieur Senghor est le mari de Madame Senghor.
3. Oui, la famille Senghor est française.
4. Oui, M. et Mme Senghor ont deux enfants. Ils ont un fils et une fille.
5. Les enfants ont ____ et ____ ans.
6. La date de l'anniversaire de la fille est ____.
7. Il y a quatre personnes dans la famille Senghor.
8. Les Senghor ont un ____.

2

1. Francine a quinze ans.
2. C'est aujourd'hui.
3. Aujourd'hui, c'est le deux août.
4. Francine donne une fête pour son anniversaire.
5. Elle invite ses amis et ses cousins à la fête.
6. Tout le monde a beaucoup de cadeaux pour Francine.
7. Oui, il y a un gâteau pour Francine.
8. Oui, le gâteau a quinze bougies.

3

1. oncle
2. tante
3. oncle
4. tante
5. cousin
6. cousine
7. grand-père
8. grand-mère

4 **Moi** Choisissez la bonne réponse.
(Choose the correct answer.)

1. Moi, je suis ____ de mes grands-parents.
   a. le petit-fils **b.** la petite-fille
2. Je suis ____ de mes parents.
   a. le fils **b.** la fille
3. Je suis ____ de mon oncle.
   a. le neveu **b.** la nièce
4. Je suis ____ de mes cousins.
   a. le cousin **b.** la cousine

5 **Une famille** This country wedding, *Une noce à la campagne,* was painted by le Douanier Rousseau in 1905. Give the people names and decide who they are in relation to one another.

Une noce à la campagne

6 **Une fête d'anniversaire** With a classmate describe some things that take place at a typical birthday party. You may want to use some of the following words.

arriver · écouter · donner · danser · inviter · préparer · regarder

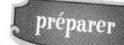

ENCORE PLUS *For more practice using words from **Mots 1**, do Activity 10 on page H11 at the end of this book.*

Art Connection

Henri Rousseau, called **le Douanier,** was born in Paris in 1844 and died there in 1910. He came from a very humble family. He spent some time in the army and worked for the municipal government in Paris. Self-taught as far as art was concerned, in 1884 he got **une carte de copiste** at the Louvre and little by little he was able to work his way into the artistic circle of the time, thanks to the **Salon des Indépendants,** where he exhibited his works. In 1899 he wrote a play and in order to subsist he gave music and art lessons. Around 1906 or 1907 he met Apollinaire, Delaunay, and Picasso and he was able to start selling his paintings to collectors. He painted many landscapes and scenes of Paris and its suburbs, as well as scenes of daily life such as ***Une noce à la campagne*** (seen here), which he painted in 1905. He also did still lifes. Rousseau was the originator of **l'art naïf**—*primitive art* in English.

National Standards

Communities

If there is a French family or family from any French-speaking country living in your area, it would be fun to have them come and speak to your students. Let the students ask them some simple questions in their limited French.

Answers to Commençons

4 *If students are boys they will answer:*

1. a **3.** a
2. a **4.** a

If students are girls they will answer:

1. b **3.** b
2. b **4.** b

5 *Answers will vary but may include:*
C'est M. Brun. C'est le grand-père.
C'est Mme Brun. C'est la grand-mère.
C'est Mme Dupont. C'est la mère, etc.

6 *Answers will vary but may include:*
Quand on donne une fête, on invite les amis. Les copains arrivent. Ils ont beaucoup de cadeaux. Il y a un gâteau. Le gâteau a des bougies.

Assessment

As an informal assessment, you may wish to use Vocabulary Transparency 4.2 and have students identify as many family members as they can.

Vocabulaire *Mots 2*

1 Preparation

Resource Manager

Vocabulary Transparencies 4.4–4.5
Audio Activities Booklet TE, pages 51–52
Audiocassette 3B/CD 3
Workbook, pages 31–32
Quiz 2, page 18
ExamView Pro®

Bellringer Review

Use BBR Transparency 4.2 or write the following on the board.
Answer.

1. **Tu habites où?**
2. **Tu quittes la maison à quelle heure le matin?**
3. **Tu arrives à l'école à quelle heure?**

2 Presentation

Step 1 Using Vocabulary Transparencies 4.4–4.5, have students repeat each word after you or Audiocassette 3B/CD 3 two or three times.

Step 2 Ask the question **Qu'est-ce que c'est?** as you point to various objects on the transparencies.

Step 3 When teaching **près de** and **loin de** on page 116, draw arrows on the board—a short one for **près de;** a long arrow for **loin de.** When teaching **autour de,** draw a circle around a house on the board as you say the phrase.

Step 4 Have students open their books to pages 116–117; ask *yes/no, either/or,* and then interrogative word questions about the illustrations. For example: **La maison a une terrasse? L'immeuble a trois étages ou quatre étages? La maison a combien de pièces? Où sont les voisins?**

Vocabulaire *Mots 2*

La maison

La vieille maison est très belle.
Il y a un jardin autour de la maison.
De la terrasse on a une vue du jardin.

L'immeuble

Le balcon donne sur la rue.
Les Briand ont un très joli appartement.
Il est dans un très beau quartier de Paris.
Leur immeuble est (tout) près d'une station de métro.
L'immeuble n'est pas loin d'une station de métro.

Attention! Il y a un nouveau code!

Reaching All Students

Total Physical Response Use desks to represent different rooms and label them. Pictures of a stove, table, television set, and telephone may be placed on the desks. Dramatize the meaning of **venez.**

(Student 1), **levez-vous, s'il vous plaît.**
Venez ici.
Allez dans la cuisine.
Préparez le dîner.
Mettez le dîner sur la table.
Mettez-vous à table.
Et maintenant, levez-vous.
Entrez dans la salle de séjour.
Mettez la télé.
(pantomime turning on the T.V.)
Asseyez-vous.
Regardez la télé.
Allez au téléphone.
Téléphonez à un ami.
Parlez. Dites «bonjour».
Merci, *(Student 1).*
Retournez à votre place et asseyez-vous.

Les voisins sont dans la cour.

Les Briand montent toujours en ascenseur.
Ils montent au troisième étage.

Les pièces de la maison

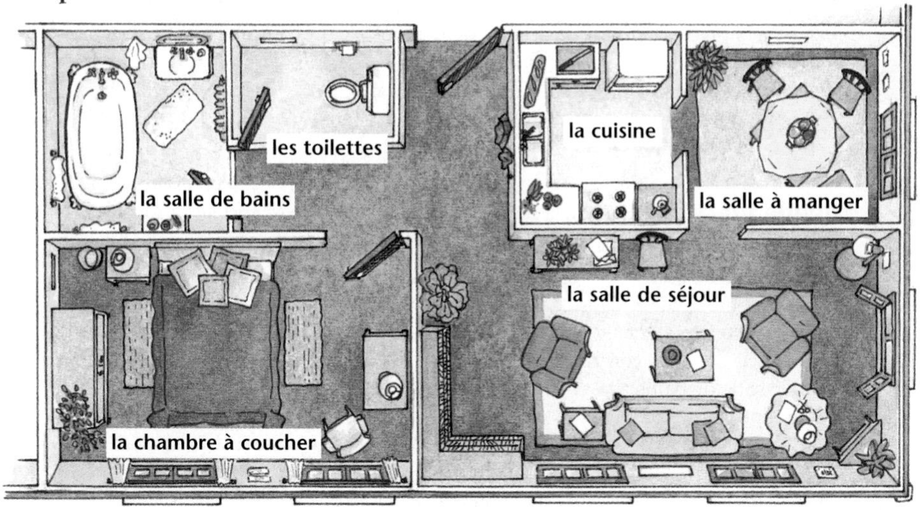

Teaching Tip: Repetition is important for introducing new material, but it can quickly become tiresome. To maintain student interest, alternate between whole-class and individual repetition. Walk around the room during repetition, and switch to another activity if you sense that students are becoming bored. Come back to repetition later.

FUN-FACTS

- Each apartment building in Paris has a code. You must know the code and punch it in at the main entrance for the door to open.
- In France the ground floor of a building is called **le rez-de-chaussée.** What the French call the "first floor," **le premier étage,** is our second floor.
- Point out to students that, in comparison to U.S. cities, French cities are very old. In many older French buildings, elevators have been installed in the stairwell since these buildings were constructed long before the invention of elevators; many apartment buildings have no elevator at all.

About the French Language

The word for the restroom, **les toilettes,** is used in the plural. In the singular, **la toilette** refers to washing and is used in the expression **faire sa toilette.** The toilet is also often referred to as **le W.C.** *(water closet).*

Reaching All Students

Additional Practice Have students work in pairs. Each student draws and labels a floor plan of his or her house or apartment. Then, without showing the drawing to their partner, students describe their house or apartment. Each student draws a floor plan according to the description provided by his or her partner. When finished, they compare the two plans and discuss the differences.

3 Practice

Commençons
Let's use our new words

Writing Development

Have students write a summary of some of the **Historiette** activities.

Learning from Photos

(page 118) Giverny is a lovely town in Normandy, not far from Paris, about halfway between Paris and Rouen. It is a small town with fewer than 600 inhabitants. Monet lived there from 1883 until his death in 1926. The gardens around the house inspired many of Monet's paintings, especially the water lilies **(les nymphéas)**. Note: In this chapter's video episode, students can take a tour of Monet's house.

Commençons
Let's use our new words

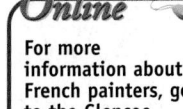

La maison de Claude Monet, Giverny

7 Historiette La maison de Monet Répondez que **oui.** *(Answer* oui.*)*

1. Monet est un artiste célèbre?
2. Il a une jolie maison?
3. Sa maison est grande?
4. Il y a un jardin autour de sa maison?
5. C'est un très beau jardin?
6. Il y a des arbres et des fleurs dans le jardin?

8 Historiette L'appartement des Lapeyre
Inventez une histoire. *(Make up a story.)*

1. La famille Lapeyre a un appartement dans un vieil immeuble à Paris?
2. Leur appartement est dans un beau quartier de Paris?
3. L'appartement est au rez-de-chaussée ou au troisième étage?
4. Leur balcon donne sur la rue ou sur la cour?
5. Il y a six pièces dans l'appartement de la famille Lapeyre?
6. Quelles pièces?
7. Les Lapeyre montent toujours à pied ou en ascenseur?
8. L'immeuble est près d'une station de métro ou loin d'une station de métro?
9. Il y a un code pour entrer dans l'immeuble?

FRENCH Online
For more information about French painters, go to the Glencoe French Web site: french.glencoe.com

9 Quelle pièce? Choisissez la bonne réponse. *(Choose the correct answer.)*

1. On regarde la télé dans ____.
   a. la salle de bains **b.** la salle à manger **c.** la salle de séjour
2. On prépare le dîner dans ____.
   a. la salle à manger **b.** la cuisine **c.** la chambre à coucher
3. On parle avec ses voisins dans ____.
   a. la salle de bains **b.** la cour **c.** la chambre à coucher
4. On dîne dans ____.
   a. la salle à manger **b.** la salle de séjour **c.** la chambre à coucher
5. On a une belle vue ____.
   a. du balcon **b.** de l'étage **c.** de l'ascenseur

ANSWERS TO Commençons

7
1. Oui, Monet est un artiste célèbre.
2. Oui, il a une jolie maison.
3. Oui, sa maison est grande.
4. Oui, il y a un jardin autour de sa maison.
5. Oui, c'est un très beau jardin.
6. Oui, il y a des arbres et des fleurs dans le jardin.

8 *Answers will vary but may include:*
1. Oui, la famille Lapeyre a un appartement dans un vieil immeuble à Paris.
2. Oui, leur appartement est dans un beau quartier de Paris.
3. Non, l'appartement n'est pas au rez-de-chaussée. L'appartement est au troisième étage.
4. Leur balcon donne sur la rue.
5. Oui, il y a six pièces dans l'appartement de la famille Lapeyre.
6. Il y a une cuisine, une salle à manger, une salle de séjour, trois chambres et une salle de bains.
7. Les Lapeyre montent toujours en ascenseur.
8. L'immeuble est loin d'une station de métro.
9. Oui, il y a un code pour entrer dans l'immeuble.

9
1. c
2. b
3. b
4. a
5. a

10 **Historiette** **Chez moi** Donnez des réponses personnelles.
(Give your own answers.)

1. Tu habites quelle rue?
2. Tu habites dans un appartement ou dans une maison privée?
3. Il y a combien de pièces dans l'appartement ou la maison?
4. Il y a combien de chambres à coucher?
5. Il y a un jardin ou un balcon?
6. La maison ou l'immeuble a un garage?
7. Il y a une voiture dans le garage?

11 **Quelle maison pour nous?** Work with a classmate. Your families plan to spend a month in France. Read the following real estate ads and discuss which house or apartment is good for your family.

Appartement

dans un bel immeuble, cinq pièces, deux chambres à coucher, une grande cuisine moderne, bien situé au centre-ville, près d'une station de métro

Très jolie villa

avec jardin et terrasse, vue sur l'océan, huit pièces, quatre chambres à coucher, garage pour deux voitures, située dans une rue très calme, loin de la ville

Petit bungalow

dans un vieux quartier, beaucoup de charme, trois pièces, une chambre à coucher, vingt minutes de la ville de Strasbourg

ENCORE PLUS *For more practice using words from **Mots 2**, do Activity 11 on page H12 at the end of this book.*

10 After completing this activity with the whole class, have students work in pairs. Partners use the questions to interview each other, taking notes. Then they report to the class on their partner's home, using the third person.

Learning from Realia

(page 119)

- The apartment is in the **7e arrondissement** of Paris near the Eiffel Tower.
- The villa is in Saint-Jean-Cap-Ferrat. Cap-Ferrat, as it is commonly called, is a famous resort that is still very peaceful. It is located on a peninsula and is therefore isolated from the busy main road between Nice and Menton on the Italian border. Many of the beautiful homes in Cap-Ferrat are owned by celebrities.
- The bungalow is in the **département** of Orne in Basse-Normandie near the city of Caen.

ANSWERS TO Commençons

10 *Answers will vary but may include:*

1. J'habite rue _____.
2. J'habite dans _____.
3. Il y a _____ pièces dans la maison.
4. Il y a _____ chambres à coucher.
5. Il y a un jardin.
6. Oui, la maison a un garage. (Non, la maison n'a pas de garage.)
7. Oui, il y a une voiture dans le garage. (Non, il n'y a pas de voiture dans le garage.)

ENCORE PLUS This *infogap* activity will allow students to practice in pairs. The activity should be very manageable for them, since all vocabulary and structures are familiar to them.

Attention!

Note that the activities are color-coded. All the activities in the text are communicative. However, the ones with blue titles are guided communication. The red titles indicate that the answers to the activity are more open-ended and can vary more. You may wish to correct students' mistakes more so in the guided activities than in the activities with a red title, which lend themselves to a freer response.

1 Preparation

Resource Manager

Audio Activities Booklet TE, pages 53–55
Audiocassette 3B/CD 3
Workbook, pages 33–35
Quizzes 3–5, pages 19–21
ExamView Pro®

Bellringer Review

Use BRR Transparency 4.3 or write the following on the board.
Write a sentence using each of the following verbs.

passer	**regarder**
étudier	**arriver**
écouter	**quitter**

2 Presentation

Avoir au présent

Step 1 Review the **il a, ils ont** forms which students already know from the **Vocabulaire** section of this chapter. Draw a stick figure on the board and label it **Robert.** Have students make up sentences with **Robert a ____.** Do the same with **Caroline et Janine ont ____.**

Step 2 Have students repeat **j'ai** after you as they point to themselves. Then have them tell some things they have.

Step 3 Have students open their books to page 120 and go through the forms of **avoir.**

Step 4 Go over Items 2–3.

Telling what you and others have
Avoir au présent

1. Study the following forms of the irregular verb **avoir** *(to have).*

AVOIR	
j' ai	nous‿avons
tu as	vous‿avez
il/elle/on‿a	ils‿/elles‿ont

2. You also use the verb **avoir** to express age.

Tu as quel âge?
Moi? J'ai quatorze ans.

3. The expression **il y a** means "there is" or "there are."

Il y a un jardin autour de la maison.
Il n'y a pas de fleurs dans le jardin.

Rappelez-vous que...
Un, une, and **des** become **de (d')** after a negative.
J'ai une sœur mais Marc n'a pas de sœur.

Continuons
Let's put our words together

12 Historiette Les Binand
Inventez une histoire.
(Make up a story.)

1. Suzanne Binand a un frère?
2. Guillaume a une sœur?
3. Monsieur et Madame Binand ont deux enfants?
4. La famille Binand a un appartement à Paris?
5. Ils ont un chat?

Reaching All Students

Kinesthetic Learners Many students learn better when they can get up and move around to use the language they are learning. You may want to do the following: Student stands up and says, **Moi, j'ai ____ ans.** *(Student 1)* goes up to another student and asks: **Et, toi** *(name),* **tu as quel âge?** Student responds. Then Student 1 says: **Nous avons (n'avons pas) le même âge.** Note: You may want to use **on** rather than **nous.**

Answers to Continuons

12 *Answers will vary but may include:*
1. Oui, Suzanne Binand a un frère.
2. Oui, Guillaume a une sœur.
3. Oui, Monsieur et Madame Binand ont deux enfants.
4. Oui, la famille Binand a un appartement à Paris.
5. Non, ils n'ont pas de chat.

Deux amis, Narbonne, France

13 **Tu as un frère?** Répétez la conversation. *(Repeat the conversation.)*

Flore: Tu as un frère?
Rémi: Non, je n'ai pas de frère, mais j'ai une sœur.
Flore: Tu as une sœur? Elle a quel âge?
Rémi: Elle a quatorze ans.
Flore: Et toi, tu as quel âge?
Rémi: Moi, j'ai seize ans.
Flore: Et… vous avez un chien?
Rémi: Non, on n'a pas de chien. Mais on a un petit chat.

14 **Rémi** Complétez d'après la conversation. *(Complete according to the conversation.)*

1. Rémi n'____ pas ____ frère.
2. Il ____ une sœur.
3. Sa sœur ____ quatorze ans.
4. Rémi ____ seize ans.
5. Rémi et sa sœur n'____ pas ____ chien.
6. Mais ils ____ un petit chat adorable.

15 **Historiette Ma famille** Donnez des réponses personnelles. *(Give your own answers.)*

1. Tu as des frères? Tu as combien de frères?
2. Tu as des sœurs? Tu as combien de sœurs?
3. Tu as un chien ou un chat?
4. Tu as des amis?
5. Tu as des cousins?
6. Tu as combien de cousins?
7. Tu as une grande famille ou une petite famille?
8. Tu as quel âge?

Un père et son fils

3 Practice

Continuons
Let's put our words together

13 **and** **14** Have students present the dialogue as a real conversation. They can dramatize it in front of the class, using as much expression as possible. Then have students retell it in narrative form. Note that the conversation reinforces the **je** and **tu** forms and that Activity 14 has students use the third person in their narration.

15 Note that this activity focuses attention on the **j'ai** form. Students get practice hearing **tu as** as they respond with **j'ai.**

Learning from Photos

(page 121)

- *(top)* Narbonne is a quiet little town in Languedoc. It is known for its cathedral of St. Just, which was begun in 1272 but never completed. It is one of the tallest Gothic cathedrals in France.
- *(top)* Have students describe the teens in the photo. Have them include their relationship to each other. Include also a description of the home behind them.
- *(bottom)* Ask students the following questions about this photo: **C'est la photo d'un père et d'un fils? Ils sont sympathiques? Le fils a quel âge? Et le père?**

Answers to Continuons

14

1. a, de
2. a
3. a
4. a
5. ont, de
6. ont

15 *Answers will vary but may include:*

1. Oui, j'ai des frères. J'ai ____ frères.
2. Non, je n'ai pas de sœurs.
3. Oui, j'ai un chien, mais je n'ai pas de chat.
4. Oui, j'ai des amis.
5. Oui, j'ai des cousins.
6. J'ai ____ cousins.
7. J'ai une ____ famille.
8. J'ai ____ ans.

3 Practice *(continued)*

Continuons
Let's put our words together

Reteaching
Have students work in groups of three. They tell one another what members of their family have and they then compare. For example, someone says that he or she has a dog. The others can say: **Ah, vous avez un chien. Nous avons un chien aussi.** or **Ah, vous avez un chien. Nous n'avons pas de chien. Nous avons un chat.**

Writing Development
Have students write a paragraph about the Ghez family based on their answers to Activity 18.

16 Dans mon sac à dos Préparez une conversation d'après le modèle. *(Make up a conversation according to the model.)*

—Tu as des livres dans ton sac à dos?
—Oui, j'ai des livres dans mon sac à dos./ Non, je n'ai pas de livres dans mon sac à dos.

17 Qu'est-ce que vous avez? Préparez une conversation d'après le modèle. *(Make up a conversation according to the model.)*

une maison ou un appartement
—Vous avez une maison ou un appartement?
—Nous avons ____.

1. une grande famille ou une petite famille
2. une grande voiture ou une petite voiture
3. un chien ou un chat
4. un PC ou un Mac

18 Historiette La famille Ghez Complétez avec **avoir.** *(Complete with* avoir.*)*

La famille Ghez __1__ un bel appartement à Nice. Leur appartement __2__ six pièces. Leur appartement __3__ un balcon. Le balcon donne sur la mer Méditerranée. Du balcon les Ghez __4__ une très belle vue sur la mer.

Il y a quatre personnes dans la famille Ghez. Halima a dix-sept ans et son frère, Ahmed, __5__ quinze ans. Halima et Ahmed __6__ un petit chat adorable.

Et toi, tu __7__ un chien ou un chat? Tu __8__ une petite ou une grande famille? Vous __9__ un appartement ou une maison?

Moi, j'__10__ quinze ans et j'__11__ un chien adorable. J'adore mon petit chien.

Answers to Continuons

16 *Answers will vary but may include:*

—Tu as beaucoup de cahiers dans ton sac à dos?
—Oui, j'ai beaucoup de cahiers dans mon sac à dos. (Non, je n'ai pas beaucoup de cahiers dans mon sac à dos. Je n'ai pas de cahiers dans mon sac à dos.)
—Tu as combien de classeurs dans ton sac à dos?
—J'ai deux classeurs dans mon sac à dos. (Je n'ai pas de classeurs dans mon sac à dos.)

17 *Answers will vary but may include:*

1. Vous avez une grande famille ou une petite famille?
   Nous avons une ____ famille.
2. Vous avez une grande voiture ou une petite voiture?
   Nous avons une ____ voiture.
3. Vous avez un chien ou un chat?
   Nous avons ____.
4. Vous avez un PC ou un Mac?
   Nous avons ____.

18

1. a
2. a
3. a
4. ont
5. a
6. ont
7. as
8. as
9. avez
10. ai
11. ai

Telling what belongs to you and others
Les adjectifs possessifs

1. You use a possessive adjective to show possession or ownership. Like other adjectives, a possessive adjective must agree with the noun it modifies.

2. The adjectives **mon** *(my)*, **ton** *(your)*, and **son** *(his/her)* each have three forms. The adjectives **notre** *(our)*, **votre** *(your)*, and **leur** *(their)* each have two forms.

SINGULIER		PLURIEL	
Masculin	Féminin	Masculin	Féminin
mon frère	ma sœur	mes frères	mes sœurs
ton frère	ta sœur	tes frères	tes sœurs
son frère	sa sœur	ses frères	ses sœurs
notre frère	notre sœur	nos frères	nos sœurs
votre frère	votre sœur	vos frères	vos sœurs
leur frère	leur sœur	leurs frères	leurs sœurs

3. **Son, sa,** and **ses** can mean "his" or "her." The adjective agrees with the item owned, not the owner.

   C'est le chien de Paul. **C'est son chien.**
   C'est le chien de Marie. **C'est son chien.**

4. You use **mon, ton,** or **son** before a feminine singular noun that begins with a vowel or silent **h.**

   son ‿n amie et mon ‿n amie

Une famille d'origine marocaine, Saint-André, France

Attention!

Liaison occurs with **mon, ton,** and **son,** as well as with all plural possessive adjectives.

mon ‿n oncle **nos ‿z amis**
ton ‿n ami **vos ‿z amis**
son ‿n école **leurs ‿z amis**

Structure

1 Preparation

Bellringer Review

Use BRR Transparency 4.4 or write the following on the board.
Write the answer.
1. **Tu as combien de frères?**
2. **Tu as combien de sœurs?**
3. **Tu as combien de copains?**
4. **Tu as combien de professeurs?**
5. **Tu as quel âge?**

2 Presentation

Les adjectifs possessifs

Step 1 Write the examples with possessive adjectives on the board. Call on individual students to read Items 1–4 aloud.

Step 2 To demonstrate **son, sa, ses,** use students' items. For example: **le livre de Michel, son livre; la calculatrice de François, sa calculatrice.**

Step 3 Continue to demonstrate the forms in this way. You and a student hold on to one book together and say **notre livre.** Then you each hold up a pencil and say **nos crayons,** etc., or **mon crayon et son crayon ➝ nos crayons.**

Reaching All Students

Additional Practice Give each student a card with a noun. List the nouns on the board. Students find out who has what by asking questions: **Jean et Luc, vous avez une radio? Non, nous n'avons pas de radio. Marie, tu as une radio? Oui, j'ai une radio.** Write the name of the possessor(s) next to the word on the board. When all have been identified, practice **qui.** For example: **Qui a une radio? Marie a une radio.**

Learning from Photos

(page 123) Saint-André is a suburb of Lille in the north of France, not far from the Belgian border. This family is of Moroccan background. People from the **Maghreb** (Morocco, Algeria, and Tunisia) make up the largest minority group in France. Students will learn a great deal about **le Maghreb** and **les Maghrébins** throughout **Bon voyage!**

3 Practice

Continuons
Let's put our words together

19 Do this activity first with books closed. Call on individual students to answer one item each. Do the activity a second time, having one student respond to several consecutive items before calling on the next student.

20 **Expansion:** Use this activity as a model interview that students can conduct with each other. Randomly assign student pairs, or assign students as pairs who don't know each other. Students should question their partner and take notes. Have them switch roles. Then each pair reports back to the class to "introduce" their partner to the class.

Writing Development
Have students write a paragraph about their family and home based on their responses to Activity 19.

Learning from Photos
(page 124) Ask questions about the house in the photo on page 124.

C'est une maison ou un appartement?
La maison est près d'une station de métro?
La maison est dans un quartier de Paris?
La maison a un ascenseur?
Il y a un jardin autour de la maison?

Continuons
Let's put our words together

19 Historiette Ta famille et chez toi Donnez des réponses personnelles. *(Give your own answers.)*

1. Où est ta maison ou ton appartement?
2. Ta maison ou ton appartement a combien de pièces?
3. Ta maison est grande ou petite? Ton appartement est grand ou petit?
4. C'est quand, ton anniversaire? Tu as quel âge?
5. Quel âge a ton frère, si tu as un frère?
6. Quel âge a ta sœur, si tu as une sœur?

Un beau chalet, Suisse

20 J'ai une question pour toi. Suivez le modèle. *(Follow the model.)*

—Où est _ta_ maison?
—Ma maison est dans la rue Jacob.

1. Qui est ____ amie?
2. Qui est ____ ami?
3. Où habitent ____ grands-parents?
4. ____ frère a quel âge?
5. ____ sœur a quel âge?
6. Où est ____ maison ou ____ appartement?
7. Tu aimes ____ cours de français?
8. ____ prof est sympa?

21 Oui! Suivez le modèle. *(Follow the model.)*

—Le frère de Marine est dans sa chambre?
—Oui, son frère est dans sa chambre.

1. Le père de Marine est dans la cuisine?
2. La sœur de Marine est blonde?
3. La sœur de Thomas est à Paris?
4. La maison de Thomas est jolie?
5. L'appartement de Marine est beau?
6. Les cousins de Thomas sont élèves?
7. Les grands-parents de Thomas ont un chien?

Answers to Continuons

19 *Students will give personal answers about their home and family.*

20 *Answers will vary but may include:*
1. Qui est ton amie? Mon amie est Cécile.
2. Qui est ton ami? Mon ami est Cédric.
3. Où habitent tes grands-parents? Mes grands-parents habitent ____.
4. Ton frère a quel âge? Mon frère a ____ ans.
5. Ta sœur a quel âge? Ma sœur a ____ ans.
6. Où est ta maison ou ton appartement? ____ est ____.
7. Tu aimes ton cours de français? Oui, j'aime mon cours de français.
8. Ton (Ta) prof est sympa? Oui, mon (ma) prof est sympa.

21
1. Oui, son père est dans la cuisine.
2. Oui, sa sœur est blonde.
3. Oui, sa sœur est à Paris.
4. Oui, sa maison est jolie.
5. Oui, son appartement est beau.
6. Oui, ses cousins sont élèves.
7. Oui, ses grands-parents ont un chien.

Structure

22 Historiette Notre école

Donnez des réponses personnelles.
(Give your own answers.)

1. Votre école est grande ou petite?
2. Votre école est près ou loin de votre maison?
3. Votre école a combien d'élèves?
4. Vos cours sont faciles ou difficiles?
5. Vos profs sont intéressants ou pas?
6. Vos classes sont grandes ou petites?

La Techno Parade, Paris

23 Historiette Leur maison

Complétez. *(Complete.)*

Fabien et Christophe sont frères. Ils sont dans __1__ chambre. Ils écoutent __2__ disques. __3__ collection de CD est surtout de la techno. __4__ amies, Catherine et Émilie, aiment aussi la techno. Fabien et Christophe, __5__ deux amies et __6__ copains écoutent souvent de la techno. Mais __7__ parents n'aiment pas du tout la techno.

24 Votre famille

Draw your own family tree and say as many things as you can about your family to your classmates.

ENCORE PLUS *For more practice using **avoir** and possessive adjectives, do Activity 12 on page H13 at the end of this book.*

22 It is recommended that you go over this activity first with books closed as students answer with the correct form of **notre / nos.** Do the activity a second time with students reading in pairs. One reads the questions, and the other responds. You can do this as a paired activity or as a round-robin class activity.

24 Students who don't wish to share this information about their own families can create an imaginary family tree using pictures of people cut out from magazines.

Assessment

As an informal assessment, check for comprehension of possessive adjectives by walking around the room, picking up various objects, and asking if the object belongs to a particular person or persons. For example: **C'est le crayon de Jacques? (Oui, c'est son crayon.) C'est ton sac à dos? (Oui, c'est mon sac à dos.) Ce sont les livres de Jules et Monique? (Oui, ce sont leurs livres)**, etc.

Reteaching

Do the following activity orally, or write the words on the board. Have students volunteer a series of nouns. Then have them use these nouns with **mon, ma, mes.** Next have them ask a question, using the same noun with **ton, ta,** or **tes.** Do the activity again with **notre / nos** and **votre / vos.**

ENCORE PLUS This *infogap* activity will allow students to practice in pairs. The activity should be very manageable for them, since all vocabulary and structures are familiar to them.

Answers to Continuons

22 *Answers will vary but may include:*
1. Mon école est grande.
2. Mon école est ____ de ma maison.
3. Mon école a ____ élèves.
4. Mes cours sont difficiles.
5. Mes profs sont intéressants.
6. Mes classes sont petites.

23
1. leur
2. leurs
3. Leur
4. Leurs
5. leurs
6. leurs
7. leurs

24 *Students will tell as much as they want in their own words about their family.*

1 Preparation

Bellringer Review

Use BRR Transparency 4.5 or write the following on the board.
Complete each sentence.

1. **On prépare le dîner dans ____.**
2. **On dîne dans ____.**
3. **On regarde la télé dans ____.**
4. **On monte au troisième étage en ____.**
5. **On monte ____ à pied.**

2 Presentation

D'autres adjectifs

Attention!

This presentation begins with the feminine forms, since students tend to have an easier time dropping the final sound in the oral form and the final letters in the written form. For example: **belle, bel, beau.**

Step 1 Lead students through the explanation on page 126. Emphasize that **beau, nouveau, vieux, petit,** and **grand** are exceptions to the usual rule of placing adjectives after the noun.

Step 2 In more able groups, you may wish to explain the difference between **nouvelle / nouveau** and **neuve / neuf** *(recently acquired and newly manufactured new).*

Describing more people and things
D'autres adjectifs

1. Most French adjectives follow the noun. Some common ones, such as **petit** and **grand,** come before the noun. The adjectives **beau** *(beautiful),* **nouveau** *(new),* and **vieux** *(old)* also come before the noun. These adjectives have several forms. Pay careful attention to both the spelling and the pronunciation of these adjectives.

SINGULIER

Féminin	Masculin (Voyelle)	Masculin (Consonne)
une belle maison	un bel appartement	un beau quartier
une nouvelle maison	un nouvel appartement	un nouveau quartier
une vieille maison	un vieil appartement	un vieux quartier

PLURIEL

Féminin	Masculin (Voyelle)	Masculin (Consonne)
de belles maisons	de beaux‿z appartements	de beaux quartiers
de nouvelles maisons	de nouveaux‿z appartements	de nouveaux quartiers
de vieilles maisons	de vieux‿z appartements	de vieux quartiers

2. In formal French, **de** is used instead of **des** with a plural adjective that precedes the noun. In informal French, people use **des.**

Attention!

Liaison occurs with **beaux, nouveaux,** and **vieux** when they come before a word beginning with a vowel or silent **h.** The **x** is pronounced as a **z.**

mes nouveaux‿z amis
les vieux‿z appartements

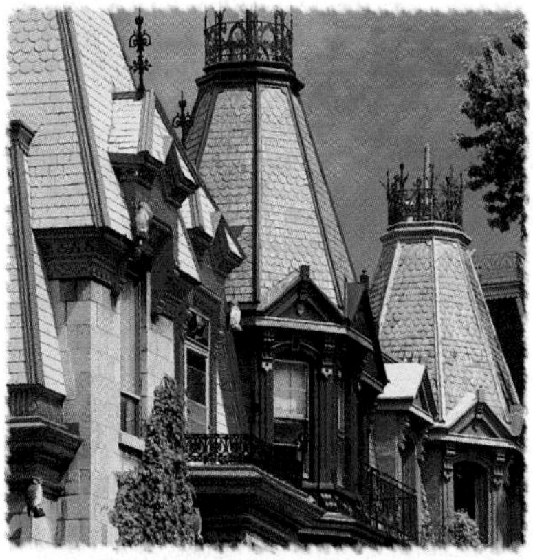

De belles maisons, Montréal, Canada

Learning from Photos

(page 126)

- Ask about the houses: **D'après vous, ce sont des vieilles maisons ou des nouvelles maisons?**
- **Le carré Saint-Louis,** where these houses are located, is a beautiful square in Montreal surrounded by large nineteenth-century homes. The area was originally a reservoir. It became a park in 1879 and attracted upper middle-class families and artists. The neighborhood today is home to many musicians, writers, and painters.

Continuons

Let's put our words together

25 Historiette Le bel appartement des Texier Complétez. *(Complete.)*

1. Les Texier ont un ____ appartement dans un ____ immeuble dans un ____ quartier de la ville. (beau, vieux, beau)
2. Il y a de ____ et de ____ quartiers à Montréal. (nouveau, vieux)
3. L'appartement des Texier a de très ____ pièces. (beau)
4. Il a de ____ pièces et un très ____ balcon. (grand, beau)
5. De l'appartement il y a une très ____ vue sur la ville. (beau)
6. Les Texier ont une ____ voiture. (nouveau)
7. Leur ____ voiture est ____. (nouveau, beau)

Attention!

You have just learned that the plural of **beau** and **nouveau** is spelled with an **x**. Almost all words in French that end in **(e)au** or **eu** are spelled with **x**, not **s**, in the plural.

un cadeau	**des cadeaux**
un beau château	**de beaux châteaux**
mon neveu	**mes neveux**

Mettez au pluriel. *(Write in the plural.)*

1. Il a un très beau cadeau pour son neveu.
   Il a de très ____ ____ pour ses ____.
2. Le beau gâteau est aussi pour son neveu.
   Les ____ ____ sont aussi pour ses ____.
3. Il visite un beau château avec son neveu.
   Il visite de ____ ____ avec ses ____.

26 Comme qui? Work with a classmate. Take turns saying whom you and your family members take after. You may wish to use the following words.

Je suis intelligent(e) comme ma mère.
Mon frère est enthousiaste comme notre père.

petit, amusant, blond, sympa, grand, beau, brun

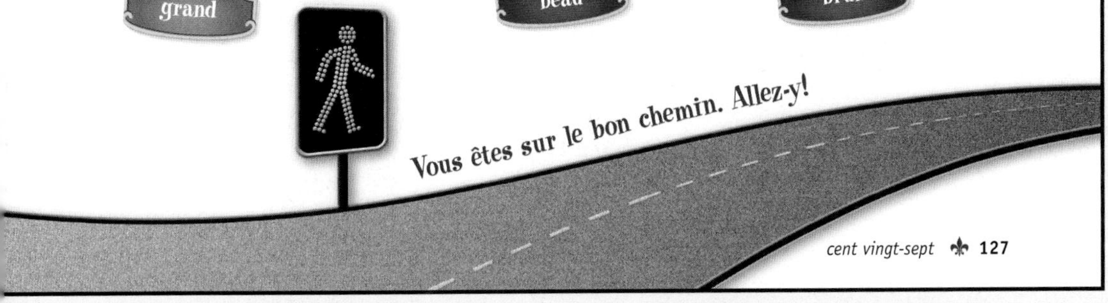
Vous êtes sur le bon chemin. Allez-y!

Structure

3 Practice

Continuons

Let's put our words together

25 Give students a few minutes to prepare this activity (without writing it). Then call on several individuals to read aloud. Have students write it for homework.

FUN-FACTS

How many students have been corrected for putting an **s** after **au**, etc., instead of an **x**!!! Yet, in old French it was written **chevaus**, not **chevaux**. The **x** replaced the **s** because at one time scribes wrote a final **s** with a long flourish, crossing the end of the preceding **u**, and this flourish was erroneously interpreted by later scribes to be an **x** and slavishly imitated. Alas!

Allez-y!
At this point in the chapter, students have learned all the vocabulary and structure necessary to complete the chapter. The conversation and cultural readings that follow recycle all the material learned up to this point.

Answers to Continuons

25
1. bel, vieil, beau
2. nouveaux, vieux
3. belles
4. grandes, beau
5. belle
6. nouvelle
7. nouvelle, belle

Answers to Attention!

1. beaux, cadeaux, neveux
2. beaux, gâteaux, neveux
3. beaux, châteaux, neveux

Conversation

1 Preparation

Resource Manager

Audio Activities Booklet TE, page 56
Audiocassette 3B/CD 3
CD-ROM

Bellringer Review

Use BRR Transparency 4.6 or write the following on the board.
Make complete sentences from the following elements.

1. **je / avoir / nouveau / ami**
2. **tu / avoir / beau / maison**
3. **nous / avoir / vieux / voiture**

2 Presentation

Step 1 Tell students they are going to hear a conversation between Vincent and Charlotte. Have them watch the conversation on the CD-ROM or listen to Audiocassette 3B/CD 3 with their books closed.

Step 2 Have them open their books and repeat the conversation after you.

Step 3 Have two students read the conversation aloud with as much expression as possible.

Step 4 After presenting the conversation, go over the **Après la conversation** activity.

Glencoe Technology

CD-ROM
On the CD-ROM, students can watch a dramatization of this conversation. They can then play the role of either one of the characters and record themselves in the conversation.

Conversation

Ma nouvelle adresse

Vincent: Tu as ma nouvelle adresse?
Charlotte: Ta nouvelle adresse? Non! Tu habites où maintenant?
Vincent: 21, avenue de la Bourdonnais.
Charlotte: Ah, avenue de la Bourdonnais. C'est dans le 7e tout près de la tour Eiffel, non?
Vincent: Oui. De notre balcon on a une très belle vue sur la tour Eiffel.
Charlotte: Génial!

Après la conversation

Répondez. *(Answer.)*

1. Vincent parle à qui?
2. Charlotte a la nouvelle adresse de Vincent?
3. Quelle est sa nouvelle adresse?
4. Où est l'avenue de la Bourdonnais?
5. Est-ce que l'appartement de Vincent a un balcon?
6. De son balcon il a une vue sur la tour Eiffel?

Answers to Après la conversation

1. Vincent parle à son amie Charlotte.
2. Non, elle n'a pas la nouvelle adresse de Vincent.
3. Sa nouvelle adresse est 21, avenue de la Bourdonnais.
4. C'est près de la tour Eiffel, dans le 7e.
5. Oui, l'appartement de Vincent a un balcon.
6. Oui, de son balcon il a une vue sur la tour Eiffel.

Parlons un peu plus
Let's talk some more

A **Appartement ou maison?** Work with a classmate. Pretend you live in Rouen. One of you lives in a house, the other lives in an apartment. Decide who lives where. Then describe your house or apartment.

B **Jeu** **Qui est qui?** Work with a classmate. Write down the first names of some of your family members. Exchange lists and then ask each other who's who.

C'est qui, Paul?
C'est mon oncle. C'est le frère de ma mère.

Prononciation

Le son /ã/

1. There are three nasal vowel sounds in French: /ã/ as in **cent**, /õ/ as in **sont**, and /ẽ/ as in **cinq.** They are called "nasal" because some air passes through the nose when they are pronounced. In this chapter, you will practice only the sound /ã/ as in **cent.**
2. Repeat the following. Notice that there is no /n/ sound after the nasal vowel.

Jean	**cent**	**grand**	**amusant**
français	**parent**	**fantastique**	

Voilà les grands-parents, les parents et les enfants.
Jean-François est fantastique. Il est français, grand, amusant.

les parents et les enfants

3 Practice

Parlons un peu plus
Let's talk some more

A Have students work in pairs. You may wish to choose a pair of students to do this activity for the class.

Prononciation

Step 1 Using Pronunciation Transparency P 4 or textbook page 129, model the key words **parents** and **enfants.** Have students repeat them in unison and individually.

Step 2 Model the words and phrases in similar fashion.

Step 3 For additional pronunciation practice, use the **Prononciation** section on Audiocassette 3B/CD 3.

Step 4 Give students the following **dictée: Jean est français. Les parents de Jean sont amusants. Ses grands-parents n'ont pas cent ans.**

Answers to Parlons un peu plus

A *Students will describe their house or apartment. They can reincorporate the vocabulary presented in this chapter.*

B *Answers will vary but may include:*
—C'est qui, Jeanne?
—C'est ma tante. C'est la sœur de ma mère.
—C'est qui, Claude?
—C'est mon grand-père. C'est le père de mon père.

Resource Manager

Audio Activities Booklet TE, pages 58–59
Audiocassette 3B/CD 3

Bellringer Review

Use BRR Transparency 4.7 or write the following on the board.
Pick out a member of your family and write three sentences to describe him or her.

National Standards

Cultures
In this reading, students will learn about the different types of housing typically found in France.

Presentation

Pre-reading

Step 1 Have students locate the **1er arrondissement** on the map of Paris, page xxxiii (French 1A, French 1B: page xxv).

Step 2 Read and discuss the Reading Strategy on page 130. Have students look at the photos.

Reading

Step 1 Lead students through the reading selection on pages 130–131 by reading aloud. Have students repeat each sentence after you.

Step 2 After every two or three sentences, ask comprehension questions. For example: **Où habitent les Duval? C'est un vieil immeuble? L'appartement a combien de pièces?**

Le Québec

Lectures culturelles

Reading Strategy

Visualizing
As you are reading, try to visualize or make a mental picture of what is being described. Allow your mind to freely develop an image. This will help you remember what you read. It may also help you identify with what you are reading.

Où habitent les Français?

Maisons et appartements

Beaucoup de Français qui habitent en ville, habitent dans un appartement. Il y a des appartements de toutes sortes: des studios, des petits appartements, des grands appartements. Pour les gens qui n'ont pas beaucoup d'argent il y a des H.L.M.[1] (Habitations à Loyer Modéré). Les H.L.M. sont généralement à l'extérieur des villes, à la périphérie ou en banlieue[2]. En banlieue, il y a aussi des petites maisons individuelles—des pavillons.

[1] H.L.M. *low-income housing*
[2] en banlieue *in the suburbs*

Une H.L.M.

Des pavillons de la banlieue parisienne

Learning from Photos

(page 130)

- *(top)* **H.L.M.** stands for **Habitations à loyer modéré.** These are government subsidized housing units for people of modest means. The majority of them are in large concrete apartment blocs, but there are also individual units, usually of more recent construction. There are some 3.5 million such units in all of France. There were one million new ones built between 1992 and 1996 (the latest figures available). The proportion of immigrant families living in an H.L.M. is high.
- *(bottom)* **Un pavillon** is a rather small, modest house with a little garden as seen in this photo.

Have students answer the following questions about the photo of the **pavillons: Les maisons sont grandes ou petites? Les maisons ont un jardin? Il y a des garages? Il y a des voitures? Les maisons sont nouvelles ou vieilles?**

La famille Duval

Les Duval habitent à Paris. Leur appartement est dans un vieil immeuble dans le premier arrondissement. Les Duval habitent dans un très beau quartier.

L'immeuble où habitent les Duval a six étages. Les Duval habitent au cinquième. Ils ont un appartement de quatre pièces: une salle de séjour, une salle à manger et deux chambres à coucher. Il y a aussi, bien sûr, une cuisine, une salle de bains, des toilettes et même une petite entrée. La salle de séjour et la salle à manger donnent sur la rue. La cuisine et les chambres à coucher donnent sur la cour. De leur balcon, les Duval ont une très belle vue sur le musée du Louvre.

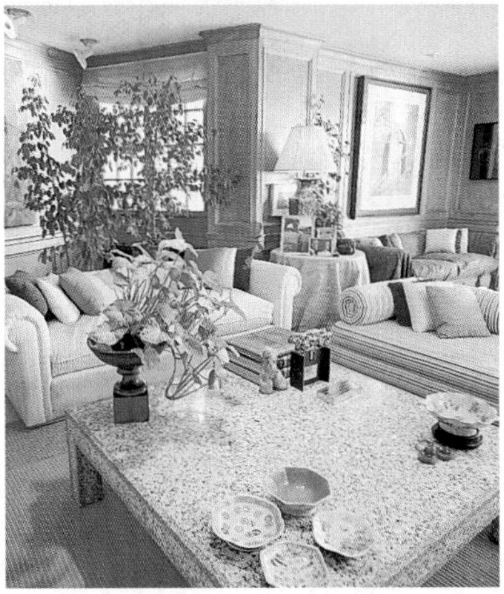

Un bel appartement à Paris

Après la lecture

A Le logement Vrai ou faux? *(True or false?)*

1. Beaucoup de Français habitent dans des appartements.
2. Il y a beaucoup de maisons individuelles dans les villes françaises.
3. Les H.L.M. sont pour les gens qui n'ont pas beaucoup d'argent, qui ne sont pas très riches.
4. Les H.L.M. sont toujours au centre-ville.
5. Le Louvre est dans le deuxième arrondissement.

B La famille Duval Répondez. *(Answer.)*

1. Où habitent les Duval?
2. Où est leur appartement?
3. Il y a combien d'étages dans l'immeuble?
4. Ils habitent au cinquième?
5. Quelles pièces donnent sur la rue?
6. Quelles pièces donnent sur la cour?
7. Du balcon de l'appartement, il y a une vue sur quel musée parisien?

Step 3 Call on some students to read aloud individually. After a student has read about three sentences, ask questions of other students to check comprehension.

Post-reading

Have students do the **Après la lecture** activities orally after reading the selection in class. Then assign these activities to be written at home. Go over them again the following day.

Après la lecture

A Expansion: After doing Activity A, you may wish to have students correct each false statement. For example: **2. Il y a beaucoup d'appartements dans les villes françaises.**

B Allow students to refer to the story to look up the answers or you may prefer to use this activity as a testing device for factual recall.

FUN-FACTS

- 56% of French families live in a private home, 44% in an apartment
- 54% of the French own their principal residence
- almost one out of five families lives in subsidized housing

Answers to Après la lecture

A

1. V
2. F
3. V
4. F
5. F

B

1. Les Duval habitent à Paris.
2. Leur appartement est dans le premier arrondissement.
3. Il y a six étages dans l'immeuble.
4. Oui, ils habitent au cinquième.
5. La salle de séjour et la salle à manger donnent sur la rue.
6. La cuisine et les chambres à coucher donnent sur la cour.
7. Du balcon il y a une vue sur le Louvre.

National Standards

Cultures
This selection familiarizes students with the different types of housing in the French-speaking world.

Attention!

This reading is optional. You may skip it completely, have the entire class read it, have only several students read it and report to the class, or assign it for extra credit.

Après la lecture

Allow students to refer to the story to look up the answers or you may use this activity as a testing device for factual recall.

Learning from Photos

(page 132)
(left) Dakar, the capital of Sénégal, is a pleasant city on the Cap Vert peninsula, the westernmost part of the African peninsula. It enjoys a temperate climate, and the city has many tree-lined streets in its relatively compact central area. It has a population of just under one million.
(top right) The thatched-roof house shown in this photo is typical of much of the rural **(la brousse)** housing found in Africa. The types of houses do, however, vary from region to region. Many houses are made out of clay and have either a clay or thatched roof.
(bottom right) The colorful wood house seen here is typical of many houses in the French Antilles.

Lecture supplémentaire 1

Le logement dans d'autres pays

Dakar, Sénégal

Une maison avec un toit de chaume, Sénégal

En Afrique

Dans les grandes villes modernes de l'Afrique Occidentale comme Abidjan ou Dakar il y a beaucoup de grands immeubles où les Ivoiriens et les Sénégalais habitent dans de très beaux appartements de grand standing. Mais dans les petits villages de la brousse[1], les gens habitent dans des petites maisons avec un toit de chaume. Voilà une maison typique de la brousse.

À la Martinique

La Martinique est une belle île francophone dans la mer des Antilles (la mer des Caraïbes). La Martinique est un département français d'outre-mer[2]. Beaucoup de Martiniquais habitent dans des maisons en bois[3]. Les couleurs des maisons martiniquaises sont très belles.

[1] brousse *bush*
[2] d'outre-mer *overseas*
[3] en bois *wooden*

Après la lecture

Le monde francophone Donnez les informations suivantes. *(Give the following information.)*

1. deux grandes villes africaines
2. une région rurale dans beaucoup de pays africains
3. un département français d'outre-mer
4. une île où il y a beaucoup de maisons multicolores en bois

Une maison en bois, Pointe-à-Pitre, Guadeloupe

Answers to Après la lecture

1. Abidjan et Dakar
2. la brousse
3. la Martinique
4. la Martinique

Les noms de famille

En France les noms de famille ont des origines très variées. Certains évoquent une caractéristique physique: **Legrand, Lebrun, Petit.**

D'autres sont des noms de profession.

D'autres sont des noms d'endroits.

D'autres encore sont des termes géographiques.

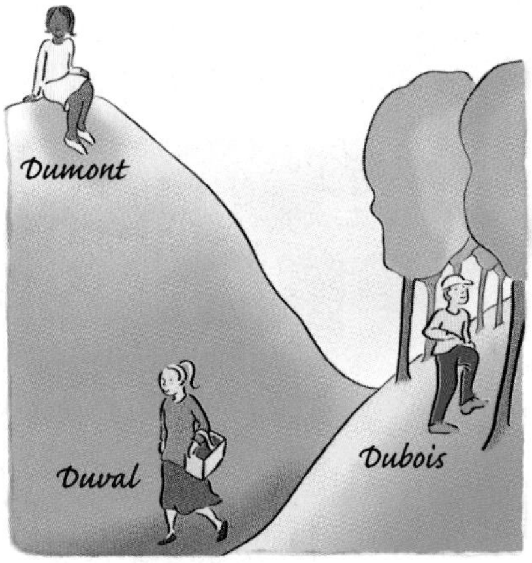

Quel est votre nom de famille?
Il signifie quelque chose de spécial?

Après la lecture

Noms de famille américains Can you think of some American family names for each of the above categories? Can you think of any other categories for American family names?

Answers to Après la lecture

- *American names that reflect professions:* **Carpenter, Baker, Shoemaker**
- *Americans of French descent sometimes have names that reflect places or geographical features:* **Dubois**
- *American family names often reflect "son of"*—**O'Reilly** *(son of O'Reilly) (Irish)* or **Peterson** *(son of Peter),* **Jensen** *(son of Jens) (Scandinavian),* **MacDonald** *(Scottish),* **-ovich** or **-ovna** on a Russian name *(son or daughter of).*

Lecture supplémentaire 2

Attention!

This reading is optional. You may skip it completely, have the entire class read it, have only several students read it and report to the class, or assign it for extra credit.

Presentation

Step 1 Have students read the selection to themselves.

Step 2 Now have students do the **Après la lecture** activity on page 133 individually.

Step 3 You may wish to ask students to share their answers and create a class list on the board.

Expansion: Use the class list of names to find more categories of names. You may even wish to have students research the origin of their family name if possible. Some American family names refer to trades that no longer exist and may not be obvious at first glance. For example: Cooper = barrel maker.

FRENCH Online

Encourage students to take advantage of this opportunity to learn more about French family names. You could do some genealogical research on the Internet, searching for a common French name, or perhaps a student has French ancestors and this family could be researched. You can do this in class or in a lab if students do not have Internet access at home.

National Standards

Connections
The photos of the famous portraits of Marie-Antoinette and her family by French artists on pages 134–135 establish a connection with two other disciplines, fine art and history, allowing students to reinforce and further their knowledge of these areas through the study of French.

Presentation

Les Beaux-Arts
Art et histoire

Step 1 Have students read the introduction in English.

Step 2 Have students read the selection quickly or have them skim it.

Step 3 You may wish to have students find and repeat all the cognates in the reading selection. Explain to them that there are two important strategies to use when reading unfamiliar material—they should learn to recognize cognates and derive meaning from context.

Step 4 Have students work in pairs to find the answers to the **Après la lecture** activity on page 135.

CONNEXIONS

Les Beaux-Arts

Art et histoire

Art and history are often closely connected. Looking at a beautiful painting brings us much enjoyment. It can also teach us a great deal about the period in which the artist produced it. A portrait, for example, shows us how people looked and dressed at the time.

Today many families keep a photo album. Prior to the invention of photography many families had a portrait done. This was particularly true of the royal families, and King Louis XVI and his queen, Marie-Antoinette, were no exception.

Marie-Antoinette à la rose

La portraitiste de Marie-Antoinette

Élisabeth Vigée-Lebrun est née[1] à Paris en 1775 (mille sept cent soixante-quinze). Elle étudie l'art auprès de son père, l'artiste Louis Vigée. La jeune Élisabeth a beaucoup de talent et en très peu de temps[2] elle a du succès. Élisabeth Vigée-Lebrun est la portraitiste de Marie-Antoinette.

Marie-Antoinette

Voici un portrait de Marie-Antoinette avec ses quatre enfants. La reine est une mère dévouée. Elle adore ses enfants.

[1] née *born*
[2] en très peu de temps *in a short time*

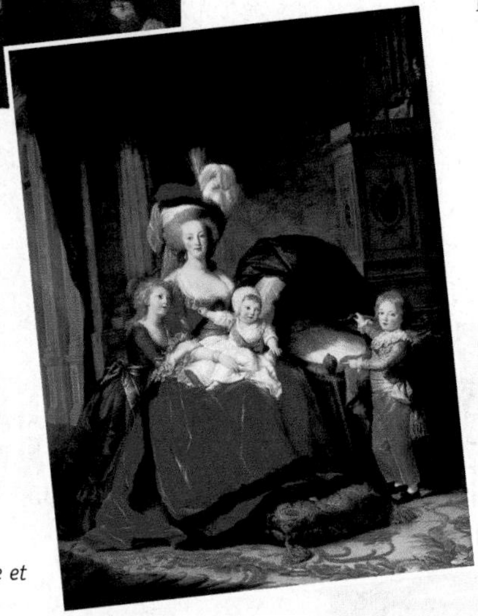

Marie-Antoinette et ses enfants

Versailles

Versailles

La famille royale habite dans le grand palais à Versailles. Mais Marie-Antoinette n'aime pas beaucoup la vie[3] au grand palais. Elle a un petit palais—le Petit Trianon. Pas loin du Petit Trianon Marie-Antoinette a un petit hameau où elle aime passer du temps. Le hameau est un petit village avec des maisonnettes (petites maisons) avec un toit de chaume. Là, Marie-Antoinette aime passer du temps avec les gens[4] simples.

La Révolution

Pendant la Révolution la famille royale est séparée et emprisonnée. Louis XVI et Marie-Antoinette sont guillotinés. *Les adieux de Louis XVI* est un tableau de l'artiste J.-J. Hauer de l'époque révolutionnaire.

[3] vie *life* [4] gens *folks, people*

Le hameau de Marie-Antoinette

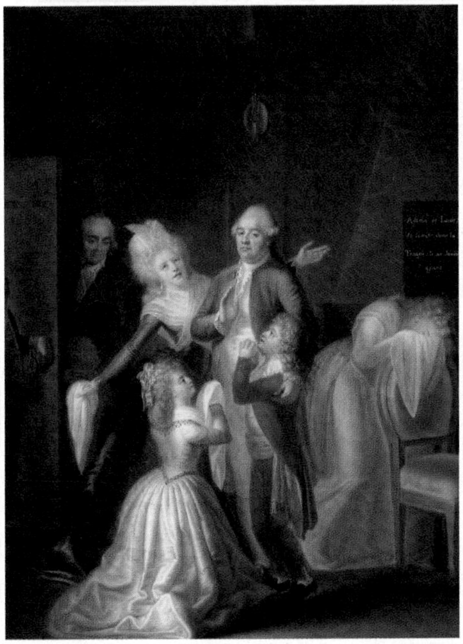

Les adieux de Louis XVI

Après la lecture

La famille royale Donnez les informations suivantes. *(Give the following information.)*

1. le nom de la portraitiste de Marie-Antoinette
2. le nom du mari de Marie-Antoinette
3. la résidence officielle de la famille royale
4. le nom du petit palais de Marie-Antoinette
5. la destinée de la famille royale

CONNEXIONS

History Connection

Louis XVI and his wife Marie-Antoinette were the last of the Bourbon monarchs to live in the great palace of Versailles. They found it too prisonlike for their tastes. Louis took refuge in the much smaller **Petit Trianon** and Marie-Antoinette went often to the small village **(le hameau)**, which her husband diligently built for her. It is said she played at being a milkmaid with **Sèvres** porcelain milk pails.

- Marie-Antoinette (Vienna 1755–Paris 1793) was the daughter of the German Emperor François I and the Austrian Arch Duchess Marie-Thérèse. She spent her childhood in Vienna, and in 1770 she married **le dauphin de France** *(crown prince),* the future Louis XVI. They had four children, two sons and two daughters. It is said that she exercised great influence over her husband, which made conciliation impossible between the monarchy and those in favor of the Revolution. The queen refused to accept the idea of a constitutional monarchy. She was taken prisoner on August 10, 1792, and was transferred on August 2, 1793, to the **Conciergerie** prison in Paris. There, she was sentenced by the Revolutionary Tribunal, accused of plotting for foreign intervention to save the monarchy. She was condemned to death and was executed (guillotined) on October 16, 1793.

Answers to Après la lecture

1. Élisabeth Vigée-Lebrun
2. Louis XVI
3. Versailles
4. le Petit Trianon
5. Louis XVI et Marie-Antoinette sont guillotinés.

Career Connection

Students who pursue careers in the humanities often need to have a reading knowledge of at least one foreign language in order to do research in their discipline. This is particularly true for students of art history, history, and literature.

C'est à vous

Use what you have learned

Recycling

These activities allow students to use the vocabulary and structure from this chapter in completely open-ended, real-life situations.

Writing Development

Have students keep a notebook containing their best written work from each chapter. These selected writings can be based on assignments from the Student Textbook and the Writing Activities Workbook. The three activities on page 137 are examples of writing assignments that may be included in each student's portfolio. In the Workbook, students will develop an organized autobiography **(Mon autobiographie).** These workbook pages may also become a part of their portfolio.

C'est à vous

Use what you have learned

PARLER **1** **Belle résidence**

✔ *Describe a home or apartment*

You are trying to sell one of the apartments or houses listed in the ads. Say as much as you can to convince your client (your classmate) to buy one.

PARLER **2** **L'immeuble**

✔ *Talk about families and where they live*

With a classmate, look at the apartment building. A different family lives on each floor. University students live in the garrets under the roof. Give each family and student a name. Say as much as you can about them and their lodgings.

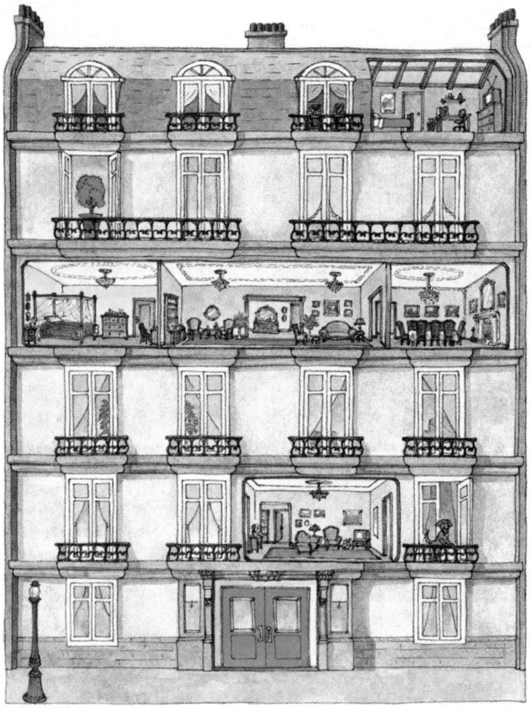

Answers to C'est à vous

1 *Answers will vary but may include:*

C'est une très belle maison. Elle a cinq pièces, une salle de bains, un jardin et une cour.

2 *Answers will vary. Let students express whatever they want to say. Encourage them to be as creative as possible.*

C'est à vous

ÉCRIRE

3 Quinze ans

✔ Invite a friend to a birthday party

A good friend will soon be fifteen. Write an invitation to his or her birthday party. You may wish to use the well-known French expression R.S.V.P.—**Répondez, s'il vous plaît.**

ÉCRIRE

4 Ma famille et moi

✔ Describe yourself and your family

You plan to spend next year as an exchange student in Toulouse, France. You have to write a letter about yourself and your family to the agency in your community that selects the exchange students. Your letter must be in French. Make your description as complete as possible.

Writing Strategy

Ordering details There are several ways to order details when writing. The one you choose depends upon your purpose for writing. When describing a physical place, it is sometimes best to use spatial ordering. This means describing things as they actually appear—from left to right, from back to front, from top to bottom, or any other logical order that works.

ÉCRIRE

5 La maison de mes rêves

Write a description of your dream house. Be as complete as you can.

Un château à Rocamadour, France

Writing Strategy

Ordering details Have students read the Writing Strategy on page 137. If students have difficulty thinking of words to describe houses, have them use the vocabulary list on page 140.

Learning from Photos

(page 137) Rocamadour is a village in central France set in a rather narrow gorge of the river Alzou. It has an interesting history. Legend has it that a certain Zacheus, who had had the honor of entertaining Jesus, came to Gaul after the crucifixion. He took the name Amadour, became a hermit, and built a shrine overlooking the river Alzou. Since then, other chapels and shrines have been built on the cliff. One contains the crypt of St. Amadour. Today the village, named Rocamadour, consists of one single street built in the Middle Ages to shelter pilgrims. Rocamadour attracts pilgrims and tourists alike and is one of the most visited sites in France.

Answers to C'est à vous

3 J'invite les amis de ____ à une fête pour son anniversaire le *(date)*. ____ a quinze ans.
Mon adresse ____________________
La date ____________________
L'heure ____________________
R.S.V.P. au *(numéro de téléphone)*

4 *Answers will vary but may include:*

J'ai quinze ans. Je suis élève dans une école américaine. Je suis grand(e) et brun(e). J'aime parler français et écouter la radio. Je déteste les examens. J'ai une sœur et un chat. Je n'ai pas de frère. Ma mère est sympa et mon père est sociable. Nous avons une belle maison. La maison a sept pièces et deux salles de bains. Il y a un jardin et un garage.

Resource Manager

Communication Transparencies
Quizzes
Test Booklet
ExamView Pro®
Situation Cards
Performance Assessment
Marathon mental Videoquiz

Assessment

This is a pre-test for students to take before you administer the chapter test. Answer sheets for students to do these pages are provided in your transparency binder. Note that each section is cross-referenced so students can easily find the material they have to review in case they made errors. You may wish to collect these assessments and correct them yourself, or you may prefer to have the students correct themselves in class. You can go over the answers orally or project them on the overhead, using your Assessment Answers transparencies.

Glencoe Technology

MINDJOGGER

You may wish to help your students prepare for the chapter test by playing the MindJogger game show. Teams will compete against each other to review chapter vocabulary and structure and sharpen listening comprehension skills.

Assessment

Vocabulaire

To review ***Mots 1,*** *turn to pages 112–113.*

1 Complétez. *(Complete.)*

1. Mes parents sont ma ____ et mon ____.
2. Les parents de mes parents sont mes ____.
3. La sœur de ma mère est ma ____.
4. Le frère de mon père est mon ____.
5. Les enfants de mes oncles et de mes tantes sont mes ____ et mes ____.

To review ***Mots 2,*** *turn to pages 116–117.*

2 Identifiez. *(Identify.)*

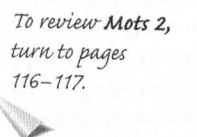

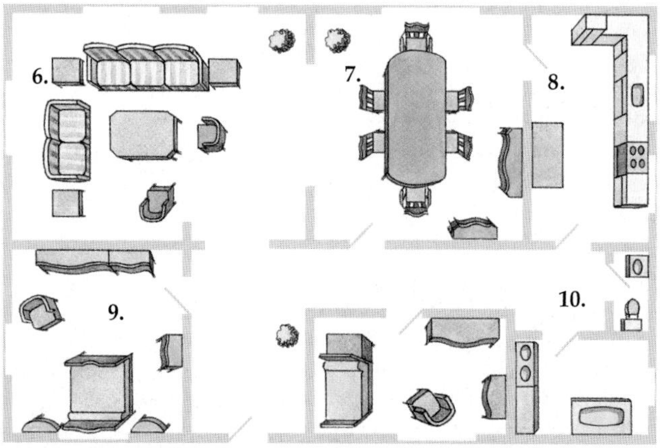

Structure

To review the verb ***avoir,*** *turn to page 120.*

3 Complétez avec «avoir». *(Complete with* avoir.*)*

11. J'____ une petite famille.
12. Marc aussi ____ une petite famille.
13. Sa sœur ____ seize ans.
14. Les parents de Marc et sa sœur ____ un appartement à Paris.
15. Vous ____ une maison ou un appartement?
16. Et toi, tu ____ une petite ou une grande famille?

Answers to Assessment

1

1. mère, père
2. grands-parents
3. tante
4. oncle
5. cousins, cousines

2

6. la salle de séjour
7. la salle à manger
8. la cuisine
9. la chambre à coucher
10. la salle de bains (les toilettes)

3

11. ai
12. a
13. a
14. ont
15. avez
16. as

4 Choisissez. *(Choose.)*

17. Où est la voiture de Serge? ___ voiture est dans le garage?
 a. Sa b. Son c. Ses
18. Où est ___ maison?
 a. ta b. ton c. tes
19. ___ anniversaire est le 4 novembre.
 a. Ma b. Mon c. Mes
20. Paul et Marc sont les frères de Sandrine? Oui, ce sont ___ frères.
 a. leurs b. son c. ses

To review possessive adjectives, turn to page 123.

5 Complétez. *(Complete.)*

21. Il y a de très ___ maisons dans notre ___ quartier. (vieux, beau)
22. Nous avons un ___ appartement avec de ___ pièces. (nouveau, beau)

To review these adjectives, turn to page 126.

Culture

6 Vrai ou faux? *(True or false?)*

23. Les pavillons sont des petites maisons en banlieue.
24. Les H.L.M. sont généralement à l'extérieur des villes.
25. Beaucoup de Français qui habitent en ville, habitent dans une maison privée.

To review this cultural information, turn to pages 130–131.

Des H.L.M.

ANSWERS TO Assessment

4	5	6
17. a	21. vieilles, beau	23. V
18. a	22. nouvel, belles	24. V
19. b		25. F
20. c		

Vocabulaire

Vocabulary Review

The words and phrases in the **Vocabulaire** have been taught for productive use in this chapter. They are summarized here as a resource for both student and teacher. This list also serves as a convenient resource for the **C'est à vous** activities on pages 136–137. There are approximately sixteen cognates in this vocabulary list. Have students find them.

Attention!

You will notice that the vocabulary list here is not translated. This has been done intentionally, since we feel that by the time students have finished the material in the chapter they should be familiar with the meanings of all the words. If there are several words they still do not know, we recommend that they refer back to the **Mots 1** and **2** sections in the chapter or go to the dictionaries at the back of this book to find the meanings. However, if you prefer that your students have the English translations, please refer to Vocabulary Transparency 4-1, where you will find all these words listed with their translations.

Vocabulaire

Identifying family members

la famille
les parents *(m. pl.)*
le père
la mère
le mari
la femme
le fils
la fille
l'enfant *(m. et f.)*
le frère
la sœur
les grands-parents *(m. pl.)*
le grand-père
la grand-mère
les petits-enfants *(m. pl.)*
le petit-fils
la petite-fille
l'oncle
la tante
le neveu
la nièce
le/la cousin(e)
un chat
un chien

Talking about family affairs or events

un anniversaire
un cadeau
un gâteau
une bougie
une fête
donner
inviter
avoir… ans
Quel âge… ?

How well do you know your vocabulary?

- Find the sixteen cognates.
- Use as many of them as you can to write a story.

Identifying the rooms of a house

une pièce
une salle de séjour
une cuisine
une salle à manger
une chambre à coucher
une salle de bains
des toilettes *(f. pl.)*

Talking about a home and the neighborhood

une maison
un appartement
un immeuble
un quartier
une station de métro
une terrasse
un jardin
un arbre
une fleur
un garage
une voiture
un balcon
une vue
le rez-de-chaussée
un étage
un escalier
un ascenseur
une entrée
un code
une cour
un(e) voisin(e)
beau, belle
nouveau, nouvelle
vieux, vieille
premier, première
deuxième
troisième
(tout) près de
loin de
donner sur
monter
à pied
en ascenseur

Other useful words and expressions

une journée
tout le monde
autour de (d')
il y a
C'est (pas) rigolo.

Technotour

BON VOYAGE!

VIDÉO • Épisode 4

Avant de visionner

In this video episode, Christine and Mme Seguin, secretary at the International Youth Institute, take a trip to Giverny.

Christine a une surprise pour Mme Seguin.

Christine et Mme Seguin dans la cuisine de la maison de Monet

FRENCH ONLINE

À découvrir

Learn more about Monet's house and Giverny, a charming village northwest of Paris, online.

Les jardins autour de la maison de Monet

FRENCH *Online*

In the Chapter 4 Internet activity, you will have a chance to learn about renting or buying a house or an apartment in a French-speaking country. To begin your virtual adventure, go to the Glencoe French Web site: **french.glencoe.com**

Technotour

Overview

This page previews two key multimedia components of the **Glencoe French** series. Each reinforces the material taught in the chapter in a unique manner.

VIDÉO

The Video Program allows students to see how the chapter vocabulary and structures are used by native speakers. For maximum reinforcement, show the video episode as a final activity for Chapter 4.

The two photos on the left show highlights from the Chapter 4 video episode. Discuss the photos with your students before viewing the episode. See the Video Activities Booklet for detailed suggestions for using this resource.

FRENCH *Online*

- The **À découvrir** photo shows Monet's home at Giverny. Students can go online to learn more about his home there.
- Teacher Information and Student Worksheets for this activity can be accessed at the Web site.

Video Synopsis

In this video episode, we see Christine with Madame Seguin, the school secretary at the International Youth Institute. She is taking Madame Seguin on a surprise trip. When Christine unfolds the blindfold, Madame Seguin finds herself in Giverny, home of Claude Monet. Christine and Madame Seguin lead us on a tour of the spectacular home of this famous painter. This leads Christine to tell us about her home in Martinique, at which point we zoom in on Christine's viewing screen to her family and a tour of Martinique—her homeland.

Révision

Preview

This section reviews the salient points from Chapters 1–4. In the **Conversation,** students will review **avoir,** addresses, and birthday vocabulary. In the **Structure** sections, they will review the present tense of **-er** verbs, **être, avoir,** articles, adjectives, and possessive adjectives.

Resource Manager

Workbook, Self-Test, pages 39–42
Test Booklet

Presentation

Conversation

Step 1 Have students open their books. Call on two students to read this short conversation aloud.

Step 2 Go over the activity in the **Après la conversation** section.

Learning from Photos

(page 142 top) Boulevard Haussmann is one of the **Grands Boulevards** of Paris. The **Grands Boulevards** form a semicircle of wide streets running from the **Place de la République** in the west to Madeleine in the east. The **Grands Boulevards** were very fashionable in the late eighteenth and early nineteenth centuries for strolling and taking in the fresh air. Today, because of the traffic, they are no longer pleasant for strolling, but they do have many stores, movie houses, theaters, and restaurants.

Révision

Conversation

Un anniversaire

Sandrine: Bonjour, Christophe. Ça va?
Christophe: Oui, ça va. Et toi?
Sandrine: Pas mal. Qu'est-ce que tu as dans ton sac?
Christophe: J'ai un cadeau pour ma sœur. C'est son anniversaire aujourd'hui.
Sandrine: Ta sœur Mélanie? Elle a quel âge?
Christophe: Elle a seize ans. Et Sandrine, tu as ma nouvelle adresse?
Sandrine: Ta nouvelle adresse? Tu n'habites pas rue de l'Odéon?
Christophe: Non, maintenant on habite dans le 5e, tout près de la station de métro Maubert-Mutualité.

Le boulevard Hausmann, Paris

La station de métro Maubert-Mutualité

Après la conversation

Répondez. *(Answer.)*

1. Sandrine parle à qui?
2. Qu'est-ce qu'il y a dans son sac?
3. C'est l'anniversaire de qui?
4. C'est quand, son anniversaire?
5. Elle a quel âge?
6. Qui a une nouvelle adresse?
7. Il habite où maintenant?
8. Il habite près de quelle station de métro?

Reaching All Students

Additional Practice Have students work together in pairs to make up their own conversations about their birthday, where they live, and their family. Have several pairs present their conversation to the class.

Answers to Après la conversation

1. Sandrine parle à Christophe.
2. Il y a un cadeau pour sa sœur.
3. C'est l'anniversaire de la sœur de Christophe.
4. C'est aujourd'hui son anniversaire.
5. Elle a seize ans.
6. Christophe a une nouvelle adresse.
7. Il habite dans le 5e.
8. Il habite près de la station Maubert-Mutualité.

Structure

Les verbes au présent

1. Review the forms of regular **-er** verbs.

PARLER	je parle, tu parles, il/elle/on parle, nous parlons, vous parlez, ils/elles parlent
AIMER	j'aime, tu aimes, il/elle/on‿aime, nous‿aimons, vous‿aimez, ils‿/elles‿aiment

2. Review the irregular verbs you have learned so far.

ÊTRE	je suis, tu es, il/elle/on‿est, nous sommes, vous‿êtes, ils/elles sont
AVOIR	j'ai, tu as, il/elle/on‿a, nous‿avons, vous‿avez, ils‿/elles‿ont

3. Review the placement of **ne (n')... pas** when expressing a negative idea.

Je ne travaille pas.
Il n'habite pas à Paris.

1 Historiette **Flore habite à Paris.**

Inventez une histoire. *(Make up a story.)*

1. Flore habite à Paris?
2. Elle quitte la maison à quelle heure le matin?
3. Et toi, tu habites où?
4. Le matin, tu arrives à l'école à quelle heure?
5. Tu parles français ou anglais à l'école?
6. Et Flore, qu'est-ce qu'elle parle?
7. Flore quitte le collège à cinq heures de l'après-midi?
8. Tes copains et toi, vous quittez l'école à quelle heure?
9. Vous travaillez après les cours?
10. Les élèves français travaillent après les cours?

Answers to Révision

1 *Answers will vary but may include:*

1. Oui, Flore habite à Paris.
2. Elle quitte la maison à sept heures et quart.
3. J'habite à ____.
4. Le matin, j'arrive à l'école à ____.
5. Je parle anglais à l'école.
6. Flore parle français.
7. Oui, Flore quitte le collège à cinq heures de l'après-midi.
8. Mes copains et moi, nous quittons l'école à trois heures et demie.
9. Oui, je travaille après les cours.
10. Les élèves français ne travaillent pas après les cours.

Révision

Presentation

Les verbes au présent

Step 1 Quickly go over the verb paradigms that appear on page 143.

Step 2 You may also write the verbs on the board and underline the endings. Have students pronounce each form after you. Repeat the **je, tu, il/elle/on, ils/elles** forms, emphasizing that they are all pronounced the same way in spite of their spelling differences.

Step 3 Ask a student to name another **-er** verb. Write its forms on the board alongside **parler** and have the class quickly repeat the verb.

Step 4 Have students repeat the forms of **avoir** and **être** after you as they read along in their books.

History Connection

Le baron Haussmann was named Prefect of La Seine by Napoléon III in 1853. Surrounded by the best architects and engineers of the time, Haussmann undertook the modernization and beautification of Paris. He designed a new city of wide boulevards and picturesque side streets. He replaced pastures to build the Champs-Élysées and the twelve avenues that form a star **(l'étoile)** around it.

(bottom) **Maubert-Mutualité** This metro stop is on the boulevard Saint-Germain.

2 Have students write a paragraph for homework (modeled after Activity 2) in which they substitute information about their own family for the information in the text.

Presentation

Les articles et les adjectifs

Step 1 Have students open their books to page 144. Read the explanation aloud with them. Have them repeat the model words and sentences after you.

Step 2 Now do Activities 3–5 on pages 145–146.

Learning from Photos

(page 144 top) Ask students the following questions about the family in the photo.

Il y a combien de personnes dans la famille? Il y a combien d'enfants? Combien de filles? Combien de garçons? La mère est blonde? Et les autres, ils sont blonds ou pas? Qui est brun? Comment est la mère? Et le père? Ils ont un chien ou un chat?

(page 144 bottom) You may wish to ask the following questions about this photo.

Les deux copains sont français ou américains? Ils sont où? La fille est blonde ou brune? Et le garçon, il est blond ou brun? Ils sont sympas?

2 **Historiette** **Une famille**

Complétez. *(Complete.)*

1. Bonjour. Moi, je ____ français. Je ____ de Paris. (être)
2. Ma famille n'____ pas très grande. Nous ____ quatre. (être)
3. J'____ une sœur. (avoir)
4. Ma sœur ____ dix ans et moi, j'____ dix-sept ans. (avoir)
5. Et vous, vous ____ quel âge? (avoir)
6. Vous ____ américain(e) ou français(e)? (être)

Une famille française avec leur chat

Les articles et les adjectifs

1. Review the following forms of the indefinite and definite articles.

un garçon	**une fille**	
des copains	**des‿écoles**	
le garçon	**la fille**	**l'ami(e)**
les copains	**les‿écoles**	**les‿ami(e)s**

2. Adjectives that end in a consonant have four forms.

Le garçon est brun.	**Les garçons sont bruns.**
La fille est brune.	**Les filles sont brunes.**

3. Adjectives that end in **e** have only two forms, singular and plural.

un ami sympathique	**des amis sympathiques**
une amie sympathique	**des amies sympathiques**

Deux copains sympathiques à Paris

Answers to Révision

2

1. suis, suis
2. est, sommes
3. ai
4. a, ai
5. avez
6. êtes

Reaching All Students

Additional Practice Have students give you adjectives that they know. Write them on the board. Then call on students to give you original sentences using these adjectives.

Révision

3 Historiette La famille de Valentin

Complétez avec **un, une** ou **des.** *(Complete with* un, une, *or* des.*)*

Valentin a une grande famille. Il a __1__ père et __2__ mère. Il a __3__ frères et __4__ sœurs? Oui, il a trois frères et quatre sœurs. Il a aussi sept cousins, mais __5__ seule cousine. Il a __6__ chien, Tifou, et __7__ chat, Pompon.

Valentin et sa famille habitent dans __8__ grande maison à Pontchartrain. Valentin est élève dans __9__ lycée de la région. Valentin est __10__ élève excellent.

4 C'est qui?

Complétez avec **le, la, l'** ou **les.** *(Complete with* le, la, l', *or* les.*)*

1. Guillaume est ____ ami de Loïc.
2. Joanne est ____ sœur de Guillaume.
3. Mais Joanne n'est pas ____ amie de Loïc.
4. Justine et Mélanie sont ____ amies de Joanne et Guillaume.
5. Marc et Jean-Paul aussi sont ____ amis de Joanne et Guillaume.
6. Guillaume est ____ frère de Joanne et Christelle.
7. Christelle est ____ cousine de Loïc.

Learning from Photos

(page 145) Have students prepare a real estate advertisement for the house in the photo.

Answers to Révision

3

1. un
2. une
3. des
4. des
5. une
6. un
7. un
8. une
9. un
10. un

4

1. l'
2. la
3. l'
4. les
5. les
6. le
7. la

Presentation

Les adjectifs possessifs

Step 1 Have students repeat the model words after you. Have them point to themselves as they say **mon, ma, mes;** to a friend as they say **ton, ta, tes;** and to a boy, then a girl as they say **son, sa, ses;** to themselves and a friend as they say **notre, nos;** to two friends as they say **votre, vos;** to two or more friends behind them *(not speaking to them)* as they say **leur, leurs.**

5 **Sa sœur aussi** Répondez d'après le modèle. *(Answer according to the model.)*

—Il est très intelligent.
—Sa sœur aussi est très intelligente.

1. Il est content.
2. Il est amusant.
3. Il est sympathique.
4. Il est énergique.
5. Il est très intéressant.
6. Il est brun.

Les adjectifs possessifs

1. Review the forms of the possessive adjectives. The adjectives **mon, ton,** and **son** have three forms.

mon‿appartement	ma maison	mes‿appartements	mes maisons
ton‿appartement	ta maison	tes‿appartements	tes maisons
son‿appartement	sa maison	ses‿appartements	ses maisons

2. The adjectives **notre, votre,** and **leur** have two forms—singular and plural.

notre appartement	notre maison	nos‿appartements	nos maisons
votre appartement	votre maison	vos‿appartements	vos maisons
leur appartement	leur maison	leurs‿appartements	leurs maisons

3. Remember that you use **mon, ton, son** before a feminine singular noun that begins with a vowel or silent **h: mon‿adresse, mon‿amie.**

La salle à manger de la maison de Monet à Giverny

Answers to Révision

5

1. Sa sœur aussi est contente.
2. Sa sœur aussi est amusante.
3. Sa sœur aussi est sympathique.
4. Sa sœur aussi est énergique.
5. Sa sœur aussi est très intéressante.
6. Sa sœur aussi est brune.

Révision

6 **Qui?** Complétez. *(Complete.)*

Julien a un frère, Paul, et une sœur, Magali. __1__ parents ont donc trois enfants. __2__ trois enfants sont Julien, __3__ frère et __4__ sœur.

—Julien, __5__ frère a quel âge?

—Euh… __6__ frère a quinze ans et __7__ sœur a neuf ans.

—Julien et Paul, comment est __8__ prof de musique?

—Qui? __9__ prof de musique? Il est très sympa. Beaucoup de __10__ profs sont sympas.

École nationale de musique et de danse, Yerres

7 **Un(e) amie** Work with a classmate. Each of you will tell about a friend. Describe your friend, some things he or she does and where he or she lives.

8 **Une conversation** Have a conversation with a classmate. Talk about your school, classes, family, and house.

LITERARY COMPANION *You may wish to read the adaptation of* La petite Fadette, *a novel by George Sand. You will find this literary selection on page 504.*

Learning from Photos

(page 147) You may want to teach students the expression **jouer de** and ask the following questions about the photo.

C'est un cours de musique?
Le garçon joue du violon?
Le prof de musique joue du violon ou du piano?
Tu joues du piano?
Tu aimes la musique?

Literary Companion

When you finish this review section, if you wish, have students read the literary adaptation of ***La petite Fadette,*** on pages 504–509. This adaptation has been done in accordance with the vocabulary and structures that students have acquired up to this point.

ANSWERS TO Révision

6

1. Ses
2. Leurs
3. son
4. sa
5. ton
6. mon
7. ma
8. votre
9. notre
10. nos

7 *Answers will vary.*

8 *Answers will vary.*

Preview

This section, **Reflets de la France,** was prepared by the National Geographic Society. Its purpose is to give students greater insight, through these visual images, into the culture and people of France. Have students look at the photographs on pages 148–151 for enjoyment. If they would like to talk about them, let them say anything they can, using the vocabulary they have learned to this point.

National Standards

Cultures
The **Reflets de la France** photos and the accompanying captions allow students to gain insights into the people and culture of France.

About the Photos

1. Champ de coquelicots en Provence Les coquelicots, or poppies, are extremely common throughout almost all regions of France. The poppies, with their beautiful red flowers, grow wild in wheat or cornfields.

2. Quart de finale de la coupe de l'UEFA à Lens The UEFA is the European Football (Soccer) Association. All the big professional teams belong to this association. The northern industrial city of Lens is in the center of an important area near Pas-de-Calais.

3. La cité médiévale de Carcassonne Carcassonne is the site of the largest medieval fortress in Europe. At night, the entire circle of towers and battlements high on a hill are brilliantly floodlit. **La Cité** is the walled city within the fortress. Parts of the walls were built by the Romans and later the Visigoths. Charlemagne laid siege to the fortress for some five years in the ninth century. In the last half of the seventeenth century, the fortress lost much of its military importance and began to fall into ruin. In 1844, the great architect Viollet-le-Duc was commissioned to rebuild the battlements and the tower. This restoration was the world's first restoration of such magnitude.

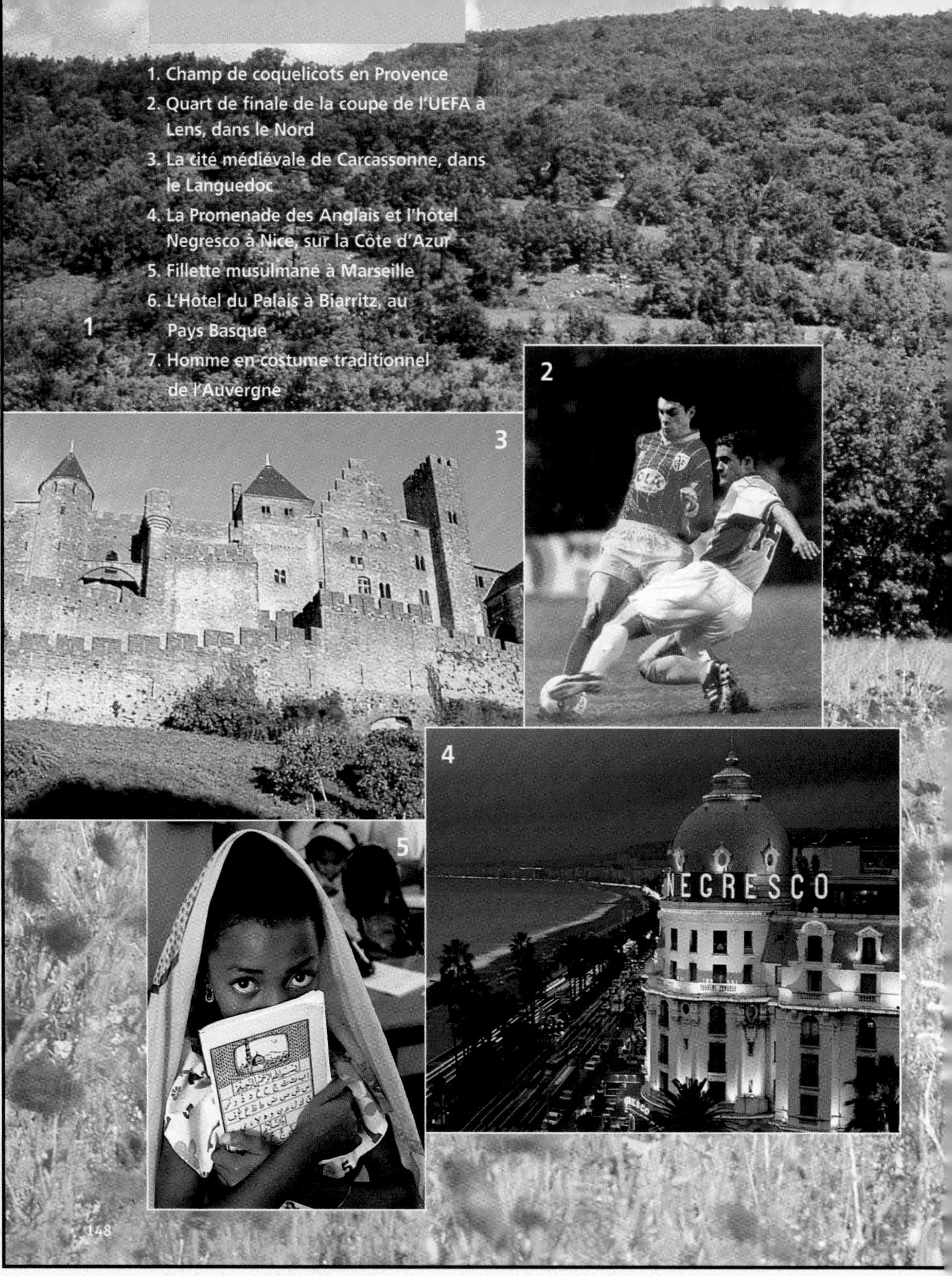

1. Champ de coquelicots en Provence
2. Quart de finale de la coupe de l'UEFA à Lens, dans le Nord
3. La cité médiévale de Carcassonne, dans le Languedoc
4. La Promenade des Anglais et l'hôtel Negresco à Nice, sur la Côte d'Azur
5. Fillette musulmane à Marseille
6. L'Hôtel du Palais à Biarritz, au Pays Basque
7. Homme en costume traditionnel de l'Auvergne

4. La Promenade des Anglais et l'hôtel Negresco à Nice, sur la Côte d'Azur Nice is often referred to as the Queen of the Riviera. Here we see the plush **Promenade des Anglais** that skirts the beautiful **Baie des Anges.** Nice has attracted visitors for more than a hundred years. The clientele of the palatial hotels lining the **Promenade des Anglais** were mostly rich foreigners and French in search of some winter sun. Today, Nice also attracts a somewhat more modest crowd. The Hôtel Negresco is synonymous with old-world elegance. It is an official historical monument.

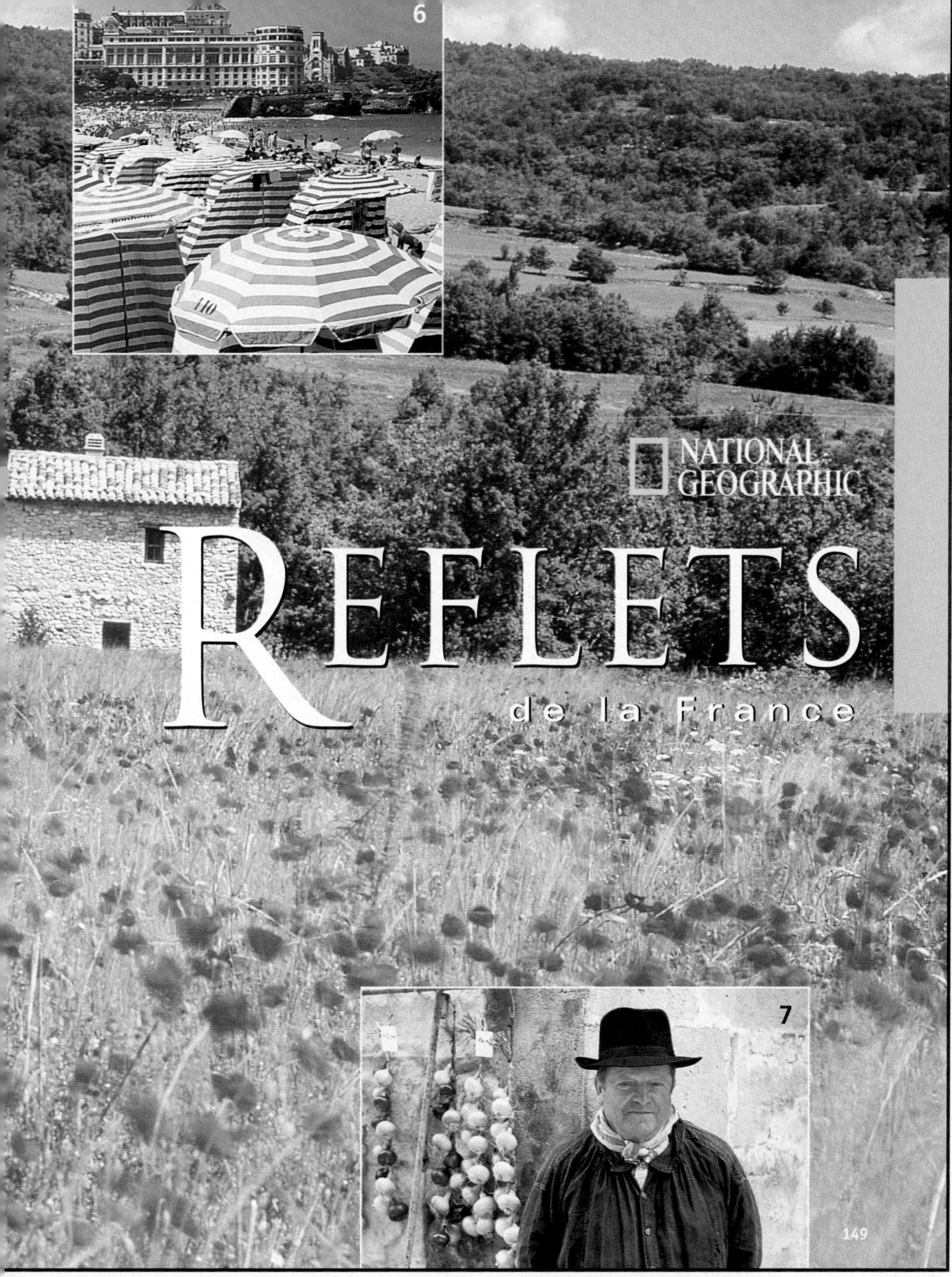

5. Fillette musulmane à Marseille Marseille, the most important port of the Mediterranean for more than two thousand years, is the third largest city in France. Since its founding by the Greeks in the year 600, Marseilles has been the home to many different ethnic groups. Today, Marseilles has a large North African **(Maghrébin)** population. The Moslem religion is the second largest in France today.

6. L'Hôtel du Palais à Biarritz Biarritz is the gateway to the French Basque country. It is a well-known beach resort and enjoys a very favorable year-round climate. The Hôtel du Palais was formerly Empress Eugénie's villa. Empress Eugénie, (1826–1920), the wife of Napoléon III, was born Eugenia María de Montijo. She was among the Spanish exiles from the Carlist wars who put Biarritz on the map when they could no longer enjoy themselves in nearby San Sebastián on the Spanish coast. Many of Europe's crowned heads have slept in the Hôtel du Palais.

7. Homme en costume traditionnel de l'Auvergne Auvergne is located mainly in the Massif Central, France's mountainous heartland in the exact center of the country. Auvergne is basically a rural area and it is often referred to as **la France profonde,** a term that is somewhat similar to "middle America."

8. Paons dans le parc du château de Valençay dans la vallée de la Loire The beautiful Loire Valley to the southwest of Paris is known as the Chateau Country because in this area there are at least a thousand châteaux. Because this area enjoys a relatively mild climate and has many lush fields and vineyards, many French consider it the garden of France. The château de Valençay resembles the beautiful and famous château de Chambord, but it is somewhat smaller. The most famous inhabitant of this château was the diplomat, bishop, and politician Talleyrand. He bought the château while he was the Foreign Minister for Napoléon. The grounds of the château de Valençay are a haven for many species of birds including peacocks, unusual ducks, and parrots.

9. Fillette en costume traditionnel au festival d'Obernai Obernai is a very picturesque Alsatian town. Sainte Odile, the patron saint of Alsace, was born in Obernai. The beautiful convent of Sainte Odile is a place of pilgrimage.

10. Le Mont-Saint-Michel Mont-Saint-Michel on the Normandy coast is often called **la merveille de l'Occident.** It is a granite offshore mount on top of which there is a Gothic abbey with a very tall spire. The first chapel was built on the mount in the eighth century, and it has been an extremely popular pilgrimage site ever since. The bay that surrounds the mount can be very dangerous. The tides are extreme and the high tide arrives at a tremendously high speed, making the mount an island. During the low tide, the water completely recedes and there are dangerous patches of quicksand.

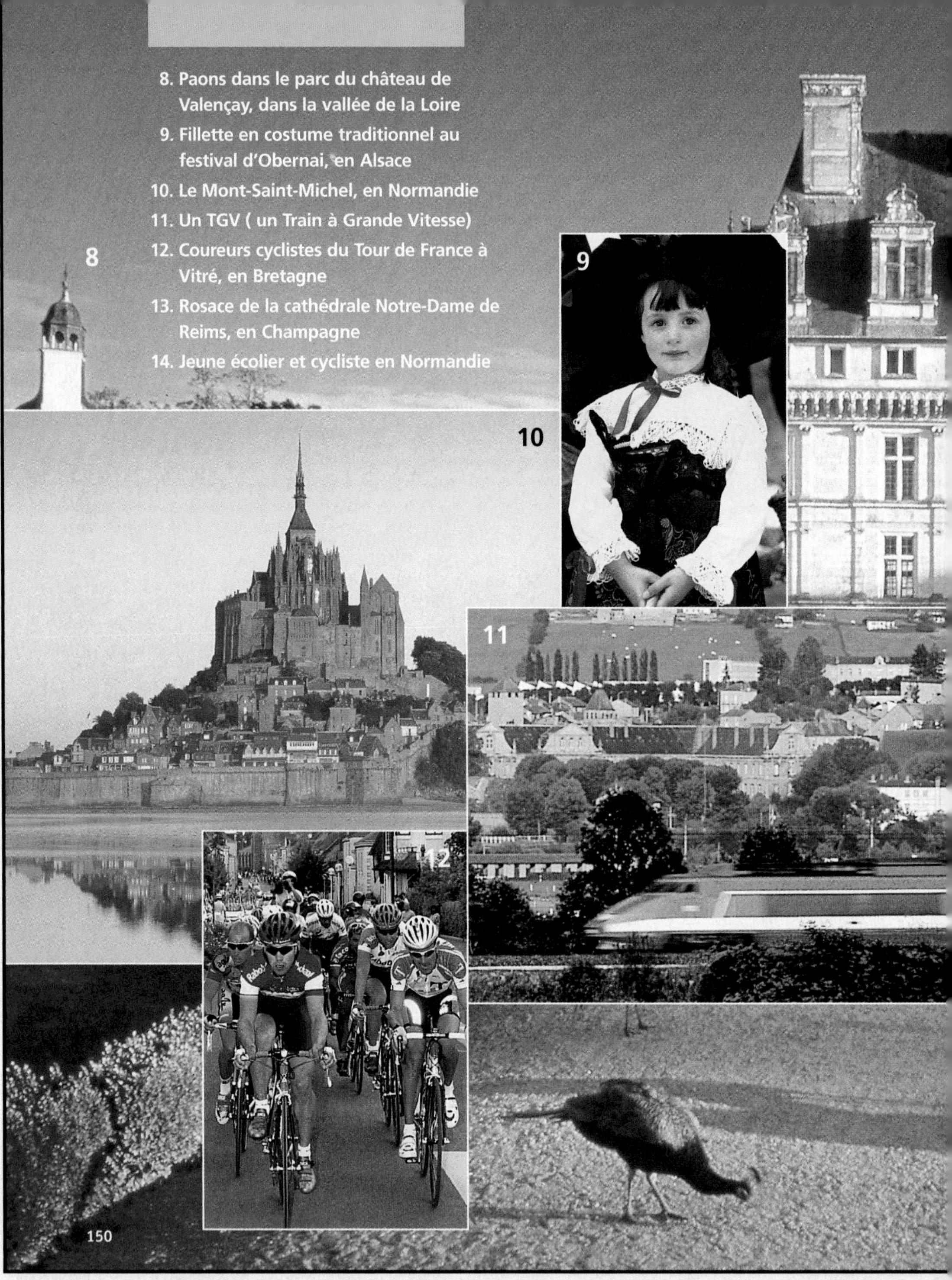
8. Paons dans le parc du château de Valençay, dans la vallée de la Loire
9. Fillette en costume traditionnel au festival d'Obernai, en Alsace
10. Le Mont-Saint-Michel, en Normandie
11. Un TGV (un Train à Grande Vitesse)
12. Coureurs cyclistes du Tour de France à Vitré, en Bretagne
13. Rosace de la cathédrale Notre-Dame de Reims, en Champagne
14. Jeune écolier et cycliste en Normandie
8
9
10
11
12
150

NATIONAL GEOGRAPHIC Teacher's Corner

Index to the NATIONAL GEOGRAPHIC MAGAZINE

The following related articles may be of interest:

- "Art Treasures from the Ice Age: Lascaux Cave," by Jean-Philippe Rigaud, October 1998.
- "Essence of Provence," by Bill Bryson, September 1995.
- "Europe Faces an Immigrant Tide," by Peter Range, May 1993.
- "Darcey: A Village That Refuses to Die," by William S. Ellis, July 1989.
- "Tour de France—An Annual Madness," by Gilbert Duclos-Lassalle, July 1989.
- "The Great Revolution," by Merle Severy, July 1989.
- "Paris: *La Belle Époque*," by Eugen Weber, July 1989.
- "The Civilizing Seine," by Charles McCarry, April 1982.

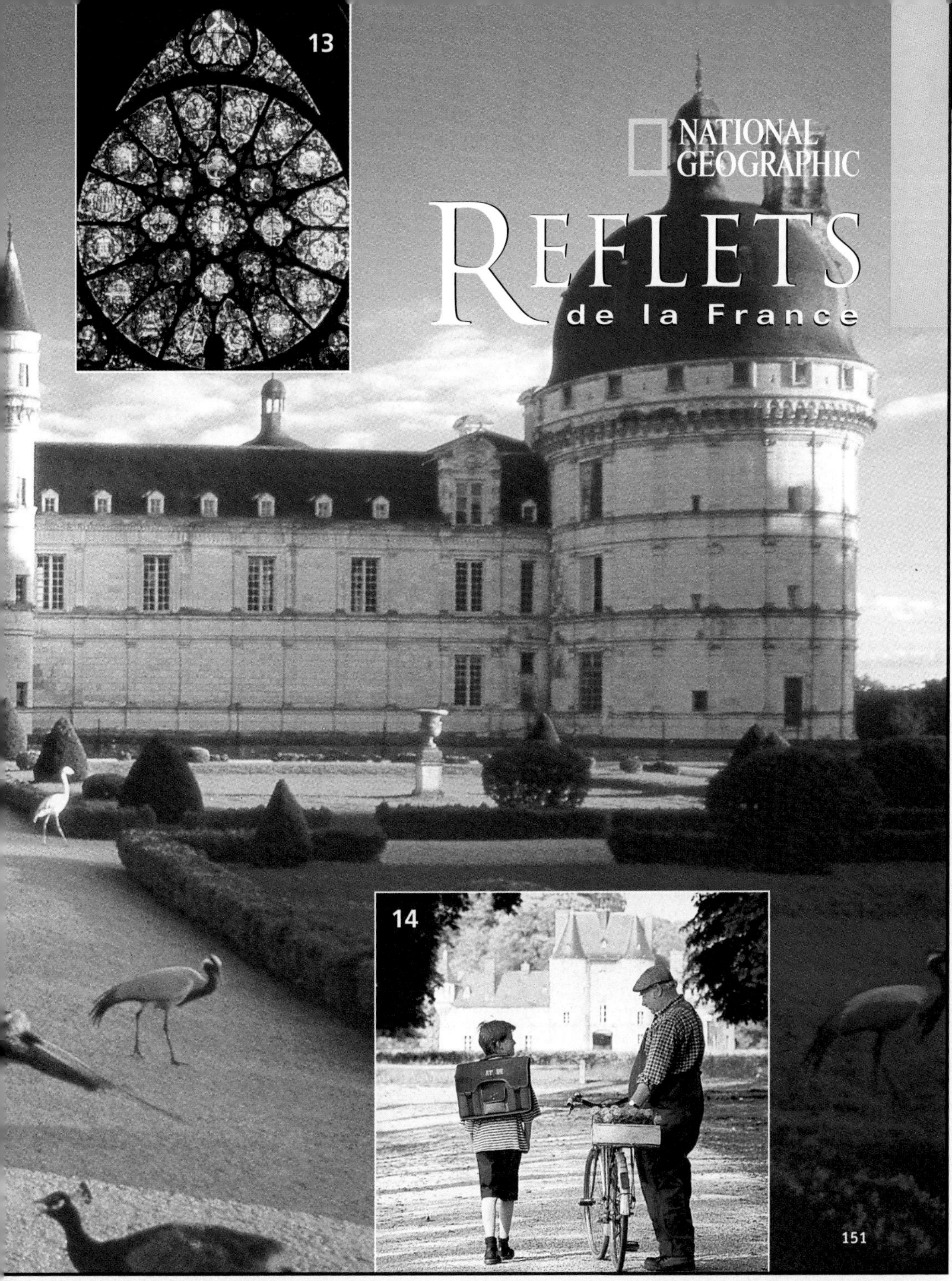

11. Un TGV The first TGV was put into service between Paris and Lyon in 1981. The **TGV Atlantique** began service in 1989 and the **TGV Nord** in 1994. New routes are added to the system as tracks are completed. For more information on the **TGV, le train à grande vitesse,** please refer to the **Lecture** on page 118 of **Bon voyage! Level 2.**

12. Coureurs cyclistes For information on the **Tour de France,** please refer to the **Lecture** on pages 344–345 of **Bon voyage!**

13. Rosace de la cathédrale Notre-Dame de Reims The cathedral at Reims is one of the greatest Gothic structures in France. It was in this cathedral that the kings of France were consecrated. The construction of the cathedral began in 1211 and ended a century later. The twin towers were completed in the fifteenth century. The enormous rose window seen here is on the cathedral's western façade as are its portals and twin towers. The interior of the cathedral is quite simple except for its majestic proportions. On one of the side chapels there are six stained glass windows by Marc Chagall.

14. Jeune écolier et cycliste en Normandie Normandy is a beautiful region of granite cliffs, sand beaches, wooded valleys, and lush meadows. It is famous for its cider, delicious butter, cheese, and cream. Normandy is also the region of William the Conqueror, Joan of Arc, the Bayeux Tapestry, Mont-Saint-Michel and the D-Day landing beaches.

Products available from GLENCOE/MCGRAW-HILL

To order the following products, call Glencoe/McGraw-Hill at 1-800-334-7344.

CD-ROMs
- Picture Atlas of the World
- The Complete National Geographic: 112 Years of National Geographic Magazine

Transparency Set
- NGS PicturePack: Geography of Europe

Products available from NATIONAL GEOGRAPHIC SOCIETY

To order the following products, call National Geographic Society at 1-800-368-2728.

Books
- National Geographic World Atlas for Young Explorers
- National Geographic Satellite Atlas of the World

Software
- ZingoLingo: French Diskette

Video
- France
- Europe

Planning for Chapter 5

SCOPE AND SEQUENCE, PAGES 152–183

Topics

- Going to a café or restaurant
- Going places

Culture

- Discussing differences between restaurants in the United States and France
- Discussing meals in France
- Dining out in France

Functions

- How to order food in a restaurant
- How to express where you are going
- How to give locations
- How to express what belongs to you

Structure

- The verb **aller** in the present tense
- **Aller** + infinitive
- Contractions with **à** and **de**
- The verb **prendre** in the present tense

National Standards

- Communication Standard 1.1 pages 156, 157, 160, 161, 163, 164, 165, 166, 167, 168, 169, 171, 178
- Communication Standard 1.2 pages 156, 157, 160, 161, 163, 164, 165, 166, 167, 168, 169, 170, 173, 174, 175, 177
- Communication Standard 1.3 pages 156, 160, 164, 165, 166, 168, 169, 179
- Cultures Standard 2.1 pages 154, 155, 159, 172–173, 174, 175
- Cultures Standard 2.2 pages 155, 174, 175
- Connections Standard 3.1 pages 176–177
- Comparisons Standard 4.1 pages 176–177
- Comparisons Standard 4.2 pages 172–173, 174
- Communities Standard 5.1 page 179

PACING AND PRIORITIES

The chapter content is color coded below to assist you in planning.

■ required ■ recommended ■ optional

Vocabulaire *(required)* *Days 1–4*

- ■ Mots 1
  - À la terrasse d´un café
- ■ Mots 2
  - Le couvert
  - Au restaurant
  - Les trois repas de la journée

Structure *(required)* *Days 5–7*

- ■ Le verbe **aller** au présent
- ■ **Aller** + infinitif
- ■ Les contractions avec **à** et **de**
- ■ Le verbe **prendre**

Conversation *(required)*

- ■ Au restaurant

Prononciation *(recommended)*

- ■ Le son **/r/**

Lectures culturelles

- ■ Au restaurant? Vraiment? *(recommended)*
- ■ Les repas en France *(optional)*
- ■ Les goûts changent *(optional)*

Connexions *(optional)*

- ■ L´arithmétique

■ **C'est à vous** *(recommended)*

■ **Assessment** *(recommended)*

■ **Technotour** *(optional)*

RESOURCE GUIDE

Section	Pages	Section Resources
Vocabulaire *Mots 1*		
À la terrasse d´un café	154–157	Vocabulary Transparencies 5.2–5.3 Audiocassette 4A/CD 4 Audio Activities Booklet TE, pages 62–64 Workbook, pages 43–44 Quiz 1, page 22 ExamView Pro®
Vocabulaire *Mots 2*		
Le couvert Au restaurant Les trois repas de la journée	158 158–159 159–161	Vocabulary Transparencies 5.4–5.5 Audiocassette 4A/CD 4 Audio Activities Booklet TE, pages 64–65 Workbook, pages 45–46 Quiz 2, page 23 ExamView Pro®
Structure		
Le verbe **aller** au présent **Aller** + infinitif Les contractions avec **à** et **de** Le verbe **prendre**	162–164 165 166–167 168–169	Audiocassette 4A/CD 4 Audio Activities Booklet TE, pages 66–68 Workbook, pages 47–50 Quizzes 3–6, pages 24–27 ExamView Pro®
Conversation		
Au restaurant	170	Audiocassette 4A/CD 4 Audio Activities Booklet TE, pages 69–70 CD-ROM
Prononciation		
Le son **/r/**	171	Pronunciation Transparency P 5 Audiocassette 4A/CD 4 Audio Activities Booklet TE, page 70
Lectures culturelles		
Au restaurant? Vraiment? Les repas en France Les goûts changent	172–173 174 175	Audiocassette 4A/CD 4 Audio Activities Booklet TE, page 71 Test Booklet, Chapter 5
Connexions		
L´arithmétique	176–177	Test Booklet, Chapter 5
C'est à vous		
	178–179	**Bon voyage!** Video, Episode 5 Video Activities Booklet, Chapter 5 French Online Activities french.glencoe.com
Assessment		
	180–181	Communication Transparency C 5 Quizzes 1–6, pages 22–27 Test Booklet, Chapter 5 ExamView Pro® Situation Cards, Chapter 5 **Marathon mental** Videoquiz

Using Your Resources for Chapter 5

Transparencies

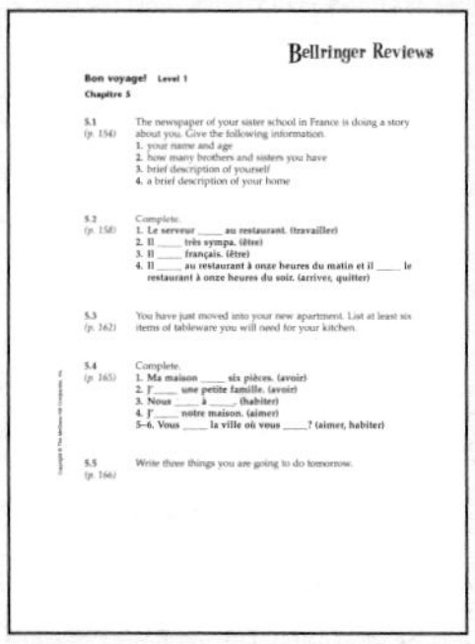
Bellringer 5.1–5.8

Vocabulary 5.1–5.5

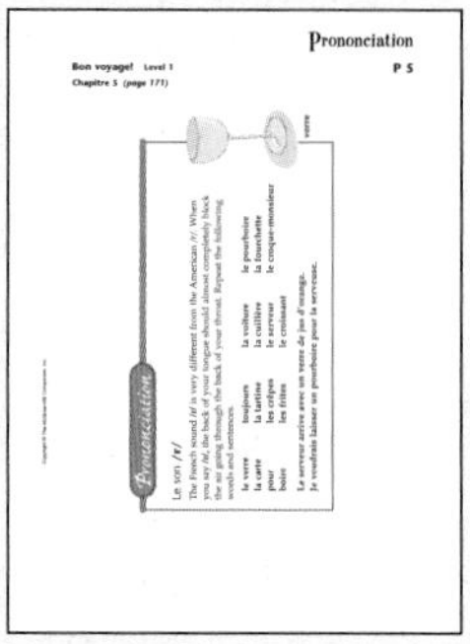
Pronunciation P 5

Communication C 5

Writing Activities Workbook

Vocabulary, pages 43–46

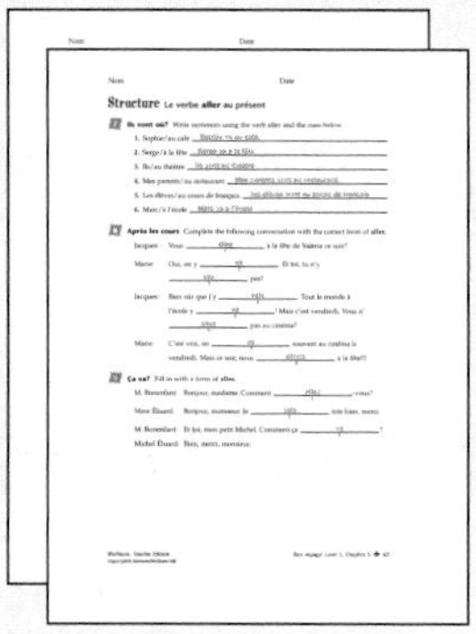
Structure, pages 47–50

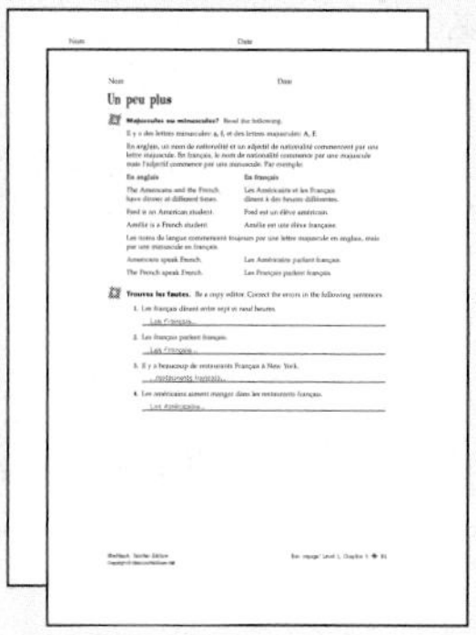
Enrichment, pages 51–54

Audio Program and Audio Activities Booklet

Vocabulary, pages 62–65

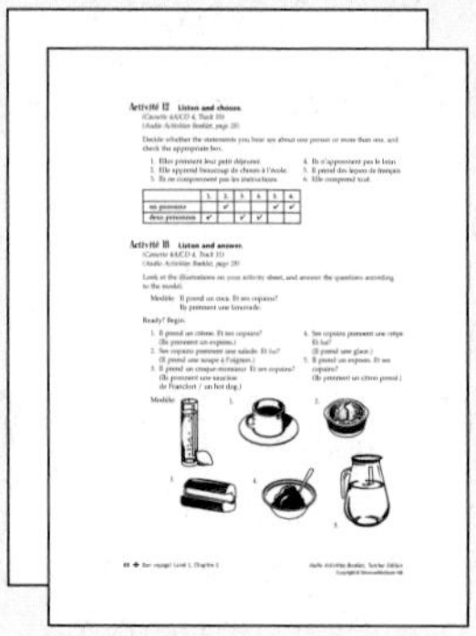
Structure, pages 66–68

Conversation, Pronunciation, pages 69–70

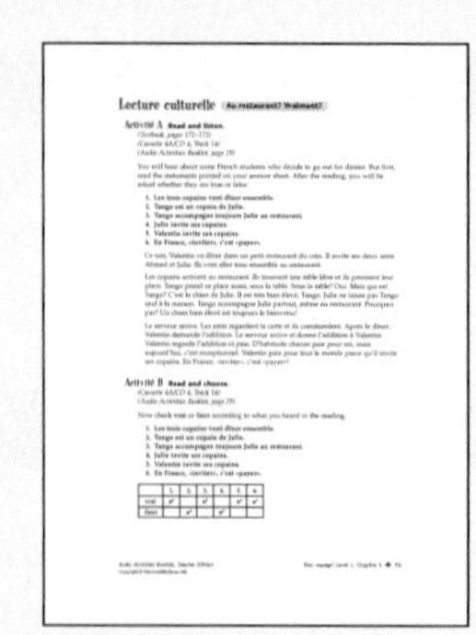
Cultural Reading, page 71

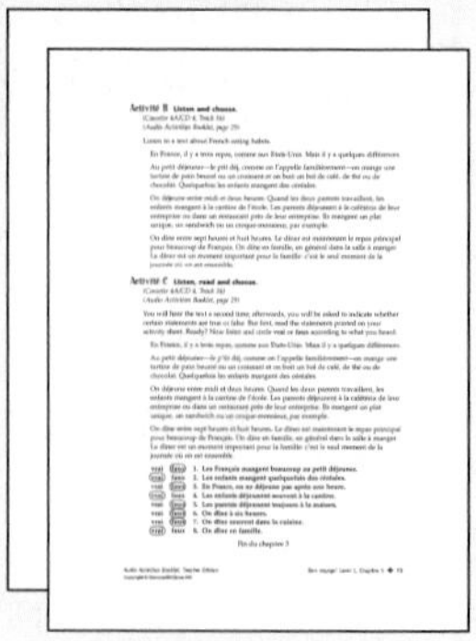
Additional Practice, pages 72–73

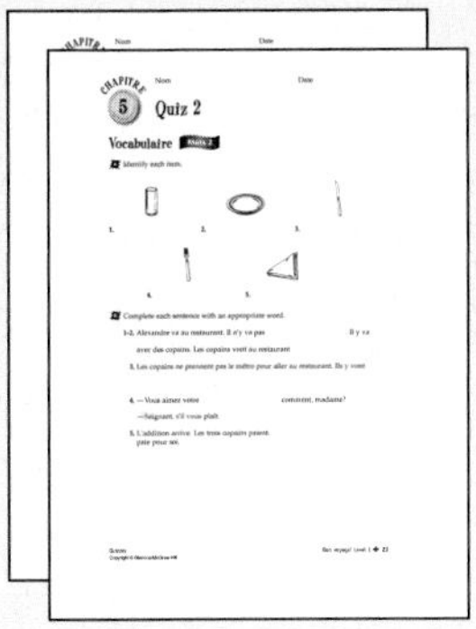

Vocabulary and Structure Quizzes, pages 22–27

Chapter Tests, Chapter 5

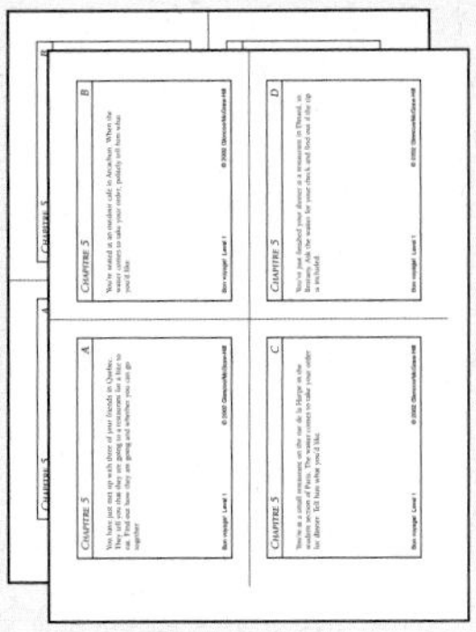

Situation Cards, Chapter 5

Timesaving Teacher Tools

Interactive Teacher Edition

Imagine having your Teacher's Edition and all resources on a CD-ROM. Click on a resource and it appears on your screen, ready to be printed, sorted, or planned.

Interactive Lesson Planner

The Interactive Lesson Planner CD-ROM helps you organize your lesson plans for a week, month, semester, or year. Look at this planning tool for easy access to your Chapter 5 resources.

ExamView Pro®

Test Bank software for Macintosh and Windows makes creating, editing, customizing, and printing tests quick and easy.

Technology Resources

FRENCH Online

In the Chapter 5 Internet activity, you will have a chance to learn more about cafés and restaurants in the Francophone world. Visit french.glencoe.com.

On the Interactive Conversation CD-ROM, students can listen to and take part in a recorded version of the conversation in Chapter 5.

NATIONAL GEOGRAPHIC SOCIETY

See the National Geographic Teacher's Corner on pages 150–151, 256–257, 396–397, 500–501 for reference to additional technology resources.

Bon voyage! Video and Video Activities Booklet.

Help your students prepare for the chapter test by playing the **Marathon mental** Videoquiz game show. Teams will compete against each other to review chapter vocabulary and structure and sharpen listening comprehension skills.

CHAPITRE 5

Preview

In this chapter, students will learn how to order food at a café or restaurant. To do this, they will learn to identify some food items, to use expressions needed for ordering food, and the verbs **aller, aller + infinitif,** and **prendre.** They will also learn some differences between eating customs in the United States and French-speaking countries.

National Standards

Communication

In Chapter 5, students will communicate in spoken and written French on the following topics:
- Ordering food at a café
- Eating habits

Students will engage in conversations, provide and obtain information, and exchange opinions as they fulfill the chapter objectives listed on this page.

CHAPITRE 5

Au café et au restaurant

Objectifs

In this chapter you will learn to:

- ✔ *order food or a beverage at a café or restaurant*
- ✔ *tell where you and others go*
- ✔ *tell what you and others are going to do*
- ✔ *give locations*
- ✔ *tell what belongs to you and others*
- ✔ *describe more activities*
- ✔ *compare eating habits in the United States and in the French-speaking world*

Vincent Van Gogh *Terrasse du café le soir*

152

Correlations to Continuum *(see page* i *for code)*

Stage I
Greet and respond. p. 163 (**14**, *p*); Engage in conversations. p. 161 (**12**, *p*); Express likes and dislikes. p. 157 (**5**, *p*); Make requests. pp. 154–155 (*i*), p. 157 (**4**, *p*), p. 178 (**1**, *m*); Obtain information. p. 161 (**13**, *p*); Provide information. p. 165 (**21**, *p*); Converse in face-to-face social interactions. p. 157 (**6**, *p*); Listen during social interactions and listen to audio or video texts. p. 183 (*p*); Use authentic materials such as menus and short narratives when reading. p. 170 (*i*), p. 171 (*p*); Write lists (menu). p. 179 (**3**, *p*); Use short sentences, learned words and phrases, simple questions, and commands when speaking. p. 171 (*m*); Understand ideas and familiar details when listening. p. 178 (**2**, *p*); Understand texts enhanced by visual clues. pp. 176–177 (*p*); Understand and convey information on food and customs. pp. 172–173 (*p*) pp. 176–177 (*p*); Demonstrate culturally acceptable behavior for Stage I functions. p. 178 (**2**); Understand most important information. p. 179 (**3**)

Stage II
Understand and express important ideas and some detail. p. 165 (**21**, *p*); Create simple paragraphs. p. 179 (**4**, *p*)

Stage III
Narrate and understand narration in the future. p. 165 (**19**, *i*), p. 165 (**21**, *p*)

CHAPITRE 5

Spotlight on Culture

Photograph This photo is of the Place du Tertre, a famous square in Montmartre that has many restaurants and cafés. The Place du Tertre attracts many artists who paint scenes of Montmartre and caricaturists. In the background, we see the lovely basilique du Sacré-Cœur.

Painting The story of the sad life of the painter Vincent Van Gogh (1853–1890) is well known. As a young man, Van Gogh worked as a missionary in a poor mining village in Belgium. His true love, however, was art and he quickly withdrew and devoted himself to his art. His early paintings were drab and depicted peasant life. Supported by his beloved brother Théo, he continued to paint. He is particularly known for his landscapes and scenes such as we see here in ***Terrasse du café le soir.***

Chapter Projects

On mange... Have students make a list of all the foods they learned in this chapter. Then have them separate the foods into two categories. *Foods I often eat* and *Foods I seldom or don't eat.*

Au café Have students who like to perform work in small groups and prepare a skit that takes place in a restaurant or café. They can present the skit to the class.

À la cantine Have students prepare a menu they would like to see in the school cafeteria.

1 Preparation

Resource Manager

Vocabulary Transparencies 5.2–5.3
Audio Activities Booklet TE, pages 62–64
Audiocassette 4A/CD 4
Workbook, pages 43–44
Quiz 1, page 22
ExamView Pro®

Bellringer Review

Use BRR Transparency 5.1 or write the following on the board.
The newspaper of your sister school in France is doing a story about you. Give the following information.

1. your name and age
2. how many brothers and sisters you have
3. brief description of yourself
4. a brief description of your home

2 Presentation

Step 1 Use Vocabulary Transparencies 5.2–5.3, point to each item, and model the individual words. Build to complete sentences.

Step 2 Have students open their books and read pages 154–155. Ask: **Karim arrive au café? Il y a des tables libres? Karim trouve une table? Le serveur arrive? Il donne la carte à Karim? Karim regarde la carte? Il a soif? Il commande une boisson?**

Step 3 More difficult questions are: **Karim arrive où? Qui arrive à la table? Qu'est-ce qu'il donne à Karim? Qu'est-ce que Karim commande? Si tu as soif, qu'est-ce que tu commandes? Si tu as faim, qu'est-ce que tu commandes?**

Vocabulaire Mots 1

À la terrasse d'un café

Karim va au café avec Maïa.
Les deux copains y vont ensemble.
Ils trouvent une table libre.

Le serveur arrive.
Il donne la carte à Karim.
Maïa regarde la carte.

Vous désirez?
Un coca, s'il vous plaît.
Et pour moi, une limonade.

Karim prend un coca.
Maïa prend une limonade.
Ils commandent une boisson (une consommation).

Reaching All Students

Total Physical Response

(Student 1), **lève-toi, s'il te plaît.**
Tu vas mimer les actions suivantes. D'accord?
Prends la carte.
Regarde la carte.
Et maintenant, donne la carte à un(e) ami(e).
Moi, je suis le serveur (la serveuse). Parle au serveur (à la serveuse).
Indique que tu as faim.
Indique que tu as soif.

Do the following as a whole-class activity. Students stand up (or raise hand) if the statement makes sense. They do nothing if it doesn't make sense.

J'ai faim. Je voudrais boire quelque chose.
J'ai faim. Je vais commander une omelette.
Je voudrais boire quelque chose. Je vais prendre une glace.
J'ai soif. Je voudrais un coca.
J'ai faim. Je voudrais un sandwich au jambon.
Moi aussi, j'ai faim. Je vais boire un coca.

J'ai soif. Je voudrais quelque chose à boire.

un citron pressé

un café (un express)

un crème

un jus de pomme

un jus d'orange

des tartines de pain beurré

un croissant

une omelette nature

une omelette aux fines herbes

un sandwich au jambon

un croque-monsieur

un sandwich au fromage

une salade verte

des frites

une soupe à l'oignon

une saucisse de Francfort, un hot-dog

J'ai faim. Je voudrais quelque chose à manger.

une crêpe

une glace au chocolat

une glace à la vanille

VOCABULAIRE

cent cinquante-cinq ✦ 155

♻ Recycling

Students will continue to work with **-er** verbs in this chapter. **Trouver, désirer, commander,** and **laisser** are new verbs. Recycled verbs are **arriver, donner, regarder, parler, inviter.**

About the French Language

At home or in a hotel, the French usually use the term **un café au lait** for their breakfast coffee with heated milk. In a café, however, they order **un crème**, or **un grand crème**, the equivalent of the large **café au lait** consumed at breakfast. ⚜

Vocabulary Expansion

You may wish to give students this additional food vocabulary.
> **une part de pizza**
> **des spaghettis**
> **des raviolis**
> **une salade de tomates**
> **une salade de thon**
> **un hamburger**

More food items will be introduced in future lessons.

♻ Recycling

Have students describe the people in the illustrations on pages 154–155.

Cognate Recognition

Students already know the French words for many foods. Have them concentrate on their pronunciation as they repeat these **Mots 1** items: **un sandwich, une salade, une omelette, une soupe, un coca, un café, un thé.**

Teacher Note: In the TPR activities, we always use **vous,** of course, when it is an entire class activity. When it involves just an individual, we sometimes use the **tu** command to give students passive exposure to this form. The use of **tu** or **vous** with individual students depends upon teacher preference.

3 Practice

Commençons
Let's use our new words

Attention!

When students are doing the **Commençons** activities, accept any answer that makes sense. The purpose of these activities is to have students use the new vocabulary. They are not factual recall activities. Thus, it is not necessary for students to remember specific factual information from the vocabulary presentation when answering. If you wish, have students use the photo on this page as a stimulus, when possible.

Historiette Each time **Historiette** appears, it means that the answers to the activity form a short story. Encourage students to look at the title of the **Historiette,** since it can help them do the activity.

2 **Expansion:** After you finish this activity, have students close their books. Say either **J'ai faim** or **J'ai soif.** The students must provide an appropriate item to order based on the statement.

Commençons
Let's use our new words

1 Historiette On va au café.

Répondez d'après les indications.
(Answer according to the cues.)

1. Pierre va où? (au café)
2. Il va au café avec qui? (Chantal)
3. Ils vont au café quand? (après les cours)
4. Les deux copains y vont ensemble? (oui)
5. Qu'est-ce qu'ils trouvent? (une table libre)
6. Qui arrive? (le serveur)
7. Il donne la carte à qui? (à Chantal)
8. Qu'est-ce que les amis commandent? (une boisson)
9. Chantal prend une limonade? (oui)
10. Qu'est-ce que Pierre prend? (un coca)

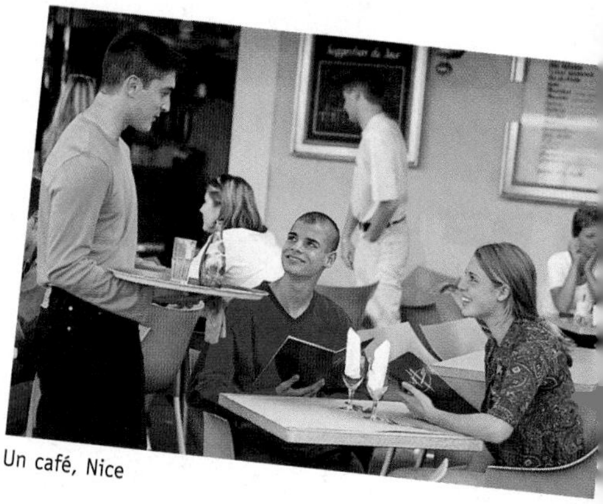

Un café, Nice

2 Tu as faim ou soif? Suivez les modèles.

(Follow the models.)

une salade
Moi, j'ai faim. Je voudrais quelque chose à manger.

un coca
Moi, j'ai soif. Je voudrais quelque chose à boire.

1. un citron pressé
2. un petit crème
3. une omelette nature
4. une limonade
5. une glace à la vanille
6. un jus d'orange
7. un croque-monsieur
8. une crêpe

3 Historiette Un beau café

Répondez d'après le dessin.
(Answer according to the illustration.)

1. C'est la terrasse d'un café ou l'intérieur d'un café?
2. Il y a beaucoup de tables occupées?
3. Il y a une table libre?
4. Qui travaille dans le café?
5. Magali a soif. Qu'est-ce qu'elle commande?
6. Rémi a faim. Qu'est-ce qu'il commande?

Answers to Commençons

1

1. Pierre va au café.
2. Il va au café avec Chantal.
3. Ils vont au café après les cours.
4. Oui, les deux copains y vont ensemble.
5. Ils trouvent une table libre.
6. Le serveur arrive.
7. Il donne la carte à Chantal.
8. Les amis commandent une boisson.
9. Oui, Chantal prend une limonade.
10. Pierre prend un coca.

2

1. Moi, j'ai soif. Je voudrais quelque chose à boire.
2. Moi, j'ai soif. Je voudrais quelque chose à boire.
3. Moi, j'ai faim. Je voudrais quelque chose à manger.
4. Moi, j'ai soif. Je voudrais quelque chose à boire.
5. Moi, j'ai faim. Je voudrais quelque chose à manger.
6. Moi, j'ai soif. Je voudrais quelque chose à boire.
7. Moi, j'ai faim. Je voudrais quelque chose à manger.
8. Moi, j'ai faim. Je voudrais quelque chose à manger.

3

1. C'est la terrasse d'un café.
2. Oui, il y a beaucoup de tables occupées.
3. Non, il n'y a pas de table libre.
4. Un serveur travaille dans le café.
5. Elle commande un jus de pomme.
6. Il commande un sandwich au jambon et des frites.

Vocabulaire

4 **À la terrasse d'un café** Suivez le modèle. *(Follow the model.)*

Client: Monsieur, s'il vous plaît!
Serveur: Oui, vous désirez?
Client: Une glace au chocolat, s'il vous plaît.

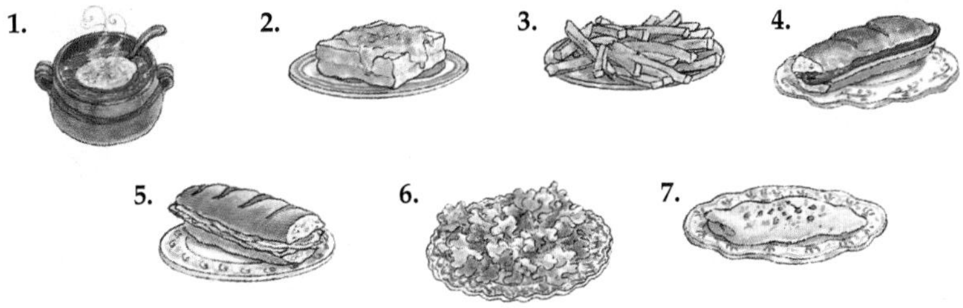

5 **J'aime ça.** Work with a classmate. Tell what snack foods and beverages you like or don't like.

6 **Au café** Work in small groups. You're in a café in Honfleur, in Normandy. One of you will be the server. Have a conversation from the time you enter the café until you leave. You will get a table, order, and talk about your friends, family, and school. The waiter will have to interrupt once in a while.

Honfleur, Normandie

7 **Jeu** **Devinette** French people often tell you: **J'ai une faim de loup!** Can you guess whether it means they are very hungry or not? You also hear: **Elle mange comme un oiseau.** Can you guess whether it means she eats a lot or very little? Are there similar expressions in English? What are they?

ENCORE PLUS *For more practice using words from **Mots 1**, do Activity 13 on page H14 at the end of this book.*

4 Use this activity as a starting point for a skit. Create a café using tables, chairs, and other props. Two students play the waiter/waitress and the customer.

6 **Expansion:** If you have access to a video camera, you may wish to have students prepare this conversation/skit, practice it, and then record it on a "set" (in another location, perhaps the school cafeteria). Then have a "movie" day complete with popcorn where the whole class watches the videotape of the different skits.

7 **Jeu** You may wish to explain that we often say, "I'm as hungry as a bear." The French say, "as a wolf" **(un loup). Elle mange comme un oiseau** is the same in both languages—"like a bird."

Writing Development

Have the students write answers to Activities 1 and 3 in paragraph form to illustrate how the answers to all the items tell a story.

Learning from Photos

(page 157) Honfleur is one of Normandy's most picturesque harbors. The scene in this photo is of **le Vieux Bassin,** which was built in the seventh century. Because of its beauty and picturesque charm, Honfleur became a favorite of artists such as Courbet, Renoir, Sisley, Cézanne, and Picasso in the nineteenth century. The artist Eugène Boudin was born in Honfleur in 1824.

Answers to Commençons

4

1. Monsieur, s'il vous plaît!
   Oui, vous désirez?
   Une soupe à l'oignon, s'il vous plaît.
2. Un croque-monsieur, s'il vous plaît.
3. Des frites, s'il vous plaît.
4. Une saucisse de Francfort, (un hot-dog) s'il vous plaît.
5. Un sandwich au jambon, s'il vous plaît.
6. Une salade verte, s'il vous plaît.
7. Une omelette aux fines herbes, s'il vous plaît.

1 Preparation

Resource Manager

Vocabulary Transparencies 5.4–5.5
Audio Activities Booklet TE, pages 64–65
Audiocassette 4A/CD 4
Workbook, pages 45–46
Quiz 2, page 23
ExamView Pro®

Bellringer Review

Use BRR Transparency 5.2 or write the following on the board.
Complete.

1. **Le serveur ______ au restaurant. (travailler)**
2. **Il ______ très sympa. (être)**
3. **Il ______ français. (être)**
4. **Il ______ au restaurant à onze heures du matin et il ______ le restaurant à onze heures du soir. (arriver, quitter)**

2 Presentation

Step 1 Review **Mots 1** by asking: **Karim va au restaurant? Il va au restaurant avec Maïa? Ils vont au restaurant ensemble? Ils trouvent une table? Le serveur arrive?**

Step 2 You may wish to present the new word at the top of this page as you set a table using real objects.

Step 3 With books closed, have students repeat the rest of the vocabulary after you or Audiocassette 4A/CD 4. Ask several students: **Tu vas commander un steak? Tu aimes ton steak comment?**

Note: A colloquial way of saying **le restaurant** is **le resto.**

Vocabulaire

Mots 2

Le couvert

Au restaurant

Alexandre va au restaurant.
Il ne va pas au restaurant tout seul.
Il y va avec des copains.
Ils n'y vont pas en voiture.
Ils ne prennent pas le bus.
Ils y vont à pied.

Alexandre prend un steak frites.

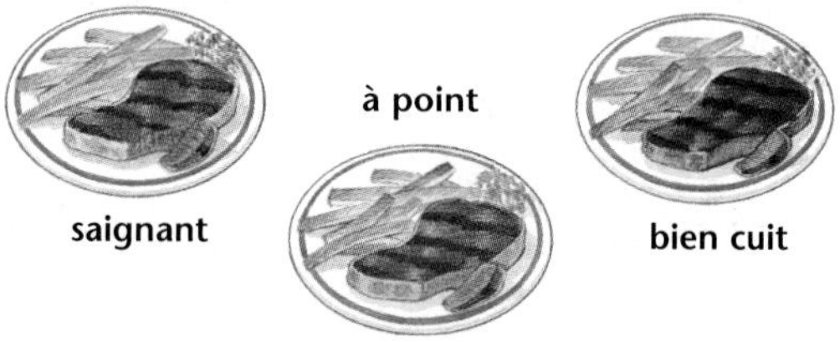

Reaching All Students

Total Physical Response Before you begin, set up a restaurant table with a place setting. Dramatize the meaning of **coupe.**

(Student 1), **lève-toi.**
Va au restaurant.
Tu trouves une table. Assieds-toi.
Et maintenant, *(Student 2),* **lève-toi. Entre dans le restaurant. Tu es le serveur/la serveuse.**
(Student 1), **demande la carte.**
Regarde la carte.
Commande un steak.
(Student 2), **sers le steak.**
(Student 1), **prends la fourchette.**
Prends le couteau.
Coupe le steak.
Mange le steak.
Demande l'addition au serveur/à la serveuse.
Paie l'addition. Donne de l'argent au serveur/à la serveuse.
Laisse un pourboire.
Levez-vous, tous les deux.
Et maintenant, retournez à vos places.

Alexandre n'invite pas ses copains.
Chacun paie pour soi.

Le service est compris.
Mais Alexandre laisse tout de même un petit pourboire.
Il laisse un peu d'argent pour le serveur.

Note

Here are some common time expressions. They range from "always" to "very seldom."

Au café...
Il y va toujours.
Il y va souvent.
Il y va quelquefois.
Il y va très peu.

Les trois repas de la journée

le petit déjeuner

On prend le petit déjeuner le matin.

le déjeuner

On déjeune entre midi et deux heures.

le dîner

On dîne le soir.

FUN-FACTS

- In France, the tip is almost always included in the check, although many people leave a little extra.
- The French tend to eat meat rare. There is a category even rarer than **saignant**, called **bleu.** The meat is almost raw.
- When people pass others in a restaurant who are eating, they often say **«Bon appétit!».**

Vocabulary Expansion

You may want to give students the following restaurant related vocabulary.

une petite cuillère
une soucoupe
du pain
de l'eau
du vin
une entrée
un dessert

FUN-FACTS

- It is difficult to make sweeping generalizations about cultural mores, but you may wish to point out to students that it is more common to see young people in France having a meal together in a nice restaurant than it is here in the United States.
- You may wish to demonstrate how French people use eating utensils, holding the fork in the left hand, and cutting with the knife in the right hand. Show how the fork in the left hand is used to bring food to the mouth, rather than switching the fork from one hand to the other as is done in the United States.

Recycling

The verbs **inviter, payer, dîner, déjeuner, aimer, avoir,** and **être** are recycled.

3 Practice

Commençons
Let's use our new words

8 After going over this activity once, call on one student to give all the answers as the rest of the class listens to the story.

Learning from Photos

(page 160 top) The bistro in this photo is in Nice on the Côte d'Azur.

Class Motivator

Un pique-nique You may want to prepare a French picnic. Take up a small collection, if it is allowed, and have students go to the store and find some things for their French picnic. Items that are not difficult to find and not very expensive are: **du pâté, une baguette, du camembert, du brie, du jambon.**

Un petit déjeuner français works well for early morning classes. Have each student bring a predetermined item: **du beurre, de la confiture** *(jam),* **une baguette, du jus d'orange, du chocolat chaud,** etc.

Commençons
Let's use our new words

8 Historiette Au restaurant Inventez une histoire. *(Make up a story.)*

1. Laurène va au restaurant?
2. Elle prend le bus pour aller au restaurant?
3. Elle a faim?
4. Elle regarde la carte?
5. Elle commande un steak frites?
6. Elle aime son steak comment?
7. Pour le dessert, elle prend une glace? À quel parfum? Au chocolat ou à la vanille?
8. Après le déjeuner, Laurène demande l'addition?
9. Le service est compris ou pas?
10. Laurène laisse un pourboire pour le serveur?
11. Elle laisse un peu d'argent ou beaucoup d'argent?

Laurène regarde la carte.

Un serveur

9 Historiette Un dîner au resto Choisissez. *(Choose.)*

1. Loïc ne va pas au restaurant ____. Il y va avec des copains.
   a. ensemble b. au cinquième c. tout seul
2. Ils n'y vont pas en voiture. Ils ne prennent pas le métro. Ils y vont ____.
   a. ensemble b. à pied c. après les cours
3. Loïc ____ un steak frites.
   a. prend b. laisse c. prépare
4. Après le dîner, Loïc demande ____.
   a. la carte b. le pourboire c. l'addition
5. Dans les restaurants en France, le service est ____.
   a. occupé b. compris c. libre
6. Le service est excellent et Loïc ____ un pourboire.
   a. laisse b. prend c. commande
7. Mais Loïc n'invite pas ses copains. ____ paie pour soi.
   a. L'addition b. Chacun c. Le serveur

Answers to Commençons

8 *Answers will vary but may include:*

1. Oui, Laurène va au restaurant.
2. Non, elle prend le métro pour aller au restaurant.
3. Oui, elle a faim.
4. Oui, elle regarde la carte.
5. Oui, elle commande un steak frites.
6. Elle aime son steak bien cuit.
7. Oui, elle prend une glace à la vanille.
8. Oui, elle demande l'addition.
9. Le service est compris.
10. Oui, Laurène laisse un pourboire pour le serveur.
11. Elle laisse un peu d'argent.

9

1. c
2. b
3. a
4. c
5. b
6. a
7. b

10 **Madame, s'il vous plaît!** Demandez à la serveuse.
(Tell the waitress what you need.)

Une serviette, s'il vous plaît, madame!

1. 
2. 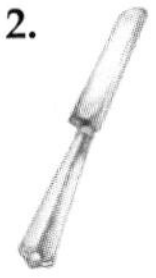
3. 
4. 
5. 

11 **Les repas** Vrai ou faux? *(True or false?)*

1. On dîne le matin.
2. En France, on déjeune entre midi et deux heures.
3. On prend une tartine et un grand crème pour le dîner.
4. On prend un croque-monsieur pour le déjeuner.
5. On prend une soupe à l'oignon pour le dessert.
6. Une fourchette, c'est pour la soupe.
7. Une assiette, c'est pour le café.
8. Une nappe, c'est pour la soupe.

12 **Au restaurant** Work with a classmate. Take turns asking each other questions about the illustration. Answer each other's questions.

13 **Qu'est-ce que tu manges?** With a classmate, take turns finding out what each of you eats for breakfast and lunch.

ENCORE PLUS *For more practice using words from **Mots 2**, do Activity 14 on page H15 at the end of this book.*

ANSWERS TO Commençons

10
1. Une fourchette, s'il vous plaît, madame!
2. Un couteau, s'il vous plaît, madame!
3. Un verre, s'il vous plaît, madame!
4. Une cuillère, s'il vous plaît, madame!
5. Une tasse, s'il vous plaît, madame!

11
1. F
2. V
3. F
4. V
5. F
6. F
7. F
8. F

12 *Answers will vary but may include:*
—La mère demande une fourchette?
—Non, elle demande une cuillère.
—La famille prend le petit déjeuner?
—Non, ils dînent au restaurant.
—Le garçon aime son steak comment?
—Il aime son steak à point.

Vocabulaire

10 With books open, partners can quiz each other on this activity, one randomly stating the numbers and asking the question, the other responding. Then they switch roles. When finished, they both write out the items, checking each other's spelling by referring to page 158.

11 **Expansion:** Have students correct the false statements.

13 **Expansion:** You may wish to have students conduct a class-wide poll and tabulate the results on the board.

National Standards

Communities

- You may wish to organize for your students a visit to a French restaurant or Bistro in your community as a class field trip. This would give students an opportunity to practice the vocabulary and structures of the chapter in a real-life setting. You could plan to simply tour the establishment or eat there depending upon cost restrictions.
- Tell students to look for the names of French foods when they go to the supermarket.

ENCORE PLUS This *infogap* activity will allow students to practice in pairs. The activity should be very manageable for them, since all vocabulary and structures are familiar to them.

1 Preparation

Resource Manager

Audio Activities Booklet TE, pages 66–68
Audiocassette 4A/CD 4
Workbook, pages 47–50
Quizzes 3–6, pages 24–27
ExamView Pro®

Bellringer Review

Use BRR Transparency 5.3 or write the following on the board.
You have just moved into your new apartment. List at least six items of tableware you will need for your kitchen.

2 Presentation

Le verbe **aller** au présent

Step 1 Write the forms of **aller** on the board and have students repeat them. Pay particular attention to the liaison.

Step 2 Lead students through Items 1–3 with individuals reading the examples.

Step 3 Have each student ask a neighbor how he or she is. That student responds and asks another student, and so on.

Attention!

The word **y** is introduced here simply as a completion to **aller,** since it is difficult to avoid. The uses of **y** are taught at a later point.

Telling and finding out where people go
Le verbe **aller** au présent

1. The verb **aller** *(to go)* is an irregular verb. Study the following forms.

ALLER			
je	vais	nous‿z‿	allons
tu	vas	vous‿z‿	allez
il/elle/on	va	ils/elles	vont

Je vais au café, mais mes parents vont au restaurant.
Tu vas au restaurant avec des copains?
Vous y allez en bus?

2. If you do not mention the place you are going to, you must put the word **y** before the verb **aller. Y** refers to a place already mentioned. **Aller** cannot stand alone.

Tu vas au café?
Oui, j'y vais et Laurent y va aussi.

Savez-vous que... ?

The expression **On y va!** means "Let's get going." As a question, it means "Should we go?"

3. As you already know, the verb **aller** is also used to express how you feel.

Ça va?	**Oui, ça va bien, merci.**
Comment tu vas?	**Très bien, merci. Et toi?**
Vous allez bien?	**Oui, je vais bien, merci. Et vous?**

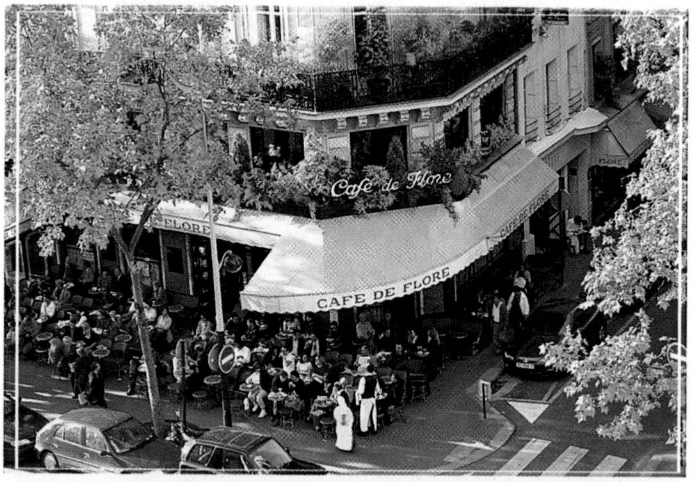

Café de Flore, Paris

Teacher Note: You may wish to write the forms of **avoir** on the board next to those of **aller,** point out the similarity between them, and have students repeat them. Draw lines through the **v** in the **je, tu, il(s), elle(s)** forms of **aller** and write a **v** over the **ll** in the **nous** and **vous** forms to further emphasize the similarity between the two verbs.

Reaching All Students

Kinesthetic Learners You may wish to play the following "ballgame" to reinforce several forms of the verb **aller.** Student 1 throws a ball to Student 2 as he or she says: **Je vais au café.** Student 2 responds: **Tu vas au café? Moi, aussi. On y va ensemble!** Student 2 then throws the ball to Student 3 who says: **Vous allez tous les deux au café? Moi aussi, j'y vais.**

Continuons

Let's put our words together

14 **Au restaurant!** Répétez la conversation avec un copain ou une copine. *(Repeat the conversation with a classmate.)*

Salut, Paul! Ça va?
Ça va, et toi?
Ça va. Tu vas où, là?
CAFE DE FLORE
Je vais au Café de Flore.
Tu y vas tout seul?
Oui. On y va ensemble?
Pourquoi pas!

15 **On va au Flore.** Complétez d'après la conversation. *(Complete according to the conversation.)*

1. Marie ____ bien.
2. Où ____ Paul?
3. Il ____ au Café de Flore.
4. Il n'y ____ pas tout seul.
5. Son amie Marie y ____ aussi.
6. Les deux copains y ____ ensemble.
7. Ils n'y ____ pas en voiture.
8. Ils y ____ à pied.

3 Practice

Continuons

Let's put our words together

14 You may wish to have students listen to the miniconversation on Audiocassette 4A/CD 4. **Expansion:** Have pairs of students present the miniconversation to the class.

15 After completing this activity, have students make up questions about Marie and Paul.

Learning from Photos

(page 162)

- The photo on page 162 is of the Café de Flore. It is next door to the café Les Deux Magots on the boulevard Saint Germain. Both of these cafés were extremely popular during the heyday of existentialism. Sartre and his left-wing intellectual friends almost lived at Les Deux Magots. The name of the café comes from a pair of Chinese figurines inside the café that are called **magots** in French.
- Ask questions about the photo on page 162: **C'est la terrasse d'un café ou c'est l'intérieur? C'est quel café? Il y a des tables libres?**

Answers to Continuons

15

1. va	**5.** va
2. va	**6.** vont
3. va	**7.** vont
4. va	**8.** vont

3 Practice *(continued)*

Continuons
Let's put our words together

16 and **17** These activities can be done in pairs, with students reporting back to the class about their partner's answers. This will practice the third person singular and plural forms.

Writing Development
Have the students write answers to Activities 16 and 17 in paragraph form to illustrate how the answers to the items tell a story.

16 **Historiette** **Oui, j'y vais.** Donnez des réponses personnelles. *(Give your own answers.)*

1. Tu vas souvent ou très peu au restaurant?
2. Tu y vas seul(e) ou avec ta famille?
3. Tu vas quelquefois dans un restaurant chinois ou italien?
4. Tu vas toujours dans le même restaurant?
5. Tu vas quelquefois au restaurant avec des copains?

17 **Historiette** **À l'école** Donnez des réponses personnelles. *(Give your own answers.)*

1. Tes copains et toi, vous allez à l'école?
2. Vous allez à quelle école?
3. Vous allez à l'école à quelle heure?
4. Vous y allez comment—à pied, en car scolaire ou en voiture?
5. Après les cours, vous allez au café?

Honfleur, Normandie

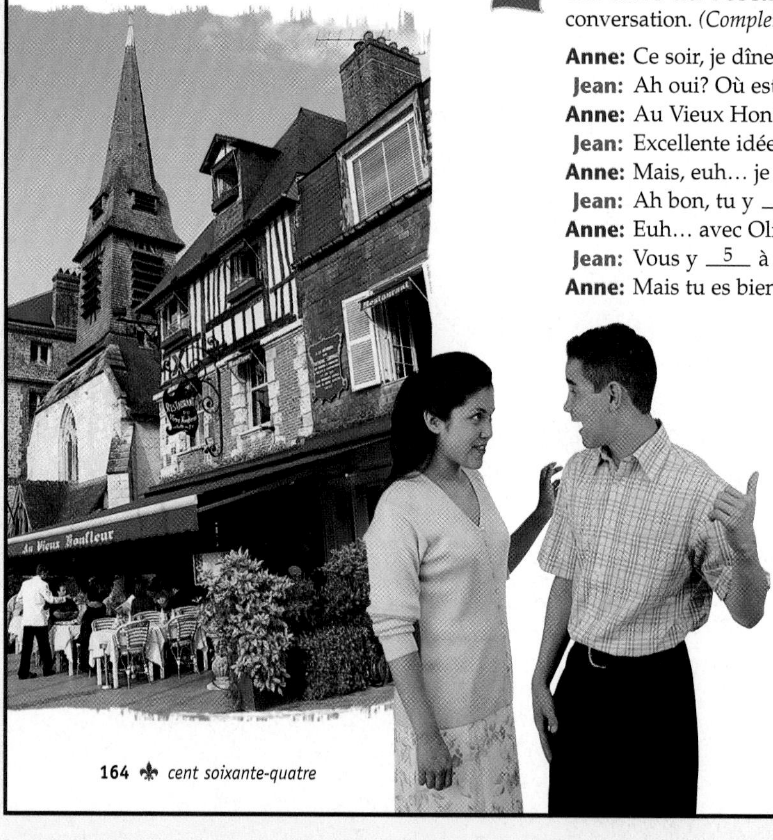

18 **On dîne au restaurant.** Complétez la conversation. *(Complete the conversation.)*

Anne: Ce soir, je dîne au restaurant.
Jean: Ah oui? Où est-ce que tu __1__?
Anne: Au Vieux Honfleur.
Jean: Excellente idée! On y __2__ ensemble.
Anne: Mais, euh… je n'y __3__ pas toute seule.
Jean: Ah bon, tu y __4__ avec qui?
Anne: Euh… avec Olivier.
Jean: Vous y __5__ à quelle heure?
Anne: Mais tu es bien indiscret!

Answers to Continuons

16 *Answers will vary but may include:*
1. Je vais souvent au restaurant.
2. J'y vais avec ma famille.
3. Oui, je vais quelquefois dans un restaurant italien.
4. Non, je ne vais pas toujours dans le même restaurant.
5. Oui, je vais quelquefois au restaurant avec des copains.

17 *Answers will vary but may include:*
1. Oui, mes copains et moi, nous allons à l'école.
2. Nous allons à ______.
3. Nous allons à l'école à sept heures et quart.
4. Nous y allons ______.
5. Non, après les cours nous n'allons pas au café.

18

1. vas
2. va
3. vais
4. vas
5. allez

Telling what's going to happen
Aller + infinitif

1. You use **aller** + an infinitive to express what is going to take place in the near future.

   Demain on va avoir un examen.
   Les élèves vont étudier.
   Je vais passer l'examen.
   L'examen va être difficile, c'est sûr!

2. To make a sentence negative, you put **ne... pas** around the conjugated form of **aller.**

   Tu ne vas pas aller au café?
   Moi, je ne vais pas regarder la télé.

Continuons
Let's put our words together

19 Ce soir! Donnez des réponses personnelles. *(Give your own answers.)*

1. Ce soir, tu vas regarder la télé?
2. Tu vas téléphoner à un copain ou une copine?
3. Tu vas préparer le dîner?
4. Tu vas aller en classe?
5. Tu vas inviter tes professeurs au restaurant?

20 Absurdités Mettez à la forme négative. *(Make the sentences negative.)*

1. Nous allons en classe pendant le week-end.
2. Les chiens et les chats vont à l'école.
3. Demain le prof de maths va parler français.
4. Vous allez déjeuner pendant le cours de géographie.
5. Ce soir, je vais parler au téléphone avec Elvis Presley.

21 Quand? Work with a classmate. Tell each other some things you like to do. Then tell when you are going to do them—**ce soir, demain, demain matin, la semaine prochaine.**

Answers to Continuons

19 *Answers will vary but may include:*
1. Non, ce soir je ne vais pas regarder la télé.
2. Oui, je vais téléphoner à une copine.
3. Oui, je vais préparer le dîner.
4. Non, je ne vais pas aller en classe.
5. Non, je ne vais pas inviter mes professeurs au restaurant.

20
1. Nous n'allons pas en classe pendant le week-end.
2. Les chiens et les chats ne vont pas à l'école.
3. Demain le prof de maths ne va pas parler français.
4. Vous n'allez pas déjeuner pendant le cours de géographie.
5. Ce soir je ne vais pas parler au téléphone avec Elvis Presley.

21 *Answers will vary but may include:*
J'aime aller au restaurant. J'aime regarder des vidéos. Ce soir je vais aller au restaurant. Demain je vais regarder des vidéos. Et toi?

Structure

1 Preparation

Bellringer Review

Use BRR Transparency 5.4 or write the following on the board.
Complete.
1. **Ma maison _____ six pièces. (avoir)**
2. **J'_____ une petite famille. (avoir)**
3. **Nous _____ à _____. (habiter)**
4. **J'_____ notre maison. (aimer)**
5–6. **Vous _____ la ville où vous _____? (aimer, habiter)**

2 Presentation

Aller + infinitif

Step 1 Have students read Items 1–2 aloud.

Step 2 Using fortune cookies or a crystal ball, pretend to predict the fortunes of several students. For example: **Delphine, tu vas être riche. Marc, tu vas aimer une jeune fille brune.** Ask the students to figure out the meanings.

Step 3 Write several sentences on the board using **aller** + infintive, but leaving out the infinitive. Ask for volunteers to fill in an appropriate infinitive. For example: **Tu vas _____ Jean et Marie? (inviter)** Call on other volunteers to make the sentences negative.

3 Practice

Continuons
Let's put our words together

20 Expansion: Have students make up other silly sentences.

1 Preparation

Bellringer Review

Use BRR Transparency 5.5 or write the following on the board.
Write three things you are going to do tomorrow.

2 Presentation

Les contractions avec à et de

Step 1 To help students understand the basic difference in meaning between **à** and **de,** draw a simple building on the board. Then draw an arrow going to the building and write **à** on the arrow. Draw an arrow coming from the building and write **de** on this arrow.

Step 2 Now lead students through Items 1–3 on page 166.

Step 3 To practice **à,** you may wish to use flashcards with locations and their definite articles written out **(l'école, le parc).** Give students a model sentence and have them change it according to the card you flash. For example: **Nous allons au parc. (Nous allons à l'école.)**

Step 4 Use the same flashcards to practice **de** with different model sentences.

Step 5 Demonstrate the possessive use of **de** by designating objects in the room and asking: **Qu'est-ce que c'est?** First model the kind of answers you are looking for. **(C'est le livre du prof.)**

Expressing direction and possession
Les contractions avec **à** et **de**

1. The preposition **à** can mean "to," "in," or "at." **À** is contracted with **le** and **les** to form one word—**au, aux.** Note that liaison occurs when **aux** is followed by a vowel.

à + le = au	Je vais au lycée.
à + les = aux	Le prof parle aux‿élèves.
à + la = à la	Tu vas à la cantine?
à + l' = à l'	Vous allez à l'école à pied?

Savez-vous que... ?
À is used in many food expressions.
une soupe à l'oignon
une omelette aux fines herbes

2. The preposition **de** can mean "of," "from," or "about." **De** contracts with **le** and **les** to form one word—**du, des.** Liaison occurs when **des** is followed by a vowel.

de + le = du	Il y a une belle vue du balcon.
de + les = des	On parle toujours des‿amis.
de + la = de la	Il arrive de la cantine.
de + l' = de l'	Je rentre de l'école.

3. The preposition **de** also indicates possession or ownership.

Le lycée de Vincent est à Paris.
C'est la voiture du professeur de Vincent.
Minou est le chat des voisins de Vincent.

Continuons
Let's put our words together

22 **Tu vas où?** Donnez des réponses personnelles. *(Give your own answers.)*

1. Quel est le nom de ton école?
2. Tu vas à l'école à quelle heure?
3. Tu vas au cours de français le matin ou l'après-midi?
4. Tu vas au cours d'anglais à quelle heure?
5. Tu aimes parler aux profs?
6. Tu aimes parler des profs aussi?
7. Tu habites près de l'école ou loin de l'école?
8. Tu rentres de l'école à quelle heure?
9. Comment est-ce que tu rentres de l'école?

Answers to Continuons

22 *Answers will vary but may include:*
1. Le nom de mon école est ______.
2. Je vais à l'école à sept heures vingt.
3. Je vais au cours de français l'après-midi.
4. Je vais au cours d'anglais à dix heures.
5. Oui, j'aime parler aux profs.
6. Oui, j'aime parler des profs aussi.
7. J'habite loin de l'école.
8. Je rentre de l'école à trois heures et demie.
9. Je rentre de l'école à pied.

23
1. au
2. au
3. au
4. au
5. aux
6. à l'
7. à la

23 Historiette Je n'y vais pas. Complétez avec à. *(Complete with* à.*)*

Ce soir, je ne vais pas __1__ (le concert). Je ne vais pas __2__ (le parc). Je ne vais pas __3__ (le collège). Je ne vais pas __4__ (le restaurant). Je ne vais pas parler __5__ (les copains). Je ne vais pas __6__ (l'anniversaire) de Julie. Je vais aller où, alors? Je vais rentrer __7__ (la maison). Pourquoi? Je suis fatigué(e)!

24 Au café Suivez le modèle. *(Follow the model.)*

une tarte aux fruits / une tarte aux pommes
—Qu'est-ce que tu vas prendre?
—Je vais prendre une tarte.
—Une tarte aux fruits ou une tarte aux pommes?
—Oh, je vais prendre une tarte ____.

1. un sandwich au jambon / un sandwich au fromage
2. une omelette au fromage / une omelette aux fines herbes
3. une soupe à la tomate / une soupe à l'oignon
4. une glace au chocolat / une glace à la vanille
5. une crêpe au chocolat / une crêpe aux fruits

25 Le dîner des copains Combinez d'après le modèle. *(Combine according to the model.)*

c'est la voiture / les parents de Vincent
C'est la voiture des parents de Vincent.

1. je vais à la table / les amis de Marc
2. ils sont à la terrasse / le café
3. nous regardons la carte / le restaurant
4. c'est le coca / l'amie de Marc
5. voilà le pourboire / la serveuse

Cellia Saubry *Coin de rue*

3 Practice

Continuons
Let's put our words together

22 Activity 22 on page 166 can be used to focus on the listening skill. Have students do this activity with their books closed.

24 You may wish to have students work in pairs to do this activity.

Writing Development

Have students write answers to Activity 23 in paragraph form to illustrate how the answers to all the items tell a story.

Answers to Continuons

24 *Answers will vary but may include:*

1. Qu'est-ce que tu vas prendre?
   Je vais prendre un sandwich.
   Un sandwich au jambon ou un sandwich au fromage?
   Oh, je vais prendre un sandwich au fromage.
2. Qu'est ce que tu vas prendre?
   Je vais prendre une omelette.
   Une omelette au fromage ou une omelette aux fines herbes?
   Oh, je vais prendre une omelette aux fines herbes.
3. Qu'est-ce que tu vas prendre?
   Je vais prendre une soupe.
   Une soupe à la tomate ou une soupe à l'oignon?
   Oh, je vais prendre une soupe à la tomate.
4. Qu'est-ce que tu vas prendre?
   Je vais prendre une glace.
   Une glace au chocolat ou une glace à la vanille?
   Oh, je vais prendre une glace à la vanille.
5. Qu'est-ce que tu vas prendre?
   Je vais prendre une crêpe.
   Une crêpe au chocolat ou une crêpe aux fruits?
   Oh, je vais prendre une crêpe au chocolat.

25

1. Je vais à la table des amis de Marc.
2. Ils sont à la terrasse du café.
3. Nous regardons la carte du restaurant.
4. C'est le coca de l'amie de Marc.
5. Voilà le pourboire de la serveuse.

1 Preparation

Bellringer Review

Use BRR Transparency 5.6 or write the following on the board.
Say when you will go to the following places: **ce soir, demain, la semaine prochaine.**

1. **l'école**
2. **la fête d'anniversaire d'une copine**
3. **le restaurant**
4. **le café**
5. **la papeterie**

2 Presentation

Le verbe **prendre**

Teaching Tips

- Have students pay particular attention to the correct pronunciation of the plural forms. This helps them to remember to double the **n** with **ils/elles.**
- It is up to the teacher to decide the level of importance of these spelling problems.
- You may want to de-emphasize the oral production of the **nous** form because of the use of **on.**

Music Connection

Put the following on an overhead and have students "sing" it with a rap beat. It reincorporates all the new structures of the chapter.

Je vais au café, au café.
Je vais prendre un café, un café au lait, au lait.
Et toi, tu voudrais un café au lait, au lait.
Tu vas avec moi au café, au café.
On y va ensemble. Pourquoi pas, pourquoi pas?
Un café, Un café, toi et moi, c'est super, super.
On y va? Oui, on y va!

Describing more activities
Le verbe **prendre**

1. The verb **prendre,** "to take," also means "to have" when used with foods. It is an irregular verb. Pay particular attention to both its spelling and pronunciation.

PRENDRE			
je	prends	nous	prenons
tu	prends	vous	prenez
il/elle/on	prend	ils/elles	prennent

Je prends le car scolaire pour aller à l'école.
Les voisins ne prennent pas l'ascenseur.
Je vais prendre un coca.

2. The verbs **apprendre** *(to learn)* and **comprendre** *(to understand)* are conjugated the same way as **prendre.**

On apprend beaucoup à l'école.
Vous comprenez le français, n'est-ce pas?

Les deux amis apprennent l'anglais.

Continuons
Let's put our words together

26 Historiette Alexandre Inventez une histoire. *(Make up a story.)*

1. Alexandre prend le car scolaire pour aller à l'école?
2. En classe, il prend des notes quand le professeur parle?
3. Il comprend bien le français?
4. Il apprend beaucoup de choses au cours de français?

Answers to Continuons

26 *Answers will vary but may include:*

1. Non, Alexandre ne prend pas le car scolaire pour aller à l'école.
2. Oui, en classe il prend des notes quand le professeur parle.
3. Oui, il comprend bien le français.
4. Oui, il apprend beaucoup de choses au cours de français.

27 *Answers will vary but may include:*

1. Je prends mon petit déjeuner à la maison.
2. Je prends l'escalier pour monter au premier étage.
3. Je prends un jus d'orange.
4. Quand j'ai faim je prends un sandwich au fromage.

Ils prennent leur petit déjeuner.

27 À l'école Donnez des réponses personnelles. *(Give your own answers.)*

1. Tu prends ton petit déjeuner à la maison ou à la cafétéria de l'école?
2. À l'école, tu prends l'escalier ou l'ascenseur pour monter au premier étage?
3. À la cafétéria de l'école, qu'est-ce que tu prends quand tu as soif?
4. Qu'est-ce que tu prends quand tu as faim?

28 Toujours à l'école Répondez. *(Answer.)*

1. La majorité des élèves prennent le car scolaire pour aller à l'école?
2. Les élèves prennent l'escalier ou l'ascenseur pour monter au premier étage?
3. En cours de français, tout le monde comprend bien quand le professeur parle?
4. Vous apprenez beaucoup de choses en cours de français?

29 Au pluriel! Mettez au pluriel. *(Make the sentences plural.)*

1. Je prends le car scolaire pour aller à l'école.
2. Je prends l'ascenseur pour monter au quatrième étage.
3. Tu prends le bus, le métro ou la voiture?
4. Tu prends beaucoup de notes en classe?
5. L'élève est très intelligent et il apprend beaucoup de choses.
6. Elle comprend bien la leçon.
7. Son copain prend un coca au café.
8. Et moi, je prends une glace au chocolat.

ENCORE PLUS *For more practice using the verbs **aller** and **prendre**, do Activity 15 on page H16 at the end of this book.*

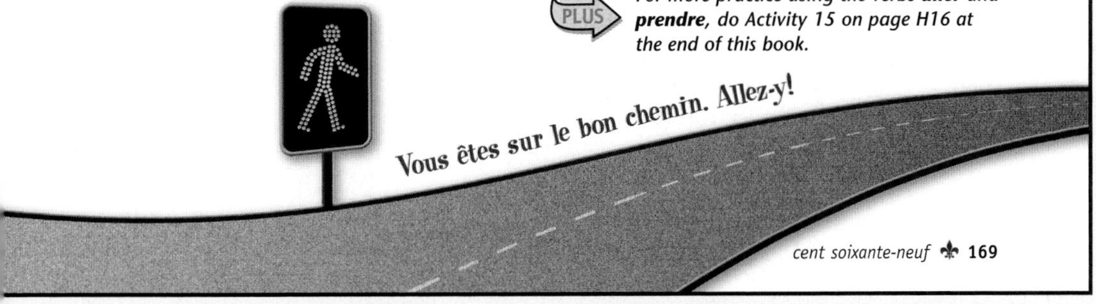
Vous êtes sur le bon chemin. Allez-y!

Answers to Continuons

28 *Answers will vary but may include:*

1. Oui, la majorité des élèves prennent le car scolaire pour aller à l'école.
2. Les élèves prennent l'escalier pour monter au premier étage.
3. Oui, tout le monde comprend bien quand le professeur parle.
4. Oui, nous apprenons beaucoup de choses en cours de français.

29

1. Nous prenons le car scolaire pour aller à l'école.
2. Nous prenons l'ascenseur pour monter au quatrième étage.
3. Vous prenez le bus, le métro ou la voiture?
4. Vous prenez beaucoup de notes en classe?
5. Les élèves sont très intelligents et ils apprennent beaucoup de choses.
6. Elles comprennent bien la leçon.
7. Ses copains prennent un coca au café.
8. Et nous, nous prenons une glace au chocolat.

Structure

3 Practice

Continuons
Let's put our words together

27 and **28** You may wish to use these activities as a starting point for a more in-depth interview between two students. You may have them report back to the class or write a report.

Learning from Photos

(page 169) Have the students look at the photo and answer the following:
Qu'est-ce qu'ils font? Qui prend le petit déjeuner? Ils sont où dans la maison? Qu'est-ce qu'ils mangent? La fille prend sa boisson dans une tasse ou un verre?

Fun Facts

Have students look carefully at the photograph on page 169. Notice that the girl is about to drink from a **bol.** French people use drinking bowls for their morning **café au lait** or **chocolat chaud.** They sometimes like to dunk their **tartine** or **baguette** into the beverage in the breakfast bowl as well as drink from it.

ENCORE PLUS This *infogap* activity will allow students to practice in pairs. The activity should be very manageable for them, since all vocabulary and structures are familiar to them.

Allez-y!
At this point in the chapter, students have learned all the vocabulary and structure necessary to complete the chapter. The conversation and cultural readings that follow recycle all the material learned up to this point.

Conversation

1 Preparation

Resource Manager

Audio Activities Booklet TE, pages 69–70
Audiocassette 4A/CD 4
CD-ROM

Bellringer Review

Use BRR Transparency 5.7 or write the following on the board.
Write an original sentence using each of the following words.

arriver	**quitter**
travailler	**rigoler**
avoir	**être**

2 Presentation

Step 1 Tell students they are going to hear a conversation between Claire, Loïc, and a waiter. Have them close their books and watch the conversation on the CD-ROM or listen as you read or play Audiocassette 4A/CD 4.

Step 2 After introducing the conversation (see suggestions in previous chapters), set up a café in the classroom and have groups of students act out the conversation for the class.

Step 3 Have students retell the conversation in their own words.

Glencoe Technology

CD-ROM
On the CD-ROM, students can watch a dramatization of this conversation. They can then play the role of either one of the characters and record themselves in the conversation.

Conversation

Au restaurant

Claire: Tu as faim?
Loïc: Oui. J'ai hyper faim! Je vais prendre un bon steak frites.
Serveur: Vous désirez?
Loïc: Un steak frites, s'il vous plaît. Saignant.
Serveur: Et pour vous, mademoiselle?
Claire: Ben, un steak aussi, mais pas de frites. Une salade verte.
Serveur: Et vous aimez votre steak comment?
Claire: À point, s'il vous plaît.
(Après le dîner)
Loïc: L'addition, s'il vous plaît!
Serveur: Oui, monsieur, j'arrive!
Claire: On laisse quelque chose? Il est sympa, le serveur.
Loïc: Oh, écoute, le service est compris.

Après la conversation

Répondez. *(Answer.)*
1. Où sont Claire et Loïc?
2. Loïc a faim?
3. Qu'est-ce qu'il va prendre?
4. Et Claire, qu'est-ce qu'elle va prendre?
5. Qu'est-ce qu'elle commande avec le steak?
6. Claire et Loïc prennent leur steak comment?
7. Après le dîner, qui demande l'addition?
8. À votre avis *(In your opinion)*, est-ce qu'ils vont laisser un pourboire?

Answers to Après la conversation

1. Claire et Loïc sont au restaurant.
2. Oui, Loïc a faim. Il a hyper faim!
3. Il va prendre un steak frites.
4. Elle va prendre un steak.
5. Elle commande une salade verte.
6. Claire prend son steak à point. Loïc prend son steak saignant.
7. Loïc demande l'addition.
8. Non, ils ne vont pas laisser de pourboire.

Parlons un peu plus
Let's talk some more

On commande? You and your friend are at a restaurant. Look at the menu and try to decide what to order. Then order. Another one of your classmates will be the server.

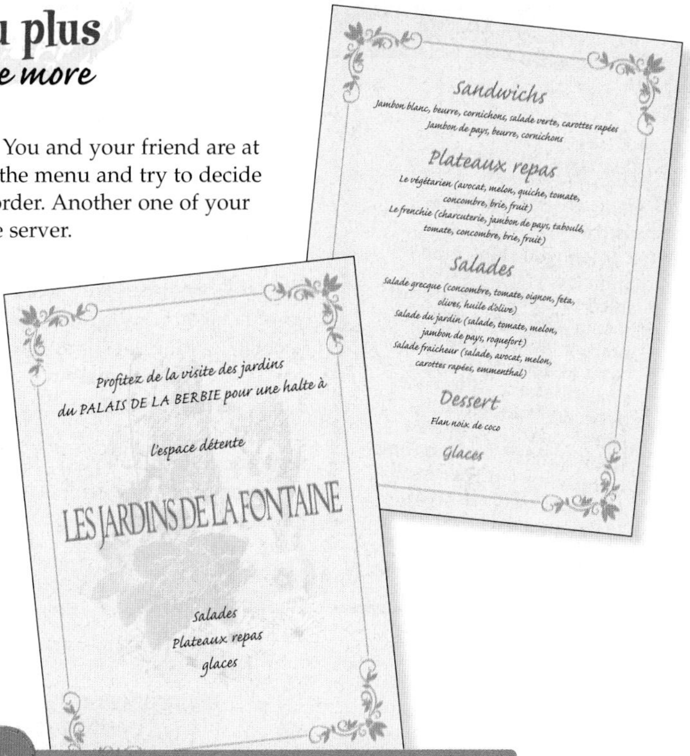
Profitez de la visite des jardins du PALAIS DE LA BERBIE pour une halte à

l'espace détente

LES JARDINS DE LA FONTAINE

Salades
Plateaux repas
glaces

Sandwichs
Jambon blanc, beurre, cornichons, salade verte, carottes rapées
Jambon de pays, beurre, cornichons

Plateaux repas
Le végétarien (avocat, melon, quiche, tomate, concombre, brie, fruit)
Le frenchie (charcuterie, jambon de pays, taboulé, tomate, concombre, brie, fruit)

Salades
Salade grecque (concombre, tomate, oignon, feta, olives, huile d'olive)
Salade du jardin (salade, tomate, melon, jambon de pays, roquefort)
Salade fraicheur (salade, avocat, melon, carottes rapées, emmenthal)

Dessert
Flan noix de coco

Glaces

Prononciation

Le son /r/

The French sound **/r/** is very different from the American /r/. When you say **/r/**, the back of your tongue should almost completely block the air going through the back of your throat. Repeat the following words and sentences.

le verre	**toujours**	**la voiture**	**le pourboire**
la carte	**la tartine**	**la cuillère**	**la fourchette**
pour	**les crêpes**	**le serveur**	**le croque-monsieur**
boire	**les frites**	**le croissant**	

Le serveur arrive avec un verre de jus d'orange.
Je voudrais laisser un pourboire pour la serveuse.

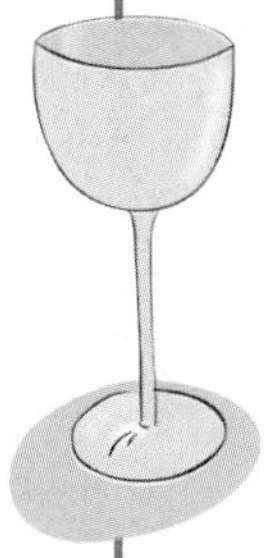
verre

ANSWERS TO Parlons un peu plus

Answers will vary but may include:
—Qu'est-ce que tu vas prendre?
—Je vais prendre le plateau végétarien. Et toi?
—Ben, une salade.
—Vous désirez?
—Le plateau végétarien, s'il vous plaît.
—Et pour vous, mademoiselle (monsieur)?
—Une salade grecque, s'il vous plaît.

Conversation

3 Practice

Parlons un peu plus
Let's talk some more

Students may want to dramatize the conversation in this activity by setting a scene in the classroom and using props. **Expansion:** Have students continue the scene, adding in a conversation about family or school between the diners while they wait for their food. At the end of the meal, the diners should request the bill and discuss leaving a tip.

Learning from Realia

(page 171) Students should be able to use this menu to order, even though they do not know the meaning of every word. You may wish to explain the following to them: **brie** and **roquefort** are two French cheeses; **cornichons** are gherkin pickles; **carottes rapées** are grated carrots. Ask students if they know what **feta** is *(Greek cheese)*. Ask them if they know what **taboulé** is *(a grain popular in dishes from the Middle East)*.

Prononciation

Step 1 Model the key word **verre** and have students repeat chorally. Then do the same for the other words and phrases.

Step 2 You may wish to give students the following **dictée: J'adore ma mère. La voiture est dans le garage. Carole arrive sur la terrasse avec un verre.**

Step 3 For additional pronunciation practice, you may wish to use Pronunciation Transparency P 5.

Resource Manager

Audio Activities Booklet TE, page 71
Audiocassette 4A/CD 4

National Standards

Cultures
The reading about restaurants and customs related to eating in restaurants give students insight into an important part of French culture.

Comparisons
The reading strategy encourages students to find practices that are similar and different from their own culture.

Presentation

Pre-reading

Step 1 Tell students they are going to read about restaurants in France.

Step 2 Read and discuss the Reading Strategy on page 172. You may wish to have students prepare a sheet with the headings "Similar" and "Different" on which they make notes about the reading.

Step 3 Have students scan the reading quickly and silently.

Reading

Step 1 Lead students through the **Lecture** on pages 172–173 by reading it aloud. Have students repeat each sentence after you.

Step 2 After every two or three sentences, ask questions such as: **Où va Valentin ce soir? Qui va au restaurant? Qui est Tango?**

Step 3 Call on some students to read aloud individually. After a student has read about three sentences, ask questions of other students to check comprehension.

Lectures culturelles

Reading Strategy

Making comparisons while reading

When you study a foreign language, you are often asked to compare customs in your country to those in another. As you read the passage, take note of similarities and differences between restaurants in France and those in the United States. Making these comparisons in your head or on paper will help clarify ideas and enable you to remember more of what you read.

Au restaurant? Vraiment?

Ce soir, Valentin va dîner dans un petit restaurant du coin[1]. Il invite ses deux amis Ahmed et Julie. Ils vont aller tous ensemble au restaurant.

Les copains arrivent au restaurant. Ils trouvent une table libre et ils prennent leur place. Tango prend sa place aussi, sous[2] la table. Sous la table? Oui. Mais qui est Tango? C'est le chien de Julie. Il est très bien élevé[3], Tango. Julie ne laisse pas Tango seul à la maison. Tango accompagne Julie partout, même au restaurant. Pourquoi pas? Un chien bien élevé est toujours le bienvenu[4]!

[1] du coin *local*
[2] sous *under*
[3] bien élevé *well-behaved*
[4] le bienvenu *welcome*

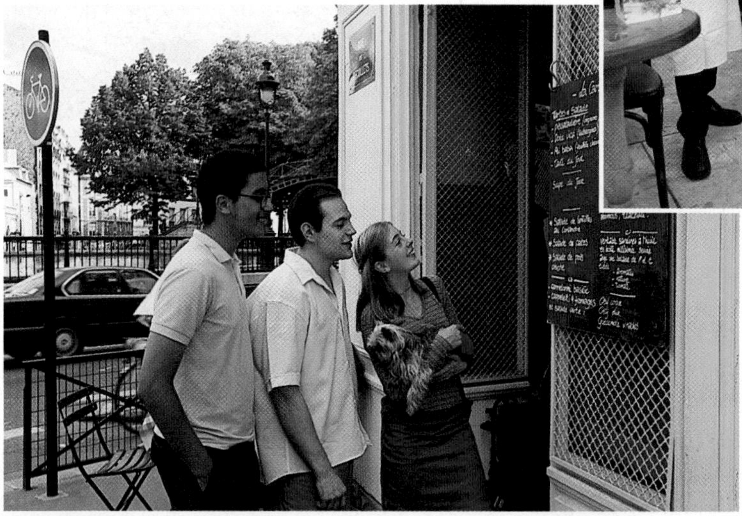

Le serveur arrive. Les amis regardent la carte et ils commandent. Après le dîner, Valentin demande l'addition. Le serveur arrive et donne l'addition à Valentin. Valentin regarde l'addition et paie. D'habitude chacun paie pour soi, mais aujourd'hui, c'est exceptionnel. Valentin paie pour tout le monde parce qu'il invite ses copains. En France, «inviter», c'est «payer»!

Après la lecture

A Valentin va au restaurant? Vrai ou faux? *(True or false?)*

1. Valentin va au restaurant tout seul.
2. Les copains entrent dans le restaurant et demandent une table au serveur.
3. Tango est un chien bien élevé.
4. Tango aussi va au restaurant.
5. Ahmed et Julie demandent l'addition.
6. Les trois amis paient l'addition.

B Des différences culturelles In this reading, there are some interesting cultural differences between France and the United States. What are they?

Post-reading

Have students do the **Après la lecture** activities on page 173 orally after reading the selection in class. Then assign these activities to be written at home. Go over them again the following day.

Après la lecture

A Expansion: After doing Activity A, you may wish to have the students correct each false statement made in the activity. For example: **1. Valentin va au restaurant avec deux copains.**

B Have students refer to the notes they made about the reading.

Learning from Photos

(page 173) Ask students the following questions about the photo.

Le restaurant est en France ou aux États-Unis?
Le chien est à la maison ou au restaurant?
Il est bien élevé?
Tu as un chien?
Tu vas au restaurant avec ton chien?

Answers to Après la lecture

A
1. F
2. F
3. V
4. V
5. F
6. F

B *Answers will vary but may include:*
It is not unusual for people to take their pet dog to the restaurant with them. A very exclusive restaurant would be an exception.

To say **Je t'invite** means you will pay for the meal.

Learning from Realia

(page 173) Le Train Bleu is a historic restaurant in the gare de Lyon. The restaurant was opened in 1901 and is decorated with gorgeous nineteenth-century frescoes.

National Standards

Cultures
This reading about dining hours and meals in France, and the related activity on page 174, give students an understanding of daily life in France.

Comparisons
This reading selection compares dining hours and eating habits in France with those of the United States.

Attention!

This reading is optional. You may skip it completely, have the entire class read it, have only several students read it and report to the class, or assign it for extra credit.

FUN-FACTS

- Latest statistics (1999) indicate that the French spend an average of 2 hours 14 minutes a day eating their meals.
- More and more French families have only one dish for dinner; that is they are skipping the **entrée** and having only **un plat principal.**
- It's becoming more common to eat on the run, in the car, at work, on the street, etc. Only 32% take their noon meal seated at a table.
- When children come from school they have a snack **(le goûter),** usually bread and chocolate or pastry.

You may wish to have students compare the above with their own habits.

Lecture supplémentaire 1

Les repas en France

La façon de manger en France change assez vite[1]. Pour le petit déjeuner, ça ne change pas vraiment; on prend toujours le petit déjeuner à la maison. C'est toujours un petit déjeuner rapide et frugal: une tartine de pain beurré et un bol de café, de thé ou de chocolat. Quelquefois, les enfants mangent des céréales.

Un restaurant aux Champs-Élysées

On déjeune entre midi et deux heures. Mais le déjeuner n'est plus[2] le repas principal parce que les enfants déjeunent à la cantine de l'école. Les parents déjeunent à la cafétéria de leur entreprise[3] ou dans un restaurant près de l'entreprise.

Le dîner est maintenant le repas principal pour beaucoup de Français. Un des parents (ou les deux) prépare le dîner dans la cuisine et la famille dîne ensemble. Souvent on mange des produits surgelés[4]. En France, il y a des plats surgelés excellents. Le dîner est un moment important pour la famille; c'est le seul moment de la journée où on est ensemble.

[1] vite *fast*
[2] n'est plus *is no longer*
[3] entreprise *firm*
[4] surgelés *frozen*

Après la lecture

Les repas Répondez. *(Answer.)*

1. En France, comment est le petit déjeuner?
2. Qu'est-ce qu'on prend pour le petit déjeuner?
3. On déjeune à quelle heure?
4. On déjeune où?
5. Quel est le repas principal?
6. Qu'est-ce qu'on prépare souvent pour le dîner?
7. Le dîner est un moment important pour la famille? Pourquoi?

Un dîner en famille

Answers to Après la lecture

1. Le petit déjeuner est rapide et frugal.
2. On prend une tartine de pain beurré et un bol de café, de thé ou de chocolat.
3. On déjeune entre midi et deux heures.
4. Les élèves déjeunent à la cantine de l'école. Les parents déjeunent à la cafétéria de leur entreprise ou dans un restaurant.
5. Le repas principal est le dîner.
6. Souvent on prépare des produits surgelés.
7. C'est le seul moment où on est ensemble.

Les goûts changent.

Au restaurant *Léon de Bruxelles*

Beaucoup de Français sont de vrais gourmets. Ils aiment manger bien. La cuisine française est excellente. Elle est célèbre dans le monde entier. Les Français continuent à apprécier leur cuisine mais ils apprécient aussi les plats d'autres pays[1]. La cuisine asiatique est très populaire: la cuisine chinoise, la cuisine thaïlandaise et aussi la cuisine vietnamienne. En France, il y a beaucoup de restaurants vietnamiens. La cuisine vietnamienne ressemble un peu à la cuisine chinoise. Il y a aussi beaucoup de restaurants algériens, tunisiens et marocains où la spécialité est toujours le couscous.

Comme aux États-Unis, il existe en France des chaînes de restaurants et des chaînes de fast-food. Certaines sont américaines, d'autres sont européennes. Elles sont françaises ou belges, par exemple, comme *Léon de Bruxelles*. Sa spécialité: les moules[2] frites, c'est-à-dire[3] des moules avec toutes sortes de sauces et des frites. C'est un plat traditionnel en Belgique.

Et la pizza? La pizza est très appréciée en France! Tout le monde aime la pizza!

[1] pays *countries*
[2] moules *mussels*
[3] c'est-à-dire *that is to say*

Les aliments préférés des jeunes de 7 à 14 ans sont:
le steak frites (51%), les hamburgers (51%), la pizza (49%), les gâteaux (37%), les spaghettis ou raviolis (32%), les sandwichs (17%).
71% des Français indiquent qu'ils préfèrent la cuisine française aux cuisines étrangères.

Après la lecture

Au restaurant en France Vrai ou faux? *(True or false?)*

1. Les Français aiment manger bien.
2. Les Français n'apprécient pas leur cuisine.
3. La cuisine asiatique est assez populaire en France.
4. Les restaurants asiatiques en France sont toujours des restaurants chinois.
5. Le couscous est une spécialité vietnamienne.
6. *Léon de Bruxelles* est une chaîne de restaurants belge en France.
7. Les Français n'aiment pas du tout la pizza.

Lecture supplémentaire 2

Attention!

This reading is optional. You may skip it completely, have the entire class read it, have only several students read it and report to the class, or assign it for extra credit.

Presentation

Step 1 Have students list or name all types of ethnic cuisine that they eat on a regular basis.

Step 2 Have students read the selection to themselves. Now have students do the **Après la lecture** activity on page 175.

Step 3 You may wish to ask students to correct the false statements.

Learning from Photos

(page 175)

- Couscous is a healthy dish made of semolina. It can be cooked in many different ways and with different ingredients. The most common meats are chicken or mutton, but fish is sometimes used. Included in the recipe are vegetables, such as zucchini, turnips, onions, chickpeas, and raisins. The couscous is served with a tasty broth to moisten the semolina and a spicy sauce or paste to be mixed into the broth. The spicy sauce is called "harissa." It is made with chili pepper and is quite hot.

Teacher Note: See more information about French foods under Fun Facts on page 177.

Answers to Après la lecture

1. V
2. F
3. V
4. F
5. F
6. V
7. F

French Online

Encourage students to take advantage of this opportunity to learn more about francophone gastronomic habits and specialties. Perhaps you can do this in class or in a lab if students do not have Internet access at home.

CONNEXIONS

Les mathématiques

L'arithmétique

When we go shopping or out to eat, it is often necessary to do some arithmetic. We either have to add up the bill ourselves or check the figures someone else has done for us. In a café or restaurant we may want to figure out what we should leave for a tip, even if **le service est compris.**

We almost never do arithmetic in a foreign language. We normally do arithmetic in the language in which we learned it. However, it is fun to know some basic arithmetical terms in case we have to discuss a problem concerning a bill, for example, with a French-speaking person.

Before we learn some of these arithmetical terms in French, let's look at some differences in numbers. Note how the numbers 1 and 7 are written in French.

Note also that the thousands are indicated by a space or a period and the decimals are indicated by a comma.

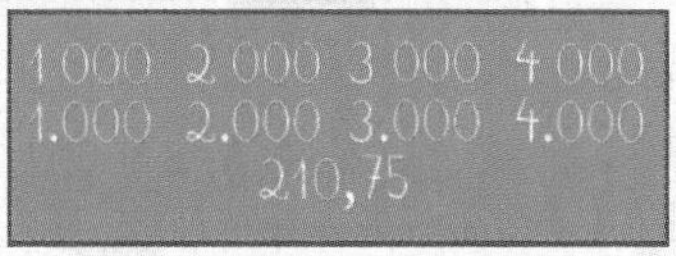

L'arithmétique

additionner	+	soustraire	−
multiplier	×	diviser	÷

Pour additionner:
Deux plus deux, ça fait quatre.
$2 + 2 = 4$

Pour soustraire:
Quatre moins deux, ça fait deux.
$4 - 2 = 2$

Pour multiplier:
Deux fois deux, ça fait quatre.
$2 \times 2 = 4$

Pour diviser:
Quatre divisé par deux, ça fait deux.
$4 \div 2 = 2$

Dix pour cent (%) de 200 euros, c'est 20 euros.

CONNEXIONS

National Standards

Connections
This reading establishes a connection with another discipline, allowing students to reinforce and further their knowledge of mathematics through the study of French.

Comparisons
Students are introduced to the different ways some numbers are handwritten, counted by hand, and the different use of the decimal point.

Presentation

Les mathématiques
L'arithméthique

Attention!

As the introduction states, one rarely does arithmetic in a foreign language. The purpose of this section is to introduce students to only the most basic and important arithmetical terms.

Note: The French way of counting on fingers is shown in the top row of the illustration on page 177.

About the French Language

Note that the word **le calcul** means "arithmetic." The terms for "calculus" are: **le calcul différentiel, le calcul intégral,** and **le calcul infinitésimal.** ⚜

Learning from Realia

(page 177) Students may ask the meaning of **M. fraich** on the receipt. It is **morue fraîche,** meaning *codfish.*

Après la lecture

A Ça fait combien? Faites les opérations suivantes à voix haute. *(Solve the following problems aloud.)*

1. $2 + 2 =$
2. $14 + 6 =$
3. $30 - 8 =$
4. $20 - 4 =$
5. $4 \times 4 =$
6. $8 \times 3 =$
7. $27 \div 9 =$
8. $80 \div 10 =$

B L'addition, s'il vous plaît! You went out to a restaurant with three friends. This is your bill. Do the following.

1. Add up to see if the total is correct.
2. Add 10 percent, even though the tip is included.
3. Calculate how much each of you owes.

LE BAR À HUÎTRES
112, Bd du Montparnasse
75014 PARIS
TEL: 01 . 43 . 20 . 71 . 01

6 Thomas

Tbl 16/1 Fct 9919 Cts 5
25 Jul 20:19
*** Réimprimée ***

Prix en Frs

3 Salade de Thon	25.00
1M. FRAICH	19.00
3 Terrine Volaille	23.00
3 SOLE MEUNIÈRE	78.00
1 Tout café	3.00
1 Café Colombie	2.00
1 Café Crème	3.00
Total	
T. V. A. 20.60%	153.00
Service 15%	22.95
Total du 153.00	

Toute l'équipe
Bar À Huîtres Montparnasse
vous remercie de votre visite.
À BIENTÔT

C Comment compter sur ses doigts Here are three different ways people count on their fingers. Which one is yours? With a classmate, choose a way that is not yours and show each other numbers. Take turns figuring out which number it is.

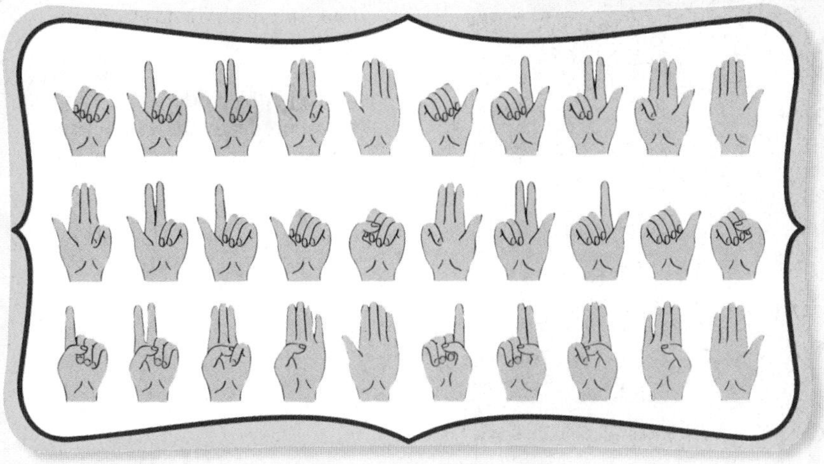

Answers to Après la lecture

A

1. Deux plus deux, ça fait quatre.
2. Quatorze plus six, ça fait vingt.
3. Trente moins huit, ça fait vingt-deux.
4. Vingt moins quatre, ça fait seize.
5. Quatre fois quatre, ça fait seize.
6. Huit fois trois, ça fait vingt-quatre.
7. Vingt-sept divisé par neuf, ça fait trois.
8. Quatre-vingts divisé par dix, ça fait huit.

B

1. Cent vingt-six plus quatre-vingt-huit, ça fait deux cent vingt-quatre...etc.
2. Dix pour cent de huit cent huit francs, ça fait quatre-vingts francs.
3. Huit cent quatre-vingt huit francs divisé par quatre, ça fait deux cent vingt-deux francs.

C *Students will try counting methods.*

Connexions

Fun-Facts

Students will learn more about regional dishes in **Bon voyage! Level 2.** However, you may wish to share the following information with them in case they go to a French restaurant.

- French cuisine is famous throughout the world. As a result, there are many French restaurants in the U.S. and in many other countries. The following is a list of dishes often found on the menu in French restaurants. Find out if the students know what any of these items are. If not, give them a brief description.

  le coq au vin: chicken cooked in a red wine sauce.

  le bœuf bourguignon: pieces of beef cooked in red wine with mushrooms, white onions, and peas.

  le pot-au-feu: a typical, home-cooked French meal with chunks of beef and marrow bones cooked in a broth with many vegetables.

  le cassoulet: a dish from the Southwest with duck, sausage, some other meats, and white beans.

  la bouillabaisse: popular in Provence, a wonderful type of fish chowder.

  le canard à l'orange: duck glazed with an orange sauce.

  le gigot d'agneau: leg of lamb. Many people eat it rare or medium in France, contrary to the U.S. custom of eating it well done.

  la salade niçoise: a salad from Provence with lettuce, tomato, onion, black olives, tuna or anchovy, hard-boiled eggs, etc. (Ask students what city **niçoise** refers to.)

  la choucroute: a specialty of Alsace-Lorraine made with sauerkraut and sausages.

Use what you have learned

Bellringer Review

Use BRR Transparency 5.8 or write the following on the board.
Answer the following questions.
1. Tu vas aller où demain?
2. Tu vas dîner au restaurant?
3. Tu vas inviter tes amis au restaurant?
4. Vous allez commander des sandwichs ou des steaks?
5. Tes amis vont aller au restaurant à pied?

Recycling

These activities allow students to use the vocabulary and structure from this chapter in completely open-ended, real-life situations.

Presentation

Encourage students to say as much as possible when they do these activities. Tell them not to be afraid to make mistakes, since the goal of these activities is real-life communication. If someone in the group makes an error, allow the others to politely correct him or her. Let students choose the activities they would like to do.

You may wish to divide students into pairs or groups. Encourage students to elaborate on the basic theme and to be creative. They may use props, pictures, or posters if they wish.

1 and **2** Let groups of students act out their conversations for this activity. Encourage them to use props and to vary the language as much as possible.

C'est à vous

Use what you have learned

PARLER

1 Au café

✔ *Order something to eat or drink in a café*

Work with a classmate. One of you is the customer and the other is the server. You order from the menu provided.

PARLER ÉCRIRE

2 À la terrasse des Deux Magots

✔ *Talk about school and teachers as you order food and drinks*

Work in groups of three or four. You're all friends sitting on the **terrasse** of the famous café **Les Deux Magots** in Paris, watching the world go by. You talk about many things—school, teachers, friends, etc. One of you will play the role of the waiter. You have to interrupt the conversation once in a while to take the orders and serve.

Answers to C'est à vous

1 *Answers will vary but may include:*
—Vous désirez, mademoiselle (monsieur)?
—Une quiche maison, s'il vous plaît.

2 *Students can say whatever they want using vocabulary they know to describe friends, teachers, school, etc.*

Learning from Photos

(page 178) Have students look at the photo on this page and say or write all they can about it.

ÉCRIRE

3 La carte

✔ Plan a menu

Write a menu in French for your school cafeteria.

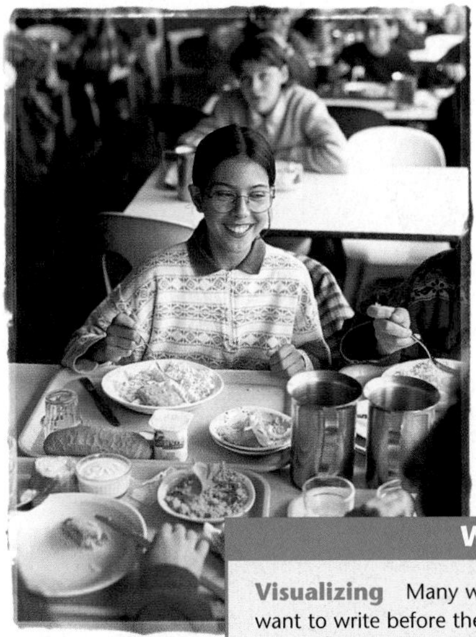

Élodie prend le déjeuner à la cantine.

Writing Strategy

Visualizing Many writers have a mental picture of what they want to write before they actually begin to write. The mental picture helps organize what they want to say. It also helps them visualize what they want to describe in their writing. Closing your eyes and visualizing what you want to write can make the writing experience more pleasant. When writing in a foreign language, you also have to restrict your mental picture to what you know how to say.

ÉCRIRE

4 Un restaurant

You have been asked to write a short article about a visit to a restaurant. Look at this illustration. Pretend this is the mental picture you have of the restaurant you are going to write about. Look at it for several minutes and then write a paragraph about it.

C'est à vous

Writing Strategy

Visualizing Have students read the Writing Strategy on page 179. If students have difficulty thinking of words relating to restaurants, have them use the vocabulary list on page 182.

Learning from Photos

(page 179) Ask the following questions about the photo on this page.

Elle est comment, Élodie?
Qu'est-ce qu'elle fait?
Elle déjeune où?
Elle déjeune avec qui?
Ils sont contents?
Qu'est-ce qu'elle mange? (un yaourt, des pâtes)
Qu'est-ce qu'il y a sur la table?

Answers to C'est à vous

3 *Answers will vary but should include vocabulary from page 182.*

Resource Manager

Communication Transparencies
Quizzes
Test Booklet
ExamView Pro®
Situation Cards
Performance Assessment
Marathon mental Videoquiz

Assessment

This is a pre-test for students to take before you administer the chapter test. Answer sheets for students to do these pages are provided in your transparency binder. Note that each section is cross-referenced so students can easily find the material they have to review in case they made errors. You may wish to collect these assessments and correct them yourself or you may prefer to have the students correct themselves in class. You can go over the answers orally or project them on the overhead, using your Assessment Answers transparencies.

Learning from Photos

(page 180) Have students describe the photo on page 180. They should describe everything they can in the scene and then imagine the conversation the people might have.

Vocabulaire

To review **Mots 1**, turn to pages 154–155.

1 Choisissez. *(Choose.)*

1. Après les cours, Michel et Chantal vont au _____.
   a. café **b.** ensemble
2. Ils trouvent _____ à la terrasse.
   a. une table libre **b.** une tartine
3. Le serveur _____ la carte à Chantal.
   a. regarde **b.** donne
4. Chantal a soif. Elle commande quelque chose à _____.
   a. manger **b.** boire
5. Michel a faim. Il prend _____.
   a. un jus d'orange **b.** une tartine de pain beurré

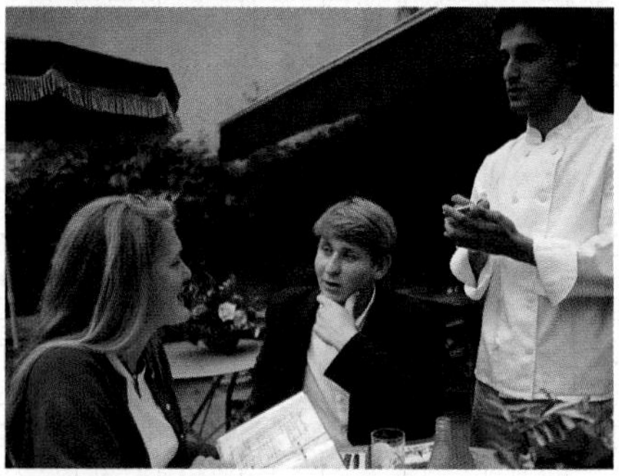

Deux amis au café

To review **Mots 2**, turn to pages 158–159.

2 Choisissez. *(Choose.)*

6. À midi, Henri va _____ au restaurant.
   a. dîner **b.** déjeuner **c.** payer
7. Il _____ le métro.
   a. prend **b.** commande **c.** laisse
8. Henri aime son steak _____.
   a. à pied **b.** à point **c.** ensemble
9. Après le déjeuner, Henri _____ l'addition.
   a. demande **b.** invite **c.** laisse
10. Dans les restaurants en France _____ est compris.
    a. le verre **b.** l'addition **c.** le service

Answers to Assessment

1

1. a
2. a
3. b
4. b
5. b

2

6. b
7. a
8. b
9. a
10. c

Reaching All Students

Additional Practice After completing Activities 1 and 2, you may wish to have students create appropriate sentences for the vocabulary words that were not used in the answers.

Assessment

Structure

3 Complétez avec «aller».
(Complete with the verb aller.*)*

11. Nous _____ à l'école en voiture?
12. Laurent, tu _____ au café?
13. Vous _____ bien, madame?

*To review the verb **aller**, turn to page 162.*

4 Choisissez. *(Choose.)*

14. Je vais _____ au café avec mes copains.
    a. déjeune b. déjeuner
15. Ils vont _____ un pourboire pour le serveur.
    a. laisser b. laissent

*To review the use of **aller** + an infinitive, turn to page 165.*

5 Complétez avec «à» ou «de».
(Complete with à *or* de.*)*

16. Les amis vont _____ café.
17. Vincent rentre _____ école à cinq heures.
18. C'est la voiture _____ père de Marie.
19. Le prof donne un examen _____ élèves.

*To review the forms of **à** and **de**, turn to page 166.*

6 Complétez avec «prendre».
(Complete with the verb prendre.*)*

20. Les copains _____ le métro.
21. Vous _____ le petit déjeuner à la maison?
22. Pour monter à l'appartement, on _____ l'ascenseur.
23. Tu _____ un sandwich à midi?

*To review the verb **prendre**, turn to page 168.*

Culture

7 Complétez. *(Complete.)*

24. Les copains _____ une table libre au restaurant.
25. Claire paie pour tout le monde. Elle _____ ses copains.

To review this cultural information, turn to pages 172–173.

Learning from Realia

(page 181)

- You may have students give the following information concerning the realia.
  le nom du restaurant,
  sa situation *(location),*
  son adresse, le numéro de téléphone, la station de métro près du restaurant
- **Reading strategy** Guessing the meaning of words in context is an important skill. Ask students what they think **angle** means based on the context. *(corner)*

Reaching All Students

For the Younger Students

- Have students make lists in their notebook of the things they would and would not order in a restaurant. Encourage them to add to these lists as they learn more foods. Tell students to learn the words for the items they order.
- Tell students they are going to open a restaurant. Have them name the restaurant and create a menu for it.

Answers to Assessment

3	4	5	6	7
11. allons	**14.** b	**16.** au	**20.** prennent	**24.** trouvent
12. vas	**15.** a	**17.** de l'	**21.** prenez	**25.** invite
13. allez		**18.** du	**22.** prend	
		19. aux	**23.** prends	

Glencoe Technology

MINDJOGGER

You may wish to help your students prepare for the chapter test by playing the MindJogger game show. Teams will compete against each other to review chapter vocabulary and structure and sharpen listening comprehension skills.

Vocabulaire

Vocabulary Review

The words and phrases in the **Vocabulaire** have been taught for productive use in this chapter. They are summarized here as a resource for both student and teacher. This list also serves as a convenient resource for the **C'est à vous** activities on pages 178–179. There are approximately thirteen cognates in this vocabulary list. Have students find them.

Attention!

You will notice that the vocabulary list here is not translated. This has been done intentionally, since we feel that by the time students have finished the material in the chapter they should be familiar with the meanings of all the words. If there are several words they still do not know, we recommend that they refer to the **Mots 1** and **2** sections in the chapter or go to the dictionaries at the back of this book to find the meanings. However, if you prefer that your students have the English translations, please refer to Vocabulary Transparency 5.1, where you will find all these words listed with their translations.

Vocabulaire

Getting along in a café or restaurant

un café
la terrasse d'un café
une table
  occupée
  libre
un serveur
une serveuse

la carte
l'addition *(f.)*
l'argent *(m.)*
le pourboire
aller
trouver une table
commander

inviter
payer
laisser
prendre
déjeuner
dîner
avoir faim

avoir soif
Vous désirez?
je voudrais
quelque chose
  à manger
  à boire
Le service est compris.

Identifying snacks and beverages

une boisson
une consommation
un coca
une limonade
un café
un express
un crème
un citron pressé
un jus de pomme

un jus d'orange
une tartine de pain
  beurré
un croissant
un sandwich
  au jambon
  au fromage
un croque-monsieur

un steak
  saignant
  à point
  bien cuit
des frites *(f. pl.)*
une soupe à l'oignon
une omelette
  nature
  aux fines herbes

une saucisse de
  Francfort, un
  hot-dog
une salade verte
une glace
À quel parfum?
  au chocolat
  à la vanille
une crêpe

Identifying a place setting

le couvert
un verre
une tasse

une fourchette
un couteau
une cuillère

une assiette
une nappe
une serviette

How well do you know your vocabulary?

- **Choose words for specific foods you enjoy.**
- **Create a menu using these words.**

Identifying meals

un repas
le petit déjeuner
le déjeuner
le dîner

Other useful words and expressions

tout(e) seul(e)
toujours
souvent

quelquefois
peu

Technotour

BON VOYAGE!

VIDÉO • Épisode 5

Avant de visionner

In this video episode, Christine and Chloé have lunch on the terrace of a café in Paris.

Chloé et Christine vont dans un café.

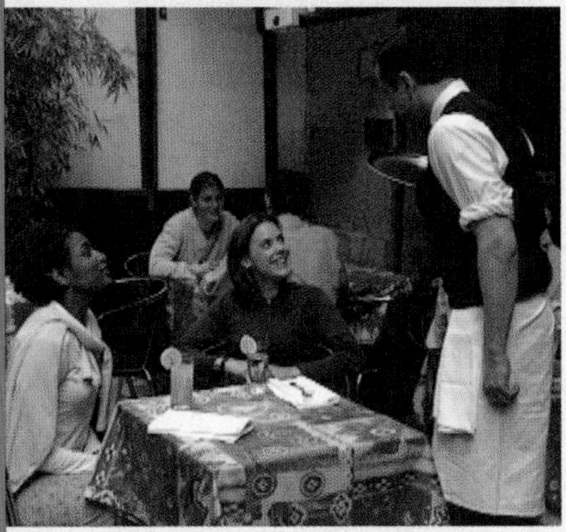

Elles commandent une boisson.

FRENCH ONLINE

À découvrir

Learn more about café life in Paris online.

Un café, Paris

FRENCH Online

In the Chapter 5 Internet activity, you will have a chance to learn more about cafés and restaurants in the Francophone world. To begin your virtual adventure, go to the Glencoe French Web site: **french.glencoe.com**

Technotour

Overview

This page previews two key multimedia components of the **Glencoe French** series. Each reinforces the material taught in the chapter in a unique manner.

VIDÉO

The Video Program allows students to see how the chapter vocabulary and structures are used by native speakers. For maximum reinforcement, show the video episode as a final activity for Chapter 5.

The two photos on the left show highlights from the Chapter 5 video episode. Discuss the photos with your students before having them view the episode. See the Video Activities Booklet for detailed suggestions for using this resource.

FRENCH Online

- The **À découvrir** photo shows a Parisian café. Students can go online to learn more about café life in Paris.
- Teacher Information and Student Worksheets for this activity can be accessed at the Web site.

Video Synopsis

In this video episode, we see Chloé and Christine stopping for a bite to eat at a café in Paris. The episode shows us random views of different cafés, giving us a feel for café life in Paris. After Chloé and Christine have something to eat, the video breaks away into a montage of various kinds of foods that are sold on the streets of Paris.

Planning for Chapter 6

SCOPE AND SEQUENCE, PAGES 184–217

Topics

- Identifying foods
- Shopping for food

Culture

- Madame Lelong shops for food
- Discussing differences between shopping for food in the United States and France
- Markets in the Francophone world

Functions

- How to identify and shop for food
- How to express what you and others are doing
- How to express what you and others have
- How to express what you and others are able to do or want to do

Structure

- The verb **faire** in the present tense
- The partitive and the definite article
- The partitive forms in the negative
- The verbs **pouvoir** and **vouloir** in the present tense

National Standards

- Communication Standard 1.1 pages 188, 189, 192, 193, 194, 195, 197, 198, 199, 200, 202, 203, 205, 212
- Communication Standard 1.2 pages 188, 189, 192, 193, 194, 195, 197, 198, 199, 200, 202, 203, 204, 207, 208, 209, 211
- Communication Standard 1.3 pages 188, 195, 212, 213
- Cultures Standard 2.1 pages 204, 206–207, 208, 209
- Cultures Standard 2.2 pages 186, 187, 189, 190, 191
- Connections Standard 3.1 pages 210–211
- Comparisons Standard 4.1 pages 210–211
- Comparisons Standard 4.2 pages 206–207, 209, 210–211
- Communities Standard 5.1 page 213

PACING AND PRIORITIES

The chapter content is color coded below to assist you in planning.
■ **required** ■ **recommended** ■ **optional**

Vocabulaire *(required)* *Days 1–4*

- ■ Mots 1
  - À la boulangerie-pâtisserie
  - À la crémerie
  - À la boucherie
  - À la poissonnerie
  - À la charcuterie
  - À l'épicerie
- ■ Mots 2
  - Au marché

Structure *(required)* *Days 5–7*

- ■ Le verbe **faire** au présent
- ■ Le partitif et l'article défini
- ■ Le partitif au négatif
- ■ Les verbes **pouvoir** et **vouloir**

Conversation *(required)*

- ■ Au marché

Prononciation *(recommended)*

- ■ Les sons **/œ́/** et **/œ̀/**

Lectures culturelles

- ■ Les courses *(recommended)*
- ■ Les grandes surfaces *(optional)*
- ■ Les marchés *(optional)*

Connexions *(optional)*

- ■ Les conversions

■ **C'est à vous** *(recommended)*

■ **Assessment** *(recommended)*

■ **Technotour** *(optional)*

RESOURCE GUIDE

SECTION	PAGES	SECTION RESOURCES
Vocabulaire *Mots 1*		
À la boulangerie-pâtisserie	186	🖥 Vocabulary Transparencies 6.2–6.3
À la crémerie	186	🎧 Audiocassette 4B/CD 4
À la boucherie	186	📘 Audio Activities Booklet TE, pages 74–76
À la poissonnerie	186	📘 Workbook, pages 55–56
À la charcuterie	186	📘 Quiz 1, page 28
À l'épicerie	186–189	💿 ExamView Pro®
Vocabulaire *Mots 2*		
Au marché	190–193	🖥 Vocabulary Transparencies 6.4–6.5
		🎧 Audiocassette 4B/CD 4
		📘 Audio Activities Booklet TE, pages 76–78
		📘 Workbook, pages 56–57
		📘 Quiz 2, page 29
		💿 ExamView Pro®
Structure		
Le verbe **faire** au présent	194–195	🎧 Audiocassette 4B/CD 4
Le partitif et l'article défini	196–197	📘 Audio Activities Booklet TE, pages 79–81
Le partitif au négatif	198–200	📘 Workbook, pages 58–61
Les verbes **pouvoir** et **vouloir**	201–203	📘 Quizzes 3–5, pages 30–32
		💿 ExamView Pro®
Conversation		
Au marché	204	🎧 Audiocassette 4B/CD 4
		📘 Audio Activities Booklet TE, pages 82–83
		💿 CD-ROM
Prononciation		
Les sons /œ/ et /œ/	205	🖥 Pronunciation Transparency P 6
		🎧 Audiocassette 4B/CD 4
		📘 Audio Activities Booklet TE, pages 83–84
Lectures culturelles		
Les courses	206–207	🎧 Audiocassette 4B/CD 4
Les grandes surfaces	208	📘 Audio Activities Booklet TE, pages 84–85
Les marchés	209	📘 Test Booklet, Chapter 6
Connexions		
Les conversions	210–211	📘 Test Booklet, Chapter 6
C'est à vous		
	212–213	📼 **Bon voyage!** Video, Episode 6
		📘 Video Activities Booklet, Chapter 6
		🖱 French Online Activities
		french.glencoe.com
Assessment		
	214–215	🖥 Communication Transparency C 6
		📘 Quizzes 1–5, pages 28–32
		📘 Test Booklet, Chapter 6
		💿 ExamView Pro®
		📘 Situation Cards, Chapter 6
		📼 **Marathon mental** Videoquiz

Using Your Resources for Chapter 6

Transparencies

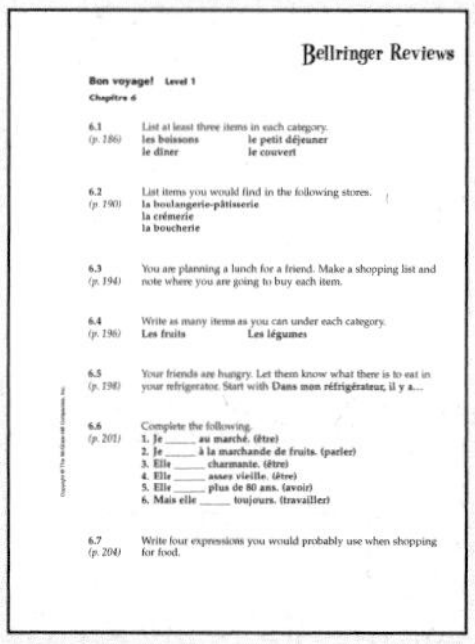

Bellringer 6.1–6.9

Vocabulary 6.1–6.5

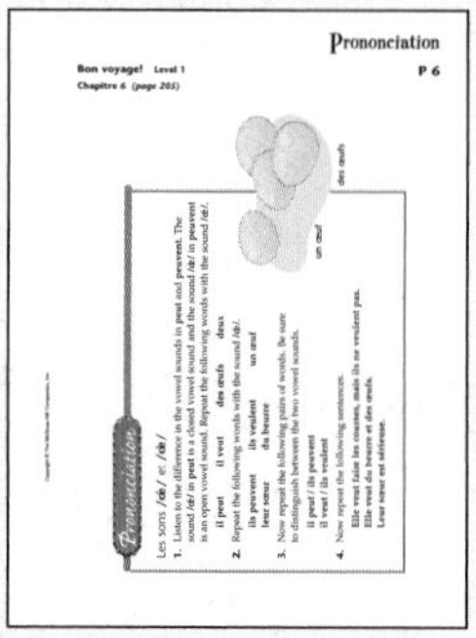

Pronunciation P 6

Communication C 6

Writing Activities Workbook

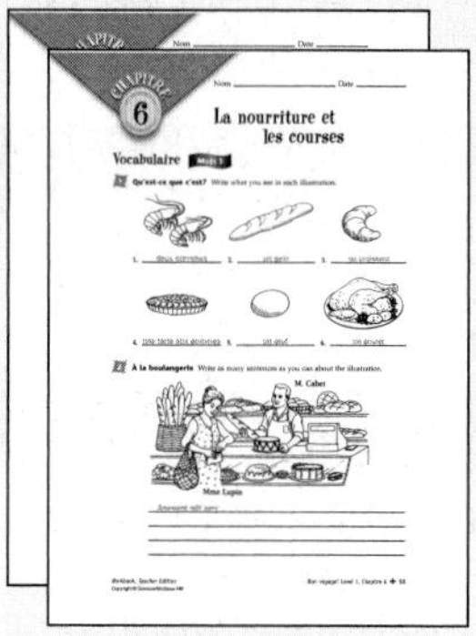

Vocabulary,
pages 55–57

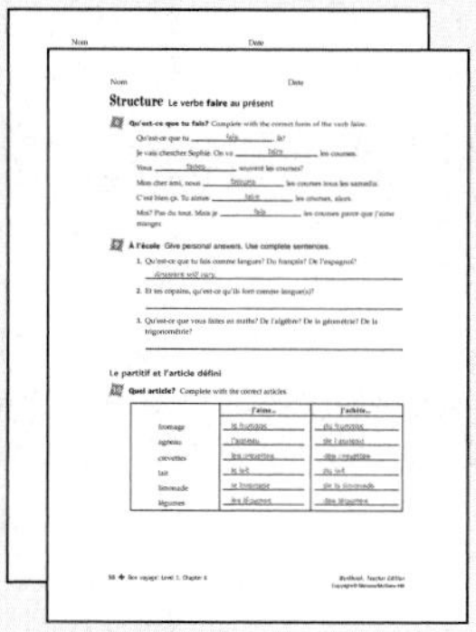

Structure,
pages 58–61

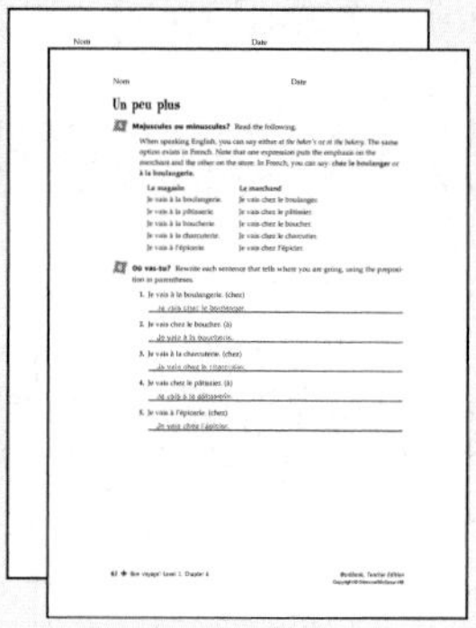

Enrichment,
pages 62–64

Audio Program and Audio Activities Booklet

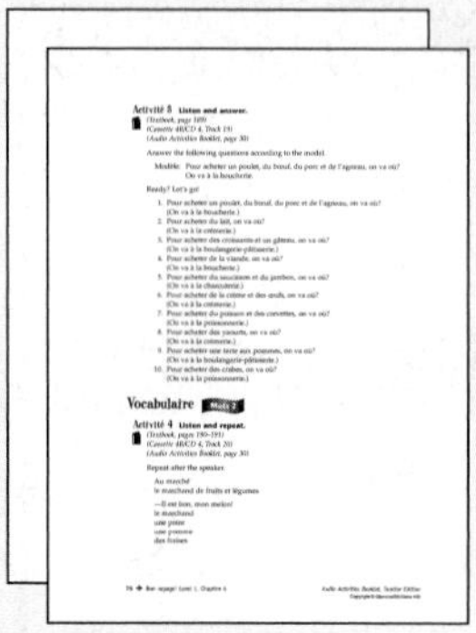

Vocabulary,
pages 74–78

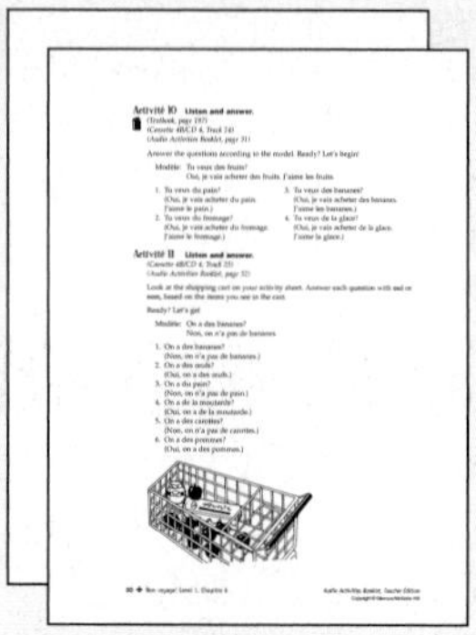

Structure,
pages 79–81

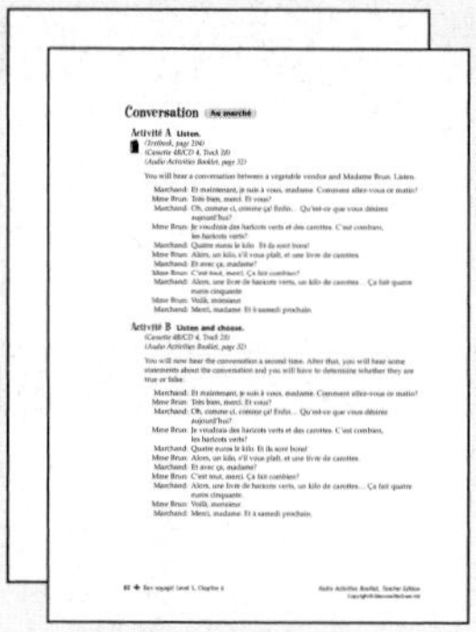

Conversation,
Pronunciation,
pages 82–84

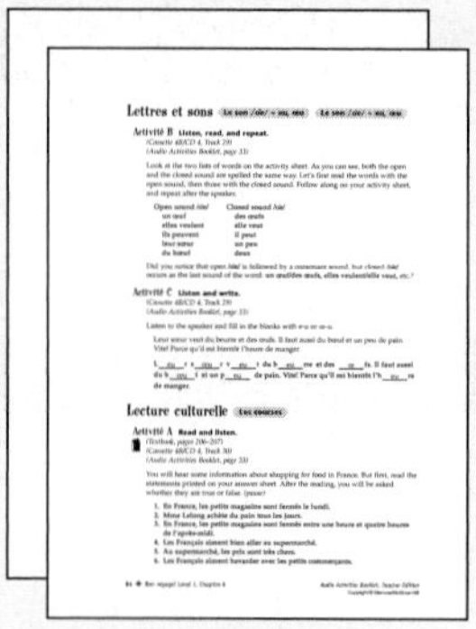

Cultural Reading,
pages 84–85

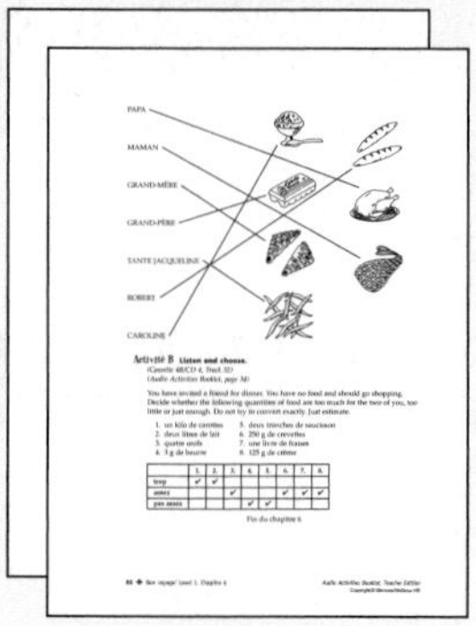

Additional Practice,
pages 85–86

Assessment

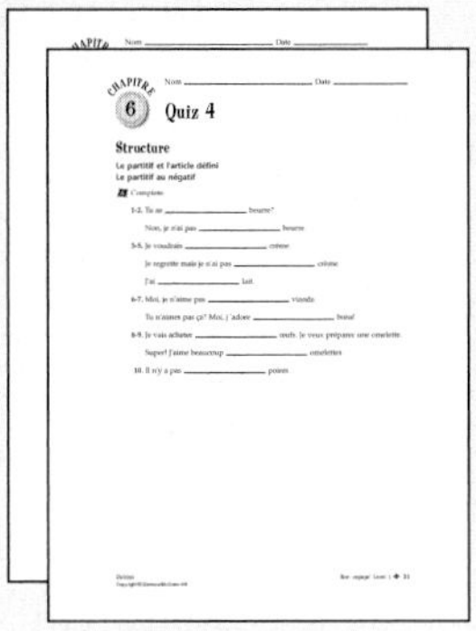

Vocabulary and Structure Quizzes, pages 28–32

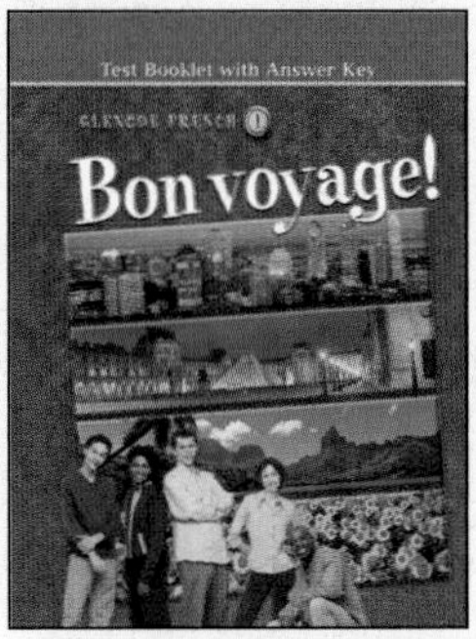

Chapter Tests, Chapter 6

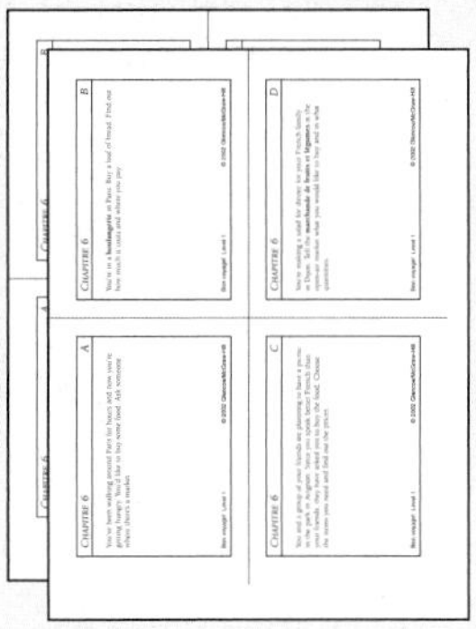

Situation Cards, Chapter 6

Timesaving Teacher Tools

Interactive Teacher Edition

Imagine having your Teacher's Edition and all resources on a CD-ROM. Click on a resource and it appears on your screen, ready to be printed, sorted, or planned.

Interactive Lesson Planner

The Interactive Lesson Planner CD-ROM helps you organize your lesson plans for a week, month, semester, or year. Look at this planning tool for easy access to your Chapter 6 resources.

ExamView Pro®

Test Bank software for Macintosh and Windows makes creating, editing, customizing, and printing tests quick and easy.

Technology Resources

FRENCH Online

In the Chapter 6 Internet activity, you will have a chance to learn more about food in the Francophone world. Visit french.glencoe.com.

On the Interactive Conversation CD-ROM, students can listen to and take part in a recorded version of the conversation in Chapter 6.

NATIONAL GEOGRAPHIC SOCIETY

See the National Geographic Teacher's Corner on pages 150–151, 256–257, 396–397, 500–501 for reference to additional technology resources.

Bon voyage! Video and Video Activities Booklet.

Help your students prepare for the chapter test by playing the **Marathon mental** Videoquiz game show. Teams will compete against each other to review chapter vocabulary and structure and sharpen listening comprehension skills.

Preview

In this chapter, students will learn vocabulary and structures associated with various foods and grocery shopping, including looking for items, expressing quantities, and talking about prices. They will also learn the forms of the irregular verb **faire** and the partitive. Students will learn to talk about what they and others can do and want to do using the verbs **pouvoir** and **vouloir.**

National Standards

Communication

In Chapter 6, students will communicate in spoken and written French on the following topics:

- Shopping for food at a market or supermarket
- French food-shopping customs

Students will engage in conversations, provide and obtain information, and exchange opinions as they fulfill the chapter objectives listed on this page.

Communities

If you have an open-air market or a French bakery in your area, a field trip to these locations would be a fun and instructive way to complete this chapter's work. Your class could plan a shopping list ahead of time for a French picnic or dinner to be prepared for the class. As you shop, have students use as much of their French vocabulary as possible. Have them compare the experience of shopping for various products from different sellers to the experience of shopping in a typical supermarket.

CHAPITRE 6

La nourriture et les courses

Objectifs

In this chapter you will learn to:

- ✔ *identify more foods*
- ✔ *shop for food*
- ✔ *tell what you or others are doing*
- ✔ *ask for the quantity you want*
- ✔ *talk about what you or others don't have*
- ✔ *tell what you or others are able to do or want to do*
- ✔ *talk about French food-shopping customs*

Paul Cézanne *Nature morte au panier*

184

Correlations to Continuum *(see page i for code)*

Stage I
Engage in conversations. p. 200 (**29**, *p*); Express likes and dislikes. p. 197 (**19**, *p*); Make requests. p. 200 (**28**, *p*); Obtain information p. 189 (**5**, *p*); Understand some ideas and familiar details. p. 189 (**4**, *p*); Listen during social interactions and listen to audio or video texts. p. 217 (*p*); Write lists. p. 205 (*p*); Use short sentences, learned words, phrases, simple questions, and commands when writing. p. 212 (**3**, *p*); Understand ideas and familiar details when listening. p. 204 (*p*); Understand texts enhanced by visual clues. pp. 210–211 (*p*); Understand and convey information about houses. p. 195 (**17**, *p*); Understand and convey information on food and customs. pp. 206–207 (*p*)

Stage II
Understand and express important ideas and some detail. p. 203 (**34**, *p*); Describe and compare. p. 195 (**17**, *p*); Use authentic materials such as advertisements when reading. p. 213 (**4**, *i*), p. 213 (**4**, *p*); Write short guided compositions. p. 213 (**5**, *p*); Demonstrate increasing fluency and control of vocabulary. p. 205

cent quatre-vingt-cinq 185

Spotlight on Culture

Photograph This photo shows a small outdoor market in Guadeloupe. Students will learn in this chapter that outdoor markets as well as indoor stores and supermarkets are common in all areas of the French-speaking world.

Painting Paul Cézanne was born in Aix-en-Provence in 1839 and he died there in 1906. The son of a baker, he received a very academic education and studied law before taking off to Paris to devote himself to painting, against the wishes of his parents. He studied the works of Delacroix, Tintoretto, and Rubens. His paintings from 1872 to 1873 assimilate Impressionist methods, but he never lost his affection for the art of the old masters. His studies of the great artists in the Louvre led him to believe that the Impressionist paintings lacked form, solidity, and structure. He spent the rest of his life trying to restore those qualities to his paintings without turning his back entirely on Impressionism. Cézanne, along with Van Gogh and Gauguin, are considered the most important of a group of artists who are now called Post-Impressionists.

Cézanne became interested in painting still-lifes because the objects could not move and he could study them closely. He often painted the same object over and over until he was completely satisfied. If a painting did not please him, he would throw it out the window or give it to his son to cut up for a jigsaw puzzle. ***Nature morte au panier*** is an example of his still-lifes.

Chapter Projects

Une fête Have students plan a menu for a French club party. They should plan who will bring the beverages and the various food items.

Au supermarché Have students check their local supermarket to find out what kind of French foods they sell. Have them report back to the class about their findings.

Tell students to remember the names of the foods they happen to like. These are the most important ones for them, since they are the very items they will want to order.

1 Preparation

Resource Manager

Vocabulary Transparencies 6.2–6.3
Audio Activities Booklet TE, pages 74–76
Audiocassette 4B/CD 4
Workbook, pages 55–56
Quiz 1, page 28
ExamViewPro®

Bellringer Review

Use BRR Transparency 6.1 or write the following on the board.
List at least three items in each category.

les boissons **le petit déjeuner**
le dîner **le couvert**

2 Presentation

Step 1 Tell students they are about to learn some new food items. Review the Chapter 5 food vocabulary using the Vocabulary Transparencies from that chapter. You may wish to have students use the words in a sentence.

Step 2 Model the new words using Vocabulary Transparencies 6.2–6.3, plastic replicas, empty containers, or large pictures of food items. Have students repeat the words and phrases after you or Audiocassette 4B/CD 4. Review by pointing to the items as you ask: **Qu'est-ce que c'est?**

Step 3 Now have students open their books and read the new words.

Step 4 Ask: **Paul fait les courses? Il fait les courses le matin? Il fait ses courses au supermarché? Il va à la boulangerie?**

Vocabulaire Mots 1

À la boulangerie-pâtisserie

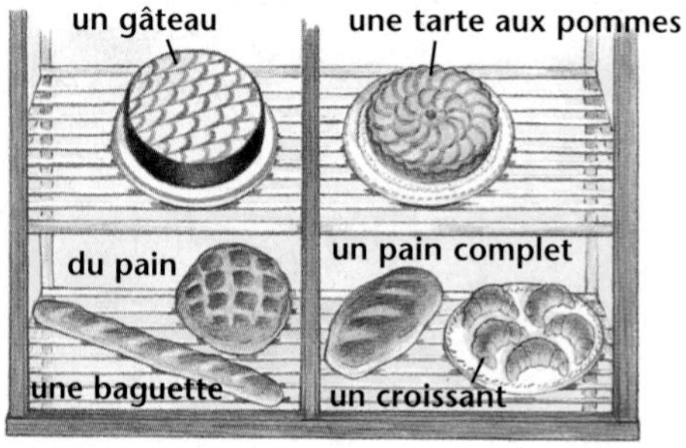

À la crémerie

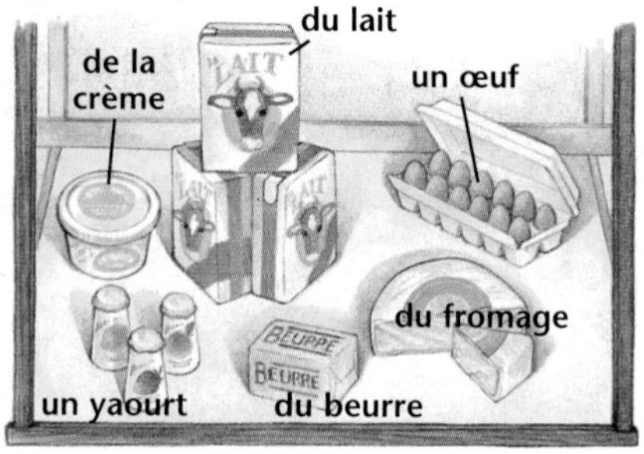

À la boucherie

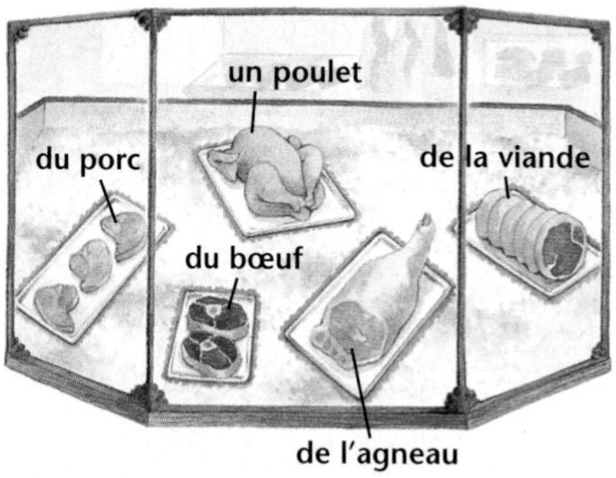

À la poissonnerie

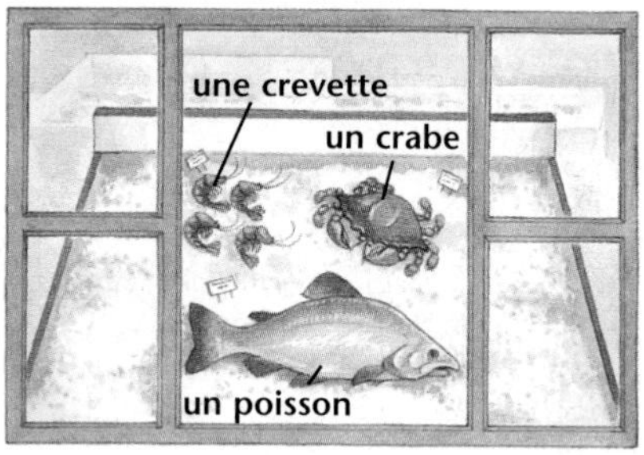

À la charcuterie

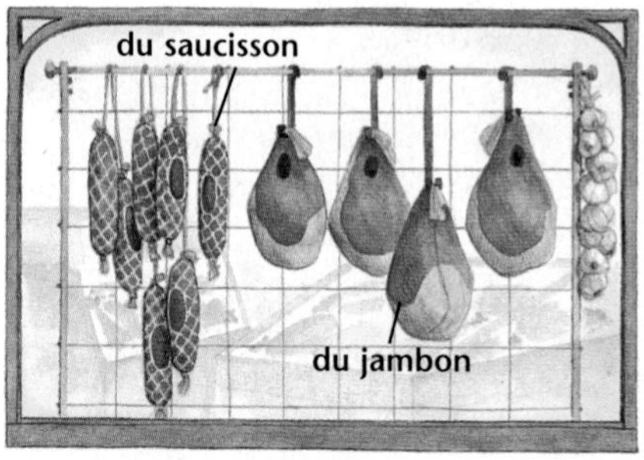

À l'épicerie

Reaching All Students

Total Physical Response Using posters or pictures of stores, get ready by setting up areas of the classroom as **la pâtisserie, la boulangerie, la poissonnerie, la boucherie, la crémerie, la charcuterie, l'épicerie.** Have pictures of food items from **Mots 1** and from Chapter 5 in each store. Dramatize the meaning of **montre-moi.**

Va à la boulangerie.
Prends une baguette.
Donne la baguette à _____.
Va à la boucherie.
Achète un poulet.
Montre le poulet à _____.
Va à la poissonnerie.
Montre-moi les crevettes.
Va à la charcuterie.
Montre-moi le saucisson.
Va à la crémerie.
Achète des œufs.
Donne les œufs à _____.
Va à l'épicerie.
Montre-moi le sel.
Va à la caisse
Paie.

Paul fait les courses.
Il va à la boulangerie.
Il va chercher du pain.

Paul est à la boulangerie.
Il veut acheter une baguette.
Il n'y a plus de baguettes.

Bon, alors un pain complet.
Et avec ça?
C'est tout, merci.

Il ne peut pas acheter de baguette.
Il achète un pain complet.

Step 5 Now ask *either/or* questions such as: **C'est un croissant ou une baguette?** For the sentences on page 187, try using question words. For example: **Qui fait les courses? Paul fait les courses quand? Il va où? Qu'est-ce qu'il achète?**

Step 6 Have students dramatize the conversation between Paul and la **boulangère.**

About the French Language

Tell students to pay careful attention to the difference in pronunciation between **un œuf** and **des œufs.**

FUN-FACTS

There are many types of French bread. **Une baguette** is used for French-style sandwiches and also sliced in half lengthwise and buttered for breakfast. **Un pain de mie,** which has a shape and texture similar to American bread, would be used to make an American-type sandwich. **Une ficelle** is a thin baguette. **Une boule** is a round loaf of crusty white bread. **Un pain complet** is an oblong loaf of whole wheat bread.

Reaching All Students

For the Younger Students Have students make a food poster. They can cut out pictures of foods from a magazine, newspaper, or supermarket flyer. Have them label the foods. You can use the posters for a bulletin board.

Kinesthetic Learners In teams of four, students sit in a circle. One student names a food item and simultaneously tosses a sponge ball to another student, who must name the place where that item can be purchased. That student then names a new item and tosses the ball to another student.

Cognate Recognition

Point out the cognates in **Mots 1: une tarte, de la crème, un yaourt, du bœuf, du porc, un crabe, du vinaigre.**

Note: At this point, students will use **acheter** only in the forms **je veux (vais) acheter** and **il/elle achète.** The special spelling and pronunciation issue will be addressed in a later chapter.

3 Practice

Commençons
Let's use our new words

Historiette Each time **Historiette** appears, it means that the answers to the activity form a short story. Encourage students to look at the title of the **Historiette,** since it can help them do the activity.

1 After doing this activity, call on a student to retell the story of the activity in his or her own words.

Writing Development
Have students write out the answers to Activities 1–2 in paragraph form.

Learning from Photos
(page 188) This **crémerie** is in Montgeron. Montgeron is a residential city in the Paris suburbs.

Commençons
Let's use our new words

1 Historiette À la crémerie
Inventez une histoire. *(Make up a story.)*

1. Madame Cadet va chercher du beurre. Elle va à la crémerie ou à la boucherie?
2. Elle veut acheter aussi du lait. Elle va à la crémerie?
3. Elle veut des œufs aussi?
4. Elle peut acheter du fromage à la crémerie?
5. Elle va acheter des yaourts pour le dessert?

Une crémerie, Montgeron, France

2 Historiette On fait les courses.
Répondez d'après les indications. *(Answer according to the cues.)*

1. Qui fait les courses? (Élodie)
2. Elle fait les courses quand? (le samedi matin)
3. Elle a un sac? (oui)
4. Elle va au supermarché? (non)
5. Elle va où? (à la boulangerie)
6. Qu'est-ce qu'elle va acheter à la boulangerie? (du pain)
7. Elle veut une baguette? (oui)
8. Il n'y a plus de baguettes? (non)
9. Alors, qu'est-ce qu'elle achète? (un pain complet)

3 À l'épicerie
Complétez d'après la photo. *(Complete according to the photo.)*

On va acheter du __1__, des __2__, de la __3__, du __4__, de l'__5__, du __6__ et du __7__.

Answers to Commençons

1
1. Elle va à la crémerie.
2. Oui, elle va à la crémerie.
3. Oui, elle veut des œufs aussi.
4. Oui, elle peut acheter du fromage à la crémerie.
5. Oui, elle va acheter des yaourts pour le dessert.

2
1. Élodie fait les courses.
2. Elle fait les courses le samedi matin.
3. Oui, elle a un sac.
4. Non, elle ne va pas au supermarché.
5. Elle va à la boulangerie.
6. Elle va acheter du pain à la boulangerie.
7. Oui, elle veut une baguette.
8. Non, il n'y a plus de baguettes.
9. Elle achète un pain complet.

3
1. lait
2. œufs
3. crème
4. poivre
5. huile
6. vinaigre
7. sel

Vocabulaire

4 **On va où?** Complétez. *(Complete.)*

1. Pour acheter un poulet, du bœuf, du porc et de l'agneau, on va ____.
2. Pour acheter du lait, on va ____.
3. Pour acheter des croissants et un gâteau, on va ____.
4. Pour acheter de la viande, on va ____.
5. Pour acheter du saucisson et du jambon, on va ____.
6. Pour acheter de la crème et des œufs, on va ____.
7. Pour acheter du poisson et des crevettes, on va ____.
8. Pour acheter des yaourts, on va ____.
9. Pour acheter une tarte aux pommes, on va ____.
10. Pour acheter des crabes, on va ____.

Une poissonnerie, Paris

5 **Les courses** You're living in Arles with a French family. You offered to do the grocery shopping. Your host gives you this list. Find out from your French brother or sister (your partner) where you go for each item.

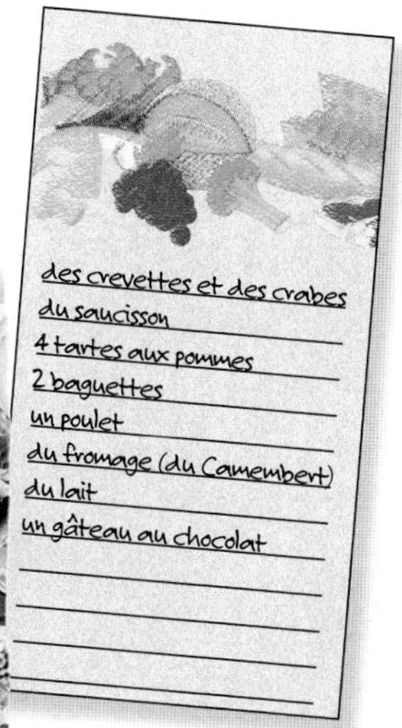

*For more practice using words from **Mots 1**, do Activity 16 on page H17 at the end of this book.*

Reteaching

Have students say whether they like or don't like each of the following items: **le pain, le lait, la crème, les œufs, les yaourts, la viande, le bœuf, le poulet.**

Assessment

As an informal assessment, check for comprehension by naming a store. Have students mention as many items as possible that can be purchased there.

This *infogap* activity will allow students to practice in pairs. The activity should be very manageable for them, since all vocabulary and structures are familiar to them.

Answers to Commençons

4

1. à la boucherie
2. à la crémerie
3. à la boulangerie-pâtisserie
4. à la boucherie
5. à la charcuterie
6. à la crémerie
7. à la poissonnerie
8. à la crémerie
9. à la boulangerie-pâtisserie
10. à la poissonnerie

5 *Answers will vary.*

Students will ask questions about where one buys certain items and then respond with the appropriate store. For example: **Pour acheter des crevettes et des crabes, on va où? On va à la poissonnerie.**

1 Preparation

Resource Manager

Vocabulary Transparencies 6.4–6.5
Audio Activities Booklet TE, pages 76–78
Audiocassette 4B/CD 4
Workbook, pages 56–57
Quiz 2, page 29
ExamView Pro®

Bellringer Review

Use BRR Transparency 6.2 or write the following on the board.
List items you would find in the following stores.
la boulangerie-pâtisserie
la crémerie
la boucherie

2 Presentation

Step 1 Model the new words, using Vocabulary Transparencies 6.4–6.5, plastic replicas, food containers, or pictures of food. Follow the procedures outlined in **Mots 1,** pages 186–187.

Step 2 Have students repeat the words and phrases after you or Audiocassette 4B/CD 4.

Au marché

le marchand de fruits et légumes

la marchande

Il est bon, mon melon!
Elle est bonne, ma salade!

des fraises

C'est combien, les carottes?
Un euro le kilo.
Alors, un kilo, s'il vous plaît.
Vous voulez autre chose?

Oui, une livre de tomates et c'est tout.
Alors ça fait deux euros cinquante.

Ariane est au marché.
Elle veut acheter des légumes.
Elle va chez la marchande de fruits et légumes.

un kilo = 1 000 (mille) grammes
une livre = 500 (cinq cents) grammes

Learning from Photos

(page 190) The market in the photos is in Charenton-le-Pont in the Val-de-Marne at the confluence of the Seine and Marne rivers. It is both a residential and industrial area.

Reaching All Students

Total Physical Response Tell students they are going to hear the names of some food items. They are to raise their right hand if it's a fruit and their left hand if it's a vegetable.

une pomme	**des fraises**
une pomme de terre	**un melon**
une carotte	**des épinards**
une poire	**des petits pois**
des haricots verts	**des bananes**
une salade	**des oignons**

On achète des épinards?

Non.

Pourquoi?

Parce que je n'aime pas ça.

un chariot

Julien et son frère sont au supermarché.
Julien veut acheter de l'eau minérale et du lait.
Il achète une bouteille d'eau minérale et un litre de lait.

Note 🎧

Many words for foods in French are cognates.

un fruit	une carotte
une banane	une tomate
une orange	un oignon

un pot de moutarde

250 grammes de beurre

un paquet de légumes surgelés

un litre de lait

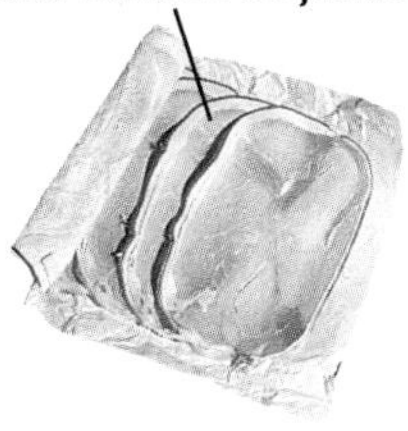

une tranche de jambon

une boîte de petits pois
une boîte de conserve

un pot de confiture

une douzaine d'œufs

une bouteille d'eau minérale

VOCABULAIRE

cent quatre-vingt-onze ✦ 191

Cognate Recognition

Point out other cognates that appear in this section: **un melon, un gramme, un litre, une bouteille, une douzaine, minérale, un paquet.**

Math Connection

Explain to students that the metric system is used in France. Students can learn about the metric system in the optional **Connexions** section of this chapter, pages 210–211.

Vocabulary Expansion

- When teaching **de l'eau minérale,** you may wish to add the expressions **gazeuse** and **plate,** since one has to state what kind of mineral water he or she wants.
- When buying something that is sold as a single unit, the word **pièce** is used. **Les melons coûtent un euro pièce.**
- You may want to teach students the following expressions useful when shopping. If the vendor wants to find out if you want something else, he or she will ask:

 Autre chose?
 Et avec ça?
 C'est tout?

You can tell what else you want or answer:·

 Rien d'autre. C'est tout, merci, or just **C'est tout.**

About the French Language

- The word **salade** can mean a salad, but is also the name given to a head of lettuce **(laitue)** used to make a green salad.
- To ask the price of something, you would ask: **C'est combien?** For example: **C'est combien, une baguette?** To find out how much you owe when you have purchased several items, you would ask: **Ça fait combien?** The vendor would say: **Les pommes de terre, les carottes et les haricots verts, ça fait deux euros quarante.**

Note: Explain to students that the definite article is used with the price of something. **Un euro la bouteille, la douzaine, le paquet.** Note the exception with **pièce—un euro pièce.** ✦

3 Practice

Commençons
Let's use our new words

6 The main objective of this activity is to give students practice using the new words with the appropriate gender marker.

7 and **8** After doing these activities, have a student retell the story of each activity in his or her own words.

Attention!

Note that the activities are color-coded. All the activities in the text are communicative. However, the ones with blue titles are guided communication. The red titles indicate that the answers to the activity are more open-ended and can vary more. You may wish to correct students' mistakes more so in the guided activities than in the activities with a red title, which lend themselves to a freer response.

Commençons
Let's use our new words

6 **Fruit(s) ou légume(s)?** Identifiez d'après le modèle. *(Identify according to the model.)*

C'est une pomme. C'est un fruit.

1. 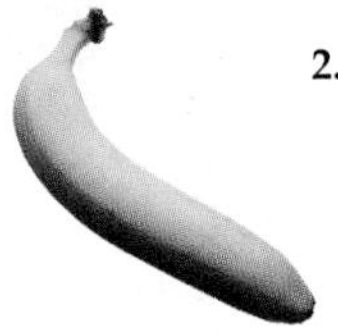
2. 
3. 
4. 
5. 
6. 
7. 
8. 

7 **Historiette** **Mathilde va au marché.** Complétez. *(Complete.)*

Mathilde veut préparer une grande salade. Elle va au marché. Elle va chez la __1__. Elle achète une __2__, des __3__ et des __4__. La marchande demande: «Vous voulez autre chose?» Mathilde répond: «Non, merci, __5__.» Elle donne de l'argent à la __6__.

8 **Historiette** **Martin va au supermarché.** Complétez. *(Complete.)*

Martin veut acheter de la moutarde, de l'eau minérale, une boîte de petits pois et un paquet de légumes surgelés. Pour acheter tout ça, il va au supermarché. Au supermarché, il prend un chariot. Il achète deux __1__ d'eau minérale, un __2__ de carottes surgelées et trois __3__ de sardines. Et autre chose aussi—un __4__ de moutarde. Martin va à la caisse. Ça __5__ combien, les bouteilles d'eau minérale, le paquet de carottes surgelées, les __6__ de sardines et le __7__ de moutarde? Ça fait onze euros cinquante.

Answers to Commençons

6

1. C'est une banane. C'est un fruit.
2. C'est un oignon. C'est un légume.
3. C'est une salade. C'est un légume.
4. C'est une orange. C'est un fruit.
5. C'est une pomme de terre. C'est un légume.
6. C'est une tomate. C'est un fruit.
7. C'est une carotte. C'est un légume.
8. C'est une poire. C'est un fruit.

7 *Answers will vary but may include:*

1. marchande de fruits et légumes
2. salade
3. tomates
4. carottes
5. c'est tout
6. marchande

8

1. bouteilles
2. paquet
3. boîtes
4. pot
5. fait
6. boîtes
7. pot

Vocabulaire

9 **C'est combien, s'il vous plaît?** Conversez d'après le modèle.
(Make up a conversation according to the model.)

—C'est combien, la boîte de petits pois?
—Un euro quatorze.

1. 

2. 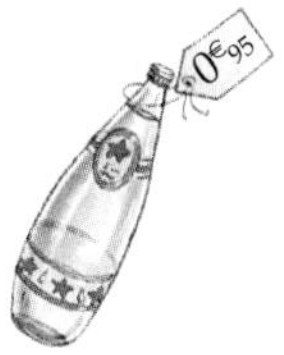

3. 

4. 

5. 

6. 

10 **Pourquoi pas?** Conversez d'après le modèle.
(Make up a conversation according to the model.)

1. Tu veux du saucisson?
2. Tu veux des fraises?
3. Tu veux des haricots verts?
4. Tu veux des petits pois?
5. Tu veux de la confiture de fraises?
6. Tu veux du poisson?

11 **À l'épicerie** You're in a grocery store in Paris. You want to buy the items on the list. Tell the clerk (your partner) how much you want of each item and find out how much it costs.

ENCORE PLUS *For more practice using words from **Mots 2**, do Activity 17 on page H18 at the end of this book.*

9 **Note:** Your students will need to know that for amounts under 1 euro, you say **cent(s)** or **centime(s).** You may wish to have students use real props and present their conversation for the class.

About the French Language

You may want to tell your students about the aspirated **h** on **haricot(s) vert(s),** which does not take **élision** or **liaison.**

11 You may wish to have students dramatize their conversation in a grocery store scene with props and play money.

Paired Activity

Have students work in pairs and find out what their partner's favorite and least favorite foods are from each of these categories: **la viande, les légumes, les fruits, les desserts, les boissons.** Then have them report their findings to the class. For example, **J'aime le poulet, mais je déteste le bœuf.** ***(À la classe)*** **Elle aime le poulet, mais elle déteste le bœuf.**

Answers to Commençons

9 *Answers will vary.*
Students will use **C'est combien** in each question and give the price in euros as follows:
—C'est combien, la douzaine d'œufs?
—Un euro quatre-vingt-dix-neuf.

10 *Students will make up conversations as follows:*
—Tu veux du saucisson?
—Du saucisson? Non.
—Pourquoi?
—Parce que je n'aime pas ça.

11 *Answers will vary. Students will use expressions such as:*
Je voudrais, C'est combien?,
Vous voulez autre chose?, Et avec ça?, Ça fait, C'est tout, rien d'autre.

Assessment

Introduce the expression **C'est vrai** and its negative. Then make true and false statements about different grocery items and where they can be found and have students elaborate. For example: **On trouve du lait à la crémerie. (C'est vrai.) On trouve de l'eau minérale à la boucherie. (Ce n'est pas vrai. On trouve de l'eau minérale à l'épicerie.)**

Structure

Telling and finding out what people do
Le verbe **faire** au présent

1. The verb **faire** *(to do, to make)* is an irregular verb. Study the following forms.

FAIRE			
je	fais	nous	faisons
tu	fais	vous	faites
il/elle/on	fait	ils/elles	font

2. You will use the verb **faire** a great deal in French. **Faire** is used in many expressions that take a different verb in English. Such expressions that cannot be translated directly from one language to another are called "idiomatic expressions." **Faire les courses** *(to go grocery shopping)* and **faire ses devoirs** *(to do homework)* are examples of idiomatic expressions. The following are some others.

Maman prépare un bon dîner. Elle aime beaucoup faire la cuisine.
Les copains vont faire un pique-nique.
Moi, je fais de l'allemand et ma sœur fait de l'espagnol.

Continuons
Let's put our words together

12 On fait les courses.
Répétez la conversation.
(Repeat the conversation.)

Éric: Salut, Anne! Ça va?
Anne: Ça va. Qu'est-ce que tu fais?
Éric: Je fais les courses.
Anne: Ben, moi aussi. Je vais au marché de la rue Dejean. On fait nos courses ensemble?
Éric: Merci, mais j'ai beaucoup de choses différentes à acheter. Je vais aller au supermarché.
Anne: Ben, je vais avec toi. C'est dans la même direction.
Éric: D'accord.

Rue Dejean, Paris

Answers to Continuons

12 *Students will repeat the conversation.*

1 Preparation

Resource Manager

Audio Activities Booklet TE, pages 79–81
Audiocassette 4B/CD 4
Workbook, pages 58–61
Quizzes 3–5, pages 30–32
ExamView Pro®

Bellringer Review

Use BRR Transparency 6.3 or write the following on the board.
You are planning a lunch for a friend. Make a shopping list and note where you are going to buy each item.

2 Presentation

Le verbe faire au présent

Step 1 Lead students through Item 1. Model the forms of **faire** and have students repeat them in unison two or three times.

Step 2 Now lead students through Item 2. Ask students personal questions practicing each different use of **faire.** For example: **Qu'est-ce que tu fais pendant le week-end? Tu fais les courses avec tes parents? Tu fais de l'histoire? Tu fais attention en cours de français?**

3 Practice

Continuons
Let's put our words together

12 This activity uses several forms of the verb **faire** in a natural context. You may wish to go over this activity once or twice orally. Then have several students retell the story in their own words.

13 **Qu'est-ce qu'ils font?** Complétez et répondez d'après la conversation.
(Complete and answer according to the conversation.)

1. Qu'est-ce qu'il ____, Éric?
2. Qu'est-ce qu'elle ____, Anne?
3. Qu'est-ce qu'ils ____, Anne et Éric?
4. Est-ce qu'ils ____ les courses ensemble?

14 **Et toi?** Donnez des réponses personnelles.
(Give your own answers.)

1. Tu fais quelquefois la cuisine chez toi?
2. Tu fais tes études dans un lycée français ou dans une école secondaire américaine?
3. Tu fais tes devoirs devant la télévision?
4. Tu fais du français?

15 **À chacun son travail** Suivez le modèle. *(Follow the model.)*

Moi, je fais le dîner. Et vous deux, qu'est-ce que vous faites?
Nous aussi, on fait le dîner.

1. Moi, je fais les courses.
2. Moi, je fais la cuisine.
3. Moi, je fais le déjeuner.
4. Moi, je fais les sandwichs.
5. Moi, je fais le gâteau.

16 **Historiette** **Mon copain Hugo** Complétez. *(Complete.)*

Hugo et moi, on est copains. Il est très intelligent. Hugo __1__ du russe. Moi aussi, je __2__ du russe. Nous __3__ du russe ensemble. Hugo et moi, nous __4__ quelquefois nos devoirs ensemble.

Hugo et son amie Marie __5__ de l'histoire avec Madame Delcourt. Qu'est-ce qu'ils __6__ au cours d'histoire? Ils apprennent beaucoup de nouvelles choses. Vous __7__ du français, n'est-ce pas? Vous __8__ du français avec qui?

17 **Nous sommes gentils.** Get together with a classmate. Discuss the things you do to help around the house. Decide who is the most helpful.

ENCORE PLUS *For more practice using the verb* ***faire****, do Activity 18 on page H19 at the end of this book.*

16 This activity recombines all forms of **faire.** It should be done with books open. Then students can retell the story in their own words.

17 You may wish to give your students the following phrases to use in the activity: **Je suis le plus gentil (la plus gentille).**

About the French Language

Explain to students that **Qu'est-ce que tu fais?, Qu'est-ce qu'elle fait?**, etc., mean *What are you doing?*, or *What is she doing?*, and that to answer the question you would often use a different verb:
Qu'est-ce que tu fais? Je regarde la télé.
Qu'est-ce qu'elle fait? Elle parle au téléphone. ✤

Learning from Photos

(page 195) Ask students what they see in the photo. You may want to give them the words: **un ananas, une mangue, un citron vert.**

Answers to Continuons

13
1. fait 3. font
2. fait 4. font

14 *Answers will vary, but all answers will be with* ***Je fais.***

15
1. —Moi, je fais les courses. Et vous deux, qu'est-ce que vous faites?
—Nous aussi, on fait les courses.
2. —Moi, je fais la cuisine. Et vous deux, qu'est-ce que vous faites?
—Nous aussi, on fait la cuisine.
3. —Moi, je fais le déjeuner. Et vous deux, qu'est-ce que vous faites?
—Nous aussi, on fait le déjeuner.
4. —Moi, je fais les sandwiches. Et vous deux, qu'est-ce que vous faites?
—Nous aussi, on fait les sandwiches.
5. —Moi, je fais le gâteau. Et vous deux, qu'est-ce que vous faites?
—Nous aussi, on fait le gâteau.

16
1. fait
2. fais
3. faisons
4. faisons
5. font
6. font
7. faites
8. faites

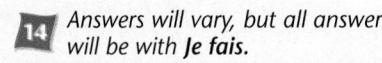

1 Preparation

Bellringer Review

Use BRR Transparency 6.4 or write the following on the board.
Write as many items as you can under each category.
Les fruits **Les légumes**

2 Presentation

Le partitif et l'article défini

Step 1 Say each of the foods below and ask students to answer with **Oui, je voudrais** (+ item) if they'd like some: **des fruits, du yaourt, du poulet, des œufs, de l'eau, du beurre, du lait, de la glace.**

Step 2 Lead students through Item 1 and discuss examples. Ask for additional examples.

Step 3 Briefly review the contractions with **de** + the definite articles (page 166).

Step 4 Lead students through Items 2–4 and discuss the examples contrasting the definite article and the partitive. For example: **J'aime les bananes. Les bananes ici sont bonnes. Je vais acheter des bananes.**

Step 5 Ask questions (such as **Qui aime le pain?, Qui a du pain?**) that contrast the definite article and the partitive.

Talking about all or some
Le partitif et l'article défini

1. In French, you use the definite article **(le, la, l', les)** when talking about something in a general sense.

Les enfants aiment le lait.	*Children like milk.*
Je déteste les œufs.	*I hate eggs.*
Je n'aime pas la salade.	*I don't like lettuce.*

2. The partitive expresses an unspecified amount. English uses "some," "any," or no word at all to express the partitive.

Do you have (any) toast?
Yes, I do. Would you like (some) jam with your toast?

3. In French, you use **de** + the definite article to express the partitive. Remember that **de** contracts with **le** and **les** to form one word, **du** and **des.**

de + le = du	Tu as du lait et du beurre?
de + les = des	Je vais acheter des fruits et des légumes.
de + la = de la	Je voudrais de la crème.
de + l' = de l'	Je voudrais de l'eau.

4. Study the following chart. It contrasts the use of a noun in the general sense with the partitive.

General Sense	Partitive
J'aime le poulet.	Je voudrais du poulet.
J'aime la viande.	Je voudrais de la viande.
J'aime l'eau minérale.	Je voudrais de l'eau minérale.
J'aime les pommes.	Je voudrais des pommes.

Note that verbs indicating likes and dislikes are followed by the definite article. All other verbs are followed by the partitive.

Il déteste la viande.	**Elle va acheter de la viande.**
J'adore le fromage.	**Tu prends du fromage?**

Class Motivator

Faisons des phrases! In teams of four, have students write as many nouns as they can think of on small bits of paper. They should write only the noun, with no article. Students place all the papers in a hat or bag and pass it around the team. Each member draws one noun and makes a sentence that uses the noun in a partitive construction. Answers may begin with: **J'ai..., Il y a..., Je vais acheter..., Je prends...,** etc.

Reaching All Students

Additional Practice You may wish to put the following on an overhead.
Je vais acheter _____ légumes et _____ fruits chez le marchand de légumes et de fruits. Ensuite, je vais aller à la boucherie où je vais acheter _____ bœuf et _____ poulet. Et comme dans la famille, on aime bien _____ fromage, je vais aller à la crémerie pour acheter _____ fromage.

Continuons

Let's put our words together

18 **Qu'est-ce que je vais acheter?** Répondez d'après le modèle. *(Answer according to the model.)*

Tu veux des fruits?
Oui, je vais acheter des fruits. J'aime les fruits.

1. Tu veux du pain?
2. Tu veux du fromage?
3. Tu veux des bananes?
4. Tu veux de la glace?

19 **J'aime tout!** Conversez d'après le modèle. *(Make up a conversation according to the model.)*

la crème
—J'aime beaucoup la crème.
—D'accord. Je vais chercher de la crème.

1. le saucisson
2. le lait
3. l'eau minérale
4. la limonade
5. le jambon
6. les pommes

20 **Historiette** **Des provisions** Complétez. *(Complete.)*

Au marché, Jean-Marc achète __1__ pain, __2__ jambon, __3__ fromage, __4__ fraises et __5__ crème. Il va préparer __6__ sandwichs au jambon et au fromage. Pour le dessert, il va préparer __7__ fraises avec __8__ crème.

21 **Historiette** **Des différences**
Complétez. *(Complete.)*

Isabelle Marquet a une sœur, Sophie. Quand les deux sœurs vont au restaurant, Isabelle commande toujours __1__ poisson. Elle aime bien __2__ poisson. Mais Sophie n'aime pas du tout __3__ poisson. Elle aime __4__ viande et elle commande toujours __5__ viande. Elle commande toujours __6__ bœuf. Et elle aime son bœuf à point, pas bien cuit!

Structure

Learning from Realia

(page 197) **La crème fraîche** is very popular in France. It is a heavy cream that has a thicker consistency than our heavy cream. Its consistency is more like that of sour cream. Although it is not sweet, it is less sour than sour cream. It is used in many recipes and is put on certain fruit desserts. Some people will add sugar to it when used with a dessert.

Note: Activity 21 is the most difficult because it indicates whether students can differentiate between speaking about an unspecified amount (partitive) and speaking in a general sense (definite).

Answers to Continuons

18

1. Oui, je vais acheter du pain. J'aime le pain.
2. Oui je vais acheter du fromage. J'aime le fromage.
3. Oui, je vais acheter des bananes. J'aime les bananes.
4. Oui, je vais acheter de la glace. J'aime la glace.

19

1. —J'aime beaucoup le saucisson.
   —D'accord. Je vais chercher du saucisson.
2. —J'aime beaucoup le lait.
   —D'accord. Je vais chercher du lait.
3. —J'aime beaucoup l'eau minérale.
   —D'accord. Je vais chercher de l'eau minérale.
4. —J'aime beaucoup la limonade.
   —D'accord. Je vais chercher de la limonade.
5. —J'aime beaucoup le jambon.
   —D'accord. Je vais chercher du jambon.
6. —J'aime beaucoup les pommes.
   —D'accord. Je vais chercher des pommes.

20

1. du
2. du
3. du
4. des
5. de la
6. des
7. des
8. de la

21

1. du
2. le
3. le
4. la
5. de la
6. du

1 Preparation

Bellringer Review

Use BRR Transparency 6.5 or write the following on the board
Your friends are hungry. Let them know what there is to eat in your refrigerator. Start with **Dans mon réfrigérateur, il y a...**

2 Presentation

Le partitif au négatif

Attention!

Although this point is not very difficult, many students do find it problematic, and for this reason we have provided eight activities to practice it.

Step 1 Lead students through Items 1–2 and the chart on page 198. Using objects in the room, review the change from **un, une,** or **des** to **de (d')** in the negative. For example (holding a pencil): **J'ai un crayon.** (Hiding the pencil): **Je n'ai pas de crayon.**

Step 2 From the chart on page 198, read the affirmative examples to the class and have students read the negative forms after you in unison. Continue with other affirmative sentences, having first the class, then individuals, give the negative.

3 Practice

Continuons

Let's put our words together

22 and **23** Have students do the activities first with books open, then with books closed.

Expressing what people don't have

Le partitif au négatif

1. All forms of the partitive, **du, de la, de l',** and **des,** change to **de (d')** after a negative.

Affirmatif		Négatif	
Je veux	du pain. de la crème. de l'eau. des carottes.	Je ne veux pas	de pain. de crème. d'eau. de carottes.

Note that the same is true after **ne... plus.**

Je ne mange plus de viande.

2. Remember that the definite article does not change in the negative.

J'aime les carottes. Je n'aime pas les carottes.

Continuons

Let's put our words together

22 Non, merci. Conversez d'après le modèle.
(Make up a conversation according to the model.)

de l'eau
—Vous voulez de l'eau?
—Non, merci. Pas d'eau pour moi.

1. du pain
2. de l'agneau
3. du porc
4. des crevettes
5. du lait
6. de la limonade

23 Qu'est-ce que tu as? Conversez d'après le modèle.
(Make up a conversation according to the model.)

des livres
—Tu as des livres?
—Non, je n'ai pas de livres. / Oui, j'ai des livres.

1. un ami
2. une amie
3. un chat
4. des cousines
5. des frères
6. des sœurs

Answers to Continuons

22

1. Vous voulez du pain?
   Non, merci. Pas de pain pour moi.
2. Vous voulez de l'agneau?
   Non, merci. Pas d'agneau pour moi.
3. Vous voulez du porc?
   Non, merci. Pas de porc pour moi.
4. Vous voulez des crevettes?
   Non, merci. Pas de crevettes pour moi.
5. Vous voulez du lait?
   Non, merci. Pas de lait pour moi.
6. Vous voulez de la limonade?
   Non, merci. Pas de limonade pour moi.

23

1. Tu as un ami?
   Non, je n'ai pas d'ami. / Oui, j'ai un ami.
2. Tu as une amie?
   Non, je n'ai pas d'amie. / Oui, j'ai une amie.
3. Tu as un chat?
   Non, je n'ai pas de chat. / Oui, j'ai un chat.
4. Tu as des cousines?
   Non, je n'ai pas de cousines. / Oui, j'ai des cousines.
5. Tu as des frères?
   Non, je n'ai pas de frères. / Oui, j'ai des frères.
6. Tu as des sœurs?
   Non, je n'ai pas de sœurs. / Oui, j'ai des sœurs.

24 **Je voudrais...** Conversez d'après le modèle.
(Make up a conversation according to the model.)

> Je voudrais du jambon, s'il vous plaît.

> Je regrette, mais il n'y a plus de jambon.

1. Je voudrais de l'eau minérale, s'il vous plaît.
2. Je voudrais de la glace à la vanille, s'il vous plaît.
3. Je voudrais des croissants, s'il vous plaît.
4. Je voudrais des fraises, s'il vous plaît.
5. Je voudrais du fromage, s'il vous plaît.

25 **Juliette fait les courses.** Répondez d'après le modèle.
(Answer according to the model.)

—**Elle va acheter du poisson à la boucherie?**
—**Non, elle ne va pas acheter de poisson à la boucherie. Elle va acheter de la viande.**

1. Elle va acheter du pain à la boucherie?
2. Elle va acheter du fromage à la boulangerie?
3. Elle va acheter des légumes à la charcuterie?
4. Elle va acheter de la viande à la crémerie?
5. Elle va acheter des œufs chez le marchand de fruits et légumes?

Une charcuterie, Conques, France

26 **Je n'aime pas ça!**
Répondez d'après le modèle.
(Answer according to the model.)

—**Tu as de la confiture?**
—**Non, je n'ai pas de confiture. Je n'aime pas la confiture.**

1. Tu as du saucisson?
2. Tu as du fromage?
3. Tu as du café?
4. Tu as de la limonade?
5. Tu as des épinards?
6. Tu as des sardines?

STRUCTURE

cent quatre-vingt-dix-neuf ✦ **199**

ANSWERS TO Continuons

24

1. Je regrette, mais il n'y a plus d'eau minérale.
2. Je regrette, mais il n'y a plus de glace à la vanille.
3. Je regrette, mais il n'y a plus de croissants.
4. Je regrette, mais il n'y a plus de fraises.
5. Je regrette, mais il n'y a plus de fromage.

25

1. Non, elle ne va pas acheter de pain à la boucherie.
2. Non, elle ne va pas acheter de fromage à la boulangerie.
3. Non, elle ne va pas acheter de légumes à la charcuterie.
4. Non, elle ne va pas acheter de viande à la crémerie.
5. Non, elle ne va pas acheter d'œufs chez le marchand de fruits et légumes.

26

1. Non, je n'ai pas de saucisson. Je n'aime pas le saucisson.
2. Non, je n'ai pas de fromage. Je n'aime pas le fromage.
3. Non, je n'ai pas de café. Je n'aime pas le café.
4. Non, je n'ai pas de limonade. Je n'aime pas la limonade.
5. Non, je n'ai pas d'épinards. Je n'aime pas les épinards.
6. Non, je n'ai pas de sardines. Je n'aime pas les sardines.

25 After completing the activity, have students do it a second time, telling where Juliette would actually buy each item.

26 Have students interview their partner using these activities and report back to the class what they find out.

Reteaching
Distribute pictures or plastic replicas of food to the class. Ask individuals questions that require negative answers. For example: **Jacques, tu as des oranges? (Non, je n'ai pas d'oranges. J'ai des pommes.) Sylvie, Marc a de l'eau minérale? (Non, il n'a pas d'eau minérale. Il a du lait.)**

Structure

28 Expansion: You may wish to provide your students with empty food containers or plastic replicas of food and have them create their own dialogues, asking questions that may be answered positively or negatively.

27 Historiette **Au supermarché** Complétez. *(Complete.)*

Quand je vais au supermarché, je n'achète pas __1__ fruits. Je n'aime pas __2__ fruits du supermarché. J'achète __3__ fruits au marché, chez le marchand de fruits et légumes. Je n'achète pas __4__ café au supermarché. Je n'achète pas __5__ viande. Je n'achète pas __6__ légumes, pas __7__ oignons. Qu'est-ce que j'achète au supermarché? J'achète seulement __8__ boîtes de conserve, __9__ bouteilles d'eau minérale, __10__ sel, __11__ poivre, __12__ vinaigre et __13__ huile.

28 **Dans le frigidaire**

Work with a classmate. Ask him or her for something you'd like to eat or drink. Your partner will check to see whether or not it's in the refrigerator. Use the model as a guide.

—Tu as de la glace au chocolat? J'adore la glace au chocolat.
—Je regrette, il n'y a plus de glace au chocolat.

29 **Un sandwich extraordinaire**

Work with a classmate. Discuss what would be a great sandwich. You may (or may not) want to use some of the following ingredients.

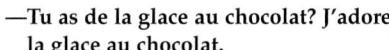

Answers to Continuons

27

1. de	**8.** des
2. les	**9.** des
3. des	**10.** du
4. de	**11.** du
5. de	**12.** du
6. de	**13.** de l'
7. d'	

28 *Answers will vary but may include:*
—Tu as des frites? J'adore les frites.
—Oui, il y a des frites.
—Tu as du jus d'orange? J'adore le jus d'orange.
—Je regrette, il n'y a plus de jus d'orange.

29 *Answers will vary but students can have fun making up horrendous combinations such as:*
un sandwich aux sardines et au chocolat

Attention!

Pay special attention to the spelling and pronunciation of the following adjectives that double the consonant in the feminine.

FÉMININ	MASCULIN
bonne(s)	**bon(s)**
canadienne(s)	**canadien(s)**
gentille(s)	**gentil(s)**
quelle(s)	**quel(s)**

Complétez. *(Complete.)*

1. Tu fais de la ____ cuisine? (bon)
2. Tu fais de ____ sandwichs? (bon)
3. Tu as des amis ____ et ____? (canadien, vietnamien)
4. Tu as des amies ____? (tunisien)
5. Tu aimes les filles qui sont ____? (gentil)
6. Tu aimes ____ profs? (quel)

Telling what one can do or wants to do
Les verbes **pouvoir** et **vouloir**

1. Study the forms of the verbs **pouvoir** *(to be able to)* and **vouloir** *(to want).*

POUVOIR		VOULOIR	
je	peux	je	veux
tu	peux	tu	veux
il/elle/on	peut	il/elle/on	veut
nous	pouvons	nous	voulons
vous	pouvez	vous	voulez
ils/elles	peuvent	ils/elles	veulent

Michel ne peut pas aller au marché à pied.
Il veut acheter des légumes et des fruits.
Vous voulez manger maintenant?
Vous pouvez si vous voulez.

Savez-vous que... ?

Je voudrais is a polite form of **je veux.** It means "I would like."

Je voudrais une livre de haricots verts, s'il vous plaît.

2. In the negative, you put **ne... pas** around the verbs **pouvoir** and **vouloir.**

Je ne veux pas manger de frites.
Ils ne peuvent pas aller au restaurant ce soir.

Structure

1 Preparation

Bellringer Review

Use BRR Transparency 6.6 or write the following on the board.
Complete the following.

1. **Je ____ au marché. (être)**
2. **Je ____ à la marchande de fruits. (parler)**
3. **Elle ____ charmante. (être)**
4. **Elle ____ assez vieille. (être)**
5. **Elle ____ plus de 80 ans. (avoir)**
6. **Mais elle ____ toujours. (travailler)**

2 Presentation

Les verbes **pouvoir** et **vouloir**

Step 1 First have students repeat the **ils/elles** forms. Then have them repeat all the singular forms. The latter all sound alike, but they are spelled differently and they drop the consonant sound heard in the **ils/elles** form.

Step 2 Now have students repeat the **nous** and **vous** forms, which again pick up the consonant sound of the infinitive. Many verbs follow this pattern in French.

Step 3 Lead students through Items 1–2 on page 201. Now do the activities that follow.

Answers to *Attention!*

1. bonne
2. bons
3. canadiens, vietnamiens
4. tunisiennes
5. gentilles
6. quels

Class Motivator

Un sandwich dégoutant After completing Activity 29 on page 200, you may wish to have a contest to see who can think of the most disgusting sandwich combination with the vocabulary they know. Have each student read the description of his or her **sandwich dégoutant** to the class and have the class vote on the top three unappetizing creations.

Structure

3 Practice

Continuons
Let's put our words together

30 This activity can be done with books either closed or open.

Learning from Photos

(page 202) Saint-Rémy-de-Provence is a quaint town at the foot of the Alpilles Mountains.

Reaching All Students

Additional Practice Have students answer according to the model:

—Moi, je ne peux pas aller au restaurant.
—Mais tes amis peuvent aller au restaurant, n'est-ce pas?

1. **Moi, je ne peux pas aller au café.**
2. **Moi je ne veux pas arriver à huit heures.**
3. **Moi, je ne veux pas préparer le dîner.**
4. **Moi, je ne peux pas faire les courses.**

Continuons
Let's put our words together

30 **Je veux bien, mais je ne peux pas.** Conversez d'après le modèle. *(Make up a conversation according to the model.)*

—Tu veux aller au restaurant?
—Je veux bien, mais je ne peux pas.

1. Tu veux aller au café?
2. Tu veux dîner avec Caroline?
3. Tu veux travailler après l'école?
4. Ta sœur veut faire les courses?
5. Elle veut aller au marché?
6. Elle veut préparer le dîner?
7. Elle veut inviter des amis?

Un marché,
Saint-Rémy-de-Provence, France

31 **Si vous voulez, vous pouvez.** Conversez d'après le modèle. *(Make up a conversation according to the model.)*

Nous voulons travailler.
Si vous voulez travailler, vous pouvez travailler.

1. Nous voulons manger maintenant.
2. Nous voulons inviter des amis.
3. Nous voulons aller au restaurant.
4. Nous voulons commander de la pizza.
5. Nous voulons regarder le film.
6. Nous voulons écouter nos CD.

Answers to Continuons

30

1. Je veux bien, mais je ne peux pas.
2. Je veux bien, mais je ne peux pas.
3. Je veux bien, mais je ne peux pas.
4. Elle veut bien, mais elle ne peut pas.
5. Elle veut bien, mais elle ne peut pas.
6. Elle veut bien, mais elle ne peut pas.
7. Elle veut bien, mais elle ne peut pas.

31

1. Si vous voulez manger maintenant, vous pouvez manger maintenant.
2. Si vous voulez inviter des amis, vous pouvez inviter des amis.
3. Si vous voulez aller au restaurant, vous pouvez aller au restaurant.
4. Si vous voulez commander de la pizza, vous pouvez commander de la pizza.
5. Si vous voulez regarder le film, vous pouvez regarder le film.
6. Si vous voulez écouter vos CD, vous pouvez écouter vos CD.

32 **Historiette** **Pas assez d'argent** Complétez avec **pouvoir** ou **vouloir.** *(Complete with* pouvoir *or* vouloir.*)*

Pierre et son frère ont faim. Ils __1__ aller dans un restaurant où ils __2__ dîner rapidement. Ils __3__ commander deux hamburgers chacun, mais ils ne __4__ pas. Pierre insiste, mais son frère ne __5__ pas: «Pas question! On n'a pas assez d'argent! Tu __6__ commander seulement un hamburger aujourd'hui.»

33 **Qui peut préparer le dîner?** Complétez. *(Complete.)*

Marie: Je voudrais bien faire le dîner ce soir, mais vraiment, je ne __1__ (pouvoir) pas.
Julien: Tu ne __2__ (pouvoir) pas? Pourquoi?
Marie: Je __3__ (être) très fatiguée! Je __4__ (être) vraiment crevée.
Julien: On __5__ (pouvoir) aller au restaurant, si tu __6__ (vouloir).
Marie: Oh, je ne __7__ (vouloir) pas aller au restaurant ce soir.
Julien: On __8__ (pouvoir) faire des sandwichs.
Marie: Oui, ou... toi, tu __9__ (pouvoir) faire le dîner.
Julien: Je __10__ (vouloir) bien, mais ce n'__11__ (être) pas une très bonne idée.
Marie: Pourquoi?
Julien: Parce que je __12__ (faire) très mal la cuisine!

34 **Pourquoi pas?** Work with a classmate. Tell each other some things you or you and your friends want to do but can't. When possible, give reasons.

ENCORE PLUS *For more practice using the verbs* ***pouvoir*** *and* ***vouloir****, do Activity 19 on page H20 at the end of this book.*

Vous êtes sur le bon chemin. Allez-y!

Answers to Continuons

32
1. veulent
2. peuvent
3. veulent
4. peuvent
5. veut
6. peux

33
1. peux
2. peux
3. suis
4. suis
5. peut
6. veux
7. veux
8. peut
9. peux
10. veux
11. est
12. fais

34 *Answers will vary.*

Structure

Reteaching

Have students write five things they want to do and five things they can do.

32 Have students retell the story in this activity.

33 You may wish to have students dramatize this dialogue with as much expression as possible.

About the French Language

In Activity 33, Marie talks about how tired **(fatiguée)** she is. To make her point she says: **Je suis vraiment crevée.** Used here, **crevé** is a colloquial expression, roughly the equivalent of "wiped out." Its literal meaning is "burst or split," but it can also mean "deflated," as in flat tire **(un pneu crevé).** ⚜

ENCORE PLUS This *infogap* activity will allow students to practice in pairs. The activity should be very manageable for them, since all vocabulary and structures are familiar to them.

Allez-y!
At this point in the chapter, students have learned all the vocabulary and structure necessary to complete the chapter. The conversation and cultural readings that follow recycle all the material learned up to this point.

1 Preparation

Resource Manager

Audio Activities Booklet TE, pages 82–83
Audiocassette 4B/CD 4
CD-ROM

Bellringer Review

Use BRR Transparency 6.7 or write the following on the board.
Write four expressions you would probably use when shopping for food.

2 Presentation

Step 1 Tell students they are going to hear a conversation between a vegetable vendor and Mme Brun. Have them close their books and watch the Conversation CD-ROM or listen as you read the conversation to them or play it on Audiocassette 4B/CD 4.

Step 2 Ask students to open their books to page 204. Have them follow along as you read the conversation or play the recorded version again.

Step 3 Set up a small fruit stand in front of the classroom and have students act out the conversation.

Step 4 Have them make up their own conversation based on the dialogue.

Glencoe Technology

On the CD-ROM, students can watch a dramatization of this conversation. They can then play the role of either one of the characters and record themselves in the conversation.

Conversation

Au marché

Marchand: Et maintenant, je suis à vous, madame. Comment allez-vous ce matin?
Mme Brun: Très bien, merci. Et vous?
Marchand: Oh, comme ci, comme ça! Enfin… Qu'est-ce que vous désirez aujourd'hui?
Mme Brun: Je voudrais des haricots verts et des carottes. C'est combien, les haricots verts?
Marchand: Quatre euros le kilo. Et ils sont bons!
Mme Brun: Alors, un kilo, s'il vous plaît, et une livre de carottes.
Marchand: Et avec ça, madame?
Mme Brun: C'est tout, merci. Ça fait combien?
Marchand: Alors, un kilo de haricots verts, une livre de carottes… Ça fait quatre euros cinquante.
Mme Brun: Voilà, monsieur.
Marchand: Merci, madame. Et à samedi prochain.

Après la conversation

Répondez. *(Answer.)*

1. Mme Brun fait ses courses?
2. Le marchand va bien?
3. Mme Brun fait ses courses au supermarché?
4. Elle parle au marchand de légumes?
5. Qu'est-ce qu'elle veut acheter?
6. Elle veut des haricots verts?
7. Ça fait combien, les haricots verts et les carottes?

Answers to Après la conversation

1. Oui, elle fait ses courses.
2. Non, il va assez bien. (Non, comme ci, comme ça).
3. Non, elle ne fait pas ses courses au supermarché. Elle fait ses courses au marché.
4. Oui, elle parle au marchand de légumes.
5. Elle veut acheter un kilo de haricots verts et une livre de carottes.
6. Oui, elle veut des haricots verts.
7. Ça fait quatre euros cinquante.

Learning from Photos

(page 204) Have students identify everything they can in the photo. You may wish to give them the additional vocabulary: **un poivron, une aubergine.**

Parlons un peu plus
Let's talk some more

Qu'est-ce qu'on va manger?
Work with a classmate. Prepare a menu in French for tomorrow's meals—**le petit déjeuner, le déjeuner et le dîner.** Based on your menus, prepare a shopping list. Be sure to include the quantities you need.

Une poissonnerie, Abidjan, Côte d'Ivoire

Prononciation

Les sons /œ́/ et /œ̀/

1. Listen to the difference in the vowel sounds in **peut** and **peuvent.** The sound /œ́/ in **peut** is a closed vowel sound and the sound /œ̀/ in **peuvent** is an open vowel sound. Repeat the following words with the sound /œ́/.

   il peut **il veut** **des œufs** **deux**

2. Repeat the following words with the sound /œ̀/.

   ils peuvent **ils veulent** **un œuf**
   leur sœur **du beurre**

3. Now repeat the following pairs of words. Be sure to distinguish between the two vowel sounds.

   il peut / ils peuvent
   il veut / ils veulent

4. Now repeat the following sentences.

   Elle veut faire les courses, mais ils ne veulent pas.
   Elle veut du beurre et des œufs.
   Leur sœur est sérieuse.

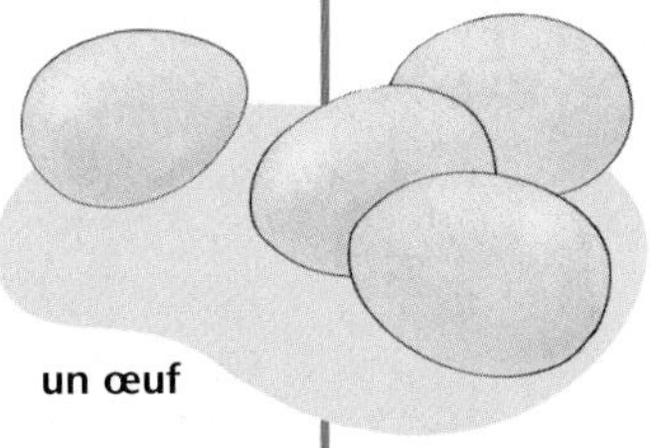
un œuf
des œufs

Answers to Parlons un peu plus

Answers will vary but may include:
Le petit déjeuner: Du café, des tartines de pain beurré, du jus d'orange.
Le déjeuner: Des sandwichs au jambon et au fromage, du coca.
Le dîner: Du poisson, des frites, une salade, une tarte aux pommes
Alors, à la boulangerie, on va acheter: une baguette, un pain complet, une tarte aux pommes.
À la charcuterie, on va acheter huit tranches de jambon
À la crémerie on va acheter une livre de fromage, du beurre,
À l'épicerie, on va acheter un paquet de café, du jus d'orange, une bouteille de coca...etc.

3 Practice

Parlons un peu plus
Let's talk some more

Have students work in pairs. You may wish to choose a pair of students to do this activity for the class.

Prononciation

Step 1 Model the key words **un œuf / des œufs** and have students repeat chorally.

Step 2 Now model the other words and phrases in similar fashion. Have students open their books to page 205. Call on individuals to read the sentences carefully.

Step 3 You may wish to give students the following **dictée: Leur sœur veut du beurre, des œufs, du bœuf et un peu de pain.**

Step 4 For additional pronunciation practice, you may wish to use Pronunciation Transparency P 6.

Learning from Photos

(page 205) This photo is of the seafood department at the supermarché Hayat in the suburban Cocody section of Abidjan. It is part of a complex that also houses a luxury hotel, swimming pool, health club, and ice skating rink.

Resource Manager

Audio Activities Booklet TE, pages 84–85
Audiocassette 4B/CD 4

National Standards

Cultures
The reading and the related activities introduce students to a French grocery shopping trip, including the different types of stores one would visit and the typical hours of operation.

Comparisons
The reading makes comparisons between French and American shopping habits and customs.

Bellringer Review

Use BRR Transparency 6.8 or write the following on the board.
Match the adjectives with the nouns. Add the correct article.

nouvelle	**appartement**
beau	**pommes**
bel	**magasin**
bonnes	**cuisine**

Le Québec

Lectures culturelles

Reading Strategy

Guessing meaning from context
It's easy to understand words you have already studied. There are also ways to understand words you are not familiar with. One way is to use the context—the way these words are used in the sentence or reading—to help you guess the meanings of those words you don't know.

Les courses

C'est aujourd'hui mardi. À dix heures du matin, comme tous les matins, excepté le lundi quand les magasins sont fermés[1], Mme Lelong quitte son appartement. Elle a son sac et elle va faire les courses. Elle fait les courses dans différents petits magasins. Elle achète du pain tous les jours. Elle va à la boulangerie où elle achète une baguette. Si elle veut de la viande, elle va à la boucherie. Si elle veut du poisson, elle peut aller à la poissonnerie, mais elle est très loin. Pour un pot de confiture ou une bouteille d'eau minérale, l'épicerie n'est pas loin. Après le déjeuner, si elle n'a pas assez de pain pour le soir, elle peut acheter une autre baguette. Mais pas avant 16 heures. Les petits magasins sont fermés tous les jours de 13 heures à 16 heures, et bien sûr le dimanche!

[1] fermés *closed*

Une boulangerie-pâtisserie, Paris

Un marchand de fruits, Paris

Presentation

Pre-reading

Step 1 Ask students who does the food shopping in their family. How many times a week? Where? Do they always go to the same store? Why? Do they chat with people who work in the stores?

Step 2 Discuss the Reading Strategy on page 206.

Reading

Step 1 Read the **Lecture** aloud, using as much expression as possible. Have students repeat each sentence after you.

Learning from Photos

(page 206) The stores in the photos on this page are in Paris. You may wish to have students identify everything they can in each photo.

Une boucherie, Domme, France

Une boulangerie, Paris

Les Français aiment bien aller chez les petits commerçants du quartier—l'épicier, le boucher, le boulanger, etc. Leurs prix sont un peu plus chers[2] qu'au supermarché, mais la qualité de leurs produits est très bonne. Il y a aussi le côté humain[3]. Les Français aiment bavarder (converser) un peu avec le marchand ou la marchande. On trouve ça sympa.

[2] Leurs prix sont un peu plus chers *Their prices are a little more expensive*
[3] côté humain *human dimension*

Après la lecture

A Madame Lelong Répondez. *(Answer.)*

1. Mme Lelong quitte son appartement à quelle heure?
2. Qu'est-ce qu'elle prend pour faire ses courses?
3. Elle fait ses courses où?
4. Elle va où pour acheter du pain?
5. Si elle veut de la viande, elle va où?
6. Si elle veut du poisson, elle peut aller où?
7. Qu'est-ce qu'elle achète à l'épicerie?
8. Quand est-ce que les magasins sont fermés?

B Stratégie de lecture Reread the Reading Strategy on page 206. You don't know the meaning of the word **commerçants.** Using the suggestion given in the Reading Strategy, can you figure out the meaning of this word?

C Les petits commerçants Expliquez. *(Explain.)*

1. Qui sont les petits commerçants du quartier?
2. Comment est la qualité de leurs produits?
3. En général, comment sont leurs prix?
4. Qu'est-ce que les Français aiment faire avec les commerçants?

Lectures culturelles

Step 2 Call on volunteers to read two to three sentences aloud at a time. Ask the other students content questions about the sentences read. Some possible questions are: **Qui quitte son appartement à dix heures? Elle va où?**

Post-reading

Have students do the **Après la lecture** activities on page 207 orally after reading the selection in class. Then assign these activities to be written at home. Go over them again the following day.

Après la lecture

A and C You may allow students to refer to the story to look up the answers or you may use this activity as a testing device for factual recall.

FUN-FACTS

The French buy bread every day at the bakery. Bread is eaten many different ways. For breakfast, slices spread with butter are dunked in coffee, tea, or hot chocolate. At lunch and dinner, it is not buttered. A piece of bread is used to push food onto the fork or to dip in gravy. The French don't cut bread; they tear a piece off and place it by the plate on the tablecloth.

Answers to Après la lecture

A

1. Madame Lelong quitte son appartement à dix heures du matin.
2. Elle prend son sac.
3. Elle fait ses courses dans différents petits magasins.
4. Elle va à la boulangerie pour acheter du pain.
5. Elle va à la boucherie.
6. Elle peut aller à la poissonnerie.
7. Elle achète un pot de confiture et une bouteille d'eau minérale.
8. Les magasins sont fermés tous les jours de 13 heures à 16 heures, et aussi le dimanche.

B

commerçants=shopkeepers. The reader can guess the meaning since the names of the types of shopkeepers follow.

C

1. Les petits commerçants du quartier sont les épiciers, les bouchers, les boulangers, etc.
2. La qualité de leurs produits est très bonne.
3. Leurs prix sont un peu plus chers.
4. Les Français aiment bavarder avec les commerçants.

Learning from Photos

(page 207 left) Domme is a medieval fortified town in Dordogne. It is situated on a steep promontory. From its well-preserved medieval ramparts there are magnificent panoramic views of the surrounding suburbs.

Lecture supplémentaire 1

National Standards

Cultures
The reading and related activities on this page introduce students to another type of food store that exists in France.

Attention!

This reading is optional. You may skip it completely, have the entire class read it, have only several students read it and report to the class, or assign it for extra credit.

Presentation

Step 1 Have students list the different types of grocery stores that exist in their area. How do they differ in size, hours of operation, and variety of goods?

Step 2 Have students read the **Lecture** quickly as they look at the photos that accompany it.

Step 3 Ask students to compare a French **hypermarché** with the types of stores in their area. Is there one they think is equivalent?

Après la lecture

Expansion: After doing the activity, you may wish to have the students correct each false statement.

Lecture supplémentaire 1

Les grandes surfaces

Beaucoup de Français font leurs courses dans les petits magasins de leur quartier. Mais beaucoup d'autres Français—surtout les gens[1] qui travaillent ou qui n'habitent pas en ville—font leurs courses dans les grandes surfaces.

Les grandes surfaces sont de grands supermarchés ou hypermarchés. Ils sont généralement situés à la périphérie des villes. Il y a toujours un grand parking parce que les clients y vont en voiture.

Dans un hypermarché on peut tout acheter: de la nourriture, mais aussi des vêtements[2], des bicyclettes, des livres, des disques et même des ordinateurs[3]. Les clients prennent des chariots pour transporter leurs achats[4]. Les grandes chaînes ont pour nom Leclerc et Carrefour.

[1] gens *people*
[2] vêtements *clothes*
[3] ordinateurs *computers*
[4] achats *purchases*

Un hypermarché, Nantes

L'intérieur d'un hypermarché

Après la lecture

Les courses Vrai ou faux? *(True or false?)*

1. Les supermarchés et les hypermarchés sont des grandes surfaces.
2. Les grandes surfaces sont situées surtout dans les grandes villes.
3. Les clients vont presque toujours à pied dans les grandes surfaces.
4. Dans un hypermarché on peut acheter toutes sortes de marchandises.

Critical Thinking Activity

Have students discuss the advantages and disadvantages of small, specialized shops and huge superstores. They can do this in French by making four lists: **Petits magasins: pour, contre; Grandes surfaces: pour, contre.**

Answers to Après la lecture

1. V
2. F
3. F
4. V

Learning from Photos

(page 208) Carrefour is the name of a popular chain of **hypermarchés.** This one is in Nantes, a large, busy, industrial city and port. The interior view is typical of a **hypermarché.**

Lecture supplémentaire 2

Les marchés

Dans les villes et les villages de France, il y a toujours un marché. Dans les grandes villes, il y a des marchés permanents temporaires. Les marchés temporaires ont lieu[1] en général deux fois par semaine, le mercredi ou le jeudi et le samedi. Ils ont lieu dans la rue ou sur une place.

Les marchés existent dans les autres pays francophones. Voici un très joli marché à Dakar. Et voici un marché à Fort-de-France. Les fruits et les légumes ont l'air[2] très bons, n'est-ce pas? Ils sont délicieux!

[1] ont lieu *take place* [2] ont l'air *look*

Sarlat-la-Canéda, Dordogne

Dakar, Sénégal

Fort-de-France, Martinique

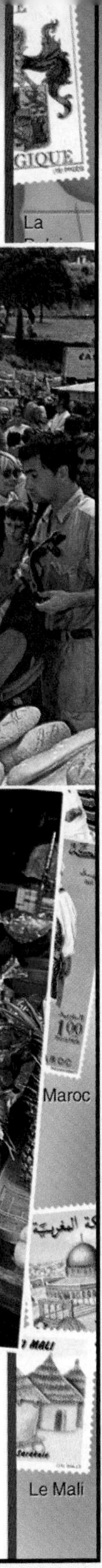

Après la lecture

Les marchés Complétez. *(Complete.)*

1. Dans les villes et les villages de France, il y a toujours un ____.
2. Les marchés peuvent être temporaires ou ____.
3. Ils peuvent avoir lieu dans ____ ou ____.
4. Ils ont lieu le ____ ou le ____ et le ____.
5. Il y a aussi des marchés dans ____.

Attention!

This reading is optional. You may skip it completely, have the entire class read it, have only several students read it and report to the class, or assign it for extra credit.

Presentation

Step 1 Before students read the selection to themselves, have them study the photos on page 209.

Step 2 Now have students do the **Après la lecture** activity on page 209.

Step 3 You may wish to ask students to describe the items they see for sale in the photos.

Learning from Photos

(page 209) The market on the left is in Dakar, Sénégal. It is very typical of the outdoor markets found in all the cities of West Africa.

Some of the markets are out in the open and some are enclosed such as the one seen here in Fort-de-France.

The market in the square in Sarlat-la-Canéda is typical of the outdoor markets in France described in the paragraph.

ANSWERS TO Après la lecture

1. marché
2. permanents
3. la rue, sur une place
4. mercredi, jeudi, samedi
5. les autres pays francophones

CONNEXIONS

National Standards

Connections
This reading about the metric system establishes a connection with another discipline, allowing students to reinforce and further their knowledge of mathematics through the study of French.

Comparisons
This reading allows students to compare the U.S. system of measurement with the metric system, which is used in most of the French-speaking world.

Attention!

The readings in the **Connexions** section are optional. They focus on some of the major disciplines taught in schools and universities. The vocabulary is useful for discussing such topics as history, literature, art, economics, business, science, etc. You may choose any of the following ways to do the readings in the **Connexions** sections.

Independent reading Have students read the selections and do the post-reading activities as homework, which you collect. This option is least intrusive on class time and requires a minimum of teacher involvement.

Homework with in-class follow-up Assign the readings and post-reading activities as homework. Review and discuss the material in class the next day.

Intensive in-class activity This option includes a pre-reading vocabulary presentation, in-class reading and discussion, assignment of the activities for homework, and a discussion of the assignment in class the following day.

CONNEXIONS

Les mathématiques

Les conversions

When you travel in many of the French-speaking countries, or almost anywhere in Europe, you need to make many mathematical conversions. The metric system, rather than the English system, is used for distance, weights, and measures.

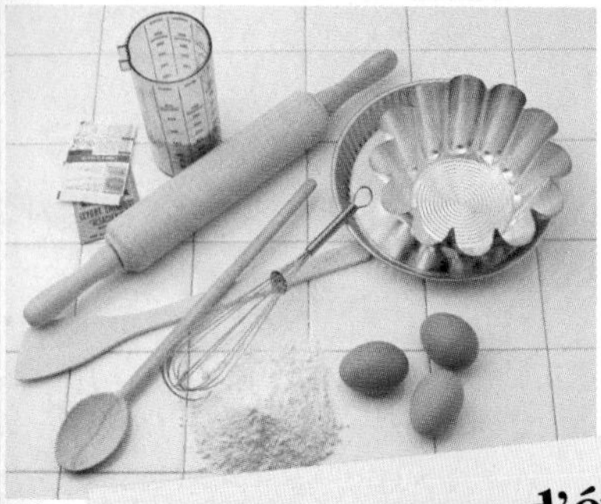

soupe d'été

Je trouve sympa de présenter la soupe avec tous ces petits morceaux de légumes. Parfois, je la sers accompagnée de croûtons de pain à l'ail et de gruyère coupé en dés. On se régale tous. Au menu, j'ai prévu une salade crue (pour la vitamine C) avec un œuf dur (pour les éléments bâtisseurs: les protéines). 1 œuf, cela peut remplacer 50 g de viande ou de poisson.

LES USTENSILES
- 1 planche à découper
- 1 cocotte
- 1 couteau de cuisine en acier inoxydable
- 1 cuillère à soupe
- 1 cuillère en bois

LES INGREDIENTS POUR 4 PERSONNES
- Pommes de terre : 250 g — 3 moyennes
- Courgettes : 250 g — 2 moyennes
- Tomates : 3 moyennes
- Oignons : 2
- Huile : 1 cuillerée à soupe
- Eau : 1 litre

Learning from Photos

(pages 210–211) Have students identify as many items as they can in the photos.

About the French Language

Croquants on the sign in the photo means *crunchy.* **Croquant** as a noun is a pejorative meaning *country bumpkin.* ✤

Le système métrique

Le système métrique est un système décimal: il a pour base 10. Les mesures ont pour base le mètre et les poids ont pour base le gramme. Pour les liquides, la base est le litre. Les unités supérieures et inférieures sont formées avec les préfixes suivants:

kilo = × 1 000	**un kilogramme = 1 000 grammes**
hecto = × 100	**un hectomètre = 100 mètres**
déca = × 10	**un décalitre = 10 litres**
déci = ÷ 10	**un décimètre = 1 mètre ÷ 10**
centi = ÷ 100	**un centilitre = 1 litre ÷ 100**
milli = ÷ 1 000	**un milligramme = 1 gramme ÷ 1 000**

Un kilogramme (un kilo) est équivalent à environ[1] deux livres[2]. Une livre est équivalente à un peu moins[3] d'un demi-kilo. Un mile américain est équivalent à environ un kilomètre et demi. Un litre est équivalent à environ un quart américain.

[1] environ *about*
[2] livres *pounds*
[3] un peu moins *a little less*

Après la lecture

Poids et mesures

Vrai ou faux? *(True or false?)*

1. Le système anglais de poids et mesures a pour base 10.
2. Les poids ont comme unité de base le litre.
3. Il y a 1 000 grammes dans un kilo.
4. Un kilo est l'équivalent d'environ deux livres anglaises.
5. Une livre américaine est l'équivalent de 500 grammes.
6. On mesure les liquides en quarts en France.
7. En France, on mesure les liquides en litres.

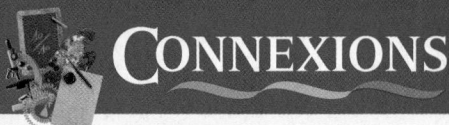

CONNEXIONS

Presentation

Les mathématiques
Les conversions

Step 1 Have students read the introduction in English on page 210.

Step 2 Have students read the selection quickly. Students should already be familiar with the metric terms used in the reading.

Après la lecture

Have a student read each sentence aloud and indicate if it is true or false. Call on more able students to correct the false statements.

FUN-FACTS

Both George Washington and Thomas Jefferson asked Congress to pass a law for a simple system of measurement, but Congress failed to enact their proposals into law. Jefferson wanted to throw out the old system and use the metric system. His proposal was turned over to a committee for study, where it eventually died.

Answers to Après la lecture

1. F
2. F
3. V
4. V
5. V
6. F
7. V

Reaching All Students

Additional Practice Have students convert the measurements in the **soupe d'été** recipe on page 210 into American Standard (quarts, cups, ounces, and so forth).

C'est à vous

Use what you have learned

Presentation

Bellringer Review

Use BRR Transparency 6.9 or write the following on the board.

Complete the following amounts with an appropriate food item.

1. un paquet	**4. une boîte**
2. un pot	**5. une tranche**
3. un kilo	**6. une bouteille**

Recycling

These activities allow students to use the vocabulary and structure from this chapter in completely open-ended, real-life situations.

Presentation

Encourage students to say as much as possible when they do these activities. Tell them not to be afraid to make mistakes, since the goal of these activities is real-life communication. If someone in the group makes an error, allow the others to politely correct him or her. Let students choose the activities they would like to do.

You may wish to divide students into pairs or groups. Encourage students to elaborate on the basic theme and to be creative. They may use props, pictures, or posters if they wish.

Learning from Photos

(page 212) Have students describe the **marché** scene. Then have them write at least five things they would expect to hear the **marchand** and a client say at this stall.

C'est à vous

Use what you have learned

PARLER

1

Au marché

✔ Buy food from a vendor at the market

Work with a classmate. You are spending a semester studying in Belgium. You are going to prepare a dinner for your Belgian family. Decide what you need to buy at the market and in what quantities. Then have a conversation with your classmate, who will be the vendor at the market.

PARLER

2

Je veux bien, mais je ne peux pas parce que...

✔ Talk about what you want to do but can't

Work in groups of three or four. Tell some things you want to do but can't do because you are going to do something else. Tell what you are going to do.

PARLER / ÉCRIRE

3

Jeu Une compétition

✔ Express quantities

Compete with a classmate. You each have two minutes. See which one of you can make up the most phrases using the following words.

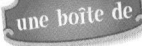

un kilo de · une livre de · un litre de · une bouteille de · une boîte de · six tranches de · un paquet de

Answers to C'est à vous

1 *Answers will vary.*

Students can use all the shopping expressions they know in their conversation

2 *Answers will vary but may include:*

Je veux regarder une vidéo et je veux téléphoner à mon copain, mais je ne peux pas. Je vais aller à la papeterie.

3 *Answers will vary but may include:*

un kilo d'agneau
une livre de beurre
un litre de jus d'orange
une bouteille d'eau minérale
un paquet de haricots verts
une boîte de conserve
six tranches de jambon

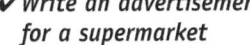

C'est à vous

ÉCRIRE

4

Une publicité

✔Write an advertisement for a supermarket

Using these French supermarket ads as a guide, write similar food advertisements in French for your local supermarket. Choose any four foods you like to advertise.

Writing Strategy

Ordering ideas You can order ideas in a variety of ways when writing. Therefore, you must be aware of the purpose of your writing in order to choose the best way to organize your material. When describing an event, it is logical to put the events in the order in which they happen. Using a sensible and logical approach helps readers develop a picture in their minds.

ÉCRIRE

5

On fait les courses.

Your class is planning a French meal. Describe the trip you take with your class to the local market or supermarket to buy the ingredients. Tell what you buy, whom you buy it from, and how much everything costs.

Un supermarché, Dakar, Sénégal

Writing Development

Have students keep a notebook containing their best written work from each chapter. These selected writings can be based on assignments from the Student Textbook and the Writing Activities Workbook. The two activities on page 213 are examples of writing assignments that may be included in each student's portfolio. In the Workbook, students will develop an organized autobiography **(Mon autobiographie).** These workbook pages may also become a part of their portfolio.

Writing Strategy

Ordering ideas Have students read the Writing Strategy on page 213. If students have difficulty thinking of words to describe their shopping expedition, have them use the vocabulary list on page 216.

Learning from Realia

Explain to students that **le lot** refers to a prepackaged quantity such as a "four-pack" or "six-pack."

Answers to C'est à vous

4 *Answers will vary but may include:*

Yaourt aux fraises
origine américaine
pots de 100 g
le lot de 4 pots
7 F
0,53€

5 *Answers will vary.*

Students can reincorporate all the vocabulary they have learned about foods and shopping for food to write an original "composition" describing whatever meal they choose.

Reaching All Students

Additional Practice Have students each make up a shopping list of all the foods they like that they might buy at a market in France. Then have them make up menus for one or two days using these foods.

Resource Manager

Communication Transparencies
Quizzes
Test Booklet
ExamView Pro®
Situation Cards
Performance Assessment
Marathon mental Videoquiz

Assessment

This is a pre-test for students to take before you administer the chapter test. Answer sheets for students to do these pages are provided in your transparency binder. Note that each section is cross-referenced so students can easily find the material they have to review in case they made errors. You may wish to collect these assessments and correct them yourself or you may prefer to have the students correct themselves in class. You can go over the answers orally or project them on the overhead, using your Assessment Answers transparencies.

Reaching All Students

Additional Practice After completing Activity 2, you may wish to have students create appropriate sentences for the vocabulary words that were not used in the answers.

Assessment

Vocabulaire

*To review **Mots 1**, turn to pages 186–187.*

1 Identifiez. *(Identify each item.)*

1. 
2. 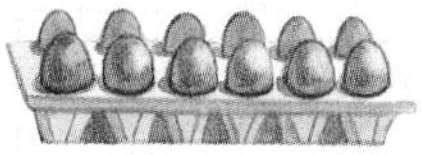
3. 
4. 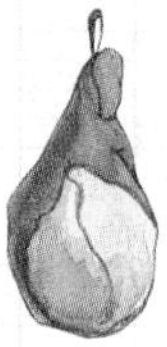

*To review **Mots 2**, turn to pages 190–191.*

2 Choisissez. *(Choose.)*

5. Une pomme et une poire sont des ____.
   a. fraises **b.** légumes **c.** fruits
6. C'est ____, un kilo de carottes?
   a. comment **b.** combien **c.** un marchand
7. Il va acheter ____ de moutarde.
   a. un paquet **b.** une boîte **c.** un pot
8. Je voudrais six ____ de jambon, s'il vous plaît.
   a. bouteilles **b.** tranches **c.** litres

Structure

*To review the verb **faire**, turn to page 194.*

3 Complétez avec «faire». *(Complete with* faire.*)*

9. Je ____ les courses le matin.
10. Mon frère ____ du latin.
11. Vous ____ vos devoirs?
12. Les élèves ne ____ pas la cuisine.

Answers to Assessment

1
1. un gâteau
2. des œufs (une douzaine d'œufs)
3. du lait
4. une poire

2
5. c
6. b
7. c
8. b

3
9. fais
10. fait
11. faites
12. font

4 Choisissez. *(Choose.)*

13. Moi, j'aime beaucoup ___ lait.
    a. le   b. du   c. de
14. Je voudrais ___ eau.
    a. d'   b. de l'   c. du
15. Il va acheter ___ fruits et ___ légumes.
    a. des   b. de   c. les

To review the partitive and the definite article, turn to pages 196, 198.

5 Récrivez au négatif. *(Rewrite the sentences in the negative.)*

16. Je vais acheter du pain.
17. Je voudrais de la crème.

6 Récrivez les phrases. *(Rewrite the sentences.)*

18. Les carottes sont très bonnes.
    Le poisson ___.
19. Tu veux quel sandwich?
    Tu veux ___ salade?

To review these special adjectives, turn to page 201.

7 Complétez. *(Complete.)*

20. Je ___ faire le travail. (pouvoir)
21. Vous ___ aller au restaurant? (vouloir)
22. Tu ___ aller au marché. (pouvoir)
23. Ils ___ parler au prof. (vouloir)

*To review the verbs **pouvoir** and **vouloir**, turn to page 201.*

Culture

8 Répondez. *(Answer.)*

24. Beaucoup de magasins sont fermés quel jour en France?
25. On peut aller où pour acheter un pot de confiture ou une bouteille d'eau minérale?

To review this cultural information, turn to pages 206–207.

Glencoe Technology

MINDJOGGER

You may wish to help your students prepare for the chapter test by playing the MindJogger game show. Teams will compete against each other to review chapter vocabulary and structure and sharpen listening comprehension skills.

Answers to Assessment

4

13. a
14. b
15. a

5

16. Je ne vais pas acheter de pain.
17. Je ne voudrais pas de crème.

6

18. Le poisson est très bon.
19. Tu veux quelle salade?

7

20. peux
21. voulez
22. peux
23. veulent

8

24. Beaucoup de magasins sont fermés le lundi. (et le dimanche)
25. On peut aller à l'épicerie pour acheter un pot de confiture ou une bouteille d'eau minérale.

Vocabulary Review

The words and phrases in the **Vocabulaire** have been taught for productive use in this chapter. They are summarized here as a resource for both student and teacher. This list also serves as a convenient resource for the **C'est à vous** activities on pages 212–213. There are approximately nineteen cognates in this vocabulary list. Have students find them.

Attention!

You will notice that the vocabulary list here is not translated. This has been done intentionally, since we feel that by the time students have finished the material in the chapter they should be familiar with the meanings of all the words. If there are several words they still do not know, we recommend that they refer to the **Mots 1** and **2** sections in the chapter or go to the dictionaries at the back of this book to find the meanings. However, if you prefer that your students have the English translations, please refer to Vocabulary Transparency 6.1, where you will find all these words listed with their translations.

Vocabulaire

Shopping for food

faire les courses *(f. pl.)*
une boulangerie
une pâtisserie
une crémerie
une boucherie
une poissonnerie
une charcuterie
une épicerie
un marché
un supermarché
le/la marchand(e)
un sac
surgelé(e)

Identifying some food

du pain
un pain complet
un croissant
une baguette
une tarte aux pommes
de la crème
du lait
du beurre
du fromage
de la confiture
un œuf
un yaourt
un poulet
de la viande
du bœuf
de l'agneau *(m.)*
du porc
du jambon
du saucisson
du poisson
une crevette
un crabe
du sel
du poivre
de l'huile *(f.)*
du vinaigre
de l'eau minérale
de la moutarde
des petits pois *(m. pl.)*
un fruit
une banane
une pomme
une orange
une poire
une fraise
un melon
un légume
une salade
une carotte
une pomme de terre
des haricots verts
des épinards *(m. pl.)*
une tomate
un oignon

Identifying quantities

un paquet
un pot
un gramme
un kilo(gramme)
une livre
un litre
une douzaine
une boîte
une bouteille
une tranche

How well do you know your vocabulary?

- Choose two foods that you like from the list.
- Tell how you buy each, for example, *une douzaine, une bouteille,* etc.

Other useful words and expressions

aller chercher
il n'y a plus de
je regrette
C'est combien?
Ça fait combien?
bon(ne)
Vous voulez autre chose?
Et avec ça?
C'est tout.
Pourquoi?
parce que

Technotour
BON VOYAGE!

VIDÉO • Épisode 6

Avant de visionner

In this video episode, Vincent and Manu go food shopping. Manu demonstrates once again how he turns a routine task into fun.

Vincent et Manu font les courses.

Manu «prépare» un repas fabuleux.

FRENCH ONLINE

À découvrir

Learn more about markets in Paris online.

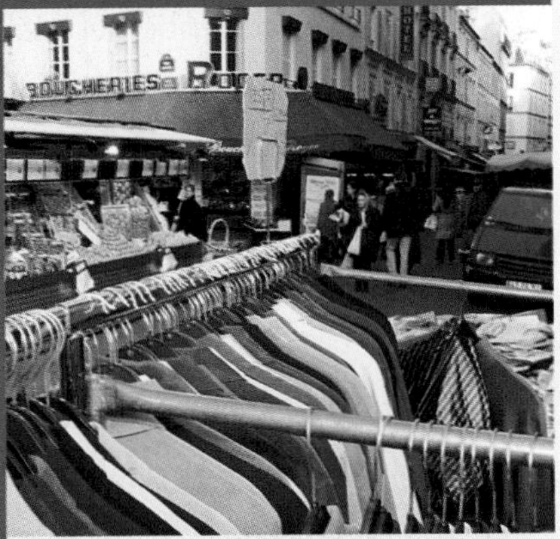

Marché Poncelet, Paris

FRENCH Online

In the Chapter 6 Internet activity, you will have a chance to learn more about food in the Francophone world. To begin your virtual adventure, go to the Glencoe French Web site: **french.glencoe.com**

Technotour

Overview

This page previews two key multimedia components of the **Glencoe French** series. Each reinforces the material taught in the chapter in a unique manner.

VIDÉO

The Video Program allows students to see how the chapter vocabulary and structures are used by native speakers. For maximum reinforcement, show the video episode as a final activity for Chapter 6.

The two photos on the left show highlights from the Chapter 6 video episode. Discuss the photos with your students before having them view the episode. See the Video Activities Booklet for detailed suggestions for using this resource.

FRENCH Online

- The **À découvrir** photo shows the Marché Poncelet in Paris. Students can go online to learn more about markets in Paris.
- Teacher Information and Student Worksheets for this activity can be accessed at the Web site.

Video Synopsis

In this video episode, Manu and Vincent purchase food from various vendors in the Marché Poncelet, and Manu entertains us with rap verses at each stop. We see that in France, people often buy items at small shops located within walking distance, rather than at large grocery stores.

Planning for Chapter 7

SCOPE AND SEQUENCE, PAGES 218–247

Topics

- Clothing
- Shopping for clothes

Culture

- Shopping for clothes in France
- Typical clothing in Africa
- Discussing clothing sizes in the United States and France
- **Reflets de l´Afrique**

Functions

- How to identify and describe articles of clothing
- How to state color and size preferences
- How to describe people's activities
- How to compare, express opinions, and make observations

Structure

- The verb **mettre** in the present tense
- Comparative adjectives
- The verbs **voir** and **croire** in the present tense

National Standards

- Communication Standard 1.1 pages 222, 223, 226, 227, 228, 229, 230, 231, 232, 235, 242
- Communication Standard 1.2 pages 222, 223, 226, 227, 228, 229, 230, 231, 232, 233, 234, 237, 238, 239, 241, 242, 243
- Communication Standard 1.3 pages 223, 226, 230, 231, 243
- Cultures Standard 2.1 pages 234, 236–237, 238, 239
- Cultures Standard 2.2 pages 238
- Connections Standard 3.1 pages 240–241
- Comparisons Standard 4.2 pages 236–237, 238, 239
- Communities Standard 5.1 page 243

PACING AND PRIORITIES

The chapter content is color coded below to assist you in planning.

■ **required** ■ **recommended** ■ **optional**

Vocabulaire *(required)* *Days 1–4*

- ■ Mots 1
  - Les vêtements sport
  - Les vêtements pour hommes
  - Les vêtements pour femmes
- ■ Mots 2
  - On fait des courses.

Structure *(required)* *Days 5–7*

- ■ Le verbe **mettre**
- ■ Le comparatif des adjectifs
- ■ Les verbes **voir** et **croire**

Conversation *(required)*

- ■ Dans une petite boutique

Prononciation *(recommended)*

- ■ Les sons **/sh/** et **/zh/**

Lectures culturelles

- ■ On fait des courses où, à Paris? *(recommended)*
- ■ Les vêtements *(optional)*
- ■ Les tailles *(optional)*

Connexions *(optional)*

- ■ La poésie

■ **C'est à vous** *(recommended)*

■ **Assessment** *(recommended)*

■ **Technotour** *(optional)*

RESOURCE GUIDE

Section	Pages	Section Resources
Vocabulaire *Mots 1*		
Les vêtements sport Les vêtements pour hommes Les vêtements pour femmes	220 221 221–223	Vocabulary Transparencies 7.2–7.3 Audiocassette 5A/CD 5 Audio Activities Booklet TE, pages 87–89 Workbook, pages 65–66 Quiz 1, page 33 ExamView Pro®
Vocabulaire *Mots 2*		
On fait des courses.	224–227	Vocabulary Transparencies 7.4–7.5 Audiocassette 5A/CD 5 Audio Activities Booklet TE, pages 89–91 Workbook, pages 67–68 Quiz 2, page 34 ExamView Pro®
Structure		
Le verbe **mettre** Le comparatif des adjectifs Les verbes **voir** et **croire**	228–229 230–231 232–233	Audiocassette 5A/CD 5 Audio Activities Booklet TE, pages 91–92 Workbook, pages 69–71 Quizzes 3–6, pages 35–38 ExamView Pro®
Conversation		
Dans une petite boutique	234	Audiocassette 5A/CD 5 Audio Activities Booklet TE, pages 92–93 CD-ROM
Prononciation		
Les sons **/sh/** et **/zh/**	235	Pronunciation Transparency P 7 Audiocassette 5A/CD 5 Audio Activities Booklet TE, pages 93–94
Lectures culturelles		
On fait des courses où, à Paris? Les vêtements Les tailles	236–237 238 239	Audiocassette 5A/CD 5 Audio Activities Booklet TE, pages 95–96 Test Booklet, Chapter 7
Connexions		
La poésie	240–241	Test Booklet, Chapter 7
C'est à vous		
	242–243	**Bon voyage!** Video, Episode 7 Video Activities Booklet, Chapter 7 French Online Activities french.glencoe.com
Assessment		
	244–245	Communication Transparency C 7 Quizzes 1–6, pages 33–38 Test Booklet, Chapter 7 ExamView Pro® Situation Cards, Chapter 7 Performance Assessment, pages 9–14 **Marathon mental** Videoquiz

Using Your Resources for Chapter 7

Transparencies

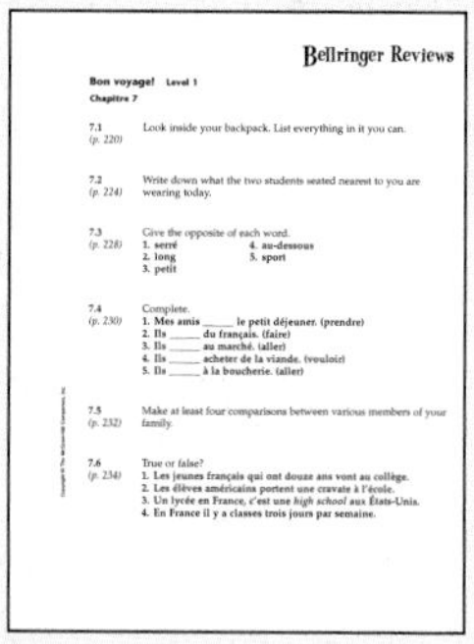

Bellringer 7.1–7.8

Vocabulary 7.1–7.5

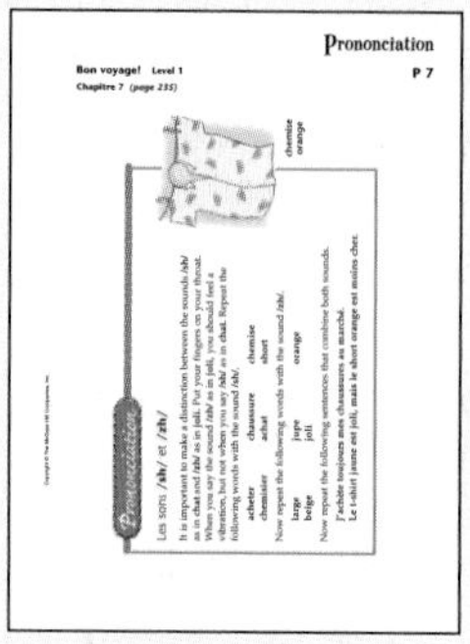

Pronunciation P 7

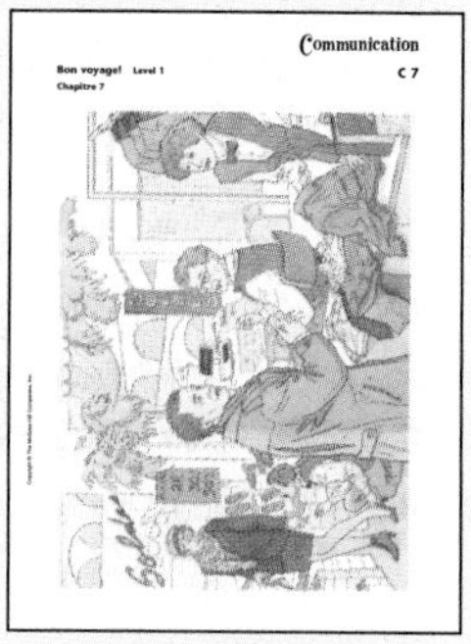

Communication C 7

Writing Activities Workbook

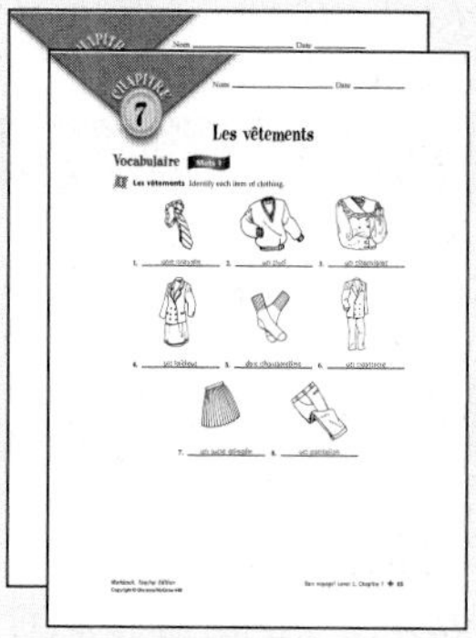

Vocabulary, pages 65–68

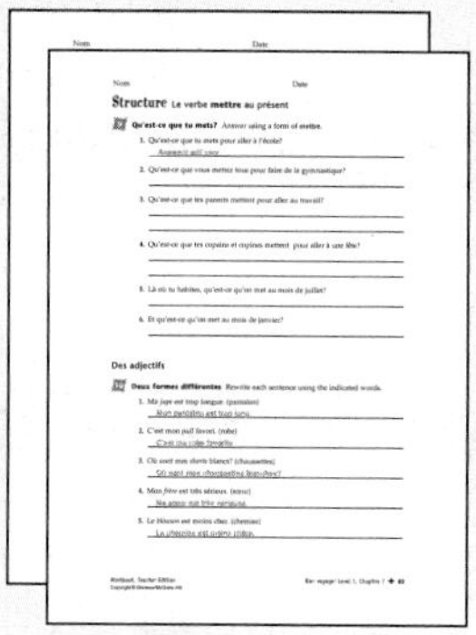

Structure, pages 69–71

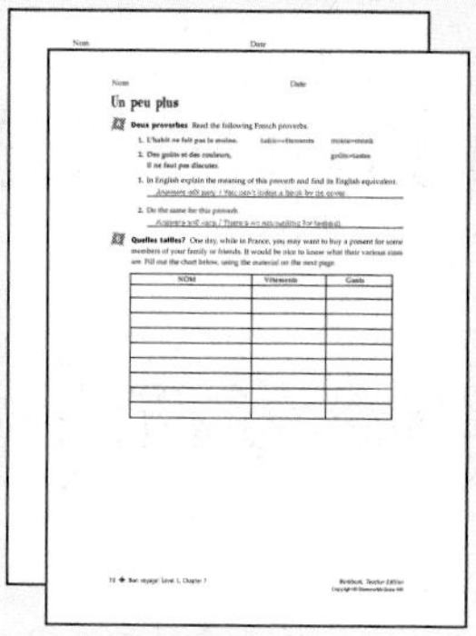

Enrichment, pages 72–74

Audio Program and Audio Activities Booklet

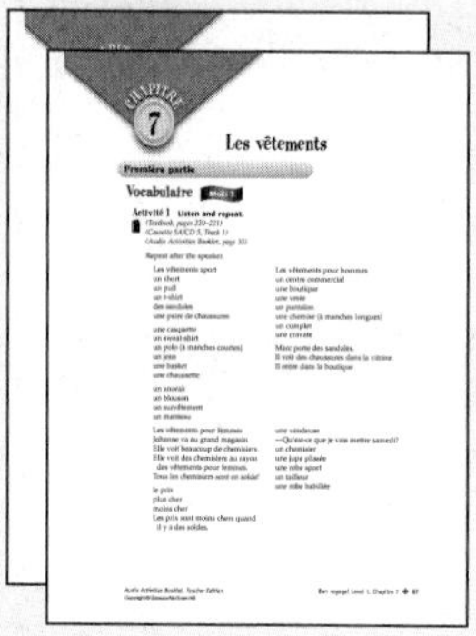

Vocabulary, pages 87–91

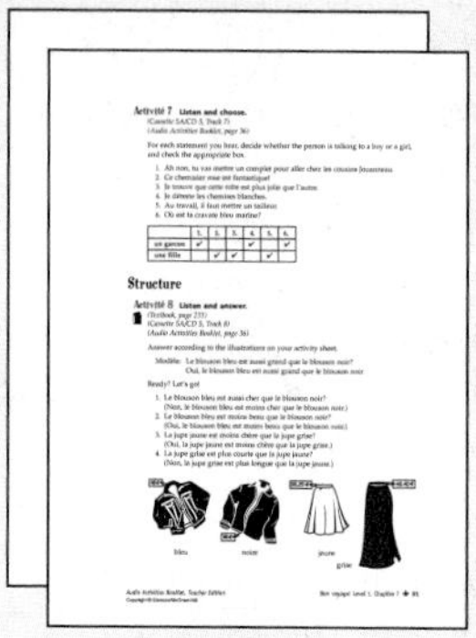

Structure, pages 91–92

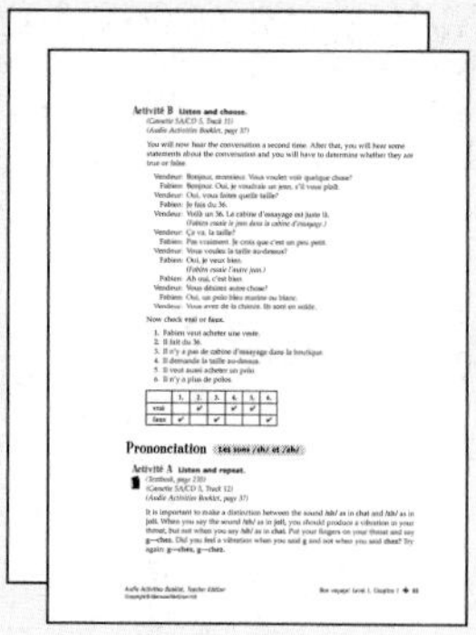

Conversation, Pronunciation, pages 92–94

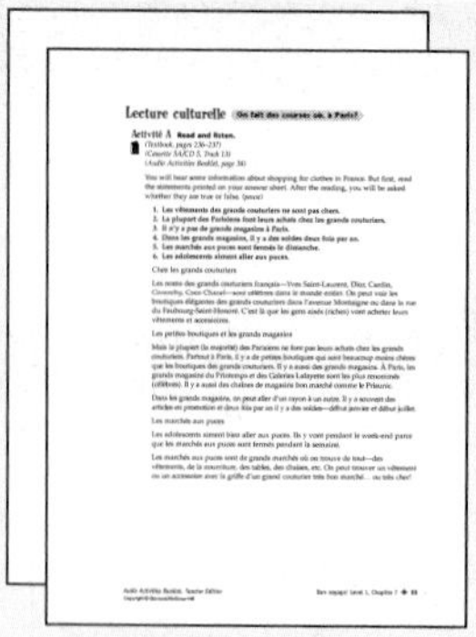

Cultural Reading, pages 95–96

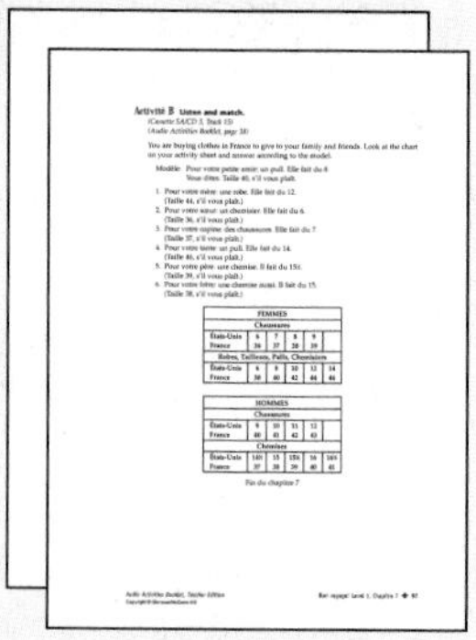

Additional Practice, pages 96–97

Assessment

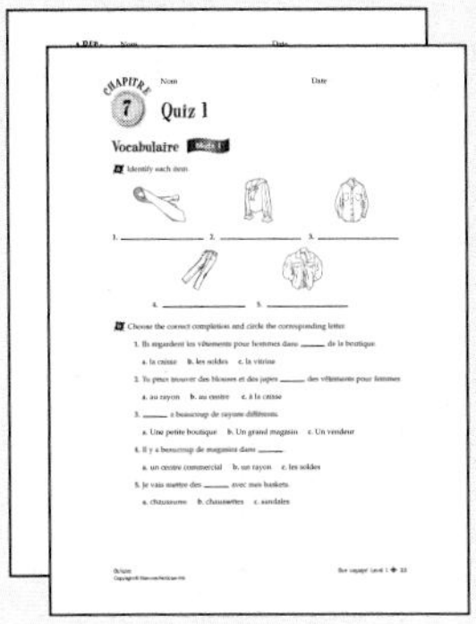

Vocabulary and Structure Quizzes, pages 33–38

Chapter Tests, Chapter 7

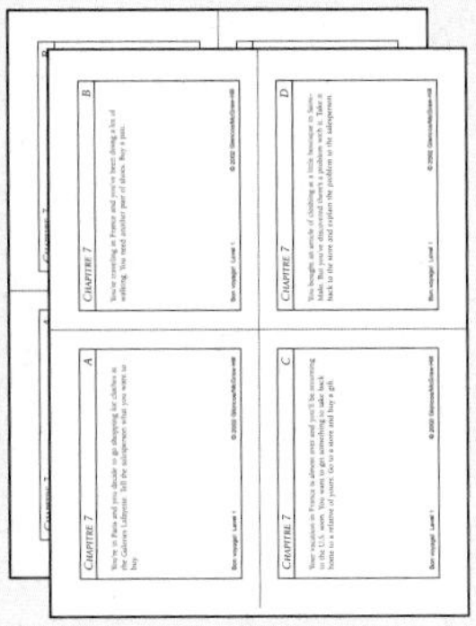

Situation Cards, Chapter 7

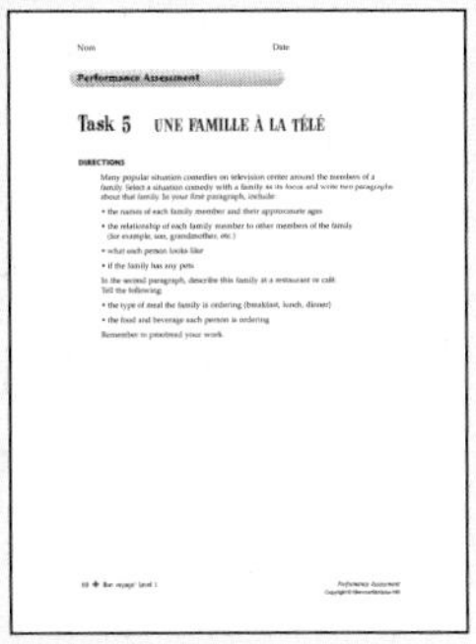

Performance Assessment, pages 9–14

Timesaving Teacher Tools

Interactive Teacher Edition

Imagine having your Teacher's Edition and all resources on a CD-ROM. Click on a resource and it appears on your screen, ready to be printed, sorted, or planned.

Interactive Lesson Planner

The Interactive Lesson Planner CD-ROM helps you organize your lesson plans for a week, month, semester, or year. Look at this planning tool for easy access to your Chapter 7 resources.

ExamView Pro®

Test Bank software for Macintosh and Windows makes creating, editing, customizing, and printing tests quick and easy.

Technology Resources

FRENCH Online

In the Chapter 7 Internet activity, you will have a chance to learn more about clothing and shopping in the Francophone world. Visit french.glencoe.com.

On the Interactive Conversation CD-ROM, students can listen to and take part in a recorded version of the conversation in Chapter 7.

NATIONAL GEOGRAPHIC SOCIETY

See the National Geographic Teacher's Corner on pages 150–151, 256–257, 396–397, 500–501 for reference to additional technology resources.

Bon voyage! Video and Video Activities Booklet.

Help your students prepare for the chapter test by playing the **Marathon mental** Videoquiz game show. Teams will compete against each other to review chapter vocabulary and structure and sharpen listening comprehension skills.

CHAPITRE 7

Preview

In this chapter, students will learn to identify, describe, and shop for clothing. They will also learn to make observations and express opinions using comparative statements about people and things. In addition, students will learn to use and conjugate verbs such as **croire, voir,** and **mettre.**

National Standards

Communication

In Chapter 7, students will communicate in spoken and written French on the following topics:
- Clothing
- Shopping for clothing

Students will engage in conversations, provide and obtain information, and exchange opinions as they fulfill the chapter objectives listed on this page.

CHAPITRE 7

Les vêtements

Objectifs

In this chapter you will learn to:

- ✔ *identify and describe articles of clothing*
- ✔ *state color and size preferences*
- ✔ *shop for clothing*
- ✔ *describe people's activities*
- ✔ *compare people and things*
- ✔ *express opinions and make observations*
- ✔ *discuss clothes and clothes shopping in the French-speaking world*

Un tissu de la Côte d'Ivoire

Correlations to Continuum (*see page* i *for code*)

Stage I

Make requests. p. 235 (**A**, *m*); Obtain information. p. 235 (**B**, *p*); Write lists. p. 243 (**4**, *p*); Understand ideas and familiar details when listening. p. 223 (**5**, *p*), p. 235 (**B**, *m*); Understand texts enhanced by visual clues. pp. 236–237 (*p*); Understand and convey information about shopping and clothes. pp. 220–221 (*i*), p. 223 (**6**, *p*); Demonstrate culturally acceptable behavior for Stage I functions. p. 242 (**1**); Understand most important information. p. 243 (**6**)

Stage II

Understand and express important ideas and some detail. p. 242 (**2**, *p*); Describe and compare. p. 230 (**16**, *i*), p. 231 (**19**, *p*); Use and understand learned expressions, sentences, and strings of sentences, questions, and polite commands when speaking and listening. p. 242 (**3**, *p*); Create simple paragraphs. p. 243 (*i*), p. 243 (**6**, *p*); Communicate effectively with some pattern of error, which may interfere slightly with full comprehension when performing Stage II functions. p. 243 (**5**)

Stage III

Express and understand opinions. p. 225 (*i*), p. 242 (**1**, *p*); Read poems. pp. 510–511 (*i*); Understand and convey information about art. pp. 240–241 (*i, p*)

CHAPITRE 7

Spotlight on Culture

Photograph Montreal, the second largest French-speaking city after Paris, is known for its long, cold winters. A virtual underground city of several stories, seen here, was built so people could go about their business without the snow and winter winds. The many malls are connected by the metro and they have more than 1,700 stores, 200 restaurants, movies, and access to hotels and the railroad station.

Weaving Many West African countries are well known for their excellent fabrics and textiles. The **Korhogo** cloth from the northern part of **Côte d'Ivoire** is considered among the best.

Chapter Projects

Des magasins In this chapter students will learn the types of stores that exist for buying clothes in France. Have students compare the shopping habits of people in France and those of people in their area. Have them tell in what types of stores they tend to shop: **une boutique, un grand magasin, un marché (aux puces), un hypermarché.**

Un magazine Some of the girls may want to read an article from **Elle**, a women's magazine also published in the United States.

Un catalogue Have students prepare a catalogue with articles of clothing taught in this chapter. Tell students to label each item. Whenever possible, have them write something about the article of clothing.

Au magasin de vêtements Have pairs of students prepare a skit that takes place at a clothing store. One student is the customer; the other is the salesclerk.

1 Preparation

Resource Manager

Vocabulary Transparencies 7.2–7.3
Audio Activities Booklet TE, pages 87–89
Audiocassette 5A/CD 5
Workbook, pages 65–66
Quiz 1, page 33
ExamView Pro®

Bellringer Review

Use BRR Transparency 7.1 or write the following on the board.
Look inside your backpack. List everything in it you can.

2 Presentation

Step 1 Identify items of clothing students are actually wearing. Have the class repeat each item after you once or twice. Ask **Qu'est-ce que c'est?** and have a student respond.

Step 2 Show Vocabulary Transparencies 7.2–7.3. Have students repeat each item after you or Audiocassette 5A/CD 5.

Step 3 Ask questions about the material on page 221, referring to the Vocabulary Transparencies. For example: **Qu'est ce que Marc porte? Qu'est-ce qu'il voit? Johanne va où? Les prix sont moins chers quand?**

Step 4 Play a game using the new vocabulary. One student describes what someone in the class is wearing and calls on classmates to guess who is being described.
Expansion: Have students recycle earlier vocabulary. Have them describe the person as well as what the person is wearing.

Vocabulaire

Mots 1

Les vêtements sport

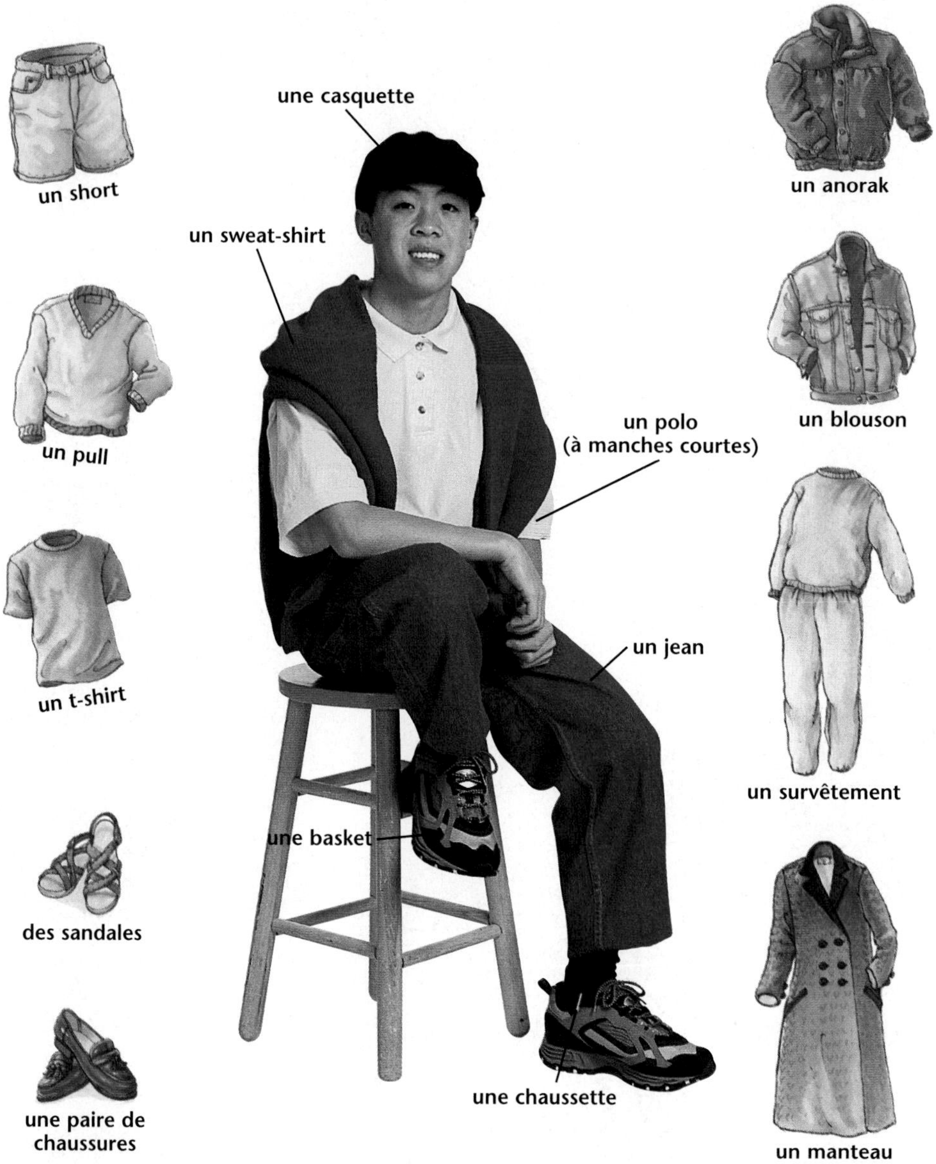

Reaching All Students

Total Physical Response You may wish to bring in a jacket to use for this activity. Dramatize the meaning of **enlévez.**

(Student 1), **venez ici, s'il vous plaît.**
Vous êtes au rayon des blousons.
Cherchez un beau blouson.
Prenez le blouson.
Essayez le blouson. Mettez le blouson.
Indiquez que vous aimez le blouson.
Et maintenant, enlevez le blouson.
(Student 2), **venez ici, s'il vous plaît.**
Vous travaillez à la caisse.
Et *(Student 1),* **allez à la caisse aussi.**
Donnez de l'argent au caissier (à la caissière).
(Student 2), **mettez le blouson dans un sac.**
Donnez le sac au client (à la cliente).
(Student 1), **prenez le sac.**
Merci *(Student 1)* **et** *(Student 2).*
Retournez à vos places, s'il vous plaît.

Les vêtements pour hommes

Marc porte des sandales.
Il voit des chaussures dans la vitrine.
Il entre dans la boutique.

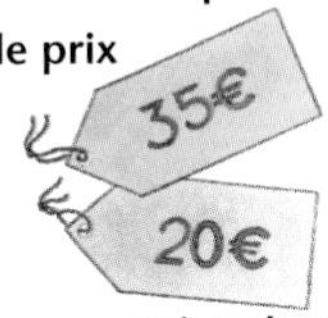

Les prix sont moins chers quand il y a des soldes.

Les vêtements pour femmes

Johanne va au grand magasin.
Elle voit beaucoup de chemisiers.
Elle voit des chemisiers au rayon des vêtements pour femmes.
Tous les chemisiers sont en solde!

Step 5 Ask personal questions about yourself and students such as: **Qui porte une jupe aujourd'hui? Je porte une cravate? Marie porte un pantalon ou une robe?** After a few such examples, see if volunteers can come up with similar questions.

Vocabulary Expansion

Many other articles of clothing will be presented in later chapters as they are needed. It is therefore recommended that you not give students an extensive list of additional vocabulary now. You may, however, wish to give them the names of a few accessories.

une ceinture
une montre
un bracelet
une bague
une boucle d'oreille
des lunettes de soleil

About the French Language

Note the invariable adjective **sport (une robe sport)** and the adjective **habillé (une robe habillée).** There is no precise French word that conveys the English "formal" or "dressy" in regard to clothing. **Habillé** is the closest approximation to "formal." Another word students will encounter frequently, if they peruse magazines, is **décontracté,** which conveys the English "casual," "informal."

Reaching All Students

Spatial Learners Have students quickly sketch some articles of clothing and identify each item they sketched.

Bodily Kinesthetic Learners Have some students come to the front of the class and tell what they're wearing.

Note: In the TPR activity on page 220, we have used the **vous** form when addressing one student. You may prefer to use **tu.**

3 Practice

Commençons
Let's use our new words

Attention!

When students are doing the **Commençons** activities, accept any answer that makes sense. The purpose of these activities is to have students use the new vocabulary. They are not factual recall activities. Thus, it is not necessary for students to remember specific factual information from the vocabulary presentation when answering. If you wish, have students use the photos on this page as a stimulus, when possible.

2 Have students practice both listening and speaking by doing this activity in pairs. One partner reads the questions while the other listens and answers with his or her book closed. Then partners switch roles. Or you can have one student read the questions to the entire class and then call on individuals to respond.

Commençons
Let's use our new words

1 Chloé et Adrien Répondez d'après les photos. *(Answer according to the photos.)*

1. Qu'est-ce que Chloé porte?
2. Et Adrien? Qu'est-ce qu'il porte?

Chloé

Adrien

2 Qu'est-ce qu'on va mettre? Répondez. *(Answer.)*

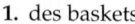

1. Ce soir M. Ben Azar va aller dans un restaurant chic. Qu'est-ce qu'il va mettre?
2. Qu'est-ce que sa femme va mettre?
3. Qu'est-ce que tu portes à l'école?
4. Qu'est-ce que tu portes à la maison?
5. Qu'est-ce qu'on porte en juillet et en août?
6. Qu'est-ce qu'on porte en décembre et janvier?
7. Qu'est-ce qu'une femme porte quand elle va travailler?
8. Qu'est-ce qu'un homme porte quand il va au travail?

3 Sport ou habillé? Identifiez. *(Tell whether each item is casual or formal.)*

1. des baskets
2. un tailleur
3. un jean
4. un complet
5. un blouson
6. une cravate
7. un polo à manches courtes
8. une chemise à manches longues
9. un survêtement
10. une jupe plissée

La vitrine d'une boutique, Paris

Answers to Commençons

1 *Answers will vary but may include:*

1. Chloé porte une robe sport, un pull et des sandales.
2. Adrien porte une casquette, un sweat-shirt, un jean et des baskets (chaussures).

2 *Answers will vary but may include:*

1. Il va mettre une chemise, un pantalon, une veste et une cravate.
2. Sa femme va mettre une robe habillée.
3. Je porte un jean, une chemise, un pull, des chaussures et un anorak.
4. Je porte un polo, un survêtement et des baskets.
5. On porte un short, un t-shirt et des sandales.
6. On porte un jean, un pull, des chaussures et un anorak ou un manteau.
7. Elle porte un tailleur.
8. Il porte un complet.

3

1. sport
2. habillé
3. sport
4. habillé
5. sport
6. habillé
7. sport
8. habillé
9. sport
10. habillé

4 **Historiette** **Au rayon des chemisiers** Inventez une histoire. *(Make up a story.)*

1. Mélanie entre dans un grand magasin ou dans une boutique?
2. La boutique est dans une rue ou dans un centre commercial?
3. Il y a des soldes aujourd'hui?
4. Il y a des chemisiers dans la vitrine?
5. Elle va au rayon des chemisiers?
6. Elle voit beaucoup de chemisiers?
7. Elle parle à la vendeuse?
8. Elle veut un chemisier à manches courtes ou à manches longues?
9. Elle veut un chemisier habillé ou sport?
10. Les chemisiers sont en solde?
11. Les vêtements sont moins chers quand ils sont en solde?

5 **C'est qui?** Work with a classmate. One of you describes what someone in the class is wearing and the other has to guess who it is. Take turns.

6 **Mon ensemble favori** Work with a classmate. Discuss what you consider an ideal outfit for school. Tell what you like to wear and what you don't like to wear. See if you are on the same wavelength.

Des jeunes habillés sport

ENCORE PLUS *For more practice using words from **Mots 1**, do Activity 20 on page H21 at the end of this book.*

Answers to Commençons

4 *Answers will vary but may include:*

1. Mélanie entre dans une boutique.
2. La boutique est dans un centre commercial.
3. Oui, il y a des soldes aujourd'hui.
4. Oui, il y a des chemisiers dans la vitrine.
5. Oui, elle va au rayon des chemisiers.
6. Oui, elle voit beaucoup de chemisiers.
7. Oui, elle parle à la vendeuse.
8. Elle veut un chemisier à manches longues.
9. Elle veut un chemisier sport.
10. Oui, les chemisiers sont en solde.
11. Oui, les vêtements sont moins chers quand ils sont en solde.

5 *Students will choose any student they wish to describe.*

6 *Students will describe what they like to wear to school.*

Vocabulaire

5 After having students work in pairs, you may wish to use this activity with the whole class.

Writing Development

Have the students write answers to Activity 4 in paragraph form to illustrate how the answers to all the items tell a story.

Assessment

As an informal assessment, you may wish to check for comprehension by using Vocabulary Transparencies 7.2–7.3. Call individuals to the screen. As classmates say words or expressions from **Mots 1**, the student at the screen points to the appropriate image.

Reteaching

Have students open their books to page 220 and write down what they wear when they do the following things.

dîner en ville
aller au café
aller à l'école
travailler dans une papeterie
travailler dans un supermarché

ENCORE PLUS This *infogap* activity will allow students to practice in pairs. The activity should be very manageable for them, since all vocabulary and structures are familiar to them.

Learning from Photos

(page 223) After presenting the vocabulary from **Mots 1**, have students look at this photograph and describe what some of the young people are wearing.

Vocabulaire
Mots 2

1 Preparation

Resource Manager

Vocabulary Transparencies 7.4–7.5
Audio Activities Booklet TE, pages 89–91
Audiocassette 5A/CD 5
Workbook, pages 67–68
Quiz 2, page 34
ExamView Pro®

Bellringer Review

Use BRR Transparency 7.2 or write the following on the board.
Write down what the two students seated nearest to you are wearing today.

2 Presentation

Step 1 Present the new vocabulary using Transparencies 7.4–7.5, following suggestions in previous chapters.

Step 2 For an activity that's fun, you may wish to bring articles of old clothing to class, or have students bring in articles of old clothing. Have students put on the wrong sizes to convey **large, serré, long, court.** They should say the appropriate phrase: **Je voudrais la taille au-dessus** or **Je voudrais la taille au-dessous.**

Step 3 Have students open their books and repeat the vocabulary after you or Audiocassette 5A/CD 5.

Step 4 Model the conversation at the bottom of page 224. Then have volunteers perform it as a demonstration of **trop** and the various adjectives, substituting different articles of clothing and sizes. Use American sizes here.

Vocabulaire
Mots 2

On fait des courses.

Il est joli, le pantalon vert. Tu ne trouves pas?
Si, j'aime beaucoup!
le shopping

Vous faites quelle pointure?
Je fais du 38.

une cabine d'essayage

Ça va, le pantalon?
Non, il est trop grand. Il est trop large. Je voudrais la taille au-dessous.
Vous faites quelle taille?
Je fais du 38.

Non, il est trop petit. Il est trop serré. Je voudrais la taille au-dessus.
essayer

Julien essaie le pantalon.

Reaching All Students

Total Physical Response Note: You may vary the articles of clothing below and their colors according to what the students are wearing.

Attention, tout le monde.
Si vous portez le vêtement que je mentionne, levez-vous.
Je vois un pantalon blanc.
Je vois un sweat-shirt noir.
Je vois une chemise bleue.
Je vois un t-shirt rouge.
Je vois une jupe verte.
Je vois un short beige.
Je vois un jean noir.
Merci bien, tout le monde! Asseyez-vous.

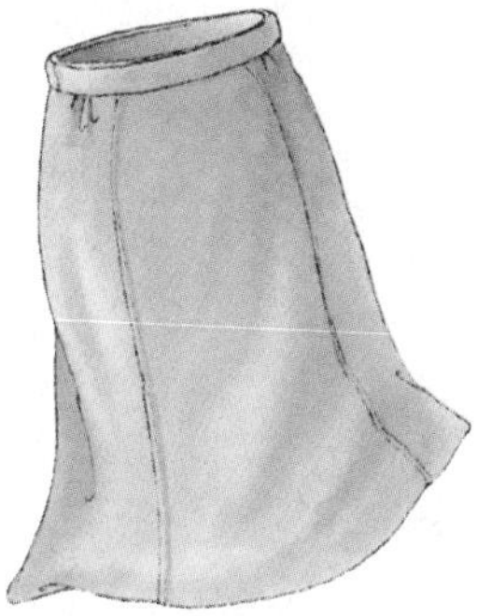

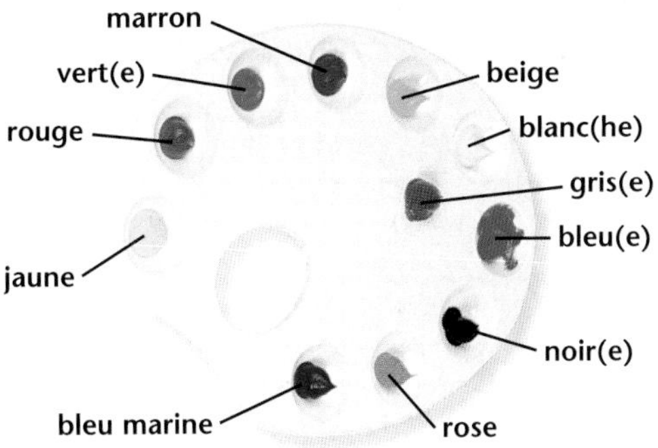

De quelle couleur est la jupe?
Elle est verte.

Et les chaussures?
Elles sont marron.

Note

The following colors are invariable. They do not change to agree with the noun they modify.

bleu marine **marron** **orange**

À mon avis, la robe rouge est plus jolie que la (robe) verte.
Moi, je crois que j'aime mieux la (robe) verte.
Moi, le rouge, c'est ma couleur favorite.

Vocabulaire

Mots 2

Step 5 Use the overhead transparency to teach the colors. Have the students repeat each color twice.

Step 6 Then go around the room and have students tell the color of articles of clothing other students are wearing: **De quelle couleur est le chemisier de ____?**

Note: Emphasize that the following colors, which are often used to describe clothes, are invariable: **bleu marine, marron, orange.** They do not agree with the feminine or plural noun they describe.

About the French Language

Point out to students that **la couleur** is feminine, but the actual colors are masculine. **Tu préfères le bleu ou le gris?**

Explain to students that the young woman in the first photo answers with **si. Si** rather than **oui** is used when you respond to a negative question. **Tu ne peux pas? Si, je peux. Ce n'est pas ta taille. Si, c'est ma taille.**

FUN-FACTS

The **grands magasins** began to appear under the Second Empire of Napoleon III, 1851–1870. This time of economic success and growth meant a large clientele with money to spend, which encouraged the development of department stores. These stores had more merchandise at lower prices than the small boutiques, previously the only place to buy clothing. The shoppers appreciated the new department stores' specialized staff, clearly marked prices, and regular sales. The first **grand magasin,** le Bon-Marché, opened in 1852. Le Printemps opened in 1865 and les Galeries Lafayette opened in 1895.

3 Practice

Commençons
Let's use our new words

7 Have students rewrite the information in the **Historiette** in their own words.

8 **Expansion:** You may wish to present the noun forms of colors: **Quelle est ta couleur favorite? C'est le bleu. Pour les chemises, c'est le blanc.**

Learning from Photos

(page 226) Have students describe the clothing in the photo.

Commençons
Let's use our new words

7 **Historiette Olivier fait des courses.** Inventez une histoire. *(Make up a story.)*

1. Olivier fait des courses?
2. Il veut acheter un blue jean?
3. Il voit un jean qu'il aime dans la vitrine?
4. Il entre dans le grand magasin?
5. Il fait quelle taille?
6. Il va essayer le jean?
7. Il est comment, le pantalon—grand, petit, juste à sa taille?
8. Il veut la taille au-dessus ou la taille au-dessous?
9. Les jeans sont en solde?
10. Ils sont moins chers quand ils sont en solde?
11. Olivier trouve que les jeans sont chers?
12. Olivier va acheter le jean?

Rayon des vêtements pour hommes, Galeries Lafayette, Paris

8 **Ta couleur favorite** Donnez des réponses personnelles. *(Give your own answers.)*

1. De quelle couleur est ton blouson favori?
2. De quelle couleur est ton jean favori?
3. De quelle couleur est ta chemise favorite ou ton chemisier favori?
4. Qu'est-ce que tu portes aujourd'hui? De quelle couleur sont tes vêtements?

9 **Mes préférences** Donnez des réponses personnelles. *(Give your own answers.)*

1. Tu aimes mieux les vêtements sport ou habillés?
2. Les baskets ou les chaussures?
3. Les chemises ou les chemisiers à manches longues ou à manches courtes?
4. Les vêtements un peu serrés ou larges?
5. Les couleurs sombres ou les couleurs claires?
6. Les vêtements chers ou pas chers?

Answers to Commençons

7 *Answers will vary but may include:*

1. Oui, Olivier fait des courses.
2. Oui, il veut acheter un blue jean.
3. Oui, il voit un jean qu'il aime dans la vitrine.
4. Oui, il entre dans le grand magasin.
5. Il fait du 40.
6. Oui, il va essayer le jean.
7. Le pantalon est petit.
8. Il veut la taille au-dessus.
9. Oui, les jeans sont en solde.
10. Oui, ils sont moins chers.
11. Non, il trouve que les jeans ne sont pas chers.
12. Oui, Olivier va acheter le jean.

8 *Answers will vary.*

Students will pick the color of their choice and make it agree with the article of clothing.

9 *Answers will vary.*

Students can select the response they wish to give.

10 **De petits problèmes** Répondez. *(Answer.)*

1. Les chaussures sont trop petites ou trop grandes?

2. La jupe est trop longue ou trop courte?

3. Le pantalon est un peu serré ou un peu large?

4. Les manches sont trop longues ou trop courtes?

5. Le tailleur est joli ou pas?

11 **Les couleurs** Complétez d'après la couleur. *(Complete with the color.)*

1. Aurélien va acheter un pantalon ____. 
2. Anne va acheter un chemisier ____. 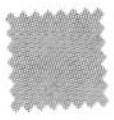
3. Fred va acheter une chemise ____. 
4. Justine va acheter une robe ____. 
5. Mélodie va acheter une jupe ____. 
6. Cyril va acheter des chaussures ____. 

12 **Jeu** **Qui porte une jupe bleue?** Study the clothing of all the students in the next row for several minutes. Then turn your back to that row. One of your classmates will mention an item of clothing and ask you who is wearing it. If you don't remember, your classmates can help you out by giving hints such as: **La personne est blonde. Elle est très amusante.**

ENCORE PLUS *For more practice using words from **Mots 2**, do Activity 21 on page H22 at the end of this book.*

Vocabulaire

10 After completing this activity, you may wish to have students quickly write a description of a ridiculous outfit. Call on volunteers to read their description to the class.

12 This is a great activity to use at the beginning or end of the class period.

Reaching All Students

For the Younger Students After doing Activity 10, you may wish to have the students sketch illustrations of the other answer given. For example, for number 1, students sketch shoes that are too large.

ENCORE PLUS This *infogap* activity will allow students to practice in pairs. The activity should be very manageable for them, since all vocabulary and structures are familiar to them.

About the French Language

You may wish to explain to students that **cher** agrees when it is an adjective.

Les jeans sont chers.
La blouse est chère.

There is no agreement when **cher** is an adverb.

Les chaussures coûtent cher.

Answers to Commençons

10

1. Les chaussures sont trop petites.
2. La jupe est trop longue.
3. Le pantalon est un peu large.
4. Les manches sont trop courtes.
5. Le tailleur n'est pas joli.

11

1. noir
2. rose
3. verte
4. bleue
5. blanche
6. marron

12 *Answers will vary but may include:*

—Elle porte un chemisier bleu.
—C'est Christelle?
—Non, elle est brune, très sociable, enthousiate…
—Ah! C'est Laurène!

1 Preparation

Resource Manager

Audio Activities Booklet TE, pages 91–92
Audiocassette 5A/CD 5
Workbook, pages 69–71
Quizzes 3–6, pages 35–38
ExamView Pro®

Bellringer Review

Use the BRR Transparency 7.3 or write the following on the board.
Give the opposite of each word.

1. serré
2. long
3. petit
4. au-dessous
5. sport

2 Presentation

Le verbe **mettre**

Step 1 When presenting the verb **mettre,** you may want to give the students first the **ils mettent** form. Have them pronounce it. Then tell them to drop the final sound and say **met.** This gives them the pronunciation for the **je, tu,** and **il** forms. Let them know that they will start to learn many verbs that drop the final sound of the **ils** form to get the sound of all the singular forms—**je, tu, il.**

Step 2 Go over the forms of the verb **mettre.** Write them on the board. Underline the double consonant in the plural forms.

Describing people's activities

Le verbe **mettre**

1. Study the forms of the verb **mettre** *(to put, to put on)* in the present tense.

METTRE			
je	mets	nous	mettons
tu	mets	vous	mettez
il/elle/on	met	ils/elles	mettent

2. Note that **mettre** has various meanings.

Il met une chemise et une cravate pour aller au travail.
Les serveurs mettent la table au restaurant.
On met la télévision pour regarder un film.

FRENCH Online

For more information about shopping for clothing in the Francophone world, go to the Glencoe French Web site: french.glencoe.com

Continuons

Let's put our words together

13 **Qu'est-ce qu'on met?** Répondez. *(Answer.)*

1. Tu mets un survêtement quand tu fais du jogging?
2. Tu mets la table pour le dîner?
3. Ton père met la télé le matin pendant le petit déjeuner?
4. Ta mère met la radio pour écouter les informations?
5. Tes copains mettent une cravate pour aller à l'école?
6. Tes copines mettent une jupe plissée pour aller à l'école?

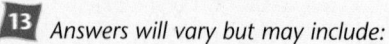

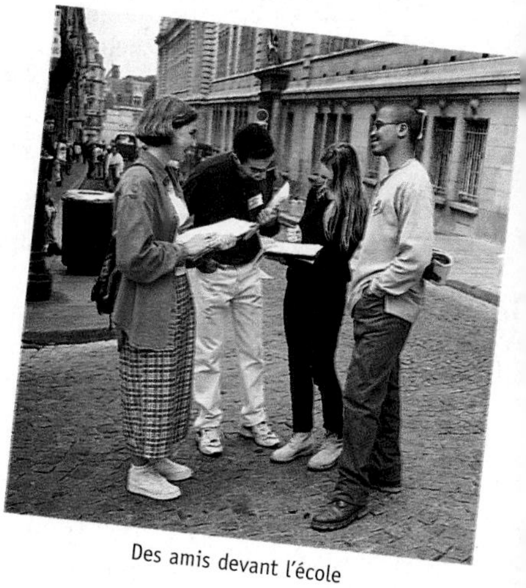

Des amis devant l'école

ANSWERS TO Continuons

13 *Answers will vary but may include:*

1. Oui, je mets un survêtement quand je fais du jogging.
2. Oui, je mets la table pour le dîner.
3. Non, mon père ne met pas la télé le matin pendant le petit déjeuner.
4. Oui, ma mère met la radio pour écouter les informations.
5. Non, mes copains ne mettent pas de cravate pour aller à l'école.
6. Oui, mes copines mettent une jupe plissée pour aller à l'école.

14 **Dans le sac à dos** Complétez avec **mettre** d'après les dessins.
(Complete with mettre *according to the illustrations.)*

1. Qu'est-ce qu'ils ____ dans leur sac à dos?
   Ils ______________.

2. Qu'est-ce que tu ____ dans ton sac à dos?
   Je ______________.

3. Qu'est-ce que vous ____ dans votre sac à dos?
   On ______________.

15 **Qu'est-ce que vous mettez?** Work with a classmate. Compare what you wear on different occasions.

- pour aller à l'école
- quand vous allez dîner chez des amis de vos parents
- pour aller au cinéma le samedi soir
- pour aller à un mariage
- pour aller dans un restaurant chic

Attention!

Pay particular attention to the spelling and pronunciation of the following adjectives. Note that the final consonant sound is pronounced in the feminine forms but not in the masculine forms.

Féminin	Masculin
sérieuse(s)	**sérieux**
longue(s)	**long(s)**
favorite(s)	**favori(s)**
blanche(s)	**blanc(s)**

Note that all forms of **cher—chère(s), cher(s)**—sound alike.

Complétez et prononcez.
(Complete and pronounce aloud.)

1. sérieux
   un élève ____ et une élève ____
2. long
   une jupe ____ et un manteau ____
3. favori
   mon pull ____ et ma robe ____
4. blanc
   une chemise ____ et un chemisier ____
5. long
   des pantalons ____ et des manches ____

ENCORE PLUS *For more practice using the verb* ***mettre****, do Activity 22 on page H23 at the end of this book.*

3 Practice

Continuons
Let's put our words together

13 You may wish to first do this activity with books closed and then again with books open.

14 Expand Activity 14 by using real clothing you put into a backpack.

Reteaching

Recycle **le couvert** vocabulary to practice the forms of **mettre:**

1. **Tu mets la table pour le dîner?**
2. **Il met les couteaux sur la table?**
3. **Toi et ta sœur, vous mettez les assiettes sur la table?**
4. **Tes frères mettent des serviettes sur la table?**

ENCORE PLUS This *infogap* activity will allow students to practice in pairs. The activity should be very manageable for them, since all vocabulary and structures are familiar to them.

Answers to Continuons

14
1. mettent, mettent des baskets
2. mets, mets un short blanc
3. mettez, met un pull vert (un sweat-shirt vert)

15 *Answers will vary but may include:*

—Pour aller à l'école je mets un polo, un jean et des baskets.
—Quand je vais dîner chez des amis de mes parents je mets un pantalon et une chemise…etc.

Answers to Attention!

1. sérieux, sérieuse
2. longue, long
3. favori, favorite
4. blanche, blanc
5. longs, longues

1 Preparation

Bellringer Review

Use the BRR Transparency 7.4 or write the following on the board.
Complete.
1. Mes amis ______ le petit déjeuner. (prendre)
2. Ils ______ du français. (faire)
3. Ils ______ au marché. (aller)
4. Ils ______ acheter de la viande. (vouloir)
5. Ils ______ à la boucherie. (aller)

2 Presentation

Le comparatif des adjectifs

Step 1 Lead students through Items 1–2 and the examples.

Step 2 Now have students make a list of words they know that can be used to describe people.

Step 3 Draw two stick figures on the board and name them. Using their list of adjectives, have students make up sentences comparing the two stick figures.

Step 4 Provide additional examples by comparing objects or students in the room. For example: **Regardez. Pierre est plus grand que Robert ou pas? (Oui, Pierre est plus grand que lui.)**

3 Practice

Continuons
Let's put our words together

16 Have students work in pairs. You may wish to extend the activity and have the students poll each other in groups of four to six and then report back their opinions. **(À notre avis…)**

Comparing people and things
Le comparatif des adjectifs

1. When you compare two or more people or things, you use **plus (+)… que, moins (−)… que,** and **aussi (=)… que.** Study the following chart.

Le jean est plus cher que le pantalon.
Le jean est aussi cher que le pantalon.
Le jean est moins cher que le pantalon.

Les sandales sont moins confortables que les baskets.
Mais elles sont plus confortables que les chaussures.

> **Attention!**
> Note the liaison with **plus** and **moins.**
> **plus‿intéressant(e)**
> **moins‿élégant(e)**

2. You use the stress pronouns **moi, toi, lui, elle, nous, vous, eux,** and **elles** after **que (qu')** when comparing people.

Elle est plus sympa que moi.
Elle est aussi sympa que lui.
Elle est moins sympa que vous.

Il est aussi intelligent que moi.
Mais il est plus intelligent qu'eux.

Continuons
Let's put our words together

16 À mon avis Donnez des réponses personnelles. *(Give your own answers.)*

1. Le français, c'est plus difficile ou plus facile que les maths?
2. Le professeur de français est plus strict, moins strict ou aussi strict que les autres professeurs?
3. Le football américain est plus amusant ou moins amusant que le basket-ball?
4. Ton école secondaire est plus grande ou moins grande que ton école primaire?
5. Ta classe de français est aussi grande ou plus petite que ta classe de sciences?

Answers to Continuons

16 *Answers will vary but may include:*
1. À mon avis, le français, (c')est plus facile que les maths.
2. À mon avis, le professeur de français est aussi strict que les autres professeurs.
3. À mon avis, le football américain est moins amusant que le basket-ball.
4. Mon école secondaire est plus grande que mon école primaire.
5. Ma classe de français est aussi grande que ma classe de sciences.

Reaching All Students

For the Younger Students After doing Activity 18 on page 231, younger students may wish to illustrate and label one or two comparisons they have made.

17 Plus ou moins que l'autre

Répondez d'après les dessins. Suivez le modèle. *(Answer according to the illustrations.)*

—Le blouson bleu est aussi grand que le blouson noir?
—Oui, le blouson bleu est aussi grand que le blouson noir.

1. Le blouson bleu est aussi cher que le blouson noir?
2. Le blouson bleu est moins beau que le blouson noir?
3. La jupe jaune est moins chère que la jupe grise?
4. La jupe grise est plus courte que la jupe jaune?

18 Ma famille et mes copains

Donnez des réponses personnelles. *(Give your own answers.)*

1. Ta sœur, elle est plus petite ou plus grande que toi? Tu es plus grand(e) ou plus petit(e) qu'elle?
2. Tu es plus patient(e) ou moins patient(e) que ton frère? Il est plus patient ou moins patient que toi?
3. Tes grands-parents sont aussi stricts que tes parents? Ils sont vraiment moins stricts qu'eux?
4. Tes copains sont plus sociables que toi? Tu es plus timide qu'eux?

19 Comparaisons

Work with a classmate. Compare people you know. You may want to use the following words.

grand · petit · sociable · intéressant · dynamique
amusant · beau · sympa · sérieux

Structure

17 After the students answer each question, you may wish to have them give all other possible answers based on their first one. For example: **2. Oui, le blouson bleu est moins beau que le blouson noir. (Non, le blouson bleu n'est pas moins beau que le blouson noir. Le blouson bleu est aussi beau que le blouson noir. Le blouson bleu est plus beau que le blouson noir.)** You may extend this activity using real items of clothing.

19 Students may also wish to compare famous people they admire.

Recycling

Activity 19 recycles and recombines the vocabulary from Chapter 1.

Assessment

As an informal assessment, you may wish to write the following words on the board:

un chien et un chat
le français et l'anglais
une boutique et un grand magasin
le prof d'anglais et le prof de biologie

Call on students to make up original sentences comparing these items.

Answers to Continuons

17

1. Non, le blouson bleu n'est pas aussi cher que le blouson noir. Le blouson bleu est moins cher que le blouson noir.
2. Oui, le blouson bleu est moins beau que le blouson noir. (Non, le blouson bleu n'est pas moins beau que le blouson noir. Le blouson bleu est aussi beau que le blouson noir. Le blouson bleu est plus beau que le blouson noir.)
3. Oui, la jupe jaune est moins chère que la jupe grise. (La jupe grise est plus chère que la jupe jaune).
4. Non, la jupe grise n'est pas plus courte que la jupe jaune. (La jupe jaune est plus courte que la jupe grise).

18 *Answers will vary but may include:*

1. Ma sœur est plus grande que moi. Je suis plus petit(e) qu'elle.
2. Je suis plus patient(e) que mon frère. Mon frère est moins patient que moi.
3. Mes grands-parents ne sont pas aussi stricts que mes parents. Oui, ils sont vraiment moins stricts qu'eux.
4. Mes copains sont plus sociables que moi. Oui, je suis plus timide qu'eux.

Structure

1 Preparation

Bellringer Review

Use BRR Transparency 7.5 or write the following on the board.
Make at least four comparisons between various members of your family.

2 Presentation

Les verbes **voir** et **croire**

Step 1 **Voir** and **croire** can be done quickly since there are only three oral forms.

Step 2 Have students read the information in the **Savez-vous que... ?** box. Give additional examples such as: **Je vois qu'il est avec Luc. Je crois qu'ils sont amis.** **Teaching Tip:** Point out to students that all forms of these verbs are pronounced the same except **vous** and **nous,** which is less important because of **on.**

3 Practice

Continuons
Let's put our words together

20 To emphasize that the questions refer to the plural "you," ask each question of two or more students who will answer the question together.

22 Be sure to have students use the appropriate form of **croire** depending upon the number of people working together. If students are working in pairs, the answer should be **Tu crois?** If they are working in groups of three or more, have two students make the statement and the third will ask **Vous croyez?**

Seeing and believing
Les verbes **voir** et **croire**

Study the forms of the verbs **voir** *(to see)* and **croire** *(to believe).*

VOIR		CROIRE	
je	vois	je	crois
tu	vois	tu	crois
il/elle/on	voit	il/elle/on	croit
nous	voyons	nous	croyons
vous	voyez	vous	croyez
ils/elles	voient	ils/elles	croient

Savez-vous que... ?

When **voir** and **croire** are followed by a clause, you must use **que (qu').**
Je vois que vous êtes content.
Je crois qu'il est content aussi.

Continuons
Let's put our words together

20 À votre avis Répondez que oui. *(Answer yes.)*

1. Vos parents croient que vous êtes intelligents?
2. Votre professeur de français croit que vous travaillez bien?
3. Vos camarades de classe croient que vous êtes sympathiques?
4. Vos grands-parents croient que vous êtes adorables?

21 Dans une boutique
Répondez que oui. *(Answer yes.)*

1. Tu vois des choses que tu aimes dans la vitrine?
2. Tu crois qu'on peut entrer dans la boutique?
3. Tu crois que tu vas acheter le pantalon noir?
4. Tu crois qu'ils vont avoir ta taille?
5. Tu vois le prix?

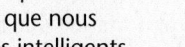

22 Vraiment? Conversez d'après le modèle. *(Make up a conversation according to the model.)*

—Il va bientôt arriver.
—Vous croyez?

1. Il va bientôt téléphoner.
2. Il va bientôt payer.
3. Il va bientôt rentrer.
4. Il va bientôt acheter une maison.

Answers to Continuons

20

1. Oui, nos parents croient que nous sommes intelligents.
2. Oui, notre professeur de français croit que nous travaillons bien.
3. Oui, nos camarades de classe croient que nous sommes sympathiques.
4. Oui, nos grands-parents croient que nous sommes adorables.

21

1. Oui, je vois des choses que j'aime dans la vitrine.
2. Oui, je crois qu'on peut entrer dans la boutique.
3. Oui, je crois que je vais acheter le pantalon noir.
4. Oui, je crois qu'ils vont avoir ma taille.
5. Oui, je vois le prix.

22

1. Il va bientôt téléphoner. Vous croyez? (Tu crois?)
2. Il va bientôt payer. Vous croyez? (Tu crois?)
3. Il va bientôt rentrer. Vous croyez? (Tu crois?)
4. Il va bientôt acheter une maison. Vous croyez? (Tu crois?)

23 **Des opinions différentes!** Complétez avec **croir.**
(Complete with croire.*)*

1. Il ____ que tout est moins cher pendant les soldes. Et vous, vous ____ ça aussi?
2. Julien ____ que l'examen va être facile, mais nous, on ____ qu'il va être difficile.
3. Tu ____ que les chats sont plus intelligents que les chiens, mais moi, je ____ que les chiens sont plus intelligents que les chats.
4. Alice ____ que Paris est près de Nice, mais nous, nous ____ que c'est loin de Nice.
5. Moi, je ____ que la cousine de Sandra est française, mais mes copains ____ qu'elle est italienne.

Attention!

Pay particular attention to the spelling of verbs that end in **-yer.**

ESSAYER	**j'essaie**	**nous essayons**
	tu essaies	**vous essayez**
	il essaie	**ils essaient**
PAYER	**je paie**	**nous payons**
	tu paies	**vous payez**
	il paie	**ils paient**

Complétez. *(Complete.)*

1. Vous ____ où? (payer)
2. On ____ à la caisse. (payer)
3. Je ____ parce que j'invite. (payer)
4. Il va ____ la chemise? (essayer)
5. Non, mais il ____ le pantalon. (essayer)

*For more practice using the verbs **voir** and **croire**, do Activity 23 on page H24 at the end of this book.*

Vous êtes sur le bon chemin. Allez-y!

Structure

About the French Language

The verbs **payer** and **essayer** can also be written with **y: je paye, j'essaye.**

Class Motivator

Qu'est-ce que tu vois?
Play "I Spy" using items in the room. The student describing a mystery item must use **voir,** and the student(s) guessing must use **croire** and **voir.** For example: **Je vois un petit objet jaune. (Je crois que tu vois un stylo-bille.) Non. (Je crois que tu vois un crayon.) Oui.**

ENCORE PLUS This *infogap* activity will allow students to practice in pairs. The activity should be very manageable for them, since all vocabulary and structures are familiar to them.

Allez-y!
At this point in the chapter, students have learned all the vocabulary and structure necessary to complete the chapter. The conversation and cultural readings that follow recycle all the material learned up to this point.

Answers to Continuons

23
1. croit, croyez
2. croit, croit
3. crois, crois
4. croit, croyons
5. crois, croient

Answers to Attention!

1. payez
2. paie
3. paie
4. essayer
5. essaie

1 Preparation

Resource Manager

Audio Activities Booklet TE, pages 92–93
Audiocassette 5A/CD 5
CD-ROM

Bellringer Review

Use BRR Transparency 7.6 or write the following on the board.
True or false?

1. **Les jeunes français qui ont douze ans vont au collège.**
2. **Les élèves américains portent une cravate à l'école.**
3. **Un lycée en France, c'est une *high school* aux États-Unis.**
4. **En France il y a classes trois jours par semaine.**

2 Presentation

Step 1 Have students open their books to page 234. Have them look at the photo and guess what the conversation is about.

Step 2 Have them watch the Conversation CD-ROM or listen to Audiocassette 5A/CD 5. Then have the class repeat the conversation after you or the audiocassette/CD. Call on two individuals to read it aloud with as much expression as possible.

Step 3 After presenting the conversation, go over the **Après la conversation** activity. If students can answer the questions with relative ease, move on. Students should not be expected to memorize the conversation.

Conversation

Dans une petite boutique

Vendeur: Bonjour, monsieur. Vous voulez voir quelque chose?
Fabien: Bonjour. Oui, je voudrais un jean, s'il vous plaît.
Vendeur: Oui, vous faites quelle taille?
Fabien: Je fais du 36.
Vendeur: Voilà un 36. La cabine d'essayage est juste là.
(Fabien essaie le jean dans la cabine d'essayage.)
Vendeur: Ça va, la taille?
Fabien: Pas vraiment. Je crois que c'est un peu petit.
Vendeur: Vous voulez la taille au-dessus?
Fabien: Oui, je veux bien.
(Fabien essaie l'autre jean.)
Fabien: Ah oui, c'est bien.
Vendeur: Vous désirez autre chose?
Fabien: Oui, un polo bleu marine ou blanc.
Vendeur: Vous avez de la chance. Ils sont en solde.

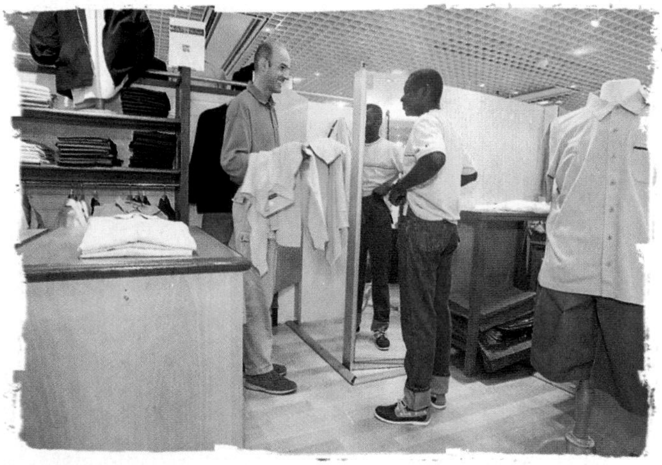

Après la conversation

Répondez. *(Answer.)*

1. À qui parle Fabien?
2. Qu'est-ce qu'il veut voir?
3. Il fait quelle taille?
4. Où est-ce qu'il essaie son jean?
5. Le jean est trop grand ou trop petit?
6. Il veut la taille au-dessus ou la taille au-dessous?
7. Il veut acheter autre chose?

Answers to Après la conversation

1. Fabien parle au vendeur.
2. Il veut voir un jean.
3. Il fait du 36.
4. Il essaie son jean dans la cabine d'essayage.
5. Le jean est trop petit.
6. Il veut la taille au-dessus.
7. Oui, il veut acheter un polo.

Glencoe Technology

CD-ROM

On the CD-ROM, students can watch a dramatization of this conversation. They can then play the role of either one of the characters and record themselves in the conversation.

Parlons un peu plus

Let's talk some more

A **Au magasin** Work with a classmate. Take turns playing the role of the salesperson and the customer in the following situations.

- **Au rayon des vêtements pour hommes** You want to buy a shirt as a gift for your father or a friend. They have his size but not the color you want.
- **Au rayon des chaussures** You are looking for a pair of brown shoes. The ones the salesperson shows you are quite expensive.

B **Jeu** **Qu'est-ce qu'il/elle porte?** Have one student leave the room while others choose a classmate to describe. The student who left comes back in and has to guess which classmate the others have chosen by asking questions about his or her clothes.

Prononciation

Les sons /sh/ et /zh/

It is important to make a distinction between the sounds **/sh/** as in **chat** and **/zh/** as in **joli.** Put your fingers on your throat. When you say the sound **/zh/** as in **joli,** you should feel a vibration, but not when you say **/sh/** as in **chat.** Repeat the following words with the sound **/sh/.**

acheter	**chaussure**	**chemise**
chemisier	**achat**	**short**

Now repeat the following words with the sound **/zh/.**

large	**jupe**	**orange**
beige	**joli**	

Now repeat the following sentences that combine both sounds.

J'achète toujours mes chaussures au marché.
Le t-shirt jaune est joli, mais le short orange est moins cher.

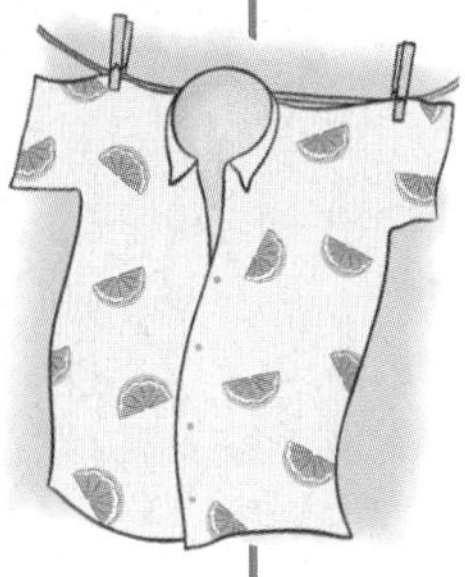

chemise orange

3 Practice

Parlons un peu plus

Let's talk some more

A Have students work in pairs. You may wish to supply students with real clothing props to use. After students have practiced their dialogues several times, you may wish to choose a pair of students to do this activity for the class.

B **Jeu** This activity is a good one to end class with.

Prononciation

Step 1 Model the key phrase **chemise orange** and have students repeat chorally.

Step 2 Now model the other words and phrases in similar fashion.

Step 3 You may wish to give students the following **dictée: Le short orange est plus large que le short beige.**

Answers to Parlons un peu plus

A **Au rayon des vêtements pour hommes** *Answers will vary depending upon the color and type of shirt students want to buy.*

Au rayon des chaussures *Answers will vary but may include:*
—Je voudrais des chaussures marron, s'il vous plaît.
—Et vous faites quelle pointure?
—Du 28.
—Voilà.
—C'est combien?
—Cent cinquante euros.
—C'est très cher.

Resource Manager

Audio Activities Booklet TE, pages 95–96
Audiocassette 5A/CD 5

Bellringer Review

Use BRR Transparency 7.7 or write the following on the board.

Complete.

1. **Je _____ (vouloir) faire les courses mais je ne _____ (pouvoir) pas parce que je n'_____ (avoir) pas le temps.**
2. **Il ne _____ (aller) pas à l'école à pied.**
3. **Il _____ (prendre) le car scolaire.**
4. **Ses amis _____ (prendre) le car scolaire aussi.**

National Standards

Cultures

This selection familiarizes students with several different types of clothes-shopping options that exist in France.

Comparisons

The readings make some comparisons between clothes shopping in France and in the United States.

Le Québec

Lectures culturelles

Reading Strategy

Scanning for specific information

Scanning for specific information means reading to find out certain details without concerning yourself with the other information in the passage. Some examples of scanning are searching a television listing to find out when certain programs are on or reading an ad to find out something specific, such as a store's hours.

On fait des courses où, à Paris?

Chez les grands couturiers[1]

Les noms des grands couturiers français—Yves Saint-Laurent, Dior, Cardin, Givenchy, Coco Chanel—sont célèbres dans le monde entier. On peut voir les boutiques élégantes des grands couturiers dans l'avenue Montaigne ou dans la rue du Faubourg-Saint-Honoré. C'est là que les gens aisés (riches) vont acheter leurs vêtements et accessoires.

Rue du Faubourg-Saint-Honoré, Paris

Magasin de la Samaritaine, Paris

Les petites boutiques et les grands magasins

Mais la plupart (la majorité) des Parisiens ne font pas leurs achats chez les grands couturiers. Partout à Paris, il y a de petites boutiques qui sont beaucoup moins chères que les boutiques des grands couturiers. Il y a aussi des grands magasins. À Paris, les grands magasins du Printemps et des Galeries Lafayette sont les plus renommés (célèbres). Il y a aussi des chaînes de magasins bon marché[2] comme le Prisunic.

Dans les grands magasins, on peut aller d'un rayon à un autre. Il y a souvent des articles en promotion[3] et deux fois par an il y a des soldes—début janvier et début juillet.

[1] grands couturiers *designers*
[2] bon marché *inexpensive*
[3] en promotion *on special*

Presentation

Pre-reading

Step 1 Ask students whether they spend their own money for clothes. Do they like malls? Why or why not?

Learning from Photos

(page 236 top) The **rue du Faubourg-Saint-Honoré** is a very elegant shopping street. Many of the **grands couturiers** have their boutiques here. *(page 236 bottom)* The Samaritaine department stores are very nice. They are not quite as upscale as the Galeries Lafayette.

Les marchés aux puces[4]

Les adolescents aiment bien aller aux puces. Ils y vont pendant le week-end parce que les marchés aux puces sont fermés[5] pendant la semaine.

Les marchés aux puces sont de grands marchés où on trouve de tout—des vêtements, de la nourriture, des tables, des chaises, etc. On peut trouver un vêtement ou un accessoire avec la griffe[6] d'un grand couturier très bon marché… ou très cher!

[4] marchés aux puces *flea markets*
[5] fermés *closed*
[6] griffe *label*

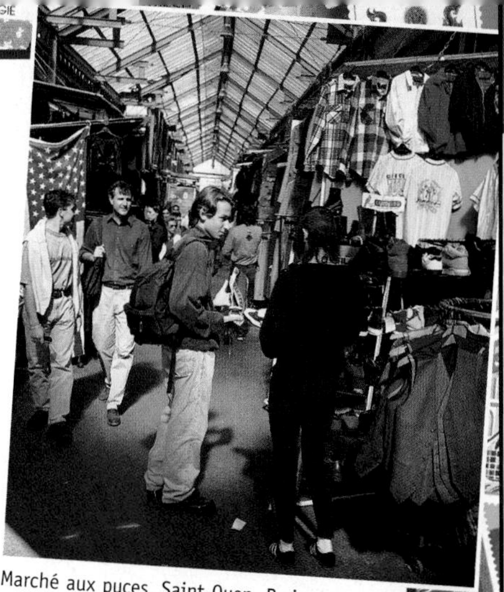

Marché aux puces, Saint-Ouen, Paris

Après la lecture

A Des informations Donnez les informations suivantes. *(Give the following information.)*

1. les noms de quelques grands couturiers français
2. les noms de quelques rues très élégantes à Paris
3. là où la plupart des Parisiens vont faire leurs achats
4. le nom d'un grand magasin parisien assez élégant
5. le nom d'une chaîne de magasins aux prix plus modestes
6. là où les adolescents aiment faire leurs achats

B Les achats Vrai ou faux? *(True or false?)*

1. La plupart des Parisiens font leurs achats chez les grands couturiers.
2. Les petites boutiques sont plus chères que les boutiques des grands couturiers.
3. Les Galeries Lafayette, c'est le nom d'un grand magasin à Paris.
4. Les grands magasins n'ont pas de soldes.
5. On va souvent au marché aux puces le lundi.
6. On peut acheter beaucoup de marchandises différentes dans un marché aux puces.

Marché aux puces, Nice

Lectures culturelles

Step 2 Share clothing ads from French magazines (***Elle, Marie-Claire, Homme,*** etc.) with students.

Step 3 Read and discuss the Reading Strategy on page 236. Have the students practice scanning for information by asking them to find the answers to questions 1 and 2, Activity A, page 237 before they begin their reading.

Reading

Step 1 Have students read the selection once quietly.

Teaching Tip: Adherence to preset time limits will encourage students to read all the material and not get "bogged down" and stop every time they think they don't know something. Encourage students to read for ideas, rather than word by word.

Step 2 Call on some students to read aloud individually. After a student has read half a paragraph, ask questions of other students to check comprehension.

Post-reading

Have students do the **Après la lecture** activities on page 237 orally after reading the selection in class. Then assign these activities to be written at home. Go over them again the following day.

Après la lecture

A Allow students to refer to the story to look up the answers or you may use this activity as a testing device for factual recall.

B Expansion: After doing Activity B, you may wish to have the students correct each statement that is false in the activity.

Answers to Après la lecture

A

1. Yves Saint-Laurent, Dior et Cardin
2. l'avenue Montaigne, la rue du Faubourg Saint-Honoré
3. des petites boutiques et les grands magasins
4. le Printemps, les Galeries Lafayette
5. Prisunic
6. les marchés aux puces

B

1. F
2. F
3. V
4. F
5. F
6. V

Learning from Photos

(page 237) The famous **marché aux puces de Saint-Ouen** is on the northern boundary of Paris. It is open on weekends and Mondays.

National Standards

Cultures
This selection familiarizes students with clothes and clothes shopping in French-speaking countries of Africa.

Learning from Photos

(page 238 top left) This photo is of the **souk** in Marrakech, Morocco. The **souk** is very often a covered market. Have students take note that the vendor is wearing Western clothes. The man is wearing a **djellaba.** The **djellaba** in Morocco very often has a hood as seen here. Most **djellabas** in Tunisia do not have a hood. It is also less common to see a man with his head covered in Tunisia than in Morocco. The woman is wearing a caftan.

The shoes in the photo are called **babouches,** a type of slipper seen frequently in the **Maghreb.** Both men and women wear **babouches.** Men's **babouches** are often plain white, while women's are often decorated with embroidery. In their home many people take off their shoes and go barefoot.

The **sifsari** worn by Tunisian women resembles a cloak or shawl. Its loose folds wrap around the woman's head and shoulders. The **sifsari** is very practical, as it can be pulled across the face, which protects the person from the wind or sand that blows in from the desert.

(page 238 bottom left) The **boubou** is worn by both men and women in West Africa. A woman's elegant **grand boubou** is a long, regal floor-length dress, often embroidered.

Lecture supplémentaire 1

Les vêtements

En Afrique du Nord

Dans les pays du Maghreb (le Maroc, l'Algérie et la Tunisie), beaucoup de gens[1] vont dans les souks pour acheter leurs vêtements. Un souk est un grand marché, souvent situé dans la médina, le vieux quartier d'une ville arabe. Dans les pays du Maghreb, beaucoup d'hommes portent un pull et un jean. Beaucoup de femmes portent une jupe et un chemisier. Mais on voit souvent des vêtements plus traditionnels. On voit des hommes qui portent une djellaba, par exemple. En Tunisie, beaucoup de femmes ont un sifsari. Le sifsari est un type de voile[2]. Le sifsari n'a pas de signification religieuse.

Deux hommes en djellaba, Tunisie

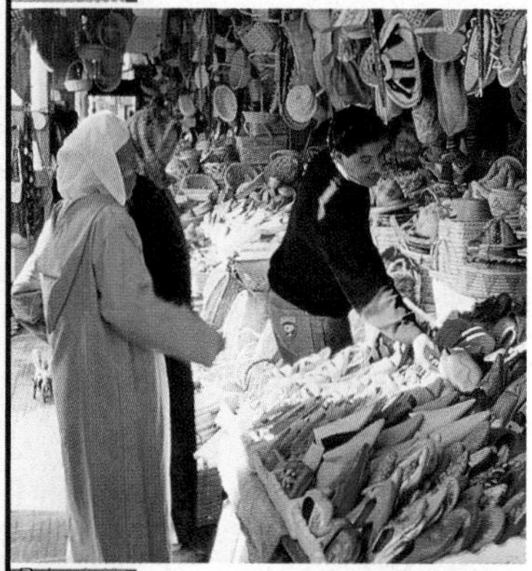

Un souk, Marrakech, Maroc

En Afrique Occidentale

Dans les pays d'Afrique Occidentale, les femmes portent souvent un boubou. Un boubou est une longue tunique ample. Les boubous sont très jolis. Les hommes aussi portent un boubou. Ils portent un boubou par-dessus[3] un pantalon et une chemise.

[1] gens *people*
[2] voile *veil*
[3] par-dessus *on top of, over*

Deux femmes en boubou, Sénégal

Après la lecture

Quel est le mot? Identifiez le mot. *(Identify the word.)*

1. un marché arabe
2. le vieux quartier d'une ville arabe
3. un vêtement masculin des pays du Maghreb
4. un type de voile tunisien
5. un vêtement porté par les hommes et les femmes en Afrique Occidentale

Answers to Après la lecture

1. un souk
2. la médina
3. une djellaba
4. un sifsari
5. un boubou

Lecture supplémentaire 2

Les tailles

En France et dans les autres pays d'Europe, les pointures et les tailles ne sont pas les mêmes qu'aux États-Unis. Voici des tableaux qui indiquent les correspondances.

FEMMES					
Chaussures					
États-Unis	6	7	8	9	
France	36	37	38	39	
Robes, Tailleurs, Pulls, Chemisiers					
États-Unis	6	8	10	12	14
France	38	40	42	44	46

HOMMES					
Chaussures					
États-Unis	9	10	11	12	
France	40	41	42	43	
Chemises					
États-Unis	$14\frac{1}{2}$	15	$15\frac{1}{2}$	16	$16\frac{1}{2}$
France	37	38	39	40	41

Si vous trouvez des chaussures que vous aimez et que vous voulez acheter, vous allez demander quelle pointure?

Si vous voyez une chemise ou un chemisier que vous voulez acheter, vous allez demander quelle taille?

Après la lecture

Moi Donnez des réponses personnelles.
(Give your own answers.)

1. Vous êtes en France. Vous voulez des chaussures. Vous faites quelle pointure?
2. Vous voulez une chemise ou un chemisier. Quelle est votre taille?

Attention!

This reading is optional. You may skip it completely, have the entire class read it, have only several students read it and report to the class, or assign it for extra credit.

Presentation

Step 1 Before doing the reading, have students make up a chart of their clothing and shoe sizes using the American system. Tell them to leave space between items—they will be making additions to their chart.

Step 2 Have students read the selection silently and study the chart. Beside each of their American sizes, have them write the equivalent European size. If their size isn't in the chart, they should extrapolate.

Step 3 Now have students answer the questions of the **Après la lecture** activity. You may wish to have students check labels on their athletic shoes. Many popular brands give both American and European sizes.

Answers to Après la lecture

Answers will vary but may include:

1. Je fais du 38.
2. Je fais du 42.

National Standards

Connections
This reading about poetry in the French-speaking world establishes a connection with another discipline, allowing students to reinforce and further their knowledge of literature through the study of French.

Attention!

The readings in the **Connexions** section are optional. They focus on some of the major disciplines taught in schools and universities. The vocabulary is useful for discussing such topics as history, literature, art, economics, business, science, etc. You may choose any of the following ways to do the readings in the **Connexions** sections.

Independent reading Have students read the selections and do the post-reading activities as homework, which you collect. This option is least intrusive on class time and requires a minimum of teacher involvement.

Homework with in-class follow-up Assign the readings and post-reading activities as homework. Review and discuss the material in class the next day.

Intensive in-class activity This option includes a pre-reading vocabulary presentation, in-class reading and discussion, assignment of the activities for homework, and a discussion of the assignment in class the following day.

CONNEXIONS

Les lettres

La poésie

A poem is a literary piece most often written in verse. The poet uses images, meter, rhythm, and sounds to evoke or suggest ideas, sensations, and emotions in the reader. Many poets say a great deal in very few words. The poem we are about to read by the French poet Apollinaire is an example.

Apollinaire (1880–1918)

Guillaume Apollinaire a une vie[1] bohème. Sa poésie reflète sa vie. Il visite beaucoup de pays européens. Les mouvements intellectuels et artistiques de son époque intéressent Apollinaire. C'est une période (avant la guerre[2] de 1914) très riche en idées. Les poètes et les artistes peintres échangent leurs nouvelles idées. Apollinaire discute ses idées avec son bon ami, le peintre Picasso.

Apollinaire est un des premiers grands poètes modernes français. Certains de ses poèmes sont des calligrammes. Le poème a la forme de l'objet que le poète décrit[3]. Le poème «La cravate» est un exemple de calligramme.

[1] vie *life*
[2] guerre *war*
[3] décrit *describes*

Pablo Picasso

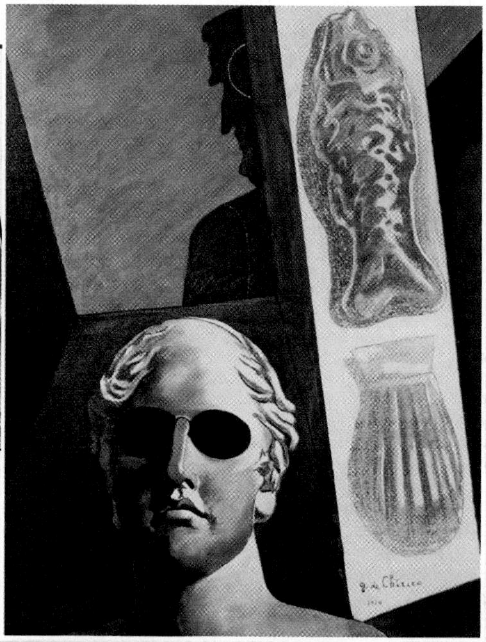

Giorgio de Chirico *Guillaume Apollinaire*

Reaching All Students

Additional Practice Bring in a copy of **Calligrammes** and share some of the other poems, such as **"Le jet d'eau"** with your students.

L A C R A V A T E
DOU
LOU
REUSE°
QUE TU
PORTES
ET QUI T'
ORNE Ô CI
VILISÉ
ÔTE- TU VEUX
LA° BIEN
SI RESPI
RER°

douloureuse *painful*

ôte-la *take it off*

respirer *breathe*

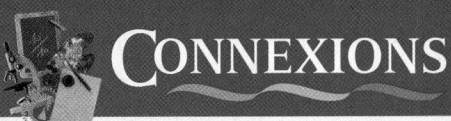

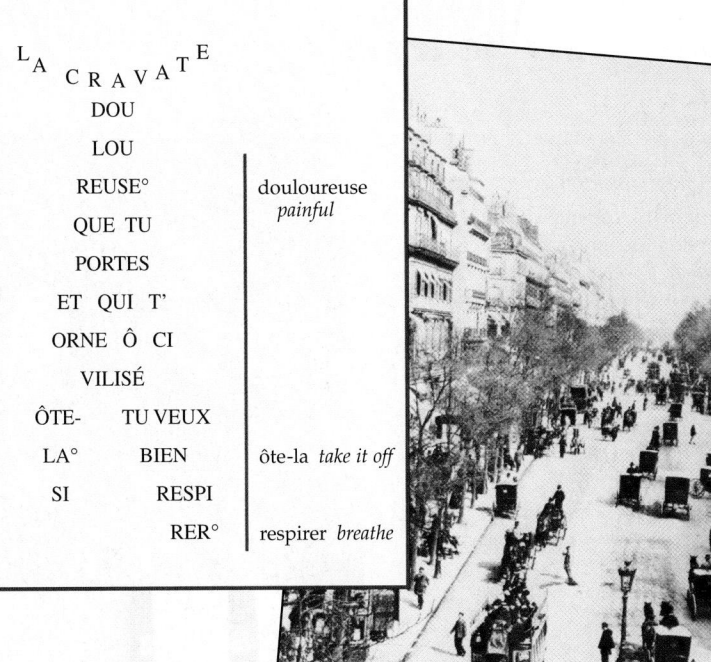

Paris vers 1900

Après la lecture

A Mes idées Répondez. *(Answer.)*

1. Si tu es un garçon, tu aimes mettre une cravate?
2. Si tu es une fille, tu trouves que c'est une bonne idée d'obliger un garçon à porter une cravate?
3. Apollinaire aime les cravates?
4. Il croit qu'on peut bien respirer si on porte une cravate?
5. Il croit que l'homme civilisé porte une cravate?

B Explication du texte Explain in English Apollinaire's ideas and tell whether you agree with him.

CONNEXIONS

Presentation

Les lettres
La poésie

Step 1 Have students read the introduction in English on page 240.

Step 2 Tell students they are going to read about a famous poet who had a very interesting life. Have students read the selection quickly or have them skim it.

Step 3 Go over the many cognates that appear in the biographical introduction.

Step 4 Have students read the biography silently, then look at the poem to figure out the order in which the words should be read.

Step 5 Read the poem to the class, then have students read it silently.

Step 6 Have students tell you the message they get from the poem.

Après la lecture

A Have students preview the questions and prepare to answer them orally.

B You may wish to have students write their response to this question.

Literature Connection

Apollinaire (1880–1918) was born of an Italian father and a Polish mother. He studied in lycées in Cannes and Nice. He revolutionized French poetry inventing new forms such as **poèmes conversations** and **calligrammes.** Some of his poems deal with themes such as modern art, and modern city life. He often omitted all punctuation from his poems. His poetic experimentation inspired surrealist poets like André Breton and Paul Éluard.

Answers to Après la lecture

A *Answers will vary but may include:*

1. Non, je n'aime pas mettre de cravate.
2. Non, ce n'est pas une bonne idée d'obliger un garçon à porter une cravate.
3. Non, il n'aime pas les cravates.
4. Non, il croit qu'on ne peut pas bien respirer si on porte une cravate.
5. Non, il croit que l'homme civilisé ne porte pas de cravate.

B *Answers will vary.*

Reaching All Students

For the Younger Students
Students may enjoy making a **mini-calligramme** of their own. Instead of a poem, students choose a vocabulary word, which they will rewrite in a form or shape that illustrates the word's meaning.

C'est à vous

Use what you have learned

Bellringer Review

Use BRR Transparency 7.8 or write the following on the board.
Use these cues to write a conversation that might take place in a department store.
1. greet the salesperson
2. say what you are looking for
3. give the size, color and style of an article of clothing
4. ask how much it is

Recycling

These activities allow students to use the vocabulary and structure from this chapter in completely open-ended, real-life situations.

Learning from Photos

(page 242) Ouagadougou, the capital of Burkina Faso, is very relaxed with lovely bicycle paths and an attractively landscaped central market, something quite unusual in West Africa. Ouagadougou is the capital of African film. The nine-day Pan-African film festival, FESPACO, is held every odd year at the end of February. It has become a major cultural event that attracts celebrities from around the world. Three famous **Burkinabé** filmmakers who enjoy international reputations are Idrissa Ouedraogo, Souleymane Cissé, and Gaston Kaboré. In the even-numbered years, this film festival is held in Tunis.

C'est à vous

Use what you have learned

PARLER

1 **Une fête**

✔ *Identify and describe articles of clothing*

You are talking with a friend after school. You are both invited to a party, but you don't know what to wear. Discuss what kind of a party it is and what would be appropriate.

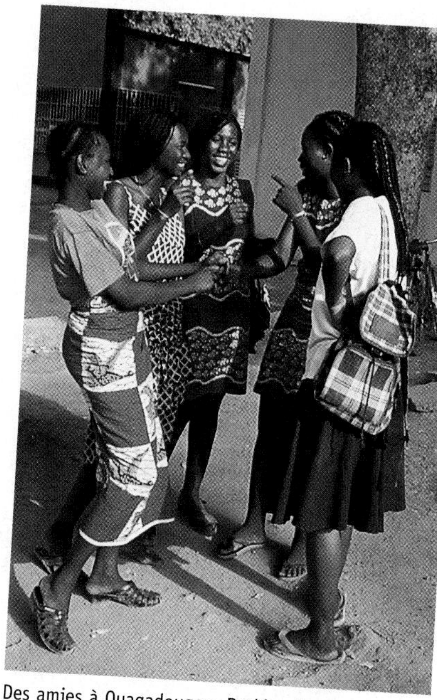

Des amies à Ouagadougou, Burkina Faso

PARLER

2 **Un nouveau look**

✔ *State your color and style preferences in clothes*

You and your partner have decided that you are going to change your style of clothes. Discuss what the new "you" is going to look like.

PARLER / ÉCRIRE

3 **Des cadeaux**

✔ *Shop for clothing*

You have just spent a few weeks in France and want to buy some gifts for family and friends back home. Make a list of what you want to buy. Go to different stores to buy the items you want. With a classmate, take turns being the customer and salesperson at the stores where you are purchasing the items on your list.

Answers to C'est à vous

1 *Answers will vary but may include:*

—Combien d'amis vont aller à la fête?
— Vingt, je crois....
—Alors, c'est une grande fête! Je ne vais pas mettre un t-shirt, un short et des baskets. Je vais mettre des vêtements habillés!
—Moi, aussi. Je vais mettre des vêtements très habillés: un jean, un polo et des sandales.
—Ce n'est pas habillé! C'est sport.
—Pour moi un jean, un polo et des sandales, c'est très habillé.

2 *Answers will vary.*

Students can use all the clothing vocabulary they know. Encourage them to be creative.

C'est à vous

ÉCRIRE

4 On commande des vêtements.

✔ *Order clothing from a catalogue and give color preferences and size*

You want to order from the catalogue to the right. Write a letter stating which items you want, what color, what size.

ÉCRIRE

5 Le catalogue

✔ *Write descriptions of clothing*

Write five descriptions for an online clothing catalogue. Describe the items, tell the sizes they come in, the colors, the occasions they could be worn for, and the prices.

REVUE DE DETAILS
NEWS MODE
Repéré aux quatre coins de la mode, tout ce qui nous plaît. De la tête aux pieds.
Coloris: noir, beige.
Tailles: du 36 au 40 pour la femme; du 40 au 45 pour l'homme.
modèle femme du 36 au 40 76,07 €
modèle homme du 40 au 45 76,07 €
l'une 15,23 €
Chemise 77% viscose, 23% polyester.
Coloris assortis. Du 37/38 au 43/44.
l'une 15,23 €
Cravate 100% soie. Coloris assortis.
(1) Robe en velours (150 €, 5 tailles, 8 coloris).
(2) Veste sur jupe en taffetas de soie (75 €, 3 tailles, 5 coloris (veste) et 150 €, du 36 au 42, en noir ou bronze (jupe)).

Writing Strategy

Clustering Most writers brainstorm ideas before they begin to write. The next logical step is to "cluster" these ideas. This is done by writing down your main ideas and drawing a box around each one. Then draw a line indicating which ideas are connected to each other. Once you do this, it is easy to add other details to each cluster of ideas. When beginning to write, sort out your clusters and present each in a logical and organized paragraph.

Quel est leur look?

ÉCRIRE

6 Le look de ton école

Write a note to your French friend describing **le look** at your school. Tell him or her what boys and girls usually wear to school and what types of clothing and colors are "in" **(à la mode).**

Answers to C'est à vous

4 *Answers will vary but may include:*

Je voudrais commander une chemise bleue. Je fais du 40. Je voudrais aussi des sandales noires—modèle homme. Je fais du 42.
Mon ADRESSE

5 *Answers will vary but may include the following.*

Idéales pour les grandes fêtes
Robes habillées
Manches longues
Coloris assortis
Petites et grandes tailles
125 €

Reaching All Students

For the Younger Students

- Have groups create a poster advertising a sale, a special designer collection, or a fashion show. They should use shopping vocabulary, colors, and the comparative of adjectives.
- Have students make collages using magazine photos, advertisements, fabrics, etc. Then have them describe their collages.
- Set up a clothing store in the room, using items of clothing or pictures from magazines. Have pairs of students make up skits between a salesperson and a customer buying a gift.

Writing Strategy

Clustering Have students read the Writing Strategy on page 243. If students have difficulty thinking of words to describe the styles at their school, have them use the vocabulary list on page 246.

National Standards

Communities
Students have learned some interesting information on modes of dress among peoples in different areas of the French-speaking world. Have students put together all the information they have learned about dress. Have them add any additional information based on anything they have learned elsewhere.

Reaching All Students

Additional Practice Display Communication Transparency C 7. Have students work in groups of five to create the conversations illustrated on the transparency. Have groups present their conversations to the class.

Resource Manager

Communication Transparencies
Quizzes
Test Booklet
ExamView Pro®
Situation Cards
Performance Assessment
Marathon mental Videoquiz

Assessment

This is a pre-test for students to take before you administer the chapter test. Answer sheets for students to do these pages are provided in your transparency binder. Note that each section is cross-referenced so students can easily find the material they have to review in case they made errors. You may wish to collect these assessments and correct them yourself or you may prefer to have the students correct themselves in class. You can go over the answers orally or project them on the overhead, using your Assessment Answers transparencies.

Assessment

Vocabulaire

To review ***Mots 1****, turn to pages 220–221.*

1 Identifiez. *(Identify.)*

1. 
2. 
3. 
4. 

To review ***Mots 2****, turn to pages 224–225.*

2 Complétez. *(Complete.)*

5. —_____, le pantalon?
—Non, il est trop grand.
6. —Vous faites quelle ____?
—Je fais du 38, pour les chemises.
7. —De quelle ____ est la jupe?
—Elle est grise.
8. —Le jean est trop petit.
—Je voudrais la taille ____.

Structure

To review the verb ***mettre****, turn to page 228.*

3 Complétez avec «mettre». *(Complete with* mettre.*)*

9. Les garçons ne ____ pas de cravate pour aller à l'école.
10. Après le dîner je ____ la télé.
11. Qu'est-ce que vous ____ quand vous faites du jogging?
12. Qu'est-ce que tu ____ dans ton sac à dos?

To review the forms of these adjectives, turn to page 229.

4 Complétez. *(Complete.)*

13. C'est ma boutique ____. (favori)
14–15. La chemise est ____ et le pantalon est ____ aussi. (blanc)
16. Elle met une robe ____. (long)

Answers to Assessment

1

1. Un blouson bleu et rouge
2. Un pull bleu (bleu clair)
3. Une jupe verte
4. Un complet gris

2

5. Ça va
6. taille
7. couleur
8. au-dessus

3

9. mettent
10. mets
11. mettez
12. mets

4

13. favorite
14. blanche
15. blanc
16. longue

5 Complétez. *(Complete.)*

17. —Jean est très sympa.
—Oui. Mais il n'est pas ___ sympa ___ toi.
18. —Ce jean ne coûte pas cher.
—Non, il est ___ cher ___ les autres.
19. —Les deux frères sont très intelligents.
—C'est vrai. Paul est ___ intelligent ___ Loïc.

To review the comparative of adjectives, turn to page 230.

6 Récrivez chaque phrase. *(Rewrite each sentence.)*

20. Je crois que oui.
Vous ___.
21. Elle voit de jolies chaussures dans la vitrine.
Elles ___.
22. Vous voyez ça?
Tu ___?

*To review the verbs **voir** and **croire**, turn to page 232.*

Culture

7 Vrai ou faux? *(True or false?)*

23. Les boutiques des grands couturiers sont très chères.
24. Un grand magasin a beaucoup de rayons différents.
25. On trouve les marchés aux puces dans les quartiers élégants de Paris.

To review this cultural information, turn to pages 236–237.

La boutique d'un grand couturier, Paris

Assessment

Glencoe Technology

MINDJOGGER

You may wish to help your students prepare for the chapter test by playing the MindJogger game show. Teams will compete against each other to review chapter vocabulary and structure and sharpen listening comprehension skills.

Learning from Photos

(page 245) Have students answer the questions about the photo:

1. **Qu'est-ce que tu vois dans la vitrine?**
2. **Les robes sont sport ou habillées?**
3. **Tu trouves que les robes sont belles?**
4. **Les robes sont de quelles couleurs?**
5. **Tu trouves que les robes sont chères? Pourquoi?**

Answers to Assessment

5

17. aussi, que (plus, que)
18. moins, que
19. plus, que (aussi, que)

6

20. Vous croyez que oui.
21. Elles voient de jolies chaussures dans la vitrine.
22. Tu vois ça?

7

23. V
24. V
25. F

Vocabulaire

Vocabulary Review

The words and phrases in the **Vocabulaire** have been taught for productive use in this chapter. They are summarized here as a resource for both student and teacher. This list also serves as a convenient resource for the **C'est à vous** activities on pages 242–243. There are approximately sixteen cognates in this vocabulary list. Have students find them.

Attention!

You will notice that the vocabulary list here is not translated. This has been done intentionally, since we feel that by the time students have finished the material in the chapter they should be familiar with the meanings of all the words. If there are several words they still do not know, we recommend that they refer to the **Mots 1** and **2** sections in the chapter or go to the dictionaries at the back of this book to find the meanings. However, if you prefer that your students have the English translations, please refer to Vocabulary Transparency 7.1, where you will find all these words listed with their translations.

Vocabulaire

Identifying articles of clothing

les vêtements *(m. pl.)*	une veste	un polo	une basket
un jean	un pantalon	un manteau	une chaussure
un short	un t-shirt	un anorak	une chaussette
une casquette	une sandale	un blouson	
un pull	un sweat-shirt	un survêtement	

Identifying men's clothing

une chemise
une cravate
un complet

Identifying women's clothing

une jupe plissée	une robe
un chemisier	un tailleur

How well do you know your vocabulary?

- Choose words that describe an outfit you would like to have.
- Describe your shopping trip to look for the outfit.

Shopping

une boutique	un vendeur	cher (chère)	trouver
un centre commercial	une vendeuse	faire des courses	mettre
un grand magasin	un rayon	essayer	
une vitrine	des soldes *(m. pl.)*	entrer (dans)	
une cabine d'essayage	le prix	porter	

Describing clothes

large	sport	à manches	la pointure
serré(e)	joli(e)	longues	la taille
habillé(e)	favori(te)	courtes	au-dessus
			au-dessous

Identifying colors

De quelle couleur?	noir(e)	rouge	marron
blanc(he)	gris(e)	beige	orange
brun(e)	bleu(e)	rose	
vert(e)	jaune	bleu marine	

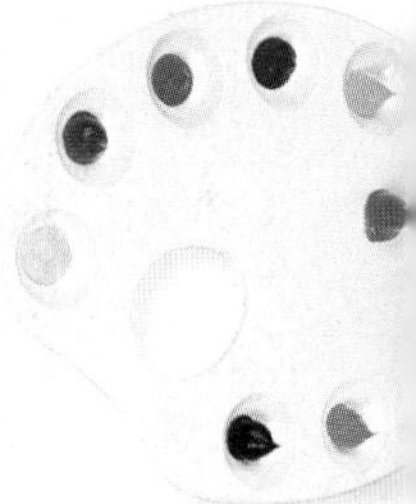

Other useful words and expressions

Vous faites quelle taille?	en solde	voir
Je fais du 40.	à mon avis	croire

Technotour

BON VOYAGE!

VIDÉO • Épisode 7

Avant de visionner

In this video episode, Christine and Chloé organize a fashion show featuring Chloé's designs.

Christine et Chloé veulent acheter une robe.

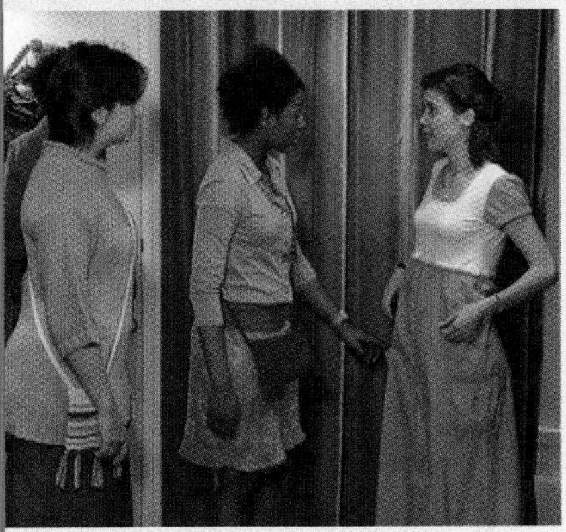

Chloé essaie une robe.

FRENCH ONLINE

À découvrir

Learn more about the world of fashion in Paris online.

Un défilé de mode à Paris

FRENCH Online

In the Chapter 7 Internet activity, you will have a chance to learn more about clothing and shopping in the Francophone world. To begin your virtual adventure, go to the Glencoe French Web site:
french.glencoe.com

Technotour

Overview

This page previews two key multimedia components of the **Glencoe French** series. Each reinforces the material taught in the chapter in a unique manner.

VIDÉO

The Video Program allows students to see how the chapter vocabulary and structures are used by native speakers. For maximum reinforcement, show the video episode as a final activity for Chapter 7.

The two photos on the left show highlights from the chapter 7 video episode. Discuss the photos with your students before having them view the episode. See the Video Activities Booklet for detailed suggestions for using this resource.

FRENCH Online

- The **À découvrir** photo shows a Paris fashion show. Students can go online to learn more about the world of fashion in Paris.
- Teacher Information and Student Worksheets for this activity can be accessed at the Web site.

Video Synopsis

In this video episode, students become aware of the wide variety of shops in Paris, from the **grands magasins** to small boutiques. Chloé and Christine visit a boutique and purchase some new clothes with help from the salesclerk. The two girls then put on a fashion show in the streets of Paris.

Preview

This section reviews the salient points from Chapters 5–7. In the **Conversation,** students will review **aller** + infinitive, irregular verbs, and food and clothing vocabulary. In the **Structure** sections, they will review the present tense of irregular verbs, the partitive, and the comparative structures.

Resource Manager

Workbook, Self-Test pages 75–78
Test Booklet

Presentation

Conversation

Step 1 Have students open their books to page 248. Call on two students to read this short conversation aloud.

Step 2 Go over the activity in the **Après la conversation** section.

Learning from Photos

(page 248 bottom) This photo shows a part of the main Galeries Lafayette building on the boulevard Haussmann in Paris.

Paired Activity

Have students work together in pairs to make up their own conversations about food shopping, food preparation, clothing shopping. Have several pairs present their conversation to the class.

Révision

Conversation

Faire la cuisine!

Julie: Tu vas préparer le déjeuner?
Miéna: Moi? Préparer le déjeuner? Tu rigoles! Je déteste faire la cuisine.
Julie: Tu veux aller au resto, alors?
Miéna: Non, je ne peux pas. Je n'ai pas le temps. Je vais manger une tranche de pizza.
Julie: Tu n'as pas le temps d'aller au resto? Pourquoi?
Miéna: Je veux acheter quelque chose pour samedi. Je vais à une fête chez une amie.
Julie: Qu'est-ce que tu vas acheter?
Miéna: Je crois que je vais acheter une robe.
Julie: Près de chez moi, il y a des soldes dans une petite boutique sympa.
Miéna: Merci, mais je vais aller aux Galeries. Je trouve toujours quelque chose là.

Galeries Lafayette, Paris

Après la conversation

Répondez. *(Answer.)*

1. Miéna va préparer le déjeuner?
2. Elle aime faire la cuisine?
3. Elle veut aller déjeuner au restaurant?
4. Elle ne peut pas aller au restaurant?
5. Qu'est-ce qu'elle va manger?
6. Qu'est-ce qu'elle veut acheter?
7. Elle va où samedi?
8. Elle va aller dans quel magasin?

Answers to Après la conversation

1. Non, elle ne va pas préparer le déjeuner.
2. Non, elle déteste faire la cuisine.
3. Non, elle ne veut pas aller déjeuner au restaurant.
4. Non, elle ne peut pas aller au restaurant.
5. Elle va manger une tranche de pizza.
6. Elle veut acheter une robe.
7. Samedi elle va à une fête.
8. Elle va aller aux Galeries Lafayette.

Reaching All Students

Additional Practice You may wish to ask students personalized questions about their food and clothing habits. For example: **Qu'est-ce que tu aimes manger? Qu'est-ce que tu prends pour le petit déjeuner? Qu'est-ce que tu portes aujourd'hui? Tu aimes mettre des vêtements habillés? Tu mets une robe/un complet pour aller à l'école? Tu achètes tes vêtements où?**

Structure

Les verbes irréguliers au présent

1. Review the following irregular verbs.

ALLER	je vais, tu vas, il/elle/on va, nous‿allons, vous‿allez, ils/elles vont
PRENDRE	je prends, tu prends, il/elle/on prend, nous prenons, vous prenez, ils/elles prennent
FAIRE	je fais, tu fais, il/elle/on fait, nous faisons, vous faites, ils/elles font
POUVOIR	je peux, tu peux, il/elle/on peut, nous pouvons, vous pouvez, ils/elles peuvent
VOULOIR	je veux, tu veux, il/elle/on veut, nous voulons, vous voulez, ils/elles veulent
METTRE	je mets, tu mets, il/elle/on met, nous mettons, vous mettez, ils/elles mettent
CROIRE	je crois, tu crois, il/elle/on croit, nous croyons, vous croyez, ils/elles croient
VOIR	je vois, tu vois, il/elle/on voit, nous voyons, vous voyez, ils/elles voient

2. Note that for all the preceding verbs except **aller,** the three singular forms sound alike. For all these verbs except **faire,** the **nous** and **vous** stems are the same.

CHAPITRES 5–7

Presentation

Les verbes irréguliers au présent

Step 1 Quickly go over the verb paradigms that appear here.

Step 2 You may also write all the verbs except **aller** on the board and underline the endings. Have students pronounce each form after you. Repeat the **je, tu, il/elle/on** forms, emphasizing that they are all pronounced the same way in spite of their spelling differences.

Révision

Learning from Photos

(page 250 top) You may wish to ask the following questions about the photo: **C'est quel grand magasin? C'est quel rayon? Il y a beaucoup de clients au rayon des vêtements pour femmes? Qui travaille dans le magasin?**

Presentation

Les contractions au et du

Step 1 Review the information regarding contractions. Have students repeat the examples after you.

Reaching All Students

Additional Practice Have students make up original sentences with **à** and or **de** using the following words:

le collège	**le magasin**
le lycée	**la papeterie**
l'école	**la caisse**
la maison	**le marché**
le café	**la boulangerie**
le restaurant	**la boucherie**
la cantine	

1 Historiette On fait des courses. Répondez d'après les indications. *(Answer according to the cues.)*

1. Tu vas aller où? (aux Galeries Lafayette)
2. Qu'est-ce que tu vas faire? (acheter un cadeau)
3. Qu'est-ce que tu veux acheter? (une chemise blanche)
4. C'est pour qui, la chemise? (mon père)
5. Il fait quelle taille? (du 39)
6. Tu vois un chemisier pour ta mère? (oui)
7. Qui met le chemisier dans un sac? (le vendeur)

Galeries Lafayette, Paris

2 Historiette À l'école Mettez au pluriel. *(Make the sentences plural.)*

1. Je vais à l'école.
2. Je prends le car pour aller à l'école.
3. Je veux poser une question.
4. L'élève peut poser des questions.
5. Sandrine croit qu'elle a la bonne réponse.
6. Elle prend ses cahiers.

Des pâtisseries

Les contractions **au** et **du**

The prepositions **à** and **de** contract with **le** to form **au** and **du,** and with **les** to form **aux** and **des.**

à + le = au	**Il va au collège.**
à + les = aux	**Le prof parle aux élèves.**
de + le = du	**Il rentre du collège.**
de + les = des	**Il parle des élèves.**

3 Où? Répondez d'après les indications. *(Answer according to the cues.)*

1. On achète des tartes où? (pâtisserie)
2. Et du saucisson? (charcuterie)
3. Et de l'eau minérale? (épicerie)
4. Et du poisson? (marché)
5. On parle a qui au marché? (marchands)

Answers to Révision

1

1. Je vais aller aux Galeries Lafayette.
2. Je vais acheter un cadeau.
3. Je veux acheter une chemise blanche.
4. La chemise est pour mon père.
5. Il fait du 39.
6. Oui, je vois un chemisier pour ma mère.
7. Le vendeur met le chemisier dans un sac.

2

1. Nous allons à l'école.
2. Nous prenons le car pour aller à l'école.
3. Nous voulons poser une question.
4. Les élèves peuvent poser des questions.
5. Elles croient qu'elles ont la bonne réponse.
6. Elles prennent leurs cahiers.

3

1. On achète des tartes à la pâtisserie.
2. On achète du saucisson à la charcuterie.
3. On achète de l'eau minérale à l'épicerie.
4. On achète du poisson au marché.
5. On parle aux marchands.

Révision

4 **D'où?** Complétez en utilisant **de** + un article défini. *(Answer with* de + *a definite article.)*

1. Mon frère rentre ____ lycée.
2. Mon autre frère rentre ____ collège.
3. Ma sœur rentre ____ école.
4. Mon autre sœur rentre ____ cantine.
5. Nous parlons tous ____ professeurs.

Le partitif

1. Remember that the partitive, "some," "any," is expressed in French by **de** + the definite article. **De** contracts with **le** to form **du** and with **les** to form **des.** In the negative, **du, de la, de l',** and **des** all become **de** or **d'.**

Je veux de l'argent.	**Je ne veux pas d'argent.**
J'ai des croissants.	**Je n'ai pas de croissants.**

2. Remember that **un** and **une** also become **de** or **d'** after a negative expression.

Tu veux un couteau?	**Tu ne veux pas de couteau?**
J'ai une serviette.	**Je n'ai pas de serviette.**

5 **Dans le chariot** Dites ce qu'il y a dans le chariot. *(Tell what is in the cart.)*

6 **Pas dans le chariot** Dites ce qu'il n'y a pas dans le chariot de l'Activité 5. *(Tell what is not in the cart in Activity 5.)*

Presentation

Le partitif

Step 1 Go through Items 1 and 2 on page 251.

Step 2 You may wish to ask students whether they would like to eat certain items or not: **Tu veux manger du gâteau? Tu veux manger du porc?**

Expansion: You may wish to tell students that **de** is also used after a quantity. Give the following examples:
une bouteille d'eau
une tranche de jambon
un pot de confiture
une douzaine d'œufs

5 Have students answer first with partitives only **(du lait)** and then have them specify amounts of each item if possible **(deux bouteilles de lait).**

Reaching All Students

For the Younger Students Have students "fill" a shopping cart with drawings or photos cut from magazines. Then have them tell what they have in their cart or write a description of their purchases.

Answers to Révision

4
1. du
2. du
3. de l'
4. de la
5. des

5
Dans le chariot il y a du pain (trois baguettes), des œufs (une douzaine d'œufs), du lait (deux bouteilles de lait), des carottes, du jambon, des yaourts (trois pots de yaourt), des bananes.

6 *Answers will vary but may include:*
Dans le chariot il n'y a pas de glace, de crème, de tomates, de moutarde, etc.

Révision

Presentation

Le comparatif

Step 1 Review Items 1 and 2.

Step 2 Use stick figures and the adjective **grand** to illustrate the comparative construction, changing the size of the figures to illustrate the following:
Jean est aussi grand que Paul.
Jean est plus grand que Paul.
Jean est moins grand que Paul.

7 J'ai faim Répondez d'après le modèle.
(Answer according to the model.)

—Tu veux du poisson?
—Non, je ne veux pas de poisson. Je n'aime pas le poisson!

1. Tu veux du bœuf?
2. Tu veux des œufs?
3. Tu veux des carottes à la crème?
4. Tu veux du poulet?
5. Tu veux de la salade?
6. Tu veux du gâteau au chocolat?

Le comparatif

1. You use the comparative to compare two people or two items.

   Aurélie est plus (aussi, moins) sportive que son frère.
   Le pantalon est plus (aussi, moins) cher que le jean.

2. You use the stress pronouns **moi, toi, lui, elle, nous, vous, eux,** and **elles** after **que (qu')** when comparing people.

   Il est moins sympa qu'elle (que toi, qu'eux).

Marie est plus fatiguée que sa sœur.

8 Cyril et moi Répondez d'après le modèle.
(Answer according to the model.)

Cyril est très sérieux.
—Il est plus sérieux que moi?
—Non, il est aussi sérieux que toi.

1. Cyril est très timide.
2. Cyril est très grand.
3. Cyril est très amusant.
4. Cyril est très patient.
5. Cyril est très beau.
6. Cyril est très sympathique.

Answers to Révision

7

1. Non, je ne veux pas de bœuf. Je n'aime pas le bœuf!
2. Non, je ne veux pas d'œufs. Je n'aime pas les œufs!
3. Non, je ne veux pas de carottes à la crème. Je n'aime pas les carottes à la crème!
4. Non, je ne veux pas de poulet. Je n'aime pas le poulet!
5. Non, je ne veux pas de salade. Je n'aime pas la salade!
6. Non, je ne veux pas de gâteau au chocolat. Je n'aime pas le gâteau au chocolat!

8

1. Il est plus timide que moi?
   Non, il est aussi timide que toi.
2. Il est plus grand que moi?
   Non, il est aussi grand que toi.
3. Il est plus amusant que moi?
   Non, il est aussi amusant que toi.
4. Il est plus patient que moi?
   Non, il est aussi patient que toi.
5. Il est plus beau que moi?
   Non, il est aussi beau que toi.
6. Il est plus sympathique que moi?
   Non, il est aussi sympathique que toi.

Révision

9 **Christelle et moi** Remplacez Cyril par Christelle dans l'Activité 8. *(Replace* Cyril *with* Christelle *in Activity 8.)*

10 **Au restaurant** With a classmate, make up a conversation between a waiter or a waitress and a customer.

Un restaurant, Paris

11 **Qu'est-ce que tu fais?** Work with a classmate. Ask each other questions about the things you do or want to do. Use the following words in the conversation.

prendre · vouloir · pouvoir · croire · faire · aller

12 **Des courses** Work with a classmate. Each of you will make up a grocery list. Exchange lists. Then tell each other where you are going to go and what you are going to do.

Literary Companion *You may wish to read the poem «Dors mon enfant», by Elolongué Epanya Yondo, who was born in Cameroun and studied in Paris. This poem is found on page 510.*

Learning from Photos

(page 253) The restaurant in this photo is on the Place des Vosges in the Marais section of Paris.

Literary Companion

When you finish this chapter, if you wish, have students read the excerpt from the poem ***«Dors mon enfant»***, on pages 510–511.

Answers to Révision

9

1. Elle est plus timide que moi?
   Non, elle est aussi timide que toi.
2. Elle est plus grande que moi?
   Non, elle est aussi grande que toi.
3. Elle est plus amusante que moi?
   Non, elle est aussi amusante que toi.
4. Elle est plus patiente que moi?
   Non, elle est aussi patiente que toi.
5. Elle est plus belle que moi?
   Non elle est aussi belle que toi.
6. Elle est plus sympathique que moi? Non, elle est aussi sympathique que toi.

10 *Answers will vary but may include:*

—Bonjour, monsieur.
—Bonjour, madame. Vous désirez?
—Je voudrais une omelette aux fines herbes, une salade verte, et une bouteille d'eau minérale, s'il vous plaît.

NATIONAL GEOGRAPHIC

Preview

This section, **Reflets de l'Afrique,** was prepared by National Geographic Society. Its purpose is to give students greater insight, through these visual images, into the culture and people of French-speaking Africa. Have students look at the photographs on pages 254–257 for enjoyment. If they would like to talk about them, let them say anything they can, using the vocabulary they have learned to this point.

National Standards

Cultures

The **Reflets de l'Afrique** photos and the accompanying captions allow students to gain insights into the people and culture of French-speaking Africa.

1. Maisons du pays Dogon au Mali
2. Masque sénoufo de la Côte d'Ivoire
3. Danse rituelle et tambourinaires du Burundi
4. Une petite fille du Mali
5. Dakar, la capitale du Sénégal
6. Youssou N'dour, le célèbre chanteur pop du Sénégal
7. Un griot raconte aux jeunes du village l'histoire de leurs ancêtres

About the Photos

1. Maisons du pays Dogon au Mali The Dogon people of Mali are extremely industrious farmers who live on and around the very rocky Bandiagara Escarpment about 100 kilometers from Mopti. The Dogon first settled around the escarpment in the fifteenth century. The houses are made of mud, with flat roofs supported by beams. The smaller buildings in the photo that have conical straw roofs are granaries. They, unlike the houses, were assembled on the ground and hoisted into place. In recent times, some of these cliff dwellings which resemble those of cliff-dwelling native Americans in the Southwest, have been abandoned. The people have moved onto the plains at the foot of the escarpment. The Dogon Country, **le pays Dogon,** has been designated a World Heritage Site for its cultural and natural significance. The Dogon people are famous for their artistic abilities. The doors of many of their houses are elaborately carved and much sought after by art collectors.

2. Masque sénoufo de la Côte d'Ivoire The **Sénoufo** people live in the northern part of **Côte d'Ivoire** in an area called Korhogo. They are renowned artisans who are separated into specific castes, such as carvers, bronze workers, and welders. **Sénoufo** masks are highly stylized. They are known for their animal masks and their facial masks. The animal masks are often very scary. The human facial masks often have a very insipid expression. The thin eyes, such as in this mask are typical.

3. Danse rituelle et tambourinaires du Burundi **Les tambourinaires,** as the players are called, play a very important role in the culture and folklore of the Burundi people. In this photograph we see a ritual dance being performed. It is a particularly interesting dance because some of the **tambourinaires** who accompany the dance beat to a basic rhythm, but others must observe the dancer, because it is the dancer who imposes rhythm, not the accompanist. The dancer indicates the changes in rhythm with gestures.

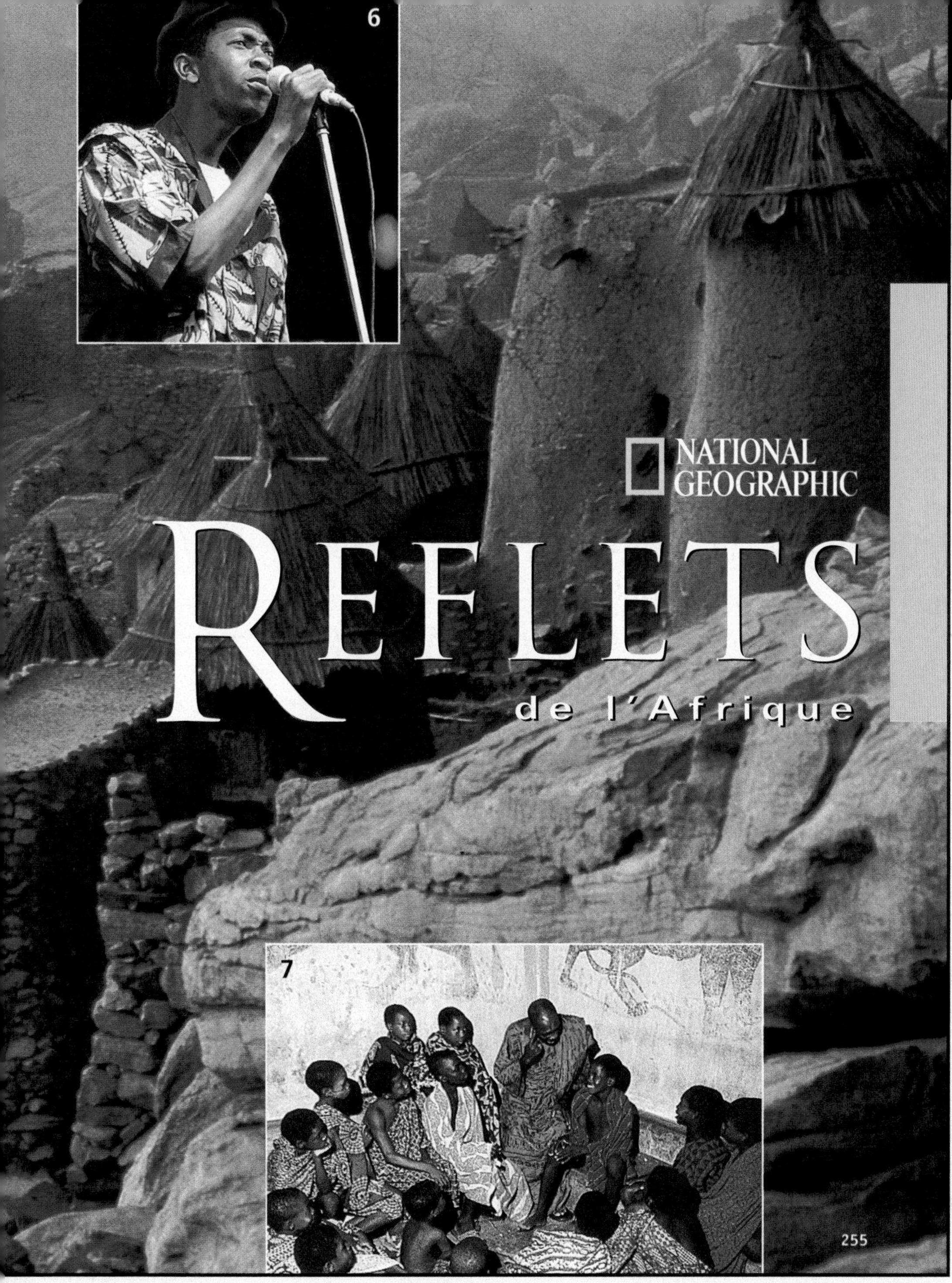

4. Une petite fille du Mali The young girl in the photo is Fulani. The Fulani are also known as the Peul or Foulbé. They are widely spread across West Africa from Nigeria to Sénégal. This girl is from Mali. The Fulani are traditionally herders and semi-nomadic. For centuries they have been cattle raisers.

It is not certain where the Fulani came from, but it appears they migrated centuries ago from Egypt. There is conjecture that they may be of Jewish origin. The Fulani are usually tall, elegant, and thin.

5. Dakar: la capitale du Sénégal Dakar is on the Cap Vert peninsula, in the westernmost part of the African continent. Dakar is considered by many to be one of the nicest cities in Africa. It enjoys a temperate climate, has a wide variety of restaurants, some lovely hotels, and many interesting things to see and do. The relatively small downtown area has many tree-lined streets that are not extremely crowded, even though the city has over a million inhabitants. Many other areas of the Center City however swarm with vendors and vehicular traffic.

6. Youssou N'dour, le célèbre chanteur pop du Sénégal Youssou N'dour is foremost among today's West African music stars. He was born in a poor section of the Medina in Dakar. (87 percent of the Senegalise population is Moslem.) Today, he is the principal interpreter of "fusion pop" music, a combination of traditional African, and Western pop, rock, and soul music. Because of his fame, N'dour is often on tour, but when at home in Dakar he and his group, **Super étoile,** perform once a week at his nightclub, **La Thiosanne.**

The film *You Africa* tells of the great success of this musician during a tour of nine West African countries. N'dour is also extremely popular in Europe.

7. Un griot raconte aux jeunes du village l'histoire de leurs ancêtres The Jeli (Jali) or **griots** in French are hereditary musicians.The **griots** have been around since the thirteenth century. The **griots** are musicians and songwriters. It is they who pass on the oral tradition and are usually the only ones who can recite family or village history. They used to entertain the royal families and sing the praises of the noble and wealthy. No festive occasion would be complete without the presence of a **griot.** Traditionally the **kora,** a harp-lute can only be played by a **griot.**

The **griots** are members of a distinct caste. Many of Mali's modern singers are members of the **griot** caste. Some of these singers are women, including Tata Bembo Kouyaté, Ami Koita, and Fanta Damba.

In Sénégal, among the Wolof people, the **griots** are the lowest of the castes, but they are highly respected, since it is they who pass on the oral tradition and know so much about everyone. The **griots** have the ears of the people and any corrupt individual has to deal with them.

8. Baobab à Madagascar The republic of Madagascar is in the Indian Ocean and is made up of one large island, Madagascar, and a smaller one, Nosy-Bé. Madagascar was declared a French colony in 1896, and General Gallieni became governor general. The country became independent in 1960.

A great deal of the territory in Madagascar is covered with forests. The baobab tree seen in the photo has an enormous trunk, up to 20 meters in circumference. It grows in the tropical regions of Africa and Australia.

9. Cueillette du thé au Burundi The economy of the Republic of Burundi in Central Africa is based almost exclusively on agriculture. The crops vary depending on the altitude. The humid, temperate climate of the middle altitude (1500–2000 meters) is favorable for cultivating tobacco, coffee, and tea. These products account for a large percentage of Burundi's exports.

10. Mosquée à Djenné, au Mali Djenné is considered one of the most interesting and picturesque towns in West Africa. It is just off the main road from Bamako to Mopti. Djenné is built on an island in the Niger River. Founded in the ninth century, it is one of the oldest towns in West Africa. Little has changed over the centuries. Almost all the houses are made of mud with thatched roofs. This elegant mosque in Djenné was built in 1905. It is a classic example of Sudanese or Sahelian mud architecture. It is a major task to keep the mosque from disintegrating each year during the rainy season. In the interior there are some 100 massive columns.

11. Abidjan en Côte d'Ivoire The coastal area of **Côte d'Ivoire** is unusual because of a lagoon, several kilometers inland. The lagoon starts at the Ghanaian border and stretches for some 300 kilometers

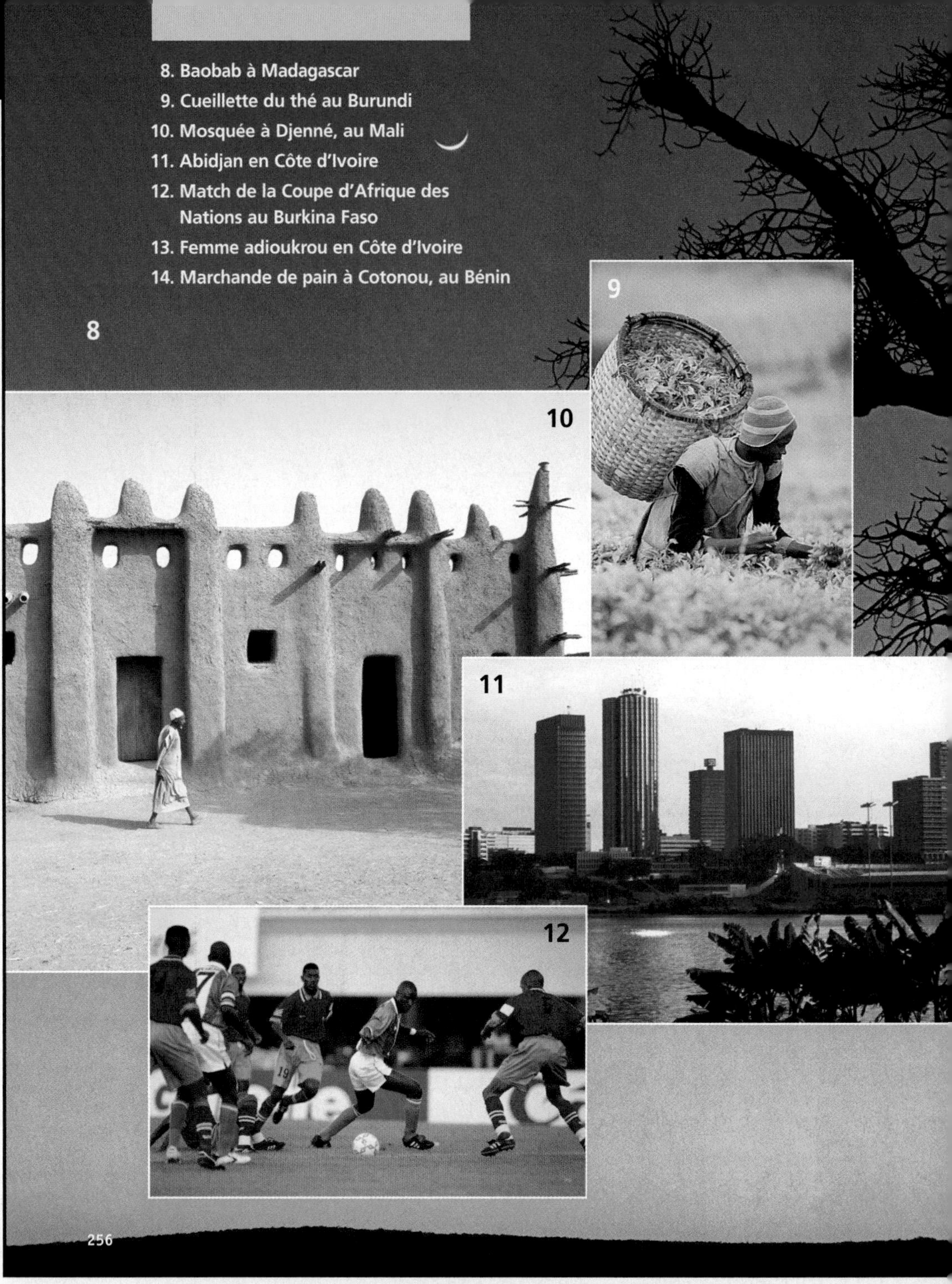
8. Baobab à Madagascar
9. Cueillette du thé au Burundi
10. Mosquée à Djenné, au Mali
11. Abidjan en Côte d'Ivoire
12. Match de la Coupe d'Afrique des Nations au Burkina Faso
13. Femme adioukrou en Côte d'Ivoire
14. Marchande de pain à Cotonou, au Bénin
8
9
10
11
12
256

NATIONAL GEOGRAPHIC Teacher's Corner

Index to the NATIONAL GEOGRAPHIC MAGAZINE

The following related articles may be of interest:

- "In Focus: Central Africa's Cycle of Violence," by Mike Edwards, June 1997.
- "Hunting the Mighty Python," by Karen Lange, May 1997.
- "Morocco: North Africa's Timeless Mosaic," by Erla Zwingle, October 1996.
- "Below the Cliff of Tombs: Mali's Dogon," by David Roberts, October 1990.
- "Africa's Sahel: The Stricken Land," by William S. Ellis, August 1987.
- "Oasis of Art in the Sahara," by Henri Lhote, August 1987.
- "Senegambia: A Now and Future Nation," by Aubine Kirtley and Michael Kirtley, August 1985.
- "Finding West Africa's Oldest City," by Roderick McIntosh and Susan McIntosh, September 1982.
- "The Ivory Coast—African Success Story," by Aubine Kirtley and Michael Kirtley, July 1982.
- "Tunisia: Sea, Sand, Success," by Mike W. Edwards, February 1980.

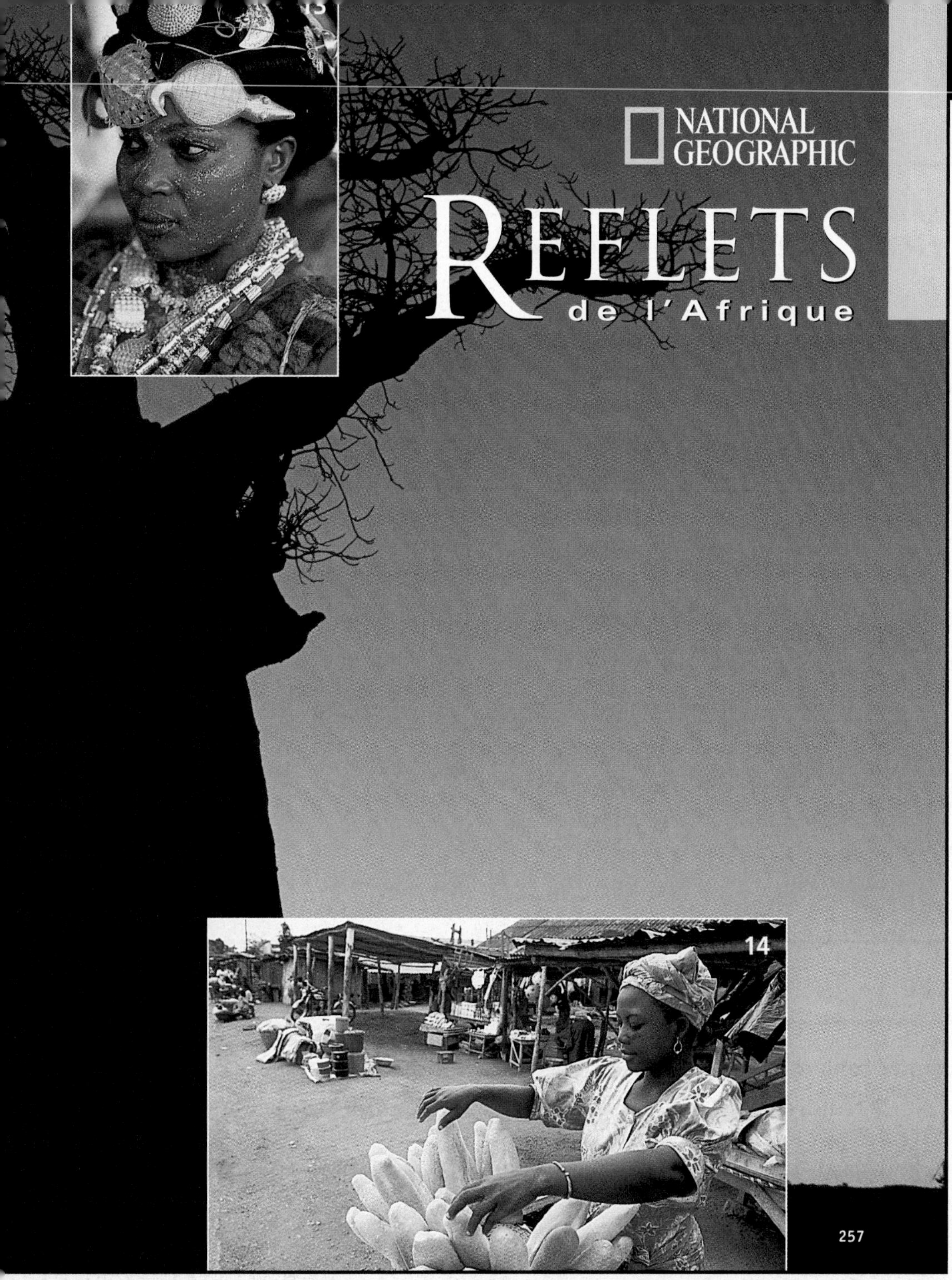

along the entire eastern half of the coast of **Côte d'Ivoire.** Abidjan, which is on the lagoon, was an unimportant town until 1951, when the French built the Vridi canal. This canal connects the lagoon with the ocean and gives Abidjan an excellent harbor. Since the opening of the canal, the population of the city has skyrocketed. It has grown from 100,000 to over 2.5 million people. The city spreads over four peninsulas around the lagoon.

Abidjan had been the capital of **Côte d'Ivoire** until 1983. In 1983 President Houphouet-Boigny declared Yamoussoukro, his native village, the official capital, but it is the capital in name only.

12. Match de la Coupe d'Afrique des Nations au Burkina Faso The game in this photo is between **Côte d'Ivoire** and Namibia. It is being played in Burkina Faso.

13. Femme adioukrou en Côte d'Ivoire In this photo we see an Adioukrou woman elegantly dressed with gold flecks on her face. She has dressed this way for a special occasion, such as a wedding or a birth. The Adioukrou people live in the Southern part of **Côte d' Ivoire** near the town of Dabousome, 49 kilometers west of Abidjan.

14. Marchande de pain à Cotonou, au Benin Street vendors and markets are commonplace in all West African cities and towns and Cotonou is no exception. The capital of Benin, Cotonou was founded in 1830. The Beninese people are quite friendly. Over half the population are members of one of five ethnic groups: the Bariba, Betamaribé, Fon, Fulani, and Yorube. Most families support themselves through agriculture. As in some other West African countries, women control the distribution of food, from transporting the produce to market, to the final barter and sale.

Products available from GLENCOE/MCGRAW-HILL

To order the following products, call Glencoe/McGraw-Hill at 1-800-334-7344.

CD-ROMs
- Picture Atlas of the World
- The Complete National Geographic: 112 Years of National Geographic Magazine

Transparency Set
- NGS PicturePack: Geography of Africa

Products available from NATIONAL GEOGRAPHIC SOCIETY

To order the following products, call National Geographic Society at 1-800-368-2728.

Books
- National Geographic World Atlas for Young Explorers
- National Geographic Satellite Atlas of the World

Software
- ZingoLingo: French Diskette

Video
- Africa

Planning for Chapter 8

SCOPE AND SEQUENCE, PAGES 258–289

Topics

- Air travel

Culture

- Madame Cadet's class spends spring break in France.
- Time differences
- Antoine de Saint-Exupéry, author and pilot

Functions

- How to check in for a flight
- How to discuss services aboard a plane
- How to describe people's activities

Structure

- Present tense of **-ir** verbs
- **Quel** and **tout**
- The verbs **sortir, partir, dormir,** et **servir** in the present tense

National Standards

- Communication Standard 1.1 pages 262, 263, 266, 267, 269, 271, 273, 274, 277, 284
- Communication Standard 1.2 pages 262, 263, 266, 267, 268, 269, 271, 273, 274, 276, 279, 280, 281, 283
- Communication Standard 1.3 pages 262, 266, 267, 269, 273, 284, 285
- Cultures Standard 2.1 pages 278–279
- Connections Standard 3.1 pages 281, 282–283
- Communities Standard 5.1 page 284

PACING AND PRIORITIES

The chapter content is color coded below to assist you in planning.
■ required ■ recommended ■ optional

Vocabulaire *(required)* *Days 1–4*
- ■ Mots 1
  - À l´aéroport
- ■ Mots 2
  - À bord

Structure *(required)* *Days 5–7*
- ■ Les verbes en **-ir** au présent
- ■ **Quel** et **tout**
- ■ Les verbes **sortir, partir, dormir,** et **servir**

Conversation *(required)*
- ■ On part pour Toulouse.

Prononciation *(recommended)*
- ■ Le son /l/ final

Lectures culturelles
- ■ On va en France. *(recommended)*
- ■ Le décalage horaire *(optional)*
- ■ Un pilote écrivain *(optional)*

Connexions *(optional)*
- ■ Le climat et le temps

■ **C'est à vous** *(recommended)*

■ **Assessment** *(recommended)*

■ **Technotour** *(optional)*

RESOURCE GUIDE

SECTION	PAGES	SECTION RESOURCES
Vocabulaire *Mots 1*		
À l'aéroport	260–263	Vocabulary Transparencies 8.2–8.3 Audiocassette 5B/CD 5 Audio Activities Booklet TE, pages 98–100 Workbook, page 79 Quiz 1, page 39 ExamView Pro®
Vocabulaire *Mots 2*		
À bord	264–267	Vocabulary Transparencies 8.4–8.5 Audiocassette 5B/CD 5 Audio Activities Booklet TE, pages 100–101 Workbook, page 80 Quiz 2, page 40 ExamView Pro®
Structure		
Les verbes en **-ir** au présent **Quel** et **tout** Les verbes **sortir, partir, dormir,** et **servir**	268–269 270–271 272–275	Audiocassette 5B/CD 5 Audio Activities Booklet TE, pages 102–104 Workbook, pages 81–83 Quizzes 3–5, pages 41–43 ExamView Pro®
Conversation		
On part pour Toulouse.	276	Audiocassette 5B/CD 5 Audio Activities Booklet TE, pages 104–105 CD-ROM
Prononciation		
Le son **/l/** final	277	Pronunciation Transparency P 8 Audiocassette 5B/CD 5 Audio Activities Booklet TE, pages 105–106
Lectures culturelles		
On va en France. Le décalage horaire Un pilote écrivain	278–279 280 281	Audiocassette 5B/CD 5 Audio Activities Booklet TE, pages 106–107 Test Booklet, Chapter 8
Connexions		
Le climat et le temps	282–283	Test Booklet, Chapter 8
C'est à vous		
	284–285	**Bon voyage!** Video, Episode 8 Video Activities Booklet, Chapter 8 French Online Activities french.glencoe.com
Assessment		
	286–287	Communication Transparency C 8 Quizzes 1–5, pages 39–43 Test Booklet, Chapter 8 ExamView Pro® Situation Cards, Chapter 8 **Marathon mental** Videoquiz

Using Your Resources for Chapter 8

Transparencies

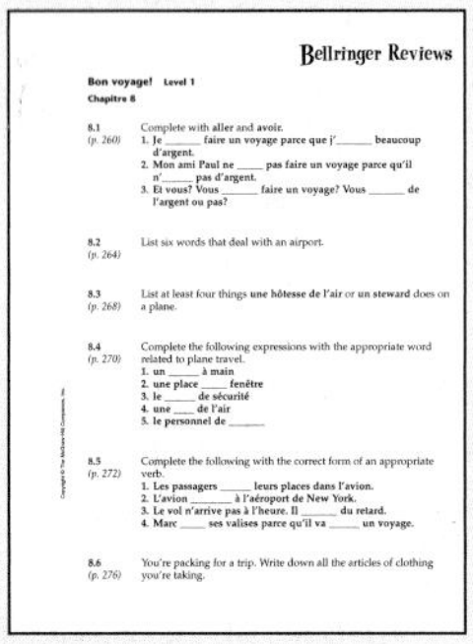
Bellringer 8.1–8.7

Vocabulary 8.1–8.5

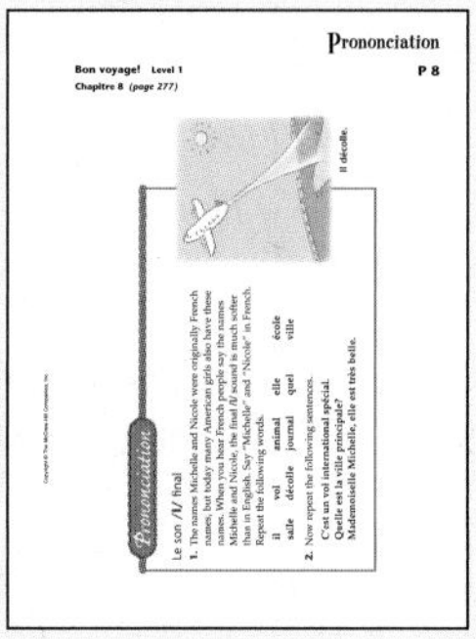
Pronunciation P 8

Communication C 8

Writing Activities Workbook

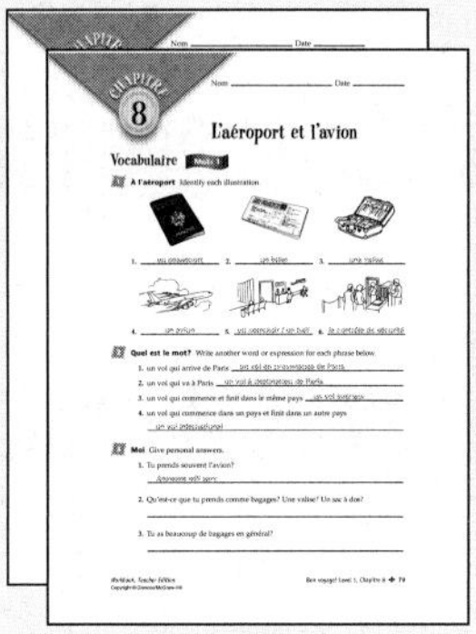
Vocabulary, pages 79–80

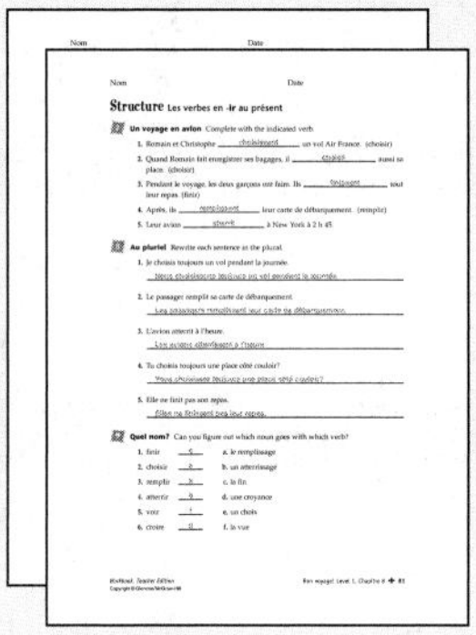
Structure, pages 81–83

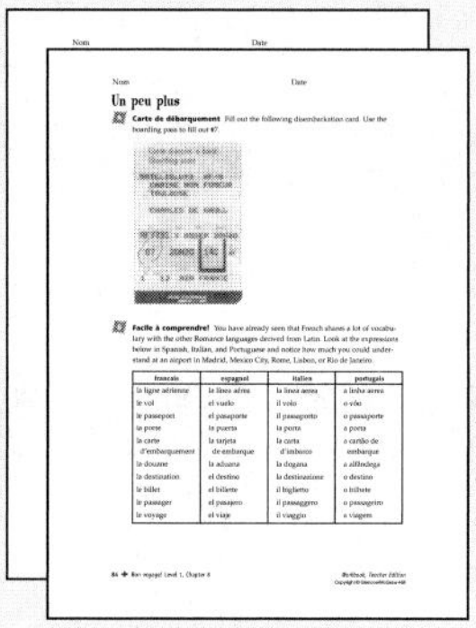
Enrichment, pages 84–86

Audio Program and Audio Activities Booklet

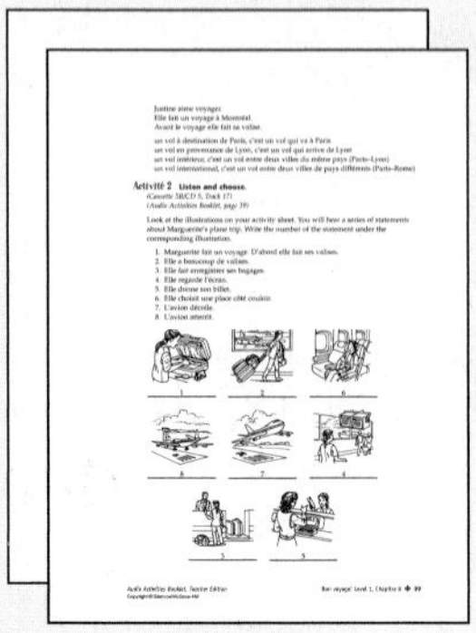
Vocabulary, pages 98–101

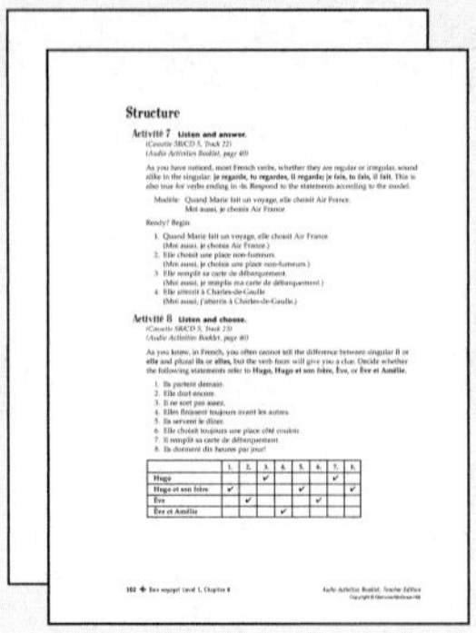
Structure, pages 102–104

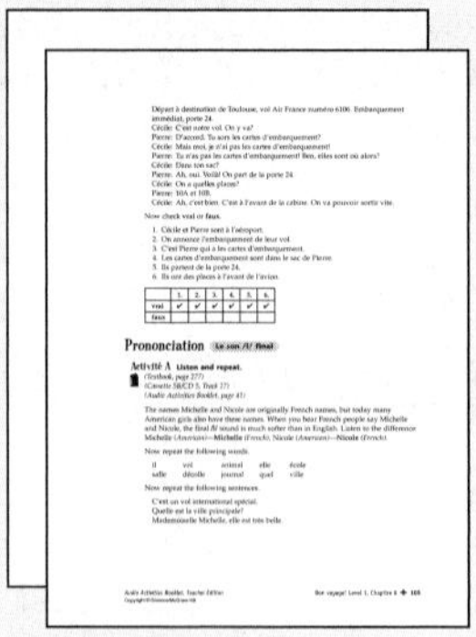
Conversation, Pronunciation, pages 104–106

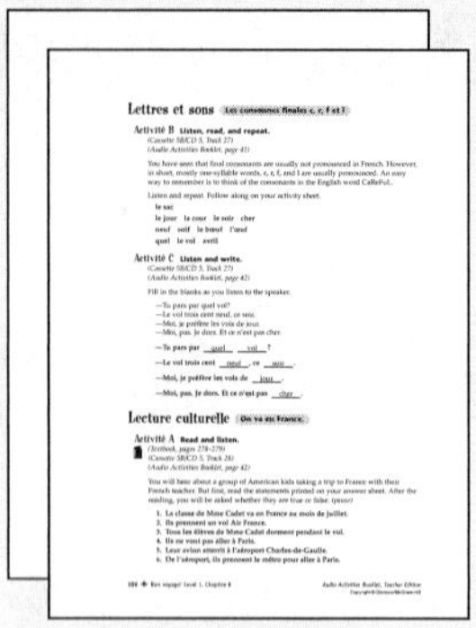
Cultural Reading, pages 106–107

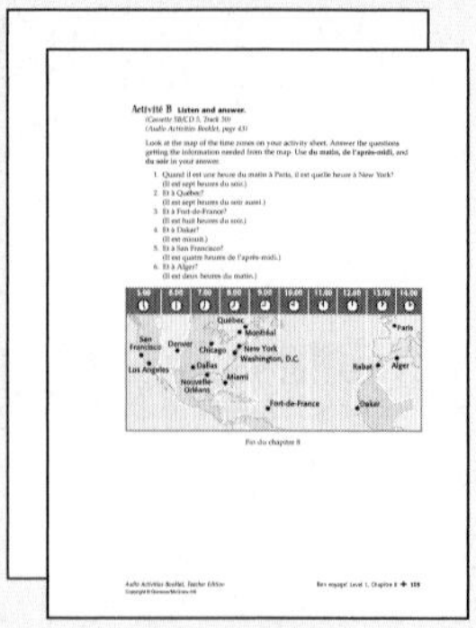
Additional Practice, pages 108–109

Assessment

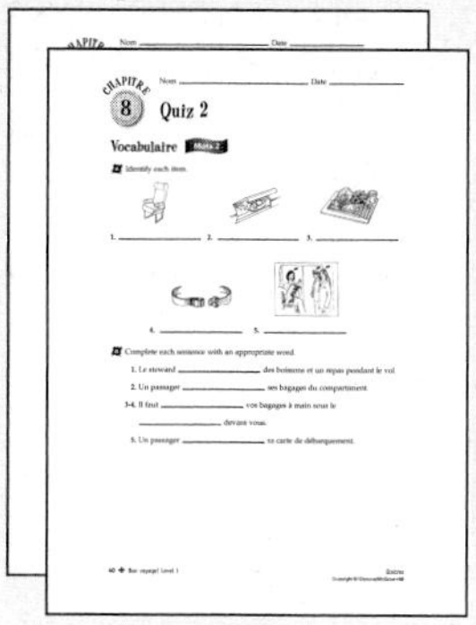

Vocabulary and Structure Quizzes, pages 39–43

Chapter Tests, Chapter 8

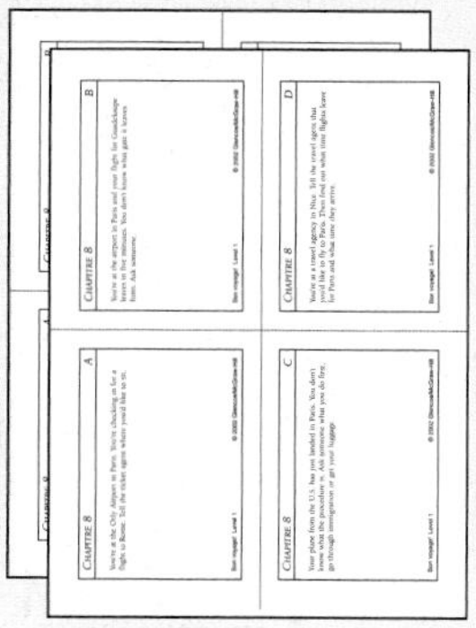

Situation Cards, Chapter 8

Timesaving Teacher Tools

Interactive Teacher Edition

Imagine having your Teacher's Edition and all resources on a CD-ROM. Click on a resource and it appears on your screen, ready to be printed, sorted, or planned.

Interactive Lesson Planner

The Interactive Lesson Planner CD-ROM helps you organize your lesson plans for a week, month, semester, or year. Look at this planning tool for easy access to your Chapter 8 resources.

ExamView Pro®

Test Bank software for Macintosh and Windows makes creating, editing, customizing, and printing tests quick and easy.

Technology Resources

FRENCH Online

In the Chapter 8 Internet activity, you will have a chance to learn more about air travel in the Francophone world. Visit french.glencoe.com.

On the Interactive Conversation CD-ROM, students can listen to and take part in a recorded version of the conversation in Chapter 8.

NATIONAL GEOGRAPHIC SOCIETY

See the National Geographic Teacher's Corner on pages 150–151, 256–257, 396–397, 500–501 for reference to additional technology resources.

Bon voyage! Video and Video Activities Booklet.

Help your students prepare for the chapter test by playing the **Marathon mental** Videoquiz game show. Teams will compete against each other to review chapter vocabulary and structure and sharpen listening comprehension skills.

CHAPITRE 8

Preview

In this chapter, students will learn to talk about traveling by air, including departing, boarding, and traveling on board. (The topic of air travel will be expanded upon in **Bon voyage! Level 2.**) They will also learn to use several important -ir verbs, to ask and answer questions using the forms of quel and tout, and to use irregular verbs such as partir.

National Standards

Communication

In Chapter 8, students will communicate in spoken and written French on the following topics:

- Checking in at the airport
- Going through security and finding their departure gate
- Being on board the airplane

Students will obtain and provide information about taking a flight and about procedures at an airport. They will learn to engage in conversations with various types of airline employees.

CHAPITRE 8

L'aéroport et l'avion

Objectifs

In this chapter you will learn to:

- ✔ *check in for a flight*
- ✔ *talk about some services aboard the plane*
- ✔ *talk about more activities*
- ✔ *ask more questions*
- ✔ *talk about people and things as a group*
- ✔ *discuss air travel in France*

René Magritte *La grande famille*

258

Correlations to Continuum *(see page i for code)*

Stage I
Engage in conversations. p. 263 (**3**, *p*); Express likes and dislikes. p. 269 (**11**, *p*); Obtain information. p. 277 (**B**, *p*); Converse in face-to-face social interactions. p. 277 (**A**, *m*); Listen during social interactions and listen to audio or video texts. p. 289 (*p*); Use authentic materials such as schedules when reading. p. 267 (**9**, *m*); Use short sentences, learned words, phrases, simple questions, and commands when speaking. p. 263 (**3**, *p*), p. 284 (**1**, *m*); Understand ideas and familiar details when listening. p. 276 (*p*); Understand and convey information on weather and seasons. pp. 282–283 (*p*); Communicate effectively with some hesitation and errors, which do not hinder comprehension. p. 274 (**24**); Understand most important information. p. 284 (**3**)

Stage II
Understand and express important ideas and some detail. p. 262 (**1**, *i*), p. 263 (**4**, *p*), p. 285 (**4**, *m*); Describe and compare. p. 271 (**18**, *p*); Use authentic materials such as tickets, brochures, and documents when reading. p. 260 (*i*), p. 284 (**2**, *p*); Write letters. p. 284 (**3**, *p*)

Stage 4
Create a series of coherent paragraphs when writing. p. 285 (**4**, *i*), p. 285 (**4**, *p*)

Stage 5
Conduct transactions and negotiations. p. 263 (**3**, *i*), p. 263 (**3**, *p*)

Assessment

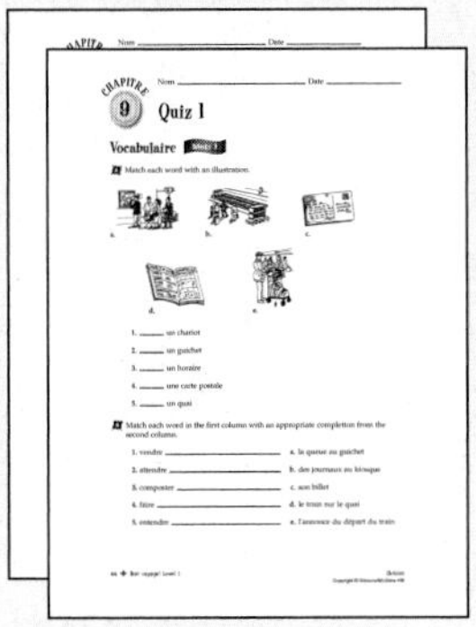

Vocabulary and Structure Quizzes, pages 44–48

Chapter Tests, Chapter 9

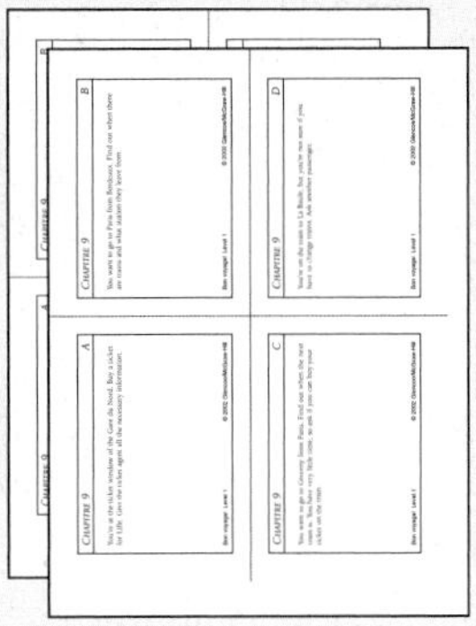

Situation Cards, Chapter 9

Timesaving Teacher Tools

Interactive Teacher Edition

Imagine having your Teacher's Edition and all resources on a CD-ROM. Click on a resource and it appears on your screen, ready to be printed, sorted, or planned.

Interactive Lesson Planner

The Interactive Lesson Planner CD-ROM helps you organize your lesson plans for a week, month, semester, or year. Look at this planning tool for easy access to your Chapter 9 resources.

ExamView Pro®

Test Bank software for Macintosh and Windows makes creating, editing, customizing, and printing tests quick and easy.

Technology Resources

FRENCH Online

In the Chapter 9 Internet activity, you will have a chance to learn more about train travel in the Francophone world. Visit french.glencoe.com.

On the Interactive Conversation CD-ROM, students can listen to and take part in a recorded version of the conversation in Chapter 9.

NATIONAL GEOGRAPHIC SOCIETY

See the National Geographic Teacher's Corner on pages 150–151, 256–257, 396–397, 500–501 for reference to additional technology resources.

Bon Voyage! Video and Video Activities Booklet.

Help your students prepare for the chapter test by playing the **Marathon mental** Videoquiz game show. Teams will compete against each other to review chapter vocabulary and structure and sharpen listening comprehension skills.

Preview

In this chapter, students will learn to communicate when traveling by train in a French-speaking country. In order to do this they will learn vocabulary related to the train station and train travel. They will learn the present tense of **-re** verbs, the demonstrative adjectives, and the verbs **dire, écrire,** and **lire.**

National Standards

Communication

In Chapter 9, students will communicate in spoken and written French on the following topics:

- Purchasing a train ticket and consulting a timetable
- Getting through a train station
- Traveling on board a train

Students will obtain and provide information about these topics and learn to engage in conversations with a ticket agent, train conductor, and fellow passengers as they fulfill the chapter objectives listed on this page.

Communities

A field trip to a local train station can be most educational after students have learned the vocabulary in this chapter. As you tour the station, have students use as much of their French vocabulary as possible. Have them compare an American train station (facilities, procedures, etc.) with a French one.

CHAPITRE 9

La gare et le train

Objectifs

In this chapter you will learn to:

- ✔ *purchase a train ticket and request information about arrival and departure*
- ✔ *use expressions related to train travel*
- ✔ *talk about people's activities*
- ✔ *point out people or things*
- ✔ *discuss an interesting train trip in French-speaking Africa*

Claude Monet *La locomotive*

290

Correlations to Continuum *(see page i for code)*

Stage I
Make requests. p. 292 (*i*), p. 305 (**18**, *p*); Obtain information. p. 309 (**B**, *p*); Understand some ideas and familiar details. p. 299 (**7**, *p*); Listen during social interactions and listen to audio or video texts. p. 321 (*p*); Use authentic materials such as schedules and charts. p. 309 (**A**, *p*); Use learned words and phrases when speaking. p. 299 (**9**, *p*); Understand ideas and familiar details when listening. p. 308 (*p*); Understand texts enhanced by visual clues. pp. 310–311 (*p*); Understand and convey information about leisure activities. p. 307 (**21**, *p*); Understand and convey information on numbers, time, and travel. pp. 314–315 (*p*); Understand most important information. p. 317 (**4**)

Stage II
Understand and express important ideas and some detail. p. 294 (**1**, *i*), p. 317 (**3**, *p*); Describe and compare. p. 316 (**1**, *p*); Use and understand expressions indicating emotion. p. 297 (*i*); Converse in face-to-face social interactions. p. 302 (**14**, *i*), p. 316 (**2**, *p*); Use and understand learned expressions, sentences, strings of sentences, questions, and polite commands when speaking and listening. p. 295 (**4**, *p*); Create simple paragraphs. p. 317 (**3**, *p*); Communicate effectively with some pattern of error, which may interfere slightly with full comprehension when performing Stage II functions. p. 316 (**1**)

Stage III
Express and understand opinions. p. 316 (**2**, *p*)

Stage V
Conduct transactions and negotiations. p. 295 (**4**, *p*)

CHAPITRE 8

Spotlight on Culture

Photograph This photo is of the Mirabel International Airport in Montréal. Mirabel serves mostly charter traffic and short-haul flights. The major international airport serving long-haul flights is Dorval International.

Painting René Magritte (1898–1967) was a Belgian painter who studied at the Académie des Beaux-Arts in Brussels. His paintings are surrealist; many are strange visual "collages," depicting the puzzling connections between perception, imagery, reality, concepts, and language.

National Standards

Communities
If your students have had little opportunity to travel, plan a field trip to a nearby airport. This is a wonderful enrichment experience for some students. As you tour the airport, have them use as much of their French vocabulary as possible.

Chapter Projects

Un passeport Have students create their own European Community passports. Have them fill out forms in French with their name, address, nationality, birth date, metric weight, etc. Students can use real photos of themselves or draw a picture. Covers can be made of construction paper.

Le décalage horaire Have students draw a map of the world and locate the time zones. Using the map on page 280, have them give the time in some major French-speaking cities, when it's noon in New York (EST).

Vocabulaire
Mots 1

1 Preparation

Resource Manager

Vocabulary Transparencies 8.2–8.3
Audio Activities Booklet TE, pages 98–100
Audiocassette 5B/CD 5
Workbook, page 79
Quiz 1, page 39
ExamView Pro®

Bellringer Review

Use BRR Transparency 8.1 or write the following on the board.
Complete with **aller** and **avoir.**

1. **Je _____ faire un voyage parce que j'_____ beaucoup d'argent.**
2. **Mon ami Paul ne _____ pas faire de voyage parce qu'il n'_____ pas d'argent.**
3. **Et vous? Vous _____ faire un voyage? Vous _____ de l'argent ou pas?**

2 Presentation

Step 1 Present the vocabulary first with books closed using Vocabulary Transparencies 8.2–8.3. Have students repeat after you or Audiocassette 5B/CD 5 as you point to the illustrations.

Step 2 After the initial presentation with the overhead transparencies, have students open their books and look at the new vocabulary words as they repeat either after you or Audiocassette 5B/CD 5.

Step 3 Point to the items on the overhead transparencies and ask the students the following types of questions: **Ce sont des valises ou des bagages à main? C'est un passeport ou un billet? Justine est où? Que fait Justine?,** etc.
Teaching Tip: Once students are familiar with the vocabulary, have a student play the teacher and ask questions of classmates.

Vocabulaire
Mots 1

À l'aéroport

Maintenant Justine est dans le hall de l'aéroport.
Elle fait enregistrer ses bagages.
L'agent vérifie son billet.

Justine choisit une place dans l'avion.
Elle demande une place côté couloir.

L'avion a du retard.
L'avion n'est pas à l'heure.

Reaching All Students

Total Physical Response Before doing this activity, dramatize the meaning of **écrivez.**

(Student 1), **levez-vous, s'il vous plaît.**
Prenez le livre de français.
Venez ici avec le livre.
Ouvrez le livre à la page 267.
Regardez la carte d'embarquement.
Allez au tableau.
Prenez le livre.
Regardez la carte d'embarquement et écrivez le nom de la compagnie aérienne au tableau.
Écrivez le numéro du vol.
Écrivez le numéro de la porte d'embarquement.
Écrivez l'heure d'embarquement.
Écrivez l'heure du départ.
Merci, *(Student 1).* **C'est très bien.**
Retournez à votre place et asseyez-vous.

L'avion part de la porte 32.

L'avion atterrit.

L'avion décolle.

Justine aime voyager.
Elle fait un voyage à Montréal.
Avant le voyage elle fait sa valise.

un vol à destination de Paris = un vol qui va à Paris
un vol en provenance de Lyon = un vol qui arrive de Lyon
un vol intérieur = un vol entre deux villes du même pays (Paris–Lyon)
un vol international = un vol entre deux villes de pays différents (Paris–Rome)

Learning from Photos

(pages 260–261) All photos on these pages were taken at the Charles-de-Gaulle airport in Roissy on the outskirts of Paris. Charles-de-Gaulle and Orly are the two major airports serving Paris.

Vocabulary Expansion

You may wish to give students the following information.

- **Une carte d'embarquement** is the most commonly used term for boarding card. You will also hear and see **une carte d'accès à bord.**
- The technical term for a plane window is **un hublot.** When asking for a window seat, however, you would request **une place côté fenêtre.**
- The large arrival-departure board you still see in some airports is **un tableau.** The TV monitor screen is called **un écran.**

About the French Language

You may wish to point out that verbs that end in **-ger,** such as **manger** (Chapter 5) and **voyager,** add an **e** in the **nous** form in order to maintain the soft consonant sound: **nous mangeons, nous voyageons.**

Reaching All Students

Total Physical Response

On va imaginer que c'est l'aéroport.
_____, vous allez à l'aéroport.
Vous avez des valises. Portez vos valises.
Allez au comptoir de la compagnie aérienne.
Faites enregistrer vos bagages.
Et maintenant, cherchez votre billet.
Vous ne trouvez pas votre billet?
Cherchez encore.
Ah, bien, vous avez votre billet.
Donnez le billet à l'agent de la compagnie.
L'agent veut voir votre passeport.
Cherchez votre passeport.
Donnez votre passeport à l'agent.
L'agent vous donne votre carte d'embarquement.
Prenez la carte.
Vérifiez le numéro du vol.
Merci, _____. Et bon voyage!
Et maintenant, retournez à votre place.

Math Connection

Have students figure out the following:

- **L'avion ne va pas arriver à l'heure, à 10 h 20. Il va arriver à 12 h 25. Il va avoir combien de retard?**
- **Notre vol ne va pas partir avant 15 h 10. Il est 13 h 30 maintenant. Il faut attendre *(wait)* combien de temps à la porte d'embarquement?**

3 Practice

Commençons

Let's use our new words

Attention!

When students are doing the **Commençons** activities, accept any answer that makes sense. The purpose of these activities is to have students use the new vocabulary. They are not factual recall activities. Thus, it is not necessary for students to remember specific factual information from the vocabulary presentation when answering. If you wish, have students use the photos on this page as a stimulus, when possible.

1 This activity uses the new verbs only in the third-person singular so students do not have to change the forms. Students will learn the other forms in the **Structure** section.

1 and **2** To focus on listening, have students keep their books closed as you ask the questions. Then have students open their books and retell the story in their own words.

Commençons

Let's use our new words

1 Historiette Un voyage à Genève.

Inventez une histoire.

1. Laurence aime voyager?
2. Elle fait un voyage à Genève?
3. Elle fait ses valises avant de partir pour l'aéroport?
4. Elle est au comptoir de la compagnie aérienne?
5. L'agent vérifie son billet et son passeport?
6. Laurence a beaucoup de bagages à main?
7. Elle fait enregistrer ses bagages?
8. Elle choisit une place dans l'avion?
9. Elle veut une place côté couloir ou côté fenêtre?
10. Elle a sa carte d'embarquement?
11. Elle va à la porte d'embarquement?

Laurence part pour Genève.

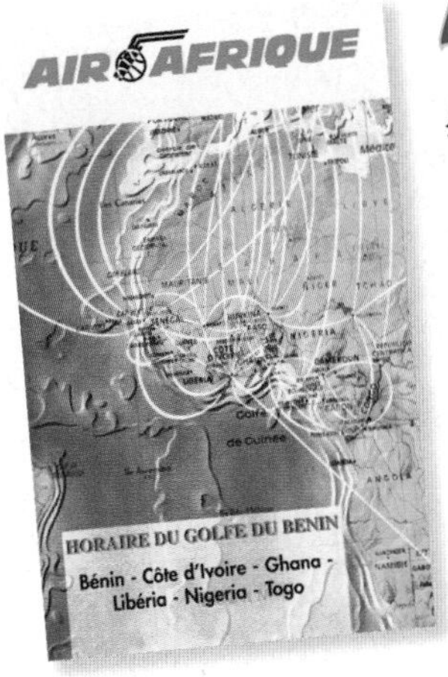

2 Historiette À l'aéroport

Répondez d'après les indications.

1. Les passagers sont où? (à l'aérogare 2)
2. Leur avion part à quelle heure? (à onze heures trente)
3. Il part de quelle porte? (trente-deux)
4. Qu'est-ce que les passagers regardent pour vérifier la porte et l'heure du départ? (l'écran)
5. Leur avion va partir à l'heure ou va avoir du retard? (va partir à l'heure)
6. Les passagers vont passer par où? (le contrôle de sécurité)
7. Qu'est-ce qu'on annonce? (le départ du vol)
8. Les passagers vont d'Abidjan à Dakar. Ils prennent un vol intérieur? (non, international)
9. L'avion est sur la piste? (oui)
10. Il va décoller ou atterrir? (décoller)
11. L'avion va atterrir à Paris? (non, à Dakar)
12. C'est un vol à destination ou en provenance de Dakar? (à destination)

Answers to Commençons

1 *Answers will vary but may include:*

1. Oui, elle aime voyager
2. Oui, elle fait un voyage à Genève.
3. Oui, elle fait ses valises avant de partir pour l'aéroport.
4. Oui, elle est au comptoir de la compagnie aérienne.
5. Oui, l'agent vérifie son billet et son passeport.
6. Non, elle a un bagage à main.
7. Oui, elle fait enregistrer ses bagages.
8. Oui, elle choisit une place dans l'avion.
9. Elle veut une place côté fenêtre.
10. Oui, elle a sa carte d'embarquement.
11. Oui, elle va à la porte d'embarquement.

2

1. Les passagers sont à l'aérogare 2.
2. Leur avion part à onze heures trente.
3. Il part de la porte trente-deux.
4. Les passagers regardent l'écran pour vérifier la porte et l'heure du départ.
5. Leur avion va partir à l'heure.
6. Les passagers vont passer par le contrôle de sécurité.
7. On annonce le départ du vol.
8. Non, ils prennent un vol international.
9. Oui, l'avion est sur la piste.
10. Il va décoller.
11. Non, l'avion va atterrir à Dakar.
12. C'est un vol à destination de Dakar.

3 **À l'aéroport** Work with a classmate. You're checking in at the airport for your flight to Fort-de-France in Martinique. Have a conversation with the airline agent (your partner) at the ticket counter.

Aéroport Charles-de-Gaulle, Roissy

4 **Un vol** Work with a classmate. Look at the following illustration. You are a passenger on this flight. Tell as much as you can about your experience at the airport.

ENCORE PLUS *For more practice using words from **Mots 1**, do Activity 24 on page H25 at the end of this book.*

Paired Activity

Have students work in pairs. One student tells the other a flight number that he or she has made up. The second student asks if the flight is leaving or arriving, then tries to guess where the flight is leaving from or going to.

Learning from Realia

(page 262) Air Afrique also has service to the United States. They fly Abidjan-Dakar-New York.

Assessment

Check for understanding by making false statements about the items on Vocabulary Transparencies 8.2–8.3. Have students correct your statements. For example: **Avant le voyage, Justine fait ses devoirs. (Non, elle ne fait pas ses devoirs. Elle fait ses valises.) C'est un tableau. (Ce n'est pas un tableau. C'est un écran.)**

Writing Development

- Have students write answers to Activities 1 and 2 in paragraph form to illustrate how the answers to all the items tell a story.
- Have students write a short paragraph describing the illustration in Activity 4.

Answers to Commençons

3 *Answers will vary but may include:*
—Bonjour, madame.
—Bonjour, monsieur. Votre billet et votre passeport, s'il vous plaît.
—L'avion va partir à l'heure ou il va avoir du retard?
—L'avion va partir à l'heure. Vous voulez une place côté couloir ou côté fenêtre?
—Côté couloir, s'il vous plaît.
—Voilà votre carte d'embarquement. L'avion va partir de la porte 50.

4 *Answers will vary.*
Students can look at the illustration and reincorporate all the vocabulary from the **Mots** section to describe it.

Reaching All Students

Linguistic and Spatial Learners Linguistic learners enjoy talking and/or writing. It is these types of students who would enjoy giving a **résumé** of the activities such as 1 and 2. On the other hand, spatial learners prefer activities such as 3 and 4. They like pictures and visual presentations.

Vocabulaire *Mots 2*

1 Preparation

Resource Manager

Vocabulary Transparencies 8.4–8.5
Audio Activities Booklet TE, pages 100–101
Audiocassette 5B/CD 5
Workbook, page 80
Quiz 2, page 40
ExamView Pro®

Bellringer Review

Use BRR Transparency 8.2 or write the following on the board.
List six words that deal with an airport.

2 Presentation

Step 1 Have students look at Vocabulary Transparencies 8.4–8.5 as they repeat each word or expression after you or the recording on Audiocassette 5B/CD 5.

Step 2 As you present the new vocabulary, you may intersperse comprehension questions. For example: **C'est un coffre à bagages? C'est un siège? Qu'est-ce que c'est? Le steward parle à un passager? Qui parle à un passager? Il faut mettre ses bagages sous le siège? Il faut mettre ses bagages dans le coffre à bagages? Il faut mettre ses bagages où?**

Step 3 Then have students open their books and read the new vocabulary aloud.

Vocabulaire *Mots 2*

À bord

Le personnel de bord:
- le pilote
- le steward
- l'hôtesse de l'air

C'est un vol non-fumeurs.

Il faut mettre vos bagages sous le siège devant vous ou dans le coffre à bagages.

L'hôtesse de l'air fait une annonce.

Reaching All Students

Total Physical Response

Vous êtes à bord d'un avion.
Montrez votre carte d'embarquement à un steward.
Cherchez votre place.
Prenez votre place.
Ah, levez-vous. Mettez votre bagage à main dans le coffre à bagages.
Et mettez votre sac sous le siège devant vous.
Et maintenant prenez votre place.
Attachez votre ceinture de sécurité.

Le steward sert des boissons à bord.
On sert un repas.

Vous ne finissez pas votre repas?
Non, merci. Je n'ai plus faim.

On ramasse les plateaux.

Un passager sort ses bagages du coffre à bagages.
Une passagère dort.
Une autre remplit sa carte de débarquement.

About the French Language

- You will hear both **le coffre à bagages** and **le compartiment au-dessus de votre tête.**
- Many languages now use the term *flight attendant.* The French still use **un steward** and **une hôtesse de l'air.**

Assessment

Check for comprehension by miming activities and having students try to guess who you are and what you are doing by asking questions. For example: Teacher mimes the action of looking at a paper. Students ask: **Vous regardez un billet? Un passeport? Une carte d'embarquement? Vous êtes un hôtesse de l'air?**

Recycling

Have students describe the people in the photos on pages 264–265.

3 Practice

Commençons
Let's use our new words

5 After completing this activity, have a student retell the story.

7 For false statements, have students supply correct information whenever possible. For example: **2. Faux. On met ses bagages à main sous le siège ou dans le coffre à bagages.**

Reaching All Students

Additional Practice Have students work in pairs to make a list of airport activities. They then decide under which of the two headings each activity belongs: **avant le départ** or **à bord de l'avion.**

Reteaching

Show Vocabulary Transparencies 8.4–8.5. Have students make up *true/false* statements about what they see. They may make up wildly illogical things that will make everyone laugh. (This is an excellent technique to check comprehension. If students laugh, you know they have understood.) Expand this activity and have the students correct the false statements.

Commençons
Let's use our new words

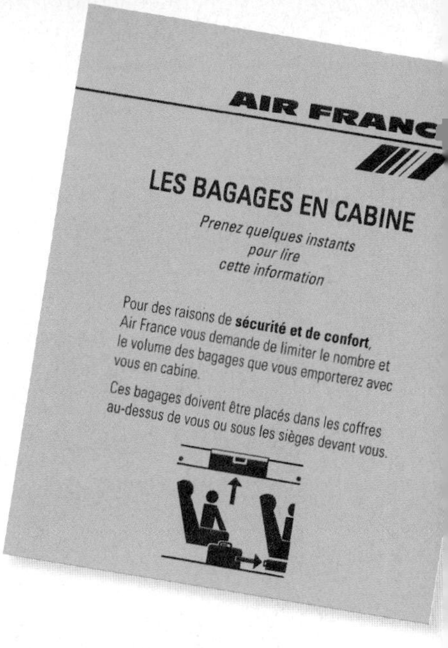

AIR FRANC
LES BAGAGES EN CABINE
Prenez quelques instants pour lire cette information
Pour des raisons de sécurité et de confort, Air France vous demande de limiter le nombre et le volume des bagages que vous emporterez avec vous en cabine.
Ces bagages doivent être placés dans les coffres au-dessus de vous ou sous les sièges devant vous.

5 **Historiette** **À bord de l'avion**
Inventez une histoire.

1. Les passagers sont à bord?
2. Le personnel de bord fait des annonces?
3. Il faut attacher sa ceinture de sécurité avant le décollage?
4. Il faut mettre ses bagages à main sous le siège?
5. On peut mettre des bagages dans le coffre à bagages?
6. Après le décollage, on sert le dîner?
7. Qui sert le dîner, le steward ou le pilote?
8. On peut fumer pendant le vol?

L'avion décolle.

6 **Antonymes** Trouvez le contraire.

1. atterrir	**a.** mettre
2. l'embarquement	**b.** à destination de
3. une hôtesse de l'air	**c.** l'atterrissage
4. en provenance de	**d.** le débarquement
5. un vol intérieur	**e.** un steward
6. embarquer	**f.** un vol international
7. l'arrivée	**g.** décoller
8. sortir	**h.** débarquer
9. le décollage	**i.** le départ

7 **À bord** Vrai ou faux?

1. Il faut passer par le contrôle de sécurité avant le vol.
2. On peut laisser ses bagages à main dans le couloir pendant le vol.
3. Il faut attacher sa ceinture de sécurité avant le décollage et l'atterrissage.
4. Il faut faire ses valises après le vol.
5. L'hôtesse de l'air ou le steward ramasse les plateaux après le repas.
6. Le pilote sert un repas et des boissons pendant le vol.
7. L'hôtesse de l'air fait une annonce.
8. Le steward dort pendant le vol.
9. Il faut remplir sa carte de débarquement.

Answers to Commençons

5 *Answers will vary but may include:*
1. Oui, les passagers sont à bord.
2. Oui, le personnel de bord fait des annonces.
3. Oui, il faut attacher sa ceinture de sécurité avant le décollage.
4. Oui, il faut mettre ses bagages à main sous le siège.
5. Oui, on peut mettre des bagages dans le coffre à bagages.
6. Oui, après le décollage on sert le dîner.
7. Le steward sert le dîner.
8. Non, on ne peut pas fumer pendant le vol.

6	7
1. g	**1.** V
2. d	**2.** F
3. e	**3.** V
4. b	**4.** F
5. f	**5.** V
6. h	**6.** F
7. i	**7.** V
8. a	**8.** F
9. c	**9.** V

8 Une carte d'embarquement This is a boarding card for a flight you are about to take. Tell a classmate (your partner) all you can about your flight based on the information on the card.

9 Arrivées Work with a classmate. Look at this arrival screen at Charles-de-Gaulle Airport. Give as much information about the flights as you can, then ask each other questions about them.

Aéroport Charles-de-Gaulle, Roissy

For more practice using words from ***Mots 2****, do Activity 25 on page H26 at the end of this book.*

8 and 9 These activities encourage students to use the chapter vocabulary in open-ended situations. It is not necessary to have all students do all activities. Let students choose the ones they wish to do.

Attention!

Note that the activities are color-coded. All the activities in the text are communicative. However, the ones with blue titles are guided communication. The red titles indicate that the answers to the activity are more open-ended and can vary more. You may wish to correct students' mistakes more so in the guided activities than in the activities with a red title, which lend themselves to a freer response.

ENCORE PLUS This *infogap* activity will allow students to practice in pairs. The activity should be very manageable for them, since all vocabulary and structures are familiar to them.

Answers to Commençons

8 *Answers will vary but may include:* C'est un vol intérieur à destination de Bordeaux. C'est le vol numéro 6117. L'avion part de la porte 24 à 8 h 55, le premier octobre. C'est un vol non-fumeurs.

9 *Answers will vary.*

1 Preparation

Resource Manager

Audio Activities Booklet TE, pages 102–104
Audiocassette 5B/CD 5
Workbook, pages 81–83
Quizzes 3–5, pages 41–43
ExamView Pro®

Bellringer Review

Use BRR Transparency 8.3 or write the following on the board.
List at least four things **une hôtesse de l'air** or **un steward** does on a plane.

2 Presentation

Les verbes en -ir au présent

Attention!

Most regular **-ir** verbs are not high-frequency words. Students will use them far less often than the **-er** verbs and the common irregular verbs.

Step 1 Write the forms of **choisir** on the board. Now pronounce the plural forms.

Step 2 Draw a line through the plural endings beginning with **ss** and pronounce what remains. What remains is the pronunciation for all the singular sounds.

Step 3 Point out the spelling of the singular endings: **-is, -is, -it.**

Structure

Describing people's activities

Les verbes en -ir au présent

1. A second group of regular verbs in French has infinitives that end in **-ir.** Verbs like **finir** *(to finish)* and **choisir** *(to choose)* are regular **-ir** verbs. They have two different stems, one for the singular and one for the plural. Study the following chart.

			FINIR		CHOISIR	
je	fin	-is	je	finis	je	choisis
tu	fin	-is	tu	finis	tu	choisis
il/elle/on	fin	-it	il/elle/on	finit	il/elle/on	choisit
nous	fin + iss	-ons	nous	finissons	nous	choisissons
vous	fin + iss	-ez	vous	finissez	vous	choisissez
ils/elles	fin + iss	-ent	ils/elles	finissent	ils/elles	choisissent

2. Other verbs that belong to this group are **atterrir** and **remplir.**

Ils remplissent une carte de débarquement.
L'avion atterrit à l'heure.

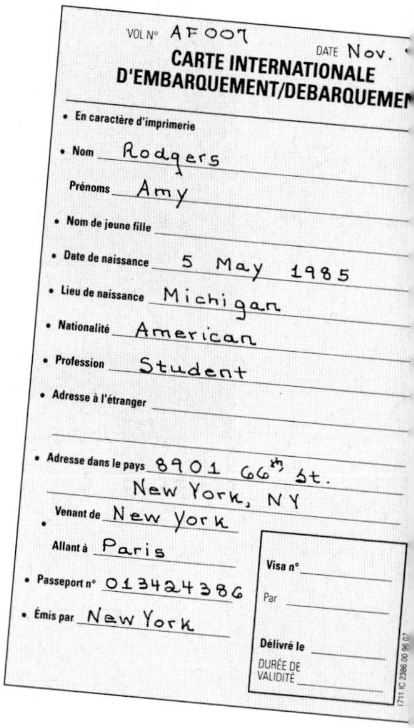
VOL N° AF007
DATE Nov.
CARTE INTERNATIONALE
D'EMBARQUEMENT/DEBARQUEME
En caractère d'imprimerie
Nom Rodgers
Prénoms Amy
Nom de jeune fille
Date de naissance 5 May 1985
Lieu de naissance Michigan
Nationalité American
Profession Student
Adresse à l'étranger
Adresse dans le pays 8901 66th St.
New York, NY
Venant de New York
Allant à Paris
Passeport n° 013424386
Émis par New York
Visa n°
Par
Délivré le
DURÉE DE VALIDITÉ

Continuons

Let's put our words together

10 Historiette Un vol pour Paris

Répondez d'après les indications.

1. Madame Lauzier choisit quelle compagnie? (Air France)
2. Elle choisit quelle classe? (la classe économique)
3. Elle choisit une place côté couloir ou côté fenêtre? (côté fenêtre)
4. Elle finit tout son repas? (non)
5. Son avion atterrit à quelle heure? (à midi)
6. Il atterrit à quel aéroport? (à Charles-de-Gaulle)
7. Qu'est-ce qu'elle remplit avant l'arrivée? (une carte de débarquement)

Answers to Continuons

10

1. Elle choisit Air France.
2. Elle choisit la classe économique.
3. Elle choisit une place côté fenêtre.
4. Non, elle ne finit pas tout son repas.
5. Son avion atterrit à midi.
6. Il atterrit à Charles-de-Gaulle.
7. Elle remplit une carte de débarquement.

11 Historiette Au restaurant Donnez des réponses personnelles.

1. En général, tu choisis des restaurants chers ou pas chers?
2. Tu choisis la spécialité de la maison?
3. Tu choisis de la viande ou du poisson?
4. Tu finis ton repas par un dessert ou du fromage?
5. Tu choisis un gâteau ou une glace?
6. Tu finis toujours tout sur ton assiette?

12 Un bon dîner Mettez au pluriel d'après le modèle.

Je choisis du bœuf et tu choisis du poisson.
Nous choisissons du bœuf et vous choisissez du poisson.

1. Je choisis un petit restaurant et tu choisis un restaurant gastronomique.
2. Je choisis un steak bien cuit et tu choisis un steak à point.
3. Je remplis mon assiette et tu remplis ton assiette.
4. Je finis mon repas par une tarte et tu finis ton repas par des crêpes Suzette.
5. Je finis mon repas par un crème et tu finis ton repas par un express.

13 Un autre vol Complétez avec **choisir** ou **remplir.**

1. Les passagers ____ un vol Air France?
2. Ils ____ une place côté fenêtre ou côté couloir?
3. Ils ____ le poulet ou le poisson pour le dîner à bord?
4. Ils ____ leur carte de débarquement pendant le vol?

ENCORE PLUS *For more practice using **-ir** verbs, do Activity 26 on page H27 at the end of this book.*

3 Practice

Continuons
Let's put our words together

12 You may wish to have students work in groups of at least four to reinforce the forms being used. Student 1 begins, points to Student 2 as he or she says **tu.** Student 2 and Student 3 say the **nous** form together, then point to Student 4 and Student 1 as they say **vous.** Students switch roles as they go through the activity. **Expansion:** Student 4 adds a statement about two other classmates not in the group: **Marie et Cécile, elles choisissent un petit restaurant...**

Writing Development
Have students write the answers to Activities 10–11 in paragraph form.

ENCORE PLUS This *infogap* activity will allow students to practice in pairs. The activity should be very manageable for them, since all vocabulary and structures are familiar to them.

Answers to Continuons

11 *Answers will vary but may include:*

1. En général, je choisis des restaurants pas chers.
2. Non, je ne choisis pas la spécialité de la maison.
3. Je choisis du poisson.
4. Je finis mon repas par un dessert.
5. Je choisis un gâteau.
6. Oui, je finis toujours tout sur mon assiette.

12

1. Nous choisissons un petit restaurant et vous choisissez un restaurant gastronomique.
2. Nous choisissons un steak bien cuit et vous choisissez un steak à point.
3. Nous remplissons notre assiette et vous remplissez votre assiette.
4. Nous finissons notre repas par une tarte et vous finissez votre repas par des crêpes Suzette.
5. Nous finissons notre repas par un crème et vous finissez votre repas par un express.

13

1. choisissent
2. choisissent
3. choisissent
4. remplissent

1 Preparation

Bellringer Review

Use BRR Transparency 8.4 or write the following on the board.
Complete the following expressions with the appropriate word related to plane travel.
1. un _____ à main
2. une place _____ fenêtre
3. le _____ de sécurité
4. une _____ de l'air
5. le personnel de _____

2 Presentation

Quel et tout

Step 1 Lead students through Items 1–2 on page 270.

Step 2 Explain the spelling, pronunciation changes, and meanings of the adjectives **quel** and **tout.**

Learning from Realia

(page 270) **La navette** is the term used for *shuttle.* This is the cover for the Paris-Bordeaux shuttle. Have students guess the meaning of **La navette.** If they need a hint, show a map of France, and emphasize that **la navette** goes back and forth between Paris and Bordeaux several times each day.

Describing people and things as a group
Quel et tout

1. You use the interrogative adjective **quel** with a noun when you want to ask "what" or "which." Note that all forms of **quel** are pronounced the same even though they are spelled differently.

	Masculin	Féminin
Singulier	quel vol quel avion	quelle compagnie quelle hôtesse
Pluriel	quels vols quels‿avions	quelles compagnies quelles‿hôtesses

2. You use **tout(e)** with the definite articles **le, la,** and **l'** to express "the whole" or "the entire." You use **tous** and **toutes** with **les** to express "all" or "every."

	Masculin	Féminin
Singulier	tout le personnel	toute la compagnie
Pluriel	tous les stewards	toutes les hôstesses

Toute la classe fait le voyage. *The whole class is taking the trip.*
Tous les élèves prennent le même vol. *All the students are taking the same flight.*
Il y a un vol tous les jours. *There is a flight every day.*

Rappelez-vous que...
The expression **tout le monde** means "everyone."
Tout le monde veut aller en France.

Continuons

Let's put our words together

14 **Quels cours?** Répondez d'après le modèle.

—Tu aimes quels cours?
—Moi? J'aime tous les cours.

1. Tu aimes quelles matières?
2. Tu aimes quelles langues?
3. Tu aimes quelles sciences?
4. Tu aimes quels livres?
5. Tu aimes quels CD?
6. Tu aimes quels profs?

15 **Quel vol?** Complétez avec **quel** et puis répondez.

1. Tu fais un voyage? ____ voyage?
2. Ton avion part à ____ heure?
3. Ton avion part de ____ porte?
4. Pendant le vol, tu vas regarder ____ film?
5. Tu vas écouter ____ cassettes?
6. Tu aimes ____ livres?

AIR FRANCE
faire du ciel le plus bel endroit de la terre
le billet électronique
si simple, si pratique
15:05 NICE
16:20 PARIS
15:45 LYON

16 **Tous les vols pour quelle ville?**
Complétez avec **tout.**

1. ____ les places sont occupées.
2. ____ l'avion est classe économique. Il n'y a pas de première classe.
3. ____ la cabine est non-fumeurs.
4. C'est vrai. Maintenant ____ les vols sont non-fumeurs.

17 **Dans l'avion** Complétez et puis répondez.

1. ____ le personnel parle ____ langues? (tout, quel)
2. ____ les stewards servent ____ boissons et ____ repas? (tout, quel, quel)
3. ____ les hôtesses font ____ annonces? (tout, quel)
4. ____ les passagers font enregistrer ____ bagages? (tout, quel)
5. ____ les vols ont ____ destination? (tout, quel)

18 **Toute la famille** Get together with a classmate. Tell each other some things that your whole family often does together. Compare notes and see if both your families do many of the same things.

Structure

3 Practice

Continuons

Let's put our words together

15, **16**, and **17** Do these activities with books open. Then assign them to be written for homework. You can go over them again the next day.

Reaching All Students

Dictée You may wish to give this dictation after doing the activities on page 271.

Quelles voitures sont françaises?
Quel livre est vieux?
Où sont toutes les filles?
Quels élèves aiment tous les profs?
Toute la classe fait tous les devoirs.

Answers to Continuons

14

1. Moi? J'aime toutes les matières.
2. Moi? J'aime toutes les langues.
3. Moi? J'aime toutes les sciences.
4. Moi? J'aime tous les livres.
5. Moi? J'aime tous les CD.
6. Moi? J'aime tous les profs.

15

1. Quel
2. quelle
3. quelle
4. quel
5. quelles
6. quels

16

1. Toutes
2. Tout
3. Toute
4. tous

17 *Answers will vary but may include:*

1. Tout, quelles
   Tout le personnel parle français, anglais et espagnol.
2. Tous, quelles, quels
   Tous les stewards servent du café et du coca, du poisson et du poulet.
3. Toutes, quelles
   Toutes les hôtesses annoncent: Il faut attacher votre ceinture de sécurité.
4. Tous, quels
   Tous les passagers font enregistrer leurs valises.
5. Tous, quelle
   Tous les vols sont à destination de Paris.

18 *Answers will vary.*

1 Preparation

Bellringer Review

Use BRR Transparency 8.5 or write the following on the board.
Complete the following with the correct form of an appropriate verb.

1. **Les passagers _____ leurs places dans l'avion.**
2. **L'avion _____ à l'aéroport de New York.**
3. **Le vol n'arrive pas à l'heure. Il _____ du retard.**
4. **Marc _____ ses valises parce qu'il va _____ un voyage.**

2 Presentation

Les verbes **sortir, partir, dormir** et **servir**

Step 1 Begin your explanation with the plural forms of these verbs. Draw a line through the last four letters and show students that what is left is the sound for all the singular forms.

Step 2 Now go over the singular forms and their spellings. Have students repeat the forms after you.

Step 3 Now lead students through the information in the **Savez-vous que... ?** box.

Describing more activities
Les verbes **sortir, partir, dormir** et **servir**

The verbs **sortir, partir, dormir**, and **servir** all follow the same pattern—the consonant sound in the infinitive is heard in the plural forms but not in the singular forms. Study the following.

SORTIR		PARTIR		DORMIR		SERVIR	
je	sors	je	pars	je	dors	je	sers
tu	sors	tu	pars	tu	dors	tu	sers
il/elle/on	sort	il/elle/on	part	il/elle/on	dort	il/elle/on	sert
nous	sortons	nous	partons	nous	dormons	nous	servons
vous	sortez	vous	partez	vous	dormez	vous	servez
ils/elles	sortent	ils/elles	partent	ils/elles	dorment	ils/elles	servent

Savez-vous que... ?

Sortir means "to go out" or "to leave."
Je sors de l'école à trois heures.
With a direct object, it means "to take out."
Je sors mes livres de mon sac à dos.

Music Connection

Have students sing this little song on page 272. Show them the picture of the windmills as you say **moulin.** Ask them what they think **meunier** means *(miller).*

Reaching All Students

Kinesthetic Learners Have students who like to perform stand up and act out Activity 21 on page 273.

Class Motivator

Have students jot down some actions that can be mimed using **sortir, partir, dormir,** and **servir.** In teams of four, each one mimes an action while the others guess what it is by asking questions. To practice **il/elle** forms, have them ask you questions about the student doing the miming. Then, each group chooses one action to mime for the class, which guesses the action using **vous.**

Continuons

Let's put our words together

19 **Historiette** **Un vol Abidjan–Paris**
Inventez une histoire.

1. M. Kuti va prendre l'avion. Il sort son billet?
2. Il sort son passeport?
3. Son avion part de quelle porte?
4. Son avion part à quelle heure?
5. À bord, on sert des boissons?
6. On sert un repas?
7. M. Kuti dort un peu pendant le vol?

M. Kuti part pour Abidjan.

20 **Historiette** **Qui part?** Donnez des réponses personnelles.

1. Tu pars pour l'école à quelle heure le matin?
2. Tu sors de la maison à quelle heure le matin?
3. Quand tu arrives à l'école, qu'est-ce que tu sors de ton sac à dos?
4. Quelquefois, tu dors un peu en classe?
5. Le week-end, tu sors avec tes copains? Qu'est-ce que vous faites?

21 **On part demain.** Répétez la conversation.

Valérie: Demain, on part pour Tunis, Marie et moi!
Philippe: Vous partez à quelle heure?
Valérie: On part à onze heures.
Philippe: Et vous partez de quel aéroport?
Valérie: D'Orly. C'est la première fois que je pars d'Orly.
Philippe: Ah oui?
Valérie: Oui, en général, nous partons toujours de Charles-de-Gaulle.

FRENCH Online
For more information on air travel in the Francophone world, go to the Glencoe French Web site: french.glencoe.com

Structure

3 Practice

Continuons

Let's put our words together

19 and **20** It is recommended that you go over these activities in class before assigning them for homework. Students can retell the stories of Activities 19 and 20 in their own words.

21 You may wish to use the recorded version of this activity.

Learning from Photos

(page 273) You may wish to ask the following questions about the photo:

M. Kuti va de Paris à Abidjan. C'est un vol intérieur ou international?
M. Kuti fait enregistrer ses bagages?
L'avion part de quelle porte d'embarquement?
Qu'est-ce que M. Kuti donne à l'agent de la ligne aérienne?
L'agent a l'air content?
Il a l'air sympathique?
Qu'est-ce que l'agent porte?
Et M. Kuti, il est content aussi?
Qu'est-ce qu'il porte?

Answers to Continuons

19 *Answers will vary but may include:*

1. Oui, il sort son billet.
2. Oui, il sort son passeport.
3. Son avion part de la porte A45.
4. Son avion part à huit heures vingt.
5. Oui, à bord on sert des boissons.
6. Oui, on sert un repas.
7. Non, M. Kuti ne dort pas pendant le vol.

20 *Answers will vary but may include:*

1. Je pars pour l'école à sept heures et demie.
2. Je sors de la maison à sept heures et demie.
3. Je sors mes cahiers et mes livres de mon sac.
4. Non, je ne dors pas en classe.
5. Oui, le week-end je sors avec mes copains. On va au café.

Reteaching

- Write the verbs **sortir, partir, dormir,** and **servir** on the board. Have students make up original sentences using these verbs.
- Students may enjoy discussing **Qui sort avec qui?** They can talk about celebrities if they feel uncomfortable talking about themselves.

3 Practice *(continued)*

22 and **23** Do these activities first orally with books open. Then have students write them for homework. Go over them again the next day.

Learning from Photos

(page 274) This photo is of Port El Kantaoui, which is located about 8 kilometers north of Sousse. It is one of Tunisia's finest beach resorts. It has an excellent beach, an 18-hole golf course, and trails for horseback riding.

22 **Après la conversation** Complétez d'après la conversation.

1. Valérie et Marie ____ pour Tunis.
2. Elles ____ en avion.
3. Leur avion ____ à onze heures.
4. Il ____ d'Orly.
5. En général, Valérie ____ d'Orly ou de Charles-de-Gaulle?

Port El Kantaoui, Tunisie

23 **Historiette** **Un petit voyage** Complétez.

1. Vous ____ quand? (partir)
2. Votre avion ____ à quelle heure? (partir)
3. Vous ____ pendant le vol? (dormir)
4. Vos copains ____? (dormir)
5. Après votre arrivée à Paris, vous ____ tout de suite? (sortir)
6. Et vos amis, ils ____ aussi ou ils ____? (sortir, dormir)

24 **Un travail** Work with a classmate. You've got a part-time job working at your local airport because you speak French. Help each of the following passengers.

- A passenger is leaving on flight 125 for Chicago. He doesn't know if it's leaving on time. Help him out.
- Another passenger is confused. He doesn't know his flight number to New York. Let him know what it is and also what time it leaves.
- An older passenger doesn't have his glasses. They are in his suitcase. He asks you to tell him what his seat number is.
- Another passenger is in a real hurry. She wants to know what gate to go to for her flight to Los Angeles. Tell her.

Answers to Continuons

22
1. partent
2. partent
3. part
4. part
5. part

23
1. partez
2. part
3. dormez
4. dorment
5. sortez
6. sortent, dorment

24 *Answers will vary but may include:*

- —Pardon, le vol numéro 125 a du retard?
  —Non, monsieur, le vol numéro 125 va partir à l'heure. Il part de la porte ____.
- —Pardon, quel est le numéro du vol à destination de New York, s'il vous plaît?
  —Monsieur, le numéro de votre vol est le ____. L'avion va partir à ____.
- —Pardon, je ne peux pas voir le numéro de ma place sur ma carte d'embarquement. Quelle est le numéro de ma place/mon siège?
  —Monsieur, vous avez la place ____.
- —Pardon, le vol à destination de Los Angeles part de quelle porte, s'il vous plaît?
  —Madame, le vol à destination de Los Angeles part de la porte ____.

Fort-de-France, Martinique

Attention!

A masculine adjective or noun that ends in **-al** changes to **-aux** in the plural.

un journal → **des journaux**

un vol international → **des vols internationaux**

but

une ville internationale → **des villes internationales**

Complétez.

La Martinique est une île __1__ (tropical) dans la mer des Caraïbes. Sa ville __2__ (principal) est Fort-de-France. À Fort-de-France, il y a plusieurs petits parcs __3__ (municipal). L'aéroport __4__ (international) est près de la ville. Tous les jours, il y a des vols __5__ (international) qui décollent et atterrissent. Il y a des vols __6__ (international) à destination de Paris et de beaucoup de villes des États-Unis comme Miami et New York.

Vous êtes sur le bon chemin. Allez-y!

Structure

Note: In general, students need a great deal of ear training before they remember to make the correct plural sound of the masculine nouns and adjectives in this **Attention!** section.

Assessment

As an informal assessment, have students quickly give the plural of the following expressions:

- **un problème local**
- **un problème médical**
- **un problème régional**
- **un problème social**
- **une organisation locale**
- **une organisation médicale**
- **une organisation régionale**
- **une organisation sociale**

Learning from Photos

(page 275) This photo shows the beautiful natural setting of Fort-de-France beneath the Pitons du Carbet on the baie des Flamands. Fort-de-France is the major city of Martinique, and it is home to approximately one-third of the island's 360,000 people.

Allez-y!
At this point in the chapter, students have learned all the vocabulary and structure necessary to complete the chapter. The conversation and cultural readings that follow recycle all the material learned up to this point.

Answers to Attention!

1. tropicale
2. principale
3. municipaux
4. international
5. internationaux
6. internationaux

1 Preparation

Resource Manager

Audio Activities Booklet TE, pages 104–105
Audiocassette 5B/CD 5
CD-ROM

Bellringer Review

Use BRR Transparency 8.6 or write the following on the board.
You're packing for a trip. Write down all the articles of clothing you're taking.

2 Presentation

Step 1 Tell students they are going to hear a conversation between Pierre and Cécile, who are about to take a trip.

Step 2 Ask students to open their books to page 276. Have them follow along as you read the conversation or play the recorded version on Audiocassette 5B/CD 5.

Step 3 Have students work in pairs to practice the conversation. Then have several pairs present it to the class.

Step 4 After presenting the conversation, go over the **Après la conversation** activity. If students can answer the questions with relative ease, move on. Students should not be expected to memorize the conversation.

Glencoe Technology

CD-ROM

On the CD-ROM, students can watch a dramatization of this conversation. They can then play the role of either one of the characters and record themselves in the conversation.

Conversation

On part pour Toulouse.

Départ à destination de Toulouse, vol Air France numéro 6106. Embarquement immédiat, porte 24.

Cécile: C'est notre vol. On y va?
Pierre: D'accord. Tu sors les cartes d'embarquement?
Cécile: Mais moi, je n'ai pas les cartes d'embarquement!
Pierre: Tu n'as pas les cartes d'embarquement! Ben, elles sont où alors?
Cécile: Dans ton sac?
Pierre: Ah, oui. Voilà! On part de la porte 24.
Cécile: On a quelles places?
Pierre: 10A et 10B.
Cécile: Ah, c'est bien. C'est à l'avant de la cabine. On va pouvoir sortir vite.

Après la conversation

Répondez.

1. Où sont Cécile et Pierre?
2. Qu'est-ce qu'on annonce?
3. Quel est le numéro de leur vol?
4. Ils vont où?
5. Ils partent de quelle porte?
6. Qui a les cartes d'embarquement?
7. Ils ont quelles places?
8. Pourquoi c'est bien d'avoir des places à l'avant de la cabine?

Answers to Après la conversation

1. Ils sont dans le hall des départs.
2. On annonce le vol.
3. Le numéro de leur vol est le 6106.
4. Ils vont à Toulouse.
5. Ils partent de la porte 24.
6. Pierre a les cartes d'embarquement.
7. Ils ont les places 10A et 10B.
8. On peut sortir vite.

Career Connection

Because of the popularity of international travel (for business and pleasure) to and from the French-speaking world, French is an important communication tool. Have students make a list of at least four professions in the travel industry for which French would be useful or necessary.

Parlons un peu plus

Let's talk some more

A **Tu vas où?** You're at the airport waiting for your flight. You strike up a conversation with the person sitting next to you (your partner). Find out information about each other's flight.

B **Un billet pour Nice** Work with a classmate. You want to fly from New York to Nice. Call the airline to get a reservation. Your partner will be the reservation agent. Before you call, think about the information you will need to give or get from the agent: date of departure, departure time, arrival time in Nice, flight number, price.

Cap Ferrat, près de Nice, France

Prononciation

Le son /l/ final

1. The names Michelle and Nicole were originally French names, but today many American girls also have these names. When you hear French people say the names Michelle and Nicole, the final /l/ sound is much softer than in English. Say "Michelle" and "Nicole" in French. Repeat the following words.

il	**vol**	**animal**	**elle**	**école**
salle	**décolle**	**journal**	**quel**	**ville**

2. Now repeat the following sentences.

   C'est un vol international spécial.
   Quelle est la ville principale?
   Mademoiselle Michelle, elle est très belle.

Il décolle.

Answers to Parlons un peu plus

A *Answers will vary but may include:*

—Vous allez où?
—Je vais à _____.
—Ah, vous prenez le vol _____. Moi aussi.
—Nous avons le même vol. Vous avez quelle place?
—Moi, j'ai la place 15C. Et vous?
—J'ai la (place) 15A. Nous sommes voisins!

B Students can ask the following types of questions. **L'agent** will answer accordingly.

Je veux aller à Nice.
Il y a un vol Paris-Nice?
Il part à quelle heure?
Il arrive à quelle heure?
Quel est le numéro du vol?
Et quel est le prix?

3 Practice

Parlons un peu plus

Let's talk some more

A and **B** Have students work in pairs. You may wish to choose a pair of students to do these activities for the class.

B You may wish to tell students that there is a 6-hour time difference between New York and Nice, or refer them to the map on page 280. You may also want to provide approximate flight costs and the exchange rate for euros before they begin.

Prononciation

Step 1 Model the key words **Il décolle** and have students repeat in unison. Then do the same for the other words and phrases.

Step 2 You may wish to give students the following **dictée:**

Le vol international décolle.
Michelle, elle est belle.

Step 3 For additional pronunciation practice, you may wish to use Audiocassette 5B/CD 5 and the Pronunciation Transparency P 8.

Learning from Photos

(page 277) Cap Ferrat is close to Nice, off the road to Menton on the Italian border. It is a very peaceful place, which has superb views over the Mediterranean, as seen in this photo. On a clear day one can see as far as the Italian Riviera. Cap Ferrat has many beautiful private homes surrounded by gardens.

Resource Manager

Audio Activities Booklet TE, pages 106–107
Audiocassette 5B/CD 5

Bellringer Review

Use BRR Transparency 8.7 or write the following on the board.
Write questions using a form of **quel.** For example: **Le garçon? Quel garçon?**

1. **Les passagers?**
2. **Les filles?**
3. **L'avion?**
4. **Ton amie?**

National Standards

Communication
The reading about traveling to Paris by plane and the related activities allow students to gain an understanding of the steps involved in this mode of transportation between the United States and France.

Lectures culturelles

Reading Strategy

Recognizing text organization

Before you read a passage, try to figure out how the text is organized. If you can follow the organization of a text, you will understand the main ideas more quickly and be able to look for certain ideas and information more easily.

On va en France.

C'est le mois d'avril et toute la classe de Madame Cadet va passer les vacances de Pâques[1] en France. Ils sont maintenant dans le hall de l'aérogare 1 de l'aéroport international JFK à New York. Ils sont au comptoir d'Air France. Ils vont prendre le vol 007. L'agent vérifie leurs billets et leurs passeports. Il donne toutes les cartes d'embarquement à Madame Cadet.

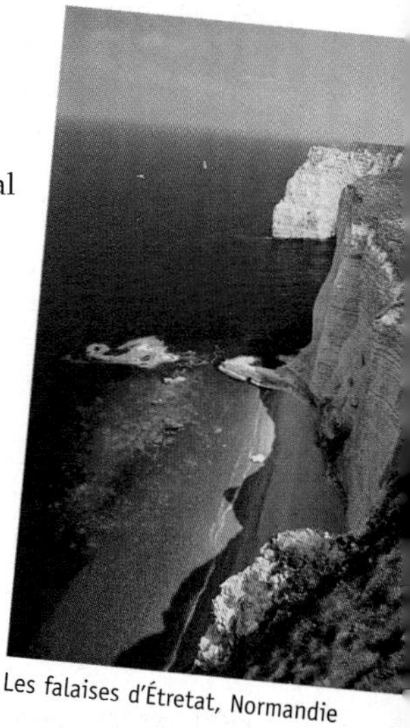
Les falaises d'Étretat, Normandie

Mont-Saint-Michel, Normandie

Les élèves passent par le contrôle de sécurité. Leur avion part de la porte A. Il part à l'heure. Il ne va pas avoir de retard. Après le décollage, le personnel de bord sert des boissons et un repas. Après le repas, il y a un film. Beaucoup de personnes ne regardent pas le film; elles dorment. Mais pas les élèves de Madame Cadet. Ils ne dorment pas. Ils parlent de leur voyage. Ils vont passer quelques jours à Paris et ensuite[2] ils vont en Normandie. Là, ils vont visiter le Mont-Saint-Michel. Avant l'arrivée à Paris, tout le monde remplit une carte de débarquement.

[1] Pâques *Easter*   [2] ensuite *then*

Presentation

Pre-reading

Step 1 Have students locate New York and Paris on a map. You may want to have students look at the photos on pages 278–279 now.

Step 2 Ask students who among them has traveled by air. Did they take a domestic or an international flight? What are some of the differences between the two? What were the good and bad points about their flights?

Step 3 Have students scan the reading quickly and silently. You may wish to tell them that the French tend to refer to JFK Airport as Kennedy Airport.

Learning from Photos

(page 278 top) Étretat is just east of the port of Le Havre. This area is famous for its spectacular white cliffs, which give it the name Alabaster Coast. Étretat is a resort town, where one can admire the incredible shapes carved into the chalk by the breaking surf.

(page 278 bottom) Mont-Saint-Michel, with its Gothic abbey and tall spire, is the third most popular tourist spot in France after Paris and Versailles. It has been a very popular pilgrimage center ever since the first chapel was built in the eighth century. Mont-Saint-Michel is connected to land during low tide. The tide comes in at an amazing speed, and there are dangerous patches of quicksand in the bay. The bay is silting up and tidal conditions are changing. Tourists are advised to pay close attention to tidal information.

À huit heures du matin, après un vol agréable, l'avion atterrit à l'aéroport Charles-de-Gaulle à Roissy. Charles-de-Gaulle est un des deux aéroports de Paris. D'abord, il faut passer au contrôle des passeports. Ensuite les formalités de douane[3] sont très simples et quarante minutes après l'atterrissage, les élèves de Madame Cadet sont dans l'autocar (le bus) qui fait la navette[4] entre l'aéroport et Paris. Tout le monde est très fatigué après le long vol. Vous croyez qu'ils vont dormir? Pas question! Le premier jour à Paris, on ne dort pas. On va visiter la belle ville de Paris.

[3] douane *customs*
[4] fait la navette *makes the run*

L'île de la Cité, Paris

Un car Air France, aéroport Charles-de-Gaulle

Tunisie

Le Maroc

Le Mali

Après la lecture

A Un voyage en France Vrai ou faux?

1. Toute la classe de Madame Cadet va à Montréal.
2. À l'aéroport, l'agent de la compagnie aérienne donne toutes les cartes d'embarquement à un des élèves de Madame Cadet.
3. L'avion pour Paris va avoir du retard.
4. Les passagers servent un bon repas après le décollage.
5. Beaucoup de passagers dorment pendant le vol.
6. Le Mont-Saint-Michel est à Paris.
7. Les formalités de douane sont très compliquées en France.
8. Quand les élèves de Madame Cadet arrivent à Paris, ils vont dormir.

B Des informations Cherchez les informations.

1. Quel est le nom d'un aéroport à New York?
2. Quel est le nom d'un des aéroports de Paris?
3. Quel est le numéro du vol des élèves de Madame Cadet?
4. Leur avion part de quelle porte?
5. Quelle est la destination de leur vol?
6. Ils arrivent à Paris à quelle heure?

Lectures culturelles

Reading

Step 1 Lead students through the **Lecture** on pages 278–279 by presenting the reading in two or three segments.

Step 2 Have one student read three sentences; then ask comprehension questions of the others. For example, questions for the second paragraph might be: **Par où passent les élèves? Leur avion part de quelle porte? L'avion part à l'heure?**, etc.

Post-reading

Step 1 Have students retell the story, changing the French class to their own and adding personalized information.

Step 2 Have students do the **Après la lecture** activities on page 279 orally after reading the selection in class. Then assign these activities to be written at home. Go over them again the following day.

Après la lecture

A Expansion: After doing Activity A, you may wish to have the students correct each false statement made in the activity. For example: **1. Toute la classe de Mme Cadet va à Paris et en Normandie.**

B Allow students to refer to the story to look up the answers, or you may wish to use this activity as a testing device for factual recall.

Answers to Après la lecture

A	B
1. F	1. JFK
2. F	2. Charles-de-Gaulle
3. F	3. 007
4. F	4. de la porte A
5. V	5. Paris
6. F	6. à huit heures du matin
7. F	
8. F	

FRENCH Online

Encourage students to take advantage of this opportunity to learn more about air travel in the Francophone world. Perhaps you can do this in class or in a lab if students do not have Internet access at home.

About the French Language

Un autobus (un bus) is used to refer to mass transportation within city limits. Any other kind of bus transportation is expressed as **un autocar (un car).**

National Standards

Cultures
This selection familiarizes students with the time difference between the U.S. and France and its effect on travelers.

Attention!

This reading is optional. You may skip it completely, have the entire class read it, have only several students read it and report to the class, or assign it for extra credit.

Presentation

Step 1 Discuss time zones and jet lag with your students. Do they know people who live in different time zones of the United States? Have they ever traveled across time zones and felt the effects of jet lag?

Step 2 Have students read the **Lecture** quickly as they look at the illustration that accompanies it.

Step 3 Ask what they learned about **le décalage horaire.**

Après la lecture

You may wish to use a toy clock to do this activity.

Lecture supplémentaire 1

Le décalage horaire

Les gens qui voyagent beaucoup souffrent souvent du décalage horaire. Le décalage horaire, qu'est-ce que c'est? C'est la différence entre l'heure d'une ville—New York, par exemple—et une autre ville comme Paris. Quand il est minuit à New York, il est six heures du matin à Paris. Les voyageurs souffrent du décalage horaire parce que quand c'est l'heure de dormir dans une ville, c'est l'heure de travailler dans une autre.

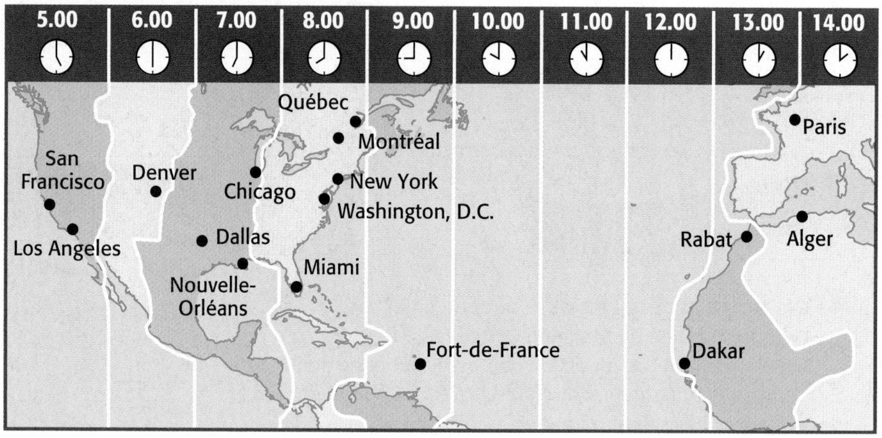

Après la lecture

Le décalage horaire Regardez la carte et répondez.

1. Quand il est midi à Washington, D.C., il est quelle heure à Paris?
2. Et à Dakar?
3. Et à Alger?
4. Et à Québec?
5. Et à Los Angeles?
6. Et à la Nouvelle-Orléans?

Answers to Après la lecture

1. Il est six heures du soir. (dix-huit heures)
2. Il est cinq heures de l'après-midi. (dix-sept heures)
3. Il est six heures du soir. (dix-huit heures)
4. Il est midi. (douze heures)
5. Il est neuf heures du matin.
6. Il est onze heures du matin.

Science Connection

To emphasize the differences between the world's time zones, you may wish to use a globe and a flashlight (for a sun). Turn out the lights and have one student hold the flashlight and another rotate the Earth. Have students indicate the progression of the "day" in France and the corresponding "day" where they live.

Un pilote écrivain

Antoine de Saint-Exupéry (1900–1944) est un écrivain (un auteur) français célèbre. Mais c'est aussi un homme d'action. Il est né[1] à Lyon en 1900. Pendant son service militaire, il apprend à piloter un avion. Il est pilote de ligne entre Toulouse et Dakar en Afrique. Il est aussi chef de l'Aéropostale (la poste par avion) à Buenos Aires. Il participe aux premiers vols France-Amérique.

Le Petit Prince est son livre le plus connu[2]. Il est connu dans le monde entier. Ses autres romans[3] reflètent sa carrière de pilote. *Courrier sud* parle de ses vols Toulouse–Dakar. *Vol de nuit* parle de trois pilotes basés à Buenos Aires. L'un d'eux est en difficulté dans le ciel[4] noir d'Amérique du Sud. *Terre des hommes* évoque le souvenir[5] de ses camarades disparus, comme Jean Mermoz, le grand aviateur français.

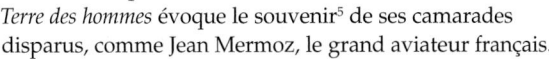

Le 13 juillet 1944, Saint-Exupéry disparaît aussi. Il disparaît dans une mission aérienne militaire au-dessus de la mer Méditerranée. Il reste[6] pour la légende le courageux, le charmant, l'exceptionnel «Saint-Ex».

Antoine de Saint-Exupéry

[1] est né *was born*
[2] le plus connu *best-known*
[3] romans *novels*
[4] ciel *sky*
[5] souvenir *memory*
[6] reste *remains*

Après la lecture

Saint-Exupéry Identifiez.
1. le nom de l'écrivain
2. la ville où il est né
3. une ville d'Amérique du Sud où il travaille
4. le nom d'un grand aviateur français

ANSWERS TO Après la lecture
1. Antoine de Saint-Exupéry
2. Lyon
3. Buenos Aires
4. Jean Mermoz

Lecture supplémentaire 2

Attention!

This reading is optional. You may skip it completely, have the entire class read it, have only several students read it and report to the class, or assign it for extra credit.

Presentation

Step 1 You may wish to ask students if any of them have ever read a novel by Antoine de Saint-Exupéry. He is often included in some of the school literature anthologies.

Step 2 Have students read the selection to themselves.

Step 3 Now have students do the **Après la lecture** activity on page 281.

Literary Companion

There is a selection by Saint-Exupéry in the literature companion on page 486 of **Bon voyage! Level 2.**

Art Connection

You may wish to show some of Saint-Exupéry's illustrations to the students. His illustrations for *The Little Prince* were even featured on the 50-franc bank note used before the recent changeover to euros. Show students his illustration of a boa constrictor eating an elephant (Chapter 1, *The Little Prince*) and ask them what they think it is. Then show the interior illustration on the next page and talk about the differences between children's and adults' perceptions.

Have students look at the stamp featured on page 258.

CONNEXIONS

National Standards

Connections
This reading about climate and weather in the French-speaking world establishes a connection with another discipline, allowing students to reinforce and further their knowledge of physical sciences through the study of French.

Attention!

The readings in the **Connexions** section are optional. They focus on some of the major disciplines taught in schools and universities. The vocabulary is useful for discussing such topics as history, literature, art, economics, business, science, etc. You may choose any of the following ways to do the readings in the **Connexions** sections.

Independent reading Have students read the selections and do the post-reading activities as homework, which you collect. This option is least intrusive on class time and requires a minimum of teacher involvement.

Homework with in-class follow-up Assign the readings and post-reading activities as homework. Review and discuss the material in class the next day.

Intensive in-class activity This option includes a pre-reading vocabulary presentation, in-class reading and discussion, assignment of the activities for homework, and a discussion of the assignment in class the following day.

Note: You may wish to have only those students interested in the particular topic read the **Connexions** selection.

CONNEXIONS

Les sciences physiques

Le climat et le temps

We often speak about the weather, especially when we are traveling. Weather can have a very positive or negative effect on our trip. When planning a vacation, for example, it's a good idea to take into account the climate of the area we are going to visit. When we talk about weather or climate, we must remember that there is a big difference between the two. Weather is the condition of the atmosphere for a short period of time. Climate refers to the weather that prevails in one area over a long period of time.

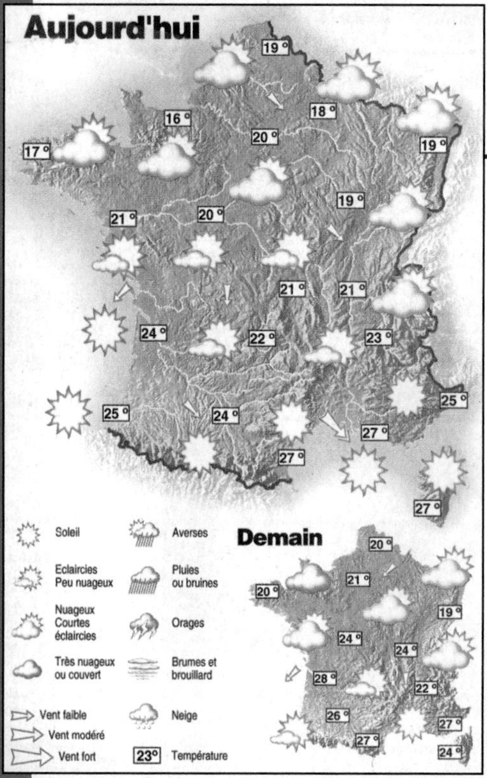

Différence entre climat et temps[1]

Il y a une grande différence entre le climat et le temps. Le temps est la condition de l'atmosphère pendant une courte période. Le temps peut changer très vite. Il peut changer plusieurs fois dans une seule journée.

Le climat, c'est le temps qu'il fait chaque année dans le même endroit[2], dans la même région.

[1] temps *weather* [2] endroit *place*

Learning from Photos

(page 283 top) Digne is a town of 16,000 inhabitants in the **département des Alpes-Hautes-Provence.** The area around Digne is known for its fruit orchards and lavender fields.

(page 283 middle) Val-d'Isère is a popular ski resort in eastern France near the Swiss border.

(page 283 bottom) This photo was taken in a rural area of Bénin. In the south of Bénin, there are two rainy seasons—April to mid-July, and mid-September to the end of October. The north has one rainy season from June to early October. The temperatures are higher in the north, reaching 46°C. In the south the temperature range is from 18° to 35°C.

Des champs de lavande, Digne, Provence

Zones climatiques

Dans le monde francophone, il y a beaucoup de zones climatiques. La France, par exemple, a un climat tempéré. Dans une région où le climat est tempéré, il y a quatre saisons: l'été, l'automne, l'hiver, le printemps. Le temps change à chaque saison.

Beaucoup de pays francophones en Afrique sont dans des zones tropicales. Le Bénin et la Côte d'Ivoire, par exemple, sont des pays tropicaux. Ils sont tout près de l'équateur. Là il fait chaud[3] toute l'année et les pluies[4] sont abondantes. Il y a deux saisons—la saison des pluies et la saison sèche[5]. Les saisons varient d'une région à l'autre.

[3] il fait chaud *it's hot* [4] pluies *rains* [5] sèche *dry*

Val-d'Isère, France

Un village de la brousse, Bénin

Après la lecture

Explication du texte

Expliquez en anglais.

1. What's the difference between weather and climate?
2. What is a characteristic of an area with a temperate climate?
3. What is a characteristic of a tropical climate?

CONNEXIONS

Presentation

Les sciences physiques

Le climat et le temps

Step 1 Have students read the introduction in English on page 282.

Step 2 As students read about these climate zones, have them locate each area being discussed, as well as the areas in the photos, on a map.

Step 3 Have students read the selection quickly or have them skim it.

Step 4 You may wish to have them find and repeat all the cognates in the reading selection. Explain to them that there are two important strategies to use when reading unfamiliar material—they should learn to recognize cognates and derive meaning from context.

Après la lecture

Discuss the answers to the activity on page 283.

Learning from Realia

(page 282) Go over the key on the map on page 282 and have students identify the different weather symbols.

Recycling

Have students say what they would wear to visit the places in each photo on page 283.

Answers to Après la lecture

Answers will vary but may include:

1. Weather refers to short-term atmospheric conditions; climate refers to long-term atmospheric conditions.
2. In a temperate climate, there are four seasons: summer, autumn, winter, and spring.
3. In a tropical climate, it is hot year-round with abundant rain.

Reaching All Students

For the Younger Students You may wish to have students draw a weather map of their area, using the terms and symbols found on page 282.

Use what you have learned

Recycling

These activities allow students to use the vocabulary and structure from this chapter in completely open-ended, real-life situations.

Presentation

Encourage students to say as much as possible when they do these activities. Tell them not to be afraid to make mistakes, since the goal of these activities is real-life communication. If someone in the group makes an error, allow the others to politely correct him or her. Let students choose the activities they would like to do.

You may wish to divide students into pairs or groups. Encourage students to elaborate on the basic theme and to be creative. They may use props, pictures, or posters if they wish.

Use what you have learned

PARLER

1 **Tu vas où?**

✔ ***Talk about a plane trip***

You just got to the airport and unexpectedly ran into a friend (your partner). Exchange information about the trip and flight each of you is about to take.

PARLER / ÉCRIRE

2 **On fait un voyage?**

✔ ***Plan a plane trip to a French-speaking destination***

Go to a travel agency in your community. Get some travel brochures and plan a plane trip. Tell all about your trip.

ÉCRIRE

3 **Un voyage en avion**

✔ ***Write about airport activities and services aboard the plane***

You have a French pen pal who is going to visit you this winter. This will be his or her first flight. Write your pen pal a letter and explain all the things he or she is going to experience before and during the flight.

Answers to C'est à vous

1 *Answers will vary depending upon what students choose to say about their trip.*

2 and **3** *Answers will vary.*

Students can come up with personal answers using all vocabulary related to travel that they have learned up to this point.

Writing Strategy

Answering an essay question When writing an answer to an essay question, first read the question carefully and determine how to structure your answer. Then restate the essay question in a single statement in your introduction. Next, support the statement with facts, details, and reasons. Finally, close with a conclusion that summarizes your answer.

ÉCRIRE

4 Un concours

In order to win an all-expense-paid trip to the French-speaking country of your choice, you have to write an essay in French and send it to the company sponsoring the trip. Read the following essay questions and then write your answers. You really want to go, so be sure to plan your answers carefully and check your work.

Tu veux aller dans quel pays?
Tu vas y aller comment?
Qu'est-ce que tu veux faire là-bas?
Qu'est-ce que tu veux apprendre?

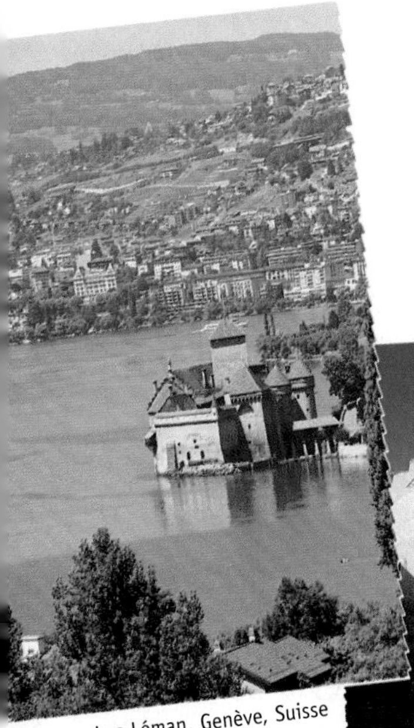
Lac Léman, Genève, Suisse

Fès, Maroc

Paris, France

Writing Development

Have students keep a notebook containing their best written work from each chapter. These selected writings can be based on assignments from the Student Textbook and the Writing Activities Workbook. The three activities on pages 284–285 are examples of writing assignments that may be included in each student's portfolio. In the Workbook, students will develop an organized autobiography **(Mon autobiographie).** These workbook pages may also become a part of their portfolio.

Writing Strategy

Answering an essay question Have students read the Writing Strategy on page 285. If students have difficulty thinking of travel vocabulary, have them use the vocabulary list on page 288.

Learning from Photos

(page 285 left) Le lac Léman is the lake in Geneva, the main French-speaking city of Switzerland. Geneva is a very cosmopolitan city. The lake is flanked by many beautiful homes.

(page 285 middle) This photo is of the Bab Bou Jeloud in central Fès. Bab means *monumental gate.* To the right of this gate one can enter the medina, the old part of the city.

(page 285 right) In this photo of Paris, we see a bateau-mouche, one of the many tourist boats that ply the Seine.

Resource Manager

Communication Transparencies
Quizzes
Test Booklet
ExamView Pro®
Situation Cards
Performance Assessment
Marathon mental Videoquiz

Assessment

This is a pre-test for students to take before you administer the chapter test. Answer sheets for students to do these pages are provided in your transparency binder. Note that each section is cross-referenced so students can easily find the material they have to review in case they made errors. You may wish to collect these assessments and correct them yourself or you may prefer to have the students correct themselves in class. You can go over the answers orally or project them on the overhead, using your Assessment Answers transparencies.

Vocabulaire

*To review **Mots 1**, turn to pages 260–261.*

1 Vrai ou faux?

1. Un bagage à main est une très grande valise.
2. Avant un voyage on fait ses valises.
3. Un vol intérieur est un vol entre deux pays.
4. Les passagers partent d'une porte d'embarquement.
5. L'avion atterrit dans le hall de l'aéroport.

*To review **Mots 2**, turn to pages 264–265.*

2 Identifiez.

8.

9.

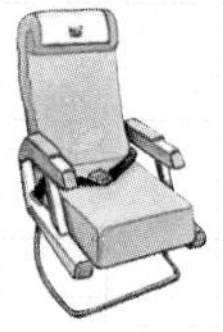

10.

Structure

*To review **-ir** verbs, turn to page 268.*

3 Complétez.

11. Je ____ mon dîner. (finir)
12. Les passagers ____ leur carte de débarquement. (remplir)
13. Il ____ sa place dans l'avion. (choisir)
14. Nous ____ nos devoirs. (finir)
15. L'avion ____ à l'heure. (atterrir)

*To review **quel**, turn to page 270.*

4 Complétez avec «quel».

16. —C'est ____ vol?
—C'est le vol pour Paris.
17. —Tu voyages avec ____ compagnie aérienne?
—Air France.
18. —Il parle de ____ hôtesses?
—Des hôtesses d'Air France.

Answers to Assessment

1
1. F
2. V
3. F
4. V
5. F

2
6. un plateau
7. une hôtesse de l'air
8. un pilote
9. un siège
10. un coffre à bagages

3
11. finis
12. remplissent
13. choisit
14. finissons
15. atterrit

4
16. quel
17. quelle
18. quelles

5 **Complétez pour indiquer *the whole* ou *every*.**

19. ____ classe va faire le voyage.
20. ____ vols n'arrivent pas à la même heure.

To review the use of **tout** with definite articles, turn to page 270.

6 **Récrivez chaque phrase.**

21. Je sers le dîner.
    Ils ________.
22. Vous sortez?
    Tu ________?
23. Ils partent demain.
    Elle ________.

To review these **-ir** verbs, turn to page 272.

Culture

7 **Vrai ou faux?**

24. Charles-de-Gaulle est le nom d'un aéroport près de Paris.
25. Le Mont-Saint-Michel est un monument célèbre à Paris.

To review this cultural information, turn to pages 278–279.

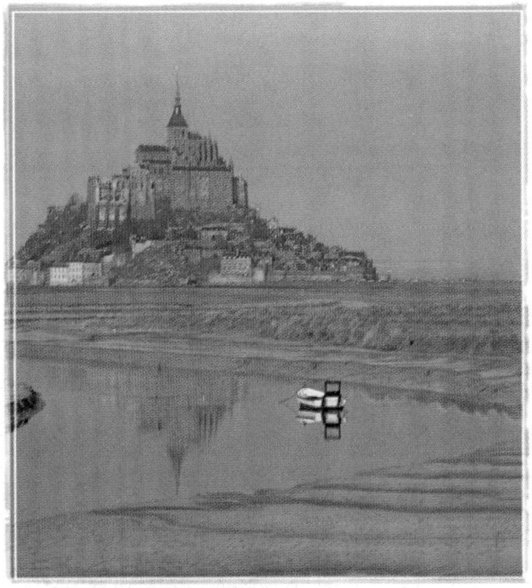

Mont-Saint-Michel

Assessment

Glencoe Technology

MINDJOGGER

You may wish to help your students prepare for the chapter test by playing the MindJogger game show. Teams will compete against each other to review chapter vocabulary and structure and sharpen listening comprehension skills.

Learning from Photos

(page 287) Students were introduced to Mont-Saint-Michel on page 278. See information on that page about this popular tourist site in France.

Answers to Assessment

5

19. Toute la
20. Tous les

6

21. Ils servent le dîner.
22. Tu sors?
23. Elle part demain.

7

24. V
25. F

Vocabulaire

Vocabulary Review

The words and phrases in the **Vocabulaire** have been taught for productive use in this chapter. They are summarized here as a resource for both student and teacher. This list also serves as a convenient resource for the **C'est à vous** activities on pages 284–285. There are approximately sixteen cognates in this vocabulary list. Have students find them.

Attention!

You will notice that the vocabulary list here is not translated. This has been done intentionally, since we feel that by the time students have finished the material in the chapter they should be familiar with the meanings of all the words. If there are several words they still do not know, we recommend that they refer to the **Mots 1** and **2** sections in the chapter or go to the dictionaries at the back of this book to find the meanings. However, if you prefer that your students have the English translations, please refer to Vocabulary Transparency 8.1, where you will find all these words listed with their translations.

Vocabulaire

Getting around an airport

un aéroport
une aérogare
un avion
un hall
un comptoir
une compagnie aérienne
un passager
une passagère
un bagage à main
une valise
un billet
un passeport
le numéro du vol
une porte d'embarquement
une carte d'embarquement
une place
côté couloir
côté fenêtre
un départ
une arrivée
une piste
le contrôle de sécurité
un vol
intérieur
international
non-fumeurs
à destination de
en provenance de
une annonce
un pays
une ville

Aboard the plane

à bord
la cabine
un siège
le couloir
une ceinture de sécurité
un coffre à bagages
un plateau
une carte de débarquement

How well do you know your vocabulary?

- Choose a word from the list.
- Have a classmate give a related word: **annonce, annoncer.**

Identifying airline personnel

un agent
le personnel de bord
un pilote
un steward
une hôtesse de l'air

Describing activities at the airport and aboard the plane

voyager
faire un voyage
faire une annonce
finir
choisir
remplir
atterrir
partir
sortir
dormir
servir
passer par
vérifier
décoller
attacher
ramasser
être à l'heure
avoir du retard
(faire) enregistrer

Other useful words and expressions

sous
il faut
faire ses valises

Technotour

BON VOYAGE!

VIDÉO • Épisode 8

Avant de visionner

In this video episode, Christine has an unusual "adventure" at the airport.

Où est Christine en réalité?

Manu est à l'aéroport avec Christine?

FRENCH ONLINE

À découvrir

Learn more about Charles-de-Gaulle airport online.

L'aéroport Charles-de-Gaulle

FRENCH Online

In the Chapter 8 Internet activity, you will have a chance to learn more about air travel in the Francophone world. To begin your virtual adventure, go to the Glencoe French Web site: **french.glencoe.com**

Technotour

Overview

This page previews two key multimedia components of the **Glencoe French** series. Each reinforces the material taught in the chapter in a unique manner.

VIDÉO

The Video Program allows students to see how the chapter vocabulary and structures are used by native speakers. For maximum reinforcement, show the video episode as a final activity for Chapter 8.

The two photos on the left show highlights from the Chapter 8 video episode. Discuss the photos with your students before having them view the episode. See the Video Activities Booklet for detailed suggestions for using this resource.

FRENCH Online

- The **À découvrir** photo on page 289 shows the Charles-de-Gaulle airport. Students can go online to learn more about this and other airports in the Francophone world.
- Teacher Information and Student Worksheets for this activity can be accessed at the Web site.

Video Synopsis

In this video episode, we find Christine, trying to write a **reportage** on Charles-de-Gaulle airport. She is extremely tired and looks like she can barely keep her eyes open. Within seconds we see Christine at the airport having a "surreal" experience as she listens to Manu's voice over the intercom. She is baffled and confused. Is she really there or is she having a dream?

Planning for Chapter 9

SCOPE AND SEQUENCE, PAGES 290–321

Topics

- Train travel

Culture

- A train trip in Africa
- Train travel in France

Functions

- How to purchase a ticket and request information
- How to use expressions related to train travel
- How to express people's activities

Structure

- Present tense of **-re** verbs
- Demonstrative adjectives
- The verbs **dire, écrire, lire** in the present tense

National Standards

- Communication Standard 1.1 pages 294, 295, 299, 301, 302, 304, 305, 306, 307, 309, 316
- Communication Standard 1.2 pages 294, 295, 298, 299, 301, 302, 304, 305, 306, 307, 308, 311, 313, 315
- Communication Standard 1.3 pages 294, 317
- Cultures Standard 2.1 pages 293, 297, 299, 308, 309, 310–311, 312–313
- Cultures Standard 2.2 pages 299, 308, 309
- Connections Standard 3.1 pages 314–315
- Comparisons Standard 4.2 pages 310–311, 312–313

PACING AND PRIORITIES

The chapter content is color coded below to assist you in planning.
■ required ■ recommended ■ optional

Vocabulaire *(required)* *Days 1–4*
- ■ Mots 1
  - À la gare
- ■ Mots 2
  - Un voyage en train
  - Dans le train

Structure *(required)* *Days 5–7*
- ■ Les verbes en **-re** au présent
- ■ Les adjectifs démonstratifs
- ■ Les verbes **dire, écrire, lire**

Conversation *(required)*
- ■ Au guichet

Prononciation *(recommended)*
- ■ Les sons **/õ/** et **/ẽ/**

Lectures culturelles
- ■ Un voyage intéressant *(recommended)*
- ■ La SNCF *(optional)*

Connexions *(optional)*
- ■ Des conversions—les horaires

■ **C'est à vous** *(recommended)*

■ **Assessment** *(recommended)*

■ **Technotour** *(optional)*

RESOURCE GUIDE

Section	Pages	Section Resources
Vocabulaire — Mots 1		
À la gare	292–295	Vocabulary Transparencies 9.2–9.3 Audiocassette 6A/CD 6 Audio Activities Booklet TE, pages 110–111 Workbook, page 87 Quiz 1, page 44 ExamView Pro®
Vocabulaire — Mots 2		
Un voyage en train Dans le train	296 296–299	Vocabulary Transparencies 9.4–9.5 Audiocassette 6A/CD 6 Audio Activities Booklet TE, pages 112–113 Workbook, page 88 Quiz 2, page 45 ExamView Pro®
Structure		
Les verbes en **-re** au présent Les adjectifs démonstratifs Les verbes **dire, écrire, lire**	300–302 303–305 306–307	Audiocassette 6A/CD 6 Audio Activities Booklet TE, pages 114–116 Workbook, pages 89–91 Quizzes 3–5, pages 46–48 ExamView Pro®
Conversation		
Au guichet	308	Audiocassette 6A/CD 6 Audio Activities Booklet TE, page 117 CD-ROM
Prononciation		
Les sons /õ/ et /ẽ/	309	Pronunciation Transparency P 9 Audiocassette 6A/CD 6 Audio Activities Booklet TE, pages 118–119
Lectures culturelles		
Un voyage intéressant La SNCF	310–311 312–313	Audiocassette 6A/CD 6 Audio Activities Booklet TE, pages 119–120 Test Booklet, Chapter 9
Connexions		
Des conversions—les horaires	314–315	Test Booklet, Chapter 9
C'est à vous		
	316–317	**Bon voyage!** Video, Episode 9 Video Activities Booklet, Chapter 9 French Online Activities french.glencoe.com
Assessment		
	318–319	Communication Transparency C 9 Quizzes 1–5, pages 44–48 Test Booklet, Chapter 9 ExamView Pro® Situation Cards, Chapter 9 **Marathon mental** Videoquiz

Using Your Resources for Chapter 9

Transparencies

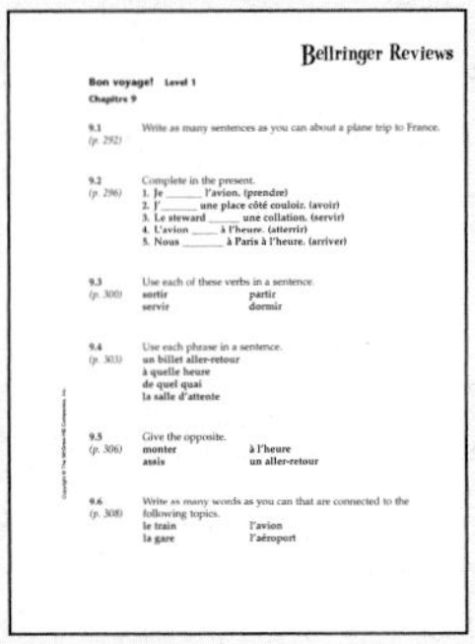

Bellringer 9.1–9.7

Vocabulary 9.1–9.5

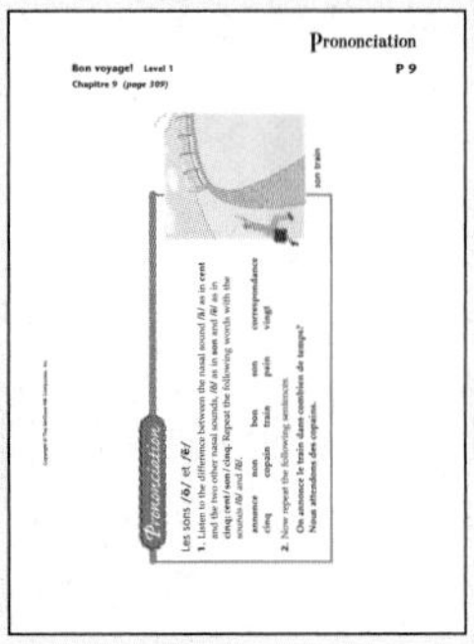

Pronunciation P 9

Communication C 9

Writing Activities Workbook

Vocabulary, pages 87–88

Structure, pages 89–91

Enrichment, pages 92–94

Audio Program and Audio Activities Booklet

Vocabulary, pages 110–113

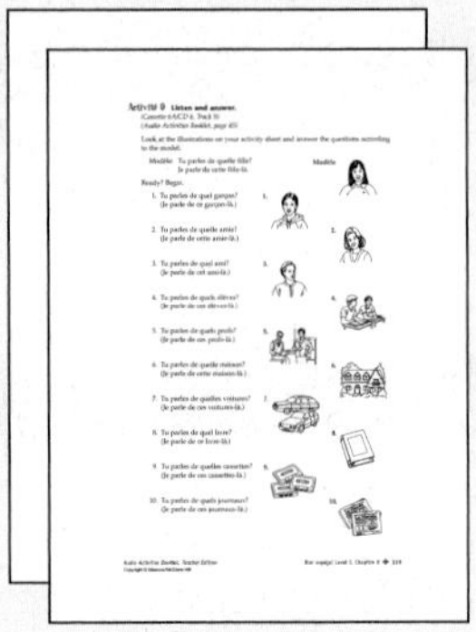

Structure, pages 114–116

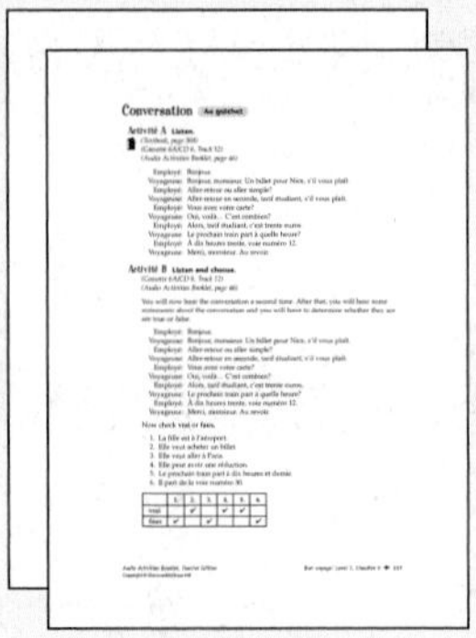

Conversation, Pronunciation, pages 117–119

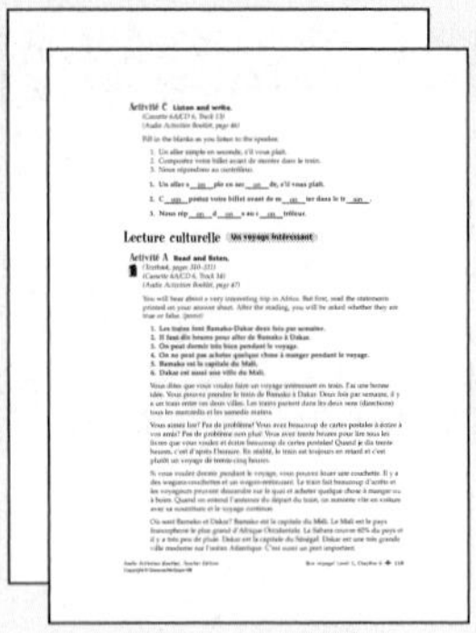

Cultural Reading, pages 119–120

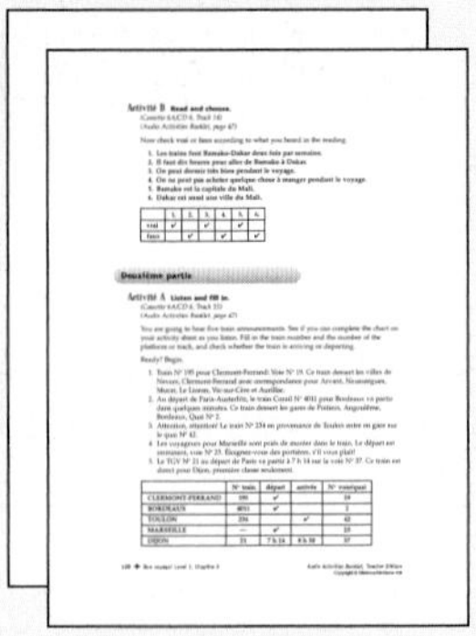

Additional Practice, pages 120–121

CHAPITRE 9

Spotlight on Culture

Photograph This train station is in the town of Montreux, in Switzerland. It is a lovely town on the shores of **Lac Léman.**

Painting In the latter part of the nineteenth century, a group of artists associated with Édouard Manet carried out their quest for realism by taking their easels, paints, and brushes outdoors to paint rather than work from sketches in their studios. These artists created a new style of painting, stressing the effects of sunlight on the subject matter. To reproduce this effect they used quick, short brushstrokes that resulted in paintings made up entirely of dabs of color. When viewed from a distance, those dabs of color blended together and created the desired effect.

In 1874 a group of artists using this new style held an exhibition of their works in Paris. Claude Monet exhibited a painting entitled ***Impression, soleil levant.*** It was this painting that gave the new movement a name—Impressionism—a term used by critics referring unkindly to the works in this exhibition.

Monet painted many outdoor scenes of beaches, rivers, bridges, cathedrals, railroad stations, etc. He did several paintings of the gare Saint-Lazare in Paris. He became interested in winter scenes in 1875, when he produced this painting, ***La locomotive*** or ***Le train dans la neige.***

Chapter Projects

Un voyage en train Have groups (or individuals) plan a rail trip through France using a guidebook, such as one from Eurail (available at many travel agencies). They should plan arrival and departure times and the length of each stop on the itinerary. They can describe their trip to the class.

Une ville Have each group or individual select one city from their itinerary and look up some information about it. They can do a brief report and either hand it in or present it to the class.

1 Preparation

Resource Manager

Vocabulary Transparencies 9.2–9.3
Audio Activities Booklet TE, pages 110–111
Audiocassette 6A/CD 6
Workbook, page 87
Quiz 1, page 44
ExamView Pro®

Bellringer Review

Use BRR Transparency 9.1 or write the following on the board.
Write as many sentences as you can about a plane trip to France.

2 Presentation

Step 1 Have students close books. Using Vocabulary Transparencies 9.2–9.3, introduce the vocabulary. Have students repeat after you or Audiocassette 6A/CD 6 as you point to the illustrations.

Step 2 Point to the items on the transparency at random and call on an individual to identify the item you are pointing to.

Step 3 When presenting the sentences on pages 292–293, ask: **Qu'est-ce qu'on vend au guichet? On vend les billets où? Qu'est-ce qu'on vend au kiosque? Qui attend le train?**, etc.

Note: The new structure points, the **-re** and irregular verbs, are introduced in these sentences in the third person. Students can immediately answer questions using the new verbs. In this way, the meaning is reinforced without the students' having to manipulate endings. They will learn to manipulate the endings in the **Structure** section of the chapter.

Vocabulaire *Mots 1*

À la gare

On vend des journaux et des magazines au kiosque.

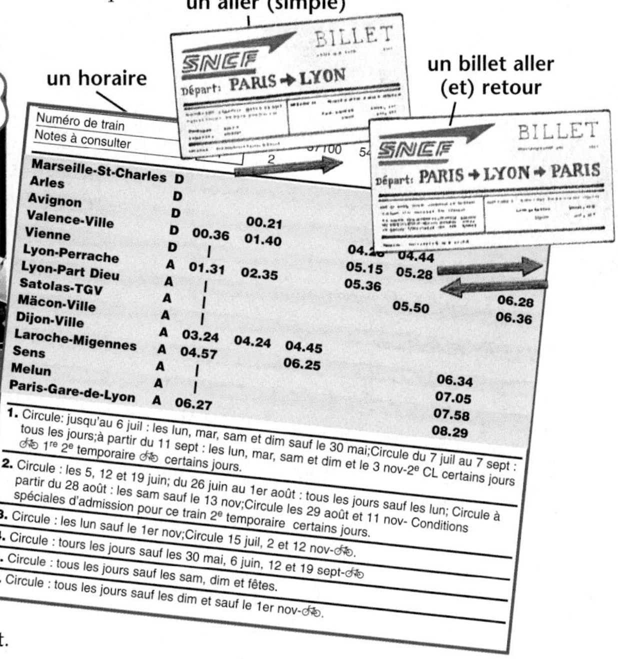

On vend les billets au guichet.
Les passagers font la queue au guichet.

Reaching All Students

Total Physical Response To get ready, have your desk be **le guichet.** One student can be **l'employé(e).** Numbers on the board can represent the **quais.** Demonstrate **monter.** A piece of paper with the word **valise** written on it can represent a suitcase.

(Student 1), **venez ici, s'il vous plaît.**
On va imaginer que c'est une gare.
Allez au guichet.
Faites la queue devant le guichet.
Sortez de l'argent.
Achetez un billet. Prenez le billet.
Cherchez le quai numéro deux.
Allez sur le quai numéro deux.
Attendez le train.
Le train arrive. Montez dans le train.
Au revoir, *(Student 1),* **et bon voyage!**
(Student 2), **venez ici, s'il vous plaît.**
Prenez cette valise. Ouvrez la valise.
Mettez un t-shirt dans la valise.
Mettez un livre dans la valise.
Fermez la valise.

Les voyageurs attendent le train.
On attend le train sur le quai.

On annonce le départ du train.
Un voyageur n'arrive pas à entendre l'annonce.

Marie est en retard.
Elle n'est pas en avance.

Cross-Cultural Comparison

Students will be unfamiliar with the action of **composter un billet.** You may wish to explain that in a French railroad station, at the entrance to the platform area, there is a machine (seen here) into which one puts his or her ticket in order to validate it. Doing so marks the ticket with the station at which the passenger boarded the train. If a ticket is not **composté,** the conductor can give you a fine.

Reaching All Students

(continued)

Allez au téléphone.
Téléphonez à un taxi.
Descendez au rez-de-chaussée.
Attendez le taxi. Le taxi arrive.
Mettez la valise dans le taxi.
Montez dans le taxi.
Descendez du taxi. Prenez la valise.
Sortez de l'argent. Payez le chauffeur.
Donnez un pourboire au chauffeur.

Vocabulaire

3 Practice

Commençons
Let's use our new words

Attention!

When students are doing the **Commençons** activities, accept any answer that makes sense. The purpose of these activities is to have students use the new vocabulary. They are not factual recall activities. Thus, it is not necessary for students to remember specific factual information from the vocabulary presentation when answering. If you wish, have students use the photos on this page as a stimulus, when possible.

Historiette Each time **Historiette** appears, it means that the answers to the activity form a short story. Encourage students to look at the title of the **Historiette,** since it can help them do the activity.

1 and **2** To focus on listening, have students keep their books closed as you ask the questions. Then have students open their books and retell the story in their own words.

Writing Development

Have students write a summary of Activities 1–2.

Commençons
Let's use our new words

1 Historiette Un voyage en train
Inventez une histoire.

1. Les voyageurs sont à la gare?
2. Ils attendent le train dans la salle d'attente?
3. On vend des billets où?
4. Où est-ce que M. Merlin prend son billet?
5. Il va faire Paris–Lyon–Paris. Il veut un billet aller-retour ou un aller simple?
6. Avant de prendre son billet, il fait la queue au guichet?
7. Les voyageurs peuvent consulter l'horaire pour vérifier l'heure du départ de leur train?
8. On annonce les départs à la gare?
9. M. Merlin arrive à comprendre l'annonce?
10. Il prend un chariot?
11. Il met ses bagages sur le chariot?
12. Son train part à l'heure ou en retard?

Gare de Lyon, Paris

2 Historiette Ton voyage en train Donnez des réponses personnelles.

1. Tu fais un voyage en train? Tu vas où?
2. Tu arrives à la gare en avance?
3. Tu prends ton billet?
4. Tu achètes un billet aller-retour ou un aller simple?
5. Tu voyages en première ou en seconde?
6. Tu consultes l'horaire?
7. Ton train part à quelle heure?
8. Ton train part de quelle voie?
9. Tu vas acheter un journal ou un magazine? Où?
10. Tu vas prendre un café au buffet de la gare?

Gare de Lyon, Paris

Answers to Commençons

1 *Answers will vary but may include:*

1. Oui, les voyageurs sont à la gare.
2. Oui, ils attendent le train dans la salle d'attente.
3. On vend des billets au guichet.
4. Il prend son billet au guichet.
5. Il veut un billet aller-retour.
6. Oui, il fait la queue au guichet.
7. Oui, ils peuvent consulter l'horaire pour vérifier l'heure du départ de leur train.
8. Oui, on annonce les départs à la gare.
9. Non, M. Merlin n'arrive pas à comprendre l'annonce.
10. Oui, il prend un chariot.
11. Oui, il met ses bagages sur le chariot.
12. Son train part à l'heure.

2 *Answers will vary but may include:*

1. Oui, je fais un voyage en train. Je vais à _____.
2. Oui, j'arrive à la gare en avance.
3. Oui, je prends mon billet.
4. J'achète un billet simple.
5. Je voyage en seconde.
6. Oui, je consulte l'horaire.
7. Mon train part à _____.
8. Mon train part de _____.
9. Je vais acheter un magazine au kiosque.
10. Non, je ne vais pas prendre de café.

Vocabulaire

3 **On attend le train.** Choisissez la bonne réponse.

1. On vend des journaux, des magazines et des cartes postales ____.
   a. au guichet b. au kiosque c. sur le quai
2. On ____ le train dans la salle d'attente.
   a. attend b. prend c. entend
3. Les voyageurs ____ l'annonce du départ de leur train.
   a. mettent b. entendent c. font
4. On fait ____ au guichet pour prendre son billet.
   a. l'annonce b. le quai c. la queue
5. Le train part ____.
   a. de la voie b. du chariot c. du kiosque
6. Il faut ____ son billet avant d'aller sur le quai.
   a. vendre b. faire c. composter

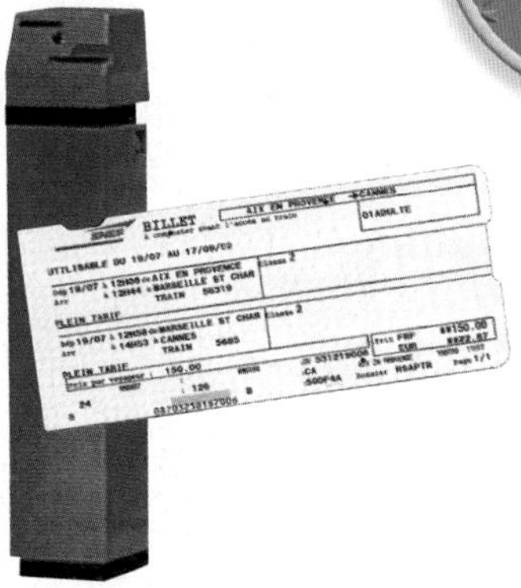

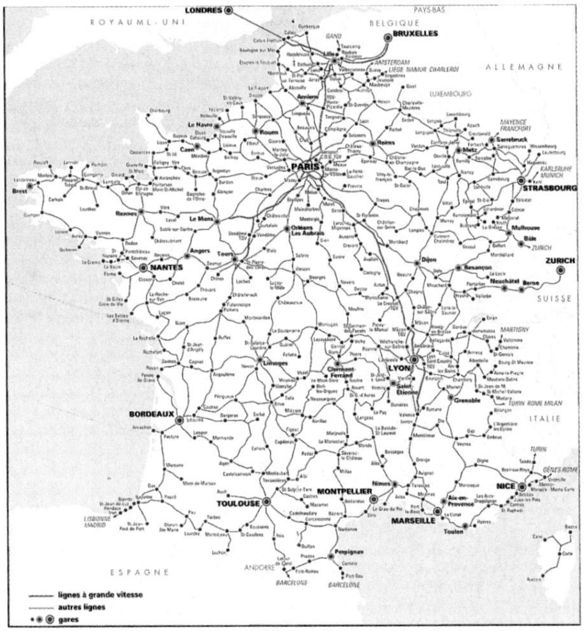

4 **La SNCF (La Société nationale des chemins de fer français)** You're in France and you want to visit one of the cities on the map. A classmate will be the ticket agent. Get yourself a ticket and ask the agent any questions you have about your train trip.

FRENCH Online

For more information on la SNCF, go to the Glencoe French Web site: french.glencoe.com

ENCORE PLUS *For more practice using words from **Mots 1**, do Activity 27 on page H28 at the end of this book.*

Vocabulaire

3 After completing this activity, you may wish to have students make appropriate sentences for the vocabulary choices which were not used in the activity. For example: **1. On vend des billets au guichet. On attend sur le quai.**

4 You may wish to have students present their dialogue to the class, complete with props.

Assessment

Check for understanding by making false statements about the items on Vocabulary Transparencies 9.2–9.3. Have students correct your statements. For example: **On vend des journaux au guichet. (Non, on vend des journaux au kiosque. On vend des billets au guichet.)**

FRENCH Online

Encourage students to take advantage of this opportunity to learn more about the French rail system. Perhaps you can do this in class or in a lab if students do not have Internet access at home.

Answers to Commençons

3
1. b
2. a
3. b
4. c
5. a
6. c

4 *Answers will vary but may include:*
—Bonjour, madame. Je voudrais un billet pour Cannes, s'il vous plaît.
—Un billet aller-retour ou un aller simple?
—Un aller-retour.
—En première ou en seconde?
—En seconde. Mon train part de quelle voie?
—Votre train part de la voie numéro douze.

Learning from Photos

(page 294) The two photos on page 294 were taken in the Gare de Lyon in Paris. Paris has six railroad stations. Trains for Lyon, Marseille, la Côte d'Azur, and Italy leave from the Gare de Lyon.

Fun Facts

The following are the five other train stations in Paris and the destinations that they serve:
Gare du Nord northern France, northern Europe, England via Calais and Boulogne
Gare Saint-Lazare Normandy and England via Dieppe
Gare de l'Est Strasbourg, Luxembourg, and central Europe
Gare d'Austerlitz Loire Valley, southwest France
Gare Montparnasse main terminus for trains to southwest France since the introduction of the **TGV-Atlantique** service.

Vocabulaire
Mots 2

1 Preparation

Resource Manager

Vocabulary Transparencies 9.4–9.5
Audio Activities Booklet TE, pages 112–113
Audiocassette 6A/CD 6
Workbook, page 88
Quiz 2, page 45
ExamView Pro®

Bellringer Review

Use BRR Transparency 9.2 or write the following on the board.
Complete in the present.

1. **Je ______ l'avion. (prendre)**
2. **J'______ une place côté couloir. (avoir)**
3. **Le steward ______ une collation. (servir)**
4. **L'avion ______ à l'heure. (atterrir)**
5. **Nous ______ à Paris à l'heure. (arriver)**

2 Presentation

Step 1 Model the new words using Vocabulary Transparencies 9.4–9.5. Have students repeat after you or Audiocassette 6A/CD 6.

Step 2 As you present the vocabulary, ask questions building from simple to more complex.
C'est le train?
Les voyageurs descendent du train?
Ils vont changer de train?
Qu'est-ce que c'est?
Qui descend du train?
Qu'est-ce qu'ils vont faire?

Step 3 Now have students open their books and read the new vocabulary.

Recycling

You may wish to review telling time and especially the 24-hour system used in travel schedules. See **Connexions** pages 314–315.

Vocabulaire
Mots 2

Un voyage en train

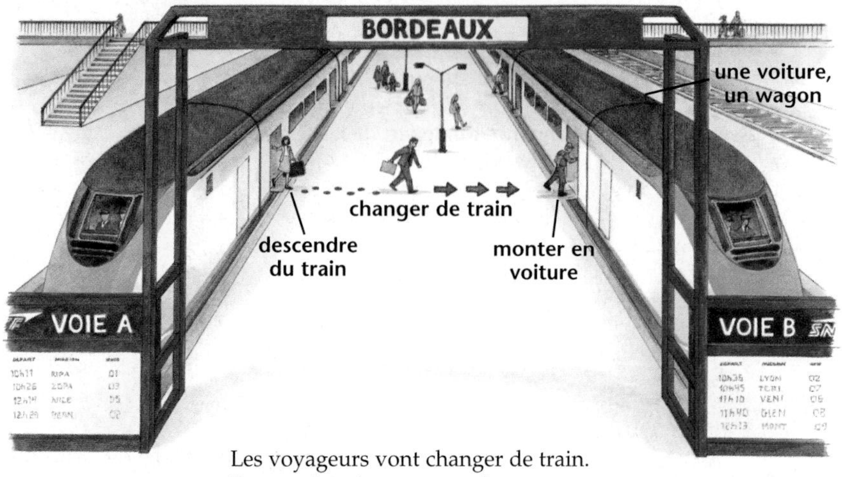

Les voyageurs vont changer de train.
Ils attendent la correspondance.
Ils ont une correspondance à Bordeaux.

Dans le train

La plupart des voyageurs sont assis.
Il y a quelques voyageurs debout.
Sylvain lit un livre.
Sa copine Christine écrit des cartes (postales).

Reaching All Students

Total Physical Response Set up an area of the classroom as a train car. Call on pairs of students, one to play the part of the passenger, the other the part of the conductor. Give the passenger a bag with the word **valise** written on it.

(Student 1), **lève-toi et viens ici, s'il te plaît.**
Va à la voie A.
Mets ta valise dans le train.
Monte en voiture.
Dis «au revoir» à tes amis.
Cherche ta place.
Assieds-toi.
Le contrôleur arrive. Sors ton billet.
Donne ton billet au contrôleur.
Reprends ton billet.
Prends ta valise. Ouvre ta valise.
Sors un livre de ta valise.
Lis ton livre.
Merci, *(Student 1).* **Retourne à ta place.**

Oui, vous descendez au prochain arrêt.

Le contrôleur contrôle les billets.
Romain a une question.
Le contrôleur répond à sa question.

le snack-bar

Je commence vraiment à perdre patience! Allez, on y va! Sinon on va rater notre train.

Jean et Thouria attendent un ami devant la gare.
Ils vont tous les trois à La Rochelle.
Jean et Thouria attendent depuis quarante-cinq minutes!
Jean dit qu'il commence à perdre patience.

Learning from Photos

(page 297) The train shown here with the conductor is a **train de banlieue.**

Vocabulary Expansion

You may wish to explain to students that in a train station they will see two arrival and two departure boards. One is for **trains de banlieue** that serve the nearby suburbs and another for **les grandes lignes**—the long-distance trains.

Assessment

Check for comprehension by miming activities and having students try to guess who you are and what you are doing by asking questions. For example: Teacher mimes the action of looking at a paper. Students ask: **Vous contrôlez un billet? Vous lisez un journal?**, etc.

Recycling

Have students say what the people might be eating or ordering in the photo of the snack-bar on page 297.

3 Practice

Commençons

Let's use our new words

5 and **6** After completing these activities, have a student or students retell the stories in their own words.

Cognate Recognition

Have students scan the vocabulary on pages 296–297 and pick out the cognates: **changer, descendre, un voyageur, un train, la patience, une minute.**

Paired Activity

Have pairs of students make up as many sentences as they can about travel. They then read their sentences to each other and decide if they deal with train travel or air travel. They should categorize their sentences under the headings Voyages en avion or Voyages en train. Finally, have them reorganize their sentences to tell two stories, one about train travel and another about air travel.

ENCORE PLUS This *infogap* activity will allow students to practice in pairs. The activity should be very manageable for them, since all vocabulary and structures are familiar to them.

Learning from Photos

(page 298) Aix-en-Provence is a beautiful city of classic buildings and historic monuments. The main avenue is the Cours Mirabeau named after the Revolution's orator, le comte de Mirabeau who lived in Aix. It is shaded with many trees and features four fountains, one seen here. Aix-en-Provence is also an important university city.

Commençons

Let's use our new words

5 Historiette De Paris à Avignon Répondez d'après les indications.

1. Pour aller à Avignon, on change de train? (non)
2. Qui monte en voiture? (les voyageurs)
3. Qui contrôle les billets? (le contrôleur)
4. Presque toutes les places sont occupées? (oui)
5. La plupart des voyageurs sont assis? (oui)
6. Il y a quelques voyageurs debout? (oui)
7. Qu'est-ce que le contrôleur contrôle? (les billets)
8. Les voyageurs descendent où? (à Avignon)

6 Historiette Aïcha prend le train. Complétez avec le mot ou l'expression qui convient.

descend	**lit**	**écrit**	**monte**	**attendre**
contrôle	**rater**	**dit**	**snack-bar**	**arrêt**

1. Aïcha fait un voyage en train. Elle ____ en voiture.
2. Le contrôleur ____ son billet.
3. Elle ____ un article dans un magazine.
4. Elle n'____ pas de cartes postales.
5. Elle a faim. Elle va au ____.
6. Aïcha ____ au contrôleur qu'elle va à Aix-en-Provence.
7. Il répond: «Il faut changer de train à Marseille. C'est le prochain ____.»
8. Elle ____ du train à Marseille.
9. À Marseille, elle va ____ sa correspondance pour Aix-en-Provence.
10. Elle ne va pas ____ le train pour Aix-en-Provence.

Aix-en-Provence, France

ENCORE PLUS *For more practice using words from **Mots 2**, do Activity 28 on page H29 at the end of this book.*

Answers to Commençons

5

1. Non, pour aller à Avignon on ne change pas de train.
2. Les voyageurs montent en voiture.
3. Le contrôleur contrôle les billets.
4. Oui, presque toutes les places sont occupées.
5. Oui, la plupart des voyageurs sont assis.
6. Oui, il y a quelques voyageurs debout.
7. Le contrôleur contrôle les billets.
8. Les voyageurs descendent à Avignon.

6

1. monte
2. contrôle
3. lit
4. écrit
5. snack-bar
6. dit
7. arrêt
8. descend
9. attendre
10. rater

7 **Toujours des questions!** Répondez.

1. Le train pour Lyon part de la voie numéro 5 à six heures trente.
   C'est le train ou l'avion qui part pour Lyon?
   Le train va où?
   Il part de quelle voie?
   Il part à quelle heure?
2. Sandrine va à Nantes et elle ne trouve pas sa place dans le train.
   Qui va à Nantes?
   Où est Sandrine?
   Qu'est-ce qu'elle ne trouve pas?

Nantes, France

8 **L'horaire** Look at the information on this schedule. Take turns with a classmate asking and answering questions about it.

MARSEILLE - ARLES - TARASCON - AVIGNON

SEMAINE

	•	◉		◉	◉	•	◉	◉	◉	•	•		◉	◉	◉	◉	◉	◉	◉	◉	•	◉	◉	◉		◉	◉	•	◉	◉	•		[illegible]
		CAR			TGV																			CAR		TGV						TGV	
			28	3		29		30			31	32							12						33	34			14	35		36	
Marseille-St-Charles			05.29		06.12	06.31	06.35	06.51			08.27	08.36	08.47	09.08	10.59		11.36	12.09			13.18	14.03	14.36		15.24			16.12		16.26	16.40	16.57	1[illegible]
Miramas			06.00		·	07.04	07.15	·	07.40		09.11	09.11	·	·	11.33		·	12.42			14.04	·	·		15.59			16.51		·	17.27	·	
Arles		06.05	06.17		06.57	07.21	07.32	07.39	08.00		09.28	09.28	09.35	·	11.51		·	12.59	13.23		14.24	14.52	15.21	15.30	16.17	16.45		17.08		·	17.49	·	1[illegible]
Arles (Le Trébon)		·	·		·	·	·	·	·		·	·	·	·	·		·	·	·		·			·	·	·		·		·	·	·	
Arles (Car. St-Gabriel)		·	·		·	·	·	·	·		·	·	·	·	·		·	·	·		·			·	·	·		·		·	·	·	
Tarascon	05.06	06.25	·	07.25	·	07.31	·	07.48	·	08.42	·	·	09.44	·	·	12.16	·	13.08	·	13.52	·	·		15.50	·	·	16.54	17.21	18.02	·	·	·	
Tarascon (Pl.Condamine)	·	·	·	·	·		·		·	·	·	·		·	·	·	·		·	·	·	·		·	·	·	·		·	·	·	·	
Graveson (Maillane)	·	·	·	·	·		·		·	·	·	·		·	·	·	·		·	·	·	·		·	·	·	·		·	·	·	·	
Graveson (Bon-Accueil)	·	·	·	·	·		·		·	·	·	·		·	·	·	·		·	·	·	·		·	·	·	·		·	·	·	·	
Graveson (La Roque)	·	·	·	·	·		·		·	·	·	·		·	·	·	·		·	·	·	·		·	·	·	·		·	·	·	·	
Rognonas (Emb.Gare)	·	·	·	·	·		·		·	·	·	·		·	·	·	·		·	·	·	·		·	·	·	·		·	·	·	·	
Rognonas (Pl.Mairie)	·	·	·	·	·		·		·	·	·	·		·	·	·	·		·	·	·	·		·	·	·	·		·	·	·	·	
Avignon (Gambetta)	·	·	·	·	·		·		·	·	·	·		·	·	·	·		·	·	·	·		·	·	·	·		·	·	·	·	
Avignon	05.18	06.55	06.33	07.40	07.13		07.50		08.16	08.55	09.45	09.45		10.11	12.09	12.29	12.41		13.42	14.04	14.42	15.10		16.20	16.34	17.03	17.10		18.14	17.30	18.07	17.57	1[illegible]

La desserte détaillée entre Marseille et Miramas figure sur la fiche horaire Marseille - Miramas via Rognac et Port de Bouc.

Voir aussi Fiche horaire Marseille - Salon - Cavaillon - Avignon.

• Du lundi au vendredi.
◉ Du lundi au samedi.

Certains trains périodiques ne figurent pas sur ce document horaire.
CAR Desserte assurée par autocar. Tarification SNCF.
TGV : réservation obligatoire.
Horaires en italiques : train soumis à des conditions d'emprunt, ou à supplément; renseignements dans les gares.
Ces horaires sont donnés sous réserve de toute modification.

3 Ne circule
12 Ne circule
14 Ne circule
17 Circule les
circule aus
24 Circule du
26 Ne circule
27 Circule les

9 **Jeu** **Les phrases** Play a game with a classmate. See who can make up the most sentences using the following words. The time limit is two minutes.

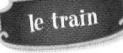

le quai · aller-retour · le contrôleur · l'annonce · assis · debout · le train · le billet · la correspondance

Answers to Commençons

7
1. C'est le train qui part pour Lyon.
   Le train va à Lyon.
   Il part de la voie numéro 5.
   Il part à six heures trente.
2. Sandrine va à Nantes.
   Elle est dans le train.
   Elle ne trouve pas sa place.

8 *Answers will vary.*

9 *Answers will vary but may include:*
Les voyageurs attendent le train sur le quai.
Je composte mon billet.
Il n'arrive pas à entendre l'annonce.
Les voyageurs attendent la correspondance.

Vocabulaire

9 You may wish to have students work in groups of four or five and have a competition between groups.

Learning from Photos

(page 299) Nantes is a large city of 245,000 inhabitants (492,000 if one includes **la communauté urbaine**). Nantes is an industrial city and is home of the last important shipyard in France—Chantiers de l'Atlantique.

Learning from Realia

(page 299) Have students note the symbols used for the different train facilities. **Vente ambulante** means that someone comes through the train car selling food and drinks. (They should recognize **vente,** since they know **vendre. Ambulante,** like ambulance, is derived from the Latin word **ambulare** meaning "to walk around.")

Math Connection

Have students look at the timetable on page 299 and tell how long some of the trips take.

Assessment

As an informal assessment, show Vocabulary Transparencies 9.4–9.5. Have students give you as many words as they can.

1 Preparation

Resource Manager

Audio Activities Booklet TE, pages 114–116
Audiocassette 6A/CD 6
Workbook, pages 89–91
Quizzes 3–5, pages 46–48
ExamView Pro®

Bellringer Review

Use BRR Transparency 9.3 or write the following on the board.
Use each of these verbs in a sentence.

sortir **partir**
servir **dormir**

2 Presentation

Les verbes en -re au présent

Step 1 Begin with the third-person plural. Write **ils attendent** and **ils vendent** on the board. Draw a line through the ending. Students now have the sound for all the singular forms. Point out that the **je** and **tu** forms take an **s.** The third person singular has no ending.

Step 2 Have students pronounce all forms of the model verbs in Item 1.

Step 3 Read Item 2 and have students repeat the sentences.

Describing more activities
Les verbes en -re au présent

1. Another group of regular verbs in French has infinitives that end in **-re.** Some verbs that belong to this group are: **vendre, attendre, descendre, répondre, entendre, perdre.**

	VENDRE	ATTENDRE
je vend -s	je vends	j' attends
tu vend -s	tu vends	tu attends
il/elle/on vend —	il/elle/on vend	il/elle/on attend (liaison n)
nous vend -ons	nous vendons	nous attendons (liaison z)
vous vend -ez	vous vendez	vous attendez (liaison z)
ils/elles vend -ent	ils/elles vendent	ils/elles attendent (liaison z)

2. **Descendre** can have several meanings. When used alone, it means "to go down" or "to get off." When used with a direct object, it means "to take down."

   Ils descendent du train.
   Ils descendent les bagages sur le quai.

Savez-vous que... ?

The verb **répondre** is followed by **à.**

Il répond à la question du contrôleur.
Il répond à l'employé.

La gare, Dakar, Sénégal

Learning from Photos

(page 300) This photo shows one of the platforms at the train station in Dakar. Trains leave from this station for Bamako (see **Lecture** on pages 310–311) and cities such as Tambacounda, Saint-Louis, and Kaolack.

You may wish to ask the students the following questions about the photo:
C'est une salle d'attente ou un quai?
Les voyageurs montent en voiture ou descendent du train?
Les voyageurs changent de train?
Il y a combien de voitures?

Continuons
Let's put our words together

10 Historiette Les voyageurs Répondez que oui.

1. Les voyageurs attendent le train?
2. Ils attendent le train dans la salle d'attente?
3. Ils perdent patience?
4. Ils entendent l'annonce du départ de leur train?
5. Ils descendent du train?

La gare Windsor, Montréal

11 Historiette Un voyage à Montréal
Répondez que oui.

1. Tu es à la gare de Grand Central à New York?
2. Tu attends le train pour Montréal?
3. Tu attends depuis une heure?
4. Tu perds patience?
5. Tu entends l'annonce du départ de ton train?
6. Tu vas sur le quai?
7. Quand tu descends du train à Montréal, tu es fatigué(e)?

12 Le train Complétez.

1. —Vous ____ depuis combien de temps? (attendre)
   —Nous ____ depuis cinq minutes. C'est tout! (attendre)
2. —Vous allez à Rennes?
   —Oui.
   —Vous ____ au prochain arrêt, alors. (descendre)
   —Ah bon? Merci.
   —Hé, les copains! On ____ au prochain arrêt! (descendre)

3 Practice

Continuons
Let's put our words together

10 and **11** These activities can be done with books open, closed, or once each way.

Writing Development
Have students write the answers to Activities 10–11 in paragraph form.

Reaching All Students

Additional Practice Have students work in groups of three. Two students question each other to find out what each is in the habit of losing. The third student listens in and reports.
(Student 1), **qu'est-ce que tu perds?**
Moi, je perds toujours ____. Et toi, qu'est-ce que tu perds?
Moi, je perds ____.
(Student 1) **perd ____ et** *(Student 2)* **perd ____. Ils (ne) perdent (pas) la même chose.**

ANSWERS TO Continuons

10

1. Oui, les voyageurs attendent le train.
2. Oui, ils attendent le train dans la salle d'attente.
3. Oui, ils perdent patience.
4. Oui, ils entendent l'annonce du départ de leur train.
5. Oui, ils descendent du train.

11

1. Oui, je suis à la gare de Grand Central à New York.
2. Oui, j'attends le train pour Montréal.
3. Oui, j'attends depuis une heure.
4. Oui, je perds patience.
5. Oui, j'entends l'annonce du départ de mon train.
6. Oui, je vais sur le quai.
7. Oui, quand je descends du train à Montréal je suis fatigué(e).

12

1. attendez, attendons
2. descendez, descend

3 Practice *(continued)*

Continuons
Let's put our words together

13 This activity should be done with books open. **Expansion:** After completing the activity, have students make up questions about the story in the activity. Then have them answer their own questions. Finally, have them retell the story in their own words.

14 Have students switch partners two or three times. You may also wish to have pairs of students present their dialogue to the class.

History Connection

Saint-Malo is one of the most-loved Breton towns. It is an ancient city on a peninsula surrounded by thirteenth-century ramparts, from the top of which there are fine views of the coast. The old city was badly bombed during the Allied invasion in August 1944. It has, however, been completely restored.

In the sixteenth century, **les marins malouins** *(sailors from Saint-Malo)*, played an important role in maritime discoveries. Jacques Cartier sailed from Saint-Malo in 1534 to explore the St. Lawrence in Canada.

Attention!

Note that the activities are color-coded. All the activities in the text are communicative. However, the ones with blue titles are guided communication. The red titles indicate that the answers to the activity are more open-ended and can vary more. You may wish to correct students' mistakes more so in the guided activities than in the activities with a red title, which lend themselves to a freer response.

13 **Historiette** **Dans la salle d'attente** Complétez.

Les voyageurs __1__ (attendre) le train dans la salle d'attente. Marc __2__ (attendre) le train pour Saint-Malo. Ah, voilà son ami, Luc.

Marc: Salut, Luc! Quelle surprise! Tu __3__ (attendre) un train?

Luc: Oui, j'__4__ (attendre) le train pour Saint-Malo.

Marc: Pas vrai? Moi aussi je vais à Saint-Malo.

Les deux garçons __5__ (entendre) l'annonce du départ de leur train. Il part de la voie numéro 5. Ils vont sur le quai. Les voyageurs qui arrivent __6__ (descendre) leurs bagages du train. Ils __7__ (descendre) leurs bagages sur le quai. Le contrôleur crie: «En voiture, s'il vous plaît!» et tout le monde qui part monte dans le train. Le contrôleur demande aux garçons où ils vont. Luc __8__ (répondre) au contrôleur. Il __9__ (répondre): «À Saint-Malo».

Saint-Malo, Bretagne, France

14 **À la gare** Work with a classmate. Pretend you are at a train station somewhere in France. Take turns asking and answering questions about your wait at the train station. You may want to use the following expressions: **attendre le train, entendre l'annonce du départ, prendre un billet, faire la queue, aller au kiosque, prendre un café au buffet de la gare.**

Answers to Continuons

13

1. attendent
2. attend
3. attends
4. attends
5. entendent
6. descendent
7. descendent
8. répond
9. répond

14 *Answers will vary but may include:*

—Tu attends le train?
—Oui, j'attends le train.
—Tu consultes l'horaire?
—Oui, on va entendre l'annonce du départ bientôt.
—Alors tu veux prendre un café au buffet de la gare?

Pointing out people and things
Les adjectifs démonstratifs

1. You use the demonstrative adjectives to point out people or things. In English, the demonstrative adjectives are "this," "these," "that," and "those." However, in French there is only one set of demonstrative adjectives. Study the following forms.

	Masculin Consonne	Masculin Voyelle	Féminin Consonne	Féminin Voyelle
Singulier	ce train	cet‿horaire	cette voiture	cette annonce
Pluriel	ces trains	ces‿horaires	ces voitures	ces‿annonces

2. The word **-là** is often attached to the noun following the demonstrative adjectives for emphasis.

—**C'est un magazine super.**
—**Ce magazine-là! Tu rigoles! Il est horrible!**

Un ancien wagon-restaurant

Learning from Photos

(page 303) Beautiful dining cars such as this one have become a thing of the past except on special trains such as the Orient Express.

Structure

1 Preparation

Bellringer Review

Use BRR Transparency 9.4 or write the following on the board.
Use each phrase in a sentence.
un billet aller-retour
à quelle heure
de quel quai
la salle d'attente

2 Presentation

Les adjectifs démonstratifs

Step 1 Go over the explanation with the class.

Step 2 Have students repeat the following sequence as you write the forms of the demonstrative adjective on the board: **cette voiture, cet horaire, ce train.** Have them take note how the sound gets softer.

Step 3 Explain that there is only one plural form: **ces voitures, ces horaires, ces trains.**

Step 4 Collect as many objects as you can that students can identify in French and put them on a table. Call some students to the table and ask them to give you specific items: **Donne-moi ce cahier. Donne-moi cette cassette.** This gives students listening practice with demonstrative adjectives. After completing the activities that follow, redo this activity as a paired activity and have the students produce all the forms of the demonstrative adjective on their own.

3 Practice

Continuons
Let's put our words together

15 This activity can be done with books closed, open, or once each way.

Learning from Photos

(page 304) Chamonix, France's oldest and largest winter resort, lies on one side of Mont Blanc. The French Alps soar to 4,807 meters (15,775 feet) and Mont Blanc is its highest peak. In the summer, Chamonix is a center for mountain climbers who scale Mont Blanc. It is also a starting place for spectacular cable car rides over a glacier called **la mer de glace** that spans 12 km to Courmayeur in Italy.

Continuons
Let's put our words together

15 Tu parles de qui ou de quoi? Suivez le modèle.

Tu parles d'une fille? De quelle fille?
De cette fille-là.

1. Tu parles d'un garçon? De quel garçon?
2. Tu parles d'une copine? De quelle copine?
3. Tu parles d'un copain? De quel copain?
4. Tu parles des élèves? De quels élèves?
5. Tu parles des filles? De quelles filles?
6. Tu parles d'un train? De quel train?
7. Tu parles d'un horaire? De quel horaire?
8. Tu parles des journaux? De quels journaux?
9. Tu parles d'un arrêt? De quel arrêt?
10. Tu parles d'une carte? De quelle carte?

16 À Grenoble ou à Chamonix? Complétez avec **ce, cet, cette** ou **ces.**

Christine: __1__ train va à Grenoble?
Contrôleur: Non, il va à Chamonix.
Christine: Et tous __2__ voyageurs, alors, ils ne prennent pas __3__ train?
Contrôleur: Non, ils attendent le train pour Grenoble.
Christine: Il va partir de __4__ quai aussi?
Contrôleur: Oui, mais pas de __5__ voie. De la voie numéro 2.

Chamonix-Mont-Blanc, France

Answers to Continuons

15

1. De ce garçon-là.
2. De cette copine-là.
3. De ce copain-là.
4. De ces élèves-là.
5. De ces filles-là.
6. De ce train-là.
7. De cet horaire-là.
8. De ces journaux-là.
9. De cet arrêt-là.
10. De cette carte-là.

16

1. Ce
2. ces
3. ce
4. ce
5. cette

17 Historiette Au kiosque

Répondez d'après les photos.

1. Ce kiosque est dans une gare ou dans la rue?
2. Qu'est-ce qu'on vend dans ce kiosque?
3. Combien coûtent ces cartes postales?
4. Ces journaux sont français ou américains?

Gare de l'Est, Paris

18 Au kiosque

You want to buy several items but you don't know how much they cost. Ask the vendor (your partner) how much they cost. Then make sure the addition is correct when he or she asks you for the sum you owe. You may want to use the following words.

du chewing-gum | un livre | un journal | un magazine | une carte postale | des kleenex

Structure

3 Practice

Continuons
Let's put our words together

18 You may wish to supply props for this activity.

Answers to Continuons

17

1. Ce kiosque est dans une gare.
2. Dans ce kiosque on vend des journaux, des magazines et des cartes postales.
3. Ces cartes postales coûtent 1 euro.
4. Ces journaux sont français.

18 *Answers will vary but may include:*

—Je voudrais un chewing-gum, une carte postale et des kleenex. C'est combien?
—C'est 3 euros.
—Comment?
—Un chewing-gum, 50 cents. Une carte postale, 1 euro. Ça fait 1 euro 50. Et puis des kleenex—1 euro 50. En tous, ça fait 3 euros.

1 Preparation

Bellringer Review

Use BRR Transparency 9.5 or write the following on the board.
Give the opposite.

monter	**à l'heure**
assis	**un aller-retour**

2 Presentation

Les verbes **dire, écrire, lire**

Step 1 Begin your explanation with the third-person plural forms of these verbs. Have students repeat them. Draw a line through **-sent** or **-vent** and have students repeat the singular forms.

Step 2 Now lead students through the information on page 306.

Teaching Tip
Tell students there are only two other verbs like **vous dites** that have the **t** sound in the **vous** form. They are **vous faites** and **vous êtes.** Have students repeat the three forms together: **vous dites, vous faites, vous êtes.**

Describing more activities
Les verbes **dire, écrire, lire**

Study the forms of the irregular verbs **dire** *(to say)*, **écrire** *(to write)*, and **lire** *(to read)*.

DIRE		ÉCRIRE		LIRE	
je	dis	j'	écris	je	lis
tu	dis	tu	écris	tu	lis
il/elle/on	dit	il/elle/on‿ₙ	écrit	il/elle/on	lit
nous	disons	nous‿z	écrivons	nous	lisons
vous	dites	vous‿z	écrivez	vous	lisez
ils/elles	disent	ils‿z/elles‿z	écrivent	ils/elles	lisent

Continuons
Let's put our words together

19 Historiette Christine et Juliette Remplacez **Christine** par **Christine et Juliette.**

Christine est dans le train. Elle lit. Elle dit que le livre qu'elle lit est très intéressant. Christine a aussi des cartes postales à écrire. Elle écrit ses cartes postales. Elle dit que ses amis, eux, n'écrivent pas. Ils lisent les cartes postales de Christine? Bien sûr qu'ils lisent ses cartes postales!

20 Petites conversations Suivez le modèle.

lire des journaux
—Tu lis des journaux?
—Oui, je lis des journaux.

1. lire le journal local
2. lire beaucoup de livres
3. lire des magazines
4. écrire des lettres aux copains
5. écrire des cartes
6. dire toujours que oui

ENCORE PLUS *For more practice using these verbs, do Activity 29 on page H30 at the end of this book.*

3 Practice

Continuons
Let's put our words together

19 Students can retell the story in Activity 19 in their own words.

20 After students work in pairs, you may wish to have them work in groups of four to practice the plural forms. For example: **Vous lisez le journal local? Oui, nous lisons le journal local.**

Answers to Continuons

19

Christine et Juliette sont dans le train. Elles lisent. Elles disent que les livres qu'elles lisent sont très intéressants. Christine et Juliette ont aussi des cartes postales à écrire. Elles écrivent leurs cartes postales. Elles disent que leurs amis, eux, n'écrivent pas. Ils lisent les cartes postales de Christine et de Juliette? Bien sûr qu'ils lisent leurs cartes postales!

20

1. Tu lis le journal local?
   Oui, je lis le journal local.
2. Tu lis beaucoup de livres?
   Oui, je lis beaucoup de livres.
3. Tu lis des magazines?
   Oui, je lis des magazines.
4. Tu écris des lettres aux copains?
   Oui, j'écris des lettres aux copains.
5. Tu écris des cartes?
   Oui, j'écris des cartes.
6. Tu dis toujours que oui?
   Oui, je dis toujours que oui.

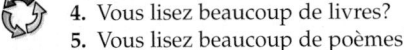

21 **Oui ou non?** Répondez.

1. Tes amis et toi, vous dites toujours des choses sérieuses?
2. Vous dites quelquefois des choses stupides?
3. Vous dites des choses amusantes?
4. Vous lisez beaucoup de livres?
5. Vous lisez beaucoup de poèmes?
6. Vous écrivez beaucoup de lettres?

La Conciergerie, Paris, France

Une jolie baie, Tahiti

22 **Tout le monde** Complétez.

1. (dire) Lui, il ____ toujours des choses stupides. Il ____ des bêtises. Ses amis ____ des bêtises aussi. Et vous, vous ____ quelquefois des bêtises aussi?
2. (dire) Lui, il ____ que oui. Ses amis ____ que oui. Et vous, qu'est-ce que vous ____?
3. (écrire) Lui, il ____ toujours des lettres. Mais ses amis n'____ pas de lettres. Ils ____ quelquefois des cartes postales. Et vous, vous ____ des lettres ou des cartes postales?
4. (lire) Lui, il ____ toujours des magazines. Ses amis ne ____ pas de magazines. Ils ____ des livres. Et vous? Vous ____ des magazines ou des livres?

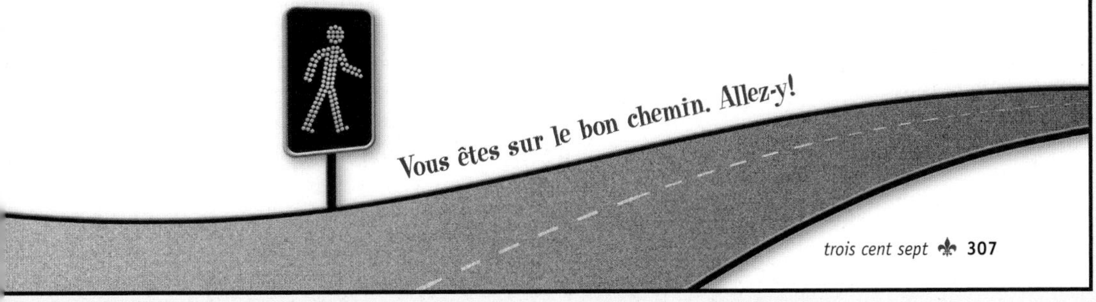
Vous êtes sur le bon chemin. Allez-y!

Structure

Learning from Photos

(page 307 left) This medieval building, La Conciergerie, was originally part of the royal palace on the Île de la Cité. It is mostly known, however, as a prison. It was the place of confinement for Danton, Robespierre, and Marie-Antoinette. It was from here that they were taken off to the guillotine. Marie-Antoinette's cell can still be visited in the Orangerie.

Assessment

Check for comprehension by having students make up sentences with the verbs **lire** and **écrire**, using things they know that they can either read or write.

Allez-y!
At this point in the chapter, students have learned all the vocabulary and structure necessary to complete the chapter. The conversation and cultural readings that follow recycle all the material learned up to this point.

Answers to Continuons

21 *Answers will vary but may include:*

1. Oui, nous disons toujours des choses sérieuses.
2. Oui, nous disons quelquefois des choses stupides.
3. Oui, nous disons des choses amusantes.
4. Oui, nous lisons beaucoup de livres.
5. Non, nous ne lisons pas beaucoup de poèmes.
6. Oui, nous écrivons beaucoup de lettres.

22

1. dit, dit, disent, dites
2. dit, disent, dites
3. écrit, écrivent, écrivent, écrivez
4. lit, lisent, lisent, lisez

Conversation

1 Preparation

Resource Manager

Audio Activities Booklet TE, page 117
Audiocassette 6A/CD 6
CD-ROM

Bellringer Review

Use BRR Transparency 9.6 or write the following on the board.
Write as many words as you can that are connected to the following topics.

le train **l'avion**
la gare **l'aéroport**

2 Presentation

Step 1 Have students close their books and listen as you either read the conversation to them or play Audiocassette 6A/CD 6.

Step 2 Ask students to open their books to page 308. Have them repeat each line once.

Step 3 Have students work in pairs to practice the conversation. Then have several pairs present it to the class.

Step 4 After presenting the conversation, go over the **Après la conversation** activity. If students can answer the questions with relative ease, move on. Students should not be expected to memorize the conversation.

Recycling

To recycle clothing vocabulary and some adjectives, have students say everything they can about the two people in the photo on page 308. Have them also list what they think is in the traveler's bag.

Conversation

Au guichet

Employé: Bonjour.
Voyageuse: Bonjour, monsieur. Un billet pour Nice, s'il vous plaît.
Employé: Aller-retour ou aller simple?
Voyageuse: Aller-retour en seconde, tarif étudiant, s'il vous plaît.
Employé: Vous avez votre carte?
Voyageuse: Oui, voilà... C'est combien?
Employé: Alors, tarif étudiant, c'est trente euros.
Voyageuse: Le prochain train part à quelle heure?
Employé: À dix heures trente, voie numéro 12.
Voyageuse: Merci, monsieur. Au revoir.

Après la conversation

Répondez.

1. La voyageuse est à la gare?
2. Elle parle à un employé de la gare?
3. Elle veut aller où?
4. Elle prend un billet aller-retour ou aller simple?
5. Elle est étudiante?
6. Elle a sa carte d'étudiante?
7. Elle a une réduction?
8. Le billet coûte combien?
9. Le prochain train part à quelle heure?
10. Il part de quelle voie?

Answers to Après la conversation

1. Oui, la voyageuse est à la gare.
2. Oui, elle parle à un employé de la gare.
3. Elle veut aller à Nice.
4. Elle prend un billet aller-retour.
5. Oui, elle est étudiante.
6. Oui, elle a sa carte d'étudiante.
7. Oui, elle a une réduction.
8. Le billet coûte trente euros.
9. Le prochain train part à dix heures trente.
10. Il part de la voie numéro 12.

Glencoe Technology

CD-ROM

On the CD-ROM, students can watch a dramatization of this conversation. They can then play the role of either one of the characters and record themselves in the conversation.

Parlons un peu plus

Let's talk some more

A **On va à Madrid.** You and a classmate are spending a semester in Paris. You will be going to Madrid for a couple of days. One of you is going to fly, and the other is going to take the train. Compare your trips: time, cost, and what you have to do the day you leave.

Réservation: 3615 3616 AF
(1,28 F TTC/mn)-**www.airfrance.fr**

Jours	Dép.	Arr.	N° Vol	Corr. Validité
PARIS				
→ Madison (WI)				-6:00
1234567	**16.00** C	**21.05**	AF380/AF8737(DL)	CVG 29/10-23/03
→ Madrid				+1:00
1234567	**07.15** F	**09.15** 1	AF1000	→ 29/10-24/03
1234567	**09.40** F	**11.40** 1	AF1300	→ 29/10-24/03
1234567	**10.45** F	**12.45** 1	AF1500	→ 29/10-24/03
1234567	**12.45** F	**14.45** 1	AF1600	→ 29/10-24/03
1234567	**14.15** F	**16.15** 1	AF1700	→ 29/10-24/03
1234567	**15.30** F	**17.30** 1	AF1800	→ 29/10-24/03
1234567	**16.30** F	**18.30** 1	AF1900	→ 29/10-24/03
1234567	**17.35** F	**19.35** 1	AF2000	→ 29/10-24/03
1234567	**19.20** F	**21.20** 1	AF2100	→ 29/10-24/03
12345-7	**20.00** F	**22.00** 1	AF2200	→ 29/10-23/03
→ Malaga				+1:00
1234567	**10.25** W	**12.45**	AF3408	→ 29/10-24/03

TRAINHOTEL Francisco de Goya
HORAIRES

	TRAIN 409		TRAIN 407
PARIS-AUSTERLITZ	19.47	MADRID-CHAMARTIN	19.00
POITIERS	22.18	VALLADOLID	21.20
VITORIA/GASTEIZ	04.12	BURGOS	22.19
BURGOS	05.21	VITORIA/GASTEIZ	23.29
VALLADOLID	06.19	POITIERS	05.45
MADRID-CHAMARTIN	08.58	PARIS-AUSTERLITZ	08.29

Circulation quotidienne.

B **Renseignements** You're at the information desk at one of the Paris train stations. You need some information. Have a conversation with the SNCF agent (your partner). You may wish to use the following expressions: **à quelle heure, le prochain train, quelle voie, quel quai, voyager en seconde, c'est combien, changer de train, attendre la correspondance.**

Prononciation

Les sons /õ/ et /ẽ/

1. Listen to the difference between the nasal sound /ã/ as in **cent** and the two other nasal sounds, /õ/ as in **son** and /ẽ/ as in **cinq: cent / son / cinq.** Repeat the following words with the sounds /õ/ and /ẽ/.

annonce	**non**	**bon**	**son**	**correspondance**
cinq	**copain**	**train**	**pain**	**vingt**

2. Now repeat the following sentences.

On annonce le train dans combien de temps?
Nous attendons des copains.

son train

Answers to Parlons un peu plus

A *Answers will vary but may include:*
—Je vais prendre le train pour aller à Madrid. Pour prendre mon billet, je fais la queue au guichet.
—Moi, je vais prendre l'avion pour aller à Madrid. À l'aéroport, je passe par le contrôle de sécurité.
—Mon train part de Paris à 19 h 47. Je vais arriver à Madrid à 8 h 58.
—Mon vol prend seulement deux heures! Un billet d'avion est plus cher.
—Le train n'est pas trop cher. Un aller-retour coûte deux cents euros.

B *Answers will vary but may include:*
—Bonjour, madame. Le train part pour Madrid à quelle heure?
—Le train part à ______.
—Et de quelle voie?
—De la voie numéro ______.
—Et il faut changer de train?
—Non, il ne faut pas changer de train.

3 Practice

Parlons un peu plus

Let's talk some more

A and **B** Have students work in pairs. You may wish to choose a pair of students to do these activities for the class.

Learning from Realia

(page 309) You may wish to ask the following questions about the schedule:

Quel est le nom de la gare à Madrid?
Quel est le nom de la gare à Paris?
Le train de Paris à Madrid part de Paris à quelle heure?
Il arrive à Madrid à quelle heure?
Il y a combien d'arrêts entre Paris et Madrid?

Prononciation

Step 1 Model the key words **son train** and have students repeat in unison after you. Model the other words in similar fashion or use Audiocassette 6A/CD 6.

Step 2 You may wish to give students the following **dictée:**
Non, les cinq copains ne vont pas voyager en train.
Mon copain annonce le départ du train.

Step 3 For additional pronunciation practice you may wish to use the Pronunciation Transparency P 9.

Resource Manager

Audio Activities Booklet TE, pages 119–120
Audiocassette 6A/CD 6

Bellringer Review

Use BRR Transparency 9.7 or write the following on the board.
Tell where you would go in a train station in the following situations:

1. **J'ai très faim. Je veux manger.**
2. **Je veux lire un journal.**
3. **Je veux écrire une carte postale.**
4. **Je veux acheter un aller simple.**
5. **Il faut attendre la correspondance.**
6. **Il faut changer de train.**

National Standards

Cultures
The reading and the related activities on pages 310–311 give students insight into train travel in western Africa.

Comparisons
The reading allows students to make comparisons between train travel in Africa, France, and the United States.

Lectures culturelles

Reading Strategy

Thinking while reading
Good readers always think as they read. They read the title and look at the visuals to determine the topic of the passage. They predict, create visual images, check for understanding, and pay close attention to each sentence in the reading.

Un voyage intéressant

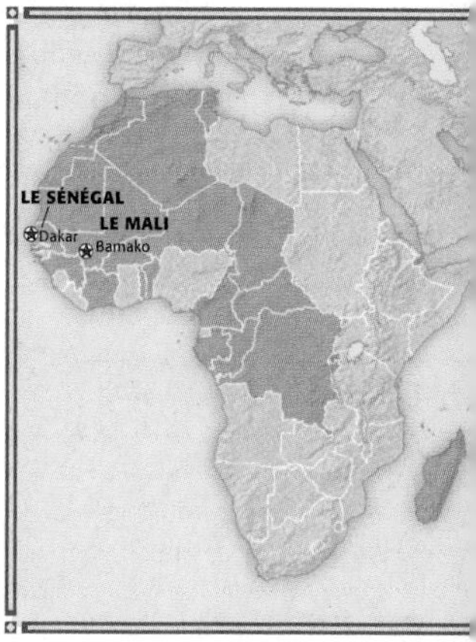

Vous dites que vous voulez faire un voyage intéressant en train. J'ai une bonne idée. Vous pouvez prendre le train de Bamako à Dakar. Deux fois par semaine, il y a un train entre ces deux villes. Les trains partent dans les deux sens (directions) tous les mercredis et les samedis matins.

Vous aimez lire? Pas de problème! Vous avez beaucoup de cartes postales à écrire à vos amis? Pas de problème non plus! Vous avez trente heures pour lire tous les livres que vous voulez et écrire beaucoup de cartes postales! Quand je dis trente heures, c'est d'après l'horaire. En réalité, le train est toujours en retard et c'est plutôt[1] un voyage de trente-cinq heures.

Si vous voulez dormir pendant le voyage, vous pouvez louer une couchette[2]. Il y a des wagons-couchettes et un wagon-restaurant. Le train fait beaucoup d'arrêts et les voyageurs peuvent descendre sur le quai et acheter quelque chose à manger ou à boire. Quand on entend l'annonce du départ du train, on remonte vite en voiture avec sa nourriture et le voyage continue.

[1] plutôt *more*
[2] louer une couchette *reserve a berth*

Le train qui fait Bamako-Dakar

Presentation

Pre-reading

Step 1 Have students study the map on page 310 and look at the photos on pages 310–311.

Step 2 Read and discuss the Reading Strategy on page 310.

Step 3 Have students scan the reading quickly and silently.

Learning from Photos

(page 310) This is a photo of the train that makes the Bamako-Dakar run twice weekly. The train has a dining car and sleeping berths **(couchettes)**. Many people, however, get their food at stations along the way. Some travelers do the trip in stages by taking the slower local train between Bamako and Kayes, which is 40 percent cheaper. They then take the omnibus to Tambacounda and the bush taxi from Tambacounda to Dakar.

Le Sahara, Mali

Où sont Bamako et Dakar? Bamako est la capitale du Mali. Le Mali est le pays francophone le plus grand d'Afrique Occidentale. Le Sahara couvre 60% du pays et il y a très peu de pluie[3]. Dakar est la capitale du Sénégal. Dakar est une très grande ville moderne sur l'océan Atlantique. C'est aussi un port important.

[3] pluie *rain*

Un marché, Mali

Après la lecture

A Bamako–Dakar Choisissez la bonne réponse.

1. Il y a un train entre Bamako et Dakar ____.
   a. une fois par semaine **b.** deux fois par semaine
2. Les trains partent ____.
   a. le matin **b.** l'après-midi
3. Les trains partent ____.
   a. le mardi et le dimanche **b.** le mercredi et le samedi
4. Le voyage entre Bamako et Dakar dure trente heures d'après ____.
   a. les contrôleurs **b.** l'horaire
5. Le train arrive presque toujours ____.
   a. en retard **b.** à l'heure
6. Beaucoup de voyageurs achètent quelque chose à manger ____.
   a. dans les gares **b.** au wagon-couchette

B Un peu de géographie Choisissez la bonne réponse.

1. **a.** Le Sahara est un grand lac.
   b. Le Sahara est un grand désert.
2. **a.** Le Sénégal est un pays désertique.
   b. Le Mali est un pays désertique.
3. **a.** Bamako est la capitale du Mali.
   b. Bamako est la capitale du Sénégal.
4. **a.** Il y a très peu de pluie à Dakar.
   b. Il y a très peu de pluie à Bamako.

Reading

Step 1 To vary the presentation of the **Lecture,** have students close books and listen as you read to them.

Step 2 Read the story again as they follow along in their books. This is beneficial for the acquisition of receptive skills.

Step 3 Call on individuals to read two or three sentences. After every two or three sentences, ask comprehension questions.

Post-reading

Have students do the **Après la lecture** activities on page 311 orally after reading the selection in class. Then assign these activities to be written at home. Go over them again the following day.

Fun Facts

Every year during December, a very interesting event takes place in Mali. The small town of Diafarabé is transformed into a center of activity and celebration as hundreds of thousands of cattle are driven south across the Niger River in search of greener pastures. It is a very happy time for herders who have been on the desolate Sahara for months. The crossing enables them to reunite with their families and gives them cause to celebrate with music and dancing. The major crossing is at Diafarabé because it is one of the narrowest places along the river. It is about 187 km east of Ségour and a 6-hour drive from Bamako. The exact date of the crossing varies because the water level is an important determinant.

Answers to Après la lecture

A	B
1. a	1. b
2. a	2. b
3. b	3. a
4. b	4. b
5. a	
6. b	

Learning from Photos

(page 311 top) In this photo we see cattle grazing on the arid Sahara desert in Mali. *(page 311 bottom)* This is a marketplace in Bamako. Have students say what people are buying in the market.

National Standards

Cultures
This selection familiarizes students with train travel in France.

Attention!

This reading is optional. You may skip it completely, have the entire class read it, have only several students read it and report to the class, or assign it for extra credit.

Presentation

Step 1 Discuss train travel in the United States with your students. Recall what they have learned about train travel in Africa. Ask students if they know the song on page 312.

Step 2 Have students read the **Lecture** quickly as they look at the photos that accompany it.

Step 3 Ask what they learned about train travel in France and the city of Avignon.

Music Connection

Have students learn the words to ***Sur le pont d'Avignon.***

Lecture supplémentaire

La SNCF
(La Société[1] nationale des chemins de fer français)

Erica Saunders est une élève américaine. Elle passe ses vacances d'été en France. En ce moment elle est à la gare de Lyon à Paris. Elle va prendre le train pour Avignon. Tous les trains qui partent de cette gare vont vers le sud. Le train est un moyen de transport très populaire en France. Il y a cinq gares à Paris. Erica va au guichet et prend son billet. Elle veut un aller-retour en seconde. Elle a de la chance parce qu'il n'y a pas de queue.

Munie de[2] son billet, Erica va sur le quai et monte dans le train. Avant d'aller sur le quai, elle composte son billet—elle passe son billet dans une machine. Ça indique où elle commence son voyage. C'est très important. Si on ne composte pas son billet, on paie une amende[3]. Erica n'attend pas longtemps. Il est 10 h 11 et le train part. Comme toujours le train part exactement à l'heure. En France, le service de la SNCF est excellent. Il y a très peu de retards.

[1] société *company*
[2] Munie de *With*
[3] amende *fine*

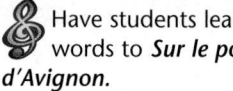

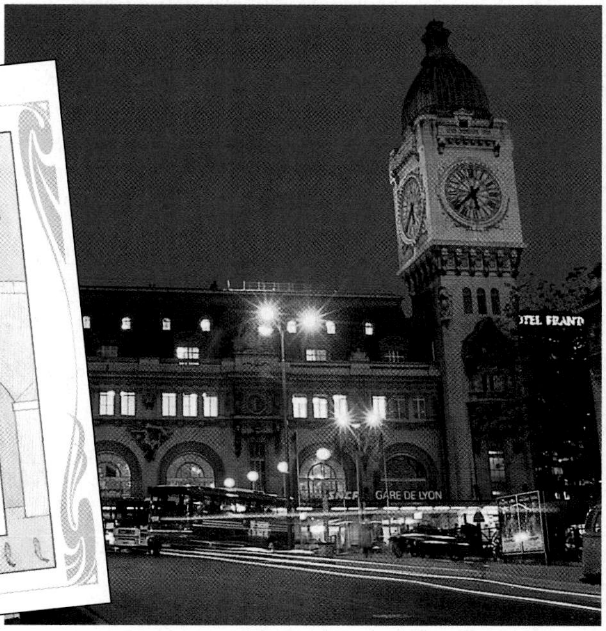

Gare de Lyon, Paris

Si Erica a faim pendant le voyage, elle peut aller au snack-bar. Là on offre de la restauration rapide—un sandwich, une pizza ou une boisson, par exemple.

Pendant le voyage, Erica lit un guide sur Avignon. Le guide répond à toutes ses questions. Elle apprend qu'Avignon est une ville de culture et de fête. Elle va visiter le célèbre palais des Papes. Elle a de la chance, parce qu'en juillet, il y a un grand festival de théâtre qui a lieu[4] dans la cour du palais… et dans toute la ville. Elle veut voir aussi le pont d'Avignon qui traverse le Rhône. Ce pont célèbre date du douzième siècle. Là, elle va chanter «Sur le pont d'Avignon». Tous les élèves américains qui font du français apprennent cette chanson.

[4] a lieu *takes place*

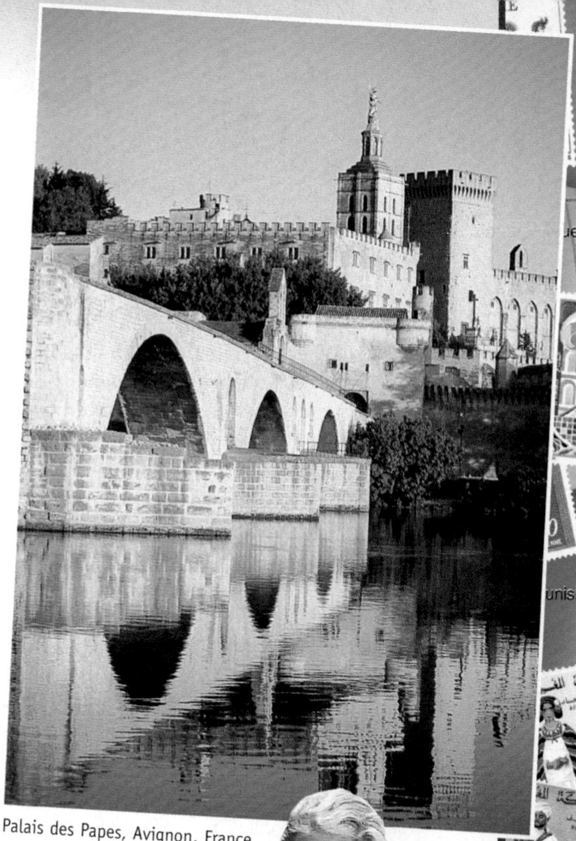

Palais des Papes, Avignon, France

Après la lecture

On va à Avignon. Répondez.

1. Qui est Erica Saunders?
2. Elle est où, en ce moment?
3. Elle va aller où?
4. Elle prend quel type de billet?
5. Le train part à quelle heure?
6. Comment est le service de la SNCF?
7. Si Erica a faim, elle peut manger où?
8. Qu'est-ce qu'elle lit pendant le voyage?
9. Qu'est-ce qu'elle veut voir à Avignon?
10. Qu'est-ce qu'il y a à Avignon pendant le mois de juillet?

Learning from Photos

(page 313) The famous Palais des Papes seen here dominates the lovely city of Avignon. Built in the Middle Ages, the papacy moved here in 1307. The Popes ruled in this palace until 1377, when they officially moved back to Rome. Several cardinals resisted and stayed in Avignon. They elected an anti-pope thus creating the Great Schism of the West, which lasted until 1449.

The bridge in the song ***Sur le pont d'Avignon*** is the half-ruined Saint Bénézet Bridge on the Rhône built in the twelfth century.

Note: Students will learn about the high-tech TGV in a subsequent lesson.

Answers to Après la lecture

1. Erica Saunders est une élève américaine.
2. Elle est en France.
3. Elle va aller à Avignon.
4. Elle prend un aller-retour en seconde.
5. Le train part à dix heures onze.
6. Le service de la SNCF est excellent.
7. Si elle a faim, elle peut manger au snack-bar.
8. Elle lit un guide sur Avignon.
9. Elle veut voir le palais des Papes et le pont d'Avignon.
10. Il y a un grand festival de théâtre pendant le mois de juillet.

National Standards

Connections
This reading about the 24-hour clock and the metric system establishes a connection with another discipline, allowing students to reinforce and further their knowledge of mathematics through the study of French.

Comparisons
This reading allows students to compare the U.S. system of distance measurement with the metric system, which is used in most of the French-speaking world.

Attention!

The readings in the **Connexions** section are optional. They focus on some of the major disciplines taught in schools and universities. The vocabulary is useful for discussing such topics as history, literature, art, economics, business, science, etc. You may choose any of the following ways to do the readings in the **Connexions** sections.

Independent reading Have students read the selections and do the post-reading activities as homework, which you collect. This option is least intrusive on class time and requires a minimum of teacher involvement.

Homework with in-class follow-up Assign the readings and post-reading activities as homework. Review and discuss the material in class the next day.

Intensive in-class activity This option includes a pre-reading vocabulary presentation, in-class reading and discussion, assignment of the activities for homework, and a discussion of the assignment in class the following day.

CONNEXIONS

Les mathématiques

Des conversions—les horaires

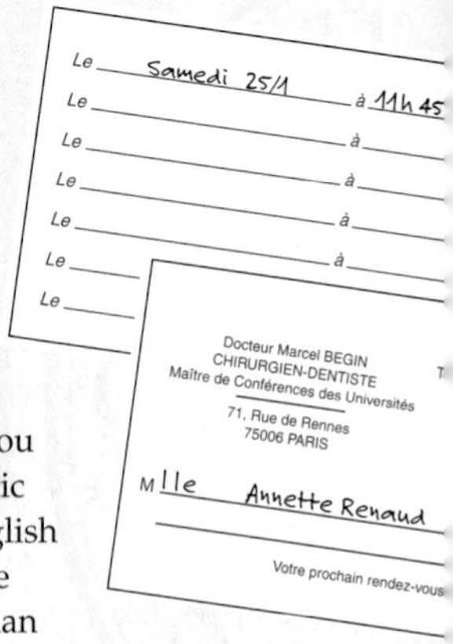

When traveling through the French-speaking countries, you will need to make some mathematical conversions. The metric system is used for weights and measures rather than the English system, which we use in the United States. For schedules, the twenty-four-hour clock is used, rather than our A.M./P.M. system of indicating time. Let's learn to make some of these conversions.

Arman *L'heure de tous*

L'heure

Il y a deux façons[1] de dire l'heure. Il y a l'heure de la conversation normale: la journée est divisée[2] en deux fois douze heures—de une heure du matin à midi et de une heure de l'après-midi à minuit. Mais il y a aussi l'heure officielle. C'est l'heure des horaires de train, d'avion, de manifestations culturelles. C'est aussi l'heure qu'on utilise quand on prend rendez-vous[3] chez le dentiste, par exemple.

[1] façons *ways*
[2] divisée *divided*
[3] prend rendez-vous *make an appointment*

Learning from Photos

(page 314 top) This clock sculpture, called **L'heure de tous,** is in front of the gare Saint-Lazare in Paris. Have students tell the times on as many clocks in the photo as they can.

Pour l'heure officielle, la journée est divisée en 24 heures, de zéro heure à 23 heures. Étudiez le tableau suivant.

HORAIRES		CONVERSATION
0.25	zéro heure vingt-cinq	minuit vingt-cinq
8.15	huit heures quinze	huit heures et quart du matin
12.00	douze heures	midi
14.00	quatorze heures	deux heures de l'après-midi
16.40	seize heures quarante	cinq heures moins vingt de l'après-midi
22.00	vingt-deux heures	dix heures du soir
23.50	vingt-trois heures cinquante	minuit moins dix

Vous voulez prendre rendez-vous chez le dentiste pour 3 h de l'après-midi. C'est quelle heure en langage officiel? Votre train part à 21 h 35. C'est quelle heure en langage courant?

Les distances

Pour mesurer la distance, le système métrique utilise le mètre et non le *yard* ni le *mile* comme en anglais. Le mètre est un peu plus d'un *yard*. Un kilomètre (1 000 mètres) est équivalent à 0,621 *mile*—un peu plus d'un demi-*mile*.

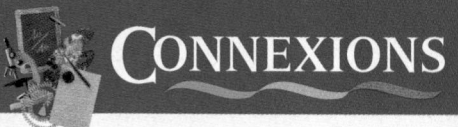

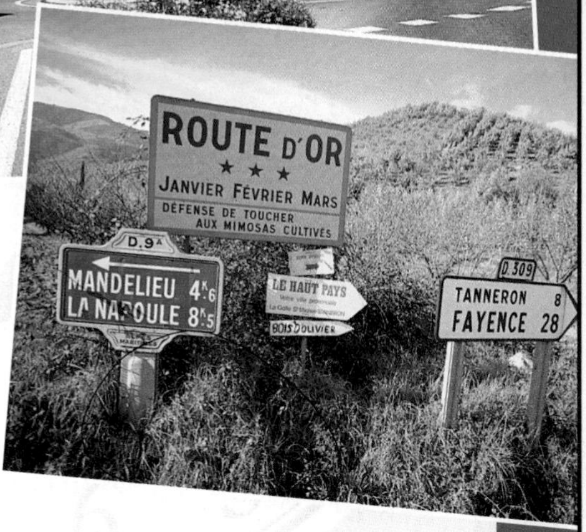

Après la lecture

A L'heure Read the departure board on page 314 and give the departure times of the trains in conversational French.

B Les distances Read these road signs. Give the approximate distance in miles to each town.

CONNEXIONS

Presentation

Les mathématiques
Des conversions—les horaires

Step 1 Have students read the introduction in English on page 314.

Step 2 Have students read the selection quickly or have them skim it.

Step 3 You may wish to have them find and repeat all the cognates in the reading selection. Explain to them that there are two important strategies to use when reading unfamiliar material—they should learn to recognize cognates and derive meaning from context.

Après la lecture

Discuss the answers to the activities on page 315.

ANSWERS TO Après la lecture

A

15 h 30 Le train part à trois heures et demie de l'après-midi.

15 h 33 Le train part à quatre heures moins vingt-sept de l'après-midi.

15 h 39 Le train part à quatre heures moins vingt et un(e) de l'après-midi.

15 h 45 Le train part à quatre heures moins le quart de l'après-midi.

15 h 48 Le train part à quatre heures moins douze de l'après-midi.

B *Answers will be as follows:*

Fayence est à 28 kilomètres. Ça fait à peu près 17 miles.

Use what you have learned

Recycling

These activities allow students to use the vocabulary and structure from this chapter in completely open-ended, real-life situations.

Learning from Photos

(page 316 middle) La gare du Palais, the train station that serves Quebec, was built in the nineteenth century; it is located in the heart of the old city. There are several trains a day between Montreal and Quebec.

Use what you have learned

PARLER

1 Le train, l'autocar ou l'avion?

✔ Discuss train, bus, and plane travel

Work in groups of three or four. Discuss the advantages **(les avantages)** and disadvantages **(les inconvénients)** of train, bus **(autocar),** or plane travel. In your discussion, include such things as speed, price, location of terminals, and anything else you consider important.

Le bus, Dakar

L'aéroport, Saint-Barthélemy, les Antilles

La gare, Québec

Un bouchon, place d'Italie, Paris

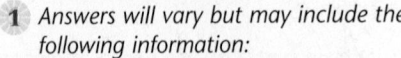

PARLER

2 Qu'est-ce qu'on va faire?

✔ Discuss what to do if you miss your train

You and a classmate are on a bus on the way to **la gare de l'Est** in Paris. There's an awful traffic jam **(un bouchon).** You know you are going to miss your train. Discuss your predicament and decide what you are going to do.

Answers to C'est à vous

1 *Answers will vary but may include the following information:*

Le train va moins rapide que l'avion.
Les gares sont dans les villes.
L'avion est plus rapide que le train.
L'avion coûte cher.
Les aéroports sont loin des villes.
L'autocar ne coûte pas cher.
L'autocar est moins rapide que le train ou l'avion.

2 *Answers will vary but may include:*

—Zut! Il y a un bouchon. Je crois qu'on va arriver à la gare en retard et on va rater le train.
—Il y a un autre train, non?
—Oui, je crois que oui.
—S'il faut attendre longtemps, on peut aller prendre quelque chose au buffet de la gare.

ÉCRIRE

3 Dans la gare

✔ Write a paragraph using expressions related to train travel

Look at the photograph and write a paragraph about it.

La gare Saint-Charles, Marseille

Writing Strategy

Writing a descriptive paragraph Your goal in writing a descriptive paragraph is to enable the reader to visualize a scene. To achieve this, you must select and organize details that create an impression. Using a greater number of specific nouns and vivid, descriptive adjectives will make your writing livelier.

ÉCRIRE

4 Un voyage fabuleux

Write about a trip you want to take. It can be a real or imaginary trip. Describe how you'll go and when. Describe in great detail how you'll get there. Describe all the things you have to do. Continue by writing about what you are going to see and do when you get there. Try to make your readers understand what it is about the place that makes you like it so much.

Writing Development

Have students keep a notebook containing their best written work from each chapter. These selected writings can be based on assignments from the Student Textbook and the Writing Activities Workbook. The two activities on page 317 are examples of writing assignments that may be included in each student's portfolio. In the Workbook, students will develop an organized autobiography **(Mon autobiographie).** These workbook pages may also become a part of their portfolio.

Writing Strategy

Writing a descriptive paragraph Have students read the Writing Strategy on page 317. If students have difficulty thinking of appropriate vocabulary, have them use the vocabulary list on page 320.

About the French Language

Another word for **bouchon** is **un embouteillage.** Have students make an association between these French terms and "bottleneck" in English. ✤

Answers to C'est à vous

3 *Answers will vary but may include:*

C'est une gare à Paris. Il y a des voyageurs sur les quais. Quelques voyageurs prennent un café au buffet de la gare. Au kiosque, quelques voyageurs achètent des journaux ou des magazines…

4 *Answers will vary.*

Students can write a composition using all the vocabulary they know about travel and the place they choose to visit.

Reaching All Students

Additional Practice Have students work in small groups and make up as many questions as possible about Communication Transparency C 9. Groups take turns asking and answering their questions.

Resource Manager

Communication Transparencies
Quizzes
Test Booklet
ExamView Pro®
Situation Cards
Performance Assessment
Marathon mental Videoquiz

Assessment

This is a pre-test for students to take before you administer the chapter test. Answer sheets for students to do these pages are provided in your transparency binder. Note that each section is cross-referenced so students can easily find the material they have to review in case they made errors. You may wish to collect these assessments and correct them yourself or you may prefer to have the students correct themselves in class. You can go over the answers orally or project them on the overhead, using your Assessment Answers transparencies.

Vocabulaire

To review **Mots 1**, *turn to pages 292–293.*

1 Répondez.

1. Qu'est-ce qu'on vend au kiosque?
2. Les voyageurs attendent le train où?
3. Qu'est-ce qu'on regarde pour vérifier l'heure du départ ou de l'arrivée d'un train?
4. On vend les billets de train où?

To review **Mots 2**, *turn to pages 296–297.*

2 Complétez d'après le dessin.

5. La plupart des voyageurs sont ____.
6. Trois voyageurs sont ____.
7. Une passagère écrit ____.
8. Un autre passager lit ____.

Structure

To review **-re** *verbs in the present, turn to page 300.*

3 Récrivez chaque phrase.

9. Ils attendent le train.
   Il ____________.
10. Tu entends l'annonce?
    Vous ____________?
11. Tout le monde perd patience.
    Je ____________.
12. Qu'est-ce qu'elle vend?
    Qu'est-ce qu'elles ____________?
13. On descend au prochain arrêt.
    Tu ____________.

Answers to Assessment

1

1. On vend des magazines et des journaux.
2. Les voyageurs attendent le train sur le quai.
3. On regarde l'horaire.
4. On vend les billets au guichet.

2

5. assis
6. debout
7. une carte postale
8. un journal

3

9. Il attend le train.
10. Vous entendez l'annonce?
11. Je perds patience.
12. Qu'est-ce qu'elles vendent?
13. Tu descends au prochain arrêt.

Assessment

4 Complétez avec «ce».

14. ____ train va à Bordeaux.
15. ____ carte postale est très jolie.
16. Notre train part de ____ voie ou de la voie 5?
17. ____ voitures sont assez vieilles.

To review demonstrative adjectives, turn to page 303.

5 Complétez.

18. J'____ des cartes postales. (écrire)
19. Ils ____ beaucoup. (lire)
20. Vous ____ que oui ou que non? (dire)
21. Vous ____ beaucoup de lettres. (écrire)
22. Tu ____ quel livre? (lire)

*To review **dire**, **écrire**, and **lire**, turn to page 306.*

Culture

6 Vrai ou faux?

23. Il y a un train deux fois par semaine entre Bamako et Dakar.
24. Ce train arrive toujours à l'heure.
25. Dakar, la capitale du Sénégal, est une très grande ville moderne sur la mer Mediterranée.

To review this cultural information, turn to pages 310–311.

La gare, Dakar, Sénégal

Learning from Photos

(page 319) This photo shows the front which is also the main entrance to the railroad station in Dakar.

Glencoe Technology

MINDJOGGER

You may wish to help your students prepare for the chapter test by playing the MindJogger game show. Teams will compete against each other to review chapter vocabulary and structure and sharpen listening comprehension skills.

Answers to Assessment

4

14. Ce
15. Cette
16. cette
17. Ces

5

18. écris
19. lisent
20. dites
21. écrivez
22. lis

6

23. V
24. F
25. F

Vocabulary Review

The words and phrases in the **Vocabulaire** have been taught for productive use in this chapter. They are summarized here as a resource for both student and teacher. This list also serves as a convenient resource for the **C'est à vous** activities on pages 316–317. There are approximately sixteen cognates in this vocabulary list. Have students find them.

Attention!

You will notice that the vocabulary list here is not translated. This has been done intentionally, since we feel that by the time students have finished the material in the chapter they should be familiar with the meanings of all the words. If there are several words they still do not know, we recommend that they refer to the **Mots 1** and **2** sections in the chapter or go to the dictionaries at the back of this book to find the meanings. However, if you prefer that your students have the English translations, please refer to Vocabulary Transparency 9.1, where you will find all these words listed with their translations.

Vocabulaire

Getting around a train station

une gare
un train
un quai
une voie
la correspondance
un horaire
un guichet
un billet
un aller simple
un aller (et) retour
en seconde
en première
un chariot
un kiosque
un journal
un magazine
une carte (postale)
une salle d'attente
un buffet

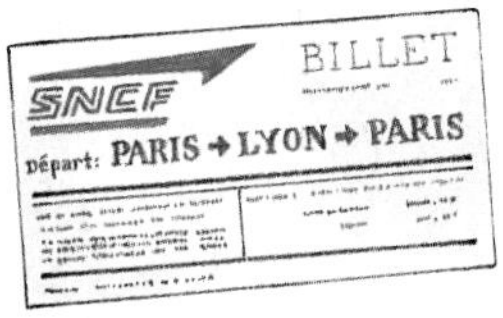

Describing activities at a train station

faire la queue
attendre
descendre
vendre
monter (en voiture)
composter
partir
changer (de)
rater

On board the train

une voiture
un wagon
assis(e)
debout
un voyageur
une voyageuse
un contrôleur
contrôler les billets
lire
dire
écrire
répondre
un snack-bar
un arrêt
au prochain arrêt

How well do you know your vocabulary?

- Choose five words from the vocabulary list.
- Use the words in original sentences to tell a story.

Other useful words and expressions

arriver à + infinitif
être en avance
être en retard
perdre patience
la plupart des
quelques
depuis

Technotour

BON VOYAGE!

VIDÉO • Épisode 9

Avant de visionner

In this video episode, Amadou and Chloé set out on a train trip to Lille. Or at least they try to.

Amadou et Chloé partent pour Lille. Ils prennent leurs billets.

Leur train part d'où?

FRENCH ONLINE

À découvrir

Learn more about train stations in Paris online.

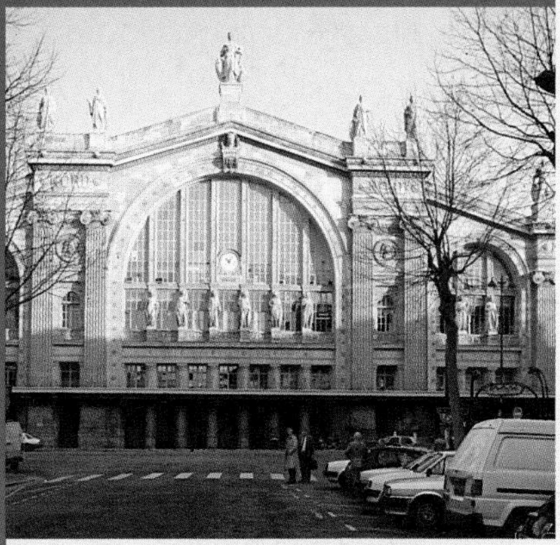

La gare du Nord, Paris

FRENCH Online

In the Chapter 9 Internet activity, you will have a chance to learn more about train travel in the Francophone world. To begin your virtual adventure, go to the Glencoe French Web site: **french.glencoe.com**

Technotour

Overview

This page previews two key multimedia components of the **Glencoe French** series. Each reinforces the material taught in the chapter in a unique manner.

VIDÉO

The Video Program allows students to see how the chapter vocabulary and structures are used by native speakers. For maximum reinforcement, show the video episode as a final activity for Chapter 9.

The two photos on the left show highlights from the Chapter 9 video episode. Discuss the photos with your students before having them view the episode. See the Video Activities Booklet for detailed suggestions for using this resource.

FRENCH Online

- The **À découvrir** photo on page 320 shows the gare du Nord train station. Students can go online to learn more about train stations in Paris.
- Teacher Information and Student Worksheets for this activity can be accessed at the Web site.

Video Synopsis

In this video episode, we are given some information about trains in France. We meet up with Chloé and Amadou at the gare du Nord in Paris. They are on their way to Lille to do a video report. They are going to take the TGV, the high-speed train. We watch Chloé attempt to purchase her ticket unsuccessfully, until a kind traveler offers his assistance. Suddenly they hear their train's departure being announced and take off in a hurry for the track. Sadly, they don't make it in time!

Planning for Chapter 10

SCOPE AND SEQUENCE, PAGES 322–353

Topics

- Sports and physical activities
- Past actions and events

Functions

- How to talk about sports and other physical activities
- How to describe past actions and events
- How to ask questions

Culture

- Popular sports in Canada and Africa
- The Tour de France bike race

Structure

- The **passé composé** of regular verbs
- **Qui, qu´est-ce que, quoi**
- The verbs **boire, devoir,** and **recevoir** in the present tense

National Standards

- Communication Standard 1.1 pages 326, 327, 330, 331, 333, 334, 335, 336, 337, 338, 339, 341, 348
- Communication Standard 1.2 pages 326, 327, 330, 331, 333, 334, 335, 336, 337, 338, 340, 343, 345, 347, 348
- Communication Standard 1.3 pages 326, 333, 338, 349
- Cultures Standard 2.1 pages 324, 325, 329, 340, 342–343, 344–345
- Connections Standard 3.1 pages 346–347
- Comparisons Standard 4.2 pages 342–343, 344–345
- Communities Standard 5.1 page 349

PACING AND PRIORITIES

The chapter content is color coded below to assist you in planning.

■ required ■ recommended ■ optional

Vocabulaire *(required)* *Days 1–4*

- ■ Mots 1
  Le foot(ball)
- ■ Mots 2
  D´autres sports d´équipe

Structure *(required)* *Days 5–7*

- ■ Le passé composé des verbes réguliers
- ■ **Qui, qu´est-ce que, quoi**
- ■ Les verbes **boire, devoir** et **recevoir** au présent

Conversation *(required)*

- ■ On a gagné!

Prononciation *(recommended)*

- ■ Liaison et élision

Lectures culturelles

- ■ Le hockey et le basket-ball *(recommended)*
- ■ Le Tour de France *(optional)*

Connexions *(optional)*

- ■ L´anatomie

■ **C'est à vous** *(recommended)*

■ **Assessment** *(recommended)*

■ **Technotour** *(optional)*

RESOURCE GUIDE

Section	Pages	Section Resources
Vocabulaire *Mots 1*		
Le foot(ball)	324–327	Vocabulary Transparencies 10.2–10.3 Audiocassette 6B/CD 6 Audio Activities Booklet TE, pages 122–124 Workbook, page 95 Quiz 1, page 49 ExamView Pro®
Vocabulaire *Mots 2*		
D´autres sports d´équipe	328–331	Vocabulary Transparencies 10.4–10.5 Audiocassette 6B/CD 6 Audio Activities Booklet TE, pages 124–126 Workbook, page 96 Quiz 2, page 50 ExamView Pro®
Structure		
Le passé composé des verbes réguliers **Qui, qu´est-ce que, quoi** Les verbes **boire, devoir** et **recevoir** au présent	332–334 335–336 337–339	Audiocassette 6B/CD 6 Audio Activities Booklet TE, pages 127–128 Workbook, pages 97–101 Quizzes 3–5, pages 51–53 ExamView Pro®
Conversation		
On a gagné!	340	Audiocassette 6B/CD 6 Audio Activities Booklet TE, page 129 CD-ROM
Prononciation		
Liaison et élision	341	Pronunciation Transparency, P 10 Audiocassette 6B/CD 6 Audio Activities Booklet TE, page 130
Lectures culturelles		
Le hockey et le basket-ball Le Tour de France	342–343 344–345	Audiocassette 6B/CD 6 Audio Activities Booklet TE, pages 130–131 Test Booklet, Chapter 10
Connexions		
L´anatomie	346–347	Test Booklet, Chapter 10
C'est à vous		
	348–349	**Bon voyage!** Video, Episode 10 Video Activities Booklet, Chapter 10 French Online Activities french.glencoe.com
Assessment		
	350–351	Communication Transparency C 10 Quizzes 1–5, pages 49–53 Test Booklet, Chapter 10 ExamView Pro® Situation Cards, Chapter 10 **Marathon mental** Videoquiz

Using Your Resources for Chapter 10

Transparencies

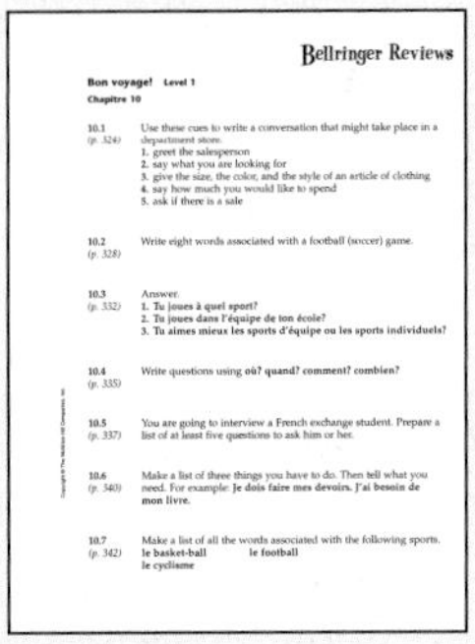

Bellringer 10.1–10.7

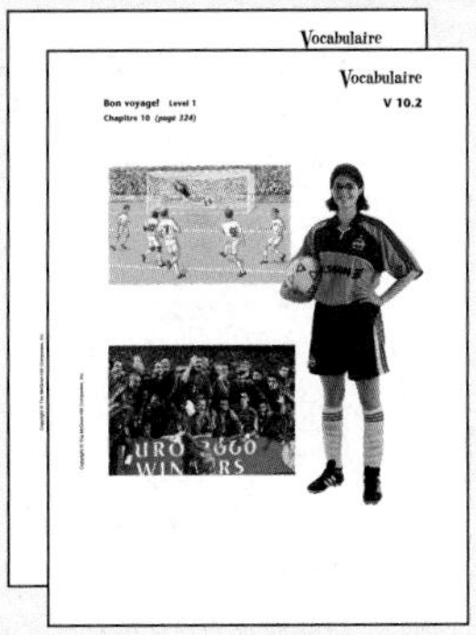

Vocabulary 10.1–10.5

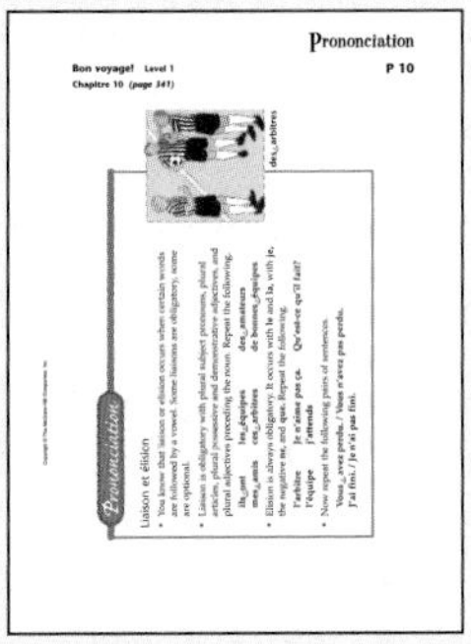

Pronunciation P 10

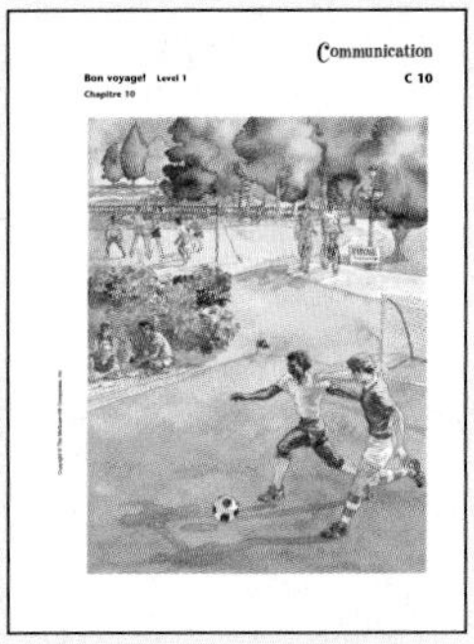

Communication C 10

Writing Activities Workbook

Vocabulary, pages 95–96

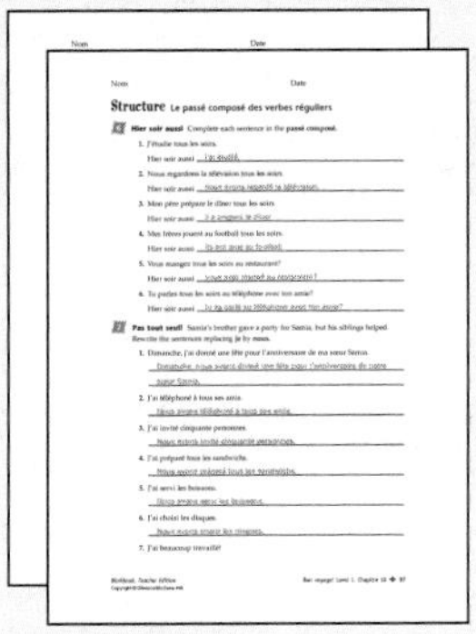

Structure, pages 97–101

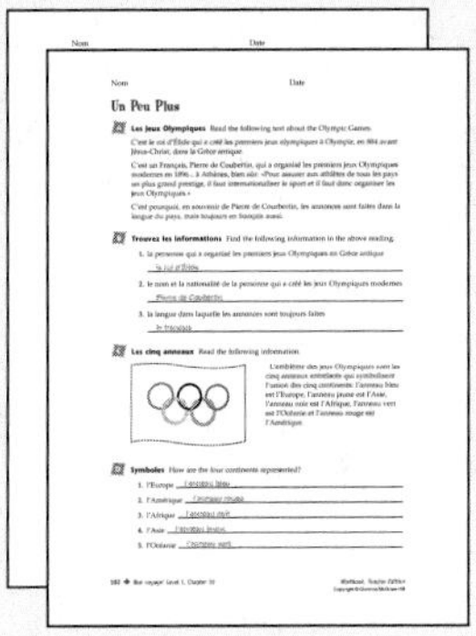

Enrichment, pages 102–104

Audio Program and Audio Activities Booklet

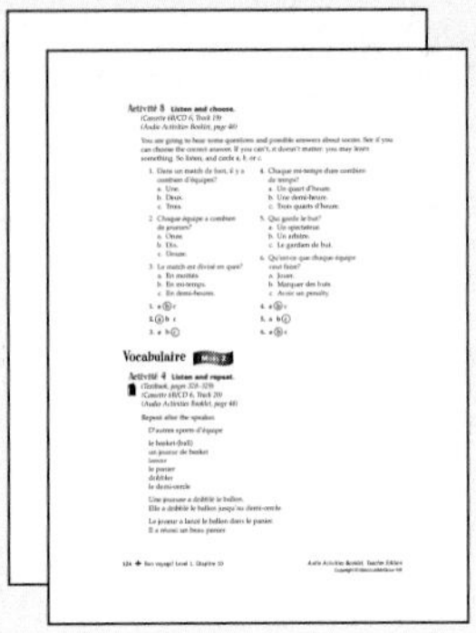

Vocabulary, pages 122–126

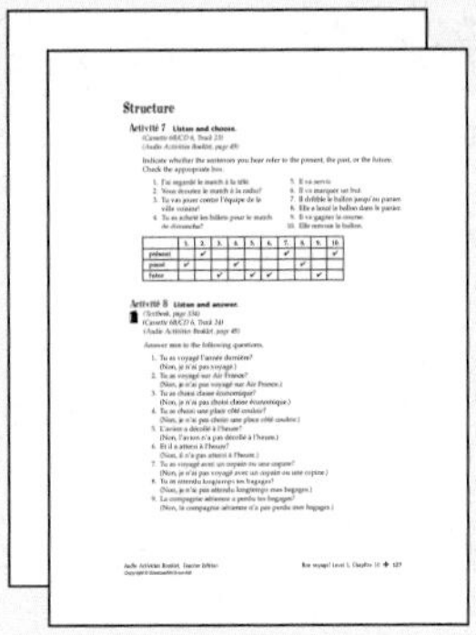

Structure, pages 127–128

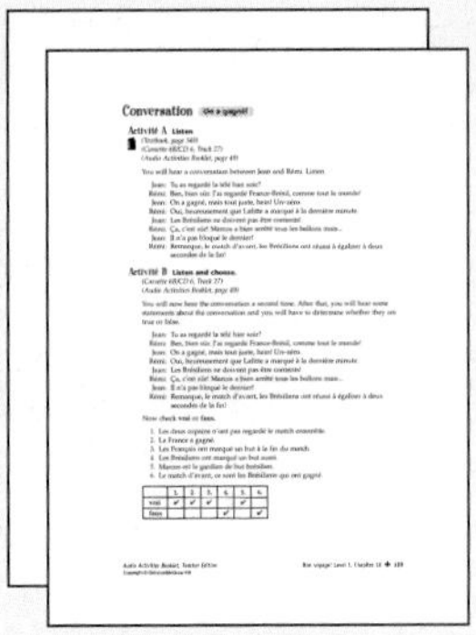

Conversation, Pronunciation, pages 129–130

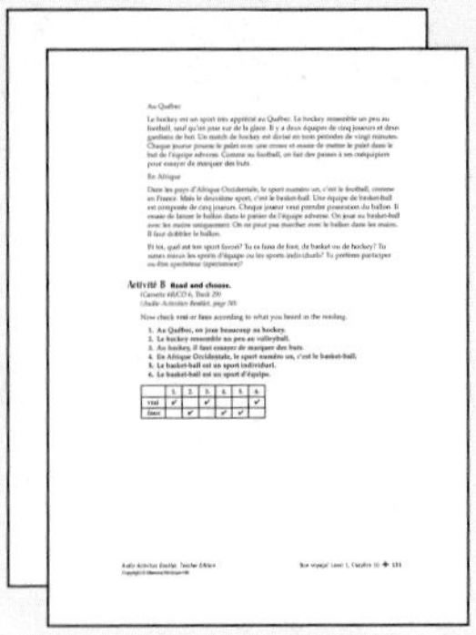

Cultural Reading, pages 130–131

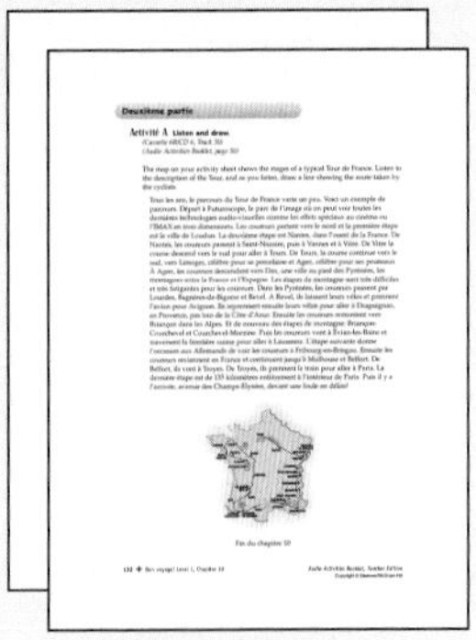

Additional Practice, page 132

Assessment

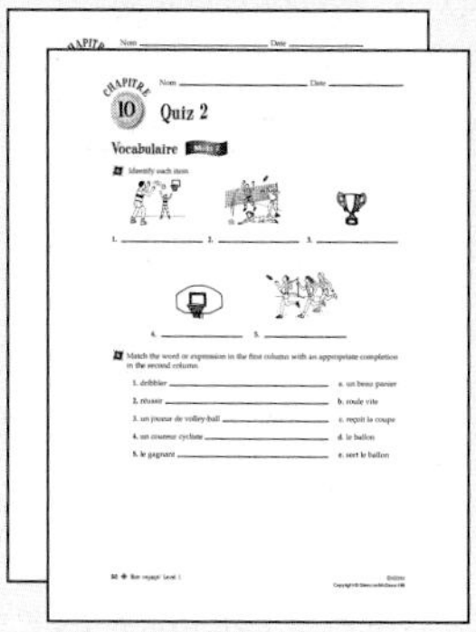

Vocabulary and Structure Quizzes, pages 49–53

Chapter Tests, Chapter 10

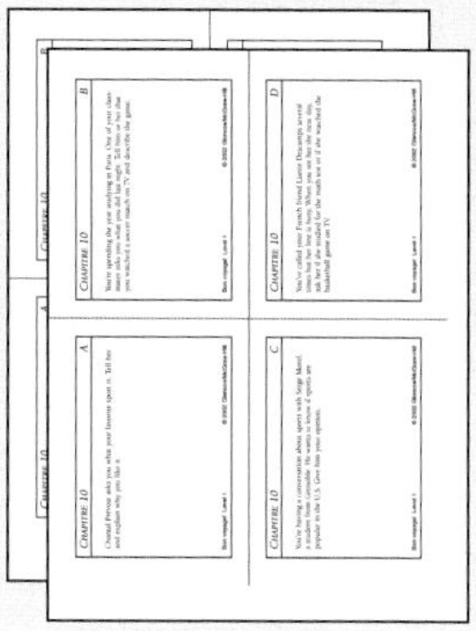

Situation Cards, Chapter 10

Timesaving Teacher Tools

Interactive Teacher Edition

Imagine having your Teacher's Edition and all resources on a CD-ROM. Click on a resource and it appears on your screen, ready to be printed, sorted, or planned.

Interactive Lesson Planner

The Interactive Lesson Planner CD-ROM helps you organize your lesson plans for a week, month, semester, or year. Look at this planning tool for easy access to your Chapter 10 resources.

ExamView Pro®

Test Bank software for Macintosh and Windows makes creating, editing, customizing, and printing tests quick and easy.

Technology Resources

FRENCH Online

In the Chapter 10 Internet activity, you will have a chance to learn more about sports in the Francophone world. Visit french.glencoe.com.

On the Interactive Conversation CD-ROM, students can listen to and take part in a recorded version of the conversation in Chapter 10.

NATIONAL GEOGRAPHIC SOCIETY

See the National Geographic Teacher's Corner on pages 150–151, 256–257, 396–397, 500–501 for reference to additional technology resources.

Bon Voyage! Video and Video Activities Booklet.

Help your students prepare for the chapter test by playing the **Marathon mental** Videoquiz game show. Teams will compete against each other to review chapter vocabulary and structure and sharpen listening comprehension skills.

CHAPITRE 10

Preview

In this chapter, students will learn to discuss and describe sports and other physical activities. To do this, they will learn basic vocabulary related to soccer, basketball, volleyball, cycling, and running. They will also learn the **passé composé** of regular verbs, review question words, and learn the present tense of the verbs **boire, devoir,** and **recevoir.**

National Standards

Communication

In Chapter 10, students will communicate in spoken and written French on the following topics:

- Describing team sports, namely, soccer, basketball, and volleyball
- Describing individual sports, namely, cycling and running

Students will also learn to narrate past events. They will obtain and provide information and engage in conversations about sports as they fulfill the chapter objectives listed on this page.

CHAPITRE 10

Les sports

Objectifs

In this chapter you will learn to:

- ✔ *talk about team sports and other physical activities*
- ✔ *describe past actions and events*
- ✔ *ask people questions*
- ✔ *discuss sports in Canada and in French-speaking Africa*

Robert Delaunay *Les coureurs*

322

Correlations to Continuum *(see page* i *for code)*

Stage I
Obtain information. p. 335 (*i*), p. 336 (**24**, *p*), p. 348 (**3**, *m*); Understand some ideas and familiar details. p. 331 (**8**, *p*); Write lists. p. 349 (**5**, *m*); Use short sentences, learned words, phrases, and simple questions when speaking. p. 348 (**2**, *p*); Understand ideas and familiar details when listening. p. 331 (**9**, *p*); Understand texts enhanced by visual clues. pp. 342–343 (*p*); Understand and convey information about leisure activities. p. 341 (**A**, *p*); Understand most important information. p. 341 (**B**)

Stage II
Understand and express important ideas and some detail. p. 327 (**4**, *p*); Describe and compare. p. 334 (**18**, *p*), p. 349 (**6**, *m*); Use and understand learned expressions, sentences, and strings of sentences, and polite commands when speaking and listening. p. 339 (**28**, *p*); Create simple paragraphs. p. 349 (**6**, *p*); Understand oral and written discourse, with few errors in comprehension when reading and demonstrate culturally appropriate behavior for Stage II functions. p. 349 (**4**)

Stage 3
Express and understand opinions. p. 331 (**10**, *p*); Narrate and understand narration in the past. p. 333 (**12**, *i*), p. 334 (**18**, *p*); Use strings of related sentences when speaking. p. 331 (**9**, *i*), p. 348 (**1**, *p*)

Stage 4
Understand and convey information on the sciences. pp. 346–347 (*i*), pp. 346–347 (*p*)

CHAPITRE 10

Spotlight on Culture

Photograph This photo shows cyclists in Paris at stage 21 of the Tour de France 2000. You can see American Lance Armstrong leading the **peloton** through Paris.

Painting Robert Delaunay was born in Paris in 1885 and died in Montpellier in 1941. He was greatly influenced by Gauguin and the neo-impressionism of Seurat. In 1912, Apollinaire defined his work as **la première manifestation de l'art inobjectif en France.** Delaunay is considered the initiator of abstract art in France. His works are also known for his use of vivid colors.

National Standards

Communities

- Try to obtain video recordings of French sporting events, such as the Tour de France or a Quebec soccer match, and view them with your students. Then have students say as much as they can about them.
- If a French person is available, have students question him or her on the physical education system in French schools, the Tour de France, and so on.
- Attend a soccer match or a basketball game with your students. Comment on the action in French and encourage them to do the same.
- Have students do some research about sports that are popular in some other areas of the world, particularly in those areas where French is spoken. One example would be **la pelote basque** played in the Basque region of France.

Chapter Projects

Les sports Have students attend one of their school's athletic events. Then have them discuss it in French. Their discussion should include the name of the sport, who the players are, how many players are on the team, and how good the team is.

Un reportage Have students prepare a TV sports broadcast in French. The broadcast can be an audio, video, or "live" broadcast.

Une interview Have students interview some of the school athletes who are taking French. They can prepare a broadcast report on the interview. If the interviewee is in the class, the interview can be done "live."

Un article Have students prepare a short sports column in French for the school newspaper. They could make this a regular feature.

Vocabulaire
Mots 1

1 Preparation

Resource Manager

Vocabulary Transparencies 10.2–10.3
Audio Activities Booklet TE, pages 122–124
Audiocassette 6B/CD 6
Workbook, page 95
Quiz 1, page 49
ExamView Pro®

Bellringer Review

Use BRR Transparency 10.1 or write the following on the board.
Use these cues to write a conversation that might take place in a department store.

1. greet the salesperson
2. say what you are looking for
3. give the size, the color, and the style of an article of clothing
4. say how much you would like to spend
5. ask if there is a sale

2 Presentation

Step 1 Tell students that the names of many sports are cognates and that they should pay particular attention to the French pronunciation.

Step 2 Present the vocabulary first with books closed using Vocabulary Transparencies 10.2–10.3. Have students repeat after you or Audiocassette 6B/CD 6 as you point to the illustrations.

Step 3 Ask questions to elicit the vocabulary. Begin with *yes/no* and *either/or* questions and progress to question-word questions. For example: **C'est un terrain de football? C'est un arbitre ou un joueur? Qui siffle?** Encourage full-sentence responses.

Vocabulaire
Mots 1

Le foot(ball)

Le gardien arrête le ballon.
Il bloque le ballon.
Le ballon n'entre pas dans le but.

Une équipe de foot a onze joueurs.

Pour jouer au football, on a besoin d'un ballon.
Et c'est tout!

Reaching All Students

Total Physical Response You will need a lightweight ball, such as one made of foam, or something to serve as an imaginary soccer ball.

(Student 1), **viens ici, s'il te plaît.**
Montre-moi ta tête. Et ton pied.
Voilà un ballon. Prends le ballon.
Donne un coup de pied dans le ballon.
(Student 2), **va chercher le ballon.**
Passe le ballon à *(Student 1).*
(Student 3), **viens ici, s'il te plaît.**
Tu es l'arbitre. Prends le sifflet.
Siffle.
Merci tout le monde. C'est très bien.
Asseyez-vous, s'il vous plaît.

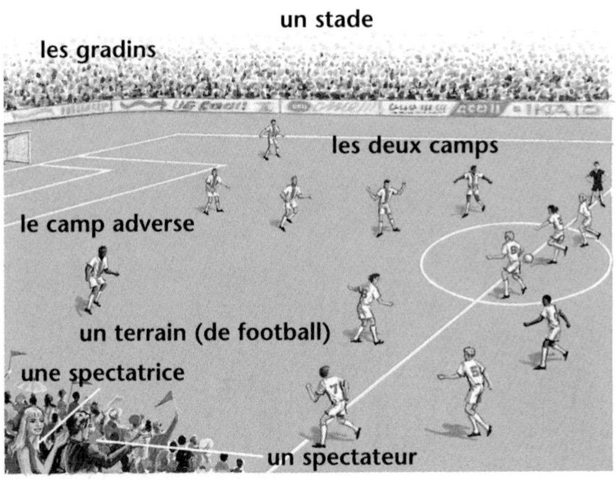

Le stade est comble.
Il y a beaucoup de monde.
Les gradins sont pleins.

Une joueuse passe le ballon à l'autre.

Hier Auxerre a joué contre Lyon.
Le match a opposé Lyon et Auxerre.
Ils ont joué au foot(ball).
Lafitte a donné un coup de pied dans le ballon.
Auxerre a gagné par 3 à 2.
Lyon a perdu.

Sissoko a envoyé le ballon dans le but.
Il a marqué un but.
Il a égalisé le score—2 à 2.

Vocabulaire

Mots 1

Teaching Tip: For the last two illustrations on page 325, make it clear that the Auxerre/Lyon match took place yesterday and the actions described are in the past. First demonstrate the meaning of **hier** by contrasting it with **aujourd'hui** and the current date or day. For example: **Aujourd'hui—mardi; hier—lundi. Aujourd'hui—le 29; hier—le 28.** Point a thumb back over one shoulder to indicate **hier** and the past in general. Use this gesture from now on to indicate or elicit past structures.

Note: The **passé composé** is presented in the **il/elle** form so you can immediately ask questions using it while presenting the new words. Students can respond to the questions without having to manipulate forms of the **passé composé**. They will learn all the forms in this chapter.

Step 4 As you go over the sentences on page 325, you may wish to ask questions such as: **Auxerre a joué contre qui? Contre quelle équipe? Quand ça? Le match a opposé quelles équipes? Qui a donné un coup de pied dans le ballon? Qui a envoyé le ballon dans le but? Il a marqué un but? Qu'est-ce qu'il a marqué? Qui a marqué le but?**

About the French Language

Explain to students that masculine nouns referring to people that end in **eur** become **euse** or **ice** in the feminine.

Reaching All Students

(Student 1), **viens ici. Tu es un spectateur/une spectatrice.**
Cherche une place dans les gradins.
Prends ta place. Regarde le match.
Quelqu'un va marquer un but. Lève-toi.
Regarde bien.
Ah, oui, il a marqué un but. Applaudis.
Merci, *(Student 1)*, **et maintenant, retourne à ta place, s'il te plaît.**

Learning from Photos

(page 324) This is a photo of the French team after winning the Euro 2000 game.

3 Practice

Commençons
Let's use our new words

Attention!

When students are doing the **Commençons** activities, accept any answer that makes sense. The purpose of these activities is to have students use the new vocabulary. They are not factual recall activities. Thus, it is not necessary for students to remember specific factual information from the vocabulary presentation when answering. If you wish, have students use the photos on this page as a stimulus, when possible.

Historiette Each time **Historiette** appears, it means that the answers to the activity form a short story. Encourage students to look at the title of the **Historiette,** since it can help them do the activity.

1 and 2 To focus on listening, have students keep their books closed as you ask the questions. Then have students open their books and retell the story in their own words.

Learning from Photos

(page 326 bottom) You may want to ask the following questions about the photo.

Il y a beaucoup de monde dans le stade?
Le stade est comble?
Les fans applaudissent leur équipe?
Ils sont contents? D'après vous, leur équipe est bonne?

Commençons
Let's use our new words

1 Historiette Un match de foot Répondez d'après les indications.

1. On a besoin de quoi pour jouer au foot? (un ballon)
2. Dans un match de foot, il y a combien d'équipes? (deux)
3. Chaque équipe a combien de joueurs? (onze)
4. Il y a combien de joueurs sur le terrain? (vingt-deux)
5. Dans un match, il y a combien de camps? (deux)
6. Le match est divisé en quoi? (en deux mi-temps)
7. Chaque mi-temps dure combien de minutes? (quarante-cinq minutes)
8. Qui garde le but? (le gardien de but)
9. Qu'est-ce que chaque équipe veut faire? (marquer des buts)
10. Qui bloque ou arrête le ballon? (le gardien de but)

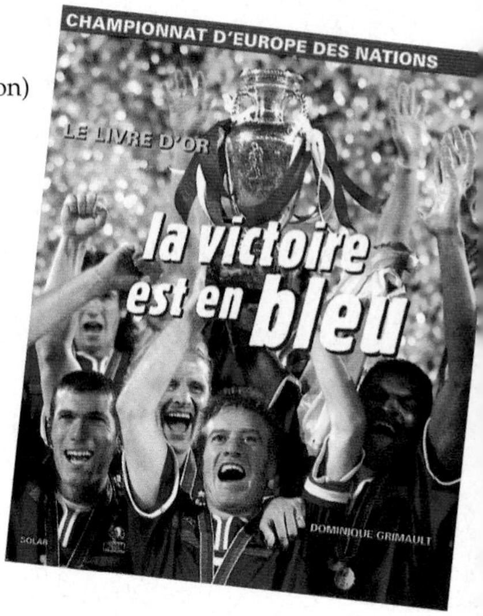

Des fanas de foot

2 Historiette Le stade est comble. Inventez une histoire.

1. Il y a beaucoup de spectateurs dans le stade aujourd'hui?
2. Les gradins sont pleins ou il y a beaucoup de places libres?
3. Le stade est comble?
4. Il y a beaucoup de monde dans le stade?
5. Le foot, c'est un sport d'équipe ou un sport individuel?

Answers to Commençons

1 *Answers will vary but may include:*
1. On a besoin d'un ballon pour jouer au foot.
2. Dans un match de foot, il y a deux équipes.
3. Chaque équipe a onze joueurs.
4. Il y a vingt-deux joueurs sur le terrain.
5. Dans un match, il y a deux camps.
6. Le match est divisé en deux mi-temps.
7. Chaque mi-temps dure quarante-cinq minutes.
8. Le gardien de but garde le but.
9. Chaque équipe veut marquer des buts.
10. Le gardien de but bloque ou arrête le ballon.

2 *Answers will vary. Students can answer in either the affirmative or the negative.*
1. Non, il n'y a pas beaucoup de spectateurs dans le stade aujourd'hui.
2. Il y a beaucoup de places libres.
3. Non, le stade n'est pas comble.
4. Non, il n'y a pas beaucoup de monde dans le stade.
5. Le foot, c'est un sport d'équipe.

Vocabulaire

3 **Auxerre contre Lyon** Répondez que oui.

1. Hier, Lyon a joué contre Auxerre?
2. Lafitte a donné un coup de tête dans le ballon?
3. Lafitte a passé le ballon à Sissoko?
4. Sissoko a marqué un but?
5. Sissoko a égalisé le score?
6. L'arbitre a sifflé?
7. Il a déclaré un penalty contre Lyon?
8. Auxerre a gagné le match?
9. Lyon a perdu le match?

4 **Un match de foot** Work with a classmate. Take turns describing the soccer game in the illustration.

ENCORE PLUS *For more practice using words from **Mots 1**, do Activity 30 on page H31 at the end of this book.*

Answers to Commençons

3

1. Oui, hier Lyon a joué contre Auxerre.
2. Oui, Lafitte a donné un coup de tête dans le ballon.
3. Oui, Lafitte a passé le ballon à Sissoko.
4. Oui, Sissoko a marqué un but.
5. Oui, Sissoko a égalisé le score.
6. Oui, l'arbitre a sifflé.
7. Oui, il a déclaré un penalty contre Lyon.
8. Oui, Auxerre a gagné le match.
9. Oui, Lyon a perdu le match.

4 *Answers will vary.*
Students will reincorporate all the vocabulary they learned in this **Mots 1** section to describe the illustration.

Vocabulaire

3 This activity allows students to practice using past participles without having to manipulate forms.

Reaching All Students

Linguistic/Spatial Learners Linguistic learners enjoy talking and or writing. It is these types of students who would enjoy giving a **résumé** of the activities such as 1 and 2. Spatial learners, on the other hand, prefer activities such as 4. They like pictures and visual presentations.

Writing Development

- Have students write answers to Activities 1 and 2 in paragraph form to illustrate how the answers to all the items tell a story.
- Have students write a short paragraph describing the illustration in Activity 4.

Cognate Recognition

Have students scan the **Mots 1** words again and then identify and pronounce each cognate.

Learning from Realia

(page 326 top) Have students read the headline on the magazine. They should understand the cognate **la victoire.** Ask them what they think the **bleu** refers to. (Refer students to the photo on page 324. Ask them what color jersey the players on the French team wear.) You may wish to tell them that the French team is often called **les Bleus.**

1 Preparation

Resource Manager

Vocabulary Transparencies 10.4–10.5
Audio Activities Booklet TE, pages 124–126
Audiocassette 6B/CD 6
Workbook, page 96
Quiz 2, page 50
ExamView Pro®

Bellringer Review

Use BRR Transparency 10.2 or write the following on the board.
Write eight words associated with a football (soccer) game.

2 Presentation

Step 1 Using Vocabulary Transparencies 10.4–10.5 and realia, have students repeat after you or Audiocassette 6B/CD 6. Stress the correct French pronunciation of words borrowed from English.

Step 2 Have students close their books. Make negative statements about the illustrations on Vocabulary Transparencies 10.4–10.5. Ask individuals to respond with an appropriate affirmative statement. For example: **Le joueur n'a pas dribblé le ballon. (Le joueur a lancé le ballon.) Le joueur n'a pas renvoyé le ballon. (Le joueur a servi.)**

Learning from Photos

After presenting the **Mots 2** vocabulary, have students say as much as they can about the painting and the photo on pages 322–323.

Vocabulaire Mots 2

D'autres sports d'équipe

Le basket(-ball)

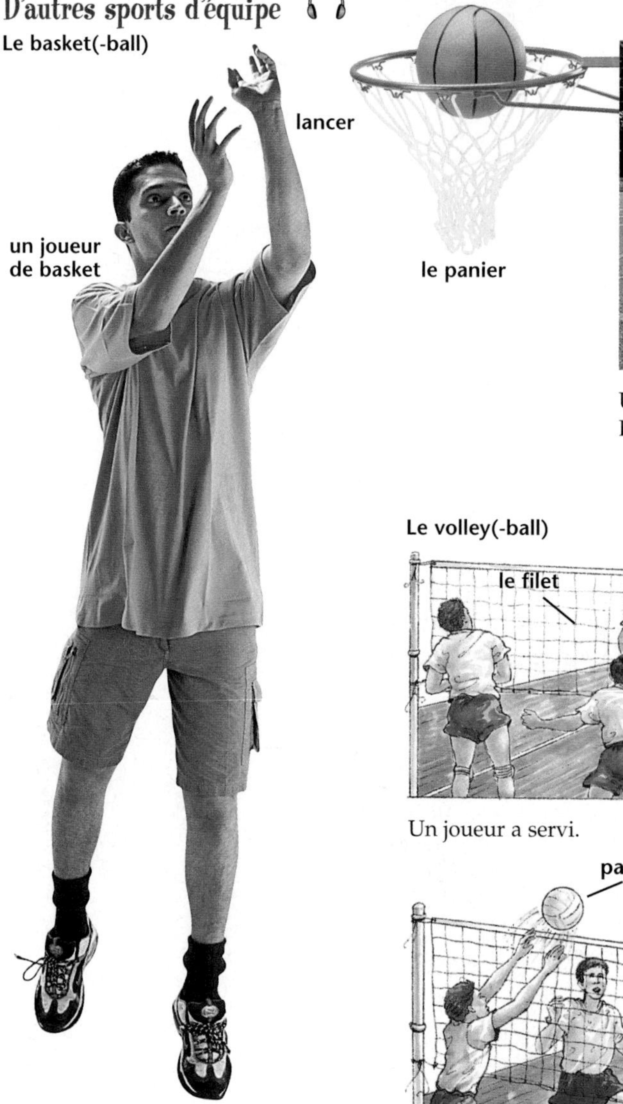

Une joueuse a dribblé le ballon.
Elle a dribblé le ballon jusqu'au demi-cercle.

Le joueur a lancé le ballon dans le panier.
Il a réussi un beau panier.

Le volley(-ball)

Un joueur a servi.

Un autre joueur a renvoyé le ballon.
Le ballon ne doit pas toucher le sol.

Reaching All Students

Total Physical Response If you wish, set up part of a mock basketball court on the floor with tape and use a toy basketball and hoop. Demonstrate the meaning of **lentement** and **vite**.

(Student 1), **viens ici, s'il te plaît.**
Tu vas jouer au basket-ball.
Dribble le ballon lentement.
Dribble le ballon vite.
Va au demi-cercle.
Lance le ballon dans le panier. Bravo! Tu as lancé le ballon dans le panier.
Merci, *(Student 1).* **Tu as très bien joué.**
Retourne à ta place, s'il te plaît.
(Student 2), **viens ici, s'il te plaît.**
Tu vas jouer au volley-ball.
Prends le ballon.
Voilà le filet.
Renvoie le ballon par-dessus le filet.
Merci, *(Student 2).* **Tu as très bien joué.**
Retourne à ta place, s'il te plaît.

Le cyclisme

une course cycliste

Le coureur roule vite.
Pendant la course, les coureurs boivent de l'eau.

L'athlétisme

un coureur **la coupe** **un gagnant**

une piste

Khalil (Numéro 27) a gagné la course.
Leblanc (N° 10) a perdu la course.

Khalil a reçu la coupe.
C'est la première fois qu'il reçoit la coupe.

Note

The following expressions are often used to express past events:

- **hier**
- **avant-hier**
- **la semaine dernière**
- **l'année dernière**

Reaching All Students

Additional Practice

- Have students work in teams of three. The first team member gives the name of a student on one of the school sports teams. The second student makes a statement about the team this person plays on. The third student says whether he or she likes or dislikes that particular sport and whether or not he or she attends the games.
- Each group chooses a leader, who asks the others what their favorite sports are and whether they prefer to play the sports, watch them on TV, or go to games. The leader takes notes and reports to the class. You can follow up with a class survey, grouping names of students on the board according to their preferences and discussing the results.

Step 3 Have students prepare questions to ask you about which sports you prefer, whether you participate in or watch them, what your favorite teams are, and so on. Hold a question-and-answer session using this material.

Learning from Photos

(page 329 middle) The woman leading the track race is French runner Patricia Djate-Taillard.

3 Practice

Commençons

Let's use our new words

5 and **6** After completing these activities as a whole-class activity, focus on the listening skill by having students do them again in pairs, with one partner reading the questions while the other listens and answers with his or her book closed.

6 **Expansion:** After completing this activity, have students use it as a model to make up six new questions about the game of soccer. Then, in pairs, they take turns asking the questions and answering.

7 **Expansion:** Have students make logical sentences with the other two words which were not the correct answer. For example: **2. Un spectateur regarde le match. Un joueur joue au volley-ball.**

Commençons

Let's use our new words

5 Historiette Un match de basket

Répondez.

1. Le basket-ball est un sport individuel ou collectif (d'équipe)?
2. Il y a cinq ou onze joueurs dans une équipe de basket?
3. Pendant un match de basket, les joueurs dribblent le ballon ou donnent un coup de pied dans le ballon?
4. Un joueur dribble le ballon jusqu'au demi-cercle ou jusqu'au panier?
5. Un joueur de basket lance le ballon dans le panier ou dans le filet?

Du sport au lycée

6 Historiette Le volley-ball Vrai ou faux?

1. Une équipe de volley-ball a six joueurs.
2. Un joueur sert.
3. Un joueur du camp adverse renvoie le ballon.
4. Quand il renvoie le ballon, le ballon peut toucher le filet.
5. On renvoie le ballon par-dessus le filet.
6. Le ballon doit toucher le sol du camp adverse.

7 Historiette Une course cycliste Choisissez.

1. Un vélo est ___.
   a. une bicyclette **b.** une voiture **c.** un stade
2. ___ roule à vélo.
   a. Un spectateur **b.** Un coureur cycliste **c.** Un joueur
3. Dans une course internationale, chaque équipe ___.
   a. reçoit une coupe **b.** représente son pays **c.** roule
4. Le gagnant de la course est ___.
   a. la coupe **b.** le champion **c.** le coureur
5. Dans une course cycliste, les coureurs roulent sur ___.
   a. des gradins **b.** un terrain **c.** une piste
6. Pendant la course les coureurs boivent ___.
   a. du vinaigre **b.** du café **c.** de l'eau

Answers to Commençons

5

1. Le basket-ball est un sport collectif.
2. Il y a cinq joueurs dans une équipe de basket.
3. Pendant un match de basket, les joueurs dribblent le ballon.
4. Un joueur dribble le ballon jusqu'au demi-cercle.
5. Un joueur de basket lance le ballon dans le panier.

6	7
1. V	1. a
2. V	2. b
3. V	3. b
4. V	4. b
5. V	5. c
6. V	6. c

8 **C'est quel sport?** Choisissez.

1. Le joueur a dribblé le ballon très vite.
2. Le joueur a donné un coup de tête dans le ballon.
3. La joueuse a réussi un beau panier.
4. La coureuse française a gagné.
5. Le gardien de but a arrêté le ballon.
6. La joueuse américaine a renvoyé le ballon par-dessus le filet.
7. Un joueur a servi.

Fabien Barthez, gardien de but de l'équipe de France

9 **Jeu** **C'est quel sport?** Work with a classmate. Give him or her some information about a sport. He or she has to guess the sport you're talking about. Take turns.

10 **Mon équipe favorite** Work with a classmate. Find out each other's favorite team. Explain why it is your favorite team. You may like to know that "baseball" is the same word in French: **le base-ball.**

Henry Rodriguez, les Expos de Montréal

FRENCH Online
For more information about team sports in the Francophone world, go to the Glencoe French Web site: french.glencoe.com

ENCORE PLUS *For more practice using words from* ***Mots 2****, do Activity 31 on page H32 at the end of this book.*

Vocabulaire

8 and **9** Use these activities as a base for a class competition. Have students write their sentences on slips of paper, collect them, put them in a bag and have one student from each team come forward to compete at a time. Reward the winning team.

10 You may wish to use this activity to do a classwide poll.

Learning from Photos

(page 331 top) The goalie shown here for the **équipe de France** is Fabien Barthez. He always insists on playing in short sleeves.

Assessment

Check comprehension by making statements about various sports and having students tell which sport you are talking about. For example: **Il a marqué un but. (C'est le foot.) Les spectateurs applaudissent quand il lance le ballon dans le panier. (C'est le basket-ball.)**

Reteaching

Have students write three sentences that can be mimed, describing the sporting activities from **Mots 1 and 2.** Then have them choose a partner who must correctly mime the activity in front of the class when it is read.

ENCORE PLUS This *infogap* activity will allow students to practice in pairs. The activity should be very manageable for them, since all vocabulary and structures are familiar to them.

Answers to Commençons

8
1. le basket-ball
2. le football
3. le basket-ball
4. l'athlétisme
5. le football
6. le volley-ball
7. le volley-ball

9 *Answers will vary but may include:*
On a besoin d'un ballon et c'est tout.
C'est le football!
On dribble le ballon jusqu'au demi-cercle.
C'est le basket-ball!

10 *Answers will vary.*
Students will describe their favorite team using the vocabulary presented in this chapter.

1 Preparation

Resource Manager

Audio Activities Booklet TE, pages 127–128
Audiocassette 6B/CD 6
Workbook, pages 97–101
Quizzes 3–5, pages 51–53
ExamView Pro®

Bellringer Review

Use BRR Transparency 10.3 or write the following on the board.
Answer.

1. **Tu joues à quel sport?**
2. **Tu joues dans l'équipe de ton école?**
3. **Tu aimes mieux les sports d'équipe ou les sports individuels?**

2 Presentation

Le passé composé des verbes réguliers

Step 1 Quickly review the forms of **avoir.**

Step 2 Show students how the past participle of regular verbs is formed. The more past participles students can repeat the better. Following are some of the regular verbs they have already learned in the present tense: **quitter, habiter, parler, passer, écouter, regarder, étudier, lever, poser, jouer, rigoler, déjeuner, travailler, acheter, payer, demander, coûter, aimer, détester, donner, inviter, trouver, commander, laisser, dîner, désirer, manger, essayer, porter, voyager, vérifier, décoller, attacher, ramasser, composter, changer, rater, contrôler, finir, choisir, remplir, atterrir, dormir, servir, attendre, vendre, répondre, perdre.**

Step 3 Guide students through Items 1–3 on page 332.

Describing past actions
Le passé composé des verbes réguliers

1. You use the **passé composé** to express an action that began and was completed in the past. To form the **passé composé,** you use the present tense of the verb **avoir** and the past participle. Study the forms of the past participle of regular verbs.

-er → é		-ir → i		-re → u	
parler	parlé	finir	fini	perdre	perdu
jouer	joué	choisir	choisi	vendre	vendu

2. Study the forms of the **passé composé.**

JOUER	CHOISIR	PERDRE
j' ai joué	j' ai choisi	j' ai perdu
tu as joué	tu as choisi	tu as perdu
il/elle/on a joué	il/elle/on a choisi	il/elle/on a perdu
nous avons joué	nous avons choisi	nous avons perdu
vous avez joué	vous avez choisi	vous avez perdu
ils/elles ont joué	ils/elles ont choisi	ils/elles ont perdu

Hier soir, j'ai téléphoné à un copain.
Après j'ai regardé un match de foot.
Mon copain aussi a regardé le match.
Malheureusement, notre équipe a perdu.

3. In the **passé composé, n'... pas** goes around the verb **avoir.**

Tu n'as pas regardé la télé?
Non, parce que je n'ai pas fini mes devoirs.

Savez-vous que... ?

When you talk about playing a sport, you use **jouer à.**

Ils ont joué au football. Mais moi, j'ai joué au base-ball.

Learning from Photos

(page 333) Have students say as much as they can about the photo on page 333 using the vocabulary from this chapter.

Continuons

Let's put our words together

11 **Participes passés** Donnez le participe passé des verbes suivants.

1. habiter
2. parler
3. écouter
4. travailler
5. remplir
6. réussir
7. servir
8. dormir
9. perdre
10. vendre
11. attendre
12. répondre

12 **Historiette** **Hier** Donnez des réponses personnelles.

1. Hier matin, tu as quitté la maison à quelle heure?
2. Tu as rigolé un peu avec les copains avant les cours?
3. Tu as parlé au prof de français?
4. Tu as passé un examen?
5. Tu as répondu à toutes les questions?
6. Tu as quitté l'école à quelle heure?
7. Tu as attendu le bus pour rentrer à la maison?

13 **Historiette** **La fête de Chloé** Complétez au passé composé.

Samedi dernier, Chloé __1__ (donner) une fête. Elle __2__ (téléphoner) à tous ses copains. Tous ses copains __3__ (répondre) au téléphone. Chloé __4__ (inviter) tous ses amis à la fête. Tous, ils __5__ (accepter) son invitation. Yves et moi, nous __6__ (préparer) des sandwichs, mais c'est Chloé qui __7__ (acheter) la nourriture et les boissons. À la fête, on __8__ (écouter) de la musique, on __9__ (danser). On __10__ bien __11__ (rigoler).

Paris-Saint-Germain contre Metz

14 **Historiette** **Un match de foot** Inventez des réponses.

1. Tu as regardé un match de foot à la télé hier soir?
2. Auxerre a joué contre Lyon?
3. L'année dernière, qui a gagné la coupe? Lyon?
4. Mais hier soir, Lyon a perdu?
5. L'arbitre a puni un joueur lyonnais?
6. Il a déclaré un penalty contre Lyon?
7. Les spectateurs ont applaudi?

3 Practice

Continuons

Let's put our words together

12, **13**, and **14** Have students retell orally the information in these activities.

Writing Development

Have students write the answers to Activities 12, 13, and 14 in paragraph form.

Reaching All Students

Additional Practice After completing Activities 11–12, you may wish to ask students additional personalized questions to further reinforce the **tu/je** questions and answers in the **passé composé: Julie, tu as téléphoné à des amis hier soir? Tu as parlé avec qui? Tu as écouté des cassettes? Tu as étudié? Qu'est-ce que tu as étudié hier soir? Tu as dîné à quelle heure? Qu'est-ce que tu as mangé? Tu as regardé la télé? Qu'est-ce que tu as regardé?**, etc.

Answers to Continuons

11

1. habité
2. parlé
3. écouté
4. travaillé
5. rempli
6. réussi
7. servi
8. dormi
9. perdu
10. vendu
11. attendu
12. répondu

12 *Answers will vary but may include:*

1. Hier matin, j'ai quitté la maison à sept heures et demie.
2. Oui, j'ai rigolé un peu avec mes copains avant les cours.
3. Non, je n'ai pas parlé au prof de français.
4. Oui, j'ai passé un examen.
5. Oui, j'ai répondu à toutes les questions.
6. J'ai quitté l'école à trois heures et quart.
7. Oui, j'ai attendu le bus pour rentrer à la maison.

13

1. a donné
2. a téléphoné
3. ont répondu
4. a invité
5. ont accepté
6. avons préparé
7. a acheté
8. a écouté
9. a dansé
10. a
11. rigolé

14 *Answers will vary but may include:*

1. Oui, j'ai regardé un match de foot à la télé hier soir.
2. Oui, Auxerre a joué contre Lyon.
3. Oui, l'année dernière Lyon a gagné la coupe.
4. Oui, hier soir Lyon a perdu.
5. Oui, l'arbitre a puni un joueur lyonnais.
6. Oui, il a déclaré un penalty contre Lyon.
7. Non, les spectateurs n'ont pas applaudi.

3 Practice *(continued)*

Continuons
Let's put our words together

15 After asking the questions and calling on individuals to respond, you may wish to have students work in pairs to do this activity. Have them do the activity first with books open, then with books closed.

16 Have students retell the **Historiette,** using **on** whenever appropriate.

17 After having students work in pairs, have them work in groups of four. Have them practice asking in the **vous** form and answering in the **nous** form. Then have them report back to the class to practice the **ils/elles** forms.

Note: The verbs are listed in Activity 18 so students do not go "off base" and try to use verbs whose participles they do not yet know or verbs that are conjugated with **être.**

Recycling

Note that Activity 15 brings back vocabulary related to air travel, and Activity 16 reviews train travel.

15 **Un voyage en avion** Répondez que non.

1. Tu as voyagé l'année dernière?
2. Tu as voyagé sur Air France?
3. Tu as choisi classe économique?
4. Tu as choisi une place côté couloir?
5. L'avion a décollé à l'heure?
6. Et il a atterri à l'heure?
7. Tu as voyagé avec un copain ou une copine?
8. Tu as attendu longtemps tes bagages?
9. La compagnie aérienne a perdu tes bagages?

16 **Historiette** **Un voyage en train** Mettez au passé composé.

J'attends le train. Ma copine Alice et moi, nous voyageons ensemble. Nous attendons le train dans la salle d'attente. J'achète un magazine au kiosque. Ma copine choisit un livre. Nous entendons l'annonce du départ de notre train. Nous trouvons la voiture numéro 11. Nous montons nos bagages dans le train. Nous trouvons nos places réservées occupées par deux personnes très désagréables! Que faire? Nous laissons nos places à ces personnes!

17 **Le voyage d'Alice** Relisez l'Activité 16 et posez des questions à Alice et sa copine sur leur voyage. Suivez le modèle.

Vous avez voyagé ensemble?

Stade de France, Paris

18 **La semaine dernière** Work with a classmate. Ask each other what you did last week. Answer each other's questions. Talk about the things you both did. You can also talk about some things your friends did. Here are some words you may wish to use: **regarder, parler, jouer, quitter, étudier, acheter, voyager, écouter, travailler, préparer, gagner, servir, dormir, attendre, perdre, répondre à.**

ENCORE PLUS *For more practice using regular verbs in the **passé composé**, do Activity 32 on page H33 at the end of this book.*

Answers to Continuons

15

1. Non, je n'ai pas voyagé l'année dernière.
2. Non, je n'ai pas voyagé sur Air France.
3. Non, je n'ai pas choisi classe économique.
4. Non, je n'ai pas choisi une place côté couloir.
5. Non, l'avion n'a pas décollé à l'heure.
6. Non, il n'a pas atterri à l'heure.
7. Non, je n'ai pas voyagé avec un copain ou une copine.
8. Non, je n'ai pas attendu longtemps mes bagages.
9. Non, la compagnie aérienne n'a pas perdu mes bagages.

16

J'ai attendu le train. Ma copine Alice et moi, nous avons voyagé ensemble. Nous avons attendu le train dans la salle d'attente. J'ai acheté un magazine au kiosque. Ma copine a choisi un livre. Nous avons entendu l'annonce du départ de notre train. Nous avons trouvé la voiture numéro 11. Nous avons monté nos bagages dans le train. Nous avons trouvé nos places réservées occupées par deux personnes très désagréables! Que faire? Nous avons laissé nos places à ces personnes!

17 and **18** *Answers will vary.*

Asking questions
Qui, qu'est-ce que, quoi

1. You use **qui** in questions when asking about a person.

   Qui va gagner? — **Paul.**
   Tu as invité qui? — **Nathalie.**

2. You use **qu'est-ce que (qu')** or **quoi** to ask "what." **Qu'est-ce que (qu')** goes at the beginning of a sentence and **quoi** at the end.

   Qu'est-ce que tu regardes? }
   Tu regardes quoi? } **Un match de foot.**

3. After a preposition, you use **qui** for people and **quoi** for things.

   Tu vas aller au match avec qui? — **Avec Loïc.**
   On joue au foot avec quoi? — **Avec un ballon.**
   Tu as besoin de quoi? — **D'un ballon.**

Continuons
Let's put our words together

Savez-vous que... ?
Qu'est-ce que tu as? can mean "What's the matter (with you)?"

19 **Qui ça?** Posez des questions avec **qui.**

1. *Marie* parle au téléphone.
2. Elle parle à *son copain Julien.*
3. Elle invite *Julien* à un match de football.
4. *Julien* veut aller au match.
5. *Ézédine* va jouer.
6. *Ézédine* est un très bon joueur.
7. Julien parle souvent d'*Ézédine.*

20 **Comment? Qu'est-ce que tu fais?** Posez des questions d'après le modèle.

J'écoute la radio.
Comment? Qu'est-ce que tu écoutes?

1. Je lis le journal.
2. Je regarde la télé.
3. Je fais des exercices.
4. J'écris une carte postale.
5. Nous voulons le journal.
6. Nous mettons la table.
7. Nous préparons le petit déjeuner.

Answers to Continuons

19

1. Qui parle au téléphone?
2. Elle parle à qui?
3. Elle invite qui à un match de football?
4. Qui veut aller au match?
5. Qui va jouer?
6. Qui est un très bon joueur?
7. Julien parle souvent de qui?

20

1. Comment? Qu'est-ce que tu lis?
2. Comment? Qu'est-ce que tu regardes?
3. Comment? Qu'est-ce que tu fais?
4. Comment? Qu'est-ce que tu écris?
5. Comment? Qu'est-ce que vous voulez?
6. Comment? Qu'est-ce que vous mettez?
7. Comment? Qu'est-ce que vous préparez?

Structure

1 Preparation

Bellringer Review

Use BRR Transparency 10.4 or write the following on the board.
Write questions using **où? quand? comment? combien?**

2 Presentation

Qui, qu'est-ce que, quoi

Step 1 Students have been hearing and using **qui** and **qu'est-ce que** for some time. This explanation is here for additional reinforcement and to assure that students understand the difference between the two. This is the first exposure to **quoi.**

Step 2 To show that **qui** is for a person and **quoi** is for a thing, draw a stick figure on the board and ask: **Qui?** Then draw a box and ask: **Quoi?**

Teaching Tip: Explain the term "object of a preposition" and provide examples in both French and English.

About the French Language

- **Tu regardes quoi?** is more colloquial than **Qu'est-ce que tu regardes?**
- **Qu'est-ce que** is also used in an exclamation. You will hear either **Qu'est-ce qu'elle est belle!** (a bit colloquial) or **Qu'elle est belle!** (more formal).

3 Practice

Continuons
Let's put our words together

19 This activity should be done with books open.

3 Practice *(continued)*

Continuons
Let's put our words together

21, **22**, and **23** Have students work in pairs. Have them practice first with books open, then have them ask each other questions with books closed. They can ask the questions in a random order.

Learning from Photos

(page 336) Ask students the following questions about the photo.
Qui dribble le ballon?
Qu'est-ce que le garçon dribble?
Il dribble quoi?
Il joue à quoi?
Il joue au basket avec quoi?
Qu'est-ce qu'il porte?

Reaching All Students

Additional Practice The more students hear and use these interrogative forms, the easier it will be for them to deal with them as they speak on their own. You may want to ask the following questions to reinforce even more use of these words.

De tous tes amis:
Qui travaille après les cours?
Qui joue au foot?
Qui joue au tennis?
Qui fait de l'espagnol?

Dans ta famille:
Qui prépare le dîner?
Qui aime les sports?

Après les cours:
Qu'est-ce que tu regardes?
Qu'est-ce que tu écoutes?
Qu'est-ce que tu aimes faire?
Tu joues au foot avec quoi?
Tu paies avec quoi?

21 Mini-conversations Posez des questions et répondez d'après le modèle.

marquer un but
—Qu'est-ce que les joueurs ont marqué?
—Ils ont marqué un but.

1. lancer le ballon
2. dribbler le ballon
3. envoyer le ballon
4. perdre le match
5. gagner la coupe
6. égaliser le score

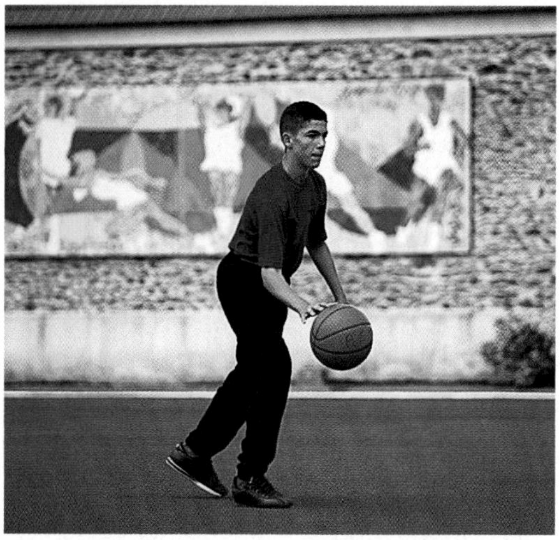

Le garçon dribble le ballon.

22 On a besoin de quoi? Conversez d'après le modèle.

—J'ai besoin d'un verre pour boire de l'eau.
—Qu'est-ce que tu dis? Tu as besoin de quoi?

1. J'ai besoin d'une télé pour regarder des vidéos.
2. J'ai besoin d'un ballon pour jouer au basket.
3. J'ai besoin d'un billet pour prendre le train.
4. J'ai besoin d'un stylo-bille pour écrire des cartes postales.
5. J'ai besoin d'un oignon pour faire la salade.

23 Je n'ai pas bien entendu. Posez des questions.

1. Il aime bien *Marie.*
2. Il parle souvent de *Marie.*
3. Il parle à *Marie* maintenant.
4. Il invite Marie à *une fête.*
5. Il parle à Marie de *la fête.*

24 Jeu Beaucoup de questions Work with a classmate. Play a guessing game. Ask as many questions as you can. See who can answer the most questions.

Answers to Continuons

21

1. Qu'est-ce que les joueurs ont lancé? Ils ont lancé le ballon.
2. Qu'est-ce que les joueurs ont dribblé? Ils ont dribblé le ballon.
3. Qu'est-ce que les joueurs ont envoyé? Ils ont envoyé le ballon.
4. Qu'est-ce que les joueurs ont perdu? Ils ont perdu le match.
5. Qu'est-ce que les joueurs ont gagné? Ils ont gagné la coupe.
6. Qu'est-ce que les joueurs ont égalisé? Ils ont égalisé le score.

22 *All answers will be:*

Qu'est-ce que tu dis? Tu as besoin de quoi?

23

1. Il aime bien qui?
2. Il parle souvent de qui?
3. Il parle à qui maintenant?
4. Il invite Marie à quoi?
5. Il parle à Marie de quoi?

24 *Answers will vary.*

Describing more activities
Les verbes **boire, devoir et recevoir** au présent

Study the forms of the irregular verbs **boire** *(to drink)*, **devoir** *(to owe)*, and **recevoir** *(to receive)*.

BOIRE		DEVOIR		RECEVOIR	
je	bois	je	dois	je	reçois
tu	bois	tu	dois	tu	reçois
il/elle/on	boit	il/elle/on	doit	il/elle/on	reçoit
nous	buvons	nous	devons	nous	recevons
vous	buvez	vous	devez	vous	recevez
ils/elles	boivent	ils/elles	doivent	ils/elles	reçoivent

Vous buvez de l'eau ou de la limonade?
Je dois beaucoup d'argent à mes parents.
Cet enfant reçoit toujours trop de cadeaux.

Savez-vous que... ?

When **devoir** is followed by another verb, it means "must" or "to have to."
Elle doit étudier parce qu'elle doit passer un examen demain.

Continuons
Let's put our words together

25 Historiette Un match de volley-ball Répondez.

1. Pendant un match de volley-ball, les joueurs reçoivent le ballon?
2. Ils doivent renvoyer le ballon?
3. Le ballon doit toucher le sol?
4. Il doit passer par-dessus le filet?
5. Après le match, les joueurs boivent de l'eau?

Elles jouent au volley-ball.

Structure

1 Preparation

Bellringer Review

Use BRR Transparency 10.5 or write the following on the board.
You are going to interview a French exchange student. Prepare a list of at least five questions to ask him or her.

2 Presentation

Les verbes **boire, devoir** et **recevoir** au présent

Step 1 Give students the **ils/elles** forms of **boire, devoir,** and **recevoir: ils boivent, ils doivent, ils reçoivent.** Have them drop the final consonant sound to get the sound for all the singular forms.

Step 2 Now go over the singular forms and their spellings. Have students repeat the forms after you.

Step 3 Call on a student to read the example sentences on page 337.

3 Practice

Continuons
Let's put our words together

25 Do this activity with books closed, calling on individuals to respond.

Answers to Continuons

25

1. Oui, les joueurs reçoivent le ballon.
2. Oui, ils doivent renvoyer le ballon.
3. Oui (Non), le ballon (ne) doit (pas) toucher le sol.
4. Oui, il doit passer par-dessus le filet.
5. Oui, après le match, les joueurs boivent de l'eau.

Learning from Photos

(page 337) Ask students the following questions about the photo.
Elles jouent à quoi?
Qui joue au volley-ball?
Qu'est-ce qu'elles renvoient?
La joueuse renvoie le ballon par-dessus quoi?

3 Practice *(continued)*

Continuons
Let's put our words together

Reteaching

Have students list the things they have to do each day, using the verb **devoir.** Have them question each other about their lists and do a class summary.

26 This activity recycles vocabulary related to beverages and birthdays.

Learning from Realia

(page 338) Have students scan the article. Ask them to locate all forms of the verb **boire.** Ask them to determine what the main idea of the article is. Look for the times of the day when drinking water is recommended. Emphasize that they do not need to know every word of a reading selection to understand the main idea.

26 Moi Donnez des réponses personnelles.

1. Tu dois boire beaucoup d'eau?
2. Tu bois de l'eau?
3. Qu'est-ce que tu bois quand tu as soif?
4. Tu dois de l'argent à tes amis?
5. Tu dois de l'argent à tes parents?
6. Tu reçois de l'argent pour ton anniversaire?
7. Tu reçois des cadeaux?

À CONSOMMER SANS MODÉRATION

C'est au cours des repas que nous consommons près de 70% de ce que nous buvons. Mais où placer les autres pauses boisson? L'idéal est de commencer par boire un verre d'eau avant le petit déjeuner pour bien drainer notre organisme. Un autre avant de passer à table remet à neuf le palais et permet de mieux jouir du goût des aliments. Enfin, un petit dernier avant de se coucher évite la trop grande concentration des urines. C'est tout? Mais non! Un verre toutes les deux heures, même sans avoir spécialement soif, cela fait du bien.

27 Pardon? Suivez le modèle.

Je bois beaucoup d'eau.
Pardon? Je n'ai pas bien entendu. Qu'est-ce que vous buvez?

1. Je bois beaucoup d'eau minérale.
2. Je dois boire beaucoup d'eau.
3. Je reçois le ballon.
4. Je dois renvoyer le ballon.

Answers to Continuons

26 *Answers will vary but may include:*

1. Oui, je dois boire beaucoup d'eau.
2. Oui, je bois de l'eau.
3. Quand j'ai soif je bois de l'eau.
4. Non, je ne dois pas d'argent à mes amis.
5. Oui, je dois de l'argent à mes parents.
6. Oui, je reçois de l'argent pour mon anniversaire.
7. Non, je ne reçois pas de cadeaux.

27

1. Pardon? Je n'ai pas bien entendu. Qu'est-ce que vous buvez?
2. Pardon? Je n'ai pas bien entendu. Qu'est-ce que vous devez boire?
3. Pardon? Je n'ai pas bien entendu. Qu'est-ce que vous recevez?
4. Pardon? Je n'ai pas bien entendu. Qu'est-ce que vous devez renvoyer?

28 **Qu'est-ce que je dois faire?** Work with a classmate. Discuss some things you should or must do. Tell if you can do them or not. If you can't, try to explain why.

Le marathon de Paris

*For more practice using **boire**, **devoir**, and **recevoir** in the present, do Activity 33 on page H34 at the end of this book.*

Vous êtes sur le bon chemin. Allez-y!

trois cent trente-neuf ❖ **339**

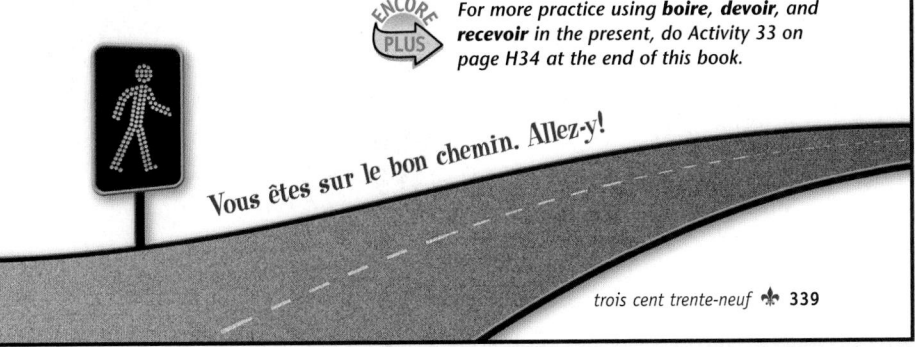

Learning from Photos

(page 339) This photo shows the runners in the Paris marathon on the Champs-Élysées in Paris.

ENCORE PLUS This *infogap* activity will allow students to practice in pairs. The activity should be very manageable for them, since all vocabulary and structures are familiar to them.

Allez-y!
At this point in the chapter, students have learned all the vocabulary and structure necessary to complete the chapter. The conversation and cultural readings that follow recycle all the material learned up to this point.

ANSWERS TO **Continuons**

28 *Answers will vary but may include:*
—Je dois acheter un cadeau pour mon frère, mais je ne peux pas parce que je n'ai pas d'argent!

1 Preparation

Resource Manager

Audio Activities Booklet TE, page 129
Audiocassette 6B/CD 6
CD-ROM

Bellringer Review

Use BRR Transparency 10.6 or write the following on the board.
Make a list of three things you have to do. Then tell what you need. For example: **Je dois faire mes devoirs. J'ai besoin de mon livre.**

2 Presentation

Step 1 Tell students they are going to hear a conversation between Jean and Rémi, who are discussing a soccer match.

Step 2 Have them watch the conversation video or listen as you read the conversation or play Audiocassette 6B/CD 6.

Step 3 Have students work in pairs to practice the conversation. Then have several pairs present it to the class.

Step 4 You may have a more able student retell the conversation in narrative form in his or her own words.

Glencoe Technology

CD-ROM
On the CD-ROM, students can watch a dramatization of this conversation. They can then play the role of either one of the characters and record themselves in the conversation.

Conversation

On a gagné!

Jean: Tu as regardé la télé hier soir?
Rémi: Ben, bien sûr. J'ai regardé France–Brésil, comme tout le monde!
Jean: On a gagné, mais tout juste, hein! Un–zéro.
Rémi: Oui, heureusement que Lafitte a marqué à la dernière minute.
Jean: Les Brésiliens ne doivent pas être contents!
Rémi: Ça, c'est sûr! Marcos a bien arrêté tous les ballons mais…
Jean: Il n'a pas bloqué le dernier!
Rémi: Remarque, le match d'avant, les Brésiliens ont réussi à égaliser à deux secondes de la fin!

Après la conversation

Répondez.

1. À qui parle Rémi?
2. Qu'est-ce qu'ils ont regardé hier?
3. Qui a gagné le match?
4. Qui a marqué le but pour la France?
5. Qui est Marcos?
6. Qu'est-ce qu'il n'a pas bloqué?
7. Dans le match précédent qui a égalisé le score?

Answers to Après la conversation

1. Rémi parle à Jean.
2. Ils ont regardé un match de football.
3. La France a gagné le match.
4. Lafitte a marqué le but pour la France.
5. Marcos est un joueur brésilien.
6. Il n'a pas bloqué le dernier ballon.
7. Les Brésiliens ont égalisé le score.

Learning from Photos

(page 340 top) The player on the right is Youri Djorkaeff, playing for France against Brazil for the World Cup. France won 3–0. This match was played in the Stade de France.

Parlons un peu plus

Let's talk some more

A **Je ne suis pas très fana de...** Work with a classmate. Tell him or her what sport you don't like to play. Tell what sport or sports you like. Then ask your classmate questions to find out what sports he or she does or doesn't like.

B **Un match de foot** You are at a soccer game with a friend (your classmate). He or she has never been to a soccer game before and doesn't understand the game. Your friend has a lot of questions. Answer his or her questions and explain the game. You may want to use some of the following words: **jouer, recevoir, donner un coup de pied, donner un coup de tête, marquer, perdre, gagner, devoir, passer, arrêter, bloquer.**

Prononciation

Liaison et élision

- You know that liaison or elision occurs when certain words are followed by a vowel. Some liaisons are obligatory, some are optional.
- Liaison is obligatory with plural subject pronouns, plural articles, plural possessive and demonstrative adjectives, and plural adjectives preceding the noun. Repeat the following.

ils$_{z}$ont	**les$_{z}$équipes**	**des$_{z}$amateurs**
mes$_{z}$amis	**ces$_{z}$arbitres**	**de bonnes$_{z}$équipes**

- Elision is always obligatory. It occurs with **le** and **la,** with **je,** the negative **ne,** and **que.** Repeat the following.

l'arbitre	**Je n'aime pas ça.**	**Qu'est-ce qu'il fait?**
l'équipe	**j'attends**	

- Now repeat the following pairs of sentences.

Vous$_{z}$avez perdu. / Vous n'avez pas perdu.
J'ai fini. / Je n'ai pas fini.

des$_{z}$arbitres

Answers to Parlons un peu plus

A *Answers will vary.*
Students will ask questions using all the sports they learned in this chapter.

B *Answers will vary.*
Students will use the expressions given to make up questions about a football (soccer) game in the present tense.

3 Practice

Parlons un peu plus

Let's talk some more

A and **B** Have students work in pairs. You may wish to choose a pair of students to do these activities for the class.

B **Expansion:** You may wish to ask students to videotape a school soccer match or one from the television to use as an audiovisual aid for their explanation.

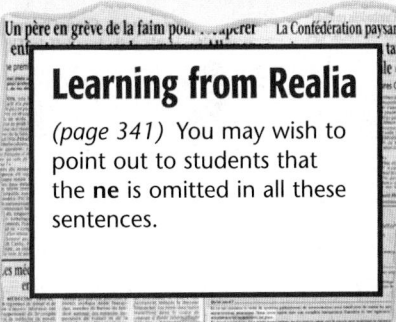

Learning from Realia

(page 341) You may wish to point out to students that the **ne** is omitted in all these sentences.

Prononciation

Step 1 Model the key word **des$_{z}$arbitres** and have students repeat in unison.

Step 2 Now lead students through the information on page 341 and model the other words, phrases, and sentences.

Step 3 You may wish to give the students the following **dictée: Mes amis ont joué. Ils ont gagné. L'arbitre a sifflé. L'équipe a marqué un but.**

Step 4 For additional pronunciation practice you may wish to use Audiocassette 6B/CD 6 and the Pronunciation Transparency P 10.

Resource Manager

Audio Activities Booklet TE, pages 130–131
Audiocassette 6B/CD 6

Bellringer Review

Use BRR Transparency 10.7 or write the following on the board.
Make a list of all the words associated with the following sports.
le basket-ball **le football**
le cyclisme

National Standards

Cultures

The reading about hockey and basketball on pages 342–343 and the related activities on page 343 give students an understanding of the importance of these sports in different parts of the French-speaking world.

Presentation

Pre-reading

Step 1 You may want to have students look at the photos on pages 342–343 now.

Step 2 Read and discuss the Reading Strategy on page 342. Have students brainstorm what they already know about hockey in Canada and basketball in Africa (or in other countries).

Step 3 Have students scan the reading quickly and silently.

Note: Have students look at the callout words in the photo on the right.

Lectures culturelles

Reading Strategy

Using background knowledge

When assigned a reading, look at the titles and the visuals to determine what the reading is about. Spend a few minutes thinking about what you already know about the topic. If you do this, the reading will be easier to understand and you will be able to figure out unfamiliar words.

Le hockey et le basket-ball

Au Québec

Le hockey est un sport très apprécié au Québec. Le hockey ressemble un peu au football, sauf[1] qu'on joue sur de la glace. Il y a deux équipes de cinq joueurs et deux gardiens de but. Un match de hockey est divisé en trois périodes de vingt minutes. Chaque joueur pousse le palet avec une crosse et essaie de mettre le palet dans le but de l'équipe adverse. Comme au football, on fait des passes à ses coéquipiers[2] pour essayer de marquer des buts.

[1] sauf *except*
[2] coéquipiers *teammates*

Turner Stevenson, les Canadiens de Montréal

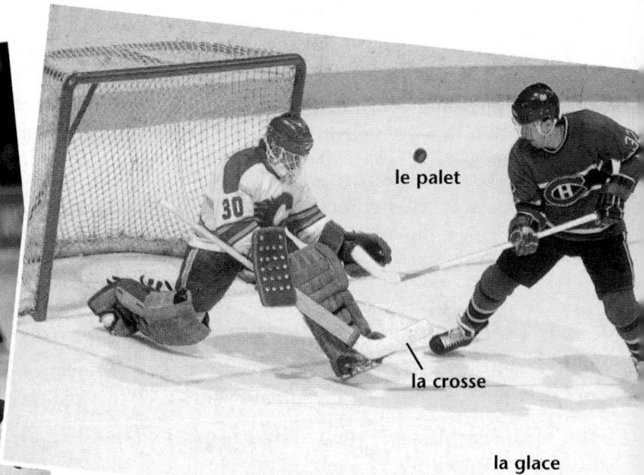

Les Canadiens de Montréal contre les Calgary Flames.

Learning from Photos

(page 342 right) The game shown in this photo was the NHL final between **les Canadiens de Montréal** and the Calgary Flames. In the photo, Claude Lemieux of Montreal is shooting. The Calgary goalie is Mike Vernon.

About the French Language

In Canada, **le palet** is called **la rondelle.**

En Afrique

Dans les pays d'Afrique Occidentale, le sport numéro un, c'est le football, comme en France. Mais le deuxième sport, c'est le basket-ball. Une équipe de basket-ball est composée de cinq joueurs. Chaque joueur veut prendre possession du ballon. Il essaie de lancer le ballon dans le panier de l'équipe adverse. On joue au basket-ball avec les mains uniquement. On ne peut pas marcher[3] avec le ballon dans les mains. Il faut dribbler le ballon.

Et toi, quel est ton sport favori? Tu es fana de foot, de basket ou de hockey? Tu aimes mieux les sports d'équipe ou les sports individuels? Tu préfères participer ou être spectateur (spectatrice)?

[3] marcher *walk*

Un match de basket: Sénégal contre Canada

Après la lecture

A Le hockey Répondez.

1. Quel est un sport très apprécié au Québec?
2. On joue au hockey sur quoi?
3. On joue au hockey avec quoi?
4. Il y a combien de joueurs dans une équipe de hockey?
5. Qu'est-ce qu'un joueur de hockey essaie de faire?
6. Qu'est-ce qu'il fait à ses coéquipiers?

B Le basket-ball Vrai ou faux?

1. Le basket-ball est très apprécié dans les pays d'Afrique Occidentale.
2. C'est le sport le plus populaire.
3. Une équipe de basket-ball a onze joueurs.
4. Un joueur de basket-ball essaie de lancer le ballon dans le panier de l'équipe adverse.
5. On joue au basket avec les mains et les pieds.

Un joueur de basket du Cameroun

Reading

Step 1 Lead students through the **Lecture** on pages 342–343 by having individuals read two or three sentences at a time. After each student reads, ask others follow-up questions.

Step 2 Ask five or six questions that review the main points. The answers will give a coherent oral review of the **Lecture.**

Step 3 Have a more able student summarize the **Lecture.** Call on slower students to answer questions about the summary. Then have a slower student orally summarize the reading based on the more able student's review.

Step 4 Have students in more able classes write their own summary of the **Lecture** in six or seven minutes.

Post-reading

Step 1 Have students work in groups to write brief news announcements for hockey and basketball and present them to the class.

Step 2 Have students do the **Après la lecture** activities on page 343 orally after reading the selection in class. Then assign these activities to be written at home. Go over them again the following day.

Answers to Après la lecture

A

1. Le hockey est un sport très apprécié au Québec.
2. On joue au hockey sur de la glace.
3. On joue au hockey avec une crosse et un palet.
4. Il y a cinq joueurs (et un gardien de but) dans une équipe de hockey.
5. Un joueur de hockey essaie de mettre le palet dans le but de l'équipe adverse.
6. Il fait des passes à ses coéquipiers.

B

1. V
2. F
3. F
4. V
5. F

Après la lecture

A Allow students to refer to the story to look up the answers or you may use this activity as a testing device for factual recall.

B **Expansion:** After doing Activity B, you may wish to have the students correct each false statement made in the activity.

National Standards

Cultures
This selection familiarizes students with the popularity of cycling in France.

Attention!

This reading is optional. You may skip it completely, have the entire class read it, have only several students read it and report to the class, or assign it for extra credit.

Presentation

Step 1 Ask students what they know about the Tour de France. Ask them if they know Lance Armstrong, shown in the photo on page 345. Have students study the map and photos on pages 344–345.

Step 2 Have students read the **Lecture** quickly.

Step 3 Ask students what new information they learned about the Tour de France.

Lecture supplémentaire

Le Tour de France

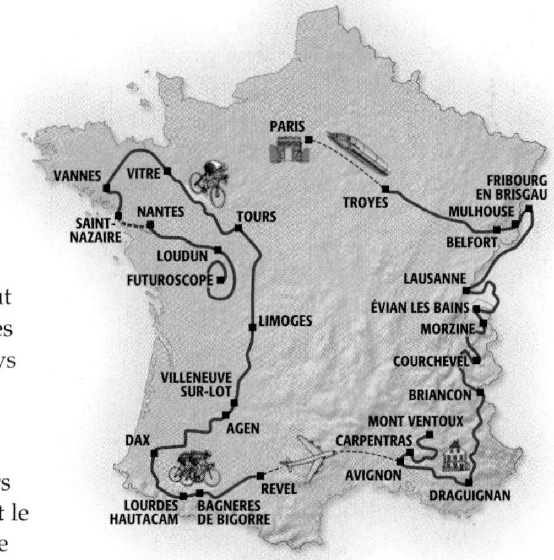

Un sport très apprécié

Un des sports les plus appréciés en France, c'est le cyclisme. Et l'événement sportif le plus populaire, c'est le Tour de France. Le Tour de France a lieu[1] tous les ans au mois de juillet. C'est une course cycliste sur un long circuit de routes françaises, tout autour du pays et quelquefois dans d'autres pays. Des coureurs cyclistes de tous les pays du monde participent au Tour de France.

Qu'est-ce que le Tour de France?

Le Tour de France est divisé en plusieurs étapes[2]. On va d'une ville à l'autre. On part le matin et on arrive le soir. Le Tour de France dure trois semaines. On donne au gagnant une coupe et le droit[3] de porter le maillot[4] jaune. Il reçoit aussi une somme d'argent.

On a organisé le premier Tour de France en 1903. C'est Maurice Garin qui a gagné le premier Tour de France. Il a fait 2 397 kilomètres en six étapes. Depuis 1903, 21 Français ont gagné le Tour de France.

Tour de France, Champs-Élysées, Paris

Lance Armstrong a gagné!

En 1999, il y a un miracle. Un Américain, Lance Armstrong, gagne le Tour de France. Le miracle, ce n'est pas qu'un Américain gagne le Tour de France. Non, un autre Américain, Greg LeMond, a gagné le Tour de France trois fois. Pourquoi un miracle? Parce que trois ans avant, à l'âge de 25 ans, Lance Armstrong a

[1] a lieu *takes place*
[2] étapes *laps*
[3] droit *right*
[4] maillot *jersey*

le cancer. Après deux opérations et quatre traitements de chimiothérapie et beaucoup de courage et de volonté[5] de sa part, le jeune Armstrong est guéri[6] et il recommence sa carrière de coureur cycliste.

Depuis cent ans, les Français appellent le vélo, «la petite reine»[7]. Ils disent que c'est la petite reine qui choisit toujours le nouveau roi du Tour de France. En 1999 et encore en 2000, elle a choisi son roi—Lance Armstrong. Et pour lui, comme pour tout le monde, c'est un vrai miracle!

[5] volonté *willpower*
[6] guéri *cured*
[7] reine *queen*

Tour de France

Lance Armstrong

La Tunisi

Le Maroc

Le Mali

Après la lecture

A Une course cycliste Vrai ou faux?

1. Le cyclisme n'est pas très apprécié en France.
2. Le Tour de France est une course cycliste.
3. Le Tour de France a lieu au mois de décembre.
4. Tous les cyclistes qui participent au Tour de France sont français.
5. Le Tour de France est divisé en deux mi-temps.
6. Pendant le Tour de France, les cyclistes roulent la nuit—de minuit à six heures.
7. Le gagnant du Tour de France reçoit une coupe et une somme d'argent.

B Un miracle Répondez.

1. Qui a gagné le Tour de France trois fois?
2. Il est de quelle nationalité?
3. Quel est le deuxième Américain qui a gagné le Tour de France?
4. Il a quel âge quand il apprend qu'il a le cancer?
5. Armstrong a recommencé à faire du vélo après combien d'opérations?
6. Quelles sont les qualités de Lance Armstrong?
7. D'après les Français, qui est la petite reine qui choisit le gagnant du Tour de France?
8. C'est une personne?
9. Elle a choisi qui en 1999 et encore en 2000?

Après la lecture

A Have students correct any false statements.

B Allow students to refer to the story to look up the answers, or you may use this activity as a testing device for factual recall.

Reaching All Students

Additional Practice Have students research the next Tour de France. Have them plot the course on a map of France. Have them research the favored teams and cyclists.

Answers to Après la lecture

A

1. F
2. V
3. F
4. F
5. F
6. F
7. V

B

1. Greg LeMond a gagné le Tour de France trois fois.
2. Il est américain.
3. Lance Armstrong est le deuxième Américain qui a gagné le Tour de France.
4. Il a vingt-cinq ans quand il apprend qu'il a le cancer.
5. Il a recommencé à faire du vélo après deux opérations.
6. Il a beaucoup de courage et de volonté.
7. La petite reine est le vélo.
8. Non, ce n'est pas une personne.
9. Elle a choisi Lance Armstrong en 1999 et encore en 2000.

National Standards

Connections
This reading on anatomy establishes a connection with another discipline. It enables students to draw from previous knowledge and to talk about a scientific topic in French.

Attention!

The readings in the **Connexions** section are optional. They focus on some of the major disciplines taught in schools and universities. The vocabulary is useful for discussing such topics as history, literature, art, economics, business, science, etc. You may choose any of the following ways to do the readings in the **Connexions** sections.

Independent reading Have students read the selections and do the post-reading activities as homework, which you collect. This option is least intrusive on class time and requires a minimum of teacher involvement.

Homework with in-class follow-up Assign the readings and post-reading activities as homework. Review and discuss the material in class the next day.

Intensive in-class activity This option includes a pre-reading vocabulary presentation, in-class reading and discussion, assignment of the activities for homework, and a discussion of the assignment in class the following day.

CONNEXIONS

Les sciences naturelles

L'anatomie

Staying in good physical condition is important for all athletes. To do so, they have to know how to care for their bodies. They also have to know something about their bone structure to avoid injuries. Athletes should have some basic knowledge of anatomy. Anatomy is the branch of science that studies the structures of humans and animals.

Before reading this selection on anatomy, study the diagrams of the human body.

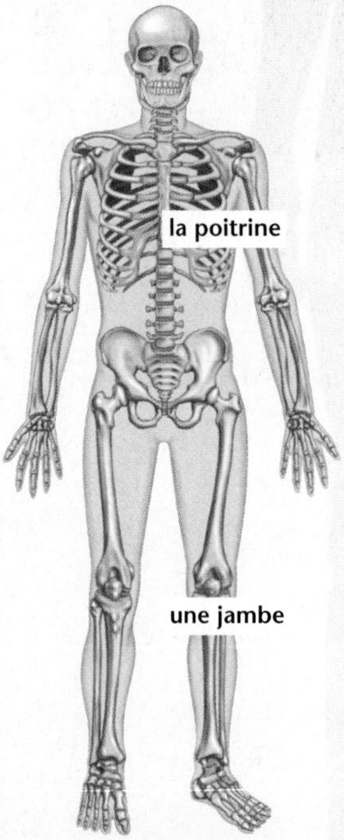

le squelette

Le corps humain

Le squelette

Le squelette humain a en tout 206 os. Il y a 32 os dans chaque bras et 31 os dans chaque jambe. Il y a plus de 600 muscles dans le corps humain. Certains muscles sont attachés à un os. Ils peuvent être attachés directement à l'os ou par l'intermédiaire d'un tendon.

En plus des muscles squelettiques, il y a de nombreux muscles internes. Le cœur, par exemple, est un muscle.

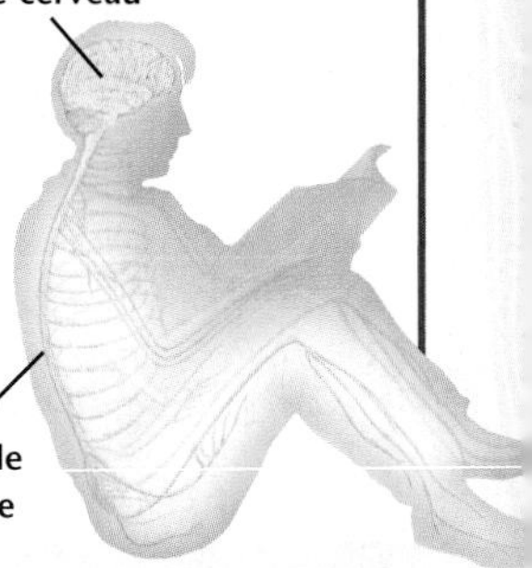

Le cerveau et le système nerveux

Le cerveau est bien protégé par la boîte cranienne[1]. Le cerveau est

[1] boîte crânienne *skull*

Learning from Photos

(page 346 middle) This photo shows Christine Aaron of France taking off after receiving the baton from Muriel Hurtis during the Women's Olympic relay qualifying round in Sydney, Australia, during the 2000 Olympics.
(page 346) Have students say everything they can about the two photos on page 346.

composé de deux hémisphères. Le tronc cérébral relie[2] le cerveau à la moelle épinière. Le tronc cérébral contient les centres nerveux qui contrôlent les fonctions automatiques telles que le rythme cardiaque et la respiration[3].

Le cœur et les poumons

Le cœur est un organe musculaire. C'est le principal organe de la circulation du sang. Le cœur est situé plus ou moins au centre de la poitrine. Les poumons sont situés de part et d'autre[4] du cœur. Le poumon est le principal organe de l'appareil respiratoire. L'air arrive dans chaque poumon par une bronche. Le sang arrive par l'artère pulmonaire. Quand il arrive, l'air est chargé de gaz carbonique. Quand le sang ressort[5] par les veines pulmonaires, il est purifié et enrichi en oxygène.

Il n'y a pas de doute, le corps humain est une machine extraordinaire!

[2] relie *connects*
[3] respiration *breathing*
[4] de part et d'autre *on each side*
[5] ressort *leaves*

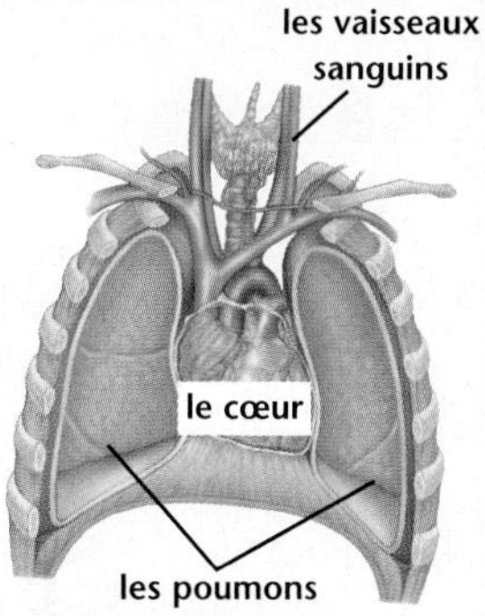

le bras

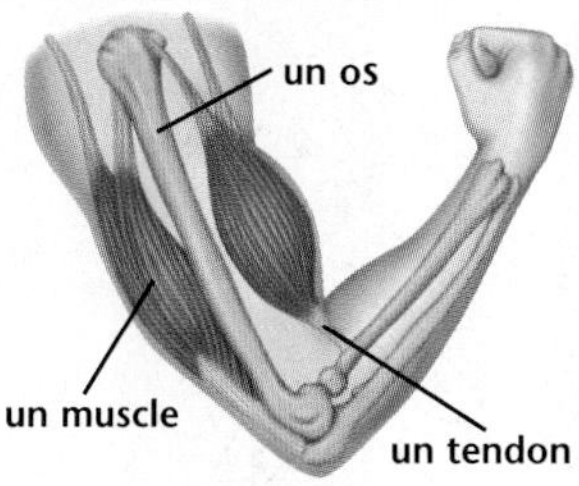

Après la lecture

A Les mots apparentés Trouvez les mots apparentés dans la lecture.

B Des informations Identifiez.

1. le nombre d'os dans chaque bras
2. le nombre de muscles dans le corps humain
3. ce qui attache un muscle à un os
4. un muscle interne très important, un muscle vital
5. ce qui protège le cerveau
6. ce qui relie le cerveau à la moelle épinière
7. ce qui contrôle les fonctions automatiques du corps humain
8. l'organe vital situé au centre de la poitrine
9. l'organe principal de l'appareil respiratoire
10. là où le sang est purifié et enrichi en oxygène

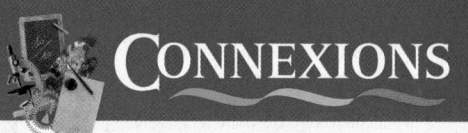

CONNEXIONS

Presentation

Les sciences naturelles
L'anatomie

Note: It is suggested that you have students who are interested in science, particularly biology, read this selection.

Step 1 Have students read the introduction in English on page 346.

Step 2 Have students look at the callout words in the illustrations to familiarize themselves with the new lexical items they will encounter in the reading.

Step 3 As students read about these parts of the body, have students study the illustrations on pages 346–347.

Step 4 Have students read the selection quickly or have them skim it.

Après la lecture

Discuss the answers to the activities on page 347.

Reaching All Students

For the Younger Students You may wish to have students draw and label an illustration of the body.

Answers to Après la lecture

A

Le squelette: squelette, humain, muscles, corps, certains, attachés, directement, intermédiaire, tendon, internes, exemple

Le cerveau et le système nerveux: composé, hémisphères, contient, centres nerveux, contrôlent, fonctions automatiques, rythme cardiaque, respiration

Le cœur et les poumons: organe, musculaire, principal, circulation, situé, respiratoire, air, artère pulmonaire, gaz carbonique, veines pulmonaires, purifié, enrichi, oxygène, doute, humain, machine, extraordinaire

B

1. 32
2. 600
3. un tendon
4. le cœur
5. la boîte crânienne
6. le tronc cérébral
7. le tronc cérébral
8. le cœur
9. les poumons
10. les poumons

C'est à vous

Recycling

These activities allow students to use the vocabulary and structure from this chapter in completely open-ended, real-life situations.

Presentation

Encourage students to say as much as possible when they do these activities. Tell them not to be afraid to make mistakes, since the goal of these activities is real-life communication. If someone in the group makes an error, allow the others to politely correct him or her. Let students choose the activities they would like to do.

You may wish to divide students into pairs or groups. Encourage students to elaborate on the basic theme and to be creative. They may use props, pictures, or posters if they wish.

C'est à vous

Use what you have learned

PARLER

1 Je suis fana de...

✔ Describe your favorite sport

Work with a classmate. Each of you will name a sport you really like and give a description of that sport.

Elles jouent au foot.

La France est victorieuse.

PARLER

2 Une interview du capitaine

✔ Ask someone questions about his or her team

You have to interview the captain of one of the school's sports teams (your classmate) for a French television station. Find out as much information as possible from him or her. Then reverse roles.

PARLER

3 Jeu Devinette

✔ Describe your favorite sports hero and ask questions about your classmates' favorites

Think of your favorite sports hero. Tell a classmate something about him or her. Your classmate will ask you three questions about your hero before guessing who it is. Then reverse roles and guess who your classmate's hero is.

Answers to C'est à vous

1 *Answers will vary but may include:*

—Je suis fana de volley-ball. Le ballon ne doit pas toucher le sol. Il faut servir le ballon par-dessus le filet.

—Je suis fana de cyclisme. Les coureurs roulent vraiment vite!

2 *Answers will vary but may include:*

—Comment est l'équipe de basket de ton école?

—Nous avons une très bonne équipe de basket. Notre équipe gagne beaucoup de matchs.

—Quelle joueuse réussit beaucoup de paniers?

—Hier, Nicole a réussi dix paniers!

—Les spectateurs ont applaudi?

—Bien sûr!

3 *Answers will vary.*

Students will make up questions using vocabulary they know to describe a person and a sport.

C'est à vous

ÉCRIRE

4 Reportage

✔ *Write a description of a sporting event*

Work in groups of three. One of you is the captain of one of the school's teams. The other two are sports reporters for a French newspaper. The two reporters will prepare an interview with the captain about the team's last game. The reporters will edit the information they get from the interview and write their report for tomorrow's paper. The report can be in the present tense.

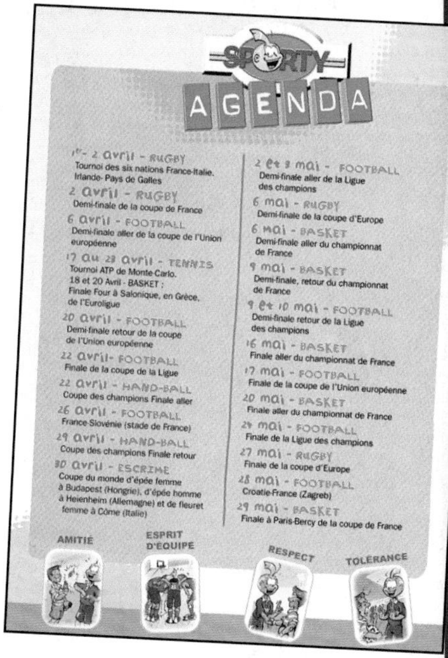

ÉCRIRE

5 Calendrier sportif

✔ *Post a schedule of sporting events*

Your French class has a Web site. Prepare your school's schedule of sporting events for the coming month in French to post at your site.

Writing Strategy

Gathering information If your writing projects deal with a subject you are not familiar with, you may need to gather information before you begin to write. Some of your best sources are the library, the Internet, and people who know something about the topic. Even if you plan to interview people about the topic, it may be necessary to do some research in the library or on the Internet to acquire enough knowledge to prepare good interview questions.

ÉCRIRE

6 La Coupe du Monde

Many of you already know that the World Cup is a soccer championship. Try to give a description of the World Cup as best you can in French. If you are not familiar with it, you will need to do some research. It might be interesting to take what you know or find out about the World Cup and compare it to the World Series in baseball. Gather information about both these championships and write a report in French.

Writing Development

Have students keep a notebook containing their best written work from each chapter. These selected writings can be based on assignments from the Student Textbook and the Writing Activities Workbook. The three activities on page 349 are examples of writing assignments that may be included in each student's portfolio. In the Workbook, students will develop an organized autobiography **(Mon autobiographie).** These workbook pages may also become a part of their portfolio.

Writing Strategy

Gathering information

Have students read the Writing Strategy on page 349. If students have difficulty thinking of sports-related vocabulary, have them use the vocabulary list on page 352.

Learning from Photos

(page 349) The young fan has his face painted in the colors of the French flag during a game against South Africa.

Resource Manager

Communication Transparencies
Quizzes
Test Booklet
ExamView Pro®
Situation Cards
Performance Assessment
Marathon mental Videoquiz

Assessment

This is a pre-test for students to take before you administer the chapter test. Answer sheets for students to do these pages are provided in your transparency binder. Note that each section is cross-referenced so students can easily find the material they have to review in case they made errors. You may wish to collect these assessments and correct them yourself or you may prefer to have the students correct themselves in class. You can go over the answers orally or project them on the overhead, using your Assessment Answers transparencies.

Vocabulaire

*To review **Mots 1**, turn to pages 324–325.*

1 Complétez.

1–2. Il y a onze ____ dans une ____ de foot.
3. Le gardien veut arrêter ou ____ le ballon.
4. Le stade est comble. Les ____ sont pleins.
5. Le joueur peut donner un coup de ____ ou un coup de tête dans le ballon.

*To review **Mots 2**, turn to pages 328–329.*

2 Identifiez.

6.

7.

8.

9.
10.
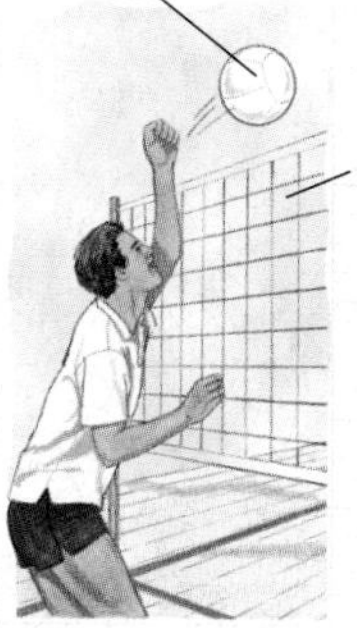

Structure

*To review the **passé composé** of regular verbs, turn to page 332.*

3 Récrivez au passé composé.

11. Je joue au foot.
12. Ils regardent le match à la télé.
13. Elle réussit un beau panier.
14. Notre équipe ne perd pas.
15. Vous finissez la course?

Answers to Assessment

1

1. joueurs
2. équipe
3. bloquer
4. gradins
5. pied

2

6. un coureur cycliste
7. le gagnant (un coureur)
8. un panier
9. un ballon
10. un filet

3

11. J'ai joué au foot.
12. Ils ont regardé le match à la télé.
13. Elle a réussi un beau panier.
14. Notre équipe n'a pas perdu.
15. Vous avez fini la course?

4 Complétez.

16. —Tu as invité ____?
 —Nathalie.
17. —____ tu as regardé à la télé?
 —La course cycliste.
18. —Pour jouer, tu as besoin de ____?
 —D'un ballon et d'un filet.

To review asking questions, turn to page 335.

5 Complétez au présent.

19. Tu ____ des cadeaux. (recevoir)
20. Je ____ beaucoup d'eau. (boire)
21. Elle ____ passer l'examen. (devoir)
22. Vous ____ combien d'argent? (recevoir)
23. Ils ____ faire attention. (devoir)

*To review **boire, devoir,** and **recevoir** in the present, turn to page 337.*

Culture

6 Identifiez.

24. un sport populaire qui est très apprécié au Québec
25. le deuxième sport dans les pays d'Afrique Occidentale

To review this cultural information, turn to pages 342–343.

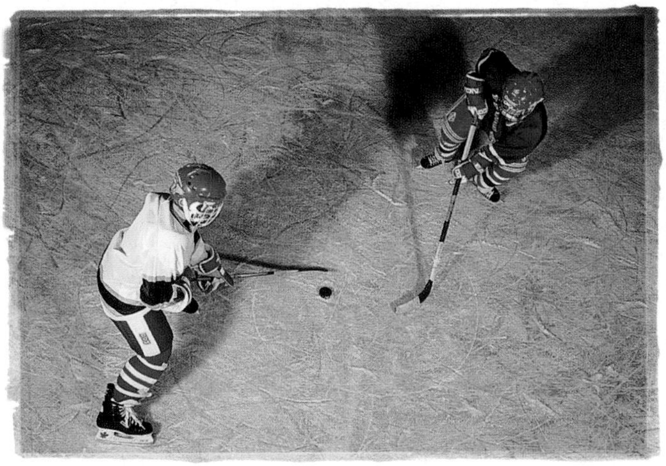

Un match de hockey

Answers to Assessment

4

16. qui
17. Qu'est-ce que
18. quoi

5

19. reçois
20. bois
21. doit
22. recevez
23. doivent

6

24. le hockey
25. le basket-ball

Vocabulary Review

The words and phrases in the **Vocabulaire** have been taught for productive use in this chapter. They are summarized here as a resource for both student and teacher. This list also serves as a convenient resource for the **C'est à vous** activities on pages 348–349. There are approximately twenty-three cognates in this vocabulary list. Have students find them.

Attention!

You will notice that the vocabulary list here is not translated. This has been done intentionally, since we feel that by the time students have finished the material in the chapter they should be familiar with the meanings of all the words. If there are several words they still do not know, we recommend that they refer to the **Mots 1** and **2** sections in the chapter or go to the dictionaries at the back of this book to find the meanings. However, if you prefer that your students have the English translations, please refer to Vocabulary Transparency 10.1, where you will find these words listed with their translations.

Vocabulaire

Describing a sports event

un stade	une joueuse	jouer (à)	gagner
des gradins *(m. pl.)*	une équipe	lancer	perdre
un spectateur	le camp (adverse)	servir	siffler
une spectatrice	un arbitre	envoyer	beaucoup de monde
un terrain	un penalty	renvoyer	comble
une piste	le score	passer	plein
un match	un(e) gagnant(e)	recevoir	contre
un joueur	une coupe	égaliser	

Describing a soccer game

le foot(ball)	un coup	bloquer
un ballon	de pied	arrêter
marquer un but	de tête	
un gardien de but	un but	

Describing a basketball game

le basket(-ball)	dribbler
un panier	réussir un beau panier
un demi-cercle	

How well do you know your vocabulary?

- Choose a sport from the list.
- Ask classmates to give a word associated with the sport you chose.

Describing a volleyball game

le volley(-ball)	le sol
un filet	

Describing a bicycle race

un vélo	un coureur cycliste	le cyclisme	rouler vite
une bicyclette	une coureuse cycliste	une course	

Describing a track event

l'athlétisme *(m.)*	un coureur
une piste	une coureuse

Expressing the past

hier	avant-hier	une fois
hier matin	la semaine dernière	
hier soir	l'année dernière	

Other useful words and expresssions

par-dessus

Technotour

BON VOYAGE!

VIDÉO • Épisode 10

Avant de visionner

In this video episode, Manu entertains the crowd with his narration of an exciting game.

Manu joue bien au basket.

Manu est fana de basket-ball. C'est son sport favori.

FRENCH ONLINE

À découvrir

Learn more about ice hockey, a popular sport in the French-speaking world, online.

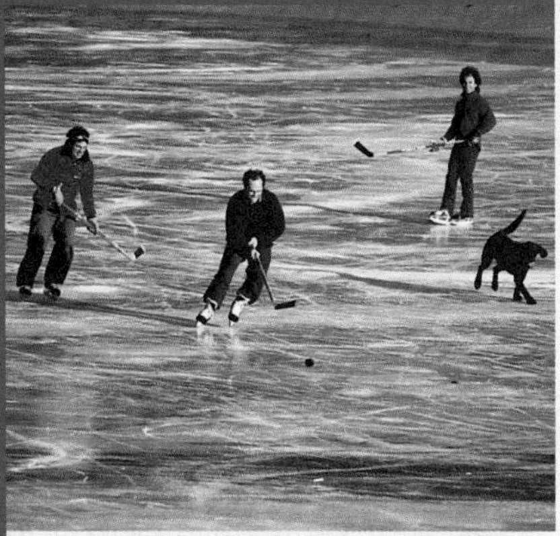

Le hockey est très populaire au Canada.

FRENCH Online

In the Chapter 10 Internet activity, you will have a chance to learn more about sports in the Francophone world. To begin your virtual adventure, go to the Glencoe French Web site:
french.glencoe.com

Technotour

Overview

This page previews two key multimedia components of the **Glencoe French** series. Each reinforces the material taught in the chapter in a unique manner.

VIDÉO

The Video Program allows students to see how the chapter vocabulary and structures are used by native speakers. For maximum reinforcement, show the video episode as a final activity for Chapter 10.

The two photos on the left show highlights from the Chapter 10 video episode. Discuss the photos with your students before having them view the episode. See the Video Activities Booklet for detailed suggestions for using this resource.

FRENCH Online

- The **À découvrir** photo on page 353 shows ice hockey. Students can go online for additional information about this popular sport in Canada.
- Teacher Information and Student Worksheets for this activity can be accessed at the Web site.

Video Synopsis

In this video episode, we find ourselves in the courtyard of the lycée Louis-le-Grand in Paris where there is a basketball game in progress. We hear Manu doing a play-by-play in a genuine sportscaster's voice. We are also exposed to Manu's "expertise" as a player in this humorous spoof. The video ends with an overview of other popular sports in the French-speaking world.

Planning for Chapter 11

SCOPE AND SEQUENCE, PAGES 354–385

Topics

- Summer activities
- Winter activities
- Discuss past actions and events

Culture

- Madame Lebrun's class spends winter vacation in Québec.
- Beaches in France
- Carnaval in Québec
- **Reflets du Canada**

Functions

- How to describe summer and winter activities
- How to describe past actions and events
- How to make negative statements

Structure

- The **passé composé** of irregular verbs
- Negative words
- The **passé composé** with **être**

National Standards

- Communication Standard 1.1 pages 358, 359, 362, 363, 365, 366, 367, 368, 370, 371, 373, 380
- Communication Standard 1.2 pages 358, 359, 362, 363, 365, 366, 367, 368, 370, 372, 375, 376, 377
- Communication Standard 1.3 pages 358, 363, 365, 370, 371, 381
- Cultures Standard 2.1 pages 363, 373, 374–375, 376, 377
- Cultures Standard 2.2 page 363
- Connections Standard 3.1 pages 378–379
- Comparisons Standard 4.2 pages 374–375, 376, 377
- Communities Standard 5.1 page 381

PACING AND PRIORITIES

The chapter content is color coded below to assist you in planning.
■ required ■ recommended ■ optional

Vocabulaire *(required)* *Days 1–4*

- ■ Mots 1
  - À la plage
  - Des activités d'été
  - Le printemps
  - L'été
- ■ Mots 2
  - Une station de sports d'hiver
  - L'automne
  - L'hiver

Structure *(required)* *Days 5–7*

- ■ Le passé composé des verbes irréguliers
- ■ Les mots négatifs
- ■ Le passé composé avec **être**

Conversation *(required)*

- ■ À la plage

Prononciation *(recommended)*

- ■ Le son **/y/**

Lectures culturelles

- ■ Un petit voyage au Canada *(recommended)*
- ■ Les grandes vacances *(optional)*
- ■ Le carnaval *(optional)*

Connexions *(optional)*

- ■ La peinture

■ **C'est à vous** *(recommended)*

■ **Assessment** *(recommended)*

■ **Technotour** *(optional)*

RESOURCE GUIDE

SECTION	PAGES	SECTION RESOURCES
Vocabulaire *Mots 1*		
À la plage	356	🔲 Vocabulary Transparencies 11.2–11.3
Des activités d'été	357	🎧 Audiocassette 7A/CD 7
Le printemps	357	📘 Audio Activities Booklet TE, pages 133–135
L'été	357–359	📘 Workbook, pages 105–106
		📘 Quiz 1, page 54
		💿 ExamView Pro®
Vocabulaire *Mots 2*		
Une station de sports d'hiver	360–361	🔲 Vocabulary Transparencies 11.4–11.5
L'automne	361	🎧 Audiocassette 7A/CD 7
L'hiver	361–363	📘 Audio Activities Booklet TE, pages 135–137
		📘 Workbook, pages 107–108
		📘 Quiz 2, page 55
		💿 ExamView Pro®
Structure		
Le passé composé des verbes irréguliers	364–366	🎧 Audiocassette 7A/CD 7
		📘 Audio Activities Booklet TE, pages 138–139
Les mots négatifs	367–368	📘 Workbook, pages 109–111
Le passé composé avec **être**	369–371	📘 Quizzes 3–5, pages 56–58
		💿 ExamView Pro®
Conversation		
À la plage	372	🎧 Audiocassette 7A/CD 7
		📘 Audio Activities Booklet TE, pages 139–140
		💿 CD-ROM
Prononciation		
Le son /y/	373	🔲 Pronunciation Transparency P 11
		🎧 Audiocassette 7A/CD 7
		📘 Audio Activities Booklet TE, pages 140–141
Lectures culturelles		
Un petit voyage au Canada	374–375	🎧 Audiocassette 7A/CD 7
Les grandes vacances	376	📘 Audio Activities Booklet TE, pages 141–142
Le carnaval	377	📘 Test Booklet, Chapter 11
Connexions		
La peinture	378–379	📘 Test Booklet, Chapter 11
C'est à vous		
	380–381	📺 **Bon voyage!** Video, Episode 11
		📘 Video Activities Booklet, Chapter 11
		🌐 French Online Activities french.glencoe.com
Assessment		
	382–383	🔲 Communication Transparencies C 11.1–11.2
		📘 Quizzes 1–5, pages 54–58
		📘 Test Booklet, Chapter 11
		💿 ExamView Pro®
		📘 Situation Cards, Chapter 11
		📘 Performance Assessment, pages 15–22
		📺 **Marathon mental** Videoquiz

Using Your Resources for Chapter 11

Transparencies

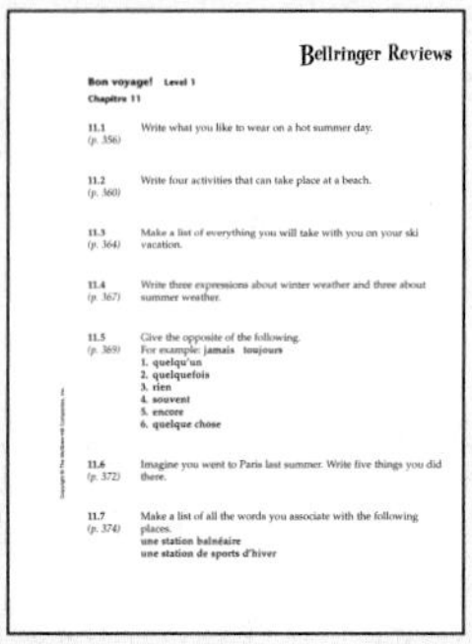
Bellringer 11.1–11.7

Vocabulary 11.1–11.5

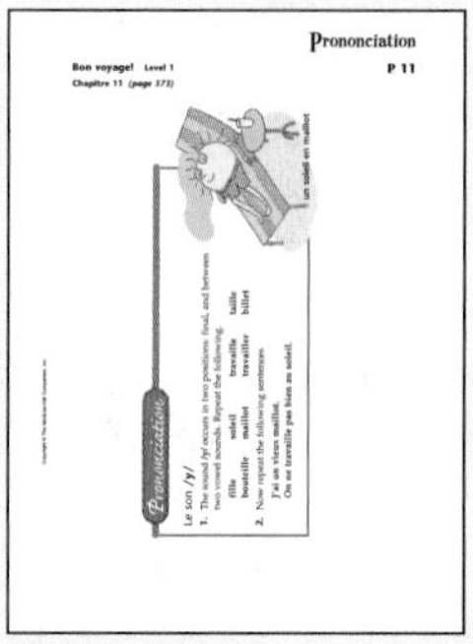
Pronunciation P 11

Communication C 11.1–11.2

Writing Activities Workbook

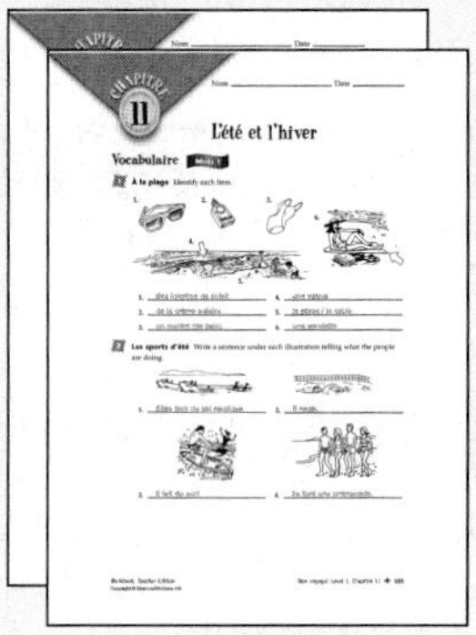
Vocabulary, pages 105–108

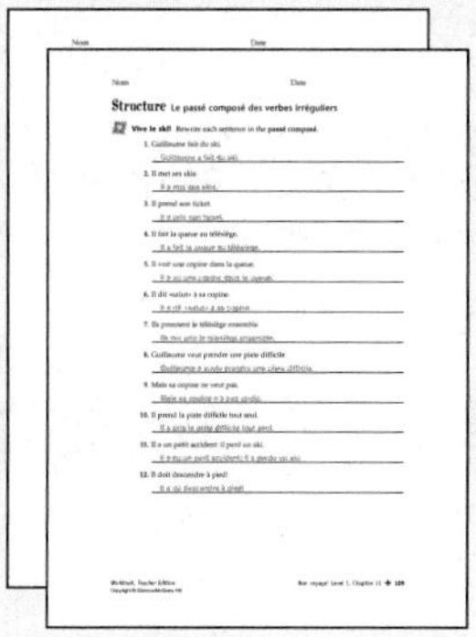
Structure, pages 109–111

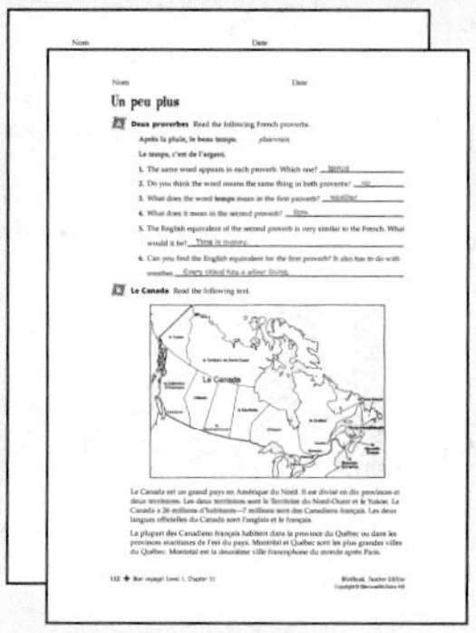
Enrichment, pages 112–114

Audio Program and Audio Activities Booklet

Vocabulary, pages 133–137

Structure, pages 138–139

Conversation, Pronunciation pages 139–141

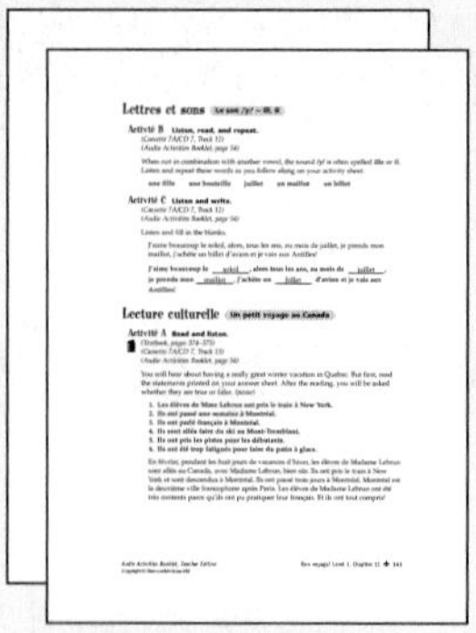
Cultural Reading, pages 141–142

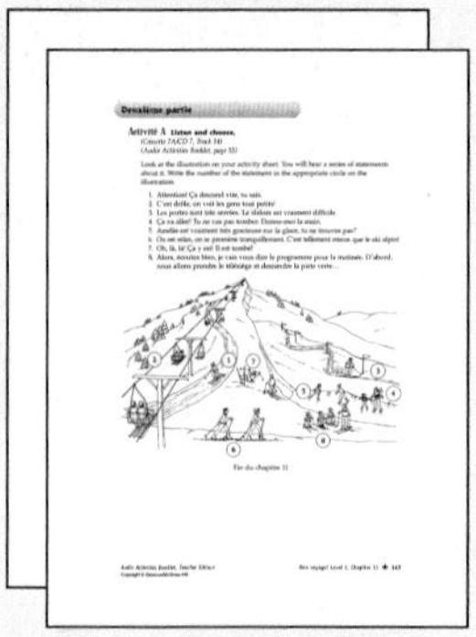
Additional Practice, page 143

Assessment

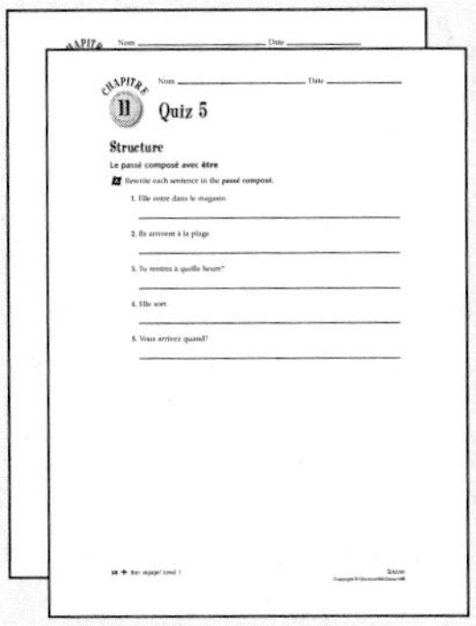

Vocabulary and Structure Quizzes, pages 54–58

Chapter Tests, Chapter 11

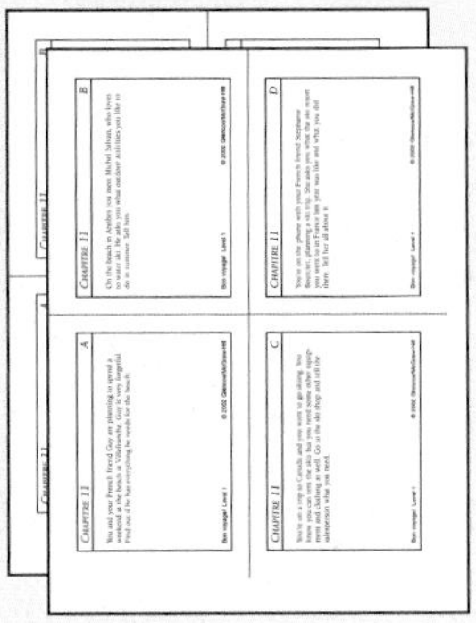

Situation Cards, Chapter 11

Performance Assessment, pages 15–22

Timesaving Teacher Tools

Interactive Teacher Edition

Imagine having your Teacher's Edition and all resources on a CD-ROM. Click on a resource and it appears on your screen, ready to be printed, sorted, or planned.

Interactive Lesson Planner

The Interactive Lesson Planner CD-ROM helps you organize your lesson plans for a week, month, semester, or year. Look at this planning tool for easy access to your Chapter 11 resources.

ExamView Pro®

Test Bank software for Macintosh and Windows makes creating, editing, customizing, and printing tests quick and easy.

Technology Resources

FRENCH Online

In the Chapter 11 Internet activity, you will have a chance to learn more about vacation spots in the Francophone world. Visit french.glencoe.com.

On the Interactive Conversation CD-ROM, students can listen to and take part in a recorded version of the conversation in Chapter 11.

NATIONAL GEOGRAPHIC SOCIETY

See the National Geographic Teacher's Corner on pages 150–151, 256–257, 396–397, 500–501 for reference to additional technology resources.

Bon Voyage! Video and Video Activities Booklet.

Help your students prepare for the chapter test by playing the **Marathon mental** Videoquiz game show. Teams will compete against each other to review chapter vocabulary and structure and sharpen listening comprehension skills.

CHAPITRE 11

Preview

In this chapter, students will learn to discuss and describe winter and summer sports. They will learn to talk about the clothing and the equipment needed for these activities. They will also learn to describe the weather during the four seasons of the year. They will learn the **passé composé** of irregular verbs that are conjugated with **avoir** and the **passé composé** of the verbs that are conjugated with **être.** They will also learn negative expressions.

National Standards

Communication

In Chapter 11, students will communicate in spoken and written French on the following topics:

- Describing winter sports, clothing and equipment
- Describing summer sports, clothing and equipment
- Describing the weather of each season

Students will also learn to narrate past events. They will obtain and provide information and engage in conversations about these sports and seasons as they fulfill the chapter objectives listed on this page.

CHAPITRE 11

L'été et l'hiver

Objectifs

In this chapter you will learn to:

- ✔ *describe summer and winter weather*
- ✔ *talk about summer activities and sports*
- ✔ *talk about winter sports*
- ✔ *discuss past actions and events*
- ✔ *make negative statements*
- ✔ *talk about a ski trip in Quebec*

Maurice Utrillo ***Montmartre sous la neige***

354

Correlations to Continuum *(see page* i *for code)*

Stage I
Write postcards. p. 381 (**4**, *p*); Use short sentences, learned words, phrases, simple questions, and commands when speaking. p. 359 (**5**, *p*); Understand and convey information about leisure activities. p. 368 (**23**, *p*); Understand and convey information on weather. p. 357 (*i*), p. 363 (**11**, *p*); Understand most important information. p. 381 (**4**)

Stage II
Understand and express important ideas and some detail. p. 363 (**12**, *p*), p. 371 (**30**, *m*); Describe and compare. p. 373 (**A**, *p*); Converse in face-to-face social interactions. p. 359 (**7**, *i*), p. 363 (**13**, *p*), p. 380 (**3**, *m*); Write short guided compositions. p. 381 (**5**, *p*); Use and understand learned expressions, sentences, strings of sentences, and questions. p. 371, (**30**, *p*); Understand and convey information about leisure activities. pp. 374–375 (*m*); Communicate effectively with some pattern of error, which may interfere slightly with full comprehension when performing Stage II functions. p. 380 (**1**)

Stage III
Narrate and understand narration in the past. p. 366 (**18**, *p*), p. 380 (**2**, *m*); Listen during face-to-face social interactions and listen to audio or video texts. p. 373 (*i*), p. 373 (**B**, *p*); Use strings of related sentences when speaking. p. 359 (**6**, *p*); Understand and convey information about art. pp. 378–379 (*p*)

Stage IV
Compare and contrast. p. 381 (**5**, *i*), p. 381 (**5**, *p*); Read short literary texts. pp. 512–514 (*i*), pp. 514–517 (*p*)

CHAPITRE 11

Spotlight on Culture

Photograph This photo is of the unspoiled island, **Île des Saintes.** The archipelago of Guadeloupe is made up of two large islands, **Basse-Terre** and **Grande-Terre,** three smaller islands, **Île des Saintes, La Désirade, and Marie-Galante,** and some other even smaller islands.

Île des Saintes is made up of eight small islands off the south coast of Guadeloupe, all of which are usually referred to as **Les Saintes.** Only two of the eight islands, **Terre-de-Haut** and **Terre-de-Bas** are inhabited. Together they have a population of about 3,260. Many of the inhabitants of **Les Saintes, les Santois,** are fair-haired, blue-eyed descendants of Breton and Norman sailors. Their main occupation is fishing. For additional information about Guadeloupe, see page 383.

Painting Maurice Utrillo was born in Paris in 1883. He suffered from alcoholism from a very young age. His devoted mother encouraged him to become an artist and he actually learned to paint on his own. He began to paint in a realistic style using somber colors. Much influenced by the works of Pissarro and Sisley, he came to use lighter colors. The period from 1907 to 1916 was known as his **période blanche.** He painted scenes of Montmartre and the Paris suburbs, using bright colors. His streets, cafés, etc., were often covered with snow as seen here. In 1934, he married another French artist, Lucie Valore. They retired to Le Vésinet but continued to produce works of art. Utrillo died in Le Vésinet in 1955.

Chapter Projects

Mes vacances Have students share their family's vacation habits by bringing in photos and vacation memorabilia. You may wish to group them according to their vacation destinations (mountains, seaside, visiting a city, etc.) and have each group tell as much as they can in French about their type of vacation.

On va en France. Have groups plan the ideal five-week vacation in France. The description should be in French and should include information about transportation, meals, and leisure activities. They may do a poster or collage to illustrate it. Students can then choose the trip they would most like to take.

En hiver ou en été Have students work in groups to prepare a brochure about a winter or summer resort in the French-speaking world. Have them describe its features and weather. They can also include some ads for things to do at the resort.

1 Preparation

Resource Manager

Vocabulary Transparencies 11.2–11.3
Audio Activities Booklet TE, pages 133–135
Audiocassette 7A/CD 7
Workbook, pages 105–106
Quiz 1, page 54
ExamView Pro®

Bellringer Review

Use BRR Transparency 11.1 or write the following on the board.
Write what you like to wear on a hot summer day.

2 Presentation

Step 1 Show Vocabulary Transparencies 11.2–11.3. Point to individual items and have the class repeat the words after you or Audiocassette 7A/CD 7.

Step 2 As an alternative, you may wish to bring in some props such as sunglasses, suntan lotion, and so on.

Step 3 During your presentation, ask: **C'est une plage? C'est une plage ou la mer? C'est une vague? Il y a des vagues dans la mer? C'est une station balnéaire? Il y a des stations balnéaires au bord de la mer? Il y a des stations balnéaires où? En été, tu vas dans une station balnéaire? Tu vas dans quelle station balnéaire? Quand tu vas à la plage, tu mets un maillot de bain? Tu mets des lunettes de soleil?**

Step 4 You may wish to call a student or two to the front of the class. Using the vocabulary transparencies, they can ask questions and call on class members to respond.

Vocabulaire
Mots 1

À la plage

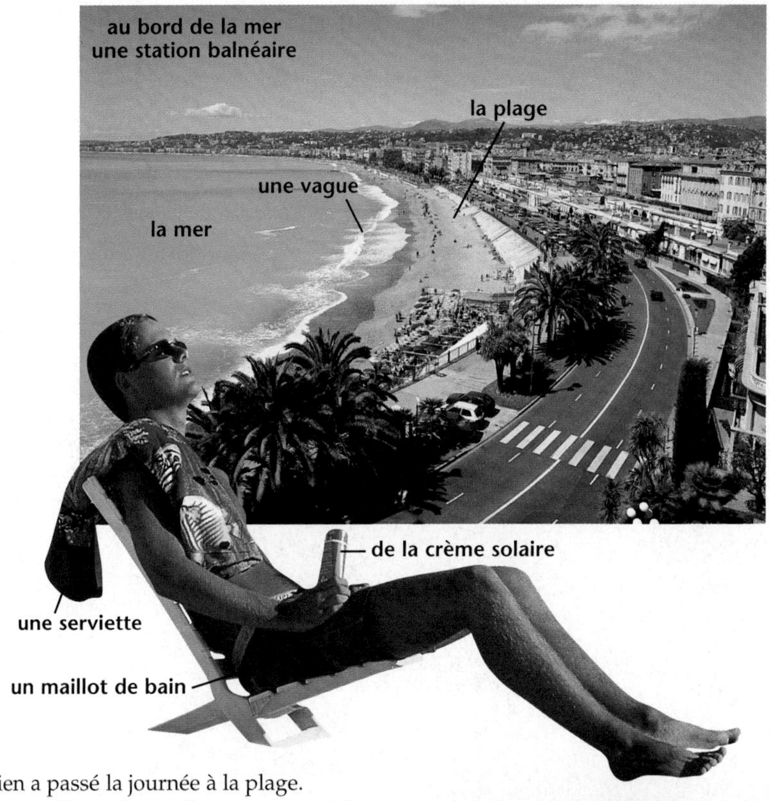

Fabien a passé la journée à la plage.
Il a apporté sa crème solaire et sa serviette.
À la plage, il faut faire attention.
Il faut mettre de la crème solaire.
Il ne faut pas rester trop longtemps au soleil.

Caroline a pris un bain de soleil.
Elle a bronzé.
Elle a mis de la crème solaire.
Elle n'a pas attrapé de coup de soleil.

Reaching All Students

Kinesthetic Learners You may wish to have students dramatize the following words or expressions: **mettre de la crème solaire, nager, plonger, faire de la planche à voile, faire du ski nautique, faire du surf, faire une promenade.**

Learning from Photos

(page 356 top) This photo is of the beautiful beach on the **Baie des Anges** in Nice. The famous street that runs along the beach is the **Promenade des Anglais.**

Des activités d'été

faire de la planche à voile

faire du ski nautique

faire du surf

faire une promenade

Cécile a plongé dans la piscine.
Laure a pris des leçons de natation.
Elle a appris à nager.

Le printemps

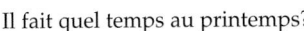

Il fait quel temps au printemps?

Il fait beau.
De temps en temps,
il y a des nuages.

Il y a du vent.
Il pleut.
Il fait mauvais.

L'été

En été il fait chaud.
Il fait du soleil.

Note: Pourquoi questions (with **parce que** responses) are the most challenging to answer. The following are some questions you may wish to ask more able students while presenting words in this section: **Il faut mettre de la crème solaire à la plage. Pourquoi? Il faut faire attention. Pourquoi? Caroline n'attrape pas de coup de soleil. Pourquoi?**

Fun-Facts

The beaches in Nice are not sandy. They have small stones or rocks called **galets.**

Vocabulary Expansion

The following are some additional weather expressions you may wish to give students. These expressions are often used for the **météo** both on TV and in the newspaper.

Le temps est ensoleillé.
Il est nuageux.
Le ciel est couvert.
Il y a des averses.
Il y a des éclaircies.

If you present the above expressions, you may wish to have the students do the following activity.

Exprimez d'une autre façon:

1. **Il fait du soleil.**
2. **Il y a des nuages.**
3. **Il pleut.**
4. **Le temps est nuageux.**
5. **Le ciel n'est pas couvert.**

Recycling

In this section, the concept of **-er** verbs is reinforced with the new verbs **bronzer, attraper, nager,** and **plonger.** In addition, the verbs **aller, faire,** and **mettre** are reintroduced. You may wish to explain that **nager** and **plonger** have the same spelling change as **manger: nous mangeons, nous nageons, nous plongeons.**

Reaching All Students

Total Physical Response

(Student 1), **levez-vous et venez ici, s'il vous plaît.**
Vous allez mimer les activités suivantes:
Nagez.
Faites du ski nautique.
Faites de la planche à voile.
Faites du surf.
Faites une promenade.
Plongez dans la piscine.
Mettez de la crème solaire.
Mettez vos lunettes de soleil.
Prenez un bain de soleil.
Vérifiez si vous attrapez un coup de soleil.
Merci, *(Student 1).* **Retournez à votre place, s'il vous plaît.**

3 Practice

Commençons
Let's use our new words

Attention!

When students are doing the **Commençons** activities, accept any answer that makes sense. The purpose of these activities is to have students use the new vocabulary. They are not factual recall activities. Thus, it is not necessary for students to remember specific factual information from the vocabulary presentation when answering. If you wish, have students use the photos on this page as a stimulus, when possible.

1, **2**, and **3** To focus on listening, have students keep their books closed as you ask the questions. Then have students open their books and retell the story in their own words.

Writing Development

Call on students to review the information in Activities 1, 2, and 3 by writing a short paragraph based on each activity.

Commençons
Let's use our new words

1 Historiette À la plage

Inventez une histoire.

1. Juliette a passé la journée à la plage?
2. Elle a beaucoup nagé?
3. Elle a pris un bain de soleil?
4. Elle a apporté de la crème solaire?
5. Elle a fait attention? Elle a mis de la crème solaire?
6. Elle a mis aussi des lunettes de soleil?
7. Elle a bronzé?
8. Elle a fait du ski nautique?
9. Elle a fait une promenade sur la plage?
10. Elle a fait de la planche à voile aussi?

Nice, France

De la crème solaire et des lunettes de soleil

2 Historiette En été

Donnez des réponses personnelles.

1. En été, tu aimes aller à la plage?
2. Tu vas dans quelle station balnéaire?
3. Tu vas à la plage quand il pleut?
4. Tu aimes nager dans la mer ou dans une piscine?
5. Tu aimes plonger?
6. Qu'est-ce que tu mets pour nager?
7. Il faut mettre de la crème solaire quand on va à la plage?
8. Et toi, tu mets de la crème solaire?
9. Tu bronzes facilement ou tu attrapes des coups de soleil?
10. Tu mets des lunettes de soleil quand tu vas à la plage?
11. Tu apportes ta serviette?

Answers to Commençons

1 *Answers will vary but may include:*

1. Oui, Juliette a passé la journée à la plage.
2. Non, elle n'a pas beaucoup nagé.
3. Oui, elle a pris un bain de soleil.
4. Oui, elle a apporté de la crème solaire.
5. Oui, elle a fait attention. Elle a mis de la crème solaire.
6. Non, elle n'a pas mis de lunettes de soleil.
7. Oui, elle a bronzé.
8. Non, elle n'a pas fait de ski nautique.
9. Oui, elle a fait une promenade sur la plage.
10. Oui, elle a fait de la planche à voile aussi.

2 *Answers will vary but may include:*

1. Oui, en été j'aime aller à la plage.
2. Je vais à ______.
3. Non, je ne vais pas à la plage quand il pleut.
4. J'aime nager dans la piscine.
5. Oui, j'aime plonger.
6. Je mets un maillot de bain.
7. Oui, il faut mettre de la crème solaire quand on va à la plage.
8. Oui, je mets de la crème solaire.
9. J'attrape des coups de soleil.
10. Oui, je mets des lunettes de soleil quand je vais à la plage.
11. Oui, j'apporte ma serviette.

3 Historiette Au bord de la mer Complétez.

1. Au bord de la mer, on va à la ____ pour nager et bronzer.
2. Il y a beaucoup de plages et de stations balnéaires sur la ____ Méditerranée.
3. Il y a de grandes ____ sur la mer ou sur l'océan, surtout quand il y a du ____.
4. Beaucoup de gens aiment prendre un ____ de soleil sur la plage.
5. Il faut mettre de la ____ si on ne veut pas attraper de coup de soleil.
6. Quand on va nager, on met un ____.
7. Quand il fait chaud à la plage, il ne faut pas ____ trop longtemps au soleil.
8. On peut faire du ____ ou du ____ sur la mer quand il fait beau.
9. Quand il fait mauvais, il y a souvent des ____ dans le ciel.
10. À Biarritz, sur l'océan Atlantique, il y a souvent des ____ qui font du surf.

Une leçon de natation

4 Qu'est-ce qu'elle a appris?

Répondez d'après la photo.

1. Jeanne a appris à nager?
2. Elle a pris des leçons de natation?
3. Elle a appris à nager dans la mer ou dans une piscine?
4. Elle a compris toutes les instructions de la monitrice?

5 On va à la plage.

Work with a classmate. You are going to spend a day or two at the beach. Go to the store to buy some things you need for your beach trip. One of you will be the salesperson and the other will be the shopper. Take turns.

Une jolie baie, Tahiti

6 Des vacances parfaites

Plan a great summer vacation. Tell your classmate where you want to go and why. Tell him or her what you do there. Then find out your classmate's summer plans.

7 Le temps au printemps ou en été

With a classmate describe the spring or summer weather where you live. Which season do you prefer? Tell why.

ENCORE PLUS *For more practice using words from **Mots 1**, do Activity 34 on page H35 at the end of this book.*

Vocabulaire

Cognate Recognition

Have students scan the **Mots 1** words again and then identify and pronounce each cognate.

Learning from Photos

(page 359) Tahiti is an island belonging to the group called **la Polynésie-Française** in the South Pacific. These islands are **un territoire d'outre-mer (un T.O.M.).** The capital of Tahiti is **Papeetee.** The island has 115,820 inhabitants, including about 5,000 Chinese. Tourism is the main industry of this tropical island.

Assessment

As an informal assessment, check for understanding by mixing true and false statements about Vocabulary Transparencies 11.2–11.3. Students either agree by saying **Je suis d'accord** or they correct the statement.

ENCORE PLUS This *infogap* activity will allow students to practice in pairs. The activity should be very manageable for them, since all vocabulary and structures are familiar to them.

Answers to Commençons

3

1. plage
2. mer
3. vagues, vent
4. bain
5. crème solaire
6. maillot de bain
7. rester
8. ski nautique, surf
9. nuages
10. surfeurs

4

1. Oui, Jeanne a appris à nager.
2. Oui, elle a pris des leçons de natation.
3. Elle a appris à nager dans une piscine.
4. Oui, elle a compris toutes les instructions de la monitrice.

5 *Answers will vary.*

Students will use shopping expressions learned in previous lessons. Some things they may want to buy are: **des lunettes de soleil, de la crème solaire, une serviette pour la plage, un maillot.**

6 *Answers will vary depending upon student preferences.*

7 *Answers will vary depending upon where students live.*

1 Preparation

Resource Manager

Vocabulary Transparencies 11.4–11.5
Audio Activities Booklet TE, pages 135–137
Audiocassette 7A/CD 7
Workbook, pages 107–108
Quiz 2, page 55
ExamView Pro®

Bellringer Review

Use BRR Transparency 11.2 or write the following on the board.
Write four activities that can take place at a beach.

2 Presentation

Step 1 To vary the procedure for presenting the vocabulary, you may wish to ask students to open their books to pages 360–361. Have them look at the illustrations as you play Audiocassette 7A/CD 7 once.

Step 2 Show Vocabulary Transparencies 11.4–11.5. Have students close their books and repeat the new words after you two or three times.

Step 3 Call a student to the front of the room. As you say a new word or phrase, have the student point to the appropriate item on the transparency.

Step 4 Have a student point to items on the transparencies as he or she asks: **Qu'est-ce que c'est?** or **C'est qui?** and calls on classmates to respond.

Step 5 Now have students read the words and sentences aloud for additional reinforcement.

Vocabulaire

Mots 2

Une station de sports d'hiver

Les skieurs ont descendu la piste verte.
La piste verte, c'est pour les débutants.

Reaching All Students

Total Physical Response

(Student 1), **venez ici, s'il vous plaît.**
Asseyez-vous, s'il vous plaît.
Mettez vos chaussures de ski.
Et maintenant, levez-vous.
Mettez votre anorak.
Mettez votre bonnet.
Mettez vos lunettes et vos gants.
Mettez vos skis.
Prenez vos bâtons.
Et maintenant, allez faire du ski!
Merci, *(Student 1)*. **Vous pouvez retourner à votre place.**
(Student 2), **venez ici, s'il vous plaît.**
Vous êtes dans une station de sports d'hiver.
Faites la queue.
Attendez le télésiège.
Le voilà, il arrive. Asseyez-vous sur le télésiège.
Maintenant vous êtes au sommet de la montagne.

Marie est débutante.
Elle n'a jamais fait de ski.
Elle tombe tout le temps.

Ce matin, elle a pris sa première leçon.
Elle a eu un très bon moniteur.

Les filles font du patin à glace avec leur mère.

L'automne

En automne il ne fait pas froid.
Il fait frais.

L'hiver

Il fait quel temps en hiver?

Il fait froid.

Il neige.

Il gèle.

Step 6 Bring magazines or catalogues to class that show ski clothing, equipment, and actions. Ask questions about the pictures. For example: **Qui descend la piste? C'est une piste verte? Elle/Il a mis quels vêtements? De quelle couleur est son écharpe? De quelle couleur est son bonnet? Et ses gants?,** etc.

Reaching All Students

For the Younger Students Have students compile a calendar using photographs, magazine pictures, postcards, or other illustrations of the weather conditions they have learned to describe. For each month of the year, they should write a sample date, a weather description, and a sentence about the illustration they have chosen. For example: **C'est aujourd'hui le 7 juillet. Il fait très chaud. Nous allons à la plage pour faire du surf.**

Learning from Photos

(page 360 bottom) The photo of the ski slopes with the downhill skiers **(le ski alpin)** was taken in **Serre-Chevalier** in the **Hautes-Alpes** region of France.

(page 360 middle right) The cross-country skiing **(le ski de fond)** photo was taken in the Laurentians **(les Laurentides)** in the **Mont-Tremblant** area of Quebec.

Reaching All Students

Total Physical Response *(continued)*

Descendez du télésiège.
Prenez un bâton dans chaque main.
Descendez! Tombez!
Regardez votre jambe.
Non, il n'y a pas de problème. Levez-vous et continuez à skier.
Merci, *(Student 2).* **Retournez à votre place.**
(Student 3), **venez ici, s'il vous plaît.**
Vous allez mimer ce que je dis.
Il fait très froid.
Mettez votre anorak.
Mettez vos patins.
Faites du patin à glace.
Tombez.
Levez-vous.
Très bien, *(Student 3).* **Merci. Maintenant, retournez à votre place.**

3 Practice

Commençons
Let's use our new words

10 After completing the activity on page 363 as a whole-class activity, have students do it again in pairs.
Expansion: Have students retell the story in their own words.

Learning from Realia
(page 362) Mont-Orford is a ski resort near Sherbrooke in Quebec.
1. Have students give the colors for the various levels.
2. **Pistes sauvages non entretenues** are natural unmaintained slopes. **Planche à neige** means *snowboard.*

Commençons
Let's use our new words

8 Historiette Dans une station de sports d'hiver
Répondez d'après les indications.

1. Les stations de sports d'hiver sont très fréquentées en quelle saison? (en hiver)
2. Quel temps fait-il en hiver à la montagne? (froid)
3. Il y a quelles catégories de pistes dans une station de sports d'hiver? (pour les skieurs débutants, pour les skieurs moyens et pour les skieurs experts)
4. Les skieurs ont fait du ski où? (sur la piste verte)
5. Qu'est-ce qu'ils ont pris pour monter au sommet de la montagne? (un télésiège)
6. Ils ont descendu quelle piste? (la piste noire)
7. Qu'est-ce qu'il y a sur les pistes noires? (beaucoup de bosses)
8. Les bosses, c'est dangereux pour les débutants? (oui, très)
9. Après le ski, ils ont mis leurs patins? (oui)
10. Ils ont fait du patin à glace où? (à la patinoire)

9 On fait du ski. Répondez d'après les dessins.

1. C'est une station balnéaire ou une station de sports d'hiver?
2. C'est une plage ou une montagne?
3. C'est la neige ou la mer?
4. C'est le sommet de la montagne ou la vallée?
5. C'est quelle saison? L'automne ou l'hiver?
6. C'est une piste ou une piscine?
7. C'est une skieuse ou une nageuse?
8. Elle fait du ski alpin ou du ski de fond?
9. Elle skie bien ou elle tombe souvent?

Answers to Commençons

8
1. Les stations de sports d'hiver sont très fréquentées en hiver.
2. En hiver à la montagne il fait froid.
3. Dans une station de sports d'hiver il y a des pistes pour les skieurs débutants, pour les skieurs moyens et pour les skieurs experts.
4. Les skieurs ont fait du ski sur la piste verte.
5. Ils ont pris un télésiège pour monter au sommet de la montagne.
6. Ils ont descendu la piste noire.
7. Il y a beaucoup de bosses sur les pistes noires.
8. Oui, les bosses, c'est très dangereux pour les débutants.
9. Oui, après le ski, ils ont mis leurs patins.
10. Ils ont fait du patin à glace à la patinoire.

9
1. C'est une station de sports d'hiver.
2. C'est une montagne.
3. C'est la neige.
4. C'est la vallée.
5. C'est l'hiver.
6. C'est une piste.
7. C'est une skieuse.
8. Elle fait du ski alpin.
9. Elle skie bien.

10 Historiette Leçons de ski

Inventez une histoire.

1. Christine a appris à faire du ski?
2. Qui a appris à Christine à faire du ski?
3. Elle a eu un très bon moniteur?
4. Christine a mis un anorak de quelle couleur?
5. Elle a mis des gants, une écharpe et un bonnet?
6. Elle a mis ses chaussures de ski et ses skis?
7. Elle a pris le télésiège?
8. Elle a descendu quelle piste?
9. Il a fait très froid? Il a neigé? Il a gelé?

11 Qu'est-ce qu'on fait?

A French exchange student (a classmate) asks you what the weather is like in your town in the summer and in the winter and what people do during these seasons. Answer his or her questions, giving as much information as possible.

12 Dans une station de sports d'hiver

Have a conversation with a classmate. Tell as much as you can about what people do at a ski resort. Find out which one of you knows more about skiing. If skiing is a sport that is new to you, tell whether you think you would like to ski.

13 Dans quelle ville?

With a classmate, look at this weather map that appeared in a Paris newspaper. You are both in Paris and you want to take a short side trip. Since you both have definite preferences concerning weather, use the map to help make a decision. Choose what city you want to go to, tell why, and explain what you are going to do there.

ENCORE PLUS *For more practice using words from* ***Mots 2****, do Activity 35 on page H36 at the end of this book.*

Vocabulaire

Assessment

- As an informal assessment, have students write three sentences describing the sporting activities from **Mots 1** and **2** that can be mimed. Then they choose a partner who must correctly mime the activity in front of the class when it is read only once or twice.
- You may also wish to check for comprehension by reading sentences, words, or expressions from **Mots 2** in random order and having individuals point to the corresponding illustration on Vocabulary Transparencies 11.4–11.5.
- Show magazine pictures that depict different types of weather. Have students say what the weather is in each one.

ENCORE PLUS This *infogap* activity will allow students to practice in pairs. The activity should be very manageable for them, since all vocabulary and structures are familiar to them.

Answers to Commençons

10 *Answers will vary but may include:*

1. Oui, Christine a appris à faire du ski.
2. Son père a appris à Christine à faire du ski.
3. Oui, elle a eu un bon moniteur.
4. Christine a mis un anorak vert.
5. Oui, elle a mis des gants, une écharpe et un bonnet.
6. Oui, elle a mis ses chaussures de ski et ses skis.
7. Oui, elle a pris le télésiège.
8. Elle a descendu la piste verte.
9. Oui, il a fait très froid. Il a gelé.

11 *Answers will vary depending on the type of weather where students live.*

12 *Answers will vary but may include:*

—Dans une station de sports d'hiver on peut faire du ski de fond ou du ski alpin. J'aime beaucoup le ski de fond.
—Et on monte au sommet comment?
—On peut prendre un télésiège. Il y a aussi de très bons moniteurs. On peut apprendre très vite.
—Moi, je ne veux pas faire de ski. Je crois que c'est trop dangereux.

13 *Answers will vary depending upon the city students choose.*

Structure

1 Preparation

Resource Manager

Audio Activities Booklet TE, pages 138–139
Audiocassette 7A/CD 7
Workbook, pages 109–111
Quizzes 3–5, pages 56–58
ExamView Pro®

Bellringer Review

Use BRR Transparency 11.3 or write the following on the board.
Make a list of everything you will take with you on your ski vacation.

2 Presentation

Le passé composé des verbes irréguliers

Note: The past participles have been grouped by their sound and spelling to make the learning easier for students.

Step 1 Explain Item 1 quickly to students. Have them repeat the **/i/** and **/ü/** sounds in isolation. Then have them repeat after you the past participles in the list.

Step 2 Write the infinitives from the chart on the board. As you write each one, have the class give you the appropriate past participle. Write it alongside the infinitive.

Step 3 In the case of the **/i/** verbs, underline the **s** and **t.** Tell students to remember the difference in spelling even though the pronunciation is the same.

Step 4 Have students read the sentences in unison or call on individuals to read.

Step 5 Lead students through Item 2.

Structure

Describing more past actions
Le passé composé des verbes irréguliers

1. You have already learned that the past participles of regular verbs end in the sounds **/é/, /i/,** and **/ü/.** The past participles of most irregular verbs also end in the sounds **/i/** or **/ü/,** even though they are not spelled the same way.

Infinitif → participe passé /i/		Infinitif → participe passé /ü/	
dire	dit	avoir	eu
écrire	écrit	croire	cru
		voir	vu
mettre	mis	boire	bu
permettre	permis	devoir	dû
		pouvoir	pu
prendre	pris	lire	lu
apprendre	appris	recevoir	reçu
comprendre	compris	vouloir	voulu

J'ai pris des leçons de natation.
J'ai appris à nager.
J'ai eu un bon moniteur.

Tu as lu son livre?
Il a écrit un livre?
Tu as compris ce qu'il a dit?

2. The verbs **être** and **faire** have irregular past participles.

être → été   faire → fait

J'ai fait un voyage à Megève l'année dernière.
J'ai été content d'apprendre à faire du ski.

Une classe de ski

FUN-FACTS

En France, les écoles primaires ont des classes de neige. Les élèves vont dans une station de sports d'hiver. Le matin, ils ont des cours de maths, d'histoire, etc. L'après-midi, des moniteurs apprennent à faire du ski aux élèves.

Il y a des classes de neige aux États-Unis?

Answers to Continuons

14

1. Oui, Gilles a mis son anorak.
2. Oui, son ami a dit «Bonne chance» à Gilles.
3. Oui, son ami a déjà fait du ski aujourd'hui.
4. Oui, Gilles a bien fait du ski.
5. Oui, il a eu un accident.
6. Oui, après l'accident il a lu un livre pour les débutants.

Continuons
Let's put our words together

14 Historiette Gilles a fait du ski.
Répondez que oui.

1. Gilles a mis son anorak?
2. Son ami a dit «Bonne chance» à Gilles?
3. Son ami a déjà fait du ski aujourd'hui?
4. Gilles a bien fait du ski?
5. Il a eu un accident?
6. Après l'accident, il a lu un livre pour les débutants?

Une vue de la ville de Québec

15 Ce matin
Donnez des réponses personnelles.

1. Tu as pris ton petit déjeuner à quelle heure ce matin?
2. Qu'est-ce que tu as bu au petit déjeuner?
3. Est-ce que tu as lu le journal ce matin? Et tes parents?
4. Est-ce que tu as reçu une lettre?
5. Est-ce que tu as vu tes copains avant les cours?
6. Est-ce que tu as dit bonjour à ton prof de français?

16 Qu'est-ce que tu as dit?
Complétez d'après le modèle.

—J'____ que j'____ ce que j'____.
—J'ai dit que j'ai lu ce que j'ai écrit.

1. Il ____ qu'il ____ ce qu'il ____.
2. Nous ____ que nous ____ ce que nous ____.
3. Tu ____ que tu ____ ce que tu ____.
4. J'____ que j'____ ce que j'____.
5. Vous ____ que vous ____ ce que vous ____.
6. Elles ____ qu'elles ____ ce qu'elles ____.

Answers to Continuons

15 *Answers will vary but may include:*

1. J'ai pris mon petit déjeuner à six heures et demie ce matin.
2. J'ai bu du jus d'orange.
3. Oui, j'ai lu le journal ce matin. Mes parents ont lu le journal aussi.
4. Oui, j'ai reçu une lettre.
5. Non, je n'ai pas vu mes copains avant les cours.
6. Oui, j'ai dit bonjour à mon prof de français.

16

1. Il a dit qu'il a lu ce qu'il a écrit.
2. Nous avons dit que nous avons lu ce que nous avons écrit.
3. Tu as dit que tu as lu ce que tu as écrit.
4. J'ai dit que j'ai lu ce que j'ai écrit.
5. Vous avez dit que vous avez lu ce que vous avez écrit.
6. Elles ont dit qu'elles ont lu ce qu'elles ont écrit.

3 Practice

Continuons
Let's put our words together

14 Have students retell orally the information in this activity.

Writing Development
Have students write the answers to Activity 14 in paragraph form.

Learning from Photos
(page 365 top) The beautiful city of Québec sits on a cliff above a rather narrow point of the Saint Lawrence River. The city is divided into the Upper Town and the Lower Town. The old town, **Le Vieux-Québec,** has many seventeenth and eighteenth century buildings and ramparts that once protected the city. UNESCO has designated **le Vieux-Québec** a World Heritage Site.

History Connection
The first European explorer to set foot on what is today Québec was the Frenchman Jacques Cartier. **La Nouvelle France** was not founded, however, until 1608 when another French explorer, Samuel de Champlain, set up a fort in Québec because of the military advantages of its location.

Fun Facts
The word **Québec** comes from the Algonquin Indian word meaning, "where the river narrows."

Approximately 96% of the people living in the area of **Québec** city (approx. 650,000) are French-speaking.

17 Have students retell the **Historiette** in their own words.

18 The verbs are given here as a guide, so students do not try to use a verb conjugated with **être.** By the end of this chapter, they will be able to use the **être** verbs. **Expansion:** After having students work in pairs, have them work in groups of four. Have them practice asking in the **vous** form and answering in the **nous** form. Then have them report back to the class to practice the **ils/elles** forms.

Learning from Photos

(page 366) Have students identify everything they can in the photo.

Chamonix is the oldest and biggest winter sports resort in France.

ENCORE PLUS This *infogap* activity will allow students to practice in pairs. The activity should be very manageable for them, since all vocabulary and structures are familiar to them.

17 Historiette À Chamonix

Complétez au passé composé.

Laurent aime beaucoup le ski. Son ami Étienne et lui __1__ (décider) d'aller faire du ski. Ils __2__ (prendre) le Guide Michelin et __3__ (lire) la description de plusieurs stations. Finalement, ils __4__ (choisir) Chamonix. Ils __5__ (avoir) de la chance. Les parents de Laurent __6__ (permettre) aux deux garçons de prendre leur voiture. La voiture, c'est plus pratique que le train! Alors les deux copains __7__ (mettre) leurs skis sur la voiture et… en route! Mais la voiture, ça n'est pas toujours plus pratique que le train: il y __8__ (avoir) une avalanche et la route __9__ (être) bloquée pendant dix heures!

Chamonix, France

18 L'été dernier

Your classmate wants to know what you did last summer. Tell him or her several things you did, using some of the verbs below. Then reverse roles.

recevoir, prendre, écrire, voir, bronzer, nager, lire, pouvoir, boire, mettre, faire

ENCORE PLUS *For more practice using irregular verbs in the* ***passé composé****, do Activity 36 on page H37 at the end of this book.*

Answers to Continuons

17

1. ont décidé
2. ont pris
3. ont lu
4. ont choisi
5. ont eu
6. ont permis
7. ont mis
8. a eu
9. a été

18 *Answers will vary.*

Students can use any or all of the verbs that appear in the list.

Making negative statements
Les mots négatifs

1. You already know the negative expressions **ne... pas** and **ne... plus.** Study the following negative expressions that function the same way as **ne... pas** and **ne... plus.**

Affirmatif	Négatif
Elle voit quelque chose.	Elle ne voit rien.
Elle voit quelqu'un.	Elle ne voit personne.
Il lit toujours.	Il ne lit jamais.
Il lit souvent.	Il ne lit jamais.
Il lit quelquefois.	Il ne lit jamais.
Il lit encore.	Il ne lit plus.

Rappelez-vous que...

Un, une, des, du, de la, de l' change to **de (d')** after **pas** and other negative expressions.

Il n'a pas d'amis.
Il ne fait jamais de sport.
Elle n'écrit plus de lettres.

2. With the exception of **personne,** the negative words go around the verb **avoir** in the **passé composé.** **Personne** goes after the past participle.

Je n'ai jamais dit ça!
On n'a plus parlé de ça. *mais* **Je n'ai vu personne.**
On n'a rien dit. **Et je n'ai parlé à personne!**

Continuons
Let's put our words together

19 Le matin, en haut de la montagne Répondez que non.

Il voit quelque chose?
Non, il ne voit rien.

1. Il dit quelque chose?
2. Il entend quelque chose?
3. Il regarde quelque chose?
4. Il voit quelqu'un?
5. Il regarde quelqu'un?
6. Il parle à quelqu'un?
7. Il attend quelqu'un?

Answers to Continuons

19

1. Non, il ne dit rien.
2. Non, il n'entend rien.
3. Non, il ne regarde rien.
4. Non, il ne voit personne.
5. Non, il ne regarde personne.
6. Non, il ne parle à personne.
7. Non, il n'attend personne.

Structure

1 Preparation

Bellringer Review

Use BRR Transparency 11.4 or write the following on the board.
Write three expressions about winter weather and three about summer weather.

2 Presentation

Les mots négatifs

Step 1 Present negative expressions by holding up an object (pencil, book, etc.) as you say: **J'ai quelque chose. (Je vois quelque chose).** Then put the object away and say: **Je n'ai rien. (Je ne vois rien).**

Step 2 Have a student stand by you as you say: **Je vois quelqu'un. J'entends quelqu'un.** Then have the person go away as you say: **Je ne vois personne. Je n'entends personne.**

Step 3 Lead students through Items 1 and 2 on page 367.

Note: Point out that the words **rien, personne,** and **jamais** can stand alone as short answers. For example: **Qu'est-ce que tu as? Rien! Qui parle? Personne. Tu y vas souvent? Non, jamais.**

3 Practice

Continuons
Let's put our words together

19 Have students do this activity once with books open and then again with one partner, asking the questions in random order while the other partner answers with books closed. Change roles.

20, **21**, **22** and **23** Do these activities first orally with books closed. Call on individuals to respond. Activities can be done again with books open for reading reinforcement.

Learning from Photos

(page 368 top) La Martinique is **un département d'outre-mer (un D.O.M.).** It is a popular winter destination for French vacationers. It is also very popular with French Canadians. The same holds true for Guadeloupe.
(page 368 bottom) Ask the students the following questions about the photo:

C'est où?
Qu'est-ce que les gens font?
Qu'est-ce qu'ils portent?
Il fait quel temps?
C'est quelle saison?

Reaching All Students

Additional Practice Write the following verbs on the board:

Je vois	**J'achète**	**J'attends**
Je veux	**J'entends**	**J'écris**
J'ai	**Je dis**	**J'apprends**

Have students use either **quelque chose** or **quelqu'un** with each verb. Then have them put the sentences in the negative with **ne... rien** or **ne... personne.**

De la planche à voile à la Martinique

20 Elle ne fait jamais de sport.

Répondez d'après le modèle.

—Jeanne adore nager.
—Elle dit ça, mais elle ne nage jamais!

1. Jeanne adore faire du surf.
2. Elle adore aller à la plage.
3. Elle adore faire de la planche à voile.
4. Elle adore faire du sport.
5. Elle adore jouer au tennis.
6. Elle adore faire du ski nautique.

21 C'est fini! Répondez que non.

1. Ta grand-mère travaille encore?
2. Ta sœur joue encore au foot?
3. Tu écris encore à ton amie Marie?
4. Tes amis et toi, vous allez encore en vacances à Chamonix?
5. Tes amis sont encore à Paris?

22 Non, non et non! Répondez que non.

1. Tu as dit quelque chose?
2. Il a vu quelque chose?
3. Ils ont acheté quelque chose?
4. Ils ont appris quelque chose?
5. Ils ont toujours fait du sport?
6. Il a vu quelqu'un?
7. Ils ont entendu quelqu'un?
8. Tu as téléphoné à quelqu'un?

23 L'été

Work with a classmate. Tell him or her some things you like to do in the summer. For some reason, you didn't get to do these things last summer. Tell what you didn't do.

Une piscine, Paris

Answers to Continuons

20

1. Elle dit ça, mais elle ne fait jamais de surf.
2. Elle dit ça, mais elle ne va jamais à la plage.
3. Elle dit ça, mais elle ne fait jamais de planche à voile.
4. Elle dit ça, mais elle ne fait jamais de sport.
5. Elle dit ça, mais elle ne joue jamais au tennis.
6. Elle dit ça, mais elle ne fait jamais de ski nautique.

21

1. Non, elle ne travaille plus.
2. Non, elle ne joue plus au foot.
3. Non, je n'écris plus à mon amie Marie.
4. Non, mes amis et moi, nous n'allons plus en vacances à Chamonix.
5. Non, mes amis ne sont plus à Paris.

22

1. Non, je n'ai rien dit.
2. Non, il n'a rien vu.
3. Non, ils n'ont rien acheté.
4. Non, ils n'ont rien appris.
5. Non, ils n'ont jamais fait de sport.
6. Non, il n'a vu personne.
7. Non, ils n'ont entendu personne.
8. Non, je n'ai téléphoné à personne.

Describing more past actions
Le passé composé avec être

1. Certain verbs form their **passé composé** with **être** instead of **avoir.** Many verbs that are conjugated with **être** express motion to or from a place.

arriver	**Il est arrivé.**
entrer	**Il est entré.**
monter	**Il est monté.**
descendre	**Il est descendu.**
aller	**Il est allé.**
partir	**Il est parti.**
sortir	**Il est sorti.**
rentrer	**Il est rentré.**

Rappelez-vous que...

Ne... pas goes around the verb **avoir** in the **passé composé.** It also goes around the verb **être** in the **passé composé.**
Il n'est pas arrivé.

2. The past participle of verbs conjugated with **être** must agree with the subject in number (singular and plural) and in gender (masculine and feminine). Note that when **on** means **nous,** the past participle agreement is the same as for **nous.** Study the following forms.

Masculin		Féminin	
je	suis parti	je	suis partie
tu	es parti	tu	es partie
il	est parti	elle	est partie
on	est partis	on	est parties
nous	sommes partis	nous	sommes parties
vous	êtes parti(s)	vous	êtes partie(s)
ils	sont partis	elles	sont parties

Note that since all the past participles of the verbs above end in a vowel, there is no difference in sound.

3. Although the following verbs do not express motion to or from a place, they are also conjugated with **être.**

rester	**Il est resté huit jours.**	*He stayed a week.*
tomber	**Il est tombé.**	*He fell.*
naître	**Elle est née en France.**	*She was born in France.*
mourir	**Elle est morte en 2000.**	*She died in 2000.*

Structure

1 Preparation

Bellringer Review

Use BRR Transparency 11.5 or write the following on the board.
Give the opposite of the following.
For example: **jamais** **toujours**
1. **quelqu'un**
2. **quelquefois**
3. **rien**
4. **souvent**
5. **encore**
6. **quelque chose**

2 Presentation

Le passé composé avec être

Note: It is up to the discretion of the teacher to decide the degree of importance to be placed on the spelling of the past participle of these verbs.

Step 1 Have students open their books to page 369. Lead them through Items 1–3. Model the examples and have students repeat chorally.

Step 2 Call on a volunteer to dramatize the verbs listed in Item 1.

Step 3 As you write the paradigm in Item 2 on the board, you may want to add the endings to the past participle with a different color chalk or underline them for emphasis.

Note: The difference between **être** and **avoir** with some of these verbs will be presented in a later chapter.

Reaching All Students

For the Younger Students/ Visual Learners **La maison du verbe être** Have students draw a cut-away side-view of a two-story house. Have them draw in the **être** verbs in appropriate locations in the house.

Some ideas include **monter/descendre** *(people going up/down stairs),* **naître** *(stork arriving at chimney with baby),* **mourir** *(gravestone in yard),* etc.

Auditory Learners Edith Piaf's classic song, *Non, je ne regrette rien,* is a wonderful way to reinforce the **ne... rien** construction. You may just play it for students to listen to, or you may want to print the lyrics with the negative constructions missing for a **dictée** exercise. Younger students may enjoy singing along!

3 Practice

Continuons
Let's put our words together

24, **25** and **26** Have students retell the activities in their own words.

27 and **29** Have students work in pairs. Have students report back to the class what they learned about their partner.

Learning from Photos

(page 370 top) Grenoble is the capital of Dauphiné in the Alps. It is a fast growing city with many new skyscrapers. It is home to several universities, and major companies that specialize in electronics, engineering, and nuclear research. Surrounded by mountains, Grenoble is a modern, cosmopolitan city.

(page 370 bottom) Villefranche on the Côte d'Azur is a lovely small town with excellent fish restaurants along the quayside. The narrow bay at Villefranche is deep enough for large ships to anchor.

Continuons
Let's put our words together

24 Historiette Un voyage à Grenoble
Répondez que oui.

1. Carine est allée à Grenoble?
2. Elle est arrivée à la gare de Lyon à 10 h?
3. Elle est allée sur le quai?
4. Elle est montée dans le train?
5. Le train est parti à l'heure?
6. Le train est arrivé à Grenoble à l'heure?
7. Carine est descendue du train à Grenoble?
8. Elle est sortie de la gare?

Un téléphérique, Grenoble

25 Historiette À l'école Donnez des réponses personnelles.

1. Tu es allé(e) à l'école ce matin?
2. Tu es arrivé(e) à quelle heure?
3. Tu es entré(e) immédiatement?
4. Tu es sorti(e) de l'école à quelle heure hier?
5. Tu es rentré(e) chez toi à quelle heure?

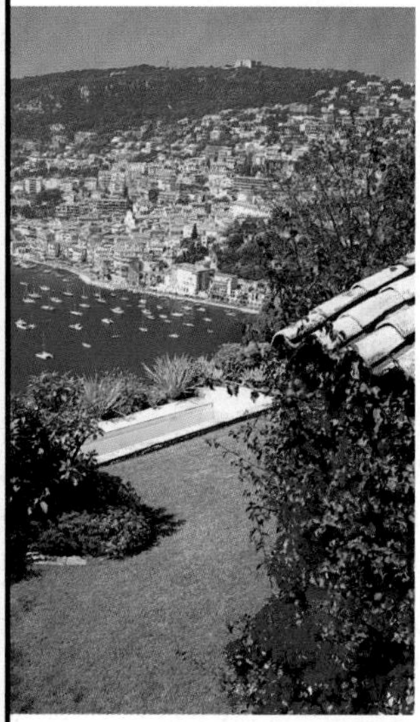
Villefranche, Côte d'Azur

26 Historiette Au bord de la mer
Mettez au passé composé.

Michel et sa sœur vont au bord de la mer. Ils partent à l'heure. Ils montent dans l'autocar. Ils arrivent à Villefranche. Ils descendent de l'autocar. Ils vont à la plage. La sœur de Michel va nager. Elle sort de l'eau. Tous les deux, ils vont au café. Ils rentrent chez eux très tard.

27 Qui est sorti? Donnez des réponses personnelles.

1. Le mois dernier, vous êtes allés au cinéma, tes copains et toi?
2. Vous y êtes allés comment? En voiture? En bus?
3. Qu'est-ce que vous avez vu comme film?
4. Vous êtes partis tous ensemble?
5. Vous êtes arrivés en retard?
6. Vous êtes allés manger et boire quelque chose après le film?
7. À quelle heure est-ce que vous êtes rentrés chez vous?

Answers to Continuons

24

1. Oui, Carine est allée à Grenoble.
2. Oui, elle est arrivée à la gare de Lyon à 10 h.
3. Oui, elle est allée sur le quai.
4. Oui, elle est montée dans le train.
5. Oui, le train est parti à l'heure.
6. Oui, le train est arrivé à Grenoble à l'heure.
7. Oui, Carine est descendue du train à Grenoble.
8. Oui, elle est sortie de la gare.

25 *Answers will vary but may include:*

1. Oui, je suis allé(e) à l'école ce matin.
2. Je suis arrivé(e) à huit heures.
3. Oui, je suis entré(e) immédiatement.
4. Je suis sorti(e) de l'école à trois heures hier.
5. Je suis rentré(e) chez moi à cinq heures.

26

Michel et sa sœur sont allés au bord de la mer. Ils sont partis à l'heure. Ils sont montés dans l'autocar. Ils sont arrivés à Villefranche. Ils sont descendus de l'autocar. Ils sont allés à la plage. La sœur de Michel est allée nager. Elle est sortie de l'eau. Tous les deux, ils sont allés au café. Ils sont rentrés chez eux très tard.

28 Une excursion Complétez en utilisant le passé composé.

Mathieu: Tu ___1___ (aller) en Normandie avec Laure. C'est ça?

Thérèse: C'est ça. Nous ___2___ (aller) au Mont-Saint-Michel.

Mathieu: Vous avez aimé?

Thérèse: Nous avons adoré! Nous ___3___ (monter) à la basilique. Heureusement, nous ___4___ (arriver) avant tous les touristes!

Mathieu: Vous ___5___ (sortir) sur la terrasse?

Thérèse: Oui. Superbe, la vue! Mais des cars entiers de touristes ___6___ (arriver), alors nous ___7___ (partir). Nous ___8___ (rentrer) à l'hôtel.

Mont-Saint-Michel, Normandie

Saint-Jean-de-Luz, Pays Basque

29 Être ou ne pas être
Donnez des réponses personnelles.

1. Tu es né(e) quel jour?
2. Tu es né(e) à l'hôpital? Dans quel hôpital?
3. Ta mère est restée combien de jours à l'hôpital?
4. Tes parents sont nés où?
5. Et tes grands-parents, ils sont nés où?
6. Ta grand-mère est morte? Et ton grand-père?

30 À Saint-Jean-de-Luz
 Work with a classmate. You both went to Saint-Jean-de-Luz, on the Atlantic Ocean, near the Spanish border, but you did not go together. Ask each other what you did there. Find out as much as you can about each other's trip.

For more practice using the **passé composé** with **être**, do Activity 37 on page H38 at the end of this book.

Vous êtes sur le bon chemin. Allez-y!

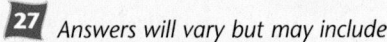

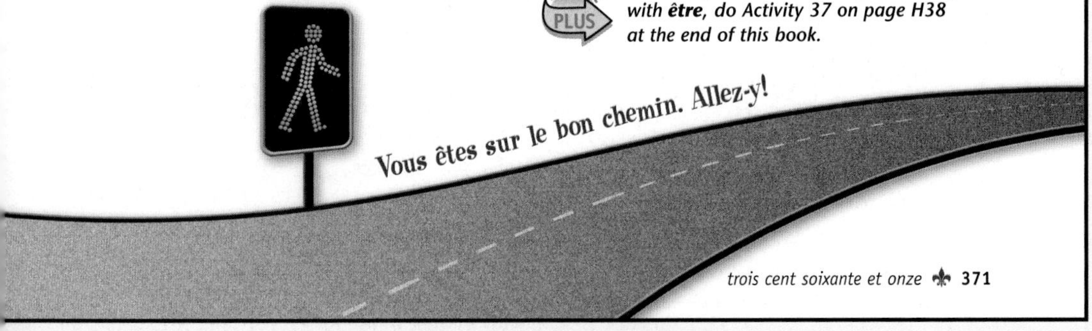

Learning from Photos

(page 371 right) Please refer to pages 278–279 for more information about Mont-Saint-Michel.

(page 371 left) Saint-Jean-de-Luz is a picturesque resort and fishing village on the Atlantic in the Basque country, very close to the Spanish border. The harbor area seen in this photo has become an important sardine-fishing port. The building in the photo is the **maison de l'Infante,** so called because it was here that the Infanta María Teresa of Spain stayed before her marriage to Louis XIV. The door through which Louis XIV passed to marry her still stands.

FUN-FACTS

Sailors from the little village of Saint-Jean-de-Luz were the first to fish the Grand Banks off Newfoundland in the sixteenth century.

 Assessment

As an informal assessment, you may wish to write the infinitives on page 369 on the board. Call on students to make up an original sentence using any verb they wish.

Allez-y!
At this point in the chapter, students have learned all the vocabulary and structure necessary to complete the chapter. The conversation and cultural readings that follow recycle all the material learned up to this point.

ANSWERS TO Continuons

27 *Answers will vary but may include:*

1. Oui, le mois dernier mes copains et moi, nous sommes allés au cinéma.
2. Nous y sommes allés en bus.
3. Nous avons vu une comédie.
4. Oui, nous sommes partis tous ensemble.
5. Non, nous ne sommes pas arrivés en retard.
6. Oui, nous sommes allés manger et boire quelque chose après le film.
7. Nous sommes rentrés chez nous à _____.

28

1. es allée
2. sommes allées
3. sommes montées
4. sommes arrivées
5. êtes sorties
6. sont arrivés
7. sommes parties
8. sommes rentrées

1 Preparation

Resource Manager

Audio Activities Booklet TE, pages 139–140
Audiocassette 7A/CD 7
CD-ROM

Bellringer Review

Use BRR Transparency 11.6 or write the following on the board.
Imagine you went to Paris last summer. Write five things you did there.

2 Presentation

Step 1 Tell students they are going to hear a conversation between Laurène and Marine, who are discussing what they did yesterday.

Step 2 Have them watch the conversation on the CD-ROM or listen as you read the conversation or play Audiocassette 7A/CD 7.

Step 3 Have students work in pairs to practice the conversation. Then have several pairs present it to the class.

Step 4 You may have a more able student retell the conversation in narrative form in his or her own words.

Glencoe Technology

CD-ROM
On the CD-ROM, students can watch a dramatization of this conversation. They can then play the role of either one of the characters and record themselves in the conversation.

Conversation

À la plage

Laurène: Qu'est-ce que tu as fait hier?
Marine: Je suis allée à la plage.
Laurène: Tu as eu de la chance. Il a fait très beau hier!
Marine: Oui, mais je suis arrivée à la plage, j'ai regardé dans mon sac et… pas de maillot!
Laurène: Ben, qu'est-ce que tu as fait, alors?
Marine: Je suis allée dans l'eau.
Laurène: Sans maillot!
Marine: Oui, mais en blue-jean! Et toi, qu'est-ce que tu as fait?
Laurène: Absolument rien. Je n'ai rien fait et je n'ai vu personne.

Après la conversation

Répondez.

1. Marine est allée où hier?
2. Il a fait beau?
3. Elle a pris son maillot?
4. Elle a nagé?
5. Elle est allée dans l'eau sans maillot?
6. Elle est allée dans l'eau comment?
7. Et Laurène, qu'est-ce qu'elle a fait hier?
8. Elle a vu quelqu'un?

Answers to Après la conversation

1. Elle est allée à la plage.
2. Oui, il a fait beau.
3. Non, elle n'a pas pris son maillot.
4. Oui, elle a nagé.
5. Oui, elle est allée dans l'eau sans maillot.
6. Elle est allée dans l'eau en blue-jean.
7. Elle n'a rien fait.
8. Non, elle n'a vu personne.

Learning from Photos

(page 372) Saint-Barthélemy is one of the islands of the French Antilles. It is only eight square miles and is quite hilly, with many small, sheltered inlets. Although it is becoming more touristy, Saint-Barthélemy is still quite unspoiled, and the island has not been over-built with high-rise condos or glitzy hotels.

Parlons un peu plus
Let's talk some more

A **Quel temps fait-il?** Work with a classmate. Pretend that one of you lives in Montreal and the other lives in Fort-de-France in Martinique. Compare what it's like on a typical day in February. Tell some things you do in February.

B **À Tahiti** Work with a classmate. Pretend you spent a week on the beach in Tahiti. Tell your partner about your vacation and answer any questions he or she may have.

Martinique
Les Plages

Vauclin / Plage de Macabou : Entrée payante, plage aménagée, sable blanc et raisiniers bord de mer, tables pour pique-nique.

Plage du Diamant / Plage de la Dizac : Plage sauvage, très ventilée, beaucoup de vagues. Littoral ombragé et aménagé. Baignade avec prudence.

Anses d'Arlets / Plage de Grande Anse et Petite Anse : Jolies plages de sable blanc, très ensoleillées. Mer très calme, peu ventée, restaurants à proximité.

Sainte-Luce : Plage de Corps de Garde et de Gros Raisin, plages animées et aménagées, tables et bancs, sable blanc.

L'Anse Céron / L'Anse Couleuvre : Belle plage aménagée et typique. Sable noir. En continuant le petit chemin pittoresque, à un kilomètre de marche, vous arriverez à l'Anse Couleuvre, plage déserte de dable noir. Eaux profondes.

Plage du Carbet / Anse Turin : Grande plage de sable noir, eaux profondes.

Prononciation

Le son /y/

1. The sound /y/ occurs in two positions: final, and between two vowel sounds. Repeat the following.

fille	**soleil**	**travaille**	**taille**
bouteille	**maillot**	**travailler**	**billet**

2. Now repeat the following sentences.

J'ai un vieux maillot.
On ne travaille pas bien au soleil.

un soleil en maillot

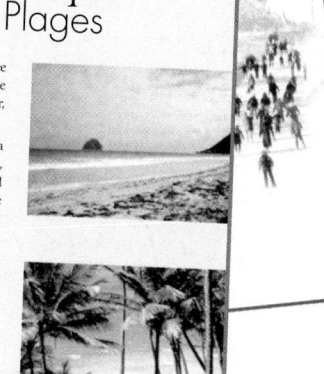

Answers to Parlons un peu plus

A *Answers will vary.*
Students will give summer weather expressions and activities when talking about Martinique and winter ones when talking about Montreal.

B *Answers will vary but may include:*
—Il a fait beau à Tahiti?
—Oui, il a fait beau. Il a fait chaud et il a fait du soleil.
—Qu'est-ce que tu as fait?
—Je suis allé(e) à la plage. J'ai appris à faire du ski nautique. J'ai beaucoup nagé aussi.

Conversation

3 Practice

Parlons un peu plus
Let's talk some more

A and **B** Have students work in pairs. You may wish to choose a pair of students to do these activities for the class.

Fun-Facts

Christopher Columbus "discovered" the island of Saint-Barthélemy in 1493. The first French colony there was wiped out by the Carib Indians. A new group of colonists from Brittany and Normandy arrived in 1694, and their industrious, friendly descendants still prosper there today.

Prononciation

Step 1 Model the key phrase **un soleil en maillot** and have students repeat in unison.

Step 2 Now lead students through the information on page 373 and model the other words and sentences.

Step 3 You may wish to give the students the following **dictée**:
La gentille fille a un billet.
Le soleil brille. La fille ne travaille pas en maillot.

Step 4 For additional pronunciation practice you may wish to use the Pronunciation Transparency P 11.

Resource Manager

Audio Activities Booklet TE, pages 141–142
Audiocassette 7A/CD 7

Bellringer Review

Use BRR Transparency 11.7 or write the following on the board.
Make a list of all the words you associate with the following places.
une station balnéaire
une station de sports d'hiver

National Standards

Cultures
The reading about a trip to Canada on pages 374–375 and the related activities on page 375 allow students to find out more about this important French-speaking country.

Presentation

Pre-reading

Step 1 You may want to have students look at the photos on pages 374–375 now.

Step 2 Read and discuss the Reading Strategy, page 374.

Step 3 Have students scan the reading quickly and silently.

Reading

Step Lead students through the **Lecture** on pages 374–375 by having individuals read two to three sentences at a time. After each one reads, ask others comprehension questions.

Step 2 Ask five or six questions that review the main points. Call on individuals to answer. Answers will give an organized summary of the **Lecture.**

Lectures culturelles

Reading Strategy

Summarizing
When reading an informative passage, we try to remember what we read. Summarizing helps us to do this. The easiest way to summarize is to begin to read for the general sense and take notes on what you are reading. It is best to write a summarizing statement for each paragraph and then one for the entire passage.

Un petit voyage au Canada

En février, pendant les huit jours de vacances d'hiver, les élèves de Madame Lebrun sont allés au Canada, avec Madame Lebrun, bien sûr. Ils ont pris le train à New York et sont descendus à Montréal. Ils ont passé trois jours à Montréal. Montréal est la deuxième ville francophone après Paris. Les élèves de Madame Lebrun ont été très contents parce qu'ils ont pu pratiquer leur français. Et ils ont tout compris!

Après trois jours à Montréal, ils sont partis pour le parc du Mont-Tremblant. Le Mont-Tremblant est une station de sports d'hiver tout près de la jolie ville de Québec. Ils sont arrivés au parc à midi. Ils ont mis leurs skis et sont montés au sommet de la montagne en télésiège. De là-haut, quelle vue superbe on a sur les montagnes et les vallées couvertes de neige! Tu n'as jamais vu de montagnes couvertes de neige? Il n'y a rien de plus beau!

Vieux-Port à Montréal

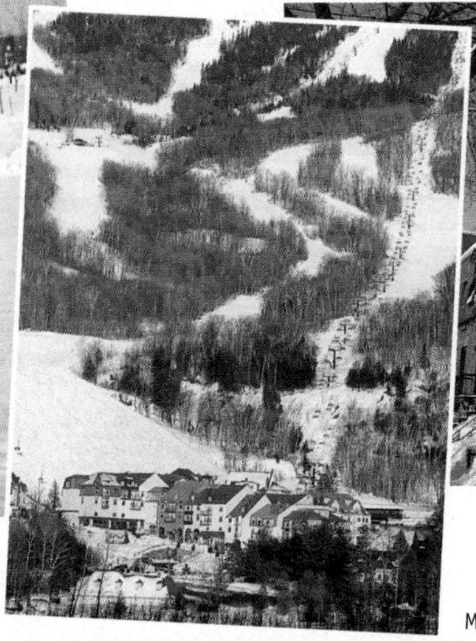
Mont-Tremblant, Québec

Une rue résidentielle, Montréal

FUN-FACTS

The color coding for the difficulty level of ski slopes is different in Canada and France.

Skieurs	Canada	France
Débutants	piste verte	piste verte
Moyens	piste jaune	piste bleue
Bons	piste rouge	piste rouge
Très bons	piste noire	piste noire

Note that the only difference is for **moyens.**

Skis aux pieds et bâtons en mains, ils ont commencé à descendre la piste. Ils ont choisi une piste verte. Au Québec, les pistes vertes sont les pistes faciles pour débutants. Après trois heures sur les pistes, ils sont allés à la patinoire où ils ont fait du patin à glace.

À neuf heures du soir, un des élèves a dit: «Moi, je n'ai jamais été aussi fatigué!» Ça a été le signal de la retraite vers les dortoirs[1]. Ils ont tous dormi comme des souches[2]!

[1] dortoirs *dormitories*
[2] souches *tree stumps*

Après la lecture

A Au Canada Répondez.

1. La classe de Madame Lebrun est allée où?
2. Ils y sont allés quand?
3. Ils y sont allés comment?
4. Ils ont pratiqué leur français où?
5. Après trois jours à Montréal, ils sont partis pour où?
6. Qu'est-ce que le Mont-Tremblant?
7. C'est près de quelle ville?
8. Ils y sont arrivés à quelle heure?
9. Ils sont montés jusqu'où?
10. Qu'est-ce qu'ils ont vu du sommet?

B Les vacances d'hiver Vrai ou faux?

1. Les élèves ont eu un mois de vacances.
2. Ils ont pris le train pour aller à Montréal.
3. Montréal est une petite ville.
4. Les élèves sont montés à skis au sommet de la montagne.
5. Pour faire du ski, ils ont mis des bâtons.
6. Ils ont pris la piste rouge pour les très bons skieurs.
7. Ils ont fait aussi du patin à glace.

Post-reading

Have students do the **Après la lecture** activities on page 375 orally after reading the selection in class. Then assign these activities to be written at home. Go over them again the following day.

Après la lecture

A Allow students to refer to the story to look up the answers or you may use this activity as a testing device for factual recall.

B **Expansion:** After doing Activity B, you may wish to have the students correct each false statement made in the activity.

Geography Connection

Mont-Tremblant is the highest peak in the Laurentian mountains. Located north of Montreal, it is the number one ski resort in eastern North America. It has 90 marked runs and more than 600 skiable acres.

FRENCH Online

Encourage students to take advantage of this opportunity to learn more about French-speaking Canada. Perhaps you can do this in class or in a lab if students do not have Internet access at home.

Answers to Après la lecture

A

1. La classe est allée au Canada.
2. Ils y sont allés en hiver.
3. Ils y sont allés en train.
4. Ils ont pratiqué leur français à Montréal.
5. Ils sont partis pour le parc du Mont-Tremblant.
6. Le Mont-Tremblant est une station de sports d'hiver.
7. C'est près de la ville de Québec.
8. Ils y sont arrivés à midi.
9. Ils sont montés au sommet.
10. Ils ont vu des montagnes couvertes de neige.

B

1. F
2. V
3. F
4. F
5. F
6. F
7. V

National Standards

Cultures
This selection familiarizes students with the traditional summer vacation in France.

Attention!

This reading is optional. You may skip it completely, have the entire class read it, have only several students read it and report to the class, or assign it for extra credit.

Presentation

Step 1 Ask students about their family vacations. Do they stay at home or go away?

Step 2 Have students read the **Lecture** quickly.

Step 3 Ask what new information they learned about **Les grandes vacances** in France.

Après la lecture

If possible, bring in pictures or slides of popular French beach or mountain vacation areas and share them with your students. Some sources for these materials might be your own collection, that of an acquaintance, your library, or a local travel agency.

Learning from Photos

(page 376) Have students identify and describe everything they can in the photos. For information on Biarritz, please see pages 71 and 149. For information on Étretat, please see page 278.

Lecture supplémentaire 1

Les grandes vacances

Le mois d'août, c'est le mois des grandes vacances en France. Beaucoup de Français quittent la ville et vont à la montagne, à la campagne[1] ou au bord de la mer.

En été, quand le soleil brille dans le ciel bleu, il est fabuleux de passer la journée à la plage. La France est un pays de plages merveilleuses. Il y a plus de mille kilomètres de côtes et des stations balnéaires tout le long de ces côtes—sur la Manche au nord; sur l'océan Atlantique à l'ouest; sur la mer Méditerranée au sud.

Étretat, Normandie

Cannes, Côte d'Azur

Biarritz, Pays Basque

Vous voulez passer une petite semaine sur une belle plage en France? Vous voulez rentrer chez vous bien bronzé(e)s? Vous allez aller où?

[1] campagne *countryside*

Après la lecture

Au bord de la mer Identifiez.

1. le mois des grandes vacances en France
2. la mer qui sépare l'Angleterre de la France
3. l'océan à l'ouest de la France
4. la mer au sud de la France

Answers to Après la lecture

1. le mois d'août
2. la Manche
3. l'Atlantique
4. la Méditerranée

Lecture supplémentaire 2

Le carnaval

La neige arrive au Québec fin novembre et reste jusqu'au mois d'avril. Les jours sont courts, froids, mais très beaux. Le soleil brille souvent dans le ciel bleu et la neige scintille[1].

En février, les Québécois sortent de chez eux pour célébrer le carnaval. Des milliers de visiteurs vont à Québec à cette époque pour célébrer le carnaval. Pendant les dix jours de festivités, il y a un grand défilé de chars[2]. On construit un magnifique palais de glace et il y a un concours[3] de sculptures de glace.

Toutes ces festivités sont orchestrées par un gigantesque bonhomme de neige appelé «Bonhomme Carnaval».

[1] scintille *sparkles*
[2] défilé de chars *float parade*
[3] concours *contest*

«Bonhomme Carnaval», Québec

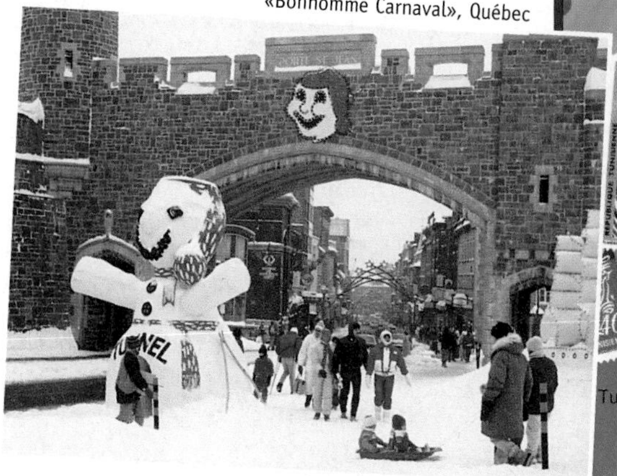

Le palais de glace, Québec

Après la lecture

Au Québec et à Québec Décrivez.

1. un jour d'hiver au Québec
2. le carnaval de Québec
3. «Bonhomme Carnaval»

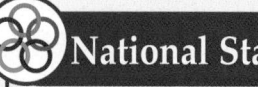

National Standards

Cultures
This selection familiarizes students with the Winter Carnival in Quebec.

Attention!

This reading is optional. You may skip it completely, have the entire class read it, have only several students read it and report to the class, or assign it for extra credit.

Presentation

Step 1 Discuss winter in the area where you live. Are there any special winter traditions related to the weather in your area?

Step 2 Have students read the **Lecture** quickly.

Step 3 Ask what new information they learned about **Le carnaval** in Quebec.

Après la lecture

After answering the questions on page 377, you may wish to have students make their own true or false statements about the reading.

Answers to Après la lecture

1. Un jour d'hiver au Québec est court et froid, mais le soleil brille souvent.
2. Le carnaval de Québec, c'est dix jours de festivités avec un grand défilé de chars.
3. «Bonhomme Carnaval» est un gigantesque bonhomme de neige.

Reaching All Students

For the Younger Students Have students paint a mural of **carnaval** activities. They can also include scenes of people skiing and skating. Have them label the activities in French. Hang the mural where it can be seen by other people in your school.

National Standards

Connections
This reading about painting and the photos of the famous works of art by French artists on pages 378–379 establish a connection with another discipline, allowing students to reinforce and further their knowledge of fine art through the study of French.

Attention!

The readings in the **Connexions** section are optional. They focus on some of the major disciplines taught in schools and universities. The vocabulary is useful for discussing such topics as history, literature, art, economics, business, science, etc. You may choose any of the following ways to do the readings in the **Connexions** sections.

Independent reading Have students read the selections and do the post-reading activities as homework, which you collect. This option is least intrusive on class time and requires a minimum of teacher involvement.

Homework with in-class follow-up Assign the readings and post-reading activities as homework. Review and discuss the material in class the next day.

Intensive in-class activity This option includes a pre-reading vocabulary presentation, in-class reading and discussion, assignment of the activities for homework, and a discussion of the assignment in class the following day.

CONNEXIONS

Les Beaux-Arts

La peinture

One may know a great deal or just a little about art. But almost everyone has at least some interest in art. How often have we heard, "I may not know anything about art, but I certainly know what I like"?

There is no doubt that France has produced many of the world's greatest artists. Do you recognize the names of these famous French artists: Renoir, Monet, Manet, Degas, Seurat, Boudin, Gauguin?

In 1874, two of these painters, Monet and Renoir, were among a group of artists who held a famous exhibition of their works in Paris. The critics laughed at their works and called the artists "Impressionists" to mock one of Monet's paintings entitled ***Impression, soleil levant***. Today, paintings by the Impressionists are among the most admired works in the history of art.

Claude Monet *La pie*

Claude Monet *La route sous la neige à Honfleur*

Les impressionnistes

On dit que les impressionnistes sont les peintres de la vie moderne. Ils ont peint la vie quotidienne[1] des gens (personnes) simples. Pour eux, tous les sujets sont bons. Ils ont peint des parcs, des gares, des usines[2]. Beaucoup de peintres impressionnistes ont préféré quitter leur atelier[3] pour aller peindre en plein air. Les scènes d'été et les scènes d'hiver sont des sujets favoris de plusieurs impressionnistes.

Voici deux tableaux de paysages d'hiver de Claude Monet—*La pie* et *La route sous la neige à Honfleur.*

[1] vie quotidienne *daily life*
[2] usines *factories*
[3] atelier *studio*

Eugène Boudin *La plage de Trouville*

Voici maintenant des scènes de plage. Eugène Boudin a peint *La plage de Trouville.*

Ce tableau *Sur la plage* a été peint par l'ami de Monet, Édouard Manet.

Georges Seurat a peint *Les baigneurs à Asnières.* Asnières est dans la banlieue[4] parisienne sur la Seine. Au fond, on voit les cheminées des usines de Clichy. Il fait très chaud et les ouvriers[5] font un petit plongeon dans la Seine.

[4] banlieue *suburbs*
[5] ouvriers *workers*

Édouard Manet *Sur la plage*

Georges Seurat *Les baigneurs à Asnières*

Après la lecture

A Un peu de géographie Find all the places mentioned where these artists painted.

B Mon tableau favori Pick your favorite painting, describe it, and explain why it is your favorite.

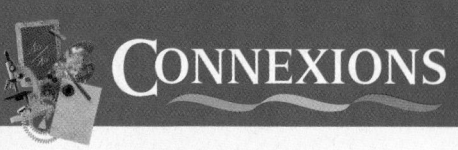

CONNEXIONS

Presentation

Les Beaux-Arts

La peinture

Step 1 Have students read the introduction in English on page 378.

Step 2 Give the students any information you like about the artists listed on page 378.

Step 3 Have students read the selection quickly or have them skim it.

Après la lecture

Discuss the answers to the activities on page 379.

Technology Option: You may wish to project Fine Art Transparencies F 16–F 20 as you do the reading. Students can also do the related activities that accompany the transparencies.

Reaching All Students

For the Younger Students You may wish to have students choose one of the paintings shown anywhere in the text and create their own "forgery" of that painting. They can research the artist and write a short paragraph about him or her (in English or French). The works of art can be hung around the room to create your own **Musée des Beaux-Arts.**

Answers to Après la lecture

A

Honfleur, une ville en Normandie
Trouville, une petite ville en Normandie sur la Manche
Asnières, une banlieue parisienne sur la Seine
Clichy, une ville dans la banlieue au nord-est de Paris

B *Answers will vary depending upon the painting the student chooses.*

Use what you have learned

Recycling

These activities allow students to use the vocabulary and structure from this chapter in completely open-ended, real-life situations.

Presentation

Encourage students to say as much as possible when they do these activities. Tell them not to be afraid to make mistakes, since the goal of these activities is real-life communication. If someone in the group makes an error, allow the others to politely correct him or her. Let students choose the activities they would like to do.

You may wish to divide students into pairs or groups. Encourage students to elaborate on the basic theme and to be creative. They may use props, pictures, or posters if they wish.

Learning from Photos

(page 380) Ask students the following types of questions about the photos.

C'est une montagne ou une plage?
C'est un skieur ou un nageur?
Il fait du ski alpin ou du ski de fond?
Qu'est-ce que le skieur porte?
Il neige ou il pleut?
Il y a de la neige?

C'est à vous

Use what you have learned

PARLER

1 La mer ou la montagne?

✔ Talk about summer or winter vacations

Work with a classmate. Tell him or her where you like to go on vacation. Tell what you do there and some of the reasons why you enjoy it so much. Take turns.

Mont-Blanc, Chamonix

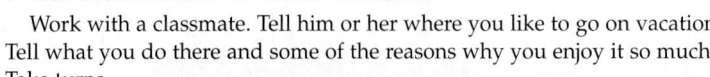

Dans les Alpes

PARLER

2 Des vacances merveilleuses

✔ Talk about vacation activities

Work with a classmate. Pretend you each had a million dollars. You went on a dream vacation. Take turns describing what you did.

PARLER

3 Le ski

✔ Talk about skiing

You're having a hot chocolate on the terrace of a chalet near the slopes of Pralognan-la-Vanoise in the French Alps. You make friends with a French skier (your classmate). Find out as much as you can about each other's skiing habits and abilities.

Answers to C'est à vous

1. *Answers will vary depending upon where students say they would like to go.*
2. *Answers will vary depending upon students' preferences.*
3. *Answers will vary depending upon students' skiing ability.*

C'est à vous

ÉCRIRE

4 Une carte postale

✔ ***Write about a summer or winter vacation destination***

Look at these postcards. Choose one. Pretend you spent a week there. Write the postcard to a friend.

Saint-Malo, Bretagne

Mont-Tremblant, Québec

Writing Strategy

Comparing and contrasting Before you begin to write a comparison of people, places, or things, you must be aware of how they are alike or different. When you compare, you are emphasizing similarities; when you contrast, you are emphasizing differences. Making a diagram or a list of similarities and differences is a good way to organize your details before you begin to write.

ÉCRIRE

5 En été et en hiver

A summer day in most parts of the world is quite different from a winter day. Write a paragraph comparing how you spend a vacation day in the summer in comparison to the way you spend a vacation day in the winter. Because of the weather, many of your activities are probably quite different. Not everything is different, however. Describe some things you do whether it's summer or winter.

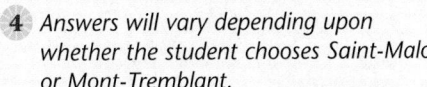

Writing Development

Have students keep a notebook containing their best written work from each chapter. These selected writings can be based on assignments from the Student Textbook and the Writing Activities Workbook. The two activities on page 381 are examples of writing assignments that may be included in each student's portfolio. In the Workbook, students will develop an organized autobiography **(Mon autobiographie).** These workbook pages may also become a part of their portfolio.

Writing Strategy

Comparing and contrasting Have students read the Writing Strategy on page 381. If students have difficulty thinking of related vocabulary, have them use the vocabulary list on page 384.

Reaching All Students

Additional Practice

Display Communication Transparencies C 11.1–C 11.2. Have students work in groups to make up as many questions as they can about the illustration. Have groups take turns asking and answering the questions.

Answers to C'est à vous

4 *Answers will vary depending upon whether the student chooses Saint-Malo or Mont-Tremblant.*

5 *Answers will vary.*

Students will compare winter and summer weather and activities, using vocabulary they have learned in this chapter and in previous ones.

Resource Manager

Communication Transparencies
Quizzes
Test Booklet
ExamView Pro®
Situation Cards
Performance Assessment
Marathon mental Videoquiz

Assessment

This is a pre-test for students to take before you administer the chapter test. Answer sheets for students to do these pages are provided in your transparency binder. Note that each section is cross-referenced so students can easily find the material they have to review in case they made errors. You may wish to collect these assessments and correct them yourself or you may prefer to have the students correct themselves in class. You can go over the answers orally or project them on the overhead, using your Assessment Answers transparencies.

Vocabulaire

*To review **Mots 1**, turn to pages 356–357.*

1 Complétez.

1. Au bord de la mer, on va à la ____.
2. Il faut mettre de la ____ quand on prend un bain de soleil.
3. Laure apprend à nager. Elle a un très bon ____.
4. Elle apprend à nager dans une ____.
5. Quand il fait mauvais, il y a souvent des nuages dans le ____.
6. Il y a beaucoup de stations balnéaires sur la ____ Méditerranée.

2 Identifiez.

7. 

8. 

9. 

10. 

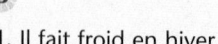

*To review **Mots 2**, turn to pages 360–361.*

3 Répondez.

11. Il fait quel temps en hiver?
12. Qui tombe souvent—un skieur débutant ou un bon skieur?

Structure

*To review irregular verbs in the **passé composé**, turn to page 364.*

4 Complétez au passé composé.

13. Il ____ des leçons de natation. (prendre)
14. Il ____ un très bon moniteur. (avoir)
15. Elles ____ un maillot de bain. (mettre)
16. J'____ une carte postale. (écrire)
17. Tu ____ le match? (voir)

Answers to Assessment

1

1. plage
2. crème solaire
3. moniteur
4. piscine
5. ciel
6. mer

2

7. un anorak
8. un bâton
9. un gant
10. une montagne

3

11. Il fait froid en hiver. (Il neige, il fait mauvais, il pleut.)
12. Un skieur débutant tombe souvent.

4

13. a pris
14. a eu
15. ont mis
16. ai écrit
17. as vu

5 Donnez le contraire.

18. Il joue toujours au foot.
19. Il entend quelque chose.
20. Il regarde quelqu'un.

To review negative statements, turn to page 367.

6 Récrivez au passé composé.

21. Elles arrivent à la plage.
22. Il part.
23. Anne et Marie, vous sortez?

*To review the **passé composé** with **être**, turn to page 369.*

Culture

7 Vrai ou faux?

24. On peut pratiquer le français au Québec parce que les Québécois parlent français.
25. Il y a beaucoup de stations de sports d'hiver dans la ville de Montréal.

To review this cultural information, turn to pages 374–375.

Le ski alpin

Answers to Assessment

5

18. Il ne joue jamais au foot.
19. Il n'entend rien.
20. Il ne regarde personne.

6

21. Elles sont arrivées à la plage.
22. Il est parti.
23. Anne et Marie, vous êtes sorties?

7

24. V
25. F

Assessment

Glencoe Technology

MINDJOGGER

You may wish to help your students prepare for the chapter test by playing the MindJogger game show. Teams will compete against each other to review chapter vocabulary and structure and sharpen listening comprehension skills.

The following is additional information about Guadeloupe.

History Connection

Guadeloupe was annexed by France in 1635. During the French Revolution, battles broke out between Royalists and Revolutionaries on the island. Britain went to the aid of the Royalists in 1794. In the same year, the French sent Victor Hugues to Guadeloupe. Hugues sent the British fleeing, abolished slavery, and guillotined the Royalist planters. Those who "kept their heads" fled to Louisiana or to the hills of **Grande-Terre** where their descendants still live. Slavery was reinstated by Napoleon, and the French and English battled over the island until 1815, when the Treaty of Paris restored Guadeloupe to France. Slavery was abolished in 1848, due to the great efforts of the Alsatian Victor Schoelcher, who actually lived on Martinique. The island was made a **département d'outre-mer (un D.O.M.)** of France in 1946, and became a **région** in 1982. It is administered by a prefect, appointed from Paris.

Vocabulaire

Vocabulary Review

The words and phrases in the **Vocabulaire** have been taught for productive use in this chapter. They are summarized here as a resource for both student and teacher. This list also serves as a convenient resource for the **C'est à vous** activities on pages 380–381. There are approximately seven cognates in this vocabulary list. Have students find them.

Attention!

You will notice that the vocabulary list here is not translated. This has been done intentionally, since we feel that by the time students have finished the material in the chapter they should be familiar with the meanings of all the words. If there are several words they still do not know, we recommend that they refer to the **Mots 1** and **2** sections in the chapter or go to the dictionaries at the back of this book to find the meanings. However, if you prefer that your students have the English translations, please refer to Vocabulary Transparency 11.1, where you will find all these words listed with their translations.

Vocabulaire

How well do you know your vocabulary?

- Choose one of the seasons from the list.
- Have a classmate make up a sentence that tells something about that season.

Going to the beach

une station balnéaire	des lunettes *(f. pl.)* de soleil
au bord de la mer	de la crème solaire
la mer	un maillot de bain
une plage	une serviette
une vague	

Describing summer activities

nager	faire du surf	la natation
plonger	faire du ski nautique	une leçon de natation
prendre un bain de soleil	faire de la planche à voile	un moniteur, une monitrice
bronzer	faire une promenade	une piscine
attraper un coup de soleil		un surfeur, une surfeuse

Going to a ski resort

une station de sports d'hiver	un télésiège	une chaussure de ski	un gant
une montagne	une piste	un bâton	un bonnet
un sommet	une bosse	une patinoire	une écharpe
un skieur, une skieuse	le ski alpin	la glace	un anorak
un(e) débutant(e)	le ski de fond	le patin à glace	
	un ski	un patin	

Describing winter activities

faire du ski	descendre une piste	faire du patin à glace
monter en télésiège	tomber	

Describing weather and seasons

le temps	Il fait quel temps... ?	Il fait beau.	Il pleut.	le ciel
le printemps	au printemps	Il fait mauvais.	Il neige.	le soleil
l'été *(m.)*	en été	Il fait chaud.	Il gèle.	un nuage
l'automne *(m.)*	en automne	Il fait froid.	le vent	
l'hiver *(m.)*	en hiver	Il fait frais.		
		Il fait du soleil.		

Other useful words and expressions

la journée	apporter	longtemps
passer	rester	de temps en temps
faire attention		tout le temps

Technotour
BON VOYAGE!

VIDÉO • Épisode 11

Avant de visionner

In this video episode, Christine experiences "almost firsthand" the wonderful world of skiing. However, it doesn't take her long to figure out that summer activities are much more to her liking.

Christine «apprend» à faire du ski.

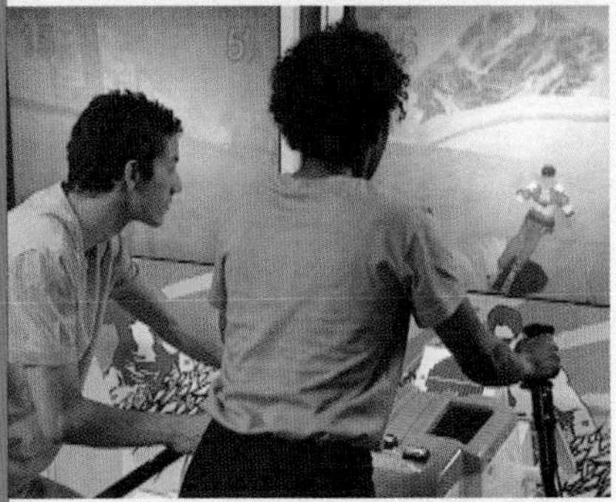

Manu est un très bon moniteur.

FRENCH ONLINE

À découvrir

Learn more about sports and leisure activities online.

La planche à voile

FRENCH Online

In the Chapter 11 Internet activity, you will have a chance to learn more about vacation spots in the Francophone world. To begin your virtual adventure, go to the Glencoe French Web site: **french.glencoe.com**

Technotour

Overview

This page previews two key multimedia components of the **Glencoe French** series. Each reinforces the material taught in the chapter in a unique manner.

VIDÉO

The Video Program allows students to see how the chapter vocabulary and structures are used by native speakers. For maximum reinforcement, show the video episode as a final activity for Chapter 11.

The two photos on the left show highlights from the Chapter 11 video episode. Discuss the photos with your students before having them view the episode. See the Video Activities Booklet for detailed suggestions for using this resource.

FRENCH Online

- The **À découvrir** photo on page 385 shows wind surfing. Students can go online to learn more about sports and leisure activities.
- Teacher Information and Student Worksheets for this activity can be accessed at the Web site.

Video Synopsis

In this video episode, we get an overview of summer and winter in some French-speaking countries. From skating and skiing to the ice sculpture contest during Carnaval, residents of Quebec city take part in many outdoor activities. The island of Martinique also provides a beautiful setting for a beach vacation. Manu tries to instruct Christine as she takes her first "ski lesson."

Révision

Preview

This section reviews the salient points from Chapters 8-11. In the **Conversation,** students will review the **passé composé,** and travel and vacation vocabulary. In the **Structure** sections, they will review the present tense of **-ir** and **-re** verbs, irregular verbs, some adjectives, the **passé composé,** and negative expressions.

Resource Manager

Workbook, Self-Test pages 115–118
Test Booklet

Presentation

Conversation

Step 1 Have students open their books to page 386. Call on two students to read this short conversation aloud.

Step 2 Go over the activity in the **Après la conversation** section.

Learning from Photos

(page 386) You may wish to ask the following questions about the photo.

Les deux copains sont où?
Qu'est-ce qu'ils font?
Qu'est-ce qu'il y a sur la plage?
Il fait quel temps?
Qu'est-ce qu'ils portent?

Presentation

Les verbes au présent

Step 1 Quickly go over the verb paradigms that appear on pages 386–387.

Révision

Conversation

En vacances

Anne: Tu es arrivé à Nice quand?
Loïc: Je suis arrivé ce matin.
Anne: Tu as pris le train ou l'avion?
Loïc: J'ai pris le train—le TGV.
Anne: Et maintenant qu'est-ce que tu vas faire?
Loïc: Absolument rien! Je ne vais rien faire. Je vais passer toute la journée à la plage et lire tous les magazines sportifs que je n'ai jamais le temps de lire.

Promenade des Anglais, Nice

Après la conversation

Répondez.

1. Loïc est arrivé à Nice quand?
2. Qu'est-ce qu'il a pris, le train ou l'avion?
3. Il a pris le TGV?
4. Qu'est-ce que Loïc va faire à Nice?
5. Il va passer toute la journée où?
6. Qu'est-ce qu'il veut lire?

Les verbes au présent

1. Review the following regular **-ir** and **-re** verbs.

FINIR	je finis, tu finis, il/elle/on finit, nous finissons, vous finissez, ils/elles finissent
VENDRE	je vends, tu vends, il/elle/on vend, nous vendons, vous vendez, ils/elles vendent

Answers to Après la conversation

1. Il est arrivé à Nice ce matin.
2. Il a pris le train.
3. Oui, il a pris le TGV.
4. Il ne va rien faire.
5. Il va passer toute la journée à la plage.
6. Il veut lire des magazines sportifs.

2. Review these other **-ir** verbs.

SORTIR	je sors, tu sors, il/elle/on sort, nous sortons, vous sortez, ils/elles sortent
PARTIR	je pars, tu pars, il/elle/on part, nous partons, vous partez, ils/elles partent
DORMIR	je dors, tu dors, il/elle/on dort, nous dormons, vous dormez, ils/elles dorment
SERVIR	je sers, tu sers, il/elle/on sert, nous servons, vous servez, ils/elles servent

3. Review the following irregular verbs.

ÉCRIRE	j'écris, tu écris, il/elle/on‿écrit, nous‿écrivons, vous‿écrivez, ils‿/elles‿écrivent
LIRE	je lis, tu lis, il/elle/on lit, nous lisons, vous lisez, ils/elles lisent
DIRE	je dis, tu dis, il/elle/on dit, nous disons, vous dites, ils/elles disent

RECEVOIR	je reçois, tu reçois, il/elle/on reçoit, nous recevons, vous recevez, ils/elles reçoivent
DEVOIR	je dois, tu dois, il/elle/on doit, nous devons, vous devez, ils/elles doivent
BOIRE	je bois, tu bois, il/elle/on boit, nous buvons, vous buvez, ils/elles boivent

CHAPITRES 8–11

Technology Connection

Le TGV—le train à grande vitesse—is an ultramodern train designed and manufactured in France. It is one of the world's fastest trains.

FUN-FACTS

The French manufacturer of the TGV is building the new train ACELA that will serve the Northeast corridor of the U.S. between Boston and Washington, D.C.

1 After going over the activity orally in class, have students retell the story in their own words.

1 **Historiette** **Un voyage en train** Complétez au présent.

Nous __1__ (partir) en voyage. Maman __2__ (attendre) devant le guichet. Elle __3__ (choisir) deux places en seconde. Maman __4__ (sortir) de l'argent et achète les billets. Nous __5__ (attendre) le train sur le quai. Le train __6__ (partir) à l'heure. Je __7__ (sortir) les billets de mon sac à dos. Je __8__ (donner) les billets au contrôleur. Nous __9__ (aller) au snack-bar. Je __10__ (choisir) un sandwich au jambon. Maman aussi __11__ (prendre) un sandwich au jambon. Le serveur __12__ (servir) Maman en premier. Nous __13__ (finir) notre sandwich. Nous commandons un express; nous __14__ (boire) notre express. Nous retournons à notre place. Nous __15__ (dormir) un peu… Et nous arrivons à Toulon. Tous les voyageurs __16__ (descendre) du train. Nous __17__ (descendre) aussi. Enfin, nous sommes en vacances!

2 **Qu'est-ce que tu fais?** Donnez des réponses personnelles.

1. Tu lis tous les magazines que tu reçois?
2. Tu écris des articles dans le journal de l'école?
3. Tu dis toujours quels sont tes projets à tes amis?
4. Tu reçois quelquefois des e-mails de tes amis?
5. Tu dois aller voir tes grands-parents de temps en temps?

3 **Qu'est-ce qu'il fait?** Refaites l'Activité 2 en remplaçant **tu** par **il,** et puis répondez.

4 **Qu'est-ce que vous faites?** Refaites l'Activité 2 en remplaçant **tu** par **vous,** et puis répondez.

Answers to Révision

1

1. partons
2. attend
3. choisit
4. sort
5. attendons
6. part
7. sors
8. donne
9. allons
10. choisis
11. prend
12. sert
13. finissons
14. buvons
15. dormons
16. descendent
17. descendons

2 *Answers will vary but may include:*

1. Non, je ne lis pas tous les magazines que je reçois.
2. Oui, j'écris des articles dans le journal de l'école.
3. Oui, je dis toujours quels sont mes projets à mes amis.
4. Oui, je reçois quelquefois des e-mails de mes amis.
5. Oui, je dois aller voir mes grands-parents de temps en temps.

3 *Answers will vary but may include:*

1. Non, il ne lit pas tous les magazines qu'il reçoit.
2. Oui, il écrit des articles dans le journal de l'école.
3. Oui, il dit toujours quels sont ses projets à ses amis.
4. Oui, il reçoit quelquefois des e-mails de ses amis.
5. Oui, il doit aller voir ses grands-parents de temps en temps.

Les adjectifs

1. Review the adjectives **quel, ce,** and **tout.**

Quel groupe?	Quels garçons?	Quelle classe?	Quelles filles?
Ce groupe?	Ces garçons?	Cette classe?	Ces filles?
Oui, tout le groupe.	Oui, tous les garçons.	Oui, toute la classe.	Oui, toutes les filles.

2. Remember that you use **cet** before a singular masculine noun that begins with a vowel or a silent **h: cet‿ami, cet‿horaire.**

5 Quels sont tes favoris? Répondez.

1. Toutes les classes sont intéressantes?
   Tu aimes cette classe aussi?
   Quelle classe est vraiment ta favorite?
2. Tu trouves tous les sports intéressants?
   Tu aimes ce sport?
   Quel est ton sport favori?
3. Tous les joueurs de cette équipe sont bons?
   Cette équipe gagne tous les matchs?
   Tous les spectateurs aiment ce sport?
   On parle de quel sport?

Ils jouent au foot.

6 Les sports

Complétez d'après les indications.

1. Tu parles de ____ équipe et de ____ match? (quel)
2. Je parle de ____ équipe, de ____ match et de ____ arbitre. (ce)
3. J'aime ____ les sports, mais pas ____ les équipes. (tout)
4. Voilà ____ les joueurs de l'équipe. (tout)
5. ____ trois joueurs sont excellents. C'est pourquoi ____ équipe gagne toujours. (ce)

Presentation

Les adjectifs

Step 1 Review the information regarding these adjectives. Have students repeat the examples after you.

5 Have students interview several different people using the questions in this activity.

Learning from Photos

(page 389) Have the students make up a conversation about a soccer **(football)** game.

Answers to Révision

4 *Answers will vary but may include:*

1. Non, nous ne lisons pas tous les magazines que nous recevons.
2. Oui, nous écrivons des articles dans le journal de l'école.
3. Oui, nous disons toujours quels sont nos projets à nos amis.
4. Oui, nous recevons quelquefois des e-mails de nos amis.
5. Oui, nous devons aller voir nos grands-parents de temps en temps.

5 *Answers will vary but may include:*

1. Oui, toutes les classes sont intéressantes.
   Oui, j'aime cette classe aussi.
   Ma classe favorite est la classe de dessin.
2. Oui, je trouve tous les sports intéressants.
   Oui, j'aime ce sport.
   Mon sport favori est le football.
3. Oui, tous les joueurs de cette équipe sont bons.
   Oui, cette équipe gagne tous les matchs.
   Oui, tous les spectateurs aiment ce sport.
   On parle du football.

6

1. quelle, quel
2. cette, ce, cet
3. tous, toutes
4. tous
5. Ces, cette

Presentation

Les verbes au passé composé

Step 1 Have students repeat the forms of **avoir** after you.

Step 2 Now have students repeat some past participles: **regardé, parlé, joué, servi, choisi, vendu, attendu.**

Step 3 Go over Items 1–2 of the explanation on page 390.

Step 4 You may wish to ask the following questions: **Hier soir, tu as regardé la télé? Ta famille a dîné à quelle heure? Tes parents ont regardé la télé aussi? Qu'est-ce que vous avez regardé?**

Les verbes au passé composé

1. The **passé composé** expresses an action begun and completed at a specific time in the past. You form the **passé composé** by using the present tense of **avoir** and the past participle. Review the regular **-er, -ir,** and **-re** verbs.

PARLER		CHOISIR		ATTENDRE	
j'	ai parlé	j'	ai choisi	j'	ai attendu
tu	as parlé	tu	as choisi	tu	as attendu
il/elle/on	a parlé	il/elle/on	a choisi	il/elle/on	a attendu
nous	avons parlé	nous	avons choisi	nous	avons attendu
vous	avez parlé	vous	avez choisi	vous	avez attendu
ils/elles	ont parlé	ils/elles	ont choisi	ils/elles	ont attendu

2. Review the verbs that have an irregular past participle.

devoir	**dû**	**recevoir**	**reçu**	**dire**	**dit**
boire	**bu**	**avoir**	**eu**	**écrire**	**écrit**
croire	**cru**				
voir	**vu**	**prendre**	**pris**	**être**	**été**
lire	**lu**	**apprendre**	**appris**	**faire**	**fait**
pouvoir	**pu**	**comprendre**	**compris**		
vouloir	**voulu**	**mettre**	**mis**		

Aéroport Charles-de-Gaulle, Roissy

7 **Historiette** **En voyage** Répondez.

1. Tu as fait tes valises?
2. Tu as pris ton billet et ton passeport?
3. À l'aéroport, tu as fait enregistrer tes bagages?
4. Tu as choisi ta place?
5. Tu as fait bon voyage?

Answers to Révision

7 *Answers will vary but may include:*

1. Oui, j'ai fait mes valises.
2. Oui, j'ai pris mon billet et mon passeport.
3. Oui, à l'aéroport j'ai fait enregistrer mes bagages.
4. Oui, j'ai choisi ma place.
5. Oui, j'ai fait bon voyage.

8 **Historiette** **C'est passé.** Complétez en utilisant le passé composé.

1. Ils ____ ce que vous ____. (croire, dire)
2. Elle ____ des leçons de natation et elle ____ toutes les instructions de son moniteur. (prendre, comprendre)
3. Nous ____ une lettre de Marianne mais nous n'____ pas ____ à sa lettre. (recevoir, répondre)
4. Il ____ des courses. Il ____ tout ce qu'il ____ dans un grand sac. (faire, mettre, acheter)
5. Chez elle, elle ____ un verre d'eau et elle ____ son journal. (boire, lire)
6. J'____ très contente de voir Sébastien, mais je n'____ pas ____ sortir avec lui. (être, vouloir)

Le passé composé avec être

1. Many verbs that express motion to or from a place are conjugated with **être** in the **passé composé.** Such verbs are: **aller, descendre, rentrer, entrer, sortir, monter, arriver,** and **partir.**

MASCULIN				FÉMININ			
ALLER		DESCENDRE		ALLER		DESCENDRE	
je	suis allé	je	suis descendu	je	suis allée	je	suis descendue
tu	es allé	tu	es descendu	tu	es allée	tu	es descendue
il	est allé	il	est descendu	elle	est allée	elle	est descendue
on	est allés	on	est descendus	on	est allées	on	est descendues
nous	sommes allés	nous	sommes descendus	nous	sommes allées	nous	sommes descendues
vous	êtes allé(s)	vous	êtes descendu(s)	vous	êtes allée(s)	vous	êtes descendue(s)
ils	sont allés	ils	sont descendus	elles	sont allées	elles	sont descendues

Note that the past participle of verbs conjugated with **être** agrees with the subject.

2. The verbs **rester, tomber, naître,** and **mourir** are also conjugated with **être.**

Il est resté huit jours.
Elle est tombée.
Elle est née le 20 décembre.
Son grand-père est mort le 2 janvier.

Révision

Presentation

Le passé composé avec être

Step 1 Have students repeat the forms of **être** after you.

Step 2 Go over Items 1–2 of the explanation on page 391.

Step 3 You may wish to ask the following types of questions: **Hier soir, tu es sorti(e) ou tu es resté(e) à la maison? Tes amis et toi, vous êtes allés au restaurant?**

Answers to Révision

8

1. ont cru, avez dit
2. a pris, a compris
3. avons reçu, avons répondu
4. a fait, a mis, a acheté
5. a bu, a lu
6. ai été, ai voulu

9 and **10** These activities can be done first with books closed. Call on individual students to respond. They can be done a second time for reading reinforcement or as a paired activity.

Presentation

Les mots négatifs

Step 1 Review the information on page 392.

Learning from Photos

(page 392) Geneva is a beautiful, sophisticated French-speaking city on **le lac Léman** (Lake Geneva) in Switzerland.

Literary Companion

When you finish this review section, if you wish, have students read the literary adaptation of *La Chanson de Roland,* on pages 512–517. The adaptation has been done in accordance with the vocabulary and structures that the students have acquired up to this point.

9 Historiette À l'école

Répondez.

1. Tu es allé(e) à l'école à quelle heure ce matin?
2. Tu es sorti(e) de la maison à quelle heure?
3. Quand tu es entré(e) dans la classe de français, tu as dit bonjour au professeur?
4. Tu es resté(e) à l'école après les cours?
5. Tu es allé(e) où après les cours?
6. Tu es rentré(e) chez toi vers quelle heure?

10 Historiette En train

Refaites les phrases avec le sujet indiqué.

1. Ils sont allés à Genève. (elles)
2. Les voyageurs sont descendus du train. (la voyageuse)
3. Elle est sortie de la gare. (il)
4. Il a cherché un taxi. (elle)
5. Elles sont rentrées à neuf heures du soir. (nous)

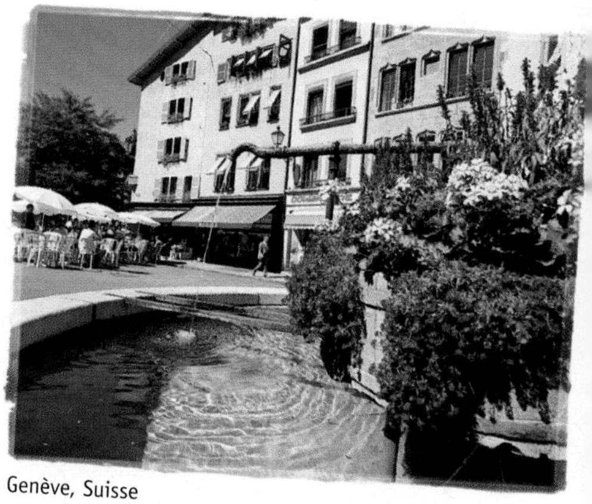

Genève, Suisse

Les mots négatifs

Review the negative words. Pay particular attention to their placement.

Je ne vais pas au café.
Je ne vais jamais au café.
Je ne vais plus au café.

Je ne suis pas allé(e) au café.
Je ne suis jamais allé(e) au café.
Je ne suis plus allé(e) au café.

Je ne vois rien et je n'ai rien vu.
Je ne vois personne et je n'ai vu personne.

LITERARY COMPANION *You may wish to read the adaptation of* **La Chanson de Roland.** *You will find this literary selection on page 512.*

ANSWERS TO Révision

9 *Answers will vary but may include:*

1. Je suis allé(e) à l'école à sept heures et demie.
2. Je suis sorti(e) de la maison à sept heures et quart.
3. Oui, quand je suis entré(e) dans la classe de français, j'ai dit bonjour au professeur.
4. Non, je ne suis pas resté(e) à l'école après les cours.
5. Je suis allé(e) dans un café après les cours.
6. Je suis rentré(e) chez moi vers cinq heures.

10

1. Elles sont allées à Genève.
2. La voyageuse est descendue du train.
3. Il est sorti de la gare.
4. Elle a cherché un taxi.
5. Nous sommes rentré(e)s à neuf heures du soir.

11 Non. Répondez que non.

1. Tu vois quelqu'un?
2. Tu entends quelqu'un?
3. Tu vois quelque chose?
4. Tu veux quelque chose?
5. Tu vas encore au café?
6. Tu arrives toujours en retard?
7. Tu as vu quelque chose?
8. Tu as dit quelque chose?
9. Tu as vu quelqu'un?
10. Tu as attendu quelqu'un?

12 Enquête sur les saisons

You want to know if your partner prefers summer or winter. On a separate sheet of paper, make a chart like the one to the right. Fill it out for both seasons. Compare your chart with your partner's and try to guess which season your partner prefers by asking questions about his or her choices.

	L'hiver	L'été
Vêtements		
Activités	le ski	le ski nautique
Équipement		
Nourriture		

13 Un match

Work with a classmate. Discuss the last sports event you saw.

14 On y va comment?

Look at these train and plane schedules. You want to go from Paris to London. With a classmate decide how you are going to get there and discuss your choice. Then tell what you are going to do there.

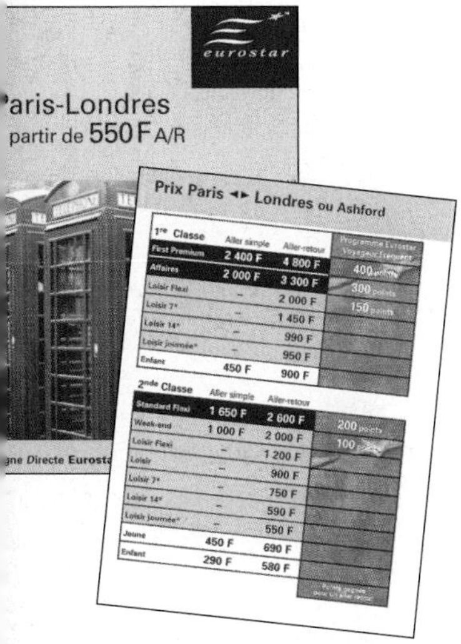

1re Classe	Aller simple	Aller-retour	Programme Eurostar Voyageur Fréquent
First Premium	2 400 F	4 800 F	400 points
Affaires	2 000 F	3 300 F	300 points
Loisir Flexi	–	2 000 F	150 points
Loisir 7*	–	1 450 F	
Loisir 14*	–	990 F	
Loisir journée*	–	950 F	
Enfant	450 F	900 F	

2nde Classe	Aller simple	Aller-retour	
Standard Flexi	1 650 F	2 600 F	200 points
Week-end	1 000 F	2 000 F	100 points
Loisir Flexi	–	1 200 F	
Loisir	–	900 F	
Loisir 7*	–	750 F	
Loisir 14*	–	590 F	
Loisir Journée*	–	550 F	
Jeune	450 F	690 F	
Enfant	290 F	580 F	

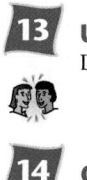

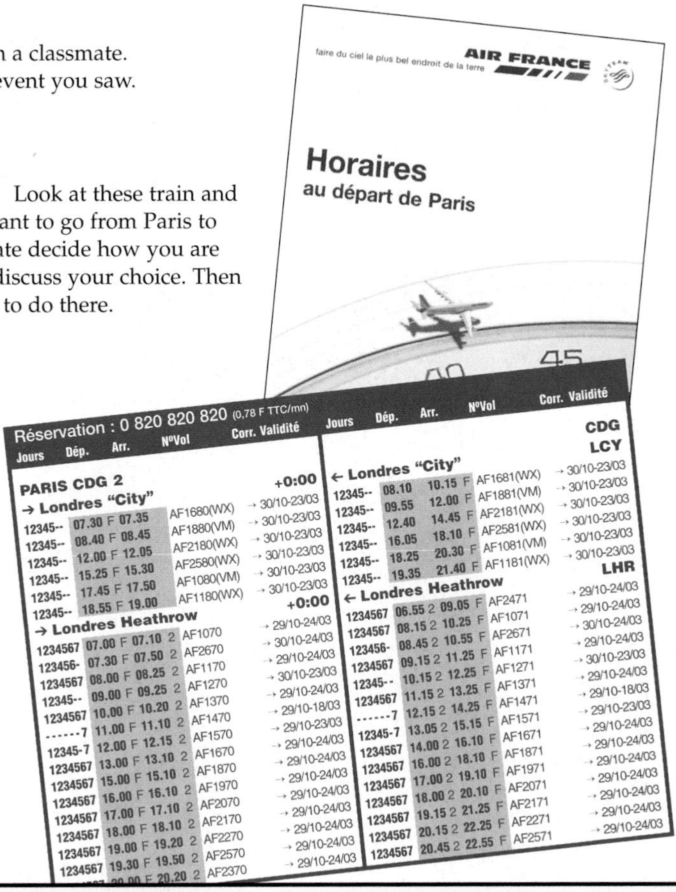

Réservation : 0 820 820 820 (0,78 F TTC/mn)

PARIS CDG 2 +0:00

Jours	Dép.	Arr.	NºVol	Corr. Validité
→ Londres "City"				
12345--	07.30 F	07.35	AF1680(WX)	→ 30/10-23/03
12345--	08.40 F	08.45	AF1880(VM)	→ 30/10-23/03
12345--	12.00 F	12.05	AF2180(WX)	→ 30/10-23/03
12345--	15.25 F	15.30	AF2580(WX)	→ 30/10-23/03
12345--	17.45 F	17.50	AF1080(VM)	→ 30/10-23/03
12345--	18.55 F	19.00	AF1180(WX)	→ 30/10-23/03
→ Londres Heathrow				+0:00
1234567	07.00 F	07.10 2	AF1070	→ 29/10-24/03
123456-	07.30 F	07.50 2	AF2670	→ 30/10-24/03
1234567	08.00 F	08.25 2	AF1170	→ 29/10-24/03
12345--	09.00 F	09.25 2	AF1270	→ 30/10-23/03
1234567	10.00 F	10.20 2	AF1370	→ 29/10-24/03
------7	11.00 F	11.10 2	AF1470	→ 29/10-18/03
12345-7	12.00 F	12.15 2	AF1570	→ 29/10-23/03
1234567	13.00 F	13.10 2	AF1670	→ 29/10-24/03
1234567	15.00 F	15.10 2	AF1870	→ 29/10-24/03
1234567	16.00 F	16.10 2	AF1970	→ 29/10-24/03
1234567	17.00 F	17.10 2	AF2070	→ 29/10-24/03
1234567	18.00 F	18.10 2	AF2170	→ 29/10-24/03
1234567	19.00 F	19.20 2	AF2270	→ 29/10-24/03
1234567	19.30 F	19.50 2	AF2570	→ 29/10-24/03
	20.00 F	20.20 2	AF2370	→ 29/10-24/03

Jours	Dép.	Arr.	NºVol	Corr. Validité
← Londres "City"				CDG LCY
12345--	08.10	10.15 F	AF1681(WX)	→ 30/10-23/03
12345--	09.55	12.00 F	AF1881(VM)	→ 30/10-23/03
12345--	12.40	14.45 F	AF2181(WX)	→ 30/10-23/03
12345--	16.05	18.10 F	AF2581(WX)	→ 30/10-23/03
12345--	18.25	20.30 F	AF1081(VM)	→ 30/10-23/03
12345--	19.35	21.40 F	AF1181(WX)	→ 30/10-23/03
← Londres Heathrow				LHR
1234567	06.55 2	09.05 F	AF2471	→ 29/10-24/03
1234567	08.15 2	10.25 F	AF1071	→ 29/10-24/03
123456-	08.45 2	10.55 F	AF2671	→ 30/10-24/03
1234567	09.15 2	11.25 F	AF1171	→ 29/10-24/03
12345--	10.15 2	12.25 F	AF1271	→ 30/10-23/03
1234567	11.15 2	13.25 F	AF1371	→ 29/10-24/03
------7	12.15 2	14.25 F	AF1471	→ 29/10-18/03
12345-7	13.05 2	15.15 F	AF1571	→ 29/10-23/03
1234567	14.00 2	16.10 F	AF1671	→ 29/10-24/03
1234567	16.00 2	18.10 F	AF1871	→ 29/10-24/03
1234567	17.00 2	19.10 F	AF1971	→ 29/10-24/03
1234567	18.00 2	20.10 F	AF2071	→ 29/10-24/03
1234567	19.15 2	21.25 F	AF2171	→ 29/10-24/03
1234567	20.15 2	22.25 F	AF2271	→ 29/10-24/03
1234567	20.45 2	22.55 F	AF2571	→ 29/10-24/03

Révision

FUN FACTS

It is now possible to travel between Paris and London without changing trains since the opening of the Eurotunnel between France and England in the spring of 1994.

Answers to Révision

11

1. Non, je ne vois personne.
2. Non, je n'entends personne.
3. Non, je ne vois rien.
4. Non, je ne veux rien.
5. Non, je ne vais plus au café.
6. Non, je n'arrive jamais en retard.
7. Non, je n'ai rien vu.
8. Non, je n'ai rien dit.
9. Non, je n'ai vu personne.
10. Non, je n'ai attendu personne.

NATIONAL GEOGRAPHIC

Preview

This section, **Reflets du Canada,** was prepared by National Geographic Society. Its purpose is to give students greater insight, through these visual images, into the culture and people of French-speaking Canada. Have students look at the photographs on pages 394–397 for enjoyment. If they would like to talk about them, let them say anything they can, using the vocabulary they have learned to this point.

National Standards

Culture

The **Reflets du Canada** photos and the accompanying captions allow students to gain insights into the people and culture of French-speaking Canada.

1. La ville de Québec vue du Saint-Laurent
2. La porte Saint-Louis à Québec
3. Le complexe Desjardins à Montréal
4. La chute Montmorency à l'est de la ville de Québec
5. Bateau de pêche dans la baie de Gaspé
6. Skieurs à Sainte-Agathe-des-Monts dans les Laurentides
7. Marionnettes sur le Vieux-Port à Montréal
1
2
3
4
5
394

About the Photos

1. La ville de Québec vue du Saint-Laurent The beautiful city of Quebec is perched on a cliff at a narrow point in the St. Lawrence River. Quebec, as can be seen in this photograph, is a split-level city, consisting of Upper Town and Lower Town. A very steep rock separates these two sections of the city. There are some twenty-five staircases that join the two "towns," as well as a funicular.

The tall building in the photograph is the beautiful Château Frontenac, Quebec City's most celebrated landmark. It stands on the site of the former administrative and military headquarters of **la Nouvelle France.** It is named after le comte de Frontenac, governor of the French colony from 1672–1698. Today the Château Frontenac is a luxury hotel.

2. La porte Saint-Louis à Québec The **porte Saint-Louis** once served as an entrance gate to the walled city. Today the gate serves as a bridge that enables people to walk on top of the ancient fortifications to tour the old city. The **porte Saint-Louis,** built in 1878, has the appearance of a medieval fortress.

3. Le complexe Desjardins à Montréal Montreal, a beautiful island city, is Quebec's largest and most important city. After Paris, it is the second largest French-speaking city in the world. The Île de Montréal is 51 kilometers long and 14 kilometers wide. The only rise in elevation is the 764 foot high Mont-Royal which gave the island its name.

The **complexe Desjardins** is in the modern downtown area. The mall or galleria area is home to many boutiques.

4. La chute Montmorency à l'est de la ville de Québec The Montmorency Falls are 10 kilometers east of Quebec City. Here the Montmorency River cascades over a cliff 274 feet high into the St. Lawrence River. During very cold weather, the falls' heavy spray freezes and forms a gigantic loaf-shaped cone called the **Pain du Sucre** by the **Québecois.** Ice climbers scale the falls in the winter months.

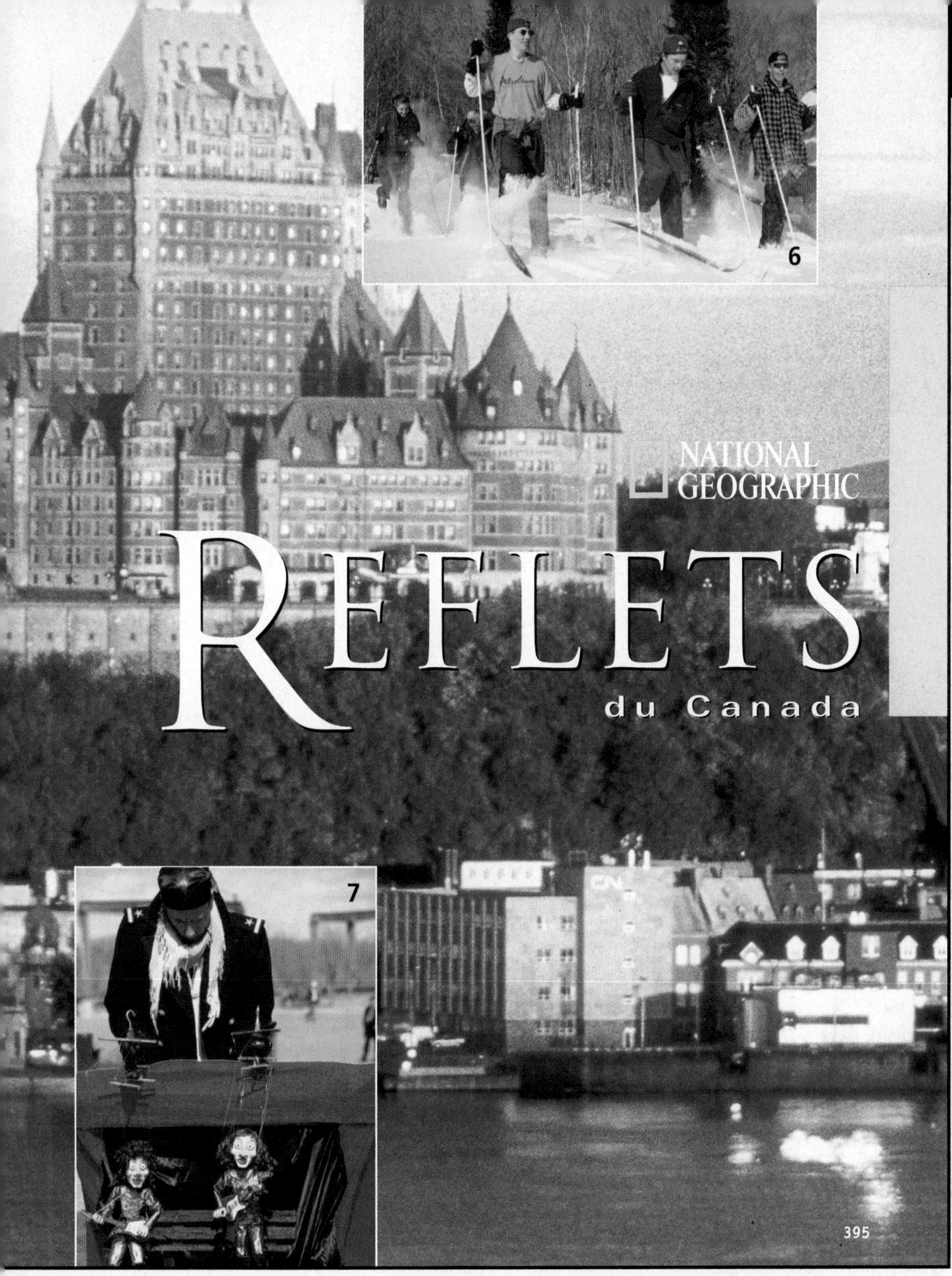

5. Bateau de pêche dans la baie de Gaspé The Gaspé Peninsula juts into the stormy Gulf of St. Lawrence. This is a very isolated region with spectacular sights, sheer cliffs, wide beaches, and tiny picturesque fishing villages.

Jacques Cartier first set foot on shore in North America in the town of Gaspé in 1534. It is said, however, that Vikings and fishermen had been there before Cartier.

6. Skieurs à Sainte-Agathe-des-Monts dans les Laurentides This town is 60 kilometers northwest of Montreal. It overlooks **le lac des Sables** and serves as a large commercial center for the many ski communities farther north. Mont-Tremblant, the highest peak in the Laurentians, and a major ski resort, is 25 kilometers north of Sainte-Agathe-des-Monts.

7. Marionnettes sur le Vieux-Port à Montréal Vieux-Port was once an important commercial port area. Today its docks are too small and its channels too shallow to accommodate mega-ships. Only a few freighters and some smaller cruise ships use the port. Today, the port is a popular waterfront recreational area with a promenade, snack bars, and cinemas. In the winter there is a giant outdoor skating rink.

8. Le Rocher Percé en Gaspésie Percé is a lovely fishing village on the Gaspé peninsula. A very famous site in this region is the Percé rock. It is a huge fossil-embedded rock offshore that the sea "pierced" thousands of years ago.

9. Détail d'un totem au musée McCord d'histoire canadienne à Montréal This museum contains exhibits that portray the life of ordinary Canadians. It is the best historical museum in all of Canada. It has exhibits of costumes and textiles, paintings, prints, drawings, and photographs.

The Algonquins and Iroquois play an important part in the history of Canada. Montreal was originally called Hochelaga and Quebec City was Stadacona. More than 1000 Iroquois greeted Cartier. It took two centuries of fierce fighting before the French made peace with the Iroquois.

In 1535, during Cartier's second voyage in the area, he found a wide river and decided to sail down it. He came to the Indian village of Stadacona. He liked the location of the village perched on the cliffs overlooking an area where the waters of the river narrowed—a **kebec** in the Algonquin language.

10. Tours et la basilique Notre-Dame de Montréal This is one of the most beautiful churches in North America. It is located in the **place d'Armes,** a square that was the sight of fierce battles with Iroquois in the 1600s, and later became the center of **la haute ville.** The towers are 228 feet high, and one holds the largest bells in North America.

11. Intérieur de la basilique Notre-Dame de Montréal The original basilica was made of wood and built in 1642. It was torn down and rebuilt three times. The present church has 3,800 seats. The church has magnificent stained

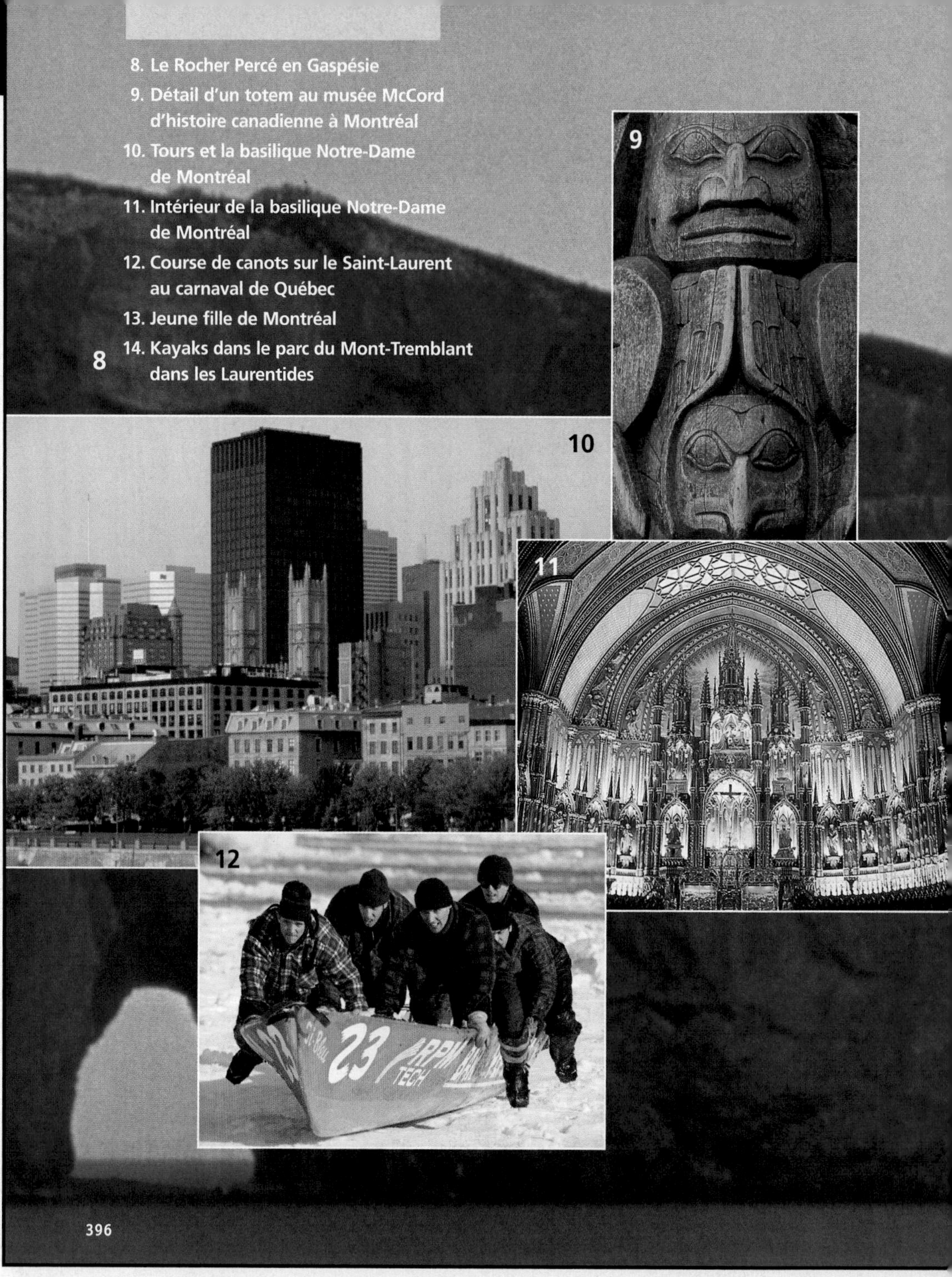

8. Le Rocher Percé en Gaspésie
9. Détail d'un totem au musée McCord d'histoire canadienne à Montréal
10. Tours et la basilique Notre-Dame de Montréal
11. Intérieur de la basilique Notre-Dame de Montréal
12. Course de canots sur le Saint-Laurent au carnaval de Québec
13. Jeune fille de Montréal
14. Kayaks dans le parc du Mont-Tremblant dans les Laurentides
8
9
10
11
12
23
396

NATIONAL GEOGRAPHIC Teacher's Corner

Index to the NATIONAL GEOGRAPHIC MAGAZINE

The following related articles may be of interest:

- "Quebec's Quandary," by Ian Darragh, November 1997.
- "James Bay: Where Two Worlds Collide," by John G. Mitchell, November 1993.
- "Montreal: Spirited Heart of French Canada," by Douglas B. Lee, March 1991.
- "Henry Hudson's Changing Bay," by Bill Richards, March 1982.
- "Quebec's Northern Dynamo," by Larry Kohl, March 1982.
- "The St. Lawrence River: Canada's Highway to the Sea," by William S. Ellis, May 1980.

glass windows and carvings in pine and walnut. The vaulted blue ceiling is studded with thousands of twenty-four karat gold stars. The pipe organ is one of the largest in the world, with more than 7000 pipes.

12. Course de canots sur le Saint-Laurent au carnaval de Québec
For more information about carnival in Quebec, please see **Lecture supplémentaire 2** on page 377.

13. Jeune fille de Montréal

14. Kayaks dans le parc du Mont-Tremblant dans les Laurentides
This park covers hundreds of square miles of mountainous wilderness. It was once home to the Algonquin Indians. The park is a vast wildlife sanctuary. It has more than 400 lakes and rivers. Moose hunting is allowed in-season and during the winter. Cross-country skiing is very popular. In the summer camping and canoeing are favorite activities.

Products available from GLENCOE/MCGRAW-HILL

To order the following products, call Glencoe/McGraw-Hill at 1-800-334-7344.

CD-ROMs
- Picture Atlas of the World
- The Complete National Geographic: 112 Years of National Geographic Magazine

Transparency Set
- NGS PicturePack: Geography of North America

Products available from NATIONAL GEOGRAPHIC SOCIETY

To order the following products, call National Geographic Society at 1-800-368-2728.

Books
- National Geographic World Atlas for Young Explorers
- National Geographic Satellite Atlas of the World

Software
- ZingoLing: French Diskette

Video
- Physical Geography of Canada

Planning for Chapter 12

SCOPE AND SEQUENCE, PAGES 398–429

Topics

- Daily routine
- Family life

Functions

- How to describe your personal grooming habits
- How to describe your daily routine
- How to talk about family life
- How to describe daily activities in the past

Culture

- The Ben Amar family's daily routine
- Discussing differences in breakfast habits among the United States, France, and Africa

Structure

- Reflexive verbs in the present tense
- Reflexive verbs in the **passé composé**

National Standards

- Communication Standard 1.1 pages 402, 403, 406, 407, 410, 411, 412, 413, 414, 415, 417, 424
- Communication Standard 1.2 pages 402, 403, 406, 407, 410, 411, 412, 413, 414, 416, 419, 421, 423
- Communication Standard 1.3 pages 402, 407, 411, 414, 425
- Cultures Standard 2.1 pages
- Cultures Standard 2.2 pages 418–419, 420–421
- Connections Standard 3.1 pages 422–423
- Comparisons Standard 4.2 pages 418–419, 420–421
- Communities Standard 5.1 page 425

PACING AND PRIORITIES

The chapter content is color coded below to assist you in planning.

■ required ■ recommended ■ optional

Vocabulaire *(required)* *Days 1–4*

- ■ Mots 1
  La routine
- ■ Mots 2
  Chez les Moulin

Structure *(required)* *Days 5–7*

- ■ Les verbes réfléchis au présent
- ■ Les verbes réfléchis au passé composé

Conversation *(required)*

- ■ Quelle interro?

Prononciation *(recommended)*

- ■ Les sons **/s/** et **/z/**

Lectures culturelles

- ■ La famille Ben Amar *(recommended)*
- ■ Le petit déjeuner *(optional)*

Connexions *(optional)*

- ■ L´écologie

■ **C'est à vous** *(recommended)*

■ **Assessment** *(recommended)*

■ **Technotour** *(optional)*

RESOURCE GUIDE

SECTION	PAGES	SECTION RESOURCES
Vocabulaire *Mots 1*		
La routine	400–403	Vocabulary Transparencies 12.2–12.3 Audiocassette 7B/CD 7 Audio Activities Booklet TE, pages 144–146 Workbook, pages 119–120 Quiz 1, page 59 ExamView Pro®
Vocabulaire *Mots 2*		
Chez les Moulin	404–407	Vocabulary Transparencies 12.4–12.5 Audiocassette 7B/CD 7 Audio Activities Booklet TE, pages 146–147 Workbook, page 121 Quiz 2, page 60 ExamView Pro®
Structure		
Les verbes réfléchis au présent Les verbes réfléchis au passé composé	408–412 413–415	Audiocassette 7B/CD 7 Audio Activities Booklet TE, pages 148–151 Workbook, pages 122–125 Quizzes 3–5, pages 61–63 ExamView Pro®
Conversation		
Quelle interro?	416	Audiocassette 7B/CD 7 Audio Activities Booklet TE, pages 151–152 CD-ROM
Prononciation		
Les sons **/s/** et **/z/**	417	Pronunciation Transparency P 12 Audiocassette 7B/CD 7 Audio Activities Booklet TE, pages 152–153
Lectures culturelles		
La famille Ben Amar Le petit déjeuner	418–419 420–421	Audiocassette 7B/CD 7 Audio Activities Booklet TE, pages 154–155 Test Booklet, Chapter 12
Connexions		
L´écologie	422–423	Test Booklet, Chapter 12
C'est à vous		
	424–425	**Bon voyage!** Video, Episode 12 Video Activities Booklet, Chapter 12 French Online Activities french.glencoe.com
Assessment		
	426–427	Communication Transparency C 12 Quizzes 1–5, pages 59–63 Test Booklet, Chapter 12 ExamView Pro® Situation Cards, Chapter 12 **Marathon mental** Videoquiz

Using Your Resources for Chapter 12

Transparencies

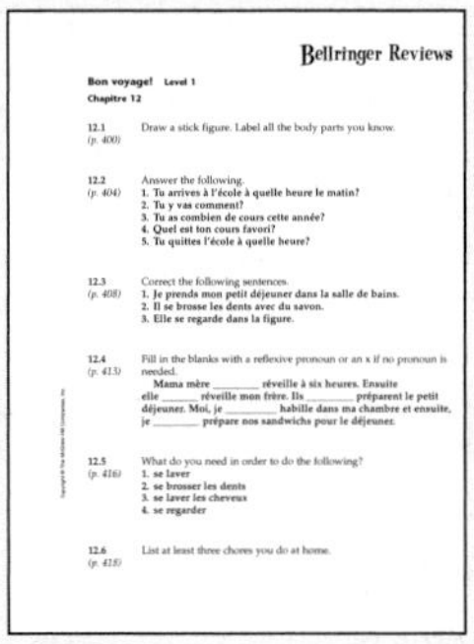

Bellringer 12.1–12.6

Vocabulary 12.1–12.5

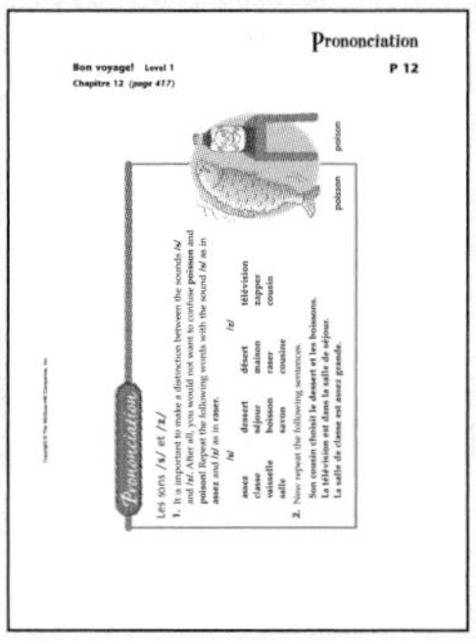

Pronunciation P 12

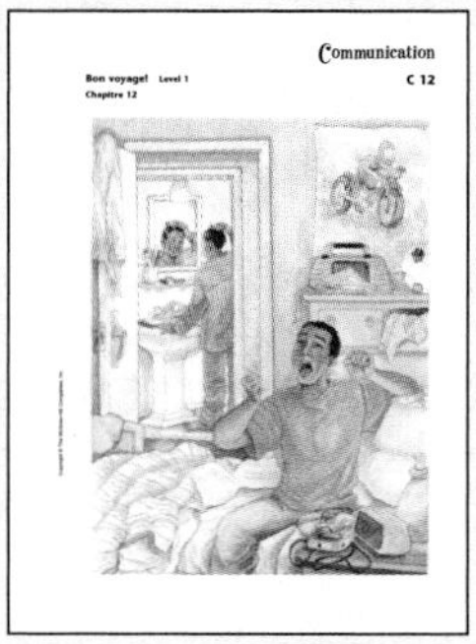

Communication C 12

Writing Activities Workbook

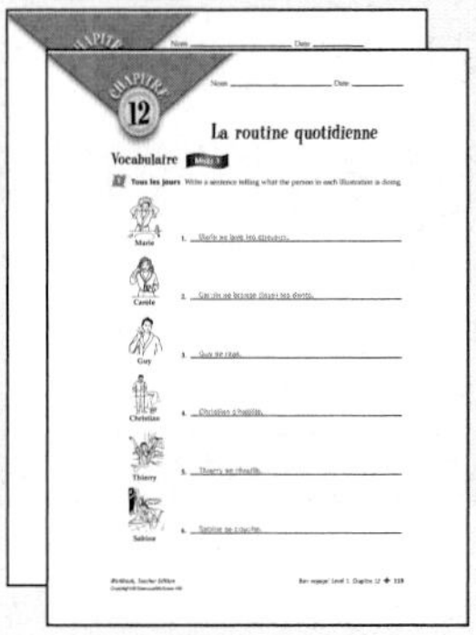

Vocabulary,
pages 119–121

Structure,
pages 122–125

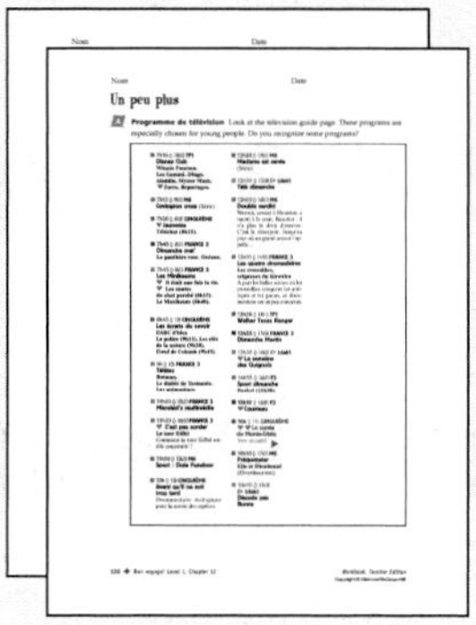

Enrichment,
pages 126–128

Audio Program and Audio Activities Booklet

Vocabulary,
pages 144–147

Structure,
pages 148–151

Conversation,
Pronunciation,
pages 151–153

Cultural Reading,
pages 154–155

Additional Practice,
page 156

Assessment

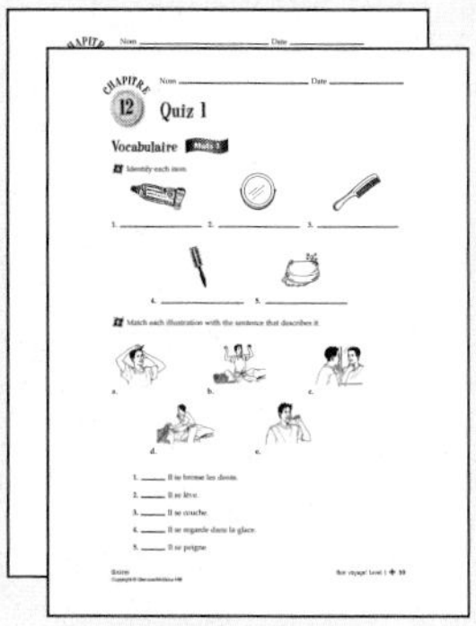

Vocabulary and Structure Quizzes, pages 59–63

Chapter Tests, Chapter 12

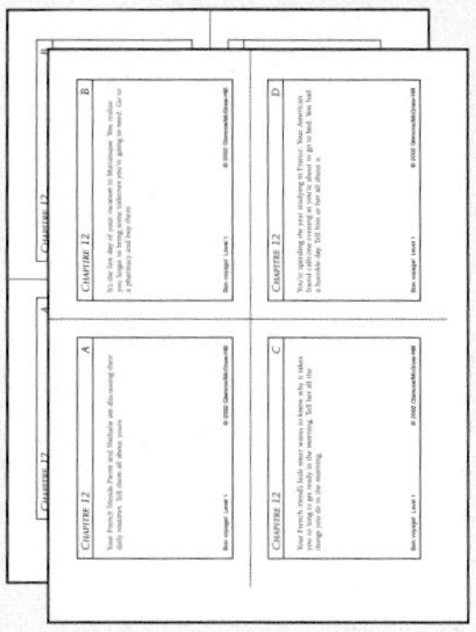

Situation Cards, Chapter 12

Timesaving Teacher Tools

Interactive Teacher Edition

Imagine having your Teacher's Edition and all resources on a CD-ROM. Click on a resource and it appears on your screen, ready to be printed, sorted, or planned.

Interactive Lesson Planner

The Interactive Lesson Planner CD-ROM helps you organize your lesson plans for a week, month, semester, or year. Look at this planning tool for easy access to your Chapter 12 resources.

ExamView Pro®

Test Bank software for Macintosh and Windows makes creating, editing, customizing, and printing tests quick and easy.

Technology Resources

FRENCH Online

In the Chapter 12 Internet activity, you will have a chance to learn more about daily life in the Francophone world. Visit french.glencoe.com.

On the Interactive Conversation CD-ROM, students can listen to and take part in a recorded version of the conversation in Chapter 12.

NATIONAL GEOGRAPHIC SOCIETY

See the National Geographic Teacher's Corner on pages 150–151, 256–257, 396–397, 500–501 for reference to additional technology resources.

Bon Voyage! Video and Video Activities Booklet.

Help your students prepare for the chapter test by playing the **Marathon mental** Videoquiz game show. Teams will compete against each other to review chapter vocabulary and structure and sharpen listening comprehension skills.

CHAPITRE 12

Preview

In this chapter, students will learn to discuss and describe their personal grooming habits, daily routine, and family life. In order to do this they will learn the reflexive verbs in the present tense and the **passé composé.**

National Standards

Communication

In Chapter 12, students will communicate in spoken and written French on the following topics:

- Daily routines
- Taking care of oneself
- Family activities and routines

Students will also learn to narrate past events. They will obtain and provide information and engage in conversations about everyday habits, including daily hygiene, as they fulfill the chapter objectives listed on this page.

CHAPITRE 12

La routine quotidienne

Objectifs

In this chapter you will learn to:

- ✔ *describe your personal grooming habits*
- ✔ *talk about your daily routine*
- ✔ *talk about your family life*
- ✔ *tell some things you do for yourself*
- ✔ *talk about daily activities in the past*
- ✔ *discuss a French family's daily routine*

Edgar Degas *Toilette matinale*

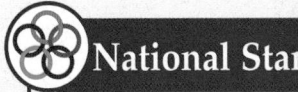

398

Correlations to Continuum *(see page i for code)*

Stage I
Understand some ideas and familiar details. p. 410 (**10**, **11**, *p*); Understand and convey information about home and schedules. pp. 400–401 (*i*), p. 407 (**7**, *p*)

Stage II
Understand and express important ideas and some detail. p. 402 (**1**, *i*), p. 403 (**4**, *p*); Describe and compare. p. 424 (**2**, *p*); Converse in face-to-face social interactions. p. 407 (**8**, *p*); Listen in social interactions and listen to audio or video texts. p. 415 (**27**, *p*); Write letters. p. 425 (**4**, *p*); Use and understand learned expressions, sentences, strings of sentences, and questions when speaking and listening. p. 407 (**9**, *p*), p. 412 (**17**, *m*); Understand and convey information about family, home, schedules, and leisure activities. pp. 418–419 (*m*); Demonstrate increasing fluency and control of vocabulary. p. 424 (**1**)

Stage III
Narrate and understand narration in the past. p. 414 (**21**, *i*), p. 415 (**26**, *p*); Converse in face-to-face social interactions and in simple transactions on the phone. p. 416 (*i*), p. 416 (*p*), p. 424 (**3**, *p*); Understand and convey information about current affairs and the environment. pp. 422–423 (*i*), pp. 422–423 (*p*); Generally choose appropriate vocabulary for familiar topics, but as the complexity of the message increases, there is evidence of hesitation and groping for words, as well as patterns of mispronunciation and intonation. p. 415 (**28**)

CHAPITRE 12

Spotlight on Culture

Photograph This photo is of the **Jardin du Luxembourg** in Paris. Paris is a city of many small and large parks.The **Jardin du Luxembourg** is one of the largest and considered one of the prettiest. Parisians use their parks as they go about their daily routine, just walking through one on their way to their next destination, stopping for a brief rest, or having a quick lunch. This park, located in the Latin Quarter, is especially popular with university students.

Painting Edgar Degas was born in Paris in 1834, and he died there in 1917. He studied law before dedicating himself to art. In his works, Degas was concerned with the line, form, and movement of the human body. This explains why so many of his famous paintings are of ballerinas. He did several paintings of **femmes à leur toilette.** As we can see in this painting, many of his poses are candid.

Chapter Projects

De bonnes habitudes Have students prepare a booklet in French on good and bad daily habits. Have them make a list of do's and don'ts. After students have prepared their own list, they can get together and compile a master list that can be used as a bulletin board display.

Publicité Have students prepare a newspaper ad for products at a drugstore.

1 Preparation

Resource Manager

Vocabulary Transparencies 12.2–12.3
Audio Activities Booklet TE, pages 144–146
Audiocassette 7B/CD 7
Workbook, pages 119–120
Quiz 1, page 59
ExamView Pro®

Bellringer Review

Use BRR Transparency 12.1 or write the following on the board.
Draw a stick figure. Label all the body parts you know.

2 Presentation

Step 1 Show Vocabulary Transparencies 12.2–12.3. Point to individual items and have the class repeat the words after you or Audiocassette 7B/CD 7.

Step 2 As an alternative, you may wish to bring in some props such as shampoo, a brush, a razor, etc.

Step 3 Act out the new words: **se réveiller, se lever, se laver, se laver les cheveux, se brosser les dents, se raser,** etc.

Step 4 As you present the new vocabulary, ask: **La fille se réveille le matin ou le soir? Ensuite, elle se lève ou elle se couche? Elle se lave la figure et les mains? Elle se brosse les dents? Elle se lave les cheveux tous les matins? Elle s'habille vite? Elle s'habille dans la salle de bains ou dans la chambre à coucher? Elle se lève ou se couche à dix heures et demie du soir?**

La routine

tôt tard

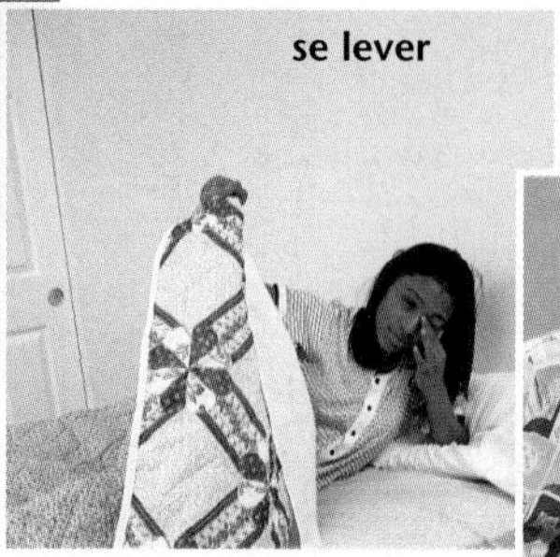

Elle se lève tôt.
Elle ne se lève pas tard.

Il se lave la figure.

du shampooing

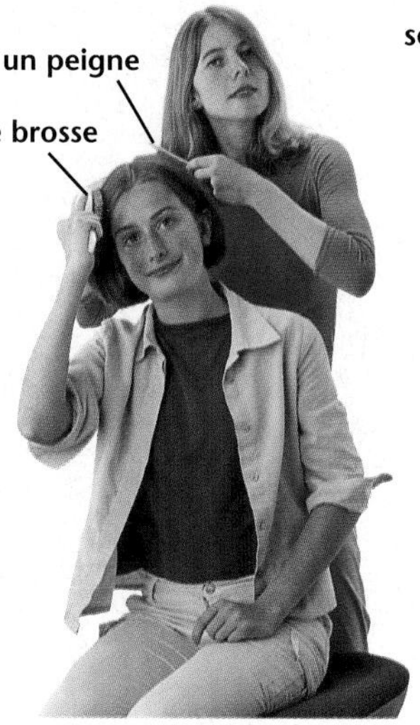

Une fille se peigne.
L'autre se brosse les cheveux.

se maquiller

s'habiller

Reaching All Students

Total Physical Response You may wish to use a chair for a bed and bring in an alarm clock as a prop. Point out that the alarm clock is called **un réveil.**

(Student 1), **viens ici, s'il te plaît.**
Il est sept heures du matin. Tu dors encore.
Tu entends le réveil.
Tu te réveilles.
Tu regardes le réveil.
Tu te lèves.
Tu vas dans la salle de bains.
Tu te laves.
Tu te brosses les dents.
Tu te regardes dans la glace.
Tu te brosses les cheveux.
Tu t'habilles vite.
Tu pars pour l'école. Au revoir et bonne journée!
Merci, *(Student 1).* **Tu peux retourner à ta place.**

se coucher

prendre une douche

prendre un bain

Elle s'appelle Mélanie.
Mélanie se réveille.
Elle se lève tout de suite.

D'abord, elle se lave.

Ensuite elle se lave les dents.

Enfin elle prend son petit déjeuner.

Elle se dépêche.

Step 5 Call out the following verbs and have students pantomime each one: **se réveiller, se lever, se laver, se laver les cheveux, se brosser les cheveux (les dents), se peigner, s'habiller, se regarder dans la glace, se maquiller.**

Step 6 Have one student ask his or her neighbor's name. **(Tu t'appelles comment?)** The students who responds then asks the next student and so on.

Reaching All Students

Kinesthetic Learners Try this activity with the class.

Attention. Levez-vous. Nous allons mimer des actions.
Réveillez-vous.
Lavez-vous la figure et les mains.
Lavez-vous les cheveux.
Rasez-vous.
Brossez-vous les dents.
Brossez-vous les cheveux.
Habillez-vous.
Couchez-vous.
Bonne nuit! Merci.
Asseyez-vous.

3 Practice

Commençons
Let's use our new words

Attention!

When students are doing the **Commençons** activities, accept any answer that makes sense. The purpose of these activities is to have students use the new vocabulary. They are not factual recall activities. Thus, it is not necessary for students to remember specific factual information from the vocabulary presentation when answering. If you wish, have students use the photos on this page as a stimulus, when possible.

Historiette Each time **Historiette** appears, it means that the answers to the activity form a short story. Encourage students to look at the title of the **Historiette,** since it can help them do the activity.

Writing Development

Have students write the answers to Activity 1 in paragraph form.

Recycling

Recycle the expression **avoir besoin de** by making statements about what people want to do and having students say what is needed to do it. For example: **Elle veut se peigner. Elle a besoin d'un peigne.** Tell students that **de** follows **avoir besoin. J'ai besoin de dentifrice. J'ai besoin d'une serviette. J'ai besoin de savon.**

Commençons
Let's use our new words

1 Historiette La matinée de Guillaume

Inventez des réponses.

1. Le matin Guillaume se réveille à six heures? Il se lève tôt ou tard?
2. Il se lève tout de suite?
3. D'abord, il va dans la salle de bains pour se laver?
4. Il se lave la figure avec un gant de toilette?
5. Ensuite, il se lave les dents avec une brosse à dents et du dentifrice?
6. Il prend un bain ou une douche?
7. Il se regarde dans la glace quand il se rase?
8. Il s'habille dans sa chambre à coucher?
9. Enfin, il prend son petit déjeuner avant d'aller à l'école?
10. Il se dépêche? Pourquoi?

Guillaume se rase.

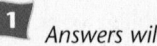

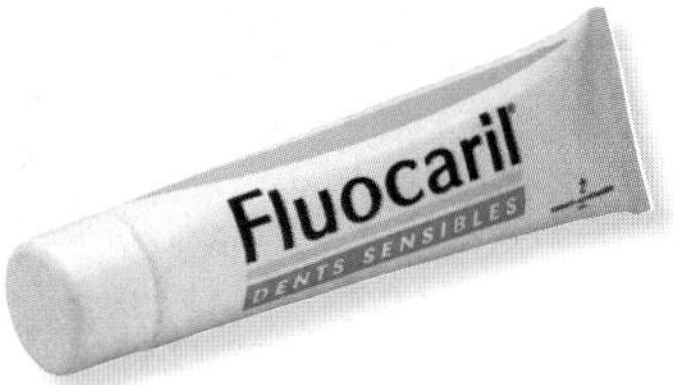

2 Dans quelle pièce? Complétez.

1. On se brosse les dents dans ____.
2. On se couche dans ____.
3. On prend une douche dans ____.
4. On se maquille dans ____.
5. On dort dans ____.
6. On prend son petit déjeuner dans ____.

Answers to Commençons

1 *Answers will vary but may include:*

1. Oui, le matin Guillaume se réveille à six heures. Il se lève tôt.
2. Oui, il se lève tout de suite.
3. Oui, d'abord il va dans la salle de bains pour se laver.
4. Oui, il se lave la figure avec un gant de toilette.
5. Oui, il se lave les dents avec une brosse à dents et du dentifrice.
6. Il prend une douche.
7. Oui, il se regarde dans la glace quand il se rase.
8. Oui, il s'habille dans sa chambre à coucher.
9. Oui, il prend son petit déjeuner avant d'aller à l'école.
10. Oui, il se dépêche. Il ne veut pas être en retard!

2

1. la salle de bains
2. la chambre à coucher
3. la salle de bains
4. la salle de bains
5. la chambre à coucher
6. la cuisine (la salle à manger)

3 **Qu'est-ce qu'il faut?** Choisissez la bonne réponse.

1. Pour se laver les dents il faut ____.
   a. de la crème b. du dentifrice c. du déodorant
2. Pour se laver la figure et les mains, il faut ____.
   a. du déodorant b. du dentifrice c. du savon
3. Pour se raser il faut ____.
   a. un rasoir b. une brosse à dents c. un peigne
4. Pour se peigner il faut ____.
   a. du shampooing b. un peigne c. du savon
5. Pour se laver les cheveux il faut ____.
   a. du déodorant b. du shampooing c. du savon
6. Pour se brosser les cheveux il faut ____.
   a. une brosse b. un peigne c. une brosse à dents

4 **Pendant la journée** Work with a classmate. Each of you will choose a family member and tell each other about that person's daily activities.

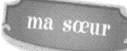

mon père   mon cousin   ma mère

ma sœur   ma cousine   mon frère

Une famille fait les courses, Yerres, France

ENCORE PLUS *For more practice using words from **Mots 1**, do Activity 38 on page H39 at the end of this book.*

Vocabulaire

Reteaching

Show Vocabulary Transparencies 12.2–12.3 and let students say as much as they can about them in their own words.

Learning from Photos

(page 403) You may wish to ask the following questions about the photograph.

Il y a combien de personnes dans cette famille?
Ils ont fait les courses?
Ils ont acheté beaucoup de choses?
Il y a beaucoup de choses dans le chariot?
Ils ont fait leurs achats dans un supermarché?
Ils y sont allés à pied?

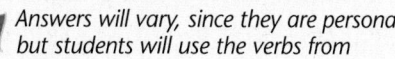

ENCORE PLUS This *infogap* activity will allow students to practice in pairs. The activity should be very manageable for them, since all vocabulary and structures are familiar to them.

Answers to Commençons

3

1. b
2. c
3. a
4. b
5. b
6. a

4 *Answers will vary, since they are personal, but students will use the verbs from **Mots 1**.*

1 Preparation

Resource Manager

Vocabulary Transparencies 12.4–12.5
Audio Activities Booklet TE, pages 146–147
Audiocassette 7B/CD 7
Workbook, page 121
Quiz 2, page 60
ExamView Pro®

Bellringer Review

Use BRR Transparency 12.2 or write the following on the board.
Answer the following.

1. **Tu arrives à l'école à quelle heure le matin?**
2. **Tu y vas comment?**
3. **Tu as combien de cours cette année?**
4. **Quel est ton cours favori?**
5. **Tu quittes l'école à quelle heure?**

2 Presentation

Step 1 Show Vocabulary Transparencies 12.4–12.5. Have students close their books and repeat the new words after you two or three times.

Vocabulaire Mots 2

Chez les Moulin

Avant le dîner, Christophe met la table.

Après le dîner, Mélanie débarrasse la table.
Et Maman fait la vaisselle.

M. Moulin a mis (a allumé) la télé.

Reaching All Students

Total Physical Response Before starting, demonstrate the meaning of **rincer.**

(Student 1), **lève-toi et viens ici, s'il te plaît.**
Imagine que c'est la table dans ta salle à manger.
Mets la table.
Et maintenant, débarrasse la table.
Rince les assiettes.
Mets les assiettes dans le lave-vaisselle.

(Student 2), **lève-toi et viens ici, s'il te plaît.**
Imagine que tu es dans la salle de séjour.
Mets la télé.
Prends la télécommande.
Zappe d'une chaîne à l'autre.
Maintenant assieds-toi.
Regarde ton émission favorite.
Et maintenant, éteins la télé.
Va te coucher.

M. Moulin a zappé pour éviter les publicités.
Il a changé de chaîne.
Il a regardé son émission favorite.
Mélanie a fait ses devoirs après le dîner.

Après l'émission M. Moulin a éteint la télé.

Mélanie a fait ses devoirs.
Elle n'a pas pu regarder le film à la télé.
Elle a enregistré le film.

Vocabulaire

Mots 2

Step 2 Ask questions about the statements on pages 404–405: **Qu'est-ce que M. Moulin a mis? Il a zappé pour éviter quoi? Qu'est-ce qu'il a regardé? Qui a fait ses devoirs?**, etc.

Step 3 After presenting the vocabulary with the transparencies, have students open their books and read the words and sentences.

Recycling

- Have students name the items in a table setting **(le couvert).**
- You may wish to ask the following questions to have students reveiw **pourquoi** and **parce que.**
  M. Moulin a zappé. Pourquoi?
  Mélanie n'a pas pu regardé la télé. Pourquoi?
  Elle a enregistré le film. Pourquoi?

3 Practice

Commençons
Let's use our new words

5 and **7** You may wish to have students write their answers to these activities in paragraph form.

6 You could use this activity as an end-of-class game. You read each description in random order and see which team/group can answer correctly with books closed.

Learning from Photos

(page 406) Ask the following questions about the photo.
Où sont le père et son fils?
Qui est à leurs pieds?
Qui regarde la télé?
Et le fils, qu'est-ce qu'il regarde?
Il lit?
Qu'est-ce que le père a dans la main?
Qu'est-ce qu'il fait avec la télécommande?

Learning from Realia

(page 406) Ask students to study the advertisement. Is it for a remote control or a cable service? Ask them what **les nouveaux pouvoirs** refers to and how much the service costs.

Commençons
Let's use our new words

5 Historiette Chez les Fauvet

Répondez d'après les indications.

1. Qui a mis la table? (Paul)
2. Qui a servi le dîner? (Mme Fauvet)
3. Qui a débarrassé la table? (M. Fauvet)
4. Qui a fait la vaisselle? (Sophie)
5. Où est-ce qu'elle a mis les assiettes, les verres et les couverts? (dans le lave-vaisselle)
6. Après le dîner, qui a mis la télé? (M. Fauvet)
7. Qu'est-ce qu'ils ont regardé à la télé? (leur émission favorite)
8. Ils ont zappé pour éviter les publicités? (oui)
9. Qui a éteint la télé? (M. Fauvet)
10. Qui est sorti après le dîner? (Sophie)
11. Elle s'est bien amusée? (oui)
12. Elle a fait ses devoirs avant de sortir? (oui)

Ils regardent la télé.

6 Quel est le mot? Complétez.

1. L'évier, le frigidaire et le lave-vaisselle se trouvent dans la ____.
2. On rince la vaisselle dans l'____, et ensuite, on met les verres, les assiettes et les couverts dans le ____.
3. Avant le dîner, on ____ la table.
4. Après le dîner, on ____ la table.
5. Quand on veut regarder la télévision, on ____ la télévision.
6. M. Fauvet n'arrive pas à trouver une émission qu'il aime. Il change souvent de ____.
7. On peut changer de chaîne avec une ____.
8. Si on n'est pas à la maison pour regarder un film, on peut ____ le film sur une cassette vidéo.
9. Pour enregistrer un film à la télé il faut avoir un ____.

Answers to Commençons

5

1. Paul a mis la table.
2. Mme Fauvet a servi le dîner.
3. M. Fauvet a débarrassé la table.
4. Sophie a fait la vaisselle.
5. Elle a mis les assiettes, les verres et les couverts dans le lave-vaisselle.
6. M. Fauvet a mis la télé.
7. Ils ont regardé leur émission favorite à la télé.
8. Oui, ils ont zappé pour éviter les publicités.
9. M. Fauvet a éteint la télé.
10. Sophie est sortie après le dîner.
11. Oui, elle s'est bien amusée.
12. Oui, elle a fait ses devoirs avant de sortir.

6

1. cuisine
2. évier, lave-vaisselle
3. met
4. débarrasse
5. met
6. chaîne
7. une télécommande
8. enregistrer
9. magnétoscope

7 Historiette **Chez moi** Donnez des réponses personnelles.

1. Tu rentres à la maison vers quelle heure?
2. Qui prépare le dîner chez toi?
3. Qui met la table?
4. Qui sert le dîner?
5. Qui débarrasse la table?
6. Qui fait la vaisselle?
7. Qu'est-ce que vous faites après le dîner?
8. Tu fais tes devoirs avant de regarder la télévision?

8 **Chez nous** Work with a classmate. Share information about what you usually do when you return home after school. Decide if much of your routine is the same.

9 **En famille** Work with a classmate. Ask each other questions about the illustration. Answer each other's questions.

ENCORE PLUS *For more practice using words from **Mots 2**, do Activity 39 on page H40 at the end of this book.*

Vocabulaire

7 You may wish to have students use this activity as the basis for a classwide poll. Tabulate the results to see who does more work, boys or girls.

9 You can do this activity in small groups or as a whole-class activity.

Assessment

Check for comprehension by reading sentences, words, or expressions from **Mots 2** in random order and having individuals point to the corresponding illustration on Vocabulary Transparencies 12.4–12.5.

ENCORE PLUS This *infogap* activity will allow students to practice in pairs. The activity should be very manageable for them, since all vocabulary and structures are familiar to them.

Answers to Commençons

7 *Answers will vary but may include:*

1. Je rentre à la maison vers cinq heures.
2. Mon père prépare le dîner chez moi.
3. Je mets la table.
4. Ma mère sert le dîner.
5. Je débarrasse la table.
6. Mon frère et moi, nous faisons la vaisselle.
7. Après le dîner on fait nos devoirs.
8. Oui, je fais mes devoirs avant de regarder la télévision.

1 Preparation

Resource Manager

Audio Activities Booklet TE, pages 148–151
Audiocassette 7B/CD 7
Workbook, pages 122–125
Quizzes 3–5, pages 61–63
ExamView Pro®

Bellringer Review

Use BRR Transparency 12.3 or write the following on the board.
Correct the following sentences.

1. **Je prends mon petit déjeuner dans la salle de bains.**
2. **Il se brosse les dents avec du savon.**
3. **Elle se regarde dans la figure.**

2 Presentation

Les verbes réfléchis au présent

Step 1 Have students make a list of the verbs learned in this chapter that describe what they do almost every morning.

Step 2 Lead students through Item 1, calling on volunteers to read the material. You may wish to give additional examples of reflexive vs. nonreflexive actions.
Je me réveille. Je réveille mon frère.
Je me lave. Je lave ma voiture.
Il se regarde. Il regarde ses copains.
Il se brosse. Il brosse son chien.

Step 3 Write the model verbs shown on page 408 on the board. Underline the reflexive pronouns.

Telling what people do for themselves
Les verbes réfléchis au présent

1. Compare the following pairs of sentences.

Paul regarde le bébé.

Paul se regarde.

Anne couche le bébé.

Anne se couche.

In the sentences on the left, one person performs the action and another receives the action. In the sentences on the right, the person performs the action and also receives the action. For this reason, the pronoun **se** must be used. **Se** refers to the subject or doer of the action and is called a "reflexive" pronoun. It indicates that the action of the verb is reflected back to the subject.

2. Each subject pronoun has its corresponding reflexive pronoun. Study the following.

SE LAVER		S'HABILLER	
je	me lave	je	m'habille
tu	te laves	tu	t'habilles
il/elle/on	se lave	il/elle/on	s'habille
nous	nous lavons	nous	nous‿z habillons
vous	vous lavez	vous	vous‿z habillez
ils/elles	se lavent	ils/elles	s'habillent

3. The reflexive pronoun cannot be separated from the verb. In the negative, **ne** comes before the reflexive pronoun and **pas** comes after the verb.

Je me réveille mais je ne me lève pas tout de suite.
On ne se lave jamais les dents avant le dîner.
Je ne me lave plus les cheveux tous les jours.

4. When a reflexive verb follows another verb, the reflexive pronoun agrees with the subject.

Je ne veux pas me lever tôt.
Vous allez vous coucher tard.

Les lavages publics du Banco, Abidjan, Côte d'Ivoire

Note: Point out to students that the forms of these verbs are the same as those of any other **-er** verb. The only addition is the pronoun.

Learning from Photos

(page 409) The **parc du Banco** is on the northwestern edge of Abidjan. It is a rainforest preserve and a pleasant place for a stroll. Near the park there is an interesting outdoor launderette. Every day some 375 washermen, called **fanicos,** get together in this small stream. They rub the clothes vigorously on large stones held in place by old car tires. Afterwards they spread the clothes over rocks and grass in an area that covers at least a half kilometer. Once the clothing is dry, they iron it and they never mix up a piece. There are strict rules imposed by the washers' trade union. It is this union that allocates positions, and anyone who does not respect the rules is fired.

The work of the **fanicos** starts at dawn when they make their rounds in various parts of Abidjan to collect the laundry. The washing in the stream starts at about 6:30 A.M. The **fanicos** are almost all **Burkinabé**—from Burkina Faso; none are Ivoirian.

3 Practice

Continuons
Let's put our words together

10 Have students practice the dialogue in pairs.

11 Go over this activity once calling on individuals to respond. Then call on just one person to answer all six questions. This will give a review in narrative form of the conversation in Activity 10.

Attention!

Note that the activities are color-coded. All the activities in the text are communicative. However, the ones with blue titles are guided communication. The red titles indicate that the answers to the activity are more open-ended and can vary more. You may wish to correct students' mistakes more so in the guided activities than in the activities with a red title, which lend themselves to a freer response.

Continuons
Let's put our words together

10 La matinée de Jean-Marc Répétez la conversation.

11 Historiette C'est malin! Répondez d'après la conversation.

1. Jean-Marc se lève à quelle heure?
2. Il se lave?
3. Il se lave les dents?
4. Il se rase?
5. Il s'habille?
6. Qu'est-ce qu'il fait en une demi-heure?

Answers to Continuons

10 *Students will repeat the dialogue.*

11

1. Il se lève à six heures et demie.
2. Oui, il se lave.
3. Oui, il se lave les dents.
4. Oui, il se rase.
5. Oui, il s'habille.
6. Il se lave, il se lave les dents, il se rase, il s'habille et il prend son petit déjeuner.

Class Motivator

Qu'est-ce que je fais? You may wish to play the following game for more practice with reflexive verbs. Write the reflexive verbs on index cards, one to a card. Put the cards in a deck. A student picks a card and pantomimes the action of the verb. Another student tells him or her what he or she is doing, using the **tu** form.

Structure

13 and **16** Have students interview many different students, using these questions as a guide.

Writing Development

Have students write the answers to Activity 12 in paragraph form.

Learning from Photos

(page 411) Have students say everything they can about the girls in the photograph.

Reaching All Students

Additional Practice Have pairs of students make sentences with the following verbs, taking turns and alternating between reflexive and nonreflexive constructions. For example: Student 1: **Je me brosse.** Student 2: **Je brosse mon chien.**

amuser
laver
peigner
réveiller
brosser

12 Historiette Caroline et Stéphanie Remplacez **Caroline** par **Caroline et Stéphanie.**

1. Caroline se réveille à sept heures.
2. Caroline se lève tout de suite.
3. Caroline se lave les dents.
4. Caroline se lave les mains et la figure.
5. Caroline se brosse les cheveux.
6. Caroline s'habille.
7. Caroline se maquille.

Les deux sœurs se maquillent.

13 Historiette Le matin Donnez des réponses personnelles.

1. Tu te lèves à quelle heure le matin?
2. Tu vas dans la salle de bains?
3. Tu te laves?
4. Tu te laves les mains et la figure?
5. Tu prends une douche ou un bain?
6. Tu te laves les cheveux avec du shampooing?
7. Tu te peignes?
8. Tu te regardes dans la glace quand tu te peignes?

14 Historiette Ma famille Remplacez **on** par **nous.**

Je m'appelle Christian. Dans la famille on se réveille tôt. On ne se lave pas le matin parce qu'on se lave le soir. Ensuite on s'habille. On prend notre petit déjeuner tous ensemble. Après, on se lave les dents. Et on se dépêche d'aller, moi à l'école, mes parents au travail.

15 Ta famille Posez des questions à Christian. Utilisez le paragraphe de l'Activité 14 comme guide. Vous pouvez utiliser les sujets suivants.

tu — tes parents — ta famille — vous

16 Historiette Dimanche Donnez des réponses personnelles.

1. Tu vas te réveiller à quelle heure dimanche?
2. Tu vas t'habiller avant de prendre le petit déjeuner?
3. Tu vas sortir avec des amis?
4. Vous allez vous habiller comment?
5. Tu vas te coucher tard?

ENCORE PLUS *For more practice using reflexive verbs, do Activity 40 on page H41 at the end of this book.*

Answers to Continuons

12

1. Caroline et Stéphanie se réveillent à sept heures.
2. Caroline et Stéphanie se lèvent tout de suite.
3. Caroline et Stéphanie se lavent les dents.
4. Caroline et Stéphanie se lavent les mains et la figure.
5. Caroline et Stéphanie se brossent les cheveux.
6. Caroline et Stéphanie s'habillent.
7. Caroline et Stéphanie se maquillent.

13 *Answers will vary but may include:*

1. Le matin, je me lève à sept heures.
2. Oui, je vais dans la salle de bains.
3. Oui, je me lave.
4. Oui, je me lave les mains et la figure.
5. Je prends une douche.
6. Oui, je me lave les cheveux avec du shampooing.
7. Oui, je me peigne.
8. Oui, je me regarde dans la glace quand je me peigne.

14

Je m'appelle Christian. Dans la famille nous nous réveillons tôt. Nous ne nous lavons pas le matin parce que nous nous lavons le soir. Ensuite nous nous habillons. Nous prenons notre petit déjeuner tous ensemble. Après, nous nous lavons les dents. Et nous nous dépêchons d'aller, moi à l'école, mes parents au travail.

3 Practice *(continued)*

Continuons

Let's put our words together

17 Have students share their findings with the class.

Attention!

Note that **se promener** is included here. Students have learned **faire une promenade.** Emphasize that the two expressions are equivalent by writing on the board:

faire une promenade = se promener

Learning from Photos

(page 412) You may wish to have students look at the photo and describe **les trois copains.**

Reaching All Students

Additional Practice

Give the correct form of the verb in parentheses.

1. tu (se lever)
2. vous (manger)
3. ils (acheter)
4. nous (nager)
5. nous (commencer)
6. elle (s'appeler)

17 **Je me réveille et...** Work in groups of three or four. Tell the order of your daily activities from morning to night. Do you all do everything in the same order? What's the most common routine? Who has the oddest routine? Describe it.

AMICO

18 **Jeu** **J'ai quelque chose.** You have something you use routinely. Tell a classmate what it is. He or she will guess what you use it for.

J'ai du dentifrice.
Tu te laves les dents.

Attention!

1. Note the changes in pronunciation and spelling of the following verbs.

SE LEVER	**nous nous levons**
je me lève	**vous vous levez**
tu te lèves	**ils se lèvent**
il se lève	
S'APPELER	**nous nous appelons**
je m'appelle	**vous vous appelez**
tu t'appelles	**ils s'appellent**
il s'appelle	

The verbs **se promener** and **acheter** have the same spelling changes as **se lever.**

2. Note the spelling of the **nous** form of verbs that end in **-ger** and **-cer: nous mangeons, nous nageons, nous voyageons, nous commençons.**

Répondez d'après le modèle.

— **Je me lève à six heures!**
— **Nous aussi, nous nous levons à six heures.**

1. Je me lève à cinq heures.
2. Je me promène un peu dans le parc.
3. Je nage dans la piscine.
4. J'achète un café et un croissant.
5. Je commence à manger mon croissant dans la rue.
6. Je mange tout mon croissant dans la rue.

Answers to Continuons

17 *Answers will vary depending upon students' routines. However, they will have many things in common.*

Answers to Attention!

1. Nous aussi, nous nous levons à cinq heures.
2. Nous aussi, nous nous promenons un peu dans le parc.
3. Nous aussi, nous nageons dans la piscine.
4. Nous aussi, nous achetons un café et un croissant.
5. Nous aussi, nous commençons à manger notre croissant dans la rue.
6. Nous aussi, nous mangeons tout notre croissant dans la rue.

Telling what people did for themselves
Les verbes réfléchis au passé composé

1. You form the **passé composé** of reflexive verbs with the verb **être.** Note the agreement of the past participle with reflexive verbs.

SE LAVER

Masculin		Féminin	
je	me suis lavé	je	me suis lavée
tu	t'es lavé	tu	t'es lavée
il	s'est lavé	elle	s'est lavée
on	s'est lavés	on	s'est lavées
nous	nous sommes lavés	nous	nous sommes lavées
vous	vous êtes lavé(s)	vous	vous êtes lavée(s)
ils	se sont lavés	elles	se sont lavées

2. Note that when a part of the body follows a reflexive verb, there is no agreement.

Agreement	No agreement
Marie s'est lavée.	Marie s'est lavé les mains.
Nous nous sommes brossés.	Nous nous sommes brossé les cheveux.

3. In the negative sentence, you put the negative words around the reflexive pronoun and the verb **être.**

Je ne me suis pas levée tard.
Mes amis ne se sont jamais amusés chez Paul.

Continuons
Let's put our words together

Papa va se réveiller?
Il s'est déjà réveillé.

19 Déjà fait Répondez d'après le modèle.

1. Papa va se lever?
2. Papa va se laver?
3. Papa va se peigner?
4. Papa va s'habiller?

Answers to Continuons

19

1. Il s'est déjà levé.
2. Il s'est déjà lavé.
3. Il s'est déjà peigné.
4. Il s'est déjà habillé.

20

1. Elle s'est déjà levée.
2. Elle s'est déjà lavée.
3. Elle s'est déjà peignée.
4. Elle s'est déjà habillée.

Structure

1 Preparation

Bellringer Review

Use BRR Transparency 12.4 or write the following on the board.
Fill in the blanks with a reflexive pronoun or an **x** if no pronoun is needed.

Ma mère ___ réveille à six heures. Ensuite elle ___ réveille mon frère. Ils ___ préparent le petit déjeuner. Moi, je ___ habille dans ma chambre et ensuite, je ___ prépare nos sandwichs pour le déjeuner.

2 Presentation

Les verbes réfléchis au passé composé

Attention!

Reciprocal verbs will be taught at a later date. Please note that we have not referred to the reflexive pronoun in Item 2 as an indirect object. This concept is quite difficult for students to understand, since with parts of the body the pronoun almost functions as a possessive. The reflexive pronoun as an indirect object in the reciprocal construction is introduced later. The importance the teacher places on the spelling of the past participle is left up to each individual's discretion.

Step 1 Review the **passé composé** with **être.**

Step 2 Lead students through Items 1–3 on page 413.

Step 3 Have students repeat the model sentences in Items 2–3 after you.

3 Practice

Continuons
Let's put our words together

19 Have students do Activity 19 on page 413 once with books open, and then again with one partner asking the questions in random order, while the other partner answers with books closed. Change roles.

20 and **23** Write answers on the board or on an overhead transparency so students can see the ending on the past participle.

21 Have students retell all the information in their own words after going over the activity in class.

Writing Development
Activity 21 can also be written as a miniconversation at home.

20 **Maman** Refaites l'Activité 19 en remplaçant **Papa** par **Maman.**

21 **Historiette** **Tôt** Donnez des réponses personnelles.

1. Tu t'es réveillé(e) tôt ce matin?
2. Tu t'es levé(e) tout de suite ou tu t'es rendormi(e)?
3. Tu as pris une douche ou tu t'es lavé seulement la figure et les mains?
4. Tu t'es habillé(e) avant ou après le petit déjeuner?
5. Tu t'es peigné(e) ou tu t'es brossé les cheveux ce matin?
6. Tu t'es lavé les dents après le petit déjeuner?
7. Tu t'es bien amusé(e) à l'école?
8. Tu t'es couché(e) à quelle heure hier soir?

22 **Nous et vous** Complétez au passé composé.

1. Ce matin, ma sœur et moi, nous ____ à sept heures. Et vous, vous____ à quelle heure? (se réveiller)
2. Nous ____ tard. Vous ____ tard? (se lever)
3. Nous ____. Vous ____ aussi? (se dépêcher)
4. Nous ____ très vite. Vous ____ vite aussi? (s'habiller)

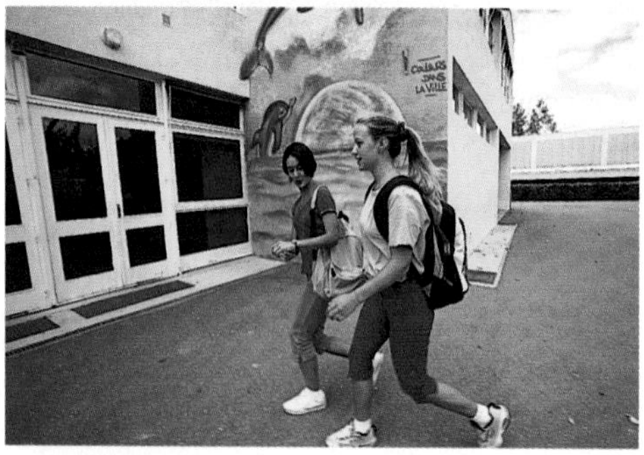

Elles se dépêchent.

23 **Mes cousins** Mettez au pluriel.

1. Il s'est levé.
2. Il s'est lavé.
3. Il s'est rasé.
4. Il s'est habillé.
5. Elle s'est levée tard.
6. Elle s'est maquillée.
7. Elle s'est vite habillée.
8. Elle s'est dépêchée.

24 **Historiette** **Ce matin** Inventez une histoire.

1. Tu t'es levé(e) à quelle heure ce matin?
2. Et ton frère, il s'est levé à quelle heure?
3. Vous vous êtes tous habillés avant le petit déjeuner?
4. Vous vous êtes lavé les dents après le petit déjeuner?
5. Tes parents se sont dépêchés pour aller au travail?

Answers to Continuons

21 *Answers will vary but may include:*
1. Oui, je me suis réveillé(e) tôt.
2. Je me suis levé(e) tout de suite.
3. Je me suis lavé seulement la figure et les mains.
4. Je me suis habillé(e) après le petit déjeuner.
5. Je me suis brossé les cheveux.
6. Oui, je me suis lavé les dents après le petit déjeuner.
7. Oui, je me suis bien amusé(e) à l'école.
8. Je me suis couché(e) à onze heures hier soir.

22
1. nous sommes réveillé(e)s, vous êtes réveillé(e)(s)
2. nous sommes levé(e)s, vous êtes levé(e)(s)
3. nous sommes dépêché(e)s, vous êtes dépêché(e)(s)
4. nous sommes habillé(e)s, vous êtes habillé(e)(s)

23
1. Ils se sont levés.
2. Ils se sont lavés.
3. Ils se sont rasés.
4. Ils se sont habillés.
5. Elles se sont levées tard.
6. Elles se sont maquillées.
7. Elles se sont vite habillées.
8. Elles se sont dépêchées.

24 *Answers will vary but may include:*
1. Je me suis levé(e) à six heures.
2. Mon frère, il s'est levé à sept heures.
3. Oui, nous nous sommes tous habillés avant le petit déjeuner.
4. Oui, nous nous sommes lavé les dents après le petit déjeuner.
5. Oui, mes parents se sont dépêchés pour aller au travail.

25 **Qu'est-ce qu'elle a fait?** Complétez.

1. Elle s'est levé__ ce matin à six heures.
2. Elle s'est lavé__ la figure.
3. Elle s'est lavé__ les dents.
4. Elle s'est amusé__ à l'école.
5. Elle s'est couché__ de bonne heure.

26 **Ce matin** Work with a classmate. Tell each other what you did this morning from the time you woke up until you left for school.

27 **On s'est bien amusé(e)s.** Choose one of the illustrations. Describe it. A classmate will tell which one you're describing and let you know whether the people had fun. Take turns.

28 **Une journée extraordinaire!** Work with a classmate. Imagine that yesterday was really a great day. Tell each other what happened.

ENCORE PLUS *For more practice using reflexive verbs, do Activity 41 on page H42 at the end of this book.*

Vous êtes sur le bon chemin. Allez-y!

Structure

3 Practice

Continuons
Let's put our words together

26 **Expansion:** Have students make up a silly version, giving illogical activities or activities out of order. Their partner points out what is not logical as they listen.

27 **Expansion:** Have students compare their day with those of the people in the illustrations.

ENCORE PLUS This *infogap* activity will allow students to practice in pairs. The activity should be very manageable for them, since all vocabulary and structures are familiar to them.

Allez-y!
At this point in the chapter, students have learned all the vocabulary and structure necessary to complete the chapter. The conversation and cultural readings that follow recycle all the material learned up to this point.

Answers to Continuons

25
1. e
2. *no agreement*
3. *no agreement*
4. e
5. e

26 *Answers will vary depending upon what individual students did.*

27 *Answers will vary but may include:*
La mère a débarrassé la table. Le père et le fils ont fait la vaisselle. Ils ne se sont pas amusés.

28 *Answers will vary depending upon what students did to have a great day.*

Conversation

1 Preparation

Resource Manager

Audio Activities Booklet TE, pages 151–152
Audiocassette 7B/CD 7
CD-ROM

Bellringer Review

Use BRR Transparency 12.5 or write the following on the board.
What do you need in order to do the following?

1. **se laver**
2. **se brosser les dents**
3. **se laver les cheveux**
4. **se regarder**

2 Presentation

Step 1 Have students listen as you read the conversation or play Audiocassette 7B/CD 7.
Step 2 Have students work in pairs to practice the conversation. Then have several pairs present it to the class.
Step 3 You may have a more able student retell the conversation in his or her own words.

Conversation

Quelle interro?

Thomas: Tu n'as pas l'air très réveillée, ce matin.
Magali: Ben, non, je n'ai pas assez dormi.
Thomas: Tu t'es couchée à quelle heure?
Magali: À trois heures du matin.
Thomas: À trois heures du mat! Ça va pas, non? Qu'est-ce que tu as fait? Tu n'as pas pu éteindre la télé, c'est ça?
Magali: La télé? Tu rigoles! L'interrogation de maths, plutôt.
Thomas: L'interro de maths? Quelle interro de maths?

Après la conversation

Répondez.

1. Magali a assez dormi hier soir?
2. Elle s'est couchée à quelle heure?
3. Elle a regardé la télévision?
4. Qu'est-ce qu'elle a fait?
5. Et Thomas, il a étudié ses maths?

About the French Language

It is very "in" to shorten words. **L'interro,** used in this conversation, is an example. Others are: **le petit déj, la télé, un appart.** Tell students to look for the word in the conversation used for "test." ⚜

Answers to Après la conversation

1. Non, elle n'a pas assez dormi hier soir.
2. Elle s'est couchée à trois heures du matin.
3. Non, elle n'a pas regardé la télévision.
4. Elle a étudié pour l'interrogation de maths.
5. Non, il n'a pas étudié ses maths.

Reaching All Students

Bodily Kinesthetic Learners
These learners like to use gestures when expressing themselves. Thomas and Magali are quite expressive in this photo. Before going over the conversation you may wish to say the following to the class: **Regardez bien la photo de Thomas et Magali. C'est Magali ou Thomas qui a quelque chose à dire à l'autre? C'est Magali ou Thomas qui a l'air un peu surpris?**

Parlons un peu plus
Let's talk some more

A **Je suis fatigué(e)!** Neither you nor your classmate look too good this morning. You both got to bed really late. Tell each other why.

B **Une journée horrible!** Work with a classmate. Imagine that yesterday was really a bad day. Tell each other what happened.

Prononciation

Les sons /s/ et /z/

1. It is important to make a distinction between the sounds /s/ and /z/. After all, you would not want to confuse **poisson** and **poison!** Repeat the following words with the sound /s/ as in **assez** and /z/ as in **raser.**

/s/		/z/	
assez	**dessert**	**désert**	**télévision**
classe	**séjour**	**maison**	**zapper**
vaisselle	**boisson**	**raser**	**cousin**
salle	**savon**	**cousine**	

2. Now repeat the following sentences.

Son cousin choisit le dessert et les boissons.
La télévision est dans la salle de séjour.
La salle de classe est assez grande.

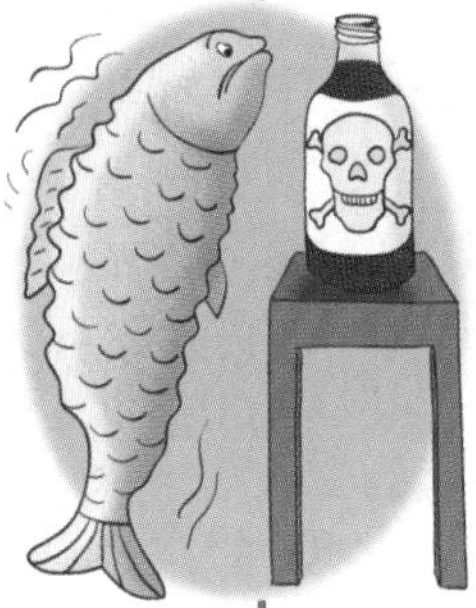

poisson poison

3 Practice

Parlons un peu plus
Let's talk some more

A **and** **B** Have students work in pairs. You may wish to choose a pair of students to do these activities for the class.

B **Expansion:** You may wish to encourage students to exaggerate as much as they can. Then have a "contest" to see whose day was the absolute worst.

Prononciation

Step 1 Model the key words **poisson/poison** and have students repeat in unison.

Step 2 Now lead students through the information on page 417 and model the other words and sentences.

Step 3 You may wish to give the students the following **dictée:**

Assez de dessert, Cassandre!
La cassette de ma cousine est dans la valise.

Step 4 For additional pronunciation practice show Pronunciation Transparency P 12 on the overhead.

Answers to Parlons un peu plus

A *Answers will vary depending upon what the students did.*

B *Answers will vary.*
Students should be able to exaggerate and have fun doing this activity.

Glencoe Technology

CD-ROM

On the CD-ROM, students can watch a dramatization of this conversation. They can then play the role of either one of the characters and record themselves in the conversation.

Resource Manager

Audio Activities Booklet TE, pages 154–155
Audiocassette 7B/CD 7

Bellringer Review

Use BRR Transparency 12.6 or write the following on the board.
List at least three chores you do at home.

National Standards

Cultures
The reading about an Algerian family living in France on pages 418-419, and the related activities on page 419, allow students to find out more about this important minority group in France.

Presentation

Pre-reading

Step 1 You may want to have students look at the photos on pages 418–419 now.

Step 2 Read and discuss the Reading Strategy on page 418.

Step 3 Have students skim the reading quickly and silently.

Reading

Step 1 Lead students through the **Lecture** on pages 418–419 by having individuals read two or three sentences at a time. After each one reads, ask others comprehension questions.

Step 2 Ask five or six questions that review the main points. The answers will give a coherent oral review of the **Lecture.**

Le Québec

Lectures culturelles

Reading Strategy

Skimming
There are several ways to read an article or a passage—each one with its own purpose. Skimming means reading quickly in order to find out the general idea of a passage. To skim means to read without paying careful attention to small details, noting only information about the main theme or topic. Sometimes a reader will skim a passage only to decide whether it's interesting enough to read in detail.

La famille Ben Amar

Les Ben Amar habitent à Saint-Quentin-en-Yvelines. C'est une ville nouvelle dans la banlieue[1] parisienne. Les Ben Amar sont des Français d'origine algérienne. En France, il y a beaucoup de gens originaires des pays du Maghreb, c'est-à-dire des trois pays francophones d'Afrique du Nord—le Maroc, l'Algérie et la Tunisie. Aujourd'hui, la deuxième religion en France, c'est la religion musulmane.

Le matin

Dans la famille Ben Amar, il y a six personnes: M. Ben Amar, sa femme et leurs quatre enfants. Ce matin, comme d'habitude, les Ben Amar se sont levés entre six heures et six heures et demie. Ils se sont lavés, peignés, habillés et ils ont pris leur petit déjeuner. Ils sont partis de chez eux vers sept heures et demie. M. Ben Amar est allé à l'usine[2] où il travaille comme contremaître[3]. Ahmed et Halima vont au collège et Aïcha est à l'école primaire. Le petit Jamal a deux ans. Il ne peut pas encore aller à l'école maternelle. Il passe la journée chez sa grand-mère qui habite dans le même immeuble. Comme beaucoup de femmes françaises, Mme Ben Amar travaille à l'extérieur. Tout est assez cher et la famille a besoin de deux salaires. Mme Ben Amar est assistante sociale[4]. Et Mima est toujours contente de garder son petit Jamal.

Les Ben Amar rentrent déjeuner? Non, ils ne rentrent pas chez eux à midi. M. et Mme Ben Amar déjeunent là où ils travaillent et les enfants déjeunent à la cantine de leur école. Le petit Jamal déjeune avec sa grand-mère.

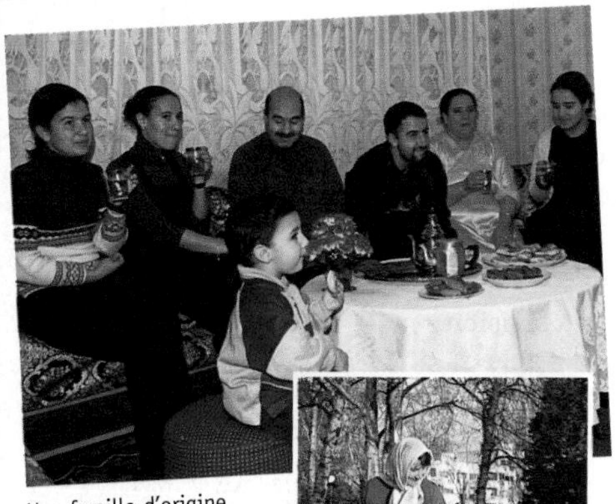
Une famille d'origine algérienne

Mima avec son petit-fils

[1] banlieue *suburbs*
[2] usine *factory*
[3] contremaître *foreman*
[4] assistante sociale *social worker*

Le soir

Le soir, les enfants rentrent de l'école vers cinq heures. Ils vont chez leur grand-mère. Ils mangent une tartine de confiture ou des petits gâteaux faits par Mima et ils font leurs devoirs. Vers sept heures et demie, leurs parents rentrent. Ce soir, Mima a préparé un bon couscous pour toute la famille. Après le dîner, Ahmed débarrasse la table, Halima aide sa mère à faire la vaisselle et M. Ben Amar regarde la télévision. Ce soir, il y a un bon film égyptien à 22 h 30. Les films égyptiens sont excellents et M. et Mme Amar aiment bien voir de temps en temps un film en arabe.

Saint-Quentin-en-Yvelines, près de Paris

Un bon couscous

Après la lecture

A Les Ben Amar Lisez rapidement le texte et trouvez les informations suivantes.

1. le nom de la petite ville où les Ben Amar habitent
2. les noms des pays du Maghreb
3. la deuxième religion en France
4. le nombre d'enfants dans la famille
5. leurs prénoms respectifs
6. l'heure où les Ben Amar se lèvent
7. comment les enfants appellent leur grand-mère

B La journée des Ben Amar Décrivez.

1. le travail de M. Ben Amar
2. le travail de Mme Ben Amar
3. le travail de la grand-mère
4. le dîner des Ben Amar
5. la soirée des Ben Amar

Lectures culturelles

Post-reading

Have students do the **Après la lecture** activities on page 419 orally after reading the selection in class. Then assign these activities to be written at home. Go over them again the following day.

Après la lecture

A and B Allow students to refer to the story to look up the answers, or you may use this activity as a testing device for factual recall.

FUN-FACTS

There are presently 4.2 million immigrants living in France.This figure does not include illegal aliens (estimates vary from 300,000 to 1 million). Approximately one-third of the immigrant population lives in the Paris area.

Over the past two decades, the number of new arrivals from other European countries has decreased, while the numbers from North Africa, West Africa, and Asia have increased. The largest single minority group in France is made up of **Maghrébins:** Algerians, Moroccans, and Tunisians, in that order.

Learning from Photos

(page 419) **Une ville nouvelle,** such as the one in the photograph, is a self-contained town built on the outskirts of a large city. It is made up of high-rise buildings, many of which are **HLM (Habitation à loyer modéré),** a French version of subsidized housing. In addition to the apartment blocks there is a mall with shops, markets, and almost always **un hypermarché** as well as schools and a post office. The **villes nouvelles** are almost exclusively inhabited by people of moderate to low income.

Answers to Après la lecture

A

1. Saint-Quentin-en-Yvelines
2. le Maroc, l'Algérie et la Tunisie
3. la religion musulmane
4. quatre
5. Ahmed, Halima, Aïcha, Jamal
6. entre six heures et six heures et demie du matin
7. Mima

B

1. M. Ben Amar est contremaître dans une usine.
2. Mme Ben Amar est assistante sociale.
3. La grand-mère garde son petit fils.
4. Les Ben Amar mangent un couscous.
5. M. Ben Amar regarde un film égyptien. Mme Ben Amar fait la vaisselle. Aïcha et Jamal vont se coucher. Halima et Ahmed font leurs devoirs.

National Standards

Cultures
This selection familiarizes students with the typical breakfasts in France and North Africa.

Comparisons
This selection compares a typical American breakfast with typical French and North African breakfasts.

Attention!

This reading is optional. You may skip it completely, have the entire class read it, have only several students read it and report to the class, or assign it for extra credit.

Presentation

Step 1 Ask students: **Qu'est-ce que tu as pris comme petit déjeuner ce matin? Tu aimes les œufs? Tu prends du jus d'orange? Tu manges des céréales avec du lait?**

Step 2 Have students read the **Lecture** quickly.

Step 3 Ask what new information they learned about **Le petit déjeuner** in France and North Africa.

Lecture supplémentaire

Le petit déjeuner

Tout le monde se réveille le matin, se lève, se lave, s'habille et… prend son petit déjeuner. On commence la journée par un bon petit déjeuner. Mais le petit déjeuner n'est pas le même partout[1].

Aux États-Unis

Aux États-Unis, on boit souvent un verre de jus de fruit—du jus d'orange, par exemple. Ensuite on mange des céréales ou des œufs—des œufs brouillés[2], des œufs sur le plat avec du bacon, des saucisses ou du jambon et du pain grillé. Avec ça, on boit du café ou du chocolat ou même un verre de lait. C'est un vrai petit déjeuner américain, mais ce n'est pas un petit déjeuner français. En France, on ne mange jamais d'œufs ni de bacon au petit déjeuner.

[1] partout *everywhere*
[2] brouillés *scrambled*

Un petit déjeuner américain—des œufs sur le plat

Une tartine

En France

Un petit déjeuner typiquement français, c'est du pain, des croissants ou des brioches avec un bol de café au lait (le lait est chaud.) Les enfants boivent souvent du chocolat chaud. On mange souvent des tartines. Une tartine, c'est une tranche de pain beurré avec de la confiture.

Un croissant et une brioche

Du droî

Des olives

Des figues et des raisins secs

Au Maghreb

En Tunisie, les enfants mangent souvent du droî pour le petit déjeuner. Le droî est de la farine de sorgho[3] cuite à l'eau bouillante[4]. On mange le droî chaud avec un peu de sucre. Les adultes mangent aussi quelquefois du droî, mais souvent ils mangent des tartines comme en France. À la campagne, on mange quelquefois des figues et des raisins secs blancs.

En Algérie, on mange des tartines et du café au lait comme en France, mais à la campagne, on mange quelquefois du fromage, des olives, du pain et de la soupe.

[3] farine de sorgho *sorghum flour*
[4] cuite à l'eau bouillante *cooked in boiling water*

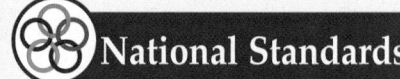

Après la lecture

Un petit déjeuner excellent Décrivez.

1. un petit déjeuner américain
2. un petit déjeuner français
3. un petit déjeuner tunisien
4. un petit déjeuner algérien

National Standards

Communities
If you have students of different ethnic backgrounds have them share with the class a typical breakfast of their culture group.

Answers to Après la lecture

1. On boit souvent du jus de fruit, et on mange des céréales ou des œufs.
2. On boit du café au lait ou du chocolat chaud et on mange des croissants, des brioches ou des tartines.
3. Les enfants mangent du droî et les adultes mangent du droî ou des tartines. À la campagne, on mange des figues et des raisins secs blancs.
4. On mange des tartines et on boit du café au lait. À la campagne on mange du fromage, des olives, du pain et de la soupe.

CONNEXIONS

National Standards

Connections
This reading about ecology establishes a connection with another discipline, allowing students to reinforce and further their knowledge of natural sciences through the study of French.

Attention!

The readings in the **Connexions** section are optional. They focus on some of the major disciplines taught in schools and universities. The vocabulary is useful for discussing such topics as history, literature, art, economics, business, science, etc. You may choose any of the following ways to do the readings in the Connexions sections.

Independent reading Have students read the selections and do the post-reading activities as homework, which you collect. This option is least intrusive on class time and requires a minimum of teacher involvement.

Homework with in-class follow-up Assign the readings and post-reading activities as homework. Review and discuss the material in class the next day.

Intensive in-class activity This option includes a pre-reading vocabulary presentation, in-class reading and discussion, assignment of the activities for homework, and a discussion of the assignment in class the following day.

CONNEXIONS

Les sciences

L'écologie

Ecology is a subject of great interest to people around the world. No one wants to wake up each morning and breathe polluted air or drink contaminated water. Unfortunately, however, much of what we do in our daily life has a negative impact on our environment. The way we dispose of waste litters fields and pollutes waterways. Factories and vehicles belch smoke and fumes that pollute the air. We are all aware that urgent and dramatic steps must be taken to avert future disasters.

L'air pollué, Lyon

L'air pur, Pays Basque

L'écologie

L'écologie, c'est l'équilibre entre les êtres vivants[1] et la nature. Le terme est maintenant synonyme de survie[2] pour beaucoup d'êtres humains à cause de problèmes écologiques très graves.

La pollution de l'air

L'air que nous respirons est souvent pollué. Le plus souvent, il est pollué par des émissions de gaz qui s'échappent des voitures

[1] êtres vivants *living beings*
[2] survie *survival*

et des camions[3]. Il est pollué aussi par la fumée qui se dégage des cheminées des usines qui brûlent[4] des substances chimiques.

La pollution de l'eau

La contamination de l'eau de nos lacs, de nos rivières et de nos mers est catastrophique dans certaines régions. Les accidents de pétroliers font que des millions de litres de pétrole se déversent[5] dans les mers et les océans. Dans les zones industrielles les usines déversent des déchets[6] industriels dans les rivières. Beaucoup de ces déchets sont toxiques et peuvent causer des maladies[7] très graves.

Le recyclage

De nos jours, il y a de grandes campagnes de recyclage. Grâce au recyclage, nous pouvons utiliser à nouveau des déchets de verre, de papier, de métal et même de plastique.

[3] camions *trucks*
[4] brûlent *burn*
[5] se déversent *are spilled*
[6] déchets *wastes*
[7] maladies *illnesses*

Le naufrage d'un pétrolier, Bretagne

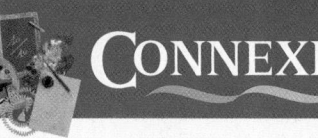

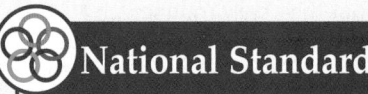

Conteneurs pour le recyclage

Après la lecture

A En français, s'il vous plaît. Trouvez l'équivalent des mots suivants dans la lecture.

1. ecology
2. ecological problems
3. chemical substances
4. air pollution
5. toxic wastes
6. recycling

B Discussion Répondez.

1. L'air est pollué là où vous habitez?
2. Il y a beaucoup d'usines près de chez vous?
3. Il y a beaucoup de voitures, d'autocars et de camions qui passent?
4. Vous recyclez? Qu'est-ce que vous recyclez? Le papier, le carton *(cardboard),* le verre… ?

CONNEXIONS

Presentation

Les sciences
L'écologie

Step 1 Have students read the introduction in English on page 422.

Step 2 Have students scan each reading section for cognates. Then have them do the reading again, this time for comprehension.

Après la lecture

A This activity encourages students to look for cognates as they read.

B This activity is designed to encourage students to think about ecological conditions in their immediate community.

National Standards

Connexions
Have students form a research partnership with the biology class to find out what people can do to conserve water, prevent pollution, and protect the environment. Then you may wish to have them design posters illustrating these issues. Students can label them in French.

Answers to Après la lecture

A
1. l'écologie
2. les problèmes écologiques
3. des substances chimiques
4. la pollution de l'air
5. des déchets industriels
6. le recyclage

B *Answers can be in the affirmative or negative depending upon where students live.*
1. Oui, l'air est pollué là où j'habite.
2. Oui, il y a beaucoup d'usines près de chez moi.
3. Oui, il y a beaucoup de voitures, d'autocars et de camions qui passent.
4. Je recycle le papier, le carton et le verre.

Reaching All Students

For the Younger Students Have students identify an ecological problem at your school or in your community. Have them make a poster in French, identifying the problem and offering some solutions to it. Hang the posters up in the classroom or around the school. You might consider doing this for Earth Day.

Use what you have learned

Recycling

These activities allow students to use the vocabulary and structure from this chapter in completely open-ended, real-life situations.

Art Connection

(page 424) Vincent Van Gogh was born in Holland. His father was a Calvinist minister. As a young man, Van Gogh worked as a lay missionary in a poor Belgian mining village. This, however, was not his vocation, and he became quite a loner and developed his interest for art. His early paintings were done in drab colors and showed peasants going about their daily routine.

In 1886 Van Gogh moved to Paris to be with his brother, Theo, an art dealer. Theo recognized his brother's artistic ability and gave him an allowance so he could continue painting. In Paris he came under the influence of the Impressionists and his colors became brighter. He became fascinated with Japanese woodcut prints, which had an effect on his paintings. He began to use large flat areas of color and tilt his subject matter, as we see in this painting, to present an unusual perspective.

Van Gogh moved to Arles in 1888 at age 35. During his stay in Arles he was extremely productive, producing ***La chambre de Vincent à Arles, Vue d'Arles aux iris, La plaine de Crau,*** and several portraits including ***L'Arlésienne*** and ***Mme Ginoux.***

Use what you have learned

PARLER

1

Ma famille

✔ Compare your family life to someone else's

Work with a classmate. Find out about some family habits in your respective homes: who does what chores, what you do after dinner, etc. Compare your findings.

Vincent Van Gogh *La chambre de Vincent à Arles*

PARLER

2

Pas la même chose

✔ Talk about your weekday and weekend routines

Most people like a change of pace on the weekend. Talk with a classmate about things that students do or don't do during the week. Your partner will say how that differs on the weekend and why. Take turns.

Pendant la semaine, on se lève tôt.
Pendant le week-end, on se lève plus tard.

PARLER

3

Quel jour!

✔ Talk about an atypical day

You have a set routine but sometimes you just can't stick to it. That was the case yesterday. Have a conversation with a friend. Use the model as a guide.

—D'habitude je me lève à sept heures.
—Tu t'es levé(e) à quelle heure hier?
—Je me suis levé(e) à dix heures et demie.

Answers to C'est à vous

1 *Answers will vary based on students' daily life.*

2 *Answers will vary but may include:*
Pendant la semaine on ne peut pas se coucher tard. Pendant le week-end on se couche plus tard.
Pendant la semaine on se lève tôt.
Pendant le week-end on se lève plus tard.
Pendant la semaine on va à l'école.
Pendant le week-end il n'y a pas classe.

3 *Answers will vary depending upon students' daily routines.*

ÉCRIRE

4 Une journée typique

✔ *Write about your daily routine*

Your Tunisian pen pal is curious about your daily routine. Write him or her an e-mail describing all the activities you do on a typical day, from the time you wake up to the time you go to bed.

Halima est de Kairouan en Tunisie

Writing Strategy

Taking notes Taking notes gives you a written record of important information you may need for later use. When taking notes from a lecture, write down key words and phrases as you continue to focus on what the speaker is saying. When the speaker has finished, go back over your notes as soon as possible, highlighting the most important points and adding details to make them as complete as possible. If necessary, rewrite your notes, organizing them so they will be of utmost use to you.

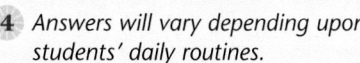

ÉCRIRE

5 Un job d'été

You are working in Quebec this summer. You are going to help take care of two small children. The children's parents give you many instructions about the children's routine and activities. Since you probably will not remember all they are telling you, you jot down notes. Take your notes and organize them to describe each child's day. Then write down your responsibilities—what it is you have to do.

Answers to C'est à vous

4 *Answers will vary depending upon students' daily routines.*

Writing Development

Have students keep a notebook containing their best written work from each chapter. These selected writings can be based on assignments from the Student Textbook and the Writing Activities Workbook. The two activities on page 425 are examples of writing assignments that may be included in each student's portfolio. In the Workbook, students will develop an organized autobiography **(Mon autobiographie).** These workbook pages may also become a part of their portfolio.

Writing Strategy

Taking notes Have students read the Writing Strategy on page 425. If students have difficulty thinking of related vocabulary, have them use the vocabulary list on page 428.

Reaching All Students

Additional Practice Display Communication Transparency C 12. Have students work in groups to make up as many questions as they can about the illustration. Have groups take turns asking and answering the questions.

Learning from Photos

(page 425) The young person in this photo is from Kairouan, Tunisia. Kairouan is an interesting city founded in 670. Kairouan is an Islamic holy city with a Great Mosque and several sanctuaries.

Resource Manager

Communication Transparencies
Quizzes
Test Booklet
ExamView Pro®
Situation Cards
Performance Assessment
Marathon mental Videoquiz

Assessment

This is a pre-test for students to take before you administer the chapter test. Answer sheets for students to do these pages are provided in your transparency binder. Note that each section is cross-referenced so students can easily find the material they have to review in case they made errors. You may wish to collect these assessments and correct them yourself or you may prefer to have the students correct themselves in class. You can go over the answers orally or project them on the overhead, using your Assessment Answers transparencies.

Vocabulaire

1 Identifiez.

1. 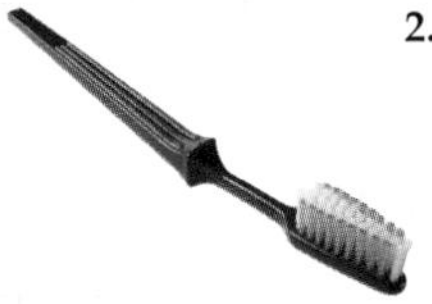
2. 
3. 
4. 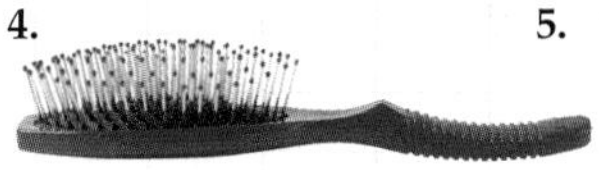
5. 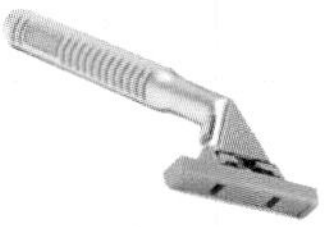

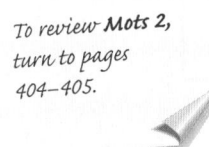

*To review **Mots 1**, turn to pages 400–401.*

2 Mettez en ordre.

6. ____	**a.** se laver
7. ____	**b.** se réveiller
8. ____	**c.** se coucher
9. ____	**d.** se lever

3 Choisissez.

*To review **Mots 2**, turn to pages 404–405.*

10. Après le dîner, il ____ la table.
    a. met **b.** débarrasse **c.** fait
11. Il lave les assiettes, les verres, etc. Il fait ____.
    a. le lave-vaisselle **b.** la vaisselle **c.** l'évier
12. Il ____ pour éviter les publicités.
    a. allume la télé **b.** fait ses devoirs **c.** zappe
13. Après son émission favorite, il a ____ la télé.
    a. éteint **b.** regardé **c.** mis

Structure

To review reflexive verbs in the present, turn to pages 408–409.

4 Complétez au présent.

14. Il ____ la figure. (se laver)
15. Elles ____ les cheveux. (se brosser)
16. Nous ____ beaucoup. (s'amuser)
17. Je ____ à onze heures. (se coucher)
18. Éric, tu ____ tous les matins? (se raser)

Answers to Assessment

1

1. une brosse à dents
2. un peigne
3. une glace
4. une brosse
5. un rasoir

2

6. b
7. d
8. a
9. c

3

10. b
11. b
12. c
13. a

4

14. se lave
15. se brossent
16. nous amusons
17. me couche
18. te rases

5 **Récrivez.**

19. Tu t'appelles comment?
    Vous ____________?
20. Nous nous levons tôt.
    Je ____________.

To review verbs with spelling changes, turn to page 412.

6 **Complétez au passé composé.**

21. Elle ____. (se laver)
22. Elles ____ les cheveux. (se laver)
23. Mes amis ____. (s'amuser)

To review reflexive verbs in the **passé composé,** turn to page 413.

Culture

7 **Identifiez.**

24. les pays du Maghreb
25. la deuxième religion en France

To review this cultural information, turn to pages 418–419.

Un marché, Alger, Algérie

FRENCH *Online*

For more information on the Maghreb, go to the Glencoe French Web site: french.glencoe.com

Assessment

Glencoe Technology

MINDJOGGER

You may wish to help your students prepare for the chapter test by playing the MindJogger game show. Teams will compete against each other to review chapter vocabulary and structure and sharpen listening comprehension skills.

Learning from Photos

(page 427) This photo is an outdoor market in Algiers, the capital of Algeria. Note the spelling of Algiers in French, **Alger.**

Answers to Assessment

5

19. Vous vous appelez comment?
20. Je me lève tôt.

6

21. s'est lavée
22. se sont lavé
23. se sont amusés

7

24. le Maroc, l'Algérie, la Tunisie
25. la religion musulmane

Vocabulary Review

The words and phrases in the **Vocabulaire** have been taught for productive use in this chapter. They are summarized here as a resource for both student and teacher. This list also serves as a convenient resource for the **C'est à vous** activities on pages 424–425. There are approximately eight cognates in this vocabulary list. Have students find them.

Attention!

You will notice that the vocabulary list here is not translated. This has been done intentionally, since we feel that by the time students have finished the material in the chapter they should be familiar with the meanings of all the words. If there are several words they still do not know, we recommend that they refer to the **Mots 1** and **2** sections in the chapter or go to the dictionaries at the back of this book to find the meanings. However, if you prefer that your students have the English translations, please refer to Vocabulary Transparency 12.1, where you will find all these words listed with their translations.

Doing daily activities

la routine
prendre un bain
prendre une douche
se réveiller
se lever
se laver
se brosser
se raser
se maquiller
se peigner
s'habiller
s'amuser
se dépêcher
se coucher

Identifying grooming articles

du savon
un gant de toilette
du shampooing
une brosse à dents
du dentifrice
une glace
un rasoir
un peigne
une brosse

Identifying more parts of the body

la figure
les cheveux *(m. pl.)*
les dents *(f. pl.)*

How well do you know your vocabulary?

- Choose an expression from the list that describes something you do as part of your daily routine.
- Ask a classmate to give words related to that particular daily activity.

Identifying household appliances

un évier
un lave-vaisselle
un frigidaire, un réfrigérateur
une télé(vision)
une télécommande
un magnétoscope

Discussing home activities

mettre la table
débarrasser la table
faire la vaisselle
faire ses devoirs
mettre la télévision
allumer
éteindre
enregistrer
zapper
changer de chaîne
une émission
une publicité
une chaîne

Other useful words and expressions

s'appeler
tôt
tard
d'abord
ensuite
enfin
tout de suite

Technotour

BON VOYAGE!

VIDÉO • Épisode 12

Avant de visionner

In this video episode, Vincent walks a sleepy Manu through the morning routine.

Manu se réveille.

Manu prend son petit déjeuner.

FRENCH ONLINE

À découvrir

Learn more about people's busy lives in Paris online.

Forum des Halles, Paris

FRENCH *Online*

In the Chapter 12 Internet activity, you will have a chance to learn more about daily life in the Francophone world. To begin your virtual adventure, go to the Glencoe French Web site:
french.glencoe.com

Technotour

Overview

This page previews two key multimedia components of the **Glencoe French** series. Each reinforces the material taught in the chapter in a unique manner.

VIDÉO

The Video Program allows students to see how the chapter vocabulary and structures are used by native speakers. For maximum reinforcement, show the video episode as a final activity for Chapter 12.

The two photos on the left show highlights from the Chapter 12 video episode. Before viewing the episode, go over the photos with your students. See the Video Activities Booklet for detailed suggestions for using this resource.

FRENCH *Online*

- The **À découvrir** photo on page 429 shows a Paris street scene. Students can learn more about people's busy lives in Paris online.
- Teacher Information and Student Worksheets for this activity can be accessed at the Web site.

Video Synopsis

In this video episode, we hear Vincent give an overview of daily life in Paris, making comparisons to other parts of the world where the hustle and bustle of daily routine is much the same. We then see him greet Madame Chentouf at Manu's house where he learns that Manu is still asleep! Vincent proceeds to walk Manu through his morning routine, casually reminding him that Christine is expecting them in half an hour.

Planning for Chapter 13

SCOPE AND SEQUENCE, PAGES 430–461

Topics

- Movies, plays, museums

Culture

- Cultural activities in France
- African music — traditional and modern

Functions

- How to discuss movies, plays, and museums
- How to express what happens to you or someone else
- How to refer to people and things already mentioned

Structure

- The verbs **savoir** and **connaître**
- The pronouns **me, te, nous, vous**
- The pronouns **le, la, les**

National Standards

- Communication Standard 1.1 pages 434, 435, 438, 439, 442, 443, 445, 446, 447, 449, 456
- Communication Standard 1.2 pages 434, 435, 438, 439, 442, 443, 445, 446, 447, 448, 451, 453, 455
- Communication Standard 1.3 pages 434, 435, 438, 441, 443, 447, 456, 457
- Cultures Standard 2.1 pages 432, 437, 439, 448, 449, 450–451, 452–453, 454–455
- Cultures Standard 2.2 pages 432, 437, 438, 439, 441, 449, 450–451, 452–453, 454–455
- Connections Standard 3.1 pages 433, 436, 437, 454–455
- Comparisons Standard 4.2 pages 449, 450–451, 452–453, 454–455
- Communities Standard 5.1 pages 456, 457

PACING AND PRIORITIES

The chapter content is color coded below to assist you in planning.

■ required ■ recommended ■ optional

Vocabulaire *(required)* *Days 1–4*

- ■ Mots 1
  - Au cinéma
  - Au théâtre
- ■ Mots 2
  - Au musée

Structure *(required)* *Days 5–7*

- ■ Les verbes **savoir** et **connaître**
- ■ Les pronoms **me, te, nous, vous**
- ■ Les pronoms **le, la, les**

Conversation *(required)*

- ■ On va au cinéma?

Prononciation *(recommended)*

- ■ Le son **/ü/**

Lectures culturelles

- ■ Les loisirs culturels en France *(recommended)*
- ■ La musique africaine *(optional)*

Connexions *(optional)*

- ■ La musique

■ **C'est à vous** *(recommended)*

■ **Assessment** *(recommended)*

■ **Technotour** *(optional)*

RESOURCE GUIDE

Section	Pages	Section Resources
Vocabulaire *Mots 1*		
Au cinéma Au théâtre	432–433 433–435	Vocabulary Transparencies 13.2–13.3 Audiocassette 8A/CD 8 Audio Activities Booklet TE, pages 157–158 Workbook, pages 129–130 Quiz 1, page 64 ExamView Pro®
Vocabulaire *Mots 2*		
Au musée	436–439	Vocabulary Transparencies 13.4–13.5 Audiocassette 8A/CD 8 Audio Activities Booklet TE, page 159 Workbook, pages 131–132 Quiz 2, pages 65 ExamView Pro®
Structure		
Les verbes **savoir** et **connaître** Les pronoms **me, te, nous, vous** Les pronoms **le, la, les**	440–441 442–443 444–447	Audiocassette 8A/CD 8 Audio Activities Booklet TE, pages 160–162 Workbook, pages 133–135 Quizzes 3–5, pages 66–68 ExamView Pro®
Conversation		
On va au cinéma?	448	Audiocassette 8A/CD 8 Audio Activities Booklet TE, page 163 CD-ROM
Prononciation		
Le son **/ü/**	449	Pronunciation Transparency P 13 Audiocassette 8A/CD 8 Audio Activities Booklet TE, page 164
Lectures culturelles		
Les loisirs culturels en France La musique africaine	450–451 452–453	Audiocassette 8A/CD 8 Audio Activities Booklet TE, pages 164–165 Test Booklet, Chapter 13
Connexions		
La musique	454–455	Test Booklet, Chapter 13
C'est à vous		
	456–457	**Bon voyage!** Video, Episode 13 Video Activities Booklet, Chapter 13 French Online Activities french.glencoe.com
Assessment		
	458–459	Communication Transparency C 13 Quizzes 1–5, pages 64–68 Test Booklet, Chapter 13 ExamView Pro® Situation Cards, Chapter 13 **Marathon mental** Videoquiz

Using Your Resources for Chapter 13

Transparencies

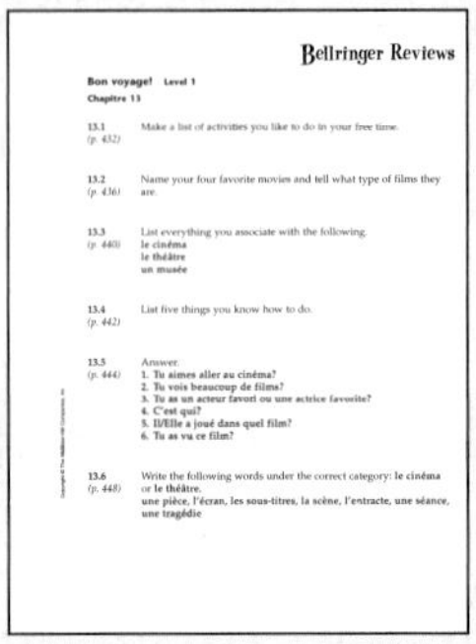

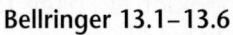

Bellringer 13.1–13.6

Vocabulary 13.1–13.5

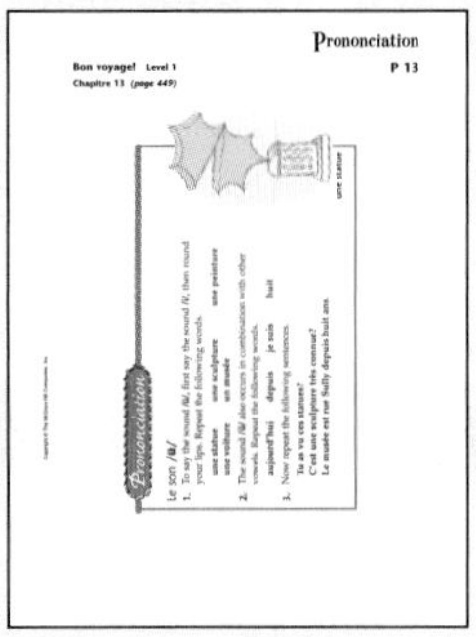

Pronunciation P 13

Communication C 13

Writing Activities Workbook

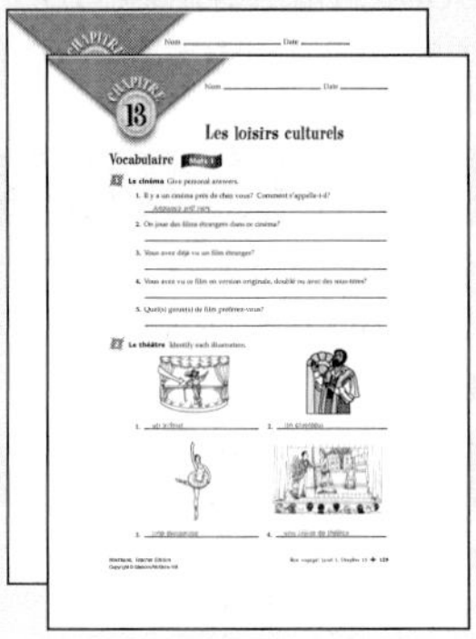

Vocabulary, pages 129–132

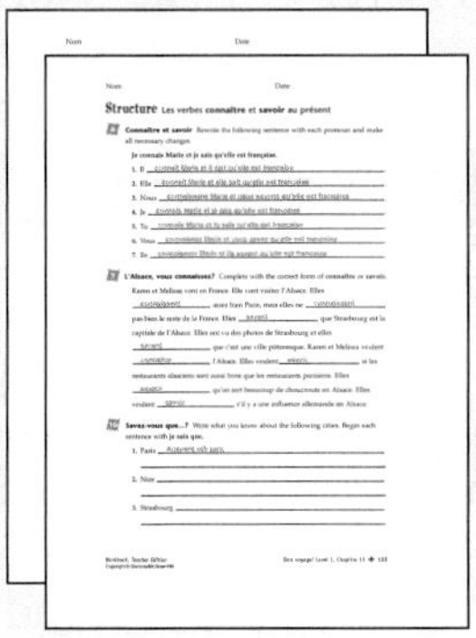
Structure, pages 133–135

Enrichment, pages 136–138

Audio Program and Audio Activities Booklet

Vocabulary, pages 157–159

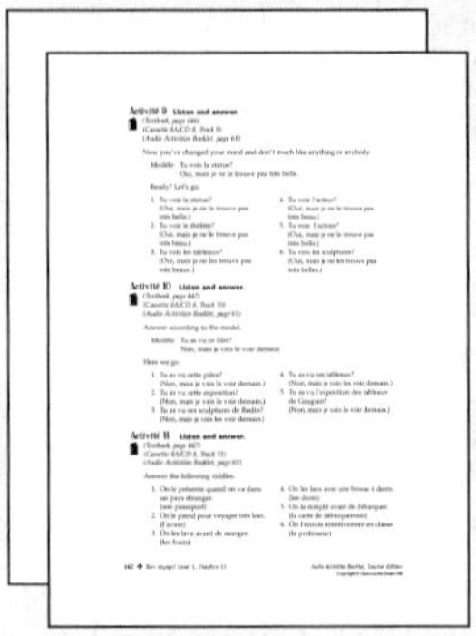
Structure, pages 160–162

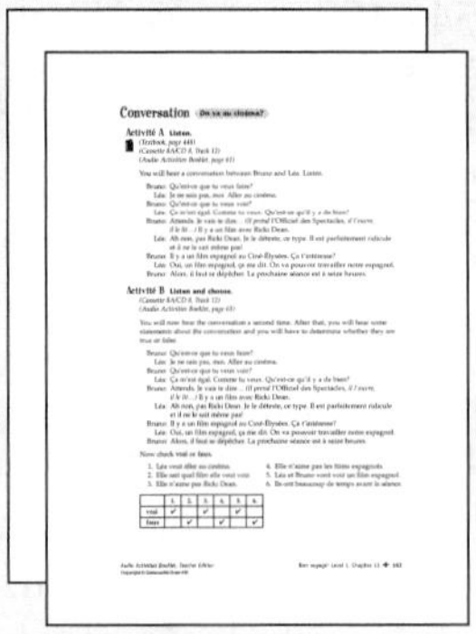
Conversation, Pronunciation, pages 163–164

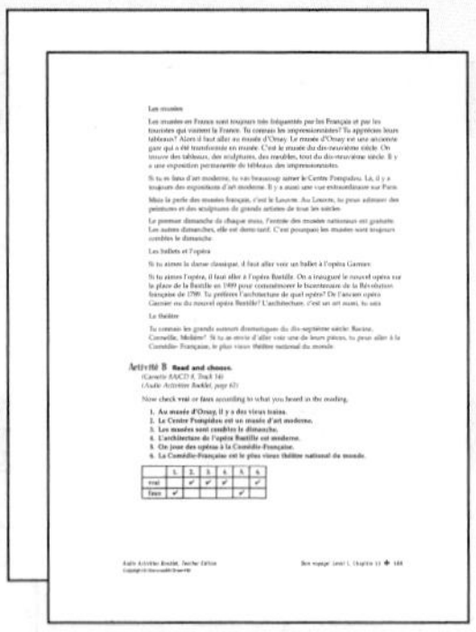
Cultural Reading, pages 164–165

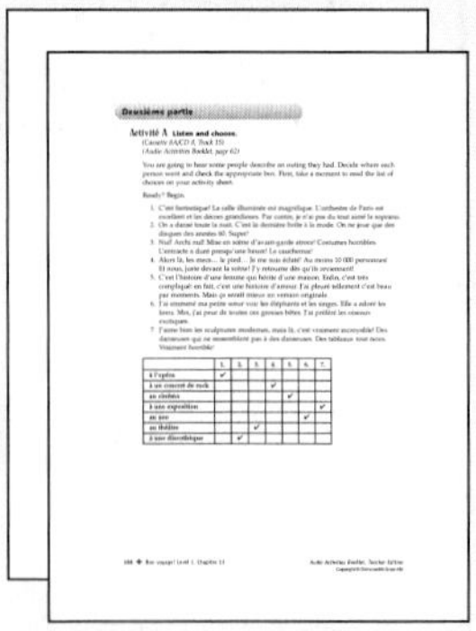
Additional Practice, pages 166–167

Assessment

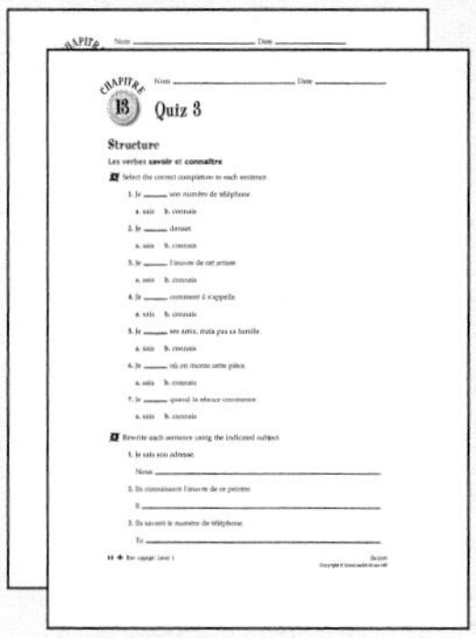

Vocabulary and Structure Quizzes, pages 64–68

Chapter Tests, Chapter 13

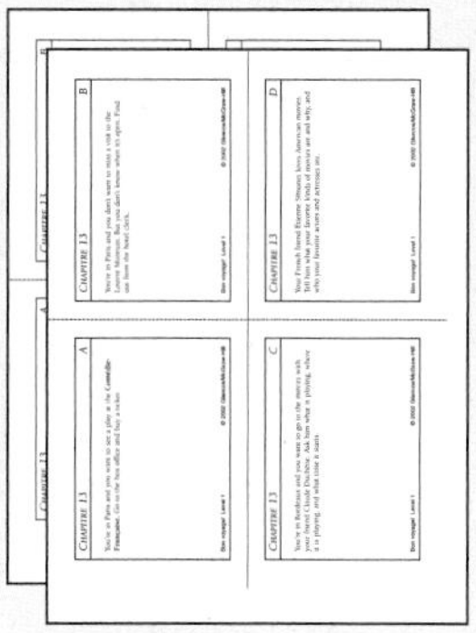

Situation Cards, Chapter 13

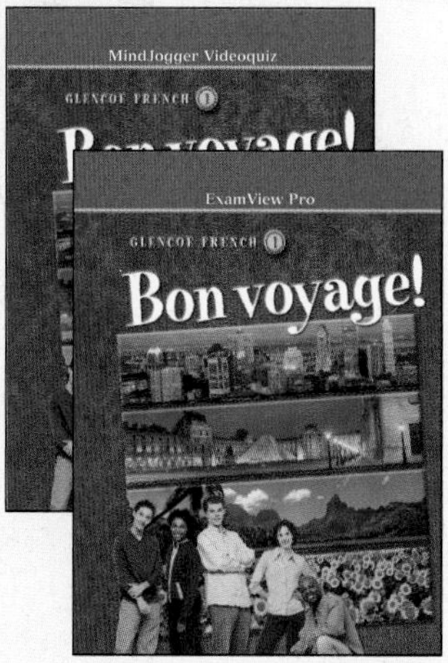

Timesaving Teacher Tools

Interactive Teacher Edition

Imagine having your Teacher's Edition and all resources on a CD-ROM. Click on a resource and it appears on your screen, ready to be printed, sorted, or planned.

Interactive Lesson Planner

The Interactive Lesson Planner CD-ROM helps you organize your lesson plans for a week, month, semester, or year. Look at this planning tool for easy access to your Chapter 13 resources.

ExamView Pro®

Test Bank software for Macintosh and Windows makes creating, editing, customizing, and printing tests quick and easy.

Technology Resources

FRENCH Online

In the Chapter 13 Internet activity, you will have a chance to learn more about cultural activities in the Francophone world. Visit french.glencoe.com.

On the Interactive Conversation CD-ROM, students can listen to and take part in a recorded version of the conversation in Chapter 13.

NATIONAL GEOGRAPHIC SOCIETY

See the National Geographic Teacher's Corner on pages 150–151, 256–257, 396–397, 500–501 for reference to additional technology resources.

Bon Voyage! Video and Video Activities Booklet.

Help your students prepare for the chapter test by playing the **Marathon mental** Videoquiz game show. Teams will compete against each other to review chapter vocabulary and structure and sharpen listening comprehension skills.

Preview

In this chapter, students will learn to discuss cultural events and express their cultural likes and dislikes. In order to do this, they will learn vocabulary associated with films, museums, and the theater. They will also learn to use the verbs **savoir** and **connaître** and the direct object pronouns.

National Standards

Communication

In Chapter 13, students will communicate in spoken and written French on the following topics:

- Going to the movies
- Visiting a museum
- Attending a theater performance

Students will also learn to tell whom and what they know. They will obtain and provide information and engage in conversations about their personal experiences with cultural events. They will also learn to use direct object pronouns.

Communities

After having learned about cultural preferences of the French, have students compare them with those of their own community.

CHAPITRE 13

Les loisirs culturels

Objectifs

In this chapter you will learn to:

- ✔ *discuss movies, plays, and museums*
- ✔ *tell what you know and whom you know*
- ✔ *tell what happens to you or someone else*
- ✔ *refer to people and things already mentioned*
- ✔ *talk about some cultural activities in Paris*

Des statues béninoises du seizième siècle

430

Correlations to Continuum *(see page i for code)*

Stage I
Understand some ideas and familiar details. p. 447 (**26**, *p*); Understand ideas and familiar details when listening. p. 441 (**14**, *p*)

Stage II
Use authentic materials, such as tickets and brochures. p. 433 (*i*), p. 439 (**10**, *p*); Write letters. p. 457 (**4**, *p*); Use and understand learned expressions, sentences, and strings of sentences when speaking. p. 439 (**9**, *m*); Understand and convey information on buildings and monuments. pp. 450–451 (*i*), pp. 450–451 (*p*); Communicate effectively with some pattern of error, which may interfere slightly with full comprehension when performing Stage II functions. p. 456 (**1**)

Stage III
Express and understand opinions. p. 435 (**6**, *i*), p. 447 (**27**, *p*); Narrate and understand narration in the future. p. 443 (**19**, *p*); Converse in face-to-face social interactions and in simple transactions on the phone. p. 439 (**10**, *i*), p. 456 (**2**, *p*); Listen during face-to-face social interactions and listen to audio or video texts. p. 448 (*i*), p. 456 (**2**, *p*); Create paragraphs when writing. p. 457 (**5**, *p*); Understand and convey information about music and art. pp. 432–433 (*i*), p. 439 (**9**, *p*), pp. 454–455 (*m*); Generally use culturally appropriate behavior in social situations. p. 449; Understand and retain most key ideas and some supporting detail when reading and listening. p. 457 (**5**)

Stage IV
Explain and support an opinion. p. 435 (**6**, *i*), p. 457 (**5**, *p*)

CHAPITRE 13

Spotlight on Culture

Photograph The Louvre is the world's largest museum, and at night, as seen here, it is beautifully illuminated by 70,000 lightbulbs. The Louvre as it stands today is the product of centuries of construction. It was originally built by Philippe-Auguste in the thirteenth century as a fortress. Throughout the centuries the palace has served many purposes, from the royal residence to empty apartments that were taken over by artists. Louis XVI and Marie-Antoinette fled from the palace, then called the **Palais des Tuileries,** in 1791, two years after the start of the Revolution. At the end of the eighteenth century, Napoleon made the Louvre into a museum, but three more French kings, Louis XVIII, Charles X, and Louis Philippe, continued to make the Louvre their home.

The Louvre's incredible collections include paintings, drawings, sculpture, furniture, coins, and jewelry. For information concerning the Pyramid, please see page 500. You may wish to see if your school district owns a video copy of the wonderful documentary called *The Louvre,* narrated in English by Charles Boyer. Although the film was made in 1978, it is a fascinating look at the origins, inhabitants, and changing face of the Louvre with amazing facts and stories.

Sculpture For much of its history, Bénin was known as Abomey, and later the kingdom of Dahomey. The cultural history of Bénin is very rich, and the art produced during the Dahomey era attracts international attention. Art served both a functional and spiritual purpose. The bronzes seen here are of leopards, and they date from the sixteenth century.

Chapter Projects

Une exposition Have groups research different French painters and/or sculptors. Each group can put on an art show, using prints of the artists' most famous works.

Au musée Visit a local museum so that students can see different styles of art and, hopefully, some work by French artists.

Un film You may wish to rent a video of a French film in **version originale** and show it to the class. Your students might enjoy the following movies: *Au revoir les enfants, Les quatre cents coups, L'enfant sauvage, Le ballon rouge, Jean de Florette, La gloire de mon père, Cyrano de Bergerac.*

1 Preparation

Resource Manager

Vocabulary Transparencies 13.2–13.3
Audio Activities Booklet TE, pages 157–158
Audiocassette 8A/CD 8
Workbook, pages 129–130
Quiz 1, page 64
ExamView Pro®

Bellringer Review

Use BRR Transparency 13.1 or write the following on the board.
Make a list of activities you like to do in your free time.

2 Presentation

Step 1 Show Vocabulary Transparencies 13.2–13.3. Point to individual items and have the class repeat the words after you or Audiocassette 8A/CD 8.

Step 2 Call on individual students to point to the corresponding illustration on the transparency as you say the word or expression.
Teaching Tip: Ask questions about students' personal preferences when practicing the vocabulary. For example: **Jacques, tu préfères les films policiers ou les documentaires? Qui aime les dessins animés?**

Step 3 After presenting the vocabulary orally, have students open their books. Call on individuals to read. Ask questions about the sentences such as: **On joue ce film étranger où? Le film est en V.O. ou on le voit avec des sous-titres?**

Step 4 Call on students to act out the short conversation.

Au cinéma

Pierre est devant le guichet.
La prochaine séance est à treize heures.

Qui joue dans ce film?
On joue un film étranger au Rex.
Le film est en V.O. (version originale).
On le voit avec des sous-titres.
Dans un autre cinéma, le film est doublé.
On peut le voir en français.

Qu'est-ce que tu veux voir?
Ça m'est égal.

Qu'est-ce qu'on joue au Rex?
Je ne sais pas. On peut regarder dans *l'Officiel des Spectacles.*
Les places coûtent combien?

Reaching All Students

Total Physical Response
(Student 1), **levez-vous, s'il vous plaît.**
Faites la queue devant le guichet.
Prenez votre billet.
Entrez dans le cinéma.
Choisissez une place.
Prenez votre place. Asseyez-vous.
Regardez le film.
Indiquez que le film est amusant.
Le film est fini. Levez-vous.
Sortez du cinéma.

un film de science-fiction

un film d'horreur

un film policier

un documentaire

un film d'amour

un dessin animé

un film d'aventures

Au théâtre

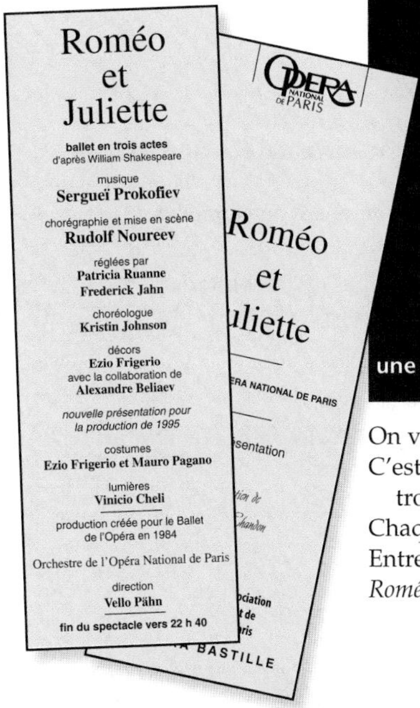

On va monter *Roméo et Juliette.*
C'est une pièce de théâtre en trois actes.
Chaque acte a deux scènes.
Entre deux actes, il y a un entracte.
Roméo et Juliette est aussi un ballet.

Voici d'autres genres de pièces:
- une tragédie
- une comédie
- un drame
- une comédie musicale

Vocabulary Expansion

You may wish to give students the following additional words.
- **un fauteuil**
- **l'orchestre**
- **le balcon**
- **un rang**
- **le rideau**
- **le lever du rideau**
- **un costume**
- **un décor**

Reaching All Students

Additional Practice Have students work in pairs to prepare a skit. One plays the part of a box office clerk at a movie theater; the other plays the part of a ticket buyer.

Class Motivator

Des films Students work in groups of four. Each person writes down the title of a movie he or she has seen recently. They put their titles together and scramble them. Each person in turn picks one and asks: **Qui a vu ce film?** and then makes up as many present-tense questions about it as possible. The student who saw the film answers. If anyone picks his or her own film, he or she tells the others about it.

Variation: Each person in turn picks one and describes the film, the actors, etc., and the others try to name the film.

Vocabulaire

3 Practice

Commençons
Let's use our new words

Historiette Each time **Historiette** appears, it means that the answers to the activity form a short story. Encourage students to look at the title of the **Historiette,** since it can help them do the activity.

1, 3, 5 With books closed, ask the questions to these activities and call on individuals to respond.

Note: Answers to these activities can be written at home.

2 and 4 Call on student(s) to retell the information in their own words. Have students open books. Call on individuals to read aloud, completing the sentences with the appropriate words.

Commençons
Let's use our new words

Le cinéma Champollion, Paris

1 Fana de cinéma ou pas?
Donnez des réponses personnelles.

1. Tu vas souvent au cinéma?
2. Qu'est-ce que tu aimes comme films?
3. Quel est ton acteur préféré? Et ton actrice préférée? Il/Elle est très connu(e)?
4. Il y a un cinéma près de chez toi?
5. La première séance est à quelle heure?
6. Où est-ce que tu achètes les billets?
7. Tu fais souvent la queue devant le guichet?
8. Dans la salle de cinéma, tu aimes mieux une place près de l'écran ou loin de l'écran?
9. Si tu vas voir un film étranger, tu aimes mieux voir le film doublé ou en version originale avec des sous-titres?

2 Historiette Au cinéma Complétez.

Ce soir, on __1__ un très bon film au Wepler. C'est un film étranger. Il n'est pas doublé. Il y a des __2__. Le film est en __3__ originale. La prochaine __4__ est à quelle heure? Les __5__ coûtent combien?

3 Tu aimes mieux quels genres de film?
Donnez des réponses personnelles.

1. Tu aimes mieux (préfères) les documentaires ou les westerns?
2. Tu aimes mieux les films policiers ou les films d'horreur?
3. Tu aimes mieux les films comiques ou les films d'amour?
4. Tu aimes mieux les films d'aventures ou les films de science-fiction?
5. Tu vas voir quelquefois des dessins animés?
6. Tu loues quelquefois des films en vidéo? Quels genres de film?

Answers to Commençons

1 *Answers will vary but may include:*

1. Oui, je vais souvent au cinéma.
2. J'aime les films policiers.
3. Mon acteur préféré est ____. Mon actrice préférée est ____. Oui, ils sont très connus.
4. Oui, il y a un cinéma près de chez moi.
5. La première séance est à 19 h.
6. J'achète les billets au guichet.
7. Oui, je fais souvent la queue devant le guichet.
8. Dans la salle de cinéma j'aime mieux une place près de l'écran.
9. Si je vais voir un film étranger, j'aime mieux voir le film en version originale avec des sous-titres.

2

1. joue
2. sous-titres
3. version
4. séance
5. places

3 *Answers will vary but may include:*

1. J'aime mieux les westerns.
2. J'aime mieux les films policiers.
3. J'aime mieux les films comiques.
4. J'aime mieux les films de science-fiction.
5. Oui, je vais voir quelquefois des dessins animés.
6. Oui, je loue quelquefois des films en vidéo. Des films policiers.

4 Des pièces et des films Complétez.

1. Au lycée les élèves ____ une pièce tous les ans.
2. On voit un film au cinéma. On voit une pièce au ____.
3. Une ____ a des actes et les actes sont divisés en ____.
4. Entre deux actes, il y a un ____.
5. Un ____ joue le rôle de Roméo.
6. Une ____ joue le rôle de Juliette.
7. Dans une comédie musicale, les ____ chantent et les ____ dansent.

5 Historiette Au théâtre Donnez des réponses personnelles.

1. Tu aimes le théâtre?
2. Tu vas souvent au théâtre?
3. Il y a un théâtre là où tu habites?
4. Ton école a un club d'art dramatique?
5. Tu es membre de ce club?
6. Le club monte combien de pièces par an?
7. Cette année, le club va monter quelle pièce?
8. C'est quel genre de pièce?
9. Il y a combien d'actes?
10. Il y a combien d'entractes?

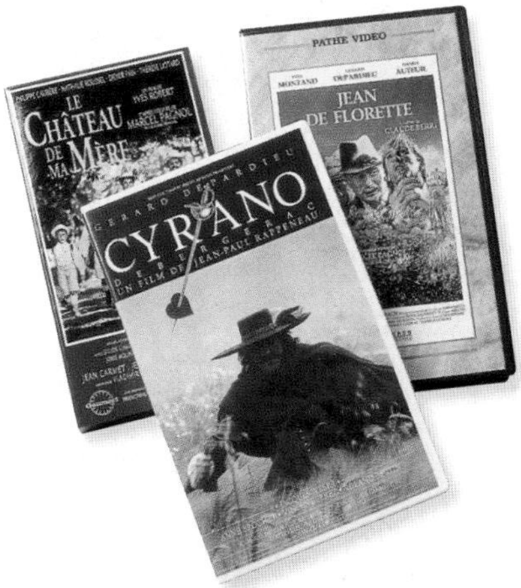

6 Mon film préféré Find out what a classmate's favorite movies are and why. Then find out which movies he or she dislikes and why. Take turns.

ENCORE PLUS *For more practice using words from **Mots 1**, do Activity 42 on page H43 at the end of this book.*

Answers to Commençons

4

1. montent
2. théâtre
3. pièce, scènes
4. entracte
5. acteur
6. actrice
7. chanteurs, danseurs

5 *Answers will vary but may include:*

1. Oui, j'aime le théâtre.
2. Oui, je vais souvent au théâtre.
3. Oui, il y a un théâtre là où j'habite.
4. Oui, mon école a un club d'art dramatique.
5. Oui, je suis membre de ce club.
6. Le club monte trois pièces par an.
7. Cette année le club va monter ____.
8. C'est ____.
9. Il y a ____ actes.
10. Il y a ____ entractes.

Vocabulaire

Writing Development

Have students write the answers to Activities 2–5 in paragraph form.

Cognate Recognition

Have students scan the **Mots 1** words again and then identify and pronounce each cognate.

Reteaching

Show Vocabulary Transparencies 13.2–13.3 and let students say as much as they can about them in their own words.

Learning from Realia

(page 435 middle) You may wish to tell students that Molière was a famous seventeenth-century dramatist whose comedies are still very much appreciated today.

ENCORE PLUS This *infogap* activity will allow students to practice in pairs. The activity should be very manageable for them, since all vocabulary and structures are familiar to them.

Attention!

Note that the activities are color-coded. All the activities in the text are communicative. However, the ones with blue titles are guided communication. The red titles indicate that the answers to the activity are more open-ended and can vary more. You may wish to correct students' mistakes more so in the guided activities than in the activities with a red title, which lend themselves to a freer response.

1 Preparation

Resource Manager

Vocabulary Transparencies 13.4–13.5
Audio Activities Booklet TE, page 159
Audiocassette 8A/CD 8
Workbook, pages 131–132
Quiz 2, page 65
ExamView Pro®

Bellringer Review

Use BRR Transparency 13.2 or write the following on the board.
Name your four favorite movies and tell what type of films they are.

2 Presentation

Step 1 Show Vocabulary Transparencies 13.4–13.5. Have students close their books and repeat the new words after you two or three times.

Step 2 Call a student to the front of the room. As you say a new word or phrase, have the student point to the appropriate item on the transparency.

Step 3 After presenting the vocabulary with the transparencies, have students open their books and read the words and sentences.

Au musée

Une exposition de peinture et sculpture

Reaching All Students

Total Physical Response Before you begin, demonstrate the meaning of **se promener.**

(Student 1), **levez-vous et venez ici, s'il vous plaît.**
Vous êtes devant le musée d'Art Moderne.
Entrez dans le musée.
Promenez-vous dans la grande salle.
Vous voyez un tableau que vous trouvez beau.
Arrêtez-vous.
Regardez le tableau.
Indiquez que vous aimez le tableau, que vous le trouvez beau.
Et voilà un autre tableau. Indiquez que vous n'aimez pas ce tableau. Vous ne le trouvez pas beau.

Je sais que le peintre s'appelle Duval.
Je ne le connais pas personnellement.
Je connais son œuvre (ses tableaux).
Ses tableaux, je les trouve extraordinaires!

Le musée n'est pas ouvert le mardi.
Il est ouvert tous les jours sauf le mardi.

Vocabulary Expansion

You may wish to give students the following additional vocabulary in order to talk about art.

une gravure
une lithographie
de la poterie
une aquarelle
un portrait
une peinture à l'huile

Cognate Recognition

Ask students to identify as many cognates as they can in **Mots 2.** Pay particular attention to their pronunciation of these cognates.

3 Practice

Commençons
Let's use our new words

8 You may wish to have students write their answers to this activity in paragraph form.

Reaching All Students

Additional Practice Have students quickly write down as many words associated with the movies, theater, or museums as they can. Then have them work in pairs, giving their partner one word at a time from their list. Their partner puts the word into a sentence.

Art Connection

Starting in 1890, Monet had built at his home in Giverny a beautiful garden and a pond, **un jardin d'eau,** which reflected his interest in Japanese art. He did many paintings of his **jardin d'eau.** Many of his paintings of **les nymphéas** *(water lilies)* can be seen today in the Orangerie in Paris.

Commençons
Let's use our new words

7 Un peu de culture Répondez d'après les dessins.

1. C'est un musée ou un théâtre?

2. Le musée est ouvert ou fermé?

3. Elle est peintre ou sculpteur?

4. C'est un tableau ou une statue?

8 Historiette Au musée
Inventez des réponses.

1. Michel sait comment s'appelle le peintre?
2. Il connaît le peintre personnellement?
3. Il connaît l'œuvre du peintre?
4. Annick sait dans quel musée il y a une exposition de Monet?
5. Elle trouve ses tableaux extraordinaires?
6. Elle connaît le musée de l'Orangerie?
7. Elle le visite souvent?
8. Elle sait que le musée est fermé le mardi?
9. Le musée de l'Orangerie est ouvert tous les jours sauf le mardi?

Claude Monet *Le bassin aux nymphéas*

Answers to Commençons

7
1. C'est un musée.
2. Le musée est ouvert.
3. Elle est sculpteur.
4. C'est un tableau.

8 *Answers will vary but may include:*
1. Non, Michel ne sait pas comment s'appelle le peintre.
2. Non, il ne connaît pas le peintre personnellement.
3. Oui, il connaît l'œuvre du peintre.
4. Oui, elle sait dans quel musée il y a une exposition de Monet.
5. Oui, elle trouve ses tableaux extraordinaires.
6. Oui, elle connaît le musée de l'Orangerie.
7. Oui, elle le visite souvent.
8. Oui, elle sait que le musée est fermé le mardi.
9. Oui, le musée de l'Orangerie est ouvert tous les jours sauf le mardi.

9 **L'art français** Work with a classmate. Discuss together what you have learned so far about French art and French artists. Find out who appreciates art more and who knows more about art.

Paul Cézanne *Pommes et oranges*

Art Connection

Early in his career, Paul Cézanne (1839–1906) also took part in the first exhibition of the Impressionists. Later studies led him to believe that Impressionist paintings lacked form, solidity, and structure. Cézanne wanted to paint nature, but he was not interested in reproducing exactly the shapes, colors, etc., found in nature. He began to experiment with still-life painting, often painting the same subject over and over until he was completely satisfied with it.

Tours et crypte archéologique de **Notre-Dame** –12 ans : gratuit

Rue de Cloître, Paris 4e. **M°**: Cité, ou **RER C**: St. Michel. Tours: **tél**: 01 44 32 16 72, groupes: 01 44 32 16 72. **Horaires**: 9h30-19h30 du 1.04 au 30.09; 10h-17h du 1.10 au 31.03. Fermeture des caisses 45mn plus tôt. Crypte: **tél**: 01 43 29 83 51. **Horaires**: 9h30-18h du 1.04 au 30.09; 10h-16h30 du 1.10 au 31.03.
Du haut des tours: une vue exceptionnelle sur la cathédrale et la ville. . . Dans la crypte archéologique: l'histoire de Paris de l'époque gallo-romaine au XIXe s.

Musée de l'**Ordre de la Libération** –12 ans : gratuit

Hôtel national des Invalides, 51 bis, boulevard de Latour-Maubourg, Paris 7e. **Tél**: 01 47 05 35 15. **M°**: Invalides. **Horaires**: 10h-17h.
Musée de la France Libre, de la Résistance et de la Déportation.

Musée d'**Orsay** – 18 ans : gratuit

1, rue de Bellechasse, Paris 7e. **Tél**: 01 40 49 48 14 . **M°**: Solférino, ou **RER C**: Musée d'Orsay. **Horaires**: 10h-18h, nocturne le jeudi jusqu' à 21h45. Le dimanche, et du 20.06 au 20.09: 9h-18h. Fermé le lundi.
Peintures impressionnistes et ensemble de la création artistique de 1848 à 1914.

10 **Renseignements** You're in Paris and you'd like to visit one of the museums listed in the brochure on the left. Call the museum and find out from the museum employee (your partner) where it's located, what time it opens and closes, what day it's closed, and how much a ticket costs. Your partner can use the information in the brochure to answer your questions.

ENCORE PLUS
*For more practice using words from **Mots 2**, do Activity 43 on page H44 at the end of this book.*

Answers to Commençons

9 *Answers will vary depending upon the painter and/or works of art the students select.*

10 *Answers will vary.*

1 Preparation

Resource Manager

Audio Activities Booklet TE, pages 160–162
Audiocassette 8A/CD 8
Workbook, pages 133–135
Quizzes 3–5, pages 66–68
ExamView Pro®

Bellringer Review

Use BRR Transparency 13.3 or write the following on the board.
List everything you associate with the following.

le cinéma
le théâtre
un musée

2 Presentation

Les verbes **savoir** et **connaître**

Step 1 Lead students through Items 1–4 and the examples.

Step 2 Make two lists on the board, one of information that follows **connaître** (names of people, cities and other places, artistic and literary works), and the other with facts that follow **savoir** (dates, times, telephone numbers, addresses, infinitives, clauses).

Step 3 Give students the following words or expressions and have them say whether they would use **savoir** or **connaître: André, sa famille, son adresse, son numéro de téléphone, le nom de son école, ses professeurs, sa ville.**

Telling whom and what you know

Les verbes **savoir** et **connaître**

1. Study the following present-tense forms of the verbs **savoir** and **connaître,** both of which mean "to know."

SAVOIR		CONNAÎTRE	
je	sais	je	connais
tu	sais	tu	connais
il/elle/on	sait	il/elle/on	connaît
nous	savons	nous	connaissons
vous	savez	vous	connaissez
ils/elles	savent	ils/elles	connaissent

Note the **passé composé** of these verbs: **j'ai su, j'ai connu.**

2. You use **savoir** to indicate that you know a fact or that you know something by heart.

Tu sais à quelle heure la séance commence?
Tu sais le numéro de téléphone de Philippe?

3. You use **savoir** + infinitive to indicate that you know how to do something.

Tu sais danser le tango?
Il ne sait pas nager.

4. **Connaître** means "to know" in the sense of "to be acquainted with." You can use **connaître** only with nouns—people, places, and things. Compare the meanings of **connaître** and **savoir** in the sentences below.

Je sais comment elle s'appelle. Nathalie. — **Je connais bien Nathalie.**
Je sais où elle habite. À Grenoble. — **Je connais bien Grenoble.**
Je sais le nom de l'auteur. Victor Hugo. — **Je connais son œuvre.**

Grenoble, France

Learning from Photos

(page 440) Please refer to page 370 for information on Grenoble.

Continuons
Let's put our words together

11 **Qu'est-ce que tu sais?** Donnez des réponses personnelles.

1. Tu sais où habite ton ami(e)? Il/Elle habite dans quelle ville?
2. Tu connais bien cette ville?
3. Tu sais où on peut bien manger pour pas cher?
4. Tu sais le nom de l'auteur de *Hamlet?*
5. Tu connais les pièces de Shakespeare?
6. Tu connais *Hamlet?*

12 **On sait tout!** Complétez.

1. Moi, je ____ où se trouve le théâtre.
2. Paul, tu ____ quel est le numéro de téléphone?
3. Nous ne ____ pas l'adresse exacte.
4. Nos amis ____ à quelle heure la pièce commence.
5. Vous ____ quelle pièce on joue en ce moment à la Comédie-Française?
6. Il faut demander à Julie. Elle ____ tout.

13 **Qu'est-ce que tu connais?** Complétez.

1. Je ____ bien la France.
2. Les élèves de Mme Benoît ____ bien la peinture française.
3. Mais ils ne ____ pas très bien la littérature française.
4. Tu ____ la culture française?
5. Et Paul, il ____ la peinture française contemporaine?
6. Vous ____ les sculptures de Rodin?
7. Nous ____ des impressionnistes comme Monet, Manet et Renoir.
8. Tu ____ l'œuvre du peintre Edgar Degas?
9. Oui, je ____ son œuvre. J'adore ses danseuses.

Edgar Degas *Deux danseuses en scène*

14 **Tu le/la connais bien!** Work with a classmate. Think of someone in the class whom you know quite well. Tell your partner some things you know about this person. Don't say who it is. Your partner will guess. Take turns.

ENCORE PLUS *For more practice using **savoir** and **connaître**, do Activity 44 on page H45 at the end of this book.*

Answers to Continuons

11 *Answers will vary but may include:*

1. Oui, je sais où habite mon amie. Elle habite à Chicago.
2. Oui, je connais bien cette ville.
3. Oui, je sais où on peut bien manger pour pas cher.
4. Oui, je sais le nom de l'auteur de *Hamlet.*
5. Oui, je connais les pièces de Shakespeare.
6. Oui, je connais *Hamlet.*

12

1. sais
2. sais
3. savons
4. savent
5. savez
6. sait

13

1. connais
2. connaissent
3. connaissent
4. connais
5. connaît
6. connaissez
7. connaissons
8. connais
9. connais

3 Practice

Continuons
Let's put our words together

11 This activity can be done with books closed, open, or once each way.

12 and **13** After doing these activities with books open, have students close their books. You give sentence fragments, and the students say a complete sentence. Example: **quel est le numéro de téléphone**
Je sais quel est le numéro de téléphone.

Reaching All Students

Additional Practice Have students write five things they know how to do using **savoir** + infinitive. Groups of students interview each other, then compile a report, and present it to the class. Students might then practice questioning techniques. For example: **Qui sait nager? Qui ne sait pas plonger? Qu'est-ce que Carole sait faire?**

ENCORE PLUS This *infogap* activity will allow students to practice in pairs. The activity should be very manageable for them, since all vocabulary and structures are familiar to them.

Art Connection

(page 441) Please refer to page 399 for information on Edgar Degas.

1 Preparation

Bellringer Review

Use BRR Transparency 13.4 or write the following on the board.
List five things you know how to do.

2 Presentation

Les pronoms me, te, nous, vous

Note: The object pronouns **me, te, nous, vous** are introduced before the third-person pronouns for two reasons. First, they are less complicated than the third-person pronouns since they are both direct and indirect objects. Second, they are the only object pronouns that are truly necessary for communication. For example, if asked a question with **te** or **vous,** one must answer with **me** or **nous.** When speaking in the third person, however, one could respond with a noun instead of a pronoun: **Tu as invité Jean? Non, je n'ai pas invité Jean.**

Step 1 Lead students through Items 1–2 on page 442.

3 Practice

Continuons
Let's put our words together

15 and **16** Ask the questions with books closed and call on students to respond. Activities can be done again with books open for additional reinforcement.

Telling who does what for whom
Les pronoms **me, te, nous, vous**

1. The pronouns **me, te, nous,** and **vous** are object pronouns.

Marie t'invite au théâtre?	**Oui, elle m'invite au théâtre.**
Elle te parle au téléphone?	**Oui, elle me parle au téléphone.**
Le prof vous regarde?	**Oui, il nous regarde.**
Il vous explique la leçon?	**Oui, il nous explique la leçon.**

2. The object pronoun **me, te, nous,** or **vous** always comes right before the verb it is linked to.

Il	me parle.
Il ne	me parle pas.
Il veut	me parler.
Il ne veut pas	me parler.

Continuons
Let's put our words together

15 Historiette **Une invitation**
Répondez que oui.

1. Jean te téléphone?
2. Il te parle longtemps?
3. Il t'invite au cinéma?
4. Il te demande quel film tu veux voir?
5. Il te paie la place?
6. Après le film il t'invite au café?

Une conversation au café

16 Historiette **En classe** Répondez que oui.

1. En classe, la prof vous parle, à toi et aux autres élèves?
2. Elle vous apprend à lire et écrire en français?
3. Elle vous explique la grammaire?
4. Elle vous présente le vocabulaire?
5. Elle vous donne beaucoup de devoirs?
6. Elle vous donne trop de devoirs?
7. Elle vous parle toujours en français?

Answers to Continuons

15

1. Oui, Jean me téléphone.
2. Oui, il me parle longtemps.
3. Oui, il m'invite au cinéma.
4. Oui, il me demande quel film je veux voir.
5. Oui, il me paie la place.
6. Oui, il m'invite au café.

16

1. Oui, la prof nous parle.
2. Oui, elle nous apprend à lire et écrire en français.
3. Oui, elle nous explique la grammaire.
4. Oui, elle nous présente le vocabulaire.
5. Oui, elle nous donne beaucoup de devoirs.
6. Oui, elle nous donne trop de devoirs.
7. Oui, elle nous parle toujours en français.

17 **Au rayon des chemisiers** Complétez avec **me** ou **vous.**

Je suis au rayon des chemisiers des Galeries Lafayette. La vendeuse __1__ parle. Elle __2__ demande:

La vendeuse: Vous désirez?
Moi: Je voudrais ce chemisier, s'il __3__ plaît. Je fais du 40.
La vendeuse: Je __4__ donne quelle couleur?
Moi: Qu'est-ce que vous __5__ proposez?
La vendeuse: Je ne sais pas. En bleu marine, il __6__ plaît?
Moi: Oui, il __7__ plaît.
La vendeuse: Mais je __8__ suggère d'essayer un 38.
Moi: D'accord. Je peux __9__ payer par carte de crédit?
La vendeuse: Mais bien sûr, mademoiselle!

18 **Pourquoi ça?** Répondez d'après le modèle.

1. Il me pose des questions!
2. Il me parle!
3. Il me téléphone!
4. Il me dit son numéro de téléphone!
5. Il me donne son adresse!

19 **Historiette** **C'est ton anniversaire.**
Inventez une histoire.

1. Tes copains vont te téléphoner le jour de ton anniversaire?
2. Ils vont te voir?
3. Ils vont t'inviter au cinéma ou au concert?
4. Ils vont te dire «Joyeux anniversaire!» ?
5. Ils vont te faire un gâteau?
6. Ils vont te donner des cadeaux?

Structure

17 After students complete filling in the blanks, have two students read the conversation aloud in front of the class.

17 and **18** Have students use the proper intonation with the questions and **pourquoi?**

Reaching All Students

Additional Practice Have students ask each other for something. For example:
Robert, tu me donnes ton crayon?
Oui, je te donne mon crayon.
Then have two students ask two others for something:
Robert et Laure, vous nous donnez ce livre?
Oui, nous vous donnons ce livre.

Answers to Continuons

17
1. me
2. me
3. vous
4. vous
5. me
6. vous
7. me
8. vous
9. vous

18
1. Il te pose des questions? Pourquoi?
2. Il te parle? Pourquoi?
3. Il te téléphone? Pourquoi?
4. Il te dit son numéro de téléphone? Pourquoi?
5. Il te donne son adresse? Pourquoi?

19 *Answers will vary but may include:*
1. Oui, mes copains vont me téléphoner le jour de mon anniversaire.
2. Oui, ils vont me voir.
3. Ils vont m'inviter au concert.
4. Oui, ils vont me dire «Joyeux anniversaire.»
5. Oui, ils vont me faire un gâteau.
6. Oui, ils vont me donner des cadeaux.

1 Preparation

Bellringer Review

Use BRR Transparency 13.5 or write the following on the board.
Answer.
1. **Tu aimes aller au cinéma?**
2. **Tu vois beaucoup de films?**
3. **Tu as un acteur favori ou une actrice favorite?**
4. **C'est qui?**
5. **Il/Elle a joué dans quel film?**
6. **Tu as vu ce film?**

2 Presentation

Les pronoms le, la, les

Step 1 Write a few example sentences from Item 1 on the board. Put a box around the noun object. Circle the object pronoun. Draw a line from the box to the circle. This helps students grasp the concept.

Step 2 Lead the students through Items 1–2 on page 444.

Referring to people and things already mentioned

Les pronoms **le, la, les**

1. You have already learned to use **le, la, l',** and **les** as definite articles. These words are also used as direct object pronouns. A direct object receives the action of the verb. A direct object pronoun can replace either a person or a thing.

Singulier	Je connais ce film.	Je le connais.
	Je connais cet acteur.	Je le connais.
	J'admire cet acteur.	Je l'admire.
	Je connais cette pièce.	Je la connais.
	Je connais cette actrice.	Je la connais.
	J'admire cette actrice.	Je l'admire.
Pluriel	Je connais les tableaux de Monet.	Je les connais.
	Je connais les pièces de Molière.	Je les connais.
	Je connais ces actrices.	Je les connais.
	J'admire ces acteurs.	Je les‿admire.

2. Just as with the pronouns **me, te, nous, vous,** the pronouns **le, la, l',** and **les** come right before the verb they are linked to.

Je le vois.
Je ne le vois pas.
Je veux le voir.
Je ne veux pas le voir.

Attention!

Note the elision and liaison with the direct object pronouns.
Vous l'admirez. **Vous les‿admirez.**

Opéra Garnier, Paris

Learning from Photos

(page 444) You will read about l'Opéra Garnier in the cultural reading on pages 450–451.

Continuons
Let's put our words together

20 Contacts Répondez d'après le modèle.

1. Tu vois toujours Sylvie?
2. Tu vois toujours tes copains tunisiens?
3. Tu vois toujours Marc?
4. Tu vois toujours tes cousines de Lyon?
5. Tu vois toujours tes professeurs de l'année dernière?

21 En version originale Complétez.

Paul: On va voir le film doublé ou en V.O.?
Annick: On va __1__ voir en V.O.
Paul: Tu connais l'actrice principale?
Annick: Tu rigoles! Bien sûr que je ne __2__ connais pas, mais je sais qui c'est!
Paul: Tu comprends l'espagnol?
Annick: Oui, je __3__ comprends un peu.
Paul: Tu __4__ comprends assez bien pour comprendre le film?
Annick: Non, mais il y a des sous-titres. Alors je __5__ lis quand je ne comprends pas les dialogues.

3 Practice

Continuons
Let's put our words together

20 Expansion: After doing this activity, have students list some of their friends and classmates. They will then follow the example of the activity, substituting the names on their lists.

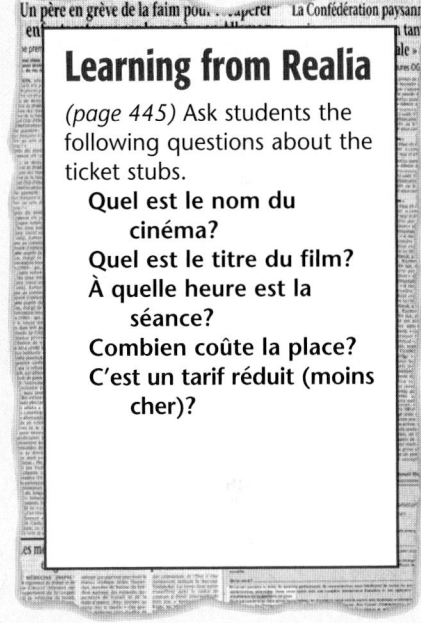

Learning from Realia

(page 445) Ask students the following questions about the ticket stubs.

Quel est le nom du cinéma?
Quel est le titre du film?
À quelle heure est la séance?
Combien coûte la place?
C'est un tarif réduit (moins cher)?

Answers to Continuons

20

1. Oui, je la vois de temps en temps.
2. Oui, je les vois de temps en temps.
3. Oui, je le vois de temps en temps.
4. Oui, je les vois de temps en temps.
5. Oui, je les vois de temps en temps.

21

1. le
2. la
3. le
4. le
5. les

Recycling

Activity 22 also reviews the adjective **beau.**

Art Connection

Pierre Auguste Renoir (1841–1919) began his career as an artist copying the masters of the eighteenth century in the Louvre. In 1863 he went to study in the Gleyre Studio where he met Monet, Sisley, and Bazille. He went to paint with them in the Forest of Fontainebleau. He became very friendly with Monet, and they started to paint some of the same themes.

Renoir exhibited in the first exhibit of the Impressionists in 1874, and shortly thereafter he produced some of his best works, including ***Bal du moulin de la Galette,*** which he painted in 1876.

The **Moulin de la Galette,** made famous by Renoir's painting, still stands surrounded by shrubs on a hill in Montmartre. In Renoir's day, it was a popular open-air cabaret. It is now privately owned.

ENCORE PLUS This *infogap* activity will allow students to practice in pairs. The activity should be very manageable for them, since all vocabulary and structures are familiar to them.

Learning from Photos

(page 446) Ask the students the following questions about the painting.

Qu'est-ce que les gens font? Ils s'amusent?

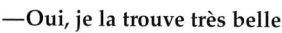

22 Tout est très beau!

Répondez d'après le modèle.

—Tu vois la statue?
—Oui, je la trouve très belle.

1. Tu vois le théâtre?
2. Tu vois les tableaux?
3. Tu vois l'acteur?
4. Tu vois l'actrice?
5. Tu vois les sculptures?

Jean-Antoine Houdon *Molière*

23 Tout n'est pas très beau.

Refaites l'Activité 22 d'après le modèle.

—Tu vois la statue?
—Oui, mais je ne la trouve pas très belle.

Pierre Auguste Renoir *Bal du moulin de la Galette*

ENCORE PLUS *For more practice using pronouns, do Activity 45 on page H46 at the end of this book.*

Answers to Continuons

22

1. Oui, je le trouve très beau.
2. Oui, je les trouve très beaux.
3. Oui, je le trouve très beau.
4. Oui, je la trouve très belle.
5. Oui, je les trouve très belles.

23

1. Oui, mais je ne le trouve pas très beau.
2. Oui, mais je ne les trouve pas très beaux.
3. Oui, mais je ne le trouve pas très beau.
4. Oui, mais je ne la trouve pas très belle.
5. Oui, mais je ne les trouve pas très belles.

24 **Demain** Répondez d'après le modèle.

—Tu as vu ce film?
—Non, mais je vais le voir demain.

1. Tu as vu cette pièce?
2. Tu as vu cette exposition?
3. Tu as vu ces sculptures de Rodin?
4. Tu as vu ces tableaux?
5. Tu as vu l'exposition des tableaux de Gauguin?

25 **Devinettes** Devinez ce que c'est.

1. On le présente quand on va dans un pays étranger.
2. On le prend pour voyager très loin.
3. On les lave avant de manger.
4. On les lave avec une brosse à dents.
5. On la remplit avant de débarquer.
6. On l'écoute attentivement en classe.

Auguste Rodin *Le penseur*

26 **Jeu** **Encore des devinettes** Work in groups and make up riddles similar to those in Activity 25. Ask other groups your riddles. The group that guesses the most riddles wins.

27 **L'artiste** Have some fun. Pretend you are an artist. Draw something. Have a classmate give a critique of your artwork. Take turns.

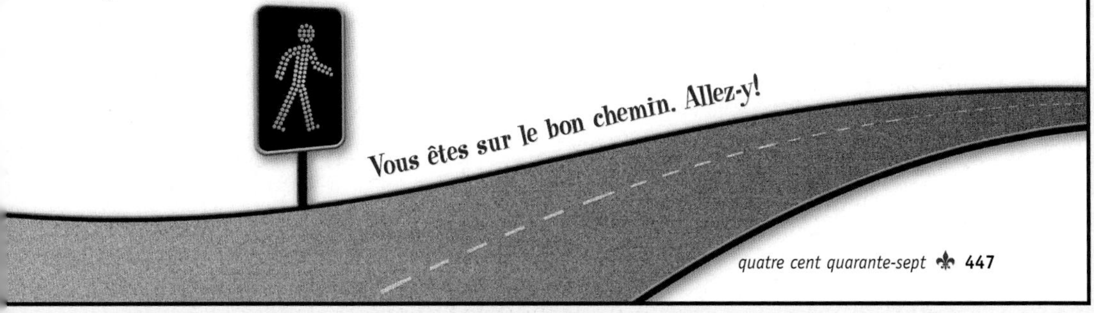
Vous êtes sur le bon chemin. Allez-y!

Structure

Art Connection

Auguste Rodin (1840–1917) dominated the world of sculpture at the end of the nineteenth century and the beginning of the twentieth century. His technique in sculpture was similar to that of the Impressionists in painting. As he modeled in wax or clay, he added pieces bit by bit to construct his forms, just as the painters added dots and dashes of paint to create their pictures.

This statue, ***Le penseur,*** is one of his most famous. This sculpture, along with others, is located in the garden of **le musée Rodin** in the **7e arrondissement** of Paris. The museum is housed in a beautiful eighteenth-century mansion that was once Rodin's studio.

Allez-y!
At this point in the chapter, students have learned all the vocabulary and structure necessary to complete the chapter. The conversation and cultural readings that follow recycle all the material learned up to this point.

Answers to Continuons

24

1. Non, mais je vais la voir demain.
2. Non, mais je vais la voir demain.
3. Non, mais je vais les voir demain.
4. Non, mais je vais les voir demain.
5. Non, mais je vais la voir demain.

25

1. son passeport
2. l'avion
3. les mains
4. les dents
5. la carte de débarquement
6. le prof, la prof

26 *Answers will vary but may include:*

On le donne à un ami pour son anniversaire. (le cadeau)
On les peigne le matin. (les cheveux)
On l'achète pour voir un film. (le billet)

27 *Answers will vary but may include:*

Je trouve ton dessin très beau. Je le trouve très intéressant.

1 Preparation

Resource Manager

Audio Activities Booklet TE, page 163
Audiocassette 8A/CD 8
CD-ROM

Bellringer Review

Use BRR Transparency 13.6 or write the following on the board.
Write the following words under the correct category: **le cinéma** or **le théâtre.**

une pièce, l'écran, les sous-titres, la scène, l'entracte, une séance, une tragédie

2 Presentation

Step 1 Tell students they are going to hear a conversation between Bruno and Léa, who are discussing going to a movie.

Step 2 Have them watch the conversation on the CD-ROM or listen as you read the conversation or play Audiocassette 8A/CD 8.

Step 3 Have students work in pairs to practice the conversation. Then have several pairs present it to the class.

Step 4 You may have a more able student retell the conversation in narrative form in his or her own words.

Glencoe Technology

CD-ROM

On the CD-ROM, students can watch a dramatization of this conversation. They can then play the role of either one of the characters and record themselves in the conversation.

On va au cinéma?

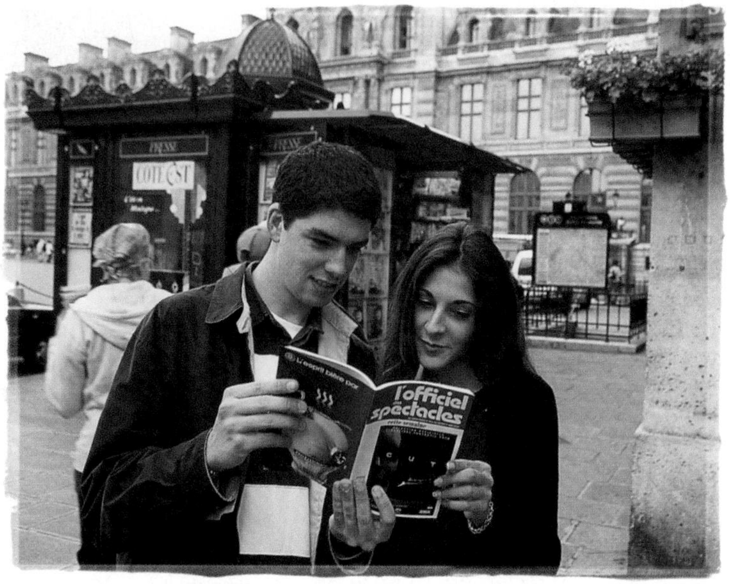

Bruno: Qu'est-ce que tu veux faire?
Léa: Je ne sais pas, moi. Aller au cinéma.
Bruno: Qu'est-ce que tu veux voir?
Léa: Ça m'est égal. Comme tu veux. Qu'est-ce qu'il y a de bien?
Bruno: Attends. Je vais te dire… *(Il prend* l'Officiel des Spectacles, *il l'ouvre et il le lit…)* Il y a un film avec Ricki Dean.
Léa: Ah non, pas Ricki Dean. Je le déteste, ce type. Il est parfaitement ridicule et il ne le sait même pas!
Bruno: Il y a un film espagnol au Ciné-Élysées. Ça t'intéresse?
Léa: Oui, un film espagnol, ça me dit. On va pouvoir travailler notre espagnol.
Bruno: Alors, il faut se dépêcher. La prochaine séance est à seize heures.

Après la conversation

Répondez.

1. Qu'est-ce que Léa veut faire?
2. Qui a *l'Officiel des Spectacles*?
3. Qui le lit?
4. Léa aime Ricki Dean? Pour quelle raison?
5. Bruno et Léa vont voir quel film?
6. Pourquoi est-ce que Léa veut voir un film espagnol?
7. Ils vont aller à quelle séance?

Answers to Après la conversation

1. Elle veut aller au cinéma.
2. Bruno a *l'Officiel des Spectacles*.
3. Bruno le lit.
4. Non, elle n'aime pas Ricki Dean parce qu'il est ridicule.
5. Ils vont voir un film espagnol.
6. Ils vont pouvoir travailler leur espagnol.
7. Ils vont aller à la séance de seize heures.

Parlons un peu plus

Let's talk some more

On va au cinéma? Look at the movie guide. Decide which movie you'd like to see and invite a classmate to see it with you. Tell your partner when and where the movie is playing, whether it is dubbed or in the original language with subtitles. Discuss whether or not you both want to see the movie or figure out an alternative.

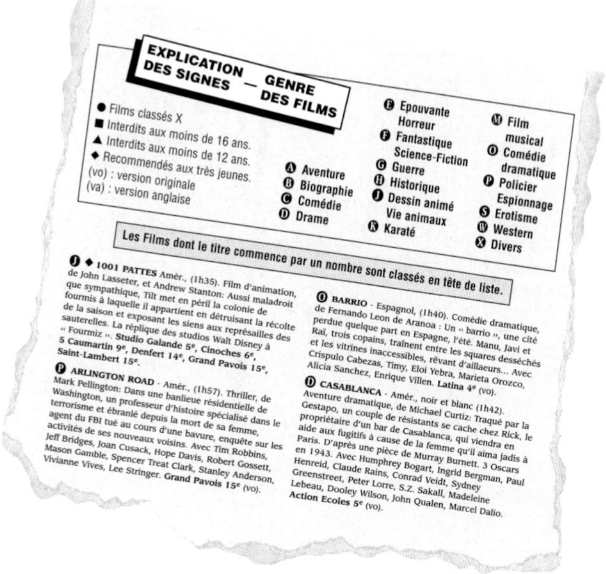

EXPLICATION DES SIGNES — GENRE DES FILMS

● Films classés X
■ Interdits aux moins de 16 ans.
▲ Interdits aux moins de 12 ans.
◆ Recommendés aux très jeunes.
(vo) : version originale
(va) : version anglaise

A Aventure
B Biographie
C Comédie
D Drame
E Epouvante Horreur
F Fantastique Science-Fiction
G Guerre
H Historique
J Dessin animé Vie animaux
K Karaté
M Film musical
O Comédie dramatique
P Policier Espionnage
S Erotisme
W Western
X Divers

Les Films dont le titre commence par un nombre sont classés en tête de liste.

J ◆ **1001 PATTES** Amér., (1h35). Film d'animation, de John Lasseter, et Andrew Stanton: Aussi maladroit que sympathique, Tilt met en péril la colonie de fourmis à laquelle il appartient en détruisant la récolte de la saison et exposant les siens aux représailles des sauterelles. La réplique des studios Walt Disney à « Fourmiz ». **Studio Galande 5e, Cinoches 6e, 5 Caumartin 9e, Denfert 14e, Grand Pavois 15e, Saint-Lambert 15e.**

P **ARLINGTON ROAD** - Amér., (1h57). Thriller, de Mark Pellington: Dans une banlieue résidentielle de Washington, un professeur d'histoire spécialisé dans le terrorisme et ébranlé depuis la mort de sa femme, agent du FBI tué au cours d'une bavure, enquête sur les activités de ses nouveaux voisins. Avec Tim Robbins, Jeff Bridges, Joan Cusack, Hope Davis, Robert Gossett, Mason Gamble, Spencer Treat Clark, Stanley Anderson, Vivianne Vives, Lee Stringer. **Grand Pavois 15e** (vo).

O **BARRIO** - Espagnol, (1h40). Comédie dramatique, de Fernando Leon de Aranoa : Un « barrio », une cité perdue quelque part en Espagne, l'été. Manu, Javi et Raï, trois copains, traînent entre les squares desséchés et les vitrines inaccessibles, rêvant d'aillaeurs... Avec Crispulo Cabezas, Timy, Eloi Yebra, Marieta Orozco, Alicia Sanchez, Enrique Villen. **Latina 4e** (vo).

D **CASABLANCA** - Amér., noir et blanc (1h42). Aventure dramatique, de Michael Curtiz: Traqué par la Gestapo, un couple de résistants se cache chez Rick, le propriétaire d'un bar de Casablanca, qui viendra en aide aux fugitifs à cause de la femme qu'il aima jadis à Paris. D'après une pièce de Murray Burnett. 3 Oscars en 1943. Avec Humphrey Bogart, Ingrid Bergman, Paul Henreid, Claude Rains, Conrad Veidt, Sydney Greenstreet, Peter Lorre, S.Z. Sakall, Madeleine Lebeau, Dooley Wilson, John Qualen, Marcel Dalio. **Action Ecoles 5e** (vo).

Prononciation

Le son /ü/

1. To say the sound /ü/, first say the sound /i/, then round your lips. Repeat the following words.

   une statue **une sculpture** **une peinture**
   une voiture **un musée**

2. The sound /ü/ also occurs in combination with other vowels. Repeat the following words.

   aujourd'hui **depuis** **je suis** **huit**

3. Now repeat the following sentences.

   Tu as vu ces statues?
   C'est une sculpture très connue?
   Le musée est rue Sully depuis huit ans.

une statue

3 Practice

Parlons un peu plus

Let's talk some more

Have students work in pairs. You may wish to choose a pair of students to do these activities for the class.

Prononciation

Step 1 Model the key word **une statue** and have the students repeat in unison.

Step 2 Now lead students through the information on page 449 and model the other words and sentences.

Step 3 You may wish to give the students the following **dictée:**

Le musée n'est pas rue Victor Hugo. Tu as bu du lait?

Step 4 For additional pronunciation practice you may wish to use the Pronunciation Transparency P 13.

ANSWERS TO Parlons un peu plus

Answers will vary.

Audio Activities Booklet TE, pages 164–165
Audiocassette 8A/CD 8

National Standards

Cultures

The reading about cultural life in France on pages 450–451 and the related activities on page 451 allow students to find out more about museums, ballet, opera, and theater in France.

Presentation

Pre-reading

Step 1 You may want to have students look at the photos on pages 450–451 now.

Step 2 Read and discuss the Reading Strategy, page 450. Have students identify the main idea of each section of the reading.

Step 3 Have students skim the reading quickly and silently.

Reading

Step 1 Lead students through the Lecture on pages 450–451 by having individuals read two to three sentences at a time. After each one reads, ask others follow-up questions.

Step 2 Ask five or six questions that review the main points. Call on individuals to answer. Answers will give an organized summary of the **Lecture.**

Reading Strategy

Identifying the main idea

When reading, it is important to identify the main idea the author is expressing. Each paragraph usually discusses a different idea. The main idea is often found in the first or second sentence in each paragraph. First, skim the passage. Once you know the main idea of the passage, go back and read it again more carefully.

Les loisirs culturels en France

Les musées

Les musées en France sont toujours très fréquentés par les Français et par les touristes qui visitent la France. Tu connais les impressionnistes? Tu apprécies leurs tableaux? Alors il faut aller au musée d'Orsay. Le musée d'Orsay est une ancienne gare qui a été transformée en musée. C'est le musée du dix-neuvième siècle[1]. On trouve des tableaux, des sculptures, des meubles[2], tout du dix-neuvième siècle. Il y a une exposition permanente de tableaux des impressionnistes.

Si tu es fana d'art moderne, tu vas beaucoup aimer le centre Pompidou. Là, il y a toujours des expositions d'art moderne. Il y a aussi une vue extraordinaire sur Paris.

Mais la perle des musées français, c'est le Louvre. Au Louvre, tu peux admirer des tableaux et des sculptures de grands artistes de tous les siècles.

Le premier dimanche de chaque mois, l'entrée des musées nationaux est gratuite. Les autres dimanches, elle est demi-tarif[3]. C'est pourquoi les musées sont toujours combles le dimanche.

[1] siècle *century*
[2] meubles *furniture*
[3] demi-tarif *half-price*

Centre Pompidou

Musée d'Orsay

Learning from Photos

(page 450 left) The **Centre Pompidou** is named after Georges Pompidou, the French president who launched the project to establish this museum of modern art. Most Parisians simply refer to it as **Beaubourg** because it is located on the plateau **Beaubourg.** The center was opened in 1977, and it soon attracted millions of visitors, five times more than had been estimated. The brightly painted exterior service pipes and the plastic tubing enclosing the escalator were in need of constant repair. In 1996 the government shut down the center for a complete renovation. It reopened in January 2000 and the total complex was greatly expanded.

(page 450 right) The **musée d'Orsay** was once a railroad station. Today it houses the world's most complete and famous collection of Impressionist paintings.

Opéra Garnier

Les ballets et l'opéra

Si tu aimes la danse classique, il faut aller voir un ballet à l'opéra Garnier.

Si tu aimes l'opéra, il faut aller à l'opéra Bastille. On a inauguré le nouvel opéra sur la place de la Bastille en 1989 pour commémorer le bicentenaire de la Révolution française de 1789. Tu préfères l'architecture de quel opéra? De l'ancien opéra Garnier ou du nouvel opéra Bastille? L'architecture, c'est un art aussi, tu sais.

Le théâtre

Tu connais les grands auteurs dramatiques du dix-septième siècle: Racine, Corneille, Molière? Si tu as envie[4] d'aller voir une de leurs pièces, tu peux aller à la Comédie-Française, le plus vieux théâtre national du monde.

[4] as envie *feel like*

Opéra Bastille

Comédie-Française

Après la lecture

A Les musées Répondez.

1. Qui fréquente les musées français?
2. Tu connais quelques peintres impressionnistes?
3. Tu apprécies leurs tableaux?
4. Tu connais leur œuvre?
5. Il y a une exposition permanente des impressionnistes dans quel musée?
6. Quel est le musée d'art moderne?
7. Quel est un autre musée très célèbre à Paris?
8. Qu'est-ce qu'il y a dans ce musée?
9. Les musées sont presque toujours combles le dimanche. Pourquoi?

B D'autres loisirs Répondez.

1. Tu es à Paris et tu veux voir un ballet. Tu vas où?
2. Tu veux voir un opéra. Tu vas où?
3. Tu veux voir une tragédie de Racine ou une comédie de Molière. Tu vas où?

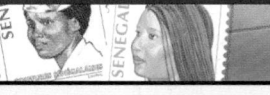

Answers to Après la lecture

A

1. Les Français et les touristes qui visitent la France fréquentent les musées français.
2. Oui, je connais quelques peintres impressionnistes.
3. Oui, je les apprécie.
4. Oui, je la connais.
5. Il y a une exposition permanente des impressionnistes au musée d'Orsay.
6. Le musée d'art moderne est le centre Pompidou.
7. Le Louvre est un autre musée très célèbre à Paris.
8. Au Louvre il y a des tableaux et des sculptures de grands artistes de tous les siècles.
9. Les musées sont combles le dimanche parce que l'entrée est gratuite ou demi-tarif.

B

1. Je vais à l'opéra Garnier.
2. Je vais à l'opéra Bastille.
3. Je vais à la Comédie-Française.

Post-reading

Have students do the **Après la lecture** activities on page 451 orally after reading the selection in class. Then assign these activities to be written at home. Go over them again the following day.

Après la lecture

A and B Allow students to refer to the story to look up the answers or you may use this activity as a testing device for factual recall.

Learning from Photos

(page 451 top) The **Opéra Garnier** is the original opera house of Paris. Built at the behest of Napoleon III, construction was begun in 1862 but not completed until 1875. It is named after its architect, Charles Garnier. It is a beautiful building with a mélange of many architectural styles. Most operas are now performed at the new **Opéra Bastille,** but there are still occasional performances at the Garnier, which is more often used for ballets.

(page 451 middle) The **Opéra Bastille** on the **place de la Bastille** was designed by the Argentine-born architect Carlos Ott. It opened in 1989 and it seats more than 3,000 people. Many Parisians are not fond of its glass façade that looks like a modern office building.

(page 451 bottom) The **Comédie-Française** theater building dates from 1790. The **Comédie-Française** Acting Company was created by Louis XIV and dates back to 1680. The **Comédie-Française** is the setting for performances of classical French dramas. The comedies of Molière and the tragedies of Racine and Corneille are performed regularly.

National Standards

Cultures
This selection familiarizes students with traditional and popular African music.

Attention!

This reading is optional. You may skip it completely, have the entire class read it, have only several students read it and report to the class, or assign it for extra credit.

Presentation

Step 1 Ask the students if they have heard any African music. You may wish to play a sample of some of the music mentioned in the **Lecture.**

Step 2 Have students read the **Lecture** quickly.

Step 3 Ask what new information they learned about African music.

La musique africaine

Un griot

Quand on parle de musique africaine, on parle de deux sortes de musique—la musique traditionnelle et la musique moderne pop. Il y a une grande différence entre les deux.

La musique traditionnelle

La musique traditionnelle est la musique de la brousse[1], des villages ruraux. Cette musique traditionnelle accompagne toutes les activités de la vie quotidienne ainsi que[2] les événements mémorables de la vie sociale. Il y a de la musique pour les femmes, par exemple, de la musique pour les jeunes, pour les chasseurs[3], etc. À toutes ces festivités, les griots, des poètes musiciens, racontent des histoires et jouent de la musique. Tous les instruments de musique sont souvent faits à la main par les griots eux-mêmes[4].

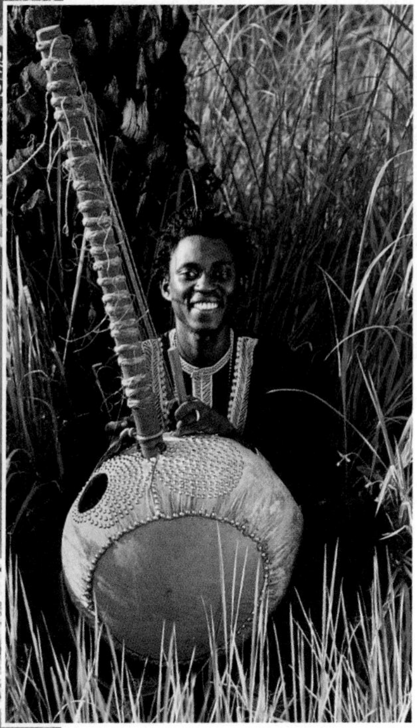
Un musicien joue du kora, Gambie

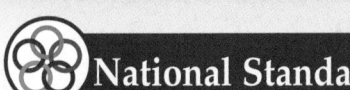

La musique moderne

La musique pop africaine est devenue[5] très populaire au-dehors des pays africains, surtout en Europe. La première fois que vous l'entendez, vous pensez que c'est un mélange de rythmes latins et afro-américains des États-Unis comme le rock et le jazz. C'est vrai. Pourquoi? Parce que la musique africaine est à l'origine de la musique latino-américaine et de la musique afro-américaine d'aujourd'hui.

[1] brousse *brush*
[2] ainsi que *as well as*
[3] chasseurs *hunters*
[4] eux-mêmes *themselves*
[5] est devenue *has become*

Learning from Photos

(page 452 top) The **griot** is a member of a caste responsible for maintaining an oral record of the tribal history in the form of music, poetry, and storytelling. Although the **griots** are the lowest of the castes, they are highly respected. As musicians and songwriters, they used to entertain the royal families. Many musicians who play the **kora**, and quite a few popular singers, are from the **griot** families.

(page 452 bottom) The **kora** is one of the most sophisticated instruments in Sub-Saharan Africa. It has twenty-one strings. The neck is made of rosewood. The neck goes into a somewhat circular gourd covered with cowhide. The **kora** is described as a harp-lute, and it is played most often in Gambia, Guinea, Mali, and Senegal.

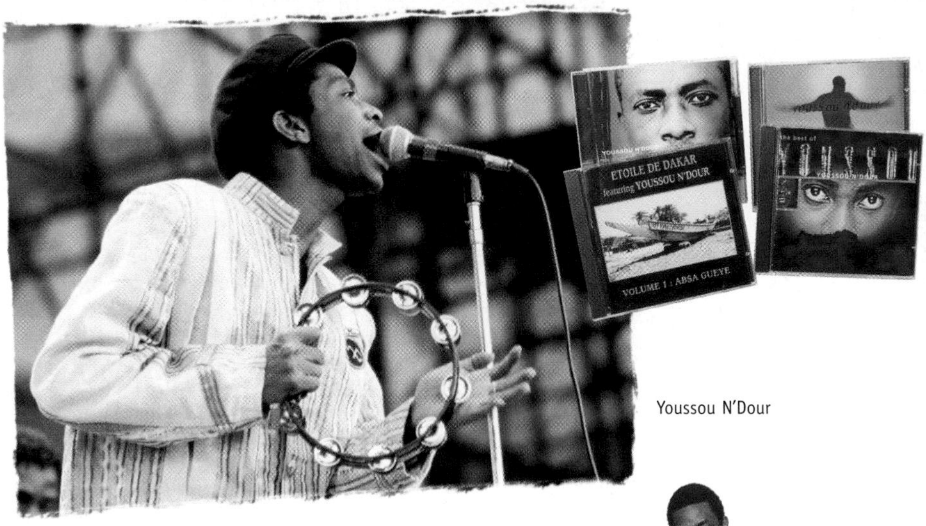

Youssou N'Dour

Le chanteur sénégalais Youssou N'Dour a un très grand succès. Il est né dans le quartier pauvre de la Médina à Dakar. Il est fils et petit-fils de griots, les poètes musiciens en Afrique. C'est lui le plus grand interprète de la musique «fusion pop». C'est une fusion d'un rythme africain, le m'balax, avec des rythmes de reggae, de rock et de jazz.

Après la lecture

La musique traditionnelle Vrai ou faux?

1. La musique traditionnelle d'Afrique, c'est la musique des grandes villes cosmopolites.
2. La musique traditionnelle varie selon l'événement.
3. Les griots sont des poètes et des musiciens.
4. Les griots jouent toujours de la guitare électrique.
5. La musique moderne africaine est très populaire aux États-Unis.
6. Le rock et le jazz ont influencé la musique africaine.
7. Youssou N'Dour est un chanteur sénégalais très connu.
8. La musique latino-américaine est une fusion de musique africaine avec du reggae, du rock et du jazz.

Après la lecture

You may wish to have students correct the false statements. You may also wish to have students research some of the types of music and musicians mentioned in the **Lecture.** They can use the Internet to do this or contact their school's music teacher for resources.

Learning from Photos

(page 453) For more information about Youssou N'Dour, please see pages 254–255.

Answers to Après la lecture

1. F
2. V
3. V
4. F
5. F
6. F
7. V
8. F

CONNEXIONS

National Standards

Connections
This reading about music on pages 454–455 establishes a connection with another discipline, allowing students to reinforce and further their knowledge of music through the study of French.

Attention!

The readings in the **Connexions** section are optional. They focus on some of the major disciplines taught in schools and universities. The vocabulary is useful for discussing such topics as history, literature, art, economics, business, science, etc. You may choose any of the following ways to do the readings in the **Connexions** sections.

Independent reading Have students read the selections and do the post-reading activities as homework, which you collect. This option is least intrusive on class time and requires a minimum of teacher involvement.

Homework with in-class follow-up Assign the readings and post-reading activities as homework. Review and discuss the material in class the next day.

Intensive in-class activity This option includes a pre-reading vocabulary presentation, in-class reading and discussion, assignment of the activities for homework, and a discussion of the assignment in class the following day.

Presentation

Les Beaux-Arts
La musique

Step 1 Have students read the introduction in English on page 454.

CONNEXIONS

Les Beaux-Arts

La musique

Like painting and literature, music is a form of art. Think of all the times you hear music each day. Music has been an integral part of the daily lives of people since the beginning of recorded history.

Before reading some general information about music, let's take a look at some of the many cognates that exist in the language of music.

un ballet

un orchestre symphonique

un opéra

une fanfare

un chœur

The names of many musical instruments are also cognates.

un piano	**un saxophone**	**une trompette**
une guitare	**une flûte**	**une clarinette**
un accordéon	**un violon**	**une harpe**

La musique

Les instruments musicaux

On classifie les instruments musicaux en quatre groupes principaux—les instruments à cordes, les instruments à vent, les instruments à percussion et les instruments à clavier.

Un orchestre ou une fanfare

Quelle est la différence entre un orchestre et une fanfare? Une fanfare n'a pas d'instruments à cordes. Il n'y a pas de violons, par exemple. Et dans une fanfare, il n'y a pas de flûtes ni de hautbois[1]. Les fanfares qui jouent de la musique pendant les événements sportifs et qui participent aux défilés[2] sont plus populaires aux États-Unis qu'en France.

[1] hautbois *oboes* [2] défilés *parades*

L'opéra *Carmen*

L'orchestre symphonique

Un orchestre symphonique est un grand orchestre composé d'instruments de tous les groupes musicaux. Une symphonie est une composition musicale pour orchestre. Une symphonie est en général une composition ambitieuse qui dure de vingt à quarante-cinq minutes.

L'opéra

Un opéra est une composition dramatique sans dialogue parlé. Dans un opéra, les acteurs chantent; ils ne parlent jamais. Ils chantent des airs d'une beauté extraordinaire. L'orchestre les accompagne. L'histoire est en général très tragique. Un opéra comique est un opéra avec des dialogues parlés. Un opéra comique n'est pas nécessairement très amusant. Un opéra bouffe est un opéra dont l'histoire est une comédie. *Carmen* de Georges Bizet et *Dialogue des Carmélites* de Francis Poulenc sont deux opéras français très célèbres.

La musique populaire

Il y a toutes sortes de musique populaire. Il y a des groupes de jazz, de rock et de rap, par exemple. De nos jours, le rap et la musique techno sont très populaires. Les chansons populaires ont souvent des thèmes romantiques. Il y a toujours une relation intime entre la musique populaire et la danse.

La chanteuse Céline Dion

Après la lecture

A Des instruments Nommez.

1. un instrument à cordes
2. quelques instruments à vent

B Vous le savez? Répondez.

1. Quelle est la différence entre un orchestre et une fanfare?
2. Qu'est-ce qu'un opéra?
3. Quels sont quelques types de musique populaire?

CONNEXIONS

Step 2 Most students will be familiar with these musical terms in English. Model the terms in French and have students repeat after you.

Step 3 Ask students to scan the readings to get the general information.

Step 4 It is suggested that you play some recordings of the types of music discussed in this section. Ask a music teacher to help you assemble some selections from the Music Department's library.

Après la lecture

A You may wish to ask students if they know how to play these (or other) instruments: **Qui sait jouer de la guitare?**

Music Connection

Georges Bizet, the French composer, wrote the music to the opera *Carmen.* It is based on the short story *Carmen*, by Prosper Mérimée, published in 1845. It is the tragic love story of the bohemian Carmen and the brigadier don José in Seville, Spain. A scene from the opera is shown above.

Learning from Photos

(page 455 middle) This photo of Céline Dion, the popular French-Canadian singer who now resides in the U.S., shows her in concert at the Centre Molson, the home of the Montreal Canadiens.

Answers to Après la lecture

A *Answers will vary but may include:*

1. un violon
2. un saxophone, une flûte, une trompette, une clarinette

B

1. La différence entre un orchestre et une fanfare est qu'une fanfare n'a pas d'instruments à cordes.
2. Un opéra est une composition dramatique sans dialogue parlé, et l'histoire est en général très tragique.
3. Quelques types de musique populaire sont le jazz, le rock, le rap et la musique techno.

Recycling

These activities allow students to use the vocabulary and structure from this chapter in completely open-ended, real-life situations.

Learning from Photos

(page 456 top) The **Maison du Roi** is opposite the town hall (also seen in the photo) in Brussels. In spite of its name, no king ever lived there. The building is a sixteenth-century palace that houses the city museum. It has an excellent collection of ceramics and silverware. Brussels is famous for both ceramics and silverware.

✔ Discuss movies, plays, and museums

Work with a classmate. Pretend you're on vacation in Brussels in Belgium. You meet a Belgian teenager (your partner) who's interested in what you do for fun in your free time. Tell him or her about your leisure activities. Then your partner will tell you about what he or she does.

Maison du Roi, Bruxelles, Belgique

PARLER

2 Une journée au musée

✔ Ask and answer questions about a museum visit

Work in groups of three or four. Several of you spent the day at a museum last Saturday. Other friends have some questions. Describe your museum visit and be sure to answer all their questions.

Musée du Louvre

ÉCRIRE

3 Une affiche

✔ Make a poster for a play

Prepare a poster in French for your school play. Give all the necessary information to advertise **le spectacle.**

Answers to C'est à vous

1. *Answers will vary depending upon student preferences.*
2. *Answers will vary depending upon whether or not students have been to a museum.*

C'est à vous

ÉCRIRE

4 Des renseignements, s'il vous plaît.

✔ *Write for information about cultural events*

You're going to spend a month in the French city of your choice. Write a letter or an e-mail to the tourist office **(le syndicat d'initiative)** asking for information about cultural events during your stay. Be sure to mention your age, what kind of cultural activities you like, and the dates of your stay.

Une colonne Morris, Paris

Les Grandes Heures du Parlement

L'Assemblée nationale présente dans l'aile du Midi du Château de Versailles un musée qui vous permet de découvrir la salle des séances du Congrès du Parlement, troisième hémicycle de la République, dans laquelle vous assisterez à un spectacle audiovisuel sur les grands débats de la Nation.

Sur le pourtour de cette salle, vous revivrez deux cents ans d'histoire parlementaire et vous vous familiariserez avec le travail au quotidien du député. Vous découvrirez l'activité internationale du Parlement français et ses liens avec les différents parlements du monde.

Prix d'entrée

Individuel:visite libre avec audioguide
Tarif normal: 4€ - Tarif réduit 3€ - Gratuit pour les scolaires

Group de 30 personnes au plus: visite commentée
Tarif normal: 40€ - Tarif réduit 30€ - Gratuit pour les scolaires

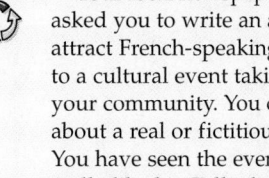

Visitez la salle
du Congrès du Parlement
au Château de Versailles
Découvrez
l'histoire du Parlement
le spectacle audiovisuel dans la salle des séances
" Les grandes heures du Parlement "
Musée présenté par l'Assemblée nationale
du mardi au samedi de 9h00 à 17h30

Writing Strategy

Persuasive writing Persuasive writing is writing that encourages a reader to do something or to accept an idea. Newspaper and magazine advertisements, as well as certain articles, are examples of persuasive writing. As you write, present a logical argument to encourage others to follow your line of thinking. Your writing should contain sufficient evidence to persuade readers to "buy into" what you are presenting. Explain how your evidence supports your argument; end by restating your argument.

ÉCRIRE

5 Un reportage

Your local newspaper has asked you to write an article to attract French-speaking readers to a cultural event taking place in your community. You can write about a real or fictitious event. You have seen the event and you really liked it. Tell why as you try to convince or persuade your readers to go see it.

Writing Development

Have students keep a notebook containing their best written work from each chapter. These selected writings can be based on assignments from the Student Textbook and the Writing Activities Workbook. The two activities on page 457 are examples of writing assignments that may be included in each student's portfolio. In the Workbook, students will develop an organized autobiography **(Mon autobiographie).** These workbook pages may also become a part of their portfolio.

Writing Strategy

Taking notes
Have students read the Writing Strategy on page 457. If students have difficulty thinking of related vocabulary, have them use the vocabulary list on page 460.

Reaching All Students

Additional Practice Display Communication Transparency C 13. Have students work in groups to make up as many questions as they can about the illustration. Have groups take turns asking and answering the questions.

Learning from Photos

(page 457) The **colonnes Morris,** such as the one seen in this photo, can be found throughout Paris. Their purpose is to advertise cultural events.

Resource Manager

Communication Transparencies
Quizzes
Test Booklet
ExamView Pro®
Situation Cards
Performance Assessment
Marathon mental Videoquiz

Assessment

This is a pre-test for students to take before you administer the chapter test. Answer sheets for students to do these pages are provided in your transparency binder. Note that each section is cross-referenced so students can easily find the material they have to review in case they made errors. You may wish to collect these assessments and correct them yourself or you may prefer to have the students correct themselves in class. You can go over the answers orally or project them on the overhead, using your Assessment Answers transparencies.

Assessment

Vocabulaire

1 Choisissez.

*To review **Mots 1**, turn to pages 432–433.*

1. On joue des films où?
   a. dans une séance
   b. dans une salle de cinéma
   c. dans un théâtre
2. Qui joue dans un film?
   a. des acteurs et des actrices
   b. des sous-titres
   c. des joueurs
3. Une pièce de théâtre est divisée en quoi?
   a. en version originale
   b. en entractes
   c. en actes et en scènes
4. Le film est doublé?
   a. Oui, il y a deux films.
   b. Non, il est en V.O.
   c. Oui, il y a des sous-titres.
5. Qu'est-ce que *l'Officiel des Spectacles?*
   a. un magazine
   b. une place
   c. un film

2 Identifiez.

*To review **Mots 2**, turn to pages 436–437.*

6. 

7. 

8. 

9. 

10. 

Answers to Assessment

1	2
1. b	6. un musée
2. a	7. une statue (une sculpture)
3. c	8. une peintre
4. b	9. un sculpteur
5. a	10. un tableau

Structure

3 Récrivez.

11. Je sais le numéro.
    Vous ________.
12. Vous connaissez mon ami?
    Il ______________?

To review the verbs **savoir** and **connaître**, turn to page 440.

4 Complétez avec «savoir» ou «connaître».

13. Je ____ son numéro de téléphone.
14. Vous ____ où il habite, non?
15. Je ____ très bien l'œuvre de cet artiste.
16. Tu ____ Paris?
17. Ils ____ danser le tango.

5 Répondez avec un pronom.

18. Il te parle au téléphone? Oui, ____.
19. Tu invites Jean? Oui, ____.
20. Tu vas inviter sa petite amie aussi? Oui, ____.
21. Le prof vous donne beaucoup de devoirs? Oui, ____.
22. Tu vois la petite fille? Oui, ____.
23. Tu connais les pièces de Molière? Oui, ____.

To review the object pronouns, turn to pages 442–444.

Culture

6 Identifiez.

24. un musée à Paris
25. un auteur français dramatique du dix-septième siècle

To review this cultural information, turn to pages 450–451.

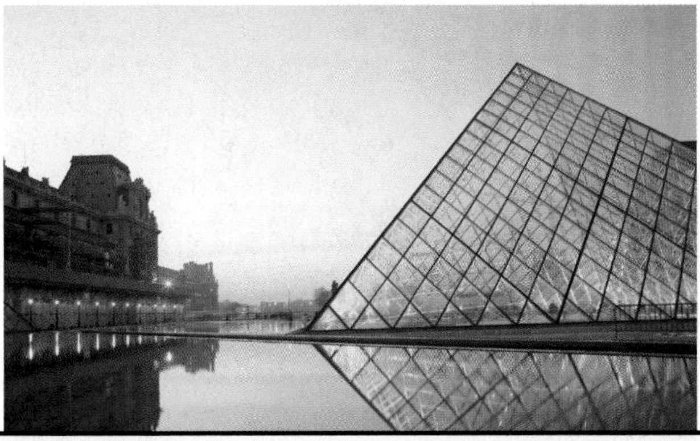

Musée du Louvre, Paris

Glencoe Technology

MINDJOGGER

You may wish to help your students prepare for the chapter test by playing the MindJogger game show. Teams will compete against each other to review chapter vocabulary and structure and sharpen listening comprehension skills.

Answers to Assessment

3

11. Vous savez le numéro.
12. Il connaît mon ami?

4

13. sais
14. savez
15. connais
16. connais
17. savent

5

18. Oui, il me parle au téléphone.
19. Oui, je l'invite.
20. Oui, je vais l'inviter aussi.
21. Oui, le prof nous donne beaucoup de devoirs.
22. Oui, je la vois.
23. Oui, je les connais.

6

24. le musée d'Orsay (le musée du Louvre, le Centre Pompidou)
25. Molière

Vocabulary Review

The words and phrases in the **Vocabulaire** have been taught for productive use in this chapter. They are summarized here as a resource for both student and teacher. This list also serves as a convenient resource for the **C'est à vous** activities on pages 456–457. There are approximately twenty-two cognates in this vocabulary list. Have students find them.

Attention!

You will notice that the vocabulary list here is not translated. This has been done intentionally, since we feel that by the time students have finished the material in the chapter they should be familiar with the meanings of all the words. If there are several words they still do not know, we recommend that they refer to the **Mots 1** and **2** sections in the chapter or go to the dictionaries at the back of this book to find the meanings. However, if you prefer that your students have the English translations, please refer to Vocabulary Transparency 13.1, where you will find all these words listed with their translations.

Discussing a movie

un cinéma
une salle de cinéma
un guichet
une place
une séance
un écran

un film comique
policier
d'horreur
de science-fiction
d'aventures
d'amour

un documentaire
un dessin animé
étranger
en V.O.
doublé
avec des sous-titres

jouer un film
louer une vidéo

Describing a play

un théâtre
une pièce
un acteur
une actrice
un chanteur
une chanteuse

un danseur
une danseuse
une scène
un acte
un entracte
une tragédie

une comédie
un drame
monter une pièce
chanter
danser

How well do you know your vocabulary?

- **Choose the name of a cultural event or artistic profession.**
- **Have a classmate tell you his or her favorite in the category you chose.**

Describing a museum visit

un musée
une exposition
un tableau
une sculpture
une statue

une œuvre
la peinture
la sculpture
une peintre
un sculpteur *(m. et f.)*

Other useful words and expressions

connaître
savoir
ouvert
fermé

célèbre
connu
sauf
ça (m')est égal

Technotour

BON VOYAGE!

VIDÉO • Épisode 13

Avant de visionner

In this video episode, Chloé visits the Musée d'Orsay and puts her artistic skills to work. She later meets up with Vincent, where they experience other cultural wonders.

Chloé visite le musée d'Orsay. Elle trouve les tableaux fabuleux.

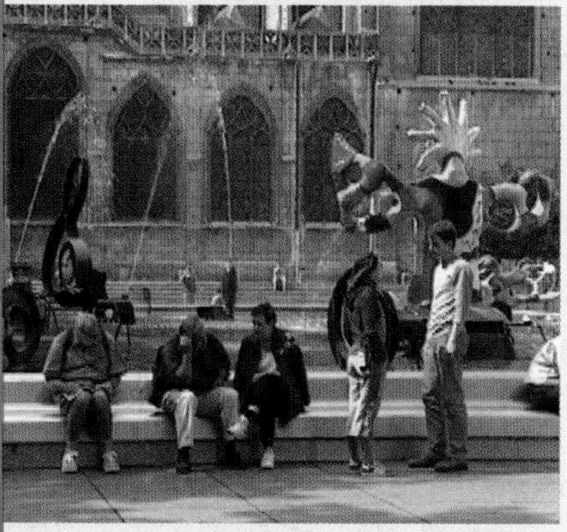

Chloé et Vincent sur la place Igor Stravinsky

FRENCH ONLINE

À découvrir

Learn more about the Centre Pompidou online.

Centre Pompidou, Paris

FRENCH Online

In the Chapter 13 Internet activity, you'll have a chance to learn more about cultural activities in the Francophone world. To begin your virtual adventure, go to the Glencoe French Web site: **french.glencoe.com**

Technotour

Overview

This page previews two key multimedia components of the **Glencoe French** series. Each reinforces the material taught in the chapter in a unique manner.

VIDÉO

The Video Program allows students to see how the chapter vocabulary and structures are used by native speakers. For maximum reinforcement, show the video episode as a final activity for Chapter 13.

The two photos on the left show highlights from the Chapter 13 video episode. Discuss the photos with your students before having them view the episode. See the Video Activities Booklet for detailed suggestions for using this resource.

FRENCH Online

- The **À découvrir** photo on page 461 shows the Centre Pompidou. Students can go online to learn more about this interesting modern art museum.
- Teacher Information and Student Worksheets for this activity can be accessed at the Web site.

Video Synopsis

In this video episode, Chloé explores aspects of cultural life in Paris. As she wanders through the **musée d'Orsay,** we catch glimpses of famous Impressionist paintings. She also talks with some other French teens about the theater and the movies. Finally, the video introduces us to the lively street performers of Paris, demonstrating the wide variety of art forms on display throughout the city.

Planning for Chapter 14

SCOPE AND SEQUENCE, PAGES 462–493

Topics

- Health and medicine
- Prescriptions

Functions

- How to describe an illness
- How to give commands
- How to refer to people, places, and things already mentioned

National Standards

- Communication Standard 1.1 pages 466, 467, 470, 471, 473, 474, 476, 477, 478, 479, 481, 488
- Communication Standard 1.2 pages 466, 467, 470, 471, 473, 474, 476, 477, 478, 479, 480, 483, 484, 485, 487
- Communication Standard 1.3 pages 466, 470, 474, 489
- Cultures Standard 2.1 pages 482–483, 484, 485–486
- Connections Standard 3.1 pages 486–487
- Comparisons Standard 4.1 page 467
- Comparisons Standard 4.2 pages 482–483, 484
- Communities Standard 5.1 page 489

Culture

- Doctors make house calls in France.
- Discussing the relationship between culture and health
- Medical services in France
- **Reflets de Paris**

Structure

- The pronouns **lui, leur**
- The verbs **souffrir** and **ouvrir**
- The imperative
- The pronoun **en**

PACING AND PRIORITIES

The chapter content is color coded below to assist you in planning.

■ **required** ■ **recommended** ■ **optional**

Vocabulaire *(required)* *Days 1–4*

■ Mots 1

On est malade.

■ Mots 2

Chez le médecin

À la pharmacie

Structure *(required)* *Days 5–7*

■ Les pronoms **lui, leur**

■ Les verbes **souffrir** et **ouvrir**

■ L´impératif

■ Le pronom **en**

Conversation *(required)*

■ Chez le médecin

Prononciation *(recommended)*

■ Les sons **/u/** et **/ü/**

Lectures culturelles

■ Une consultation *(recommended)*

■ Culture et santé *(optional)*

■ Les services médicaux en France *(optional)*

Connexions *(optional)*

■ La diététique

■ **C'est à vous** *(recommended)*

■ **Assessment** *(recommended)*

■ **Technotour** *(optional)*

RESOURCE GUIDE

Section	Pages	Section Resources
Vocabulaire *Mots 1*		
On est malade.	464–467	Vocabulary Transparencies 14.2–14.3 Audiocassette 8B/CD 8 Audio Activities Booklet TE, pages 168–170 Workbook, pages 139–140 Quiz 1, page 69 ExamView Pro®
Vocabulaire *Mots 2*		
Chez le médecin À la pharmacie	468–469 469–471	Vocabulary Transparencies 14.4–14.5 Audiocassette 8B/CD 8 Audio Activities Booklet TE, pages 171–172 Workbook, page 140 Quiz 2, page 70 ExamView Pro®
Structure		
Les pronoms **lui, leur** Les verbes **souffrir** et **ouvrir** L´impératif Le pronom **en**	472–473 474 475–477 478–479	Audiocassette 8B/CD 8 Audio Activities Booklet TE, pages 173–175 Workbook, pages 141–145 Quizzes 3–6, pages 71–74 ExamView Pro®
Conversation		
Chez le médecin	480	Audiocassette 8B/CD 8 Audio Activities Booklet TE, pages 175–176 CD-ROM
Prononciation		
Les sons **/u/** et **/ü/**	481	Pronunciation Transparency P 14 Audiocassette 8B/CD 8 Audio Activities Booklet TE, page 176
Lectures culturelles		
Une consultation Culture et santé Les services médicaux en France	482–483 484 485	Audiocassette 8B/CD 8 Audio Activities Booklet TE, page 177 Test Booklet, Chapter 14
Connexions		
La diététique	486–487	Test Booklet, Chapter 14
C'est à vous		
	488–489	**Bon voyage!** Video, Episode 14 Video Activities Booklet, Chapter 14 French Online Activities french.glencoe.com
Assessment		
	490–491	Communication Transparency C 14 Quizzes 1–6, pages 69–74 Test Booklet, Chapter 14 ExamView Pro® Situation Cards, Chapter 14 Performance Assessment, pages 23–28 **Marathon mental** Videoquiz

Using Your Resources for Chapter 14

Transparencies

Bellringer 14.1–14.8

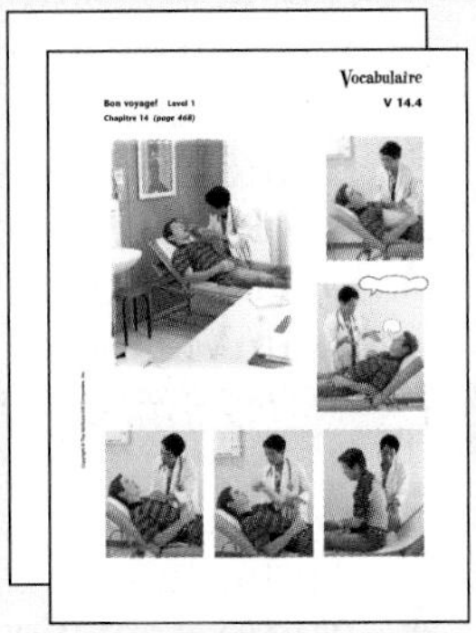

Vocabulary 14.1–14.5

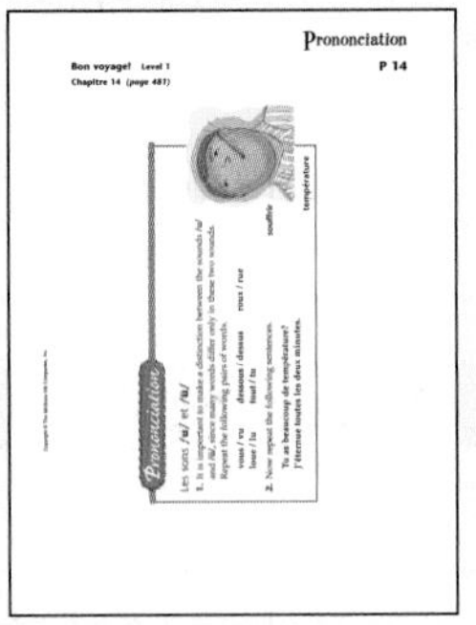

Pronunciation P 14

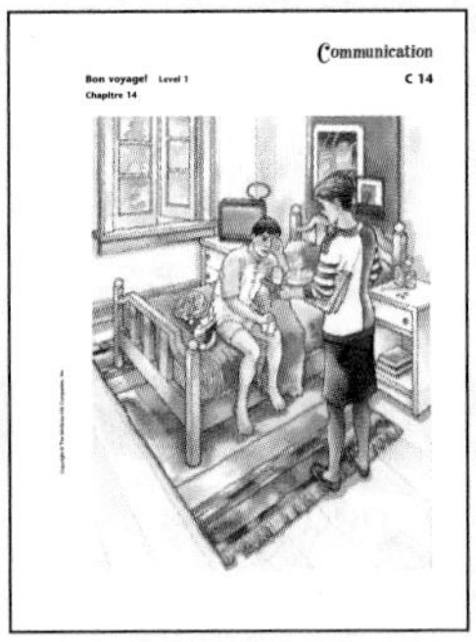

Communication C 14

Writing Activities Workbook

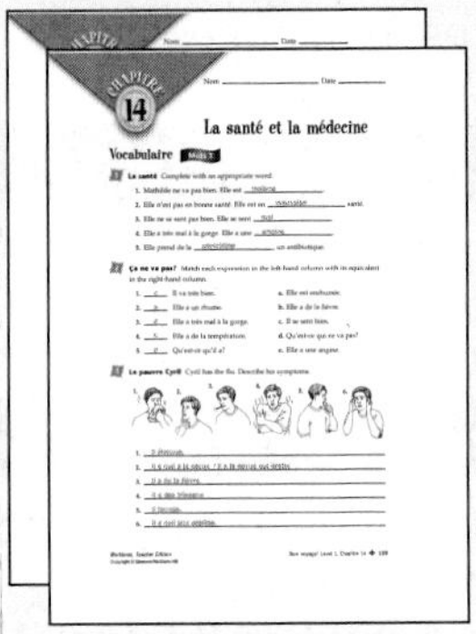

Vocabulary, pages 139–140

Structure, pages 141–145

Enrichment, pages 146–148

Audio Program and Audio Activities Booklet

Vocabulary, pages 168–172

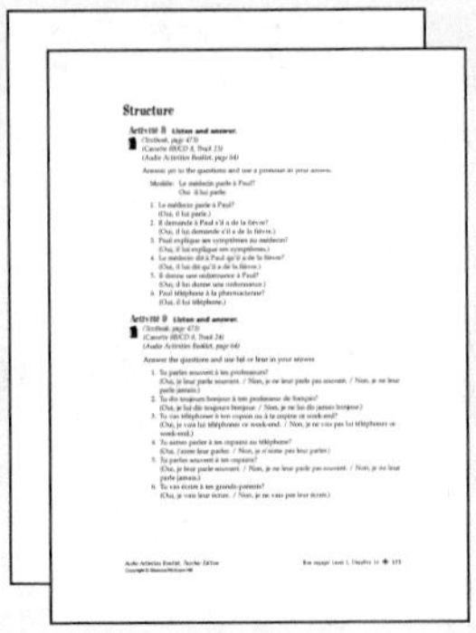

Structure, pages 173–175

Conversation, Pronunciation, pages 175–176

Cultural Reading, page 177

Additional Practice, page 178

Assessment

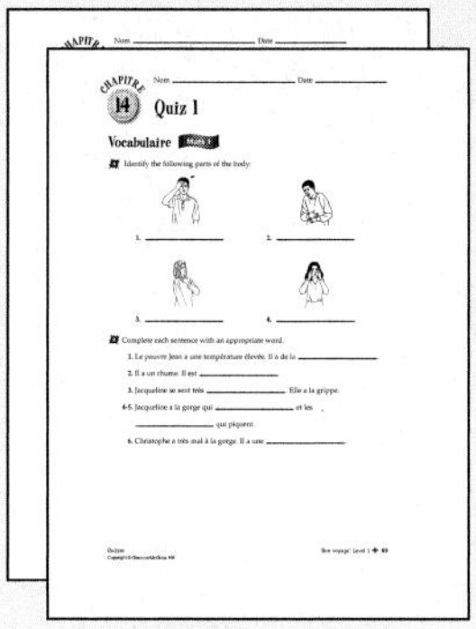

Vocabulary and Structure Quizzes, pages 69–74

Chapter Tests, Chapter 14

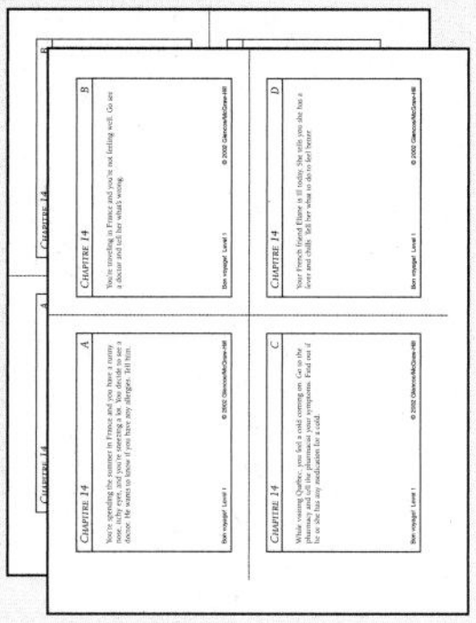

Situation Cards, Chapter 14

Performance Assessment, pages 23–28

Timesaving Teacher Tools

Interactive Teacher Edition

Imagine having your Teacher's Edition and all resources on a CD-ROM. Click on a resource and it appears on your screen, ready to be printed, sorted, or planned.

Interactive Lesson Planner

The Interactive Lesson Planner CD-ROM helps you organize your lesson plans for a week, month, semester, or year. Look at this planning tool for easy access to your Chapter 14 resources.

ExamView Pro®

Test Bank software for Macintosh and Windows makes creating, editing, customizing, and printing tests quick and easy.

Technology Resources

FRENCH Online — In the Chapter 14 Internet activity, you will have a chance to learn more about health and medicine in the Francophone world. Visit french.glencoe.com.

On the Interactive Conversation CD-ROM, students can listen to and take part in a recorded version of the conversation in Chapter 14.

NATIONAL GEOGRAPHIC SOCIETY — See the National Geographic Teacher's Corner on pages 150–151, 256–257, 396–397, 500–501 for reference to additional technology resources.

Bon Voyage! Video and Video Activities Booklet.

Help your students prepare for the chapter test by playing the **Marathon mental** Videoquiz game show. Teams will compete against each other to review chapter vocabulary and structure and sharpen listening comprehension skills.

CHAPITRE 14

Preview

In this chapter, students will learn to talk about routine illnesses and to describe their symptoms to a doctor. In order to do this, they will learn vocabulary associated with medical exams, prescriptions, and minor ailments such as colds, the flu, and headaches. Students will learn the indirect object pronouns **lui** and **leur,** the **present** and **passé composé** of verbs like **ouvrir** and **souffrir,** and the imperative forms of verbs.

National Standards

Communication

In Chapter 14, students will communicate in spoken and written French on the following topics:

- Describing symptoms of minor ailments
- Getting a prescription at a pharmacy

Students will obtain and provide information and engage in conversations about their personal health. They will also learn to tell others what to do. Students will also learn to use indirect object pronouns.

CHAPITRE 14

La santé et la médecine

Objectifs

In this chapter you will learn to:

- ✔ *explain a minor illness to a doctor*
- ✔ *have a prescription filled at a pharmacy*
- ✔ *tell for whom something is done*
- ✔ *talk about some more activities*
- ✔ *give commands*
- ✔ *refer to people, places, and things already mentioned*
- ✔ *discuss medical services in France*

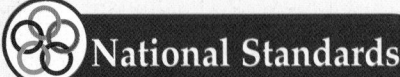

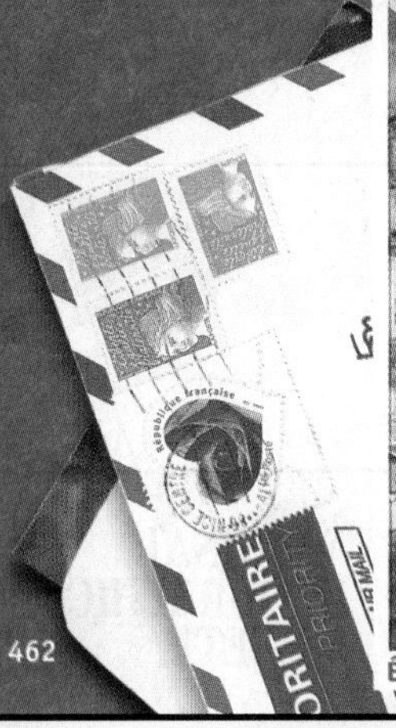

Édouard Vuillard *Le docteur Viau dans son cabinet*

462

Correlations to Continuum (*see page* i *for code*)

Stage I
Understand some ideas and familiar details. p. 467 (**4**, *p*), p. 479 (**27**, *m*); Write notes. p. 489 (**4**, *m*); Use short sentences, learned words, phrases, and simple questions when speaking. p. 467 (**5**, *p*); Understand ideas and familiar details when listening. p. 471 (**9**, *p*), p. 480 (*m*); Understand and convey information about health. pp. 464–465 (*i*), p. 466 (**3**, *p*), pp. 482–483 (*m*); Understand most important information. p. 489 (**4**)

Stage II
Understand and express important ideas and some detail. p. 471 (**12**, *p*); Converse in face-to-face social interactions. p. 481 (**A**, *p*); Listen in social interactions and listen to audio or video texts. p. 488 (**1**, *p*); Write short guided compositions. p. 489 (**5**, *m*); Understand and convey information about health. pp. 486–487 (*p*); Communicate effectively with some pattern of error, which may interfere slightly with full comprehension when performing Stage II functions. p. 488 (**1**); Understand oral and written discourse, with few errors in comprehension when reading and demonstrate culturally appropriate behavior for Stage II functions. p. 489 (**1**)

Stage III
Converse in face-to-face social interactions and in simple transactions on the phone. p. 471 (**10**, *p*); Use strings of related sentences when speaking. p. 473 (**16**, *p*), p. 488 (**3**, *m*)

Stage IV
Give and understand advice and suggestions. p. 475 (*i*), p. 481 (**B**, *p*), p. 488 (**2**, *m*); Read short literary texts. pp. 518–520 (*i*), pp. 520–523 (*p*)

Stage V
Convince and persuade. p. 489 (**5**, *i*), p. 489 (**5**, *p*)

CHAPITRE 14

Spotlight on Culture

Photograph This old-style pharmacy is on the lovely **rue des Francs-Bourgeois,** one of the main, though narrow, streets in the Marais section of Paris. The sign with the serpent is called **un caducée.** It is a symbol for pharmacists and physicians.

Painting Édouard Jean Vuillard (1868–1940) was a painter, watercolorist, and engraver. He also became a decorator, and he worked for **le Théâtre-Libre.** He also did some large murals. He was a friend of many symbolist painters, but in his own paintings he preferred intimate scenes with a bourgeois background. He enjoyed doing street scenes and portraits. In this painting we see Doctor Viau in his dental surgical suite.

Chapter Projects

La santé Obtain a video on first aid, health, or nutrition in French or English from the health department in your school or county. Use it as a springboard for discussing health and illnesses with the new vocabulary from this chapter.

Le corps humain Have students create a poster of a human body like the kind in doctors' offices, labeling in French as many external and internal body parts as they can. This poster can be displayed in your classroom. You may wish to refer students to pages 346–347.

Vocabulaire
Mots 1

1 Preparation

Resource Manager

Vocabulary Transparencies 14.2–14.3
Audio Activities Booklet TE, pages 168–170
Audiocassette 8B/CD 8
Workbook, pages 139–140
Quiz 1, page 69
ExamView Pro®

Bellringer Review

Use BRR Transparency 14.1 or write the following on the board.
Draw a stick figure of a person and label all the body parts you can.

2 Presentation

Teaching Tip: You may wish to bring a handkerchief, tissues, and throat lozenges to class to use in the presentation of the **Mots 1** vocabulary.

Step 1 Point to yourself to model the following parts of the body: **la bouche, le nez, la gorge, l'oreille, les yeux, le ventre.**

Step 2 Use gestures to teach the following expressions: **avoir de la fièvre; avoir des frissons; il est très malade; il n'est pas en bonne santé; il a mal au ventre; il tousse; il éternue; il a mal à la tête; il a mal aux oreilles; elle a le nez qui coule; elle a les yeux qui piquent; elle a la gorge qui gratte.**

Step 3 Have students repeat the cognates carefully after you or Audiocassette 8B/CD 8. These are the words they are most likely to anglicize.

Note: Remind students that in French the definite article is usually used when talking about parts of the body. Introduce the plural of **un œil (les yeux).**

Vocabulaire
Mots 1

On est malade.

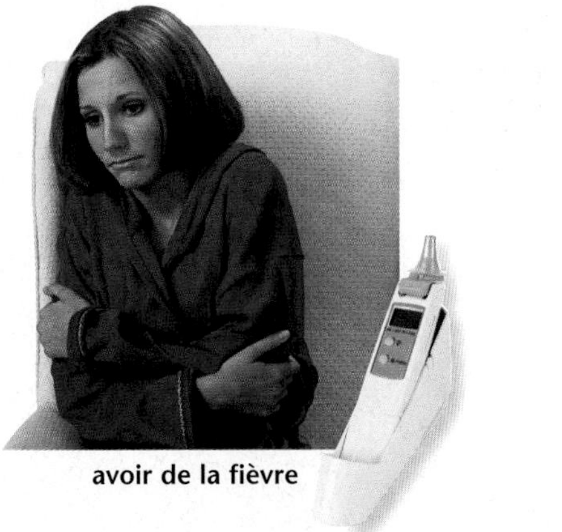
avoir de la fièvre

Paul a un rhume.
Il est enrhumé.
Il éternue.
Il a besoin d'un kleenex ou d'un mouchoir.

David tousse.

Reaching All Students

Total Physical Response Before you begin, demonstrate the meaning of **toucher.**
(Student 1), **venez ici, s'il vous plaît.**
Montrez-moi votre bouche.
Montrez-moi votre main.
Montrez-moi votre nez.
Montrez-moi votre pied.
Montrez-moi votre ventre.
Montrez-moi votre gorge.
Montrez-moi vos yeux.
Levez la main.
Ouvrez la bouche.
Fermez les yeux.
Mettez la main sur la tête.
Touchez vos pieds avec vos mains.
Merci, *(Student 1).* **Retournez à votre place et asseyez-vous, s'il vous plaît.**

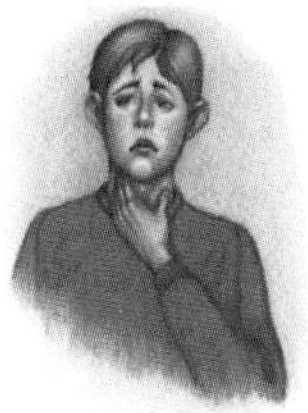

Christophe a très mal à la gorge.
Il a une angine.

Martin n'est pas en bonne santé.
Il est en mauvaise santé.
Il est très malade, le pauvre.
Il ne se sent pas bien. Il se sent très mal.

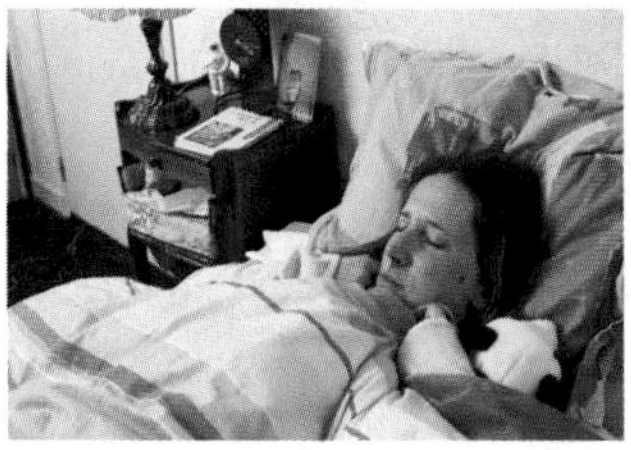

La pauvre Miriam, qu'est-ce qu'elle a?
Elle a la grippe.
Elle a de la fièvre.
Elle a des frissons.

Note

Study the following cognates related to health and medicine:

allergique	un sirop
bactérien(ne)	de l'aspirine
viral(e)	une infection
une allergie	de la pénicilline
un antibiotique	la température

Elle a mal à la tête.

Elle a mal au ventre.

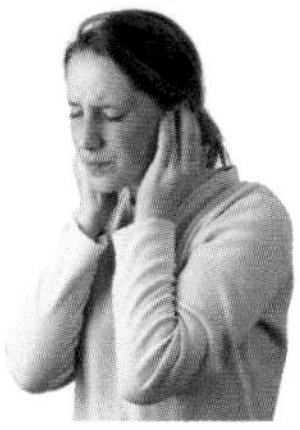

Elle a mal aux oreilles.

Elle a le nez qui coule.

Elle a les yeux qui piquent.

Elle a la gorge qui gratte.

Step 4 Ask several volunteers to come to the front of the room. Have each one mime a different ailment. The rest of the class describes the symptoms and suggests what he or she needs. Use as many props as possible. Guide the class with questions when necessary. For example: **La pauvre Isabelle! Elle a un rhume. Elle a besoin de quoi? Elle a besoin de beaucoup de kleenex.**

Step 5 Ask each volunteer to recapitulate his or her illness, symptoms, and needs. Cue key words or ask the class for help as necessary. For example: **J'ai un rhume. J'ai le nez qui coule. J'ai besoin d'aspirine,** etc.

Vocabulary Expansion

Tourists often experience stomach problems. If you wish, you may give the students the following useful words and expressions.

Vous avez des nausées (mal au cœur)?
Vous avez la diarrhée?
Vous êtes constipé(e)?
Vous vomissez?

FUN-FACTS

You may wish to introduce the colloquial expression **Mon œil!** to students. It means, "Come on, do you think I'm going to believe that?" When people say it, they usually put their finger up to their eye.

Class Motivator

Jacques a dit Students will enjoy playing the French version of "Simon says." Call the first round yourself and have students act out the following:

Jacques a dit: Vous avez mal à la tête.
Jacques a dit: Mettez les mains sur la tête.
Jacques a dit: Toussez.
Jacques a dit: Éternuez.

Then call on students to lead the game.

About the French Language

The word **angine** can sometimes cause confusion. When used alone it means a bad sore throat. Angina *(heart pain)* is **une angine de poitrine.**

3 Practice

Commençons
Let's use our new words

Attention!

When students are doing the **Commençons** activities, accept any answer that makes sense. The purpose of these activities is to have students use the new vocabulary. They are not factual recall activities. Thus, it is not necessary for students to remember specific factual information from the vocabulary presentation when answering.

Historiette Each time **Historiette** appears, it means that the answers to the activity form a short story. Encourage students to look at the title of the **Historiette,** since it can help them do the activity.

2 and **3** Do these activities first with books closed. Ask the questions and call on individuals to answer. Students can write the activities for homework. Go over them the next day with books closed.

Expansion: Have students retell the information in Activities 2 and 3 in their own words.

Writing Development

Have students write the answers to Activities 2–3 in paragraph form.

Commençons
Let's use our new words

1 Qu'est-ce que c'est?
Identifiez.

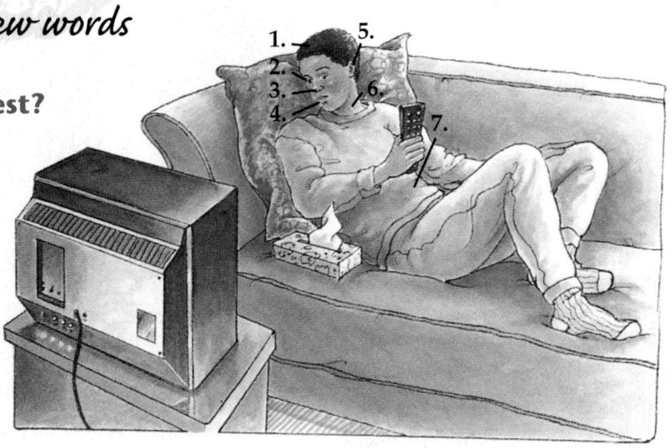

2 Historiette Qu'est-ce qu'il a?
Inventez une histoire.

1. David est malade?
2. Il ne se sent pas bien?
3. Qu'est-ce qu'il a?
4. Il a de la fièvre et des frissons?
5. Il a la gorge qui gratte?
6. Il a les yeux qui piquent et le nez qui coule?
7. Il a mal à la tête?
8. Il a mal au ventre?
9. Il a mal aux oreilles?

3 Historiette La santé Donnez des réponses personnelles.

1. Tu es en bonne santé ou en mauvaise santé?
2. Quand tu es enrhumé(e), tu as le nez qui coule?
3. Tu as les yeux qui piquent?
4. Tu as la gorge qui gratte?
5. Tu tousses?
6. Tu éternues?
7. Qu'est-ce qu'on te dit quand tu éternues?
8. Tu as mal à la tête?
9. Tu ne te sens pas bien?
10. Tu as de la fièvre quand tu as un rhume?
11. Et quand tu as la grippe, tu as de la fièvre?
12. Quand tu as de la fièvre, tu as quelquefois des frissons?

Answers to Commençons

1

1. la tête
2. l'œil
3. le nez
4. la bouche
5. l'oreille
6. la gorge
7. le ventre

2 *Answers will vary but may include:*

1. Oui, David est malade.
2. Il ne se sent pas bien.
3. Il a un rhume.
4. Oui, il a de la fièvre et des frissons.
5. Oui, il a la gorge qui gratte.
6. Oui, il a les yeux qui piquent et le nez qui coule.
7. Oui, il a mal à la tête.
8. Oui, il a mal au ventre.
9. Oui, il a mal aux oreilles.

3 *Answers will vary but may include:*

1. Je suis en bonne santé.
2. Oui, quand je suis enrhumé(e), j'ai le nez qui coule.
3. Oui, j'ai les yeux qui piquent.
4. Oui, j'ai la gorge qui gratte.
5. Non, je ne tousse pas.
6. Oui, j'éternue.
7. On me dit «À tes souhaits!»
8. Oui, j'ai mal à la tête.
9. Non, je ne me sens pas bien.
10. Non, je n'ai pas de fièvre quand j'ai un rhume.

Vocabulaire

4 On a mal. Complétez.

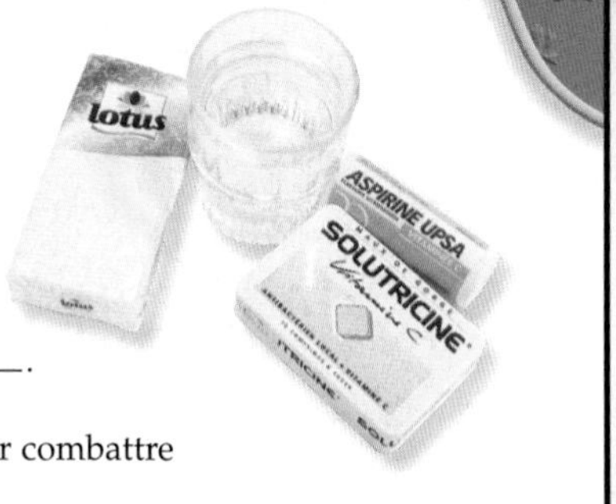

1. On prend de l'aspirine quand on a mal à la ____.
2. Si on a très mal à la gorge, on a une ____.
3. La ____ est un antibiotique.
4. L'aspirine et les antibiotiques sont des ____.
5. On ne peut pas prendre de pénicilline quand on est ____ à la pénicilline.
6. Si on a une température de 40° Celsius, on a de la ____.
7. Quand on est toujours malade, on est en ____.
8. On donne des antibiotiques comme la pénicilline pour combattre des infections bactériennes, pas des infections ____.
9. Quand on a le nez qui coule, on a besoin d'un ____ ou d'un ____.
10. Quand on a un rhume, on ____ et on ____.
11. Quand on est enrhumé ou quand on écoute la musique trop fort, on a mal aux ____.

5 Qu'est-ce que tu as? Work with a classmate. Ask him or her what the matter is. Your classmate will tell you. Then suggest something he or she can do to feel better. Take turns.

6 Devinette Have some fun! Work with a classmate and look at the following illustrations and French sayings. Together come up with some English equivalents.

Je ne suis pas dans mon assiette aujourd'hui.

Tu vas vite être sur pied.

Il a une fièvre de cheval.

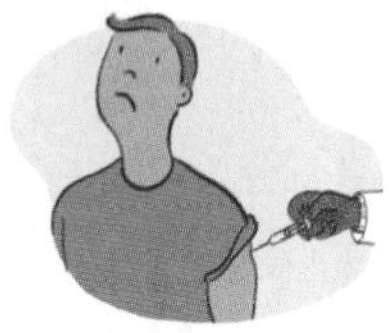

Ça fait mal. Aïe aïe aïe!

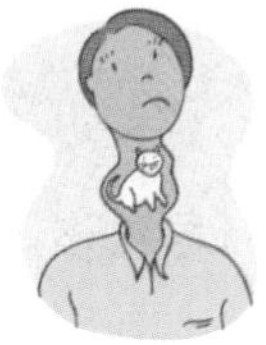

J'ai un chat dans la gorge.

ENCORE PLUS *For more practice using words from **Mots 1**, do Activity 46 on page H47 at the end of this book.*

6 Expansion: Practice the expressions in this activity by miming or supplying the literal statement and having students supply the informal expression. For example: **Je ne peux pas parler. (Vous avez un chat dans la gorge.) Je ne me sens pas bien. (Vous n'êtes pas dans votre assiette.)** Clutch your arm and say **«Aïe!» (Ça fait mal.)**

Reteaching

Show Vocabulary Transparencies 14.2–14.3 and let students say as much as they can about them in their own words.

Vocabulary Expansion

Tell students the word "sofa" is the same in French: **un sofa**, but one also frequently hears **un canapé** or **un divan.**

ENCORE PLUS This *infogap* activity will allow students to practice in pairs. The activity should be very manageable for them, since all vocabulary and structures are familiar to them.

Answers to Commençons

(continued)

11. Oui, quand j'ai la grippe j'ai de la fièvre.
12. Oui, quand j'ai de la fièvre j'ai quelquefois des frissons.

4

1. tête
2. angine
3. pénicilline
4. médicaments
5. allergique
6. fièvre
7. mauvaise santé
8. virales
9. kleenex, mouchoir
10. tousse, éternue
11. oreilles

5 *Answers will vary but may include:*

—Qu'est-ce que tu as?
—Je ne sais pas. J'ai le nez qui coule et la gorge qui gratte.
—Je crois que tu es enrhumé! Tu as besoin de beaucoup de kleenex!

6 *Answers will vary but may include:*

1. I don't feel so hot today.
2. You'll be back on your feet in no time.
3. He has a high fever.
4. That hurts! Ow, ow, ow!
5. I have a frog in my throat. (I have a scratchy throat.)

Vocabulaire *Mots 2*

1 Preparation

Resource Manager

Vocabulary Transparencies 14.4–14.5
Audio Activities Booklet TE, pages 171–172
Audiocassette 8B/CD 8
Workbook, page 140
Quiz 2, page 70
ExamView Pro®

Bellringer Review

Use BRR Transparency 14.2 or write the following on the board.
Write down what part(s) of the body you associate with the following.

1. **des lunettes**
2. **un bonnet de ski**
3. **un kleenex**
4. **des chaussures**

2 Presentation

Step 1 Have students keep their books closed. Dramatize the following expressions from **Mots 2: ouvrir la bouche; examiner la gorge; souffrir; tousser; respirer à fond.** Ask students to imitate each of your dramatizations and repeat each corresponding word.

Step 2 As you present the new words in sentences, ask questions such as:
Qui examine le malade? Qui ouvre la bouche? Qu'est-ce que le médecin examine?

Vocabulaire *Mots 2*

Chez le médecin

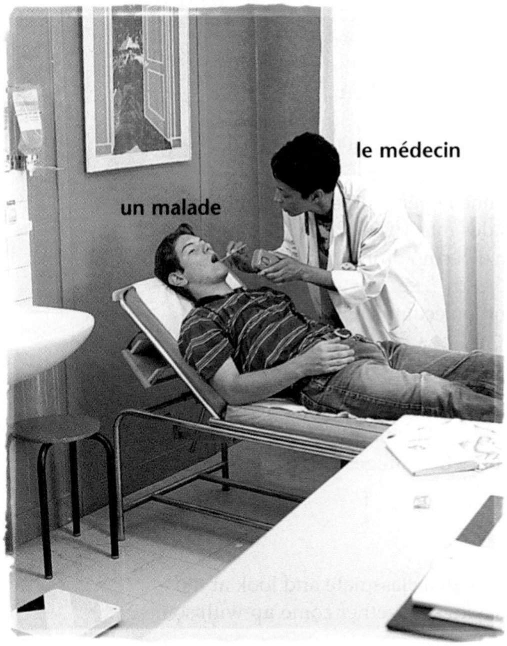
le médecin
un malade

Le médecin examine le malade.
Le malade ouvre la bouche.
Le médecin examine la gorge du malade.

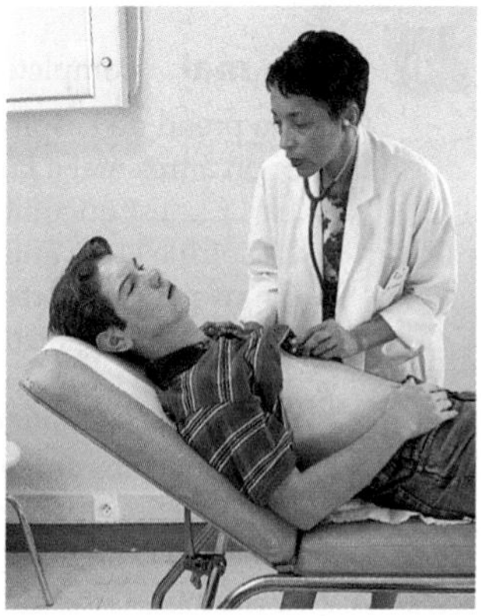

Elle ausculte le malade.
Il souffre, le pauvre.

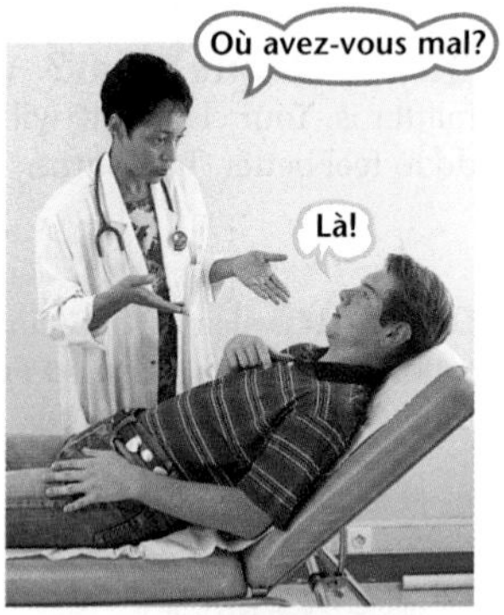
Où avez-vous mal?
Là!

Le médecin parle.

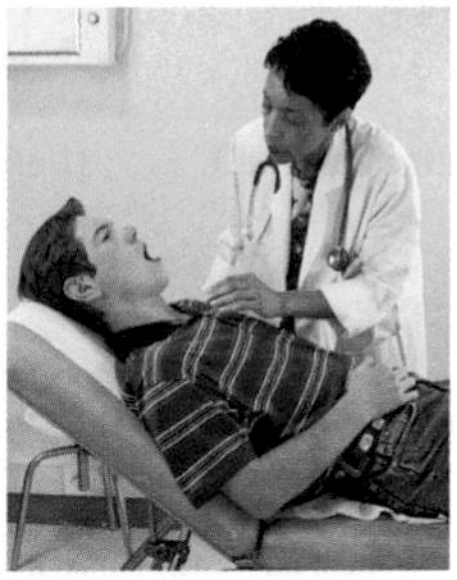

Ouvrez la bouche!

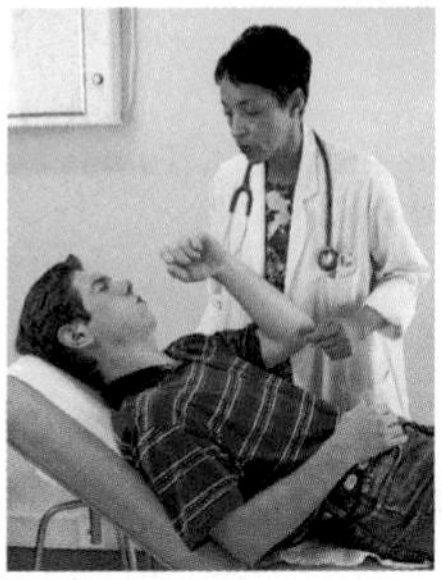

Toussez!

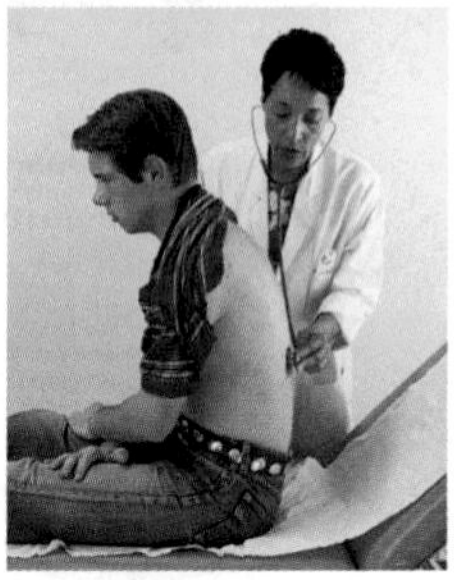

Respirez à fond!

Reaching All Students

Total Physical Response

(Student 1), **levez-vous et venez ici, s'il vous plaît.**
Vous allez chez le médecin. Moi, je suis le médecin. Je vais vous examiner.
Je vais vous ausculter. Respirez à fond.
Encore une fois.
(Student 1), **asseyez-vous, s'il vous plaît.**
Ouvrez la bouche.
Dites «Ah».
Ouvrez les yeux.
Et maintenant, fermez les yeux.
Merci, *(Student 1)*. **C'est très bien. Vous êtes un(e) bon(ne) patient(e). Retournez à votre place, s'il vous plaît.**
(continued)

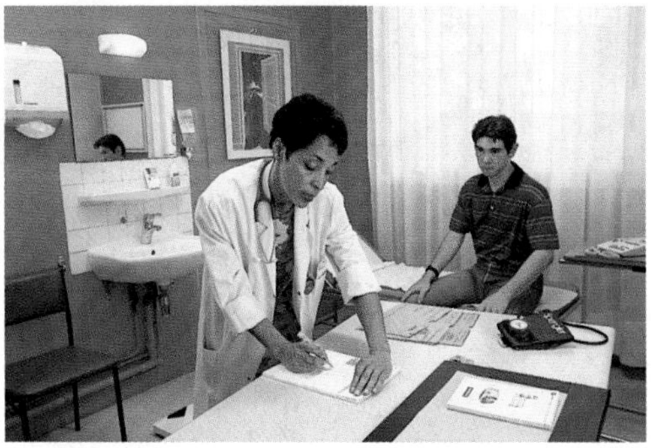

Le médecin fait un diagnostic.
Sébastien a une sinusite aiguë.
Le médecin lui prescrit des antibiotiques.
Elle lui fait une ordonnance.

une ordonnance

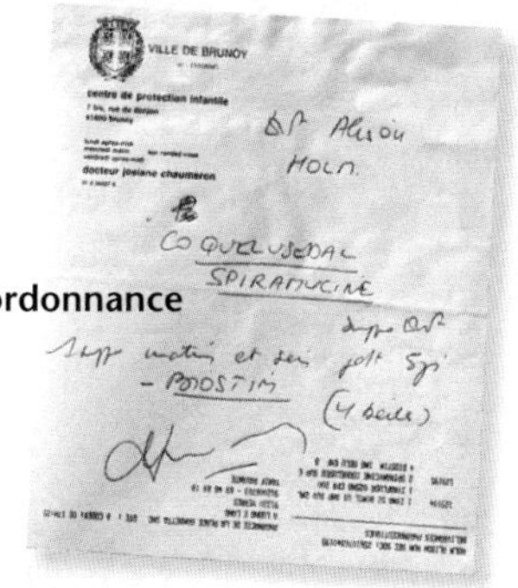

À la pharmacie

Qu'est-ce que la pharmacienne donne à Sébastien?
Elle lui donne des médicaments.

Sébastien prend les médicaments.
Il va mieux.

Recycling

Bring back previously learned vocabulary by asking **Tu as mal où?** and pointing to your hand, foot, eyes, ear, nose, stomach, head, or throat. Have students respond using the correct word.

Step 3 Have students open their books. Have them read along and repeat the new material after you or Audiocassette 8B/CD 8.

Reaching All Students

Bodily Kinesthetic Learners Have students get up and dramatize many of the expressions in this vocabulary section.

Vocabulary Expansion

You may wish to give students the following expressions related to physical exams.
prendre la tension
prendre le pouls
faire une piqûre
faire une prise de sang
faire un électrocardiogramme

Reaching All Students

Total Physical Response

(Student 2), **venez ici, s'il vous plaît.**
Vous allez mimer ce que je dis.
Respirez à fond.
Toussez.
Éternuez.
Vous avez mal à la tête.
Vous avez de la fièvre.
Vous avez des frissons.
Vous avez les yeux qui piquent.
Vous avez le nez qui coule.
Prenez un kleenex.
Prenez un comprimé.
Merci, *(Student 2).* **Très bien. Retournez à votre place, s'il vous plaît.**

3 Practice

Commençons
Let's use our new words

8 You may wish to have students write their answers to this activity in paragraph form.

Learning from Photos

(page 470 bottom) This green type of cross with neon lights is the symbol in France for a pharmacy. When a pharmacy in France is closed for a holiday, late hour, etc., there is always a notice on the door informing you of the nearest open pharmacy—**la pharmacie de garde.**

Paired Activity

Have students work in pairs. Have them take turns telling each other that they think they have the flu or a bad cold. They should explain why they think they are sick by explaining their symptoms. The partner should respond by giving advice.

Attention!

Note that the activities are color-coded. All the activities in the text are communicative. However, the ones with blue titles are guided communication. The red titles indicate that the answers to the activity are more open-ended and can vary more. You may wish to correct students' mistakes more so in the guided activities than in the activities with a red title, which lend themselves to a freer response.

Commençons
Let's use our new words

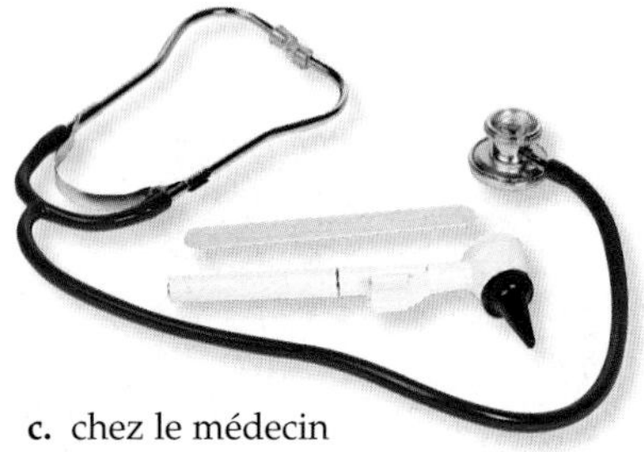

7 Il est malade. Choisissez.

1. Où est le malade?
   a. au travail **b.** à la crémerie **c.** chez le médecin
2. Qui souffre?
   a. le médecin **b.** le malade **c.** le pharmacien
3. Qu'est-ce que le médecin examine?
   a. la fièvre **b.** la grippe **c.** la gorge
4. Qu'est-ce que le malade ouvre?
   a. le ventre **b.** la bouche **c.** l'oreille
5. Quand le médecin l'ausculte, comment respire le malade?
   a. à fond **b.** rien **c.** bien
6. Qui est-ce que le médecin ausculte?
   a. le malade **b.** le pharmacien **c.** la pharmacienne
7. Que fait le médecin?
   a. des comprimés **b.** des médicaments **c.** des diagnostics
8. Qu'est-ce qu'il a, le malade?
   a. une cassette **b.** une sinusite aiguë **c.** un grand nez
9. Que fait le médecin?
   a. un pharmacien **b.** une ordonnance **c.** des antibiotiques
10. Qu'est-ce qu'elle prescrit?
   a. des yeux **b.** des ordonnances **c.** des comprimés

Une pharmacie

8 Historiette Chez le médecin
Donnez des réponses personnelles.

1. Tu vas chez le médecin quand tu es malade?
2. Le médecin te demande où tu as mal?
3. Qu'est-ce que tu réponds au médecin?
4. Quand tu as une angine, tu as mal où?
5. Qu'est-ce que le médecin te dit quand il t'ausculte?
6. Le médecin fait un diagnostic?
7. Il te prescrit des antibiotiques?
8. Tu vas à la pharmacie pour acheter des médicaments?
9. Tu prends quelquefois de l'aspirine? Quand?
10. Pour avaler des comprimés, qu'est-ce que tu bois?
11. Après quelques jours, tu vas mieux?

Answers to Commençons

7

1. c
2. b
3. c
4. b
5. a
6. a
7. c
8. b
9. b
10. c

8 *Answers will vary but may include:*

1. Oui, je vais chez le médecin quand je suis malade.
2. Oui, le médecin me demande où j'ai mal.
3. Je lui réponds: «J'ai mal à la gorge».
4. Quand j'ai une angine, j'ai mal à la gorge.
5. Quand le médecin m'ausculte il me dit: «Respirez à fond».
6. Oui, le médecin fait un diagnostic.
7. Oui, il me prescrit des antibiotiques.
8. Oui, je vais à la pharmacie pour acheter des médicaments.
9. Oui, je prends quelquefois de l'aspirine quand j'ai de la fièvre.
10. Pour avaler des comprimés, je bois de l'eau.
11. Oui, après quelques jours je vais mieux.

9 **Je ne suis pas dans mon assiette.** Work with a classmate. Yesterday you did something that made you feel ill today. Using the first list below, tell a classmate what you did. He or she has to guess what's wrong with you, choosing from the second list.

trop regarder la télé
—Hier, j'ai trop regardé la télé.
—Tu as mal aux yeux.

lire pendant six heures
manger trop de chocolat
passer beaucoup d'examens
faire une longue promenade
étudier jusqu'à trois heures du matin
écouter de la musique trop fort
jouer dans la neige en t-shirt

être enrhumé(e)
avoir mal aux yeux
avoir mal aux pieds
être fatigué(e)
avoir mal aux oreilles
avoir mal à la tête
avoir mal au ventre

HÔPITAL SAINT-PIERRE

Dr Monique Dumas
Généraliste

01.43.25.31.96

Dr Paul Forêt
Oculiste

01.43.36.97.64

Dr André Simonet
Oto-rhino-laryngologiste

01.43.55.41.71

Dr Nicole Habib
Gastroentérologue
01.43.89.39.25

10 **Qu'est-ce que tu as?** You were absent from school today. Your classmate, a French exchange student, is concerned about you and calls to find out how you are feeling. Let him or her know and tell all that you are doing to get better.

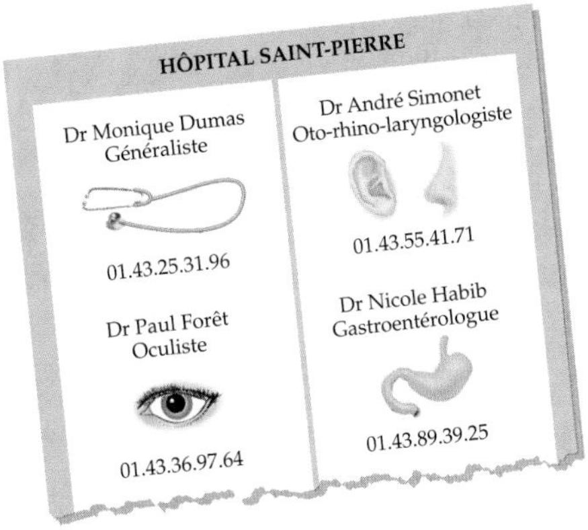

11 **Quel médecin?** While on a trip to France, you get sick. Describe your symptoms. A classmate will look at the list of doctors at the Hôpital Saint-Pierre and tell you which one to call and what the phone number is.

—J'ai mal à la gorge.
—On va appeler le docteur Simonet au 01.43.55.41.71.

12 **Au cabinet de consultation** Work with a classmate. You're sick. The doctor (your partner) will ask you questions about your symptoms. Answer the doctor's questions as completely as you can. Then reverse roles.

 For more practice using words from **Mots 2**, do Activity 47 on page H48 at the end of this book.

Assessment

As an informal assessment, you may wish to check comprehension by asking students interrogative-word questions about the illustrations on Vocabulary Transparencies 14.4–14.5. For example: **Il y a combien de malades chez le médecin? Le médecin examine qui? Elle ausculte qui? Que fait le malade? Quel est le diagnostic du médecin? Pourquoi? Elle prescrit quoi?**

ENCORE PLUS This *infogap* activity will allow students to practice in pairs. The activity should be very manageable for them, since all vocabulary and structures are familiar to them.

ANSWERS TO **Commençons**

9 *Answers will vary but may include:*
—J'ai lu pendant six heures.
—Tu as mal aux yeux.
—J'ai mangé trop de chocolat.
—Tu as mal au ventre.
—J'ai passé beaucoup d'examens.
—Tu as mal à la tête.
—J'ai fait une longue promenade.
—Tu as mal aux pieds.
—J'ai étudié jusqu'à trois heures du matin.
—Tu es fatigué(e).
—J'ai écouté de la musique trop fort.
—Tu as mal aux oreilles.
—J'ai joué dans la neige en t-shirt.
—Tu es enrhumé(e).

10 *Answers will vary depending upon the illness the students make up.*

11 *Answers will vary but may include:*
—J'ai mal au ventre.
—On va appeler le docteur Habib au 01 43 89 39 25.

1 Preparation

Resource Manager

Audio Activities Booklet TE, pages 173–175
Audiocassette 8B/CD 8
Workbook, pages 141–145
Quizzes 3–6, pages 71–74
ExamView Pro®

Bellringer Review

Use BRR Transparency 14.3 or write the following on the board.
You don't want to go to school today. Try to convince your mom or dad that you are sick. Be as descriptive as possible.

2 Presentation

Les pronoms lui, leur

Step 1 Write the sentences in Item 1 on the board. Use arrows as in the examples to help students understand the concept of direct versus indirect objects. As students look at these sentences, say: **Remarquez. Il ne lance pas Luc. Il lance le ballon. Il lance le ballon à qui? Il lance le ballon à Luc. «Le ballon», c'est l'objet direct. «Luc», c'est l'objet indirect.**

Step 2 Lead students through Items 1–2 and the accompanying examples.

Note: Be sure students learn that **lui** and **leur** are both masculine and feminine.

Step 3 You may wish to write the example sentences from Item 2 on the board and underline the indirect object once and the direct object twice.

Structure

Telling what you do for others
Les pronoms **lui, leur**

1. You have already learned the direct object pronouns **le, la,** and **les.** Now, you will learn the indirect object pronouns **lui** and **leur.** Observe the difference between a direct and an indirect object in the following sentences.

Paul lance le ballon à Luc.

Paul lance → le ballon.

Paul lance → le ballon ↗ à Luc.

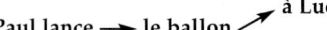

In the preceding sentence, **le ballon** is the direct object because it is the direct receiver of the action of the verb. What does Paul throw? The ball. The indirect object indicates to whom the ball was thrown. **Luc** is the indirect object of the verb. To whom does Paul throw the ball? To Luc. Note that the indirect object is preceded by the preposition **à—à Luc.**

2. The indirect object pronouns in French are **lui** and **leur.** Note that the masculine and feminine forms are the same. Study the following chart.

Singulier	Le médecin parle à Pierre. Le médecin parle à Marie.	} Il lui parle.
Pluriel	Le médecin parle à ses patients. Le médecin parle à ses patientes.	} Il leur parle.

Just like the direct object pronouns, the indirect object pronouns **lui** and **leur** come right before the verb they are linked to.

Je	lui parle.
Je ne	lui parle pas.
Je veux	lui parler.
Je ne veux pas	lui parler.

Rappelez-vous que...
The object pronouns **me, te, nous, vous** are both direct and indirect.
Je te vois.
Je te parle.

Continuons
Let's put our words together

Pour
te souhaiter
une meilleure
santé

13 **Historiette** **Une consultation**
Répondez en utilisant un pronom.
1. Le médecin parle à Paul?
2. Il demande à Paul s'il a de la fièvre?
3. Paul explique ses symptômes au médecin?
4. Le médecin dit à Paul qu'il a de la fièvre?
5. Il donne une ordonnance à Paul?
6. Paul téléphone à la pharmacienne?

14 **Un match de foot** Complétez avec **lui** ou **leur.**
1. Il lance le ballon à Marianne? Oui, il ___ lance le ballon.
2. Les joueurs parlent à l'arbitre? Oui, ils ___ parlent.
3. Et l'arbitre parle aux joueurs? Oui, il ___ parle.
4. L'arbitre explique les règles aux joueuses? Oui, il ___ explique les règles.
5. L'employée au guichet parle à un spectateur? Oui, elle ___ parle.

15 **Personnellement** Répondez en utilisant **lui** ou **leur.**
1. Tu parles souvent à tes professeurs?
2. Tu dis toujours bonjour à ton professeur de français?
3. Tu vas téléphoner à ton copain/ta copine ce week-end?
4. Tu aimes parler à tes copains au téléphone?
5. Tu parles souvent à tes copains?
6. Tu vas écrire à tes grands-parents?

16 **Des cadeaux pour tout le monde?** Work with a classmate. Describe your favorite friends or relatives. Then tell what you buy or give to each one as a gift.

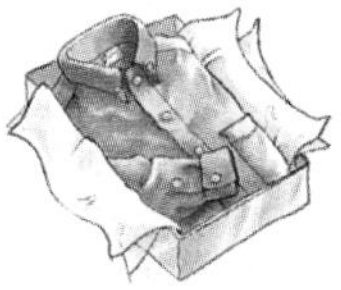

ENCORE PLUS *For more practice using using **lui** and **leur**, do Activity 48 on page H49 at the end of this book.*

Step 4 You may wish to give some additional sentences and have students indicate if the object is direct or indirect. For example: **J'écris une lettre. Une lettre? J'écris à mon ami. Mon ami? Je lis un livre. Un livre? Je lis à mon petit frère. Mon petit frère? J'achète un cadeau. Un cadeau? J'offre le cadeau à ma mère. Ma mère?**

3 Practice

Continuons
Let's put our words together

13 and **15** Do these activities first with books closed, calling on individuals to respond to each question. Activities can be done again with books open for additional reinforcement.

14 and **16** These activities have to be done with books open.

ENCORE PLUS This *infogap* activity will allow students to practice in pairs. The activity should be very manageable for them, since all vocabulary and structures are familiar to them.

Answers to Continuons

13
1. Oui, le médecin lui parle.
2. Oui, il lui demande s'il a de la fièvre.
3. Oui, Paul lui explique ses symptômes.
4. Oui, le médecin lui dit qu'il a de la fièvre.
5. Oui, il lui donne une ordonnance.
6. Oui, Paul lui téléphone.

14
1. lui
2. lui
3. leur
4. leur
5. lui

15
1. Oui, je leur parle souvent.
2. Oui, je lui dis toujours bonjour.
3. Oui, je vais lui téléphoner.
4. Oui, j'aime leur parler au téléphone.
5. Oui, je leur parle souvent.
6. Oui, je vais leur écrire.

16 *Answers will vary but may include:*
Papa, il aime le chocolat. Je lui achète une boîte de chocolats.
Maman, elle aime voyager en France. Je lui achète un livre sur la France.
Ma sœur, elle aime la musique. Je lui achète un CD.

1 Preparation

Bellringer Review

Use BRR Transparency 14.4 or write the following on the board.
Your friend seems to get things mixed up when he or she speaks French. Correct your friend's statements.

1. **La pharmacienne m'ausculte.**
2. **J'ai le nez qui pique et les yeux qui coulent.**
3. **J'ai mal à la tête. Elle est très rouge.**
4. **Je ne suis pas dans mon verre.**

2 Presentation

Les verbes souffrir et ouvrir

Note: This material should be rather easy since students have already had a great deal of practice with the **-er** verbs. Since all of these verbs, except for **ouvrir,** are of fairly low frequency, it is suggested that you go over them quickly.

Step 1 Lead students through Items 1–2. Have them repeat the forms after you.

Step 2 Explain to students that as with any regular **-er** verb the **je, tu, il, ils** forms of these verbs are all pronounced the same.

Expansion: You may wish to explain to students that **couvrir, découvrir,** and **offrir** follow the same pattern as **ouvrir** and **souffrir.**

3 Practice

Continuons
Let's put our words together

17 You may wish to have students retell the activity in their own words.

Describing more activities
Les verbes **souffrir** et **ouvrir**

1. The verbs **souffrir** and **ouvrir** are conjugated the same way as regular **-er** verbs in the present.

SOUFFRIR		OUVRIR	
je	souffre	j'	ouvre
tu	souffres	tu	ouvres
il/elle/on	souffre	il/elle/on	ouvre
nous	souffrons	nous	ouvrons
vous	souffrez	vous	ouvrez
ils/elles	souffrent	ils/elles	ouvrent

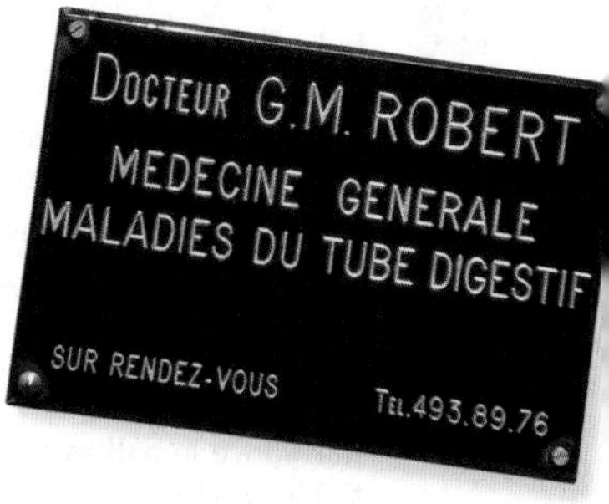

2. Note the past participles.

souffrir → souffert	**Ils ont beaucoup souffert.**
ouvrir → ouvert	**Il a ouvert la bouche.**

Continuons
Let's put our words together

17 Historiette Elle est malade.
Inventez des réponses.

1. Caroline souffre d'une angine?
2. Quand tu souffres d'une angine, tu as mal où?
3. Caroline va chez le médecin?
4. Quand le médecin lui examine la gorge, Caroline ouvre la bouche?
5. Le médecin lui donne une ordonnance?
6. Caroline va à la pharmacie?
7. Elle donne l'ordonnance au pharmacien?
8. Le pharmacien lui donne un paquet de comprimés?
9. Caroline ouvre le paquet?
10. Elle avale un comprimé?
11. Elle ne souffre plus?

À la pharmacie

Answers to Continuons

17 *Answers will vary but may include:*

1. Oui, Caroline souffre d'une angine.
2. Quand je souffre d'une angine j'ai mal à la gorge.
3. Oui, Caroline va chez le médecin.
4. Oui, quand le médecin lui examine la gorge, Caroline ouvre la bouche.
5. Oui, le médecin lui donne une ordonnance.
6. Oui, Caroline va à la pharmacie.
7. Oui, elle lui donne l'ordonnance.
8. Oui, le pharmacien lui donne un paquet de comprimés.
9. Oui, Caroline l'ouvre.
10. Oui, elle l'avale.
11. Non, elle ne souffre plus.

Telling people what to do
L'impératif

1. You use the imperative to give commands and make suggestions. The forms are usually the same as the **tu, vous,** and **nous** forms. Note that the **nous** form means "Let's . . ."

PARLER	FINIR	ATTENDRE
Parle à ton prof!	Finis tes devoirs!	Attends ton ami.
Parlez à votre prof!	Finissez vos devoirs!	Attendez votre ami.
Parlons à notre prof!	Finissons nos devoirs!	Attendons notre ami.

2. Note that with **-er** verbs, you drop the final **s** of the **tu** form. The same is true for **aller** and verbs like **ouvrir.**

   Regarde!
   Va voir le médecin!
   Ouvre la bouche!

3. In negative commands, you put the **ne... pas** or any other negative expression around the verb.

   Ne respirez plus!
   Ne dis rien.

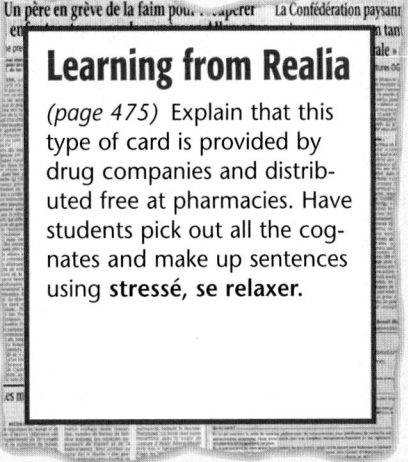

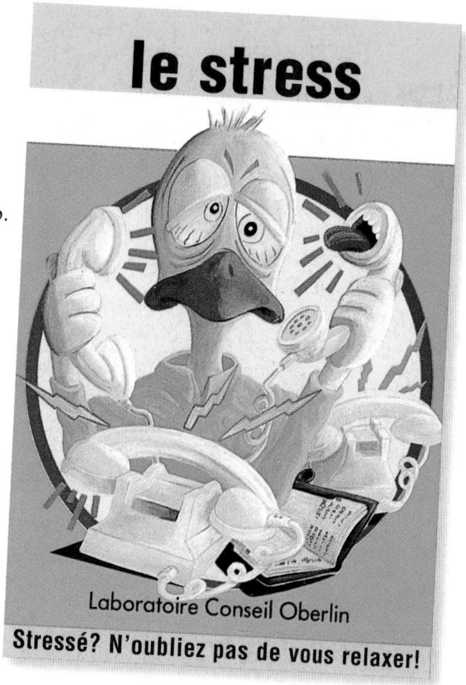

le stress
Laboratoire Conseil Oberlin
Stressé? N'oubliez pas de vous relaxer!

1 Preparation

Bellringer Review

Use BRR Transparency 14.5 or write the following on the board.
Complete the sentences with the correct form of **ouvrir, souffrir,** or **offrir.**

1. **Tu _____ un cadeau à ta mère?**
2. **Elle _____ le livre à la page 12.**
3. **Ils sont très malades. Ils _____ beaucoup.**
4. **J'ai _____ le réfrigérateur.**

2 Presentation

L'impératif

Note: Students should have little trouble learning the imperative since they are already familiar with the verb forms. The only thing that will be new to them is the dropping of the **s** in the spelling of the **tu** form of **-er** verbs.

Step 1 Have students open their books to page 475. Lead them through Items 1–3.

Step 2 Illustrate the difference between singular and plural imperatives by giving commands to one student and to groups or pairs of students. For example: **Yvonne, prends ton livre de français. Va au tableau. Ouvre le livre à la page 15. Guillaume et Martine, sortez.**

Step 3 Practice the negative forms by calling out TPR commands and having students change them to the negative. Then reverse the procedure.

Learning from Realia

(page 475) Explain that this type of card is provided by drug companies and distributed free at pharmacies. Have students pick out all the cognates and make up sentences using **stressé, se relaxer.**

3 Practice

Continuons
Let's put our words together

18 and **19** You may wish to have students work in pairs and then in groups. The recipient(s) of the command should show comprehension by miming the activity suggested in the command.

Reaching All Students

Additional Practice
Students work in groups of three. One student tells another what to do. That student dramatizes the command. The third student describes the scene. Rotate roles.

Student 1: *(Student 2),* **ouvre la bouche.**
(Student 2 dramatizes)
Student 3: *(Student 2)* **ouvre la bouche, mais moi, je n'ouvre pas la bouche.**

Learning from Realia

(page 476) Ask students what the important message is on the cover of this brochure.

Continuons
Let's put our words together

18 La loi, c'est moi! Donnez un ordre à un copain ou à une copine d'après le modèle.

—regarder
—Regarde!

1. téléphoner à Jean
2. passer l'examen
3. parler français
4. travailler plus
5. préparer le dîner
6. ouvrir la porte
7. mettre la table
8. choisir un film
9. faire le travail
10. écrire l'exercice

Hôpitaux de Toulouse
La Santé sans tabac
Avec l'aimable autorisation de la M.N.H.
Afin de protéger votre santé et par mesure de sécurité, nous vous prions de ne pas fumer. Merci de votre compréhension
Décret n°92/478 du 29-5-92 Règlement intérieur du CHU de TOULOUSE

19 Et vous aussi
Donnez un ordre d'après le modèle.

—regarder
—Regardez.

1. téléphoner à Jean
2. passer l'examen
3. parler français
4. travailler plus
5. préparer le dîner
6. ouvrir la porte
7. mettre la table
8. choisir un film
9. faire le travail
10. écrire l'exercice

Answers to Continuons

18	19
1. Téléphone à Jean!	1. Téléphonez à Jean!
2. Passe l'examen!	2. Passez l'examen!
3. Parle français!	3. Parlez français!
4. Travaille plus!	4. Travaillez plus!
5. Prépare le dîner!	5. Préparez le dîner!
6. Ouvre la porte!	6. Ouvrez la porte!
7. Mets la table!	7. Mettez la table!
8. Choisis un film!	8. Choisissez un film!
9. Fais le travail!	9. Faites le travail!
10. Écris l'exercice!	10. Écrivez l'exercice!

Structure

20 Ne fais pas ça! Donnez un ordre à un copain ou à une copine d'après le modèle.

—**regarder**
—**Ne regarde pas!**

1. lire le journal
2. écrire une lettre
3. prendre le métro
4. attendre devant la porte
5. descendre
6. aller plus vite
7. faire attention
8. entrer
9. sortir

YEUX ROUGES,
YEUX IRRITES
DÉCOUVREZ CE COLLYRE EN MONODOSES!
Une monodose stérile, pratique, évitant la contamination
Ceci est un médicament. Lire attentivement la notice. Pas en-dessous de 36 mois. Contre-indiqué en cas de glaucome. Demandez conseil à votre pharmacien.
ANTALYRE®
Collyre en monodoses

21 Ne faites pas ça!

Refaites l'Activité 20 d'après le modèle.

—**regarder**
—**Ne regardez pas!**

22 Allons-y! Répondez d'après le modèle.

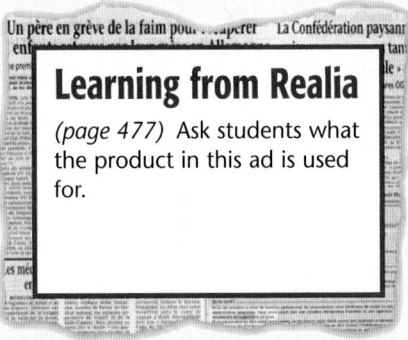

On invite Marie?
D'accord, invitons Marie!

1. On va à la plage?
2. On nage?
3. On fait du ski nautique?
4. On prend notre petit déjeuner?
5. On dîne au restaurant?
6. On sort?

23 Jeu Jacques a dit...

This game is called "Simon Says" in English. Play in groups of five people or more. Give orders to your classmates. If you say **Jacques a dit** first, they have to obey the order. If you don't say **Jacques a dit** first, they should not obey your order. If they do, they are eliminated.

ENCORE PLUS *For more practice using the commands, do Activity 49 on page H50 at the end of this book.*

Assessment

As an informal assessment, you may wish to have students quickly make up as many commands as they can. If they can make up logical (and reasonable) commands, you could comply. For example: Students say **Ouvrez la porte.** You open the door.

Learning from Realia

(page 477) Ask students what the product in this ad is used for.

ENCORE PLUS This *infogap* activity will allow students to practice in pairs. The activity should be very manageable for them, since all vocabulary and structures are familiar to them.

Answers to Continuons

20

1. Ne lis pas le journal!
2. N'écris pas de lettre!
3. Ne prends pas le métro!
4. N'attends pas devant la porte!
5. Ne descends pas!
6. Ne va pas plus vite!
7. Ne fais pas attention!
8. N'entre pas!
9. Ne sors pas!

21

1. Ne lisez pas le journal!
2. N'écrivez pas de lettre!
3. Ne prenez pas le métro!
4. N'attendez pas devant la porte!
5. Ne descendez pas!
6. N'allez pas plus vite!
7. Ne faites pas attention!
8. N'entrez pas!
9. Ne sortez pas!

22

1. D'accord, allons à la plage!
2. D'accord, nageons!
3. D'accord, faisons du ski nautique!
4. D'accord, prenons notre petit déjeuner!
5. D'accord, dînons au restaurant!
6. D'accord, sortons!

1 Preparation

Bellringer Review

Use BRR Transparency 14.6 or write the following on the board.

You are babysitting a five-year-old. Write six things you tell him or her to do or not do.

2 Presentation

Le pronom en

Step 1 Have students open their books to page 478. Lead them through the explanation.

Step 2 Read the sample sentences with **en** and have students repeat them in unison.

3 Practice

Continuons
Let's put our words together

24 This can be done as a paired activity.

Referring to people, places, and things already mentioned
Le pronom en

1. The pronoun **en** is used to replace a noun that is introduced by **de** or any form of **de—du, de la, de l', des. En** refers mostly to things.

Tu as de l'aspirine?	Oui, j' en‿ai.
Il parle de sa santé?	Oui, il en parle.
Vous sortez de l'hôpital?	Oui, j' en sors.
Tu prends des médicaments?	Oui, j' en prends.

2. You also use the pronoun **en** with numbers or expressions of quantity. Note that in this case **en** refers not only to things but also to people.

Tu as des frères?	**Oui, j'en ai deux.**
Il prend combien de comprimés?	**Il en prend trois par jour.**
Il a combien de CD?	**Il en a beaucoup.**

3. Just like other pronouns, **en** comes directly before the verb whose meaning it is linked to.

Il en parle.
Il n'en parle pas.
Il veut en parler.
Il ne veut pas en parler.

Savez-vous que... ?

En comes after **y** in the expression **il y a.**
Il y en a deux.
Il y en a beaucoup.
Il n'y en a pas.

Continuons
Let's put our words together

24 Historiette La fête de Laurence Répondez.

—Laurence sert du coca?
—Oui, elle en sert.

1. Elle sert de l'eau minérale?
2. Elle sert des sandwichs?
3. Elle sert de la pizza?
4. Elle sert de la salade?
5. Elle sert du fromage?
6. Elle sert des chocolats?
7. Elle sert de la glace?
8. Elle sert de la mousse au chocolat?

Answers to Continuons

24

1. Oui, elle en sert.
2. Oui, elle en sert.
3. Oui, elle en sert.
4. Oui, elle en sert.
5. Oui, elle en sert.
6. Oui, elle en sert.
7. Oui, elle en sert.
8. Oui, elle en sert.

25 Dans le frigo Répondez d'après le modèle.

du coca
—Il y a du coca dans ton frigo?
—Non, il n'y en a pas.

1. de l'eau minérale
2. de la glace
3. des légumes surgelés
4. du jambon
5. des tartes
6. de la viande

Viva
YOP

26 Historiette Tu es malade?

Répondez d'après le modèle.

Tu manges du chocolat? (trop)
Oui, j'en mange trop!

1. Tu prends combien de comprimés? (trois)
2. Tu bois de l'eau? (un litre)
3. Tu manges des fruits? (beaucoup)
4. Tu lis des magazines? (deux ou trois)
5. Tu regardes des vidéos? (trop)

27 Devinettes Devinez ce que c'est.

1. On en prend quand on est malade.
2. On en boit beaucoup quand on a de la fièvre.
3. On en utilise pour se laver les mains.
4. On en met sur une brosse à dents pour se laver les dents.
5. On en donne au vendeur quand on achète quelque chose.

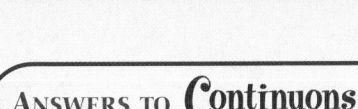

Vous êtes sur le bon chemin. Allez-y!

Structure

25 You may wish to remind students to answer questions based on what is or is not in the refrigerator.

Expansion: Ask additional questions about what is or is not in the refrigerator:

Il y a des yaourts?
Oui, il y en a.

Il y a des pommes?
Non, il n'y en a pas.

Allez-y!
At this point in the chapter, students have learned all the vocabulary and structure necessary to complete the chapter. The conversation and cultural readings that follow recycle all the material learned up to this point.

Answers to Continuons

25

1. Oui, il y en a.
2. Non, il n'y en a pas.
3. Non, il n'y en a pas.
4. Non, il n'y en a pas.
5. Non, il n'y en a pas.
6. Oui, il y en a.

26

1. J'en prends trois!
2. Oui, j'en bois un litre!
3. Oui, j'en mange beaucoup!
4. Oui, j'en lis deux ou trois.
5. Oui, j'en regarde trop.

27

1. des comprimés
2. de l'eau
3. du savon
4. du dentifrice
5. de l'argent

1 Preparation

Resource Manager

Audio Activities Booklet TE, pages 175–176
Audiocassette 8B/CD 8
CD-ROM

Bellringer Review

Use BRR Transparency 14.7 or write the following on the board.
Rewrite the following sentences with a pronoun.

1. **Le médecin examine *le malade.***
2. **Le malade ouvre *la bouche.***
3. **Le malade lit *l'ordonnance.***
4. **Il donne *l'ordonnance* au pharmacien.**
5. **Le pharmacien donne *les médicaments* au malade.**

2 Presentation

Step 1 Tell students they are going to hear a conversation between Sylvie and her doctor.

Step 2 Have them listen as you read the conversation or play Audiocassette 8B/CD 8.

Step 3 Have students work in pairs to practice the conversation. Then have several pairs present it to the class.

Conversation

Chez le médecin

Sylvie: Bonjour, docteur.
Médecin: Bonjour, Sylvie. Alors, qu'est-ce qui ne va pas?
Sylvie: Je ne sais pas… Je ne me sens pas bien du tout.
Médecin: Tu as mal où?
Sylvie: Ben, j'ai mal un peu partout, mais surtout à la gorge.
Médecin: Tu as mal à la tête?
Sylvie: Oui, à la tête aussi. Et j'ai froid, j'ai des frissons…
Médecin: Tu dois avoir de la fièvre. Ouvre la bouche, s'il te plaît. Dis «Aaa… »
Sylvie: Aaa…
Médecin: Tu as la gorge très rouge. C'est certainement une angine.
Sylvie: Une angine!
Médecin: Oui, mais ce n'est pas grave. Je vais te donner des antibiotiques. Tu vas en prendre trois par jour pendant une semaine.

Après la conversation

Répondez.

1. Qui est malade?
2. Quels sont ses symptômes?
3. Elle a mal où?
4. Sylvie ouvre la bouche. Pourquoi?
5. Qu'est-ce que le médecin lui donne?
6. Sylvie doit prendre combien de comprimés par jour?
7. Pendant combien de temps?

Glencoe Technology

CD-ROM
On the CD-ROM, students can watch a dramatization of this conversation. They can then play the role of either one of the characters and record themselves in the conversation.

Answers to Après la conversation

1. Sylvie est malade.
2. Elle a froid et elle a des frissons.
3. Elle a mal partout, mais surtout à la gorge et à la tête.
4. Elle ouvre la bouche parce que le médecin veut examiner sa gorge.
5. Le médecin lui donne des antibiotiques.
6. Elle doit en prendre trois par jour.
7. Pendant une semaine.

Learning from Photos

(page 480) You may wish to ask the following questions about the photo:
Qui examine la malade?
Elle lui parle?
La malade explique ses symptômes au médecin?
Qu'est-ce qu'elle lui dit? Elle a mal où?

Parlons un peu plus
Let's talk some more

 A **Tu dois ou tu ne dois pas être médecin.** Work with a classmate. Interview each other and decide who would make a good doctor. Make a list of questions for your interview. One question you may want to ask is: **Tu as beaucoup de patience ou très peu de patience?**

B **Je suis très malade.** Imagine you're sick with a cold, the flu, or a sore throat. Tell the doctor (your partner) what your symptoms are. He or she makes a diagnosis and tells you what to do to get better. Use the model as a guide.

> J'ai de la fièvre et des frissons.

> Vous avez la grippe. Restez au lit et prenez de l'aspirine.

Prononciation

Les sons /u/ et /ü/ 🎧

1. It is important to make a distinction between the sounds /u/ and /ü/, since many words differ only in these two sounds. Repeat the following pairs of words.

vous / vu	dessous / dessus	roux / rue
loue / lu	tout / tu	

2. Now repeat the following sentences.

 Tu as beaucoup de température?
 J'éternue toutes les deux minutes.

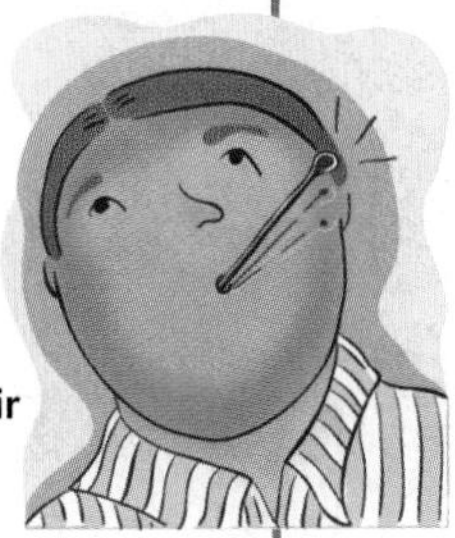

souffrir

température

Practice

Parlons un peu plus
Let's talk some more

Have students work in pairs. You may wish to choose a pair of students to do these activities for the class.

Prononciation

Step 1 Model the key words **souffrir** and **température** and have the students repeat in unison.

Step 2 Now lead students through the information on page 481 and model the other words and sentences.

Step 3 You may wish to give the students the following **dictée:**
 Il est descendu à l'avenue Victor-Hugo.
 Vous avez vu la rue.
 Au-dessous ou au-dessus?

Step 4 For additional pronunciation practice you may wish to use Pronunciation Transparency P 14.

Answers to Parlons un peu plus

A *Answers will vary but may include:*

—Tu aimes la biologie et la chimie?
—Oui, j'aime beaucoup ces matières.
—Tu es bon étudiant/bonne étudiante?
—Oui, j'aime bien étudier.
—Tu es sociable?
—Oui, je suis très sociable!

B *Answers will vary but may include:*

—J'ai le nez qui coule et la gorge qui gratte.
—Vous êtes enrhumé. Vous avez un virus. Je ne vous donne pas d'antibiotiques parce que vous n'avez pas d'infection bactérienne. Buvez du jus d'orange et beaucoup d'eau. Et vous pouvez prendre un sirop pour la gorge.

Resource Manager

Audio Activities Booklet TE, page 177
Audiocassette 8B/CD 8

Bellringer Review

Use BRR Transparency 14.8 or write the following on the board.
Choose the correct completion.

ouvre **avale**
respire **souffre**
prend

1. **Il_____ la bouche.**
2. **Il est très malade. Il _____ beaucoup.**
3. **Il _____ à fond.**
4. **Il _____ les comprimés avec de l'eau.**
5. **Il _____ ses médicaments.**

National Standards

Cultures
The reading about a visit with the doctor on pages 482–483 and the related activities give students an understanding of health services in France.

Comparisons
The reading will allow students to make comparisons between the French and American medical systems.

Presentation

Pre-reading
Step 1 Read and discuss the Reading Strategy, page 482. Have students skim the questions in the **Après la lecture** activities.

Step 2 Have students skim the reading quickly and silently.

Reading
Step 1 Have individuals read two or three sentences at a time. After each one reads, ask others comprehension questions.

Lectures culturelles

Reading Strategy

Identifying important concepts

A quick way to identify the important concepts in a passage is to first read the questions that follow it. This will tell you what ideas the author is emphasizing and what type of information you should look for as you read.

Une consultation

La pauvre Mélanie. Elle est très malade! Elle tousse. Elle éternue. Elle a mal à la tête. Elle a de la température. Elle a des frissons. Elle n'est pas du tout dans son assiette. Elle veut appeler le médecin, mais c'est le week-end et son médecin ne donne pas de consultations le week-end. La seule solution, c'est d'appeler S.O.S. Médecins.

S.O.S. Médecins est un service qui envoie des médecins à domicile[1]. Un médecin arrive chez Mélanie et l'examine. Elle l'ausculte, elle lui prend sa température. Elle lui dit qu'elle a la grippe. Mais ce n'est pas grave. Elle va être vite sur pied. Le médecin lui fait une ordonnance. Elle prescrit des

[1] à domicile *to the home*

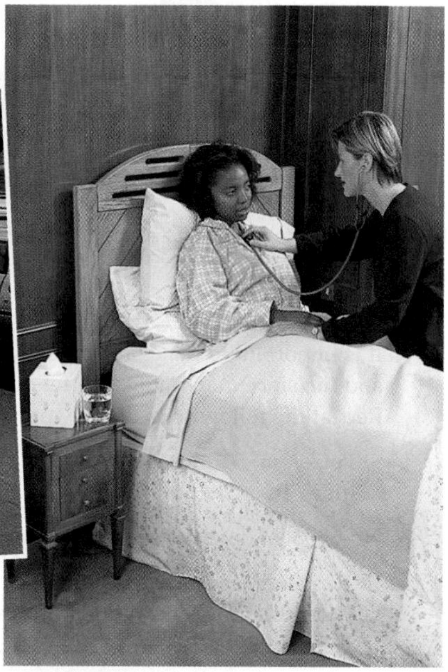

Le médecin ausculte la malade.

antibiotiques: trois comprimés par jour pendant une semaine. Mélanie va en prendre un à chaque repas.

Mélanie paie le médecin. Mais en France, la Sécurité Sociale rembourse les honoraires des médecins, c'est-à-dire l'argent qu'on donne aux médecins. Les honoraires et tous les frais[2] médicaux sont remboursés de 80 à 100% (pour cent) par la Sécurité Sociale.

[2] frais *expenses*

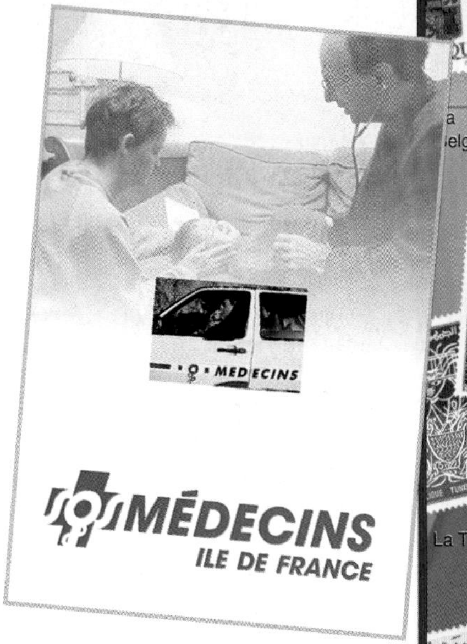

Après la lecture

A Autrement dit Dites d'une autre manière.

1. Mélanie a *de la fièvre.*
2. Elle *ne se sent pas bien.*
3. Elle veut *téléphoner au* médecin.
4. Le médecin *ne voit pas de malades* le week-end.
5. S.O.S. Médecins envoie des médecins *chez les malades.*
6. Le médecin *écoute la respiration de* Mélanie.
7. La grippe n'est pas une maladie *alarmante.*
8. Mélanie va vite *se sentir mieux.*

B Vous avez compris? Répondez.

1. Mélanie est très malade?
2. Elle a beaucoup de fièvre?
3. Elle a mal au ventre?
4. Elle veut aller chez le médecin?
5. Son médecin donne des consultations tous les jours?
6. Mélanie téléphone à qui?
7. Le médecin lui prescrit de l'aspirine?
8. Les frais médicaux ne sont pas remboursés en France?

C En France Qu'est-ce que vous avez appris sur les médecins et les services médicaux en France?

Step 2 Ask five or six questions that review the main points. The answers will give a coherent oral review of the **Lecture.**

Post-reading

Have students do the **Après la lecture** activities on page 483 orally after reading the selection in class. Then assign these activities to be written at home. Go over them again the following day.

Après la lecture

A and B Allow students to refer to the story to look up the answers or you may use this activity as a testing device for factual recall.

About the French Language

Explain to students that **les honoraires** is the term used for the fees of professionals such as doctors and lawyers.

Answers to Après la lecture

A

1. Mélanie a de la température.
2. Elle n'est pas du tout dans son assiette.
3. Elle veut appeler le médecin.
4. Le médecin ne donne pas de consultations le week-end.
5. S.O.S. Médecins envoie des médecins à domicile.
6. Le médecin ausculte Mélanie.
7. La grippe n'est pas une maladie grave.
8. Mélanie va être vite sur pied.

B

1. Oui, Mélanie est très malade.
2. Non, elle a un peu de fièvre.
3. Non, elle n'a pas mal au ventre.
4. Oui, elle veut aller chez le médecin.
5. Non, son médecin ne donne pas de consultations le week-end.
6. Mélanie téléphone à S.O.S. Médecins.
7. Non, le médecin ne lui prescrit pas d'aspirine.
8. Si, les frais médicaux sont remboursés en France.

C *Answers will vary but may include:*
En France les médecins viennent chez vous. Mais vous devez payer le médecin après la consultation. Les honoraires et les frais médicaux sont remboursés par la Sécurité Sociale.

National Standards

Cultures
This selection familiarizes students with cultural differences dealing with health matters.

Comparisons
This selection makes a comparison between typical health concerns of Americans and French people.

Attention!

This reading is optional. You may skip it completely, have the entire class read it, have only several students read it and report to the class, or assign it for extra credit.

Learning from Realia

(page 484) Point to the rabbit and say: **C'est un lapin. Qu'est-ce qu'il a, le lapin? Qu'est-ce qu'il a mangé? Il a mangé trop de carottes? Tu aimes les carottes? Tu manges beaucoup de carottes? On dit que les carottes sont bonnes pour les yeux?**

Lecture supplémentaire 1

Culture et santé

La culture influence la santé et la médecine? Certainement. Par exemple, en France tout le monde parle de son foie[1]. Les Français disent souvent, «J'ai mal au foie.» Aux États-Unis, on n'entend jamais dire ça. Pourquoi? Parce qu'aux États-Unis, une maladie du foie, c'est grave. Mais quand un Français dit qu'il a mal au foie, il veut dire tout simplement qu'il a un trouble digestif. Rien de grave. Il n'est peut-être pas dans son assiette aujourd'hui, mais il va vite être sur pied!

Aux États-Unis, par contre, on parle beaucoup d'allergies. De nombreux Américains souffrent d'une petite allergie. Les symptômes d'une allergie ressemblent aux symptômes d'un rhume. On éternue et on a souvent mal à la tête. Une allergie, c'est désagréable, mais ce n'est pas grave. En France, on parle moins souvent d'allergies. Pourquoi? Qui sait? Vive la différence!

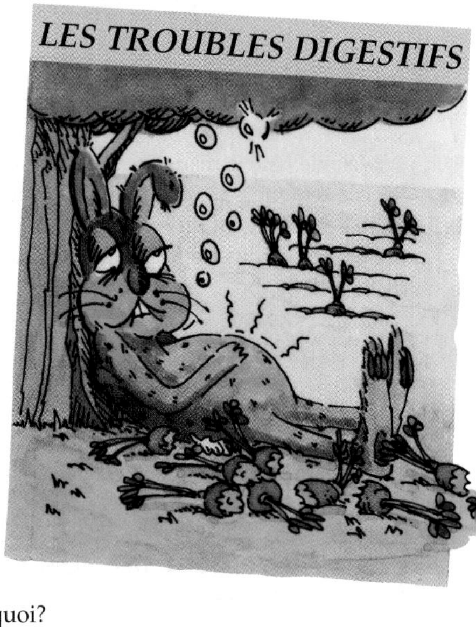

[1] foie *liver*

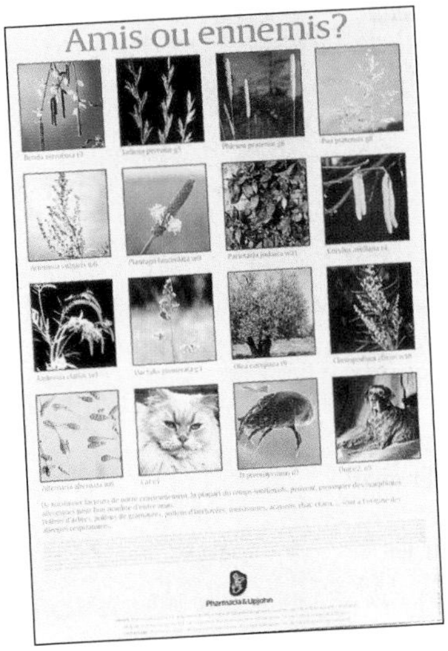

Après la lecture

Des différences Répondez.

1. On dit souvent qu'on a mal au foie dans quel pays?
2. Que veut dire un Français quand il dit qu'il a mal au foie?
3. Et pour un Américain, qu'est-ce que cela veut dire «J'ai mal au foie»?
4. Qui parle souvent d'allergies?
5. Quels sont les symptômes d'une allergie?

Answers to Après la lecture

1. en France
2. qu'il a un trouble digestif
3. que c'est une maladie grave
4. les Américains
5. On éternue, on a les yeux qui piquent et on a mal à la tête.

Lecture supplémentaire 2

Les services médicaux en France

En France, il y a de grands hôpitaux avec tout l'équipement haut de gamme[1] nécessaire à la pratique d'une médecine moderne. On compte plus de 3 500 établissements de soins polyvalents[2]. Il y a à peu près 900 établissements hospitaliers publics et plus de 2 500 cliniques privées. Beaucoup de ces cliniques ressemblent à des hôtels.

En France, on fait beaucoup de recherches médicales et pharmaceutiques. C'est à l'Institut Pasteur de Paris que le docteur Montagnier a isolé le virus du sida. Aujourd'hui à l'Institut Pasteur on continue à faire des recherches contre cette terrible maladie.

[1] haut de gamme *state of the art*
[2] soins polyvalents *general care*

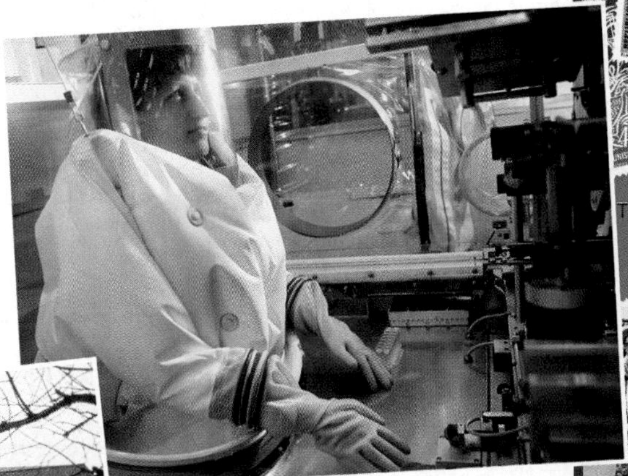

Un laboratoire de recherche à l'Institut Pasteur

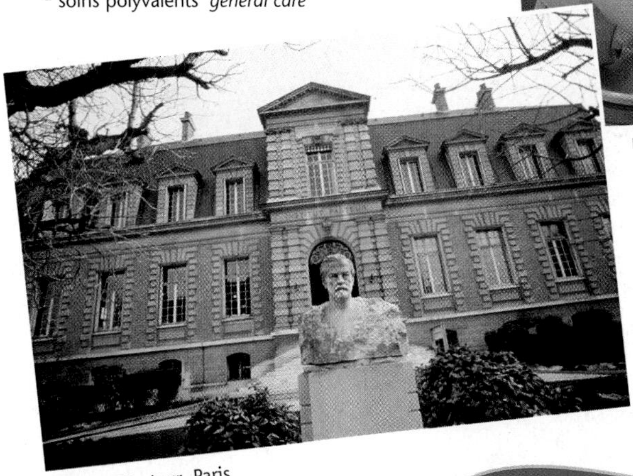

L'Institut Pasteur, Paris

Après la lecture

Des mots apparentés Trouvez les mots apparentés dans la lecture.

National Standards

Cultures
This selection familiarizes students with medical services in France.

Attention!

This reading is optional. You may skip it completely, have the entire class read it, have only several students read it and report to the class, or assign it for extra credit.

Presentation

Have students skim the selection to get the general information.

Learning from Photos

(page 485) Louis Pasteur, who did research that led to the pasteurization process, founded the Institute that bears his name in 1887–1889. It is still a very important center of medical research. The institute also houses a museum that has an exact replica of Pasteur's laboratory.

Answers to Après la lecture

hôpitaux, l'équipement, nécessaire, pratique, moderne, compte, établissements, publics, cliniques, privées, ressemblent, hôtels, recherches, médicales, pharmaceutiques, l'Institut, isolé, le virus, continue, terrible

National Standards

Connections
This reading about nutrition establishes a connection with another discipline, allowing students to reinforce and further their knowledge of natural sciences through the study of French.

Attention!

The readings in the **Connexions** section are optional. They focus on some of the major disciplines taught in schools and universities. The vocabulary is useful for discussing such topics as history, literature, art, economics, business, science, etc. You may choose any of the following ways to do the readings in the **Connexions** sections.

Independent reading Have students read the selections and do the post-reading activities as homework, which you collect. This option is least intrusive on class time and requires a minimum of teacher involvement.

Homework with in-class follow-up Assign the readings and post-reading activities as homework. Review and discuss the material in class the next day.

Intensive in-class activity This option includes a pre-reading vocabulary presentation, in-class reading and discussion, assignment of the activities for homework, and a discussion of the assignment in class the following day.

CONNEXIONS

Les sciences naturelles

La diététique

Good nutrition is very important. What we eat can determine if we will enjoy good health or poor health. For this reason, it is most important to have a balanced diet and avoid the temptation to eat "junk food."

Read the following information about nutrition in French. Before reading this selection, however, look at the following groups of related words. Often if you know the meaning of one word you can guess the meaning of several words related to it.

individuel, individu
actif, activité
consommation, consommer, consommateur
adolescent, adolescence
âge, âgé

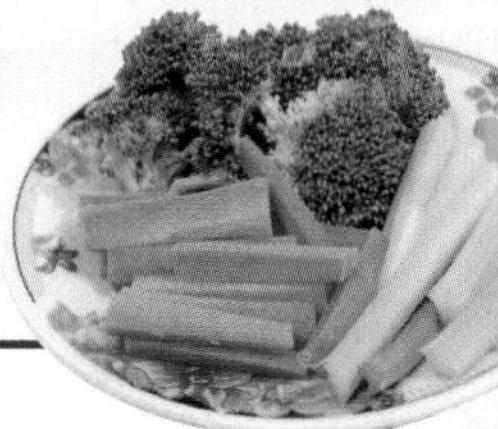

Un bon régime[1]

Il est très important d'avoir une alimentation équilibrée[2] pour être en bonne santé. Un régime équilibré comporte une variété de légumes et de fruits, des céréales, de la viande et du poisson.

Tout le monde a besoin de calories, mais le nombre idéal dépend de l'individu—de son métabolisme, de sa taille, de son âge et de son activité physique. Les adolescents, par exemple, ont besoin de plus de calories que les personnes âgées. Ils ont besoin de plus de calories parce qu'ils sont plus actifs et ils sont en période de croissance[3].

Les protéines

Les protéines sont particulièrement importantes pour les enfants et les adolescents parce qu'ils sont en pleine croissance. Les protéines aident à fabriquer des cellules. La viande et les œufs contiennent des protéines.

[1] régime *diet* [2] équilibrée *balanced* [3] croissance *growth*

Class Motivator

Des aliments Those students who are interested in nutrition may prepare a food chart with the following headings:

Aliments hauts en calories
Aliments bas en calories
Graisses
Hydrates de carbone
Vitamine A
Vitamine B
Vitamine C
Vitamine D
Vitamine E

Under each heading they can put photos or drawings of the appropriate foods labeled in French that they have already learned to identify.

Les glucides (les hydrates de carbone)

Les glucides (les pommes de terre, les pâtes comme les spaghettis, le riz[4]) sont la source d'énergie la plus efficace pour le corps humain.

Les lipides (les graisses)

Les lipides sont aussi une bonne source d'énergie. Mais pour les personnes qui ont un taux de cholestérol élevé[5], les graisses ne sont pas bonnes. Il faut faire un régime sans graisse. Il faut les éliminer.

Les minéraux

Beaucoup de minéraux sont essentiels pour le corps humain. Le calcium est absolument nécessaire pour les os[6] et les dents.

L'eau

L'eau est absolument essentielle au corps humain qui est fait de 65% d'eau.

Les vitamines

Les vitamines sont indispensables au bon fonctionnement du corps humain. Ce tableau indique la source de quelques vitamines importantes.

Vitamines	Sources
A	légumes, lait, quelques fruits
B	viande, œufs, céréales, légumes verts
C	fruits, tomates, salade verte
D	lait, œufs, poisson
E	huiles, légumes, œufs, céréales

[4] riz *rice* [5] élevé *elevated, high* [6] os *bones*

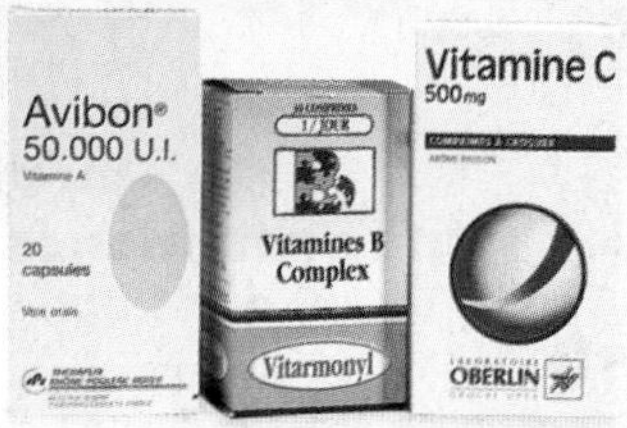

Après la lecture

A La diététique Répondez.

1. Qu'est-ce qu'on doit manger tous les jours?
2. Le nombre de calories pour chaque individu dépend de quoi?
3. Qui a particulièrement besoin de calories? Pourquoi?
4. Quelle est une source importante d'énergie?
5. Pourquoi faut-il contrôler la consommation de graisses?
6. Quel est un minéral important pour les os et les dents?
7. Qu'est-ce qui est indispensable au bon fonctionnement du corps humain?

B Assez de vitamines? Faites une liste de tout ce que vous avez mangé hier. Vous avez eu toutes les vitamines nécessaires?

CONNEXIONS

Presentation

Les sciences naturelles

La diététique

Step 1 Have students read the introduction in English on page 486.

Step 2 Ask students to scan the reading on pages 486–487.

Après la lecture

A Students can refer to the reading to answer these questions if necessary.

Recycling

This reading serves to review and reinforce the names for many foods.

Reaching All Students

Additional Practice Have students write out a balanced menu for **le petit déjeuner, le déjeuner,** and **le dîner.**

Answers to Après la lecture

A

1. Tous les jours on doit manger une variété de légumes et de fruits, des céréales, de la viande ou du poisson.
2. Le nombre de calories pour chaque individu dépend de son métabolisme, de sa taille, de son âge et de son activité physique.
3. Les adolescents ont particulièrement besoin de calories parce qu'ils sont actifs et en période de croissance.
4. Les lipides (les glucides) sont une source importante d'énergie.
5. Il faut contrôler la consommation de graisses pour ne pas avoir un taux de cholestérol élevé.
6. Le calcium est un minéral important pour les os et les dents.
7. Les vitamines sont indispensables au bon fonctionnement du corps humain.

B *Answers will vary depending upon what the students ate.*

C'est à vous

Use what you have learned

Recycling

These activities allow students to use the vocabulary and structure from this chapter in completely open-ended, real-life situations.

Presentation

Encourage students to say as much as possible when they do these activities. Tell them not to be afraid to make mistakes, since the goal of these activities is real-life communication. If someone in the group makes an error, allow the others to politely correct him or her. Let students choose the activities they would like to do.

You may wish to divide students into pairs or groups. Encourage students to elaborate on the basic theme and to be creative. They may use props, pictures, or posters if they wish.

C'est à vous

Use what you have learned

PARLER

1 **Tout le monde est malade.**

✔ ***Describe cold symptoms and minor ailments***

Work with a classmate. Choose one of the people in the illustrations. Describe him or her. Your partner will guess which person you're talking about and say what's the matter with the person. Take turns.

1.

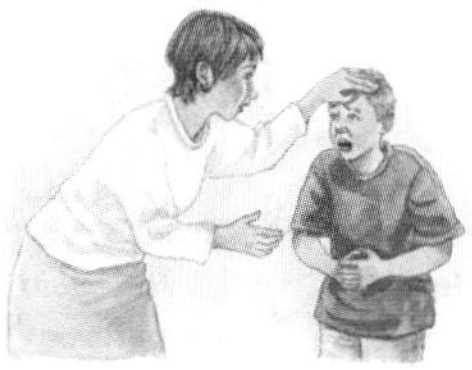

2.

3.

4.

PARLER

2 **Une ordonnance**

✔ ***Discuss a prescription with a pharmacist***

You are in a pharmacy in Bordeaux. Your classmate will be the pharmacist. Make up a conversation about your prescription. Explain why and how you have to take the medicine.

PARLER

3 **Jeu** **Je suis malade comme un chien!**

✔ ***Talk about how you are feeling***

Work with a partner. Make gestures to indicate how you're feeling today. Your partner will ask you why you feel that way. Tell him or her. Be as creative and humorous as possible.

ANSWERS TO C'est à vous

1 *Answers will vary but may include:*

—Le pauvre! Il a très mal au ventre. Il a aussi de la fièvre. Sa mère va téléphoner au médecin.
—C'est le dessin numéro 1. Il a la grippe.

2 *Answers will vary but may include:*

—J'ai une angine. Le médecin m'a donné cette ordonnance.
—Ah, oui. C'est un très bon antibiotique.
—Il faut prendre combien de comprimés?
—Trois par jour. Et vous allez être vite sur pied.

3 *Answers will vary but may include:*

Student points to his or her stomach.
—Tu as mal au ventre?
—Oui. Hier je suis allé(e) à une fête et j'ai beaucoup mangé. Je sais que j'ai mangé trop de gâteau au chocolat.

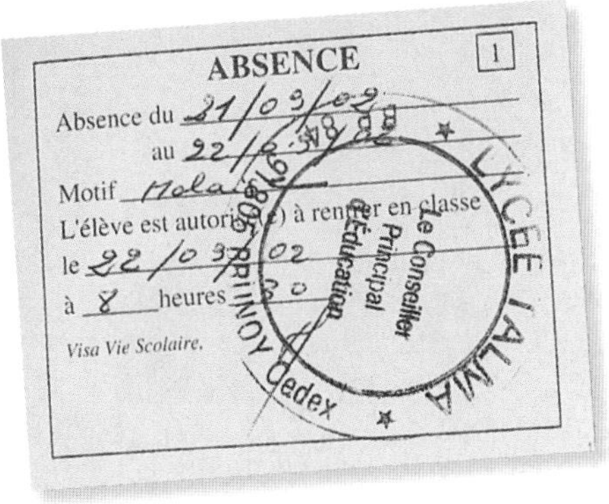

ÉCRIRE

4 Excusez-moi...

✔ *Write a note describing a minor illness*

You're supposed to take a French test today but you're not feeling well. Write a note to your French teacher explaining why you can't take the test, and mention some symptoms you have.

Une ambulance du SAMU

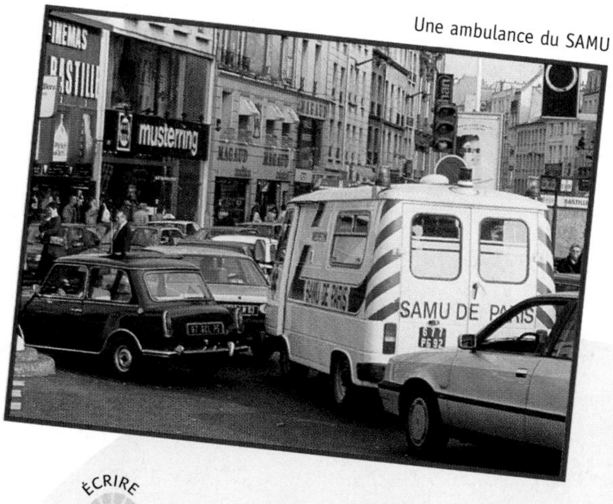

Writing Strategy

Writing a personal essay In writing a personal essay, a writer has several options: to tell a story, describe something, or encourage readers to think a certain way or to do something. Whatever its purpose, a personal essay allows a writer to express a viewpoint based on his or her own experience. Your essay will be much livelier if you choose interesting details and vivid words to relay your message.

ÉCRIRE

5 Des bénévoles

Your French club has a community service requirement. You have decided to work in the emergency room **(le service des urgences)** at your local hospital. You serve as a translator or interpreter for patients who speak only French. Write a flyer for your French club. Tell about your experience with one or more patients. Give your feelings about the work you do and try to encourage other club members to volunteer their services, too.

Answers to C'est à vous

4 *Answers will vary.*

5 *Answers will vary.*

Writing Development

Have students keep a notebook containing their best written work from each chapter. These selected writings can be based on assignments from the Student Textbook and the Writing Activities Workbook. The two activities on page 489 are examples of writing assignments that may be included in each student's portfolio. In the Workbook, students will develop an organized autobiography **(Mon autobiographie).** These workbook pages may also become a part of their portfolio.

Writing Strategy

Taking notes Have students read the Writing Strategy on page 489. If students have difficulty thinking of related vocabulary, have them use the vocabulary list on page 492.

Reaching All Students

Additional Practice Display Communication Transparency C 14. Have students work in groups to make up as many questions as they can about the illustration. Have groups take turns asking and answering the questions.

Reaching All Students

For the Younger Students Have students make colorful get-well cards using some of the expressions they have learned. If someone they know is ill, they can send him or her the cards.

Resource Manager

Communication Transparencies
Quizzes
Test Booklet
ExamView Pro®
Situation Cards
Performance Assessment
Marathon mental Videoquiz

Assessment

This is a pre-test for students to take before you administer the chapter test. Answer sheets for students to do these pages are provided in your transparency binder. Note that each section is cross-referenced so students can easily find the material they have to review in case they made errors. You may wish to collect these assessments and correct them yourself or you may prefer to have the students correct themselves in class. You can go over the answers orally or project them on the overhead, using your Assessment Answers transparencies.

Assessment

Vocabulaire

To review **Mots 1**, *turn to pages 464–465.*

1 Choisissez.

a.

b.

c.

d.

1. ____ Elle a mal à la tête.
2. ____ Elle a mal au ventre.
3. ____ Elle tousse.
4. ____ Elle est enrhumée.

2 Identifiez.

To review **Mots 2**, *turn to pages 468–469.*

3 Complétez.

8. Le médecin ____ le malade.
9. Le malade ouvre la ____ quand le médecin lui examine la gorge.
10. Le médecin fait un ____. Il dit que Nathalie a une sinusite aiguë.
11. Le médecin lui fait une ____ pour des antibiotiques.
12. Elle va à la ____ pour acheter ses médicaments.

Answers to Assessment

1	2	3
1. c	**5.** la tête	**8.** examine
2. a	**6.** l'oreille	**9.** bouche
3. d	**7.** la gorge	**10.** diagnostic
4. b		**11.** ordonnance
		12. pharmacie

Assessment

Structure

4 Complétez.

13. Le médecin parle au malade?
 Oui, il ____ parle.
14. Le médecin donne une ordonnance à ses patients?
 Oui, il ____ donne une ordonnance.
15. Paul donne son ordonnance à la pharmacienne?
 Oui, il ____ donne son ordonnance.

*To review **lui** and **leur**, turn to page 472.*

5 Complétez.

16. Ils ____ beaucoup, les pauvres. (souffrir)
17. J'____ le livre à la page 100. (ouvrir)
18. Vous ____ la bouche quand le médecin vous examine? (ouvrir)

*To review **souffrir** and **ouvrir**, turn to page 474.*

6 Complétez avec l'impératif.

19. (ouvrir) Paul, ____ ton livre.
 Luc et Louise, ____ vos livres aussi.
20. (attendre) Carole, ____ un moment.
 Sandrine et Maïa, ____ avec Carole.
21. (dire) Luc, ____ au médecin où tu as mal.
 Vous deux, ____ au médecin où vous avez mal.

To review commands, turn to page 475.

7 Répondez avec un pronom.

22. Tu as de l'aspirine?
 Oui, __________.
23. Tu as douze comprimés?
 Oui, __________.
24. Tu peux sortir de l'hôpital demain?
 Oui, __________.
25. Il a beaucoup d'argent?
 Oui, __________.

*To review the use of **en**, turn to page 478.*

Glencoe Technology

MINDJOGGER

You may wish to help your students prepare for the chapter test by playing the MindJogger game show. Teams will compete against each other to review chapter vocabulary and structure and sharpen listening comprehension skills.

Answers to Assessment

4

13. lui
14. leur
15. lui

5

16. souffrent
17. ouvre
18. ouvrez

6

19. ouvre, ouvrez
20. attends, attendez
21. dis, dites

7

22. Oui, j'en ai.
23. Oui, j'en ai douze.
24. Oui, je peux en sortir.
25. Oui, il en a beaucoup.

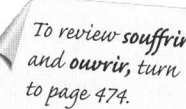

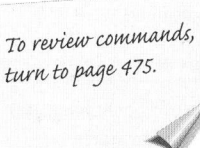

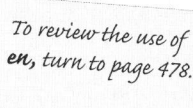

Vocabulaire

Vocabulary Review

The words and phrases in the **Vocabulaire** have been taught for productive use in this chapter. They are summarized here as a resource for both student and teacher. This list also serves as a convenient resource for the **C'est à vous** activities on pages 488–489. There are approximately sixteen cognates in this vocabulary list. Have students find them.

Attention!

You will notice that the vocabulary list here is not translated. This has been done intentionally, since we feel that by the time students have finished the material in the chapter they should be familiar with the meanings of all the words. If there are several words they still do not know, we recommend that they refer to the **Mots 1** and **2** sections in the chapter or go to the dictionaries at the back of this book to find the meanings. However, if you prefer that your students have the English translations, please refer to Vocabulary Transparency 14.1, where you will find all these words listed with their translations.

Vocabulaire

Describing minor health problems

la santé
  en bonne santé
  en mauvaise santé
une infection
un frisson
la grippe
un rhume
une angine
une sinusite aiguë
une allergie
un mouchoir
un kleenex
se sentir bien
  mal
être enrhumé(e)
tousser
éternuer
avoir mal
  à la tête
  au ventre
  aux oreilles
  à la gorge
avoir de la fièvre
  le nez qui coule
  les yeux qui piquent
  la gorge qui gratte
malade
viral(e)
bactérien(ne)
allergique

Speaking with the doctor

le médecin
le/la malade
un diagnostic
une ordonnance
souffrir
ouvrir
examiner
ausculter
respirer
prescrire

How well do you know your vocabulary?

- **Find as many cognates as you can in the list.**
- **Use five cognates to write several sentences.**

Identifying more parts of the body

la tête
un œil, des yeux
le nez
la bouche
une oreille
la gorge
le ventre

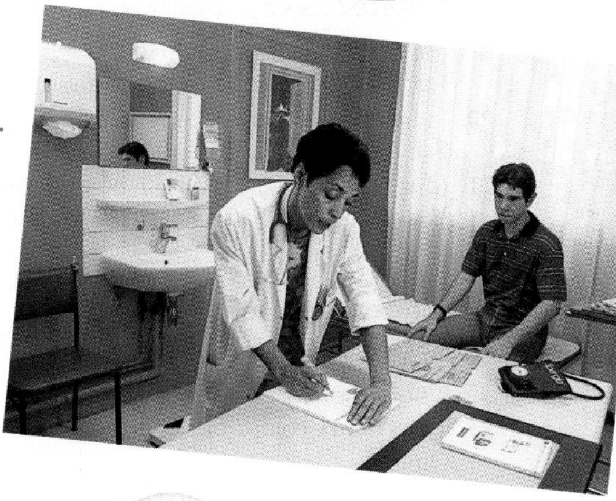

Speaking with a pharmacist

un(e) pharmacien(ne)
une pharmacie
un médicament
un comprimé
un antibiotique
un sirop
de la pénicilline
de l'aspirine *(f.)*
avaler

Other useful words and expressions

À tes souhaits!
Qu'est-ce qu'il a?
le/la pauvre
à fond

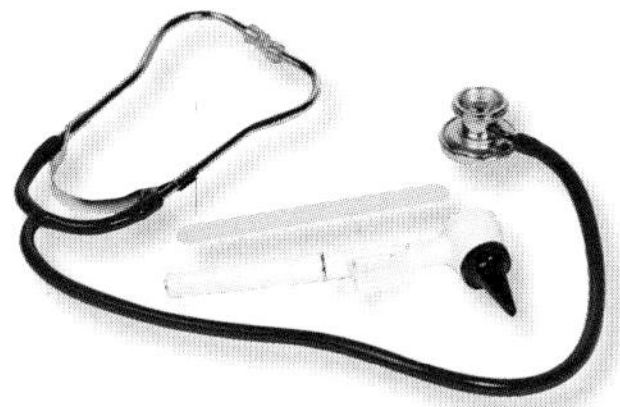

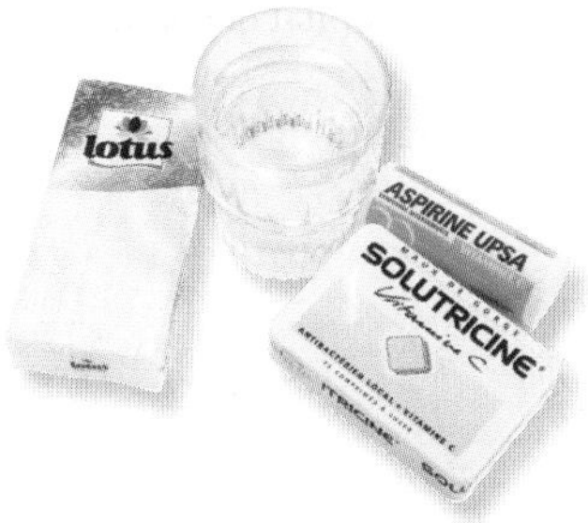

BON VOYAGE!

VIDÉO • Épisode 14

Avant de visionner

In this video episode, Vincent experiences a strange nightmare. The next day he pays a visit to his doctor.

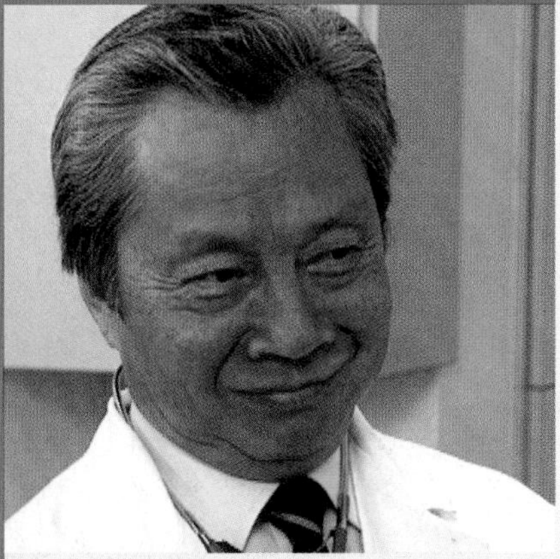

Le docteur Nguyen est très sympa.

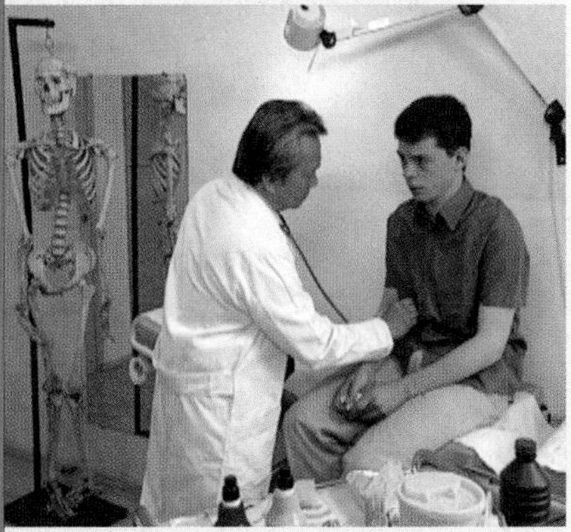

Vincent n'est pas en bonne santé.

FRENCH ONLINE

À découvrir

Learn more about l'Institut Pasteur online.

L'Institut Pasteur

FRENCH Online

In the Chapter 14 Internet activity, you will have a chance to learn more about health and medicine in the Francophone world. To begin your virtual adventure, go to the Glencoe French Web site: **french.glencoe.com**

Technotour

Overview

This page previews two key multimedia components of the **Glencoe French** series. Each reinforces the material taught in the chapter in a unique manner.

VIDÉO

The Video Program allows students to see how the chapter vocabulary and structures are used by native speakers. For maximum reinforcement, show the video episode as a final activity for Chapter 14.

The two photos on the left show highlights from the Chapter 14 video episode. Discuss the photos with your students before having them view the episode. See the Video Activities Booklet for detailed suggestions for using this resource.

FRENCH Online

- The **À découvrir** photo on page 493 shows the **Institut Pasteur.** Students can go online to learn more about this important research institute.
- Teacher Information and Student Worksheets for this activity can be accessed at the Web site.

Video Synopsis

In this video episode, Vincent has a bad dream about the famous Paris catacombs. The video flashes from these ancient skeletons to one in a doctor's office. Vincent explains his symptoms, and the doctor conducts a routine examination. Vincent is relieved to receive a diagnosis of the flu and not something more serious.

Preview

This section reviews the salient points from Chapters 12–14. In the **Conversation,** students will review movie and health vocabulary. In the **Structure** sections, they will review the present and **passé composé** of reflexive verbs and object pronouns.

Resource Manager

Workbook, Self-Test, pages 149–152
Test Booklet

Presentation

Conversation

Step 1 Have students open their books to page 494. Call on two students to read this short conversation aloud.

Step 2 Go over the activity in the **Après la conversation** section.

Learning from Realia

(page 494) You may wish to ask the following questions about the poster.

Quel est le titre du film?
Comment s'appelle le film en anglais?
Qui sont les acteurs principaux du film?
Qui sont les actrices principales du film?
C'est quel genre de film?
Tu as vu ce film?

Conversation

On va au cinéma?

Céline: Tu as déjà vu *Autant en emporte le vent* avec Clark Gable et Vivien Leigh?
Thomas: Non, mais c'est un classique.
Céline: Tu veux le voir? On le joue au Champollion en version originale.
Thomas: Je voudrais bien, mais je ne peux pas. Je dois me coucher de bonne heure ce soir.
Céline: Pourquoi? Tu ne te sens pas bien?
Thomas: Non, pas très bien. Je ne sais pas ce que j'ai… Je suis fatigué, j'ai mal à la tête… Je crois que j'ai la grippe.

Après la conversation

Répondez.

1. Céline parle à qui?
2. Elle lui parle de quoi?
3. Thomas a déjà vu *Autant en emporte le vent*?
4. Il croit que c'est un bon film?
5. On joue *Autant en emporte le vent* dans quel cinéma?
6. Pourquoi est-ce que Thomas ne peut pas aller au cinéma?
7. Qu'est-ce qu'il a?

Answers to Après la conversation

1. Céline parle à Thomas.
2. Elle lui parle d'un film.
3. Non, il n'a pas vu *Autant en emporte le vent.*
4. Il croit que c'est un bon film.
5. On joue *Autant en emporte le vent* au Champollion.
6. Thomas ne peut pas aller au cinéma parce qu'il ne se sent pas bien.
7. Il a la grippe.

Reaching All Students

Additional Practice You may wish to ask students personalized questions about their movie viewing habits.

Tu aimes quel genre de film? Quel est ton film favori? Quel acteur ou quelle actrice joue dans ce film?

Révision

Structure

Les verbes réfléchis

1. The subject of a reflexive verb both performs and receives the action of the verb. For this reason, an additional pronoun is used. It is called a reflexive pronoun. Review the following forms.

SE LAVER		S'HABILLER	
je	me lave	je	m'habille
tu	te laves	tu	t'habilles
il/elle/on	se lave	il/elle/on	s'habille
nous	nous lavons	nous	nous‿habillons
vous	vous lavez	vous	vous‿habillez
ils/elles	se lavent	ils/elles	s'habillent

2. Reflexive verbs are conjugated with **être** in the **passé composé.** Note that there is no agreement when the verb is followed by a noun referring to a part of the body.

Elle s'est brossée. — **Elle s'est brossé les cheveux.**
Elle s'est maquillée. — **Elles se sont maquillé les yeux.**
Ils se sont lavés. — **Ils se sont lavé les dents.**

1 Historiette Ce matin Répondez que oui.

1. Il s'appelle Arnaud?
2. Qu'est-ce qu'il fait le matin? Il se dépêche?
3. Il se lève à sept heures?
4. Il s'habille vite?
5. Et toi, tu te lèves à sept heures?
6. Tu te laves les mains et la figure?
7. Tes parents se dépêchent le matin?

Presentation

Les verbes réfléchis

Step 1 Quickly go over the verb paradigms that appear here.

Step 2 Review the **passé composé** and the rules for agreement of the past participle.

Learning from Photos

(page 495) Have students identify the objects.

Paired Activity

Have students work together in pairs to make up their own conversations about going to see a movie. Have them discuss their choices and come to a decision about which movie to see.

Answers to Révision

1

1. Oui, il s'appelle Arnaud.
2. Oui, il se dépêche.
3. Oui, il se lève à sept heures.
4. Oui, il s'habille vite.
5. Oui, je me lève à sept heures.
6. Oui, je me lave les mains et la figure.
7. Oui, mes parents se dépêchent le matin.

Révision

Presentation

Les pronoms

Step 1 Review the information regarding the use of object pronouns. As you go over the explanation, write the examples on the board. Underline the noun object and circle the object pronoun. Draw a line from one to the other.

Step 2 Have students repeat the examples on page 496.

Reaching All Students

Additional Practice

Give students the following nouns and have them make up questions with **tu vois** and a direct object pronoun. For example:

Le livre?
Tu le vois?

- **Les billets?**
- **La lettre?**
- **Le magazine?**
- **Les cassettes?**
- **La vidéo?**
- **La photo?**
- **Le stylo?**
- **Le CD?**
- **La calculatrice?**
- **Les cartes postales?**

2 Historiette La routine Complétez en utilisant le passé composé.

Ce matin, je __1__ (se réveiller) tôt et je __2__ (se lever) tout de suite. Je __3__ (se laver) la figure et les mains et, après le petit déjeuner, je __4__ (se brosser) les dents.

Mes deux copains Sandrine et Sylvain __5__ (se lever) tard ce matin. Ils __6__ (se dépêcher) pour arriver à l'école à l'heure.

Et vous, vous __7__ (se lever) tard ou tôt ce matin? Vous __8__ (se dépêcher)?

Les pronoms

1. The pronouns **me, te, nous,** and **vous** can be either direct or indirect objects.

OBJET DIRECT:	**Il me voit.**	**Elle t'invite à la fête.**
	Ils nous regardent.	**Je vous connais.**
OBJET INDIRECT:	**Tu me parles?**	**Elle te dit quoi?**
	Il nous téléphone.	**Je vous réponds que oui.**

2. The pronouns **le, la,** and **les** are direct objects. They can replace either a person or a thing.

Jean? Je le connais.	**Son collège? Je ne le connais pas.**
Marie? Je la connais.	**Sa voiture? Je la vois.**
Tes copains? Je les connais.	**Leurs billets? Je les ai.**

3. **Lui** and **leur** are indirect objects. They replace **à** + a person.

Je téléphone à Jean.	**Je lui téléphone.**
Il lit la lettre à Anne.	**Elle lui lit la lettre.**
Elle parle aux élèves.	**Elle leur parle.**

4. The pronoun **en** replaces **de (du, de la, de l', des)** + a thing.

Tu as de l'aspirine?	**Oui, j'en ai.**
Il prend des antibiotiques?	**Non, il n'en prend pas.**

Remember that with numbers and expressions of quantity **en** refers not only to things but also to people: **Tu as des frères? Oui, j'en ai deux.**

5. Object pronouns always come directly before the verb they are linked to.

Il me téléphone.	**Il va lui téléphoner.**
Elle en achète.	**Il ne va pas leur parler.**
Il ne la regarde pas.	

ANSWERS TO Révision

2

1. me suis réveillé(e)
2. me suis levé(e)
3. me suis lavé
4. me suis brossé
5. se sont levés
6. se sont dépêchés
7. vous êtes levé(e)(s)
8. vous êtes dépêché(e)(s)

3 Vraiment? Complétez avec **me, te, nous** ou **vous.**

1. —Je vous connais, vous deux.
   —Vraiment? Tu ____ connais?
2. —On va te téléphoner.
   —Vraiment? Vous allez ____ téléphoner?
3. —Je t'aime!
   —Vraiment? Tu ____ aimes?
4. —Elle nous invite, ma sœur et moi.
   —Vraiment? Elle ____ invite?
5. —Elle t'invite aussi.
   —Vraiment? Elle ____ invite aussi?
6. —Il vous regarde fixement, ta sœur et toi.
   —Vraiment? Il ____ regarde fixement?

Musée du Louvre, Paris

4 Jean et ses amis Refaites les phrases en utilisant des pronoms.

1. Je connais *Jean,* mais je ne connais pas *ses amis.*
2. Je ne vois pas souvent *Caroline,* mais je parle *à sa sœur* tous les jours.
3. Jean m'invite à sa fête et je veux apporter un cadeau *à ses parents.*
4. J'aime beaucoup *Virginie et ses amis.* Je vais téléphoner *à Virginie* pour les inviter tous.
5. J'aime beaucoup *ses CD.* Je vais acheter trois *CD.*

5 Questions Répondez en utilisant un pronom.

1. Tu lis ce magazine?
2. Tu achètes les billets?
3. Tu vas voir cette pièce de théâtre?
4. Tu veux voir ces deux films?
5. Tu aimes mieux voir les films en version originale ou doublés?
6. Tu vois beaucoup de films américains?

6 Une journée typique Work with a classmate.

Compare a typical day in your life with a typical day in your partner's life.

7 On s'amuse. Work with a classmate.

Discuss what you do when you have free time. Do you like to do the same activities?

Literary Companion *You may wish to read the adaptation of* Le Comte de Monte-Cristo. *You will find this literary selection on page 518.*

Art Connection

(page 497 top) The people in the photo are admiring ***La Joconde*** *(Mona Lisa)* in the Louvre museum. Leonardo Da Vinci *(Léonard de Vinci)* painted this portrait of the noble Florentine Mona Lisa in 1504. It became the prototype of a Renaissance portrait. The famous smile is the subject of many commentaries.

As you can observe in the photo, the painting is protected by thick glass and has a barrier around it to prevent people from approaching too close.

Literary Companion

When you finish this review section, if you wish, have students read the literary adaptation of ***Le Comte de Monte-Cristo,*** on pages 518–523. The adaptation has been done in accordance with the vocabulary and structures that the students have acquired up to this point.

Answers to Révision

3

1. nous
2. me
3. m'
4. vous
5. m'
6. nous

4

1. Je le connais, mais je ne les connais pas.
2. Je ne la vois pas souvent, mais je lui parle tous les jours.
3. Jean m'invite à sa fête et je veux leur apporter un cadeau.
4. Je les aime beaucoup. Je vais lui téléphoner pour les inviter tous.
5. Je les aime beaucoup. Je vais en acheter trois.

5

1. Oui, je le lis.
2. Oui, je les achète.
3. Oui, je vais la voir.
4. Oui, je veux les voir.
5. J'aime mieux les voir en version originale.
6. Oui, j'en vois beaucoup.

Preview

The section **Reflets de Paris** was prepared by National Geographic Society. Its purpose is to give students greater insight, through these visual images, into the culture and people of Paris, France. Have students look at the photographs on pages 498–501 for enjoyment. If they would like to talk about them, let them say anything they can, using the vocabulary they have learned to this point.

National Standards

Cultures
The **Reflets de Paris** photos and the accompanying captions allow students to gain insights into the people and culture of Paris, the City of Light.

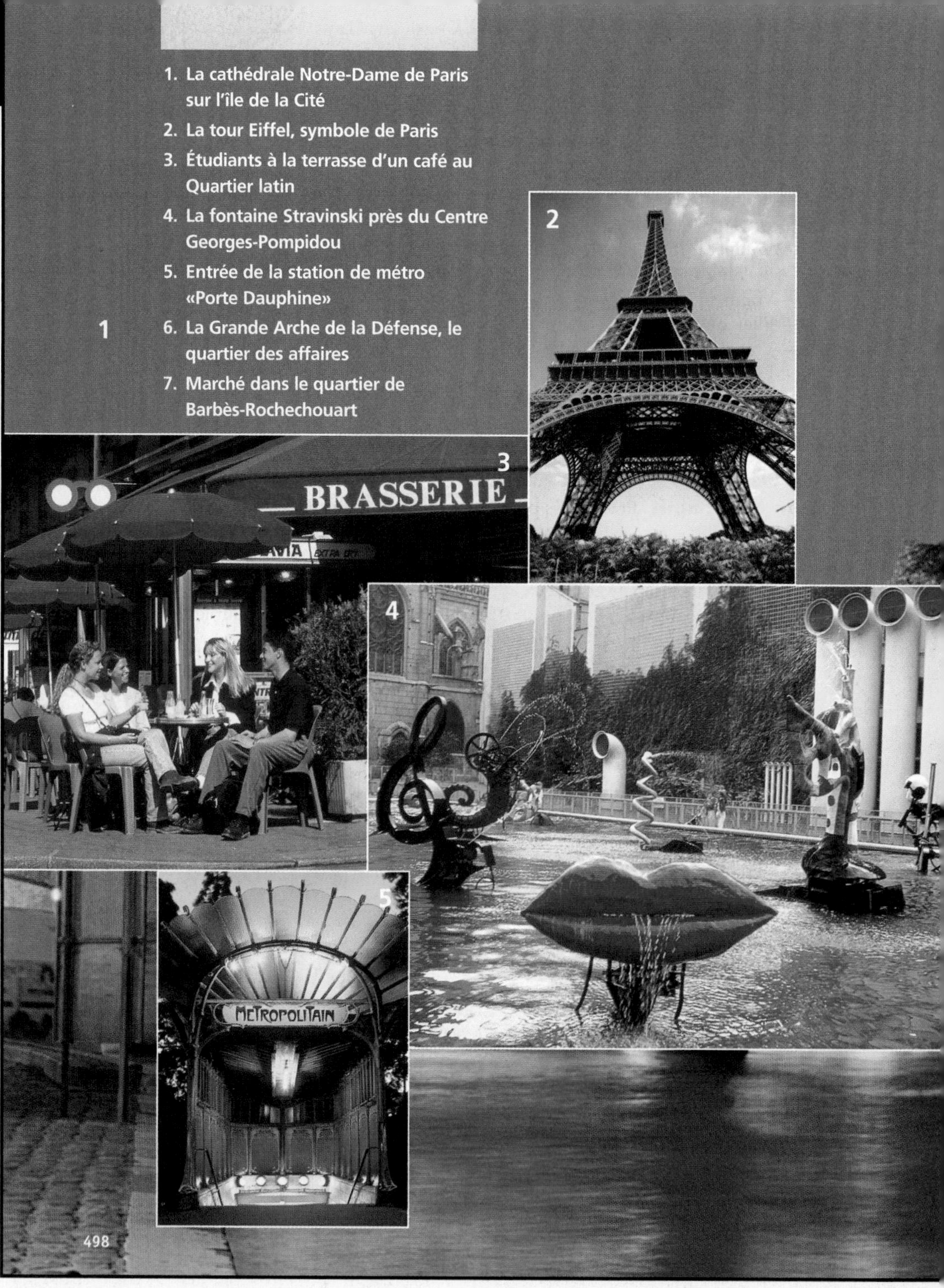

1. La cathédrale Notre-Dame de Paris sur l'île de la Cité
2. La tour Eiffel, symbole de Paris
3. Étudiants à la terrasse d'un café au Quartier latin
4. La fontaine Stravinski près du Centre Georges-Pompidou
5. Entrée de la station de métro «Porte Dauphine»
6. La Grande Arche de la Défense, le quartier des affaires
7. Marché dans le quartier de Barbès-Rochechouart

498

About the Photos

1. La cathédrale Notre-Dame de Paris sur l'île de la Cité Construction of the magnificent **cathédrale Notre-Dame de Paris** in the center of Paris on the île de la Cité, was begun in 1163 and completed around 1250. Various changes were made during the seventeenth century.

The cathedral has three main entrances, each surrounded by magnificent carvings, many of which are nineteenth-century copies of the originals. There are twin towers: the south one has the great bell of Notre-Dame that was tolled by Victor Hugo's fictional hunchback Quasimodo.

Among other things, the cathedral is famous for its rose windows. This photo of the cathedral gives students a good view of the spires and the **arcs boutants,** or flying buttresses.

2. La tour Eiffel, symbole de Paris The Eiffel Tower is the most famous landmark of Paris. It was designed by Gustave Eiffel for the World Exhibition of 1889, the centennial of the French Revolution. (He also designed the frame for the Statue of Liberty in New York.) Many artists and intellectuals of the day ridiculed the "metal monster." It remains, however, the number one tourist attraction of Paris. The tower has 15,000 pieces of metal and 2,500,000 rivets. It now stands more than 1,000 feet high since television relays were added.

3. Étudiants à la terrasse d'un café au Quartier latin The Latin Quarter on the left bank across from the île de la Cité, is known as the "bohemian" or student quarter of Paris. La Sorbonne, a part of the **Université de Paris,** is in the Latin Quarter, because until the Revolution studying and speaking Latin were university traditions.

The Latin Quarter has many cafés and restaurants frequented by university students.

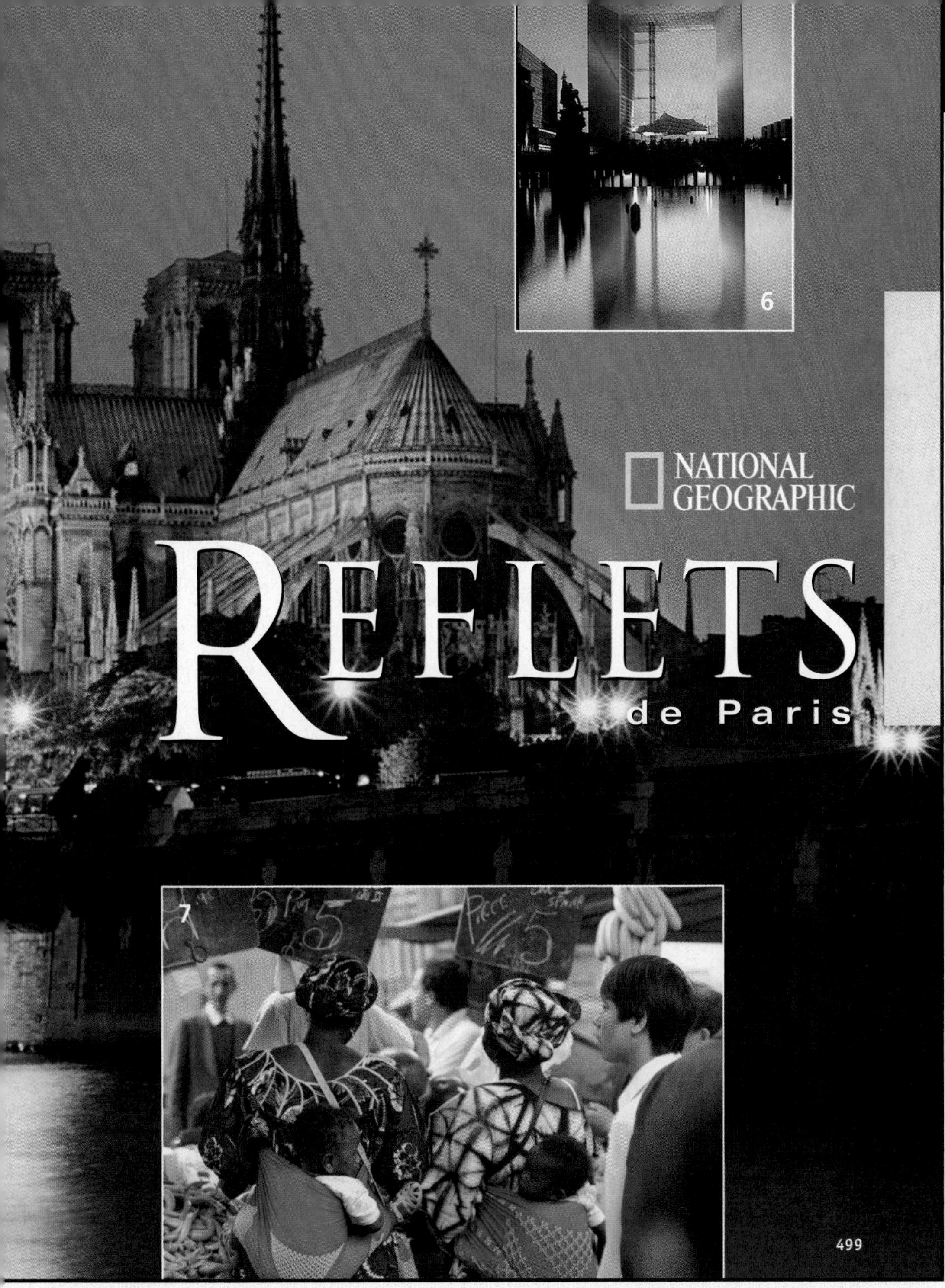

6

7

6. La Grande Arche de la Défense, le quartier des affaires La Défense is an area just west of Paris, across the Seine from the upscale area of Neuilly. In the past twenty years, La Défense has been transformed into an interesting area of high rises that showcase state-of-the-art engineering and futuristic architectural designs. Most of these high rises are mainly office buildings. La Grande Arche, designed by the Danish architect Otto Spreckelsen, is a colossal office building that was inaugurated for the seventeenth Summit of Industrial Countries in July 1989. La Grande Arche is as wide as the Champs-Élysées; this giant cube could hold Notre-Dame cathedral and its spires.

7. Marché dans le quartier de Barbès-Rochechouart The Barbès Rochechouart area of Paris is just to the northwest of the gare du Nord near Montmartre. It is a working-class area and home to many new immigrants.

4. La fontaine Stravinski près du Centre Georges-Pompidou Parisians often call the **Centre Pompidou Beaubourg,** the name of the district in which it is located. It is claimed that the **Centre Pompidou** has the largest collection of modern art in the world.

Near the **Centre Pompidou** is the **Fontaine Stravinski.** The extremely imaginative and colorful statues were done by the French artist, Niki de Saint-Phalle, in collaboration with her husband, Jean Tinguely, the Swiss sculptor. The statues evoke the works *Le sacre du printemps* and *L'oiseau de feu* of the famous composer Igor Stravinsky.

5. Entrée de la station de métro «Porte Dauphine» The Porte Dauphine station entrance shown here has the typical design of older stations. These older entrances feature curly green **Art-Nouveau** railings and archways, and the full title: **Métropolitain.** The entrances to the newer stations have a large yellow **M** within a circle.

NATIONAL GEOGRAPHIC

8. L'Arc de Triomphe sur la place Charles-de-Gaulle The grand Arc de Triomphe stands in the center of a hectic and incredible traffic circle. From it, twelve avenues branch off in all directions, one of which is the Champs-Élysées. The roundabout from which the avenues branch out is called today place Charles de Gaulle. Its previous name was **l'Étoile.** Napoleon proposed building the Arc de Triomphe in 1806 after the victory at the battle of Austerlitz.

9. La pyramide du musée du Louvre The glass pyramid in the Cour Napoléon in front of the Louvre by the American architect I. M. Pei, was commissioned by former president François Mitterrand, and unveiled in March 1989. Below the pyramid there is a large museum shop, a café, and a restaurant. Standing at the pyramid one can look straight ahead and capture one of the most beautiful views in the world—a vista stretching from the Arc de Triomphe du Carrousel, les Tuileries, la place de la Concorde, les Champs-Élysées, l'Arc de Triomphe to the new giant Grande Arche de la Défense.

When the pyramid was first unveiled, its modernistic look in the midst of such classical architecture as that of the Louvre and its courtyard caused a furor. The furor over the years has subsided, and many compare the reaction to that caused by the Eiffel Tower a century earlier.

10. Horloge de l'ancienne gare d'Orsay transformée en musée The gare d'Orsay was used as a train station for routes between Paris and the Southwest of France. By 1939, however, it had become too small for mainline travel, and the lines to the Southwest were transferred to the gare d'Austerlitz. The gare d'Orsay became a terminal for trains to the suburbs until it closed in 1960. In the late 1970s, former president Valéry Giscard d'Estaing ordered that the building be turned into a museum. It opened

8. L'Arc de Triomphe sur la place Charles-de-Gaulle
9. La pyramide du musée du Louvre
10. Horloge de l'ancienne gare d'Orsay transformée en musée
11. Petits bateaux à voiles au jardin du Luxembourg
12. Lampadaires sur le pont Alexandre III
13. Enfant avec pains
14. La Joconde par un jeune artiste de la rue

NATIONAL GEOGRAPHIC Teacher's Corner

Index to the NATIONAL GEOGRAPHIC MAGAZINE

The following related articles may be of interest:

- "Paris: *La Belle Époque,*" by Eugen Weber, July 1989.
- "The New, the Enduring Paris," by James L. Stanfield, July 1989.
- "Letters from France," by Don Belt, Cathy Newman, Cliff Tarpy, July 1989.
- "A Castle Under the Louvre," by Peter Miller, July 1989.
- "The Fantastic Flight of Cote d'Or," by Cynthia Shields, December 1983.
- "The Civilizing Seine," by Charles McCarry, April 1982.
- "Pompidou Center, Rage of Paris," by Cathy Newman, October 1980.

as the musée d'Orsay in 1986, and it is devoted to the arts spanning the years 1848–1914. Most of its collections are French. The chief artistic attraction is the collection of Impressionist and post-Impressionist works.

11. Petits bateaux à voiles au jardin du Luxembourg For a large commercial city, Paris has many open spaces. This is because of the many parks that are in the city. With its ponds, fountains, hedges, and rows of trees with gravel walks, **le jardin du Luxembourg** is one of the prettiest parks in the city.

12. Lampadaires sur le pont Alexandre III The **Pont Alexandre III** is one of the most photographed of all of the bridges across the Seine. It is lined with bronze lamps that epitomize the **fin-de-siècle** style of the **Belle Époque.** The bridge was built for the 1900 World's Fair and was named after the visiting Russian Czar.

13. Enfant avec pains In this photo, we see a young boy with loaves of bread. In Paris, as in any other French city or town, it is common to see people walking home with their fresh bread.

14. *La Joconde* par un jeune artiste de la rue Near the museums, and in some other areas of the Quartier latin, it is not unusual to see young artists or art students reproducing famous works on the sidewalk with chalk. Those passing by will often leave a coin to "help out" the artist.

Products available from
GLENCOE/MCGRAW-HILL

To order the following products, call Glencoe/McGraw-Hill at 1-800-334-7344.

CD-ROMs
- Picture Atlas of the World
- The Complete National Geographic: 112 Years of National Geographic Magazine

Transparency Set
- NGS PicturePack: Geography of North America

Products available from
NATIONAL GEOGRAPHIC SOCIETY

To order the following products, call National Geographic Society at 1-800-368-2728.

Books
- National Geographic World Atlas for Young Explorers
- National Geographic Satellite Atlas of the World

Software
- ZingoLing: French Diskette

Video
- France
- Europe

Preview

All literary selections are optional. You may wish to skip them or present them very thoroughly. In some cases you may have students read the selection quickly just to get a general idea of the selection.

Attention!

The exposure to literature early in one's study of a foreign language should be a pleasant experience. As students read these selections, it is not necessary for them to understand every word. Explain to them that they should try to enjoy the experience of reading literature in a new language. As they read they should look for the following:

- Who the main characters are
- What they are like
- What they are doing—the plot
- What happens to them—the outcome of the story

Literary Companion

Literary Companion

These literary selections develop reading and cultural skills and introduce students to French literature.

La petite Fadette 504
George Sand

«Dors mon enfant» 510
Elolongué Epanya Yondo

La Chanson de Roland 512
Auteur anonyme

Le Comte de Monte-Cristo .. 518
Alexandre Dumas

La petite Fadette

National Standards

Cultures

Students experience, discuss, and analyze an adaption of the novel *La petite Fadette* by George Sand.

Attention!

This literary selection is optional. You may wish to present it after students have completed Chapters 1–4, as they will have acquired the vocabulary and structures necessary to read the selection by this point.

You may present the piece thoroughly as a class activity or you may have some or all students merely read it on their own. If you present it as a class activity, you may wish to vary presentation procedures from section to section. Some options are:

- Students read silently.
- Students read after you in unison.
- Call on individuals to read aloud.
- When dialogue appears in the story, call on students to take parts.

With any of the above procedures, intersperse some comprehension questions. Call on a student or students to give a brief synopsis of a section in French.

Note: The following teaching suggestions are for a thorough presentation of *La petite Fadette.*

La petite Fadette George Sand

Vocabulaire

Les jumeaux sont semblables.
Ils ont les yeux bleus.
Ils sont forts.

Il y a deux autres garçons dans la famille.
L'aîné a cinq ans.
Le cadet a deux ans.

Il est triste. Il pleure.

Le petit garçon a peur.

Les paysans travaillent dans les champs.
La petite fille est très pauvre.

Elle est (tombe) malade.

Le Berry, France

Activités

A **Historiette** **Les jumeaux**
Répondez.

1. Les deux frères sont jumeaux?
2. Ils sont très semblables?
3. Ils ont les yeux bleus?
4. Ils sont forts ou faibles?
5. Le cadet a cinq ans ou deux ans?
6. Et l'aîné, il a quel âge?

B **Quel est le mot?** Complétez.

1. Des ____ sont des frères qui ont le même âge.
2. Le petit garçon est triste. Il ____.
3. Il pleure aussi quand il a ____.
4. Les jumeaux sont blonds et ils ont les yeux bleus. Ils sont très ____.
5. M. et Mme Gaillard ont deux enfants. L'____ a quinze ans et le ____ a huit ans.
6. M. et Mme Gaillard ____ dans les champs. M. et Mme Gaillard sont des ____.
7. La petite fille n'est pas riche. Elle est ____.
8. La petite fille est ____. Elle a la grippe.

Teaching Vocabulary

Step 1 Present the new vocabulary on pages 504–505 using the teaching suggestions given in the regular chapters in this textbook.
Teaching Tips: You may use some students as models to reinforce **Ils ont les yeux bleus. Ils sont forts.**

You can also use dramatizations to teach **pleurer, peur, triste, malade, pauvre.** For **pauvre** you can show empty pockets.

Step 2 Quickly go over Activities A and B with the class.

Reaching All Students

Multi-Sensory Learning
Have a student or students stand up and act out the following:

Il a peur.
Il est triste.
Il pleure.
Il est fort.
Il est malade.

Answers to Activités

A

1. Oui, les deux frères sont jumeaux.
2. Oui, ils sont très semblables.
3. Oui, ils ont les yeux bleus.
4. Ils sont forts.
5. Le cadet a deux ans.
6. L'aîné a cinq ans.

B

1. jumeaux
2. pleure
3. peur
4. semblables
5. aîné, cadet
6. travaillent, paysans
7. pauvre
8. malade

Discussing Literature

Introduction

Step 1 You may go over the Introduction with students or you may omit it and just have the students read the story.

Step 2 You can ask the following questions about the Introduction:

Quel est le vrai nom de George Sand?
Elle est de Paris?
Elle passe son enfance où?
Le Berry c'est quel genre de région? C'est une région rurale, industrielle ou urbaine?
George Sand a un bon mariage?
George Sand a combien d'enfants?

Step 3 Ask students the following question in English:

Does a pastoral novel, called **un roman champêtre** in French, take place in a large city or in the country?

La petite Fadette

Step 1 Before reading this selection you may wish to give students the following brief introduction in English to set the scene and help students understand the story.

"We are going to read a story about twin brothers who live in a rather poor, rural area of France. Something is going to happen that makes the twins very sad. Later one of the twins is actually going to become jealous of his brother. As you read, look for reasons for this sadness and jealousy. Then a very interesting person is going to come on the scene who will improve the situation."

Step 2 Since this reading is rather long, you may wish to go over only certain sections orally and have students read the other parts silently.

INTRODUCTION Le vrai nom de George Sand (1804–1876) est Aurore Dupin. Elle est née[1] à Paris, mais elle passe son enfance à Nohant, dans le Berry. Le Berry est une région rurale.

George Sand a un mariage malheureux. Séparée de son mari, elle rentre à Paris avec ses deux enfants. Ses romans les plus connus[2] sont des romans champêtres[3]. Dans ses romans, elle montre un grand intérêt pour les paysans du Berry. *La petite Fadette* est un roman champêtre publié en 1849.

[1] née *born*
[2] romans les plus connus *best-known novels*
[3] champêtres *pastoral*

La petite Fadette

1

Le père Barbeau habite à la Cosse. Le père Barbeau est un homme important. Il a deux champs. Il cultive ses deux champs pour nourrir° sa famille. Il a aussi une maison avec un jardin. C'est un homme courageux et bon. Il aime beaucoup sa famille—sa femme, la mère Barbeau, et ses trois enfants.

C'est alors que le père Barbeau et la mère Barbeau ont deux garçons à la fois°: deux beaux jumeaux. Il est impossible de distinguer les jumeaux l'un de l'autre parce qu'ils° sont très semblables. Sylvinet est l'aîné et Landry est le cadet.

nourrir *to feed*
à la fois *at the same time*
parce qu'ils *because they*

2

Les deux garçons grandissent° sans problème. Ils sont blonds avec de grands yeux bleus. Ils parlent avec la même voix°. Ils sont très amis. Ils sont toujours ensemble.

Les enfants ont maintenant 14 ans. Le père Barbeau dit qu'ils ont l'âge de travailler. Mais il n'y a pas assez de travail pour les deux garçons chez les Barbeau. Le père décide d'envoyer° un des garçons chez un voisin, le père Caillaud. Le père Caillaud habite à la Priche.

grandissent *grow up*
voix *voice*
envoyer *to send*

Les jumeaux sont très tristes. Être séparés, c'est horrible. Sylvinet commence à pleurer et Landry pleure aussi.

—Mais, le père Caillaud n'habite pas très loin, dit Landry.

—C'est vrai. Je vais chez le père Caillaud…

—Non, Sylvinet. Pas toi, moi! Je vais chez le père Caillaud!

Donc Landry quitte la maison de son père… Maintenant, il travaille chez le père Caillaud. Le père Caillaud est content que Landry travaille pour lui. Landry est très fort.

Le père Caillaud aime beaucoup Landry. Il traite Landry comme un de ses enfants. Landry aussi aime beaucoup le père Caillaud. Il est content de travailler à la Priche. Mais Sylvinet n'est pas content. Il est jaloux de Landry.

3

Françoise Fadet est une petite fille très pauvre. Elle habite avec sa grand-mère et son petit frère handicapé. Ils habitent près de la rivière°, pas très loin de la Priche. On appelle Françoise «la petite Fadette». La petite Fadette est très solitaire. Elle n'est pas comme les autres enfants. Elle est assez différente des autres. Les autres enfants ont peur de la petite Fadette. Certains détestent la petite fille.

Un jour, Landry rentre à la Priche et rencontre° la petite Fadette qui pleure.

—Pourquoi° tu pleures comme ça?

—Parce qu'on me déteste.

—C'est un peu ta faute°, Fadette.

—Ma faute? Pourquoi?

—Parce que tu es toujours très sale° et désagréable avec les autres.

rivière *river*

rencontre *meets*

Pourquoi *Why*

faute *fault*

sale *dirty*

Émile Lambinet *Écouen, près de Paris*

The following are some suggestions for presenting each section:

Section 1

A. Draw the Barbeau "family tree" on the board as students encounter each member of the family.

B. To help with comprehension of paragraph 2, you can say **Oh là là. Il est très difficile de distinguer les deux frères?** (with a mysterious look): **C'est qui? C'est Landry ou c'est Sylvinet? Ah, oui. C'est Landry.**

Section 2

A. **Les deux garçons grandissent.** Draw stick figures on the board. Each one gets a little bigger.

B. **Voix**—talk in a dramatic voice

C. **Pleurer**—cry. **Triste**—make a sad expression. **Content**—make a happy face. **Fort**—pretend to show arm muscles.

Section 3

Solitaire—look dejected and lonely. **Peur**—expression of fear. **Détestent**—look at someone with a mean look.

Art Connection

Émile Lambinet is one of the lesser-known artists from the "Generation of 1830," a group who followed the principles of the so-called Barbizon school. Barbizon is a small village that borders on the forests of Fontainebleau. In the 1830s, landscape painters such as Camille Corot and Théodore Rousseau visited the Barbizon area frequently. The surrounding scenery was the subject of the painters of this group. Some of Lambinet's works are a part of the Otto and Anna Monsted art collection that hangs in the Aarhus Kunstmuseum in Aarhus, Denmark.

Après la lecture

A. Activities A, B, and C can be done after reading Sections 1 and 2.
B. Activity D can be done after Section 2.
C. Activity E can be done after Section 3.

Art Connection

Adolphe-William Bouguereau (1825–1905) was born at La Rochelle. He also lived in Bordeaux and Paris and spent time in Italy and Brittany. Like many painters of his time, Bouguereau made a careful study of form and technique. Before beginning a painting he would master the history of his subject and do numerous sketches. Hallmarks of his work are the tenderness with which he portrays children (he had several of his own) and family scenes, his passion for the classics, and his love of rich colors.

Landry, lui, ne trouve° pas la petite Fadette désagréable. Il trouve même qu'elle est intelligente et intéressante. La petite Fadette trouve Landry très beau. Elle aime Landry. Landry et la petite Fadette sont souvent ensemble et Landry change la personnalité de la petite Fadette.

Le jumeau de Landry, Sylvinet, est très jaloux de Landry et la petite Fadette. Il tombe très malade. Sa famille est désespérée. Mais qui sauve Sylvinet? La petite Fadette, l'amie de son frère Landry. Maintenant, tout° est possible, même le mariage de Landry et de la petite Fadette.

trouve *finds*

tout *everything*

William Bouguereau *Jeune fille au panier de fruits*

Answers to Après la lecture

A

1. Ils ont trois enfants.
2. Oui, ils ont des jumeaux.
3. L'aîné, c'est Sylvinet.
4. Le cadet, c'est Landry.
5. Ils sont blonds, avec de grands yeux bleus.
6. Ils sont blonds.
7. Ils ont les yeux bleus.
8. Oui, ils ont la même voix.

B

Le père Barbeau est un homme important. Il est courageux et bon. Il aime sa famille. Il cultive deux champs pour nourrir sa famille.

C

Les jumeaux Barbeau sont blonds. Ils ont les yeux bleus. Ils sont très semblables et ils parlent avec la même voix.

Après la lecture

A **Les enfants Barbeau** Répondez.

1. M. et Mme Barbeau ont combien d'enfants?
2. Ils ont des jumeaux?
3. L'aîné, c'est Sylvinet ou Landry?
4. Et le cadet?
5. Comment sont les jumeaux?
6. Ils sont bruns ou blonds?
7. Ils ont les yeux de quelle couleur?
8. Ils ont la même voix?

B **Le père Barbeau** Décrivez le père Barbeau.

C **Les jumeaux** Décrivez les jumeaux Barbeau.

D **Séparation** Complétez.

1. Quand les enfants ont ____ ans, le père Barbeau dit qu'ils ont l'âge de ____.
2. Le père Barbeau décide d'envoyer un enfant chez un ____, le père Caillaud.
3. Le père Caillaud ____ à la Priche.
4. Les jumeaux sont très ____ parce qu'ils vont être séparés.
5. Ils sont très tristes et ils ____.
6. ____ travaille chez le père Caillaud.
7. Le père Caillaud ____ beaucoup Landry. Il ____ Landry comme un de ses enfants.

E **La petite Fadette** Répondez.

1. Avec qui habite la petite Fadette?
2. Elle habite où?
3. Comment est la petite Fadette?
4. Qui a peur de la petite Fadette?
5. La petite Fadette pleure. Pourquoi?
6. Elle parle à qui?
7. Landry trouve la petite Fadette comment?
8. Qui change la personnalité de la petite Fadette?
9. Qui tombe malade?
10. Qui sauve Sylvinet?

ANSWERS TO Après la lecture

D

1. quatorze, travailler
2. voisin
3. habite
4. tristes
5. pleurent
6. Landry
7. aime, traite

E

1. Elle habite avec sa grand-mère et son petit frère handicapé.
2. Elle habite près de la rivière, pas très loin de la Priche.
3. Elle est très solitaire est assez différente des autres.
4. Les autres enfants ont peur de la petite Fadette.
5. Parce qu'on la déteste.
6. Elle parle à Landry.
7. Il trouve qu'elle est intelligente et intéressante.
8. Landry change la personnalité de la petite Fadette.
9. Sylvinet tombe très malade.
10. La petite Fadette sauve Sylvinet.

«Dors mon enfant» Elolongué Epanya Yondo

Vocabulaire

une revue un magazine
l'avenir le futur

Gerard Sekoto *Jeune fille à l'orange*

Activité

Un oranger Répondez.

1. Un oranger, c'est un fruit ou un arbre?
2. L'orange, c'est le fruit de l'oranger?
3. Tu aimes les oranges?
4. Tu aimes le jus d'orange?
5. Il y a des orangers dans les régions tropicales?
6. C'est beau un oranger fleuri?

INTRODUCTION La poésie africaine francophone est la poésie écrite par des Africains de langue française. La poésie africaine francophone est riche et variée. Deux écrivains de langue française célèbres sont Léopold Sédar Senghor et Aimé Césaire. Ces deux écrivains créent dans les années 30 le mouvement de «la négritude». La négritude, c'est «l'ensemble des valeurs culturelles de l'Afrique noire.»

En 1947, Alioune Diop fonde à Paris la revue *Présence Africaine.* La revue publie les œuvres[1] d'écrivains africains francophones et diffuse le concept de la négritude.

[1] œuvres *works*

«Dors mon enfant»

National Standards

Communication
Students experience, discuss, and analyze the poem ***«Dors mon enfant»*** by Elolongué Epanya Yondo.

Attention!

This literary selection is optional. You may wish to present it after students have completed Chapters 5–7, as they will have acquired the vocabulary and structures necessary to read the selection by this point.

You may present the piece thoroughly as a class activity or you may have some or all students merely read it on their own. If you present it as a class activity, you may wish to vary presentation procedures from section to section. Some options are:

- Students read silently.
- Students read after you.
- Call on individuals to read aloud.
- When dialogue appears in the story, call on students to take parts.

Teaching Vocabulary

Note: It is not necessary for students to become as thoroughly familiar with this vocabulary as with the vocabulary in a typical chapter. It is presented to help students understand the reading.

Step 1 Quickly go over the activity with the class.

Introduction

Step 1 Have students read the introduction quickly to get a general idea of the **négritude** movement of poets from Africa and the Caribbean.

Answers to Activité

Answers will vary but may include:

1. Un oranger, c'est un arbre.
2. L'orange, c'est le fruit de l'oranger.
3. Oui, j'aime les oranges.
4. Oui, j'aime le jus d'orange.
5. Oui, il y des orangers dans les régions tropicales.
6. Oui, un oranger fleuri est beau.

History Connection

Elolongué Epanya Yondo was greatly influenced by the **négritude** movement of the 30s, 40s and 50s. It began among French-speaking African and Caribbean writers living in Paris. The **négritude** movement was a protest against French colonial rule and the policy of assimilation.

In his collection of poems, ***Kamerun! Kamerrun!***, published in 1960, Elolongué Epanya Yondo exalts the ideal of the possibility of a future Cameroonian nation, and describes a proud and glorious past.

Aujourd'hui, *Présence Africaine* est une maison d'édition[2] qui publie les œuvres d'écrivains africains.

«Dors mon enfant» est tiré de[3] *Kamérun! Kamérun!* du poète Elolongué Epanya Yondo. Elolongué Epanya Yondo est né au Cameroun en 1930. Il va étudier à Paris où il habite chez Alioune Diop. Elolongué Epanya Yondo veut inspirer un esprit de solidarité chez ses compatriotes pour établir un avenir[4] solide sans oublier[5] les traditions passées.

[2] maison d'édition *publishing house*
[3] tiré de *taken from*
[4] avenir *future*
[5] sans oublier *without forgetting*

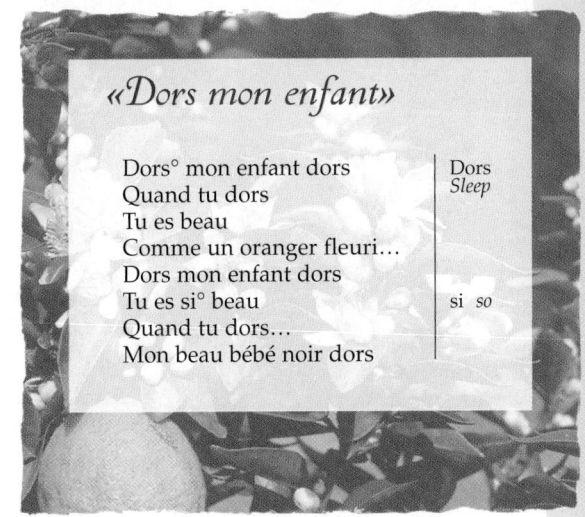

«Dors mon enfant»

Dors° mon enfant dors
Quand tu dors
Tu es beau
Comme un oranger fleuri…
Dors mon enfant dors
Tu es si° beau
Quand tu dors…
Mon beau bébé noir dors

Dors *Sleep*
si *so*

Elizabeth Barakah Hodges *Madone noire*

Après la lecture

Dors mon enfant Répondez.

1. Qui parle dans le poème?
2. La mère trouve son enfant beau?
3. Elle compare son enfant à quel arbre?
4. Un oranger est un bel arbre?
5. Un oranger est beau surtout quand il fleurit?
6. La mère compare son enfant à un bel oranger fleuri?
7. Le petit enfant est de quelle race?
8. C'est un bébé ou un petit garçon?

Note: The following teaching suggestions are for a thorough presentation of ***«Dors mon enfant»***.

Step 1 Have students close their books. Read the poem aloud to the class as you pretend you are rocking a baby in your arms.

Step 2 Now have students open their books. Have them read the poem silently to themselves.

Step 3 Have the class read the poem aloud in unison. The gentility and the simplicity of the words and the rhythm of the lines convey the feeling of deep love a mother has for her child.

Art Connection

Gerard Sekoto is one of South Africa's most noted painters. He was born in 1913 in what is today the Mpumalanga Province of South Africa. He started to paint there before moving to Johannesburg and later to Cape Town. His work during his days in Johannesburg and Cape Town is characterized by a strong representation of the human condition. Sekoto achieved most of his international success before leaving for Paris in 1947. In Paris, his work began to show the influence of Impressionism and Cubism. Although he never returned to South Africa, his subject matter remained mostly South African. He died in Paris in 1993.

Art Connection

Elizabeth Hodges was born to an artistic family in Columbia, South Carolina. For many years, she taught high school and college before devoting herself to painting. She signs many of her paintings as Elizabeth Barakah Hodges. Barakah, her name in Hebrew, reflects her Jewish heritage.

Answers to *Après la lecture*

1. C'est la mère qui parle dans le poème.
2. Oui, la mère trouve son enfant beau.
3. Elle compare son enfant à un oranger.
4. Oui, un oranger est un bel arbre.
5. Oui, un oranger est beau surtout quand il fleurit.
6. Oui, la mère compare son enfant à un bel oranger fleuri.
7. Le petit enfant est noir.
8. C'est un bébé.

La Chanson de Roland

National Standards

Cultures
Students experience, discuss, and analyze an adaption of the famous French epic poem, ***La Chanson de Roland.***

Attention!

This literary selection is optional. You may wish to present it after students have completed Chapters 8–11, as they will have acquired the vocabulary and structures necessary to read the selection by this point.

You may present the piece thoroughly as a class activity or you may have some or all students merely read it on their own. If you present it as a class activity, you may wish to vary presentation procedures from section to section. Some options are:

- Students read silently.
- Students read after you in unison.
- Call on individuals to read aloud.
- When dialogue appears in the story, call on students to take parts.

With any of the above procedures, intersperse some comprehension questions. Call on a student or students to give a brief synopsis of a section in French.

La Chanson de Roland **Auteur anonyme**

Vocabulaire

C'est un champ de bataille.
Les deux armées ont une bataille.

Les guerriers luttent.
Un guerrier est plus fort que l'autre.
Un guerrier est blessé.

Le guerrier sonne du cor.
Ça fait du bruit.

Reaching All Students

Multi-Sensory Learners The following words or expressions can be easily dramatized:

blessé	(play injured)
lutter	(pretend to fight)
sonner du cor	(blow into your hands)
du bruit	(make a loud noise)
frapper	(bang something on table)
cacher	(hide something)
briser	(break something)

Have students mimic the following:

Tu es un roi.
Tu es fort.
Tu luttes.
Tu sonnes du cor.
Tu as une épée.
Tu frappes ton épée contre la table.
Tu es blessé(e).

Le guerrier frappe son épée contre le rocher.
Il veut briser son épée.

Il se couche sous un arbre.
Il cache l'épée sous lui.

une lutte une bataille, un combat
du bruit un son désagréable
la guerre Deux armées qui luttent font la guerre.
gagner la bataille être victorieux, sortir victorieux d'une bataille

Activités

A Historiette **Sur le champ de bataille** Répondez.

1. Il y a des guerriers sur le champ de bataille?
2. Ils luttent?
3. C'est l'armée du roi?
4. Un guerrier est plus fort que l'autre?
5. Un guerrier est blessé?
6. Il a une épée à la main?
7. Il a un cor à la ceinture?
8. Est-ce qu'un guerrier sonne du cor?
9. Ça fait du bruit quand il sonne du cor?
10. Un guerrier frappe son épée contre un rocher?
11. Il cache son épée?
12. Il cache son épée où?

B **Quel est le mot?** Complétez.

1. Un ____ est un ancien instrument musical.
2. Une ____ est une ancienne arme.
3. Une ____, c'est un groupe de guerriers ou de soldats.
4. Le guerrier qui ____ la bataille est victorieux.

Note: The following teaching suggestions are for a thorough presentation of *La Chanson de Roland.*

Teaching Vocabulary

Step 1 Present the new vocabulary on pages 512–513 using the teaching suggestions given in the regular chapters in this textbook.

Step 2 Students merely need to be familiar with the vocabulary to help them understand the story. This vocabulary does not have to be a part of their active, productive vocabulary.

Answers to Activités

A

1. Oui, il y a des guerriers sur le champ de bataille.
2. Oui, ils luttent.
3. Oui, c'est l'armée du roi.
4. Oui, un guerrier est plus fort que l'autre.
5. Oui, un guerrier est blessé.
6. Oui, il a une épée à la main.
7. Oui, il a un cor à la ceinture.
8. Oui, un guerrier sonne du cor.
9. Oui, ça fait du bruit quand il sonne du cor.
10. Oui, un guerrier frappe son épée contre un rocher.
11. Oui, il cache son épée.
12. Il cache son épée sous lui.

B

1. cor
2. épée
3. armée
4. gagne

Discussing Literature

Introduction

It is recommended that you go over the Introduction with the class, since it will help them understand the reading selection.

History Connection

Depending on your school curriculum, students may or may not be familiar with European history. If they are not, you may wish to give them the following brief historical introduction.

The Romans gave the name Gaul to the two regions of Europe that had been occupied by the Celts. It included what is today France, Belgium, Switzerland, and the Left Bank of the Rhine. The Romans ruled Gaul for four centuries. They were then attacked by people who came from Germany. One group was the Franks.

The Franks chose their kings from members of the **famille mérovingienne.** The name comes from the name of a famous king from this family, Mérovée. Mérovée's grandson, Clovis I, was another famous Mérovingien king. He converted to Catholicism. After his baptism, the name **la Gaule** was changed to **la France.** The descendents of Clovis were all bad rulers, and in 752 the Franks began to choose their kings from the **famille carolingienne.** The most famous of the Carolingian kings was Charlemagne, who ruled from 768–814. In 800, Charlemagne was crowned Holy Roman Emperor by the Pope. During his reign, Charlemagne ordered many brave warriors to combat. The most famous of these warriors was his nephew, Roland.

La Chanson de Roland **Auteur anonyme**

INTRODUCTION *La Chanson de Roland* est un poème épique qui date de la fin du onzième siècle[1]. C'est le premier poème de ce genre qui est écrit en français et pas en latin. L'auteur est anonyme, c'est-à-dire qu'il est inconnu. Le poème raconte la guerre de Charlemagne en Espagne. Charlemagne passe sept années victorieuses en Espagne. Il reste une seule ville à prendre. C'est Saragosse. Roland est un chevalier[2] dans l'armée de Charlemagne. Il veut continuer la guerre pour prendre Saragosse. Mais un autre chevalier dans l'armée de Charlemagne, Ganelon, veut faire la paix[3] avec le roi de Saragosse. Il veut rentrer en France. On va voir ce qui arrive[4].

[1] siècle *century*
[2] chevalier *knight*
[3] faire la paix *make peace*
[4] ce qui arrive *what happens*

Roland et Durendal

1

Nous sommes en 771. Les Français s'appellent les Francs. Le roi des Francs, c'est Charlemagne. Il a une très grande armée composée de guerriers nobles et braves. Un de ces guerriers s'appelle Roland. Roland est le neveu de Charlemagne. Il est fort et grand comme un géant. Il est fier° et très courageux.

Un jour Charlemagne donne à son neveu deux merveilleux cadeaux: un cor magique et une épée dorée°. Roland est très fier des cadeaux de son oncle. Partout où il va il garde avec lui le cor et l'épée. Il aime son épée comme une amie. Il donne un nom à son épée: «Durendal».

fier *proud*
dorée *gilded*

Avec sa belle épée, Durendal, Roland lutte contre les ennemis de Charlemagne. Il est extraordinaire sur le champ de bataille avec son cor à la ceinture et son épée à la main. Sa belle épée dorée brille dans le soleil et protège Roland dans ses combats. Il est victorieux dans beaucoup de batailles.

Charlemagne et Roland

2

Un jour Roland est dans un pays étranger loin de la France. Il lutte contre un guerrier blond inconnu. Les deux guerriers sont forts et très braves. Ils

Reaching All Students

Multi-Level Abilities This selection lends itself to be made into a skit or play. Have groups of more able students rewrite each section in dialogue form. They may also want to make use of some monologue. Then have the groups present their "play" to the class.

Here's an example of what can be done with Section 1.

Charlemage: Je suis Charlemagne. Je suis le roi de France. Ah, voici mon neveu. Bonjour, Roland.
Roland: Bonjour, mon oncle.
Charlemagne: Roland, je suis très fier de toi. Tu es un homme fort et courageux.
Roland: Merci, mon oncle.
Charlemagne: Roland, j'ai des cadeaux pour toi. Un cor et une épée.
Roland: Merci, mon oncle. J'aime beaucoup ces cadeaux.
Charlemagne: Je suis content.
Roland: Je vais toujours garder mon cor et mon épée avec moi. Je vais donner un nom à mon épée. Durendal, tu es mon amie.

luttent tous les deux avec beaucoup de courage. Leur combat commence le matin et continue toute la journée. Les deux hommes sont très fatigués. Ils sont épuisés mais ils continuent à lutter. Pendant la bataille l'épée du guerrier blond se brise°. Quand Roland voit que l'épée de son adversaire est brisée, il jette Durendal à terre°. Et la bataille continue. Les deux guerriers luttent toute la nuit. Mais le guerrier blond est blessé. Aussitôt° Roland arrête le combat et aide le guerrier blessé.

—Je m'appelle Roland et je suis le neveu de Charlemagne. On ne va pas continuer à lutter. Je veux être ton ami. Quel est ton nom?

—Olivier, répond le guerrier blond.

Les deux guerriers décident d'être amis. Désormais° ils vont toujours être ensemble. Ils ne sont plus ennemis. Ils sont comme deux frères.

se brise *breaks*
jette... à terre *throws . . . on the ground*
Aussitôt *Immediately*
Désormais *From then on*

3

778: Charlemagne et ses guerriers sont en Espagne où ils luttent victorieusement contre les Sarrasins. La bataille est presque finie. Il reste une seule ville à prendre, Saragosse. Roland veut aller à Saragosse pour prendre la ville mais un autre chevalier, Ganelon, ne veut pas y aller. Il veut faire la paix avec le roi de Saragosse, Marsile, et rentrer en France. La décision est prise. On va traverser les Pyrénées et rentrer en France. En fait, Ganelon est un traître qui veut la mort° de Roland. Il révèle aux Sarrasins le chemin° que Charlemagne va prendre pour traverser les Pyrénées.

Charlemagne s'engage dans° les montagnes à la tête de son armée. Ganelon l'accompagne. Roland et Olivier font partie de l'arrière-garde. Les soldats de Marsile sont cachés° dans les montagnes à Roncevaux. Ils laissent passer Charlemagne et les hommes qui sont avec lui. Mais quand Roland et ses hommes arrivent, ils attaquent. Ils jettent des rochers énormes sur les guerriers. Les Francs luttent avec grand courage, mais hélas, ils sont vingt mille contre cent mille. Olivier demande à Roland de sonner du cor pour appeler Charlemagne à l'aide. Mais Roland est fier, il veut lutter seul. Les Francs sont écrasés°. Seuls Olivier et Roland restent en vie°. Ils veulent continuer la bataille mais ils sont blessés et ils sont très faibles.

Roland sonne du cor.

mort *death*
chemin *route*
s'engage dans *heads into*
cachés *hiding*
écrasés *crushed*
en vie *alive*

La Chanson de Roland

History vs. Fiction or Legend
On August 15, 778, the rear guard of Charlemagne's army was returning from battle in Spain, when they were ambushed in the town of Roncevaux by some Basque highlanders. Many of the soldiers lost their lives, including Roland. These events reappear in ***La Chanson de Roland,*** but history has been transformed into legend. In the story, the battle at Roncevaux is the result of treason, and the aggressors are no longer Basque Christians, but Moors. ***La Chanson de Roland*** was inspired by the French campaigns against the Moors (Moslems) in Spain during the eleventh century. The Moors occupied Spain from 811–1492. At the time, the Moors were called Sarrasins in many areas, including France.

Geography Connection

You may wish to point out to students on a map where the action of ***La Chanson de Roland*** takes place. (Roncevaux [Roncesvalles] in the Pyrenees, and Zaragoza in Spain.)

Note: As you read many parts of this selection, you can dramatize the meaning of many sentences as suggested in the vocabulary section.

Step 1 Tell students they are going to read an epic poem about Charlemagne's war in Spain.

Step 2 You may wish to have students take a few minutes to read the selection silently before going over it orally in class.

Step 3 Call on a more able student to give a synopsis of each section. This helps the less able students to understand the selection.

Après la lecture

Each activity goes with a section of the story.

4

Roland ne veut pas laisser Durendal aux mains de ses ennemis. Il essaie de briser son épée. Il frappe son épée contre un rocher. Le rocher est dur° mais l'épée est dure aussi. Roland frappe encore mais en vain. Il ne peut pas briser son épée.

Roland va mourir°. Il se couche sous un arbre et met sa belle épée sous lui. Là, ses ennemis ne peuvent pas trouver son amie Durendal. Enfin Roland prend son cor et sonne. Il appelle Charlemagne. Il sait qu'il va mourir.

Mais Charlemagne est très loin. Il est dans une plaine en France. Il croit entendre le cor de Roland.

—Écoute! dit-il à Ganelon. C'est Roland qui sonne du cor. Il demande notre aide.

—Mais non, ce sont des bergers° qui jouent de la flûte dans la montagne, répond Ganelon.

L'armée de Charlemagne continue son voyage. Roland sonne encore.

—Je suis sûr que c'est le cor de Roland. On fait demi-tour° et on va à son aide, dit Charlemagne.

—Mais Roland est brave, dit Ganelon. Il est fort et il a des hommes avec lui. Il n'a pas besoin de nous. Notre armée est fatiguée. On ne peut pas faire demi-tour.

Le pauvre Roland est désespéré et il sonne une dernière fois°.

—C'est Roland. C'est sûr. Il a besoin de notre aide. Demi-tour, immédiatement! crie Charlemagne.

Charlemagne et ses guerriers font demi-tour. Ils arrivent dans la vallée où est l'arrière-garde. Mais il est trop tard. Tous les guerriers francs sont morts. Charlemagne trouve les corps de Roland et d'Olivier l'un près de l'autre. Roland a sonné du cor si longtemps et si fort que les veines de ses tempes° ont éclaté°.

Charlemagne et son armée attaquent l'armée de Marsile. L'ennemi est finalement écrasé. Charlemagne sort victorieux et la mort de Roland et de ses hommes est vengée.

Voilà l'histoire de Roland, le noble guerrier.

dur *hard*
mourir *to die*
bergers *shepherds*
fait demi-tour *turn around*
dernière fois *last time*
tempes *temples*
ont éclaté *burst*

La mort de Roland

ANSWERS TO Après la lecture

A

1. Charlemagne est le roi des Francs en 771.
2. Oui, il a une très grand armée.
3. Les soldats de Charlemagne sont nobles et braves.
4. Roland est le neveu de Charlemagne.
5. Charlemagne donne un cor magique et une épée dorée à Roland.
6. Roland donne le nom de «Durendal» à son épée.

B

1. b
2. b
3. b
4. b
5. b
6. b
7. a
8. b

C

1. vrai
2. faux
3. faux
4. vrai
5. faux
6. vrai
7. vrai
8. faux
9. faux
10. vrai

Après la lecture

Portrait de Charlemagne

A **Charlemagne** Répondez.

1. Qui est le roi des Francs en 771?
2. Il a une grande armée?
3. Comment sont les soldats de Charlemagne?
4. Qui est Roland?
5. Qu'est-ce que Charlemagne donne à Roland?
6. Roland donne un nom à son épée? Quel nom?

B **Un combat** Choisissez la bonne réponse.

1. Un jour Roland lutte contre ____.
   a. un ami brun **b.** un étranger blond
2. Ils luttent ____.
   a. en France **b.** dans un pays étranger
3. Pendant la bataille l'épée ____ se brise.
   a. de Roland **b.** de l'étranger blond
4. ____ jette son épée à terre.
   a. L'inconnu blond **b.** Roland
5. ____ est blessé.
   a. Roland **b.** Le guerrier inconnu
6. Roland ____ le guerrier.
   a. n'aide pas **b.** aide
7. Roland veut être ____ du guerrier blond.
   a. l'ami **b.** l'ennemi
8. Les deux vont être ____.
   a. des neveux **b.** comme des frères

Monument de Charlemagne à Roncevaux

C **En Espagne** Vrai ou faux?

1. Charlemagne et son armée luttent en Espagne.
2. Ils luttent contre les Romains.
3. Les soldats de Charlemagne prennent la ville de Saragosse.
4. Roland veut prendre la ville de Saragosse.
5. Un autre chevalier, Ganelon, veut prendre Saragosse aussi.
6. Marsile est le roi de Saragosse.
7. Charlemagne et ses guerriers décident de rentrer en France.
8. Ganelon est un ami de Roland.
9. Roland et Ganelon font partie de l'arrière-garde.
10. L'armée de Marsile attaque Roland et ses hommes.

D **Un résumé** Give a brief synopsis of the end of the story in English.

ANSWERS TO **Après la lecture**

D

Answers will vary but may include:
Roland, knowing he is about to die, tries to break his sword rather than leave it to his enemies. He is unable to break it, so he hides it under his body. Roland sounds his horn for Charlemagne, who is far away in France. Charlemagne thinks he hears Roland's horn, but is contradicted by the traitor Ganelon. Upon hearing the horn a third time, Charlemagne turns around to go to Roland's aid, but it is too late, Roland is dead. Charlemagne and his army attack Marsile's army and avenge Roland's death.

Le Comte de Monte-Cristo

National Standards

Cultures
Students experience, discuss, and analyze an adapted excerpt from the novel ***Le Comte de Monte-Cristo*** by Alexandre Dumas.

Attention!

This literary selection is optional. You may wish to present it after students have completed Chapters 12–14, as they will have acquired the vocabulary and structures necessary to read the selection by this point.

You may present the piece thoroughly as a class activity or you may have some or all students merely read it on their own. If you present it as a class activity, you may wish to vary presentation procedures from section to section. Some options are:

- Students read silently.
- Students read after you in unison.
- Call on individuals to read aloud.
- When dialogue appears in the story, call on students to take parts.

With any of the above procedures, intersperse some comprehension questions. Call on a student or students to give a brief synopsis of a section in French.

Le Comte de Monte-Cristo Alexandre Dumas

Vocabulaire

Le jeune marin va se marier.
Il regarde sa fiancée avec amour.
Ils célèbrent leurs fiançailles.

On emmène le criminel en prison.
On l'enferme dans une cellule.

Le prisonnier est désespéré.
Il frappe sur la porte.
Il crie.

Il s'est évadé de prison.

Ils ont jeté le sac à la mer.

Il a trouvé un trésor.

Activités

A **Le marin** Répondez d'après les indications.

1. Le jeune homme est un soldat ou un marin? (un marin)
2. Il est marié? (non)
3. Il va se marier? (oui)
4. Il adore sa fiancée? (oui)
5. Qu'est-ce qu'il a pour sa fiancée? (de l'or)
6. Qu'est-ce qu'ils célèbrent? (leurs fiançailles)

B **La prison** Vrai ou faux?

1. Il y a des cellules dans une prison.
2. On emmène les criminels en prison.
3. Les cellules de prison sont très belles et agréables.
4. On enferme les gardiens dans des cellules.
5. Les gardiens travaillent dans une prison. Ils surveillent les prisonniers.
6. De temps en temps, un prisonnier complètement désespéré frappe sur la porte de sa cellule.
7. Les gardiens font des trous dans les murs.
8. Pour s'évader de prison, les prisonniers creusent un tunnel.

C **Un trésor** Répondez que oui.

1. C'est une île?
2. Il y a une grotte sur l'île?
3. Il y a un coffre à l'entrée de la grotte?
4. Le coffre est plein d'or et de pierres précieuses?
5. Il y a un bateau dans la mer?
6. Quelqu'un jette un sac à la mer?

Note: The following teaching suggestions are for a thorough presentation of ***Le Comte de Monte-Cristo.***

Teaching Vocabulary

Step 1 Present the new vocabulary on pages 518–519 using the teaching suggestions given in the regular chapters in this textbook.

Step 2 Students merely need to be familiar with the vocabulary to help them understand the story. This vocabulary does not have to be a part of their active, productive vocabulary.

Step 3 To review the **passé composé** as you present this vocabulary, you may wish to ask the following questions.

On a emmené le criminel en prison?
On l'a enfermé dans une cellule?
Un autre prisonnier a fait un trou dans le mur?
Il a creusé un tunnel?
Il a frappé sur la porte?
Il a crié?
Il s'est évadé de prison?
Ils ont mis quelque chose dans un sac?
Ils ont jeté le sac à la mer?
Il a trouvé un trésor?

Answers to Activités

A

1. Le jeune homme est un marin.
2. Non, il n'est pas marié.
3. Oui, il va se marier.
4. Oui, il adore sa fiancée.
5. Il a de l'or pour sa fiancée.
6. Ils célèbrent leurs fiançailles.

B

1. vrai
2. vrai
3. faux
4. faux
5. vrai
6. vrai
7. faux
8. vrai

C

1. Oui, c'est une île.
2. Oui, il y a une grotte sur l'île.
3. Oui, il y a un coffre à l'entrée de la grotte.
4. Oui, le coffre est plein d'or et de pierres précieuses.
5. Oui, il y a un bateau dans la mer.
6. Oui, quelqu'un jette un sac à la mer.

Discussing Literature

Introduction

It is recommended that you go over the Introduction with the class, since it will help them understand the reading selection.

Le Comte de Monte-Cristo

Step 1 You may wish to have students take a few minutes to read each paragraph silently before going over it orally in class.

Step 2 Since this reading is rather long, you may wish to go over only certain sections orally and have students read the other parts silently.

Step 3 Call on a more able student to give a synopsis of each paragraph. This helps less able students understand the selection.

The following are some suggestions for presenting each section:

Section 1 Tell students to look for the following information as they read:

A. some personal characteristics of the young sailor

B. why this young man has some enemies who conspire against him

Section 2 Tell students to pay particular attention to three things Dantès and his new friend talk about.

Ask students whom each sentence describes, Dantès or Faria:

C'est un abbé.
Il est jeune.
Il a à peu près 60 ans.
Il est marseillais, c'est-à-dire, de Marseille.
Il est italien.
Il est en mauvaise santé.
Il sait où il y a un trésor.

INTRODUCTION Il y a deux Alexandre Dumas—Dumas père et Dumas fils. Les deux sont écrivains. Le père est connu surtout pour ses romans[1] d'aventures et le fils est connu surtout pour ses pièces de théâtre.

Alexandre Dumas (1802–1870) père est né à Villers-Cotterêts dans le nord de la France. Son père est général dans l'armée française et sa mère est de Saint-Domingue dans la mer des Caraïbes. Alexandre Dumas a écrit des centaines[2] de romans. Ses romans ont procuré du plaisir à des lecteurs[3] innombrables dans le monde entier. *Le Comte de Monte-Cristo* est un de ces romans.

[1] romans *novels* [2] centaines *hundreds* [3] lecteurs *readers*

Le Comte de Monte-Cristo

1

1815: Edmond Dantès est un jeune marin marseillais. Dantès est un jeune homme honnête et courageux. Il n'est pas riche, mais il est heureux°. Il a une fiancée, Mercédès. Il travaille pour M. Morrel, un homme bon et juste qui le traite comme son fils.

heureux *happy*

Mais il y a trois hommes qui n'aiment pas le jeune marin. Ces trois hommes, Fernand Mondego, Danglars et Villefort sont des ennemis dangereux. Fernand est jaloux de Dantès parce qu'il aime Mercédès. Danglars travaille aussi pour M. Morrel. Mais Danglars falsifie les comptes° de M. Morrel et Dantès le sait. Donc Danglars veut éliminer Dantès. Villefort lui aussi veut éliminer Dantès pour des raisons politiques. Les trois hommes conspirent contre Dantès. Ils l'accusent de comploter° contre le roi° et d'être pour le retour de Napoléon sur le trône. Leur accusation est totalement fausse. Le jeune Dantès est innocent, mais il est tout de même arrêté parce que ses ennemis—et Villefort en particulier—ont beaucoup d'influence. Il est arrêté pendant une fête en l'honneur de ses fiançailles avec Mercédès. Sans explication, on l'emmène en prison sur l'île du château d'If tout près de Marseille. Là on l'enferme dans une petite cellule froide et sombre. Le pauvre Dantès ne comprend pas. Il est désespéré. Il frappe contre la porte. «Pourquoi suis-je en prison?» crie-t-il. Mais il n'y a pas de réponse. Personne ne l'entend. Chaque jour, Dantès attend sa liberté, mais en vain. Le temps passe. Pendant quatre ans, Dantès reste seul dans sa cellule.

comptes *accounts*

comploter *conspiring*

contre le roi *against the king*

Dantès en prison

Château d'If

2

Un jour, il entend un bruit° de l'autre côté du mur de sa cellule. C'est un autre prisonnier qui creuse un tunnel. Cet homme arrive à faire un trou dans le mur de la cellule de Dantès et à entrer dans sa cellule. Les deux hommes sont fous° de joie. Le nouvel ami de Dantès est un abbé°, l'abbé Faria. L'abbé Faria est un intellectuel italien d'environ soixante ans. Il raconte à Dantès ses occupations en Italie et Dantès lui raconte ses voyages. Les deux amis font le projet° de s'évader de prison. Mais l'abbé n'est pas en bonne santé. Il sait qu'il ne va pas avoir la force de s'évader avec Dantès. Il lui révèle alors l'existence d'un trésor fabuleux caché° sur une petite île de la mer Méditerranée. Cette île s'appelle l'île de Monte-Cristo. Il donne un document à Dantès qui explique comment trouver le trésor.

bruit *noise*
fous *crazy*
abbé *abbot*
projet *plan*
caché *hidden*

3

Peu de temps après les gardiens de la prison trouvent l'abbé Faria mort° dans sa cellule. Ils mettent son corps dans un sac. Il vont le jeter à la mer. Mais pendant la nuit, Dantès prend la place de Faria et se met dans le sac. Les gardiens jettent le sac à la mer et Dantès est libre! Il ouvre le sac et commence à nager. Il nage longtemps dans une mer très agitée. Finalement, il est recueilli° par un bateau. Il est sauvé!

Maintenant Dantès est un homme libre! Il part à la recherche du trésor. Après de nombreuses aventures, il arrive enfin sur l'île de Monte-Cristo. Il a quelques difficultés à trouver le trésor qui est bien caché. Finalement il découvre dans une grotte un coffre avec de l'or et des pierres précieuses—des diamants, des rubis et des perles de toute beauté. Edmond Dantès est très riche! Il change de nom. Il prend le nom de l'île où il a trouvé le trésor. Le comte de Monte-Cristo est né.

mort *dead*
recueilli *picked up*

Ils jettent le sac à la mer.

Section 3 You may wish to ask the following questions concerning this section to help students figure out how Dantès gets in the sack.

Qui est mort dans sa cellule?
Qui le trouve?
Ils mettent son corps où?
Ils vont jeter le sac où?
Ils le jettent à la mer immédiatement?
Ils laissent le sac dans la cellule?
Pendant la nuit, qui se met dans le sac?
Quand les gardiens jettent le sac à la mer, qui est dans le sac?
Qui est libre?

Section 4 Have students recall or look up the names of Dantès' three enemies in Section 1.

About the French Language

You may wish to explain to students that when conversation is interspersed with the paragraph, the speaker and verb are inverted.

_______, **crie-t-il.**
_______, **dit-elle.**
_______, **répondent-ils.**

4

Le Comte de Monte-Cristo va à Paris où il achète une maison splendide. Il voyage à Rome et en Grèce. Il est invité à toutes les fêtes. Il devient° vite célèbre. Tout le monde veut faire la connaissance de cet homme mystérieux et fabuleusement riche. Mais le Comte de Monte-Cristo n'a qu'une° idée. Il veut se venger°. Il retrouve Fernand qui s'est marié avec Mercédès. Fernand est devenu très riche, lui aussi. Il a pris le nom de Comte de Morcerf. Il retrouve Danglars et Villefort. Évidemment personne ne le reconnaît. Un à un, le comte de Monte-Cristo se venge de ses ennemis. Mercédès quitte Fernand et va dans un couvent. Fernand meurt°. Danglars est ruiné et Villefort devient fou°. Mais la vengeance ne satisfait pas le comte de Monte-Cristo. Il ne se sent pas libre. Au contraire, il se sent angoissé et plein de doutes. Il décide de tout abandonner. Il laisse sa fortune à Maximilien Morrel, le fils de son ancien patron°. Puis il s'embarque sur un bateau pour une destination inconnue en compagnie d'Haydée, une très belle jeune fille.

devient *becomes*
n'a qu'une *has only one*
se venger *to get revenge*
meurt *dies*
devient fou *goes crazy*
ancien patron *former boss*

Château d'If

Après la lecture

A **Edmond Dantès** Vrai ou faux?

1. Edmond Dantès est un jeune soldat parisien.
2. Il est très riche.
3. Il va se marier avec sa fiancée Mercédès.
4. Il n'a pas d'ennemis.
5. Il y a des hommes qui sont jaloux de Dantès.
6. Ils l'accusent d'un crime.
7. Dantès n'est pas un criminel.
8. Les gardiens savent qu'ils libèrent Dantès.
9. Dantès reste longtemps en prison.

Answers to Après la lecture

A

1. faux
2. faux
3. vrai
4. faux
5. vrai
6. vrai
7. vrai
8. faux
9. vrai

B En prison Répondez.

1. Un jour, qu'est-ce que Dantès entend?
2. Quel est ce bruit?
3. Qui est le nouvel ami de Dantès?
4. Quel projet font les deux amis?
5. Qui est malade?
6. Qu'est-ce que l'abbé révèle à Dantès?
7. Où est caché le trésor?
8. Qu'est-ce que le document de l'abbé Faria explique?

C Des années ont passé. Choisissez.

1. Les gardiens trouvent ____ mort.
   a. Dantès b. l'abbé Faria c. M. Morrel
2. Ils le trouvent dans ____.
   a. un tunnel b. un trou c. sa cellule
3. Les gardiens mettent ____ dans un sac.
   a. le document b. l'abbé Faria c. Dantès
4. Les gardiens jettent le sac ____.
   a. dans le tunnel b. à la mer c. dans une grotte
5. Dantès est sauvé par ____.
   a. un homme libre b. un bateau c. une île
6. Quand Dantès arrive sur l'île de Monte-Cristo, il cherche ____.
   a. l'abbé Faria b. le trésor c. le document
7. Il découvre le trésor ____.
   a. dans la mer b. dans le bateau c. dans une grotte
8. Des diamants et des rubis sont ____.
   a. de l'or b. des perles c. des pierres précieuses

Une cellule au château d'If

D À Paris

1. Décrivez tout ce que Dantès fait à Paris.
2. Comparez la vie d'Edmond Dantès et la vie du Comte de Monte-Cristo.

Answers to Après la lecture

B

1. Un jour, Dantès entend un bruit de l'autre côté du mur.
2. C'est un autre prisonnier qui creuse un tunnel.
3. Le nouvel ami de Dantès est l'abbé Faria.
4. Les deux amis font le projet de s'évader de prison.
5. L'abbé est malade.
6. L'abbé révèle l'existence d'un trésor.
7. Le trésor est caché sur une petite île de la mer Méditerranée.
8. Le document de l'abbé explique comment trouver le trésor.

C

1. b
2. c
3. b
4. b
5. b
6. b
7. c
8. c

D *Answers will vary but may include:*

1. Il achète une maison splendide, il voyage, il va à des fêtes, il devient célèbre.
2. Edmond Dantès travaille beaucoup mais il est pauvre. Il est honnête et courageux. Il est heureux.
   Le Comte de Monte-Cristo est riche et célèbre, mais il n'est pas heureux. Il veut se venger.

Handbook

InfoGap Activities H2
These communicative activities review and reinforce the vocabulary and structure just learned

Study Tips H51
These helpful study hints aid in the learning of new material

Verb Charts H68
French-English Dictionary H72
English-French Dictionary H96
Index H120

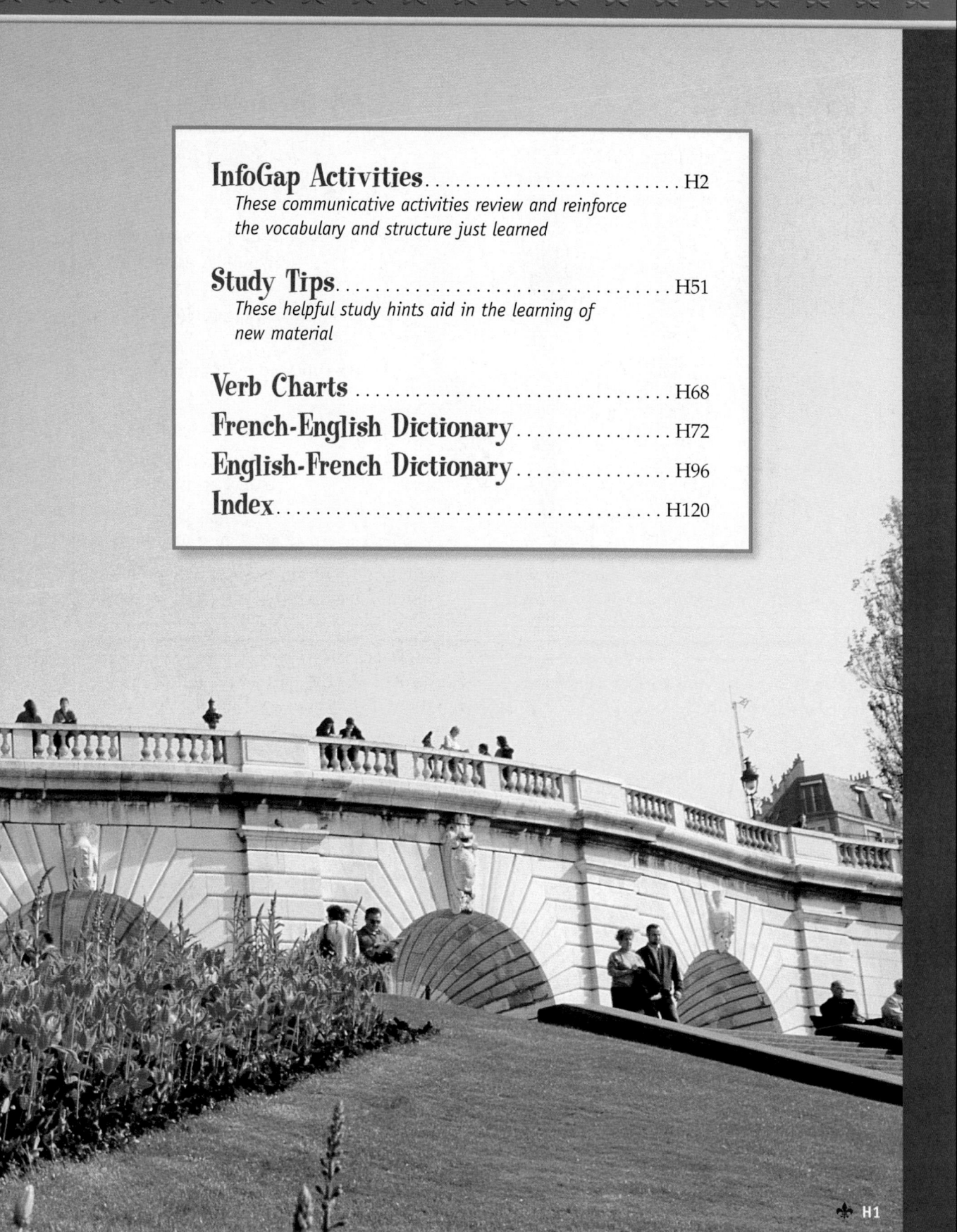

Activity 1

CHAPITRE 1, Mots 1, pages 18–19

Élève A Ask your partner the following questions. Correct answers are in parentheses.

1. Comment est Sophie, petite ou grande?
   (Sophie est petite.)
2. Comment est Sylvie?
   (Elle est grande.)
3. Il est d'où, Olivier?
   (Il est de Nice.)
4. Luc est américain ou français?
   (Il est français.)
5. Comment est Olivier, brun ou blond?
   (Il est brun.)
6. Qui est de Montréal?
   (Sylvie est de Montréal.)

Élève A Answer your partner's questions based on the pictures below.

Sophie / Paris

Sylvie / Montréal

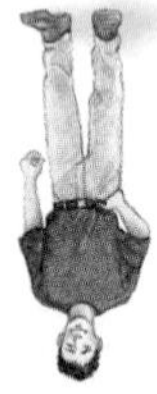
Olivier / Nice

Luc / Lyon

Élève B Answer your partner's questions based on the pictures below.

Sophie / Paris

Sylvie / Montréal

Olivier / Nice

Luc / Lyon

Élève B Ask your partner the following questions. Correct answers are in parentheses.

1. Comment est Olivier, petit ou grand?
   (Olivier est petit.)
2. Comment est Luc?
   (Luc est grand.)
3. Elle est d'où, Sophie?
   (Elle est de Paris.)
4. Qui est de Lyon?
   (Luc est de Lyon.)
5. Sophie est française ou américaine?
   (Elle est française.)
6. Comment est Luc, brun ou blond?
   (Il est blond.)

Activity 2

CHAPITRE 1, Mots 2, pages 22–23

Élève A Ask your partner the following questions. Correct answers are in parentheses.

1. Qui est Luc?
   (Luc est le frère de Nathalie.)
2. Qui est Philippe?
   (Philippe est l'ami de Nathalie.)
3. Carol est élève dans une école américaine?
   (Oui, Carol est élève dans une école américaine.)
4. Bruno est élève dans un collège français?
   (Oui, Bruno est élève dans un collège français.)

Élève A Answer your partner's questions based on the pictures below.

Nathalie et Luc Simonet

Nathalie Simonet et Philippe Latour

Carol Smith

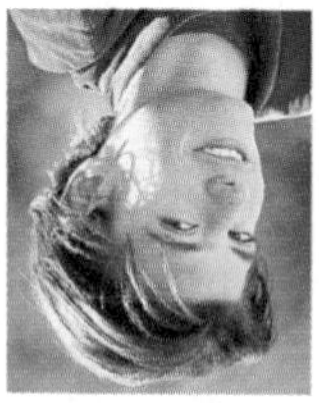
Bruno Lapierre

Élève B Answer your partner's questions based on the pictures below.

Nathalie et Luc Simonet

Nathalie Simonet et Philippe Latour

Carol Smith

Bruno Lapierre

Élève B Ask your partner the following questions. Correct answers are in parentheses.

1. Qui est Nathalie?
   (Nathalie est la sœur de Luc.)
2. Nathalie est sympathique?
   (Oui, Nathalie est très sympathique.)
3. Carol est américaine?
   (Oui, Carol est américaine.)
4. Bruno est français?
   (Oui, Bruno est français.)

Activity 3

CHAPITRE 1, Structure, pages 26–33

Élève A Read your partner the following false statements. Correct answers are in parentheses.

1. Meg Ryan est brune.
   (Non, elle n'est pas brune. Elle est blonde.)
2. Charles de Gaulle est américain.
   (Non, il n'est pas américain. Il est français.)
3. Oprah Winfrey est timide.
   (Non, elle n'est pas timide. Elle est sociable.)
4. Napoléon est très grand.
   (Non, il n'est pas très grand. Il est assez petit.)

Élève A Correct your partner's statements based on the pictures below.

Meg Ryan

Charles de Gaulle

Oprah Winfrey

Napoléon Bonaparte

Élève B Correct your partner's statements based on the pictures below.

Meg Ryan

Charles de Gaulle

Oprah Winfrey

Napoléon Bonaparte

Élève B Read your partner the following false statements. Correct answers are in parentheses.

1. Meg Ryan est timide.
   (Non, elle n'est pas timide. Elle est dynamique.)
2. Charles de Gaulle est petit.
   (Non, il n'est pas petit. Il est grand.)
3. Oprah Winfrey est française.
   (Non, elle n'est pas française. Elle est américaine.)
4. Napoléon est américain.
   (Non, il n'est pas américain. Il est français.)

Activity 4

CHAPITRE 2, Mots 1, pages 50–51

Élève A Ask your partner the following questions. Correct answers are in parentheses.

1. Le cours de français est facile?
   (Oui, le cours de français est facile.)
2. Le prof est très sympathique?
   (Oui, le prof est très sympathique.)
3. Les élèves sont françaises ou américaines?
   (Les élèves sont françaises.)
4. Les élèves sont amies?
   (Oui, les élèves sont amies.)

Élève A Answer your partner's questions based on the picture below.

Élève B Answer your partner's questions based on the picture below.

Élève B Ask your partner the following questions. Correct answers are in parentheses.

1. Les élèves sont dans le même lycée?
   (Oui, les élèves sont dans le même lycée.)
2. Les élèves sont dans la salle de classe?
   (Oui, les élèves sont dans la salle de classe.)
3. Les élèves sont sympathiques?
   (Oui, les élèves sont sympathiques.)
4. Le cours de français est difficile?
   (Non, le cours de français n'est pas difficile.) or *(Non, le cours de français est facile.)*

Activity 5

CHAPITRE 2, Mots 2, pages 54–55

Élève A Ask your partner the following questions. Correct answers are in parentheses.

1. Guy est fort en mathématiques?
   (Oui, il est fort en mathématiques.)
2. Guy est très fort en sciences naturelles?
   (Non, il n'est pas fort en sciences naturelles.) or *(Non, il est mauvais en sciences naturelles.)*
3. Il est mauvais en géométrie?
   (Non, il n'est pas mauvais en géométrie.) or *(Non, il est fort en géométrie.)*
4. L'économie est une science naturelle?
   (Non, l'économie n'est pas une science naturelle.) or *(Non, l'économie est une science sociale.)*

Élève A Answer your partner's questions based on the report card below.

Marie Dauphin

Les langues:	
Le français	A−
L'anglais	B+
Les sciences sociales:	
L'histoire	D
La géographie	C+
D'autres matières:	
La musique	A

Élève B Answer your partner's questions based on the report card below.

Guy Laurent

Les sciences naturelles:	
La biologie	C−
La chimie	D
Les mathématiques:	
La géométrie	A
Le calcul	B+
Les sciences sociales:	
L'économie	B

Élève B Ask your partner the following questions. Correct answers are in parentheses.

1. Marie est très forte en sciences sociales?
   (Non, elle est mauvaise en sciences sociales.) or *(Elle n'est pas forte en sciences sociales.)*
2. Le cours de français est très difficile?
   (Non, le cours de français est très facile.) or *(Non, le cours de français n'est pas difficile.)*
3. Marie est mauvaise en histoire?
   (Oui, Marie est mauvaise en histoire.)
4. L'anglais est une science sociale?
   (Non, l'anglais est une langue.) or *(Non, l'anglais n'est pas une science sociale.)*

Activity 6

CHAPITRE 2, Structure, pages 60–63

Élève A Answer your partner's questions in complete sentences, using either **Oui** or **Non.**

Élève A Ask your partner the following questions. Correct answers are in parentheses.

1. La salle de classe est petite?
   (Oui, la salle de classe est petite.) or *(Non, la salle de classe n'est pas petite.)*
2. Les élèves sont intelligents?
   (Oui, les élèves sont intelligents.) or *(Non, les élèves ne sont pas intelligents.)*
3. Le lycée est grand?
   (Oui, le lycée est grand.) or *(Non, le lycée n'est pas grand.)*
4. Vous deux, vous êtes élèves dans un lycée français?
   (Oui, nous sommes élèves dans un lycée français.) or *(Non, nous ne sommes pas élèves dans un lycée français.)*
5. Tu es fort(e) en maths?
   (Oui, je suis fort[e] en maths.) or *(Non, je ne suis pas fort[e] en maths.)*

Élève B Answer your partner's questions in complete sentences, using either **Oui** or **Non.**

Élève B Ask your partner the following questions. Correct answers are in parentheses.

1. La prof est patiente?
   (Oui, la prof est patiente.) or *(Non, la prof n'est pas patiente.)*
2. Les élèves sont sympas?
   (Oui, les élèves sont sympas.) or *(Non, les élèves ne sont pas sympas.)*
3. Le prof est intéressant?
   (Oui, le prof est intéressant.) or *(Non, le prof n'est pas intéressant.)*
4. Vous êtes copains?
   (Oui, nous sommes copains.) or *(Non, nous ne sommes pas copains.)*
5. Tu es fort(e) en histoire?
   (Oui, je suis fort[e] en histoire.) or *(Non, je ne suis pas fort[e] en histoire.)*

Activity 7

CHAPITRE 3, Mots 1, pages 82–83

Élève A Ask your partner the following questions. Correct answers are in parentheses.

1. Les élèves sont où?
   (*Les élèves sont dans la cour.*)
2. Ils parlent entre les cours?
   (*Oui, ils parlent entre les cours.*)
3. Ils étudient dans la cour?
   (*Non, ils n'étudient pas dans la cour.*)
4. Les copains rigolent?
   (*Oui, ils rigolent.*)

Élève A Answer your partner's questions based on the picture below.

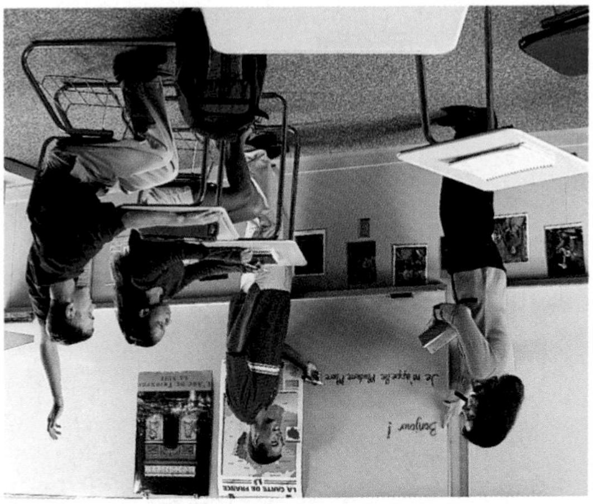

Élève B Answer your partner's questions based on the picture below.

Élève B Ask your partner the following questions. Correct answers are in parentheses.

1. Les élèves passent la journée à l'école?
   (*Oui, ils passent la journée à l'école.*)
2. Ils regardent la prof?
   (*Oui, ils regardent la prof.*)
3. Un élève pose une question?
   (*Oui, il pose une question.*)
4. Les élèves déjeunent pendant le cours?
   (*Non, ils ne déjeunent pas pendant le cours.*)

Activity 8

CHAPITRE 3, Mots 2, pages 86–87

Élève A Ask your partner the following questions. Correct answers are in parentheses.

1. Camille est à la papeterie?
   (Oui, elle est à la papeterie.)
2. Elle achète des fournitures scolaires?
   (Oui, elle achète des fournitures scolaires.)
3. Elle achète un classeur et une calculatrice?
   (Oui, elle achète un classeur et une calculatrice.)
4. Elle paie où?
   (Elle paie à la caisse.)

Élève A Answer your partner's questions based on the picture below.

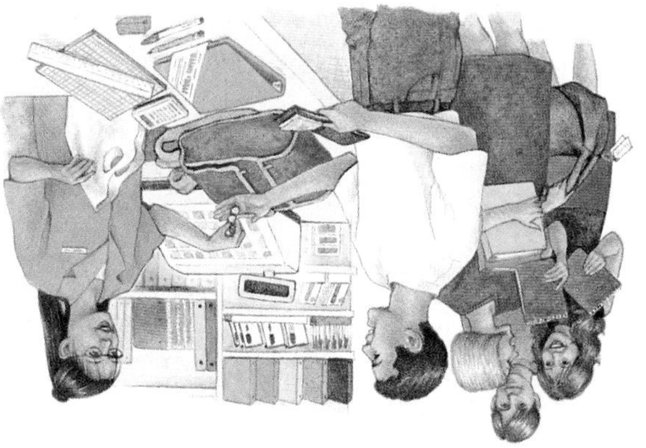

Marc Sophie

Élève B Answer your partner's questions based on the picture below.

Camille

Élève B Ask your partner the following questions. Correct answers are in parentheses.

1. Sophie travaille après les cours?
   (Oui, elle travaille après les cours.)
2. Elle travaille où?
   (Elle travaille dans une papeterie.)
3. Marc achète un sac à dos?
   (Oui, il achète un sac à dos.)
4. Il achète un classeur?
   (Oui, il achète un classeur.)

Activity 9

CHAPITRE 3, Structure, pages 90–93

Élève A Answer your partner's questions using the correct form of the verb below.

1. arriver
2. poser
3. rigoler
4. parler
5. travailler

Élève A Ask your partner the following questions. Possible responses are in parentheses.

1. Tu quittes la maison à quelle heure le matin?
   (Je quitte la maison à sept heures et demie.)
2. Qui écoute quand le prof parle?
   (Les élèves écoutent quand le prof parle.)
3. On parle français en Belgique?
   (Oui, on parle français en Belgique.)
4. Vous étudiez quelle langue?
   (Nous étudions le français.)
5. Vous détestez les examens?
   (Oui, nous détestons les examens.) or
   (Non, nous ne détestons pas les examens.)

Élève B Answer your partner's questions using the correct form of the verb below.

1. quitter
2. écouter
3. parler
4. étudier
5. détester

Élève B Ask your partner the following questions. Possible responses are in parentheses.

1. On arrive à l'école à quelle heure?
   (On arrive à l'école à huit heures.)
2. Qui pose des questions?
   (Les élèves posent des questions.) or
   (Le prof pose des questions.)
3. Vous rigolez dans la cour?
   (Oui, nous rigolons dans la cour.) or
   (Non, nous ne rigolons pas dans la cour.)
4. Tu parles beaucoup au téléphone?
   (Oui, je parle beaucoup au téléphone.) or
   (Non, je ne parle pas beaucoup au téléphone.)
5. Tu travailles après les cours?
   (Oui, je travaille après les cours.) or
   (Non, je ne travaille pas après les cours.)

Activity 10

CHAPITRE 4, Mots 1, pages 112–113

Élève A Read your partner the following statements. He or she will fill in the blank. Correct answers are in parentheses.

1. Le frère de mon père est mon ______.
   (oncle)
2. La mère de mon cousin est ma ______.
   (tante)
3. Le mari de ma mère est mon ______.
   (père)
4. La mère de mon père est ma ______.
   (grand-mère)
5. Le fils de ma tante est mon ______.
   (cousin)

Élève A Complete your partner's statements with the name of the relative.

Élève B Complete your partner's statements with the name of the relative.

Élève B Read your partner the following statements. He or she will fill in the blank. Correct answers are in parentheses.

1. La sœur de ma mère est ma ______.
   (tante)
2. La femme de mon père est ma ______.
   (mère)
3. La fille de mes parents est ma ______.
   (sœur)
4. Les parents de ma mère sont mes ______.
   (grands-parents)
5. Les enfants de mon oncle sont mes ______.
   (cousins)

Activity 11

CHAPITRE 4, Mots 2, pages 116–117

Élève A Ask your partner the following questions. Correct answers are in parentheses.

1. On regarde la télé dans la salle de bains ou la salle de séjour?
   (On regarde la télé dans la salle de séjour.)
2. On dîne dans la chambre à coucher ou la salle à manger?
   (On dîne dans la salle à manger.)
3. Le balcon donne sur la cour ou sur la cuisine?
   (Le balcon donne sur la cour.)
4. On habite au troisième étage d'un immeuble ou d'une maison?
   (On habite au troisième étage d'un immeuble.)
5. La voiture est dans la cuisine ou le garage?
   (La voiture est dans le garage.)

Élève A Now answer your partner's questions.

Élève B Answer your partner's questions.

Élève B Ask your partner the following questions. Correct answers are in parentheses.

1. On parle avec les voisins dans la cour ou la salle de bains?
   (On parle avec les voisins dans la cour.)
2. On prépare le dîner dans l'ascenseur ou la cuisine?
   (On prépare le dîner dans la cuisine.)
3. On monte à l'appartement dans le métro ou l'ascenseur?
   (On monte à l'appartement dans l'ascenseur.)
4. Les toilettes sont dans l'appartement ou dans la cour?
   (Les toilettes sont dans l'appartement.)
5. On habite dans un quartier ou dans une entrée?
   (On habite dans un quartier.)

Activity 12

CHAPITRE 4, Structure, pages 120–125

Élève A Ask your partner the following questions. Correct answers are in parentheses.

1. Marc a quel âge?
   (Il a quinze ans.)
2. Tes grands-parents ont une maison?
   (Non, ils ont un joli appartement.)
3. Tu as quel âge, toi?
   (J'ai ——— ans.)
4. Qui a deux chiens?
   (La prof de maths a deux chiens.)
5. Quel âge ont tes grands-parents?
   (Ils ont quatre-vingts ans.)

Élève A Use the chart below to answer your partner's questions. Reminder: **toi** is you.

Paul	15 ans	Une sœur
Tes grands-parents	75 ans	Un chien
Toi	?	Des profs intéressants
Tes cousines	16 ans	Deux chats
Marie	14	Une petite famille

Élève B Use the chart below to answer your partner's questions. Reminder: **toi** is you.

Marc	15 ans	Une sœur
Tes grands-parents	80 ans	Un joli appartement
Toi	?	Des profs intéressants
La prof de maths	35	Deux chiens
Sophie	14	Une petite famille

Élève B Ask your partner the following questions. Correct answers are in parentheses.

1. Qui a des profs intéressants?
   (Moi, j'ai des profs intéressants.)
2. Tes cousines ont combien de chats?
   (Mes cousines ont deux chats.)
3. Tes grands-parents ont quel âge?
   (Mes grands-parents ont soixante-quinze ans.)
4. Qui a une petite famille?
   (Marie a une petite famille.)
5. Paul a un frère ou une sœur?
   (Paul a une sœur.)

Activity 13

CHAPITRE 5, Mots 1, pages 154–155

Élève A You are the server in a French café. Ask your partner what he or she wants to order. Correct answers are in parentheses.

1. Vous désirez?
   (Un citron pressé, s'il vous plaît.)
2. Vous désirez?
   (Un croissant, s'il vous plaît.)
3. Vous désirez?
   (Une salade verte, s'il vous plaît.)
4. Vous désirez?
   (Un café, s'il vous plaît.) or *(Un express, s'il vous plaît.)*
5. Vous désirez?
   (Une tartine de pain beurré, s'il vous plaît.)

Élève A Now your partner is the server. Use the following picture menu to give your order.

1. 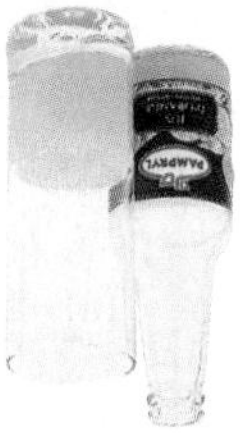

2. 

3. 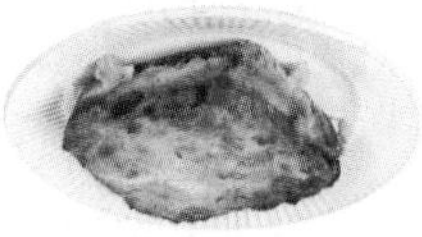

4. 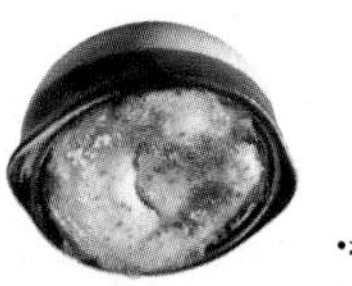

5. 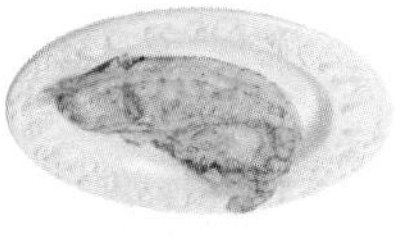

Élève B Your partner is the server in a French café. Use the following picture menu to give your order.

1. 

2. 

3. 

4. 

5. 

Élève B Now you are the server. Ask your partner what he or she wants to order. Correct answers are in parentheses.

1. Vous désirez?
   (Un jus d'orange, s'il vous plaît.)
2. Vous désirez?
   (Une saucisse de Francfort, s'il vous plaît.) or *(Un hot-dog, s'il vous plaît.)*
3. Vous désirez?
   (Un croque-monsieur, s'il vous plaît.)
4. Vous désirez?
   (Une soupe à l'oignon, s'il vous plaît.)
5. Vous désirez?
   (Une omelette nature, s'il vous plaît.)

Activity 14

CHAPITRE 5, Mots 2, pages 158–159

Élève A Ask your partner the following questions. Correct answers are in parentheses.

1. Un couteau, c'est pour la soupe?
   (Non, une cuillère, c'est pour la soupe.)
2. Un verre, c'est pour le café?
   (Non, une tasse, c'est pour le café.)
3. Une soupe à l'oignon, c'est pour le dessert?
   (Non, une glace au chocolat, c'est pour le dessert.)
4. Un couteau, c'est pour le steak?
   (Oui, un couteau, c'est pour le steak.)
5. Un verre, c'est pour la limonade?
   (Oui, un verre, c'est pour la limonade.)

Élève A Use the pictures below to answer your partner's questions.

1. 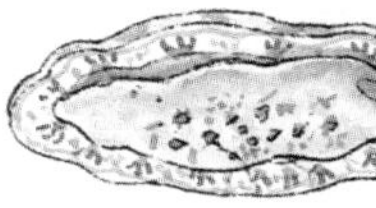
2. 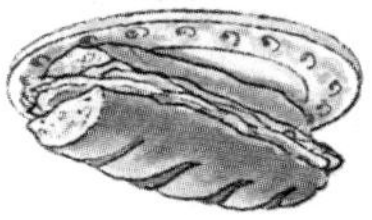
3. 
4. 
5. 

Élève B Use the pictures below to answer your partner's questions.

1. 
2. 
3. 
4. 
5. 

Élève B Now ask your partner the following questions. Correct answers are in parentheses.

1. On prend un croissant pour le dîner?
   (Non, on prend une omelette pour le dîner.)
2. On prend une crêpe pour le déjeuner?
   (Non, on prend un sandwich au jambon pour le déjeuner.)
3. C'est un pourboire ou une fourchette?
   (C'est un pourboire.)
4. C'est un steak saignant ou bien cuit?
   (C'est un steak bien cuit.)
5. C'est une assiette ou une serviette?
   (C'est une serviette.)

Activity 15

CHAPITRE 5, Structure, pages 162–169

Élève A Ask your partner the following questions. Correct answers are in parentheses.

1. Les copains vont où?
   (Ils vont à l'école.)
2. Ils y vont comment?
   (Ils y vont en voiture.)
3. Tu vas où?
   (Je vais à la papeterie.)
4. Tu y vas à pied?
   (Non, j'y vais en bus.)

Élève A Answer your partner's questions based on the cues below.

1. l'école
2. à pied
3. le café
4. le métro

Élève B Answer your partner's questions based on the cues below.

1. l'école
2. en voiture
3. la papeterie
4. en bus

Élève B Ask your partner the following questions. Correct answers are in parentheses.

1. Vous allez où?
   (Nous allons à l'école.)
2. Vous y allez comment?
   (Nous y allons à pied.)
3. Tu vas où?
   (Je vais au café.)
4. Tu prends le bus pour aller au café?
   (Non, je prends le métro.)

Activity 16

CHAPITRE 6, Mots 1, pages 186–187

Élève A Ask your partner the following questions. Correct answers are in parentheses.

1. Pour acheter du pain, on va où?
   (On va à la boulangerie-pâtisserie.)
2. Pour acheter du lait, on va où?
   (On va à la crémerie.)
3. Pour acheter une tarte aux pommes, on va où?
   (On va à la boulangerie-pâtisserie.)
4. Pour acheter du jambon, on va où?
   (On va à la charcuterie.)
5. Pour acheter de la crème, on va où?
   (On va à la crémerie.)

Élève A Use the following pictures to answer your partner's questions.

Élève B Ask your partner the following questions. Correct answers are in parentheses.

1. Pour acheter de la viande, on va où?
   (On va à la boucherie.)
2. Pour acheter du poisson, on va où?
   (On va à la poissonnerie.)
3. Pour acheter du poivre, on va où?
   (On va à l'épicerie.)
4. Pour acheter du porc, on va où?
   (On va à la boucherie.)
5. Pour acheter des crevettes, on va où?
   (On va à la poissonnerie.)

Élève B Answer your partner's questions based on the pictures below.

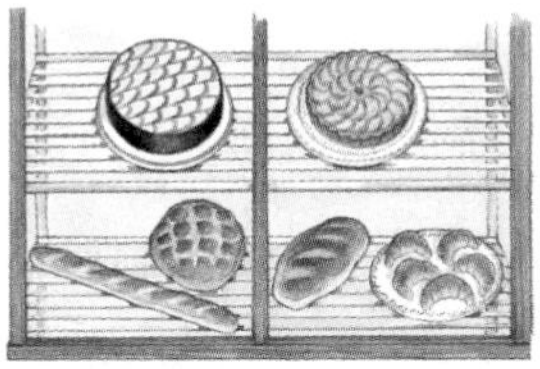

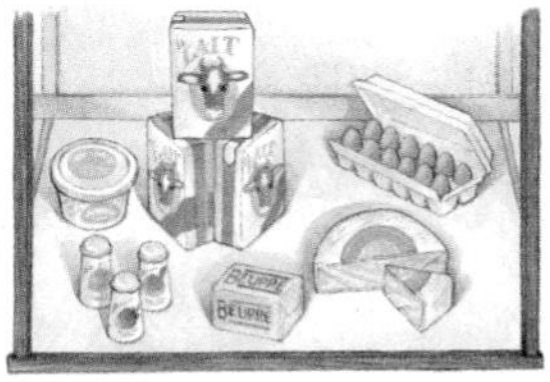

Activity 17

CHAPITRE 6, Mots 2, pages 190–191

Élève A You play the part of the vendor. Ask your partner the following questions. Correct answers are in parentheses.

1. Vous voulez de la confiture?
   (Oui, je voudrais un pot de confiture, s'il vous plaît.)
2. Vous voulez des légumes surgelés?
   (Oui, je voudrais un paquet de légumes surgelés, s'il vous plaît.)
3. Vous voulez des petits pois?
   (Oui, je voudrais une boîte de petits pois, s'il vous plaît.)
4. Vous voulez du lait?
   (Oui, je voudrais un litre de lait, s'il vous plaît.)
5. Vous voulez du jambon?
   (Oui, je voudrais une tranche de jambon, s'il vous plaît.)

Élève A Answer your partner's questions based on the information below.

un pot

250 grammes

une douzaine

une boîte

une bouteille

Élève B Answer your partner's questions based on the information below.

un pot

un paquet

une boîte

un litre

une tranche

Élève B Now you are the vendor. Ask your partner the following questions. Correct answers are in parentheses.

1. Vous voulez de la moutarde?
   (Oui, je voudrais un pot de moutarde, s'il vous plaît.)
2. Vous voulez du beurre?
   (Oui, je voudrais deux cent cinquante grammes de beurre, s'il vous plaît.)
3. Vous voulez des œufs?
   (Oui, je voudrais une douzaine d'œufs, s'il vous plaît.)
4. Vous voulez des petits pois?
   (Oui, je voudrais une boîte de petits pois, s'il vous plaît.)
5. Vous voulez de l'eau minérale?
   (Oui, je voudrais une bouteille d'eau minérale, s'il vous plaît.)

Activity 18

CHAPITRE 6, Structure, pages 194–195

Élève A Ask your partner the following questions. Correct answers are in parentheses.

1. Qui fait le déjeuner?
   (Moi, je fais le déjeuner.)
2. Qui fait du français?
   (Nous faisons du français.)
3. Qui fait des études?
   (Tu fais des études.)
4. Qui fait les exercices?
   (Alain et Eric font les exercices.)
5. Qui fait le gâteau?
   (Vous faites le gâteau.)

Élève A Use the information in the chart below to answer your partner's questions.

Qui?	**Activité**
Moi, je	(faire) les courses
Hugo et Marie	(faire) un pique-nique
Nous	(faire) de l'allemand
Vous	(faire) la cuisine
Tu	(faire) les devoirs

Élève B Use the information in the chart below to answer your partner's questions.

Qui?	**Activité**
Moi, je	(faire) le déjeuner
Nous	(faire) du français
Tu	(faire) des études
Alain et Eric	(faire) les exercices
Vous	(faire) le gâteau

Élève B Ask your partner the following questions. Correct answers are in parentheses.

1. Qui fait les courses?
   (Moi, je fais les courses.)
2. Qui fait un pique-nique?
   (Hugo et Marie font un pique-nique.)
3. Qui fait de l'allemand?
   (Nous faisons de l'allemand.)
4. Qui fait la cuisine?
   (Vous faites la cuisine.)
5. Qui fait les devoirs?
   (Tu fais les devoirs.)

Activity 19

CHAPITRE 6, Structure, pages 201–203

Élève A Ask your partner the following questions. Correct answers are in parentheses.

1. Qui veut aller au restaurant?
   (Moi, je veux aller au restaurant.)
2. Qui peut travailler après l'école?
   (Il peut travailler après l'école.)
3. Qui veut inviter des amis?
   (Tu veux inviter des amis.)
4. Qui veut manger maintenant?
   (Nous voulons manger maintenant.)
5. Qui peut regarder le film?
   (Vous pouvez regarder le film.)
6. Qui veut aller au marché?
   (Pierre veut aller au marché.)
7. Qui veut écouter des CD?
   (Eric et Michel veulent écouter des CD.)

Élève A Use the information in the chart below to answer your partner's questions.

Qui?	Activité
Moi, je	(pouvoir) regarder le film
Elle	(vouloir) aller au restaurant
Nous	(pouvoir) faire des sandwichs
Ils	(vouloir) écouter des CD
Tu	(pouvoir) manger maintenant
Alain	(pouvoir) aller au marché
Hugo et Marie	(pouvoir) inviter des amis

Élève B Use the information in the chart below to answer your partner's questions.

Qui?	Activité
Moi, je	(vouloir) aller au restaurant
Il	(pouvoir) travailler après l'école
Tu	(vouloir) inviter des amis
Nous	(vouloir) manger maintenant
Vous	(pouvoir) regarder le film
Pierre	(vouloir) aller au marché
Eric et Michel	(vouloir) écouter des CD

Élève B Ask your partner the following questions. Correct answers are in parentheses.

1. Qui peut regarder le film?
   (Moi, je peux regarder le film.)
2. Qui veut aller au restaurant?
   (Elle veut aller au restaurant.)
3. Qui peut faire des sandwichs?
   (Nous pouvons faire des sandwichs.)
4. Qui veut écouter des CD?
   (Ils veulent écouter des CD.)
5. Qui peut manger maintenant?
   (Tu peux manger maintenant.)
6. Qui peut aller au marché?
   (Alain peut aller au marché.)
7. Qui peut inviter des amis?
   (Hugo et Marie peuvent inviter des amis.)

Activity 20

CHAPITRE 7, Mots 1, pages 220–221

Élève A Ask your partner the following questions. Correct answers are in parentheses.

1. Marc porte un anorak?
   (Oui, il porte un anorak.)
2. Marc porte un blouson?
   (Non, il voit un blouson dans la vitrine.)
3. Marc porte un pull?
   (Oui, il porte un pull.)
4. Marc porte un t-shirt?
   (Non, il voit un t-shirt dans la vitrine.)
5. Marc porte une paire de chaussures?
   (Oui, il porte une paire de chaussures.)
6. Marc porte un survêtement?
   (Non, il voit un survêtement dans la vitrine.)

Élève A Use the information in the chart below to answer your partner's questions.

Elle porte...	Elle voit... dans la vitrine.
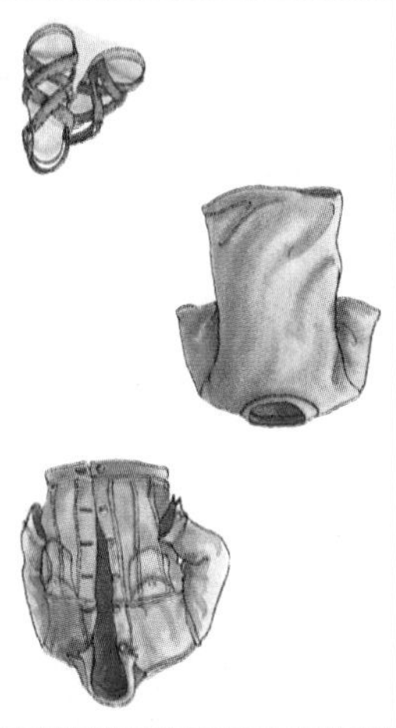	

Élève B Ask your partner the following questions. Correct answers are in parentheses.

1. Chloé porte des sandales?
   (Oui, elle porte des sandales.)
2. Chloé porte un anorak?
   (Non, elle voit un anorak dans la vitrine.)
3. Chloé porte un blouson?
   (Oui, elle porte un blouson.)
4. Chloé porte une paire de chaussures?
   (Non, elle voit une paire de chaussures dans la vitrine.)
5. Chloé porte un t-shirt?
   (Oui, elle porte un t-shirt.)
6. Chloé porte un manteau?
   (Non, elle voit un manteau dans la vitrine.)

Élève B Use the information in the chart below to answer your partner's questions.

Il porte...	Il voit... dans la vitrine.
	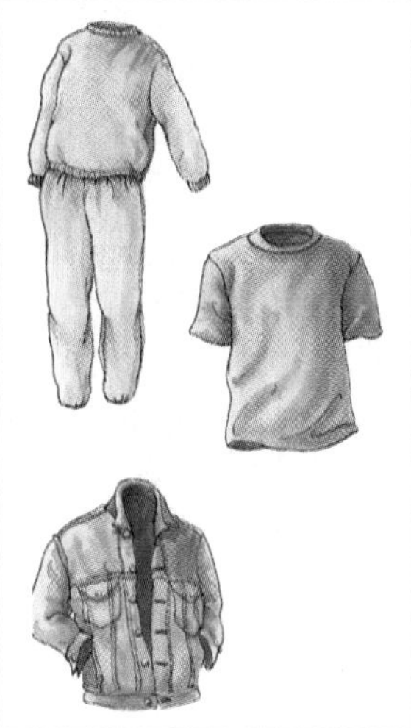

Activity 21

CHAPITRE 7, Mots 2, pages 224–225

Élève A Find out your partner's opinion of different clothing items. Correct answers are in parentheses.

1. Il est joli, le pull bleu. Tu ne trouves pas?
   (Non, il est trop serré.)
2. Il est joli, le manteau gris. Tu ne trouves pas?
   (Non, il est trop long.)
3. Il est joli, l'anorak rouge. Tu ne trouves pas?
   (Non, il est trop cher.)
4. Elle est jolie, la jupe verte. Tu ne trouves pas?
   (Non, elle est un peu courte.)
5. Elles sont jolies, les chaussures marron. Tu ne trouves pas?
   (Oui, c'est ma couleur favorite.)

Élève A Use the information below to answer your partner's questions.

trop grand

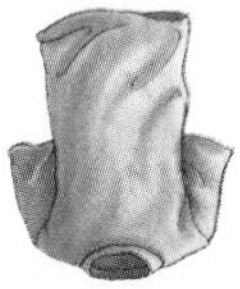

trop petit

trop chères

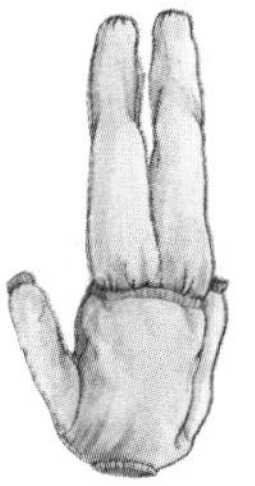

un peu large

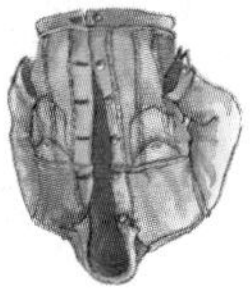

Oui, c'est ma couleur favorite.

Élève B Use the information below to answer your partner's questions.

trop serré

trop long

trop cher

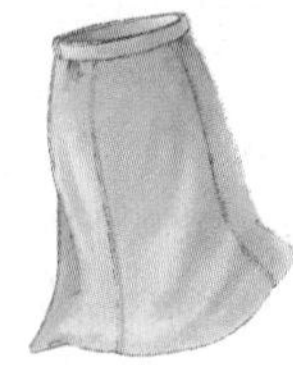

un peu courte

Oui, c'est ma couleur favorite.

Élève B Find out your partner's opinion of different clothing items. Correct answers are in parentheses.

1. Il est joli, le short vert. Tu ne trouves pas?
   (Non, il est trop grand.)
2. Il est joli, le t-shirt orange. Tu ne trouves pas?
   (Non, il est trop petit.)
3. Elles sont jolies, les sandales bleues. Tu ne trouves pas?
   (Non, elles sont trop chères.)
4. Il est joli, le survêtement jaune. Tu ne trouves pas?
   (Non, il est un peu large.)
5. Il est joli, le blouson bleu. Tu ne trouves pas?
   (Oui, c'est ma couleur favorite.)

Activity 22

CHAPITRE 7, Structure, pages 228–229

Élève A Ask your partner the following questions. Correct answers are in parentheses.

1. Qui met un short?
   (Moi, je mets un short pour faire du jogging.)
2. Qui met la radio le matin?
   (Mes copains mettent la radio le matin.)
3. Qui met une cravate?
   (Mon père met une cravate pour aller au travail.)
4. Qui met la table?
   (Vous mettez la table pour le dîner.)
5. Qui met un jean?
   (Tu mets un jean pour aller au cinéma.)
6. Qui met un complet?
   (Nous mettons un complet pour aller à un mariage.)

Élève A Use the information in the chart below to answer your partner's questions.

Qui?	Activité
Moi, je	(mettre) la télé le matin
Les serveurs	(mettre) la table au restaurant
Ma mère	(mettre) une jupe pour aller au marché
Nous	(mettre) des chaussettes rouges
Tu	(mettre) des baskets pour faire du jogging
Vous	(mettre) un pantalon pour aller à l'école

Élève B Use the information in the chart below to answer your partner's questions.

Qui?	Activité
Moi, je	(mettre) un short pour faire du jogging
Mes copains	(mettre) la radio le matin
Mon père	(mettre) une cravate pour aller au travail
Vous	(mettre) la table pour le dîner
Tu	(mettre) un jean pour aller au cinéma
Nous	(mettre) un complet pour aller à un mariage

Élève B Ask your partner the following questions. Correct answers are in parentheses.

1. Qui met la télé?
   (Moi, je mets la télé le matin.)
2. Qui met la table?
   (Les serveurs mettent la table au restaurant.)
3. Qui met une jupe?
   (Ma mère met une jupe pour aller au marché.)
4. Qui met des chaussettes rouges?
   (Nous mettons des chaussettes rouges.)
5. Qui met des baskets?
   (Tu mets des baskets pour faire du jogging.)
6. Qui met un pantalon?
   (Vous mettez un pantalon pour aller à l'école.)

Activity 23

CHAPITRE 7, Structure, pages 232–233

Élève A Your partner tells you what he or she thinks about articles of clothing. Use the chart below to give your partner the correct information. Begin your response with **Non, je vois que...**

confortables	les baskets + +		les chaussures + +
cher	l'anorak $ $ $	le blouson $	le manteau $ $ $ $ $ $

Élève A Read the statements about clothing to your partner. Your partner does not agree with what you believe to be true. Correct answers are in parentheses.

1. Moi, je crois que le polo est plus grand que le t-shirt.
   (Non, je vois que le t-shirt est plus grand que le polo.) or *(Non, je vois que le polo est plus petit que le t-shirt.)*
2. Moi, je crois que la chemise est plus grande que le polo.
   (Non, je vois que la chemise est aussi grande que le polo.)
3. Moi, je crois que la jupe plissée est moins élégante que le chemisier.
   (Non, je vois que la jupe plissée est aussi élégante que le chemisier.)

Élève B Your partner tells you what he or she thinks about articles of clothing. Use the chart below to give your partner the correct information. Begin your response with **Non, je vois que...**

grand(e)	le t-shirt + + + + +	la chemise + + +	le polo + + +
élégant(e)	la jupe plissée + +		le chemisier + +

Élève B Read the statements about clothing to your partner. Your partner does not agree with what you believe to be true. Correct answers are in parentheses.

1. Moi, je crois que les chaussures sont moins confortables que les baskets.
   (Non, je vois que les chaussures sont aussi confortables que les baskets.)
2. Moi, je crois que le blouson est aussi cher que l'anorak.
   (Non, je vois que le blouson est moins cher que l'anorak.) or *(Non, je vois que l'anorak est plus cher que le blouson.)*
3. Moi, je crois que l'anorak est plus cher que le manteau.
   (Non, je vois que le manteau est plus cher que l'anorak.) or *(Non, je vois que l'anorak est moins cher que le manteau.)*

Activity 24

CHAPITRE 8, Mots 1, pages 260–261

Élève A Make the following statements to your partner. He or she will add the location where the activity takes place. Correct answers are in parentheses.

1. Le passager vérifie la carte d'embarquement.
   (Le passager vérifie la carte d'embarquement à la porte d'embarquement.)
2. Le passager demande une place.
   (Le passager demande une place côté couloir.)
3. Le passager vérifie son billet.
   (Le passager vérifie son billet au comptoir de la compagnie aérienne.)
4. Le passager va passer par le contrôle de sécurité.
   (Le passager va passer par le contrôle de sécurité dans l'aérogare.)

Élève A Your partner will make a statement about an activity. Tell where each activity takes place according to the chart below.

Activité	Où
prendre un vol	à l'aéroport
vérifier l'heure du départ	sur l'écran
décoller	sur la piste
faire enregistrer ses bagages	au comptoir de la compagnie aérienne

Élève B Your partner will make a statement about an activity. Tell where each activity takes place according to the chart below.

Activité	Où
vérifier la carte d'embarquement	à la porte d'embarquement
demander une place	côté couloir
vérifier son billet	au comptoir de la compagnie aérienne
passer par le contrôle de sécurité	dans l'aérogare

Élève B Make the following statements to your partner. He or she will add the location where the activity takes place. Correct answers are in parentheses.

1. Le passager va prendre un vol.
   (Oui, le passager va prendre un vol à l'aéroport.)
2. Le passager vérifie l'heure du départ.
   (Oui, le passager vérifie l'heure du départ sur l'écran.)
3. L'avion décolle.
   (Oui, l'avion décolle sur la piste.)
4. Le passager fait enregistrer ses bagages.
   (Oui, le passager fait enregistrer ses bagages au comptoir de la compagnie aérienne.)

Activity 25

CHAPITRE 8, Mots 2, pages 264–265

Élève A Ask your partner the following questions. Correct answers are in parentheses.

1. Il faut attacher sa ceinture de sécurité quand?
   (avant le décollage)
2. Qui sert les boissons?
   (le steward)
3. On peut fumer quand?
   (après le vol)
4. On ramasse les plateaux quand?
   (après le repas)
5. Il faut un passeport quand?
   (pour un vol international)
6. Il faut mettre vos bagages à main où?
   (sous le siège devant vous)

Élève A Answer your partner's questions. Choose from the answers below.

1. avant le vol / après le vol
2. le passager / le pilote
3. avant le vol / pendant le vol
4. avant le décollage / pendant le décollage
5. dans la cabine / dans le coffre à bagages
6. le pilote / le passager

Élève B Answer your partner's questions. Choose from the answers below.

1. avant le décollage / après le décollage
2. le steward / le pilote
3. pendant le vol / après le vol
4. après le repas / pendant le repas
5. pour un vol intérieur / pour un vol international
6. sous le siège devant vous / dans le couloir

Élève B Ask your partner the following questions. Correct answers are in parentheses.

1. Il faut faire ses valises quand?
   (avant le vol)
2. Qui remplit sa carte de débarquement?
   (le passager)
3. On sert un repas quand?
   (pendant le vol)
4. Il faut mettre ses bagages sous le siège quand?
   (avant le décollage)
5. Les toilettes sont où?
   (dans la cabine)
6. Qui dort pendant le vol?
   (le passager)

Activity 26

CHAPITRE 8, Structure, pages 268–269

Élève A Ask your partner the following questions. Correct answers are in parentheses.

1. Qu'est-ce que vous faites?
   (Nous remplissons la carte de débarquement.)
2. Qu'est-ce-que l'hôtesse fait?
   (Elle sert le dîner.)
3. Qu'est-ce que fait l'avion?
   (L'avion atterrit.)

Élève A Answer your partner's questions according to the illustrations.

1.

2.

3.
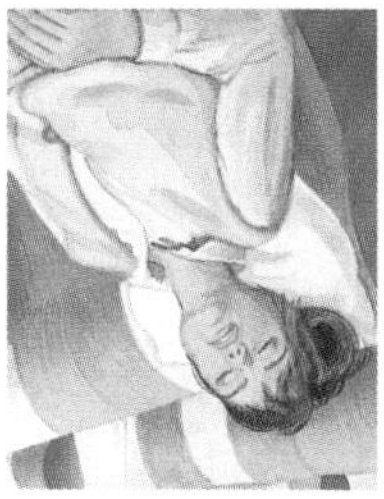

Élève B Answer your partner's questions according to the illustrations.

1.
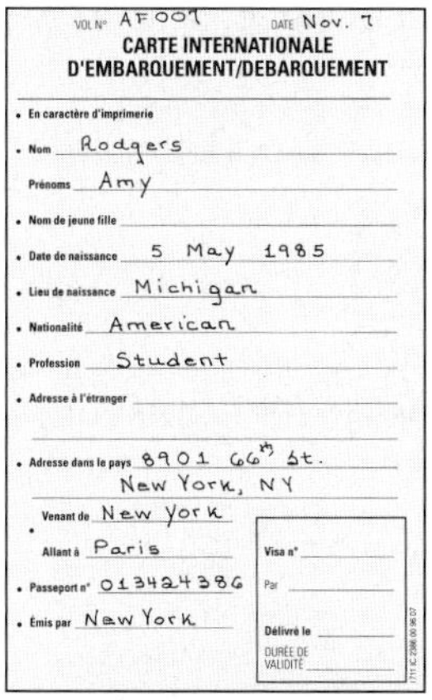

2.

3.

Élève B Ask your partner the following questions. Correct answers are in parentheses.

1. Qu'est-ce que le steward fait?
   (Il sert des boissons.)
2. Qu'est-ce que le passager fait?
   (Il sort ses bagages du coffre à bagages.)
3. Qu'est que tu fais pendant le vol?
   (Je dors pendant le vol.)

Activity 27

CHAPITRE 9, Mots 1, pages 292–293

Élève A Ask your partner the following questions. Correct answers are in parentheses.

1. Que font les passagers?
   (Les passagers font la queue.)
2. Qu'est-ce que Ahmed achète?
   (un billet)
3. Il achète son billet où?
   (au guichet)
4. Tu achètes un billet Paris-Lyon-Paris?
   (Oui, un aller-retour.)
5. Tu achètes un billet Paris-Lyon?
   (Oui, un aller simple.)

Élève A Look at the picture below; then choose the best response from the options given to answer your partner's questions.

1. un journal / un billet
2. le guichet / la voie
3. au buffet / au kiosque
4. sur le quai / dans la salle d'attente
5. au buffet de la gare / au guichet

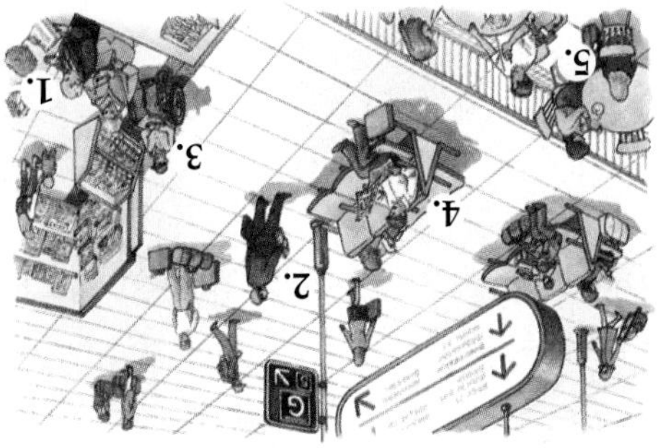

Élève B Ask your partner the following questions. Correct answers are in parentheses.

1. Qu'est-ce que Monsieur Roget achète?
   (un journal)
2. Qu'est-ce que Monsieur Laporte regarde?
   (la voie)
3. Monsieur Boucher fait la queue où?
   (au kiosque)
4. Monsieur Longtemps attend le train où?
   (dans la salle d'attente)
5. Paul prend une boisson où?
   (au buffet de la gare)

Élève B Look at the pictures below; then choose the best response from the options given to answer your partner's questions.

1. Ils attendent le train. / Ils font la queue.
2. un billet / une carte postale
3. au kiosque / au guichet
4. Oui, un aller simple. / Oui, un aller-retour.
5. Oui, un aller simple. / Oui, un aller-retour.

Activity 28

CHAPITRE 9, Mots 2, pages 296–297

Élève A Ask your partner the following questions. Correct answers are in parentheses.

1. Les voyageurs sont debout dans le wagon?
   (Non, ils sont assis.)
2. Anne lit le journal?
   (Non, elle écrit une carte postale.)
3. Paul et Sylvie sont où?
   (Ils sont devant la gare.)
4. Ils attendent une amie?
   (Oui, ils attendent une amie.)
5. Paul commence à perdre patience?
   (Oui, il commence à perdre patience.)

Élève A Answer your partner's questions based on the pictures below.

1–2.

3–5.

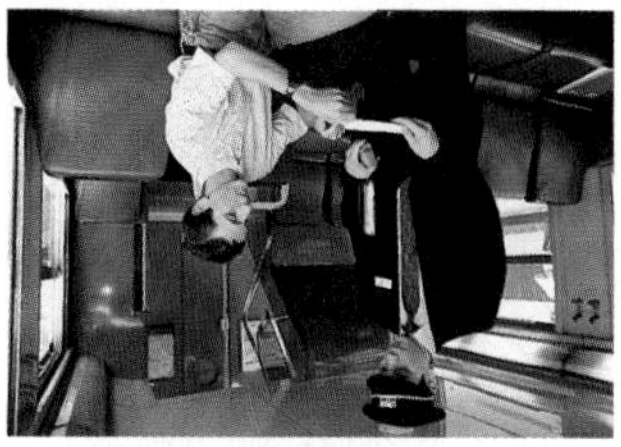

Élève B Ask your partner the following questions. Correct answers are in parentheses.

1. Madame Renoir est assise?
   (Non, elle est debout.)
2. Pierre écrit des cartes postales?
   (Non, il lit le journal.)
3. Le passager est debout?
   (Non, il est assis.)
4. Le contrôleur contrôle les boissons?
   (Non, il contrôle les billets.)
5. Toutes les places sont occupées?
   (Non, toutes les places ne sont pas occupées.)

Élève B Answer your partner's questions based on the pictures below.

1–2.

3–5.

Activity 29

CHAPITRE 9, Structure, pages 300–307

Élève A Say each of the following words to your partner. He or she will make a sentence using the word and one of the verbs listed. Possible answers are in parentheses.

1. le train
   (J'attends le train.) or
   (Je descends du train.)
2. les annonces
   (J'entends les annonces.)
3. un ami
   (J'attends un ami.) or
   (J'écris à un ami.)
4. des choses amusantes
   (Je dis des choses amusantes.) or
   (J'écris des choses amusantes.)
5. les bagages
   (Je descends les bagages.) or
   (J'attends les bagages.)

Élève A Your partner will say a word or phrase. Use the word with one of the verbs below to make a statement about what you do.

Example: You hear: **Le train.**
You respond: **J'attends le train.** *or* **Je descends du train.**

vendre	**descendre**	**répondre**	**perdre**	**lire**

Élève B Your partner will say a word or phrase. Use the word with one of the verbs below to make a statement about what you do.

Example: You hear: **Le train.**
You respond: **J'attends le train.** *or* **Je descends du train.**

attendre	**descendre**	**entendre**	**écrire**	**dire**

Élève B Say each of the following words to your partner. He or she will make a sentence using the word and one of the verbs listed. Possible answers are in parentheses.

1. des cartes postales
   (Je vends des cartes postales.) or
   (Je lis des cartes postales.)
2. la voiture
   (Je descends de la voiture.) or
   (Je vends la voiture.)
3. la question
   (Je réponds à la question.) or
   (Je lis la question.)
4. patience *(Je perds patience.)*
5. des magazines
   (Je lis des magazines.) or
   (Je vends des magazines.)

Activity 30

CHAPITRE 10, Mots 1, pages 324–325

Élève A Ask your partner the following questions. Correct responses are in parentheses.

1. Est-ce que Rennes joue contre Auxerre?
   (Non, Rennes joue contre Lille.)
2. Il y a beaucoup de spectateurs dans le stade?
   (Oui, il y a beaucoup de spectateurs dans le stade.)
3. Le gardien de but, il bloque le ballon?
   (Non, il ne bloque pas le ballon.)
4. Le ballon entre dans le but?
   (Oui, le ballon entre dans le but.)

Élève A Answer your partner's questions based on the illustration.

Élève B Answer your partner's questions based on the illustration.

Élève B Ask your partner the following questions. Correct responses are in parentheses.

1. Un joueur a donné un coup de tête dans le ballon?
   (Non, un joueur a donné un coup de pied dans le ballon.)
2. Il y a beaucoup de places libres dans les gradins?
   (Non, les gradins sont pleins.)
3. Le gardien arrête le ballon?
   (Non, le gardien n'arrête pas le ballon.)
4. Le joueur a marqué un but?
   (Oui, le joueur a marqué un but.)

Activity 31

CHAPITRE 10, Mots 2, pages 328–329

Élève A Read the following statements to your partner, some of which are false. Your partner will correct them. The correct answers are in parentheses.

1. Le basket-ball est un sport individuel.
   (Non, le basket-ball est un sport d'équipe.)
2. Il y a onze joueurs dans une équipe de basket.
   (Non, il y a cinq joueurs dans une équipe de basket.)
3. Les joueurs dribblent le ballon pendant un match de basket.
   (Oui, …)
4. Une joueuse lance le ballon dans le panier pendant un match de basket.
   (Oui, …)
5. Les joueurs de basket donnent un coup de pied au ballon.
   (Non, les joueurs de basket dribblent le ballon.)

Élève A Listen to the statements made by your partner, some of which are false. Correct the false statements.

Élève B Listen to the statements made by your partner, some of which are false. Correct the false statements.

Élève B Read the following statements to your partner, some of which are false. Your partner will correct them. The correct answers are in parentheses.

1. Le volley-ball est un sport individuel.
   (Non, le volley-ball est un sport d'équipe.)
2. Il y a cinq joueurs dans une équipe de volley-ball.
   (Non, il y a six joueurs dans une équipe de volley-ball.)
3. Une joueuse de volley-ball sert le ballon.
   (Oui, …)
4. Une joueuse de volley-ball renvoie le ballon par-dessus le filet.
   (Oui, …)
5. Quand on renvoie le ballon il peut toucher le filet.
   (Non, quand on renvoie le ballon il ne peut pas toucher le filet.)

Activity 32

CHAPITRE 10, Structure, pages 332–334

Élève A Ask your partner who did the following activities. Correct answers are in parentheses.

1. Qui a joué au foot?
   (Chloé a joué au foot.)
2. Qui a perdu le match?
   (Tu as perdu le match.)
3. Qui a regardé le match?
   (Les spectateurs ont regardé le match.)
4. Qui a choisi une place?
   (Moi, j'ai choisi une place.)
5. Qui a dansé?
   (Nous avons dansé.)

Élève A Your partner wants to know who did the activities below. Answer based on the information in the chart.

Qui?	Activité
Les spectateurs	attendre longtemps
L'arbitre	voyager
Nous	gagner la coupe
Tu	finir le match
Julien	lancer le ballon

Élève B Your partner wants to know who did the activities below. Answer based on the information in the chart.

Qui?	Activité
Chloé	jouer au foot
Tu	perdre le match
Les spectateurs	regarder le match
Moi, je	choisir une place
Nous	danser

Élève B Ask your partner who did the following activities. Correct answers are in parentheses.

1. Qui a attendu longtemps?
   (Les spectateurs ont attendu longtemps.)
2. Qui a voyagé?
   (L'arbitre a voyagé.)
3. Qui a gagné la coupe.
   (Nous avons gagné la coupe.)
4. Qui a fini le match?
   (Tu as fini le match.)
5. Qui a lancé le ballon?
   (Julien a lancé le ballon.)

Activity 33

CHAPITRE 10, Structure, pages 337–339

Élève A Ask your partner who does the following activities. Correct answers are in parentheses.

1. Qui doit passer un examen?
   (Nathalie doit passer un examen.)
2. Qui reçoit le ballon?
   (Tu reçois le ballon.)
3. Qui boit de la limonade?
   (Les enfants boivent de la limonade.)
4. Qui doit être content?
   (Vous devez être contents.)
5. Qui boit du lait?
   (Moi, je bois du lait.)

Élève A Your partner wants to know who does the following. Answer based on the information in the chart.

Qui?	Activité
Rémi	boire du coca
Tu	devoir étudier
Les copains	recevoir un cadeau
Moi, je	boire de l'eau
Nous	devoir travailler

Élève B Your partner wants to know who does the following. Answer based on the information in the chart.

Qui?	Activité
Nathalie	devoir passer un examen
Tu	recevoir le ballon
Les enfants	boire de la limonade
Vous	devoir être contents
Moi, je	boire du lait

Élève B Ask your partner who does the following activities. Correct answers are in parentheses.

1. Qui boit du coca?
   (Rémi boit du coca.)
2. Qui doit étudier?
   (Tu dois étudier.)
3. Qui reçoit un cadeau?
   (Les copains reçoivent un cadeau.)
4. Qui boit de l'eau?
   (Moi, je bois de l'eau.)
5. Qui doit travailler?
   (Nous devons travailler.)

Activity 34

CHAPITRE 11, Mots 1, pages 356–357

Élève A Ask your partner the following questions. Correct answers are in parentheses.

1. Marc fait de la planche à voile?
   (Oui, Marc fait de la planche à voile.)
2. Il pleut?
   (Non, il fait beau.)
3. Sandrine fait une promenade?
   (Non, elle fait du ski nautique.)
4. Les amis sont où?
   (Les amis sont à la plage.)
5. Ils vont faire du surf?
   (Oui, ils vont faire du surf.)

Élève A Answer your partner's questions based on the picture below.

Élève B Answer your partner's questions based on the pictures below.

1–2.

3.

4–5.

Élève B Ask your partner the following questions. Correct answers are in parentheses.

1. Jeanne a passé la journée à la piscine?
   (Non, elle a passé la journée à la plage.)
2. Elle a mis un maillot de bain?
   (Oui, elle a mis un maillot de bain.)
3. Elle a mis de la crème solaire?
   (Oui, elle a mis de la crème solaire.)
4. Il a fait mauvais temps?
   (Non, il a fait beau.)
5. Elle a pris un bain de soleil?
   (Oui, elle a pris un bain de soleil.)

Activity 35

CHAPITRE 11, Mots 2, pages 360–361

Élève A Ask your partner the following questions. Correct answers are in parentheses.

1. Qu'est-ce qu'on prend pour monter au sommet?
   (On prend un télésiège.)
2. Quel temps fait-il à la montagne?
   (Il fait froid.)
3. Il y a beaucoup de neige?
   (Oui, il y a beaucoup de neige.)
4. On fait du ski à la montagne?
   (Oui, on fait du ski à la montagne.)

Élève A Answer your partner's questions based on the picture below.

Élève B Answer your partner's questions based on the picture below.

Élève B Ask your partner the following questions. Correct answers are in parentheses.

1. Pauline a mis un anorak de quelle couleur?
   (Elle a mis un anorak bleu.)
2. Elle est bonne en ski?
   (Non, elle est débutante.)
3. Elle apprend à faire du ski?
   (Oui, elle apprend à faire du ski.)
4. Elle a eu un bon moniteur?
   (Oui, elle a eu un bon moniteur.)

Activity 36

CHAPITRE 11, Structure, pages 364–366

Élève A Read your partner the following statements. Correct responses are in parentheses.

1. Je fais un voyage en hiver.
   (J'ai fait un voyage en hiver l'année dernière.)
2. Je prends des leçons de ski alpin.
   (J'ai pris des leçons de ski alpin l'année dernière.)
3. J'apprends à faire du patin à glace.
   (J'ai appris à faire du patin à glace l'année dernière.)
4. Je dis "Merci" au moniteur.
   (J'ai dit "Merci" au moniteur l'année dernière.)
5. Je mets un bonnet.
   (J'ai mis un bonnet l'année dernière.)
6. Je lis un livre pour les débutants.
   (J'ai lu un livre pour les débutants l'année dernière.)

Élève A Your partner will tell you what he or she is doing today. Use the **passé composé** of the verb below to tell him or her you did the same thing last year **(l'année dernière).**

1. apprendre
2. prendre
3. mettre
4. faire
5. avoir
6. boire

Élève B Your partner will tell you what he or she is doing today. Use the **passé composé** of the verb below to tell him or her you did the same thing last year **(l'année dernière).**

1. faire
2. prendre
3. apprendre
4. dire
5. mettre
6. lire

Élève B Read your partner the following statements. Correct responses are in parentheses.

1. J'apprends à faire du ski.
   (J'ai appris à faire du ski l'année dernière.)
2. Je prends le télésiège.
   (J'ai pris le télésiège l'année dernière.)
3. Je mets un anorak.
   (J'ai mis un anorak l'année dernière.)
4. Je fais du ski de fond.
   (J'ai fait du ski de fond l'année dernière.)
5. J'ai un bon moniteur.
   (J'ai eu un bon moniteur l'année dernière.)
6. Je bois du chocolat chaud.
   (J'ai bu du chocolat chaud l'année dernière.)

Activity 37

CHAPITRE 11, Structure, pages 369–371

Élève A Read your partner the following statements. Correct responses are in parentheses.

1. J'arrive au bord de la mer.
   (Hier, je suis arrivé[e] au bord de la mer.)
2. Je monte dans le train.
   (Hier, je suis monté[e] dans le train.)
3. Je vais à la montagne.
   (Hier, je suis allé[e] à la montagne.)
4. Je sors de la gare.
   (Hier, je suis sorti[e] de la gare.)
5. Je tombe sur la glace.
   (Hier, je suis tombé[e] sur la glace.)

Élève A Your partner will tell you what he or she is doing today. Use the **passé composé** of the verb below to tell him or her you did the same thing yesterday **(hier).**

1. partir
2. descendre
3. rentrer
4. entrer
5. aller

Élève B Your partner will tell you what he or she is doing today. Use the **passé composé** of the verb below to tell him or her you did the same thing yesterday **(hier).**

1. arriver
2. monter
3. aller
4. sortir
5. tomber

Élève B Read your partner the following statements. Correct responses are in parentheses.

1. Je pars à l'heure.
   (Hier, je suis parti[e] à l'heure.)
2. Je descends du train.
   (Hier, je suis descendu[e] du train.)
3. Je rentre à l'hôtel.
   (Hier, je suis rentré[e] à l'hôtel.)
4. J'entre dans la classe de français.
   (Hier, je suis entré[e] dans la classe de français.)
5. Je vais à la plage.
   (Hier, je suis allé[e] à la plage.)

Activity 38

CHAPITRE 12, Mots 1, pages 400–401

Élève A Read your partner the following statements. He or she will tell you how people use the items in the daily routine. Correct responses are in parentheses.

1. Il faut une brosse à dents. Il faut du dentifrice.
   (Elle se brosse les dents.)
2. Il faut un peigne.
   (Elle se peigne.)
3. Il faut un rasoir. Il faut une glace.
   (Il se rase.)

Élève A Your partner will read you a statement about daily routine. Use the picture cues to tell him or her which products or equipment are needed.

1.

2.
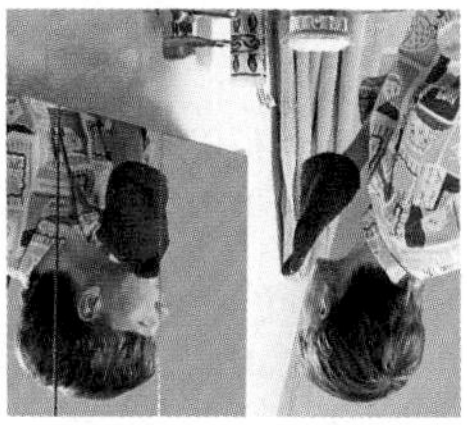

3.

Élève B Your partner will tell you which products or equipment are needed in a daily routine. Use the picture cues to tell him or her what people use the items for.

1.

2.

3.

Élève B Read your partner the following statements about daily routine. He or she will tell you what products or equipment are needed. Correct responses are in parentheses.

1. Elle se brosse les cheveux.
   (Il faut une brosse.)
2. Il se lave.
   (Il faut du savon. Il faut un gant de toilette.)
3. Il se lave les cheveux.
   (Il faut du shampooing.)

Activity 39

CHAPITRE 12, Mots 2, pages 404–405

Élève A Ask your partner the following questions. Correct answers are in parentheses.

1. Qui regarde la télé?
   (Christophe et Julie regardent la télé.)
2. Qui regarde son émission favorite?
   (Christophe regarde son émission favorite.)
3. Qui peut changer de chaîne?
   (Christophe peut changer de chaîne.)
4. Julie fait ses devoirs?
   (Non, Julie ne fait pas ses devoirs.)
5. Christophe s'est bien amusé?
   (Oui, il s'est bien amusé.)

Élève A Answer your partner's questions based on the pictures below.

1–2.

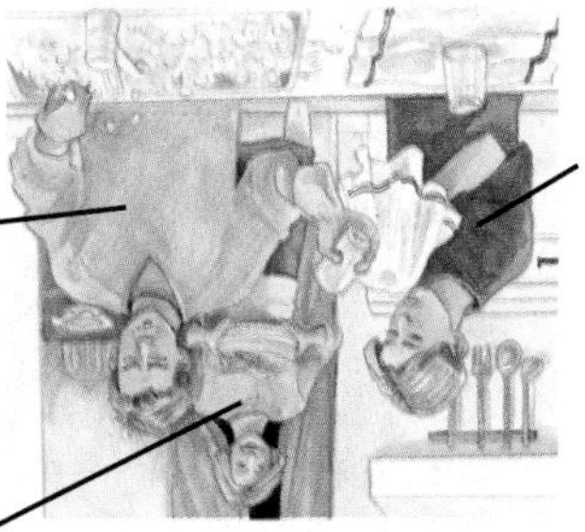

3–5.

Élève B Answer your partner's questions based on the picture below.

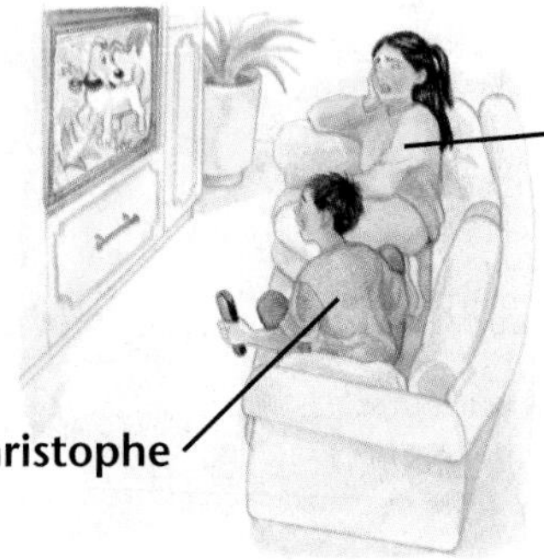

Élève B Ask your partner the following questions. Correct answers are in parentheses.

1. Qui débarrasse la table après le dîner?
   (Mme Fauvet débarrasse la table après le dîner.)
2. Qui fait la vaisselle?
   (M. Fauvet et Jean font la vaisselle.)
3. Qui fait ses devoirs?
   (Paul fait ses devoirs.)
4. Qui est sorti?
   (Sophie est sortie.)
5. Sophie s'est bien amusée?
   (Oui, elle s'est bien amusée.)

Activity 40

CHAPITRE 12, Structure, pages 408–412

Élève A Ask your partner the following questions. Correct answers are in parentheses.

1. Qui se maquille?
   (Sophie se maquille.)
2. Qui se réveille tôt?
   (Vous vous réveillez tôt.)
3. Qui se regarde dans la glace?
   (Moi, je me regarde dans la glace.)
4. Qui s'habille?
   (Les enfants s'habillent.)
5. Qui se promène dans le parc?
   (Nous nous promenons dans le parc.)

Élève A Answer your partner's questions based on the information in the chart below.

Qui?	Activité
Moi, je	se lever tôt
Les étudiants	se coucher tard
Paul	se raser
Nous	se brosser les dents
Tu	se peigner

Élève B Answer your partner's questions based on the information in the chart below.

Qui?	Activité
Sophie	se maquiller
Vous	se réveiller tôt
Moi, je	se regarder dans la glace
Les enfants	s'habiller
Nous	se promener dans le parc

Élève B Ask your partner the following questions. Correct answers are in parentheses.

1. Qui se lève tôt?
   (Moi, je me lève tôt.)
2. Qui se couche tard?
   (Les étudiants se couchent tard.)
3. Qui se rase?
   (Paul se rase.)
4. Qui se brosse les dents?
   (Nous nous brossons les dents.)
5. Qui se peigne?
   (Tu te peignes.)

Activity 41

CHAPITRE 12, Structure, pages 413–415

Élève A Ask your partner the following questions. Correct answers are in parentheses.

1. Qui s'est maquillé?
   (Sophie s'est maquillée.)
2. Qui s'est réveillé tôt?
   (Vous vous êtes réveillé[s] tôt.)
3. Qui s'est regardé dans la glace?
   (Moi, je me suis regardé[e] dans la glace.)
4. Qui s'est habillé?
   (Les enfants se sont habillés.)
5. Qui s'est promené dans le parc?
   (Nous nous sommes promenés dans le parc.)

Élève A Answer your partner's questions based on the information in the chart below.

Qui?	Activité
Moi, je	se lever tôt
Les étudiants	se coucher tard
Paul	se raser
Nous	se brosser les dents
Tu	se peigner

Élève B Answer your partner's questions based on the information in the chart below.

Qui?	Activité
Sophie	se maquiller
Vous	se réveiller tôt
Moi, je	se regarder dans la glace
Les enfants	s'habiller
Nous	se promener dans le parc

Élève B Ask your partner the following questions. Correct answers are in parentheses.

1. Qui s'est levé tôt?
   (Moi, je me suis levé[e] tôt.)
2. Qui s'est couché tard?
   (Les étudiants se sont couchés tard.)
3. Qui s'est rasé?
   (Paul s'est rasé.)
4. Qui s'est brossé les dents?
   (Nous nous sommes brossé les dents.)
5. Qui s'est peigné?
   (Tu t'es peigné[e].)

Activity 42

CHAPITRE 13, Mots 1, pages 432–433

Élève A Ask your partner the following questions. Correct answers are in parentheses.

1. Qu'est-ce que tu aimes comme film?
   (J'aime les documentaires.)
2. Qu'est-ce qu'on monte?
   (On monte Roméo et Juliette.)
3. Tu aimes mieux aller au cinéma ou louer des vidéos?
   (J'aime mieux louer des vidéos.)

Élève A Answer your partner's questions according to the illustrations.

1. 

2. 

3. 

Élève B Answer your partner's questions according to the illustrations.

1. 

2. 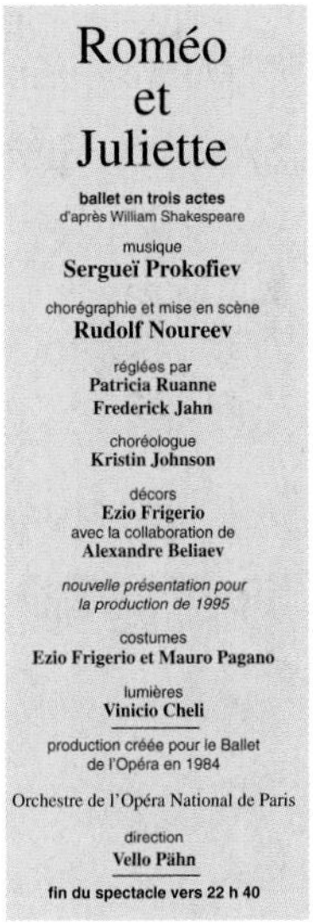

3. 

Élève B Ask your partner the following questions. Correct answers are in parentheses.

1. Qu'est-ce que tu aimes comme film?
   (J'aime les dessins animés.)
2. Tu as déjà vu le chanteur?
   (Non, mais j'ai déjà vu la danseuse.)
3. Tu vas voir une pièce de théâtre?
   (Non, je vais voir un film au cinéma.)

Activity 43

CHAPITRE 13, Mots 2, pages 436–437

Élève A Ask your partner the following questions. Correct answers are in parentheses.

1. C'est un musée ou un théâtre?
   (C'est un musée.)
2. Le musée est ouvert ou fermé?
   (Le musée est ouvert.)
3. Il y a beaucoup de tableaux ou de statues au musée?
   (Il y a beaucoup de tableaux.)

Élève A Answer your partner's questions according to the illustration.

Élève B Answer your partner's questions according to the photograph.

Élève B Ask your partner the following questions. Correct answers are in parentheses.

1. Elle est peintre ou sculpteur?
   (Elle est peintre.)
2. Il est peintre ou sculpteur?
   (Il est sculpteur.)
3. Qu'est-ce que qu'il y a au musée?
   (Il y a une exposition de peinture et sculpture au musée.)

Activity 44

CHAPITRE 13, Structure, pages 440–441

Élève A You are familiar with some people, places, and things, but your partner knows some facts or information he or she wants to share with you about them. Make your statement and your partner will respond. Correct responses are in parentheses.

1. Je connais Nathalie.
   (Je sais qu'elle habite à Grenoble.)
2. Je connais *Hamlet.*
   (Je sais que c'est une pièce de Shakespeare.)
3. Je connais Paris.
   (Je sais que c'est la capitale de la France.)
4. Je connais l'œuvre de Degas.
   (Je sais que Degas est un peintre français.)
5. Je connais Paul.
   (Je sais quel est son numéro de téléphone.)

Élève A Your partner and some of his or her friends are familiar with certain people, places, and things, but you and your friends have some facts or information to share. Add your comment according to the cues. Begin your statements with **Nous savons…**

1. …qu'ils sont très beaux.
2. …quelle pièce on joue en ce moment.
3. …où se trouve le théâtre.
4. …qu'elles savent danser le tango.
5. …qu'elles sont célèbres.

Élève B Your partner and some of his or her friends are familiar with certain people, places, and things, but you and your friends have some facts or information to share. Add your comment according to the cues. Begin your statements with **Nous savons…**

1. …qu'elle habite à Grenoble.
2. …que c'est une pièce de Shakespeare.
3. …que c'est la capitale de la France.
4. …que Degas est un peintre français.
5. …quel est son numéro de téléphone.

Élève B You are familiar with some people, places, and things, but your partner knows some facts or information he or she wants to share with you about them. Make your statement and your partner will respond. Correct responses are in parentheses.

1. Nous connaissons les tableaux de Monet, Manet et Renoir.
   (Nous savons qu'ils sont très beaux.)
2. Nous connaissons les pièces de Molière.
   (Nous savons quelle pièce on joue en ce moment.)
3. Nous connaissons la Comédie Française.
   (Nous savons où se trouve le théâtre.)
4. Nous connaissons des danseuses.
   (Nous savons qu'elles savent danser le tango.)
5. Nous connaissons les sculptures de Rodin.
   (Nous savons qu'elles sont célèbres.)

Activity 45

CHAPITRE 13, Structure, pages 442–446

Élève A Ask your partner the following questions. Correct answers are in parentheses.

1. Tu connais les tableaux de Monet?
   (Oui, je les connais.)
2. Tu vois la sculpture moderne?
   (Non, je ne la vois pas.)
3. Tu sais le nom du film?
   (Oui, je le sais.)
4. Tu lis les sous-titres?
   (Non, je ne les lis pas.)
5. Tu veux voir la pièce?
   (Oui, je veux la voir.)

Élève A Your partner will ask a question. Respond according to the cues, using the correct object pronoun.

1. Oui…
2. Non…
3. Oui…
4. Oui…
5. Oui…

Élève B Your partner will ask a question. Respond according to the cues, using the correct object pronoun.

1. Oui…
2. Non…
3. Oui…
4. Non…
5. Oui…

Élève B Ask your partner the following questions. Correct answers are in parentheses.

1. Tu m'invites au cinéma?
   (Oui, je t'invite.)
2. Ce film te plaît?
   (Non, ce film ne me plaît pas.)
3. Je te parle au téléphone avant le film?
   (Oui, tu me parles au téléphone avant le film.)
4. Le prof nous donne beaucoup de devoirs?
   (Oui, le prof nous donne beaucoup de devoirs.)
   or
   (Oui, le prof vous donne beaucoup de devoirs.)
5. Julie vous dit quand le musée est fermé?
   (Oui, Julie nous dit quand le musée est fermé.)
   or
   (Oui, Julie me dit quand le musée est fermé.)

Activity 46

CHAPITRE 14, Mots 1, pages 464–465

Élève A Read your partner the following statements. He or she will tell you each person's symptoms. Possible responses are in parentheses.

1. Miriam n'est pas en bonne santé.
   (Elle a mal aux oreilles.)
2. Elle a besoin d'un mouchoir.
   (Elle a le nez qui coule.) or *(Elle a un rhume.)*
3. Anne est très malade, la pauvre.
   (Elle a des frissons.) or *(Elle a de la fièvre.)*
4. David ne se sent pas bien.
   (Il tousse.)

Élève A Use the pictures below to tell your partner about each person's symptoms.

1.

2.

3.
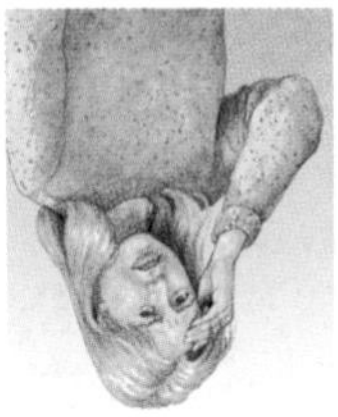

4.

Élève B Use the pictures below to tell your partner about each person's symptoms.

1.
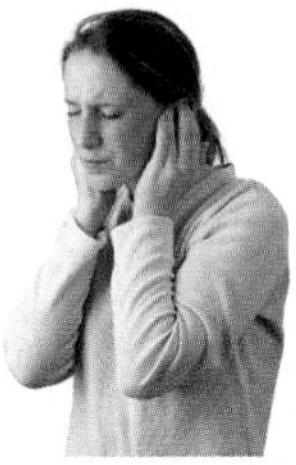

2.

3.

4.

Élève B Read your partner the following statements. He or she will tell you each person's symptoms. Possible responses are in parentheses.

1. Pauline est malade.
   (Elle est enrhumée.) or *(Elle éternue.)*
2. Martine est en mauvaise santé.
   (Elle a un rhume.) or *(Elle tousse.)*
3. Juliette ne se sent pas bien.
   (Elle a mal à la tête.)
4. Jeanne est très malade, la pauvre.
   (Elle a mal au ventre.)

Activity 47

CHAPITRE 14, Mots 2, pages 468–469

Élève A You are the doctor and your partner, the patient, needs help. Ask him or her the following questions.

1. Où avez-vous mal?
   (J'ai mal au ventre.)
2. Qu'est-ce que vous avez?
   (J'ai une angine.)
3. Qu'est-ce que vous avez?
   (J'ai une sinusite aiguë.)
4. Qu'est-ce que vous avez?
   (J'ai un chat dans la gorge.)
5. Où avez-vous mal?
   (J'ai mal à la tête.)

Élève A Answer your partner's questions according to the cues below.

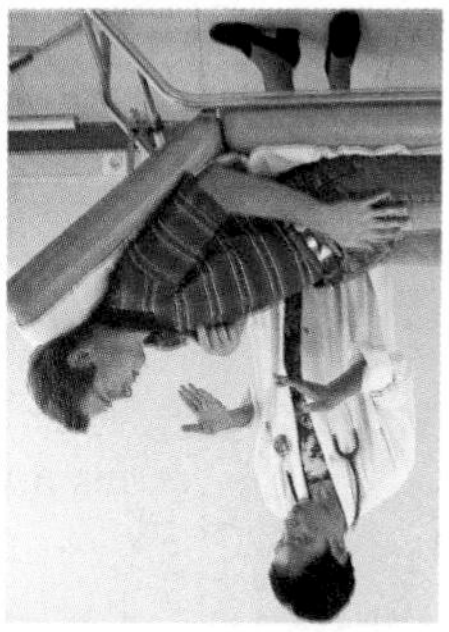

1. des frissons
2. aux oreilles
3. une allergie
4. une fièvre de cheval
5. une infection

Élève B Answer your partner's questions according to the cues below.

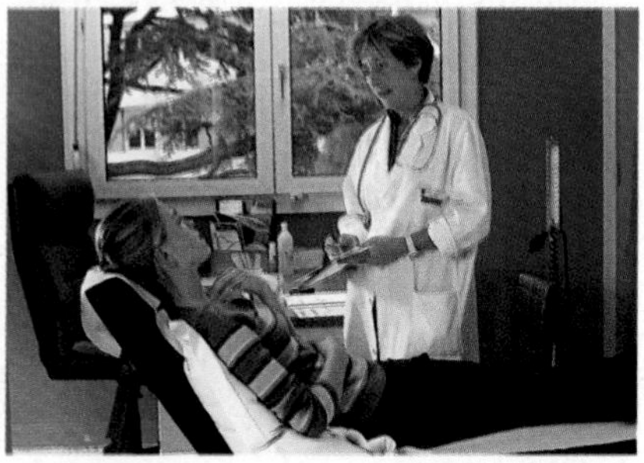

1. au ventre
2. une angine
3. une sinusite aiguë
4. un chat dans la gorge
5. à la tête

Élève B You are the doctor and your partner, the patient, needs help. Ask him or her the following questions.

1. Qu'est-ce que vous avez?
   (J'ai des frissons.)
2. Où avez-vous mal?
   (J'ai mal aux oreilles.)
3. Qu'est-ce que vous avez?
   (J'ai une allergie.)
4. Qu'est-ce que vous avez?
   (J'ai une fièvre de cheval.)
5. Qu'est-ce que vous avez?
   (J'ai une infection.)

Activity 48

CHAPITRE 14, Structure, pages 472–473

Élève A Ask your partner the following questions. Correct answers are in parentheses.

1. Tu parles souvent à ta copine?
   (Oui, je lui parle souvent.)
2. Les joueurs lancent le ballon à l'arbitre?
   (Oui, ils lui lancent le ballon.)
3. Le médecin prescrit des antibiotiques aux malades?
   (Oui, il leur prescrit des antibiotiques.)
4. Tu vas acheter un cadeau à ton frère?
   (Oui, je vais lui acheter un cadeau.)
5. Le pharmacien donne des médicaments à ta mère?
   (Oui, il lui donne des médicaments.)

Élève A Answer your partner's questions using **lui** or **leur**.

1. Oui, je ______ dis bonjour.
2. Oui, il ______ vend des billets.
3. Oui, il ______ fait une ordonnance.
4. Oui, ils ______ téléphonent.
5. Oui, elle ______ dit qu'il a de la fièvre.

Élève B Answer your partner's questions using **lui** or **leur.**

1. Oui, je ______ parle souvent.
2. Oui, ils ______ lancent le ballon.
3. Oui, il ______ prescrit des antibiotiques.
4. Oui, je vais ______ acheter un cadeau.
5. Oui, il ______ donne des médicaments.

Élève B Ask your partner the following questions. Correct answers are in parentheses.

1. Tu dis bonjour à tes amis?
   (Oui, je leur dis bonjour.)
2. L'employé vend des billets à ton père?
   (Oui, il lui vend des billets.)
3. Le médecin fait une ordonnance à Marie?
   (Oui, il lui fait une ordonnance.)
4. Les malades téléphonent au professeur?
   (Oui, ils lui téléphonent.)
5. Sa mère dit à Paul qu'il a de la fièvre?
   (Oui, elle lui dit qu'il a de la fièvre.)

Activity 49

CHAPITRE 14, Structure, pages 475–477

Élève A Ask your partner the following questions. Correct answers are in parentheses.

1. Finir les devoirs?
   (Finis tes devoirs!)
2. Préparer le dîner?
   (Prépare le dîner!)
3. Choisir un film?
   (Choisissons un film!)
4. Travailler plus?
   (Travaille plus!)
5. Dîner au restaurant?
   (Dînons au restaurant!)

Élève A Answer your partner's questions based on the information in the chart below.

Personne(s)	Activité
tu	prendre le métro
vous	attendre devant la porte
tu	faire du ski
tu	sortir ce soir
vous	regarder le film

Élève B Answer your partner's questions based on the information in the chart below.

Personne(s)	Activité
tu	finir les devoirs
tu	préparer le dîner
nous	choisir un film
tu	travailler plus
nous	dîner au restaurant

Élève B Ask your partner the following questions. Correct answers are in parentheses.

1. Prendre le métro?
   (Prends le métro!)
2. Attendre devant la porte?
   (Attendez devant la porte!)
3. Faire du ski?
   (Fais du ski!)
4. Sortir ce soir?
   (Sors ce soir!)
5. Regardez le film?
   (Regardez le film!)

This guide is designed to help you achieve success as you embark on the adventure of learning another language. There are many ways to learn new information. You may find some of these suggestions more useful than others, depending upon which style of learning works best for you. Before you begin, it is important to understand how we acquire language.

Receptive Skills

Each day of your life you receive a great deal of information through the use of language. In order to obtain (get, receive) this information, it is necessary to understand the language being used. It is necessary to understand the language in two different ways. First you must be able to understand what people are saying when they speak to you. This is referred to as oral or listening comprehension. Oral comprehension or listening comprehension is the ability to understand the spoken language.

You must also be able to understand what you read. This is referred to as reading comprehension. Reading comprehension is the ability to understand the written language.

Listening comprehension and reading comprehension are called the *receptive skills.* They are receptive skills because as you listen to what someone else says or read what someone else has written you receive information without having to produce any language yourself.

It is usually very easy to understand your native language or mother tongue. It is a bit more problematic to understand a second language that is new to you. As a beginner, you are still learning the sounds of the new language, and you recognize only a few words. Throughout **Bon voyage!** we will give you hints or suggestions to help you understand when people are speaking to you in French or when you are reading in French. Following are some general hints to keep in mind.

Hints for listening comprehension

When you are listening to a person speaking French, don't try to understand every word. It is not necessary to understand everything to get the idea of what someone is saying. Listen for the general message. If some details escape you, it doesn't matter. Also, never try to translate what people are saying in French into English. It takes a great deal of experience and expertise to be a translator. Trying to translate will hinder your ability to understand.

Hints for reading comprehension

Just as you will not always understand every word you hear in a conversation, you will not necessarily understand every word you encounter in a reading selection, either. In **Bon voyage!,** we have used only words you know or can easily figure out in the reading selections. This will make reading comprehension much easier for you. However, if at some time you wish to read a newspaper or magazine article in French, you will most certainly come across some unfamiliar words. Do not stop reading. Continue to read to get the "gist" of the selection. Try to guess the meanings of words you do not know.

Productive Skills

There are two productive skills in language. These two skills are speaking and writing. They are called productive skills because it is you who has to produce the language when you say or write something. When you speak or write, you have control over the language and which words you use. If you don't know how to say something, you don't have to say it. With the receptive skills, on the other hand, someone else produces the language that you listen to or read, and you have no control over the words they use.

There's no doubt that you can produce your native language easily. You can say a great deal in your "mother tongue." You can write, too, even though you may sometimes make errors in spelling or punctuation. In French, there's not a lot you can say or write as a beginner. You can only talk or write about those topics you have learned in French class.

HINTS FOR SPEAKING Try to be as accurate as possible when speaking. Try not to make mistakes. However, if you do, it's not the end of the world. French people will understand you. You're not expected to speak a language perfectly after a limited time. You have probably spoken with people from other countries who do not speak English perfectly, but you can understand them. Remember:

- Keep talking! Don't become inhibited for fear of making a mistake.
- Say what you know how to say. Don't try to branch out in the early stages and attempt to talk about topics or situations you have not yet learned in French.

HINTS FOR WRITING There are many activities in each lesson of **Bon voyage!** that will help you speak and write in French. When you have to write something on your own, however, without the guidance or assistance of an activity in your book, be sure to choose a topic for which you know the vocabulary in French. Never attempt to write about a topic you have not yet studied in French. Write down the topic you are going to write about. Then think of the words you know that are related to the topic. Be sure to include some action words (verbs) that you will need.

From your list of words, write as many sentences as you can. Read them and organize them into a logical order. Fill in any gaps. Then proof your paragraph(s) to see if you made any errors. Correct any that you find.

When writing on your own, be careful not to rely heavily, if at all, on a bilingual dictionary. It's not that bilingual dictionaries are bad, but when you look up a word you will very often find that there are several or many translations for the same word. As a beginning language student, you do not know which translation to choose; the chances are great that you will pick the wrong one.

As a final hint, never prepare your paragraph(s) in English and attempt to translate word for word. Always write from scratch in French.

*In each chapter of **Bon voyage!**, you will learn how to say and write new words. In Chapter 1, you learn how to describe a person. It won't be long before you'll be able to talk about many things in French. **Bon voyage!***

Chapitre 1

Vocabulaire

Mots 1 & 2 *(pages 18–25)*

1. Repeat each new word in the **Mots** section as many times as possible. The more you use a word, the more apt you are to remember it and keep it as part of your active vocabulary.
2. Read the words as you look at the illustrations.
3. If you're the type who has to write something down in order to remember it, copy each word once or twice.
4. Do these activities diligently. They provide you with the opportunity to use your new words many times.
5. This may sound strange, but it's a good idea to read these exercises aloud at home or when using the CD-ROM.
6. When doing the vocabulary activities by yourself or for homework, try to do each item orally before writing the answer.
7. After doing any activity that says **Historiette,** read all the answers aloud. Each time you do this, you will be telling a story in French. It's an excellent way to keep using the material you are learning.

Classroom suggestion Listen to what your classmates say when they respond in class. Do not tune them out. Paying attention to them allows you additional opportunities to hear your new words. The more you hear them, the more likely you are to learn and retain them.

Structure

Les adjectifs *(page 28)*

Pay particular attention to the final sound of many of the descriptive words you are learning. Remind yourself that you hear the final consonant sound of many descriptive words when you are describing a girl. You do not hear the sound when describing a boy.

Hint for spelling What letter do you delete from the feminine form? Remember that you delete the **e** that follows the consonant when referring to a male.

***Le verbe* être** *(pages 30–33)*

1. **Être** is the first verb you are learning in French. Throughout your study of French, you will continue to learn many more verbs. Verbs are extremely important in French. At this point, you know three verb forms:
   je suis when talking about yourself
   tu es when talking to someone
   il/elle est when talking about someone

Get off to a good start! Learn these three simple forms and remember them.

2. As you do the activities, don't try to use words you don't know in French. For example, you may want to talk about someone who is very outgoing, but you don't know a French equivalent for "outgoing." Give the message using what you do know. For example, you can say: **Jean n'est pas timide, pas du tout.** You can also say: **Marie, elle est timide? Non, pas du tout. Marie n'est pas timide.** Using **ne... pas** with a word you know, you can convey the meaning you wish even though you do not know the precise word.

Classroom suggestion Listen to your classmates as they respond to the structure activities. Remember, the more you hear a form, the more readily you will be able to use it.

3. After doing any activity that says **Historiette,** read all the answers aloud. Each time you do this, you will be telling a story in French. It's an excellent way to keep using the material you are learning.

Lecture culturelle

Un garçon et une fille (pages 36–37)

1. Always read the Reading Strategy at the beginning of the **Lecture culturelle.** Practice these strategies and try applying them to other selections you read in French. The Reading Strategy on page 36 talks about cognates and how they help you guess the meanings of words you do not know. For example, you read: **Jean est un garçon français. Il est très intelligent, très capable.** You have probably never seen or used the word **capable** in French. However, you can guess its meaning because it is a cognate of the English word *capable.*

   In addition, it is used in apposition to **intelligent.** When you see a word or expression followed by a comma and then another word (in apposition), the word in apposition almost always clarifies the precise word and has the same or similar meaning.

2. Let's look at another way to guess meaning: **Jean est intelligent et il est aussi très sage. Il est prudent.** You don't know the word **sage,** but its meaning is clarified by **prudent.** Which of the following do you think **sage** means? *Talented? Wise, smart? Nice?* Hopefully you chose *wise, smart.* Think about how and why you arrived at this correct answer.

HINTS FOR WRITING As you complete your first chapter in French, you are able to write a description of a person. At this point, you cannot tell what the person does because you don't have the necessary vocabulary. So avoid this. However, you are able to tell what he or she is like. Write down the words you know in order to write your description. Do not think of words in English. Try to think only of the words you know in French. Begin to write your description. Remember what you learned about **e** if your description is of a female.

VOCABULAIRE *(page 46)*
As you complete the chapter, look at the reference vocabulary list. If there are several words you don't remember, go back to the **Mots 1** and **Mots 2** sections and review. If there are only one or two, you can choose to look them up in the dictionaries beginning on page H72 at the end of this book.

CHAPITRE 2

Get off to a good start! Do your French homework diligently and study for a short period of time each day. Do not skip some days and then try to cram. It doesn't work when studying a foreign language.

In each lesson of **Bon voyage!** you will learn a very manageable amount of new material. Since French is a romance language, much of the new material will involve word endings. Study each small set of new endings on a daily basis, and you'll have no problem. Don't wait until you have lots of them and try to cram them in all at once.

Vocabulaire

Mots 1 & 2 *(pages 50–57)*

1. In Chapter 1, you learned that adjectives describing something feminine end in **e.** The final consonant is pronounced. The **e** is dropped and the consonant is not pronounced when describing something masculine. In Chapter 2, you have four new words that reinforce the same concept: **fort, mauvais, strict,** and **intéressant.**

   Elle est forte en maths.
   Il est fort en maths.
   La classe est intéressante.
   Le cours est intéressant.

HINT FOR PRONOUNCING NEW WORDS
Imitate the pronunciation of your teacher or the audiocassettes or CDs to the best of your ability. Try to acquire the best pronunciation possible.

H54

However, don't be worried if you have a slight American accent. There are three levels of pronunciation.

- **Near-native** Try to pronounce like a native. Strive for a near-native pronunciation.
- **Accented but comprehensible** Many people have an accent when they speak a foreign language. You can tell they are not native speakers, but in spite of their accent, you can understand them. If you have such an accent, don't be concerned.
- **Very accented and incomprehensible** Some people have such a strong accent that it's impossible to understand what they're saying. If you have such a strong accent, it will be necessary to repeat and imitate more carefully.

Always remember to listen carefully, repeating as accurately as possible, and you'll succeed in acquiring acceptable pronunciation.

HINT FOR SPEAKING Listen to your teacher pronounce new words or phrases and then repeat them several times. Once you know how to pronounce the words, read the words in your book. If you try to read a word in French before ever having pronounced it, the spelling will most probably interfere with your pronunciation. Always try to listen, repeat, and then read.

2. The vocabulary in **Mots 2** should be very easy to recognize and learn because many words are cognates. A cognate is a word that looks alike in both English and French and has the same meaning in both languages. In the early lessons of **Bon voyage!** we have used many cognates to help you acquire a substantial vocabulary quickly and easily. However, be careful with the pronunciation of cognates. Even though they look alike and mean the same thing in both languages, they can be pronounced very differently.

Structure

Le pluriel: articles, noms et adjectifs

(pages 58–60)

When listening, you will not hear the **s** ending for the plural of a descriptive word. When speaking, you will not pronounce the **s.** However, when writing, you have to remember to write the **s** for plural words.

Les garcons intelligents
Les filles intelligentes

Le verbe être *au pluriel* *(pages 60–63)*

In this lesson, you learn three new verb forms:

nous sommes when talking about yourself and someone else
vous êtes when talking to two or more people
ils/elles sont when talking about two or more people

Go over these three forms until you feel confident that you know them.

Conversation

(page 66)

When you listen to people speak, you will notice that they often use little words or expressions that you will never see in written form. *Yeah* and *ya' know* are examples in English. You can often guess the meaning of these expressions by the speaker's tone of voice. In this conversation, listen to the tone of voice when the young woman says **Ben oui.** Do you think **Ben oui** means *No* or *Yeah?*

Lecture culturelle

Le français aux États-Unis *(pages 68-69)*

1. Read the Reading Strategy at the beginning of the **Lecture culturelle.** Look at the title of the reading on page 68. It lets you know immediately the general topic you'll be reading about.
2. Read the three subtitles or heads in the passage. They give you a more specific idea of what you'll be reading. Without having read

the reading selection, you now have some understanding of what the reading is about. This will make comprehension much easier.

3. After looking at the title and subtitles, you may very quickly skim the reading. Rather than trying to remember all the information, look at the comprehension questions that follow it. Then go back to the reading and look for the specific factual information called for.

CHAPITRE 3

Vocabulaire

Mots 1 & 2 *(pages 82-89)*

1. Look at each photo or illustration carefully.
2. Read the labels. What does each word refer to?
3. Each word is then used in a meaningful context in a complete sentence. Repeat the individual words and then the sentences.
4. Note that in Activity 4 on page 85, the answer to the question word **qu'est-ce que (qu')** is always a thing. Therefore you should be able to guess the meaning of this question word. Does it mean *who* or *what?*
5. On page 86, after you have practiced your new words, cover up the words as you look at the drawing or photo of each classroom item. See how many you remember. If you don't remember many, you'll have to practice the words some more.

HINT Always pay careful attention to both the pronunciation and the spelling of your new words. You have now seen more than one form of certain verbs. For example: **Ils jouent. Il joue. Ils regardent. Il regarde.** Have you noticed that there is no difference in pronunciation between **regardent** and **regarde** even though they are written differently?

HINT FOR SPEAKING Whenever possible, read all the answers aloud to any activity labeled **Historiette.** Every time you do, you'll be telling a story on your own with the guidance of the activity in the text. This is an easy and useful way to get yourself speaking lots of French.

Structure

Les verbes réguliers en -er *au présent*

(pages 90–93)

1. Now that you know the word **on,** which almost always replaces **nous,** you will see that you really only have to pronounce two forms of a regular **-er** verb. When speaking, whether the subject of the sentence is **je, tu, il, on, elle, ils,** or **elles,** the verb sounds the same. Only the **vous** form has a different pronunciation. This makes spoken French quite easy.

1	2
je parle	
tu parles	**vous regardez**
il/elle/on parle	
ils/elles parlent	

2. However, when you write, remember that there are spelling changes.

   je parle
   tu parles
   il/elle/on parle
   ils/elles parlent

HINT Note that the structure activities in your book build from easy to more complex. In the beginning activities, you very often have to use only one verb form. For example, in Activity 13 on page 91, you only use the **il** form. However, in Activity 20 on page 93, you have to use all forms of the verb.

3. When doing Activity 21 on page 93, remember to use only French that you know. Refer to the list of words given here. This list will prevent you from thinking about things you cannot yet say in French.

La négation des articles indéfinis *(page 94)*
Try to condense a grammatical rule into one easy sentence that you can remember easily: **Un, une,** and **des** all become **de** after **ne... pas.**

Verbe + infinitif *(page 95)*
Note that the infinitive form of the verb used after a verb is pronounced the same as the **vous** form: **Vous travaillez.**
J'aime travailler.
Travaillez and **travailler** are pronounced the same. When writing, remember the difference in spelling:
Vous travaillez? Moi, j'aime travailler.
Vous rigolez? Moi, j'aime rigoler.

Conversation

(page 96)

1. This conversation should be very easy for you. You have already learned all the French that is used in the conversation. When practicing this conversation with a classmate, feel free to make as many changes as you want, as long as they make sense.
2. In the conversation, you hear Carol say, **C'est pas vrai.** In spoken French, **ne** is often dropped from the expression **ne... pas.**
3. Note also that Cedric says **Si, c'est vrai.** When someone tells you **no** in French and you want to contradict, you say **si** rather than **oui.**

Lecture culturelle

Une journée avec Jacqueline *(pages 98–99)*

1. Look at the photos on pages 98–99. These photos let you know the reading is about:
   a. shopping for clothes
   b. going to school
   c. making a meal
2. Skim the reading selection and look for the important information such as:
   - Who's the story about?
   - Where does she live and go to school?
   - What are her school hours?
3. Factual recall is an important reading skill. First, find the facts in the reading and then commit them to memory. Activity B tells you what factual information to look for.

VOCABULAIRE *(page 108)*
As you complete the chapter, look at the reference vocabulary list. If there are several words you don't remember, go back to the **Mots 1** and **Mots 2** sections and review. If there are only one or two, you can choose to look them up in the dictionaries beginning on page H72 at the end of this book.

CHAPITRE 4

Vocabulaire

Mots 1 & 2 *(pages 112–120)*

1. In **Mots 1**, remember to listen to the words and repeat orally before reading them. Many names for family members are cognates. Be careful to repeat them correctly.

HINT If you're the type of learner who has to write something before you can remember, copy the words in the **Mots** section once or twice. Use the following learning sequence: *listen, repeat, read, write.*

2. Activity 2 on page 114 helps you review several important question words. The answer in parentheses tells you the meaning of the question word for that sentence. Look at the following question words and answers:

Quand?	**aujourd'hui**
Qu'est-ce que?	**une fête, des cadeaux**
Qui?	**ses cousins, ses cousines**

Decide which question words mean *who, what,* and *when.*

3. Activity 4 on page 115 helps you with productive skills. Remember that when you speak or write about yourself, you must always use the masculine form if you are a male and the feminine form if you are a female.

4. After you have learned the new words in **Mots 2,** look at each illustration, cover up the sentences, and say as much as you can about the illustration. If you can describe the illustration, you know your vocabulary. If you cannot describe it, you have to study some more.

HINT Read or say aloud all the answers to the **Historiette** activities to give you practice in telling coherent stories in French.

Structure

Le verbe **avoir** *(pages 120–122)*

So far, you have learned one irregular verb in French, the verb **être.** All forms of **être** are different. You will now learn your second irregular verb, **avoir**. All forms of **avoir** are also different.

1. Familiarize yourself with the forms of **avoir** as you go over the explanation in class.
2. Do the activities diligently. They give you the opportunity to use and learn the new verb forms without having to memorize them one by one.
3. Do the activities orally and in writing.
4. After doing the activities, reread the grammar explanation. See if you can give the forms of **avoir** on your own without reading them.

REVIEW You know that **un, une,** and **des** all change to **de** after **ne... pas.** The activities on pages 120–122 will help you review this point as you talk about your own home and family.

Conversation

(page 128)

Pay careful attention when you listen to the conversation on the CD-ROM or when other students are repeating it in class. The more you hear spoken French, the easier it will be for you to understand.

Lecture culturelle

Où habitent les Français? (page 130–131)

1. Read the title. When you finish this reading, what will you be able to tell?
   a. where France is
   b. who the French are
   c. where the French people live
2. As you read each paragraph, draw a mental picture of what you're reading. To help you draw your mental picture, look at the photographs, too.

C'est à vous

(pages 136–137)

In Activity 5 on page 137, you are going to write about your house or a house of your dreams.

1. Picture the house.
2. In French, think of or write a list of words you can use to identify parts of the house.
3. In French, think about or write a list of words you can use to describe a house or rooms of a house.
4. Organize your story. Divide the house into parts, such as living area, sleeping area, first floor, second floor. You may even want to make a drawing of your house. Write a few sentences about each area.
5. Put the sentences in a logical order.
6. Add a few sentences to describe the area around your house.

CHAPITRE 5

Vocabulaire

Mots 1 & 2 *(pages 154–161)*

1. It can be fun to study with a classmate.You can do the following.
   - Ask one another questions in French about the illustrations.
   - Have a contest. See who can give more French words describing the illustrations in a three-minute period.
   - Tell your friend which of the items you would order if you were at a café.

2. Activity 1 on page 156 helps you reinforce the meaning of the important question words:

où	**au café**
qui	**Chantal, le serveur**
qu'est-ce que	**une table libre, une boisson**
quand	**après les cours**

3. Act out Activity 4 on page 157 with a classmate. The more you practice speaking French together, the better you'll be able to communicate.

Structure

Le verbe aller *(pages 162–164)*

You will now learn your third irregular verb. Make an association with another irregular verb you have already learned. Repeat the following out loud.

je vais → **j'ai**
tu vas → **tu as**
il va → **il a**
ils vont → **ils ont**

The forms of **aller** almost sound like the forms of **avoir** with a **v** sound.

HINT The more you practice speaking French, the better. When doing your homework, go over all the activities aloud. Don't just do your French homework silently.

Aller + *infinitif* *(page 165)*

1. The concept of an infinitive after a verb is not new to you. You already know how to express what you like to do:
   J'aime manger.
   J'aime aller au restaurant.
2. Now, using the same type of construction, you will be able to tell what you are going to do.
   J'aime manger et je vais manger quelque chose.
   J'aime aller au restaurant et je vais aller au restaurant vendredi.

Conversation

(page 170)

Listen carefully to the conversation. You can listen to your teacher or use the CD-ROM. Listen more than once. Each time listen for a different bit of information.

- Where are Claire and Loïc?
- What do they order?
- Why is there a possible disagreement?

Lecture culturelle

Au restaurant? Vraiment? (pages 172–173)

1. Making comparisons while reading is an important reading comprehension skill. In this reading, you learned about a cultural difference that's quite interesting. What is it? You may want to share this information with family or friends who don't know any French.
2. Finding the main idea is another important reading comprehension skill. As you read, look for the main idea in the second paragraph. What is it? What is the main idea in the third paragraph?

C'est à vous

(pages 178–179)

In Activity 4 on page 179, you're going to write about a restaurant in French.

1. Get a mental picture of the restaurant.
2. Write words you know in French to describe a restaurant and restaurant activities.
3. List items that people may order.
4. Put these words into sentences. Your first paragraph will describe the restaurant. Your second paragraph will tell what your "characters" order. Decide who pays to finish your article.

CHAPITRE 6

Vocabulaire

Mots 1 & 2 *(pages 186–193)*

1. Try to use your French as often as possible. When you see a food item at home or in a

store that is labeled in French, say the French word to yourself. You'll learn to identify many more food items as you continue with your study of French.

2. As you complete the activities, answer each question orally before you write the answers for homework. Try reading your written responses aloud for Activities 2 and 3 on page 188. Activity 2 reviews the questions words **qui, qu'est-ce que, quand, où.**
3. On your own, review the foods you have learned by putting them with an appropriate package or container. For example:
   un paquet de fromage
   un paquet de six tranches de jambon
   un pot de confiture
   un paquet de légumes surgelés

HINTS Note that Activity 10 on page 193 points out that in spoken French, you can omit the **ne** in the expression **ne... pas.**

Be sure you understand the meaning of **pourquoi** and **parce que** when you finish this activity.

Structure

Le verbe faire *au présent* *(pages 194–195)*

1. Look at the forms of the verb **faire.** Repeat them aloud, then copy them.
2. When you complete homework activities, go back to the verb chart. Cover the verb forms and see if you can say the forms without looking at them.

Le partitif et l'article défini *(pages 196–197)*

1. Always try to make what you are learning as simple as possible. If you're talking about something in general, you use **le, la, les.** If you're talking about "some" or "any," you use **du, de la,** or **des.**
2. When doing Activities 18 and 19 on page 197, pay particular attention to the contrast between the general sense and the partitive. You want to buy some (partitive) of the things you like (in general).

Le partitif au négatif *(pages 199–201)*

This concept of **de** is not new. Just remember **du, de la, de l',** and **des** all change to **de** after **ne... pas.** It's really simple, but you have to keep reminding yourself.

HINT Pay close attention as you and your classmates participate in each of these activities. The more you hear **j'ai du** (or **de la, des)** versus **je n'ai pas de,** the easier it will be for you to use the partitive.

HINTS FOR SPEAKING AND WRITING
Listen carefully for the difference in pronunciation between **bonne, bon,** and **gentille, gentil** as explained on page 201. Repeat the words carefully. Repeat the model sentences aloud, then copy them. Pay particular attention to the doubling of the consonant.

Les verbes pouvoir *et* vouloir

(pages 201–203)

Pay attention to the similarity between the forms of **pouvoir** and **vouloir.**

REVIEW Using the infinitive after a helping verb is not new. Remember:
J'aime dîner au restaurant.
Je vais dîner au restaurant.

Conversation

(page 204)

1. Intonation is the melody of a language. Intonation is produced by the rise and fall of the voice. Each language has its own intonation patterns. English intonation is very different from French intonation. Pay special attention to the rise and fall of the speakers' voices as you listen to the conversations on the audiocassette or CD or CD-ROM.
2. Try to imitate the native speakers' intonation as accurately as possible. If you do, you'll sound much more French. Don't be inhibited. Pretend you are acting while you imitate the intonation.

Lecture culturelle

Les courses *(pages 206–207)*

You may not know the meaning of a certain word you come across in a reading selection. However, you can often guess the meaning of the word by the way it is used in the context of the sentence. A new word in this reading is **les commerçants.** Guess what it means by the context of these sentences:

Les Français aiment bien aller chez les petits commerçants du quartier—l'épicier, le boucher, le boulanger, etc.

The fact that the word **commerçants** is followed by the words **l'épicier, le boucher, le boulanger** helps you figure out the meaning of **commerçants.** What do you think the word **commerçants** means in this context?

a. office workers
b. shopkeepers
c. commercials

CHAPITRE 7

Vocabulaire

Mots 1 & 2 *(pages 220–227)*

1. Look at illustrations in **Mots 1** and repeat each word aloud.
2. Write each word for additional reinforcement.
3. When you have finished studying the vocabulary, determine how much you remember. Say to yourself or aloud all the items you know for boy's clothing, girl's clothing, and unisex clothing. When you get dressed in the morning for school, notice how many words you know in French for those items you are wearing.
4. Before you write the answers to the vocabulary activities, work with a friend. Go over each exercise together orally. Then, each of you can write your answers. If you wish, you can check each other's work.
5. After studying the vocabulary in **Mots 2,** make a list of the things that you would most probably want to say in French to a salesperson when shopping for clothes.

REVIEW These vocabulary activities contain many adjectives, or descriptive words. Remember that many adjectives have an **e** when used with a feminine noun. They drop the **e** when used with a masculine noun.

La jupe est	**verte.** **grise.** **petite.** **grande.** **bleue** **jolie.**	**Le blouson est**	**vert.** **gris.** **petit.** **grand.** **bleu.** **joli.**

Structure

Le verbe **mettre** *(pages 228–229)*

1. Remember that you hear and pronounce the **t** in the plural forms of **mettre.** You do not hear or pronounce the **t** in the singular forms.
2. Do the **Attention** activity on page 229 aloud at least twice. As you do, pay very careful attention to pronunciation as well as spelling.

Le comparatif des adjectifs *(pages 230–231)*

1. Remember to make the association that **plus** (+) is more; **moins** (−) is less, and **aussi** (=) is the same. All three words are followed by **que.**
2. As you do these activities, pay particular attention to each adjective.

Les verbes **voir** *et* **croire** *(pages 232–233)*

1. Note that many forms of **voir** and **croire** are pronounced the same.

je crois	**tu crois**	**il croit**	**ils croient**
je vois	**tu vois**	**il voit**	**ils voient**

Conversation

(page 234)

This conversation should be very easy for you. You have already learned all the French that is used in the conversation. When practicing this

conversation with a classmate, feel free to make as many changes as you want, as long as they make sense.

Lecture culturelle

On fait les courses où, à Paris?
(pages 236–237)

1. Look at the photos on pages 236–237. These photos let you know what the reading is about.
2. Look at the titles. They will give you an idea of what you'll be reading about.
3. Quickly scan the reading to get a general idea of what it's all about.
4. Activity A on page 237 will help you practice factual recall. To recall certain facts, it is often necessary to go back over the reading selection and look for details.
5. Drawing conclusions from a reading selection is another important reading comprehension skill. Based on what you read, draw a personal conclusion. Where would you shop in Paris? Why?

VOCABULAIRE *(page 246)*
As you complete the chapter, look at the reference vocabulary list. If there are quite a few words you don't know, go back to the **Mots 1** and **Mots 2** sections and review.

CHAPITRE 8

Vocabulaire

Mots 1 & 2 *(pages 260–267)*

1. Repeat each new word in the **Mots** sections several times. Look at the photo or illustration as you pronounce the word.
2. Some of you may remember information more easily after writing it down. Try copying each vocabulary word once or twice.
3. You may want to do the activities aloud with a friend as a paired activity. Then, individually write the answers and check each other's work.
4. Listen carefully to what your classmates say when they respond in class. The more you hear people use the new words, the more likely you are to remember them.

Structure

Les verbes en* -ir *au présent *(pages 268–269)*
The **je, tu,** and **il/elle/on** forms of many French verbs are all pronounced the same, even though they are spelled differently. The **-is** and **-it** endings are pronounced the same.

Quel *et* tout *(pages 270–271)*
In spoken French, **quel** is very easy. You pronounce all forms the same. Pay particular attention to the different spellings.

***Les verbes* sortir, partir, dormir *et* servir**
(pages 272–275)
To learn the oral forms of many French verbs, pronounce the **ils/elles** form first. Then drop the final consonant sound and you have the pronunciation for the **je, tu, il/elle/on** forms.

ils sor~~tent~~	**je sors, tu sors, il sort**
ils par~~tent~~	**je pars, tu pars, il part**
ils dor~~ment~~	**je dors, tu dors, il dort**
ils ser~~vent~~	**je sers, tu sers, il sert**

Conversation

(page 276)
Listen carefully to the native speaker's intonation or melody on the audiocassette, CD, CD-ROM, or video. Then, imitate the natives' intonation as closely as you can when you repeat.

Lecture culturelle

On va en France. *(pages 278–279)*

1. To figure out the organization of this reading, scan the passage and look for the following information:
   - Who's going where and how?
   - What do they do when they arrive?
2. Sequencing events is an important reading comprehension skill. Sequence the events in this reading selection. Then see if you came up with a sequence similar to the following:

- **La classe de Madame Cadet est dans le hall de l'aérogare.**
- **Les élèves sont dans l'avion.**
- **Ils arrivent à l'aéroport à Paris.**
- **Ils visitent la belle ville de Paris.**

3. See if you can do all of Activity A on page 279 without referring to the reading for answers.
4. Activity B deals with factual recall. See how many of the facts you remember. Go back to the reading selection and find those you do not remember.

CHAPITRE 9

Vocabulaire

Mots 1 & 2 *(pages 292–299)*

1. Listen to the new words in **Mots 1** and repeat them orally before reading them.
2. Answer Activities 1 and 2 on page 294 however you wish. The more information you can give the better.
3. A good way to remember vocabulary is to group words in some meaningful way. For example, you can group cognates, synonyms, or antonyms. An antonym is a word that means the exact opposite of another. There are quite a few words in **Mots 2** for which you know the antonyms.

   Match the following antonyms.

1. monter	**poser une question**
2. assis	**descendre**
3. lit	**terminer, finir**
4. répondre à la question	**debout**
5. commencer	**écrit**

4. Activity 7 on page 299 helps you review the following question words: **qui, qu'est-ce que, où, quel.**

Structure

Les verbes en* -re *au présent *(pages 300–302)*
Remember to drop the final sound of the **ils/elles** form to get the pronunciation for the **je, tu, il/elle/on** forms of the verb.

ils ven~~dent~~	**je vends, tu vends, il/elle/on vend**
ils atten~~dent~~	**j'attends, tu attends, il/elle/on attend**
ils descen~~dent~~	**je descends, tu descends, il/elle/on descend**
ils enten~~dent~~	**j'entends, tu entends, il/elle/on entend**

Remember the **je, tu, il/elle/on** forms of these verbs are all pronounced the same.

HINT When doing these activities on your own, go over them first orally. Then write the answers.

Les adjectifs démonstratifs *(pages 303–305)*
Pronounce the following forms aloud and note how the final **t** sound becomes softer. When used before a masculine noun that begins with a consonant, the final **t** sound is dropped.

cette announe	**cet horaire**	**ce train**
cette gare	**cet aeroport**	**ce billet**

***Les verbes* dire, écrire, lire** *(pages 306–307)*

1. Again remember to drop the final sound of the **ils/elles** form to get the pronunciation for **je, tu, il/elle/on.**

ils di~~sent~~	**je dis, tu dis, il dit**
ils li~~sent~~	**je lis, tu lis, il lit**
ils écri~~vent~~	**j'écris, tu écris, il écrit**

2. Pay particular attention to **vous dites.** Other similar verb forms you have learned are:
   vous faites
   vous êtes

Conversation

(page 308)
You have not learned the expression **tarif étudiant,** but it's easy to guess its meaning through association with other words. **Tarif** is a word that also exists in English. **Étudiant,** a word that is related to the verb **étudier,** is a close cognate of *student.*

Study Tips

Lecture culturelle

Un voyage intéressant *(pages 310–311)*
Always locate the area of the world you are reading about. Look at the map on page 310. Locate the countries of Mali and Sénégal. Locate the cities of Bamako and Dakar.

VOCABULAIRE *(page 320)*
After going over the vocabulary you need when traveling by train, think about a plane trip in French to review the words you already know about this topic.

CHAPITRE 10

Vocabulaire

Mots 1 & 2 *(pages 324–331)*

1. Look at each photo or illustration carefully.
2. Read the labels. What does each word refer to?
3. The words are then used in a meaningful context in a complete sentence. Repeat the sentence aloud as you look at the illustration.
4. To help you learn vocabulary, work with a friend or classmate. Have a contest. See who can say the most about each illustration or photo.
5. It is important to review the question words in French often. Activity 1 on page 326 reviews the following question words: **quoi, combien, qui, qu'est-ce que.**

Structure

Le passé composé des verbes réguliers
(pages 332–334)

1. The formation of the past tense, the **passé composé,** in French is very easy.
   - Review the forms of the verb **avoir.**
   - To form the past participle of all regular verbs, you only have to remember three vowel sounds: /é/, /i/, /ü/
2. Using the **passé composé** in the negative is simple. Think of **ne… pas** as the bread of a sandwich. The filling for the sandwich is the verb **avoir.**

Les verbes* boire, devoir *et* recevoir *au présent *(pages 337–339)*
Remember once again to drop the final sound of the **ils/elle** form of these verbs to get the pronunciation of the **je, tu, il/elles/on** forms.

ils boi~~vent~~	**je bois, tu bois, il/elle/on boit**
ils doi~~vent~~	**je dois, tu dois, il/elle/on dois**
ils reçoi~~vent~~	**je reçois, tu reçois, il/elle/on reçoit**

Conversation

(page 340)
The activity **Après la conversation** enables you to practice question words.

Lecture culturelle

Le hockey et le basket-ball *(pages 342–343)*
Before reading this selection, sit back and think for a moment about what you know concerning hockey and basketball. Make a mental picture of each game. This will help you understand the reading selection.

VOCABULAIRE *(page 352)*
Look at each word and see if you can use it in a short sentence.

CHAPITRE 11

Vocabulaire

Mots 1 & 2 *(pages 356–363)*

1. For **Mots 1**, after going over the new vocabulary, review immediately. Sit back for a moment and say aloud or to yourself five words or expressions associated with the beach.
2. Pretend you are on the beach. Think of three things you would like to do while on the beach. Start your sentences with **Je voudrais…**
3. After completing each activity on pages 358–359, read all the answers aloud or

silently. You're not only reading a story with words you know; you're also having another opportunity to use your new words.

4. In **Mots 2,** when learning the winter weather expressions, review the summer expressions on pages 356–357.
5. As you do the activities on pages 362–363, work with a classmate. Take turns asking and answering the questions orally. Then write your answers individually. Correct each other's work.

Structure

Le passé composé des verbes irréguliers *(pages 364–366)*

1. Past participles of regular verbs have only three sounds:

-er	/é/
-ir	/i/
-re	/ü/

2. Remember that participles of all irregular verbs, except **être** and **faire,** have only two of these sounds: /i/ and /ü/. /Ü/ is always spelled the same, but **i** is sometimes spelled **-is** and sometimes **-it.**
3. When reading or writing the activities on pages 365–366, pay particular attention to the spelling of past participles with the /i/ sound.

Les mots négatifs *(pages 367–368)*

To learn the meaning of the negative words, pay particular attention to the opposites.

Oui, quelque chose.	**Non, rien.**
Oui, quelqu'un.	**Non, personne.**
Oui, toujours.	**Non, jamais.**
Oui, souvent.	**Non, jamais.**
Oui, quelquefois.	**Non, jamais.**

Le passé composé avec être *(pages 369–371)*

1. If necessary, quickly review the verb **être.**

je suis	**nous sommes**
tu es	**vous êtes**
il/elle/on est	**ils/elles sont**

HINTS FOR SPEAKING AND WRITING Past participles that end in a vowel (/é/, /i/, /ü/) sound the same in all forms. Even though all forms are pronounced the same, you must pay particular attention to the spelling of these past participles when writing. They add **e** for the feminine and **s** for the plural.

parti /i/
partis /i/
partie /i/
parties /i/

2. In the activities on pages 370–371, pay particular attention to the spelling of the past participle.

Lecture culturelle

Un petit voyage au Canada *(pages 374–375)*

1. Skim the selection quickly to get a very general idea of what it's about.
2. Scan the selection to look for specific information.
   - Who went where? When? How?
   - What did they see and do?
3. Which statement best summarizes the first paragraph?
   a. **C'est le mois de février.**
   b. **La classe de Madame Lebrun a pris le train.**
   c. **La classe de Madame Lebrun est allée au Canada.**
4. Which statement best summarizes the second paragraph?
   a. **Ils ont passé trois jours à Montréal.**
   b. **Ils sont allés à une très belle station de sports d'hiver.**
   c. **Ils ont mis leurs skis.**

Inference is an important reading comprehension skill. In this selection, we learn the students are really tired and they sleep like logs. The reading doesn't actually tell us why they are so tired, but you can figure it out from the information you read.

5. Why are the students so tired?
   a. They didn't sleep the night before the trip.
   b. They were anxious to get back to the dorms.
   c. They were worn out from all their activities.

CHAPITRE 12

Vocabulaire

Mots 1 & 2 *(pages 400–407)*

1. In **Mots 1,** to make it easier to remember the meaning of the new words, they are put in a logical sequence of events:
   se reveiller, se lever, se laver (la figure, les cheveux), se peigner, se maquiller, s'habiller
2. Activity 2 on page 402 helps you review the rooms of a house:
   la cuisine, la salle à manger, le salon, la chambre à coucher, la salle de bains
3. Matching synonyms and/or antonyms can often help you remember words.

   Match the antonyms *(opposites)* in **Mots 2.**

1. Il a mis la table.	**Il a débarrassé la table.**
2. Il a allumé la télé.	**Il a éteint la télé.**

   Match the synonyms.

1. un frigidaire	**mettre la télé**
2. le salon	**un réfrigérateur**
3. allumer la télé	**changer de chaine**
4. zapper	**la salle de séjour**

Structure

Les verbes réfléchis au présent
(pages 408–412)

1. Remember that if a person is doing something to or for himself or herself, the verb in French is a reflexive verb, and you must use the additional pronoun.
2. You have already learned all the verb endings that are used in these activities. The only new concept is the use of the reflexive pronoun. Pay particular attention to this pronoun as you do these activities.

Les verbes réfléchis au passé composé
(pages 413–415)
Since the past participle of almost all reflexive verbs ends in a vowel, all forms are pronounced the same. However, in writing, the plural and feminine endings must be added.

CHAPITRE 13

Vocabulaire

Mots 1 & 2 *(pages 432–439)*

1. Remember to listen to the words and repeat them orally before reading them.
2. After you have gone over the new vocabulary, see how many words you remember. Think of seven words about a movie. Think of five words about a play.
3. Go over each activity orally before you write the answers.

Structure

***Les verbes* savoir *et* connaître** *(pages 440–441)*

1. Simplify the grammatical rule: just remember that **savoir** means to know something simple, and **connaître** means to know or be familiar with something complex.
2. When doing these activities, pay particular attention to the object of each verb to determine the use of **savoir** or **connaître.**

***Les pronoms* me, te, nous, vous**
(pages 442–443)
Remember that the pronouns **me, te, nous,** or **vous** are part of the "filling in the sandwich." **Ne... pas** is the bread that goes around the filling.

	me parle	
Il ne	**te parle**	**pas.**
	nous parle	
	vous parle	

***Les pronoms* le, la, les** *(pages 444–447)*
As you do these activities, determine which word is the direct object before trying to replace it with **le, la,** or **les.** Do each activity orally before you write it.

Conversation

(page 448)

1. An important skill in understanding a foreign language is to guess the meaning of words from the context in which they occur. In this conversation, you will hear and use the expression **travailler notre espagnol.** This is new to you, but you can figure it out from the context.

   In this conversation, **travailler** means which of the following?
   - a. **parler**
   - b. **comprendre**
   - c. **pratiquer**

2. Note how Lea says **ça me dit** in response to the question **ça t'intéresse?** Do you think **ça me dit** has the same meaning as the phrase **ça m'intéresse?**

Lectures culturelle

Les loisirs culturels en France *(pages 450–451)*

Identifying the main idea is an important comprehension skill. Read the title and subtitles. What do you think is the main idea of this reading?
- a. **Il y a des musées et des théâtres en France.**
- b. **Les Français apprécient les loisirs culturels.**
- c. **L'entrée des musées est gratuite le premier dimanche du mois.**

VOCABULAIRE *(page 460)*

Read the list of words and determine how many you know. Many of these words are easy to remember because they are cognates.

CHAPITRE 14

Vocabulaire

Mots 1 & 2 *(pages 464–471)*

1. Whenever you have the chance to review, do so. As you do **Mots 1,** think of all the parts of the body you have learned in French.
2. To determine if you know your new vocabulary from **Mots 2,** see whether you can do the following:
   - Tell three things a patient may do in a doctor's office.
   - Tell three things the doctor may do.
   - Tell three things a doctor may say to a patient.

Structure

***Les pronoms* lui, leur** *(pages 472–473)*

Here's an easy way to tell the difference between a direct object and an indirect object. A direct object answers the question *who(m)* or *what.*

Who(m) did you see?	I saw the doctor.
What did you take?	I took the medicine.

If it cannot answer the question *who(m)* or *what,* the object is indirect.

***Les verbes* souffrir *et* ouvrir** *(page 474)*

Review the forms of a regular **-er** verb. Compare them to the verb **ouvrir.**

j'écoute	**j'ouvre**
tu écoutes	**tu ouvres**
il écoute	**il ouvre**
nous écoutons	**nous ouvrons**
vous écoutez	**vous ouvrez**
ils écoutent	**ils ouvrent**

L'impératif *(pages 475–477)*

Remember, you use the command (imperative) to tell someone what to do. You merely use the **tu** or **vous** form of the verb to form the command. Just remember that you drop the final **s** from the **tu** form of regular **-er** verbs.

***Le pronom* en** *(pages 478–479)*

You will hear and use the word **en** quite frequently in French. Pay careful attention to the explanation of the use of this word.

VERBS RÉGULIERS			
INFINITIF	**parler** *to speak*	**finir** *to finish*	**répondre** *to answer*
PRÉSENT	je parle tu parles il parle nous parlons vous parlez ils parlent	je finis tu finis il finit nous finissons vous finissez ils finissent	je réponds tu réponds il répond nous répondons vous répondez ils répondent
IMPÉRATIF	parle parlons parlez	finis finissons finissez	réponds répondons répondez
PASSÉ COMPOSÉ	j'ai parlé tu as parlé il a parlé nous avons parlé vous avez parlé ils ont parlé	j'ai fini tu as fini il a fini nous avons fini vous avez fini ils ont fini	j'ai répondu tu as répondu il a répondu nous avons répondu vous avez répondu ils ont répondu

VERBES AVEC CHANGEMENTS D'ORTHOGRAPHE			
INFINITIF	**acheter**[1] *to buy*	**appeler** *to call*	**commencer** *to begin*
PRÉSENT	j'achète tu achètes il achète nous achetons vous achetez ils achètent	j'appelle tu appelles il appelle nous appelons vous appelez ils appellent	je commence tu commences il commence nous commençons vous commencez ils commencent
INFINITIF	**manger**[2] *to eat*	**payer**[3] *to pay*	**préférer**[4] *to prefer*
PRÉSENT	je mange tu manges il mange nous mangeons vous mangez ils mangent	je paie tu paies il paie nous payons vous payez ils paient	je préfère tu préfères il préfère nous préférons vous préférez ils préfèrent

[1] *Verbes similaires:* **se lever, se promener**
[2] *Verbes similaires:* **nager, voyager**
[3] *Verbes similaires:* **essayer, renvoyer, employer, envoyer**
[4] *Verbes similaires:* **célébrer, espérer, suggérer**

VERBES IRRÉGULIERS			
INFINITIF	**aller** *to go*	**avoir** *to have*	**conduire** *to drive*
PRÉSENT	je vais tu vas il va nous allons vous allez ils vont	j'ai tu as il a nous avons vous avez ils ont	je conduis tu conduis il conduit nous conduisons vous conduisez ils conduisent
PASSÉ COMPOSÉ	je suis allé(e)	j'ai eu	j'ai conduit
INFINITIF	**connaître** *to know*	**croire** *to believe*	**devoir** *to have to, to owe*
PRÉSENT	je connais tu connais il connaît nous connaissons vous connaissez ils connaissent	je crois tu crois il croit nous croyons vous croyez ils croient	je dois tu dois il doit nous devons vous devez ils doivent
PASSÉ COMPOSÉ	j'ai connu	j'ai cru	j'ai dû
INFINITIF	**dire** *to say*	**dormir** *to sleep*	**écrire** *to write*
PRÉSENT	je dis tu dis il dit nous disons vous dites ils disent	je dors tu dors il dort nous dormons vous dormez ils dorment	j'écris tu écris il écrit nous écrivons vous écrivez ils écrivent
PASSÉ COMPOSÉ	j'ai dit	j'ai dormi	j'ai écrit
INFINITIF	**être** *to be*	**faire** *to do, to make*	**lire** *to read*
PRÉSENT	je suis tu es il est nous sommes vous êtes ils sont	je fais tu fais il fait nous faisons vous faites ils font	je lis tu lis il lit nous lisons vous lisez ils lisent
PASSÉ COMPOSÉ	j'ai été	j'ai fait	j'ai lu

INFINITIF	**mettre** *to put*	**ouvrir**[5] *to open*	**partir** *to leave*
PRÉSENT	je mets tu mets il met nous mettons vous mettez ils mettent	j'ouvre tu ouvres il ouvre nous ouvrons vous ouvrez ils ouvrent	je pars tu pars il part nous partons vous partez ils partent
PASSÉ COMPOSÉ	j'ai mis	j'ai ouvert	je suis parti(e)
INFINITIF	**pouvoir** *to be able to*	**prendre**[6] *to take*	**recevoir** *to receive*
PRÉSENT	je peux tu peux il peut nous pouvons vous pouvez ils peuvent	je prends tu prends il prend nous prenons vous prenez ils prennent	je reçois tu reçois il reçoit nous recevons vous recevez ils reçoivent
PASSÉ COMPOSÉ	j'ai pu	j'ai pris	j'ai reçu
INFINITIF	**savoir** *to know*	**servir** *to serve*	**sortir** *to go out*
PRÉSENT	je sais tu sais il sait nous savons vous savez ils savent	je sers tu sers il sert nous servons vous servez ils servent	je sors tu sors il sort nous sortons vous sortez ils sortent
PASSÉ COMPOSÉ	j'ai su	j'ai servi	je suis sorti(e)
INFINITIF	**venir**[7] *to come*	**voir** *to see*	**vouloir** *to want*
PRÉSENT	je viens tu viens il vient nous venons vous venez ils viennent	je vois tu vois il voit nous voyons vous voyez ils voient	je veux tu veux il veut nous voulons vous voulez ils veulent
PASSÉ COMPOSÉ	je suis venu(e)	j'ai vu	j'ai voulu

[5] *Verbes similaires:* **couvrir, découvrir, offrir, souffrir**
[6] *Verbes similaires:* **apprendre, comprendre**
[7] *Verbes similaires:* **devenir, revenir**

VERBES AVEC ÊTRE AU PASSÉ COMPOSÉ

aller *(to go)*	je suis allé(e)
arriver *(to arrive)*	je suis arrivé(e)
descendre *(to go down, get off)*	je suis descendu(e)
entrer *(to enter)*	je suis entré(e)
monter *(to go up)*	je suis monté(e)
mourir *(to die)*	je suis mort(e)
naître *(to be born)*	je suis né(e)
partir *(to leave)*	je suis parti(e)
passer *(to go by)*	je suis passé(e)
rentrer *(to go home)*	je suis rentré(e)
rester *(to stay)*	je suis resté(e)
retourner *(to return)*	je suis retourné(e)
revenir *(to come back)*	je suis revenu(e)
sortir *(to go out)*	je suis sorti(e)
tomber *(to fall)*	je suis tombé(e)
venir *(to come)*	je suis venu(e)

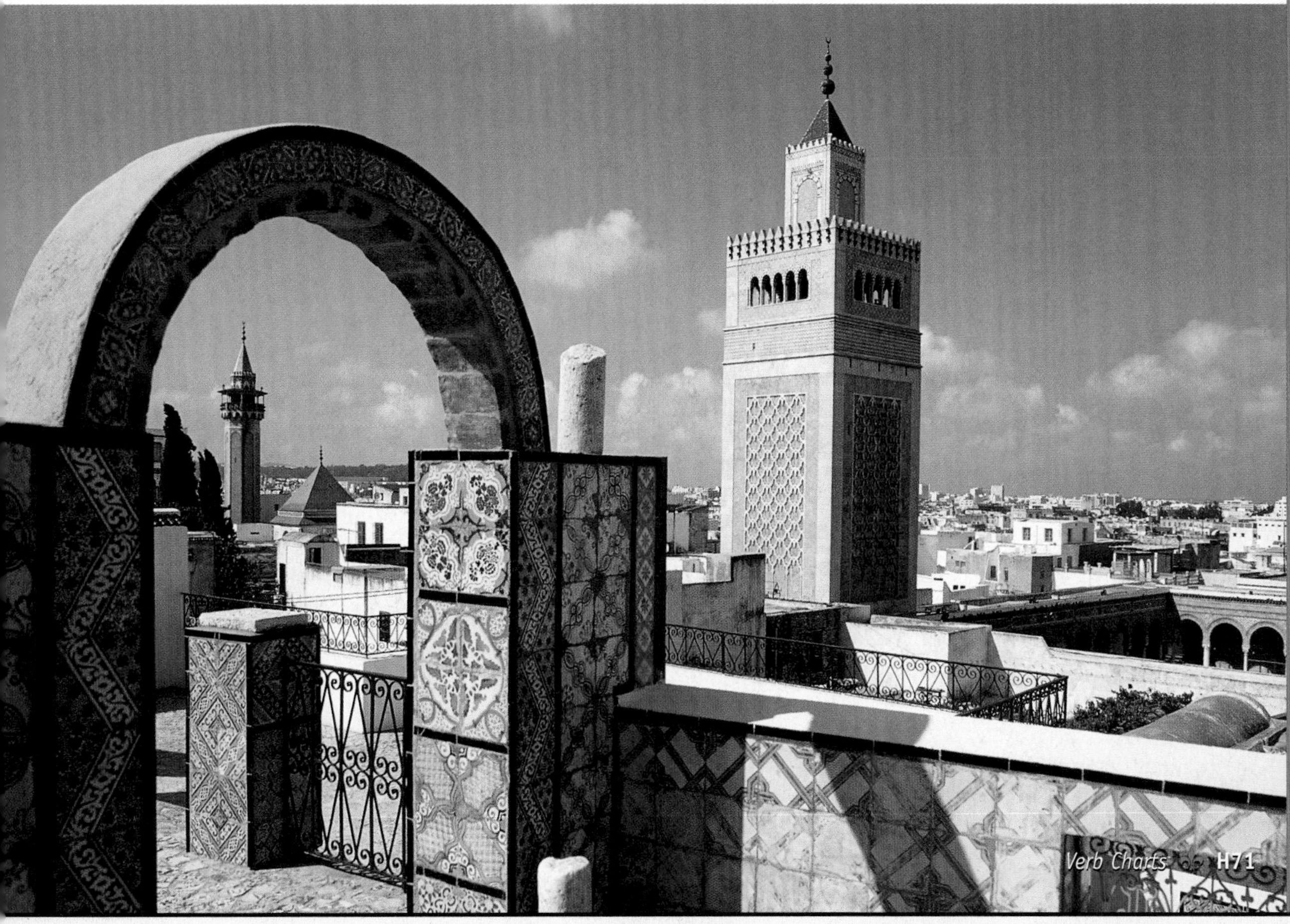

French-English Dictionary

This French-English Dictionary *contains all productive and receptive vocabulary from the text. The numbers following each productive entry indicate the chapter and vocabulary section in which the word is introduced. For example,* ***2.2*** *means that the word first appeared in* ***Chapitre 2, Mots 2. BV*** *refers to the introductory* ***Bienvenue*** *lessons.* ***L*** *refers to the optional literary readings. If there is no number or letter following an entry, this means that the word or expression is there for receptive purposes only.*

A

à at, in, to, **3.1**
À bientôt! See you soon!, **BV**
à bord (de) on board, **8.2**
à cause de because of
À demain. See you tomorrow., **BV**
à destination de to *(destination)*, **8.1**
à domicile to the home
à l'heure on time, **8.1**
à mon (ton, son, etc.) avis in my (your, his, etc.) opinion, **7.2**
à nouveau again
à peu près about, approximately
à pied on foot, **4.2**
à point medium-rare *(meat)*, **5.2**
À tout à l'heure. See you later., **BV**
abandonner to abandon
l' **abbé** *(m.)* priest
abondant(e) plentiful
absolument absolutely
accessible accessible
l' **accessoire** *(m.)* accessory
l' **accident** *(m.)* accident
accompagner to accompany, to go with
l' **accordéon** *(m.)* accordion
l' **accusation** *(f.)* accusation
accuser to accuse
l' **achat** *(m.)* purchase
faire des achats to shop
acheter to buy, **3.2**
l' **acte** *(m.)* act, **13.1**
l' **acteur** *(m.)* actor, **13.1**
actif, active active
l'**action** *(f.)* action
l'**activité** *(f.)* activity
l' **actrice** *(f.)* actress, **13.1**
l' **addition** *(f.)* check, bill *(restaurant)*, **5.2**
additionner to add
admirer to admire
l' **adolescent(e)** adolescent, teenager
adorable adorable, **4.1**
adorer to love
l' **adresse** *(f.)* address
l' **adulte** *(m. et f.)* adult
l' **adversaire** *(m. et f.)* adversary, opponent
adverse opposing, **10.1**
aérien(ne) air, flight *(adj.)*
l' **aérogare** *(f.)* airport terminal, **8.1**
l' **aéroport** *(m.)* airport, **8.1**
l' **affiche** *(f.)* poster
africain(e) African
l' **Afrique** *(f.)* Africa
afro-américain(e) African-American
l' **âge** *(m.)* age, **4.1**
Tu as quel âge? How old are you?, **4.1**
âgé(e) old
l' **agent** *(m.)* agent *(m. and f.)*, **8.1**
agité(e) choppy, rough *(sea)*
l' **agneau** *(m.)* lamb, **6.1**
agréable pleasant
l' **aide** *(f.)* aid, help
à l'aide de with the help of
aider to help
aigu(ë) acute, severe, **14.2**
aimer to like, love, **3.1**
aimer mieux to prefer, **7.2**
l' **aîné(e)** older, **L1**
ainsi que as well as
l' **air** *(m.)* air; melody
avoir l'air to look
aisé(e) well-to-do
l' **album** *(m.)* album
l' **algèbre** *(f.)* algebra, **2.2**
l' **Algérie** *(f.)* Algeria
algérien(ne) Algerian
l' **aliment** *(m.)* food
l' **alimentation** *(f.)* nutrition, diet
l' **Allemagne** *(f.)* Germany
l' **allemand** *(m.)* German *(language)*, **2.2**
aller to go, **5.1**
aller chercher to go (and) get, **6.1**
aller mieux to feel better, **14.2**
Allez! Come on!, **9.2**
Qu'est-ce qui ne va pas? What's wrong?
l' **aller** *(m.)* going
l'aller (simple) one-way ticket, **9.1**

le billet aller (et) retour round-trip ticket, **9.1**
l' **allergie** *(f.)* allergy, **14.1**
allergique allergic, **14.1**
allumer to turn on *(appliance)*, **12.2**
alors so, then, well then, **BV**
ambitieux, ambitieuse ambitious
l' **amende** *(f.)* fine
américain(e) American, **1.1**
l' **Amérique** *(f.)* **du Sud** South America
l' **ami(e)** friend, **1.2**
l' **amour** *(m.)* love, **L4**
ample large, full
amusant(e) funny; fun, **1.1**
s' **amuser** to have fun, **12.2**
l' **an** *(m.)* year, **4.1**
avoir... ans to be . . . years old, **4.1**
l' **analyse** *(f.)* analysis
analyser to analyse
analytique analytical
l' **anatomie** *(f.)* anatomy
ancien(ne) old, ancient; former
l' **angine** *(f.)* throat infection, tonsillitis, **14.1**
l' **anglais** *(m.)* English *(language)*, **2.2**
anglais(e) English
l' **Angleterre** *(f.)* England
l' **animal** *(m.)* animal
l' **année** *(f.)* year
l'année dernière last year
l' **anniversaire** *(m.)* birthday, **4.1**
Bon (Joyeux) anniversaire! Happy birthday!
l' **annonce** *(f.)* announcement, **8.2**
annoncer to announce, **9.1**
anonyme anonymous
l' **anorak** *(m.)* ski jacket, **7.1**
l' **antibiotique** *(m.)* antibiotic, **14.1**
Antilles: la mer des Antilles Caribbean Sea
l' **antonyme** *(m.)* antonym
l' **appareil** *(m.)* apparatus
apparenté: le mot apparenté cognate
l' **appartement** *(m.)* apartment, **4.2**
appeler to call
s' **appeler** to be called, be named, **12.1**
applaudir to applaud
apporter to bring, **11.1**
apprécier to appreciate
apprendre (à) to learn (to), **5;** to teach
apprendre à quelqu'un à faire quelque chose to teach someone to do something
après after, **3.2**
d'après according to
l' **après-midi** *(m.)* afternoon, **3.2**
arabe Arab
l' **arabe** *(m.)* Arabic *(language)*
l' **arbitre** *(m.)* referee, **10.1**
l' **arbre** *(m.)* tree, **L3**
l' **architecture** *(f.)* architecture
l' **argent** *(m.)* money, **5.2**
l' **arme** *(f.)* weapon
l' **armée** *(f.)* army, **L3**
l' **arrêt** *(m.)* stop, **9.2**
arrêté(e) arrested
s' **arrêter** to stop, **10.1;** to arrest
l' **arrière** *(m.)* rear, back, **8.2**
l' **arrière-garde** *(f.)* rear guard
l' **arrivée** *(f.)* arrival, **8.1**
arriver to arrive, **3.1;** to happen
arriver à (+ *inf.*) to manage to, to succeed in, **9.1**
l' **arrondissement** *(m.)* district (in Paris)
l' **artère** *(f.)* artery
l' **article** *(m.)* article
l' **artiste** *(m. et f.)* artiste
l'artiste peintre *(m. et f.)* painter
artistique artistic
l' **ascenseur** *(m.)* elevator, **4.2**
asiatique Asian
l' **aspirine** *(f.)* aspirin, **14.1**
assez fairly, quite; enough, **1.1**
l' **assiette** *(f.)* plate, **5.2**
ne pas être dans son assiette to be feeling out of sorts, **14.1**
assis(e) seated, **9.2**
l' **assistante sociale** *(f.)* social worker
l' **atelier** *(m.)* studio *(artist's)*
l' **athlétisme** *(m.)* track and field, **10.2**
l' **atmosphère** *(f.)* atmosphere
attaché(e) attached
attacher to fasten, **8.2**
attaquer to attack
attendre to wait (for), **9.1**
attente: la salle d'attente waiting room, **9.1**
l' **attention** *(f.)* attention
Attention! Careful! Watch out!, **4.2**
faire attention to pay attention; to be careful, **11.1**
atterrir to land, **8.1**
l' **atterrissage** *(m.)* landing *(plane)*
attraper un coup de soleil to get a sunburn, **11.1**
au bord de la mer by the ocean; seaside, **11.1**
au contraire on the contrary
au fond in the background
au revoir good-bye, **BV**
au-dessous (de) below
la taille au-dessous the next smaller size, **7.2**
au-dessus (de) above
la taille au-dessus the next larger size, **7.2**
aujourd'hui today, **BV**
auprès de with
ausculter to listen with a stethoscope, **14.2**
aussi also, too, **1.1;** as *(comparisons)*, **7**; so

l' **auteur** *(m.)* author *(m. and f.)*
l'auteur *(m.)* **dramatique** playwright
l' **autocar** *(m.)* bus, coach
automatique automatic, autonomic
l' **automne** *(m.)* autumn, **11.2**
autour de around, **4.2**
autre other, **L1**
autre chose something else
Autre chose? Anything else? *(shopping)*, **6.2**
d'autres some other, **2.2**
l'un... l'autre one . . . the other
autrement dit in other words
l' **avalanche** *(f.)* avalanche
avaler to swallow, **14.2**
avance: en avance early, ahead of time, **9.1**
avant before
avant de (+ *inf.*) before (+ *verb*)
l' **avant** *(m.)* front, **8.2**
avant-hier the day before yesterday, **10.2**
avec with, **3.2**
Avec ça? What else? *(shopping)*, **6.1**
l' **avenir** *(m.)* future, **L2**
l' **aventure** *(f.)* adventure
l' **avenue** *(f.)* avenue
l' **aviateur, l'aviatrice** aviator
l' **avion** *(m.)* plane, **8.1**
en avion by plane
l' **avis** *(m.)* opinion, **7.2**
à mon avis in my opinion, **7.2**
avoir to have, **4.1**
avoir l'air to look
avoir... ans to be . . . years old, **4.1**
avoir besoin de to need, **10.1**
avoir de la chance to be lucky, to be in luck
avoir envie de to want (to), to feel like
avoir faim to be hungry, **5.1**
avoir une faim de loup to be very hungry
avoir lieu to take place
avoir mal à to have a(n) . . . -ache, to hurt, **14.1**
avoir peur to be afraid, **L1**
avoir du retard to be late *(plane, train, etc.)*, **8.1**
avoir soif to be thirsty, **5.1**

B

le **baccalauréat** French high school exam
la **bactérie** bacterium
bactérien(ne) bacterial, **14.1**
les **bagages** *(m. pl.)* luggage, **8.1**
le bagage à main carry-on bag, **8.1**
le coffre à bagages baggage compartment, **8.2**
la **baguette** loaf of French bread, **6.1**
le **baigneur, la baigneuse** bather
le **bain** bath, **12.1**
prendre un bain to take a bath, **12.1**
prendre un bain de soleil to sunbathe, **11.1**
la salle de bains bathroom, **4.2**
le **balcon** balcony, **4.2**
le **ballet** ballet
le **ballon** ball *(soccer, etc.)*, **10.1**
la **banane** banana, **6.2**
la **banlieue** suburbs
la **base** base; basis
à base de based on
le **base-ball** baseball
basé(e) based
la **basilique** basilica
la **basket** sneaker; running shoe, **7.1**
le **basket(-ball)** basketball, **10.2**
la **bataille** battle, **L3**
le champ de bataille battlefield, **L3**
le **bateau** boat, **L4**
le **bâton** ski pole, **11.2**
bavarder to chat
beau (bel), belle beautiful, handsome, **4.2**
Il fait beau. It's nice weather., **11.1**
beaucoup a lot, **3.1**
beaucoup de a lot of, many, **3.2**
le **beau-père** stepfather, **4.1**
la **beauté** beauty
de toute beauté of great beauty
le **bébé** baby
beige *(inv.)* beige, **7.2**
belge Belgian
la **Belgique** Belgium
la **belle-mère** stepmother, **4.1**
ben *(slang)* well
ben oui yeah
le/la **bénévole** volunteer
le **berger, la bergère** shepherd, shepherdess
le **besoin** need
avoir besoin de to need, **10.1**
la **bêtise** stupid thing, nonsense
le **beurre** butter, **6.1**
le **bicentenaire** bicentennial
la **bicyclette** bicycle, **10.2**
bien fine, well, **BV**
bien cuit(e) well-done *(meat)*, **5.2**
bien élevé(e) well-behaved; well-mannered
bien sûr of course
eh bien well
bientôt soon
À bientôt! See you soon! **BV**
le/la **bienvenu(e)** welcome

le **billet** ticket, **8.1**
le billet aller (et) retour round-trip ticket, **9.1**
la **biologie** biology, **2.2**
biologique biological
le/la **biologiste** biologist
blanc, blanche white, **7.2**
blessé(e) wounded, **L3**
bleu(e) blue, **7.2**
bleu marine *(inv.)* navy blue, **7.2**
le **bloc-notes** notepad, **3.2**
blond(e) blond, **1.1**
bloquer to block, **10.1**
le **blouson** (waist-length) jacket, **7.1**
le **blue-jean** (pair of) jeans
le **bœuf** beef, **6.1**
bohème bohemian
boire to drink, **10.2**
quelque chose à boire something to drink
le **bois** wood
la **boisson** beverage, drink, **5.1**
la **boîte: la boîte de conserve** can of food, **6.2**
la boîte crânienne skull
boiteux, boiteuse lame
le **bol** bowl
bon(ne) correct; good, **6.2**
Bon! Okay!, Right!, **6.1**
bon marché *(inv.)* inexpensive
de bonne heure early
le **bonhomme de neige** snowman
bonjour hello, **BV**
le **bonnet** ski cap, hat, **11.2**
le **bord: à bord (de)** aboard *(plane, etc.)*, **8.2**
au bord de la mer by the ocean, seaside, **11.1**
la **bosse** mogul *(ski)*, **11.2**
la **botanique** botany
le **boubou** boubou *(long, flowing garment)*
la **bouche** mouth, **14.1**
le **boucher, la bouchère** butcher
la **boucherie** butcher shop, **6.1**
la **bougie** candle, **4.1**
la **boulangerie-pâtisserie** bakery, **6.1**
la **bouteille** bottle, **6.2**
la **boutique** shop, boutique, **7.1**
le **bras** arm
le **Brésil** Brazil
le/la **Brésilien(ne)** Brazilian *(person)*
la **Bretagne** Brittany
breton(ne) Breton, from Brittany
le/la **Breton(ne)** Breton *(person)*
briller to shine
la **brioche** sweet roll
briser to break, **L3**
se **briser** to break
la **bronche** bronchial tube
bronzer to tan, **11.1**
la **brosse** brush, **12.1**
la brosse à dents toothbrush, **12.1**
se **brosser** to brush, **12.1**
la **brousse** bush *(wilderness)*
le **bruit** noise, **L3**
brûler to burn
brun(e) brunette; dark-haired, **1.1**
le **buffet** train station restaurant, **9.1**
le **bungalow** bungalow
le **bus** bus, **5.2**
le **but** goal, **10.1**
marquer un but to score a goal, **10.1**

C

ça that, **BV**
Ça fait… euros. It's (That's) . . . euros., **6.2**
Ça fait mal. It (That) hurts., **14.1**
Ça va. Fine., Okay., **BV**
Ça va? How's it going?, How are you? *(inform.)*, **BV;** How does it look?, **7.2**
C'est ça. That's right., That's it.
le **cabaret** cabaret
la **cabine** cabin *(plane)*, **8.1**
la cabine d'essayage fitting room
cacher to hide, **L3**
le **cadeau** gift, present, **4.1**
le **cadet, la cadette** younger person, **L1**
le **café** café **BV;** coffee, **5.1**
la **cafétéria** cafeteria
le **cahier** notebook, **3.2**
la **caisse** cash register, checkout counter, **3.2**
le **calcium** calcium
le **calcul** arithmetic, **2.2**
le calcul différentiel differential calculus
le calcul intégral integral calculus
la **calculatrice** calculator, **3.2**
le **calendrier** calendar, schedule
le **calligramme** picture-poem
calme quiet, calm
la **calorie** calorie
le/la **camarade** companion, friend
le/la camarade de classe classmate
le **camembert** Camembert cheese
le **camion** truck
le **camp** side *(in a sport or game)*, **10.1**
le camp adverse opponents, other side, **10.1**
la **campagne** country(side); campaign
canadien(ne) Canadian, **6**
la **cantine** school dining hall, **3.1**
capable able
la **capitale** capital
le **car** bus *(coach)*
la **caractéristique** characteristic
Caraïbes: la mer des Caraïbes Caribbean Sea
cardiaque cardiac
le **carnaval** carnival *(season)*
la **carotte** carrot, **6.2**
la **carrière** career

la **carte** menu, **5.1;** map; card
la carte de crédit credit card
la carte de débarquement landing card, **8.2**
la carte d'embarquement boarding pass, **8.1**
la carte postale postcard, **9.1**
le **carton** cardboard
la **casquette** cap, baseball cap, **7.1**
casse-pieds pain in the neck *(slang)*
la **cassette** cassette, tape **3.1**
la cassette vidéo videocassette, **12.2**
le **catalogue** catalog
catastrophique catastrophic
la **catégorie** category
cause: à cause de because of
causer to cause
le **CD** CD, **3.1**
le **CD-ROM** CD-ROM
ce (cet), cette this, that, **9**
ce soir tonight
la **ceinture** belt, **L3**
la ceinture de sécurité seat belt, **8.2**
célèbre famous
célébrer to celebrate, **L4**
la **cellule** cell, **L4**
celte Celtic
celtique Celtic
cent hundred, **2.2**
pour cent percent
les **centaines** *(f. pl.)* hundreds
le **centilitre** centiliter
le **centre** center
le centre commercial shopping center, mall, **7.1**
le **centre-ville** downtown
le **cercle** circle
les **céréales** *(f. pl.)* cereal, grains
certainement certainly
certains some
le **cerveau** brain
c'est it is, it's, **BV**
C'est combien? How much is it?, **3.2**
C'est quel jour? What day is it? **BV**
C'est tout. That's all., **6.1**
c'est-à-dire that is
chacun(e) each (one), **5.2**
la **chaîne** chain; TV channel, **12.2**
la **chaise** chair
la **chambre à coucher** bedroom, **4.2**
le **champ** field, **L1**
le champ de bataille battlefield, **L3**
champêtre pastoral
le/la **champion(ne)** champion
la **chance** luck
avoir de la chance to be lucky, to be in luck
la **chanson** song
chanter to sing, **13.1**
le **chanteur, la chanteuse** singer, **13.1**
chaque each, every
le **char** float
la **charcuterie** deli(catessen), **6.1**
charger to load
le **chariot** shopping cart, **6.2;** baggage cart, **9.1**
charmant(e) charming
le **charme** charm
le **charpentier** carpenter
le **chasseur, la chasseuse** hunter
le **chat** cat, **4.1**
avoir un chat dans la gorge to have a frog in one's throat, **14.1**
le **château** castle, mansion
chaud(e) warm, hot
Il fait chaud. It's hot. *(weather)*, **11.1**
la **chaussette** sock, **7.1**
la **chaussure** shoe, **7.1**
les chaussures de ski ski boots, **11.2**
le **chef** head, boss
le **chemin** route; road; path
la **cheminée** chimney
la **chemise** shirt, **7.1**
le **chemisier** blouse, **7.1**
cher, chère dear; expensive, **7.1**
chercher to look for, seek
aller chercher to go (and) get, **6.1**
le **chevalier** knight
les **cheveux** *(m. pl.)* hair, **12.1**
chez at (to) the home (business) of, **3.2**
le **chien** dog, **4.1**
la **chimie** chemistry, **2.2**
la **chimiothérapie** chemotherapy
chimique chemical
le/la **chimiste** chemist
chinois(e) Chinese
le **chœur** choir
choisir to choose, **8.1**
le **cholestérol** cholesterol
la **chose** thing
ciao good-bye *(inform.)*, **BV**
le **ciel** sky, **11.1**
le **cinéma** movie theater, movies, **13.1**
le **circuit** circuit
le **cirque** circus
la **circulation** circulation
citer to cite, mention
le **citron pressé** lemonade, **5.1**
le/la **civilisé(e)** civilized person
clair(e) light *(color)*
la **clarinette** clarinet
la **classe** class, **2.1**
la classe économique coach class *(plane)*
la salle de classe classroom, **2.1**
le **classeur** loose-leaf binder, **3.2**
classifier to classify
classique classical
le **classique** classic
le **clavier** keyboard
le/la **client(e)** customer
le **climat** climate
climatique climatic
la **clinique** clinic
le **clown** clown

le **club d'art dramatique** drama club
le **coca** cola, **5.1**
le **code** code, **4.2**
le **coéquipier, la coéquipière** teammate
le **cœur** heart
le **coffre** chest, **L4**
le coffre à bagages (overhead) baggage compartment, **8.2**
le **coin: du coin** neighborhood *(adj.)*
la **collection** collection
le **collège** junior high, middle school, **1.2**
le/la **collégien(ne)** middle school/junior high student
le **combat** fight, battle, **L3**
combien (de) how much, how many, **3.2**
C'est combien? How much is it (that)?, **3.2**
comble packed *(stadium)*, **10.1**
la **comédie** comedy, **13.1**
comique comic; funny, **13.1**
le film comique comedy, **13.1**
commander to order, **5.1**
comme like, as; for; since
comme ci, comme ça so-so
commémorer to commemorate
commencer to begin, **9.2**
comment how, what, **1.1**
Comment ça? How is that?
le/la **commerçant(e)** shopkeeper
la **compagnie** company
la compagnie aérienne airline, **8.1**
en compagnie de in the company of
la **comparaison** comparison
comparer to compare
le/la **compatriote** compatriot
la **compétition** contest
le **complet** suit *(man's)*, **7.1**
complet, complète full, complete
le pain complet whole-wheat bread
complètement completely, totally
compléter to complete
compliqué(e) complicated
comploter to conspire
comporter to call for, require
composé(e) composed
le **compositeur, la compositrice** composer
la **composition** composition
composter to stamp, validate *(a ticket)*, **9.1**
comprendre to understand, **5**
le **comprimé** pill, **14.2**
compris(e) included, **5.2**
Le service est compris. The tip is included., **5.2**
le **compte** account
compter to count
le **comptoir** counter, **8.1**
le **comte** count, **L4**
le **concept** concept
le **concert** concert
le **concert-bal** concert and ball
le **concours** competition, contest
la **condition** *(f.)* condition
la **confiture** jam, **6.2**
confortable comfortable
la **connaissance: faire la connaissance de** to meet
connaître to know, **13.2**
connecter to connect
connu(e) well-known; famous, **13.1**
le (la) plus connu(e) best-known
la **conserve: la boîte de conserve** can of food, **6.2**
la **consommation** drink, beverage, **5.1**
conspirer to plot
construire to build
la **consultation** medical visit
donner des consultations to have office hours *(doctor)*
consulter to consult
le **contact** contact
la **contamination** contamination
contenir to contain
content(e) happy, glad
le **continent** continent
continuer to continue
le **contraire** opposite
contre against, **10.1**
par contre on the other hand, however
le **contremaître, la contremaîtresse** foreman, forewoman
le **contrôle** check, control
le contrôle des passeports passport check
le contrôle de sécurité security *(airport)*, **8.1**
contrôler to check; to control
le **contrôleur** conductor *(train)*, **9.2**
la **conversation** conversation
converser to converse
la **conversion** conversion
convient: qui convient that is appropriate
le **copain** friend, pal *(m.)*, **2.1**
la **copine** friend, pal *(f.)*, **2.1**
le **cor** horn, **L3**
sonner du cor to blow a horn, **L3**
la **cornemuse** bagpipes
le **corps** body
la **correspondance** correspondence; connection *(between trains)*, **9.2**
corriger to correct
cosmopolite cosmopolitan
la **côte** coast
la Côte d'Azur French Riviera
la Côte d'Ivoire Ivory Coast
le **côté** side
côté couloir aisle *(seat)*, **8.1**
côté fenêtre window *(seat)*, **8.1**

coucher to put (someone) to bed, **12**
se **coucher** to go to bed, **12.1**
la **couchette** berth *(on a train)*
couler to flow
avoir le nez qui coule to have a runny nose, **14.1**
la **couleur** color, **7.2**
le **couloir** aisle, corridor, **8.2**
le **coup: le coup de soleil** sunburn, **11.1**
donner un coup (de pied, de tête, etc.) to kick, hit (with one's foot, head, etc.), **10.1**
la **coupe** winner's cup, **10.2**
la **cour** courtyard, **3.2;** court
le **courage** courage
courageux, courageuse courageous, brave
le **coureur, la coureuse** runner, **10.2**
le coureur (la coureuse) cycliste racing cyclist, **10.2**
le **cours** course, class, **2.1**
en cours de (français, etc.) in (French, etc.) class
la **course** race, **10.2**
la course cycliste bicycle race, **10.2**
les **courses** *(f. pl.)*: **faire des courses** to go shopping, **6.1**
court(e) short, **7.2**
le **couscous** couscous
le/la **cousin(e)** cousin, **4.1**
le **couteau** knife, **5.2**
coûter to cost, **3.2**
Ça coûte combien? How much does this cost?, **3.1**
le **couturier** designer *(of clothes)*
le **couvent** convent
couvert(e) covered
le **couvert** table setting; silverware, **5.2**
couvrir to cover
le **crabe** crab, **6.1**
la **cravate** tie, **7.1**
le **crayon** pencil, **3.2**
créer to create
la **crème** cream
la crème solaire suntan lotion, **11.1**
le **crème** coffee with cream *(in a café)*, **5.1**
la **crémerie** dairy store, **6.1**
le **créole** Creole *(language)*
la **crêpe** crepe, pancake, **BV**
creuser to dig, **L4**
crevé(e) exhausted
la **crevette** shrimp, **6.1**
crier to shout, **L4**
le/la **criminel(le)** criminal, **L4**
croire to believe, think, **7.2**
la **croissance** growth
le **croissant** croissant, crescent roll, **5.1**
le **croque-monsieur** grilled ham and cheese sandwich, **5.1**
la **crosse** hockey stick
la **cuillère** spoon, **5.2**
la **cuisine** kitchen, **4.2;** cuisine *(food)*
faire la cuisine to cook, **6**
cuit(e) cooked
bien cuit(e) well-done *(meat)*, **5.2**
cultiver to cultivate
la **culture** culture
culturel(le) cultural
le **cyclisme** cycling, bicycle riding, **10.2**
le/la **cycliste** cyclist, bicycle rider
cycliste bicycle, cycling *(adj.)*, **10.2**
le coureur (la coureuse) cycliste bicycle racer, **10.2**
une course cycliste bicycle race, **10.2**

D

d'abord first, **12.1**
d'accord okay, all right *(agreement)*
être d'accord to agree, **2.1**
dangereux, dangereuse dangerous
dans in, **1.2**
la **danse** dance
danser to dance, **13.1**
le **danseur, la danseuse** dancer, **13.1**
la danseuse ballerina, **13.1**
d'après according to
la **date** date
dater de to date from
d'autres some other, **2.2**
de from, **1.1;** of, belonging to, **1.2;** about
de bonne heure early
de la, de l' some, any, **6**
De quelle couleur est... ? What color is . . . ?, **7.2**
de temps en temps from time to time, occasionally
le **débarquement** landing, deplaning
débarquer to get off *(plane)*
débarrasser la table to clear the table, **12.2**
debout standing, **9.2**
le **début** beginning
le/la **débutant(e)** beginner, **11.2**
le **décalage horaire** time difference
le **décalitre** dekaliter
le **déchet** waste
décider (de) to decide (to)
la **décision** decision
la décision est prise the decision is made
déclarer to declare, call
le **décollage** takeoff *(plane)*
décoller to take off *(plane)*, **8.1**
découvrir to discover
décrire to describe
le **défilé** parade
définir to define
la **déformation** alteration
se **dégager** to be given off

dehors: au dehors de outside
déjà already; ever; yet, **BV**
déjeuner to eat lunch, **3.1**
le **déjeuner** lunch, **5.2**
le petit déjeuner breakfast, **5.2**
délicieux, délicieuse delicious
demain tomorrow, **BV**
À demain. See you tomorrow., **BV**
demander to ask (for), **3.2**
demi(e) half
et demie half past *(time)*, **BV**
le **demi-cercle** semi-circle; top of the key *(on a basketball court)*, **10.2**
le **demi-frère** half brother, **4.1**
la **demi-heure** half hour
la **demi-sœur** half sister, **4.1**
le **demi-tarif** half price
le **demi-tour** about-face
faire demi-tour to turn around
la **dent** tooth, **12.1**
le **dentifrice** toothpaste, **12.1**
le/la **dentiste** dentist
le **déodorant** deodorant
le **départ** departure, **8.1**
le **département d'outre-mer** French overseas department
se **dépêcher** to hurry, **12.1**
dépendre (de) to depend (on)
depuis since, for, **9.2**
dernier, dernière last, **10.2**
derrière behind
désagréable disagreeable, unpleasant
descendre to get off *(train, bus, etc.)*, **9.2;** to take down, **9;** to go down, **9**
désertique desert *(adj.)*
désespéré(e) desperate, **L4**
désirer to want, **5.1**
désormais from then on
le **dessert** dessert
le **dessin** art, **2.2;** drawing, illustration
le dessin animé cartoon, **13.1**
la **destination** destination
à destination de to *(destination)*, **8.1**
la **destinée** destiny
détester to hate, **3.1**
déverser to spill
se déverser to be spilled
deuxième second, **4.2**
devant in front of, **8.2**
devenir to become
deviner to guess
la **devinette** riddle
le **devoir** homework *(assignment)*
faire ses devoirs to do homework, **12.2**
devoir to owe, **10;** must, to have to (+ *verb*), **10.2**
dévoué(e) devoted
d'habitude usually, **12.2**
le **diagnostic** diagnosis, **14.2**
le **dialecte** dialect
le **dialogue** dialog
le **diamant** diamond
dicter to dictate
la **différence** difference
différent(e) different, **8.1**
difficile difficult, **2.1**
la **difficulté** problem, difficulty
être en difficulté to be in trouble
diffuser to spread, to propagate
le **dîner** dinner, **5.2**
dîner to eat dinner, **5.2**
le **diplôme** diploma
dire to say, tell, **9.2**
Ça me dit! I'd like that!
directement directly
la **direction** direction
discuter to discuss
disparaître to disappear
disparu(e) disappeared, lost
le **disque** record
la **disquette** diskette
distinguer to distinguish, to tell apart
divers(e) various
divisé(e) divided
diviser to divide
la **djellaba** djellaba *(long, loose garment)*
le **document** document
le **documentaire** documentary, **13.1**
le **doigt** finger
le **dollar** dollar, **3.2**
le **dolmen** dolmen
le **domaine** domain, field
le **domicile: à domicile** to the home
donc so, therefore
les **données** *(f. pl.)* data
donner to give, **4.1**
donner un coup de pied to kick, **10.1**
donner une fête to throw a party, **4.1**
donner sur to face, overlook, **4.2**
dont of which
doré(e) golden
dormir to sleep, **8.2**
le **dortoir** dormitory
la **douane** customs
doublé(e) dubbed *(movies)*, **13.1**
la **douche** shower, **12.1**
douloureux, douloureuse painful
le **doute** doubt
la **douzaine** dozen, **6.2**
le **drame** drama, **13.1**
dribbler to dribble *(basketball)*, **10.2**
le **droit** right
du coin neighborhood *(adj.)*
dur(e) hard
durer to last
dynamique dynamic, **1.2**

E

l' **eau** *(f.)* water, **6.2**
l'eau bouillante boiling water
l'eau minérale mineral water, **6.2**
l' **échange** *(m.)* exchange
échanger to exchange

s' **échapper** to escape
l' **écharpe** *(f.)* scarf, **11.2**
éclaté(e) burst
l' **école** *(f.)* school, **1.2**
l'école primaire elementary school
l'école secondaire junior high, high school, **1.2**
l' **écologie** *(f.)* ecology
écologique ecological
l' **économie** *(f.)* economics, **2.2**
économique: la classe économique coach class *(plane)*
écouter to listen (to), **3.1**
l' **écran** *(m.)* screen, **8.1**
écrasé(e) crushed
écrire to write, **9.2**
l' **écrivain** *(m.)* writer *(m. and f.)*, **L2**
efficace efficient
égal(e): Ça m'est égal. I don't care., It's all the same to me., **13.1**
égaliser to tie *(score)*
égoïste egotistical, **1.2**
égyptien(ne) Egyptian
l' **élément** *(m.)* element
l' **élève** *(m. et f.)* student, **1.2**
élevé(e) high
bien élevé(e) well-behaved
éliminer to eliminate
l' **e-mail** *(m.)* e-mail
l' **embarquement** *(m.)* boarding, leaving
embarquer to board *(plane, etc.)*
l' **émission** *(f.)* program, show *(TV)*, **12.2**
emmener to send, **L4**
l' **emploi** *(m.)* **du temps** schedule
l' **employé(e)** employee *(m. and f.)*
emprisonné(e) imprisoned
en in, **3.2;** by, **5.2**
en avance early, ahead of time, **9.1**
en avion plane *(adj.)*, by plane
en ce moment right now
en classe in class
en fait in fact
en général in general
en l'honneur de in honor of
en particulier in particular
en plein air outdoors
en plus de besides, in addition
en première (seconde) in first (second) class, **9.1**
en provenance de arriving from *(flight, train)*, **8.1**
en retard late, **9.1**
en solde on sale, **7.1**
en vain in vain
en ville in town, in the city
en voiture by car, **5.2**
encore still, **11;** another; again
s' **endormir** to fall asleep
l' **endroit** *(m.)* place
l' **énergie** *(f.)* energy
énergique energetic, **1.2**
l' **enfance** *(f.)* childhood
l' **enfant** *(m. et f.)* child, **4.1**
enfermer to shut up
enfin finally, at last, **12.1**
s' **engager dans** to head into
l' **ennemi(e)** *(m. et f.)* enemy
énorme enormous
l' **enquête** *(f.)* inquiry, survey
enregistrer to tape, **12.2**
(faire) enregistrer to check *(baggage)*, **8.1**
enrhumé(e): être enrhumé(e) to have a cold, **14.1**
enrichi(e) enriched
l' **ensemble** *(m.)* outfit; whole, entirety
ensemble together, **5.1**
ensuite then *(adv.)*, **12.1**
entendre to hear, **9.1**
enthousiaste enthusiastic, **1.2**
entier, entière entire, whole
l' **entracte** *(m.)* intermission, **13.1**
entre between, among, **3.2**
l' **entrée** *(f.)* entrance, **4.2;** admission
l' **entreprise** *(f.)* firm
entrer to enter, **7.1**
environ about
envoyer to send, **10.1**
l' **épée** *(f.)* sword, **L3**
l' **épicé(e)** spicy
l' **épicerie** *(f.)* grocery store, **6.1**
les **épinards** *(m. pl.)* spinach, **6.2**
épique epic
l' **époque** *(f.)* period, times
épuisé(e) exhausted
l' **équateur** *(m.)* equator
l' **équilibre** *(m.)* balance
équilibré(e) balanced
l' **équipe** *(f.)* team, **10.1**
l' **équipement** *(m.)* equipment
l' **escalier** *(m.)* staircase, **4.2**
l' **espagnol** *(m.)* Spanish *(language)*, **2.2**
l' **esprit** *(m.)* spirit
essayer to try on, **7.2;** to try
essentiel(le) essential
et and, **BV**
établir to establish
l' **établissement** *(m.)* establishment
l' **étage** *(m.)* floor *(of a building)*, **4.2**
l' **étape** *(f.)* stage, lap
les **États-Unis** *(m. pl.)* United States
l' **été** *(m.)* summer, **11.1**
en été in summer, **11.1**
éteindre to turn off *(appliance)*, **12.2**
éternuer to sneeze, **14.1**
étranger, étrangère foreign, **13.1**
être to be, **1.1**
être d'accord to agree, **2.1**
être enrhumé(e) to have a cold, **14.1**

ne pas être dans son assiette to be feeling out of sorts, 14.1
l' **être** *(m.)* being
l'être humain human being
l' **étudiant(e)** *(university)* student
l' **étude** *(f.)* study
étudier to study, **3.1**
l' **euro** *(m.)* euro, **6.2**
l' **Europe** *(f.)* Europe
européen(ne) European
s' **évader** to escape, **L4**
l' **événement** *(m.)* event
évidemment evidently
l' **évier** *(m.)* kitchen sink, **12.2**
éviter to avoid, **12.2**
évoquer to evoke
exact(e) exact
exactement exactly
l' **examen** *(m.)* test, exam, **3.1**
passer un examen to take a test, **3.1**
réussir à un examen to pass a test
examiner to examine, **14.2**
excellent(e) excellent
excepté(e) except
l' **exception** *(f.)* exception
exceptionnel(le) exceptional
l' **excursion** *(f.)* excursion, outing
exécuter to carry out
l' **exemple** *(m.)* example
par exemple for example
l' **exercice** *(m.)* exercise
l' **existence** *(f.)* existence
exister to exist, to be
expert(e) expert *(adj.)*
l' **explication** *(f.)* explanation
expliquer to explain
l' **exposition** *(f.)* exhibit, show, **13.2**
l' **express** *(m.)* espresso, black coffee, **5.1**
l' **expression** *(f.)* expression
expulser to expel, banish
l' **extérieur** *(m.)* exterior, outside
à l'extérieur outside, outside the home
extraordinaire extraordinary, **13.2**

F

la **fable** fable
fabriquer to build
fabuleusement fabulously
fabuleux, fabuleuse fabulous
facile easy, **2.1**
la **façon** way, manner
faible weak, **L1**
faim: avoir faim to be hungry, **5.1**
faire to do, make, **6.1**
Ça fait mal. It (That) hurts., **14.1**
faire du (+ nombre) to take size (+ number), **7.2**
faire des achats to shop
faire attention to pay attention, **6;** to be careful, **11.1**
faire des courses to go shopping, **7.2**
faire les courses to do the grocery shopping, **6.1**
faire la cuisine to cook, **6**
faire ses devoirs to do homework, **12.2**
faire enregistrer to check (luggage), **8.1**
faire des études to study
faire du français (des maths, etc.) to study French (math, etc.), **6**
faire du jogging to jog
faire la navette to go back and forth, make the run
faire une ordonnance to write a prescription, **14.2**
faire partie de to be a part of
faire de la planche à voile to go windsurfing, **11.1**
faire une promenade to take a walk, **11.1**
faire la queue to wait in line, **9.1**
faire du ski nautique to water-ski, **11.1**
faire du surf to go surfing, **11.1**
faire la vaisselle to do the dishes, **12.2**
faire les valises to pack (suitcases), **8.1**
faire un pique-nique to have a picnic
faire un voyage to take a trip, **8.1**
Il fait quel temps? What's the weather like?, **11.1**
Vous faites quelle pointure? What size shoe do you take?, **7.2**
Vous faites quelle taille? What size do you take (wear)?, **7.2**
fait(e) à la main handmade
falsifier to falsify
la **famille** family, **4.1**
le nom de famille last name
le/la **fana** fan
la **fanfare** brass band
fantastique fantastic
la **farine de sorgo** sorghum flour
le **fast-food** fast-food restaurant
fatigué(e) tired
faut: il faut one must, it is necessary to, **8.2**
il ne faut pas one must not, **11.1**
la **faute** fault, mistake
faux, fausse false
favori(te) favorite, **7.2**
la **femme** woman, **7.1;** wife, **4.1**
la **fenêtre** window
côté fenêtre window *(seat) (adj.)*, **8.1**
fermé(e) closed, **13.2**

le **festival** festival
la **festivité** festivity
la **fête** party, **4.1**
de fête festive
donner une fête to throw a party, **4.1**
la **feuille de papier** sheet of paper, **3.2**
le **feutre** felt-tip pen, **3.2**
les **fiançailles** *(f. pl.)* engagement, **L4**
le/la **fiancé(e)** fiancé(e), **L4**
le **fichier** file *(computer)*
fier, fière proud
la **fièvre** fever, **14.1**
avoir de la fièvre to have a fever, **14.1**
avoir une fièvre de cheval to have a high fever, **14.1**
la **figue** fig
la **figure** face, **12.1**
le **filet** net *(volleyball, etc.)*, **10.2**
la **fille** girl, **1.1;** daughter, **4.1**
le **film** film, movie, **13.1**
le film d'amour love story, **13.1**
le film d'aventures adventure movie, **13.1**
le film comique comedy, **13.1**
le film étranger foreign film, **13.1**
le film d'horreur horror film, **13.1**
le film policier detective movie, **13.1**
le film de science-fiction science-fiction movie, **13.1**
le film en vidéo movie video, **13.1**
le **fils** son, **4.1**
la **fin** end
finalement finally
finir to finish, **8.2**
fixement: regarder fixement to stare at
la **fleur** flower, **4.2**
fleuri(e) in bloom, **L2**
fleurir to bloom
le **fleuve** river
la **flûte** flute
le **foie** liver
avoir mal au foie to have indigestion
la **fois** time *(in a series)*, **10.2**
à la fois at the same time
deux fois twice
la **fonction** function
le **fonctionnement** functioning
fond: au fond in the background
respirer à fond to breathe deeply, **14.2**
au fond de at the bottom of
fonder to found
le **foot(ball)** soccer, **10.1**
le football américain football
la **force** strength
la **formalité** *(f.)* formality
la **forme** form, shape
former to form
fort hard *(adv.)*
fort(e) strong, **2.2**
fort(e) en maths good in math, **2.2**
la **fortune** fortune
fou, folle crazy; insane
la **fourchette** fork, **5.2**
la **fourniture** supply
les fournitures scolaires school supplies, **3.2**
la **fracture** fracture *(of bone)*
frais: Il fait frais. It's cool. *(weather)*, **11.2**
les **frais** *(m. pl.)* expenses; charges
la **fraise** strawberry, **6.2**
le **français** French *(language)*, **2.2**
le/la **Français(e)** Frenchman (-woman)
français(e) French, **1.1**
la **France** France
francophone French-speaking
frapper to hit, **L3;** to knock, **L4**
fréquenter to frequent, patronize
le **frère** brother, **1.2**
le **frigidaire** refrigerator, **12.2**
les **frissons** *(m. pl.)* chills, **14.1**
les **frites** *(f. pl.)* French fries, **5.1**
froid(e) cold
Il fait froid. It's cold. *(weather)*, **11.2**
le **fromage** cheese, **5.1**
la **frontière** border
frugal(e) light, simple
le **fruit** fruit, **6.2**
la **fumée** smoke
fumer to smoke
la **fusion** fusion
le **futur** future, **L2**

G

le/la **gagnant(e)** winner, **10.2**
gagner to earn; to win, **10.1**
le **gant** glove, **11.2**
le gant de toilette washcloth, **12.1**
le **garage** garage, **4.2**
le **garçon** boy, **1.1**
garder to guard, watch; to keep
le **gardien** guard, **L4**
le gardien de but goalie, **10.1**
la **gare** train station, **9.1**
gastronomique gastronomic, gourmet
le **gâteau** cake, **4.1**
le **gaz** gas
le gaz carbonique carbon dioxide
le/la **géant(e)** giant
geler to freeze
Il gèle. It's freezing. *(weather)*, **11.2**
le **général** general, 7
en général in general
généralement generally
le **genre** type, kind, **13.1**
les **gens** *(m. pl.)* people
gentil(le) nice *(person)*, **6.2**
la **géographie** geography, **2.2**

la **géométrie** geometry, **2.2**
gigantesque gigantic
la **glace** ice cream, **5.1;** ice, **11.2;** mirror, **12.1**
le **glucide** carbohydrate
la **gomme** eraser, **3.2**
la **gorge** throat, **14.1**
avoir un chat dans la gorge to have a frog in one's throat, **14.1**
avoir la gorge qui gratte to have a scratchy throat, **14.1**
avoir mal à la gorge to have a sore throat, **14.1**
le **gourmet** gourmet
grâce à thanks to
le **gradin** bleacher *(stadium),* **10.1**
la **graisse** fat
la **grammaire** grammar
le **gramme** gram, **6.2**
grand(e) tall, big, **1.1;** great
le grand magasin department store, **7.1**
de grand standing luxury *(adj.)*
la grande surface large department store; large supermarket
grandir to grow (up) *(children)*
la **grand-mère** grandmother, **4.1**
le **grand-père** grandfather, **4.1**
les **grands-parents** *(m. pl.)* grandparents, **4.1**
gratter to scratch, **14.1**
gratuit(e) free
grave serious
la **Grèce** Greece
la **griffe** label
le **griot** griot *(African musician-entertainer)*
la **grippe** flu, **14.1**
gris(e) gray, **7.2**
la **grotte** cave, **L4**
le **groupe** group
guéri(e) cured
la **guerre** war, **L3**
le **guerrier** warrior, **L3**
le **guichet** ticket window, **9.1;** box office, **13.1**
le **guide** guidebook
guillotiné(e) guillotined
la **guitare** guitar
le/la **guitariste** guitarist
la **gymnastique** gymnastics, **2.2**

H

habillé(e) dressy, **7.1**
s' **habiller** to get dressed, **12.1**
habiter to live *(in a city, house, etc.),* **3.1**
haïtien(ne) Haitian
le **hall** lobby, **8.1**
le **hamburger** hamburger
le **hameau** hamlet
handicapé(e) handicapped
le **hardware** *(computer)* hardware
les **haricots** *(m. pl.)* **verts** green beans, **6.2**
la **harpe** harp
haut: en haut de la montagne at the top of the mountain
haut de gamme state of the art
le **hautbois** oboe
l' **hectomètre** *(m.)* hectometer
l' **hémisphère** *(m.)* hemisphere
le **héros** hero
l' **heure** *(f.)* time *(of day),* **BV;** hour, **3.2**
à l'heure on time, **8.1**
à quelle heure? at what time?, **2**
À tout à l'heure. See you later., **BV**
de bonne heure early
Il est quelle heure? What time is it?, **BV**
heureusement fortunately
heureux, heureuse happy
hier yesterday, **10.1**
avant-hier the day before yesterday, **10.2**
hier matin yesterday morning, **10.2**
hier soir last night, **10.2**
l' **histoire** *(f.)* history, **2.2;** story
l' **hiver** *(m.)* winter, **11.2**
l' **H.L.M.** low-income housing
le **hockey** hockey
l' **homme** *(m.)* man, **7.1**
honnête honest
les **honoraires** *(m. pl.)* fees *(doctor)*
l' **hôpital** *(m.)* hospital
l' **horaire** *(m.)* schedule, timetable, **9.1**
horrible horrible
hospitalier, hospitalière hospital *(adj.)*
le **hot-dog** hot dog, **5.1**
l' **hôtel** *(m.)* hotel
l' **hôtesse** *(f.)* **de l'air** flight attendant *(f.),* **8.2**
l' **huile** *(f.)* oil, **6.1**
humain(e) human
l' **hydrate** *(m.)* **de carbone** carbohydrate
hyper: J'ai hyper faim. I'm super hungry.
l' **hypermarché** *(m.)* large department store/ supermarket

I

idéal(e) ideal
l' **idée** *(f.)* idea
identifier to identify
il y a there is, there are, **4.1**
l' **île** *(f.)* island, **L4**
immédiat(e) immediate
immédiatement immediately
immense immense
l' **immeuble** *(m.)* apartment building, **4.2**
important(e) important
impossible impossible
les **impressionnistes** *(m. pl.)* Impressionists *(painters)*
l' **imprimante** *(f.)* printer
inaugurer to inaugurate
inconnu(e) unknown
l' **indication** *(f.)* cue

indiquer to indicate, show
indiscret, indiscrète indiscreet
indispensable indispensable
l' **individu** *(m.)* individual
individuel(le) individual
industriel(le) industrial
l' **infection** *(f.)* infection, **14.1**
inférieur(e) lower
infini(e) infinite
l' **influence** *(f.)* influence
influencer to influence
l' **information** *(f.)* information
les informations *(f. pl.)* news *(TV)*
l' **informatique** *(f.)* computer science, **2.2**
innocent(e) innocent
innombrable countless
insister to insist
inspirer to inspire
les **instructions** *(f. pl.)* instructions
l' **instrument** *(m.)* instrument
l'instrument à clavier keyboard instrument
l'instrument à cordes string instrument
l'instrument à percussion percussion instrument
l'instrument à vent wind instrument
intellectuel(le) intellectual
l' **intellectuel(le)** intellectual
intelligent(e) intelligent, **1.1**
intéressant(e) interesting, **1.1**
intéresser to interest
l' **intérêt** *(m.)* interest
intérieur(e) domestic *(flight)*, **8.1**
international(e) international, **8.1**
interne internal
l' **interprète** *(m. et f.)* interpreter
l' **interro(gation)** *(f.)* quiz
intime intimate
inventer to make up
inviter to invite, **4.1;** to pay for someone's meal, **5.2**
isoler to isolate
l' **italien** *(m.)* Italian *(language)*, **2.2**
italien(ne) Italian
l' **Ivoirien(ne)** *(m. et f.)* Ivorian *(inhabitant of Côte d'Ivoire)*

J

jaloux, jalouse jealous
jamais ever
ne... jamais never, **11.2**
la **jambe** leg
le **jambon** ham, **5.1**
janvier *(m.)* January, **BV**
le **jardin** garden, **4.2**
jaune yellow, **7.2**
le **jazz** jazz
je I, **1.2**
Je t'en prie. You're welcome. *(fam.)*, **BV**
je voudrais I would like, **5.1**
Je vous en prie. You're welcome. *(form.)*, **BV**
le **jean** jeans, **7.1**
jeter to throw, **L4**
le **jeu** game
jeune young
les **jeunes** *(m. pl.)* young people
le **jogging: faire du jogging** to jog
la **joie** joy
joli(e) pretty, **4.2**
jouer to play, **3.2;** to show *(movie)*; to perform, **13.1**
jouer à (un sport) to play (a sport), **10.1**
le **joueur, la joueuse** player, **10.1**
le **jour** day, **BV**
huit jours a week
de nos jours today, nowadays
tous les jours every day, **13.2**
le **journal** newspaper, **9.1**
la **journée** day, **3.1**
Belle journée! What a nice day!, **4.2**
Joyeux anniversaire! Happy birthday!
le **jumeau, la jumelle** twin, **L1**
la **jupe** skirt, **7.1**
le **jus** juice, **5.1**
le jus d'orange orange juice, **5.1**
le jus de pomme apple juice, **5.1**
jusqu'à (up) to, until, **10.2**
juste just, **2.1**
juste à sa taille fitting (him/her) just right
juste là right there
tout juste just barely

K

le **kilo(gramme)** kilogram, **6.2**
le **kilomètre** kilometer
le **kiosque** newsstand, **9.1**
le **kleenex** tissue, **14.1**

L

là there
là-haut up there
le **laboratoire** laboratory
le **lac** lake
laisser to leave *(something behind)*, **5.2;** to let, allow
laisser un pourboire to leave a tip, **5.2**
le **lait** milk, **6.1**
lancer to throw, to shoot *(ball)*, **10.2**
le **langage: en langage courant** commonly known as
la **langue** language, **2.2**
la langue maternelle mother tongue
large loose, wide, **7.2**
le **latin** Latin, **2.2**
latin(e) Latin

latino-américain(e) Latin American
laver to wash, **12**
se **laver** to wash oneself, **12.1**
le **lave-vaisselle** dishwasher, **12.2**
la **leçon** lesson, **11.1**
le **lecteur, la lectrice** reader
la **lecture** reading
la **légende** legend
le **légume** vegetable, **6.2**
la **lettre** letter
lever to raise, **3.1**
lever la main to raise one's hand, **3.1**
se **lever** to get up, **12.1**
la **liaison** liaison, linking
libérer to free
la **liberté** freedom
libre free, **5.1**
le **lieu** place
avoir lieu to take place
la **ligne** line
la **limite** limit
la **limonade** lemon-lime drink, **BV**
le **lipide** fat
le **liquide** liquid
lire to read, **9.2**
le **litre** liter, **6.2**
la **littérature** literature, **2.2**
la **livre** pound, **6.2**
le **livre** book, **3.2**
local(e) local
le **logement** housing
le **logiciel** computer program
loin far (away)
loin de far from, **4.2**
le **long: le long de** along
long(ue) long, **7.1**
longtemps (for) a long time, **11.1**
trop longtemps (for) too long, **11.1**
le **look** style
louer to rent, **13.1**
les **lunettes** *(f. pl.)* **de soleil** sunglasses, **11.1**
la **lutte** fight, battle, **L3**
lutter to fight, **L3**
le **lycée** high school, **2.1**
le/la **lycéen(ne)** high school student

M

la **machine** machine
Madame (Mme) Mrs., Ms., **BV**
Mademoiselle (Mlle) Miss, Ms., **BV**
le **magasin** store, **3.2**
le grand magasin department store, **7.1**
le **magazine** magazine, **9.1**
le **Maghreb** Maghreb
magique magic *(adj.)*
le **magnétoscope** VCR, **12.2**
magnifique magnificent
le **maillot** jersey
le maillot de bain bathing suit, **11.1**
la **main** hand, **3.1**
fait(e) à la main handmade
maintenant now, **2.2**
mais but, **2.1**
Mais oui (non)! Of course (not)!
la **maison** house, **3.1**
la maison d'édition publishing house
la **maisonnette** cottage
la **majorité** majority
mal badly, **14.1**
avoir mal à to have a(n) . . . -ache, to hurt, **14.1**
Ça fait mal. It (That) hurts., **14.1**
Où avez-vous mal? Where does it hurt?, **14.2**
Pas mal. Not bad., **BV**
le/la **malade** sick person, patient, **14.2**
malade ill, sick, **L1, 14.1**
la **maladie** illness, disease
malheureusement unfortunately
malheureux, malheureuse unhappy
malin (maligne): C'est malin! Very clever! *(ironic)*
la **maman** mom
la **Manche** English Channel
la **manche** sleeve, **7.1**
à manches longues (courtes) long- (short-) sleeved, **7.1**
manger to eat, **5.1**
la salle à manger dining room, **4.2**
la **manifestation culturelle** cultural event
le **manteau** coat, **7.1**
se **maquiller** to put on makeup, **12.1**
le/la **marchand(e) (de fruits et légumes)** (produce) seller, merchant, **6.2**
la **marchandise** merchandise
le **marché** market, **6.2**
bon marché inexpensive
le marché aux puces flea market
marcher to walk
le **mari** husband, **4.1**
le **mariage** marriage; wedding
marié(e) married
se **marier** to get married, **L4**
le **marin** sailor, **L4**
le **Maroc** Morocco
marocain(e) Moroccan
marquer un but to score a goal, **10.1**
marron *(inv.)* brown, **7.2**
marseillais(e) from Marseille
martiniquais(e) from or of Martinique
le **mat** *(fam.)* morning
le **match** game, **10.1**
les **mathématiques** *(f. pl.)* mathematics, **2.2**
les **maths** *(f. pl.)* math, **2.2**
la **matière** subject *(school)*, **2.2;** matter
le **matin** morning, **BV**
du matin A.M. *(time)*, **BV**
mauvais(e) bad; wrong, **2.2**
Il fait mauvais. It's bad weather., **11.1**
le **médecin** doctor *(m. and f.)*, **14.2**
chez le médecin at (to) the doctor's office, **14.2**

la **médecine** medicine *(medical profession)*
médical(e) medical
le **médicament** medicine, **14.1**
la **médina** medina
le **mélange** mixture
le **melon** melon, **6.2**
même *(adj.)* same, **2.1;** *(adv.)* even
tout de même all the same, **5.2**
la **mer** sea, **11.1**
la mer des Antilles Caribbean Sea
la mer des Caraïbes Caribbean Sea
la mer Méditerranée Mediterranean Sea
merci thank you, thanks, **BV**
la **mère** mother, **4.1**
merveilleux, merveilleuse marvelous
le **message** message
la **mesure** measurement
mesurer to measure
le **métabolisme** metabolism
le **métal** metal
le **mètre** meter
le **métro** subway, **4.2**
la station de métro subway station, **4.2**
mettre to put (on), to place, **7.1;** to turn on *(appliance)*, **7**
mettre la table to set the table, **7**
les **meubles** *(m. pl.)* furniture
le **microbe** microbe, germ
microbien(ne) microbial
le **microprocesseur** microprocessor
le **microscope** microscope
midi *(m.)* noon, **BV**
mieux better, **7.2**
aimer mieux to prefer, **7.2**
aller mieux to feel better, **14.2**
militaire military
mille (one) thousand, **3.2**
le **milligramme** milligram
le **million** million
le **minéral** mineral
minuit *(m.)* midnight, **BV**
la **minute** minute, **9.2**
le **miracle** miracle
la **mi-temps** half *(sporting event)*
la **mode: à la mode** in style
le **modèle** model
le **modem** modem
moderne modern
modeste modest; reasonably priced
la **moelle épinière** spinal cord
moins less, **7.1;** minus
plus ou moins more or less
le **mois** month, **BV**
le **moment** moment, time
en ce moment right now
le **monde** world
beaucoup de monde a lot of people, **10.1**
tout le monde everyone, everybody, **1.2**
le **moniteur** *(computer)* monitor
le **moniteur, la monitrice** instructor, **11.1**
Monsieur *(m.)* Mr., sir, **BV**
le **mont** mount, mountain
la **montagne** mountain, **11.2**
monter to go up, **4.2;** to get on, get in, **9.2**
monter une pièce to put on a play, **13.1**
montrer to show
la **mort** death
le **mot** word
le mot apparenté cognate
le **mouchoir** handkerchief, **14.1**
la **moule** mussel
mourir to die, **11**
la **moutarde** mustard, **6.2**
le **mouvement** movement
moyen(ne) average, intermediate
le **moyen de transport** mode of transportation
multicolore multicolored
multiplier to multiply
muni(e) de with
municipal(e) municipal
le **mur** wall, **L4**
le **muscle** muscle
musculaire muscular
le **musée** museum, **13.2**
musical(e) musical
le/la **musicien(ne)** musician
la **musique** music, **2.2**
musulman(e) Moslem
mystérieux, mystérieuse mysterious
le **mythe** myth

N

nager to swim, **11.1**
naître to be born, **11**
la **nappe** tablecloth, **5.2**
la **natation** swimming, **11.1**
national(e) national
nationalité *(f.)* nationality
la **nature** nature
nature plain *(adj.)*, **5.1**
naturel(le) natural
la **navette: faire la navette** to go back and forth, make the run
naviguer sur Internet to surf the Net
ne: ne... jamais never, **11.2**
ne... pas not, **1.2**
ne... personne no one, nobody, **11**
ne... plus no longer, no more, **6.1**
ne... que only
ne... rien nothing, **11**
né(e): elle est née she was born
nécessaire necessary
nécessairement necessarily
négatif, négative negative
la **négritude** black pride
la **neige** snow, **11.2**
neige *(inf.* **neiger**): **Il neige.** It's snowing., **11.2**
nerveux, nerveuse nervous

n'est-ce pas? isn't it?, doesn't it (he, she, etc.)?, **2.2**
le **neveu** nephew, **4.1**
le **nez** nose, **14.1**
avoir le nez qui coule to have a runny nose, **14.1**
ni... ni neither . . . nor
la **nièce** niece, **4.1**
noble noble
noir(e) black, **7.2**
le **nom** name; noun
le nom de famille last name
le **nombre** number
nombreux, nombreuse numerous
nommer to name, mention
non no
non plus either, neither
non-fumeurs non-smoking *(section)*, **8.1**
le **nord** north
nord-africain(e) North African
normal(e) normal
la **note** note; grade
nourrir to feed
la **nourriture** food, nutrition
nouveau (nouvel), nouvelle new, **4.2**
à nouveau again
la **Nouvelle-Angleterre** New England
La **Nouvelle-Orléans** New Orleans
le **nuage** cloud, **11.1**
la **nuit** night
nul(le) *(slang)* bad
le **numéro** number
le numéro de téléphone telephone number

O

ô oh
l' **objet** *(m.)* object
obligatoire mandatory
obliger to oblige, force
observer to observe
occidental(e) western
occupé(e) occupied, taken, **5.1;** busy
l' **océan** *(m.)* ocean
l'océan Atlantique Atlantic Ocean
l' **œuf** *(m.)* egg, **6.1**
l'œuf à la coque poached egg
l'œuf brouillé scrambled egg
l'œuf sur le plat fried egg
l' **œuvre** *(f.)* work(s) *(of art or literature)*, **13.1**
officiel(le) official
l' **oignon** *(m.)* onion, **5.1**
l' **oiseau** *(m.)* bird
l' **olive** *(f.)* olive
l' **omelette** *(f.)* omelette, **5.1**
l'omelette aux fines herbes omelette with herbs, **5.1**
l'omelette nature plain omelette, **5.1**
on we, they, people, **3.2**
On y va? Let's go.; Shall we go?
l' **oncle** *(m.)* uncle, **4.1**
l' **opéra** *(m.)* opera
l'opéra comique light opera
l'opéra bouffe comic light opera
l' **opération** *(f.)* operation
opposer to oppose, **10.1**
l' **or** *(m.)* gold, **L4**
l' **orange** *(f.)* orange, **6.2**
orange *(inv.)* orange *(color)*, **7.2**
l' **oranger** *(m.)* orange tree, **L2**
l' **orchestre** *(m.)* orchestra
l'orchestre symphonique symphony orchestra
orchestrer to orchestrate
ordinaire ordinary
l' **ordinateur** *(m.)* computer
l' **ordonnance** *(f.)* prescription, **14.2**
faire une ordonnance to write a prescription, **14.2**
l' **oreille** *(f.)* ear, **14.1**
avoir mal aux oreilles to have an earache, **14.1**
l' **organe** *(m.)* organ *(of the body)*
organiser to organize
l' **organisme** *(m.)* organism
l' **orgue** *(m.)* organ *(musical instrument)*
oriental(e) eastern
originaire de native of
l' **origine** *(f.)*: **d'origine américaine (française, etc.)** from the U.S. (France, etc.)
orner to decorate
l' **os** *(m.)* bone
ôter to take off *(clothing)*
ou or, **1.1**
où where, **1.1**
d'où from where, **1.1**
oublier to forget
l' **ouest** *(m.)* west
oui yes, **BV**
ouvert(e) open, **13.2**
l' **ouvrier, l'ouvrière** worker
ouvrir to open, **14.2**
l' **oxygène** *(m.)* oxygen

P

le **pain** bread, **6.1**
le pain complet whole-wheat bread
le pain grillé toast
la tartine de pain beurré slice of bread and butter
la **paire** pair, **7.1**
la **paix** peace
le **palais** palace
le **palet** puck
le **panier** basket, **10.2**
réussir un panier to make a basket *(basketball)*, **10.2**
le **pantalon** pants, **7.1**
papa dad
la **papeterie** stationery store, **3.2**
le **papier** paper, **3.2**

la feuille de papier sheet of paper, **3.2**
Pâques Easter
le **paquet** package, **6.2**
par by, through
par exemple for example
par semaine a (per) week, **3.2**
le **parc** park
parce que because
par-dessus over *(prep.)*, **10.2**
pardon excuse me, pardon me
les **parents** *(m. pl.)* parents, **4.1**
parfait(e) perfect
parfaitement perfectly
le **parfum** flavor
parisien(ne) Parisian
le **parking** parking lot
parler to speak, talk, **3.1**
parler au téléphone to talk on the phone, **3.2**
les **paroles** *(f. pl.)* words, lyrics
la **part: de part et d'autre** on each side
de sa part on his (her) part
participer (à) to participate (in)
particulièrement particularly
la **partie** part
faire partie de to be a part of
partir to leave, **8.1**
partout everywhere
pas not, **2.1**
pas du tout not at all, **3.1**
Pas mal. Not bad., **BV**
Pas question! Out of the question! Not a chance!
le **passager, la passagère** passenger, **8.1**
la **passe** pass
passé(e) past
le **passeport** passport, **8.1**
passer to spend *(time)*, **3.1;** to go (through), **8.1;** to pass, **10.1**
passer un examen to take an exam, **3.1**
les **pâtes** *(f. pl.)* pasta
la **patience** patience, **9.2**
le **patin** skate; skating, **11.2**
faire du patin à glace to ice-skate, **11.1**
la **patinoire** skating rink, **11.2**
le/la **patron(ne)** boss
pauvre poor, **14.1, L1**
Le/La pauvre! Poor thing!, **14.1**
le **pavillon** small house, bungalow
payer to pay, **3.2**
le **pays** country, **8.1**
le **paysage** landscape
le/la **paysan(ne)** peasant, **L1**
le **peigne** comb, **12.1**
se **peigner** to comb one's hair, **12.1**
peindre to paint
le/la **peintre** painter, artist, **13.2**
la **peinture** painting, **13.2**
le **penalty** penalty *(soccer)*
pendant during, for *(time)*, **3.2**
la **pénicilline** penicillin, **14.1**
penser to think
perdre to lose, **9.2**
le **père** father, **4.1**
la **période** period
la **périphérie** outskirts
la **perle** pearl
permanent(e) permanent
permettre to permit, allow
la **personnalité** personality
la **personne** person
ne... personne no one, nobody, **11**
personnel(le) personal
le **personnel de bord** flight crew, **8.2**
personnellement personally, **13.2**
petit(e) short, small, **1.1**
le petit ami boyfriend
la petite amie girlfriend
le petit déjeuner breakfast, **5.2**
les petits pois *(m.)* peas, **6.2**
la **petite-fille** granddaughter, **4.1**
le **petit-fils** grandson, **4.1**
les **petits-enfants** *(m. pl.)* grandchildren, **4.1**
le **pétrole** oil
le **pétrolier** oil tanker
peu (de) few, little
à peu près about, approximately
un peu a little, **2.1**
un peu de a little
en très peu de temps in a short time
très peu seldom, **5.2**
peur: avoir peur to be afraid, **L1**
pharmaceutique pharmaceutical
la **pharmacie** pharmacy, **14.2**
le/la **pharmacien(ne)** pharmacist, **14.2**
le **phénomène** phenomenon
la **photo** photograph
la **phrase** sentence
le/la **physicien(ne)** physicist
la **physique** physics, **2.2**
physique physical
le **piano** piano
la **pie** magpie
la **pièce** room, **4.2;** play, **13.1**
la pièce de théâtre play, **13.1**
le **pied** foot, **10.1**
à pied on foot, **4.2**
donner un coup de pied to kick, **10.1**
être vite sur pied to be better soon, **14.1**
la **pierre** stone
la pierre précieuse gem, **L4**
le/la **pilote** pilot, **8.2**
piloter to pilot, to fly
piquer to sting, **14.1**
la **piscine** pool, **11.1**
la **piste** runway, **8.1;** track, **10.2;** ski trail, **11.2**
pittoresque picturesque
la **pizza** pizza, **BV**
la **place** seat *(plane, train, movie, etc.)*, **8.1;** place; square

la **plage** beach, **11.1**
la **plaine** plain
le **plaisir** pleasure
la **planche à voile: faire de la planche à voile** to windsurf, **11.1**
la **plante** plant
le **plastique** plastic
le **plat** dish *(food)*
le **plateau** tray, **8.2**
plein(e) full, **10.1**
pleurer to cry, **L1**
pleut (*inf.* **pleuvoir**): **Il pleut.** It's raining., **11.1**
plissé(e) pleated, **7.1**
le **plongeon** dive
plonger to dive, **11.1**
la **pluie** rain
la **plupart (des)** most (of), **9.2**
le **pluriel** plural
plus plus; more, **7.1**
en plus de in addition to
ne… plus no longer, no more, **6.1**
plus ou moins more or less
plus tard later
plusieurs several
plutôt rather
le **poème** poem
la **poésie** poetry
le **poète** poet *(m. and f.)*
le **poids** weight
point: à point medium-rare *(meat)*, **5.2**
la **pointure** size *(shoes)*, **7.2**
Vous faites quelle pointure? What (shoe) size do you take?, **7.2**
la **poire** pear, **6.2**
le **poisson** fish, **6.1**
la **poissonnerie** fish store, **6.1**
la **poitrine** chest
le **poivre** pepper, **6.1**
la **politesse** courtesy, politeness, **BV**
politique political
pollué(e) polluted
la **pollution** pollution
le **polo** polo shirt, **7.1**
la **pomme** apple, **6.2**
la tarte aux pommes apple tart, **6.1**
la **pomme de terre** potato, **6.2**
le **pont** bridge
pop pop *(music)*
populaire popular, **1.2**
le **porc** pork, **6.1**
le **port** port, harbor
la **porte** gate *(airport)*, **8.1;** door, **L4**
porter to wear, **7.1**
le/la **portraitiste** portraitist
portugais(e) Portuguese
poser une question to ask a question, **3.1**
la **position** position
posséder to possess, own
la **possession** possession
la **poste** mail
la poste par avion airmail
le **pot** jar, **6.2**
le **poulet** chicken, **6.1**
le **poumon** lung
pour for, **2.1;** in order to
pour cent percent
le **pourboire** tip *(restaurant)*, **5.2**
pourquoi why, **6.2**
pourquoi pas? why not?
pousser to push
pouvoir to be able to, can, **6.1**
pratique practical
la **pratique** practice
pratiquer to practice
précédent(e) preceding
préféré(e) favorite
préférer to prefer, **6**
le **préfixe** prefix
premier, première first, **4.2**
en première in first class, **9.1**
prendre to have *(to eat or drink*, **5.1;** to take, **5.2;** to buy
prendre un bain (une douche) to take a bath (shower), **12.1**
prendre un bain de soleil to sunbathe, **11.1**
prendre le petit déjeuner to eat breakfast, **5.2**
prendre possession de to take possession of
prendre rendez-vous to make an appointment
prendre le métro to take the subway, **5.2**
le **prénom** first name
préparer to prepare
près de near, **4.2**
prescrire to prescribe, **14.2**
présenter to present; to introduce
presque almost
prie: Je vous en prie. You're welcome., **BV**
primaire: l'école *(f.)* **primaire** elementary school
principal(e) main, principal
le **printemps** spring, **11.1**
au printemps in the spring
la **prison** prison, **L4**
le **prisonnier, la prisonnière** prisoner, **L4**
privé(e) private
le **prix** price, cost, **7.1**
le **problème** problem
prochain(e) next, **9.2**
procurer to provide
le **produit** product
le/la **prof** teacher *(inform.)*, **2.1**
le **professeur** teacher *(m. and f.)*, **2.1**
professionnel(le) professional
la **programmation** programming
le **programme** program
le **projet** plan
la **promenade: faire une promenade** to take a walk, **11.1**
promotion: en promotion on special, on sale
proposer to suggest
protéger to protect
la **protéine** protein
provenance: en provenance de arriving from *(train, plane, etc.)*, **8.1**

les **provisions** *(f. pl.)* food
public, publique public
la **publicité** commercial *(TV),* **12.2;** advertisement
publier to publish
les **puces** *(f. pl.):* **le marché aux puces** flea market
le **pull** sweater, **7.1**
pulmonaire pulmonary
punir to punish
purifié(e) purified

Q

le **quai** platform *(railroad),* **9.1**
la **qualité** quality
quand when, **4.1**
le **quart: et quart** a quarter past *(time),* **BV**
moins le quart a quarter to *(time),* **BV**
le **quartier** neighborhood, district, **4.2**
quatrième fourth
que as; that; than *(in comparisons),* **7.2**
québécois(e) from or of Quebec
quel(le) which, what
quelque some *(sing.)*
quelque chose something, **11**
quelque chose de spécial something special
quelque chose à manger something to eat, **5.1**
quelquefois sometimes, **5.2**
quelques some, a few *(pl.),* **9.2**
quelqu'un somebody, someone, **10.1**
la **question** question, **3.1**
Pas question! Out of the question! Not a chance!
poser une question to ask a question, **3.1**
la **queue** line, **9.1**
faire la queue to wait in line, **9.1**
qui who, **1.1;** whom, **10;** which, that
quitter to leave *(a room, etc.),* **3.1**
quoi what *(after prep.)*
quotidien(ne) daily, everyday

R

la **race** race
raconter to tell (about)
la **radio** radio, **3.2**
le **raisin sec** raisin
la **raison** reason
ramasser to pick up, **8.2**
le **rap** rap *(music)*
rapide quick, fast
rapidement rapidly, quickly
le **rapport** relationship; report
se **raser** to shave, **12.1**
le **rasoir** razor, shaver, **12.1**
rater to miss *(train, etc.),* **9.2**
le **rayon** department *(in a store),* **7.1**
le rayon des manteaux coat department, **7.1**
la **réalité** reality
recevoir to receive, **10.2**
la **recherche** research
à la recherche de in search of
recommencer to begin again
reconnaître to recognize
la **récré** recess, **3.2**
la **récréation** recess, **3.2**
récrire to rewrite
recueillir to pick up
le **recyclage** recycling
la **réduction** discount
refléter to reflect
le **réfrigérateur** refrigerator, **12.2**
regarder to look at, **3.1**
regarder fixement to stare at
le **reggae** reggae
le **régime** diet
faire un régime to follow a diet
la **région** region
la **règle** ruler, **3.2;** rule
regretter to be sorry, **6.1**
régulier, régulière regular
la **reine** queen
la **relation** relationship
relier to connect
religieux, religieuse religious
remarquer to notice
rembourser to pay back, reimburse
remonter to get back on
remplacer to replace
remplir to fill out, **8.2**
rencontrer to meet
le **rendez-vous: prendre rendez-vous** to make an appointment
se **rendormir** to fall asleep again
rendre to give back
rendre bien service to be a big help
renommé(e) renowned
les **renseignements** *(m. pl.)* information
rentrer to go home; to return, **3.2**
renvoyer to return *(volleyball),* **10.2**
le **repas** meal, **5.2**
répéter to repeat
répondre (à) to answer, **9.2**
le **reportage** news article
représenter to represent
réservé(e) reserved
respectif (respective) respective
la **respiration** breathing; respiration
respiratoire respiratory
respirer to breathe, **14.2**
respirer à fond to breathe deeply, **14.2**
ressembler à to resemble
ressortir to leave
le **restaurant** restaurant, **5.2**
la **restauration** food service
la restauration rapide fast food
rester to stay, remain, **11.1**
il reste there remains

le **retard** delay
avoir du retard to be late *(plane, train, etc.),* **8.1**
en retard late, **9.1**
le **retour** return
la **retraite** retreat; retirement
retrouver to meet, get together with
réussir to succeed
réussir un panier to make a basket *(basketball),* **10.2**
réussir à un examen to pass an exam
réveillé(e) awake
se **réveiller** to wake up, **12.1**
révéler to reveal
la **révolution** revolution
révolutionnaire revolutionary
la **revue** magazine, **L2**
le **rez-de-chaussée** ground floor, **4.2**
le **rhume** cold *(illness),* **14.1**
riche rich
ridicule ridiculous
rien nothing
rigoler to joke around, **3.2**
Tu rigoles! You're kidding!, **3.2**
rigolo funny, **4.2**
rincer to rinse
la **rivière** river
le **riz** rice
la **robe** dress, **7.1**
le **rocher** rock, boulder, **L3**
le **roi** king, **L3**
le **rôle** role
le **roman** novel
romantique romantic
rose pink, **7.2**
rouge red, **7.2**
rouler (vite) to go, drive, ride (fast), **10.2**
la **route** road
la **routine** routine, **12.1**
royal(e) royal
le **rubis** ruby
la **rue** street, **3.1**
ruiné(e) ruined
rural(e) rural
le **russe** Russian *(language)*
le **rythme** rhythm

S

le **sac** bag, **6.1**
le sac à dos backpack, **3.2**
saignant(e) rare *(meat),* **5.2**
la **saison** season
la **salade** salad, **5.1;** lettuce, **6.2**
le **salaire** salary
sale dirty
la **salle** room
la salle à manger dining room, **4.2**
la salle d'attente waiting room, **9.1**
la salle de bains bathroom, **4.2**
la salle de cinéma movie theater, **13.1**
la salle de classe classroom, **2.1**
la salle de séjour living room, **4.2**
Salut. Hi.; Bye. **BV**
la **salutation** greeting
les **sandales** *(f. pl.)* sandals, **7.1**
le **sandwich** sandwich, **BV**
le **sang** blood
sans without
la **santé** health, **14.1**
la **sardine** sardine
satisfaire to satisfy
la **sauce** sauce
la **saucisse** sausage
la saucisse de Francfort hot dog, **BV**
le **saucisson** salami, **6.1**
sauf except, **13.2**
sauvegarder to safeguard, to save
sauver to save
le **savant** scientist
savoir to know *(information),* **13.2**
le **savon** soap, **12.1**
le **saxophone** saxophone
la **scène** scene, **13.1**
les **sciences** *(f. pl.)* science, **2.1**
les sciences naturelles natural sciences, **2.1**
les sciences sociales social studies, **2.1**
scientifique scientific
scintiller to sparkle
scolaire school *(adj.),* **3.2**
le **sculpteur** sculptor *(m. and f.),* **13.2**
la **sculpture** sculpture, **13.2**
la **séance** show(ing) *(movie),* **13.1**
sec, sèche dry
second(e) second
secondaire: l'école *(f.)* **secondaire** junior high, high school, **1.2**
seconde: en seconde in second class, **9.1**
secret, secrète secret
le **séjour** stay
la salle de séjour living room, **4.2**
le **sel** salt, **6.1**
selon according to
la **semaine** week, **3.2;** allowance
la semaine dernière last week, **10.2**
la semaine prochaine next week
par semaine a (per) week, **3.2**
semblable similar, **L1**
le/la **Sénégalais(e)** Senegalese *(person)*
le **sens** direction; meaning
se **sentir** to feel *(well, etc.),* **14.1**
séparer to separate
sérieux, sérieuse serious, **7**
serré(e) tight, **7.2**
le **serveur, la serveuse** waiter, waitress, **5.1**
le **service** service, **5.2**
Le service est compris. The tip is included., **5.2**
la **serviette** napkin, **5.2;** towel, **11.1**
servir to serve, **8.2; 10.2**
seul(e) alone, **5.2;** single; only *(adj.)*
tout(e) seul(e) all alone, by himself/herself, **5.2**

seulement only *(adv.)*
le **shampooing** shampoo, **12.1**
le **shopping** shopping, **7.2**
le **short** shorts, **7.1**
si if; yes *(after neg. question)*, **7.2**; so *(adv.)*
le **sida (syndrome immuno-déficitaire acquis)** AIDS
le **siècle** century
le **siège** seat, **8.2**
siffler to (blow a) whistle, **10.1**
le **sifsari** type of veil worn by North African women
le **signal** sign
la **signification** meaning, significance
signifier to mean
simple simple
l'aller (simple) one-way ticket, **9.1**
simplement simply
sinon or else, otherwise, **9.2**
la **sinusite** sinus infection, **14.2**
le **sirop** syrup, **14.1**
le **site** Web site
situé(e) located
le **ski** ski, skiing, **11.2**
faire du ski to ski, **11.2**
faire du ski nautique to water-ski, **11.1**
le ski alpin downhill skiing, **11.2**
le ski de fond cross-country skiing, **11.2**
le **skieur, la skieuse** skier, **11.2**
le **snack-bar** snack bar, **9.2**
sociable sociable, outgoing, **1.2**
social(e) social
la **société** company
la **sœur** sister, **1.2**
le **software** software
soi oneself, himself, herself
soif: avoir soif to be thirsty, **5.1**
le **soin** care
de soins polyvalents general care
le **soir** evening , **BV**
ce soir tonight
du soir in the evening, P.M., **BV**
le soir in the evening, **5.2**
le **sol** ground, **10.2**
le **soldat** soldier, **L3**
les **soldes** *(m. pl.)* sale *(in a store)*, **7.1**
le **soleil** sun, **11.1**
au soleil in the sun, **11.1**
Il fait du soleil. It's sunny., **11.1**
le soleil levant rising sun
la **solidarité** solidarity
solide solid
solitaire lonely
la **solution** solution
sombre dark
la **somme** sum
le **sommet** summit, mountaintop, **11.2**
le **son** sound, **L3**
le **sondage** survey, opinion poll
sonner du cor to blow a horn, **L3**
la **sorte** sort, kind, type
sortir to go out; to take out, **8.2**
sortir victorieux (victorieuse) to win (the battle)
la **souche** tree stump
dormir comme une souche to sleep like a log
souffrir to suffer, **14.2**
souhait *(m.)*: **À tes souhaits!** God bless you! Gesundheit!, **14.1**
le **souk** North African market
la **soupe** soup, **5.1**
la soupe à l'oignon onion soup, **5.1**
la **source** source
la **souris** mouse
sous under, **8.2**
les **sous-titres** *(m. pl.)* subtitles, **13.1**
soustraire to subtract
souterrain(e) underground
le **souvenir** memory
souvent often, **5.2**
les **spaghettis** *(m. pl.)* spaghetti
spécial(e) special
la **spécialité** specialty
le **spectateur, la spectatrice** spectator, **10.1**
splendide splendid
le **sport** sport, **10.2**
le sport collectif team sport
le sport d'équipe team sport, **10.2**
les sports d'hiver winter sports, **11.2**
sport *(inv.)* casual *(clothes)*, **7.1**
sportif, sportive athletic
le **squelette** skeleton
squelettique skeletal
le **stade** stadium, **10.1**
standing: de grand standing luxury
la **station** station, **4.2;** resort
la station balnéaire seaside resort, **11.1**
la station de métro subway station, **4.2**
la station de sports d'hiver ski resort, **11.2**
la **station-service** gas station
la **statue** statue, **13.2**
le **steak frites** steak and French fries, **5.2**
le **steward** flight attendant *(m.)*, **8.2**
stocker to store
la **stratégie** strategy
strict(e) strict, **2.1**
le **studio** studio (apartment)
stupide stupid
le **stylo-bille** ballpoint pen, **3.2**
la **substance** substance
le **succès** success
le **sucre** sugar
le **sud** south
suggérer to suggest
suite: tout de suite right away

suivant(e) following
suivre to follow
le **sujet** subject
super terrific, super
superbe superb
supérieur(e) higher
le **supermarché** supermarket, **6.2**
sur on, **4.2**
donner sur to face, overlook, **4.2**
sûr(e) sure, certain
bien sûr, of course
le **surf: faire du surf** to go surfing, **11.1**
le **surfeur, la surfeuse** surfer, **11.1**
surgelé(e) frozen, **6.2**
la **surprise** surprise
surtout especially, above all; mostly
surveiller to watch
le **survêtement** warmup suit, **7.1**
la **survie** survival
le **sweat-shirt** sweatshirt, **7.1**
sympa *(inv.)* nice (*abbrev. for* **sympathique**), **1.2**
sympathique nice *(person)*, **1.2**
la **symphonie** symphony
le **symptôme** symptom
le **synonyme** synonym
le **système** system
le système métrique metric system

T

la **table** table, **5.1**
le **tableau** painting, **13.2;** chart
la **taille** size *(clothes)*, **7.2**
juste à sa taille fitting (him/her) just right
la taille au-dessous next smaller size, **7.2**
la taille au-dessus next larger size, **7.2**
Vous faites quelle taille? What size do you take/wear?, **7.2**
le **tailleur** suit *(woman's)*, **7.1**
le **talent** talent
le **tango** tango
la **tante** aunt, **4.1**
tard late, **12.1**
plus tard later
le **tarif** fare
la **tarte** pie, tart, **6.1**
la tarte aux pommes apple tart, **6.1**
la **tartine** slice of bread with butter or jam
la tartine de pain beurré slice of bread and butter, **5.1**
la **tasse** cup, **5.2**
le **taux** level
la **techno** techno *(music)*
la **télé** TV, **12.2**
à la télé on TV, **12.2**
télécharger to download
la **télécommande** remote control, **12.2**
le **téléphone** telephone, **3.2**
le numéro de téléphone telephone number
téléphoner to call (on the telephone)
téléphonique telephone *(adj.)*
le **télésiège** chairlift, **11.2**
la **tempe** temple
la **température** temperature, **14.1**
tempéré(e) temperate
temporaire temporary
le **temps** weather, **11.1;** time
de temps en temps from time to time, **11.1**
l'emploi *(m.)* **du temps** schedule
en très peu de temps in a short time
Il fait quel temps? What's the weather like?, **11.1**
le **tendon** tendon
le **terme** term
le **terrain de football** soccer field, **10.1**
la **terrasse** terrace, patio, **4.2**
la terrasse d'un café sidewalk café, **5.1**
la **terre** earth, land
à terre on the ground
terrible terrible
la **tête** head, **10.1**
avoir mal à la tête to have a headache, **14.1**
le **texte** text
thaïlandais(e) Thai
le **thé** tea
le **théâtre** theater, **13.1**
la pièce de théâtre play, **13.1**
le **thème** theme
timide shy, timid, **1.2**
tirer to take, to draw
les **toilettes** *(f. pl.)* bathroom, toilet, **4.2**
le **toit** roof
le toit de chaume thatched roof
la **tomate** tomato, **6.2**
tomber to fall, **11.2**
tomber malade to get sick, **L1**
tôt early, **12.1**
totalement totally
toucher to touch, **10.2**
toujours always, **4.2;** still
la **tour** tower
la tour Eiffel Eiffel Tower
le **tour: à son tour** in turn
À votre tour. (It's) your turn.
le/la **touriste** tourist
tous, toutes *(adj.)* all, every, **2.1, 8**
tous (toutes) les deux both
tous les jours every day, **13.2**
tousser to cough, **14.1**
tout *(pron.)* all, everything
C'est tout. That's all., **6.1**
en tout in all
pas du tout not at all, **3.1**
tout(e) *(adj.)* the whole, the entire; all, any
tout le monde everyone, everybody, **1.2**
tout *(adv.)* very, completely, all, **4.2**

À tout à l'heure. See you later., **BV**
tout autour de all around *(prep.)*
tout de même all the same, **5.2**
tout près de very near, **4.2**
tout(e) seul(e) all alone, all by himself/herself, **5.2**
tout de suite right away
toxique toxic
la **tradition** tradition
traditionnel(le) traditional
la **tragédie** tragedy, **13.1**
tragique tragic
le **train** train, **9.1**
le **traitement** treatment
traiter to treat
le **traître, la traîtresse** traitor
la **tranche** slice, **6.2**
transformer to transform
transporter to transport
le **travail** work
travailler to work, **3.1;** to practice
traverser to cross
très very, **BV**
le **trésor** treasure, **L4**
la **trigonométrie** trigonometry, **2.2**
triste sad, **L1**
troisième third, **4.2**
la **trompette** trumpet
le **tronc cérébral** brain stem
le **trône** throne
trop too *(excessive)*, **2.1**
trop de too many, too much
tropical(e) tropical, **9**
le **trou** hole, **L4**
le **trouble digestif** indigestion, upset stomach
trouver to find, **5.1;** to think *(opinion)*, **7.2**
le **t-shirt** T-shirt, **7.1**
la **tunique** tunic
la **Tunisie** Tunisia
tunisien(ne) Tunisian
le **tunnel** tunnel, **L4**
le **type** type; guy *(inform.)*
typique typical
typiquement typically

U

l' **un(e)... l'autre** one . . . the other
un(e) à un(e) one by one
unique single, only one
l'enfant unique only child
uniquement solely
l' **unité** *(f.)* unit
l' **université** *(f.)* university
l' **usine** *(f.)* factory
utiliser to use

V

les **vacances** *(f. pl.)* vacation
en vacances on vacation
les grandes vacances summer vacation
la **vague** wave, **11.1**
le **vaisseau sanguin** blood vessel
la **vaisselle** dishes, **12.2**
faire la vaisselle to do the dishes, **12.2**
le **val** valley
la **valeur** value
la **valise** suitcase, **8.1**
faire les valises to pack, **8.1**
la **vallée** valley
la **vanille: à la vanille** vanilla *(adj.)*, **5.1**
varié(e) varied
varier to vary
la **variété** variety
la **veine** vein
le **vélo** bicycle, bike, **10.2**
le **vendeur, la vendeuse** salesperson, **7.1**
vendre to sell, **9.1**
vengé(e) avenged
la **vengeance** vengence
se **venger** to get revenge
le **vent** wind, **11.1**
Il y a du vent. It's windy., **11.1**
le **ventre** abdomen, stomach, **14.1**
avoir mal au ventre to have a stomachache, **14.1**
vérifier to check, verify, **8.1**
la **vérité** truth
le **verre** glass, **5.2**
vers toward
la **version originale** original language version *(of a movie)*, **13.1**
vert(e) green, **5.1**
la **veste** (sport) jacket, **7.1**
les **vêtements** *(m. pl.)* clothes, **7.1**
la **viande** meat, **6.1**
victorieux, victorieuse victorious
la **vidéo** video, **3.1**
la cassette vidéo videocassette, **12.2**
le film en vidéo movie video, **13.1**
la **vie** life
en vie alive
vieille old *(f.)*, **4.2**
vietnamien(ne) Vietnamese, **6**
vieux (vieil) old *(m.)*, **4.2**
la **villa** house
le **village** village, small town
la **ville** city, town, **8.1**
en ville in town, in the city
le **vinaigre** vinegar, **6.1**
violent(e) violent; rough
le **violon** violin
viral(e) viral, **14.1**
le **virus** virus
visionner to view
visiter to visit *(a place)*, **13.2**
vital(e) vital
la **vitamine** vitamin
vite fast *(adv.)*, **10.2**
la **vitrine** (store) window, **7.1**
vivant(e) living
Vive... ! Long live . . . !, Hooray for . . . !

voici here is, here are, **4.1**
la **voie** track *(railroad)*, **9.1**
voilà there is, there are; here is, here are *(emphatic)*, **1.2**
le **voile** veil
voir to see, **7.1**
le/la **voisin(e)** neighbor, **4.2**
la **voiture** car, **4.2**
en voiture by car, **5.2;** "All aboard!"
la **voix** voice
le **vol** flight, **8.1**
le vol intérieur domestic flight, **8.1**
le vol international international flight, **8.1**
le **volley(-ball)** volleyball, **10.2**
la **volonté** willpower
voudrais: je voudrais I would like, **5.1**
vouloir to want, **6.1**
le **voyage** trip, **8.1;** voyage
faire un voyage to take a trip, **8.1**
voyager to travel, **8.1**
le **voyageur, la voyageuse** traveler, passenger, **9.1**
vrai(e) true, real, **2.2**
vraiment really, **1.1**
la **vue** view, **4.2**

W

le **wagon** *(railroad)* car, **9.2**
le **wagon-couchette** sleeping car
le **wagon-restaurant** dining car
le **week-end** weekend
le **western** Western movie

Y

le **yaourt** yogurt, **6.1**
les **yeux** *(m. pl; sing.* **œil***)* eyes, **14.1, L1**
avoir les yeux qui piquent to have itchy eyes, **14.1**

Z

zapper to zap, to channel surf, **12.2**
la **zone** zone
la **zoologie** zoology
Zut! Darn!, **BV**

This English-French Dictionary *contains all productive vocabulary from the text. The numbers following each entry indicate the chapter and vocabulary section in which the word is introduced. For example,* ***2.2*** *means that the word first appeared in* ***Chapitre 2, Mots 2. BV*** *refers to the introductory* ***Bienvenue*** *lessons.* ***L*** *refers to the optional literary readings. If there is no number or letter following an entry, this means that the word or expression is there for receptive purposes only.*

A

a un, une, **1.1**
a week par semaine, **3.2**
a lot beaucoup, **3.1**
to **abandon** abandonner
abdomen le ventre, **14.1**
able capable
to be able to pouvoir, **6.1**
aboard à bord (de), **8.2**
about *(on the subject of)* de; *(approximately)* à peu près
about-face le demi-tour
above au-dessus (de)
above all surtout
absolutely absolument
accessible accessible
accessory l'accessoire *(m.)*
accident l'accident *(m.)*
to **accompany** accompagner
according to d'après; selon
accordion l'accordéon *(m.)*
account le compte
accusation l'accusation *(f.)*
to **accuse** accuser
act l'acte, *(m.)*, **13.1**
action l'action *(f.)*
active actif, active
activity l'activité *(f.)*
actor l'acteur *(m.)*, **13.1**
actress l'actrice *(f.)*, **13.1**
acute aigu(ë), **14.2**
to **add** additionner
to **admire** admirer
admission l'entrée *(f.)*
adolescent l'adolescent(e)
adorable adorable, **4.1**
address l'adresse *(f.)*
adult l'adulte *(m. et f.)*
adventure l'aventure *(f.)*
adversary l'adversaire *(m. et f.)*
advertisement la publicité
afraid: to be afraid avoir peur, **L1**
Africa l'Afrique *(f.)*
African africain(e)
African-American afro-américain(e)
after après, **3.2**
afternoon l'après-midi *(m.)*, **3.2**
five o'clock in the afternoon cinq heures de l'après-midi, **BV**
again encore; à nouveau
against contre, **10.1**
age l'âge *(m.)*, **4.1**
agent *(m. and f.)* l'agent *(m.)*, **8.1**
to **agree** être d'accord, **2.1**
aid l'aide *(f.)*
AIDS le sida
air *(adj.)* aérien(ne)
air l'air *(m.)*
air terminal l'aérogare *(f.)*, **8.1**
airline la compagnie aérienne, **8.1**
airmail la poste par avion
airplane l'avion *(m.)*, **8.1**
airport l'aéroport *(m.)*, **8.1**
airport terminal l'aérogare *(f.)*, **8.1**
aisle le couloir, **8.2**
aisle seat (une place) côté couloir, **8.1**
alas hélas
album l'album *(m.)*
algebra l'algèbre *(f.)*, **2.2**
Algeria l'Algérie *(f.)*
algerian algérien(ne)
alive en vie
all tout(e), tous, toutes, **2.1**
All aboard! En voiture!
all alone tout(e) seul(e), **5.2**
all around tout autour de
all the same tout de même, **5.2**
in all en tout
all right *(agreement)* d'accord, **2.1**
not at all pas du tout
That's all. C'est tout., **6.1**
allergic allergique, **14.1**
allergy l'allergie *(f.)*, **14.1**
to **allow** laisser; permettre
almost presque
alone seul(e), **5.2**
all alone tout(e) seul(e), **5.2**
along le long de
already déjà, **BV**
also aussi, **1.1**
always toujours, **4.2**
a.m. du matin, **BV**
ambitious ambitieux, ambitieuse
American *(adj.)* américain(e), **1.1**
among entre, **3.2**
to **analyse** analyser
analysis l'analyse *(f.)*
analytical analytique

and et, **BV**
animal l'animal *(m.)*
to **announce** annoncer, **9.1**
announcement l'annonce, *(f.)*, **8.2**
anonymous anonyme
another un(e) autre; encore
answer la réponse
to **answer** répondre (à), **9.2**
antibiotic l'antibiotique *(m.)*, **14.1**
antonym l'antonyme *(m.)*
Anything else? Avec ça?, **6.1;** Autre chose?, **6.2**
apartment l'appartement *(m.)*, **4.2**
apartment building l'immeuble *(m.)*, **4.2**
apparatus l'appareil *(m.)*
to **applaud** applaudir
apple la pomme, **6.2**
apple tart la tarte aux pommes, **6.1**
appointment le rendez-vous
to make an appointment prendre rendez-vous
to **appreciate** apprécier
April avril *(m.)*, **BV**
arrival l'arrivée *(f.)*, **8.1**
Arab arabe
Arabic *(language)* l'arabe *(m.)*
architecture l'architecture *(f.)*
arithmetic le calcul
to **arrest** arrêter
arrested arrêté(e)
arm le bras
army l'armée *(f.)*, **L3**
around autour de, **4.2**
to **arrive** arriver, **3.1**
arriving from *(flight)* en provenance de, **8.1**
art le dessin *(m.)*, **2.2**
artery l'artère *(f.)*
article l'article *(m.)*
artist l'artiste *(m. et f.)*; le/la peintre *(painter)*
artistic artistique
Asian asiatique
as aussi *(comparisons)*, **7;** comme
as . . . as aussi... que, **7**
as well as ainsi que
the same . . . as le (la, les) même(s)... que
to **ask (for)** demander, **3.2**
to ask a question poser une question, **3.1**
aspirin l'aspirine *(f.)*, **14.1**
at à, **3.1;** chez, **3.2**
at last enfin, **12.1**
at the home (business) of chez, **3.2**
at what time? à quelle heure?, **2**
athletic sportif, sportive
Atlantic Ocean l'océan Atlantique
atmosphere l'atmosphère *(f.)*
attached attaché(e)
to **attack** attaquer
attention l'attention *(f.)*
August août, *(m.)*, **BV**
aunt la tante, **4.1**
author l'auteur *(m.)*
automatic automatique
autumn l'automne *(m.)*, **11.2**
au pair au pair
avalanche l'avalanche *(f.)*
avenged vengé(e)
avenue l'avenue *(f.)*
average moyen(ne)
aviator l'aviateur *(m.)*, l'aviatrice *(f.)*
to **avoid** éviter, **12.2**
awake réveillé(e)

B

baby le bébé
back l'arrière *(m.)*, **8.2**
background le fond
backpack le sac à dos, **3.2**
bacon le bacon
bacterial bactérien(ne), **14.1**
bacterium la bactérie
bad mauvais(e), **2.2;** nul(le) *(slang)*
It's bad weather. Il faut mauvais., **11.1**
Not bad. Pas mal., **BV**
badly mal, **14.1**
bag le sac, **6.1**
baggage les bagages *(m. pl.)*, **8.1**
baggage cart le chariot, **9.1**
baggage compartment le coffre à bagages, **8.2**
bagpipes la cornemuse
bakery la boulangerie-pâtisserie, **6.1**
balance l'équilibre *(m.)*
balanced équilibré(e)
balcony le balcon, **4.2**
ball *(soccer, etc.)* le ballon, **10.1**
ballerina la danseuse, **13.1**
ballet le ballet
ballpoint pen le stylo-bille, **3.2**
banana la banane, **6.2**
base la base
baseball le base-ball
baseball cap la casquette, **7.1**
based basé(e)
based on à base de
basilica la basilique
basis la base
basket le panier, **10.2**
basketball le basket (-ball), **10.2**
bath le bain, **12.1**
to take a bath prendre un bain, **12.1**
bather le baigneur, la baigneuse
bathing suit le maillot (de bain), **11.1**
bathroom la salle de bains, les toilettes *(f. pl.)*, **4.2**
battle la bataille, **L3**
battlefield le champ de bataille, **L3**
to **be** être, **1.1**
to be able to pouvoir, **6.1**
to be afraid avoir peur, **L1**
to be better soon être vite sur pied, **14.1**

to be born naître, **11**
to be called s'appeler, **12.1**
to be careful faire attention, **11.1**
to be early être en avance, **9.1**
to be given off se dégager
to be hungry avoir faim, **5.1**
to be in luck avoir de la chance
to be late être en retard, **9.1;** avoir du retard *(plane, train, etc.)*, **8.1**
to be lucky avoir de la chance
to be named s'appeler, **12.1**
to be on time être à l'heure, **8.1**
to be part of faire partie de
to be sorry regretter, **6.1**
to be thirsty avoir soif, **5.1**
to be . . . years old avoir... ans, **4.1**
beach la plage, **11.1**
bean: green beans les haricots verts *(m. pl.)*, **6.2**
beautiful beau (bel), belle, **4.2**
beauty la beauté
because parce que
because of à cause de
to **become** devenir
bed: to go to bed se coucher, **12.1**
bedroom la chambre à coucher, **4.2**
beef le bœuf, **6.1**
before avant; avant de
to **begin** commencer, **9.2**
to begin again recommencer
beginner le/la débutant(e), **11.2**
beginning le début
beige beige *(inv.)*, **7.2**
being l'être *(m.)*
human being l'être humain *(m.)*
Belgian belge
Belgium la Belgique
to **believe** croire, **7.2**
below au-dessous (de)
belt la ceinture, **L3**
seat belt la ceinture de sécurité, **8.2**
berth (on a train) la couchette
better *(adv.)* mieux, **7.2**
to feel better aller mieux, **14.2**
between entre, **3.2**
beverage la boisson; la consommation, **5.1**
bicentennial le bicentenaire
bicycle la bicyclette, **10.2;** le vélo, **10.2**
bicycle race la course cycliste, **10.2**
bicycle racer le coureur (la coureuse) cycliste, **10.2**
big grand(e), **1.1**
bike le vélo, **10.2**
biological biologique
biologist le/la biologiste
biology la biologie, **2.2**
bird l'oiseau *(m.)*
birthday l'anniversaire *(m.)*, **4.1**
Happy birthday! Bon (Joyeux) anniversaire!
black noir(e), **7.2**
black pride la négritude
bleacher le gradin, **10.1**
to **block** bloquer, **10.1**
blond blond(e), **1.1**
blood le sang
blood vessel le vaisseau sanguin
bloom: in bloom fleuri(e), **L2**
to **bloom** fleurir
blouse le chemisier, **7.1**
to **blow a whistle** siffler, **10.1**
to **blow a horn** sonner du cor, **L3**
blue bleu(e), **7.2**
navy blue bleu marine *(inv.)*, **7.2**
to **board** *(plane)* embarquer
boarding l'embarquement *(m.)*
boarding pass la carte d'embarquement, **8.1**
boat le bateau, **L4**
body le corps
bohemian bohème
boiling bouillant(e)
bone l'os *(m.)*
book le livre, **3.2**
border la frontière
boss le chef; le/la patron(ne)
botany la botanique
both tous (toutes) les deux
bottle la bouteille, **6.2**
boulder le rocher, **L3**
boutique la boutique, **7.1**
bowl le bol
box office le guichet, **13.1**
boy le garçon, **1.1**
boyfriend le petit ami
brain le cerveau
brain stem le tronc cérébral
brass band la fanfare
brave courageux, courageuse; brave
Brazil le Brésil
Brazilian *(person)* le/la Brésilien(ne)
bread le pain, **6.1**
loaf of French bread la baguette, **6.1**
slice of bread and butter la tartine de pain beurré
whole-wheat bread le pain complet
to **break** briser
breakfast le petit déjeuner, **5.2**
to eat breakfast prendre le petit déjeuner, **5.2**
to **breathe** respirer, **14.2**
to breathe deeply respirer à fond, **14.2**
Breton breton(ne)
bridge le pont
to **bring** apporter, **11.1**
Brittany la Bretagne
bronchial tube la bronche
brother le frère, **1.2**

brown brun(e), marron *(inv.)*, **7.2**
brunette brun(e), **1.1**
brush la brosse, **12.1**
to **brush** *(one's teeth, hair, etc.)* se brosser (les dents, les cheveux, etc.), **12.1**
to **build** construire; fabriquer
bungalow le bungalow
to **burn** brûler
burst éclaté(e)
bus le bus; l'autocar *(m.)*
by bus en bus
bush *(wilderness)* la brousse
busy occupé(e)
but mais, **2.1**
butcher le boucher, la bouchère
butcher shop la boucherie, **6.1**
butter le beurre, **6.1**
to **buy** acheter, **3.2**
by par
Bye. Salut., **BV**

C

cabaret le cabaret
cabin *(plane)* la cabine, **8.1**
café le café, **BV**
cafeteria la cafétéria
cake le gâteau, **4.1**
calcium le calcium
calculator la calculatrice, **3.2**
calculus: differential calculus le calcul différentiel
integral calculus le calcul intégral
calendar le calendrier
to **call** appeler; *(on the telephone)* téléphoner
to call a penalty déclarer un penalty
calm calme
calorie la calorie
Camembert cheese le camembert
campaign la campagne
can pouvoir, **6.1**
can of food la boîte de conserve, **6.2**
Canadian *(adj.)* canadien(ne), **6**
candle la bougie, **4.1**
cap la casquette, **7.1**
capital la capitale
car la voiture, **4.2;** *(railroad)* le wagon
by car en voiture, **5.2**
dining car le wagon-restaurant
sleeping car le wagon-couchette
carbohydrate la glucide; l'hydrate *(m.)* de carbone
carbon dioxide le gaz carbonique
card la carte
cardboard le carton
cardiac cardiaque
care le soin
general care *(adj.)* de soins polyvalents
to **care: I don't care.** Ça m'est égal., **13.1**
career la carrière
Careful! Attention!, **4.2**
Caribbean Sea la mer des Caraïbes, la mer des Antilles
carnival *(season)* le carnaval
carpenter le charpentier
carrot la carotte, **6.2**
carry-on bag le bagage *(m. pl.)* à main, **8.1**
to **carry out** exécuter
cartoon le dessin animé, **13.1**
cash register la caisse, **3.2**
cassette la cassette, **3.1**
castle le château
casual *(clothes)* sport *(adj. inv.)*, **7.1**
cat le chat, **4.1**
catalog le catalogue
catastrophic catastrophique
category la catégorie
to **cause** causer
cave la grotte, **L4**
CD le CD, **3.1**
CD-ROM le CD-ROM
to **celebrate** célébrer, **L4**
cell la cellule, **L4**
Celtic celte, celtique
center le centre
centiliter le centilitre
century le siècle
cereal les céréales *(f. pl.)*
certainly certainement
chain la chaîne
chairlift le télésiège, **11.2**
champion le/la champion(ne)
to **change** changer (de), **9.2**
channel *(TV)* la chaîne, **12.2**
to channel surf zapper, **12.2**
characteristic la caractéristique
charges les frais *(m. pl.)*
charm le charme
charming charmant(e)
chart le tableau
to **chat** bavarder
check *(in restaurant)* l'addition *(f.)*, **5.2**
to **check** vérifier, **8.1;** contrôler
to check *(luggage)* (faire) enregistrer, **8.1**
checkout counter la caisse, **3.2**
chest le coffre, **L4**
cheese le fromage, **5.1**
chemical chimique
chemist le/la chimiste
chemistry la chimie, **2.2**
chemotherapy la chimiothérapie
chest la poitrine
chewing gum le chewing-gum
chic chic *(inv.)*
chicken le poulet, **6.1**
child l'enfant *(m. et f.)*, **4.1**
childhood l'enfance *(f.)*
chills les frissons *(m. pl.)*, **14.1**
Chinese chinois(e)
chocolate le chocolat; *(adj.)* au chocolat, **5.1**

choir le chœur
cholesterol le cholestérol
to **choose** choisir, **8.1**
choppy *(sea)* agité(e)
circle le cercle
circuit le circuit
circulation la circulation
circus le cirque
to **cite** citer
city la ville, **8.1**
in the city en ville
civilized civilisé(e)
clarinet la clarinette
class *(people)* la classe, **2.1;** *(course)* le cours, **2.1**
in class en classe
in (French, etc.) class en cours de (français, etc.)
in first (second) class en première (seconde), **9.1**
classical classique
to **classify** classifier
classmate le/la camarade de classe
classroom la salle de classe, **2.1**
to **clear the table** débarrasser la table, **12.2**
clever: Very clever! *(ironic)* C'est malin!
climate le climat
climatic climatique
clinic la clinique
closed fermé(e), **13.2**
clothes les vêtements *(m. pl.)*, **7.1**
cloud le nuage, **11.1**
clown le clown
coach l'autocar *(m.)*
coat le manteau, **7.1**
code le code, **4.2**
coffee le café, **5.1**
black coffee l'express *(m.)*, **5.1**
coffee with cream le crème, **5.1**
cola le coca, **5.1**
cold froid(e) *(adj.)*; *(illness)* le rhume, **14.1**
It's cold (weather). Il fait froid., **11.2**
to have a cold être enrhumé(e), **14.1**
collection la collection
color la couleur, **7.2**
What color is . . . ? De quelle couleur est... ?, **7.2**
comb le peigne, **12.1**
to **comb one's hair** se peigner, **12.1**
Come on! Allez!, **9.2**
comedy la comédie, **13.1;** le film comique, **13.1**
musical comedy la comédie musicale, **13.1**
comfortable confortable
comic comique, **13.1**
to **commemorate** commémorer
commercial *(TV)* la publicité, **12.2**
companion le/la camarade
company la société
in the company of en compagnie de
to **compare** comparer
comparison la comparaison
compatriot le/la compatriote
complete complet, complète
to **complete** compléter
completely complètement
complicated compliqué(e)
composed of composé(e) de
composer le compositeur, la compositrice
composition la composition
computer l'ordinateur *(m.)*
computer science l'informatique *(f.)*, **2.2**
concept le concept
concert le concert
condition la condition
conductor *(train)* le contrôleur, **9.2**
to **connect** connecter; relier
connection *(between trains)* la correspondance, **9.2**
to **conspire** comploter
to **consult** consulter
contamination la contamination
to **contain** contenir
contest la compétition, le concours
continent le continent
to **continue** continuer
contrary: on the contrary au contraire
to **control** contrôler
convent le couvent
conversation la conversation
to **converse** converser
conversion la conversion
to **cook** faire la cuisine, **6**
cooked cuit(e)
cool: It's cool (weather). Il fait frais., **11.2**
correct bon(ne), **6.2**
correspondence la correspondance
corridor le couloir, **8.2**
cosmopolitan cosmopolite
cost le prix, **7.1**
to **cost** coûter, **3.2**
coast la côte
cottage la maisonnette
to **cough** tousser, **14.1**
count le comte, **L4**
to **count** compter
counter le comptoir, **8.1**
countless innombrable
country le pays, **8.1**
country(side) la campagne
courage le courage
courageous courageux, courageuse
course le cours, **2.1**
of course bien sûr; mais oui
of course not mais non
court la cour
courtesy la politesse, **BV**
courtyard la cour, **3.2**
couscous le couscous
cousin le/la cousin(e), **4.1**
to **cover** couvrir
covered couvert(e)
crab le crabe, **6.1**
crazy fou, folle
cream la crème

coffee with cream le crème, **5.1**
to **create** créer
credit card la carte de crédit
Creole *(language)* le créole
crepe la crêpe, **BV**
criminal le/la criminel(le), **L4**
croissant le croissant, **5.1**
to **cross** traverser
crushed écrasé(e)
to **cry** pleurer, **L1**
cue l'indication *(f.)*
to **cultivate** cultiver
cultural culturel(le)
cultural event la manifestation culturelle
culture la culture
cup la tasse, **5.2**
winner's cup la coupe, **10.2**
cured guéri(e)
customer le/la client(e)
customs la douane
cycling le cyclisme, **10.2;** *(adj.)* cycliste
cyclist *(in race)* le coureur (la coureuse) cycliste, **10.2**

D

dad papa
daily quotidien(ne)
dairy store la crémerie, **6.1**
dance la danse
to **dance** danser, **13.1**
dancer le danseur, la danseuse, **13.1**
dangerous dangereux, dangereuse
dark sombre
dark haired brun(e), **1.1**
Darn! Zut!, **BV**
data les données *(f. pl.)*
date la date
What is today's date? Quelle est la date aujourd'hui?, **BV**
to **date from** dater de
daughter la fille, **4.1**
day le jour, **BV;** la journée, **3.1**
the day before yesterday avant-hier, **10.2**
every day tous les jours
What a nice day! Belle journée!, **4.2**
What day is it today? C'est quel jour aujourd'hui?, **BV**
dear cher, chère
death la mort
decaliter le décalitre
December décembre *(m.)*, **BV**
to **decide (to)** décider de
decimal *(adj.)* décimal(e)
decision la décision
the decision is made la décision est prise
to **declare** déclarer
to **decorate** orner
delay le retard
delicatessen la charcuterie, **6.1**
delicious délicieux, délicieuse
dentist le/la dentiste
deodorant le déodorant
department (in a store) le rayon, **7.1**
coat department le rayon des manteaux, **7.1**
department store le grand magasin, **7.1**
large department store la grande surface
departure le départ, **8.1**
to **depend (on)** dépendre (de)
deplaning le débarquement
descendant le/la descendant(e)
to **describe** décrire
description la description
desert le désert; *(adj.)* désertique
designer *(clothes)* le couturier
desperate désespéré(e), **L4**
dessert le dessert
destination la destination
destiny la destinée
devoted dévoué(e)
diagnosis le diagnostic, **14.2**
dialect le dialecte
dialogue le dialogue
diamond le diamant
to **die** mourir, **11**
diet l'alimentation *(f.)*; le régime
to follow a diet faire un régime
difference la différence
different différent(e), **8.1**
difficult difficile, **2.1**
difficulty la difficulté
to **dig** creuser, **L4**
dining car la voiture-restaurant
dining hall *(school)* la cantine, **3.1**
dining room la salle à manger, **4.2**
dinner le dîner, **5.2**
to eat dinner dîner, **5.2**
diploma le diplome
direction la direction; le sens
directly directement
dirty sale
disagreeable désagréable
to **disappear** disparaître
discount la réduction
to **discover** découvrir
to **discuss** discuter
disease la maladie
dish *(food)* le plat
dishes la vaisselle, **12.2**
to do the dishes faire la vaisselle, **12.2**
dishwasher le lave-vaisselle, **12.2**
diskette la disquette
to **distinguish** distinguer
district le quartier, **4.2;** *(Paris)* l'arrondissement *(m.)*
dive le plongeon
to **dive** plonger, **11.1**
to **divide** diviser
to **do** faire, **6.1**
to do the grocery shopping faire les courses, **6.1**

doctor le médecin (*m. et f.*), **14.2**
at (to) the doctor's office chez le médecin, **14.2**
document le document
documentary le documentaire, **13.1**
dog le chien, **4.1**
dollar le dollar, **3.2**
domain le domaine
domestic (*flight*) intérieur(e), **8.1**
door la porte, **L4**
dormitory le dortoir
doubt le doute
to **download** télécharger
downtown le centre-ville
dozen la douzaine, **6.2**
drama le drame, **13.1**
drama club le club d'art dramatique
dramatic dramatique
drawing le dessin
dress la robe, **7.1**
dressed: to get dressed s'habiller, **12.1**
dressy habillé(e), **7.1**
to **dribble** (*basketball*) dribbler, **10.2**
to **drink** boire, **10.2**
something to drink quelque chose à boire
drink la boisson; la consommation, **5.1**
druid le druide
dry sec, sèche
dubbed (*movie*) doublé(e), **13.1**
during pendant, **3.2**
dynamic dynamique, **1.2**

E

each (*adj.*) chaque
each (one) chacun(e), **5.2**
ear l'oreille (*f.*), **14.1**
earache: to have an earache avoir mal aux oreilles, **14.1**
early en avance, **9.1;** de bonne heure; tôt, **12.1**
to **earn** gagner
Easter Pâques
eastern oriental(e)
easy facile, **2.1**
to **eat** manger, **5.1**
to eat breakfast prendre le petit déjeuner, **5.2**
to eat lunch déjeuner, **3.1**
ecological écologique
ecology l'écologie (*f.*)
economics l'économie (*f.*), **2.2**
efficient efficace
egg l'œuf (*m.*), **6.1**
fried egg l'œuf sur le plat
poached egg l'œuf à la coque
scrambled egg l'œuf brouillé
egotistical égoïste, **1.2**
Egyptian égyptien(ne)
electric électrique
electronic électronique
element l'élément (*m.*)
elevator l'ascenseur (*m.*), **4.2**
to **eliminate** éliminer
else: something else autre chose
Anything else? Avec ça?, **6.1;** Autre chose?, **6.2**
e-mail l'e-mail (*m.*)
emission l'émission (*f.*)
employee (*m. and f.*) l'employé(e)
end la fin
enemy l'ennemi(e) (*m. et f.*)
energetic énergique, **1.2**
energy l'énergie (*f.*)
engagement les fiançailles (*f. pl.*), **L4**
England l'Angleterre (*f.*)
English anglais(e)
English (*language*) l'anglais (*m.*), **2.2**
English Channel la Manche
enormous énorme
enough assez, **1.1**
enriched enrichi(e)
to **enter** entrer, **7.1**
enthusiastic enthousiaste, **1.2**
entire entier, entière
entrance l'entrée (*f.*), **4.2**
epic (*adj.*) épique
equation l'équation (*f.*)
equator l'équateur (*m.*)
equipment l'équipement (*m.*)
equivalent l'équivalent (*m.*)
eraser la gomme, **3.2**
to **escape** s'échapper; s'évader, **L4**
especially surtout
espresso l'express (*m.*), **5.1**
essential essentiel(le)
to **establish** établir
establishment l'établissement (*m.*)
euro l'euro (*m.*)
Europe l'Europe (*f.*)
European (*adj.*) européen(ne)
evening le soir, **BV**
in the evening le soir, **5.2**
in the evening (P.M.) du soir, **BV**
event l'événement (*m.*)
ever jamais
every tous, toutes, **2.1, 8;** chaque
every day tous les jours, **13.2**
everybody tout le monde, **1.2**
everyday quotidien(ne)
everyone tout le monde, **1.2**
everything tout
everywhere partout
evidently évidemment
to **evoke** évoquer
exact exact(e)
exactly exactement
exam l'examen (*m.*), **3.1**
to pass an exam réussir à un examen
to take an exam passer un examen, **3.1**
to **examine** examiner, **14.2**

example: for example par exemple
excellent excellent(e)
except excepté(e); sauf, **13.2**
exception l'exception *(f.)*
exceptional exceptionnel(le)
exchange l'échange *(m.)*
to **exchange** échanger
excursion l'excursion *(f.)*
excuse me pardon
to **execute** exécuter
exercise l'exercice *(m.)*
exhausted crevé(e); épuisé(e)
to **exist** exister
exhibit l'exposition *(f.)*, **13.2**
existence l'existence *(f.)*
to **expel** expulser
expenses les frais *(m. pl.)*
expensive cher, chère, **7.1**
expert *(adj.)* expert(e)
to **explain** expliquer
explanation l'explication *(f.)*
expression l'expression *(f.)*
exterior l'extérieur *(m.)*
extraordinary extraordinaire
eye l'œil *(m., pl.* yeux*)*, **14.1**
to have itchy eyes avoir les yeux qui piquent, **14.1**
eyes les yeux *(m. pl.)*, **L1**

F

fable la fable
fabulous fabuleux, fabuleuse
face la figure, **12.1**
to **face** donner sur, **4.2**
factory l'usine *(f.)*
fairly assez, **1.1**
fall *(season)* l'automne *(m.)*, **11.2**
to **fall** tomber **11.2**
to fall asleep s'endormir
to fall asleep again se rendormir
false faux, fausse
to **falsify** falsifier
family la famille, **4.1**
famous célèbre; connu(e), **13.1**
fan le/la fana
fantastic fantastique
far (away) loin
far from loin de, **4.2**
fare le tarif
fast *(adj.)* rapide; *(adv.)* vite **10.2**
to **fasten** attacher, **8.2**
fast-food *(adj.)* de restauration rapide
fast-food restaurant le fast-food
fat la graisse; le lipide
father le père, **4.1**
fault la faute
favorite favori(te); préféré(e)
February février *(m.)*, **BV**
to **feed** nourrir
to **feel** *(well, etc.)* se sentir, **14.1**
to feel better aller mieux, **14.2**
to feel like avoir envie de
to feel out of sorts ne pas être dans son assiette, **14.1**
fees *(doctor)* les honoraires *(m. pl.)*
felt-tip pen le feutre, **3.2**
festival le festival
festive de fête
festivity la festivité
fever la fièvre, **14.1**
to have a fever avoir de la fièvre, **14.1**
to have a high fever avoir une fièvre de cheval, **14.1**
few peu (de)
a few quelques, **9.2**
fiancé(e) le/la fiancé(e), **L4**
field le champ, **L1;** le domaine
fig la figue
fight le combat, **L3;** lutte, **L3**
to **fight** lutter, **L3**
file *(computer)* le fichier
to **fill out** remplir, **8.2**
film le film, **13.1**
adventure film le film d'aventures, **13.1**
detective film le film policier, **13.1**
foreign film le film étranger, **13.1**
horror film le film d'horreur, **13.1**
science fiction film le film de science-fiction, **13.1**
finally enfin, **12.1;** finalement
to **find** trouver, **5.1**
fine ça va, bien, **BV**
fine l'amende *(f.)*
finger le doigt
to **finish** finir, **8.2**
firm l'entreprise *(f.)*
first premier, première *(adj.)*, **4.2;** d'abord *(adv.)*, **12.1**
in first class en première, **9.1**
fish le poisson, **6.1**
fish store la poissonnerie, **6.1**
fitting room la cabine d'essayage
flavor le parfum
flea market le marché aux puces
flight le vol, **8.1**
domestic flight le vol intérieur, **8.1**
flight attendant l'hôtesse *(f.)* de l'air, le steward, **8.2**
flight crew le personnel de bord, **8.2**
international flight le vol international, **8.1**
float le char
floor *(of a building)* l'étage *(m.)*, **4.2**

ground floor le rez-de-chaussée, **4.2**
flower la fleur, **4.2**
flu la grippe, **14.1**
flute la flûte
to **fly** *(plane)* piloter
to **follow** suivre
following suivant(e)
food la nourriture; l'aliment *(m.)*; les provisions *(f. pl.)*
food service la restauration
foot le pied, **10.1**
on foot à pied, **4.2**
football le football américain
for pour; *(time)* pendant, **3.2;** depuis, **9.2**
for example par exemple
foreign étranger, étrangère, **13.1**
foreman, forewoman le contremaître, la contremaîtresse
to **forget** oublier
fork la fourchette, **5.2**
form la forme
to **form** former
formality la formalité
former ancien(ne)
fortune la fortune
fortunately heureusement
to **found** fonder
fourth quatrième
fracture la fracture
France la France
free libre, **5.1;** gratuit(e)
to **free** libérer
freedom la liberté
freezing: It's freezing (weather). Il gèle., **11.2**
French français(e) *(adj.)*, **1.1;** *(language)* le français, **2.2**
French fries les frites *(f. pl.)*, **5.1**
Frenchman (-woman) le/la Français(e)
French-speaking francophone
to **frequent** fréquenter
Friday vendredi *(m.)*, **BV**
friend l'ami(e), **1.2;** *(pal)* le copain, la copine, **2.1;** le/la camarade
from de, **1.1**
from then on désormais
front l'avant *(m.)*, **8.2**
in front of devant, **8.2**
frozen surgelé(e), **6.2**
fruit le fruit, **6.2**
full plein(e), **10.1;** complet, complète
fun amusant(e), **1.1**
to have fun s'amuser, **12.2**
function la fonction
functioning le fonctionnement
funny amusant(e), **1.1;** rigolo, **4.2;** comique, **13.1**
furniture les meubles *(m. pl.)*
fusion la fusion
future l'avenir *(m.)*, le futur, **L2**

G

game le match, **10.1;** le jeu
garage le garage, **4.2**
garden le jardin, **4.2**
gas le gaz
gas station la station-service
gate *(airport)* la porte, **8.1**
gem la pierre précieuse, **L4**
general le général
generally généralement
geography la géographie, **2.2**
geometry la géometrie, **2.2**
germ le microbe
German *(language)* l'allemand *(m.)*, **2.2**
Germany l'Allemagne *(f.)*
Gesundheit! À tes souhaits!, **14.1**
to **get** recevoir, **10.2**
to get back on remonter
to get dressed s'habiller, **12.1**
to get married se marier, **L4**
to get sick tomber malade, **L1**
to get a sunburn attraper un coup de soleil, **11.1**
to get off a plane débarquer
to get off *(bus, train, etc.)* descendre, **9.2**
to get on (board) monter, **9.2**
to get up se lever, **12.1**
giant le/la géant(e)
gift le cadeau, **4.1**
gigantic gigantesque
girl la fille, **1.1**
girlfriend la petite amie
to **give** donner, **4.1**
to give back rendre
glad content(e)
glass le verre, **5.2**
glove le gant, **11.2**
to **go** aller, **5.1**
to go (in a car, etc.) rouler, **10.2**
to go aboard s'embarquer sur
to go down descendre, **9**
to go fast rouler vite, **10.2**
to go (and) get aller chercher, **6.1**
to go home rentrer, **3.2**
to go out sortir, **8.2**
to go surfing faire du surf, **11.1**
to go to bed se coucher, **12.1**
to go through security *(airport)* passer par le contrôle de sécurité, **8.1**
to go up monter, **4.2**
to go windsurfing faire de la planche à voile, **11.1**
to go with accompagner
Should we go? On y va?
goal le but, **10.1**
to score a goal marquer un but, **10.1**

goalie le gardien de but, **10.1**
God bless you! À tes souhaits!, **14.1**
gold l'or *(m.)*, **L4**
golden doré(e)
good bon(ne), **6.2**
good in math fort(e) en maths, **2.2**
good-bye au revoir; ciao *(inform.)*, **BV**
gourmet le gourmet
grade la note
grains les céréales *(f. pl.)*
gram le gramme, **6.2**
grammar la grammaire
granddaughter la petite-fille, **4.1**
grandfather le grand-père, **4.1**
grandmother la grand-mère, **4.1**
grandparents les grands-parents *(m. pl.)*, **4.1**
grandson le petit-fils, **4.1**
gray gris(e), **7.2**
great grand(e)
Greece la Grèce
green vert(e), **5.1**
green beans les haricots *(m. pl.)* verts, **6.2**
greeting la salutation
grilled ham and cheese sandwich le croque-monsieur, **5.1**
griot le griot
grocery store l'épicerie *(f.)*, **6.1**
ground le sol, **10.2**
ground floor le rez-de-chaussée, **4.2**
on the ground à terre
group le groupe
to **grow (up)** grandir
growth la croissance
guard le gardien, **L4**
to **guard** garder
to **guess** deviner
guide(book) le guide
guillotined guillotiné(e)
guitar la guitare
guitarist le/la guitariste
guy le type
gymnastics la gymnastique, **2.2**

H

hair les cheveux *(m. pl.)*, **12.1**
Haitian haïtien(ne)
half *(sporting event)* le mi-temps
half demi(e)
half brother le demi-frère, **4.1**
half hour la demi-heure
half past *(time)* et demie, **BV**
half price le demi-tarif
half sister la demi-sœur, **4.1**
ham le jambon, **5.1**
hamburger le hamburger
hamlet le hameau
hand la main, **3.1**
handicapé(e) handicapped
handkerchief le mouchoir, **14.1**
handmade fait(e) à la main
handsome beau (bel), **4.2**
happy content(e); heureux, heureuse
Happy birthday! Bon (Joyeux) anniversaire!
harbor le port
hard dur(e); *(adv.)* fort
hardware (computer) le hardware
harp la harpe
hat *(ski)* le bonnet, **11.2**
to **hate** détester, **3.1**
to **have** avoir, **4.1**; *(to eat or drink)* prendre, **5.1**
to have a(n) . . . -ache avoir mal à (aux)... , **14.1**
Have a nice day! Belle journée!, **4.2**
he il, **1.1**
head la tête, **10.1**; *(of department or company)* le chef
to **head into** s'engager dans
headache: to have a headache avoir mal à la tête, **14.1**
health la santé, **14.1**
to be in good (poor) health être en bonne (mauvaise) santé, **14.1**
to **hear** entendre, **9.1**
heart le cœur
high élevé(e)
hello bonjour, **BV**
to **help** aider
help l'aide *(f.)*
to be a big help rendre bien service
with the help of à l'aide de
hemisphere l'hémisphère *(m.)*
here is, here are voici, **4.1**; *(emphatic)* voilà, **1.2**
hero le héros
hi salut, **BV**
to **hide** cacher, **L3**
high élevé(e)
high school le lycée, **2.1**
higher supérieur
his sa, son, ses
history l'histoire *(f.)*, **2.2**
to **hit** frapper, **L3**; donner un coup (de pied, de tête, etc.), **10.1**
hockey le hockey
hockey stick la crosse
hole le trou, **L4**
home: at (to) the home of chez, **3.2**
to go home rentrer, **3.2**
homework *(assignment)* le devoir
to do homework faire ses devoirs, **12.2**
honest honnête
horrible horrible
hospital l'hôpital *(m.)*; *(adj.)* hospitalier, hospitalière
hot chaud(e)
hot chocolate le chocolat
hot dog la saucisse de Francfort, **BV**
It's hot (weather). Il fait chaud., **11.1**

hotel l'hôtel *(m.)*
house la maison, **3.1;** la villa
publishing house la maison d'édition
small house le pavillon
housing le logement
how comment, **1.1**
How are you? Ça va? Comment vas-tu? Comment allez-vous?, **BV**
How's it going? Ça va?, **BV**
How long have you been waiting? Tu attends depuis combien de temps?
how much, how many combien (de), **3.2**
How much is it? C'est combien?, **3.2**
human humain(e)
human being l'être humain *(m.)*
hundred cent, **2.2**
hundreds les centaines *(f. pl.)*
hungry: to be hungry avoir faim, **5.1**
I'm super hungry. J'ai hyper faim.
hunter le chasseur, la chasseuse
to **hurry** se dépêcher, **12.1**
to **hurt** avoir mal à, **14.1**
It (That) hurts. Ça fait mal., **14.1**
husband le mari, **4.1**

I

I je, **1.2**
ice la glace, **11.2**
ice cream la glace, **5.1**
idea l'idée *(f.)*
ideal idéal(e)
identify identifier
if si
ill malade, **L1, 14.1**
illness la maladie
illustration le dessin
immediate immédiat(e)
immediately immédiatement
immense immense
important important(e)
impossible impossible
Impressionists les impressionnistes *(m. pl.)*
imprisoned emprisonné(e)
in dans, **1.2;** à, **3.1;** en, **3.2**
in addition to en plus de
in fact en fait
in first (second) class en première (seconde), **9.1**
in front of devant, **8.2**
in general en général
in particular en particulier
in search of à la recherche de
in vain en vain
In what month? En quel mois?, **BV**
inaugurate inaugurer
included compris(e), **5.2**
The tip is included. Le service est compris., **5.2**
to **indicate** indiquer
indigestion le trouble digestif
to have indigestion avoir mal au foie
indiscreet indiscret, indiscrète
indispensable indispensable
individual l'individu *(m.)*; *(adj.)* individuel(le)
industrial industriel(le)
inexpensive bon marché *(inv.)*
infection l'infection *(f.)*, **14.1**
infinite infini(e)
influence l'influence *(f.)*
to **influence** influencer
information l'information *(f.)*
innocent innocent(e)
inquiry l'enquête *(f.)*
insane fou, folle
to **insist** insister
to **inspire** inspirer
instructions les instructions *(f. pl.)*
instructor le moniteur, la monitrice, **11.1**
instrument l'instrument *(m.)*
keyboard instrument l'instrument à clavier
percussion instrument l'instrument à percussion
string instrument l'instrument à cordes
wind instrument l'instrument à vent
intellectual intellectuel(le)
intelligent intelligent(e), **1.1**
interest l'intérêt *(m.)*
interesting intéressant(e), **1.1**
intermediate moyen(ne)
intermission l'entracte *(m.)*, **13.1**
internal interne
international international(e), **8.1**
interpreter l'interprète *(m. et f.)*
intimate intime
to **introduce** présenter
to **invite** inviter, **4.1**
island l'île *(f.)*, **L4**
to **isolate** isoler
Italian *(adj.)* italien(ne)
Italian *(language)* l'italien *(m.)*, **2.2**
to **itch** piquer **14.1**
to have itchy eyes avoir les yeux qui piquent, **14.1**
Ivory Coast la Côte d'Ivoire

J

jacket le blouson, **7.1**
(sport) jacket la veste, **7.1**
ski jacket l'anorak *(m.)*, **7.1**

H106

jam la confiture, **6.2**
January janvier *(m.)*, **BV**
jar le pot, **6.2**
jazz le jazz
jealous jaloux, jalouse
jeans le jean, **7.1;** le blue-jean
jersey le maillot
to **jog** faire du jogging
to **joke around** rigoler, **3.2**
joy la joie
juice le jus, **5.1**
  apple juice le jus de pomme, **5.1**
  orange juice le jus d'orange, **5.1**
July juillet *(m.)*, **BV**
June juin *(m.)*, **BV**
junior high student le/la collégien(ne)
just juste, **2.1**
  fitting (him/her) just right juste à sa taille
  just barely tout juste

K

to **keep** garder
key la clé; le demi-cercle *(basketball)*, **10.2**
keyboard le clavier
to **kick** donner un coup de pied, **10.1**
to **kid: You're kidding!** Tu rigoles!, **3.2**
kilogram le kilo(gramme), **6.2**
kilometer le kilomètre
kind la sorte; le genre, **13.1**
king le roi, **L3**
kitchen la cuisine, **4.2**
  kitchen sink l'évier *(m.)*, **12.2**
knife le couteau, **5.2**
knight le chevalier
to **knock** frapper, **L4**
to **know** connaître (*be acquainted with*); savoir *(information)*, **13.2**

L

label la griffe
laboratory le laboratoire
lake le lac
lamb l'agneau *(m.)*, **6.1**
lame boiteux, boiteuse
land la terre
to **land** atterrir, **8.1**
landing l'atterrissage *(m.)*; le débarquement
landing card la carte de débarquement, **8.2**
landscape le paysage
language la langue, **2.2**
lap *(race)* l'étape *(f.)*
large grand(e); ample
last dernier, dernière, **10.2**
  last name le nom de famille
  last night hier soir, **10.2**
  last week la semaine dernière, **10.2**
  last year l'année *(f.)* dernière
to **last** durer
late en retard, **9.1;** *(adv.)* tard, **12.1**
  to be late être en retard, **9.1;** avoir du retard *(plane, train, etc.)*, **8.1**
later plus tard
  See you later. À tout à l'heure., **BV**
Latin le latin, **2.2**
Latin *(adj.)* latin(e)
  Latin American latino-américain(e)
to **learn (to)** apprendre (à), **5**
to **leave** partir, **8.1;** ressortir
  to leave (a room, etc.) quitter, **3.1**
  to leave (something behind) laisser, **5.2**
  to leave a tip laisser un pourboire, **5.2**
leg la jambe
legend la légende
lemonade le citron pressé, **5.1**
lemon-lime drink la limonade, **BV**
less moins, **7.1**
  less than moins de
  less . . . than moins... que, **7**
lesson la leçon, **11.1**
to **let** laisser
  Let's go. On y va.
lettuce la salade, **6.2**
level le taux
liaison la liaison
life la vie
light *(color)* clair(e)
like comme
to **like** aimer, **3.1**
  I'd like that! Ça me dit!
  I would like je voudrais, **5.1**
  What would you like? *(café, restaurant)* Vous désirez?, **5.1**
limit la limite
line la ligne; *(of people)* la queue, **9.1**
  to wait in line faire la queue, **9.1**
linked en liaison
linking la liaison
liquid le liquide
to **listen (to)** écouter, **3.1**
  to listen with a stethoscope ausculter, **14.2**
liter le litre, **6.2**
literature la littérature, **2.2**
little: a little un peu, **2.1;** un peu de
to **live** *(in a city, house, etc.)* habiter, **3.1**
liver le foie
living vivant(e)
  living room la salle de séjour, **4.2**
to **load** charger
lobby le hall, **8.1**
local local(e)
located situé(e)
lonely solitaire
long long(ue), **7.1**
  (for) a long time longtemps, **11.1**
  (for) too long trop longtemps, **11.1**

Long live . . . ! Vive... !
longer: no longer ne... plus, **6.1**
to **look** *(seem)* avoir l'air
to **look at** regarder, **3.1**
to look at oneself se regarder
to look at one another se regarder
to **look for** chercher
loose *(clothing)* large, **7.2**
loose-leaf binder le classeur, **3.2**
to **lose** perdre, **9.2**
to lose patience perdre patience, **9.2**
lot: a lot beaucoup, **3.1**
a lot of beaucoup de, **3.2**
a lot of people beaucoup de monde, **10.1**
to **love** aimer, **3.1;** adorer
love l'amour *(m.)*, **L4**
lower inférieur(e)
low-income housing l' H.L.M.
luck la chance
to be in luck avoir de la chance
lucky: to be lucky avoir de la chance
luggage les bagages *(m. pl.)*, **8.1**
lunch le déjeuner, **5.2**
to eat lunch déjeuner, **3.1**
lung le poumon
luxury *(adj.)* de grand standing
lyrics les paroles *(f. pl.)*

M

ma'am madame, **BV**
machine la machine
magazine le magazine, **9.1, L2;** la revue, **L2**
Maghreb le Maghreb
magic *(adj.)* magique
magnificent magnifique
magpie la pie
mail la poste
main principal(e)
majority la majorité
to **make** faire, **6.1;** fabriquer
to make a basket *(basketball)* réussir un panier, **10.2**
to make up inventer
mall le centre commercial, **7.1**
man l'homme *(m.)*, **7.1**
to **manage to** arriver à, **9.1**
mandatory obligatoire
manner la façon
many beaucoup de, **3.2**
map la carte
March mars *(m.)*, **BV**
market le marché, **6.2**
flea market le marché aux puces
marriage le mariage
married marié(e)
to get married se marier, **L4**
marvelous merveilleux, merveilleuse
masculine masculin(e)
math les maths *(f. pl.)*, **2.2**
mathematics les mathématiques *(f. pl.)*, **2.2**
matter: What's the matter with you? Qu'est-ce que tu as?, **10**
May mai *(m.)*, **BV**
meal le repas, **5.2**
to **mean** signifier
meaning la signification; le sens
to **measure** mesurer
measurement la mesure
meat la viande, **6.1**
medical médical(e)
medicine *(medical profession)* la médecine; *(remedy)* le médicament, **14.1**
medina la médina
Mediterranean Sea la mer Méditerranée
medium-rare *(meat)* à point, **5.2**
to **meet** rencontrer; retrouver *(get together with)*; faire la connaissance de
melody l'air *(m.)*
melon le melon, **6.2**
memorable mémorable
memory le souvenir
to **mention** citer
menu la carte, **5.1**
merchandise la marchandise
merchant le/la marchand(e), **6.2**
produce merchant le/la marchand(e) de fruits et légumes, **6.2**
message le message
metabolism le métabolisme
metal le métal
meter le mètre
metric system le système métrique
microbe le microbe
microbial microbien(ne)
microprocessor le microprocesseur
microscope le microscope
middle school student le/la collégien(ne)
midnight minuit *(m.)*, **BV**
military militaire
milk le lait, **6.1**
milligram le milligramme
million le million
mineral le minéral
mineral water l'eau *(f.)* minérale, **6.2**
minus moins
minute la minute, **9.2**
miracle le miracle
mirror la glace, **12.1**
Miss (Ms.) Mademoiselle (Mlle), **BV**
to **miss** *(train, etc.)* rater, **9.2**
mistake la faute
mixture le mélange
model le modèle
modem le modem
modern moderne
modest modeste
mogul la bosse, **11.2**
mom la maman
moment le moment
Monday lundi *(m.)*, **BV**
money l'argent *(m.)*, **5.2**
monitor *(computer)* le moniteur

month le mois, **BV**
more *(comparative)* plus, **7.1**
more or less plus ou moins
no more ne... plus, **6.1**
more . . . than plus... que, **7**
morning le matin, **BV;** le mat *(fam.)*
in the morning le matin
in the morning (A.M.) du matin, **BV**
Morocco le Maroc
Moroccan marocain(e)
Moslem musulman(e)
most (of) la plupart (des), **9.2**
the most . . . le (la, les) plus...
mother la mère, **4.1**
mother tongue la langue maternelle
mount le mont
mountain le mont; la montagne, **11.2**
to (in) the mountains à la montagne
mountaintop le sommet, **11.2**
mouse la souris
mouth la bouche, **14.1**
movement le mouvement
movie le film, **13.1**
detective movie le film policier, **13.1**
movies le cinéma, **13.1**
movie theater le cinéma, la salle de cinéma, **13.1**
movie video le film en vidéo, **13.1**
science-fiction movie le film de science-fiction, **13.1**
Mr. Monsieur *(m.)*, **BV**
Mrs. (Ms.) Madame (Mme), **BV**
multicolored multicolore
to **multiply** multiplier
municipal municipal(e)
muscle le muscle
muscular musculaire
museum le musée, **13.2**
music la musique, **2.2**
musical musical(e)
musical comedy la comédie musicale, **13.1**
musician le/la musicien(ne)
mussel la moule
must devoir, **10.2**
one must il faut, **8.2**
one must not il ne faut pas, **8.2**
mustard la moutarde, **6.2**
my ma, mon, mes, **4**
mysterious mystérieux, mystérieuse
myth le mythe

N

name le nom
first name le prénom
last name le nom de famille
My name is . . . Je m'appelle... , **BV**
What's your name? Tu t'appelles comment?, **BV**
napkin la serviette, **5.2**
national national(e)
nationality la nationalité
native of originaire de
natural naturel(le)
natural sciences les sciences naturelles *(f. pl.)*, **2.1**
nature la nature
navy blue bleu marine *(inv.)*, **7.2**
near près de, **4.2**
very near tout près, **4.2**
necessarily nécessairement
necessary nécessaire
it is necessary il faut, **8.2**
need le besoin
to **need** avoir besoin de, **10.1**
neighbor le/la voisin(e), **4.2**
neighborhood le quartier, **4.2;** *(adj.)* du coin
nephew le neveu, **4.1**
nervous nerveux, nerveuse
net le filet, **10.2**
never ne... jamais, **11.2**
new nouveau (nouvel), nouvelle, **4.2**
New England la Nouvelle-Angleterre
New Orleans La Nouvelle-Orléans
news *(TV)* les informations *(f. pl.)*
news article le reportage
newspaper le journal, **9.1**
newsstand le kiosque, **9.1**
next prochain(e), **9.2**
nice *(person)* sympa, **1.2;** aimable; sympathique; gentil(le), **6.2**
It's nice weather. Il fait beau., **11.1**
niece la nièce, **4.1**
night la nuit
last night hier soir, **10.2**
no non
no longer ne... plus, **6.1**
no more ne... plus, **6.1**
no one ne... personne, **11;** personne ne...
no smoking (section) (la zone) non-fumeurs, **8.1**
noble noble
nobody ne... personne, **11;** personne ne...
noise le bruit
nonsmoking *(section)* non-fumeurs, **8.1**
noon midi *(m.)*, **BV**
north le nord
North African nord-africain(e)
nose le nez, **14.1**
to have a runny nose avoir le nez qui coule, **14.1**
not ne... pas, **1.2;** pas, **2.1**
isn't it?, doesn't it (he, she, etc.)?, n'est-ce pas?, **2.2**
not at all pas du tout, **3.1**
not bad pas mal, **BV**

note la note
notebook le cahier, **3.2**
notepad le bloc-notes, **3.2**
nothing ne... rien, **11**
to **notice** remarquer
noun le nom
novel le roman
November novembre *(m.)*, **BV**
now maintenant, **2.2**
  right now en ce moment
nowadays de nos jours
number le nombre; le numéro
  telephone number le numéro de téléphone
numerous nombreux, nombreuse
nutrition l'alimentation *(f.)*

O

oboe le hautbois
object l'objet *(m.)*
to **oblige** obliger
to **observe** observer
occupied occupé(e)
ocean l'océan *(m.)*
o'clock: It's . . . o'clock. Il est... heure(s)., **BV**
October octobre *(m.)*, **BV**
of *(belonging to)* de, **1.2**
  of course bien sûr
  Of course (not)! Mais oui (non)!
Off (they) go! En route!
office: to have office hours *(doctor)* donner des consultations
often souvent, **5.2**
official officiel(le)
oil l'huile *(f.)*, **6.1;** le pétrole
  oil tanker le pétrolier
okay *(health)* Ça va.; *(agreement)* d'accord, **BV**
  Okay! Bon!, **6.1**
old vieux (vieil), vieille, **4.2;** âgé(e); ancien(ne)
  How old are you? Tu as quel âge? *(fam.)*, **4.1**
older l'aîné(e), **L1**
omelette (with herbs/plain) l'omelette *(f.)* (aux fines herbes/nature), **5.1**
on sur, **4.2**
  on board à bord de, **8.2**
  on foot à, **4.2**
  on sale en solde, **7.1**
  on time à l'heure, **8.1**
  on Tuesdays le mardi, **13.2**
oneself soi
one-way ticket l'aller simple *(m.)*, **9.1**
onion l'oignon *(m.)*, **5.1**
only seulement; *(adj.)* seul(e)
open ouvert(e), **13.2**
to **open** ouvrir, **14.2**
opera l'opéra *(m.)*
  light opera l'opéra comique
operation l'opération *(f.)*
opinion l'avis *(m.)*, **7.2**
  in my opinion à mon avis, **7.2**
opponent l'adversaire *(m. et f.)*
  opponents le camp adverse, **10.1**
to **oppose** opposer, **10.1**
opposing adverse, **10.1**
opposite le contraire
or ou, **1.1**
  or else sinon, **9.2**
orange *(fruit)* l'orange *(f.)*, **6.2;** *(color)* orange *(inv.)*, **7.2**
  orange tree l'oranger *(m.)*, **L2**
orchestra l'orchestre *(m.)*
  symphony orchestra l'orchestre symphonique
to **orchestrate** orchestrer
order: in order to pour
to **order** commander, **5.1**
ordinary ordinaire
organ *(of the body)* l'organe *(m.)*; *(musical instrument)* l'orgue *(m.)*
organism l'organisme *(m.)*
to **organize** organiser
original language version *(of a film)* la version originale, **13.1**
other autre
  in other words autrement dit
  on the other hand par contre
  some other d'autres, **2.2**
otherwise sinon, **9.2**
our notre, nos, **4**
outing l'excursion *(f.)*
outdoors en plein air
outgoing sociable, **1.2**
outfit l'ensemble *(m.)*
outside *(n.)* l'extérieur *(m.)*; *(adv.)* à l'extérieur; *(prep.)* au dehors de
  to work outside the home travailler à l'extérieur
outskirts la périphérie
over *(prep.)* par-dessus, **10.2**
to **overlook** donner sur, **4.2**
overseas *(adj.)* d'outre-mer
oxygen l'oxygène *(m.)*
to **owe** devoir, **10**
to **own** posséder

P

to **pack** *(suitcases)* faire les valises, **8.1**
package le paquet, **6.2**
packed *(stadium)* comble, **10.1**
pain in the neck *(slang)* casse-pieds
painful douloureux, douloureuse
to **paint** peindre
painter l'artiste peintre *(m. et f.)*, le/la peintre, **13.2**
painting la peinture, **13.2;** le tableau, **13.2**
pair la paire, **7.1**
pal le copain, la copine, **2.1**
palace le palais
pancake la crêpe, **BV**

pants le pantalon, **7.1**
paper le papier, **3.2**
sheet of paper la feuille de papier, **3.2**
parade le défilé
pardon me pardon
parents les parents *(m. pl.)*, **4.1**
Parisian *(adj.)* parisien(ne)
park le parc
parking lot le parking
part la partie
to be part of faire partie de
to **participate (in)** participer (à)
party la fête, **4.1**
to throw a party donner une fête, **4.1**
pass la passe
to **pass** passer, **10.1**
to pass an exam réussir à un examen
passenger le passager, la passagère, **8.1;** *(train)* le voyageur, la voyageuse, **9.1**
passport le passeport, **8.1**
passport check le contrôle des passeports
past passé(e)
pasta les pâtes *(f. pl.)*
path le chemin
patience la patience, **9.2**
to lose patience perdre patience, **9.2**
patient le/la malade, **14.2;** *(adj.)* patient(e), **1.1**
patio la terrasse, **4.2**
to **pay** payer, **3.2**
to pay attention faire attention
to pay back rembourser
peace la paix
pear la poire, **6.2**
pearl la perle
peas les petits pois *(m. pl.)*, **6.2**
peasant le/la paysan(ne), **L1**
pen: ballpoint pen le stylo-bille, **3.2**
felt-tip pen le feutre, **3.2**
penalty *(soccer)* le penalty
pencil le crayon, **3.2**
penicillin la pénicilline, **14.1**
people les gens *(m. pl.)*
pepper le poivre, **6.1**
percent pour cent
perfect parfait(e)
perfectly parfaitement
to **perform** jouer, **13.1**
period l'époque *(f.)*; la période
permanent permanent(e)
to **permit** permettre
person la personne
personal personnel(le)
personality la personnalité
personally personnellement, **13.2**
pharmaceutical pharmaceutique
pharmacist le/la pharmacien(ne), **14.2**
pharmacy la pharmacie, **14.2**
phenomenon le phénomène
photograph la photo
physical physique
physicist le/la physicien(ne)
physics la physique, **2.2**
to **pick up** ramasser, **8.2;** recueillir
picnic le pique-nique
picturesque pittoresque
pie la tarte, **6.1**
pill le comprimé, **14.2**
pilot le/la pilote, **8.2**
airline pilot le/la pilote de ligne
to **pilot** piloter
pink rose, **7.1**
pizza la pizza, **BV**
place l'endroit *(m.)*; la place
to take place avoir lieu
to **place** mettre, **7.1**
plain la plaine
plan le projet
plane l'avion *(m.)*, **8.1**
by plane en avion
plant la plante
plastic le plastique
plate l'assiette *(f.)*, **5.2**
platform *(railroad)* le quai, **9.1**
to **play** jouer, **3.2**
to play *(a sport)* jouer à, **10.1**
play la pièce (de théâtre), **13.1**
to put on a play monter une pièce, **13.1**
player le joueur, la joueuse, **10.1**
playwright l'auteur *(m.)* dramatique
pleasant agréable
please s'il vous plaît *(form.)*, s'il te plaît *(fam.)*, **BV**
pleasure le plaisir
pleated plissé(e), **7.1**
plentiful abondant(e)
to **plot** conspirer
plus plus
p.m. de l'après-midi; du soir, **BV**
poem le poème
poet *(m. and f.)* le poète
politeness la politesse, **BV**
political politique
polluted pollué(e)
pollution la pollution
polo shirt le polo, **7.1**
pool la piscine, **11.1**
poor pauvre, **L1, 14.1**
Poor thing! Le/La pauvre!, **14.1**
pop *(music)* pop
popular populaire, **1.2**
pork le porc, **6.1**
port le port
Portuguese portugais(e)
position la position
to **possess** posséder
possession la possession
postcard la carte postale, **9.1**
poster l'affiche *(f.)*
potato la pomme de terre, **6.2**
pound la livre, **6.2**

practical pratique
practice la pratique
to **practice** pratiquer; travailler
preceding précédent(e)
to **prefer** préférer, **6**
prefix le préfixe
to **prepare** préparer
to **prescribe** prescrire, **14.2**
prescription l'ordonnance *(f.)*, **14.2**
to write a prescription faire une ordonnance, **14.2**
present le cadeau, **4.1**
to **present** présenter
pretty joli(e), **4.2**
price le prix, **7.1**
priest l'abbé *(m.)*
principal principal(e)
printer l'imprimante *(f.)*
prison la prison, **L4**
prisoner le prisonnier, la prisonnière, **L4**
private individuel(le); privé(e)
problem le problème; la difficulté
product le produit
professional professionel(le)
program le programme; *(TV)* l'émission *(f.)*, **12.2;** *(computer)* le logiciel
programming la programmation
protein la protéine
proud fier, fière
public public, publique
to **publish** publier
to **punish** punir
purchase achat *(m.)*
purified purifié(e)
to **push** pousser
to **put (on)** mettre, **7.1**
to put on makeup se maquiller, **12.1**
to put (someone) to bed coucher, **12**
to put on a play monter une pièce, **13.1**

Q

quality la qualité
quarter: quarter after *(time)* et quart, **BV**
quarter to *(time)* moins le quart, **BV**
Quebec: from or of Quebec québécois
queen la reine
question la question, **3.1**
to ask a question poser une question, **3.1**
quick rapide
quickly rapidement
quite assez, **1.1**
quiz l'interro(gation) *(f.)*

R

race *(human population)* la race; *(competition)* la course, **10.2**
bicycle race la course cycliste, **10.2**
radio la radio, **3.2**
rain la pluie
to **rain: It's raining.** Il pleut., **11.1**
to **raise** lever
to raise one's hand lever la main, **3.1**
raisin le raisin sec
rap *(music)* le rap
rapidly rapidement
rare *(meat)* saignante(e), **5.2**
rather plutôt
razor le rasoir, **12.1**
to **read** lire, **9.2**
reader le lecteur, la lectrice
reading la lecture
real vrai(e), **2.2**
reality la réalité
really vraiment, **1.1**
rear l'arrière *(m.)*, **8.2**
rear guard l'arrière-garde *(f.)*
reason la raison
to **receive** recevoir, **10.2**
recess la récré(ation), **3.2**
to **recognize** reconnaître
record le disque
recycling le recyclage
red rouge, **7.1**
referee l'arbitre *(m.)*, **10.1**
to **reflect** refléter
refrigerator le frigidaire, **12.2;** le réfrigérateur, **12.2**
reggae le reggae
region la région
to **reimburse** rembourser
relationship la relation
religious religieux, religieuse
to **remain** rester, **11.1**
remote control la télécommande, **12.2**
renowned renommé(e)
to **rent** louer, **13.1**
to **replace** remplacer
to **represent** représenter
research la recherche
to **resemble** ressembler à
reserved réservé(e)
respective respectif, respective
respiration la respiration
respiratory respiratoire
restaurant le restaurant, **5.2**
train station restaurant le buffet, **9.1**
retreat la retraite
return le retour
to **return** rentrer, **3.2;** *(volleyball)* renvoyer, **10.2**
revolution la révolution
revolutionary révolutionnaire
rhythm le rythme
rice le riz
rich riche
riddle la devinette
ridiculous ridicule
right le droit
right away tout de suite
right there juste là
to **rinse** rincer
river le fleuve; rivière
Riviera *(French)* la Côte d'Azur
road la route; le chemin

rock le rocher, **L3;** *(music)* le rock
role le rôle
romantic romantique
roof le toit
thatched roof le toit de chaume
room *(in house)* la pièce, **4.2;** la salle
dining room la salle à manger, **4.2**
living room la salle de séjour, **4.2**
round-trip ticket le billet aller-retour, **9.1**
route le chemin
routine la routine, **12.1**
royal royal(e)
ruby le rubis
ruined ruiné(e)
rule la règle
ruler la règle, **3.2**
runner le coureur, **10.2**
running shoe la basket, **7.1**
runny: to have a runny nose avoir le nez qui coule, **14.1**
runway la piste, **8.1**
rural rural(e)
Russian *(language)* le russe

S

sad triste, **L1**
to **safeguard** sauvegarder
sailor le marin, **L4**
salad la salade, **5.1**
salami le saucisson, **6.1**
salary le salaire
sale: on sale en solde, **7.1;** en promotion
sales les soldes *(m. pl.)*, **7.1**
salesperson le vendeur, la vendeuse, **7.1**
salt le sel, **6.1**
same même, **2.1**
all the same tout de même, **5.2**
It's all the same to me. Ça m'est égal., **13.1**
sandals *(f. pl.)* les sandals, **7.1**
sandwich le sandwich, **BV**
grilled ham and cheese sandwich le croque-monsieur, **5.1**
sardine la sardine
to **satisfy** satisfaire
Saturday samedi *(m.)*, **BV**
sauce la sauce
sausage la saucisse
to **save** sauver; sauvegarder
saxophone le saxophone
to **say** dire, **9.2**
scarf l'écharpe *(f.)*, **11.2**
scene la scène, **13.1**
schedule l'emploi *(m.)* du temps; l'horaire *(m.)*, **9.1**
sports schedule le calendrier sportif
school l'école *(f.)*, **1.2;** *(adj.)* scolaire, **3.2**
elementary school l'école primaire
junior high/high school l'école secondaire, **1.2**
high school le lycée, **2.1**
school supplies la fourniture scolaire, **3.2**
science les sciences *(f. pl.)*, **2.1**
natural sciences les sciences naturelles, **2.1**
social sciences les sciences sociales, **2.1**
scientific scientifique
scientist le savant
to **score a goal** marquer un but, **10.1**
to **scratch** gratter, **14.1**
screen l'écran *(m.)*, **8.1**
sculptor le sculpteur *(m. et f.)*, **13.2**
sculpture la sculpture, **13.2**
sea la mer, **11.1**
by the sea au bord de la mer, **11.1**
seashore le bord de la mer, **11.1**
seaside resort la station balnéaire, **11.1**
season la saison
seat le siège, **8.2;** la place *(plane, train, movie, etc.)*, **8.1**
seated assis(e), **9.2**
second *(adj.)* deuxième, **4.2;** second(e)
in second class en seconde, **9.1**
secret *(adj.)* secret, secrète
security (airport) le contrôle de sécurité, **8.1**
to **see** voir, **7.1**
See you later. À tout à l'heure., **BV**
See you soon! À bientôt!, **BV**
See you tomorrow. À demain., **BV**
seldom très peu
to **sell** vendre, **9.1**
seller le/la marchand(e), **6.2**
produce seller le/la marchand(e) de fruits et légumes, **6.2**
semi-circle le demi-cercle, **10.2**
to **send** envoyer, **10.1;** emmener, **L4**
separate séparer
September septembre *(m.)*, **BV**
serious sérieux, sérieuse, **7;** grave
to **serve** servir, **8.2; 10.2**
service le service, **5.2**
to **set the table** mettre la table, **7**
several plusieurs
Shall we go? On y va?
shampoo le shampooing, **12.1**
shape la forme
to **shave** se raser, **12.1**
shaver le rasoir, **12.1**
she elle, **1.1**
sheet of paper la feuille de papier, **3.2**
shepherd le berger
shepherdess la bergère
to **shine** briller
shirt la chemise, **7.1**
shoe la chaussure, **7.1**

to **shoot** *(ball)* lancer, **10.2**
shop la boutique, **7.1**
to **shop** faire des achats
shopkeeper le/la commerçant(e)
shopping le shopping, **7.2**
to do the grocery shopping faire les courses, **6.1**
to go shopping faire des courses, **7.2**
shopping cart le chariot, **6.2**
shopping center le centre commercial, **7.1**
short petit(e), **1.1;** court(e), **7.1**
in a short time en très peu de temps
shorts le short, **7.1**
to **shout** crier, **L4**
show *(TV)* l'émission *(f.)*, **12.2**
show(ing) *(movies)* la séance, **13.1**
to **show** montrer; *(movie)* jouer
shower la douche, **12.1**
to take a shower prendre une douche, **12.1**
showing *(movies)* la séance, **13.1**
shrimp la crevette, **6.1**
shy timide, **1.2**
sick malade, **14.1, L1**
to get sick tomber malade, **L1**
sick person le/la malade, **14.2**
side le côté; *(in a sporting event)* le camp, **10.1**
sidewalk café la terrasse (d'un café), **5.1**
sign le signal
significance la signification
similar semblable, **L1**
simple simple
simply simplement
since *(time)* depuis, **9.2**
to **sing** chanter, **13.2**
singer le chanteur, la chanteuse, **13.1**
single unique; seul(e)
sink *(kitchen)* l'évier *(m.)*, **12.2**
sinus infection la sinusite, **14.2**
sir monsieur, **BV**
sister la sœur, **1.2**
to **sit: Where would you like to sit?** Qu'est-ce que vous voulez comme place?, **8.1**
size *(clothes)* la taille; *(shoes)* la pointure, **7.2**
the next larger size la taille au-dessus, **7.2**
the next smaller size la taille au-dessous, **7.2**
to wear size (number) faire du (nombre), **7.2**
What size do you wear? Vous faites quelle taille (pointure)?, **7.2**
skate le patin, **11.2**
to **skate (ice)** faire du patin (à glace), **11.1**
skating le patin
to go skating faire du patin, **11.1**
skating rink la patinoire, **11.2**
skeletal squelettique
skeleton le squelette
ski le ski, **11.2**
ski boot la chaussure de ski, **11.2**
ski cap le bonnet, **11.2**
ski jacket l'anorak *(m.)*, **7.1**
ski pole le bâton, **11.2**
ski resort la station de sports d'hiver, **11.2**
ski trail la piste, **11.2**
to **ski** faire du ski, **11.2**
skier le skieur, la skieuse, **11.2**
skiing le ski, **11.2**
cross-country skiing le ski de fond, **11.2**
downhill skiing le ski alpin, **11.2**
skirt la jupe, **7.1**
skull la boîte crânienne
sky le ciel, **11.1**
to **sleep** dormir, **8.2**
to sleep like a log dormir comme une souche
sleeping car le wagon-couchette
sleeve la manche, **7.1**
long-(short-)sleeved à manches longues (courtes), **7.1**
slice la tranche, **6.2**
slice of bread with butter or jam la tartine
slice of bread and butter la tartine de pain beurré
small petit(e), **1.1**
smoke la fumée
to **smoke** fumer
snack bar *(train)* le snack-bar, **9.2**
sneaker la basket, **7.1**
to **sneeze** éternuer, **14.1**
snow la neige, **11.2**
to **snow: It's snowing.** Il neige., **11.2**
snowman le bonhomme de neige
so alors, **BV;** donc; si *(adv.)*
soap le savon, **12.1**
soccer le foot(ball), **10.1**
soccer field le terrain de football, **10.1**
sociable sociable, **1.2**
social social(e)
social sciences les sciences sociales *(f. pl.)*, **2.1**
social worker l'assistante sociale *(f.)*
sock la chaussette, **7.1**
software le software
soldier le soldat, **L3**
solely uniquement
solid solide
solidarity la solidarité
solution la solution
some du, de la, de l', des, **6;** *(adj.)* quelques *(pl.)*, **9.2;** *(pron.)* certains
some other d'autres, **2.2**
somebody quelqu'un, **10.1**

someone quelqu'un, **10.1**
something quelque chose, **11**
something else autre chose
something special quelque chose de spécial
something to drink quelque chose à boire
sometimes quelquefois, **5.2**
son le fils, **4.1**
song la chanson
soon bientôt
See you soon. À bientôt., **BV**
sore throat: to have a sore throat avoir mal à la gorge, **14.1**
sorry: to be sorry regretter, **6.1**
so-so comme ci, comme ça
sound le son, **L3**
soup la soupe, **5.1**
source la source
south le sud
South America l'Amérique *(f.)* du Sud
spaghetti les spaghettis *(m. pl.)*
Spanish espagnol(e)
Spanish *(language)* l'espagnol *(m.)*, **2.2**
to **sparkle** scintiller
to **speak** parler, **3.1**
special spécial(e)
specialty la spécialité
spectator le spectateur, la spectatrice, **10.1**
to **spend** *(time)* passer, **3.1**
to **spill** déverser
spinach les épinards *(m. pl.)*, **6.2**
spinal cord la moelle épinière
spirit l'esprit *(m.)*
splendid splendide
spoon la cuillère, **5.2**
sport le sport, **10.2**
team sport le sport collectif; le sport d'équipe, **10.2**
winter sports les sports d'hiver, **11.2**
spring *(season)* le printemps, **11.1**
square la place
stadium le stade, **10.1**
stage *(of a race)* l'étape *(f.)*
staircase l'escalier *(m.)*, **4.2**
to **stamp** *(a ticket)* composter, **9.1**
standing debout, **9.2**
to **stare at** regarder fixement
state of the art haut de gamme
station la station, **4.2**
gas station la station-service
subway station la station de métro, **4.2**
stationery store la papeterie, **3.2**
statue la statue, **13.2**
stay le séjour
to **stay** rester, **11.1**
steak and French fries le steak frites, **5.2**
stepfather le beau-père, **4.1**
stepmother la belle-mère, **4.1**
still toujours; encore, **11**
stomach le ventre, **14.1**
stomachache: to have a stomachache avoir mal au ventre, **14.1**
stone la pierre
stop l'arrêt *(m.)*, **9.2**
to **stop** s'arrêter, **10.1**
store le magasin, **3.2**
department store le grand magasin, **7.1**
to **store** stocker
story l'histoire *(f.)*
strategy la stratégie
strawberry la fraise, **6.2**
street la rue, **3.1**
strength la force
strict strict(e), **2.1**
strong fort(e), **2.2**
student l'élève *(m. et f.)*, **1.2;** *(university)* l'étudiant(e)
studio *(artist's)* l'atelier *(m.)*
studio *(apartment)* le studio
study l'étude *(f.)*
to **study** étudier, **3.1;** faire des études
to study French *(math, etc.)* faire du français (des maths, etc.), **6**
stupid stupide
stupid thing la bêtise
style le look
in style à la mode
subject le sujet; *(in school)* la matière, **2.2**
substance la substance
subtitles les sous-titres *(m. pl.)*, **13.1**
to **subtract** soustraire
subway le métro, **4.2**
subway station la station de métro, **4.2**
to **succeed in (doing)** arriver à (+ *inf.*), **9.1**
success le succès
to **suffer** souffrir, **14.2**
sugar le sucre
to **suggest** proposer; suggérer
suit *(men's)* le complet; *(women's)* le tailleur, **7.1**
suitcase la valise, **8.1**
sum la somme
summer l'été *(m.)*
in summer en été, **11.1**
summit le sommet, **11.2**
sun le soleil, **11.1**
in the sun au soleil, **11.1**
to **sunbathe** prendre un bain de soleil, **11.1**
sunburn le coup de soleil, **11.1**
Sunday dimanche *(m.)*, **BV**
sunglasses les lunettes *(f. pl.)* de soleil, **11.1**
sunny: It's sunny. Il fait du soleil., **11.1**
suntan lotion la crème solaire, **11.1**
super super
superbe superbe
supermarket le supermarché, **6.2**

supply la fourniture
school supplies la fourniture scolaire, **3.2**
sure sûr(e)
surfer le surfeur, la surfeuse, **11.1**
surfing le surf, **11.1**
to go surfing faire du surf, **11.1**
to **surf the Net** naviguer sur Internet
surprise la surprise
survey le sondage
survival la survie
to **swallow** avaler, **14.2**
sweater le pull, **7.1**
sweatshirt le sweat-shirt, **7.1**
to **swim** nager, **11.1**
swimming la natation, **11.1**
sword l'épée *(f.)*, **L3**
symphony la symphonie
symptom le symptôme
syrup le sirop, **14.1**
system le système
metric system le système métrique

T

table la table, **5.1**
table setting le couvert, **5.2**
tablecloth la nappe, **5.2**
to **take** prendre, **5.2**
What size do you take? Vous faites quelle taille (pointure)?, **7.2**
to take down descendre, **9**
to take an exam passer un examen, **3.1**
to take off *(airplane)* décoller, **8.1**
to take place avoir lieu
to take possession of prendre possession de
to take size *(number)* faire du (nombre), **7.2**
to take the subway prendre le métro, **5.2**
to take a trip faire un voyage, **8.1**
to take a walk faire une promenade, **11.1**
taken occupé(e)
talent le talent
to **talk** parler, **3.1**
to talk on the phone parler au téléphone, **3.2**
tall grand(e), **1.1**
to **tan** bronzer, **11.1**
tango le tango
tape la cassette, **7.1**
to **tape** enregistrer
tart la tarte, **6.1**
apple tart la tarte aux pommes, **6.1**
tea le thé
to **teach (someone to do something)** apprendre (à quelqu'un à faire quelque chose)
teacher le/la prof *(inform.)*, **2.1;** le professeur, **2.1**
team l'équipe *(f.)*
teammate le coéquipier, la coéquipière
techno (music) la techno
teenager l'adolescent(e)
telephone le téléphone, **3.2;** *(adj.)* téléphonique
telephone number le numéro de téléphone
to **tell** dire, **9.2**
to tell (about) raconter
temperate tempéré
temperature la température
temple la tempe
temporary temporaire
ten dix, **BV**
tendon le tendon
term le terme
terrace la terrasse, **4.2**
terrible terrible
terrific super; terrible
test l'examen *(m.)*, **3.1**
to take a test passer un examen, **3.1**
to pass a test réussir à un examen
text le texte
Thai thaïlandais(e)
than *(in comparisons)* que, **7.2**
thank you merci, **BV**
thanks merci, **BV**
thanks to grâce à
that ça; ce (cet), cette, **9**
that is c'est-à-dire
That's all. C'est tout., **6.1**
That's it., That's right. C'est ça.
thatched roof le toit de chaume
the le, la, les, **1.1**
theater le théâtre, **13.1**
their leur(s), **4**
theme le thème
then alors, **BV;** ensuite, **12.1**
there là; y, **5.2**
there are il y a, **4.1**
there is il y a, **4.1**
therefore donc
they ils, elles, **2;** on, **3.2**
thing la chose
to **think** croire, **7.2;** *(opinion)* trouver, **7.2**
third troisième, **4.2**
thirsty: to be thirsty avoir soif, **5.1**
this ce (cet), cette
thousand mille, **3.2**
throat la gorge, **14.1**
throat infection l'angine *(f.)*, **14.1**
to have a frog in one's throat avoir un chat dans la gorge, **14.1**
to have a sore throat avoir mal à la gorge, **14.1**
throne le trône
through par
to **throw** lancer, **10.2**
to throw a party donner une fête, **4.1**
Thursday jeudi *(m.)*, **BV**
ticket le billet, **8.1**
one-way ticket l'aller (simple), **9.1**
round-trip ticket le billet aller (et) retour, **9.1**

ticket window le guichet, **9.1**
to **tie** *(score)* égaliser
tie la cravate, **7.1**
tight serré(e), **7.2**
time *(of day)* l'heure *(f.)*, **BV;** *(in a series)* la fois, **10.2;** le temps
(for) a long time longtemps, **11.1**
at the same time à la fois
at what time? à quelle heure?, **2**
in a short time en très peu de temps
on time à l'heure, **8.1**
time difference le décalage horaire
times l'époque *(f.)*
What time is it? Il est quelle heure?, **BV**
timetable l'horaire *(m.)*
tip *(restaurant)* le pourboire, **5.2**
to leave a tip laisser un pourboire, **5.2**
The tip is included. Le service est compris., **5.2**
tired fatigué(e)
tissue le kleenex, **14.1**
to à, **3.1;** à destination de *(plane, train, etc.)*, **8.1;** *(in order to)* pour
(up) to jusqu'à
toast le pain grillé
today aujourd'hui, **BV;** de nos jours
together ensemble, **5.1**
tomato la tomate, **6.2**
tomorrow demain, **BV**
See you tomorrow. À demain., **BV**
tonight ce soir
tonsillitis l'angine *(f.)*, **14.1**
too *(also)* aussi, **1.1;** *(excessive)* trop, **2.1**
too many, too much trop de
tooth la dent
toothbrush la brosse à dents, **12.1**
toothpaste le dentifrice, **12.1**
totally complètement; totalement
to **touch** toucher, **10.2**
tourist le/la touriste
toward vers
towel la serviette, **11.1**
tower la tour
Eiffel Tower la tour Eiffel
town la ville, **8.1;** le village
in town en ville
small town le village
toxic toxique
track la piste, **10.2;** *(railroad)* la voie, **9.1**
track and field l'athlétisme *(m.)*, **10.2**
tradition la tradition
traditional traditionel(le)
tragedy la tragédie
tragic tragique
train le train, **9.1**
train station la gare, **9.1**
train station restaurant le buffet, **9.1**
traitor le traître, la traîtresse
to **transform** transformer
to **transport** transporter
traveler le voyageur, la voyageuse, **9.1**
tray le plateau, **8.2**
treasure le trésor, **L4**
to **treat** traiter
treatment le traitement
tree l'arbre *(m.)*, **L3**
trigonometry la trigonométrie, **2.2**
trip le voyage, **8.1**
to take a trip faire un voyage, **8.1**
tropical tropical(e)
trouble: to be in trouble être en difficulté
truck le camion
true vrai(e), **2.2**
trumpet la trompette
truth la vérité
to **try on** essayer, **7.2**
T-shirt le t-shirt, **7.1**
Tuesday mardi *(m.)*, **BV**
tunic la tunique
Tunisian tunisien(ne)
tunnel le tunnel
turn: It's your turn. À votre tour.
to **turn around** faire demi-tour
to **turn off** *(appliance)* éteindre, **12.2**
to **turn on** *(appliance)* mettre, **7;** allumer, **12.2**
TV la télé, **12.2**
on TV à la télé, **12.2**
twin le jumeau, la jumelle, **L1**
type le type, la sorte, le genre, **13.1**
typical typique
typically typiquement

U

uncle l'oncle *(m.)*, **4.1**
under sous, **8.2**
underground souterrain(e)
to **understand** comprendre, **5**
unfortunately malheureusement
unhappy malheureux, malheureuse
unit l'unité *(f.)*
United States les États-Unis *(m. pl.)*
university l'université *(f.)*
unknown inconnu(e)
until jusqu'à
up there là-haut
upset stomach le trouble digestif
to **use** utiliser
usually d'habitude, **12.2**

V

vacation les vacances *(f. pl.)*
on vacation en vacances
summer vacation les grandes vacances

valley la vallée; le val
value la valeur
vanilla *(adj.)* à la vanille, **5.1**
varied varié(e)
variety la variété
various divers(e)
VCR le magnétoscope, **12.2**
to **vary** varier
vegetable le légume, **6.2**
veil le voile
vein la veine
vengence la vengeance
to **verify** vérifier, **8.1**
very très, **BV;** tout
very near tout près, **4.2**
very well très bien, **BV**
victorious victorieux, victorieuse
video la vidéo, **3.1**
movie video le film en vidéo, **13.1**
videocassette la cassette vidéo, **12.2**
Vietnamese vietnamien(ne), **6**
view la vue
village le village
vinegar le vinaigre, **6.1**
violent violent(e)
violin le violon
viral viral(e)
virus le virus
to **visit** *(a place)* visiter
vitamin la vitamine
voice la voix
volleyball le volley (-ball), **10.2**
volunteer le/la bénévole
voyage le voyage

W

to **wait (for)** attendre, **9.1**
to wait in line faire la queue, **9.1**
waiter le serveur, **5.1**
waiting room la salle d'attente, **9.1**
waitress la serveuse, **5.1**
walk la promenade, **11.1**
to take a walk faire une promenade, **11.1**
to **walk** marcher
wall le mur, **L4**
to **want** désirer, vouloir, avoir envie de
war la guerre, **L3**
warm chaud(e)
warmup suit le survêtement, **7.1**
warrior le guerrier, **L3**
to **wash** se laver, **12.1**
to wash one's hair (face, etc.) se laver les cheveux (la figure, etc.), **12.1**
washcloth le gant de toilette, **12.1**
waste le déchet
to **watch** surveiller
Watch out! Attention!, **4.2**
water l'eau *(f.)*, **6.2**
to **water-ski** faire du ski nautique, **11.1**
way la façon
we nous, **2;** on, **3.2**
weak faible, **L1**
weapon l'arme *(f.)*
to **wear** porter, **7.1**
What size do you wear? Vous faites quelle taille?, **7.2**
weather le temps, **11.1**
It's nice (bad) weather. Il fait beau (mauvais)., **11.1**
What's the weather like? Il fait quel temps?, **11.1**
Web site le site
wedding le mariage
Wednesday mercredi *(m.)*, **BV**
week la semaine, **3.2**
a week huit jours
a (per) week par semaine, **3.2**
last week la semaine dernière, **10.2**
next week la semaine prochaine
weekend le week-end
weight le poids
welcome le/la bienvenu(e)
Welcome! Bienvenue!
You're welcome. Je t'en prie. *(fam.)*, **BV;** Je vous en prie. *(form.)*, **BV**
well bien, **BV;** eh bien; ben *(slang)*
well then alors, **BV**
well-behaved bien élevé(e)
well-done *(meat)* bien cuit(e), **5.2**
well-known connu(e), **13.1**
well-to-do aisé(e)
west l'ouest *(m.)*
western occidental(e)
western *(movie)* le western
what qu'est-ce que, **3.2;** quel(le), **6;** quoi *(after prep.)*
What color is . . . ? De quelle couleur est... ?, **7.2**
What is . . . like? Comment est... ?, **1.1**
What is it? Qu'est-ce que c'est?, **3.2**
What is today's date? Quelle est la date aujourd'hui?, **BV**
What's your name? Tu t'appelles comment?, **BV**
when quand, **4.1**
where où, **1.1**
from where d'où, **1.1**
which quel(le), **6**
to **whistle** siffler, **10.1**
white blanc, blanche, **7.2**
who qui, **1.1**
whole *(adj.)* entier, entière; *(n.)* l'ensemble *(m.)*
whole-wheat bread le pain complet
whom qui, **10**
why pourquoi, **6.2**
why not? pourquoi pas?
wide large, **7.2**
wife la femme, **4.1**
to **win** gagner, **10.1;** sortir victorieux (victorieuse)

wind le vent, **11.1**
window *(seat)* (une place) côté fenêtre, **8.1**
window *(store)* la vitrine, **7.1**
windsurfing la planche à voile, **11.1**
  to go windsurfing faire de la planche à voile, **11.1**
windy: It's windy. Il y a du vent., **11.1**
winner le/la gagnant(e), **10.2**
  winner's cup la coupe, **10.2**
winter l'hiver *(m.)*
with avec, **3.2;** auprès de; muni(e) de
without sans
woman la femme, **7.1**
wood le bois
word le mot
  words *(of song, etc.)* les paroles *(f. pl.)*
work le travail; *(of art or literature)* l'œuvre *(f.)*, **13.1**
worker l'ouvrier, l'ouvrière
world le monde
wounded blessé(e)
to **write** écrire, **9.2**
  to write a prescription faire une ordonnance, **14.2**
writer l'écrivain *(m.)*, **L2**
wrong mauvais(e), **2.2**
  What's wrong? Qu'est-ce qui ne va pas?
  What's wrong with him? Qu'est-ce qu'il a?, **14.1**

Y

yeah ben oui
year l'an *(m.)*, **4.1;** l'année *(f.)*
  to be . . . years old avoir... ans, **4.1**
yellow jaune, **7.2**
yes oui, **BV;** si *(after neg. question)*, **7.2**
yesterday hier, **10.1**
  the day before yesterday avant-hier, **10.2**
yogurt la yaourt, **6.1**
you tu, **1;** vous, **2**
young jeune
  young people les jeunes *(m. pl.)*
younger le cadet, la cadette, **L1**
your ton, ta, tes; votre, vos, **4**

Z

to **zap** zapper, **12.2**
zero zéro
zone la zone
zoology la zoologie

Index

à contractions with definite articles, **166 (5)**

adjectives agreement with singular nouns, **28 (1);** agreement with plural nouns, **58 (2);** comparative of, **230 (7);** demonstrative, **ce, cet, cette, ces, 303 (9);** ending in **-al, 275 (8);** irregular, **126 (4);** possessive, **123 (4);** position of, **126 (4); 100 (4); 138 (5); tout, toute, tous, toutes, 270 (8)**

agreement adjectives with singular nouns, **28 (1),** adjectives with plural nouns, **58 (2);** definite and indefinite articles with singular nouns, **26 (1);** definite and indefinite articles with plural nouns; **58 (2);** subject and past participles, **413 (12);** subject and verb, **30 (1); 60 (2)**

aller passé composé 369 (11); present tense, **162 (5);** with expressions of health, **162 (5);** with infinitive to express near future, **165 (5);** with **y, 162 (5)**

apprendre passé composé, 364 (11); present tense, **168 (5)**

articles *(see **definite articles, indefinite articles,** and **partitive**)*

au, aux contractions of **à** + definite articles, **166 (5)**

aussi… que 230 (7)

avoir formation of **passé composé** with, **332 (10); passé composé, 364 (11);** present tense, **120 (4);** to express age, **120 (4)**

beau 126 (4)

boire passé composé, 364 (11); present tense **337 (10)**

ce, cet, cette, ces 303 (9)

colors 225 (7)

commands *(see **imperative**)*

comparative of adjectives 230 (7)

comprendre passé composé, 364 (11) present tense, **168 (5)**

connaître present tense, **440 (12);** vs. **savoir, 440 (12)**

contractions au, aux, 166 (5); du, des, 166 (5)

croire passé composé, 364 (11); present tense, **232 (7)**

dates days of the week, **10 (BV);** months of the year, **10 (BV)**

de after **pas** to replace indefinite article, **120 (4);** after **pas** to replace the partitive, **198 (6);** contractions with definite articles, **166 (5);** to indicate possession, **166 (5);** with plural adjectives, **126 (4)**

definite articles gender and agreement with noun, **26 (1);** plural, **58 (2);** singular, **26 (1);** vs. the partitive, **196 (6)**

demonstrative adjectives 303 (9)

des contraction of **de** + **les, 166 (5);** partitive **196 (6);** plural indefinite article, **94 (3)**

devoir passé composé, 364 (11); present tense **337 (10)**

dire passé composé, 364 (11); present tense **306 (9)**

direct object pronouns le, la, les, 444 (13); me, te, nous, vous, 442 (13)

dormir present tense, **272 (8)**

du contraction of **de** + **le, 166 (5);** partitive **196 (6)**

écrire passé composé, 364 (11); present tense, **306 (9)**

elision 26 (1); 90 (3); 94 (3)

en 478 (14)

-er verbs *(see **present tense** and **passé composé**)*

être formation of **passé composé** with, **369 (11); passé composé** of, **364 (11);** present tense: plural forms, **60 (2);** present tense: singular forms **30 (1)**

faire expressions with, **194 (6); passé composé, 364 (11);** present tense **194 (6)**

future expressed with **aller** + infinitive, **165 (5)**

gender of adjectives, **28 (1);** of definite articles, **26 (1);** of indefinite articles, **26 (1);** of nouns, **26 (1)**

il y a 120 (4)

imperative formation and use of, **475 (14)**

indefinite articles gender and agreement with noun, **26 (1);** in negative sentences, **94 (3);** plural, **76 (3);** singular, **26 (1)**

indefinite pronoun on, 90 (3)

indirect object pronouns lui, leur, 472 (14); me, te, nous, vous, 442 (13)

infinitives with **aller** to express near future, **165 (5);** with other verbs, **95 (3)**

-ir verbs *(see* ***present tense*** *and* ***passé composé****)*

irregular verbs *(see individual verb entries)*

liaison 26 (1); 90 (3); 123 (4); 126 (4); 230 (7)

lire passé composé, 364 (11); present tense, **307 (9)**

mettre passé composé, 364 (11) present tense **228 (7)**

moins... que, 230 (7)

mourir passé composé, 369 (11)

naître passé composé, 369 (11)

negation ne... jamais, ne... personne, ne... rien, 367 (11); ne... pas, 33 (1); 165 (5); of indefinite articles, **94 (3);** of the partitive, **196 (6)**

nouns ending in **-al:** singular and plural, **275 (8)**

nouveau 126 (4)

numbers cardinal, 0–69, **10 (BV); 23 (1);** 70–100, **55 (2);** 101–1000, **87 (3)**

object pronouns *(see* ***direct object pronouns, indirect object pronouns, en, y****)*

on 90 (3)

partir passé composé, 369 (11); present tense, **272 (8)**

partitive 196 (6)

passé composé verbs conjugated with **avoir, 332 (10);** with **être, 369 (11);** *(see also individual verb entries)*

past participles agreement with subject, **413 (12);** of irregular verbs, **364 (11);** of regular verbs, **332 (10)**

past time expressions 329 (10)

plural of adjectives, **58 (2);** of adjectives like **beau, nouveau, vieux, 126 (4);** of definite articles, **58 (2);** of indefinite articles, **58 (2);** of nouns, **45 (2);** of subject pronouns, **60 (2)**

plus... que 230 (7)

possession with **de, 166 (5);** *(see also* ***possessive adjectives****)*

possessive adjectives 123 (4)

pouvoir passé composé, 364 (11), present tense **201 (6)**

prendre passé composé, 364 (11); present tense **168 (5)**

present tense of **-er** verbs, **90 (3);** of **-ir verbs 268 (8);** of **-re** verbs, **300 (9);** of reflexive verbs, **408 (12);** of verbs with spelling changes, **233 (7), 412 (12);** *(see also individual verb entries)*

pronouns direct object pronouns, **442 (13); 444 (13); en, 478 (14);** indirect object pronouns, **442 (13), 472 (14); on, 90 (3);** reflexive pronouns, **408 (12);** subject pronouns: singular, **30 (1);** plural, **60 (2); y, 165 (5)**

quel, quelle, quels, quelles 270 (8)

qui interrogative pronoun, **335 (10)**

quoi 335 (10)

-re verbs *(see* ***present tense*** *and* ***passé composé****)*

recevoir passé composé, 364 (11); present tense, **337 (10)**

reflexive verbs passé composé, 413 (12); present tense, **408 (12)**

savoir present tense, **440 (12);** vs. **connaître, 440 (12)**

sortir passé composé, 369 (11); present tense, **272 (8)**

spelling changes, verbs with, 233 (7), 412 (12)

subject pronouns on, 72 (3); plural, **46 (2);** singular, **30 (1); tu** vs. **vous, 64 (2)**

time past time expressions, **329 (10);** telling time, **12 (BV)**

tout, toute, tous, toutes 270 (8)

tu vs. vous 64 (2)

verbs followed by infinitives **95 (3)**

verbs *(see individual verb entries)*

vieux 126 (4)

voir passé composé, 364 (11); present tense, **232 (7)**

vouloir je voudrais, 201 (6); passé composé, 364 (11); present tense, **201 (6)**

vous vs. tu 64 (2)

weather expressions summer, **357 (11);** winter, **361 (11)**

y with **aller, 165 (5)**

Credits

COVER (t to b)Reflexion/International Stock, Oleg Cajko/Panoramic Images, Oleg Cajko/Panoramic Images, David L. Brown/Panoramic Images, (students)Philippe Gontier; **iv** (l)U-AT/The Stock Market, (r)Mark Burnett; **v** (l)Larry Hamill, (r)Travelpix/FPG; **vi** (tl)Timothy Fuller, (tr)Jonny Andre/Photo 20-20, (bl)Zepher Images/Sunset; **vii** (l)John Evans, (r)Mark Antman/Scribner; **viii** Timothy Fuller; **ix** (tl)Greg Bond, videographer, South Park Productions, Inc., (tr bl)Larry Hamill; **x** (tl)Moulo/Sunset, (tr)Musée d'Orsay, Paris/Lauros-Giraudon, Paris/SuperStock, (b)PhotoDisc; **xi** Owen Franken/Stock Boston; **xii** (tr)Larry Hamill, (b)David H. Endersbee/Stone; **xiii** (tl)Timothy Fuller, (bl)Larry Hamill, (br)Jeff Kaufman/FPG; **xiv** Doug Pensinger/AllSport; **xv** (t)Paul Hardy/The Stock Market, (b)Timothy Fuller; **xvi** (tl tr)Timothy Fuller, (b)Curt Fischer; **xvii** (l)Timothy Fuller, (r)Mark Burnett; **xviii** Timothy Fuller; **xix** Massino Listri/CORBIS; **xxxvi** (tr)Chris Sorenson/The Stock Market, (cl)Mark Antman/The Image Works, (bl)Mark Burnett; **xxxvii** (tr c)Larry Hamill, (bl)Walter Bibikow/FPG, (bc)Michele Burgess/The Stock Market, (br)Alain Even/DIAF; **xl–1** (bkgd xl/2)Curt Fischer, (xl/1)David Florenz/Option Photo, (xl/3)Photobank USA/Sunset, (xl/4)Michael Krasowitz/FPG, (1/5) Curt Fischer, (1/6)Robert Fried Photography, (1/7)Timothy Fuller, (1/8)Gio Barto/The Image Bank, (1/9)Larry Hamill; **2** Larry Hamill; **3** (tl tc bc)Larry Hamill, (tr bl)Catherine et Bernard Desjeux, (br)Timothy Fuller; **4** (l)Timothy Fuller, (r)Catherine et Bernard Desjeux; **5** Timothy Fuller; **6** Larry Hamill; **7** Mark Burnett; Larry Hamill; **9** (tl)Ilico/Wallis Phototheque, (tr cl bl br)John Evans, (cc)LCI/Wallis Phototheque, (cr)Ange/Wallis Phototheque; **11** (tl tr)Ken Karp, (bl)Jean-Daniel Sudres/DIAF, (br)U-AT/The Stock Market; **13** Mark Burnett; **14** Larry Hamill; **15** (t)Mark Burnett; **16–17** Catherine et Bernard Desjeux, **16** (b)Bridgeman Art Library; **18** Larry Hamill; **19** Timothy Fuller; **20** (tr c br)Larry Hamill, (bl)Jill Connelly/The Image Works; **21** (tl)Pacha/CORBIS, (tr)Bettman/CORBIS, (bl)Mitchell Gerber/CORBIS, (br)Christie's Images/CORBIS; **22** (tl tr br)Larry Hamill, (bl)John Evans, (br,inset)Dale Durfee/Stone; **23** (l)John Evans, (r)file photo; **24** (tl)Curt Fischer, (tr)Robert Fried Photography, (bl)Garufi/Wallis Phototheque, (br)Telegraph Colour Library/FPG; **25** (t)RAGA-France/The Stock Market, (bl)Dannic/DIAF, (br)Goumare/Wallis Phototheque; **26** Pascal Crapet/Stone; **27** P. Wysocki/S. Frances/Hémisphères Images; **28** Wayne Rowe; **31** (t)Peter McCabe/The Image Works, (bl br)Monika Graff/The Image Works; **32** (t)Larry Hamill, (b)Claudie/Sunset, (b,inset)Wayne Rowe; **33** Owen Franken/CORBIS; **34** (t)Travelpix/FPG, (b)Larry Hamill; **35** Bruno de Hogues/Stone; **36** (l)Fernand/Sunset, (r)Robert Holmes/CORBIS; **37** (t)Chris Sorenson/The Stock Market, (b)David Simson/Stock Boston; **38** (t)C. Capel/Sunset, (t,inset)Brian A. Vikander, (b)Yvan Travert/DIAF, (b,inset)Mark Antman/The Image Works; **39** (t)Private collection/The Bridgeman Art Library, (b)Jean-Daniel Sudres/DIAF; **40–41** (bkgd)Fototeca Storica Nazionale/PhotoDisc; **40** (t)Camille Moirenc/DIAF, (b)Sitki Tarlan/Panoramic Images; **41** (t)Doug Armand/Stone, (b)Ric Ergenbright/CORBIS; **42** (t)Larry Hamill, (c)Peter McCabe/The Image Works, (b)Chris Duranti/Wallis Phototheque; **44** Ozu Kiki/La Phototheque/SDP; **45** J. Brun/Explorer; **46** (t)Robert Holmes/CORBIS, (b)Larry Hamill; **47** (tl bl)Greg Bond, videographer, South Park Productions, Inc., (r)Curt Fischer; **48–49** Larry Hamill, (b)Barnes Foundation, Merion PA/SuperStock; **50** Christine et Bernard Desjeux; **51** (t)Larry Hamill, (b)Timothy Fuller; **52** (t)Marge/Sunset, (b)Timothy Fuller; **53** John Evans; **54** Curt Fischer; **55** John Evans; **56 57 59**(t)Larry Hamill; **60** (l)Monika Graff/The Image Works, (c)Ken Karp; **63** (t)Robert Fried Photography, (b)Photobank/Sunset; **65** (tl)Zephyr Images/Sunset, (tc)Sierpinski/DIAF, (tr)Robert Fried Photography, (bl)Sylva Villerot/DIAF, (bc)Stuart Cohen/The Image Works, (br)Robert Fried Photography; **66** Larry Hamill; **68** (tl)Michele Burgess/The Stock Market, (tr)Larry Hamill, (b)Beryl Goldberg; **69** (t)David Grunfeld/The Image Works, (b)SuperStock; **70** (t)Larry Hamill, (b)Curt Fischer; **71–72** (bkgd)The Studio Dog/PhotoDisc, **71** (tl)Larry Hamill, (tr)Stephane Cande/Mission/Wallis Phototheque, (b)Robert Holmes/CORBIS; **72** (l)Jean-Paul Garcin/DIAF, (r)Art Wolfe/Stone; **73** (t)Beryl Goldberg, (b)Mark Burnett; **74** Larry Hamill; **75** (t b)Larry Hamill, (b,inset)Capel/Sunset; **77** Jenny Andre/Photo 20–20; **78** (t)Larry Hamill, (b)Curt Fischer; **79** (tl b)Greg Bond, videographer, South Park Productions, Inc., (tr)Robert Holmes/CORBIS; **80–81** Bob Handelman/Stone, **80** (b)Musée du Louvre, Paris/SuperStock; **82** Larry Hamill; **83** Alain Le Bot/DIAF; **84** (t)R. Lucas/The Image Works, (b)Larry Hamill; **85** Ken Karp; **86** (alpha order, top to bottom a b)Aaron Haupt, (c f l m)Curt Fischer, (d e g h i j k)Amanita Pictures; **87** Larry Hamill; **88** (t c)Amanita Pictures, (b)Valerie Simmons; **89** Amanita Pictures; **91** (t)John Evans, (bl br)Ken Karp; **92** (t)Matthieu Colin/Hémisphères Images, (bl br)Ken Karp; **94** Beryl Goldberg; **96** (t)Larry Hamill, (b)John Evans; **98** (tr)Robert Fried Photography, (bl)John Evans, (br)Hartmut Krinitz/Hémisphères Images; **99** Larry Hamill; **100** (l)Beryl Goldberg, (tr)Guido Cozzi/Agence ANA; **101** (t)Larry Hamill, (b)Christian Roger; **102–103** (bkgd)PhotoDisc, **102** Cheryl Fenton; **103** Ed Taylor Studio/FPG; **104 105** Larry Hamill; **107** Mark Antman/Scribner; **109** (tl br)Greg Bond, videographer, South Park Productions, Inc., (r)Philip Gould/CORBIS; **110** (b)Metropolitan Museum of Art, New York/SuperStock; **112** (tl tr cl br)Larry Hamill, (bl)PhotoDisc; **113** Timothy Fuller; **114** (t)Mark Burnett; **115** Giraudon/Art Resource, New York; **117** Larry Hamill; **118** Karin Ansara/Wallis Phototheque; **119** (l)Grant V. Faint/The Image Bank, (c)Stéphane Frances/Hémisphères Images, (r)Claude/Sunset; **121** (t)Michelle Chaplow, (b)Zephyr Images/Sunset; **123** Michelle Chaplow; **124** Pawel Wysocki/Hémisphères Images; **125** Daniel Thierry/DIAF; **126** Walter Bibikow/FPG; **128** Larry Hamill; **129** (r)Ken Karp; **130** (l)Pratt-Pries/DIAF, **131** (t)Weststock/Sunset, (b)Sandra Baker/Liaison Agency; **132** (tl)SuperStock, (tr)Jean-Daniel Sudres/DIAF, (br)LCI/Wallis Phototheque; **134–135** (bkgd)CORBIS, **134** (t)Lauros-Giraudon/Art Resource, New York, (b)Réunion des Musées Nationaux/Art Resource, New York; **135** (t)David Noble/FPG, (c)Desvignes/Sunset, (b)Gianni Dagli Orti/CORBIS; **137** Travelpix/FPG; **139** Curt Fischer; **140** (t)Timothy Fuller, (bl)Pratt-Pries/DIAF, (br)Travelpix/FPG, **141** (tl bl)Greg Bond, videographer, South Park Productions, Inc., (tr)Dave G. Houser; **142** (t)Larry Hamill, (b)Mark Burnett; **143** Wayne Rowe; **144** (t)Timothy Fuller, (b)Larry Hamill; **145** R. Rozencwajg/DIAF; **147** Larry Hamill; **148–149** (bkgd)Michael Busselle/Stone, (148/2)Laurent Rebours, AP/Wide World Photos, (148/3)Bernard Boutrit/Photo Researchers, (148/4)Marie-José Jarry & Jean-François Tripelon/Agence Top/National Geographic Image Collection, (148/5)Steve McCurry/National Geographic Image Collection, (149/6)P. Bennett/AA Photo Library, (149/7)Martha Bates/Stock Boston; **150–151** (bkgd)Chad Ehlers/Stone, (150/9)Steve Vidler/Leo de Wys Stock Photo Agency, (150/10)Patrick Ingrand/Stone, (150/11)Patrick Zachmann/Magnum, (150/12)Christophe Ena, AP/Wide World Photos, (151/13)Craig Aurness/CORBIS, (151/14)Suzanne & Nick Geary/Stone; **152–153** (bkgd) John Lawrence/Stone; **152** (b)Erich Lessing/Art Resource; **155** (l to r,alpha c d)Timothy Fuller, (o)Aaron Haupt, (others)John Evans; **156** Timothy Fuller; **157** Gérard Gsell/DIAF; **158** Larry Hamill; **159** (l)John Evans, (c r)Aaron Haupt; **160** (t)Timothy Fuller, (b)Curt Fischer; **162** H. Gyssels/DIAF; **164** (l)Eve Morcrette/Wallis Phototheque, (c)file photo; **166** Gerard Lacz/Sunset; **167** (l)Bill Deering/FPG; **168** James Davis/International Stock; **169 170** Larry Hamill; **172** (l)Timothy Fuller, (r)Christine et Bernard Desjeux; **173** (l)Wayne Rowe; **174** (l)Bob Krist/The Stock Market, (tr)Larry Hamill, (br)Explorer/Photo Researchers; **175** (tl)Quinard/Wallis Phototheque, (tr)Robert Fried Photography; **176–177** (bkgd)Sami Sarkis/PhotoDisc; **178** (b)Larry Hamill; **179** David Simson/Stock Boston; **180** Wayne Rowe; **182** (t)Gerard

Lucz/Sunset, (others)John Evans; **183** (tl b)Greg Bond, videographer, South Park Productions, Inc., (r)Bruno De Hogues/Stone; **184–185** SuperStock; **184** (b)Musée d'Orsay, Paris/Lauros-Giraudon, Paris/SuperStock; **187** (tl bl br)Larry Hamill, (tr)Curt Fischer; **188** (t)Larry Hamill, (b)Mark Burnett; 189 (t)Curt Fischer, (b)Wayne Rowe; **190** Larry Hamill; **191** (t)Timothy Fuller, (bl)Terry Sutherland, (others)Larry Hamill; **192** PhotoDisc; **193** (l)Peter McCabe/The Image Works, (r)Monika Graff/The Image Works; **194** Larry Hamill; **195** (t)Larry Hamill, (l)Monika Graff/The Image Works, (r)Ken Karp; **197** (tl tr)Monika Graff/The Image Works, (c)J.-Ch. Gerard/DIAF, (bl)Moulo/Sunset; **199** (tl tr)Monika Graff/The Image Works, (b)Beryl Goldberg; **200** Larry Hamill, (inset)Curt Fischer; **202** (t)Michael Busselle/CORBIS, (b)Ken Karp; **204** Timothy Fuller; **205** Andrew Payti; **206** (l)George Gibbons/FPG, (r)Larry Hamill; **207** (l)Michael Busselle/Stone, (r)Christophe Duranti/Wallis Phototheque; **208** (l)Alain Le Bot/DIAF, (r)Laurent Giraudou/Hémisphères Images; **209** (tr)Chad Ehlers/International Stock, (l)Andrew Payti, (br)Robert Fried Photography; **210–211** (bkgd)PhotoLink/PhotoDisc, **210** (tl)Charlie Abad/SDP, (tr)Lee Snider/The Image Works, (br)Mark Antman/The Image Works; **211** (t)Mark Antman/The Image Works, (b)Spot/SDP; **212** Todd Gipstein/CORBIS; **213** M. Huet/Hoa Qui; **215** Larry Hamill; **216** (t)Moulo/Sunset, (bl)Terry Sutherland, (bc br)Larry Hamill; **217** (tl bl)Greg Bond, videographer, South Park Productions, Inc., (tr)Gilles Serrano/Liaison Agency; **218–219** Mark Gibson/Photo 20-20, **218** (b)Werner Forman Archive/Museum fur Volkerkunde, Berlin/Art Resource, New York; **220** John Evans; **221 222** (tl b)Larry Hamill, (tr)Timothy Fuller; **223** Iconos/DIAF; **224** Larry Hamill; **225** (t)John Evans, (b)Timothy Fuller; **226** (t)Larry Hamill, (b)Japack/Sunset; **228** Beryl Goldberg; **231** Larry Hamill; **232** Chris/Sunset; **234** Larry Hamill; **235** Michael Dwyer/Stock Boston; **236** (t)Robert Holmes/CORBIS, (b)Tim Gibson/Envision; **237** (t)Curt Fischer, (b)Owen Franken/Stock Boston; **238** (t)H. Rogers/TRIP, (tl)Gossler/Schuster/Explorer, (bl)Jose Nicolas/Hémisphères Images; **239** Japack/Sunset; **240–241** (bkgd)Geoff Butler, **240** (l)FPG, (r)Archivo Iconografico, S.A./CORBIS; **241** Bettmann/CORBIS; **242** Beryl Goldberg; **243** Sylva Villerot/DIAF; **245** Wayne Rowe; **246** (t)Larry Hamill, (b)John Evans; **247** (tl bl)Greg Bond, videographer, South Park Productions, Inc., (tr)Shinichi Kanno/FPG; **248** (t)Larry Hamill, (b)Tim Gibson/Envision; **250** (t)Bertrand Rieger/Hémisphères Images, (b)Steven Needham/Envision; **252** Larry Hamill; **253** Timothy Fuller; **254–255** (bkgd)Steven Rothfeld/Stone, (254/2)M & E Bernheim/Woodfin Camp & Associates, (254/3)Bruno De Hogues/Stone, (254/4)Photri/Microstock, (254/5)Nik Wheeler/CORBIS, (255/6)Tim Hall/Retna, (255/7)M & E Bernheim/Woodfin Camp & Associates; **256–257** (bkgd)Kevin Schafer/CORBIS, (256/9)Bruno De Hogues/Stone, (256/10)Betty Press/Woodfin Camp & Associates, (256/11)Giacomo Pirozzi/Panos Pictures, (256/12)TempSport/CORBIS, (257/13)Carol Beckwith & Angela Fisher; (257/14)Caroline Penn/Panos Pictures; Tibor Bognar/The Stock Market, **258** (b)Private collection/Lauros-Giraudon, Paris/SuperStock; **260** (tl tr)Larry Hamill, (c)Marc Thomas, (bl)Curt Fischer, (br)C Squared Studios/PhotoDisc; **261** (tl tr)Larry Hamill, (c)Trompas/Sunset, (bl)Barret/Wallis Phototheque; **262** (t)courtesy Air France; **263** Owen Franken/Stock Boston; **264** (t)courtesy Air France, (b)Giraudon/Wallis Phototheque; **265** (t)Stéphane Frances/Hémisphères Images, (b)DeRichemond/The Image Works; **266** (b)Barret/Wallis Phototheque; **267** (b)Larry Hamill; **269** (l)Monika Graff/The Image Works, (r)Ken Karp; **273** Larry Hamill; **274** Oldrich Karasek/Stone; **275** Pictor; **276** (t)David Barnes/The Stock Market, (b)Larry Hamill; **277** Shaun Egan/Stone; **278** (t)Marge/Sunset, (b)Telegraph Colour Library/FPG; **279** (t)Jeremy Walker/Stone; (b)Timothy Fuller; **281** (t)Archive Photo/Archive France, (b)Editions Gallimard; **282–283** (bkgd)Siede Preis/PhotoDisc; **283** (t)ZEFA London/The Stock Market, (c)Gerard Gsell/DIAF, (b)J. Du Sordet/Agence ANA; **284** (r)José Fuste/The Stock Market; **285** (l)D. Cordier/Sunset, (c)Jacques Sierpinski/DIAF, (r)David H. Endersbee/Stone; **287** X. Richer/Hoa-Qui; **288** (b)courtesy Air France; **289** (tl bl)Greg Bond, videographer, South Park Productions, Inc., (tr)Adam Woolfit/CORBIS; **290–291** Jeff Kaufman/FPG, (b)AKG London; **292 293** Timothy Fuller; **294** (l)Larry Hamill, (r)Wayne Rowe; **295** Beryl Goldberg; **297** Timothy Fuller; **298** Photobank/Sunset; **299** (t)Jacques Loic/La Phototheque SDP; **300** Andrew Payti; **301** The Purcell Team/CORBIS; **302** David Ball/DIAF; **303** Pascal Hinous/Top Agence; **304** (tl tr)Ken Karp, (b)Arnaud Fevrier/DIAF; **305** Timothy Fuller; **307** (l)J. Du Sordet/Agence ANA, (r)José Fuste/The Stock Market; **308** Timothy Fuller; **310** Stéphane Frances/Hémisphères Images; **311** (t)Henneghien/Agence ANA, (b)Alain Even/DIAF; **312** (r)J.P. Porcher/Sunset; **313** (t)John Elk/Stone, (b)Timothy Fuller; **314–315** (bkgd)The Studio Dog/PhotoDisc, **314** (t)Mark Antman/The Image Works, (bl br)Larry Hamill; **315** (t)Jeanetta Baker/Photobank/Sunset, (b)Graham Finlayson/Woodfin Camp & Associates; **316** (tr)Andrew Payti, (cl)Robert Fried Photography, (cr)Beryl Goldberg, (bl)P. Dannic/DIAF; **317** (t)Camille Moirenc/Wallis Phototheque; **319** Andrew Payti; **320** (l)Timothy Fuller, (r)Arnaud Fevrier/DIAF; **321** (tl bl)Greg Bond, videographer, South Park Productions, Inc., (tr)Bernard Regent/DIAF; **322–323** Doug Pensinger/Allsport; **322** (b)Museum of Modern Art, Troyes, France/Lauros-Giraudon, Paris/SuperStock; **324** (l)Ben Radford/AllSport, (r)Timothy Fuller; **325** (tr)Bob Thomas/Stone, (br)Timothy Fuller; **326** (t)Temp Sport/CORBIS, (b)AFP/CORBIS; **328** (tl tc)Timothy Fuller, (tr)KS Studio; **329** (t)Timothy Fuller, (b)Wally McNamee/CORBIS; **330** Beryl Goldberg; **331** (t)Gerard Vandystadt/Agence ANA, (b)AP Photo/Ryan Remiorz/Photo Archive; **333** (b)Reuters News Media Inc./CORBIS; **334** Haslin/Tempsort/NewSport Photography, Inc.; **335** (l)Peter McCabe/The Image Works, (r)Ken Karp; **336** Timothy Fuller; **337** S.T.F./Sunset; **338** (bl)Ken Karp, (br)Monika Graff/The Image Works; **339** Claude Abron/Liaison Agency; **340** (t)Reuters/Charles Platiau/Archive Photos, (b)Larry Hamill; **342** (l)Robert LaBerge/AllSport, (r)David E. Klutho/*Sports Illustrated;* **343** (t)Reuters/Petar Kujundzic/Archive Photos, (b)Aaron Haupt; **344 345** Doug Pensinger/AllSport; **346–347** (bkgd)M. Freeman/PhotoLink/PhotoDisc, **346** (t)Pictor, (b)AFP/CORBIS; **348** (l)F.Stock/Sunset, (r)Bob Martin/*Sports Illustrated;* **349** (b)Simon Bruty/*Sports Illustrated;* **351** Curt Fischer; **352** (t)Reuters News Media, Inc/CORBIS, (b)Robert LaBerge/AllSport; **353** (tl bl)Greg Bond, videographer, South Park Productions, Inc., (tr)Henry T. Kaiser/Pictor; **354–355** Sylvain Grandadam/Stone; **354** (b)Galerie Daniel Malinque, Paris, FR/The Bridgeman Art Library; **356** (t)Paul Hardy/The Stock Market, (cb)Timothy Fuller; **357** (l)Laborde/Wallis Phototheque, (lc)Chris Harvey/Stone, (rc)Timothy Fuller, (r)SuperStock; **358** (t)Adina Tovy/Photo 20-20, (b)Larry Hamill; **359** (t)Timothy Fuller, (b)José Fuste/The Stock Market; **360** (tl)Richard Lucas/The Image Works, (cl)Jonathon Rawle/Stock Boston, (cr)Bonnie Kamin/PhotoEdit, (bl)Rosine Mazin/DIAF, (r)John Evans; **361** Huet/Wallis Phototheque; **364** S.T.F./Sunset; **365** Cosmo Condina/Stone; **366** Karl Weatherly/Corbis; **367** Monika Graff/The Image Works, **368** (l)Tristian Vigouroux/Wallis Phototheque, (r)Beryl Goldberg; **370** (t)J. Sierpinski/DIAF, (b)Marge/Sunset; **371** (l)Jo Labbe/Wallis Phototheque, (r)Robert Fried Photography; **372** (t)Robert Fried Photography, (b)Aaron Haupt; **374** (l)Dave G. Houser/CORBIS, (c)Alec Ptlowany/Masterfile, (r)Patrick Frilet/Hémisphères Images; **375** Zephyr Images/Sunset; **376** (tl)Marge/Sunset, (bl)Stéphane Frances/Hémisphères Images, (r)Nik Wheeler/CORBIS; **377** (tl)Patrick Frilet/Hémisphères Images, (tr)Stuart Cohen/The Image Works, (bl)Mark Antman/The Image Works; **378–379** (bkgd)Farinaz Taghavi/PhotoDisc, **378** (t)Erich Lessing/Art Resource, New York, (b)Giraudon/Art Resource, New York; **379**

H12

Credits

Erich Lessing/Art Resource, New York; **380** (t)Marge/Sunset, (b)Picturesque/Sunset; **381** (l)Michael Busselle/Stone, (r)SuperStock; **383** Mauritius/La Phototheque SDP; **384** (t)Larry Hamill, (b)John Evans; **385** (tl bl)Greg Bond, videographer, South Park Productions, Inc., (tr)Superstock; **386** Timothy Fuller; **388** Mark Burnett; **389** Robert Fried Photography; **390** Beryl Goldberg; **392** Joachim Messerschmidt/FPG; **394–395** (bkgd)Ed Simpson/Stone, (394/2)Maggie Steber, (394/3)Yves Marcoux/Stone, (394/4)George F. Mobley, (394/5)Michael Melford, (395/6)Anna Clopet/CORBIS, (395/7)Dave G. Houser/CORBIS, **396–397** (bkgd)Chris Cheadle/Stone, (396/9)Museé McCord, (396/10)Hubert Stadler/CORBIS, (396/11)Cosmo Condina/Stone, (396/12)AFP/CORBIS, (397/13)Jocelyn Boutin, (397/14)Wolfgang Kaehler/CORBIS; **398** (b)Christie's Images; **398–399** SuperStock; **400** (tc)John Evans, (others)Timothy Fuller; **401** Timothy Fuller; **402** (tl)file photo, (tr)Chris Duranti/Wallis Phototheque; **403** Frederick/Sunset; **404 405 406** Timothy Fuller; **407** Michelle Garrett/CORBIS; **409** Andrew Payti; **411 412**(tr)Timothy Fuller, (l c)Ken Karp; **413** (l)Robert Fried Photography, (r)Ken Karp; **414** Timothy Fuller; **416** Larry Hamill; **418** Catherine et Bernard Desjeux; **419** (t)P. Moulu/Sunset, (b)Pratt-Pries/DIAF; **420** (t)Chad Slattery/Stone, (b)Rick Souders/Index Stock; **421** (tl)Timothy Fuller, (tr cr)Aaron Haupt, (cl bl br)Mark Burnett; **422–423** (bkgd)PhotoLink/PhotoDisc, **422** (t)Roy/Sunset, (b)Jonathan Blair/CORBIS; **423** (t)Martin Rogers/Stock Boston, (b)de Richemond/The Image Works; **424** (t)Mark Antman/The Image Works, (bl br)Ken Karp; **425** M. Granitsas/The Image Works; **426** (tl tc)Curt Fischer, (tr)file photo, **426** (bl br)Cheryl Fenton; **427** Carton/Pitch; **428** Timothy Fuller; **429** (tl b)Greg Bond, videographer, South Park Productions, Inc., (tr)Morcrette/Wallis Phototheque; **430–431** Mark Burnett; (b)British Museum, London/Bridgeman Art Library, London/SuperStock; **432 433**(t)Timothy Fuller, (bl)SuperStock, (br)Pictor; 434 (t)Timothy Fuller, (b)John Evans; **435** (l)Collections de la Comedie-Francaise, (r)Mark Burnett; **437** Timothy Fuller; **438** Giraudon/Art Resource, New York; **439** © Photo RMN—Hervé Lewandowski/Musée D'Orsay; **440** Jacques Sierpinski/DIAF; **441** Scala/Art Resource, New York; **442** Timothy Fuller; **443** (tl)file photo, (tr)Monika Graff/The Image Works; **444** Yann Arthus-Bertrand/CORBIS; **445** (tl)Monika Graff/The Image Works, (tr)Peter McCabe/The Image Works; **446** (t)J. Marc Lallemand/Wallis Phototheque, (b)© Photo RMN—Hervé Lewandowski/Musée D'Orsay; **447** Vanni/Art Resource, New York; **448** Larry Hamill; **450** (l)Derek Croucher/The Stock Market, (r)Larry Hamill; **451** (t)AFP/CORBIS, (c)Ramsay/Wallis Phototheque, (b)Gérard Lacz/Sunset; **452** (t)Jason Laure, (b)Hilarie Kavanagh/Stone; **453** (tl b)K. N'Dour/Liaison Agency/Neal Preston/CORBIS, (tr)Mark Burnett; **454–455** (bkgd)Steve Cole/PhotoDisc, **455** (t)Robbie Jack/CORBIS, (c)AFP/CORBIS, (b)Stephane Cardinale/CORBIS/Sygma; **456** (t)Robert Fried Photography, (b)Larry Hamill; **457** (t)Timothy Fuller; **459** Curt Fischer; **460** (t)Mark Burnett, (bl)Robbie Jack/CORBIS, (br)Larry Hamill; **461** (tl b)Greg Bond, videographer, South Park Productions, Inc., (tr)Zefa/Index Stock; **462–463** Stefano Bianchetti/CORBIS, **462** (b)Roger-Viollet, Paris/The Bridgeman Art Library; **464** (tr)John Evans, (tr,inset br)Aaron Haupt, (others)Timothy Fuller; **465** Timothy Fuller; **466** Curt Fischer; **467** Mark Burnett; **468 469** (tl bl br)Timothy Fuller, (tr)Larry Hamill; **470** (t)John Evans, (b)Timothy Fuller; **472** (l)Catherine et Bernard Desjeux, (c)Image Club Graphics; **473** (r)Catherine et Bernard Desjeux; **474** (t)Timothy Fuller, (b)Larry Hamill; **477** Ken Karp; **479** (t)Adina Tovy/Photo 20-20, (bl)Monika Graff/The Image Works, (br)Ken Karp; **480** Timothy Fuller; (l)Monika Graff/The Image Works, (r)Ken Karp; **482 484** (l)Timothy Fuller; **485** (l)CH. Vioujard/Liaison Agency, (r)SuperStock; **486–487** (bkgd)Mitch Hrdlicka/PhotoDisc; **486** (l)Curt Fischer, (cr)Mark Burnett, (b)Clasen/Wallis Phototheque; **487** (t)Catherine Panchout/Stone, (b)Larry Hamill; **489**(t)Larry Hamill, (b)P. Wysocki/Explorer; **490** Curt Fischer; **492** (t)Timothy Fuller, (bl)John Evans, (br)Mark Burnett; **493** (tl bl)Greg Bond, videographer, South Park Productions, Inc., (r)Mark Burnett; **494** Everett Collection; **495** Timothy Fuller; **497** (t)Larry Hamill, (b)Owen Franken/CORBIS; **498–499** (bkgd)PhotoDisc; (498/2)PhotoDisc, (498/3)Stephen Studd/Stone, (498/4)Photri Inc., (498/5)Bob Handelman/Stone, (499/6)Chad Ehlers/Stone, (499/7)David Turnley/CORBIS; **500–501** (bkgd)Jean-Marc Truchet/Stone, (500/9)Chris Ladd/FPG International, (500/10)Franck Eustache/Archipress, (500/11)Theo Westenberger, (500/12)Patrick Ingrand/Stone, (501/13)Harvey Lloyd/Peter Arnold, Inc., (501/14)Kim Hart/Black Star Publishing/PictureQuest; **502–503** Massimo Listri/CORBIS; **505** Jean-Daniel Sudres/DIAF; **506** Archiv/Photo Researchers, Inc; **507** Scala/Art Resource, New York; **508** Christie's Images; **510** Bridgeman Art Library; **511** (t)H. Reinhard/Sunset, (b)Elizabeth Barakah Hodges/SuperStock; **513** Giraudon, Paris/Art Resource, New York; **514** (t)Stock Montage/SuperStock, (b)AKG London; **515 516** AKG London; **517** (t)Art Resource, New York, (b)Nik Wheeler/CORBIS; **520** (t)Hulton-Deutsch Collection/CORBIS, (b)Giraudon/Art Resource, New York; **521** AKG London; **522** Franz-Marc Frei/CORBIS; **523** Marc Garanger/CORBIS; **524–H1** Suzanne & Nick Geary/Stone; **H3** (tl tr)Larry Hamill, (bl)John Evans, (br)Garufi/Wallis Phototheque; **H4** (tl)Pacha/CORBIS, (tr)Bettmann/CORBIS, (bl)Mitchell Gerber/CORBIS, (br)Christie's Images/CORBIS; **H5** Larry Hamill; **H8** John Evans; **H14** EleveA (tl)Aaron Haupt, (br)Timothy Fuller, (others)EleveB (all)John Evans; **H18** EleveA (t)Terry Sutherland, (others)Larry Hamill, EleveB (tl)Timothy Fuller, (others)Larry Hamill; **H27** EleveA Stéphane Frances/Hémisphères Images, EleveB Trompas/Sunset; **H28 H29** Timothy Fuller; **H35** EleveA Adina Tovy/Photo 20-20, EleveB (tl)Laborde/Wallis Phototheque, (tr)Chris Harvey/Stone, (b)Timothy Fuller; **H36** Richard Lucas/The Image Works; **H39** Timothy Fuller; **H43** EleveA (t)Timothy Fuller, (b)Pictor, EleveB John Evans; **H44** Timothy Fuller; **H47** (tl tr)Timothy Fuller, (bl)John Evans, (br)Aaron Haupt; **H48** Timothy Fuller; **H71** Roberto M. Arakaki/International Stock.

In appreciation

Special thanks to the following for their cordial assistance and participation in the photo illustrations:

Aeroport Charles De Gaulle; Affinage du Val d'Yerres, Montgeron, Air Afrique, Air France, Banque de France, Café Les Deux Magots, Paris, Cafeteria Flunch Evry, Centre Commercial des Halles, Paris, Club Hyppique, Varennes Jarcy, Colleg de Montois, Donnemarie-Dontilly, College Pasteur de Brunoy, Cora Boussy Saint Antoine, Crep' Yerres, Creperie au Mystere de Carnac, Montgeron, Cuisines AJ, Yerres, Docteur Ponnoussamy, Electro Star, Bonneuil, Espace Photo, Vigneux, Fermelec de L'essonne, Galeries Lafayette, Hippopotamus, Horizon F.M., International School of Paris, Kosque du Palais Royal, Paris, Laboratoire d'Analyses Medicales des Godeaux, Le Restaurant Mona Lisa, Lycee Janson de Sailly, Lycee Louis-le-Grand, Maison de la Presse Montgeron, Maison de la Presse S.G.E.C., Evry, Marche des Champs Elysees, Musée d'Orsay, Paris, Musée du Louvre, Paris, Nicolas Dupont-Aignan/Depute Maire de Yerres, Pharmacie des Godeaux, Yerres, Pharmacie Laurence Dony, Yerres, Piscine de Brunoy, RATP, Relais-H Gare de Lyon, Restaurant Chez Paul, Restaurant le Clos Saint Jacques, Paris, Restaurant Procope, SAMU de Paris, SNCF-TGV, Yerres Ecole National de Musique et de Danse.

Glencoe would like to acknowledge the artists and agencies who participated in illustrating this program: Domenick D'Andrea; Fanny Mellet Berry represented by Anita Grien; Len Ebert; Carlos Lacamara; Jane McCreary; Ortelius Design; Carol Strebel; Shannon Stirnweis; Joseph Hammond, Susan Jaekel and DJ Simison represented by Ann Remen-Willis.